Life, One Big Existential Crisis

by
Kerry Louise Stalker

Grosvenor House
Publishing Limited

All rights reserved
Copyright © Kerry Louise Stalker, 2023

The right of Kerry Louise Stalker to be identified as the author of this
work has been asserted in accordance with Section 78
of the Copyright, Designs and Patents Act 1988

The book cover is copyright to Kerry Louise Stalker

This book is published by
Grosvenor House Publishing Ltd
Link House
140 The Broadway, Tolworth, Surrey, KT6 7HT.
www.grosvenorhousepublishing.co.uk

This book is sold subject to the conditions that it shall not, by way of
trade or otherwise, be lent, resold, hired out or otherwise circulated
without the author's or publisher's prior consent in any form of binding or
cover other than that in which it is published and
without a similar condition including this condition being imposed
on the subsequent purchaser.

A CIP record for this book
is available from the British Library

ISBN 978-1-83975-362-6
eBook ISBN 978-1-83975-435-7

This is dedicated to my mum, who is an absolute trooper and takes life right on the chin. No meds, no mind-altering substances of any kind, ever. On the contrary, the experience of real, unadulterated, challenging and testing life. In her opinion, there's more valleys than mountain tops.

Nietzsche said, 'To live is to suffer, to survive is to find some meaning in the suffering'. Not dissimilar, George Orwell said, 'Most people get a fair amount of fun out of their lives, but on balance life is suffering, and only the very young or very foolish imagine otherwise'. Henry David Thoreau concedes, 'The mass of men lead lives of quiet desperation' (he said that over 100 years ago).

This is also dedicated to brother-bear, and my dad. Thanks Dad for the funds to enable my profession as a 'gentleman's scientist'. I also want to 'high five' my furry boys' aka jazz kats. Aldous Huxley advised, 'If you want to write, keep cats', and Eckhart Tolle (author of 'The Power of Now') said, 'I have lived with several Zen masters – all of them cats' (p.157).

And to all my brothers and sisters, also on this journey and equally thinking 'shut the front door'. This life is truly crazy and then we die.

'The Truth is also seeking the seeker'.

An Existential Crisis

Contents

Rationale

Foreword — ix

Introduction — xiii

PART 1

Chapter 1: What's the Point? — 5
Chapter 2: Existential Roots — 49
Chapter 3: Idealism versus Materialism — 75
Chapter 4: Mental Case? — 103
Chapter 5: The Curious Unconscious — 162
Chapter 6: Carl Gustav Jung — 181
Chapter 7: Altered States of Consciousness — 206
Chapter 8: The Spirit World — 252
Chapter 9: Can we Communicate with the Dead? — 291
Chapter 10: Doreen Irvine — 300
Keith and Melody Green Excerpt — 310

PART 2

Chapter 11: Biblical His-Story — 315
Chapter 12: Luciferian Philosophy — 359
Chapter 13: Secret Societies — 388
Chapter 14: The Royal Family — 422
Chapter 15: The One World Order — 452
Chapter 16: The Biblical Forecast — 482
Chapter 17: The Alien Deception — 520
Chapter 18: Creation versus Evolution — 555
Chapter 19: Who is God? — 596

Chapter 20: Battle for the Mind	632
God's Love Letter	665
Conclusion	667
Appendix: Ecclesiastes by King Solomon	669
References	679
About the Author	683

The Rationale for this work is,

'You Choose Your Choice'

'The last one to know about the sea is the fish'. (Chinese proverb)

Foreword

With regards to the title of this book, (for those not familiar with the term), an existential crisis uncoils when we freak out regarding the possible meaninglessness of life. We can feel overwhelming anxiety and nausea at the futility of it all. It appears we're here for a look around, and then we're toast. Hence, it seems pointless, with no intrinsic value. It's said we only get one chance at life, and so we have to make it count. But does it matter, does anything really matter? Death is another source of angst, since no-one really knows what happens when we die.

Bertrand Russell (1872-1970), renowned for representing scientific humanism, spoke about the night of nothingness. He said, 'There is no darkness without, and when I die there will be darkness within. There is no splendour, no vastness, anywhere; only triviality for a moment, and then nothing'. Whilst arguably palatable, this comfortably materialistic 'theory' conflicts with reports from those who die, sometimes for days, then return and insist that consciousness survives death.

It's understood that secular humanism usurped God, since religion is irrelevant at best and harmful at worst. Suicide bombers, enough said. Thus, human reason and scientific technology became the authority on life, and psychiatry our moral cornerstone. It's contended that people cling onto religion and spiritualism, because like a balm, it soothes existential panic and dread. Or maybe there's more to it. Maybe we've been led to believe this supposition?

It appears the universe has evolved to think about itself, at least through us, since it's innate to ask the Big Questions. Namely, where are we, what's the point, and what happens when we die. It seems we're predisposed to literally look up and wonder? Like, when we're not distracted, and on our own, away from the crowd, we look up to the expansive night sky and twinkling stars with earnest wonder. The core of us needs to know.

The world is so intoxicatingly beautiful, yet so evil, particularly behind the scenes. Indeed, life is like one big motion picture. We're part of the greatest show on Earth, but no-one's watching except us? Quantum physics however tells us someone is watching, as consciousness is part of the bigger picture. It's possible some ten year old kid is playing a computer game in his basement which conjures up our reality. We're living in a simulation?

We're 'educated', courtesy of the state, to believe that we're here because of a massive explosion that happened eons ago. An insane amount of energy appeared from nowhere, for no reason, despite the first rule of thermodynamics that states energy can't be created or destroyed. But like other important details, like the biogenesis law, that life can only come from existing life, we park these inconvenient truths.

So, from nothing, came everything. And we came from pond scum. Our brains, the most complex structure in the universe, evolved from goo. Incredibly sophisticated DNA codes randomly organised themselves. It's literally insane how many conditions are required for life, despite billions of years. It's statistically impossible. But miraculously we're here. It's noted, the God hypothesis remains off the table. Intelligent design is not accepted as an alternative scientific theory. So, we're either a happy or not so happy accident, depending on perspective.

We also apparently live on a spinning globe that circles the sun, and spins through the universe at insane speeds. Once the telescope established that no heaven was 'visible' around the solar system, the idea was superseded in mainstream science. Thus, it's purported there is no heaven up there or hell below us. John Lennon's song 'Imagine' embedded this idea in our minds, in addition to the seemingly noble aspiration for the world to live as 'One'. So, there is no God but there might be aliens?

It would appear that nothing is at it appears to be. Like, it doesn't feel like we're zipping through space, and surely it would be tricky for planes to land on a moving earth? And the sun appears to circle the earth, moving from east to west, like the moon. And the stars never change. Hence, they've been named since the beginning of time.

But moreover, as Bertrand Russell states, 'physicists assure us there is no such thing as matter, and psychologists assure us there is no such thing as mind' (cited in 'In Praise of Idleness', 1935 p.159-160). Atomic physics destroyed the illusion of matter, (since matter is largely empty space), and neuroscience destroyed the illusion of self and freewill. Mental activity is reduced to physical activity of the body. As it transpires, our brains choose our choice before the thought ever enters our mind. Consciousness appears to be some kind of by-product. This seems counterintuitive since we have an overwhelming sense that 'we' choose. So, we don't have a soul, and 'mind' is more of a concept.

Russell concedes this is an unprecedented occurrence, since back in the day, people believed they were a soul/mind. They were told that, but now we're told the diametric opposite, and we believe that? It's conveyed we're smarter now, more evolved than Neanderthals living in caves. Our science and technology is immense. Or maybe we're not smarter now. Maybe the ancients were smarter as they were closer to the truth than us? Hence, modern physics is now confirming the wisdom of cabala, Jewish mysticism, regarding the fact we live in a multidimensional universe. It would appear we're a subset of a far larger reality. And the ancients knew this. They were au fait with other dimensions.

We 'see' almost nothing, less than 1% of the electromagnetic spectrum (we only see visible light), which corroborates with the cabala that states we see 1% of reality and 99% is hidden. Science has created a religion, atheism, out of the observable, which is ironically couched in the unobservable, like dark matter and energy (which constitutes 95% of the universe).

Russell Di-Carlo (author) wrote, 'materialistically bound, traditional science assumes that anything that cannot be measured, tested in a laboratory, or probed by the five senses or their technological extensions simply doesn't exist. It's not 'real'. The consequence: all of reality has been collapsed into physical reality. Spiritual, or what I would call non-physical, dimensions of reality have been run out of town' (cited in Tolle, 2011 p.XVIII).

Scott Peck (1936-2005), psychiatrist and author, similarly said, 'The use of measurement has enabled science to make enormous strides in understanding the material universe. But by virtue of its success, measurement has become a kind of scientific tool. The result is an attitude on the part of many scientists of not mere scepticism but outright rejection of anything that cannot be measured. It is as if they were to say, "what we cannot measure, we cannot know; there is no point worrying about what we cannot know; therefore, what cannot be measured is unimportant and unworthy of investigation". Because of this attitude many scientists exclude from their serious consideration all matters that are – or seem to be – intangible. Including, of course, the matter of God' (Along the Road Less Travelled and Beyond, 1997 p.245).

The invisible world, (by its very nature), cannot be explained by science whose means of investigations are limited i.e. it can't be observed, weighed, measured. It's like the elephant in the room. Paul McKenna concedes, 'As so often in the realm of the paranormal, we find an unwillingness to accept what we do not understand'. And further, 'some of the most fascinating and mysterious secrets of our universe are being ignored by scientists for no better reason than that they do not fit with the current paradigm – the mindset of the scientific community' (p.63 and p.73). However, it seems this rhetoric is changing, with the advance of modern physics?

Nikola Tesla (1856-1943), scientific genius, said, 'The day science begins to study non-physical phenomena, it will make more progress in one decade than in all previous centuries of existence'. But moreover, Tesla admitted he was given inventions from the spirit world. He said on his deathbed, that he would leave a pad of paper and pen by his bedside, before he went to bed, and in the morning, inventions would be written down for him (not in his handwriting). So, that's weird? And it's also bemusing that the two most famous rocket scientists, Werner Von Braun and Hermann Oberth, claimed they 'were helped from people from other worlds'. It seems there are aliens?

Fundamentally, it seems we've been lied to. As Jonathan Black highlights, in his book 'The Secret History of the World' (2010), 'Could the very people who have done most to form today's scientifically orientated and materialistic world view secretly have believed something else? Newton, Kepler, Voltaire, Paine, Washington, Franklin, Tolstoy, Dostoyevsky, Edison, Wilde, Gandhi, Duchamp: could it be true that they were initiated into a secret tradition, taught to believe in the power of mind over matter and that they were able to communicate with incorporeal spirits?' (p.20)

But people are beginning to wake up? We're beginning to realise there's more going on than what we 'see'. Paracelsus (1493-1541), alchemical genius, said, 'anyone who peremptorily denies the existence of anything beyond the horizon of his understanding, because it doesn't harmonise with his or sciences accepted opinions, is arguably a slave to those opinions he has accepted'.

In the Bible, in Proverbs 18:13, we're told, 'He that answereth a matter before he heareth it, it is folly and shame unto him'. Like, how many people have an opinion on the Bible, yet they've never read it? This is not accidental siblings.

Einstein said, 'Condemnation without investigation is the height of ignorance'. He also said, 'Be a loner. That gives you time to wonder, to search for the truth. Have holy curiosity. Make your life worth living'.

Look up.

Child Abuse

'We are programmed to believe our presidents are men of honour, men of great integrity. Our presidents are rotten bastards – they are paedophiles, they are drug addicts, they practice high magic, they practice ritual. They think nothing of live sacrifice of children'. Cisco Wheeler (2009)

Introduction

My starting point is I want to know the truth. Like, are our leaders' haunted perverts that worship Satan? And who is God exactly, given the myriad conjectures. And who else is out there, doing the astral fandango on non-physical dimensions.

And respectively share this truth. Yet I have been consistently told (during my journey writing this book) that no-one cares. The sentiment seems to be that people don't care that they've been indoctrinated with lies about the most important aspects of life. They're happy to be distracted by facebook and football and soul-destroying soaps.

But we're not happy, as evidenced by depressing mental health statistics. It seems that in our vacant alpha state, we follow the script we've been given, coupled with our conditioned dopamine (feel-good brain chemical). We get a dopamine hit when 'EastEnders' plays its intro music. We're chuffed our favourite 'programme' is starting. And we get a hit knowing that 'our friends' on facebook 'like' the fact we're having macaroni and cheese for dinner.

But arguably more disconcerting, (and regardless of whether we're happy or not), is that we know we're being hoodwinked, as everybody knows? The cat is out the bag. Thus, we know we're programmed, hypnotically entranced, through the TV 'programmes' we watch daily. We know 'the news' supports governments and international corporations, because they have the same owners (the media is essentially a monopoly). In the US, news anchors literally read the same script.

And we know that much of 'the news' we receive is manufactured using advertising companies, who get nicely paid to manage our perception of events. Like the Rendon Group (PR firm), for example, was paid $23 million by the Central Intelligence Agency (CIA) to create anti-Saddam propaganda. Apparently after 9/11 PR became a $200 billion industry.

We know that propaganda is used to manipulate us into illegal wars for corporate gain, and governments use 'false flags' to surreptitiously set others up. Like, Hitler classically set fire to the Reichstag, his own government building, and blamed it on the communists. And in Operation Himmler, Nazis (dressed in Polish uniforms) faked attacks on their own people and resources and blamed the Poles as a pretext for starting WW2.

It's understood Hitler was a pioneer in the art of war, including terrorism. He recognised that 'fear of attack' (technique) scares us into trusting our governments to protect us, which enables them to achieve their political goals i.e. we support a war we would otherwise oppose. Hitler said, 'terrorism is the best political weapon for nothing drives people harder than the fear of sudden death'. Stalin conceded, 'the easiest way to gain control of a population is to carry out acts of terror. The public will clamour for such laws if their personal security is threatened'.

It's literally one big set up and they have the audacity to bang on about fake news. Like, in the early 1950s, Israeli agents planted bombs in several buildings in Egypt, including the US diplomatic facilities, then left behind 'evidence' implicating the Arabs as the culprits. They got caught when one of the bombs detonated prematurely, allowing the Egyptians to identify the bombers. Russian KGB apparently conducted a wave of bombings in Russia in order to justify war against Chechnya and put Vladimir Putin in power. And the Turkish government were caught bombing its own and blaming it on a rebel group to justify a crackdown on that group.

Or, like the Gulf of Tonkin incident in Vietnam, whereby US military alleged their US destroyers were fired upon by North Vietnamese (they weren't), to enable the most heinous atrocities, including the illegal use of Agent Orange. That was evil?

Lest we forget Operation Northwoods, the CIA plan to launch a wave of terrorist attacks on US soil (e.g. Washington DC, Miami), and blame Castro, to provide a pretext for invading Cuba. They proposed shooting innocent Americans on the streets, (with people being framed for crimes they didn't commit), sinking boats carrying refugees from Cuba, and blowing up a ship in Guantanamo Bay. Using phony evidence, all of it would be pinned on Castro. The idea was to trick people and the international community into war against him. But moreover, they also had elaborate plans for destroying US planes.

Like, the plan to stage a Cuban attack on a US Air Force plane, whereby the pilot, under a fake name, would report that he was under attack and then stop transmitting. He would then fly back to base, the plane would be repainted with a new number, and he would resume his real name. Wreckage would be presented to confirm it was a Cuban attack. Another plan was to fake an attack on a civilian plane carrying American college students. This plane would be replaced (intercepted) with a CIA drone, painted to look like the civilian plane. The drone would send out a distress signal that it was under attack by Cuba, and then get blown up. It's understood JFK wasn't up for this plan, and other insidious plans, hence he met his demise (courtesy of the CIA) with a magical bullet.

It's duly noted, the CIA invented the term 'conspiracy theorist', to undermine the credible questioners who were challenging the mainstream JFK Jackanory. And since then, anyone who challenges the mainstream account is labelled a conspiracy theorist. But we know mainstream is lame-stream, created by presstitutes. Hence, these are conspiracy facts. William Casey, former CIA director, notably said in the first staff meeting in 1981, 'We'll know our disinformation program is complete when everything the American public believes is false'. Say what?

So, we know that wars are by design, and we've maimed and killed untold millions for untold billions. And there's many ways to skin a cat, like training and funding terrorist groups, mercenaries, to use as a proxy war. Like the 'Bay of Pigs' fiasco in Cuba, whereby the CIA trained and funded a counter-revolutionary group to overthrow Castro, which failed miserably. Castro was like a cat with 600 lives (he apparently faced more than 600 assassination attempts).

And so it continues, that is, the removal of regimes contrary to global corporate interest. It's politics, and there's nothing new under the sun? Divide and conquer is the ultimate strategy. It bodes well to capitalise on differences including sectarian.

But then 9/11 landed, which changed everything. And unlike the aforementioned, the CIA weren't involved? But rather it was nineteen hijackers, radical Muslims who liked cocaine, strippers, and booze. And weirdly, at least seven of them are still alive. In his book 'The David Icke Guide to the Global Conspiracy' (2007) Icke states, 'No Arab names appear in the passenger lists issued by the airlines, but, within days of the attacks, the FBI were able to name nineteen hijackers and produce their photographs. Seven of these 'hijackers' have since been found to be still alive and yet the FBI has never changed its list of those it claims were responsible' (p.341). Like, apparently Mohammed Atta, the lead hijacker, phoned his dad the next day. So, he was one of the survivors?

And suffice to say, it's nothing short of ridiculous that the US President continued to listen to a story about a pet goat for half an hour (he was conveniently in a classroom in Florida), after being told America was under attack. And the book was upside down. He didn't seem surprised at all. The plan was underway?

The world knows about the cosy relationships between the Bin Laden family, the innermost circle of the Saudi royal family, and the Bush family, and the subsequent cosy profits. Lest we forget the mint made in American and United Airlines shares, as investors foreseen the share price would plummet. And the Pentagon's Budget Analysts office was conveniently destroyed, after Donald Rumsfeld announced $2.3 trillion was missing the day before. You couldn't make it up. The evidence overwhelmingly suggests we were lied to, as we were regarding the 'Weapons of Mass Destruction' (WMD) in Iraq. Indeed, does any rational person actually believe the official stories?

Bush was told (under no uncertain terms) Saddam Hussein had no WMD when he started in office in 2001 (after he seemingly fixed his win and got egged at his inauguration). But then, after 9/11 which had nothing to do with Saddam, we were told that within forty-five minutes we could all be on chemical Shit Street. Propaganda enabled us to annihilate Iraq.

And we know that Dr David Kelly, UN weapons inspector, didn't top himself. After telling Her Majesty's Government there were no WMD in Iraq, he told David Broucher, a former British Ambassador, 'I will probably be found dead in the woods'. And he was. Not dissimilar to Princess Diana, who predicted she'd be bumped off in a car crash. And she was.

It's noted, Hitler is often quoted for saying, 'if you tell a big enough lie and tell it frequently enough, it will be believed'. Vladimir Lenin conceded, 'a lie told often enough becomes the truth'. Like, the terms 'terrorism' and '9/11' on repeat on 'the news'? Repetition is the most basic form of mind control.

So, we know 9/11 was far less about Islam and much more about American hegemony. As Russell Brand (2014) highlights, 'what is irrefutable is that America has a long history of carrying out invasions to impose the will of its corporate clientele' (p.312). In his book '9-11' (2001), Noam Chomsky said, 'the US itself is a leading terrorist state', and in 2013 he said, 'Obama, first of all, is running the biggest terrorist operation that exists, maybe in history'. He also said, 'when foreign policy refers to a situation as stable, its technical meaning is that it's firmly under US control'.

It's notably an uncomfortable irony that the west has been outraged by public beheadings, since this is common practice in Saudi Arabia, our ally in the 'War on Terror'. The severed head is usually sewn back on, and sometimes crucifixion is ordered for public displaying of the beheaded body. According to the UN, beheading is prohibited under International Law under all circumstances, and yet Saudi Arabia is a member of the UN's Human Rights Council. It's also noted, whilst the 9/11 hijackers were largely Saudi Arabian, Saudi Arabia wasn't on the radar unlike other Arab nations.

And we know the 'War on Terror', which includes 'rogue countries' and 'invisible enemies' like biological warfare (manufactured diseases), doesn't end until they achieve their stated globalist Big Brother goal. Namely, the infamous New World Order (NWO). The global government, with one army or global militarised police, one economy, and one cashless currency linked to a centralised bank via a chip. The UN New World Order project, founded in 2008, aims to achieve its global goals by 2030.

Rumour has it that we're destined to become micro-chipped zombies of the state, and we'll love our servitude. It's said that after 9/11 George Orwell's dystopian '1984' was realised, as surveillance replaced privacy. Like, we know everything we do is recorded e.g. our phone calls, emails, purchases, internet searches, location. It's understood China provides the blueprint for the NWO, in terms of its insane surveillance and authoritarian control.

However, it's also purported that our tyrannical NWO will arise like a phoenix from the ashes of WW3. And further, as outlined by HG Wells, in his book 'The New World Order' (1940), the global government is couched in a secular global religion. Thus, 'conspiracy theorists' predictions mirror what the Bible tells us about the beast system in the 'end times'. We're forewarned about the One World Order, and that we'll need to take the 'mark of the beast' (RFID chip?) in order to buy or sell.

Evil follows biblical prophecy to the letter. Like, we're told Israel would return home in the end times, and this was achieved by WW2. No-one cared about the Jews having a national home until the horrors of the holocaust. This in turn creates chaos in the Middle East, which precipitates WW3, the premise for the NWO. So, God has prepped His people about the order of events. And now we're watching it unfold?

But furthermore, the Bible tells us the antichrist will rule from the third temple in Jerusalem. He will declare himself to be God and mandate that all worship him. The NWO is thus both political and spiritual. And the world needs to be ready for this charmer. We need to be 'enlightened' to know that Lucifer is God. Thus, there's a reason we're being programmed to migrate towards Hinduism and Buddhism, to like yoga and have Buddha statues in our garden. There's a reason Hellywood endorses the cabala. Hellywood also serves to distract us. In Roman times, the herd were placated with bread and circuses, and today it's TV and pizza.

But maybe we should care that society is hiding God, and Satanists rule the world. Noam Chomsky said, 'The general population doesn't know what is happening, and it doesn't even know that it doesn't know'. Or maybe it doesn't care, as it's too subdued in its alpha state?

'Truthers' speak about when they woke up and realised what's really going on. It's like being born again into truth. But it's highlighted there's degrees of being awake. Thus, people might accept that intelligence agencies execute the deep state's nefarious agenda, but the idea that the puppeteers sexually abuse and sacrifice kids to Satan is too much of a stretch? Like, the notorious Bush family and the royals? The idea that they worship Lucifer, disguised by a Christian front, is too outlandish.

And yet the Luciferians have publicised their beliefs and agenda. Like, in 1888 Helena Blavatsky, dubbed grandmother of the New Age, published 'The Secret Doctrine'. She revealed the Luciferian doctrine, which had been concealed for millennia in secret societies and mystery schools. So, we know. In Mark 4:22 Jesus said, 'For everything that is hidden will eventually be brought into the open, and every secret will be brought to light'.

Hitler endorsed Blavatsky's teachings, which corroborates with the Masonic teaching, that Lucifer is God (Blavatsky was an honorary 33rd degree mason). And this is the religion of the UN, the steppingstone to global government. Moreover, Luciferians are actively chanting for their messiah Maitreya to come (see UN website). That is, the antichrist?

In short, we know that Hitler didn't lose WW2 but rather the Third Reich went underground and became the Fourth Reich. We also know that Hitler didn't commit suicide in a bunker in Berlin in 1945, as CIA files revealed they were looking for him in South America in 1955. However, at the time of investigation, Hitler could no longer be prosecuted as a war criminal because it had been ten years since the end of WW2.

Whilst it's generally understood that a bunch of Nazis, including Hitler, went to South America and Antarctica, we know top Nazi scientists and engineers (1,600 and their families) were snaffled into the US under Operation Paperclip after WW2. Not long after this, the CIA was created in 1947, and then NASA aka Never A Straight Answer, and then DARPA came into being in 1958. DARPA, the Defense Advanced Research Projects Agency, develops technology for the military. A lot has happened since WW2. The plan is ramping up.

I started writing this book, affectionately but frustratingly known as 'the never-ending story', to address the mind and the reality of the spirit world. But just like the next person, I've gone down the proverbial rabbit hole. Hence, the book is massive, and hence there's two parts. The first part is contentiously normal.

Thus, we question 'what's the point?', as we reflect on modern lifestyles, if there is no point. We consider existentialism (a philosophy of existence), which insists on authentically thinking for ourselves. The herd or crowd is held in contempt for not thinking. We consider the prospect of soul survival, and also mental health, since society is literally swimming in psychiatric theories. We then consider the curious unconscious, altered states of consciousness, the reality of non-physical (spiritual) dimensions, and witchcraft. The mind is the common thread that links the chapters. Part 1 is the foundation for Part 2. I pray that you can bear with me, as it can be quite the snore at times.

Then in Part 2, it gets infinitely more interesting, as we consider what's really going on. And the bemusing part is God's word seems true. It appears there really is a battle between good and evil, between God and His angels, and the Devil and his minions, and it's being played out on our turf.

As it transpires, the truth is stranger than fiction. And the greatest trick the Devil ever pulled was convincing the world he doesn't exist. Life really is this insane. Depending on how awake the reader is, will correlate to how life changing this book is. So, buckle up and enjoy the ride.

PS. Brazilian author Paulo Coelho said, 'writing reveals the personality', so I hope I don't offend you with mine. Ever so candidly, and in line with existentialism, I merely call a spade a spade.

PART 1

'Choose Life. Choose a job. Choose a career. Choose a family. Choose a fucking big television, choose washing machines, cars, compact disc players and electrical tin openers. Choose good health, low cholesterol, and dental insurance. Choose fixed interest mortgage repayments. Choose a starter home. Choose your friends. Choose leisurewear and matching luggage. Choose a three-piece suite on hire purchase in a range of fucking fabrics. Choose DIY and wondering who the fuck you are on a Sunday morning. Choose sitting on that couch watching mind-numbing, spirit-crushing game shows, stuffing fucking junk food into your mouth. Choose rotting away at the end of it all, pishing your last in a miserable home, nothing more than an embarrassment to the selfish, fucked up brats you spawned to replace yourselves. Choose your future. Choose life...'

Irvine Welsh, 'Trainspotting' (1993)

'We are born naked, wet and hungry. Then things get worse'. (Chinese proverb)

1

What's the Point?

We could argue there is none. Apparently 80% of people in the UK believe life has no meaning or point. But we all get here at some stage. It's just a matter of time and it would be egocentric to suggest otherwise. As highlighted in 'Trainspotting', we live this life, do DIY on a Sunday, buy, for the most part, unnecessary material clobber, replicate a couple of brats to replace ourselves, before pissing out our last in a miserable nursing home. And sweet like a lemon for the dodgers (the workshy), the nursing home is the same irrespective of whether we've worked all our days or not. And yes, the 'waiting place', if we make it there, truly sucks. What a way to spend our 'last days'. In a honking home complete with a bunch of strangers who have deteriorating mental and physical capacities. And the 'care' can be shocking. Perhaps carers should be motivated beyond inherent decency (minimum wage) to want to wipe someone else's arse?

We check out our stars for a glimmer of hope in our otherwise mundane lives, and then worse is looking up to pointless stars for direction. Like, glamour model Katie Price (the 'Pricey'), iconic or symbolic of contemporary British society, who was reported saying at a press conference in 2012, 'I f****d Alex up the a**e with a vodka bottle'. Apparently, her ex-husband Alex Reid, who's alter-ego is Roxanne, can't get enough up there (LOL). Lovely, the Pride of Britain. We seem to adulate the beautiful and dirty rich. Like, Kim Kardashian, who became a household name after her sex-tape was conveniently leaked. We want to be them? We want to be WAGS? Presumably, the suffragettes are turning in their graves.

So, 'Choose Life', but what sense do we make in post-modern post-Christian Britain? Russell Brand (2014) said, 'In the United Kingdom, the Scottish want out, the Welsh want out, even the English want nothing to do with it' (p.274). What does that say, bugger the Queen and the political system? Lest we forget, the west is the best.

Not to bring on the 'doom factor', but who hasn't flirted with the idea of not being here. For most of us, it's school, work, pension, death. We're told the two sure things in life are death and taxes. The latter is however dodged by the dodgers, which includes the high rolling bigwigs. We're brainwashed into being fear abiding consumers. Cancer lurks round the corner for us all, as do mental health problems. Apparently the 21st century is the Age of Paranoia, or is it me?

Depression, anxiety, substance misuse, and Attention Deficit Hyperactivity Disorder (ADHD) for kids, are particularly prevalent. We're told that 1:4 adults have a mental health problem (1:6 are diagnosed with depression), and 1:8 young people have a mental health problem. Estimates vary, but research suggests that

20% of children have a mental health problem in any given year, and about 10% at any one time. Perhaps, (unlike cancer), mental health problems contain some kind of contagion? It can however always be worse. Like in America, 70% of adults are on prescription drugs and even more kids have ADHD. It's normal to be 'sick'?

Indecision is also symptomatic of the 21st century. It's said we have too many choices. Douglas Coupland, in his book 'Generation X' (1991), pertains to 'option paralysis' to refer to the tendency, when given unlimited choices, to make none (p.161). Coupland notably coined the term Generation X to refer to overeducated underachievers born 1965-1980. We came after the post-war baby boomers, and unlike the baby boomers, we're workshy. It's highlighted that self-obsessed millennials, the so-called 'snowflake generation', are even more feckless and scared of hard graft.

We're told people are stressed out. Statistics speak volumes. Many of us are not happy campers, but rather huge discontentment is commonplace in society. Indeed, there's no shortage of depressed, confused and crazy people out there. Prisons are bursting at the seams and schools can be shocking places. It's shocking that schools need to have metal detectors and police onsite? And kids have sex in the toilets, and take illegal drugs?

It's only taken one generation (seventy years) for society to change from god-fearing to self-pleasing. So, we'll look at modern lifestyles, and how we got here. This unavoidably leads to ethical issues, including addictions. The government insists more mental health services are vital, but treating symptoms is not treating the cause. It seems society and 'the system' are funky? Fortunately however, most people follow the script they've been given. They play the prescribed roles. Like, pay our taxes and abide by the law. Thus, the following is a Generation X reflection on the social problems the system highlights.

It's said the feral culture began circa 1997, which includes our knife culture, and the birth of ladettes. Thus, cheers to the Spice Girls for girl power, as girls equally take no prisoners. Apparently female direct aggression increased to match males, and we match male stamina and bravado. We've become more aggressive, out of control, with debt maxed, disordered eating, a heavy ladette drinking and drugs culture, complete with casual sex. And we've become sexual predators like men, because it's all awesome?

The rise in female crime is associated with the liberalisation of women. There is no difference between men and women. We all please ourselves. Indeed, it's said we're living in a 'Me' generation, a culture of narcissism. And that our moral values are in decline, which includes manners, the building blocks of civilised society. Or perhaps our moral consideration depends upon the neighbourhood we're from?

It seems our Generation X-rated ways of being have been infectious. Since the early 1990s, drink, drugs, obesity, and violence has increased. We're party to a drink and drugs epidemic. In 2004 Tony Blair called alcoholism the 'new British disease'. There was a 40% increase in binge drinking from 1995-2004. There's more knife crimes and drunken fuelled violence, and we're choked up with social problems.

Resources such as A&E services, ambulance services, social work and police are massively drained by problems associated with drink, drugs, and aggression. It's said there's an epidemic of violence in the UK. Every minute assault is reported to the cops. 999 calls doubled from 1989-1999, and doubled again the followed decade from 1999-2009, largely as a result of antisocial behaviour and binge drinking. Suffice to say, how demoralising and oppressive for the workers who have to suck-up ('tolerate') abusive behaviour on a daily basis.

So, it seems society's unruly behaviour is much the same today. The same shady antics roll on. Anti-Social Behavioural Orders (ASBOs) continue to be seen as a badge of honour, like getting street cred from the number of times spent inside. And it's a small joke that 60% of ASBOs are violated, and prisons are equally ineffective. It's understood that prisons don't rehabilitate people, but rather effectively spread the offending disease among inmates.

In essence, there's no shame in not giving a rat's ass. It's a given. This was epitomised by the England riots in 2011, when the youth of today went on a rampage. There was no ideology per se, other than feck em and get yourself some designer threads. It's said this antisocial behaviour is underpinned by cultural factors like criminality, hooliganism, breakdown of social morality, and gang culture. But it can equally be understood as precipitated by increasing inequality and financial divergence?

Or perhaps life is increasingly forbidding, as reflected in the nation's deteriorating mental health. Or are doctors better at diagnosing 'illness'? It seems the most notable difference today is the mobile phone addiction (social media) and the explosion of transgenderism and sexual fluidity. Sexual orientation/identity is no longer innate and unchangeable. Like, singer Sam Smith, for example, identifies as Non-Binary Gender Queer. Sometimes he feels like a man, and sometimes he feels like a woman. And that's okay. It seems we're obsessed with our identity.

It's also noted, that the paradox of self and society, (however sick, dysfunctional and miserable), is that we both shape and are shaped by it. Or maybe it's by design? Maybe we've been programmed to think the way we do?

Record numbers are depressed, and depression remains the World Health Organisation's (WHO) biggest concern. Millions are on antidepressants at a cost of hundreds of millions every year. But perhaps we can wonder if 'medical' doctors are qualified and equipped to prescribe regarding the mind and not organic illness? We hear about 'chemical imbalances', but it's not that straight forward with mental health, as thoughts affect the brain, and there is no disease as such.

And with regards to ADHD, as we'll get to when we address mental health, apparently Dr Leon Eisenberg, the scientific father of ADHD, said on his deathbed, 'ADHD is a prime example of a fictitious disease'. Unbelievable. Like depression, ADHD is a multibillion-dollar industry.

Back in the day, we used to go to the doctor when we were physically unwell, but increasingly we attend for mental relief. We need something to help alleviate our morbid thoughts and feelings of sheer desperation. Suicidal thoughts seep into our mind like poisonous tendrils. But why are so many of us not okay, and flirting heavily with checking out?

More than a million people die by suicide every year, making it the 10th leading cause of death worldwide. Up to 90% of people who commit suicide have a mental health problem. Alcoholics and 'the depressed' are most at risk. But moreover, a WHO report (2012) revealed that in the last 45 years suicide rates have increased by 60% worldwide. Chinese women are notably killing themselves at an astronomical rate, some 500 daily.

On our own soil, suicide is the number one cause of death for men under 45 (the most common method is hanging). Apparently, someone successfully commits suicide in the UK every one-two hours. Suicide attempts are up to twenty times more frequent than completed suicide. Apparently, women are three times more likely to attempt suicide, but men are three times more likely to succeed. And twice as many women are prescribed antidepressants, which helps? Or maybe not, as suicidal thoughts are a side-effect of these drugs. Increasing numbers of kids also have 'suicidal ideation'.

It's noted, that should we require any support, there's 'chatting to death' internet sites. These pro-suicide chatrooms enable remote strangers to encourage each other to take the fatal plunge. It seems ironic that this provides solace. There's also websites offering tips on how to top our self, suicide manuals, and we can even purchase 'death in a bag' online. The latter is a jiffy bag that contains a suicide kit, and the promise of 'painless deliverance'. All we need is £50 and a photocopy of our passport (no proof of terminal illness or psychiatric assessment is required).

And how sad, that some two hundred funerals (in the UK) go unattended every month. People are decomposing for however long, until the smell catches on. The irony of desperate loneliness amid billions is second to none. It's said we're living in the 'Age of Loneliness'. There's an epidemic of loneliness in Britain, (the UK is the loneliness capital of Europe), and this silent illness is killing us.

Apparently, doctors have quantified the effects of the 'loneliness disease', warning that lonely people are twice as likely to die prematurely as those who do not suffer feelings of isolation. The dramatic consequences on health include disrupted sleep, raised blood pressure, lower immunity, depression, lower overall subjective wellbeing, increased heart and stroke risk. It's apparently more worrying for our health than obesity. And it's as bad as badass smoking.

It seems many of us don't care about being here, and it would appear many don't care if we are either. As my friend says, if we could click our fingers and die, how many would be here? It's easy to kill ourselves, if we really want to, but it's not that easy, which depending on perspective, is just as well? But that would constitute an existential crisis, having necked two hundred pills and wondering if we've made the right decision. Not dissimilar from having surgically changed gender, and thinking, 'whoops', wrong move? 'Sex change regret' is notably not uncommon.

But how awful, having genuinely attempted not to be here, only to wake up in a hospital ward because 'we care' in Britain. Or maybe that's not strictly true, as many A&E staff get exasperated with the same punters (the same troubled souls) coming through the revolving door having attempted to check out. It's the same for those perpetually seeking medical attention having self-harmed. It's said we're 'disorder culture'.

Valium aka vallies (Diazepam, a benzodiazepine) were 'mother's little helper' in the seventies since its work, cook, clean, and the same again. As Jack Nicholson said in 'The Witches of Eastwick' (1987), 'there's always more dishes to do tomorrow'. 'Meds' kept her sane, as they placated her life force that screamed there must be more to living than this. Valium was launched in 1968 and by 1978 it was the best-selling pharmaceutical in the world, (which was sweet for shareholders, like having shares in Viagra when that exploded onto the market). They were marketed for anxiety, as daytime sedatives and sleeping pills, but the covert subtext was a 'cure for all life's discomforts'.

However, whilst America seemed less worried about the mass tranquilisation of society, (shockers), there was a backlash in conservative Britain and 'zonked out' mamas became an issue for the women's movement. Stepford wives indeed. These pills were not prescribed to treat an abnormal state of mind but rather to neutralise a women's complaint about her life-space. It seems the issue at hand, is whether being subdued and *comfortably numb* is immoral?

As it transpired, it was all good until it wasn't. People began to complain that they were robbed of normal emotions during drugged up years. They felt like they'd been 'living in cotton-wool'. Hence, the negative image of doctors that began to circulate as 'pill pushers'. And hence, the subsequent Benzodiazepine Act which provided grounds to sue doctors for negligence i.e. careless prescribing.

Perhaps it's more about choice. That is, those who had no choice but to take these meds for their 'life-space illness', felt cheated, compared to those who knew the script but wanted the drugs. Perhaps the doctors and patients could have played a better game i.e. doctor in the role of drug-dealer, offering this medication, and it's the patient's choice. Because the result has been that the complainers have spoiled it for the rest of us.

It's also noted, that besides being mega addictive, because life's considerably nicer with Valium, this 'medication' didn't cure anxiety. One has to keep popping the pills or the anxiety rebounds, and with a vengeance. The symptoms the drug was supposed to make better, got worse. They're not like antibiotics that cure an illness. So, perhaps it's better for desperate housewives to take antidepressants instead?

But equally, is work so joyous (it's rhetorical). If it didn't suck, phoning in sick wouldn't be so tempting. We're 'sick note generation' and cost the taxpayer billions. Working Dolly Parton's *9-5* is overrated and equates to Groundhog-Day, with the light at the end of the tunnel being retirement and pensions[1]. You blink and you miss the weekend and then it's back to work. A good day at work passes 'quickly', which effectively means we're wishing our life away. Living for the weekends and again blink, where's it gone? Holidays aka jolly-days are the same. You know you've been on holiday given the remnants of a tan and perhaps a souvenir or three. But a few days back at work and you're really questioning if you've been away. It feels like a dream or mirage.

Albeit it would appear our 'Brits abroad' Kodak moments, make life worth living. Such evidence can then be flaunted on facebook and other social plugs (extension of the ego). We like to let others know we're having a good time. It's duly noted, the 'selfie' craze further highlights our narcissism, and then there's belfies (bum selfies), LOL. Suffice to say, the impressions we endeavour to create are sculpted and well-crafted. And everyone 'likes' the 'likes', otherwise, why do it? As the more 'likes' we get suggests we're liked more? As mentioned, we get a dopamine kick, hence it's addictive. So, we've been socially engineered to become narcissists? Social media has also revealed there's a lot of nasty bastardos 'out there', as evidenced by vitriolic forums.

It's noted however, that fake-book, as my friend calls it, is not for everyone (only three billion of us). As it transpires, looking at others' seemingly awesome lives can make us feel crap about our own comparatively sad lives. It seems we're happy for others, if we're on the same happy page, but if we're not, why would we want to see others doing what we'd like to be doing? It makes us feel worse because their photos, 'happy faces', rub it in? It also goes without saying that no good can come from spying on others. It's surely a form of self-harm? I've heard there's rehab for it (LOL).

A study at the University of Salford found that 50% of social media users believed social networking had a negative effect on their lives and was damaging for self-esteem. Depression, and increased anxiety and guilt were common side effects of social networking. It's mental, (pun intended), that 'facebook depression' and 'social media depression' are actual terms. So, we give ourselves depression? It's also understood that DARPA

---

[1] The movie Groundhog Day, starring Bill Murray, entails him reliving the same day every day. Every day starts at 6am with the same song on the clock radio.

(who created the internet) created facebook, and the CIA gave it to Mark Suckerberg to sensor us. We hand them all our personal information on a plate, complete with 'happy faces'.

So, we work, even if it does entail having a face like a bag of spanners, because (in the absence of having a rich spouse or parent), we have to. And also if we value holidays, as generally speaking, people can't afford holidays on benefits. But it seems for the vast majority we'd rather not work. Polls consistently highlight that 80-90% hate their job. Whilst it would seem the trick is to secure employment that we like, perhaps even the best job would still be less than ideal, as it still equates to work and is therefore intrinsically distasteful.

So, whilst not undermining those who actually like their work, it seems that for average Jo Munter, it's about clinging to our lottery ticket with desperate hope that we can escape the drudge. And yet studies have revealed that having won the lottery, baseline happiness returns to normal after a year. Thus, the cliché that money doesn't make us happy is true.

It seems that both working and not working gives us the pip, but not working is better? It seems that once we get over the ambition/career lark (and/or take up drugs including pharmaceuticals), and realise that 'everything is meaningless says the teacher' (says King Solomon, allegedly the wisest man ever), who cares? It would appear 'pride' in work has been replaced by apathy? But someone has to work, and someone has to care.

Hence, the injustice of paying taxes no-end so the great unwashed can take it even easier and watch daytime drivel on their massive TV's. Or bask in the sun with tins of cider. This crack has not been received well by taxpayers for a long time. Indeed, the dodgers on 'Benefits Street', who exhibit no desire to work and resort to shoplifting, get on the taxpayer's goat. God's commandment, 'thou shalt not steal', is clearly disregarded, as shoplifting is one of Britain's most common crimes. Apparently, a theft takes place every ten seconds, with eleven thousand crimes committed every day, and four million offences every year. Apparently, Britain has the most shoplifters in Europe, and the most NEDS. It seems we've historically been trendsetters, as NEDS are catching on worldwide.

As it transpired however, the 'glory days' for shaders conveying disability were over after the economic crash of 2008. No good can come from the 'fit test' replacing the 'sick test', and the billions cut in disability benefits (circa 2012). My good friend was on benefits for more than twenty years, and now he only has hustling for a living. It's also noted, that whilst the government refuted allegations that they introduced sanctions, apparently sanctions were applied, like 80% of disabled people had to get back to work. On the surface, the endeavour seemed to be about weeding out the genuine from the disingenuous, but both are caught in the net. Increased poverty is precipitating more suicides (people are doing away with themselves to escape poverty). Living on benefits is depressing.

It further has to be noted, that workshy Dee White and her merry wo/men did not cause the cutbacks and austerity measures. But rather, it seems we've been programmed to focus on the gangsters, to distract us from the real culprits, namely, the banksters. Hence, the numerous 'programmes' regarding so-called 'subsidy junkies' and 'benefit lovers'.

As Russell Brand (2014) highlights, 'Immigrants did not cause the financial crisis. Benefit cheats did not get multi-million dollar bonuses. Disability claimants did not knowingly fracture the planet's stability' (p.88). Greedy bankers made hundreds of billions in the run up to the 2008 crash, and then we reimbursed them with hundreds of billions to pay off their debt. We were explicitly told there would be 'cutbacks, closures, jobs will be lost'. Bankers were irresponsible, taking risky wagers, but it was our job to clean it up.

The government insists they don't want to leave a legacy of debt for future generations, but it seems our debt (circa £2 trillion) is by design, as we'll get to. It's also highlighted that the super-rich are getting richer, and the poor poorer. The robust middle class required for economic growth is being superseded by growing disparity between the rich and poor. And this is reflected in our changing landscapes i.e. our cities increasingly feature charity shops, pound-lands, and betting shops. It's said that if this trend continues, the super-rich will need super protection, as it's always possible we'll want to rob them. Cities and towns are also dying a commercial death, (an obscene amount of shops are closing every month), as people increasingly buy their goods online.

Following Margaret Thatcher's 'trickledown' monetarist economics from 1979, the middle class has been shrinking with the wealth going to the rich. President Ronald Regan employed the same model across the pond, to enhance the elite's money, so called Reaganomics. The trickledown theory is the idea that tax breaks and other economic benefits provided to businesses and upper income levels will inevitably benefit poorer members of society by improving society as a whole. Their cash trickles down to the rest of us. So, Maggie reduced tax from 83% to 60% for the wealthy, conveying that lower taxes would stimulate growth, but as it transpired after three decades of low taxes, the rich have doubled their income and the rest have stagnated. It's also pointed out that tax avoidance was Government policy.

With regards to the despairing situation of living on benefits, it seems the question is do we want to change our reality, and can we? Structuralism posits that the structures in society create us. That is, we're social products of the environments we live in (we'll get to this in the next chapter). But 'conservatively' it could be argued that social mobility is possible, given our opportunities, education and employment. Theoretically, we could live the American Dream. If we work hard enough, we will (eventually) reap the rewards?

Indeed, it could be argued, particularly from those living in poorer countries, that living in the UK equates to Willy Wonka's golden ticket. There's a reason economic migrants flock to our shores. Great Benefits Britain is the best. There's a huge safety-net for us all. Our basic needs are met, regardless. That is, regardless of having no beans to rub together, and an inability to contribute, we're housed, fed, clothed, educated, and receive quality health care which is 'free at the point of consumption'.

Our comprehensive welfare system ensures that we're looked after from cradle to grave. It was allegedly inspired by William Beveridge's revolutionary vision to 'slay the five giants', namely, Want, Disease, Ignorance, Squalor and Idleness. 'The Beveridge Report' (1942) was then implemented by the post-war Labour government in 1945. The system required full employment and steady economic growth. We would all contribute to the money pot and we would all benefit. It seemed too good to be true, but the truth is we don't all want to make an effort?

It's highlighted however, that it was foreseen the system would result in debt. David Icke explains that whilst 'on the surface' the report was admirable in many ways, it has created dependency (increasing debt) on the increasingly privatised welfare state. And further, that Beveridge was merely a figurehead, as the plan was conjured up by other political parties. Apparently, the phrase 'from the cradle to the grave' was Winston Churchill's (conservative). Thus, the system was not some nice Labour idea as we're led to believe. State assets are sold to reduce debt, and the result is we're at the mercy of private companies whose sole interest rests with share price and making mo money. Fundamentally, all paths lead to the banksters, as we'll get to.

However, it seemed like a good idea, and at that time people were more ethical? The 'system' was based on the nuclear family, where husbands worked and wives raised the children, and at a time when values and morals, including pride prevailed. People were on the same page. They had pulled together through the second ghastly world war, and there was community spirit. Hard work and honour were valued. Our grandparents and great grandparents gave a rat's ass (and bonus, we're not speaking German).

So, there was shame in not working, and there was no time to be depressed. At that time, there was a clear line between the sane and insane. And not wanting to be crazy kept people sane. Or at least acting sane, which equally works since its 'observable' behaviour that's medicalised and institutionalised. Homosexuality was illegal and considered a mental illness, so few campers were setting their tents up. Indeed, sodomy warranted the death penalty until 1861. And now, who doesn't like a stick in the mud? It's interesting to note, that lesbians weren't recognised, as the Sexual offences Act 1967 decriminalised homosexual acts in private between two men aged 21+, as only men could be gay. [LOL].

Society has thus changed considerably since the system was implemented, including the breakdown of families. Back in the day, broken families were largely unheard of, and now they're the norm. Marriage was a promise to live together 'til death do us part' but who cares if there is no God to judge. 'Science' (and wars) convinced us there is no God. Darwin assured us we came from monkeys, and Freud insisted that we're at the mercy of our sexual impulses.

Thus, forget duty, sacrifice and obligation if you want to be with someone else. The marriage certificate can be rendered a mere piece of paper. It's highlighted that weddings are pantomime not sacrament. Perhaps we can wonder what marriage means to people, besides ironic white dresses, and an expensive party? So, whilst divorce previously happened to the 'unlucky' few, it grew exponentially in the seventies (after laws made it easier), and now almost half of marriages end in divorce.

So, family breakdown landed, leaving lots of messed up kids in its wake. Emotional and behavioural problems doubled between 1974 and 1999. And so, it continues. 'Man deserts' notably refer to areas/neighbourhoods where more than 75% of kids are growing up without dads. 1:4 families in Britain have the father absent, which is more than the rest of Europe.

As mentioned, children are increasingly afflicted with mental health problems. And how sad, that a UNICEF study revealed that British kids are the unhappiest in Europe. Teenagers are in despair. Apparently, they're more damaged and unhappy than ever, with a reality that includes knives, drugs and alcohol. Nearly half of 16/17 years olds have suffered from depression, and wish they were someone else. And self-harming is through the roof.

It's highlighted the decline of extended families has also negatively impacted on kids in urban society. But it's equally noted that grandparents are increasingly looking after their grandchildren because the substance misusing parents are too useless. The dark side of family life thus includes violence, aggression, depression, and substance misuse. Its mental, parents batter their kids, and increasingly kids batter their parents. Apparently 1:10 parents are routinely battered by their offspring, which is mostly mums, as it's usually mums who are left to bring up the kids.

To cut the story short then, the family constellation 'the system' was based on has deviated from the American Dream. And it's contended the 'system' has undermined individual and family responsibilities. Take some parents who dump their kids outside social work departments refusing to look after them anymore. Unbelievable. They're their kids. Suffice to say, this is most nippy from a social worker's point of view, especially at 4:55pm on a Flyday. Apparently, a child is taken into care every fifteen minutes.

It seems we create problems for ourselves, or our social structures create problems for us. Like, substance misuse translates to mental health problems. A deviant lifestyle becomes a 'disease'. People become incapacitated and need help. Besides benefits, hundreds of millions of taxpayers hard earned cash is spent on drink and drug treatments, including rehab, which more often than not, doesn't work. It's said people change, when it's more painful to stay the same i.e. the payoffs not enough. Increasing numbers are dying from illegal drugs. Most deaths are due to opiates, like heroin, but cocaine deaths have doubled in the last three years.

It's also noted, that prisoner's aka cuff-bags secured compensation for going cold turkey in prison. In 2008 it was ruled that denying prisoners heroin and other drugs such as methadone to 'treat their addiction' was illegal. It's beautiful, insiders who couldn't get golden brown secured retribution from Gordon Brown. Chris Huhne (MP) said, 'some of these claims seem to be little more than a shameless cashing in on this country's compensation culture'. It's asserted that we're familiar with 'our rights', but less so our responsibilities.

It's also noted, that despite its fruitfulness compared to methadone programmes, outrage was expressed by the public at the prospect of providing free heroin for addicts. Taxpaying Brits thought, what gall? Like, in Sweden and Switzerland, for example, patients are administered heroin four times daily in health clinics. Bloods are regularly checked to ensure they're not taking additional substances, and the result is they're more likely to want to come off the drugs. Maybe it would become a chore going to the surgery four times a day, but you would for free heroin. Maybe there's a hint of reverse psychology involved, and even heroin can lose its sparkle? The NHS is now trying this strategy as a 'last resort' bid to combat the highest drug death rates in Europe.

Thus, with regards to structuralism and the great unwashed, it's argued 'the system' has effectively created our 'something for nothing' culture. It's contended we've created a dodgy underclass amid the paradigm of deserving and undeserving poor. The 'underclass' is characterised as feckless, unwilling to work, associated with lone parenthood and crime. It's also noted however, that politicians inadvertently (?) created sickness to mask unemployment figures back in the day. They 'figured' it looked better for people to be sick, than unemployed.

Perhaps we've come full circle to the question of who actually wants to work (alarm clocks are dreadful, and it's worse when it's freezing). My social worker friend regards being a 'Job Seeker' as a rite of passage. And whilst we can milk it, we have to work eventually? As for those caught in the so-called poverty-trap, (rational but not necessarily ethical people), where's the incentive to get out of bed and work our ass-cheeks off for buttons, when we can get by on benefits and watch daytime TV? As Scott Peck asserts, 'we're innately lazy'.

And whilst someone has to do it, work can make us sick e.g. stress, backache, anxiety, dread. And there's lack of motivation (laziness?), apathy, despondency, no will to live, which is illness. Maybe some people are allergic to work, or we have a phobia?

In the Bible, Thessalonians 3:19, we're told '…we gave you this rule: "The one who is unwilling to work shall not eat"'. And Proverbs 6:6 states, 'Take a lesson from the ants you lazybones – learn from their ways and be wise! Even though they have no prince, governor or ruler to make them work, they labour hard all summer, gathering food for the winter. But you lazybones, how long will you sleep? When will you wake up?' King Solomon notably wrote Proverbs. He also wrote, in Proverbs 26:13, 'The lazy person is full of excuses, saying 'I can't go outside because there might be a lion on the road! Yes, I'm sure there is a lion out there'.

We've arguably had it all on a plate, and taken it for granted? Some of us literally haven't had to work for anything. Like, our free education, which some might chop off their right arm for, and yet we don't seem to care that much? As stated, schools can be shocking places. It remains to be seen that truanting is still cool, and being impudent and threatening to teachers. Drugs are more prevalent, and kids are more sexualised. They know anal is better as there's no chance of pregnancy. Maybe if we had to pay for education, we'd make more of an effort?

Or take our free health care. Maybe if we had to pay for it (beyond general taxation) we would take greater care of our health? We might be less inclined to smoke, drink, eat excessive pies, take drugs, and get into fights that require patching up? We know the consequences of lifestyle choices, because we're educated, and still we choose to harm our health. Our fag packets are a constant reminder that 'smoking kills'. But then we rationalise that life kills, as we all get a one-way ticket.

Maybe our carefree or careless attitude is because the NHS is always there to fall back on, should the proverbial s-h-i-t hit the fan? Not that triple bypasses or liver transplants sound like a hoot, but we're pro-instant gratification, not delayed. Our lack of respect for our beloved NHS is also evidenced by the millions wasted on missed NHS appointments, and meds. It's estimated that each year £100-£800 million worth of dispensed NHS medicines go unused and are ultimately discarded. Maybe if we had to pay for our appointments, we would turn up. The same applies to other services, like counselling. And maybe if we had to pay for our meds, we wouldn't waste them?

Benefits Street does however go somewhere in progressing community spirit, as there's a sense of belonging. We're on the same 'looked after' page, and know where to get cheap fish and trainers (and drugs). Or we can fulfil the American Dream? Perhaps we have a margin of freedom within the structures imposed upon us. And whilst it's considerably less likely, (since the 7% of those who attend fee-paying schools become 70/80% of the highest earners), some do triumph through adversity, including dodgy neighbourhood, school and family. They're driven. Their life-force compels them? Maybe we need a purpose beyond our next deal?

So, besides mental health problems, or part of it, substances are quite the feature of modern lifestyles. Thus, unlike those who take life right on the chin, including my mum (single sober parent who worked fulltime to provide for my brother and I), there's the rest of us who anesthetise ourselves to some extent through life. But seriously, how many would be up for living in the absence of antidepressants and other mood-altering drugs, including a wine or three, that alleviate everyday living. On the contrary, as John Lennon sang, *'whatever gets you thru the night, it's alright'.*

Albeit drink to good health my arse. Drink to liver cirrhosis, sweating, shaking, convulsions, insomnia, throwing up bile if nothing else, feeling doomed up, anxiety and dodgy guts. All booze-bags (me included) know about the squits. When I was alcohol counselling, clients often phoned up to cancel their appointment because they couldn't get off the toilet. On one occasion, an angry client phoned up, (a so-called 'crisis call'), ranting on about how she shit in a vase and broke it, which resulted in slashing her arse and a trip to A&E, and did I know what that was like?

There's record numbers drinking themselves to death. More than 30,000 people die from alcoholism every year and alcohol misuse costs the NHS circa £3 billion a year. According to government statistics, most people drink, and many (75-80%) drink too much. 1.4 million are registered as alcohol dependent, and more than eight million are binge drinkers. It seems we like to slurp our prescribed weekly (14-21) units in one sitting, and have next week's allowance.

As touched on, women are drinking more than ever. Alas the rise in ADHD behaviour? ADHD is symptomatic of Foetal Alcohol Spectrum Disorder (FASD). It's understood that mum's who drink during pregnancy fry their baby's brain, and as a result kids have varying degrees of physical, mental and intellectual impairment. It's the same with drugs (alcohol is a drug), but alcohol's the worst.

And suffice to say, no good can come from smoking. Besides yellow teeth, ming breath, coughing up chunks of phlegm, and breathing problems, there's amputations, cancer, strokes etc. It costs the NHS £2 billion for smoking related illnesses. In fairness however, it seems boozers and smokers (unlike drug users) pay for their healthcare through tax. 80% of the price of a packet of cigarettes consists of taxation. Thus, whilst we're advised not to smoke, and drink small units, it's fortuitous that we scaffold the NHS?

Besides legal drugs (like alcohol, caffeine and nicotine), and what we can procure from our GPs, our favourite recreational drugs are cannabis, cocaine, ecstasy, poppers, amphetamines, and ketamine, which is a horse tranquilliser. [Poppers (amyl-nitrate), a muscle relaxant, help expand the anus, for those partial to the anal canal]. But there's literally thousands of different drugs, for myriad different experiences (we're spoiled for choice). We pay for particular moods/feelings i.e. hallucinogens, stimulants, euphoric, emotional, spiritual, concentration. Whilst cannabis is our favourite recreational drug in the UK and worldwide, ecstasy has been one of the most popular party drugs since the 1980s (use was the highest in the UK and US in the late 1990s and early 2000s).

Pills are like Pringles, once you pop, you can't stop. As Voltaire (French philosopher) infamously said, 'the superfluous, a very necessary thing'. Describing ecstasy, in his book Ecstasy, Irvine Welsh wrote 'I didn't seem to walk but to float within my own mystical aura. It was like I knew everybody though, all those strangers. We shared an insight and intimacy that nobody who hadn't done this in this environment could ever know about. It was like we were altogether in our own world, a world far away from hate and fear.' Taking crack and heroin however, seems to up the ante. Heroin is commonly described as the best 'feeling' in the world. So, it's probably wise not to take it, as we'll probably want to take it again, and again?

Whilst heroin used to be cool, like in the US in the sixties, these days it tends to be associated with deprivation. We don't regard heroin users as cool jazz cats, but rather 'junkies' (which notably comes from Americans selling their junk metal to pay for heroin). Volatile Substance Misuse aka buzzing is similarly associated with deprived areas. Apparently 1:5 teenagers have experimented with this. It's the most common form of substance misuse among eleven/twelve year olds, and second only to cannabis by age fifteen (apparently the average kid tries puff aged thirteen). My friend used to regularly conk out when we did this. Its madness, people die instantly (at least one a week).

'Experimentation' typifies teenagers, and evidently, we aspire to be *in with the in-crowd'*. Ergo we do what everyone else is doing? So, in terms of structuralism, we arguably choose our choice but the 'structures' in society signpost that drugs are cool. And we all want to be cool, because it's cool to be cool. Indeed, my chum's mantra was '2 COOL 4U' (LOL).

It's thus noted, that drugs are embedded within a cultural context which gives meaning, and they're tied in with personal image, identity and peer association. Take cannabis, for example, which became illegal in 1928, and which achieved cult status in the sixties, as reflected by popular culture and music etc. Millions have tried puff and habitual smokers have increased more than 1000% since the 1970s. The message is that cannabis is cool. Like, Snoop Dogg loves to smoke weed, and he's cool? And crack is also cool?

Suffice to say, rising materialism and the cult of celebrity further contribute to an erosion of children's values and morals. But who cares what others think, given 'in group' respect, where groups validate and affirm our values and beliefs. It seems drugs are glamorised, inspired by those we idolise, and going to the toilet to powder our nose is fabulous? But moreover, there's a reason people take drugs. They're awesome? Paulo Mantegazza, who wrote a book on coca (1859), declared he would rather have ten years of a life on coca than a life of a million centuries without coca. It would appear people increasingly concur, as drug use continues to rise.

Russell Brand (2014) asserts, 'the War on Drugs has been lost. People like taking drugs and that's that...' (p.343). He observes that drug use among the young is extremely prevalent (p.264). My mate (the hustler) used to joke that he had a phobia about being straight, which used to seem funny in our twenties. But as it transpires, it's not funny in our forties, as he smokes heroin every day, and has done for years. He typifies the story of someone who had everything going for him e.g. looks, brains, personality, and agile like a cat.

In my mum's generation, a small proportion of people took drugs. It was for the most part deemed ethically wrong. Indeed, my mum remains shocked at the lack of inherent morality when it comes to taking drugs. And my friend's mum wonders why life is so intolerable that we 'need' to consume excessive drugs and alcohol. This is however ironic since she admits that she often feels like checking out (her son's lifestyle arguably doesn't help, but rather it's another problem in the mix).

Russell Brand (2014) asserts, 'drugs and alcohol are not our problem, reality is our problem; drugs and alcohol are our solution to that problem' (p.9). It seems life is better with drugs and alcohol? Substances offer a beautiful escape, from emotional pain to boredom, and they make nightclubs tolerable. Life's considerably more palatable with the edge removed.

And for teenagers, it's increasingly normal, as everyone's doing it. Well, not everyone, but a lot are. The cool people are. And also because, (through the lens of a teenager), we don't care? The law is overrated, and we're increasingly ambivalent about living or dying? Like many sex-workers using heroin claim they're past caring, and are prepared not to use a condom for extra cash. They say they don't care if they die. And the way to feel better is drink and drugs, hence the vicious cycle.

Psychiatry informs that many people with mental health problems are masked through self-medication, which means even more of us have issues. Evidence says depressed people are more likely to use alcohol, tobacco and drugs. Suffice to say, we can rationalise our habits, and self-medication is rational. Thus, why be miserable, if we can drown our sorrows and smoke them into oblivion (it's a no-brainer). Parties for one are arguably better than willing death. And yet we know, what goes up, must come down, and we'll feel worse when we come back to reality. Drink and drugs birth depression and anxiety. And we equally know that if we're depressed, or anxious, and we're using substances to cope, we need proper medical help? Thus, we're back to antidepressants?

Or even better, ketamine, which is regarded as a 'miracle cure' for depression. Scientists hailed the scientific discovery of ketamine for depression as 'ground-breaking'. The drug works quickly, producing a dramatic improvement in mood (sufferers symptoms cleared within hours), and can work on people who haven't gotten better with other depression treatments. Thus, while we're warned about the physical, psychological and criminal dangers of this class B drug, the scientific community are chuffed. Besides the inability to move, this horse tranquilliser can make us feel detached from our body and surroundings. We 'melt' and our problems disappear down the 'K-hole'.

Perhaps we need to redress what we think about substances? Lest we forget that Selective Serotonin Reuptake Inhibitors (SSRI) antidepressants are essentially a mild version of disco biscuits. They both block the reuptake of serotonin (happy hormone), but with ecstasy there's a massive rise in serotonin. It seems like a double standard that cigarettes and alcohol, which are more detrimental to our health and more addictive than Valium and other drugs, are legal? Thus, it's legal to get intoxicated on booze, with people metamorphosing into the Hulk, but it's illegal to smoke some spliffs. Cops universally concede that it's easier to contend with someone who's been on the Bob Marley cigarettes, than someone's who been on the sauce.

And whilst doctors can prescribe Valium, it's illegal to poach her off the streets. The same goes for ketamine. And it's like we're told not to take cocaine, but they plough ADHD kids with it e.g. Ritalin. But what if booze is not our bag and we want to dull our senses, or indeed brighten them with a few lines of cheeky Charlie? Is that immoral, like the zonked-out Stepford wives, and should that be illegal?

Boundaries seem blurred between what's okay and what's not, and then there's the law. Fundamentally, doctors are the gatekeepers, and if we want psychoactive drugs, we need to have some kind of mental illness. Otherwise we need to go undercover to an undisclosed location. So, despite our notorious binge drinking car-crash culture, it seems drugs remain illegal because they're considered morally wrong. And which is a small joke, given the vast numbers that consume them, including cops, judges and politicians. All walks of life take drugs, from the rich to the poor, to those above the law.

Maybe we don't want people to take drugs if we're not taking them, because we're doing the right thing and adhering to the law? Maybe there's a sense of injustice because we're all supposed to. Rules are rules. But then we're back to questioning why cigarettes and alcohol are okay. And maybe we'd like some of the (free) drugs given to those with mental health problems e.g. Valium, ketamine, meths, lithium. Certainly, I've thought, 'share them out', when looking at friends and 'service users' pleasantly pickled. Indeed, it might be quite fine to get some ketamine off our GP.

Whilst substances are tricksters, it seems most people can use substances and still function, so we don't have a genetic deficiency, like say 'alcoholics'? It's rumoured that we're at the mercy of our genes e.g. alcohol gene. And such genetic predispositions undermine self-control, which is otherwise psychological competence? It's like we're led to believe that mental health problems are due to dodgy genes. But we're also creatures of habit, and unhealthy 'habits' or 'diseases' ooze from the cervices of our societal structures.

It's also duly noted, that it works out well for the trusty pharmaceutical industry that addictions are classified as mental illness, as they can provide a plethora of treatments, whereas there's no money to be made with Abstinence Based Recovery. With the latter however, we need to cultivate some will to live. And maybe we have the depression gene? Or maybe we have an addictive personality, which explains why we can't curb our greediness, or something else.

Either way, we learn these addictions. Like, no one likes smoking to begin with. It's gross. But we persevere (because it's cool?), until we're hooked on the 'feel good' chemical factor. We learn that we want to feel good.

And when we know how good we can feel, we can't not know, and life seems even more joyless without additional chemical joy.

Perhaps, as scientists suggest, some of us are born with fewer dopamine receptors and need drugs for the same pleasure. It's possible we've inherited a gene that stops us from experiencing joy as others do. Maybe this gene is like the depression gene? Hence, we need substances to top up our levels. Like, cocaine, heroin, cannabis, amphetamines, nicotine and alcohol, as these all raise dopamine levels by either increasing the amount released or blocking re-absorption. Heroin and cocaine facilitate more, hence they're more addictive. Experts circularly inform that when we have extra dopamine, we have less cravings for other substances we're addicted to, because we're happier. So, it's beneficial to take sanitised dopamine, but not from the streets?

Interestingly, an experiment was carried out with rats. Thus, they had an electric current applied to the part of the brain associated with dopamine release, and they were given a lever to control the electric current. The rats pressed the lever 2,000 times an hour, for hours at a time, and with the choice of food or lever, they chose to starve themselves. Rats were also exposed to an electrified grid which produced immense pain to their feet, and whilst they would rather die of starvation than cross the grid, they would for the dopamine pedal. These rats relentlessly endured electric shocks in order to administer the dopamine. They were prepared to do what it took for that 'rush'.

The interesting part however, is that when the rats were placed in a luxury rat park with jogger wheels, plants, warm nests, nice food, copious space, mountain scenery and streams painted on the walls, they barely touched the dopamine pedal. Perhaps, we're more like the caged rats? It's also noted, that presumably scientists who conduct animal experiments are sadists.

When it comes to substances, it seems the trick is to have a focus beyond them i.e. structure and boundaries e.g. no wine before 5pm, and at least two alcohol free days a week. The drug of choice cannot take the lead role in our cage. The biggest drinkers in the UK include doctors, dentists and cops. Apparently, the highest earners, those earning £40,000 and above, are more likely to be frequent 'binge' drinkers.

It's beautiful, the GPs dish out antidepressants to placate the punters, and then consume a couple of bottles of cabernet sauvignon to placate themselves. Suicide rates for UK doctors are double the national average, and they're well aware that alcohol is a depressant. For others, the first thing they do after work is roll a joint and put the kettle on. Many limit drink and drugs to the weekend, and others are placated 24/7 by pharmaceuticals.

When it comes to alcohol problems, the definition is, it's a problem if it's causing problems in our life i.e. financial, relationships, work. Alcohol is the same as any other drug in terms of it being about our relationship with it i.e. there's use and abuse. If no problems arise and we're not offending anyone, then it's not healthy, but it's not a problem. So, it's okay if we sully the bed, as long as no-one sees?

It's understood there's a difference between our binge drinking culture (i.e. at the weekends) and going to the shop first thing in the morning to get voddy for the body, as the latter has a problem. But then, there's the despairing situation of being addicted to say, heroin. A man I counselled, who was both alcohol and drug dependent, injected heroin into his eyeballs because he literally had nowhere else to jab himself. Russell Brand (2014) speaks about the 'indignity of active addiction', 'the despair of hopelessness', and 'the inexhaustible cycle of incremental self-immolation'. How badly do we need to feel good? It seems boozers are however less desperate than heroin users for their fix, as they're less likely to kill or sell their granny?

It seems fair to say, the addictive nature of drink and drugs is self-explanatory. We like it so we do it again and again, and sometimes continue to the point of having a problem with it. I appreciated Paul Gascoigne's comment, (who has battled with alcohol and drugs long-time), when asked on a chat-show why he abuses alcohol, and he replied that he doesn't blame anyone or anything, but rather drinks because he likes it. And when sober, and despite everything (i.e. how crazy it gets), he's honest enough to admit that he would love a drink. Gazza's been in rehab several times, and he's apparently died three times while undergoing treatment for alcoholism. He was featured in the Sun newspaper, stroking a chicken in a garden pub (September 2014), with the caption stating, 'Oh no Gazza, not again!' It's easy done.

So, people can abstain, like Russell Brand (his addictions included sex and heroin), but they're far more likely to relapse. Hence, the argument that addiction is not an illness but rather moral weakness. Oscar Wilde said, 'the only way to get rid of temptation is to yield to it...I can resist everything but temptation'. A drugs report (findings from New York and Chicago) stated, 'it is inescapable that delinquency both preceded and followed addiction to heroin use'. It is, after all, illegal.

It's noted, that in the eighteenth century, drug and alcohol addictions were considered a moral issue, whereas in the nineteenth century, they were rendered a disease. The 'moral model' of human behaviour is based on the notion of freewill, whereas with the 'disease model' or 'medical model' freewill is superseded by determinism. Interestingly, while there was no disease as such, no physical cause was apparent, but physical malfunctions or 'symptoms' were, evoked the notion of 'mental illness'. We'll get back to this however in chapter 4.

With addictions, the luxury of choice is replaced by compulsion. Our capacity is diminished i.e. we've lost control and rational choice. We're bound to dreadful habits that rob us of life. And there is no peace, as we're always thinking about them. Apparently, heroin users spend 70% of the day thinking about their next fix. They effectively steal our freedom.

However, there also seems to be degrees of freedom, until there's not. I coined the term 'Ten to Ten Syndrome' (given 10pm liquor laws), ironically when I was an alcohol counsellor, to describe the jittery dilemma, the sweating and rationalising, of whether or not to drink. And before I knew it, I'd be at the shop buying wine. And I'd drink, all the while realising how boring and pointless it was. I later discovered, those endeavouring to abstain from drinking are equally familiar with this anxious time. Hence, support buddies (from support groups), phone each other and keep chatting until it's after 10pm. And woo hoo, another day sober. And then the next day, to drink or not to drink, that is the mo fo question.

This element of freedom is however a luxury, as like a black hole, an addiction can seem inescapable. Like for Bill Wilson (1895-1971), cofounder of Alcoholics Anonymous (AA) and the 'Twelve Step Program'. He said he realised that he couldn't help himself, and his alcohol addiction was beyond his control. He ruined his promising career on Wall Street, damaged his marriage, and was hospitalised several times. His doctor explained to him that alcoholism is an illness, as opposed to moral failing i.e. no willpower. Wilson was apparently elated to find out he was suffering from an illness. At any rate, the doctor's advice was to abstain.

But Wilson was unable to abstain, presumably because he had this illness? And since no-one else could help him, he cried out to God for help. He said that whilst lying in bed, depressed and despairing, he cried out, 'I'll do anything! Anything at all! If there be a God, let Him show Himself!' He then experienced a 'Hot Flash' spiritual conversion which involved the sensation of a bright light, a feeling of ecstasy and absolute serenity. It would appear God answered.

Perhaps we could find sanctuary with God, and perhaps that's the divine design? Maybe we've been looking in the wrong places. It's highlighted that substance misuse can be understood as spiritual yearning. Like, Russell Brand said he was in spiritual pain. He pertains to the pain beneath the drink and drugs. Psychiatrist Carl Jung notably recommended religious faith as a cure for alcoholism, and apparently had an indirect role in establishing AA.

Active addictions are beyond exasperating. But unlike alcohol, drugs are illegal, so there's a criminal element. However, as Brand contends, criminalising the addiction or 'disease' is futile and actually complicates the issue. Apparently £4 billion a year is spent on criminalising drugs (which is ineffective as being illegal doesn't deter people from taking drugs), whereas £1 billion is spent 'helping' addicts. The result is financially challenged people from the ghettos partake in the 'revolving door' with regards to being caught with a small amount of brown sugar, prison, and the same again. It's arguably madness.

There's also the compelling argument for legalising and taxing drugs. We can but wonder if society would go more nuts? Brand highlights that countries like Portugal and Switzerland, who have introduced progressive and tolerant drug laws, have seen crime plummet and drug-related deaths significantly reduced. It seems the issue is whether or not drugs constitute a criminal or health problem, or a spiritual problem? In the absence of spiritual fulfilment, we live in a pleasure seeking, pain avoiding culture. Hence, we want drugs?

However, besides drink and drugs, too many are eating pies no-end. Record numbers of westerners are eating themselves to death. Like alcoholism, 30,000 people die a year from obesity. And like drinking, it's extremely easy to shovel food into the hole. On a TV programme I watched about overeaters, an 'Overeaters Anonymous' member likened overeaters to crack addicts. She said cheesecake for them is like crack cocaine for a crack addict. However, another member (like Gazza taking responsibility) advised that she didn't blame anyone for becoming obese, as she ate the food, and no-one forced it down.

It's explained that junk foods stimulate the reward system in the brain in the same way as drugs like cocaine, and whereas eating an apple might cause a moderate release of dopamine, cheesecake releases much more. Carbohydrates and sugars release 'feel good' chemicals, hence emotional munching to feel better. Apparently rats that were given access to high-fat foods showed similar characteristics to those hooked on cocaine and heroin, and found it hard to quit even when given electric shocks.

It costs the NHS billion's annually for obesity related health problems. 1:4 Brits are obese, and it's the same for kids, and more than 60% are overweight. Obesity is overtaking smoking as the main cause of strokes. And there's an epidemic of diabetes type II on account of obesity/lifestyle (every five minutes someone in the UK is diagnosed with diabetes). Millions are spent on gastric bands and bypasses, with thousands undergoing these surgical procedures, despite the complications e.g. uncontrolled vomiting, severe cramps, blood clots, dumping syndrome, diarrhoea, and hernias.

Thus, like other lifestyles that engender disease, we can be incapacitated, unable to work and in receipt of benefits, on morbidly obese grounds. And how sad, that some people are too fat to leave their homes. In December 2014 The European Court of Justice ruled that obesity can constitute a disability. Unsurprisingly, there were mixed views about this ruling. One girl I read about, who is obese, stated it wasn't her fault (hence disability) because she's addicted to coca cola. It presumably bodes well however that we have the poor man's version of coca cola, (prior to 1903 it contained a significant dose of cocaine), as presumably there'd be even more coca cola addicts?

Scotland, aka the 'Sick Man of Europe', has the most obesity in Europe. And no danger, apparently 7/10 Scot's pets eat too much. [Apparently Scotland spends more on alcohol, illegal drugs, and gambling than the rest of Britain. And the alcohol death rate is double the rest of UK]. But America trumps the world with its share of porkers. So, we indulge in a sedentary lifestyle and fatty diet, and grow like Babushka Dolls.

Or maybe we have the fat gene? Indeed, apparently millions of Brits carry the greediness (rogue/FTO) gene. Scientists inform that diets are essentially doomed because excessive munching is driven by a deep fundamental genetic process. Thus, rather than greed being one of the seven deadly sins, if we're feeling greedy, we can blame our genes. It also however stands to reason, that our greediness could be countered by exercise? Or maybe we have a sloth gene? Hence, we'd rather get liposuction than exercise, as exercise requires effort (in 2013 there was a 41% rise in liposuction).

Foods not love but it's something to do just like drinking, drugs, and smoking no-end. And what's with 'feeders'? Besides 'fat fetish' (attraction to fat people), some kinky people get sexual gratification from the process of helping others gain body fat.

Addictions appear to motivate us, (they're better than nothing?), but they underpin sadness and loneliness? It seems we need something to 'keep us going'? Like, holidays keep some people going. Some people depend on others as their lifeline (is that the definition of relationships or co-dependency?). Affairs keep others going. Feeling that older, younger, or morbidly obese person can make people feel alive. Or getting whipped to hell and back, or smeared with faeces.

For others, the opiate might be money, power and status. Apparently super-yacht owners, competitively plagued by the need to have the biggest boat in the world, get their boats extended to preside (my diamond encrusted ring-piece is bigger than yours). And as counterintuitive as it might seem, some people live to work, and like to be defined by their work. Or it might be striving to be beautiful, and undergoing countless operations to that end.

And then there's gambling. The adrenaline rush associated with the possibility of pulling off a big win is often described by gamblers as an unbeatable feeling. Interestingly, a gambling addict, namely, Graham Calvert, tried to sue William Hill for letting him lose two million in six months. But to no sympathetic avail. His gambling spree resulted in him losing his marriage, livelihood, and health. But the court ruled that William Hill had no legal responsibility to protect its customers from the consequences of their gambling.

Compulsive gambling is similar to a chemical addiction and is regarded as mental illness. It seems the responsibility for our behaviour 'lies' within the structures of society, but we're left with the problem? Gambling addicts are increasing, which includes 11-16 year olds. On the plus side however, gambling generates billions for the economy. Our gambling and betting industry is a key contributor to the UK economy.

Compulsive stealing is on the same chemically addictive page, but it drains the economy. It only benefits the thief, or not if they have a mental illness? Apparently, the difference between emotional stealing and kleptomania is that with kleptomania the person is secure, not insecure. Emotional stealing is more like hoarding to fill an emotional void. Kleptomania seems naughtier?

People are also increasingly addicted to video games, the internet, and their phones. Indeed, the mobile phone addiction is apparently more addictive than nicotine, and harder to quit than heroin. Lest we forget retail therapy, which guarantees shoppers two hits of dopamine. The first dopamine release comes when they find something they want to buy, and the second comes when they actually pay for it. Shopaholics Anonymous notably provides counselling for shoplifting addictions, compulsive shopping addictions, and overspending.

It seems mad that people buy and steal items that they then have to hide from others. And society concedes this behaviour is peculiar. Hence, we call it 'illness'. And some people are addicted to lying, which is a whole other 'pathological' fantasy. It seems that we can be addicted to literally anything. As conveyed, it seems we're desperately seeking happiness and pleasure? Perhaps we all need a dopamine lever.

As touched on in the Foreword, secular humanism usurped religion. According to sociologists, 'secularisation' is the rise of scientific rationalism and technology, which is characterised by an increased tendency towards atheism and agnosticism. The 'secularisation thesis' is the belief that as societies progress i.e. 'modernise', religion loses its authority in all aspects of social life and governance. In short, no-one cares what the church thinks about anything. God's not in charge, but rather we are.

It's highlighted the critical shift in the last hundred years has been the move away from moral regulation by churches to a more secular mode of organisation through medicine, education and psychology. GPs and psychiatrists are the voice of wisdom, and they're trained to be non-judgemental, unlike religion? It's duly noted however, that secular humanism evolved from Christian values. Jesus loved people and insisted 'judge, lest we be judged'. It's also highlighted there's been a historic significant shift from protestant self-denial to hedonism with a credit society. Society promotes consumerism and pleasure, which is good for the economy?

Secularisation in Britain was however part of a much larger social and 'cultural revolution' that began in the sixties, when we binned the shackles of religion in favour of promiscuity ('free love') and drugs. The world was changing. The contraceptive pill was introduced, (coupled with provocative clothing like the mini-skirt), and the church retreated into the recesses of society. There was a spirit of rebellion. It's asserted, that 'thanks to the sixties, we're all shamefully selfish'. This era spurred on the self-absorbed 'me generation'. And whilst seemingly liberating and progressive, it has nevertheless led to the postmodern condition 'nihilism'.

Nihilism comes from nihil, which is Latin for nothingness. This 'condition' is characterised by a sense of uncertainty, meaninglessness, doubt in traditional values, and spiritual malaise. Life seems pointless and morality does not inherently exist. It seems that having written off God, we're left with a God-shaped hole that drink, drugs, pies, sex, gambling etc attempt to fill? As Blaise Pascal (1623-1662), mathematician and theologian, said, 'There is a God-shaped vacuum in the heart of each man which cannot be satisfied by any created thing but only by God the Creator, made known through Jesus Christ'.

Nihilism is used in association with 'anomie' to explain society's general mood of despair. Anomie, which is Greek for 'without law', was popularised by the French sociologist Emile Durkheim (1858-1917). He referred to anomie as the destructive chaos that creeps in at the margins of life. He observed that without moral regulation and structure, (as society provides little moral guidance), people feel alienated from each other's thinking. And this leads to norm-less-ness, disillusionment and isolation. We also no longer have the right to morally judge, as values are relative. Thus, it's none of our business what deviant people do with their pets?

Durkheim warned us that individualism (i.e. please yourself and 'do your own thing') would result in the disintegration of society, and he predicted the pathological outcome would be an increase in modern times of suicide, alcohol and crime. It seems he was right.

It's understood that in the absence of being shaped by religion, secular culture primarily shapes our emotions, which includes fear and depression. The media (including movies and popular music) provides us with morals and ideals, whether consciously or unconsciously absorbed. The entertainment industry is the 'culture creator'. The TV gives us our sense of reality, including 'the news'. Television tells-a-vision. David Icke refers to the TV as the 'resident hypnotist in the corner of the room', and states 'how appropriate that we call television output television *programmes*' (p.525-526).

Apparently, crime-fears are rising because of TV programmes and soaps that dramatize real life i.e. highlighting all social problems, psychos and weirdoes. It's said these digital reflections hold up a cracked mirror to society. But moreover, they also seem to legitimise behaviour. That is, we rationalise it's the same deviance happening everywhere, so who cares? It's said we're desensitised to what's right and wrong, as we're immersed with murder, violence and sex on TV. It's said that human nature is running wild, which is evidenced by the degeneration of attitudes and behaviours, the epidemic of adultery, the increase in crime, disrespectful youngsters and coveters.

It further seems pertinent to note, that religious philosophies predicted these wayward times. Like, the prophecy of Shambala (Buddhist BEF 700 CE), for example, states, 'People will no longer have any religion to which they can turn for solace or liberation: the doctrines of materialism will overwhelm their minds and drive them to struggle for their own selfish ends. The lust for power and wealth will prevail over teachings of compassion and truth'. And the Lotus Sutra 13 states, 'In the evil age to come, living beings will decrease in good qualities and increase in utter ignorance, coveting gain and honours, developing their evil qualities, and being far removed from deliverance'.

It's foreseen that in the 'end days' (eschatology is the study of end-times), we become degenerates. Like, in the Bible, 2 Timothy 3:1-5, we're told, 'But mark this: There will be terrible times in the last days. For people will love only themselves and their money. They will be boastful, proud, abusive, disobedient to their parents, ungrateful, unholy, unloving, unforgiving, slanderous, without self control, brutal, not lovers of the good, treacherous, rash, conceited, lovers of pleasure rather than lovers of God – having a form of godliness but denying its power'. So, we're here? Islam concedes that we become debauched in the last days i.e. cheating, lying, selfishness, and sexual immorality increase. Many Muslims believe we're living in the last days.

Anomie is likened to soul sickness in society. Community spirit has been replaced by cities full of dispirited strangers. Apparently, paranoia is twice as high as rural areas, and at least 25% have an irrational fear. No-one speaks to their neighbours, since besides the weather, what is there to speak about? It's like the forced conversations we have to endure with hairdressers etc? It seems we're on the same page that small talk is overrated. Hence, people are perpetually on their phones, and no-one's talking anymore. But maybe it's good for us to talk to each other i.e. it's healthy? And maybe we're losing the art of conversation? And what does anyone talk about in any case. Football, soaps or 'Netflix', and we parrot 'the news'?

It's also highlighted that people are increasingly using email and texting to opt out of 'talking' situations, and this is causing us to become more insular. It's 'easier' to text than speak? It's less hassle and less anxiety? And then some of us anxiously scrutinise the messages we've sent, to reassure ourselves they're fine. Suffice to say, embarking down this path can lead us to 'one is the loneliest number'. About 10% of people in the UK have no friends, so we might as well party for one? Or watch 'Friends' and pretend we have some, (my cats are my friends), or go 'online'.

But for those who do have an urban family to play with, and henceforth 'do have a life', according to what society calls a life, it seems to be going out and getting wrecked? That is, before we settle down to family life. The sentiment is *'enjoy yourself'* and consumerism is good. We can enjoy that churches are now clubs, and *sisters are doing it for themselves*.

A survey in 2017 revealed that 31 is the average age at which people stop clubbing, and it was considered 'tragic' to still be clubbing at 37. It's highlighted that people in their twenties don't want to see people in their forties and fifties in clubs. It seems Generation X has reluctantly passed on the 'YOLO' (You Only Live Once) baton? We have to make the most of our window?

So, what is a good night out? Drink, drugs, dancing, sex? [As mentioned, drugs help the otherwise monotony]. Russell Brand (2014) poetically raps, 'drink some cider, get inside her', and 'do a gram, drop a pill, download an app, eat some crap, get a slap, mind the gap, do a line, instagram, little grope in the cab' (p.60). And for some, it's fighting, and waking up in A&E or the police station. Fun aside, people can be brutal. Sometimes people just smack someone else in the face because they can. They actively look for fights. Philip Hensher wrote an article for 'The Independent' (7 January 2000) entitled 'My Perfect Night Out: Sex, Drugs, Dancing and Fighting', which typifies 'good nights'.

Thus, he describes his Hogmanay, which lasted for eighteen hours, from 6pm to lunchtime the next day. During which time he drank three bottles of wine on a completely empty stomach. He went to a succession of parties, French kissed four strangers and a policeman, committed an indeterminate number of criminal acts, had sex in the lavatories of a club, pissed on Starbucks window, shared a spliff with a very famous model, got into a fight, walked five miles and danced for seven or possibly eight hours. He states, 'in short, I had a completely champion time'. But he insists his good time wouldn't live up to his reckless friend, who never thought he had a really good night out unless it ended up in casualty and securing the attention of professional medical assistance.

We're notorious, and we're not any better behaved on holiday. It's said we forget to pack our morals. It's estimated 40,000 illegal pills are consumed every night in Ibiza. No danger. And it truly is sex on the beach, lest we forget 'Sticky Vicky' in Benidorm (LOL).

So, we're also preoccupied with sex, another source of pleasure. It's said, 'art is a mirror of its age' and sex sells everything. Even milk is advertised using a skimpily clad broad featuring a milk moustache. Is there any need? It's understood that beautiful people inspire us to buy products (because we'll be like them?) and also that adverts home in on sex and relationships etc to market their products, as they realised we care more about people than products. But every music video is the same, leaving very little for the imagination. I'm so beyond bored of it. Indeed, I couldn't help but wonder, is there more to life than Sex in the City? And for sure, I've seen an obscene amount of SJP and her buds.

It's highlighted that TV innocence dissipated from the 60s, and sex was out in the open from the 70s/80s. And it came with a pornified twist. Sex on the beach landed with American wet-dream 'Baywatch' in the late 80s, (Extras were playboy playmates), and then came no holds barred 'Sex and the City' in the late 90s. Like soaps, the latter reflected 'real life' relationships and entanglements, 'human emotion in the city', but it was considerably more glamorous. Like, they lived in New York, (not Coronation Street), and walked in fabulous Jimmy Choo's. Is it fabulous to pay £500 for shoes, or 20K for a handbag aka piece of cow hide dyed gold with a Fendi label? Or are we victims of advertising? It's noted, that our 'programmes' foster materialism, as well as sex.

In essence, the societal sentiment is sex is all good if people enjoy themselves and 'protect' themselves. We're 'liberated' and there is no judgement. But moreover, it seems this instinct has been sold to us as a 'physical need'? Hence, any port will do in a storm, and beggars can't be choosers? We can use each other. A friend of mine from uni said he put a pillow over a girl's face during intercourse, because he found her so unattractive. Sex is advertised as a mechanical means to a satisfying end. 'Love Sex: Durex'.

As it transpires however, we don't actually need to have sex (anymore than we need to fight). That's what gets me about the number of unwanted kids. It's like, stop having sex then, and cultivate some self-control? Take a Valium? Or maybe the need for sex is like other 'chemical' addictions ergo wild horses won't stop us? My Hindu-esque friend, who abstains from having sex despite being married, because of his pursuit for purity, says sex is like an itch that you have to keep scratching. It's the same for masturbation.

It's purported that women are more promiscuous than men. It seems we learned from the best? And from the feminist angle, why not be sexually liberated. Why not emancipate ourselves from sexual slavery. Like 'Samantha Jones' in Sex and the City, who epitomised this sentiment and was iconic of female sexual liberation. Or maybe the 'sex in the city' crack is overrated? More than 50% of women regret one-night stands (needless to say they're invariably coupled with liquor). And then there's 'the walk of shame' the next day. It's appears however, that the walk of shame scenario is dying a death, as people increasingly opt for 'half-night stands' (it appears breakfast is overrated).

It's highlighted that dating apps like Tinder make sex super accessible, as people can hook up for sex, minus the sleepovers. And that way people can avoid the awkwardness the following morning (the 'small talk' LOL), and also wake up in their own bed, which is always a bonus. And whilst it's asserted that women are again following in men's footsteps by leaving before morning, it's retorted that they're leaving early because they're not satisfied. It seems sex has never been so disposable, meaningless and empty?

It seems Freud's supposition that most people feel guilt about sex their entire lives is no longer valid (Freud was obsessed with our sexual inhibition). It hasn't been for a long time. On the contrary, no one cares. Indeed, people boast about their sexual conquests and risqué behaviours. It seems we like to push the boundaries? We have a hyper-sexualised society and there's intrinsically no morality about it. Love and sex divorced a long time ago. They're apparently two separate 'constructs' i.e. emotional and physical, and we don't need to mix them up.

However, unlike sex, we do need love (babies literally die without love). And it's possible this sexualised behaviour is a counterfeit to real love and intimacy? Maybe love and sex do belong together, and the joining of our bodies symbolises this? It's always possible society has taken something beautiful and massively cheapened it? It seems we've trivialised the 'intimacy' of sex?

According to scientists, whenever a woman has sex her body produces a chemical which causes her to emotionally attach. This chemical may account for how much we think of someone after having sex just once. There's an illusion of closeness yet with little groundwork done in terms of getting to know each other. We don't know the person, but at some level we do. We know them intimately. At some metaphysical level, it's possible our souls have intertwined? Fundamentally, we give our 'self' to someone, and it's said our bodies make a promise whether we do or not.

Thus, maybe we should be forewarned about this chemical, and its potential to confuse our perception of sex and love i.e. we may read into something that's not there, and we may become slightly deranged. Maybe condom packets could feature a mental health warning (like cigarette packets), that sex might affect our emotions. Thus, whilst we're informed about protection on a physical level, it seems we're less informed about protection on an emotional level. Maybe this chemical accounts for why my friend describes one night stands as, 'it's like giving away a piece of your soul each time'.

So, whilst we're brainwashed to believe that we're 'liberated', maybe we're not? People can feel cheap and cheated, which is damaging for self-esteem. And perhaps we can wonder how the village bike, (where everyone's had a ride), really feels within her inner most self. Lest we forget that diamonds have no value except that placed upon them. I remember thinking it was sad when my friend from university told me that she felt like a pair of legs and a hole. It seems so many girls don't realise their worth? Or maybe we don't need to read into sex so much. It's just sex. But it can also be grim. Like having sex with someone, you don't want to have sex with, but feeling compelled to go through with it. Lying there and taking it because it's only manners? And suffice to say, not everyone is clean, and STDs are pretty gross. Crabs (LOL).

It's also noted, that teenagers' sex lives reflect adult sex lives. Kids seem to be growing up faster than ever, but perhaps they're not ready for 'grown up' behaviours, and the emotions that accompany these? From twelve years old, kids can see a GP and in confidence, hence without parental consent, secure contraception. Contemplating kids having sex that young seems preposterous. They're so young with their baby faces and bodies. And yet we all knew kids at school who were getting nasty that young.

As touched on, there's much pressure on kids to be deviant and this includes underage sex. Being a virgin is not cool (the cool people are not virgins). I heard at my secondary school, that kids get battered if they're a virgin. Sexual promiscuity, for the most part, elicits a positive peer response. Any hole's a goal. Britain has more sexually active under-18s than any other country in Europe. We also have the highest number of teenage mothers and the highest teenage abortion rate in Western Europe. Teenage abortions are disturbingly high (1:3 teenage pregnancies are terminated). Nearly a quarter of all abortions are carried out on girls under 20.

Thus, so much for the 'get it on' condom campaigns etc, given the record numbers of abortions and STDs. Hundreds of millions have been spent on sex education and it's not working. That's not strictly true however, as British kids are highly informed about sex and contraception. I suspect that has something to do with society legitimising it at some level. That is, adults acknowledging that kids are having sex, and whilst illegal, the covert subtext is to be sensible about it. There's enough unwanted kids in society. But seriously, what does giving under 16s free condoms say, if not, 'knock your-self out'.

Masturbation is also now being taught as part of sex education, particularly for girls, as this has historically been taboo. There is no shame in masturbation. It's healthy to masturbate? It's also highlighted there's a sexting epidemic, with teens sharing graphic pictures from 12/13 years old. Apparently, they're inspired by 'celebs' naked selfies and sex scenes in videos. They think it's grown up, and the popular girls do it. They feel confident and sexy, but it can backfire, with repercussions including anxiety, depression and feeling suicidal.

So, sex is not all fun and games, as sometimes 'accidents' happen. It's like Russian roulette. Most of the time we get away with it, but not every time. Men are literally loaded guns and on occasion unwanted babies are conceived. The absolute worst thing that could possibly happen happens. Imagine the desperation pre-abortion days, using knitting needles or throwing oneself down the stairs. It seems the most sensible option is securing the morning-after pill, following any 'accidents'. But not everyone's so quick off the mark. Or some people take a chance, hoping the laws of probability will be favourable?

It's arguably a paradox that it's considered 'preventative' to secure the morning-after pill. It's not preventative if a baby has been conceived. It's the same as abortion, the only difference is when taking the morning after pill, one doesn't know if they're pregnant (maybe, maybe not). Interestingly, the contraceptive pill doesn't prevent conception but rather prevents the fertilised egg from embedding in the womb. Thus, the number of babies conceived and eradicated must be immense.

Before abortion was legalised, many deaths arose from backstreet abortions. And duty-bound doctors bore this ethical burden. Then in 1938 the landmark Bourne case landed. A young woman was gang raped by a group of soldiers and the doctor agreed to terminate the pregnancy on the grounds that it would preserve the mental health of the young woman. The doctor was prosecuted but a judge subsequently ruled the pregnancy would have been tantamount to wrecking her life. Thus, a precedent was set, whereby abortion would be legal if it preserved the woman's mental wellbeing.

Then the feminist movement pioneered 'a woman's right to choose'. Abortion is marketed, 'every child a wanted child, every abortion a wanted abortion'. It's extremely rare for a woman to be refused an abortion. Only 1% of abortions are on the grounds that the child would be born disabled. Most abortions are carried out on 'healthy' babies for social reasons. 1:4 babies conceived today are aborted, and gender abortions are not illegal. With respect to the latter, it's estimated some 4,000 kids are aborted a year, so-called female foeticide, as girls are surplus to requirements and evidently disposable (most gender abortions are associated with ethnic communities).

It's said that many people (more so teenagers) use abortion as contraception, so-called 'lifestyle abortions'. 1:3 women have had abortions, and thousands have had more than four abortions. There's been millions of abortions since the Abortion Act was introduced in 1967. Having binned God, it was no longer a moral issue. There is no judgement. No-one cares? Besides perhaps, that abortions cost the NHS millions every year.

200,000 foeti are aborted in Britain each year, and it's estimated some 56 million abortions take place worldwide. That's over 100,000 babies per day. Indeed, abortion is the single greatest cause of death of human beings today. Russia has the highest number of abortions in the world, with abortions consistently outnumbering live births by 2:1. It seems foeti can be likened to a tumour that needs to be cut out?

Whilst polls suggest that most people don't regret their decision, it's still something significant that happened? Maybe there's a sense of loss or emptiness? And perhaps people might subsequently wonder if 'it' was a boy or girl, and what they would be like? As with everything in life however, it depends on mindset. Hence, it stands to reason, that it's psychologically healthier to rationalise that 'it's' a blob of cells rather than a baby?

It seems the issue is when is a baby a baby? Like, from conception when life begins (apparently there's a flash of light when ova meets sperm). Or when it has a heartbeat circa four weeks old, or when it's more human like? 'It's' called a foetus, which is Latin for little child, at nine weeks. This also questions the ethics of snowflake babies, IVF babies on ice? The millions that are surplus to requirements are used in scientific experiments, destroyed, or sold on the black market.

Apparently, a fertilised ovum is 1/10mm in diameter, which is the size of a talcum powder particle. The zygote, the first cell, has the full DNA blueprint and births trillions of other cells, producing its tiny body and beating heart. From 6-12 weeks, all of the baby's features develop e.g. tiny fingers with tiny fingernails, the mouth, the nose, the ears, the eyes (with its own unique iris, like its unique fingerprints). There's recognisably human behaviour by 13 weeks, as the foetus can yawn and rub its eyes. At 15 weeks the foetus gains the sense of taste. At 18 weeks s/he begins to hear. And at 23 weeks the foetus can be seen sucking its thumb, turning somersaults, playing with its toes, and smiling. And then it can be game over.

Terminations are legal until 24 weeks, which is the highest in Europe. This limit was set in 1990, as it was previously 28 weeks. The assumption is that foeti don't (consciously) feel pain, which relies on the neural structure not being established until 26 weeks. However, other research informs that foeti feel pain from 20 weeks, and even 18 weeks.

It's also duly noted, that in one ward, people are aborting babies up to 24 weeks, and in another ward, medical staff are saving babies born prematurely. With medical advances and specialist neonatal units, the majority of babies (75%) born at 23 weeks survive outside the womb. And there is growing evidence that foeti are able to sustain life from 20 weeks. In 2007, a study published in the British Journal of Obstetrics and Gynaecology revealed that one in thirty babies aborted after 16 weeks gestation is born alive.

If we 'catch it' early enough (up to 9 weeks), we can have an abortion pill. Taking a pill to make it all go away seems like the most palatable option. Like the morning after pill, it's almost like it didn't happen? With a vacuum abortion or suction aspiration (from 7-15 weeks) the foetus is literally vacuumed out the womb via a tube/cannula. The suction is apparently 29 times more powerful than a vacuum cleaner. If they're small enough, they can remain intact when sucked out, with their heart still beating.

I watched a horrendous documentary about this when Britain was deliberating whether or not to cut the abortion limit in 2007. These perfectly formed babies came out alive, complete with raw pink skin and tiny screams, and continued breathing. And I watched these nurses battering the wretched teeny tiny babies over the head with a spatula to end, quicker, their tragic little lives. It was truly horrific. [It was so horrific it inspired my painting]. It would seem the legal duty of care towards a live born baby who survives an abortion is thus somewhat violated? If they don't come out whole, they're dismembered i.e. their tiny heads are ripped off, legs, arms etc.

In the next trimester (from 15 weeks of pregnancy), it gets worse with the Dilation and Evacuation procedure. Because the baby is too large to fit through the cervix, the abortionist has to tear the body apart with pliers, pulling each part through the cervix, limb by limb. The spine must also be snapped, and the skull crushed to remove these pieces. The vacuum is also used to suck all debris out. With a late surgical abortion (20-24 weeks), the foetus receives a lethal injection (known as feticide) to stop its heartbeat. Or with a late medical abortion, the same drugs that are used in early medical abortions are administered. The baby is again broken into pieces and removed.

Abortion in the last trimester is horrendous. With the Partial Birth Abortion, Dilation and Extraction method, the abortionist uses forceps to manoeuvre the foetus into a breech position, and pulling the alive and moving baby out by the feet, the abortionist removes the brain (which kills them) while the head is in the birth canal, and then the baby is extracted. When the brain is suctioned out, it causes the skull to collapse which allows the foetus head to pass more easily through the birth canal. In some countries, abortions are legal up to the time of birth, and in some states in America, like New York. There's also debate about permitting infanticide, which is killing the child after birth.

It's interesting to note however, that whilst abortion is the mother's right, some children in the US afflicted with FASD have sued their mums for drinking when pregnant. Women can be criminalised for behaviours that are harmful to the foetus, like drinking excessive alcohol, which is challenging because it suggests the foetus has some rights?

The prospect of criminal prosecution for drinking mums also surfaced in the UK. In 2014 a landmark case arose, as a North West England council sought criminal injuries compensation for a six year old girl with 'growth retardation'. But despite the lifelong damage the mother inflicted on her child after drinking heavily throughout her pregnancy, the court ruled that the mother did not commit a criminal offence. The rational was, the time at which the grievous bodily harm was done occurred when the child was in the womb, and at that stage the child did not have a legal personality as to constitute a person. It was agreed for the purposes of the law, that the unborn baby was a 'unique organism' but not a person. Lord Justice Treacy ruled, 'A mother who is pregnant and who drinks to excess despite knowledge of the potential harmful consequence to the child of doing so is not guilty of a criminal offence under the law if her child is subsequently born damaged as a result'.

It seems we've separated sex from babies, as well as love? It seems sex has less to do with procreation, and more to do with pleasure? Apparently, the majority of teenage mums are reluctant to breastfeed because their breasts are seen as sex symbols. And elective Caesarean sections are growing in popularity, (which is four times more dangerous than normal delivery), as no good can come from a wizard's sleeve. And it's too hard to push the baby out?

So, we're big fans of casual sex, and we're most partial to porn. The latter includes politicians, as it was discovered in 2013 when official records revealed that nearly 300,000 attempts were made to access porn websites from computers within the Houses of Parliament that year. This figure equates to more than 800 attempts per day. Politicians clearly need to schedule in time for a tug (LOL). It seems some restraint was exercised in 2014, as it was revealed that 250,000 attempts were made, which is 700 times a day. Maybe they had more work to do?

So, porn is another popular addiction. Apparently more than one third of the internet's content is pornographic (there's hundreds of millions of porn web pages). Apparently a third of daily downloads are pornographic, and 2.5 billion emails per day are pornographic. Just lest I be judged, but that's shocking and proper skanky. The word porneia notably refers to sexual immorality or sex without marriage. 10% of adults admit having an internet sex addiction, nearly a third of these are women, and the numbers are rising.

A sexual addiction is defined as a pattern of sexual behaviour which feels out of control. It could involve sex with a partner, but it may be viewing porn, masturbating, visiting prostitutes, or using sex chat lines. Sexual addiction therapists are reporting a dramatic increase in the numbers of people seeking treatment, which is largely attributed to the readily available internet porn. People can become preoccupied about spending time online to engage in sexual activities, and will feel anxious if unable to do so. Research has shown that dopamine lies at the heart of porn addiction.

Apparently porn releases more dopamine than sex and the effects last longer (hence, its appeal). As a result, people can become physically and psychologically dependent. It's said porn addicts get the same buzz as alcoholics when they get their fix. Research shows that our brain physically changes by overdosing on porn. The brain is an extraordinary plastic machine, as well get to. But it's noted, that what we feed our minds with, physically affects our brain. The non-material affects the material?

Like other addictions, those plagued by a sex-addiction (i.e. however many hours a day) build up a tolerance. Users report that it takes longer to get aroused and they require progressively harder, more extreme footage for boners. What was once exciting becomes mundane, and sometimes people will cross an unexpected line, and view illegal images, in the never-ending quest for the more extreme images needed to induce an excitement reaction. People can subsequently feel guilty and ashamed after viewing explicit content on the internet. We're not proud of our addictions, or how low we stoop.

Surveys reveal that the vast majority of sex and relationship therapists are also seeing an increase in relationship problems caused by porn. Cybersex addicts become less able to have intimate and satisfying sexual relationships in real life. Physical interaction pales in comparison to the sort of sexual fulfilment they can achieve online, and most will avoid sexual interaction with their partners. Marriage therapists report that problems with internet pornography are now a regular cause for divorce between clients. Although many cybersex addicts dismiss claims of infidelity, partners feel differently, claiming they feel in competition with online parties.

Porn is also normalised for teenagers, particularly teenage boys. Teens are encouraged to appear experienced about porn, including aggressive or violent porn. Most kids have seen porn by thirteen. [One of my mates said he's noticed how porn's changed over time, becoming more hardcore]. But again, research shows it's detrimental to their ability to form relationships as it provides a distorted view of sex. They can have difficulty sustaining mutual loving relationships, and otherwise normal intimacy.

At school they speak about who does anal, and who's the best at oral etc. Forget personality, girls are sexual objects. The societal message is sex is good, and it's better to have sex than not have sex, and those (girls) who are better at sex are better. Porn perpetuates a sexually toxic environment, as people act out what they've seen. It's therefore commendable for girls to act as porn-stars? It's good for boys/men to splash or hose all over their young pretty faces? Porn's designed to give the impression girls like it, and to accept what's literally coming. Soak it up.

Maybe girls/women are pressured into mimicking porn-stars, or maybe they like it? Maybe it's empowering to say, 'treat me like I'm your bitch', and 'treat me like I'm your ho'? It seems people like to lose themselves and adopt a 'ho' persona, as this alter ego turns them on. It's sexy? They get off on tapping into their inner dirty little girl, which is all the grimmer, when they're still girls. So, acting like a porn-star is empowering, or we're brainwashed to think its empowering? The erotic payoff seems huge.

Whilst we'll get to psycho-politics later, which conveys power and control in relationships, it's duly noted, this underpins interesting dynamics in the bedroom, or wherever else one is commanded to play this game. Like, Christian Grey's 'red room of pain'. And maybe we wouldn't mind getting a hiding from that particular domestic abuser, because he's a handsome billionaire? It's noted, that E.L James 'Fifty Shades of Grey' made quite the impact on society. Ann Summers sales rocketed, as did our appetite for bondage. It's also understood that porn has led to the sodomy and rimming (sphincter licking) revolution.

Since Hitler's quite the feature, it seems pertinent to note that he was partial to porn and had quite the collection of porn on his bookcase. It's claimed he liked young women to urinate and defecate on him. We can but wonder what our leaders are into? Like, Russell Brand (2014) said 'Napoleon wrote his missus filthy letters insisting that she kept her privates unkempt and unwashed' (p.263). [LOL].

Apparently, Hitler begged a well-known film actress, Renate Mueller, to beat him (she had accompanied him to his quarters one evening). Renate confided in a director that Hitler fell to his knees and begged to be beaten, and shortly after relating this, she fell out of the window in a hotel in Berlin. Her death was ruled a suicide. Apparently six out of seven women who had some sort of relationship with Hitler 'committed suicide'. A journalist, Fritz Gerlich, knew that one of his lovers Geli Raubal was murdered (she allegedly shot herself in the chest). He claimed to have conclusive proof but was killed before he could print it and all his documents were burned. Its purported Hitler contracted syphilis off a Jewish prostitute (karma?), but we'll get back to Hitler.

So, the sex industry is booming. It seems we're never sated, but rather always want/need more? Besides porn, there's gentleman's clubs and paying for an erection. My mum's bud notably realised the urban legend, namely, he went to a gentleman's club, wearing beige chinos, and he came out the club with skid marks on them. [Lovely]. Sex clubs, privately organised orgies and sex parties are becoming increasingly common. It seems we've progressed beyond the keys in a bowl caper, the seventies swinging initiative (couples put their keys in a bowl or bag and randomly select a set which determines who they have sex with). And sex toys etc are big business (sex dolls also help combat loneliness).

Prostitution is dubbed 'the world's oldest profession'. And why not sell sex and use our bodies as a cash cow? Indeed, some sex workers, like high-class call girls, regard their work as epitomising feminine empowerment. They even seem glamorous? They're the clever ones. Why not get paid for half-night stands? It's also noted, that whilst many immigrants use this type of work to support their families back home, most prostitutes in the UK are not victims of human trafficking, but rather choose to sell sex and do so freely.

Whilst it's argued that prostitution is a 'victimless crime', as it involves consenting adults, it seems society remains ambivalent about its ethical stance. Thus, prostitution is technically legal in the UK, so working as an outcall escort is legal, but other related activities such as soliciting for sex in a public place, kerb crawling, keeping brothels, and pimping are outlawed. Making porn is notably legal because they're 'actors' (LOL).

It seems some affairs are best left private, and we don't want to see prostitutes doing business on our streets and in public places. Like drugs however, this legality doesn't deter people, and criminalising this activity arguably doesn't help. Life could be made a lot safer for sex-workers on the streets. In their line of work, most get raped, they're victimised 8-10 times a year, and their mortality rate is 40% higher than the non-prostitute. Apparently, most customers don't care what gender the sex-worker is, as it's more about power and degradation.

It's highlighted that sex can be sold when understood in terms of pleasure. Hence, non-marital sex, loveless sex, sex that satisfies hedonistic desires, can be capitalised on. Sexual gratification can be exploited. It's a service, (supply and demand), like any other? An estimated one in ten British men regularly pays for sex. And many sex workers take pride in their work. They pride themselves on being good at their job, insisting they give it 100%. Presumably like most products and services, we get what we pay for?

However, contrary to the liberal stance, the 'asymmetry thesis' presupposes that markets in sex and reproduction is worse than treating any other capacities as commodities. It's understood that by virtue of working, we're all essentially prostituting ourselves. As Karl Marx said, we're all prostitutes sold into slavery. We're some company's gimp. But using our bodies in this intimate way takes it to a new unethical level. There's something intuitively not peaceful about it?

And moreover, whilst the liberals maintain its freewill, perhaps it's less free when we consider how many sex workers were sexually abused as children. At a Barnardos conference I attended regarding the sexual exploitation of children and young people, I heard that 90% of sex workers were sexually abused as children. However hard up, I don't know how punters using sex workers can feel okay about this. The sex worker has been robbed and damaged. Most 'normal' people don't choose this occupation. It's not the childhood dream. Perhaps, when already 'dirty', people deduct that they may as well use their predicament for their own ends and treat their bodies as a cash-cow? It's thus contended that commercial sex harms these individuals, and society. And regarding those hard-up, there's always life-like Hustler dolls with her three orifices. Or sex bots?

So, there's no shortage of seedy people whose seedy eyes light up with seediness, like our politicians. But then there's getting chuffed with kids. Like our politicians? Lest we forget the Westminster paedo-ring cover-up in the 80s. How convenient that the evidence, more than a hundred files containing allegations of child abuse, was destroyed. Suffice to say, there's been an overwhelming number of paedo's coming out of the woodwork of late, which besides politicians includes childhood legends like Jimmy Savile and Rolf Harris. And how ironic that Sa-vile granted kids their dreams on his TV show 'Jim'll Fix It', and that Harris was campaigning against child sexual abuse at the height of his offending.

More recently there was the Pizza-gate scandal in 2016, when wikileaks exposed John Podesta's (Hillary Clinton's campaign manager) emails, which revealed a child sex ring in Washington DC. And then there's royal paedos, like the late Lord Mountbatten and Prince Andrew ('allegedly'), and their BFF links with paedos, like Savile and Jeffrey Epstein. However, we'll get back to these freaks later, as it ties in with Satanic Ritual Abuse, as in Savile's sordid case.

It's also well known that paedophilia is rampant in Hollywood. Corey Feldman, for example, has long said paedophilia is the biggest problem facing Hollywood. He said, 'I can tell you the number one problem was and is and always will be paedophilia'. He alleged the darkest secret in Tinseltown was not the casting couch, but the paedo-ring. He said, 'It's all done under the radar. It's the big secret. I was surrounded by them when I was fourteen years old. Literally. They were everywhere, like vultures'. His friend, the late Corey Haim, was sodomised at age eleven by some dirty pervert.

More than 90% of victims know their abuser, but child sexual abuse remains largely a hidden crime, with experts agreeing that the incidence is far greater than what is reported to the authorities. For uncle Sneaky's who don't want to risk using their relatives, or spend time grooming other kids, there's sex tourism e.g. holidaying in Cambodia or Thailand. [It seems ironic that not wearing underwear in Thailand is a criminal offence?]. Like one of my regular customers at the café I worked at, bought a twelve year old girl in Thailand. My boss told me he regaled about how he and his friend used her for their three week vacation.

The dark side of global travel is thus the exploitation of children in many tourist destinations by travelling sex-offenders. UNICEF estimates that every year, two million children globally are affected by sexual exploitation. Apparently, virgins are in high demand, but sex-offenders have a penchant for little boys. And not that I can understand why someone would sexually abuse kids, but it seems babies takes this to a new disturbing level. It was pointed out to me that babies are tighter. There's no shortage of sick puppies out there.

It's also noted, that whilst the terms sex offender and paedophile are often used interchangeably, there's a difference, namely, a sex offender has been convicted of a sex-related crime, which may or may not involve a child, whereas paedophile is reserved for people sexually attracted to pre-pubescent kids. Paedophilia is thus regarded as a psychological disorder, as it's not 'normal' to lust after kids. And unlike a sex offender, a paedophile may not have committed a crime as such i.e. they haven't acted on their desires.

Moreover, unlike those who relish in abusing kids, many paedos are haunted by their sexual attraction for kids. They hate their affliction and are often suicidal. They know it's wrong but can't help the way they feel. This despairing attraction is beyond their control (so they're born that way or made that way?). Hence, we can but have compassion for them, 'there but for the grace of God, go I'. Russell Brand (2014) highlights, 'when paedophiles talk about their obsession they always say they have no choice and the urge is overwhelming. And he asserts, 'it's unlikely that there's anyone in the world who can't identify with that urge or obsession: the distinction is object' (p.252).

Unlike paedos per se then, sex offenders often target teenagers. Some like kids who are going through puberty. It's highlighted they either rationalise it's okay to target young people, or they don't care. And then there's say teachers, who fall in love with their pupils (*Hey! Teachers! Leave them kids alone),* and pupils who become infatuated with their teachers. Is that wrong, as they also can't help it? Perhaps we should also feel sorry for these kiddy-fiddlers. It can be a challenge, particularly when kids start developing, and filling out. Like, jailbait Britney Spears in her school uniform, singing 'hit me baby one more time'?

So, kids are in demand. Like women, they're a commodity. Hence, thousands of women and children (fresh meat) are delivered to Britain every year to become sex-slaves. Human trafficking is the most profitable crime after drugs. It's also a multibillion-dollar industry. And like drugs, these operations are conducted at the highest levels of intelligence i.e. CIA black operations. Thus, we'll get back to this in Part 2.

For those unable to access kids, there's no shortage of kiddy porn. There's hundreds of millions of indecent pictures of kids online. It's highlighted that pervs or the 'unwell' not only get aroused looking at hardcore vile images/footage of kids, and new-born babies, but also kids subjected to very extreme acts of violence and abuse. Apparently, some people think children posing in provocative positions, rather than suffering horrific abuse, is more okay. It seems we each have our own level of what's acceptable to us. And some people cross darker lines.

Thus, beyond lust, and other kinky fetishes like asphyxiation (turning off the gas), is disgust. Like, a smear campaign and necrophilia? For the average bear however, it seems we have no idea just how infernally perverted some people are. 'Oh my' Christian Grey is a tame version of events.

It seems the world is spellbound, lost and depraved. And sex is intrinsically in the mix. But haunted perverts aside, and as touched on, there seems to be a sadness and emptiness about using people for sex. And whilst the erotic offerings may be enticing, it seems they're not fulfilling, like all substances, period. As Russell Brand (2014) said of his sex addiction, 'it became a joyless trudge through flesh' (p.257).

But moreover, it seems there's something sacred and esoteric about sex. Hence, sex magic practices (as we'll get to). And perhaps we can wonder if there's something sacred about virginity. It seems 'something' changes when the seal is broken? Vernon (2012) wrote, 'To be human is to hold some things as sacred. Not to do so would make us less than human' (p.96). It's always possible there's more to sex, at some metaphysical level, and as also mentioned, we literally need love. And whilst it's not for me, maybe rimming for hours on end is the ultimate demonstration of love?

For most people i.e. those not paying for sex, or torturing others into it, we have to make an effort to attract someone. Like, a bee to a flower, or a moth to flame. We need some kind of pizzazz, or at least look the part. Fortunately, this doesn't require much mulling over because society tells us what's 'in fashion'. We're told what to wear, and how to style our hair, so we can be a generic homogenised version of everyone else.

And how grim that Chanel boasted its 'globalisation of fashion'. It's duly noted, the world increasingly reflects western culture, as we're exposed to and affected by the same-ish media, and given the implication that materialism equals success. Cultural diversity is dying a death, as we're all merging to become blah Chanel.

Thus, people want tattoos, because tattoos are smart, like smart phones are smart. Or we're brainwashed to want these things, because we see cool people with them? It seems we're all about packaging in our depthless society, and we're brainwashed to be image conscious. It's imperative that we're attractive and fashionable.

Feminists say that as a backlash to feminism and women's breach of the power structure, society became obsessed with looks since beauty was the last of the old feminine ideologies. Introducing women as simply attractive mortals is to sustain their vulnerability by forcing their self-esteem to be subject to criticism. [See Naomi Wolf's 'The Beauty Myth: How Images of Beauty Are Used Against Women' (1990)].

So, from the 1980s supermodels landed, coupled with the boom of the cosmetic industry and the rise in eating disorders. Circa 3 million Brits are diagnosed with an eating disorder but many more (undiagnosed) have issues with food. Most eating disorders develop during adolescence. About 10% are diagnosed with anorexia nervosa (voluntary starvation). At least half never recover from this 'illness', which has the highest mortality rate of any mental illness. And about 40% suffer from bulimia nervosa. It's noted, whilst the anorexic will restrict calories and skip meals, for the bulimic the trick is to binge and purge. Our thoughts insist we can't gain weight, and we must obey our thoughts, like all addictions?

Anorexia/bulimia has trebled in the last decade and is especially high in adolescence. Whilst it most commonly affects girls and women, it has become more common in boys and men in recent years. Eating disorders are second only to depression as the most common new mental health problem for teenage girls. Experts highlight the increasing pressure to 'be perfect and look perfect' is now so severe that it threatens the mental health of an entire generation. Suffice to say, social media is exacerbating the unhealthy obsession with body image.

It does however seem ironic that girls aspire to look like super-models, who literally soil themselves walking down the catwalk on account of the laxatives they've taken to keep them super skinny. 'Get the London Look'. It's purported the toilets are minging behind the scenes (splashed with liquid brown). Being so slim, starving ourselves, betrays the stomach. Skinny birds are arguably victims. And yet it's also true, as Kate Moss said, 'nothing tastes as good as skinny feels'.

It's also noted, that the pressure to be slim, coupled with our social drinking culture, has led to a new eating disorder, namely, drunkorexic. Thus, we pick our battle with calories (since no one wants to be a heifer), binning food in favour of drink to keep the stealth svelte figure. The ethos has however always been that food is a waste of good drink. Eating is cheating. And we can always take class A's like Kate Moss, to get her figure.

And yet the irony is, for as much as we want to be skinny, it appears we also want to have a fat arse like Kim Kardashian (LOL). Hence, increasing numbers are undergoing butt 'augmentation' surgery. They get implants or transfer fat (the fat transfer procedure is commonly known as a Brazilian butt lift). To surgically transport fat around our bodies suggests we're the butt of the joke. Butt augmentation is the most dangerous cosmetic procedure but we're all about the butts, because society tells us.

But how sad is the aspiration to be a size zero, and how sad that a third of girls by age ten are worried about their body image. Given the stigma attached to looks, kids want their jug lugs and dodgy moles rectified. And no good can come from a skewed tooth to gum ratio. It seems most of us could benefit from some tweaking. Like, otherwise beautiful Iranian women, who have the most nose jobs (Iran is the nose job capital of the world), look better having reshaped their 'dodgy' nose (shaved off some bone).

And Asian people look better with the appearance of bigger (more western) eyes, having reduced the 'excess' skin in the upper eyelids. Eyelid plastic surgery has become the most popular of all facial cosmetic surgery procedures selected by Asian patients. Breast augmentation remains popular (because mammary size is very important), and there's been a labiaplasty boom in recent years, because our mud-flaps are the wrong size (LOL). It seems evident porn has propelled this demand, as who knew what anyone else's muff looked like?

There's no end to what we can perfect e.g. shorten our toes so they look cute in sandals, use fillers to 'enhance' our face and plump our lips (and our feet to endure high heels). Or have Dimpleplasty (dimple surgery) to be beautiful like Cheryl Tweedy and Ariana Grande. Blacks (and coloured people) bleach their skin, and the lily-white burn theirs chasing the tangerine dream. We bleach our teeth and anus with hydrogen peroxide, since we're all about the blinding smile (on both counts), and we wear other people's hair. Lovely. And we're all buying into it, literally. Like, 'nails' are big business. They're also important? Like the sex industry, the cosmetic industry is booming. It rakes in billions.

The 'beauty myth' (the homage paid to women's physical beauty to impede them) has however backfired on our male counterparts. Men are increasingly dissatisfied with their body shape and appearance e.g. their beer bellies, moobs, eye bags, sagging jowls and angry brow, receding hairline and going bald. The latter is tough. Apparently one of the biggest thing's men worry about is how their hair and clothes make them look.

Like women, it's commendable for men to be well groomed and wax their ass, crack and sack. It stands to reason that men need to be an acceptable height, but increasingly they're feeling the pressure to have chiselled abs, big arms, and muscular chests. It seems they aspire to look like Neanderthals? People are increasingly obsessed with their bodies, and even addicted to muscles. Increasing numbers of boys and men have an 'Adonis complex', where in addition to the egg whites and protein shakes, increasing numbers are taking steroids.

It seems with enough money people can look good, (or at least plastically good), and therefore feel good? It appears we don't feel good if we look bad, which blows if we look bad. It seems we're captivated by beautiful people, whereas munters blend into the background (in the absence of having a colourful personality). And we compare ourselves to beautiful people. We want their mathematical symmetry and airbrushed glossiness. And courtesy of the cosmetic industry, the average bear can have a taste of that adulation.

It seems everyone wants to be attractive, as survival of the fittest is survival of the most attractive. Attractiveness is valued in society. It entails more friends, employment opportunities, success, and romantic offers. And it's no revelation that kids don't befriend others on account of their appearance, and 50% of teenagers are bullied because of their looks.

But moreover, some people have a fear of ugliness, so called Cacophobia. The Elephant Man didn't stand a chance. 'Ugly people' get abused and battered (punched, kicked and spat on), like disabled people. It's highlighted that unlike racism and sexism, disablism (discrimination) is not in public consciousness. And no danger, a growing number of parents are turning to plastic surgery to 'help' their 'Down's Syndrome' children look normal from the 'outside'.

Body Dysmorphic Disorder (BDD), which involves an abnormal preoccupation with a perceived defect in one's appearance, highlights how self-esteem ties in with body image. And there's a BDD pandemic. Apparently 1:50 have BDD and it affects wo/men equally. Whilst we can all feel like a munter from time to time, for someone with BDD, they always feel like a munter. Rather than vanity, BDD is more about anxiety, as they spend time worrying about their appearance.

So, unlike those who look in the mirror and think 'yum', (those whose mirror you'd like to borrow), people spend hours every day looking in the mirror and criticising their looks. They're obsessed with their looks but not self-obsessed? For those plagued with the exhausting rigmarole of being perfectly groomed every day, depression ensues. Almost a third attempt suicide, and a third develop substance misuse problems.

Beauty and fashion are seen as central components of identity, particularly for young wo/men, but what about the person behind the physical, the superficial surface. What is beauty? Apparently, Socrates was extremely ugly but 'perfectly delightful' inside. And Jesus' looks wasn't His strong point. It's duly noted, that vain means 'empty, nothing'.

It's also clear that beauty is youth i.e. bald in the right places ('eew'), no wrinkles, no fat, no cellulite etc, or as feminists say, no power and easier to dominate. Perhaps men don't want an equal, but rather someone young and bald to dominate. It's noted, that unlike Brazilian waxes, which at least left a hint of age in terms of a landing strip, Hollywood waxes (full wax) are most popular. Girls as young as nine are getting bikini waxes. Indeed, they're offered cut price waxing. It's argued however that bikini waxing offers are cultural driven abuse i.e. the shrieks (pain), but also that girls aren't celebrating their aging body. And whilst society (porn) brainwashes us to this baldy end, I suspect that Kate Bush may make a comeback.

So, we want to look young because younger people are more attractive? Every box of Botox is notably tested on mice (nice). They're paralysed for days before they die. It's also interesting to note, that Botoxed frozen faces makes it harder to read others' emotions. Our facial muscles mirror others' expressions, but with Botox our muscles respond less, making emotions harder to identify, which makes us more autistic. And how literally sad, apparently Kim Kardashian doesn't smile because it gives her wrinkles.

Age appears to be currency. And as my mum says, we become invisible after 40. The shelf life for even the prettiest, including actresses and popstars, is limited. Although fair play to Madge (Madonna) hanging on with her pink leotard and giving credence to her camel toe. In his book 'Generation X' (1991), Douglas Coupland pertains to 'Dorian Graying' as the unwillingness to gracefully allow one's body to show signs of aging (p190).

It's almost as if aging is a disease, as opposed to normal development? Like the menopause, hence the provision of Hormone Replacement Therapy (HRT). HRT doesn't cure an 'illness', but merely delays the inevitable. And HRT is most popular, despite the increased risk of breast and ovarian cancer, and depression. HRT is notably harvested from the urine of pregnant mares. The mares are kept in cramped conditions, in the dark, with next to no water as strong piss is best. They are pregnant for 11 months, and the foals are slaughtered as crap meat, and then this process is repeated. HRT costs the NHS £2 billion a year.

Aging men are also becoming sick. Apparently one million men 'suffer' from the male menopause, so called andropause. A deficiency of testosterone gives rise to tiredness, moodiness, loss of libido, weight gain, and other symptoms, hence the provision of Testosterone Replacement Therapy. It seems we want to stay forever young, and we entertain a dismal view on aging. But maybe we should value age? We've earned our silver stripes and whiskers of wisdom.

Sociologists say we provide the 'gaze' and we adhere to a 'sexual fix'. That is, socially constructed models regarding sexuality, what we are and what we want to attract. Feminists contended that women were typically the objects, rather than the possessors of gaze i.e. the male gaze. But it seems men are increasingly objectified?

Rather than the mind being the most sexual organ, the ethos is, 'if you've got it, flaunt it'. More is more, and imagination is overrated. Hence, cleavages are consistently on display. And with regards to post-feminism and utilising our femininity or being empowered through sexuality, it's transpired that the jokes on us. Women have effectively become sex symbols, and this sexual identity is what men want. So, Sex and the City, and we're told its good fun. Dancing on stage, with the moves like Jagger, and providing the gaze. [See painting 'The Gaze'].

It seems society is obsessed with sexual relationships and espouses romantic love. It's like we inherit a mindset (from Disney movies?), that mandates we must have a partner. And so, the quest for true love begins. We need to find someone to complete us and make us whole. It's my suspicion however, that the predominant focus on our love lives, (inspired by celebrities' love lives), is another distraction to keep us from questioning the point of this existence. Surely there's more to life? Let's remind ourselves it's the 21st century, and a woman needs a man like a fish needs a bike. To fall in love is amazing but there's also the potential of looking into the same face and desiring to suffocate it with a pillow.

In theory marriage is a beautiful thing i.e. security, no broken hearts or STDs, but as Proverbs 21:19 states, 'it is better to live alone in the desert than with a crabby, complaining wife' (or husband). Thus, we've been warned. And further, maybe the 'top shelf' isn't so bad given 25% of women and 7% of men suffer domestic abuse, and there is no excuse. Two women are killed by a current or former partner every week. Women are more likely to be smacked about when pregnant, and women with disabilities are most vulnerable. Bugger that. Indeed, I'm all for reframing the crack: the top shelf is the penthouse.

It's also highlighted there's a growing abusive epidemic with teenagers. Feminists argue that men threatened by women's success, and feeling lost with regards to what was stereotypically their place in the world, manifest their anguish through anger. It's reported that all women are subjected to some form of sexism, and 60% of women will be physically or sexually abused.

However, (and parking the dark side of relationships), it seems Disney has left an imprint on us, and so we put ourselves out there. We get dolled up and throw some shapes on the dance floor. A blur happens and we wake up the next day with a kebab in our handbag, in conjunction with flashbacks of carnage from the night before. As highlighted, it seems the endeavour is to 'have fun', and then at some point, find 'the one' to ultimately start a family, which is the point of life?

With regards to modern lifestyles and 'What's the Point?', Russell Brand (2014) said, 'I used to believe in a system that I was born into: aspire, acquire, consume, get famous and glamorous, get high and mighty, get paid and laid. I wanted choice, freedom, power, sex and drugs and I used them and they used me' (p.9). And he later comments, 'I'm not a total idiot. If taking drugs worked I'd still be doing it, if promiscuous sex was continually fulfilling Id've carried on, if fame and money were the answer I'd hurl this laptop out the window and get on with making movies. They don't work, inspite of what I was told, and there's a reason for that...' (p.51).

But moreover, whilst we're led to believe that secularisation naturally birthed our postmodern society, it seems it's been engineered. Nothing is quite as it appears. Like, we know that history is written by the winners. The focus on self is by design. We're driven by what we want, and what we want is marketed to us. Money makes the world go round. Life is commerce? Soul sickness is also profitable e.g. addictions and other mental health problems.

At its most basic level, we don't need much 'stuff'. And we also don't need to work so much. As Bertrand Russell advocated, we could all work four hours a day. People would be less stressed, and more importantly, it would free up time to question the point, to discover the meaning of life? But it appears the powers that be, don't want us to question? They want us to be dumbed down and distracted by BS? Undermining critical thinking makes us easier to control.

Whilst we'll get back to Masonic witch Alice Bailey, not least because her Luciferian New Age philosophy is the UN philosophy (i.e. evolution, reincarnation, astrology and meditation), it seems pertinent to note her 'Ten Point Charter' as this has shaped our current state of affairs. It was designed to create a New World Order. Her strategy to change a nation from being Christian to Luciferian was to target children from 1945. She said, don't bother with the old people, as they're too stuck in the old traditions and they will not change.

Thus, she advised governments to take God and prayer out of the education system, and free kids from the bondage of Christian culture; reduce parental authority over children and promote excessive child rights; destroy the traditional family structure by promoting sexual promiscuity; make abortion legal and easy; make divorce easy; encourage homosexuality; debase art and make it run mad; use media to promote a change in mindsets; promote other faiths to oppose Christianity, and create an interfaith to usher in the new world religion; get governments to make all these law and get the church to endorse these changes to usher in the New World Order.

Fundamentally, the breakdown of the family would result in broken kids (drugs would be our new BFF). It's said that Christianity is the last stronghold against the programme. Hence, yoga is promoted as an alternative spiritual path to God. As touched on, the NWO is both political and spiritual. We need to be primed to accept Lucifer.

So, Bailey recognised the best way to control us, is to control our perception. And our perception can be controlled by information i.e. media and education. Social norms could be revised using the press, radio, TV, cinema, and other public 'entertainment'. Like, it's purported the Beatles, for example, wasn't a spontaneous rebellion by youth against the old social system, but rather a carefully crafted plot in cohort with the Tavistock clinic. The name 'Beatles' apparently comes from the scarab beetle, which is an Egyptian symbol for rebirth, as we'll get back to.

The Tavistock Clinic was founded in 1921, by British intelligence and psychiatry, and was funded by the Royal Institute for International Affairs. One of their primary objectives was mass mind control e.g. through movies, music, and drugs. As it transpires, we're predictable and programmable, and we embody a herd instinct, which they capitalised on. So, they conspired against the youth. They were after the kids. Thus, rock and roll, and pop music was introduced, with drugs like LSD. And words like 'cool' and 'teenager' were introduced just before the Beatles arrived on the scene.

They recognised how music creates emotions e.g. melancholy, enthusiasm. It conditions us. Thus, music was instrumental (pun intended) to the revolution. But moreover, music has the power to create characters. We identify with music and musicians? Like, the Beatles and the Rolling Stones? We want to be cool like them? Like, the Beatles made LSD look cool. Unlike 'old boring parents', teenagers knew the song 'Lucy in the Sky with Diamonds' was a reference to LSD. Or rather, Lucy refers to Lucifer in the sky (as we'll get to).

Bands like the Beatles and the Rolling Stones were perfect for leading us astray. Hence, the Tavistock Clinic enabled their sojourn to the US. It's understood they wanted to distract people from actually caring about issues, like anti-Vietnam and civil rights movements. In addition to providing us with idols, musicians were also instrumental to dishing out CIA supplied drugs, like LSD. So, the Cultural Revolution was a ploy to ruin kids. It became cool to piss, snort, smoke, and inject our money and health away. And 'free love' is awesome. We became less than cheap, as we give ourselves freely. Like, Mick Jagger and David Bowie were lovers (why not).

Moreover, at the heart of this New Age is Satanist Aleister Crowley's philosophy, namely, 'Do what thou wilt shall be the whole of the law'. John Lennon said, 'The whole Beatles idea was to do what you want… do what thou wilst, as long as it doesn't hurt somebody'. It's noted, that Crowley features on the Beatle's Sergeant Pepper's album, along with Carl Jung, and Satanists Karl Marx and Albert Pike (freemasonry hero). But the plot thickens, as apparently John Lennon wanted to blow the whistle. He wanted to tell the masses that social engineering goes back to Tavistock? Hence, the CIA bumped him off.

Furthermore, kids of military parents became stars (they were pimped out). Like, the Doors, the Monkeys, Mamas and Papas, Byrds, Eagles, Crosby, Nash and Stills. So, the music industry wasn't organic but rather an intelligence operation. It's reported, these bands were rigged to be successful e.g. connections, fans, promoters, places to play, contracts, instruments to play. The same happens today. That is, manufactured 'artists' and their crap music, and pointless 'celebrities' (like Kim Kardashian) continue to be pushed on us. And we idolise them? It seems if we listen to crap songs for long enough, we eventually like them?

It's highlighted that rap evolved from rock and roll. And rap is cool? It's cooler than heavy metal music, for example, which blatantly promotes Satanism. It seems music and characters have deteriorated over time? Like, Madonna's music was edgy in the eighties, but now we have skanky Miley Cyrus, Nicky Minaj, Cardi B and Lil Wayne, whose music videos are essentially soft porn. The message is that drink, drugs, sex, parties, and money are awesome. After the psychedelic sixties, the CIA flooded the streets with cocaine and heroin (from the 80s), but we'll get back to this.

It's noted, that Bailey's plan mirrors Vladimir Lenin's (1870-1924) ideology to infiltrate the west. The short version was thus, 'Corrupt the young, get them away from religion, encourage their interest in sex. Make men superficial by focussing their attention on sports, sensual entertainments and other trivialities. Always preach true democracy but seize power as fast and as ruthlessly as possible. Encourage government extravaganza, destroy its credit, encourage disorders and foster a lenient attitude towards disorders. By specious argument, cause the breakdown of the old moral values: honesty, sobriety and self restraint'. So, it's not an accident that society is the way it is.

It's also noted, that Aldous Huxley's 'Brave New World' (1931) parodies today's 'modern society'. Unlike George Orwell's tyrannical 1984, Huxley's dystopian world uses pleasurable diversions to create a citizenry too distracted to notice the chains that bind them. Like, drugs, entertainment, technology, and porn. The state uses 'non-stop distractions' to drown the minds of people into a sea of irrelevance. Like, following 'stars' on social media? Psychiatrists recognised that we can be conditioned through positive reinforcements (like facebook likes). They ruled covertly, as people were controlled, yet they 'felt free'. 'They were doing what they wanted'. The question of 'freedom' never arises.

In Brave New World, Soma is used to condition people into subservient compliant behaviour (like, the Stepford wives). This super-drug was ingested daily by citizens for the benefit of the state. The daily Soma ration was an insurance against personal maladjustment, social unrest, and the spread of subversive ideas. It also offered a 'holiday from reality', depending on the dose. It stimulated feelings of euphoria and pleasant hallucinations, and acted as a powerful sleep aid. It also increased suggestibility, which increased the effects of propaganda used to brainwash citizens.

In addition to Soma, sexual promiscuity was promoted by the state as another tactic to ensure people enjoy their servitude. The slogan was 'everyone belongs to everyone else'. The constant access to sexual gratification ensured that citizens were too distracted to pay attention to the reality of their situation. YOLO was drilled into people's minds from a young age. And with the institutions of monogamy and the family abolished, everyone was able to indulge in their sexual impulses without hindrance. So, Huxley predicted the future?

Huxley stated, (in a speech for Tavistock Group, California medical school, in 1961), 'There will be, in the next generation or so, a pharmacological method of making people love their servitude, and producing dictatorship without tears, so to speak, producing a kind of painless concentration camp for entire societies, so that people will in fact have their liberties taken away from them, but will rather enjoy it, because they will be distracted from any desire to rebel by propaganda or brainwashing, or brainwashing enhanced pharmacological methods. And this seems to be the final revolution'.

Besides our meaningless existence, it can always be worse. We just have to look at others' lives. More than a billion can't access safe drinking water, and half of the world's population live on less than £1 a day. The poorest countries in the world are notably poorer today than they were in the 1960s. It's estimated a billion go to sleep hungry every day. It's crazy, whilst we're dying of over-indulgence in the west, which includes eating too many pies, our brothers and sisters are starving to death and have no medicine. They're literally dying every other second on account of starvation and diseases that could be prevented or cured.

It's duly noted, that anorexia is virtually unknown in places where food is hard to come by. It seems to be an affliction of affluence. As discussed, we're blessed with so much in the UK, and it seems we create many of our problems? Others are begging because they're starving and have nothing to feed their children, not because they 'need' heroin (people won't die without heroin).

And to add insult to injury, in addition to our wasted meds, is our waste of food. Apparently a third of our food is wasted, which costs billions. It's criminal that food's binned amid the starving. Like, the retarded fishing quotas, which resulted in thousands of fish being killed every day, but thrown back into the sea, because they were surplus to requirements. [Besides suffocating to death, often the fish are so squashed in the nets, their eyes and stomachs pop out]. Surely there's a better way of managing our food e.g. order food in advance, which would help prevent all animals, fish and birds being slaughtered in vain.

But seriously, why are we so wasteful, because we can be? The earth's resources are being unduly depleted due to the free market, and the economics is arguably mad. Like, we import and export a similar quantity of the same commodity e.g. fish. Russell Brand (2014) notes that America exports the same amount of beef as it imports every year, stating, 'flying beef around the world, like a dead, carved up rent boy, because it serves the agenda of big business to the detriment of the planet and it's people doesn't require the contemplation of a sociological or economic genius, we just have to stop doing it' (p.87). He also points out that apples grown in Britain are flown to South Africa to be cleaned and waxed, and then flown back to Britain.

David Icke (2007) pertains to the stock piling that took place in the eighties, in response to the change in legislation, whereby farmers got paid for all their produce irrespective of whether they sold it or not. Hence, they produced shed loads, and hence it was an economic disaster, as one would expect? The outraged public had to foot the bill, and (conveniently) small and independent farmers went bust and were taken over by corporations. But moreover, (besides the globalist takeover), he points out the irony, that popstars were singing 'Feed the World' (1985) in the face of massive surpluses of food mountains. Thus, rather than giving our African siblings our surplus food, we watched them starve (on our TVs).

It's also noted, there would be more land for food if we stopped eating cows. James Lovelock (Gaia Theory) said, 'if we gave up eating beef we would have roughly 20-30 times more land for food than we have now'. Do we need to eat animals? It's pretty gross.

But moreover, our western countries have fleeced Africa and co from the start. Our politics created their dire straitjacket. We've created their debt and inability to feed themselves, despite having the resources to, because they owe us. And yet all we've done is rob them e.g. their gold, diamonds, oil, food, and even their people for slaves.

Vernon (2012) highlights, 'As we who live in a world that is ruled by the institutions of free markets can see very clearly, competition is a formula that can improve goods and services, but it must also pay the price of greed, selfishness, exploitation, injustice and violence' (p.184). And Russell Brand (2014) quotes (economist) John Keynes, who said 'capitalism is the extraordinary belief that the nastiest of men for the nastiest of motives will somehow work for the benefit of all'.

Suffice to say, it's all about the coin. The 21st century is the most unequal period in history. According to Oxfam, the world's 26 richest people own as much as the poorest 50% (circa 3.5 billion). But we'll get back to these fat cats, as it's possible they're part of a conspiracy. It's possible these globalists have a dastardly plan, and the devil financially rewards his people. Whilst Russell Brand (2014) states, 'the masters of the universe are just experts at Hungry Hippo', it seems the picture is much darker.

It's duly noted, that there's few players i.e. it's really a corporate oligarchy, and that free trade enables corporations to manufacture in the poorest countries (e.g. Asia) at the lowest price, and sell in the richest countries at the highest possible price[2]. Thus, both people in rich and poor countries are exploited for maximum profit. As Russell Brand (2014) highlights, 'when Nike moved from the US to Asia shoe prices did not drop, instead profit margins rose' (p.281).

It's also highlighted that our self-sufficiency is being undermined, with dependency created on the global economy. And no good can come from dependency because it underpins control? Martin Luther King junior said, 'eating breakfast this morning, you depended on half the world' (e.g. our orange juice, coffee, tea etc). We can but wonder how would we survive without it? And what life is like for those who provide our orange juice, coffee, and clothes. How are the sweat shops these days?

It also seems pertinent to acknowledge animals, who have no voice, and who we treat as commodities to be used. Besides our beloved cats and dogs, including pet fish or birds or rabbits and guinea pigs, we don't seem to care about the torture that takes place in say factory farms? Apparently, the UK munches one billion farm animals every year, and about 1,500 million sea fish and 80 million farmed salmon. It seems we have little regard for their life, that is, before we eat them. There's a cognitive dissonance. Animals feel pain, like our pets.

It's also noted, (like premature babies can be saved or killed), we torture some animals and help save the lives of others e.g. RSPCA. And further, there's no shortage of twisted Brits (thousands) who use pets for sex. People use websites to upload pictures and discuss preferences. Dogs, horses, cows, and sheep are among the animals targeted.

As for other animal torture, (besides eating them and using them for sex), millions squared of procedures are carried out for biomedical research and testing every year (largely mice, rats, hamsters and other rodents, but also fish, birds, frogs, dogs, cats, rabbits, guinea pigs, and monkeys). Before their deaths, some are forced to inhale toxic fumes, others are immobilized in restraint devices for hours, some have holes drilled into their skulls, and others have their skin burned off, or their spinal cords crushed.

In addition to the torment of the actual experiments, animals in laboratories are deprived of everything that is natural and important to them. They're confined to barren cages, socially isolated, and psychologically traumatized. Animals used in experiments are treated like disposable laboratory equipment. Like, pigs are shot so British army medics can learn to treat battle wounds. Unbelievable.

And every year around 40 million animals are killed for their fur. That's one every second. Fur farming includes fur from foxes, minks, raccoons, chinchillas, and rabbits (it takes up to 15 foxes to make a coat). Many of the animals are not killed outright, but rather they have their skins ripped from their bodies when still alive and conscious. How can anyone feel good wearing fur? Or feathers that have been ripped out a living bird? In many countries' animals are caught in vicious traps, where they spend hours or even days in agony. Some animals chew off their limbs in a desperate attempt to escape the pain of the trap.

Like animals, some people's lives are truly horrific (besides the poverty, disease, and starvation). Like those sold into slavery and butchered for their organs. Or take Congolese women for example, who are repeatedly raped every day. Apparently, the soldiers consider it their right, and often rape women using their guns and

---

[2] Arcadia, for example, a British multinational retail company, owns Burton, Dorothy Perkins, Evans, Miss Selfridge, Topshop, Topman, Wallis, BHS, and the chain Outfit, which sells lines from other group chains.

knives (leaving them not only massively traumatised but also with incontinence problems). Bloody awful, and we can but wonder is this evil or ignorance? The prevalence and intensity of rape in the Congo is described as the worst in the world. But what's most touching, is when asked what they would like done to their abusers, most of them choose to forgive (Jesus in action).

But rape, (which is less about sex and more about power), is rampant worldwide. In the UK an estimated 95,000 rapes take place each year. Yet just over a fifth are reported and only 1% of rapists are convicted. 9:10 know their attacker. It truly is a man's world. And we could really hate man. Or it's not their fault because they're social products? Or people choose to be good or evil?

The world is characterised by corruption, oppression, conspiracy, injustice, war and genocide. We steal, kill and rape on an unprecedented level. How we treat (torture) vulnerable others, including animals, can be diabolical. The twentieth century was marked by global violence and mass death. Humans killed more than 100 million fellow humans in the twentieth century alone. 50 million people were murdered in China, Russia, and other countries, to further the cause of communism. The human race is messed up, or we're unwittingly led into this anarchy?

As touched on, we're increasingly suspicious of 'the news' and we know our leaders are not to be trusted. As Wheeler (2009) said, 'While stationed with Army Intelligence in a high level analysis facility during the Vietnam War, I realised our government routinely, daily lies to us. In fact, it is a rarity when government officials tell 'the truth, the whole truth, and nothing but the truth'' (p.281). Hence, do we care about the millions maimed in Vietnam because of Agent Orange, or that more than 1:5 Iraqis have lost family members through war?

For most of us in the comfortable west, it seems we watch 'the news' and then we switch off. Or we switch over to something more 'entertaining'. Terrorists and 'countries of concern' are tentatively keeping us on our toes, but we're not at war (yet). Thus, we might feel bad for a moment or three but ever so quickly we're back to us. It seems we're largely consumed with ourselves and what's going on in our lives e.g. our next hairstyle, holiday, car, or kitchen sink. We might placate ourselves with our charity donations?

It's not our city that's just been bombed the shit out of. It's not our dead family and friends we have to crawl over to scamper for refuge. My refugee buds described this; can you imagine. They were from Somalia and said, 'anyone's president who has a gun'. We're not listening to sirens and bombs going off no-end. And yet, despite knowing the insanely horrific lives others lead, we can still sleep?

Perhaps we all have blood on our hands, as part of the system? Edmund Burke said, 'it is necessary only for the good man to do nothing for evil to triumph'. And Gandhi said, 'you must be the change you wish to see in the world'. Like, don't wear fur? The paradox of responsibility is notably that we are responsible for everything and at the same time we cannot be responsible for everything.

And it's not strictly true that we can sleep, as apparently a third of Britons struggle to get to sleep and five million have insomnia. The NHS spends millions on sleeping pills annually and apparently 'tiredness' costs the economy an estimated £1.6 billion a year. But that's not because we're worried about the rest of humanity but rather because we're self-absorbed and stressed? Like, we're anxious about our appearance?

Maybe we're being deliberately distracted by 'first world problems' and 'western' mental health problems? Maybe we become so consumed with how dreadful our life seems to be, that we forget how dreadful it is for others (like walking miles for water). It's all about us?

Hence, another problem that's promulgated is there's too many of us. And yet apparently, we could all fit into the state of Texas, with our houses. Not so charming Prince Philip notoriously said in 1988, 'In the event that I am reincarnated, I would like to return as a deadly virus, to contribute something to solving overpopulation'. Something like the corona virus? The human population has increased almost exponentially in the last 100 years and it's predicted there will be 9.7 billion people by 2050. Thus, our basic economic problem, namely, infinite wants and finite resources, is increasingly a problem. Or is it capitalism?

It seems our planet is in peril and its exacerbating. Besides the war on oil, there's food and water shortages aka more wars. It's predicted that over the next 20-40 years, the world will become more stressed, which does not bode well for our mental state. We're already using our planets natural resources (her forests, fisheries and croplands) at a rate that is unsustainable, and our waste is inexcusable.

It's highlighted however that the globalists are on a mission to curb the numbers e.g. through vaccinations, sterilisation, toxic food and drink (and water), drugs, chemtrails. Chemtrails are notably chemical and biological agents sprayed into the sky by aircrafts. It's understood our skies have been sprayed with heavy metals (like barium, aluminium and strontium) for two decades, which is linked to neurological disorders including Attention Deficit Disorder, Alzheimer's, Autism, Parkinson's, and dementia. The list goes on. Or this is all conspiracy?

And there's our tumultuous (changeable and violent) weather. We're told that global warming is primarily caused by human-induced emissions of greenhouse gases. So, we're to blame for higher average temperatures, freak storms, hurricanes, earthquakes, rising sea levels, droughts? Others however say it's a hoax, like James Delingpole (British journalist). He claims, 'climate change is the biggest scam in the history of the world'. And this fraud has cost taxpayers trillions i.e. providing grants to scientists whose research supports global warming. It's noted, that mainstream science is driven by funds, not necessarily an open mind.

Delingpole analysed e-mails among leading climate scientists that had been hacked and posted on the web, and he discovered a pattern of purposeful and coordinated efforts to manipulate the data. These include supporting the claims of a sudden and dangerous increase in the earth's temperature; not disclosing private doubts about whether the world was actually heating up; suppressing evidence that contradicts the hypothesis of anthropogenic global warming; disguising the facts around the Medieval Warm Period, when the earth was warmer than it is today; and suppressing opposition by squeezing dissenting scientists out of the peer review process. Like others, he asserts there's been no global warming since 1998. Hence, the preferred term is 'climate change'.

It's also highlighted that warming is caused by other environmental factors, like a stronger sun, for example, which happens as it goes through cycles. Hence, the Medieval Warm Period. The sea produces the most CO2, which happens when it warms up (when it cools, it absorbs CO2). So, it's always possible CO2 does not cause the warming but rather the warming causes the CO2. It seems carbon dioxide has been demonised. Yet Nature needs carbon dioxide to breathe. And there's only 0.04%.

Dr Timothy Francis Ball, who studied the climate for forty-two years, concedes climate change is a hoax, and the 'greatest deception in history'. He said weather is always changing and it's within its natural variability. He equally pertains to the manipulation of data, which is motivated by political and financial opportunities. Carbon dioxide is isolated as the problem, which means ignoring 95% of other gases. It's understood scientists only look at human causes to merit changing behaviours.

Patrick Moore, one of the founders of Greenpeace, agrees. He wrote to The Royal Society arguing there was no scientific proof that mankind was causing global climate change and believes that it 'has a much better correlation with changes in solar activity than CO_2 levels'. It's also noted, that sea levels are not rising because of melting ice. They've remained essentially unchanged for the last hundred years.

But furthermore, it's understood that not all natural disasters are natural, given the staggering amount of weather modification and geo-engineering programs. Like, in the UK, Project Cumulus was involved in cloud seeding experiments from 1949-1952, which resulted in the Lynmouth flood disaster in 1952. Thirty-five people died and many buildings and bridges were seriously damaged. According to the BBC, 'North Devon experienced 250 times the normal August rainfall in 1952'.

Cloud seeding changes the weather by creating or dispersing clouds, by releasing chemicals into the atmosphere by pilots (largely silver iodide, potassium iodide and ice). Whilst cloud seeding is usually used to create rain or snow, apparently hail and fog suppression are widely practiced in airports. Or take beloved Wills and Kate, who paid to have no clouds on their royal wedding day in 2011. Cloud-bursting companies guarantee 100% clear skies, stating you can't put a price on perfection, although you can, because prices start from £100,000. But maybe we shouldn't be spraying shiz into our skies and interfering with our weather. Like, pilots are spraying chemicals to block out the sun, so-called solar engineering, to prevent so-called global warming.

It's noted, that weather warfare has been used as early as Vietnam, when the US ran a cloud seeding program, namely, Operation Popeye (1967-1972). This weather modification program was used in Vietnam, Cambodia and Laos to induce rain and extend the monsoon season. It befitted the US to make their turf muddy. Whilst a treaty was signed in 1978 to ban weather warfare, its understood countries worldwide are engineering the weather for whatever nefarious purposes. Like, a 1996 official US Air Force document described the artificial creation of floods, hurricanes, droughts, earthquakes, storms, fog and precipitation, by the military. Being able to control the weather is a Weapon of Mass Destruction.

Like, HAARP (High Frequency Active Auroral Research Program), for another example, modifies the weather by shooting microwaves into the ionosphere (sixty miles above earth). This can create earthquakes, tsunamis, hurricanes, and volcanic activity. Like, the Venezuelan president, Hugo Chavez, insisted in 2010 the US triggered the earthquake in Haiti. So, perhaps we should focus on the climate changers and address the root of the problem. US President Lyndon Johnson (who replaced JFK) is renowned for saying (in 1962), 'He who controls the weather will control the world'.

It's said global warming is not about science, but politics and expanding the power of the elites. Global warming is a global problem that requires a global solution. Climate change affects everyone. And we need global problems to necessitate a global government. Like, global pandemics, global recession, and global war? Suffice to say, there's growing distrust of governments and scientists, given the bribes and profits at stake. Scientists are not necessarily ethical people. Lest we forget they create bioterrorism, like Ebola, anthrax, and corona viruses. They create plagues and pestilences. They torture people and animals.

It seems pertinent to note, (in tandem with secular reports), the Bible forewarns us there will be increasing wars, revolutions, plagues, epidemics, chronic famines, earthquakes, tsunamis, religious deception, and strange occurrences in space in the last days. So, we could be living in the last days? The prophecy of Shambala (Buddhist, BEF 700 CE) similarly predicted perilous times, stating, 'Drought, famine, disease and war will sweep the world...Nation will fight nations, and the larger will devour the smaller'.

Malcolm Muggeridge (1903-1990), British journalist, said, 'What is called Western Civilisation is an advanced state of decomposition, and another Dark Ages will soon be upon us, if, indeed, it has not already begun. With the media, especially television, governing all our lives, as they indubitably do, it is easily imaginable that this might happen without our noticing...by accustoming us to the gradual deterioration of our values'. It's said we're being subtly mind controlled, like a frog slowly boiling in a pot.

Yet more people are waking up to the lies we've been told? Our hypnosis is beginning to break down, as we're exposed to truth? Like, we understand our culture has been created and the aforementioned 'popstars' are essentially gimps working for the system. We no longer trust 'the news' and science as gospel? We're questioning the narrative we've been spoon-fed through media and education. Like, it appears we live on a flat stationary earth, and Darwinism doesn't add up?

Respectively, Muggeridge said, 'I myself am convinced that the theory of evolution, especially to the extent to which it has been applied, will be one of the greatest jokes in the history books of the future. Posterity will marvel that so very flimsy and dubious an hypothesis could be accepted with the incredible credulity it has'. So, Muggeridge knew better.

And we didn't go to the moon? The moon is apparently 240,000 miles away, and the furthest we've been since the alleged moon landings (since the sixties) is 400 miles away (the International Space Station is 250 miles away). One would think we would have returned many times by now, not least because our technology is infinitely superior?

Albert Camus (1913-1960), (existential) philosopher and author, said 'I see many people die because they judge that life is not worth living. I see others paradoxically getting killed for the ideas or illusions that give them a reason for living… I therefore conclude that the meaning of life is the most urgent of questions'. He also said, 'It is in the struggle of good and evil that life has its meaning'. Maybe life is a moral experiment? And we're not doing very well? Indeed, it's contended that the world grows more cynical, apathetic, disillusioned, uncaring and selfish, every day.

The script is, we reproduce (like animals) and perpetuate existence. But there is no real meaning or point. Hence, we might as well 'enjoy our time' aka 'good food, good wine, good time'. Maybe 'religion is the opiate of the masses', as Karl Marx said, or maybe we prefer opium? Maybe life is so unpleasant we need to invent supernatural stories to cling to, or placate ourselves with drugs. Substances help eliminate time, which could be considered otherwise precious. Benjamin Franklyn said, 'Does thou love life? Then do not squander time, for that is the stuff life is made of'. Or maybe we don't care? It seems we increasingly don't. The K-hole is better?

People also say they've no time to be depressed. No time to reflect and ponder. Like a hamster on a wheel (on speed), they can't come off. If they do, they may well confront depression. But maybe that's also a cop out. As Ferris Buler told us, on his 'day off' back in 1986, 'if you don't stop and look around once in a while you could miss it'. Surely, we should think about that which is most important. Namely, what's the point?[3]

---

[3] I'd question the sanity of someone who's never questioned, what's the point?

An Existential Portrait

'The play of life keeps going on, and on, and on. A never ending circle. There is no escape. And the person responsible for everything in my life is the face I see in the mirror every morning... the one who had big hopes and dreams. I waken up each morning and wonder if today will be different. So often it feels off track, empty and numb, superficial and pointless. How long do I try to convince myself, when madness is all around. We have to keep up facades, even when we don't feel fully alive. Everything appears fine watching it from the outside, but inside it is a different story. We have to ride the waves or drown beneath them. The choice is ours. We cry out to God for relief... but all we hear is silence. Is He listening? Has He abandoned us?

Do we endure it because the opportunity for things to be better is round the corner... only we can't see round the corner. Is waiting a necessary part? There have been so many times I didn't know what to do or where to turn. I had to tie a knot at the end of my rope and hold on, but I'm still here, even though I've felt like giving up. Still, I can't live a positive life with a negative mind. They say every situation is a lesson and the obstacles we overcome serve to make us stronger and help to make us more understanding and compassionate. As Robert Broult said, 'where hope would otherwise become hopelessness it becomes faith', and an unknown author said, 'some see a hopeless end while others see an endless hope'. Hope is certainly my best friend'.

By my wonderful mum, Lynda Stalker

'No one comes back from the dead, no one has entered the world without crying; no one is asked when he wishes to enter life, nor when he wishes to leave'. Soren Kierkegaard

I'm like you. I'm passing through. I'm here now, and just like that, I vanish like a fart in the wind.

2

Existential Roots

So, we're born, unlike millions of foeti each year. We could deduct that we're lucky to be here, but the depressed would dispute this. Indeed, the depressed (the mental lepers) may resonate with Nietzsche's deduction, namely, it's 'best not to be born but second best is to die quickly'. We didn't ask to be here, nor did we choose the bodies or environments we were born into. I didn't choose my white female body coupled with my British passport aka silver spoon up my ass, anymore than the little Somali dude chose to be born with no limbs and bake in the sun with flies in his eyes. That's consciously not our choice.

But regardless, we're here now, and the starting point (for existentialists) is the human experience. We can only be-here-now when we accept that right now is instantaneous moment by moment, real living experience. This very moment is the only real thing.

So, what does it mean to be alive, to be consciously aware that we're living now? In an existential nutshell, we get our life, we choose our choices, and we die. And unless we're some genius who contributed to mankind, no-one (besides our loved ones) will care that we were here. King David's 'three score and ten' (seventy) years equates to 25,568 days, to mince around. So what now, before we're clutching our chest on the way out. What to do with our time, besides drink, smoke and mainline heroin?

I've migrated towards existentialism since I'm all for advocating 'you choose your choice'. Rather than too many cop outs, it's about being responsible for the choices we make. This philosophy maintains that what we are (our essence) is the result of our choices (our existence), and hence Sartre's assertion that 'existence precedes essence' rather than the reverse. Sartre said, 'man is nothing else than what he makes of himself' and 'man is fully responsible for his nature and his choices'.

Essence or nature comes from free choice, where we each fashion our own unique individuality. This premise enshrines John Locke's (1602-1794) tabula rasa concept aka we're born a blank slate (tabula rasa is Latin for blank slate). This maintains that human development is primarily influenced by environment. Genetically this is not the case given genetic predispositions, but still we choose our choice?

George Kelly (1905-1966), clinical psychologist, famously said 'all men are scientists', because we test reality using hypotheses. We explore our world, make hypotheses about it, and alter those hypotheses in light of experience. Experience in life is thus similar to testing ideas about events or hypotheses in experiments.

Sartre (a movie buff) observed no preordained script in life. For him, we're like actors thrust onto a stage, but we haven't learned our lines or script, and despite no direction, we must nevertheless decide for ourselves how to live. For Sartre, man exists, encounters himself, surges up in the world and defines himself afterwards. We exist before we can ex-ist and reflect on who we are. We exist in-situation, and thus transcending our existence, we engage with ex-isting, in the sense of standing outside our self and looking in.

Sartre said, 'as far as men go, it is not what they are that interests me, but what they can become'. And he acknowledged, 'we do not know what we want and yet we are responsible for what we are – that is the fact'. So, we are what we make ourselves to be. We get our deal but it's what we do with our deal that counts. Voltaire likewise said, 'each player must accept the cards life deals him or her: but once they are in hand, he or she alone must decide how to play the cards in order to win the game'.

In tandem with philosophers who say that life must be understood backwards, we'll start with Jean Paul Sartre (1905-1980), known as the Pope of Existentialism, because he pope-ularised the movement after WW2. And then we'll get to the fathers of Existentialism, namely, Soren Kierkegaard (1813-1855), followed in close pursuit by Friedrich Nietzsche (1844-1900). It's noted that, whilst differing in their doctrines, existentialists shared the belief that philosophical thinking begins with the human subject, not merely the thinking subject, but the acting, feeling, living human individual. And unlike much philosophy that undermines feelings and emotions, existentialists place great significance on emotions as these summon awareness (they scream at us).

An existential thinker therefore draws his or her entire existence into their philosophical reflection. The key word is existence which is not the same thing as being alive. There are many living beings (e.g. plants and animals) but they don't consciously think about what existence implies. They simply exist and roll with their instincts. Like, hippos basking in the river. Only conscious beings can be observers and reflect. We can stop and look around, take timeout to examine our lives, to date.

So, with self-awareness, we know that we know. Self-awareness is the capacity for introspection i.e. we examine our thoughts and actions. Virginia Woolf said, 'without self-awareness we are babies in the cradles'. 'Psychological mindedness' refers to our capacity for self-examination, reflection and introspection. But it also includes having insight into other's intentions and motives. We can infer what others are thinking?

The 'theory of mind' is that children develop minds, and recognise that others equally have minds, which are full of thoughts, memories, emotions, dreams and wishes. It's said that if you treat a child as if they have a mind, their mind magically forms. Autism is notably defined as having a lack of theory of mind. As Scott Peck said, autism is narcissism in the extreme.

So, what sense do we make of existence? What do we infer about ourselves, others, and the nature of reality? For 'atheist' Nietzsche, (who founded atheist existentialism), there is no God, and for 'Christian' Kierkegaard (who founded theistic existentialism), there is a God. Christianity notably means to have a personal relationship with God through Christ. Christians believe the Bible is God's word. It's the treasure map to the Kingdom of Heaven. And we have this time, (while we're still breathing), to figure out this conundrum for ourselves. That is, is there a God, and rationale for existence? And if so, perhaps we'd like to hear it? Or are we placing our faith in the allegedly clever materialist scientists, and hoping they're right?

I like to romanticise about the existentialists, basking in their post WW2 freedom, listening to jazz, raking on fags (when smoking was healthy), and discussing the nature of human beings, existence, and the point. Sartre notably viewed jazz as a representation of freedom and authenticity. When asked what jazz might be, Louis Armstrong said, 'if you still have to ask...shame on you'. It was a creative time couched in a culture of freedom. People were free and had choice. And choice is liberating. In its French expression, existentialism was a child of liberation.

According to the likes of Sartre, wo/men could do whatever they wanted, and be whoever they wanted to be. A *brand new start* can happen anywhere and at any time. We can change our minds and reinvent ourselves. Jane Fonda said, 'my great asset is that I am constantly changing' (cited in Sue Atkinson, 'Climbing out of Depression', 2005 p.188). Good for her. Or take Lady Gaga, for example, who presents herself however she chooses, or rather the company that owns her?

Sartre was also insistent that we stop lying to ourselves. There's always a choice. We don't have to stay in some job, or live in some house, in some country, with some miserable partner. But rather we choose to, for whatever reason, probably financial?

It's understood the one factor that most discourages people from experiencing themselves as free is money. We're controlled by debt. But like Jesus, Sartre insisted we don't need 'stuff'. And like Jesus, he equally had nothing e.g. no house, car, wife, kids, and apparently he burned all his books on one occasion. He condemned capitalism, which he felt steered us into working an insane amount of hours to buy 'stuff' we're brainwashed into buying. We're dictated to, but we don't have to go along with the 'programme' at hand. Sartre spent his life challenging traditional thinking and testing the limits. His revelation of 'no set path to follow' was radical at the time, unlike today?

Sartre embodied freedom. And that included sexual freedom, despite his lifelong partner, Simone de Beauvoir (1906-1986), who was buried beside him. Indeed, he was quite the lothario, and often kept beautiful company e.g. models. And yet Sartre always felt ugly (he frequently described himself as ugly), and aware of his downfall (?) he famously said, 'hell is other people'. He was aware that we can't escape the gaze. He was 5 foot 3, and had a wandering eye (squint), so he capitalised on his brain.

But Sartre was cool. He was a rebel with a just cause. Not dissimilar to Che Guevara, who he met in Cuba in 1960, along with Castro and other leaders in the revolution (apparently the FBI kept tabs on Sartre). In his Parisian way, Sartre was also revolutionary? We don't need to conform to the prescription (the checklist, milestones and boxes). We're free. Like Voltaire said, 'Man is free at the moment he wishes to be'. Our freedom is all encompassing. We don't have to care what others think, but rather be true to ourselves. And there was a growing consensus that we were free from God's opinion.

For Sartre, there is no God. But rather, each of us necessarily plays God to others, where 'others' are reduced to mere characters in our drama, in the sense that our life is a play that we direct. Sartre proclaimed that we are the authors of the play of our own lives. Rhonda Byrne, author of 'The Secret' (2006), concedes, 'you are the designer of your destiny. You are the author. You write the story. The pen is in your hand, and the outcome is whatever you choose'. Our identity is the autobiography, metaphorically speaking, that we write as we move through life. We're a story in the process of being written.

Thus, we make up the rules, not God. Sartre, who insisted on freedom, made assertions like, 'if God is real, man is not free' and 'if man is free, God is not real'. It seems society was disillusioned with God, as where was

God in war, in the holocaust? And moreover, 'science' was rejecting God, which was refreshing as there's no condemnation? We were no longer constrained by society or the church i.e. the moral standards imposed upon us.

Whilst we'll get back to Nietzsche, it seems pertinent to note his most famous pronouncement, namely, 'God is Dead'. By that he meant that modern science has rendered belief in the divine irrelevant. Humans are reduced to a mere product of nature, a mistake. But this came at a cost, given the implication that we are without intrinsic value or ultimate hope, namely, nihilism. Thus, whilst advocating the 'death of God', Nietzsche was nevertheless disturbed by the rain cloud of nihilistic doom, that he saw enveloping European society. He recognised that life would be deemed pointless, and he observed that as people come to reject religion, they end up rejecting any ultimate values.

[This famous dictum 'God is Dead' notably featured on Life magazine in the movie 'Rosemary's Baby' (1968). Rosemary's baby is of the Devil's seed. This film that we'll get back to, was written and directed by paedo Roman Polanski (he was accused of raping a thirteen year old girl, having first supplied her with sedatives). His pregnant wife, actress Sharon Tate, was murdered by members of the 'Manson Family', the cult of mind-controlled Satanist, Charles Manson, a year after it was released. However, I digress].

Darwin equally recognised that by writing off God, nihilism would loom over us. Thus, he sat on his theory of Natural Selection (he refrained from getting it published) for over twenty years. Apparently, he didn't want to kill God.

With no God, society is devoid of any meaning, and there are no universal overarching moral codes to guide our actions. Such freedom could be extremely dangerous. Nietzsche argued that if God doesn't exist then everything is permitted. Traditional morality disappears. We can do whatever we want. If someone annoys us, we could kill them? Thus, Nietzsche's self-appointed task was to combat the nihilism this event entailed and promote wo/man to create our own 'divinely inspired' values.

Nietzsche was the first philosopher to study nihilism and whilst he wrote extensively about it, as he was concerned about the effects on society and culture, he did not advocate it. For him, nihilism was a disease. He was insistent that life is meaningful, (which is ironic because he was a sickly and depressed man who self-medicated with huge doses of opium and other sedatives). But it's up to us to cultivate purpose and meaning. Existentialism thus challenges nihilism. The emphasis was on finding an alternative to the void that was left by God's absence. It seems scientific humanism is the 21st century religion, our current (divinely inspired) values. But it's increasingly eastern philosophy?

So, Sartre was on the same page as Nietzsche, and he was having none of the church. And whilst he was accused of moral corruption, it seems Sartre said what others were thinking. That is, he spoke to those who recognised the façade of going to church when their heart wasn't in it? God knows how many people were going to church who weren't Christians. As the late Keith Green (musician) said, 'Going to church doesn't make you a Christian anymore than going to McDonald's makes you a hamburger'. And how otherwise boring going to church, unless it's real historic supernatural truth?

But Sartre's outspoken atheism still seemed rebellious, hence he was cool? And it was also cool that he chose to smoke, drink, take drugs, and sleep around. Why not? He was free and we should all be free. It's our fundamental right to choose our choice, and do whatever we want (on the premise we don't harm others, including kids and animals). It's understood God designed us to have freewill.

Freedom constitutes the ultimate value for existentialists, and Sartre insisted everyone has a right to liberty. Hence, our duty is to ensure that others enjoy freedom, as we do. Sartre advocated that humans are responsible for humans, stating, 'you are responsible for the period of history that you are living in. You have not only the right to choose, but the duty to choose and if you are surrounded by poverty, by war, by oppression, by cruelty – that is what you have chosen'.

Terrorists (like Palestinians) were seen as desperately oppressed. Sartre maintained that terrorism is the only means which 'underdogs' have to revolt. He described terrorism as the poor man's atomic bomb. Terrorists are victims of whatever regime. Take beloved but terrorist Mandela. He had to break a few eggs, (and spend a lifetime in a tiny jail cell), as that racist crack was not okay.

Sartre's philosophy envisaged culture as a very fluid concept. Neither predetermined, nor definitely finished, but rather culture was always conceived as a process of continual invention and reinvention. The only thing constant is change. Einstein conceded, 'to have a better life, we must continue to keep choosing how we are living'.

So, we're responsible for our state of affairs. Our freely chosen actions have value. Like, we let our governments represent us? We let heinous atrocities happen on our watch. Thus, whilst the newfound freedom rocked, it came at a cost, namely, responsibility. We're responsible for our choices (choosing not to choose is a choice). We have the power to change the direction society is taking us, but it's easier to let the state dictate to us, than we dictate to the state? It's easier to have no responsibility, relinquish our power, so we're not accountable?

Sartre recognised the state is the biggest threat to freedom, and he was up for overthrowing the state. As it transpires then, freedom is more of a burden, than a luxury. It's highlighted, that once we're aware that we're free, we feel anxiety and dread, as there's no one else to blame.

So, Sartre insisted on being truthful with ourselves. The emphasis is on authenticity. It's our duty to be honest? Sartre's 'bad faith' is living inauthentically, and in his view the inauthentic person is living a lie. We lie to ourselves that we don't have freedom to choose other choices. We choose to believe we're not free. Sartre's notion of radical freedom stipulates that everyone always has a choice, and every act is a free act. Thus, when people say they had 'no choice' but to do something, they are lying to themselves.

He recognised that such 'bad faith' seems to be our 'natural' disposition. That is, to flee from our freedom and lie to ourselves. Nietzsche similarly said, 'the lie is a condition of life'. But Sartre insists 'we are without excuse'. Hence, he held those, who acted like they had no choice and were not really free, in contempt. We're always free to change our situations, so we can't complain? It's also highlighted that no-one can make us feel happy, sad, or angry, but us. We could choose different emotional responses or choose not to care.

Sartre took no prisoners. There were no excuses for the weak-willed dieters, drinkers, smokers, drug-takers, adulterers, gamblers, Master Baters etc, who protest we won't (or don't want to) do whatever but know we will. Excuses are planned. We deceive ourselves with the same consciousness. It's a cynical lie. As the truth is, we decide. Our 'personality' is our underlying instinct that urges our decision. In counselling we notably assess 'motivation for change'. Do people want to change, or does it seem like too much effort? Can we help ourselves? Morality is arguably a choice, and mental health arguably requires discipline.

Sartre further condemned those who made up excuses and explanations for what they had or hadn't done, to convince others that they're not responsible for their actions. It's like we play a self-defeating game? We pretend to ourselves and others. But Sartre wasn't buying it. Sartre observed that bad faith plagued society. In his words, 'bad faith is knowledge that is ignorant and ignorance that knows better'. Thus, actions speak louder than words.

It seems apposite to note Thomas Szasz's vantage (1920-2012), a psychiatrist who was anti-psychiatry. In 'The Untamed Tongue: A Dissenting Dictionary' (1990) he wrote, 'The concept of disease is fast replacing the concept of responsibility. With increasing zeal Americans use and interpret the assertion "I am sick" as equivalent to the assertion "I am not responsible": Smokers say they are not responsible for smoking, drinkers that they are not responsible for drinking, gamblers that they are not responsible for gambling, and mothers who murder their infants that they are not responsible for killing. To prove their point — and to capitalize on their self-destructive and destructive behaviour — smokers, drinkers, gamblers, and insanity acquitees are suing tobacco companies, liquor companies, gambling casinos, and physicians. Can American society survive this legal-psychiatric assault on its moral and political foundations?'

Szasz maintains addiction is individual election (he advocates society should permit a free-trade in dangerous drugs, with restrictions like alcohol and tobacco), and he also insists that suicide is a fundamental liberty. He thus recommends a policy of total non-intervention towards suicide and addiction, as these are our rights. In tandem with the existentialists, he said 'People often say that this or that person has not yet found himself. But the self is not something one finds; it is something one creates'. We'll get back to Szasz.

The observation is thus, we primarily live in a world without thinking. Before we ever start thinking, we are already living, and we are fundamentally living inauthentically. We passively accept the values and beliefs that have been handed down to us. We incessantly pick up and disseminate attitudes, behaviours, stereotypes and attributions, basically regurgitating what we've been spoon fed. We're expected to behave the way we've been shown, no questions asked?

Respectively, Sartre stressed it's imperative to question everything. He insisted we need to think against/criticise everything that has ever been 'given' to us. This includes 'education' and 'the news'. Sartre said, 'I think against myself'. To be authentic therefore means to think for ourselves. It's refusing to take things for granted, like we've been told the truth? It involves recognising the belief system that has been passed down to us, and really questioning if all the 'isms' (e.g. racism, sexism, ageism, disablism, anti-Semitism) and the rest we've been programmed with, make sense. Like, it's okay to factory farm animals and torture them in sadistic experiments?

We like to think we think for ourselves, yet psychological experiments consistently show we're conformists of the highest order. For (quirky) example, take applause, and the fact it's not so much to do with the act but rather how much others are clapping. Psychologist Solomon Asch's (1951) famous experiment shows how social pressure from a majority group can affect a person to conform. The 'majority' influences our beliefs and opinions.

Thus, participants were shown a target line, which they have to match with one of three lines. One is the same length, one clearly shorter, and the other longer. Confederates (pretending to be real participants) go first, providing the blatantly wrong answer, and participants tend to concur despite knowing otherwise. Apparently, people conform for two main reasons, namely, because they want to fit in with the group (normative influence), and because they believe the group is better informed (informational influence). Most of them said they went along with the group for fear of being ridiculed or thought 'peculiar'.

It's also pertinent to note, Stanley Milgram's famous Experiment (1963), which demonstrates 'The Perils of Obedience', to authority figures. Inspired by the Germans in WW2, Milgram was interested in seeing how easily ordinary people could be influenced into committing atrocities. Thus, participants (volunteers) were told they were partaking in scientific research to improve memory. They were (unknowingly) paired up with a confederate 'Mr Wallace', and whilst they draw straws to see who becomes the 'learner' and the 'teacher', the outcome is fixed because the participant is the teacher, who has to administer electric shocks to the learner. The learner is strapped to a chair with electrodes attached to his arms in the room next door, and each time he provides a wrong answer (the teacher asks words in a word game), the teacher is told to increase the voltage by the doctor.

It's crazy, as the teachers can hear 'Mr Wallace' screaming, and shouting to get out, but because the authority figure, the man in the white coat, tells them to continue, most people do. Experts estimated 1-3% of subjects would not stop giving shocks to potentially fatal levels (450 volts), as it was thought psychopathic to do so, but as it transpired 65% never stopped giving shocks. All participants continued to 300 volts. This experiment horrified America, as they realised decent American citizens were equally capable of committing crimes against their conscience, as Germans had under the Nazis.

So, we choose our potentially psychopathic choices. And we have to take responsibility for our actions, like Nazi war criminals? They can't blame Hitler? Besides the freedom, and the burden of the freedom, Sartre recognised the 'absurdity' of life. He recognised the nihilism, the absolute meaninglessness of life. And he recognised the sense of alienation in modern society i.e. city dwellers. He observed that wo/men feel 'alien' in a world without meaning, yet he surmised there is no point or meaning.

He noted that we eat and drink to preserve our existence and yet there's no point. And yes, we are alone. We come into this world on our own, and we leave this world on our own. Our sense of alienation creates feelings of despair, boredom, nausea, and absurdity. And contrary to mental health 'professionals', (at least) for Sartre it's perfectly normal to be bored and depressed. It's part of the human condition.

And it may well come to surface that we face the ultimate either/or, namely, choosing whether to live or die. Death offers freedom from a mindset of despair, with the irony being that we create our mindset. We choose what we think about, including suicide. It's duly noted, the prospect of suicide can ironically serve as a coping strategy. We can kill ourselves if it gets that bad. Nietzsche similarly arrived at this deduction, stating 'it is always consoling to think of suicide: in that way one gets through many a bad night'. He also famously said, 'what doesn't kill you makes you stronger'.

It seems we need to cultivate or conjure up reason not to end our life. Or get some meds pronto. Eckhart Tolle (2011) asserts that if a situation is intolerable and makes us unhappy, we have three options (besides topping ourselves), namely: remove our self from the situation, change it, or accept it totally, surrender and free our-self internally. Latterly, this involves harnessing a Buddhist mindset and transcending this reality. It seems our soul is screaming for meaning?

Existentialists actively look for meaning, and despite being unpleasant, painful emotions can provide the right catalyst for serious reflection and change in our life. Emotion literally means 'disturbance'. The word comes from Latin 'emovere', meaning to disturb. Depression and anxiety, for example, can be triggers telling us something needs to change? Thus, however unpopular, given it flies in the face of all treatment of depression today, one of the major tenets of existential psychology provides that despair and crisis are not necessarily bad things to be tranquilised and cured as quickly as possible (much to the dismay of Big Pharma). 'Therapeutic despair' holds tremendous possibility for self-acceptance, growth, and positive change.

Psychiatrist Donald Winnicott (1896-1971) asserted 'depression has within it the germ of recovery'. He said, 'If we experience nothingness while finding the courage to go on with life, we gain affirmation both of the power of being and also of the fact that the power and worth of existing or being gives some meaning to our lives even while we're experiencing nothingness' (cited in Cook, 1999 p.58).

Maybe, as Thomas Moore (psychotherapist, monk and author) argues, the word 'depression' is too clinical, and essentially reductionist for something that makes us question the very meaning of life. He cautions that we do ourselves a disservice when we treat our feelings of despair and emptiness as deviations from the healthy, normal life we idealise. And he cautions labelling difficult emotions as sick.

Moore believes we live in an age that has suffered a 'loss of soul', and this is manifested by depression, addictions, obsessions, and violence. But he believes the cause of these symptoms is linked to a deeper crisis of meaning. And this can be missed because the medical approach to such symptoms is to alleviate them (with pills), and not to try and understand them. He suggests that rather than depression, we might be experiencing a 'Dark Night of the Soul'. The Spanish mystic and poet John of the Cross (1541-1597) referred to the Dark Night of the Soul as a period of sadness, loss, trial, frustration, failure. He wrote the account, Dark Night of the Soul, after a period in prison in solitary confinement.

In his book 'Dark Night of the Soul' (2004), Moore states a dark night may be a period of apparent lifelessness that precedes a new birth of meaning. He points out that whilst depression is a label and a syndrome, a dark night is a meaningful event. He states, 'Depression is a psychological sickness, whereas a dark night is a spiritual challenge'. He advocates that a Dark Night of the Soul is a normal part of life, a natural process of change. Darkness has transformative power, like alchemy. And like grief, which is a process and more than just an emotion, a dark night can be a painful restructuring that necessitates change.

He highlights, 'if the dark night is to be as beautiful and powerfully life-giving as John of the Cross says it is, then you have to grasp the special enlightenment offered by the dark' (p.108). He contends that 'dark nights of the soul can play a role in transcending mediocrity, where accepting mediocrity involves giving up the possibility of living an outstanding life'. The trouble is however, 'a dark night of the soul is dark because it doesn't give us any assurance that what is happening makes sense and will ultimately be beneficial'.

Sartre concedes, 'life begins on the other side of despair'. But as an atheist, he considered it futile searching for the meaning of life in general. The twentieth century is meaningless, an accident of chemical combinations. But moreover, besides 'the depressed' willing death, others experience overwhelming anxiety about the prospect of death and the pointlessness of existence. Hence, it gets worse (?), as with no meaning or philosophy of life to cling to, and knowing that we're alive now but will one day die, gives rise to angst. Like, one of my chums seriously freaks out at the prospect of not being here, and there's nothing she can do about that apart from not think about it.

Sartre relayed that we experience a sense of dread and feel nauseous aka an existential crisis. This sense of dread or angst can lead to religious faith, as Kierkegaard spells out and which we'll get to later, but not for Sartre. For Sartre, the individual is solely responsible for giving life meaning. Life is what we make it.

In his first novel 'Nausea' (1938), Sartre writes about a thirty-year-old man, who's struggling to restore a sense of meaning to his life. Disenchanted with life, he wanders the streets and cafes, acutely aware of his nausea. He's basically having an existential crisis and is regularly afflicted with nausea attacks. He feels nausea whenever he suddenly becomes aware of life's meaninglessness and absurdity. Indeed, he gets disgusted at the absurdity. Life bores him and he tries to make time pass. Like, he eats, for example, not because he's hungry, but rather to pass the time. He's aware that he's free to choose but he has no enthusiasm about anything, but rather seems to exist passively.

Durant said, 'to say that we are free is merely to mean that we know what we are doing' (cited in Harris, 1972 p.237). In fairness, life is completely absurd if there is no point. And it's no revelation that 'research' shows bored people eat more.

Sartre believed in human freedom and freewill, and whilst Nausea is arguably depressing, it urges us to give our existence meaning. For Sartre, the fact life is meaningless gives us scope to make it meaningful. He was sensitive to the unfulfilled potential of human beings. But furthermore, beyond this merely being our prerogative, he believed that life must have meaning, it's an imperative. Thus, rather than viewing our freedom and independence positively, Sartre viewed it as a curse. He emphasised the burden of individual freedom, since it's up to us (and no-one else) to find meaning, since to exist is to create our own life. Sartre said, 'Man is condemned to be free; because once thrown into the world, he is responsible for everything he does'.

We're essentially depicted as hostage to our own freedom, adrift a godless universe. And each one of us must find our own existential way. We are self-acting agents, and choice by choice, we 'become' who we are. He said, 'humans are nothing: no ordained plan of what they ought to be. They will not be anything until later, and they will be what they make of themselves later'.

Thus, it seems freedom offers boundless possibilities but being aware that we're responsible for our choices can be a chore. Like, we could be a jazz musician if we got off our arses. The fact that we're free to change our situation, makes it worse? It can make us want to flee this responsibility. Like sleep, drink, or take drugs? Sartre highlights that when confronting anxiety-related emotions, we become aware of our freedom. He used the word anguish to describe the realisation that we have total freedom of choice, and there are no constraints on us bar those we choose to impose.

For Sartre, human beings live in anguish, not because life is dreadful, but rather we're condemned to be free. The anguish of existence is that everything is terrifyingly possible because nothing is preordained. Kierkegaard called this awesome sense of freedom and responsibility, which is simultaneously attractive and repulsive, 'ambivalence dread'.

It's noted, the existentialist distinguishes anguish from fear. Thus, fear has a definite object e.g. we're afraid to fall off the cliff, whereas anguish is the awareness that we could throw ourselves off the cliff. So, anguish is a good thing because it engenders freedom? It gives us the opportunity to redirect ourselves back to authenticity. More generally, whilst there's nothing we can do about our pending demise, or the fact there is no ultimate meaning (at least for Sartre), if we want otherwise (day to day) meaning in our life, we need to make it happen. Like, devise goals for ourselves. If we don't, we may well declare we're bored.

So, besides the anxiety, nausea, dread, depression, anguish etc, boredom is a major existential problem for the psyche. We get so very bored. As Iggy Pop said, 'they say that death kills you, but death doesn't kill you.

Boredom and indifference kill you. I need more'. We can justify that it drives us to destructive behaviours such as overeating, gambling, alcohol and drug abuse. Boredom's associated with depression and anxiety, hence the urge to eradicate it. Albert Camus said, 'The truth is that everyone is bored, and devotes himself to cultivating habits'.

It's highlighted that we live in the 'Age of Distraction'. And we've become passive recipients of stimulation e.g. we put the TV on, or play a computer game. We need to be entertained. Maybe worrying about drivel, or creating problems (however unconsciously), prevents boredom? My bud from Zambia ('brother from the Zed') maintains that people in Africa have more sex because of boredom. Getting nasty gives them something to do (LOL).

Blaise Pascal was also interested in people's quiet struggle with the apparent meaninglessness of life and the use of diversion to escape from boredom. He said, 'Men seek rest in a struggle against difficulties; and when they have conquered these, rest becomes insufferable'. It's truly ironic. We aspire to have free time and when we secure it, we don't know what to do with ourselves. Like, people moan about their work, but they're bored when they don't work. Nietzsche said, 'a subject for a great poet would be God's boredom after the seventh day of creation'. And Chuck Palahniuk (author) said, 'did perpetual happiness in the Garden of Eden maybe get so boring that eating the apple was justified?'

Apparently, pilots report being proper bored, and boredom can make pilots lose attention. In one study, 30% of co-pilots who woke up after a nap reported seeing the other pilot asleep too (safe). Maybe the world would be a better and less tedious place, if people devoted their time to prayer instead of boredom?

Sociologists Cohen and Taylor, in their book 'Escape Attempts: The Theory and Practice of Resistance in Everyday Life' (1976), highlight how we endeavour to escape the banality of everyday life. The solution to our boredom and oppressive routine is often an escape attempt. At the very least, daydreaming can rescue us from the despair of the mundane e.g. at the office. Cohen and Taylor explain that 'escape attempts' include 'activity enclaves' such as hobbies, games, gambling and sex; 'new landscapes' which they associate with holidays, popular cultural interests, and art; and 'mindscaping' which involves the use of hallucinogenic drugs and therapy.

The trouble is however, that these endeavours merely reveal our limitations at escaping, since we always return to being in itself. That is, here and now, and not wasted or consumed with some distraction. Such escape attempts are but an imaginative way of realising the precincts of our world. Cohen and Taylor highlight that escape attempts metaphorically describe society as a prison without walls. The assumption being that prison life is a severe form of society. We're essentially trapped (we're hostages). The ultimate escape is death, or maybe not, if there's life after death?

Sociologists highlight that we hide from death. We live in a death denying culture because death's a source of fear and anxiety for those who want to live. Life is for the living, and as discussed, we can get our freak on at the prospect of not being here. It's duly noted, fear of death births myriad 'mental health problems'. Feeling out of control can lead to all kinds of craziness. I take solace in my mum's view of death, namely, death is like catching a train. Some get the earlier one and others get the later one. And we can but wonder where the boogie train is going?

Suffice to say, death is the weirdest. Like, being in the home of the recently deceased, and seeing their reading glasses and word puzzles, food in the fridge and cupboards, clothes in the wardrobe etc, but the person who should be there has literally vanished. Poof they've gone. And it's also the weirdest doing the 'shake in vac' with their ashes over some memorial site e.g. 'garden of remembrance'. Or maybe we'll hang onto their ashes, as it's better than nothing?

For others however, death is a muse. Like Scott Peck (1998) said, 'More than anything else, my romance with death has given me a sense of the meaningfulness in life. Death is a magnificent lover' ('Further Along the Road Less Travelled' p.49). He recommends taking up a serious relationship with the end of our existence. He wrote, 'Like any great love, death is full of mystery and that's where much of the excitement comes from. Because as you struggle with the mystery of your death, you will discover the meaning of your life'. Thus, excluding the looming inevitability of death from awareness effectively limits consciousness.

Tolle (2011) similarly advised, 'One of the most powerful spiritual practices is to meditate deeply on the mortality of physical forms, including your own. This is called: Die before you die' (p.163). And Socrates said, 'Death may be the greatest blessing of all human blessings'. God knows. We'll all find out soon enough. It's also noted, that nothing focuses a person's priorities in life, like learning they're about to die. Hence, existentialists don't shy away from death. Zarathustra, who was a muse for Nietzsche, said 'He who fears death is already dead'.

For existentialists, death allows us to grasp the meaning of life. We need to accept and embrace the inevitability of death to appreciate and understand life. Once we realise that at some point, we will no longer be, (that we'll truffle shuffle off this mortal coil), we gain insight into what it means to exist. And thus, with death's counsel, we can make the most of our time.

Martin Heidegger (1889-1976), another existential philosopher, said the constant fear of death and the anxieties of life help man to ask the central question 'what is it to be?' He conceded that asking this all important question required standing back and actually existing free from absorption and distraction. For Heidegger, the mystery of life was linked to the individual's confrontation and consideration of the temporary nature of our existence. Time and human existence are inextricably linked. Like Sartre, Heidegger equally viewed our 'being' as a process of 'becoming' and rejected a fixed human essence.

Apparently, Sartre was inspired by Heidegger, and Heidegger was inspired by Kierkegaard, the first existentialist philosopher. In Kierkegaard's first published work 'Either/Or: A Fragment of Life' (1843) he wrote, '…even the richest personality is nothing before he has chosen himself, and on the other hand even what one might call the poorest personality is everything when he has chosen himself; for the great thing is not to be this or that but to be oneself, and this everyone can be if he wills it'.

So, we are what we will, and then our time ends. As Sartre said, 'One always dies too soon or too late. And yet, life is there, finished: the line is drawn, and it must all be added up. You are nothing other than your life'. He said, 'In life, a man commits himself, draws his own portrait, and there is nothing but that portrait'. And then, that portrait is taken to a charity shop, along with the person's belongings. No-one cares, it's done. Throw it in the trash.

Both Heidegger and Sartre were notably fascinated with phenomenology, which is a theory of consciousness. Phenomenology looks at the relationship between the world and the senses that experience the world. The focus is on the human experience, as knowledge and experience are part of the same reality. Our senses collaborate to give us meaning in our inner world, and our perceptions are completely individual and personal.

Freud and the role of the unconscious are parked. Sartre was notably suspicious of the Freudian unconscious for its threat to individual freedom.

Existentialism thus comes from phenomenology. 'Existential phenomenology' attempts to characterise the nature of a person's experience of his world and himself. It's interesting to note, that when Sartre was asked what existentialism was, he would say he didn't know. But rather he believed in a philosophy of existence that had reliance on phenomenology, and he couldn't be hooped going into that.

For existentialists then, life equates to a beginning and an end, a 'time' to spend on earth. We get a body that roots us to the here and now, this time and place (hence the time-bound nature of the human condition). And we know ourselves through our bodies. For the duration of our life, we remain implicated in bodily desires, gratifications, frustrations, and subjection to dangers, until the curtain finally comes down, on our own particular show. Our essence is embodied. And it's anyone's guess what happens to our essence when it's disembodied.

But moreover, embodiment provides a base from which we can be with other human beings. And whilst our embodied self is personal, no wo/man's an island. But rather, we 'become' through the medium of others. This seems prudent to note, with respect to the 'Mental Case?' chapter, because the contention is that personality arises through interpersonal relationships. And personality is how we see the world. Hence, deviant personalities suggest dodgy programming? Or perhaps deviance is a sane reaction to the absurdity?

John Mbiti (1970), philosopher and writer, said, 'I am because we are, and because we are therefore I am'. It would appear this is a spin on Descartes' 'I think therefore I am' axiom. Existentialism notably has reliance on Descartes eminent 'I think therefore I am' maxim, as its starting point of existential philosophical meaning. But we'll get to this. My friend says, 'I breathe therefore I am'.

Ronald David Laing (1927-1989), Scottish psychiatrist referred to as 'controversial philosopher of madness', states, 'We must begin with the concept of man in relation to other men and from the beginning 'in a world, with the realisation that man does not exist without 'his' world'' (cited in 'The Divided Self', 1960, p.20). He thus maintains we are 'separates' not 'isolates'. Our relatedness to others is an essential facet of our being, as is our separateness, and whilst we need others to become who we are, we don't need any particular person for the making of who we are.

Laing points out that 'one chooses the point of view or intentional act within the overall context of what one is 'after' with the other' (p.22). Behaviour is contextual. We act and react, relentlessly, until we're no longer here. Ontology is the study of being. Hence, the great Ontological Question is 'what is the meaning of being (of life)'. It teaches us that our 'being' is both personal and social, as these are interlocking aspects of human experience. Thus, we are a 'being-in-the-world'. Sartre said, 'Being is. Being is in itself. Being is what it is'. Heidegger pertained to 'being, spatiality and being with' as a process of self-identification of self and other, and between internal and external.

Social interaction is the reflective medium that allows us to perceive our self-conception. We know what we're like through others. We each comprise our own unique medley of characteristics, traits and attributes, which manifest through interaction, and which reveal the 'type of person' we are e.g. angry, kind, compassionate, sensitive, aggressive, sad, funny, laidback or uptight. We know what we are because of what we're not. Hence, the world is like a mirror reflecting our perception. And people we are in relationships with are like a mirror, reflecting our beliefs, where simultaneously we are mirrors reflecting their beliefs. Hence, relationships are the most powerful tool for growth.

The process of becoming is thus interaction with others, and our ongoing interaction with our personal and social circumstances i.e. making sense of the situations we encounter. But moreover, as Heidegger says, we're thrown into society, which comprises our straitjacket. ['Into this house we're born, into this world we're thrown', and we become *riders on the storm*]. And until we see the existential light, and think for ourselves, we're inauthentic social products, like automatons.

Sociologists explain that society is a system of interrelationships which connects individuals together. We're linked through roles and rules, our contemporary values and norms. Society and identity are interwoven by patterns of culture. 'We' create culture to define reality and that culture defines us. Or rather, 'culture creators' provide our narratives, which define us?

In 'Person to Person' (1967), psychologist Carl Rogers wrote, 'Normal' making ourselves what other people are is too hard. I am linked with many people through my surface or mask or disguise by approved actions…the way I eat and speak…according to a formula…playing a role. This is a veneer…even if I have done this for a long time the surface seems real to me…it is more like apples bobbing in a tub of water…skin touching skin…with no awareness of the flesh or core. We are all apples. Not satisfied with being an apple? Just do what the other apples are doing and you will be okay. Not to do that is bad'.

But the authentic task at hand is to define our own roles and rules, not inauthentically play the role we've been given. Hence, Sartre was on mission to burn the straitjacket Heidegger pertained to. We don't have to play the roles that society gives us and tick all the boxes e.g. education, career beyond mere job, money, success, smart house and possessions, including car and phone, partner(s), marriage, kids, grandkids, friends, attractiveness, tattoos (LOL), popularity, sanity.

But it seems we want to? Our self-worth is sandwiched between these boxes. Hence, it's an 'imperative' to tick them for the sake of our mental health? We need to be at least normal, but ideally better than normal. No good can come from being ostracised from mainstream (lame-stream) society. Carl Jung said, 'To be normal is the ideal aim of the unsuccessful'.

Heidegger believed people in cities lose touch with individuality, and they're forced to conform to patterns of mass behaviour. He observed that we feel anxiety if we're not a sheep, doing what the sheep do, and so we're inauthentic (I'm paraphrasing). And yet ironically, Heidegger was a Nazi fascist. He wasn't popular after the war, but apparently Sartre and his Jewish mistress, Hannah Arendt, did much to restore his reputation.

It seems bemusing to think that we use other people as criteria to judge ourselves. That other people provide the benchmark, and our self-esteem comes from how we compare. Self-esteem notably comes from 'to estimate'. It's measured by how we perceive ourselves. 'Being' on display means that we instantly form opinions of each other. We judge at first glance. Sociologists call any group that individuals use as a standard for evaluating themselves a 'reference group'. Like, people look like shaders or weirdoes. 'Stereotypes' are regarded as psychological shortcuts.

So, we all fall into a group by virtue of our appearance and manner, but most people seem normal? Ironically, whilst we're fixated on the norm, it seems most people say they're not normal. And many of us feel like weirdoes? Presumably, that's in part due to the number of things (society tells us) we can potentially have wrong with us. Arthur Schopenhauer (German philosopher) said, 'we forfeit 'three quarters' of ourselves to be like other people'. We're all subject to appraisal, because we collectively call it into 'being'. We're obsessed with the boxes?

Sartre noted that self-consciousness needs the other to prove/display its own existence. He argued that self-consciousness is only possible when one is compelled to self-awareness with the reflective activity forced upon him by the 'look' of the other. That is, we become self-conscious when we're aware of others' awareness of us. And nice, 'Freak Shows' took place from 1840-1940.

As mentioned, Sartre was afflicted with issues relating to body image and self-esteem therein. He was familiar with the discomfort of people looking at him. Feeling shame or embarrassment is being aware that others are looking at us, judging us. It's being aware of someone else's point of view or imagining what they're thinking. And then there's social anxiety? It's therefore tempting to blend in like a chameleon, which can be a challenge for transgendered men and women. Unless we reclusively stay indoors, there's no escaping the gaze and 'being-for-others'.

In his poem, 'To a Louse', Robbie Burns spoke about 'the gift to see ourselves as others see us'. Whilst we have some insight into this, since we're living it, we don't really know. We see our reflection in the mirror, and think, there you are, that's you staring back. Or like in photos and footage. That's me, the human object that I am. And that's our voice on recordings, on answer messages, irrespective of not sounding like that in our heads. That's how we sound. That's how we look. Picasso (1881-1973) said, 'who sees the human face correctly: the photographer, the mirror, or the painter?

It's noted, that mirror self-recognition is considered to be a sign of self-awareness. It's said that to be able to see ourselves, means we have a sense of self. Humans pass the test at eighteen months. Apparently, dolphins and great apes are able to recognise themselves in a mirror, unlike my jazz cats.

At a new job I started, the manager enquired about my dietary requirements, and having advised him I'm a vegetarian, he said 'you look like a vegetarian'. What does a vegetarian look like? LOL. And in hindsight, I remember thinking, since I knew he was gay, that I could have said 'and you look like a homo'. LOL. I actually wouldn't have known his sexual orientation. My gaydar is rubbish.

So, we're all human objects in someone else's visual field, hence we're all objectified. It's a two-sided dynamic. We stare at others, and others stare at us. And whilst it's said being objectified can seem threatening, we objectify ourselves. We construct an idea of ourselves, to be an object in the world. This in turn works out well for the cosmetic industry. It's sweet that we aspire to be a prettier/sexier object. That we succumb to socially constructed 'desire' (blinding smiles included). Our body is essentially an outfit (flesh coat) to embody our essence. But outfits are judged and there's money to be made. As discussed, it seems we're obsessed with our appearance. Indeed, for some victims, it's a mental illness. Surely some ketamine would help?

Carl Rogers' starting point is, 'this is me, but who am I?' So, who are we, besides the face we see in the mirror? In addition to our 'self-image' obsession, (or part of it), it seems we're also obsessed with identity politics and defining/labelling ourselves. Identity politics is underpinned by 'facticity', which denotes the inescapable givens of existence that we can't change e.g. the time we were born, our parents, race, nationality, biological sex, talents, limitations, our former choices. It's duly noted, that gender reassignment defies the gender 'box', as we can become the opposite sex if we choose?

Sartre highlights that facticity signifies all of the concrete details against the background of which human freedom exists and is limited. Facticity is thus both a limitation and a condition of freedom i.e. it's a limitation in the sense that we didn't choose our facticity (e.g. birthplace) and a condition in the sense that our values most likely depend on it. Thus, it seems we have factical freedom as opposed to absolute freedom. It's the cards we've been dealt.

But moreover, it seems we like to make distinctions. Like, we're conservative or labour, nationalist or globalist, vegetarian, animal activist, LGBTQ+, feminist, Muslim, Christian, witch, black, white, yellow, purple, bipolar, schizophrenic. Or maybe the powers that be have propelled this self-obsession to encourage dissent. Identifying with certain groups, exclusive political alliances, creates division.

It would appear the 'divide and rule' strategy continues to control us, despite us knowing better? Despite recognising how incomprehensible it is that something like skin colour has been so problematic over the years. That wars have persistently ensued because of skin colour. It's noted, that white supremacists introduced races in the 1800s. Like, Caucasians are white, Asians are yellow, Malaysians are brown, American Indians are red, and Africans are black. This 'scientific' racism was inspired by Darwin's theory of 'favoured races'. It underpinned racial inferiority and superiority, and the world adopted this racist thinking. In his book, 'The Descent of Man' (1871), Darwin referred to black people as 'savage races' and stated they're closer to apes than whites (p.201). [Nice].

Thus, whilst on the noble surface, marginalised groups have been heard through 'consciousness raising', it seems there's been an agenda. Hence, billionaire George Soros, for example, funds and creates social revolutions through his 'Open Society Foundations'. Riots are not therefore spontaneous uprisings but rather organised and funded. Like, protestors are paid at 'Black Lives Matter'. People can 'rent a mob'. Agent provocateurs, including cops, covertly create chaos for political goals. It's like Antifa, the left wing anti-fascist political activist movement in the US, aims to achieve political objectives through the use of direct action rather than through policy reform. It's like 'terrorists' are armed and funded by the west.

Soros is regarded as one of the world's foremost philanthropists. He benevolently gives away millions to allegedly help civil rights groups. As it transpires however, he was a double agent Jew (he grassed up other Jews during WW2), and he's a key player in the world stage. So, we're being pitted against each other. Indeed, it's said we're more divided than ever. We continue to be distracted by BS and fight amongst ourselves instead of paying attention to what the puppeteers are doing. As highlighted in the movie 'The Hunger Games', never forget who the real enemy is. But we'll get to this.

So, whatever identity we have is imposed from outside or is sustained by our ongoing, self-defining choices. Identity is essentially a concept of synthesis. It's the process whereby we integrate our various statuses, roles, and diverse experiences into a coherent image of self. Our self is made and makes itself in the circumstances in which we live. We are therefore both a social and self-construction, since we are active and conscious agents of our identity.

As the existentialists highlight, identity is not fixed, but rather every moment, every second, we continue to redefine ourselves. Being here now is always dynamic and underway, and never static and complete. We're always a work in process (progress?), as we're constantly processing ourselves. And like Fonda and Gaga, we can reinvent, repackage, ourselves at any time. Like, we could become a Muslim and adopt the letter box look. Or become a Rasta, or whatever.

Social Identity Theory states that our identity results from a fundamental tension between the need to be like others but a corresponding need to be different. The creation of identity is therefore a collective affair in the sense that we negotiate the different messages that come from parents, siblings, TV, friends, culture. Identities evolve and entail a process of reflection, which enables us to adjust them in relation to society. They are fundamentally a process of self/other negotiation.

It seems pertinent to note, given our gender fluid culture, that Simone de Beauvoir applied existentialism to feminism. Since Sartre advocated that wo/man has no basic nature, and we create ourselves, Beauvoir denied the existence of a basic 'female nature' or 'male nature'. She asserted that society creates sexism based on perception of the sexes. She formulated that 'one is not born, but rather becomes, a woman'. This suggests that woman or man is a social construct or idea, and also that gender is an aspect of identity which is 'gradually acquired'.

In her book 'The Second Sex' (1949) she highlights that men behave as if they are the subjects, treating women as their objects (the male gaze). This in turn undermines and even deprives women of the responsibility for their own lives. But for Beauvoir, women are as free and independent as they choose to be. Albeit, perhaps not in Saudi Arabia?

But moreover, besides the advances of feminism, it seems anything goes in our post post-modern era? Like, men become women, and vice versa. Or people dress like the opposite sex, no questions asked. It's mainstream, normalised, no one cares. Choose your choice?

The role of expression conveys impressions of self. How we think about ourselves and life in general, fashions how we live it. Identity is stylistic self-expression, where we extend the presentation of self i.e. beyond clothes and shoes including 'labels', our weight/physique, make-up, hairstyle, perfume, piercings and tattoos, by the music and art we like, the restaurants we dine in, the clubs we're seen in, the cars we drive, and the area/house we live in.

The concept of individualism is thus reinforced by capitalism (and a credit society) i.e. we buy (create) our self and lifestyle. Indeed, it's contended 'I shop therefore I am'. We want just as we're brainwashed to. Yet despite the quintessential airbrushed façade, the idea that materialism and consumerism equate to happiness is an illusion. Statistically we've never been more depressed.

Social roles are acquired and achieved i.e. social class, power, and image. Status is a position in society. And money is a measure of success in life. Hence, the royal family hit the jackpot, by virtue of being born into royal bodies? So, we perspire to aspire, but as Russell Brand (2014) asserts, 'achieving status and honour are entrenched in toxic structures'.

Moreover, a role is more than a mask. We live through our perspective. We are our values, opinions, beliefs and attitudes. [Opinions are primarily cognitive and transient, whereas attitudes are opinions that are evaluative and emotional, and hence harder to change]. And we express what we think. Everyone speaks about everyone else. Conversation is the ultimate sphere in which all judging and evaluating takes place. Assessments are negotiated and shared agreements are reached i.e. norms. We can equally wonder, when stripped of whatever superimposed roles and identity, who are we? When we're butt naked, the Queen included.

Furthermore, perhaps we should challenge the norms we've accepted. As we've been deliberately led to collectively create them. We're being fashioned into particular social products for a particular reason, because someone benefits e.g. cosmetic industry, pharmaceutical industry, entertainment industry. Like fashion designers design our clothes, social engineers provide our narrative. It's like wars are fashioned because it pays.

But life could be completely different. Like, we could be happy without 'stuff'. We could be happy with each other and nature. Perhaps as Bertrand Russell advocated, we could work four hours a day. We could enjoy life, which is not sitting in like a loner watching TV or playing computer games no end. We could sack our government and royal family, since bugger being 'subjects of the crown'. But many people like the royals because they're programmed to. They like watching their royal weddings and family celebrations. We're programmed to love our servitude? Maybe we should rethink the purpose of the royal family, who made their mint through exploitation, slavery, and heroin sales.

So, we're told the script, which includes important events, 'dates for our diaries'. Like, Valentine's Day, Easter, Father and Mother's days, Birthdays, Halloween, Bonfire night, and Christmas, which are all capitalised on. And the same the next year, and the next, no questions asked. Everyone does the same thing, as we're compelled to. It's arguably a contrived snore.

Like with Christmas, for example, the 'Christmas' tree goes up. People buy 'stuff' for others, which they often don't want or need, and send cards. The season, whilst allegedly jolly, invariably stresses people out. And it can compound the loner's loneliness. Then the big day arrives, after months of anticipation. And it's never worth the build up? Everyone has turkey and trimmings. What's with that? There's often liquor induced carnage, and besides the Queen's speech, viewers tune into watch their favourite soaps etc, the 'Christmas specials' (LOL). We're programmed to succumb to this nonsense, and we enjoy it because we're programmed to? It's another distraction that we welcome. Maybe we should rethink 'traditions'?

It's too ironic, as besides the fact that few believe in Jesus so why would they celebrate Christmas, Christmas has nothing to do with Christ. It's Saturnalia, the Roman festival of Saturn worship, which is the diametric opposite of Christ. Christmas celebrates the birth of the sun god (25th December) not the Son of God. A couple of centuries before Christ, people would exchange gifts, 'eat, drink and be merry'. This par excellence shows our inauthenticity?

The Bible also rejects the Christmas tree as pagan. It gets weirder, as it's said the Christmas tree is a symbol of the Tree of Life (Jesus is referred to as the Tree of Life) within us and its illumination symbolises our illumined consciousness, which means our inner senses are fully open and active. But we'll get back to this curiousness. And then on Boxing Day, the shoppers get high on bargains. It seems the jokes on us. It's also noted, that Valentine's Day, Easter and Halloween are pagan celebrations. So, we're inadvertently, inauthentically, paying homage to Satan (Santa)?

Maybe we should think twice about going along with what Kierkegaard calls the 'crowd' and the 'plebs', and Nietzsche calls the 'herd'. The crowd is basically public opinion in the widest sense. It's the ideas that a given age takes for granted i.e. the ordinary and accepted way of doing things. It's the mainstream page that most normal people are on. But it's a complacent attitude of conformity. And the result is, the individual gets lost in the crowd, and lives life without sincerity i.e. without any real deep feeling, thinking or believing[4].

---

[4] I like the word sincere, which comes from Latin sine (sin), which is without, and cera (cere), which comes from wax. Unscrupulous marble workers, pottery makers or brick layers would cover imperfections with wax, but then the sun would melt the wax exposing the imperfections. Hence, when something was claimed to be sine cera, it was an important guarantee.

The crowd is thus a reference to thinking, acting, speaking, dressing, and so forth, as 'they do'. In essence, we don't think for ourselves. In his book '1984', George Orwell conceded that the unthinking masses are like cattle, which is 85% of the population.

For Kierkegaard, 'The objective truths of science and history, however well-established, are in themselves matters of indifference; they belong to the crowd'. Kierkegaard proposed that each individual, not society or religion, is solely responsible for giving meaning to life, and living it passionately and sincerely. That is to say, authentically. In tandem with postmodernism, which postulates that truth is individual and subjective, Kierkegaard claimed that 'subjectivity is the truth'. As it transpired, modernism, which asserts that absolute answers can be found in science and the material world, was usurped by postmodernism.

Thus, it doesn't matter what others think, it's what we think that counts. We have to figure out the truth for ourselves. Kierkegaard said what characterised the crowd was their idle chatter. He deducted 'the crowd is untruth'. Truth is not consensus. Lest we forget that we're deliberately lied to, scientifically and historically. We're being played like a fiddle.

Nietzsche reached the same conclusion. He called the crowd, or mass society, the 'herd'. Herd mentality refers to those who stop thinking for themselves and let others think for them. Like sheep, sheeple just follow where they are being led, blindly and without reflection. Sheeple are however worse than sheep, as we don't require a sheepdog to herd us, as we do it to ourselves.

For Nietzsche, the so-called autonomous, self-legislating individual is nothing but a herd animal that has trained itself to docility and unfreedom by conforming to the universal standards of morality. He said, 'Morality is the herd-instinct in the individual'. And, 'It is not the ferocity of the beast of prey that requires a moral disguise but the herd animal with its profound mediocrity, timidity and boredom with itself'.

Nietzsche distinguishes between 'slave' morality, which is obedience and submission, and 'master' morality, which creates its own values beyond good and evil. The master transcends the mediocrity of the common person. The master is noble and strong, and thinks for himself.

Nietzsche conceived of a world 'Beyond Good and Evil'[5]. He believed everything, good and evil, is perception and he criticised philosophers for the dogmatic dualism they accepted i.e. the good man is the opposite of the evil man. On the contrary, good and evil can be conceived as different manifestations of the same basic impulses that seek expression. They're aspects of our being and are inherently not to be judged. Nietzsche said, 'there is no such thing as moral phenomena, but only a moral interpretation of phenomena'.

So, there are no moral absolutes, as there is no distinction between good and evil, and we're led by instincts? There is no right or wrong? Absolutes are notably unchangeable truths from which we can reason from cause to effects. The words good and evil require an a priori value judgement i.e. good and evil are objective truths/facts irrespective of experience. Like, paedophilia and sacrificing babies is evil.

'Perspectivism' was a key idea developed by Nietzsche. That is, all ideations take place from particular perspectives. This implies that no way of seeing the world can be seen as definitively 'true'. Truth is separated from any particular vantage point, and is essentially created by integrating different vantage points together.

---

[5] See 'Beyond Good and Evil: Prelude to a Philosophy of the Future' (1886).

Take an acrimonious couple, for example, the truth of their problems lies somewhere in the middle of their perspectives. So, truth is somewhere between at least two versions of a particular account.

Nietzsche observed that people always adopt perspective by default, whether they are aware of it or not. And the concepts of one's existence are defined by the circumstances surrounding that individual. Nietzsche's deduction was thus, truth is made by and for individuals and peoples. He said, 'you have your way. I have my way. As for the right way, the correct way, and the only way, it does not exist'. So, we basically make it up as we go along.

However, Nietzsche's conclusion, 'there are no facts, only interpretations', and 'there are no eternal facts, as there are no absolute truths', might be misguided. It's always possible there is objective truth beyond our manmade subjective truths. Like, God's word, the Bible, is eternal absolute truth? And it's possible that truth doesn't change but rather perspectives vary. Like, 'science' claims we're a material brain not a soul, but maybe an unchangeable truth is that we are a soul, and we have a body?

Science also tells us it's irrational to believe in creator God? It's more rational to believe in the scientific impossibility that everything came from nothing, and we evolved from goo by way of the zoo? Maybe Nietzsche was wrong to declare the death of God. As maybe God does exist a priori.

The Ontological Argument for God notably uses the method of a priori proof. It states if we can conceive of God, then God must exist. If God were simply an idea, it would be a contradiction because a God that existed would be greater than the idea of one. But if God is one 'than which no greater can exist' then God must inevitably exist. Atheist and evolutionist Richard Dawkins says the 'bare assertion fallacy' is ludicrous (LOL).

Nietzsche condemned those who looked up to the sky for answers. He criticised those for being more interested in the heavens and divine imaginings than the real world i.e. traditional philosophy and Christianity. He was concerned with this life, in this world. He said, 'do not listen to those who offer you supernatural expectations' and 'be true to the world'. Albeit it seems the real world resonates of a pseudo world in the sense that the herd aren't living existentially?

Nietzsche's advice 'become what you are' concerns living the truth about ourselves and our condition as human beings. To be true to ourselves gives rise to being a 'free spirit' or 'true individual'. Free spirits dare to question opinions and assumptions, as a means to finding our own way. Given Nietzsche's atheism, he spoke of free spirits as a challenge to wo/men to assume divine prerogatives. It's duly noted, that to complement someone as a 'free spirit' is a New Age cliché. It's like saying someone is an 'old soul', which suggests they're wise because of their previous lives. Or maybe they're not wise, if they keep reincarnating?

Nietzsche placed the human condition between animal and superman. He explained that 'man is an evaluating animal', hence, the onus in on us (on-us) to create our own life-affirming morals and life enhancing aesthetic values. Fundamentally, the challenge is to become a superman. Nietzsche believed in the 'will to power', which is the driving force of the human character. He said, 'the world itself is the will to power – and nothing else! And you yourself are the will to power and nothing else!' The will to power embodies the free-spirited aspiration to become 'super' wo/men.

The responsibility rests with the agent (our authenticity). So, rather than rolling over and claiming 'it was', Nietzsche transforms this mindset into 'I' willed it so. Such 'will to power' is thus a central tenet of Nietzsche's philosophy. We will to do what we choose. Freud's pleasure principle (minimise pain and maximise pleasure) can be seen as a 'will to pleasure'. But rather than willing whatever in a degenerate or hedonistic way, Nietzsche saw the driving force, the will to power, as instrumental to achievement, ambition, and reaching the highest possible position in life. These are manifestations of the will to power.

It remains to be seen that consciousness is always intentional. It always intends or is directed towards goals. Be it I choose to lie in bed all day. I choose not to answer my phone. I choose not to deal with reality. Or alternatively I want to fly to the moon. Aim for the stars and all that jazz. What dreams did we have before they got choked up in life? Szasz highlights we can choose to drown, drink, dope ourselves to perdition, or choose to become president of the USA. Fundamentally we either accept our fate or create our destiny. It's said, between tomorrow's dream and yesterday's regrets, is today's opportunity. Choice is a function of the present. Or is it a matter of brain chemicals?

It's noted, that 'the will to power' regarding self-mastery and psychology paved the way for 'self-making' therapy. Freewill transforms into willpower. It's argued that without Nietzsche, there would be no Freud. In essence then, Nietzsche loved power. He viewed power as good, and weakness as bad. He said, 'What is good?' All that heightens the feeling of power, the will to power, power itself. What is bad? All that is born of weakness'. And for him, the church was born of weakness.

Nietzsche believed the Christian system of faith was not only incorrect but harmful to society. For Nietzsche, the church suppressed the will to power, and it allowed the weak to rule the strong. But furthermore, Nietzsche perceived active pity for failures and all the weak, as more harmful than any vice. According to Nietzsche, pity is nothing less than the multiplication of suffering, in that it allows us to suffer along with those for whom we feel pity. It depresses us, sapping us of our strength and will to power. We are deprived of strength when we feel pity, and for Nietzsche, Christianity is the religion of pity. It appears no good can come from sympathy or empathy?

To combat what he called 'slave morality', he sought to effect a 'revaluation of all values' i.e. a new system of values devoid of God. A free spirit is thus the embodiment of a transvaluation of all values, which comes from the will to power. Contrary to church suppression, he wanted to liberate the life force of the strongest.

'Being' anti-Christ and anti the church, Nietzsche maintained that every man should be a god to himself. Indeed, Nietzsche thought of himself as a god, a Christ figure. He said, 'There cannot be a God because if there were one, I could not believe that I was not He'. He even (audaciously) went to the extent of seeing himself as taking on the suffering of mankind. Thus, contrary to Lord Jesus, Nietzsche is our saviour. He set us free? The church gave the moral truth, but we can have our own self-appointed truth. It's our will be done, not God's will.

Thus, Nietzsche considered himself to be the great liberator, insisting that we think for our-self. He wanted wo/men to bin the shackles of misguided Christian morality and become supermen, free and titanic. Nietzsche affirms, 'everything is possible' when we become god. Heidegger also advocated that people ought to abandon their humanist and Christian ideas, so not to be weakened by them.

It was notably this 'legacy of supermen' that primed anti-Semitism. Hitler believed in literal supermen, and he used some of Nietzsche's aphorisms. Hitler believed extra-terrestrial gods created the Aryan race. He promulgated that Germans were descendants of this superior Aryan race (tall with blonde hair and blue eyes).

They were more evolved (it seemed obvious?) and different from 'monkey-men' (all other races are sub-human and genetically inferior). And this master-race was destined to the rule the world. The Nazis were also attracted by Nietzsche's attack on the church, as they had their own religion to replace it, namely, the Luciferian New World Order religion (which we'll get to). The swastika (ancient Hindu symbol) would replace the cross.

Apparently, Nietzsche's avid Nazi sister tried to promote him as a Nazi philosopher, but in fairness to Nietzsche, he was a firm anti-nationalist and hater of anti-Semitism. Group mentality was the antithesis of Nietzsche's rationale. He said, 'in individuals, insanity is rare, but in groups, parties, nationals and epochs, it is the rule'. Like, Germany's collective adoration for psycho Hitler.

With regards to Nietzsche's hatred of Christianity, it seems pertinent to note, that Nietzsche's father was a preacher, but he died when Nietzsche was only four. And then to make matters worse, his little brother died six months later. Nietzsche in turn questioned why God punished him with so much suffering. He was serious at a young age and preferred solitude, that is, to give himself over to himself. He studied theology but gave this up and later declared himself the antichrist, in conjunction with his book entitled 'The Antichrist' which outlines his philosophy as discussed. Those seeking God provoked laughter in Nietzsche. He would muse in turn, 'where is God?'

Interestingly, Nietzsche wrote 'The Parable of the Madman' (1882), which told the story of a madman who cried incessantly 'I seek God! I seek God!' The unbelievers around the man laughed and mocked him saying things like 'why, is He lost? Has He strayed away like a child? Does He keep Himself hidden? Is He afraid of us? Has He emigrated? In response, the madman declares 'God is dead. God remains dead. And we have killed Him. We're all His murderers'. The interesting or ironic part is that Nietzsche fulfilled the parable. He was (or became) the madman who proclaimed the death of God.

Nietzsche entered the land of madness and stayed there for the last ten years of his life. Apparently, he had a mental breakdown when he saw a horse being whipped and he threw his arms around it to protect it. He collapsed founded on profound pity for the horse, yet until then Nietzsche stoically denounced pity. Hence, this profound sympathy (God like love?), was an interesting turn of events. It's tragic that he lost his mind but beautiful that emotionalism, genuine empathy, finally gripped him in the face of his otherwise rational philosophical repose. It's said that after the horse incident, Nietzsche returned to his boarding house and danced naked, and began to believe he was Jesus, Napoleon, Buddha and other historical figures.

It's widely reported that he contracted syphilis from a brothel. Others however argue that this was a smear campaign against him, given his association with Nazis, and that his madness derived from a brain tumour, or dementia, or manic-depression (bipolar disorder) with bouts of psychosis. Either way, he was declared clinically insane and moved into an asylum. Albeit, and perhaps not so insane, he advised that one can 'find refuge in madness'.

And last but not least, and in tandem with, 'the last shall be first, and the first last' (Matthew 20:16), is Kierkegaard. Unlike the former, Kierkegaard believed in God, and therefore had an answer for the otherwise absurdity of life. There is a God and a purpose. Life's not meaningless. Indeed, life is precious. Kierkegaard said we should view life like an egg-timer, as we watch the precious sands of time slipping away, irretrievably gone for good.

As touched on, Kierkegaard claimed truth is subjective, and cannot be determined by anyone else because the most important questions are questions of morality (like adultery, abortion, and animal cruelty?).

For Kierkegaard, to 'exist' is always to be confronted with the question of meaning, and listening to the voice of God is the ultimate source of meaning. It seems the authentic endeavour is thus to ex-ist and reflect on whether God is or isn't true, taking our entire existence into our philosophical reflection.

Philosophers have forever mused whether or not God exists, but we can never know. We can't prove God exists, so it's up to each person to decide for themselves. We need to park the crowd and the plebs, and on our own, in honest solitude, think deeply and sincerely for ourselves. Irrespective of how irrational Christianity might appear to others, what matters most is, is Christianity true for you?

For Kierkegaard, whether or not Christianity is true is the most important question of our lives because it's a matter of life and death. And since we can never know, it is a matter of faith. But for Kierkegaard this makes sense, because requiring proof detracts from our faith, which results in a loss of passion. If Christianity had required reason, it would not require faith. Ergo faith goes beyond the intellect. It surpasses reason and knowledge. Kierkegaard said, 'doubt is conquered by faith, just as it is faith which has brought doubt into the world'.

He said, 'if I am capable of grasping God objectively, I do not believe, but precisely because I cannot do this I must believe. If I wish to preserve myself in faith I must constantly be intent upon holding fast the objective uncertainty, so as to remain out upon the deep, over seventy thousand fathoms of water, still preserving my faith'. Rollo May (1909-1994), existential psychologist and author, concedes, 'the relationship between commitment and doubt is by no means an antagonistic one. Commitment is healthiest when it is not without doubt, but in spite of doubt' (The Courage to Create, 1975 p.21).

Kierkegaard proposed that the individual passed through three 'stages on life's way' to becoming a true self, namely, aesthetic, ethical and religious stages. These stages are styles of living or spheres of existence. In the aesthetic realm, the emphasis is on enjoyment and pleasure. Having fun in beautiful places with beautiful people is good, and boredom is bad. This stage is defined by pleasure and pain, which comes from sensory experience. The aesthetic is essentially a slave to their own moods and desires (their flesh). So, we can fart about at this narcissistic stage, but it's vacuous and unfulfilling. It's meaningless and ultimately boring. It's said that everyone who lives aesthetically is in despair, whether they know it or not.

The ethical stage is characterised by seriousness and consistency of moral choices. More specifically, the ethical realm starts with the realisation that we choose our choice. We're responsible for our choices, so the ethical person does 'the right thing' e.g. says 'no' to drugs? Someone might move from the aesthetic stage to the ethical stage upon parenthood, as they have to do the right thing by their kids i.e. it's no longer just about them anymore. Unlike the focus being on pleasure and pain, the focus at the ethical stage is on good and evil.

Kierkegaard's 'Either/Or' notably portrays these two opposing life views, namely, hedonistic or ethical and duty bound. And the book's central concern, as posited by Aristotle, is 'How should we live?' The crux of the matter is, we either please ourselves or we do the right thing. We can choose to be a moral person, but alas responsibility is not nearly as pleasing, as pleasing ourselves. Why not enjoy our time. Why ruefully subject ourselves to the mundane. It seems society's focus is on the pursuit of pleasure and happiness, and Immanuel Kant's (1724-1804) 'sense of duty' is overrated.

Do we care to 'will' the right actions, particularly if there is no God? The answer to the Nietzschean question of 'why be moral?' is because 'it makes you happy'. Really? It's truly beyond me, why the world's not more nuts given the vast numbers that don't believe in God. Freud's pleasure principle is rational. And why not kill someone if they annoy us?

So, contrary to the aesthetic who relishes pleasure, the ethical person abstains, but it can suck. Living by the law of morals can be boring and joyless. It's depressing (hence the role of 'legitimate medication'). Indeed, the ethical stage can be so dire straits it births angst, that infamous sense of dread, emptiness and anxiety, aka an existential crisis. But according to Kierkegaard, angst is contentiously positive. There is hope because when one is at this stage, they find themselves in an 'existential situation'. They can now make the leap to the highest plane of existence, the religious stage, which for Kierkegaard is Christianity.

Kierkegaard spoke about the 'conversion experience' where the decisive move is not purely intellectual but a matter of will, feelings and passion. It's a 'process of highest inwardness'. It entails an attitude towards transcendence as the deepest potentiality of our existence, where transcendence is the absolute other that grounds our existence. This supernatural awareness goes beyond all understanding. This 'leap of faith' constitutes the highest form of individuation. It's a game changer.

Kierkegaard acknowledged it can be 'terrible to jump into the open arms of the living God' but it is the only path to redemption. Jesus said He is the way, and we either believe Him or we don't. Thus, you either make the leap of faith or you don't. No-one can do it for you. It's your choice.

But at your peril, since as Kierkegaard cautions, 'Once having chosen to play the ethical game, as it were, one cannot reconsider and return to the purely aesthetic without qualification. You have lost your innocence, literally, and now can resume your hedonistic behaviour only as an immoral person. By parity of reasoning, it would seem, the lonely individual who had made the leap of religious faith cannot backslide to the merely aesthetic or even to the purely ethical, without incurring the penalty of sin'.

Thus, beyond aesthetically reflecting on pain and pleasure, and ethically reflecting on good and evil, the focus at this stage is sin and grace. And fundamentally, we can't 'know' God and then return to the 'world' innocently. Unless we get a lobotomy, (and unlike Neo who has the option of choosing the blue pill to stay in the illusion of the matrix), we can't not know what we know, which includes God[6]. In the Bible, 2 Peter 2:22 states that returning to the world, having known the Lord, is like a 'dog returning to its vomit' and 'a washed pig returns to the mud'.

It's arguably better to be ignorantly, blissfully hedonistic, than incur sin? But pleasures are fleeting, and then we're back to tedious meaninglessness. In his poem 'Tam O'Shanter', Robbie Burns wrote, 'But pleasures are like poppies spread, you seize the flower, its bloom is shed; or like the snow falls in the river, a moment white-- then melts for ever'. So, whilst glimpses of pleasure are better than the boring ethical stage, there's the opportunity of 'being' in relationship with God. This is the ultimate adventure for those willing to take that chance and jump. Fly like an eagle.

For Kierkegaard, the one who walks alone with God has become a true self, a fully free and realised human being. The religious sphere correlates to spiritual growth. Our (spiritual) self continues to grow in relationship with God. When we ask God into our hearts, God the Holy Spirit comes (the third person of the Godhood),

---

[6] In the movie 'The Matrix', the character Neo, played by Keanu Reeves has the choice of taking the blue pill to remain in the artificial reality forever, or take the red pill and escape into the real world.

who convicts us with truth. Thus, by acting on our convictions, and taking responsibility and committing to truth, we become our true authentic self.

Kierkegaard acknowledged that Christianity was both so overwhelming and so irrational that it had to be an either/or. It seems irrational that the Godman Jesus came to Earth to tell us about the Kingdom of God and how best to live? And then He died for our sins to make it possible. Jesus took it for the team, as someone had to pay for our sin. Holy God cannot abide sin. Thus, whilst we're responsible for our choices, we can be forgiven for our wrong doings, if we're humble enough to ask. It's noted, that historical accounts verify the Bible, that a man named Jesus walked the earth two thousand years ago, performed myriad miracles, was crucified under Pontius Pilate and then resurrected (there is no body).

But furthermore, if we believe it's real, this ken should be reflected in our passion and sincerity. Having a relationship with God is life changing. It's literally mind-blowing. Thus, Kierkegaard had no time for 'Sunday Christianity' or lukewarm Christians. He observed a culture devoid of passion and commitment, and asserted 'the whole of Europe is on the road to bankruptcy'. As touched on, it seems the sheeple went to church because everyone else did, without actually reflecting why they went? Attending church was the 'done' thing, the ethical thing. It seems people were more ethical in the days of yore?

Kierkegaard thus believed the church (entire Christendom) can distract people from our personal relationship with God. No good can come from the crowd, even if they do go to church. In the religious life, one is ruled by total faith in God. Pascal said, 'Faith is different from proof; the latter is human, the former is a Gift from God'. So, God gives us the gift of faith. But do we want this gift?

Pascal also presented his wager, (known as Pascal's wager), that humans all bet with their lives that God exists or does not exist. And he posits that given the possibility that God actually does exist, and assuming the infinite gain or loss associated with belief in God or with unbelief, a rational person should live as if God exists and seek to believe in God. If God does not actually exist, such a person will only have a finite loss i.e. some pleasure, luxury etc. My chum deducted this as a kid. She figured it's better to believe in God, than not to believe. We've all heard about hell? It's sensible to get fire insurance?

In summary, existentialism is a humanist, person-centred philosophy. As Sartre said, 'existentialism is humanism', as existentialists begin with humanity itself. The focus is on the individual's pursuit of identity and meaning amidst the social and economic pressure of mass society for superficiality and conformism. Anxiety is a response to freedom and possibility. But most people don't want freedom. They want security so they cling to the crowd. It's safer to do what others do.

As Kierkegaard notes, most choose not to be a self but to be the crowd, as they lack the strength to endure the anxiety to be a self. But to choose this, is to choose despair, which is defined as 'sickness of the spirit'. He highlights that most people go through the motions, but they're not truly living but rather dead. And further, the man who has no self has failed as a human being.

Kierkegaard said, 'Every human being...has a natural need to formulate a life-view, a conception of the meaning of life and its purpose'. And whilst we all have a life-view, an idea of the point of existence, not everyone consciously forms their own. But rather, most people passively adopt themselves to society's impositions, values and moulds of behaviour. The endeavour is therefore to think for ourselves. Oscar Wilde said, 'to disagree with three-fourths of the British public is one of the first requisites of sanity'. And Vivienne Westwood succinctly put it, 'If you think something is right because everyone else believes it, you are not thinking'.

As touched on in the last chapter, structuralism and post-structuralism ensued. Structuralism focused on the way that human experience and behaviour is determined by various structures, and it rejected the existential concept of human freedom and choice, which is the heart of existential philosophy. Structuralists argued that impersonal and necessary structures unconsciously guide and limit our reasoning processes and practices. So, we don't think per se. The thorny problem was thus the responsibility of the agent in a structuralist world, since as social products e.g. NEDS, how can we be held responsible for the very conditioning that has fashioned us into this kind of person?

Post-structuralism, closely related to postmodernism, is a response to structuralism. Thus, rather than looking at what binds us together, post-structuralists tend to focus on our differences. They focus on the individual operating within the structure. This is arguably existentialism in disguise. It's compatibly contended that as social products we're a mixture of both structuralism and existentialism.

What I appreciate about existentialism, or existential psychology, as Hoeller (1990) encapsulates, 'it rescues psychology from being drowned in a sea of theories that have lost contact with the everyday world and givens of experience' (p.5). Our feelings of despair, boredom, absurdity, anguish, depression etc make sense. They're normal? For existentialists, the problem is existence.

I also appreciate the honesty. Sartre maintained the choice of authenticity, (not lying to ourselves), is a moral one. People are considered moral subjects: self-governing, self-monitoring, self-reflecting, and self-evaluating. Indeed, the world felt like they'd lost their moral compass when Sartre became the late Sartre. And it seems he took his uncompromising philosophy of freedom with him, as we no longer want the burden or responsibility of freedom? And we're too subdued in our alpha state to care about the direction society takes?

Regarding 'mental health', (as we'll get to), it seems important to recognise what we can and can't control, and making sure that what we can, doesn't get assigned to that which we cannot. Rather than 'bad faith', like 'I can't help it, that's the way I am', it's often that we don't want to change. Like, we could arguably stop drinking, smoking, and eating copious amounts of pies?

So, we choose our choice, but then there's mental health problems? Like, the depressed can't get out their bed, and the anxious can't leave their home. But physically they can. So, is it that they can't or really don't want to (squared and to the power of infinity)? Laurel Lee (author) said, 'I know I am not seeing things as they are, I am seeing things as I am'.

It's understood there's power in language (words have power). Hence, if we believe we can or we can't, we're right. The social psychological principle states, 'I believe what I hear myself say'. It's also understood, there's a stream of choices before one 'becomes' debilitated or addicted. We're not sane then crazy. It's cumulative. There's a build-up and we choose our choice on a slippery slope. 'The Serenity Prayer', adopted by AA and other 'twelve step programs' states, 'God, grant me the serenity to accept the things I cannot change, the courage to change the things I can, and the wisdom to know the difference'.

We embody the freedom to change. As Michael Jackson, who conversed with the *man in the mirror*, said, 'make that change'. So, we can 'become' a Nietzschean superhero, or we can jump into the arms of the living God and 'become' a Christian, or neither. It's our choice.

By virtue of our depression and suicide rate (worldwide), it seems many are caught up in the nihilistic cloud of doom that permeates society. It's generally assumed that life is without objective meaning, purpose or intrinsic value. There is no God? There is no point in getting out of bed, unless we have to ethically attend to kids, which we have brought into the world to perpetuate this purposeless and painful existence?

It's contended that the lack of taste for mystery gives rise to despondency. Sue Atkinson (2005) quotes psychiatrist Robin Skynner's observation, namely, 'I've always been struck by the way so many patients, if they do well in therapy, develop an interest in the meaning and purpose of life' (p.144). It seems we're designed to ask the big questions? The late Stephen Hawking said, 'I want to understand the world and know the answers to the big questions, it keeps me going' (fair play).

Meaning in life gives will to live, will to power? It seems however that we've inauthentically allowed others, (so called 'intellectuals'), to do our thinking for us. And maybe their thinking is funky. Maybe they're on the highway to hell? We've been educated by the 'crowd' to believe that it's irrational to believe in God. But maybe untold souls, bewitched by materialism, will discover that Kierkegaard was right to have faith, and Nietzsche was wrong to declare the death of God. And it will be too late, as we only get one shot at life.

As George Monbiot (British writer and political activist) asserted, 'Tell people something they know already and they will thank you for it. Tell them something new and they will hate you for it' (cited in David Icke, 2007 p. 573). But that's the existential point, to step aside from the crowd and plebs, and endeavour to think for ourselves.

Black (2010) wrote, 'PLATO SAID THAT ALL PHILOSOPHY BEGINS with wonder. Modern science is killing off wonder, by telling us that we know it all. Modern science is killing off philosophy, by encouraging us not to ask the big Why questions. These questions are strictly meaningless, they say. Just get on with it. Today's scientists try to insist that theirs is the only way to interpret the basic condition of human existence. They like to dwell on what they know. In their view, the known is like a vast continent occupying nearly everything there is... Science is *not* certain. It is a myth like any other, representing what people in the deepest parts of themselves *want* to believe' (p.548/549).

In the Bible, James 4:14 states, 'Yet you do not know what tomorrow will bring. What is your life? For you are a mist that appears for a little time and then vanishes'. The biggest mystery in life is what happens next.

"To be or not to be"... that truly is the question

3

Idealism versus Materialism

Materialism and idealism are the two camps in the great ontological debate, which concerns itself with the nature of existence. Death is clearly a challenge to our physical existence and there's no denying, as Bertrand Russell duly observed 'when I die, I rot'. But what if science, materialism, that which advocates that the mind is the brain, and hence when our brain dies, we die, are wrong?

The materialist view which stipulates that life ends with the death of a body is the dominant, contemporary idea. Existence is physical and the basis of reality is matter. But what if we do have a soul? What if there is something more going on with consciousness, that which appears transcendent. Jainism, the Uttaradhyayana Sutra 18:13 states, 'a wise man believes in the existence of the soul, he avoids the heresy of the non-existence of the soul...' Would you sell your soul, like in Hollywood?

Consciousness is associated with a core self, a sense of being here now, but to date it remains extremely perplexing for science. Contrary to materialism, idealism advocates the essence of our existence is consciousness. Idealists view consciousness, our internal subjective reality, as ultimately real. For materialists, mind comes from matter, but perhaps matter comes from mind? It's arguably more rational that God's mind created our physical world. Or maybe there is no matter, and all matter is in the mind? Reality exists in the mind. As the philosopher George Berkeley (1985-1753) posited, 'If a tree falls in a forest and no one is around to hear it, does it make a sound?'

Philosophically, consciousness itself is nothing until it has perceived something, because consciousness is always conscious of something. Contrary to realism, which states physical reality exists independent of observation, it seems the zeitgeist ('spirit of the times') is panpsychism, which is the doctrine that consciousness is in everything. The cosmos doesn't exist without some type of consciousness witnessing it. It appears we're being groomed for the cabala.

I remember resonating with Cartesian Dualism, which argues for mind-body separation, when I was studying philosophy as an undergraduate student at university. And concluded, for-real we can appreciate the mind as a separate entity. Lying in a pitch-black room, anaesthetised up so we don't feel our bodies and given drugs that erase all memory including knowledge that we even have a body, it's possible to think that we're just a mind. All we have to do is close our eyes and imagine. Hence, my resonance with Rene Descartes (1596-1650) founding principle 'je pense donc je suis. Cogito, ergo sum'. And in English, 'I think therefore I am'.

Descartes, the father of modern philosophy and rationalism, decided to doubt everything that could possibly be doubted. He deducted that senses can be deceptive and the source of illusions e.g. phantom limbs[7]. And when we dream, we feel like we're experiencing reality. Ergo, like others before him, he questions, 'How can you be certain your whole life is not a dream?' However, by virtue of doubting, he deducted that he must exist. He thus developed a rationalist philosophy, a closed system of reasoning without the necessity of reference to the realm of the senses.

In Nausea, Sartre said, 'I am. I am, I exist, I think, therefore I am; I am because I think, why do I think? I don't want to think any more, I am because I think that I don't want to be, I think that I . . . because . . . ugh!' (LOL).

So, unlike materialism where the mind is the brain, Cartesian dualism argues for the independence of the mind since the mind thinks on its accord. We're thinking beings. Unlike the body, the mind is non-physical and non-spatial. Descartes argued that the psychic space inside our heads is infinite and ethereal, and it seems obvious it is made of different stuff than organs. Love and anger, he noted, can't be weighed and measured.

Descartes was bemused by how a non-material mind can produce movements in a material body. He maintained, 'I know myself as a thought…' Descartes insisted on the fundamental division between the 'I' and the world. Identity equated with mind rather than whole body. People (adults) feel ageless which correlates with the soul not the body. It's like our soul exists outside of time?

The supposition that we're isolated souls existing within bodies agreed with his catholic beliefs. Descartes was a devout Roman catholic and espoused the ontological argument for God. But moreover, according to Descartes, only humans have a soul, which distinguishes us from animals who only have a body. This resulted in horrendous consequences for animals, as they were treated like they don't have feelings or experience pain.

A somewhat interesting prospect, although not founded, was the idea that the soul weighed 21 grams. This was made popular in the 2003 movie '21 Grams'. This notion came about in 1901 when Dr Duncan MacDougall hypothesised that the soul had mass, and thus when the soul departed the body, so did the mass. To test the hypothesis MacDougall weighed six patients while they were in the process of dying from tuberculosis in an old age home. The determination of the soul weighing 21 grams was based on the average loss of mass in the six patients within moments after death. As it transpires, his results have never been reproduced, and instead his assertion is generally regarded as scientifically worthless.

But moreover, Descartes rediscovered the ancient esoteric idea of the pineal gland as the gateway between the corporeal body and the immaterial mind. The brain meets the mind in the pineal gland. The pineal gland, named because it looks like a pinecone, (like the huge pinecone in the Vatican courtyard, and like Buddha's pinecone head), is the tiny structure deep in the middle of the brain (between the two hemispheres).

The pineal gland is like our inner eye. Like, when we imagine/visualise something in our minds. The interior of the pineal gland has retinal tissue composed of rods and cones (photoreceptors), like the eye, and it's also wired into the visual cortex of the brain. As a result of the nerve connections with the retina, it's known as the 'third eye'.

The third eye is represented by the bindis Hindu gods and goddesses feature between their eyebrows. Like Hindu mystics, Descartes believed the pineal gland to be 'the seat of the soul'. He believed this is the place in

---

[7] With phantom limbs, the part of the brain formerly activated by the limb can continue to be activated.

which all our thoughts are formed, and it's where we receive our messages from the Divine. In addition to his Roman Catholic faith, Descartes spent years researching the Rosicrucian secret society, which we'll get to.

Scientists haven't fully sussed out the pineal gland. They know it regulates melatonin, where high levels prevail at night and low levels during the day. [Serotonin is converted into melatonin in the pineal gland]. Melatonin is called the 'Dracula hormone' because darkness signals to the pineal gland to make melatonin and light signals for it to stop. People take melatonin to help them sleep e.g. the jet lagged and ADHD kids who can't sleep on account of Ritalin. And many report having vivid dreams and nightmares. Melatonin is apparently in cherries, bananas, grapes, rice and cereals, herbs, olive oil, wine, and beer.

So, the pineal gland has to do with our sleep patterns. And it calcifies and diminishes in size in teenage years. It's purported that fluoride in water is the chief cause of calcification of the pineal gland. Apparently, Hitler pioneered adding fluoride to water in the Nazi concentration camps, as it kept the prisoners docile and easier to manage. Fluoridated water is however just one of the many chemical assaults on our brains. It's like, people are 'happier' with lithium infused water. Hence, governments are flirting with the idea of introducing lithium into the water supply, which parallels with Huxley's soma? It will help prevent suicide and make us more subservient?

The pineal gland seems to be an interesting piece of kit, not least because it can be manipulated to produce Altered States of Consciousness (ASC). Meditation, for example, can cause the release of melatonin, to induce 'hallucinations'. The pineal gland is viewed esoterically as the organ of perception of higher worlds. This inner eye provides perception beyond ordinary sight. It's associated with religious visions, clairvoyance, the ability to observe chakras and auras (subtle energies), and Out of Body Experiences (OBEs).

The practice of activating the pineal gland comes from ancient pagans, Babylonians, Egyptians, Greeks, Gnostic and cabalist traditions (all of which we'll get to). The forced opening of the pineal gland enables access to the spiritual realm, replete with spiritual entities. It's understood these intelligent entities operate on a different frequency. Hence, we don't 'normally' see them. Like a radio, we're tuned into our own particular frequency and broadcast. When it comes to the pineal gland, there's more going on than meets the eye. The mystery schools secret is the pineal gland is our spiritual eye.

Moreover, the pineal gland also secretes Dimethyltryptamine (DMT) aka the 'spiritual molecule'. It's structurally analogous to serotonin and melatonin, and is similarly connected with dreaming. Higher levels prevail until adolescence, when the pineal gland calcifies and shrinks. It's referred to as the spiritual molecule because it produces near death and mystical experiences. People experience visions, voices, disembodied consciousness, novel insights, and powerful emotions, including an overwhelming sense of significance. It can literally change people's lives, as they realise materialism is wrong.

Whilst it occurs in trace amounts in humans and animals, it's widespread throughout the plant kingdom (it's in hundreds of plants). DMT is the key ingredient in the Amazonian shamanistic brew ayahuasca. When ingested, DMT is like a psychedelic drug, which shamans use to contact the spirit world e.g. for healing and divination purposes. The shamans speak about 'seeing the gods'. People taking DMT report encountering beings, most commonly serpents.

Whilst we'll get back to ASC in another chapter, it seems pertinent to note, Dr Rick Strassman's clinical research into DMT, which was approved and funded by the US Government. [See his book 'DMT: The Spirit Molecule: A

Doctor's Revolutionary Research into the Biology of Near-Death and Mystical Experiences' (2000)]. Thus, from 1990-1995 he injected sixty volunteers with DMT. All volunteers (consistently) experienced visual imagery with eyes open or closed. And many reported convincing encounters with intelligent beings that appeared in a variety of forms. Such as gnomes, elves, fairies, goblins, spiders, reptiles, hybrid monsters, Hindu gods, native Indians, and 'grey aliens'.

Strassman believes that 'alien abduction experiences' are brought on by accidental releases of DMT. Whilst DMT is present in us all, apparently 2% have high enough levels, naturally occurring in the brain, to birth spontaneous and involuntary trance states. It's suggested DMT could account for psychosis.

Many volunteers however refused to believe these experiences were hallucinations or dreams, as they seemed too real. This was confirmed by the fact that creatures they'd met before, on former trips to 'DMT space', remembered their names. Hence, they were real, independent entities.

Strassman talked to them during the encounters, and they were aware that they were in two worlds. They could see the spirit world overlaid the physical world. They were aware that they were visiting this higher plane, like intruders. But moreover, it wasn't all happy days, as subjects were commonly raped and traumatised. There's apparently benevolent and malevolent entities or 'energies', so this place is not without its perils.

It's also pertinent to note, that the pineal gland is regarded as an organ of telepathic communication. The pineal gland is apparently like an antenna that picks up thought vibrations. And unlike our five senses, our sixth sense aka intuition, doesn't need an external opening as thought vibrations permeate matter like an x-ray. Thus, we receive thoughts, visions, information, through our third eye?

So, Descartes 'knew' the pineal gland connects to the spirit world. But that aside, Descartes' dualism was always the mainstream dream until the onslaught of materialism. In tandem with the church, people believed they had a soul. They were told that, just as the voice of reason tells us the opposite today.

But it arguably 'feels like' we're a soul living in this temporal body? It feels like our body is our house and we're tucked up inside. We're a person inside with thoughts and feelings, dreams and passions. We experience our inner world and have an overwhelming sense of self. We seem to think from our heads, above and behind our eyes. And our eyes enable our soul to look out and see the world. And people can see glimpses of our soul through our eyes? In essence, it was intuitive to think of ourselves as embodied souls. Like, the Greek philosophers, who were renowned for dualistic thinking about a separate and eternal soul.

Like Socrates (470BC-399BC), the Father of Greek philosophy, hypothesised that the soul is immortal. He surmised that death is not the end of existence, but rather it's merely separation of the soul from the body. Socrates, who taught Plato, who in turn taught Aristotle, are the three great classical philosophers, so we can reflect on their vantage, their rational worldview. Unlike religion, which could be mythical, these clever and rational philosophers really thought about the nature of reality. And they rationally assumed mind preceded matter. This makes the most sense? It was generally agreed that someone had to be responsible for creating the world. Some great mind, 'the God', must have moved things into being. Thus, 'Logos' (word) was considered the First Cause or Prime Mover.

Philosophy notably means 'love of wisdom'. Thus, a philosopher is someone who loves wisdom. As it transpires however, nothing is as it seems, as wisdom is also associated with the serpent. The serpent is the symbol of wisdom. And the serpent is associated with sun worship, as we'll get to in Part 2. As it transpired, Aristotle tutored Alexander the Great, who was curiously known as the serpent's son. Alex, Greek King of Macedonia, seemed to be an existentialist. He was memorably quoted for saying, 'there is nothing impossible to him who will try', and yet he also succumbed to the existential boredom factor, and died prematurely of boredom and alcoholism at 32 years young.

Socrates endeavoured to think for himself. He insisted the unexamined life isn't worth living. Yet he equally submitted the wise man knows he knows nothing. Socrates believed that before humans can understand the world, they need to understand themselves. We need to 'know thyself'. And the only way to accomplish that is through rational thought. He said, 'to find yourself, think for yourself'.

Socrates viewed the soul as having two parts, namely, the irrational part which contains emotions and desires, and the rational part which is our true self. In everyday experience, the irrational soul is drawn into the physical body by its desires. It merges with the body so that our perception of the world is limited to that delivered by our physical senses. Alternatively, the rational soul perceives the world in a spiritual manner. But, 'to know the world in this way requires that one first knows oneself as a soul'.

The rational soul is beyond our conscious knowledge, but it can communicate with us through dreams, images, and other means. The aim is thus to refine and extract the rational soul from the bondage of the physical body, replete with its desires and emotions. But moreover, Socrates believed we have an innate need for moral development, which requires connecting with the rational soul. Perhaps we can rationally rise above our desires and emotions. Perhaps our moral instinct can override our animal instincts?

Ethically fibrous Socrates insisted on truth and honesty. He professed 'there is only one good, knowledge, and one evil, ignorance'. A virtuous man does what is right, whereas evil is committed out of ignorance (or inauthentic thinking?). For Socrates, virtue is supreme good and knowledge. He said, 'he who knows good will do good'. The right insight will give birth to the right action. Contrary to the sophists, (his contemporaries), who like Nietzsche insisted there are no absolute norms for what is right and wrong, Socrates believed that true knowledge and moral virtues are innate. They're inscribed on our souls.

Real understanding comes from within. We can know truth from innate reason. We can know right from wrong, if we think about it. Our moral instinct tells us, which could be God's voice? Hence, he insisted that some such norms, namely, right and wrong, are universally valid. Like, we know it's wrong to murder. And it's wrong to lie? Perhaps morals aren't relative? Or the moral of the story is the Golden Rule (always treat others as you would like to be treated) is absolute?

Socrates believed that no-one could be happy if they acted against their better judgement. He couldn't calibrate how anyone could be happy 'deep down' if they knew what they were doing was wrong. Paracelsus concedes, 'we should do that which our conscience teaches, for no other reason but because our conscience teaches it'. We don't feel happy betraying our conscience. We're not content or at peace.

Like, how can we be happy having an affair if we know it seriously wounds our partner? Or having learned about factory farming, how can anyone eat factory farmed pork sausages or hamburgers or chicken in good conscience? And people should know 'deep down' that it's not okay to use animals as sex toys. Thus, whilst we can attribute some foul play to ignorance, for those who know better, it's no route to happiness. Socrates valued his conscience and truth more than life. He said, 'if I do not reveal my views on justice in words, I do so by my conduct'.

But moreover, Socrates was a master of the art of discourse. He had faith in human reason and challenged people to think critically. He enabled them to use their own reason to ascertain right from wrong, through his questioning and probing. Rather than professing to have all the answers, he would act like he knows nothing, and merely ask questions to spark discussions. Socratic irony is notably the profession of ignorance and of willingness to learn, used as a ploy to spur others to discover their own ignorance through their attempts to explain a word or concept. Socratic questioning is a 'technique' used in psychotherapy.

So, he used irony to great effect, and cleverly and covertly backed others into a corner (LOL). He believed everyone could know the truth if they used their common sense. Thus, he forced people, by way of their common sense, to be ethical. Interestingly, Socrates said his 'art' was like that of a midwife (his mum was a midwife) in that he helped others 'give birth' to the correct insight. Learning cultivates our soul, as we make our implicit understanding of truth explicit. Ergo, we can cultivate a good soul by making the right choices.

However, not everyone appreciated Socrates' radical philosophical musings, not least the Greek officials. He criticised all forms of injustice and corruption, including the death penalty. Hence, he was charged with corrupting Athens youth and blaspheming local gods. It wasn't okay to denounce the gods of the state. But Socrates was honest, and he didn't believe in the gods of the Athenians, which included Zeus, Poseidon, Aphrodite, Apollo, Hermes, Dionysus, Artemis, etc. They seemed fictitious? And yet priests at the temples would offer animal sacrifices to them.

But moreover, he believed he spoke on behalf of something greater than himself. He felt he had a mission from 'the God' to be a gadfly to the corrupt officials in Greece. Someone had to hold up a mirror to them? And someone had to remind the Athenians about innate moral truth?

Furthermore, Socrates believed he had a good daemon, which prevented him from doing wrong. Daemon is Greek for knowledge and daemons are nature spirits. The word genius is derived from daemon. These ethereal beings speak through our minds. They prompt us through hunches and intuition, and they can be a force for good or evil. Like, the Bible tells us about angels and demons, and the Koran refers to jinn. It's noted, that daemon became demon with the advent of Judeo-Christian language in the second century. Demons are not the same as angels, but we'll get to all this.

So, Socrates said he had a divine voice within him, who told him what was right, and he had no choice but to challenge people on their incorrect thinking. Presumably he would be considered psychotic today? He said that inner conscience never told him what to do but rather spoke to him if what he was proposing to do was wrong. This admission didn't help his case. They weren't at all pleased with his talk of daemons, introducing these 'strange new gods'.

Despite assuring the jury that he only acted in the best interests of the state, there was a marginal majority, and the result was Socrates drank the poison (hemlock). He refused to retract his beliefs. It's understood he had a more sincere belief that any of his accusers. Socrates mused about an afterlife whereby good souls are rewarded, and bad souls punished. Like, perhaps good souls' transit to the divine, whereas bad souls become wandering phantoms. Apparently, he postulated to Plato, that maybe deity forgives sin. He just wasn't sure how. It's noted, Jesus didn't incarnate until four hundred years later.

Plato (427-347BC) was 29 when Socrates died. This injustice evidenced the conflict between society (i.e. the herd) and the true or ideal society. Alternatively, Plato's utopian society would be governed by reason, by philosophers who know better. Like, Atlantis was ruled by ten philosopher kings, who told the masses what to do for their own benefit. Whilst it's believed that Plato birthed the legend of Atlantis, he claimed that Egyptian records were translated circa 590-580BC. So, it was a real place, submerged in the Atlantic Ocean?

Atlantis was a highly advanced society and the ten kings were Poseidon and Cleito's giant kids, (five sets of male twins). As it transpired however, the inhabitants became greedy, petty, and morally bankrupt, so the gods destroyed Atlantis with a flood, which happened 9000 years before Plato arrived. However, we'll get back to 'Atlantis'.

Interestingly, Socrates never wrote a single word down his entire life. His philosophy and life have largely been relayed to us by Plato. Hence, it's difficult to distinguish between their teachings. Plato published Socrates 'Apology', which is Plato's version of the speech given by Socrates as he defended himself before the jury.

Whilst primarily a philosopher, Plato looked to the heavens as he sought life's answers. He recognised that some kind of divine architect must have fashioned the eternal universe. Thus, God is the Primary Cause or unmoved mover (a priori argument). He observed the beauty of Nature and believed this evidenced God. God could be seen in creation. He believed God is the source of all goodness, like beauty, truth, virtue, and excellence. God was not a personal God, but rather a transcendent high God, beyond human comprehension. And this Supreme Being, who emanates qualities, is all good, just and perfect.

Before we continue with Plato's theory however, it seems pertinent to interject regarding the difference between pantheism and theism. Thus, for pantheists, Creator is creation i.e. everything is God, which includes us, and the maggots. Alternatively, theists view God as separate from His creation. In tandem with the Bible, Paracelsus said, 'God is greater than Nature, for Nature is His product'. So, we're not God, and neither are the maggots. Unlike theism, which holds that God intervenes and even manifests in the universe, deism believes that God doesn't intervene. So, He was the Prime Mover, but that's where His activity ended. In his book, 'The God Delusion' (2006), Richard Dawkins stated, 'Pantheism is sexed up atheism. Deism is watered-down theism'.

Plato also believed two worlds coexist, (so called metaphysical dualism), namely, the ideal realm and the realm of the senses. Plato's heaven or ideal realm is perfect and eternal, which contrasts to the physical world, which is imperfect and in a constant state of flux. Everything withers and dies in the material realm, but the ideas that spawned all physical existence never die. Plato submitted that God created our physical world, based on the ideal realm. This God, who Plato called the Demiurge, is an artisan like figure, a sculptor.

Thus, perfect ideas in the ideal realm, became imperfect forms in the material realm. And unlike physical forms, the idea that everything came from is eternal and immutable. For example, there's a perfect idea for a cat, which inspired physical cats. And whilst cats all die, the cat idea will never die. Ideas are archetypes, timeless moulds, or blueprints. Perfect ideas are therefore superior to everything in the sensory world. They're more real than all material nature. Plato believed there were a limited number of ideas i.e. a certain amount of variety created.

So, Plato believed there was a higher reality behind the material world, that he called the 'world of ideas'. We can't however see it, because we live in the world of the senses, and our senses can't perceive the world of ideas. Our material body is inseparably bound to the world of the senses, so we don't know there's this other world. The world we see around us is only a shadow of reality. Everything we perceive, all physical objects (creatures etc), are but mere shadows or reflections of this higher world.

He portrays this concept in his classic 'Allegory of the Cave', which illustrates how what we assume to be real can so easily turn out to be an illusion[8]. Thus, men are depicted as prisoners in a cave. They're chained and bound in position, so they can only see the back wall of the cave. They've been shackled there all their lives and thus have only ever seen the shadows cast on the cave wall (there's a fire in situ to enable the shadows). And since they've only ever seen shadows of forms, they believe this is all there is. But if they could free themselves from their position and turn round, they would see the real animals and flowers etc that the cave shadows are but a poor reflection of.

The relationship between the darkness of the cave and the world beyond corresponds to the relationship between the forms of the natural world and the world of ideas. In other words, we're literally in the dark about higher realms. We think we're living in the real world, but we only see the shadows of reality, not its essence. It's also implied that life equates to a jail sentence? We're like prisoners, chain and shackled. Death is freedom?

Like Socrates, Plato taught that we have an immortal soul. So, whilst our body dies, 'we' do not die. But rather, our soul is released, separated from the body, and survives death. Plato compared the soul to a person driving a chariot pulled by two flying horses. One horse is beautiful and noble, and wants to fly to heaven. This horse is our finer spirit. The other horse is ugly and bad. It represents our base nature, driven by passions and irrationality. The soul is our rational self, which tries to keep control between these two horses pulling in opposite directions. Like, a good and bad daemon tugging on the bit. It seems the body is the problem because of its desires?

However, Plato further conceived of a threefold division of the soul, where each of the soul faculties has an ideal or virtue. Thus, 'reason' belongs to the soul. We 'think' with our reason and it aspires to wisdom. Hence, the virtue is wisdom. Our soul has spirit/energy or 'will' which aspires to courage. Hence, the virtue is courage. And it embodies desire and 'appetite', which must be curbed to exercise temperance. Hence, the virtue is temperance and submission to control. All three parts must harmonise and function as a unity to bestow a virtuous individual. Plato believed God designed the world with a purpose or goal, which is for man to become as good as God. Alas however, we live in an imperfect world.

Plato also believed the soul existed before it inhabited the body. So, before we were physically born, we existed in the world of perfect ideas, but when we're born, we forget this. He highlighted that childbirth, for example, was so traumatic that we forget all knowledge. Hence, for Plato, all learning is a form of remembering what was known before the soul came into the body. We recognise imperfect forms in our material reality, and we have an inner knowing (an inkling), that we were once in a world of ideas. There is some kind of recollection, which stirs in our soul a 'longing to return to its true origin'. We're aware that we're living in an imperfect world and we yearn to go home. Plato calls this yearning Eros (love). He maintains the soul longs to be free from the world of the senses aka the shackles of the body.

Plato believed that the soul was fundamentally pure but becomes deformed through association with the body. He observed that just as the body is prone to disease, so is the soul vulnerable to injustice and ignorance etc. Death therefore sets us free, enabling our souls to journey back to the truly real existence found among the forms. The world of ideas seems like a good idea, unlike the physical world?

---

[8] The 'Allegory of the Cave' is presented in 'Republic', which also describes his 'ideal' or utopian state.

Plato theorised that the soul is in a constant cycle of being trapped in a human body, escaping the body at death, and returning to the realm of forms, and back to a human body. It's said that Plato's belief in reincarnation was a product of his time. The ancient Greeks believed that the soul about to be reincarnated drank from the river Lethe (forgetfulness) which explained why people have no recollection of their former lives. But he further asserted that wicked souls would become animals, like donkeys. There was however the possibility that philosophy could provide deliverance from bodily imprisonment, with philosophers joining the company of the gods. It was possible to ensure our own redemption i.e. breaking the cycle through philosophical cleverness or 'wisdom'?

As it transpires, Plato was a mystic. He 'knew' there was a spiritual plane of existence, beyond our material world. He knew we have a spirit body (the 'noble horse') that can fly to heaven. According to Bill Cooper (author/researcher), Plato was initiated into the mystery schools in Egypt. He was in the great pyramid for three days and three nights, in the sarcophagus no less, during which time he was imparted secret knowledge that he had to protect. Presumably, he manipulated his pineal gland or took some hallucinogenic potion to access the spirit world?

Like Socrates, Plato also entertained dialogue with daemons, which he located on earth. He called this host of invisible beings intelligent and wise, and curiously said they assist in the governments of the world. And like Socrates, who spoke of demons influencing the possessed aka the insane, Plato conceded that demons obsessed mortals. However, we'll get back to this infernal prospect.

So, Plato engaged with gods, spirits and angels that exist on otherwise unknowable planes or dimensions. He believed there's unknowable transcendent God, but a knowable spiritual realm. It seems the 'forms' he pertained to, were entities he encountered in the spirit world? Maybe the world of ideas isn't a good idea. It gets crazy up there, like DMT space?

Aristotle (384-322BC) had a different take on the nature of souls, and unlike his predecessors, he didn't believe in life after death. Contrary to Plato, who believed souls are immortal and exist apart from the body, Aristotle believed that all living beings have souls, but there is no separate, immortal soul. He argued that the real us (our soul) and our form (our body) are inseparable. The soul is the form of a living body i.e. we have the souls of humans, cats have the souls of cats, and sharks have the souls of sharks. Form enables function, and soul enables life. Soul can be seen as 'breath of life' that pervades all living things.

Aristotle thus perceived soul as life principle and not separate from the body. And when we perish, we lose our form and therefore soul (the soul 'does not remember'). So, rather than being embodied souls, we're 'ensouled' bodies. Soul can be seen as personality or essence i.e. cat personality or shark personality. Thus, whilst cats and sharks have their own unique personality, they all behave like cats and sharks. Like we have our own unique personality, but we're all human. We have the same human instincts and needs.

Unlike Plato, who promulgated the notion that knowledge gained through the senses always remains impure and confused, and that the contemplative soul must turn away from the world to acquire 'true knowledge', Aristotle placed much more value on knowledge gained from the senses. For Aristotle, Nature is the real world, and all we know is reality perceived through the senses. Aristotle also rejected Plato's theory of forms. He regarded Plato as trapped in a mythical world that confused imagination with reality, and argued that Plato was 'doubling the number of things'. So, Aristotle wasn't initiated?

Rather than having certain innate ideas, and the supposition that nothing exists in the natural world that has not first existed in the realm of ideas, Aristotle countered, 'there is nothing in the mind except what was first in the senses'. The human soul thus contains reflections of the natural world and objects therein. Aristotle was an advocate of tabula rasa. Thus, unlike rationalists Socrates, Plato and Descartes, Aristotle was more an empiricist, believing that experience is the ultimate source of knowledge.

Indeed, Aristotle pioneered empiricism, the idea that we need to observe and measure the universe to understand it i.e. the scientific method. He was much more interested in nature and natural processes. He's regarded as the first biologist/scientist, having created the terms that scientists continue to use today. He scientifically categorised nature into categories, and sub-categories. He observed that we sense reality, and with our innate power to reason, we organise all sensory impressions into categories and classes e.g. plant, animal, human.

He asserted this capacity to reason and think rationally sets us apart from animals. It's our defining characteristic. Thus, whilst he contends that plants and animals are ensouled because they're living beings, he concedes that humans have an intellectual soul. It seems having an intellectual soul parallels with the existential difference between being alive and existing.

Presumably, this inspired the idea that only humans have souls, because souls contain minds i.e. self-awareness and our ability to reason, which animals don't appear to have. But souls are personalities, and animals have personalities. And they feel pain and sorrow. Like, elephants cry, bury their dead, and they remember. And apparently cows are very emotional. Like other animals, they have their 'favourites' as demonstrated by grooming, and they're known to hold grudges for months and even years. So, they have conscious minds and choose their choice?

Aristotle concurred that God was the 'Prime Mover', setting the celestial bodies in motion. And God is the unmoved mover i.e. God's moves without being moved (God's not moved by any prior action). He argued that the Prime Mover had to be immaterial, because matter is capable of being acted upon, and hence it has the potential to change. He therefore deducted that the activity of God must be purely spiritual and intellectual. That is, the activity of God is thought.

As mentioned, Aristotle wondered 'how should we live' and 'what does it require to live a good life?' His answer is that man can only achieve happiness by using all his abilities and capabilities. Aristotle held that there are three forms of happiness and these need to be in balance. Thus, the first form of happiness is a life of pleasure and enjoyment. The second form of happiness is a life as a free and responsible citizen. And the third form of happiness is a life as a thinker and philosopher.

Aristotle believed thought took place in the heart. He believed that the heart is the source of consciousness i.e. intelligence, emotion, and sensation. He regarded the heart as the most important organ of the body and the seat of the soul. Aristotle said, 'educating the mind without educating the heart is no education at all'.

It seems there's something very special about the heart, beyond pumping blood around the body. Like, alchemists knew the heart was an organ of perception. Paracelsus said, 'the human heart is a great thing, so great that no-one can fully express its greatness… if we only knew all the powers of the human heart, nothing would be impossible for us'. And Pascal said, 'the heart has reasons that reason knows not of'. In the Bible, in

Proverbs 4:23, we're told, 'Above all else, guard your heart, for it affects everything you do'. To have a broken heart means to have a broken spirit.

Like Aristotle, the Egyptians also credited the heart with intelligence and thought. Hence, it was carefully preserved during the mummification process, whereas the brain was scooped out through the nose (lovely) and discarded. In Egyptian religion, the heart was the key to the afterlife. The 'heart' of the soul would be placed on a great golden scale balanced against the white feather of Ma'at - the Egyptian concept of truth, harmony, order, law, morality, and justice. If the soul's heart was lighter than the feather, then the soul was allowed to enter the realm of the dead. But if the heart proved heavier, it was thrown to the floor of the Hall of Truth where it was devoured by Amenti (a god with the face of a crocodile, front of a leopard and the back of a rhinoceros) and the individual soul then ceased to exist. There was no 'hell' for the ancient Egyptians. Their 'fate worse than death' was non-existence. And their heaven was the underworld?

It seems pertinent to note, that whilst the brain trumps with 100 billion neurons (brain cells), the heart has some 40,000 neurons that can sense, feel, learn, and remember. This is fascinating with regards to recipients of heart donors i.e. inheriting new 'tastes' and it raises the 'character implant' debate. The heart is considered the small brain (the heart's complex nervous system is like a little brain). It's like there's mind consciousness and heart consciousness. The heart and brain maintain a continuous two-way dialogue, each influencing the other's functioning. But apparently the heart sends more information to the brain, than the brain sends to the heart. The signals the heart sends to the brain can influence perception, emotional processing, and higher cognitive functions.

Apparently when we experience positive emotions like compassion and appreciation, our heart processes these emotions, and the heart's rhythm becomes more coherent and harmonious. Science documentary filmmaker, David Malone, in the film 'Of Hearts and Minds', said 'it is our heart working in tandem with our brain that allows us to feel for others...it is ultimately what makes us human...Compassion is the heart's gift to the rational mind'. Compassion is our heart's response to others. It seems we're designed to have compassion?

Hippocrates (460-370BC) is usually accredited with being the first to argue the brain is the most important organ for sensation, thought, emotion and cognition. He recognised the unique nature of the brain, with intellect seen to be in the head. He said, 'Men ought to know that from the brain, and from the brain alone, arise our pleasures, joys, laughter and jests, as well as our sorrows, pains, griefs and tears. Through it, in particular, we think, see, hear and distinguish the ugly from the beautiful, the bad from the good, the pleasant from the unpleasant... I hold that the brain is the most powerful organ of the human body...wherefore I assert that the brain is the interpreter of consciousness'.

Hippocrates, the Father of medical practice, did not attribute causes of death to the influence of supernatural forces but rather sought observable natural factors. He endeavoured to find natural explanations for sickness and health. And he deducted that moderation and healthy lifestyles were the most essential safeguards against sickness. It's all about a 'balance'. It's duly noted, it was Hippocrates who pioneered medical ethics in terms of the Hippocratic Oath which pledges to do no harm and to maintain the privacy of patients.

Like Hippocrates, Democritus (460-370 BC), who many consider to be the 'Father of modern science', also argued for the brain. Regarding morality, Democritus said, 'Good means not merely not to do wrong, but rather not to desire to do wrong'. Apparently, Plato disliked him so much he wished for all his books to be burned. And apparently Nietzsche said 'Plato was a bore'. So, there's that.

But moreover, Democritus formulated atomic theory as a philosophical concept. He assumed everything was built by tiny invisible blocks or units called atoms. And these are eternal units of matter since 'nothing can come from nothing'. He deducted that nature is built of different atoms that join and separate again. That is, atoms create forms and forms die, and new forms are created. So, atoms are indestructible. They have always been, and always will be, in motion. And between atoms, lies empty space. He said, 'Nothing exists except atoms and empty space; everything else is opinion'.

He observed that everything in nature acts mechanically. Thus, everything that happens has a natural cause, which is inherent in the thing itself. Whilst Democritus was a materialist and didn't believe in a soul per se, he did however believe that the soul consisted of 'soul atoms'. His conjecture was that when a person dies, their soul atoms disperse in all directions, but that these soul atoms could become part of a new soul formation. Hence, no immortal soul as such, but rather souls live and die.

Besides the soul aspect, this is essentially the page we're on today. Scientists understand that atoms make up everything in the universe. The solid world is made up of atoms which have no solidity. The structure of everything is energy. And energy can't be created or destroyed. It can only change form. It's noted, the nucleus of every atom of every living thing consists of particles known as protons and neutrons, and around the nucleus are electrons revolving constantly at very high speeds. The movement of electrons create electrical energy permeating every life form. So, we're electric. It's also noted, the heart has a more electric electromagnetic field than the brain.

However, contrary to the Greek philosophers, the contemporary consensus is there was no Prime Mover. But rather, an insane amount of energy magically appeared from nowhere for no reason. And we evolved from stardust. There is no soul and the mind is associated with the brain. However, before we get to the current material paradigm, it seems pertinent to consider Scripture's view of man, Paracelsus', and the yogi's for good measure.

Thus, rather than dualism i.e. mind and body, scripture teaches about the tripartite man, that is, body, soul and spirit. We have a threefold nature of being i.e. physical, non-physical, and metaphysical. Our soul is our personality i.e. mind, will, emotions. Our body houses our soul, which is rooted in the sensory world, with its desires. Unlike our soul which is conscious, our spirit is unconscious. It's like an internal advisor to the conscious soul. It's the seat of our moral character. It's more than our conscience however, because it's our link to God. God speaks to His people in their spirit. People get revelation/insight in their spirit. It seems our spirit is our distinguishing human feature. Thus, unlike animals, we can have an intellectual relationship with God? We're also made in God's image, which sets us apart from animals.

In Hebrew, nephesh is soul, and ruach is spirit. [In Latin, spiritus is breath, and anima is soul. Anima animates the body, but it's also referred to as breath. The Greek word for spirit and breath is pneuma, (hence 'pneumatic tyres'), and psyche is soul]. God provides nephesh to all living beings. Like, He breathed into Adam and Adam became a living soul. Whilst Nephesh translates to breath or soul, blood can also be said to be nephesh because blood contains life. The Bible tells us the life is in the blood (life is in the DNA). It seems a blood sacrifice is literally a soul sacrifice?

But moreover, it seems animals do have a soul. We have the same nephesh animating our body. Ecclesiastes 3:19 states, 'Surely the fate of human beings is like that of the animals; the same fate awaits them both: As one dies, so does the other. All have the same breath; humans have no advantage over animals'.

And when God takes His breath back, (His Spirit, Life Force), we die. We return to the dust from whence we came. Genesis 3:19 and Ecclesiastes 3:20 tell us that we're dust, we come from dust, and we return to dust. It's noted, that God created Adam from the dust of the ground, which contains all the elements required for life e.g. carbon, nitrogen, hydrogen, oxygen, phosphorus. God then caused Adam to go into a deep sleep (which suggests He performed an operation) and removed one of Adam's ribs (DNA) to create Eve. Something from him, for him, but perfectly made for each other. His soulmate?

Job 4:18 also highlights we're dust, stating we're crushed as easily as moths. He said, 'They are alive in the morning, but by evening they are dead, gone forever without a trace. Their tent collapses; they die in ignorance'. Death translates to giving up the breath, ghost or spirit. The question is thus, what happens to the soul we've cultivated during our time here?

Some advocate that our soul goes to sleep, so-called soul sleep. When nephesh (breath) departs at death, we go into a deep sleep i.e. we're unconscious. It's said the dead know nothing. Their thoughts and plans perish when they die. God's spirit is like an umbilical cord that gives our soul life, and when our life support is cut off, we're dead, or in deep slumber. Nephesh returns with life at the resurrection, when we're raised from the dead. We're resurrected for 'Judgement Day', when we have to give an account of ourselves, our souls. Thus, lifeless souls are awoken from their deathly slumber. They get resurrection bodies which are ensouled once again.

It's purported that early Christians taught soul sleep, and that Christianity was corrupted by Greek teachings about an immortal soul e.g. Plato. Contrary to Plato however, the Bible doesn't teach reincarnation. We live once and then we face our Maker. Jesus notably said, 'I am the Resurrection and the Life' (John 11:25).

Others say we go to Hades/Sheol (Greek/Hebrew), which is essentially a holding place for souls (until Judgement Day), deeper underground. This abode of the dead has two areas, namely, paradise and a place of torment, which are separated by an impassable gulf. In Luke 16:19-31, we're told about a rich man who was in the place of torment, and he was in agony because of the fire. He was desperate for a droplet of water. The rich man wanted to tell his brothers about this reality, to warn them. So, we're conscious and depending on which side we land on, we can be very thirsty.

Others say believers in Christ go to be with Jesus. As Paul said, 'Absent from the body, present with the Lord'. And when Stephen was dying, he said 'Lord Jesus, receive my spirit'. It's further said, that when Jesus died, He went to the paradise underground, affectionately known as 'Abraham's bosom', and took the saints who were abiding there with Him into heaven (the damned souls remain in Sheol). So, the paradise underground is empty? It's noted, the Bible speaks about three heavens. The first heaven is the 'air' (our atmosphere), the second heaven is the stars etc ('outer space'), and the third heaven is God's abode. But we'll get back to this.

It's said that unlike animals, whose soul belongs to the body i.e. they're ensouled bodies, our soul belongs to the spirit. Thus, when their body dies, their soul dies. But maybe not. Maybe their souls are sleeping until they're breathed into again. The Bible tells us about a new heaven and earth, (when this earth has passed away), and presumably God will want to furnish the new earth with animals and birds etc. So, maybe people do see their beloved pets etc again? Surely innocent animals that inherited a harsh life and death, through no fault of their own, deserve some recompense i.e. eternity in heaven on earth? God's word tells us He knows every sparrow that falls to the ground. So, He cares.

But moreover, it seems that animals don't have a spirit body like us? In 1 Corinthians 15:44 we're told, 'There is a natural body and a spiritual body'. But as Dr Rebecca Brown, author of 'Prepare for War' (1987), highlights, 'this is a much overlooked verse'. She asserts that few people other than Satanists and those involved in practices like astral projection realise this.

Our physical bodies have a corresponding light spiritual body. So, we're body, soul, spirit (breath) and spirit body, which is a ghost like see-through version of us. Brown notes that New Agers refer to this as our 'higher self' or 'god force', and often references are made to spiritual energy or vibrations. It seems our spirit body houses our soul when our physical body dies? And we can separate our spirit body from our physical body through certain occult practices.

Whilst we'll get back to the biblical version of events, it seems pertinent to note, that something catastrophic went down eons ago. There's a backdrop to our reality, and current state of decomposition. Thus, Adam and Eve were living the good life in paradise, which included walking and talking with God. They lived in both a spiritual and physical world, and they were consciously aware of both their physical and spiritual bodies. They were clothed in light. But they betrayed God, and everything changed. They were cut off from God, and death (entropy) landed.

Brown explains, their souls controlled both their spiritual and physical bodies, but at the fall spiritual death landed. They were no longer aware of their spirit body and could no longer communicate with God as they had done. God severed the link between the spirit and the soul, and they lost the freedom of being and moving in two worlds at once. Our spirit bodies are the link between us and the spirit world. But these are out of action.

It's postulated that Adam and Eve had their pineal gland fully functioning in the Garden of Eden and after the fall it was closed off to prevent humans from interacting with the spiritual dimensions. After Adam, all humankind was born spiritually dead. Thus, we're dualists (or were) deducting that we only have a body and a soul. Our spirit however recognises there's something wrong. There's something missing, some kind of disconnect. We know life isn't supposed to be like this, marred with death and sin? Our spirit longs to reconnect with God, albeit not necessarily consciously. Hence, we fill our spiritual void with rubbish.

Having lost their garments of light, they became aware of their nakedness and covered themselves with fig leaves. The spiritual world was separated from the physical world and became 'invisible'. Thus, materialists assume we live in a material world. But the spirit world is still there. We just don't have the senses to perceive it, or we do, but they've been closed off. It would appear this is for the best, as by all accounts the spirit world sounds insane. Hence, God put a dimensional wall in place and told His kids not to engage with spiritual beings. They do not have our best interests at heart. On the contrary. It seems the spirit world has something to do with the dark energy and matter we can't 'see'?

We become spiritually alive when we ask God to come into our hearts. But we are not to reactivate our spirit bodies. He closed down our third eye for a reason. But moreover, as Dr Rebecca Brown highlights, 'Satan's goal is to teach humans to regain the conscious control of their spiritual bodies. Many do. Once this is achieved, these people can perceive the spirit world as well as the physical world. They can talk freely with demons, leave their physical bodies with their spirit bodies, and with full conscious awareness go places and do things with, what seems to be the average human, supernatural power. They can levitate objects without ever touching them physically, light candles without a match, create physical healings, etc' (p.253-254). She states, 'there's a phenomenal amount of power and intelligence in the spirits of humans, especially when those spirit bodies are under the control of their souls'.

Self-control of the spirit body is achieved through occult practices, such as meditation, hypnosis, visualisation, kundalini yoga, trance dancing, mantra repetition etc. Brown explains that when people submit themselves to these practices, they invite a demon that will act as a bridge, linking their soul to their spirit body, enabling them to enter the spirit world. Sorcery, which includes psychedelic drugs, also violates the veil that's in situ. Like with DMT, people can be catapulted into DMT space, which is the spirit world aka the second heaven? People can leave their physical bodies and travel in their astral bodies (so called astral projection).

Thus, as Brown highlights, human spirits (like witches) can torment and afflict people, just as demon spirits do. It's understood much happens on the astral plane. She affirms we can't see them because physical eyes can't see them. Only a spirit can see a spirit. However, we'll get back to these precarious practices.

Paracelsus advised, 'The spirit of man comes from God, and when the body dies the spirit returns to God. The body comes from nature and returns to it'. Paracelsus conceived of man as a twofold being, visible (material) and invisible (spiritual), which are linked together by a soul. The internal living man is made from the breath of God. Neither the external nor the astral man is the real man, but rather the real man is the soul in connection with the divine spirit.

The invisible body is the one which is spoken of as constituting our corporeal form on the day of resurrection. The inner man is the source of thought and imagination, and the outer man may act what the inner man thinks. The physical body is merely a corpse without the inner ethereal man. So, for Paracelsus, spirit (breath) goes back to God at death, and our spirit body is lying dormant without life. And this spirit body is reanimated at the resurrection.

Like Paracelsus, classical, medieval, renaissance, neo-Platonists, theosophists and Rosicrucian philosophy taught the astral body is an intermediate body of light linking the rational soul to the physical body. They understood the astral world or spirit world was an intermediate dimension between the earth and the divine. And this astral world can only be accessed via our astral bodies. It seems the astral world is Plato's world of ideas? For Yogis, the astral world is a general term that refers to all the planes above the physical world, and we go there when we die. Our soul encased in its astral body passes out of the physical body.

According to Yogi Philosophy, we have a body and soul, but we are a spirit possessing a soul. The real self is pure spirit, a spark of the divine fire, a ray from the central sun. Our divine spark is our inheritance from the divine power, but it's encased in sheaths. Our soul has several vehicles of expression, which have different degrees of density. Like, our body is the lowest form of expression, then our astral body etc. They teach that man is a sevenfold creature. The body is a temple of the living spirit. Bodies come and go, as they espouse reincarnation, but our soul is eternal.

All life is animated with primal creative energy, chi/prana, which underpins the great truth of oneness (monism). All is One and One is God. We're all one energy dancing for itself? They endorse pantheism which stipulates that creation is creator. Everything in existence is divine and can be worshipped as such.

Our conscious mind corresponds to our intellect, and our subconscious mind corresponds to our instinctive mind. The instinctive mind is the seat of our appetites, passions, desires, instincts, sensations, and emotions. This is manifested in both animals and people alike. On the physical plane, we long to please our flesh and carnal desires. Thus, intelligence, which includes self-consciousness and introspection, separates man from the brute. For yogis, the body should not rule the mind, but the mind should rule the body. Humans can however behave like animals despite our intellect. Our intellect can be pulled down by our brute nature.

But moreover, our spiritual mind, which is unconscious like our instinctive mind, prompts the intellect to think about truth. The spiritual mind is the spirit's means of communication with intellectual consciousness. It passes truths down to the intellect, which results in a struggle between our two natures.

The yogi emphasis is on spiritual evolution. Spiritual consciousness is a 'process of illumination', and we spiritually evolve through endless lifetimes. It's noted, that unlike traditional teachings on reincarnation, which maintains we can reincarnate as animals after death, the 'western' version is that we can only progress. Thus, we'll never reincarnate as animals because they're below our evolutionary advancement.

This therefore contrasts with Siddhaswarupananda Paramahamsa's advice in 'Reincarnation Explained' (1987), namely, that people who act like beasts with other humans, like 'the pigs in India who enjoy the smell and taste of stool, and enjoy licking anuses and vaginas', cultivate animal consciousness and return as animals. He wrote, 'Humans who engage in the licking of vaginas, penises, and anuses and whose sole lives are centred around sexual enjoyment are no doubt cultivating the subtle bodies of beasts. And God will give them what they want' (p.51). LOL. This does not bode well for our current generation.

When we die, we apparently go to the plane of slumber for a snooze (there's many sleepers there). The period of soul slumber is like the existence of the babe in its mother's womb. Our memory of our past life fades during this period of rest, leaving its impression on our soul. Just like in this life, we forget many things, but they inform our character. As we awaken, our astral body or 'shell' slips away from us, and our soul, clothed in finer undergarments, passes onto its spiritual destination. This is determined by how spiritually evolved we are.

Basically, the less dense or coarse our soul is, the better, as higher planes become increasingly more etherealised. It's like net curtains that range in thickness. Thus, those on higher planes can visit those on lower planes, but those on lower planes can't visit higher planes, because their souls are too coarse and dense to pass through the ethereal veil. Those at the lowest planes are the most gross, animal like and undeveloped. They're vile and like to play pranks on us. Hence, the veil is a good call to restrain this nefarious lot.

It's explained that above our physical plane of existence, is the astral plane, which is separated by a veil. Then above this spiritual plane is the 'world of shells'. This is where 'empty' astral bodies or shells are dumped. Apparently, they float by and they're gross (eerie) to look at. Like our physical bodies however, they do eventually disintegrate i.e. astral atoms disperse. Then above that plane is the plane of slumber. And above that, is the spirit world proper. Thus, the sub-astral world, immediately above our material plane, is not the real astral world but rather our extended astral turf.

Apparently, the astral world has seven great planes, sometimes referred to by Hindus as 'seven heavens', but each great plane has myriad sub-planes. So, we spend time learning truths where we're placed or drawn to, in the company of like-minded others. Those with the same level of spiritual development are notably called our 'soul group'. Then we reincarnate again on the physical plane. And so on, to enhance our souls.

So, it's possible, we do have a soul that operates the body? As Paracelsus the great Magus said, 'the mind is not created by the brain, neither is love or hate created by the heart; but mind acts through the brain, and love and hate have their origin in the will'. Maybe we have an inner wo/man that thinks thoughts, which materialise in our brain. Neurophysiologist Sir John Eccles (1903-1997) famously said, 'the brain is a machine that a ghost can operate'. And Tesla said, 'My brain is only a receiver. In the universe there is a core from which we obtain knowledge, strength and information. I've not penetrated into the secrets of this core but I know that it exists'.

Yogis highlight the spiritual mind is the source of inspiration for artists. People sense things in their spirit or spirit body. Like, God communicates with us through our spirit. Daemons or higher intelligences can project thoughts and ideas into our minds? As highlighted, consciousness is the greatest mystery of science. We don't know how it works, but we know the brain is involved.

Ancient Taoists notably believed the human body was controlled by two separate brains, namely, the cerebral brain and the brain in the abdomen. Both brains have a nervous system and are equally important. The cerebral brain is operated by the Central Nervous System (brain and spinal cord) and the brain in the abdomen is operated by the Autonomic Nervous System, which is responsible for the majority of physiological changes associated with emotional reactions. The cerebral brain has a mind like a library containing all knowledge, experience and education, and the soul resides in the brain in the abdomen.

So, the stomach is the seat of the soul. The anatomical name for the abdominal nervous system is the solar plexus (found in the torso, beneath the heart and behind the stomach) and this has nerves radiating to the organs. The solar plexus makes itself known when we feel sick to our stomachs, experience butterflies, nervousness, un-ease, and dread.

It's purported the brain in the gut plays a major role in human happiness and misery, and the two brains interact, where if one is upset, it upsets the other. Our second brain apparently contains 100 million neurons, and it produces every type of neurotransmitter found in the cranial brain, including serotonin and dopamine. Indeed, the belly brain produces 95% of serotonin in our bodies. We therefore need to take care of both our brains (and the heart brain). It's said that the brain in the gut accounts for why antidepressants cause nausea or abdominal upset in millions of people who take them.

It's duly noted, that before the seventeenth century, before materialism materialised, science and religion were integrated. They met and married through philosophy. God was the central reality, and religion harmonised with science in relation to the unseen order of things. The purpose of religion was to connect with God, to realign. But then the Age of Enlightenment landed, the Age of alleged Reason. And with the advance of knowledge through the scientific method, people exasperated with superstition, became intolerant. The telescope established there was no heaven 'visible' up there. Religion was a fairy-tale? There is no God, or hell, or spirits?

Society was in a state of reform, with the focus on reason and individualism, rather than tradition. The result was science and religion divorced. Natural knowledge became firmly rooted as the province of science and supernatural knowledge became the province of religion. Science got the natural kids, and religion got the supernatural kids.

As it transpired, Descartes' Cartesian Dualism effectively helped religion and science to co-exist at this testing time, when their relationship was fraught with difficulties. It allowed scientists to proceed without being burned at the stake for heresy. Descartes' two separate realms, namely, the mental (thinking) and physical (body), enabled placing science and religion into two different realms. The physical realm, matter and energy, could be measured and studied by science (since everything in this realm operates purely by mechanical properties). This also includes the body, since the body is a biological machine.

And the mental realm, the mind and soul, which are viewed as being transcendent to physical reality, could be best served by religion and philosophy. The properties of the mental realm cannot be measured and hence are alleged not to exist physically. They therefore fall outside of the realm of science. Suffice to say, the view of the body as a machine has led to a very mechanical approach to medicine.

The mind/brain split was substantiated with the birth of modern science. Such physical and non-physical thinking paved the way for the dichotomy of seeing mental distress and disorder as either the result of a faulty brain or a faulty mind. That is, as something organic and neurological or something psychological. Such dichotomies persist today. Hence, the professions of psychiatry aka physical treatments for the brain, since brain affects mind, and psychotherapy aka the talking cure, since mind affects brain. It seems to be a chicken and an egg situation. With regards to the 'chicken and egg' quandary, Plato would say the idea of chicken came before both the chicken and egg. Or God created the hen first.

Today we understand the mind to be a product of the brain. The brain and mind appear to be the same thing, monism, but with two different languages, namely, physical and psychological. Rather than the mind floating aimlessly about the ether, somewhere in the Outer Hebrides, and communicating with the body through say the pineal gland, it's understood that the brain structure is in place for a mind. The brain births the mind.

Science explains that the electrical firing of millions of tiny neurons produces our private, subjective, conscious experience. Indeed, apparently more than 500 trillion connections perform a dazzling array of complex mental processes every second. Our bioelectric brain generates and regulates our sensations, perceptions, thoughts and reason, emotion, attention, learning and memory. It's the key to our being. Life happens in the brain.

The adult brain comprises 2% of our body weight but it requires 20% of energy. And 80% of brain energy is used to provide power, like batteries, for electrical signals in axons (part of brain cells). Apparently, the brain uses 12 watts of power to electrically relay messages between brain cells and the body (neurons generate and suppress electrical and chemical signals). It's noted, the human body consists of 70% ionised water (which makes us conductive). Our blood is more than 80% water, and our brain consists of 75% water. Our consciousness is online when we're awake and goes offline when we sleep. Our brain however never slumbers, as there's always fireworks.

The fact the brain is intimately involved in consciousness is evidenced by changes in the brain which cause changes in consciousness. Like, brain damage can reduce/distort consciousness, and drink/drugs affect consciousness. Stimulating certain areas of the brain can induce specific experiences such as hallucinations, physical sensations, and emotional reactions. Part of the brain, the somatosensory cortex, has a map of the body and by stimulating any part of it causes a sensation as though the corresponding part of the body is being touched e.g. if the motor cortex is touched, part of the body moves, or if the visual cortex is touched, things are seen.

Brains can also be probed to induce spiritual experience and phenomenon. Like, neuroscientist professor Persinger's 'God Helmet' creates religious experiences, (such as feelings of ecstasy, sensing a presence, hearing voices, and seeing visions), by stimulating temporal lobes with complex magnetic fields. So, our brains are responsible for spiritual phenomenon? This confirms there is no 'spirit world'?

In 1934 neurosurgeon Wilder Penfield (1891-1976) further demonstrated that memories are physically stored. When he stimulated a particular part of the brain, a memory popped into the patient's mind, memories about things or events that were otherwise not recalled. And when he stimulated the same small area again, the same memory popped back into the patient's mind. It's apparently phenomenological, in the sense that it feels like it's really happening and feels exactly how it did at the time. If we were bored (which is existentially probable), we could probe our brain and have phenomenological trips to the past. We could probe the same area for particularly awesome memories/experiences.

It's also noted, the brain is an extraordinary plastic and responsive machine. Some regions of the brain literally grow in response to the information storage demands placed on them. Neurogenesis is the growth of new brain cells. For example, brain scans have shown that taxi drivers in London have a bigger hippocampus, the part of the brain that stores working memories into long-term explicit memories. It stores detailed mental maps, and this spatial information leads to a bigger hippocampus. It seems immaterial thoughts (information) physically alter our brain. Like, overdosing on porn causes physical changes to the brain. It's said the brain is like a muscle.

Regarding consciousness then, our brain receives information from our senses and decodes it. Sensations are messages from the senses. Besides the traditional five senses, we have other senses like heat, cold, gravitation, acceleration. Sensory transduction involves converting the incoming energy, i.e. light, sound, touch, or smell (currency of information), into electrical signals. Like, the eardrum transforms the vibration of sound into electrical signals that are sent to the brain, enabling hearing. And then there's clever cochlear implants, a small microphone that captures sound waves and transforms these into electrical impulses.

With vision, everything we see meets the eye in the form of light waves. We see things because light reflects off the surface of objects, hits the retina in our eye and the resulting electrical impulses are processed in the brain. Data through the eye-optic-nerve is translated into images and then into consciousness. It's noted, that soundwaves are slower than light-waves, hence we see lightening before we hear thunder.

Thus, we 'see' the physical world with our brain not our 'eyes'. What we think we 'see' is a pulse of energy to a completely dark part of the brain. When we look at a tree, for example, the image we see is not 'out there' but in our brains. Thus, our reality is essentially a series of electrical stimuli to the brain. And we can't see most of our reality because we can only see 'luminous matter' (visible light). Like, we can't see dark energy/matter because it doesn't reflect light.

As the existentialists alluded to, we make sense of our sensations, through our perceptions. Perceptions are the brain's educated guesses about what the combined senses are telling it. And experience educates sensory perception. Like, touch educates vision. It's highlighted we don't appreciate depth (3D) until we touch things. Until then, we have a 2½D sketch in our mind. Perception is defined as the process through which sensations are interrupted, using knowledge of the world, so they become meaningful experiences. Our life experience provides us with a reservoir of stored information for our brains to draw on.

But moreover, it's possible to perceive what is not sensed, not to perceive what is sensed, and to construct more than one perception from the same sensation. Take blind-sight, for example, which is the ability to see although without the actual experience of seeing. Those with this condition deny consciously seeing anything, yet they correctly guess the colour of stimuli they can't see. Some show pupil dilation and other emotional responses to stimuli. This implies a dissociation between vision and consciousness. Sensory data flows through the senses and the brain tries to look for patterns/meanings. Or we might see, hear, and smell things that others don't i.e. hallucinations.

That curiousness aside, the brain is programmed with a certain sense of reality and actively seeks to reaffirm this. Apparently more than 50% of perceived experience received by the brain is edited to fit a preconceived idea. It's highlighted this bodes well for the social engineers. It's sweet that the herd and plebs reaffirm the programme they've been given despite evidence to the contrary?

Such 'confirmation bias', however unconscious, thus avoids contradictory evidence and opinions. Like, if we don't believe in God, (or want to), we'll look for information to confirm this. And vice versa, we can find evidence for God. Like, the physical universe? Or like, when we fall in love, we're convinced the object of our desire has no flaws. Or, if we're depressed or angry, we might look for evidence to confirm our depression and anger. The brain omits or adds information to construct a reality or experience that fits with beliefs.

For the purposes of example, read the following sentence and count the F's: Finished flies are the result of years of scientific study combined with the experience of years[9]. Thus, we see what we want to see or what we're programmed to see. We can also think of optical illusions, which involve visual deception (see photos). Thus, our eyes see something, but the image tricks our brain that it sees something else. We're duped.

But moreover, the conscious mind receives a mere fraction of what passes through the senses, which it edits, whereas the unconscious sees all. This was brought to light when subliminal advertising was exposed in the 1950s, when some TV and movie theatre adverts were found to be transmitting split-second images that the conscious mind couldn't see to stimulate a desire for a product. For example, coca cola would flash on the screen and whilst it wasn't consciously seen, suddenly people were parched and in want of (what's the

---

[9] There's six but most people see three, and seeing four is rare. Our brain does not process the 'of' so it gets deleted.

chances) coca cola. Subliminal advertising was thus ruled as a threat to human freedom and banned. Subliminal notably means 'below threshold', so subliminal stimuli are any sensory stimuli below an individual's threshold for conscious perception.

Despite the practice being banned, it's understood we continue to receive subliminal messages. How would we consciously know? Subliminals are usually planted in the 'back of our mind' and we're left with 'feelings'. It's purported that our subconscious is frequently being filled with suggestions that can alter our perception of things. Subliminal messages are calculated to induce a particular reaction. That is, we're primed to have particular thoughts and emotional patterns, to be controlled.

Disney, for example, is notorious for using subliminal sexual images, which is even weirder since these movies are aimed at kids. Like, sex is written in the clouds, and genitals etc are depicted. It's said this contributes to our hyper-sexualised society, as our unconscious is bombarded with sexual imagery. So, besides being conditioned by the conscious content i.e. the overt 'programme', we're covertly conditioned by its unconscious content. Our perceptions are also 'subliminally' manipulated by other nefarious practices, like Google search engines, news feeds and suggestions. But moreover, social media platforms like Facebook, Twitter and YouTube actively remove information to control our perception. Like, 'conspiracy theories' about 9/11.

It's highlighted, that so much is implanted that we're not aware of. We absorb endless messages that filter into our conscious minds as thoughts, perceptions, and decisions that we naively think are ours i.e. regarding our fears, wants, desires, and acceptance. But they're not. They've been given to us. And we suck it all up in our alpha state. So, what we expose ourselves to affects us e.g. music, movies, computer games.

Several studies have linked viewing violence, for example, with an increased risk for aggression, anger, and failing to understand the suffering of others. Viewers are less likely to help others, feel sympathetic toward victims, and express empathy. It's also understood that we're being deliberately desensitised, which starts from childhood. Cartoons, for example, like Tom and Jerry, can be brutal. It seems we don't think about the content because it's a cartoon? It's also noted, that our brain treats violence on TV as real, and stores this as long term memories (like Post-Traumatic Stress Disorder), so that's not good for our mental wellbeing?

As mentioned, repetition is the most basic form of mind control. Like, we're conditioned by 'the news'. And like, choruses in songs. With the Jackson's song 'Enjoy Yourself', for example, the message 'enjoy yourself' is implanted in our brains. It's also noted, that some songs literally trigger us to get out our seat and start dancing. Like, David Bowie's song *'Let's Dance'*, makes us want to put our red shoes on and dance the blues. It's like we're hypnotised? As touched on, music is an extremely powerful method of mind control.

But it gets more sinister with back-masking, which is deliberately planting messages into songs that the unconscious mind receives. Apparently, our brains register words backwards and forwards. Like, Led Zeppelin's 'Stairway to Heaven', for example, when played backwards, features satanic messages, like 'my sweet Satan' and '666', that we're not consciously aware of but our brains are. It's like the Beatles song 'Helter Skelter' says 'Satan' when played in reverse. And Jay-Z's song 'Lucifer' says '666 murder murder Jesus 666'.

It's also noted, that movies and music videos are full of symbolism. Symbolism is a secret language used by those who know what the signs, symbols and numbers etc mean. Like, freemasons have their own secret language. But it seems the masses are beginning to recognise the occult symbols that society is saturated in e.g. the pyramid with the all-seeing eye? As touched on, this is not an accident because they want us to know. Everything that was hidden is being brought to light.

Whilst we'll get back to this, it's further noted, that Hollywood and the music industry use predictive programming, which is known as lesser magic. Thus, they show us a glimpse of the future, so we're prepared and accept what's coming e.g. Orwell's 1984 dystopian society. It's like alien movies groom us into accepting ETs. And we were told in advance about the recent corona virus. Like Event 201, held in October 2019, was a global pandemic exercise modelling a 'fictional corona virus'. And in 2017, Dr Fauci said there would be a surprise outbreak during Trump's administration. And he should know, given he worked on creating corona viruses (the US gave $7 million to the Wuhan Institute of Virology). However, I digress.

'Perceptual or inattentional blindness' illustrates how the brain is highly selective in deciding which elements of sensory information are consciously perceived. Classically shown in Daniel Simons and Christopher Chabris's 'Selective Attention Test' (1999), subjects are asked to count the number of passes between basketball players. As the players pass the basketballs around, a gorilla strolls into the middle of the action, faces the camera and thumps its chest, then leaves. But as a result of the participant's concentration on the passes, on average half fail to see the gorilla walking by.

The brain is so engaged with the counting task it decides not to bother itself generating a conscious picture of the gorilla, despite a substantial part of the brain's visual system absorbed with the gorilla's presence. The gorilla is literally airbrushed out the conscious (picture). We assume that we have a detailed inner representation in our heads, but it would appear not. The brain fills in the gaps as we don't always see things, like the gorilla. Hence, the visual experience is continuous scenery even though we can't see all of it.

It seems there is no conscious perception without attention. When we look around a room, we only see the very few things we pay attention to, and despite the way it feels, we do not really see anything else. The gist is retained hence the phenomenal experience of continuity without too much confusion. This explains why we can walk down the same street a hundred times, only to notice something we've never seen before. Again, we've airbrushed it out, as it's unimportant. Or sometimes I can be looking for one cat in a particular room, and not see my other cat sitting there, and yet it feels like I am taking in 100% of the room.

Or we're not aware of a clock ticking, until we are. We 'hear' background information, but we don't really listen until our attention is summoned. Like, we hear our name mentioned, our ears prick up, stand to attention. Or we buy a new car (or become infatuated with someone who has a particular car), and suddenly these cars are everywhere.

It's said we have an inbuilt radar system, which is part of our Reticular Activating System (RAS), located in the oldest part of the brain (in the brainstem within the reptilian brain). This acts as a gateway between our conscious mind and unconscious mind. It's said that our sudden alertness to things that are particular to us e.g. our name mentioned in a room that's crowded with 'blur' noise, is because we've subconsciously instructed our RAS to listen out for our name.

The RAS is responsible for our sleeping, eating, arousal and motivation. It's the RAS that wakes us up. It picks up signals like light coming through the curtains or bird noises or a full bladder. It tells the higher centres of the brain where our consciousness resides. It's highlighted that when we make goals, we give the RAS something to focus on. We can programme it. It's like our instinctive mind?

Whilst some claim there can be no consciousness without attention, others disagree. It's said, 'highway hypnosis', for example, shows how driver's consciousness can be fully focussed elsewhere yet they demonstrate attention. They have no recollection of driving during that time, because they're in a hypnotic state, yet they drive safely.

It's understood the conscious and subconscious minds are able to concentrate on different things. And that driving a car is a manifestation of automaticity. Once we learn to do something, and we've practised it many times, it becomes an automatic response pattern. Like walking, talking, riding a bike, and assembly line work. We don't have to think about it. These skills become hardwired into the brain and become unconscious. Thus, our mind can focus on other activities while undertaking an automatised activity, like holding a conversation while driving. It's said the unconscious mind is far more powerful than the conscious mind. Apparently only 5% of our lives are controlled by conscious thought.

But moreover, it seems our power to direct our attention is something that our conscious mind does. It seems like we have a mind that chooses what to pay attention to? We think about whatever and execute our actions. As touched on, it feels like we're an embodied soul. It feels like we're a 'self' that thinks thoughts. We perceive that 'we' have consciousness, ('a stream of consciousness'), hold opinions, have passions, and make decisions. And we have self-consciousness, which presupposes there's a self to know, to be conscious of.

However, we're told this is a fallacy. Science tells us we're deluded, as there is no self or separate mind. We're told the argument for a non-physical, self-conscious mind that is separate from the unconscious physical brain is nonsense. There is no satisfactory explanation regarding how a separate mind interacts with the brain, or the world for that matter.

Conscious perceptions are assembled from sensory input in the cerebral cortex, but since information from the senses is distributed all over the place for different purposes, it's contended there is no central place for 'I'. So, there is no mind that emerges from the brain. But rather consciousness comes from neural activity.

It's understood that consciousness (self-awareness) consists of complex thought processes, which are separate yet function together. Like an orchestra, functions of particular brain regions play together. Thus, consciousness is the performance of billions of neurons acting in concert. Brain cells are also likened to ants in a colony. They follow chemical signals, and each has their own particular job to do. Perhaps consciousness could be likened to synergy i.e. the creation of the whole is greater than the sum of its parts?

Whilst there is no specific site in the brain for consciousness i.e. 'consciousness centre', it seems to be more localised in the frontal lobes, which are at the front of both cerebral hemispheres, than anywhere else. [Both hemispheres have conscious awareness of things, but the left is more verbal and expresses its awareness in words, whereas the right is more creative and pictorial]. The frontal lobes seem instrumental in defining personality, (more than other regions of the brain), as evidenced by frontal lobe disorders. Thus, people can have a sudden and dramatic change in their personality e.g. loss of social awareness, disinhibition, emotional instability, aggression, irritability, impulsiveness, including spending money impulsively, and sexually inappropriate behaviour.

It's noted, when people are manic or psychotic, the frontal lobes are working overtime. In addition to brain damage, tumours of frontal lobes will often manifest themselves in diminished awareness of alertness, which results in diminished capacity to solve complex problems.

So, there is no inner me or inner you, with a mind that thinks thoughts. But rather the frontal cortex creates an awareness of the 'self' in relation to the world. It's responsible for executive functions, like attention span, decision making, volitional behaviour, and planning for the future. Consciousness is an inseparable part of our ability to perceive, think and feel. So, it's not an extra ingredient but rather a by-product. It seems this puts a bullet in the theory of mind? And the concept of 'self' is just that. It's a concept as there is no self.

Vernon (2012) wrote, 'To be a self is to be an assembly of cells, not a creature with a soul' ('The Big Questions: God' p.195). He quotes Francis Crick (one of the discoverers of DNA) who said, '"You", your joys and your sorrows, your memories and ambitions, your sense of identity and freewill, are in fact no more than the behaviour of a vast assembly of nerve cells and their associated molecules'. The self is reduced to particular brain processes. 'We' are a bundle of processes (sensations) happening until our neurons stop firing.

Contrary to 'ego theorists' (dualism is an ego theory), 'bundle theorists' argue that the self is not an entity but more like a bundle of sensations. David Hume (1711-1776), Scottish philosopher, was a bundle theorist. He maintained the perception we have of an inner self or ego is in reality a long chain of simple impressions. He said the ego is 'nothing but a bundle or collection of different perceptions, which succeed each other with an inconceivable rapidity, and are in a perpetual flux and movement'.

Rather than a self per se, it appears we're a transient self endlessly created for each object with which the brain interacts. Our life is a series of impressions that seem to belong to us but are really just tied together through memory and other such relationships. The illusion of continuity occurs because each temporary self comes along with memories that give an impression of continuity.

Hume described the mind as 'a kind of theatre, where several perceptions successively make their appearance; pass, repass, slide away, and mingle in an infinite variety of postures and situations.' It's like a movie, which is a collection of instants. It's made up of single pictures, but in reality, the pictures are not connected. So, there is no stream of consciousness, only fleeting events and delusions of self.

The capacity for thought and autobiographical memory gives rise to the autobiographical self. Our language spins the story of a self and so we become to believe there is one. But really there is no inner self but only multiple parallel processes that give rise to a benign inner illusion. In essence, the self provides a useful fiction. Thus, for Hume, we have no underlying 'personal identity' beneath or behind these perceptions and feelings which come and go.

It's noted, that Buddha was the first bundle theorist, as he believed the self to be an illusion. Russell Brand (2014) concurs, 'The self is a construction. We have memories, feelings, opinions and beliefs. This 'self' that we hold in consciousness is temporary and it is an illusion'. And yet, as mentioned, we have an overwhelming sense of self. It seems 'we' are an accumulation of our memories, with experience building on experience, each day shaping the next, and shaping 'us'. However, with materialism, we're told that thought itself is the thinker.

But furthermore, it's promulgated we have no freewill. Scientists observe that freewill is nothing more than a by-product of the workings of a vast assembly of nerve cells. So, like the self, freewill is an illusion. It seems the existentialists were wrong. We're not free to choose our choice?

Brain scans show that choices are determined before we actually make them. The point in time when we think we have willed an action occurs after the brain has initiated the action. Hence, freewill is incompatible with neuroscience findings. Like, with movement, experiments have shown that brain processes planned the movement before the person had the conscious desire to move. The conscious thought to do something comes about half a second later than the action itself. In brain terms this is a long time. A lot of neural processing must have happened before the person consciously decided to move.

Thus, our brain (brain processes) plans for an action, which in turn gives rise to thoughts about that action, and then the action happens, and we presume we consciously created the action. Like, we assume we choose to say phone someone, but it's really brain activity that plans the action, which gives rise to thinking about phoning whoever. So, our brain chooses. 'We' do not choose.

This contradicts our most basic assumption about willed action. That is, believing our decision to act starts off the whole process. It's said consciousness arrives too late to be a voluntary action, hence our actions are determined. Rather than freewill, (self-conscious thought and choosing our choice), all events are determined by prior events. Determinism stipulates life is causally determined. It's the idea that every effect is connected by physical laws to a cause. Hence, determinists believe the future is fixed because of absolute causality. If the past were different, the present and future would also be different.

It seems counterintuitive to think we don't choose. And it's bemusing to think that the future is set. It's weird to think all our future states of mind and subsequent behaviours are determined. Like, what we're munching or wearing or whatever, next week or next year, is determined. And our death is determined?

It's duly noted, whilst operating external devices with thoughts is possible i.e. controlling robotic arms with thoughts, scientists nevertheless insist that doesn't prove there's a self in control. Such technology notably blows the clever cochlear implant out the water. To reach for an object, one 'imagines' moving the arm (electrodes are placed on the motor cortex) and that intention is translated computationally into a specific reaching movement of the arm. This technology allows the patient to coordinate their movements with their own thoughts, despite the disconnection of the biological link between their brain and spinal cord. It's said using bionic limbs is like learning to reach, walk, etc again.

It's bemusing that we can move bionic limbs with our thoughts. It questions what other machinery is operable by thoughts? And what is the military thinking about? Like, downloading consciousness onto computers or avatars i.e. new bodies? Perhaps 'souls' could live forever? Perhaps we could cryogenically freeze our heads, which is cheaper than freezing the whole body, until they figure out the technology to reanimate us. Weirdly some people want to live forever? Suffice to say, technology is immense, and we don't know the half of it. However, we'll get back to this.

The idea that the power of consciousness, choosing our choice, is a useless by-product or epiphenomenon, massively threatens human responsibility. It suggests we're not responsible for our actions? 'We're' not responsible for what our brain does. It's also said, that if everyone lost their belief in freewill, it could affect the way we behave. It's said those who reject freewill are more likely to cheat at things, for example, and are also less concerned about punishing other wrongdoers. It's seems we're given a neuroscientific license to please ourselves even more?

However, while scientists contend that consciousness can't initiate an action, they do however propose that it could prevent it. Thus, we don't have freewill but rather free-don't. This has important implications, namely, we cannot consciously control our dispositions or impulses, but we can consciously prevent them being acted out. So, for example, we should not be held responsible for merely imagining wanting to kill, rape or steal, because these impulses are not under conscious control, but we can be expected to prevent ourselves from doing such things. We essentially have a conscious veto. Presumably such wayward thoughts come from our unconscious? Or are daemons responsible?

It would appear we find ourselves at a junction. Science tells us there is no self with freewill, and there is no life after death. We're a brain that thinks thoughts, and then we die. There's nothing personal about it. Life is one big accident. So, there's that. Or do we listen to the voice of wisdom? Do we pay attention to our spirit tugging at our heartstrings?

In a mechanical vision, subjective experiences, including love, are reduced to physical and chemical processes. It seems life is even more pointless? However, as Vernon (2012) points out, 'brain science is condemned to remain on the outside, looking in, whereas the human individual can directly inspect the contents of their mind'. And maybe love is more than brain chemicals? Maybe love is the most important aspect to our reality. And maybe it's the only thing that ultimately matters. Vernon also highlights, 'brain science, for all its insights, changes its mind almost every week' (p.133). LOL.

It's also noted, that our brains make decisions we're not conscious of, until we are, which affect our brain e.g. take drugs, which affects our consciousness. It seems the brain knows consciousness is a source of pain, hence the great escape attempts. It equally seems paradoxical that our brain chooses, we do not choose, what to believe regarding idealism or materialism? Our brain decides whether or not it believes in God?

Jane Goodall (author) said, 'how sad it would be... if our left brains were literally to dominate the right so that logic and reason triumphed over intuition and alienated us absolutely, from our innermost being, from our hearts, our souls' (cited in Vernon, 2012, p.155).

CS Lewis (who intellectually battled with Christianity but finally succumbed to its higher reason) is often credited with saying, 'You don't have a soul, you are a soul. You have a body'. But apparently, it's not his quote. Maybe we are a spiritual being having a human physical experience. And perhaps the purpose of our life (God's breath) is to create our soul? Maybe physical existence is a breeding ground for souls. And the soul we cultivate, the character we 'become', is subject to appraisal by 'the God'? Perhaps the fact that we intuitively feel like a self that chooses, and it seems like there's some moral game taking place, is because we do and there is? Maybe we should trust our senses?

Moore (2012) highlights a letter by Keats, which said being intelligent is not enough – your intelligence has to be converted into a soul. He wrote, 'Do you not see how necessary a world of pains and troubles is to school an intelligence and make it a soul? Call the world if you Please 'The Vale of Soul-making' (p.29).

They do have souls

A Quote from the film 'Adaptation' (2002)

The character, Charlie Kaufman (played by John Cusack) said to himself:

'Do I have an original thought in my head? My bald head. Maybe if I were happier, my hair wouldn't be falling out. Life is short. I need to make the most of it. Today is the first day of the rest of my life. I'm a walking cliché. I really need to go to the doctor and have my leg checked. There's something wrong. A bump. The dentist called again. I'm way overdue. If I stop putting things off, I would be happier. All I do is sit on my fat ass. If my ass wasn't fat I would be happier. I wouldn't have to wear these shirts with the tails out all the time. Like that's fooling anyone. Fat ass. I should start jogging again. Five miles a day. Really do it this time. Maybe rock climbing. I need to turn my life around. What do I need to do? I need to fall in love. I need to have a girlfriend. I need to read more, improve myself. What if I learned Russian or something? Or took up an instrument? I could speak Chinese. I'd be the screenwriter who speaks Chinese and plays the oboe. That would be cool. I should get my hair cut short. Stop trying to fool myself and everyone else into thinking I have a full head of hair. How pathetic is that? Just be real. Confident. Isn't that what women are attracted to? Men don't have to be attractive. But that's not true. Especially these days. Almost as much pressure on men as there is on women these days. Why should I be made to feel I have to apologize for my existence? Maybe it's my brain chemistry. Maybe that's what's wrong with me. Bad chemistry. All my problems and anxiety can be reduced to a chemical imbalance or some kind of misfiring synapses. I need to get help for that. But I'll still be ugly though. Nothing's gonna change that'.

'Men are so necessarily mad, that not to be mad would amount to another form of madness'.
Blaise Pascal

Everyone's normal until you get to know them. Normal is a spin on a washing machine.

4

Mental Case?

There's an epidemic of mental health problems. Depression and anxiety, for example, are rampant. But there's so many disorders, hundreds, with new ones created all the time. Take Narcissistic Personality Disorder, for example, (which replaced the old school term megalomaniac), which pertains to those with an over-inflated sense of importance. No danger, there's a 'medical' diagnosis for someone who's a legend in their own mind. Multiple Personality Disorder however takes the concept of an alter-ego to a whole new level, as people exhibit an array of different personalities known as 'alters'.

Obsessive Compulsive Disorder (OCD) seems popular, an avatar of anxiety, a need for control through compulsions, like excessive cleaning or hoarding. Sufferers are plagued with a never-ending stream of intrusive thoughts. Then there's mental illness like schizophrenia and psychosis. People can see or hear things that others don't, and there's also delusions of grandeur and truly believing one is say Napoleon or the Queen of Sheba. Or less pleasant are paranoid delusions that the world is out to get us. It seems we're increasingly paralysed by fear? Einstein said the best question we can ask ourselves is, 'is this a friendly universe?'

The Diagnostic and Statistical Manual of Mental Disorders (DSM) aka 'psychiatry's bible' provides standard criteria for the classification of mental disorders. And we all arguably have something? We're all a standard deviation away from madness? It's duly noted, that some mental dis-ease seems more mental than others. Like, we can all relate to depression and anxiety, to some extent, but 'hallucinations' and multiple personalities seem pretty crazy? It seems we're all at risk of being mental, because it comes with the human condition. But there's a dastardly progression from mental health problems to mental illness to mental disease?

As mentioned, it's always possible material scientists are out their depth when it comes to the mind. And it's also possible Sartre was right that depression, anxiety, anguish, boredom, alienation, absurdity etc is normal, as our soul is screaming for meaning. As psychiatrist Eric Fromm said, 'It is the fully sane person who feels isolated in the insane society'. The existential claim is that much mental illness is grounded in nihilism. It matters that there's no point? For existentialists, life is suffering, responsibility and truth.

Whilst psychology gives us feedback i.e. signs and symptoms, it's highlighted that every diagnosis in the DSM is negative and attributes responsibility to the person. The person is blamed for not being okay, as opposed to the system that births not okay-ness. The DSM undermines society's contribution. Like, the breakdown of the family, and the garbage we're conditioned with.

The contention is thus, that most mental illness makes sense. Like, it makes sense that soldiers suffer from Post-Traumatic Stress Disorder (PTSD). And it makes sense that people are depressed? Life's not all sunshine and rainbows. Moreover, the fundamental point is, we're always thinking. Buddha said, 'What we are today comes from our thoughts of yesterday, and our present thoughts build our life of tomorrow. Our life is the creation of our mind'. And also, 'All that we are is the result of what we have thought'.

When it comes to questioning the origin of mental health problems and illness then, where best to start but the beginning? 'Postmodern' philosopher Jacques Derrida (1930-2004) notably pertained to deconstructionism. That is, to understand the structure of something, we need to understand its genesis. Thus, we'll start with the birth of personality, and take it from there.

Lest it be said, whilst I advocate that we choose our choice, we nevertheless have to hope for 'good enough' parenting and not too mental a reality to give us a chance, a reasonable hand to start the game. Existentially it's what we do with the hand that counts but there's also taking the piss with some mental families.

Thus, we have to hope for reasonable care whilst growing in the womb. It's a hit if our mums don't smoke as we're less likely to get asthma etc and be born premature (which can impact on intelligence?). It's also a bonus if they refrain from drinking or taking drugs since that fries our brain and as a result it's highly likely we'll be diagnosed with ADHD and behaviour problems. Stress also causes harm to the developing foetus, so we'd hope our mum has minimal stress. And we'd hope she actually wants us. How dreadful, not to be wanted. Our self-esteem is dunted before we're even out.

And we'd hope to acquire model genes. Genes (in our DNA) are the blueprint for our physical development through our lifespan. Our bodies are controlled by genes, and the environment controls genes, as genes respond to life. Gene regulation (i.e. genes switch on and off) allows cells to react quickly to changes in their environments. Whilst society seems to suggest we're at the mercy of our genes, it's not as straight forward as we're led to believe?

Like, people with the gene that predisposes them to breast cancer, for example, may not get breast cancer, and those without this gene can get breast cancer. Or people might inherit the 'TOWIE' gene ('The Only Way is Essex' 'programme') that raises the risk of sunbed addiction. People with one variant were up to fourteen times more likely to get hooked. Or they could be sensible enough not to use sunbeds? It seems there's genes for everything? This includes the god gene, VMAT2, which predisposes us to religious belief. But moreover, it seems even more precarious when it comes to mental health, particularly since attitudes and beliefs are not in the genes.

It's also understood that early childhood affects gene expression. Like, abuse activates or deactivates genes, putting that person on a different developmental trajectory. Different environmental and lifestyle factors can alter how our genes behave, without actually changing our genetic makeup. Like, people can become schizophrenic as a result of dodgy environments and funky early adaptation. Research shows we can switch genes on and off by our thoughts. Our thoughts can trigger particular genes into action, which is social pathology?

It's like stress plays a huge role in mental illness, and stress comes from perception. It's our reaction to 'stressors' in our environment. Stress is notably not a mental state but rather the non-specific response of the body to any demands (stressors) made on it. So, we don't want to be a stress cat, or we can't help it?

Thus, we arrive, and need to be looked after i.e. held, comforted, fed, and changed. In fairness, that's the least the natives can do, since we didn't ask to be here. Primary or basic emotions are a set of emotions present at birth or emerging early in the first year. Like, babies look interested, fearful, disgusted, joyful, sad or angry. Babies learn to negotiate their needs, like screaming to secure attention. It's like ringing a bell.

Whilst we're each a snowflake, babies' temperaments are categorised as easy, slow-to-warm up, or difficult (which means they cry a lot). Right from the beginning, infants show distinct styles of responding to the environment. Crucially, we need to be able to trust that our needs will be met, as this enables feeling safe and secure in the world, whereas failure to develop trust results in fear. And fear comes in many forms i.e. unease, worry, anxiety, nervousness, tension, dread, phobia etc. We have an intrinsic need to be loved, to connect with others, and to feel a sense of belonging and acceptance.

Research informs that from about six months old we develop 'internal working models' of self in relation to others. These mental representations illustrate how our sense of self is a product of how we're treated by our caregivers i.e. are we liked, loved, of interest, ignored, hurt or abused? Our sense of self develops in tandem with neural networks aka pathways in the brain. And the first two years are critical for brain development. At birth, our brain is a quarter of its adult size, by age three it's 90% formed, and it's fully formed by five years old.

Loving attachments with caring adults strongly stimulate a child's brain, causing synapses (the gaps between brain cells) to grow and existing connections to get stronger. Bonding releases endogenous (homemade) opiates. And positive interaction enhances self-esteem and self-worth. Alternatively, adverse attachments can cause problems such as intellectual delays, impaired cognitive functioning, demanding of attention but no genuine attachments.

In essence, if a child shows a particular range of needs and behaviours, evidence suggests these are typically associated with particular parenting and care-giving styles. If we're loved and our needs are met, we become cooperative. Whereas if our needs aren't met, different traits surface. Peter Fonagy (clinical psychologist) states, 'the child's strategy will inevitably be a reflection of the caregiver's behaviour towards them'. Attachment behaviour is any type of behaviour that gets the child into proximity with the parent.

Thus, attachments are critical as they affect behaviour. Dodgy attachments can translate to dodgy behaviour. According to psychiatrists, at least 50% of kids have insecure attachments, and 85% of families are dysfunctional. Happy days. It seems dysfunction is the new normal? Maybe psychiatrists should widen their margins regarding what's normal?

Attachment theory is based around the poles of attachment and separation, and recognises how relationships are shaped by the threat and need for security. It further relates the quality of early attachments to emotional functioning throughout life, in the sense that these are a template for future relationships. We carry this perspective of self/others into subsequent relationships. Fonagy highlights 'early infant attachment patterns seem to predict behaviour in school and later in the way individuals talk and think about themselves, and perhaps how they relate intimately to others'.

It's also noted, that children are highly responsive to the modelling of emotional expressiveness, and they partake in social referencing i.e. picking up on cues and body language. They observe emotional expressions and 'take on' other's emotional states through contagion. Role modelling is hugely important, since monkey see, inauthentic monkey do. Children emulate adults, and thus mental health problems or dysfunctional ways of being can be contagious in the sense of being learned. It's also highlighted that unconscious 'imprinting' takes place during the first few years of life e.g. we imprint our parent's relationship, how they treat each other.

Secondary emotions or more complex emotions emerge with cognitive abilities. We could say they're learned, as they're embedded in a cultural context. Thus, we have raw emotions like fear, but what triggers them is learned e.g. we learn to be afraid of rattlesnakes. So, we adapt to our environment. Like little sponges, we soak it all up. And our little personalities come into 'being' as we're shaped by demands placed upon us. We have to learn the rules i.e. what's right and wrong, and internalise these values into our personality. We have to keep up with the programme. But that doesn't undermine that we're self-acting agents?

It seems pertinent to note, that contrary to Freud's deduction that the propensity to make bonds was secondary or consequential to the instinct to feed, we're designed to attach, and this is not dependent on physical care. Harlow's monkeys illustrated this and thus the 'cupboard love theory' (attachment through munch) was binned. As every psychology student knows, the chimps were fed by a metal structure but didn't attach to that but rather snuggled up with Bobo, the terry towel structure.

Interestingly however, although these chimps formed attachments to Bobo, they were crap at mothering their own chimps which in turn highlights that mothering is not instinctive as previously assumed. We learn from our mums how to be mums. We have to be shown love, so that we too can love.

Whilst we'll get back to Freud, when we address the 'curious unconscious', we'll start with his theory of personality. For Freud, the personality consists of our ego, superego and id, and these psychic structures are forever enmeshed in a battle of the wills. The ego is basically our personality. It's our identity, our centre of consciousness. But it's influenced by the id and superego. The id is the source of our basic impulses and drives, and is present from birth, whereas we don't develop the superego, which is like our conscience, until several years later. Freud basically reduced man's constitution to animal instincts, like hunger, sex, and aggression. And we do what it takes to get our needs met?

So, Freud proposed that as babies we're all id. We're impulsive and demanding, as we want our needs met. The id seeks immediate pleasure and gratification. Whilst we carry the id or 'pleasure principle' all our lives, we learn to regulate our desires and adjust to our surroundings. We learn that we can't scream until we get what we want. Unless we're autistic, we tend to grow out of narcissism. Thus, our ego begins to form, which incorporates this regulative function.

And on the premise moral development isn't stunted on account of adverse home dynamics, we go onto develop our superego from three-five years old, (we stop babbling out loud and develop inner speech). This internal censor or watchdog is a force for good. It's our moral compass, and it inspires positive aspirations. Thus, the ego, which is here and now, concerns itself with managing the demands of the id and superego.

It's an interesting observation that the ego attempts to exact a balance between the hedonistic id and the moralistic superego. Like, if we're tempted to do something, like smoke a crack-pipe, our impulsive id is chomping at the bit, whereas the superego is telling us, no good can come from it. Or maybe our battle is we really want to lie in bed, but know we shouldn't. It's a challenge. To use a religious analogy, the id can be regarded as the naughty angel, the superego the good angel, and 'we' decide who to listen to.

Whilst we'll also get back to Jung in the next chapter, it's noted that he proposed every personality has a 'Persona' (literally a mask worn by Greek actors). It's our mask that we wear every day, pretending to be who we are. It's referred to as a social archetype or conformity archetype, as it forms in early childhood out of a need to conform to the wishes or expectations of parents, peers and teachers. It's imperative that we build acceptable traits into our persona, to be socially adept, to be 'normal'? Unacceptable traits are alternatively banished into the unconscious, or the 'shadow', as Jung calls it. But we'll get to this curious realm.

We can also consider Eric Berne's takeaway on personality, as his model is commonly used in therapy. Berne endorsed Freud's psychic structure i.e. ego, superego and id. But he divided the ego into three identifiable 'ego states', namely, child, adult and parent. He observed that we use these ego states when we interact with others. We're a mixture of these ego states, (ways of being), which fluctuate endlessly.

He explains the child ego state is born when we're born. We have feelings and emotions in response to external events. We're free but we learn to adapt. Hence, our child ego state has two natures, namely, free and adapted. We internalise the messages we're bombarded with from parents (role models), which can be critical or nurturing, and this creates our parent ego state. Thus, our parent ego state has two natures, namely, critical and nurturing. But from about from one year old, in tandem with our gross motor skills, we learn to do things by ourselves e.g. control a cup we're drinking from or grab a toy. Thus, our adult ego state begins to form. We begin to think and evaluate for ourselves. So, the parent is taught, the child feels, and the adult learns.

These states of mind and related patterns of behaviour present as consistent patterns of behaviour and bear no relation to age or role. Rather these are the structures of the personality. For example, we might be a 'nurturing parent', if we comfort our friend, or tell them to put a coat on because it's cold outside. Or we might be a 'critical parent' if we reproach them for being stupid, and not having gloves and a scarf. Or we might be a critical parent to ourselves. Like, we tell ourselves we're rubbish.

When gripped by 'feelings' the child has taken over. Like, we're crying because we're not okay (we're 'cry babies'), or having temper tantrums. Thus, we might need the rational adult to step in and instruct us to get a grip. Moreover, the free child in us says 'why not' to adventure, whereas the adapted child in us says 'better not'.

It's also noted, that if we act like a child, we might elicit a parent response from others. And vice versa, if we act like a parent, we might elicit childlike behaviour from others. There's also adults who like to regress to childlike behaviour, to be a little boy or girl? Which is slightly creepy? Like kinky adults, who dress up as babies and pretend to be them. It seems the best interaction is adult to adult? The adult in us is the 'grown up' rational person. Berne insists that everyone has a good functional 'adult' or rational intelligible ego. The only question is whether or not it's being used.

Berne identified five 'drivers' that motivate and shape us into being. Namely, Be Perfect, Be Strong, Hurry Up, Please Others, and Try Hard. These drivers are seeking to help the child become socially functional, but they're also at the root of dysfunctional behaviour. Like, if kids aren't praised for adequate behaviour, the child can go overboard doing things. We might find we have problems later in life with an over-exaggerated need or compulsion to please people.

It's highlighted that 'people pleasers' learn in childhood that their needs are met (we survive) by taking care of others. The pleaser projects an image of being helpful, in order to be seen as indispensable (we earn love). 'Perfectionists' experienced much criticism and judgement in childhood, hence they learn to be perfect (sticking to the rules) to prevent condemnation. It seems our need to please people, be perfect, stress about time, try hard, and be strong is a condition of our worth? Carl Rogers' pertained to 'conditions of worth', asserting if there's too many conditions, the self isn't worth much.

It's said we don't change our basic personality type over our lifetime, but we can become more conscious of it and moderate it. We can choose another way of responding? Like, we can actively defy our need to please people or be perfect. We can live with imperfections. We also don't have to try that hard. We can be deliberately untimely. And we can cry if we want to. We don't have to be strong. We can rationally override our instinct to behave in a certain way? Like, 'controllers' could lighten up with their controlling antics? Maybe we could choose to be a breezy B personality type instead of anal A? Or that's only possible with Valium and Ketamine?

Type A individuals are identified as aggressive, ambitious, controlling, highly competitive, preoccupied with status, and impatient. Whereas Type B's are relaxed, less stressed, flexible, emotional and expressive, and have a laid-back attitude. Type B's are more about living in the moment, whereas Type A's are a heart attack waiting to happen.

The theory of Type A personality notably emerged in the 1950s when cardiologists Mayer Friedman and Ray Rosenman observed the correlation between personality and heart disease. Type C has since been added, which exhibits both tendencies of Type A and Type B. And there's also a Type D personality, known as 'distressed' or 'disease prone'. This defines people who tend to be worried, irritable, and express a great deal of negative emotions. They tend to experience stress-related illness, and they're also linked to coronary heart disease.

Whilst there's myriad personality types, which suggests we like to define ourselves; psychologists are partial to The Big Five Personality Theory. Personality types are distinguished from personality traits in that there's different types of personality e.g. introvert or extravert, whereas with trait theories, introversion and extraversion are part of a continuum.

The Big Five personality traits are thus: Openness (inventive/curious versus consistent/cautious); Conscientious (efficient/organised versus easy going/careless); Extraversion (outgoing/energetic versus solitary/reserved); Agreeableness (friendly/compassionate versus analytical/detached); Neuroticism (sensitive/nervous versus secure/confident). Beneath each global trait are clusters of correlated and more specific traits which found the tension that exists within each polarity.

It's duly noted, that personality tests are increasing being used to vet candidates in the hiring process. Like, Myers-Briggs sixteen personality types, for example, which are actually more like horoscopes e.g. the nurturer, artist, protector, scientist, giver, idealist or visionary (her philosophy was inspired by Jung).

There's also a difference between personality and character. Thus, our personality is our identity, our distinctive personal qualities and traits, which are on display, whereas our character reveals what we are inside. Our character refers to our morals and beliefs that define how we behave with others and ourselves. It determines how we react to whatever situation or event (our thinking style). Both our personality and character develop through the interaction of our temperament, which is inherited, and environment.

And we're part responsible for them, as active agents of our identity? As existentially explicated, we come into 'being' in context. Our personality and character surges up. But this is where the trouble begins, as people have problems with these. People's characters and personalities are not okay. Indeed, the most common psychiatric disorder is personality disorders. These are diagnosed in about 50% of 'patients'.

Like other 'illnesses', personality disorders are classed as mild, moderate and severe. And it's not uncommon to be diagnosed with more than one. Whilst people diagnosed with mild personality disorders usually live 'normal lives', at stressful times their symptoms can become more pronounced. But it gets worse, as there's no real cure, and many people don't even know they have a personality disorder. No danger, they think they're 'normal' (LOL). Like, some highly successful business people, for example, show all the signs of a personality disorder e.g. they behave ruthlessly towards others, totally disregard their feelings, and deliberately isolate themselves. But being successful, their behaviour is accepted. It's like psychos in banking is normal, but we'll get back to psychos.

The DSM groups personality disorders into 'clusters'. Thus, Cluster A pertains to 'odd and eccentric' behaviour, Cluster B defines 'dramatic, emotional or erratic' behaviour, and Cluster C categorises 'anxious or fearful' behaviour. And within these clusters are the various personality disorders. Like, under Cluster A we find 'Paranoid Personality Disorder' (self-explanatory), 'Schizoid Personality Disorder' (cold, distant, reclusive, introverted), and 'Schizotypal Personality Disorder' (like the former but additionally has chaotic thoughts and views).

Cluster B covers 'Borderline Personality Disorder' aka 'Emotionally Unstable Personality Disorder' (manipulative, often self-harm, feel empty and abandoned, moody, angry, act impulsively, abnormal emotional reactions), Antisocial Personality Disorder (violent, aggressive, no remorse, bloated self-image, manipulative), Narcissistic Personality Disorder (abnormally high opinion of self and resent those who fail to admire them, lack empathy), and Histrionic Personality Disorder (obsessed with appearance and demand attention, 'praise me', and behaviour often seen as shallow and over the top).

And Cluster C has Dependent Personality Disorder, Avoidant Personality Disorder, and Obsessive-Compulsive Personality Disorder (anxious, indecisive, inflexible and need to be in control, perfectionism), which is different from OCD. OCD is an anxiety disorder as we'll get to.

In essence, someone with a personality disorder 'doesn't seem right'. They're not 'normal' like the rest of us. Their interpersonal functioning and impulse control is askew e.g. they might be intense, inappropriate, self-centred, overly suspicious, emotional or anal. They can be rigid and unbending in the way they think and act, which can cause considerable personal and social disruption to their lives. Their inflexibility comes about because the way they think makes sense for them. It's their personality and how they see the world.

Before personality disorders were invented, presumably we'd refer to 'challenging' others as difficult, weird, a pain in the hoop, a drama queen etc. Suffice to say, we all have opinions on each other. And we can all be weird. We'll notably get back to Multiple Personality Disorder at the end, because this is a particularly interesting disorder, and quite unlike other 'personality disorders'.

It's understood that dysfunctional childhoods give rise to dysfunctional 'ways of being'. Confused minds develop in confused environments. Hence, about 80% of people with Borderline Personality Disorder, for example, experienced trauma in childhood. Too many people have been seriously psychologically damaged. Not undermining radical freedom then, but some people have a lot of issues to deal with. The experts further inform that we may be genetically vulnerable to personality disorders, which seems a weird conjecture to think about?

It's generally recognised that people have difficulties because they haven't learned (at an earlier age) how to act or react appropriately. It's contended psychological disorders reflect an internalisation of adverse attachment experiences, particularly those that undermine self-reliance and feelings of security. But resilience can be fostered. We can change our thinking and learn new behaviours? We can learn social skills, like how to behave appropriately? It can be seen as a maturation process, where the cost is usually worth the benefit.

Whilst those with a personality disorder can be perceived as manipulative, strategic and calculated, their behaviour could be the result of limited coping strategies and communication skills. It thus seems there's a difference between those who are A-holes, because they can be, and those who don't know any better. Besides personality disorders, there's also character disorders.

Scott Peck highlights that most people who see a psychiatrist are suffering from either a neurosis or a character disorder. These are disorders of responsibility and are opposite in nature. Thus, 'neurotic' people assume too much responsibility for everyone and everything, compared to 'character disordered' people who don't take enough responsibility for themselves or anything. The neurotic person is obsessed with 'shoulds' and 'oughts', whereas the self-image of the latter is someone with no power or choice, whose behaviour is directed by outside forces, totally beyond their control. Hence, they maintain they 'can't', 'couldn't', 'have to', or 'had to'.

However, he also highlights that many individuals have both a neurosis and a character disorder (i.e. in different areas of their lives), hence the term 'character neurotic'. He notes that few of us can escape being neurotic or character disordered to some degree, as we figure out what we are and are not responsible for. He states, 'it is said that neurotics make themselves miserable; those with character disorders make everyone else miserable'.

It seems bemusing to assert that someone's character or personality is disordered? But for many people, identifying their disorders is helpful as it gives them a compass to work with. Their dodgy behaviour is not uncommon. Many people have similar issues, given similar dysfunction. Hence, the ascribed label.

However, before we get to diagnosing behaviour as 'mental illness', it seems pertinent to continue with Berne's 'Transactional Analysis' theory. Because Berne maintains we're OK. And that's a good thing? Berne's philosophy insists that everyone has the capacity to think. People decide their own destiny, and these decisions can be changed. Berne was an existentialist. Maybe the concept of 'mental illness' isn't entirely helpful? But rather, understanding context is.

Berne was interested in how we've been programmed, since past interactions give rise to present life positions. We are the 'presenting past' and analysing our social interaction helps explain behaviour. 'Life positions' are our windows onto the world. They're our perceived place in the world. They're our basic beliefs (convictions) about our self and others, which are used to justify decisions and behaviour.

The crux of the matter is, are we okay and what about others? The 'okay corral' notably depicts the four basic life positions, namely, I'm okay, you're okay; I'm not okay, you're okay; I'm okay, you're not okay; and I'm not okay, and neither are you.

So, maybe our conviction is that we're not OK, but everyone else is? It's understood we all experience not OK-ness in childhood, regardless of quality parenting. But Harris (1972) states that the life position 'I'm not OK, you're OK' comes first and persists for most people throughout life (p.48). So, most of us are in the same boat, thinking we're not OK and everyone else is. Being not OK is normal by default?

Berne recognised that we have three emotional needs, namely, we need stimulation, (because we get very bored), we need structure and attention. It's interesting how much attention we need and why? Like with kids, it's understood that negative attention is better than no attention. It's also noted, that no-one says or does anything for no reason. The faces we pull, the grunts and groans, the huffs and cream puffs, are all passively aggressively making a point. We don't sigh or act tired, or act distant, or say 'I'm not saying anything' for no reason. Or maintain we're fine, when we've clearly got a cob on. There might be some residue, (lurking resentment), from a previous altercation.

Berne states all transactions (interactions) are designed to achieve responses. We get 'strokes', which is a unit of recognition. But moreover, Berne pertains to 'the games people play'. Game playing is one of the devices we adopt as young children to get our ego's needs met. Indeed, attachment behaviour can be seen as seductive coy ploy. The way we interact and behave, including the games we play, reflect our emotional needs. Harris (1972) notably compares games with some comedian's comment, namely, 'it's better to have halitosis than no breath at all' (p.117).

Games entail a discrepancy between what's happening on the social level and what's happening at the psychological level. At the psychological level, secret messages are communicated and exposed as the true intentions. Such covert messages are usually conveyed by non-verbal cues. What's going on beneath the surface is revealed by incongruities of speech and behaviour. Berne (1964) asserts, 'many games are played most intensely by disturbed people; generally speaking, the more disturbed they are, the harder they play' (Games People Play p.153). Edward Albee's play 'Who's Afraid of Virginia Woolf' (1962), the drunken drama and games of Martha and George, par excellence conveys the games people play. And the point is to win the game?

So, we play games, (however unconsciously), because we're not OK. Like, the infamous 'one up' aka 'Mine is Better' game, provides temporary relief and superiority, but it really means I'm not as good as you. Games result in payoffs but they're negative, because they're not being played with the person, but rather the parents or parental figures of childhood. The person playing the game is transferring their issues onto the person they're transacting with. Thus, they're pointless and their recurrence promotes damaging life positions.

But moreover, with games we're looking for a particular response. Games are used repeatedly to achieve certain outcomes. The most common games are reflected in Stephen Karpman's 'Drama Triangle' (Karpman was Berne's protégé), which is a social model of human interaction. It models the connection between personal responsibility and power in conflicts, and the destructive and shifting roles people play.

The three positions or roles that comprise the triangle are victim, persecutor, and rescuer. Thus, the victim is helpless and unable to make decisions or think for themselves. They're 'not OK' and may seek a rescuer to confirm their belief that they can't cope. They may enjoy the rescuer's sympathy, the 'positive strokes', which is the plus side to not being OK. Unlike the victim, the rescuer is OK. The rescuer may feel guilty if they don't rescue the victim, but rescuing can keep the victim dependent, which maybe the rescuer likes? Maybe they like to feel needed, like people pleasers? Persecutors put others down and belittle them. They're OK, unlike inferior others. Or maybe they're not OK?

All three Drama Triangle roles are inauthentic. And when we're in one of these roles, we're responding to the past rather than to the here-and-now. Thus, we've learned to be the victim, the rescuer or the persecutor? It's noted, playing the victim is a common game. But some people take it to new levels, getting typecast as always the victim. It's also noted, that rescuers often find themselves in caring professions such as counselling or social work.

With games however, there's an element of surprise. The drama or confusion comes about from shifting position or role i.e. persecutor becomes victim, or victim becomes persecutor. [TV soaps use this model to create drama]. Like, players of 'Poor Me' portray 'I can't think' or 'help myself', but if they get confronted, they may switch to persecutor by becoming angry or accusing e.g. 'should have known better than to think I'd get any help from you'. The player of 'Do Me Something' seeks covertly to manipulate others into thinking and acting for him, again the victim role, but which can be switched into 'See What You Made Me Do'.

Or the rescuer, having suggested myriad options to the victim, can switch to persecutor like 'See How Hard I've Tried'. 'Martyrs' often arise with co-dependent relationships, where there is an exaggerated sense of responsibility for the other. This role is both rescuer and victim. Attention is focused on the other and caretaking is compulsive. There is a need to rescue that person, but it seems this stems from a fear of abandonment on behalf of the martyr and a need for control.

There's so many games including 'You Can't Make Me', 'There I Go Again', 'Why Does This Have to Happen to Me', 'I'll Show Them', but one of my favourites (perversely) is 'Now I've got you, Son of a Bitch'. Not even funny, but that's why games perpetuate. The switch is made when the victim has secured sufficient residue from previous encounters aka altercations. It's like we collect all the perceived injustices in a jar, and then when the jar's full we triumphantly smash it. But, like the one-upmanship, after the initial joy dissipates, we're left feeling worse.

Or one I made up, namely, 'I Didn't Ask to be Born', where victim becomes persecutor. I've admittedly said this on more than one occasion (as a late teenager) to my mum. The most common game played between spouses is, 'if it weren't for you, I could be doing whatever'. It's seems we like to blame others because we're not OK, and we're rejecting our freedom? Games protect the integrity of the not OK position without the threat of uncovering the position.

It would appear Sartre's right, that we're actors on a stage. And we mix it up by playing games? It makes for a more interesting existence. Indeed, we're cautioned that bailing from games, (because they're destructive), can result in a loss of excitement. It's understood that we can't change others, but we can recognise what we get out of games, and change the responses we give and bail.

Like Sartre, Canadian sociologist Erving Goffman (1922-1982) believed that when we're born, we're thrust onto a stage called everyday life. He developed the concept of 'dramaturgy', which is the idea that everyday life is like a never-ending play in which people are actors. We play for an audience, including the cheap seats at the back.

Like Berne, Goffman analysed social interaction. And it seems Goffman was the ultimate 'people watcher'. He would go to parties and sit in the background, the periphery, and observe human interaction. He explained that our socialisation consists of learning how to play our roles. We enact our roles in the company of others, who are in turn enacting their roles in interaction with us. Goffman recognised that we're comprised of various social selves, which elicit different behaviours e.g. the daughter, sister, friend, mother, employee, neighbour, spouse or ex. They're like different facets of our personality.

In his play, 'As You Like It', Shakespeare conceded, 'All the world's a stage. And all the men and women merely players; They have their exits and their entrances. And one man in his time plays many roles'.

Goffman conceptualised 'impression management' and 'self presentation'. Impression management is a conscious or unconscious process in which we attempt to influence the perception of our image. We regulate information e.g. we're motivated to tell particular stories about ourselves. We care about what people think so we endeavour to be our best or worst self (depending on what we want them to think). It's always possible we might want to convey we're a nutter? So, we attempt to manage the impressions we give.

Goffman observed the discrepancy between the impressions we give and those given off, with the latter not intended. Unlike the impressions we give, we cannot control the impressions we give off. They're unintentional. They're defined as facial expressions or expressions that are given off while a person presents him or herself. For example, we may act confident but other signs betray that we're not e.g. we're sweating and twitching. It seems we like to pretend. Like, we might pretend we're okay, when flirting heavily with suicide. Or we may get more out of not being okay i.e. attention.

Psychologists refer to 'self-monitoring' which is how much we monitor (regulate and accommodate) our behaviour in social situations i.e. we're high or low self-monitors. Self-monitors try to understand how individuals and groups will perceive their actions. It's defined as a personality trait, as some personality types act spontaneously, whereas others consciously control and adjust their behaviour.

High self-monitors have more dating and sexual relationships, and they're more likely to take on leadership roles. But they're also more susceptible to herd mentality. And like chameleons blending into their situations, they're more likely to change their opinions and beliefs depending on who they're talking to. Low self-monitors are more consistent (genuine?) throughout all situations. They don't change who they are because the situation calls for it.

It's bemusing that we amend or bend ourselves. Like, a Scottish girl I met, who had a Scottish accent, started speaking with an English accent when we met a group of English accented people. Some people put on a posh or chavy voice, depending on the company. And what's the 'telephone voice' all about (LOL).

It seems odd or surreal that everyday life is a mixture of metagames, impersonated roles, coercive roles, and similar ironies. It seems fake? People might exaggerate or even lie to sound more impressive. Russell Jacoby said, 'the role is a façade, consciously assumed so as to hide the real self...the neat division between roles and real selves reduces society to a masquerade party' (cited in Sedgwick, 'Psycho Politics', 1982 p.112). Paramahansa (Indian yogi and guru) concedes, 'play your part in life, but never forget it is only a role'.

It's also noted, that we're all mere people until we play a role or put a 'uniform' on and 'become' someone. Like, the infamous Stanford Prison Experiment' (1971), led by psychology professor Philip Zimbardo, illustrates the potency of sticking a uniform on. Indeed, participants became so deranged the experiment had to be disbanded after six days, as opposed to the proposed two weeks.

Thus, a group of male students were divided into the roles of Prisoner and Warden, and put into a prison-like environment. But the Wardens got overexcited with their power, including Zimbardo who made himself a Warden (LOL). It shows how quickly we accept the roles that are ascribed to us. Like NEDS? It stands to reason then, that only role-less encounters would be authentic? But many people like their roles, particularly if they embody power, because power means control? As Nietzsche insisted, power is good, and weakness is bad.

Psycho-politics illustrates how power and control is exercised, consciously or unconsciously. In his book 'On Personal Power' (1977), Rogers defined 'psycho-politics' as the processes of highly complex interactions and the effects of these elements as they exist in relationships between persons, between a person and a group, or between groups. We all partake in a political order which reflects the way we exercise control over one another. The exercise of power is to attempt to influence by one's own actions. And we all have a certain amount of power to exert? Even otherwise powerless political prisoners could go on hunger strike.

And infants are not powerless. They can exercise power through tantrums, and protest by holding their breath. Apparently, I was partial to holding my breath as an infant. And on one occasion, when I wasn't allowed to take my doll into the pool, I held my breath to the point of turning blue, going limp, and my eyes rolled to the back of my head. It seems we learn how to play this game early on. And that game is about power and control. My mum caved and I was allowed to take my doll into the pool.

Rogers states, 'Politics, in present-day psychological and social usage, has to do with power and control: with the extent to which person's desire, attempt to obtain, possess, share, or surrender power and control over others and/or themselves. It has to do with the manoeuvres, the strategies and tactics, witting or unwitting, by which such power and control over one's life and others' lives is sought and gained – or shared or relinquished. It has to do with the locus of decision making power: who makes decisions which, consciously or unconsciously, regulate or control the thoughts, feelings or behaviour of others or oneself'.

So, communication generally forms patterns (verbal and non-verbal), which expresses power and control in relationships. These patterns of communication give evidence of interpersonal operating rules, revealing who's getting the respect and why i.e. with regards to sexuality, power, dependence, assertiveness and separateness. This is apparent within the micro-world of family but also within our larger social order. Like, intimate political structures underpin the relations of authority i.e. between doctor and patient, parent and child, man and woman, employer and employee (aka identity politics). We know our place?

In her novel 'We Need to Talk About Kevin' (2003) Lionel Shriver wrote, '...the bickering of the playground perfectly presages the machinations of the boardroom, that our social hierarchies are merely an extension of who got picked for the kickball team, and that grownups still get divided into bullies and fatties and cry babies' (p.173).

But it's a dynamic power structure, as things can always change. New information, for example, can be added which changes everything. The balance of power can shift. Someone independent can become dependent (e.g. sickness), and vice versa. Dependent children become independent adults. Someone financially solvent can become insolvent. Good looks fade.

It seems the ideal is to be independent? To be dependent on others, at least psychologically, seems parasitic? It's said if we depend on many, they all become subtle masters. Apparently Passive Dependency Personality Disorder is the most common psychological disorder. Dependent people need to 'filled'. But such dependence has no choice or freedom. With regards to how we live without someone, we do, because we keep breathing.

To confront or criticise is to exercise power/leadership, which is difficult for 'people pleasers'. And yet for certain others, who don't have the people pleasing problem, they seem to thrive on confrontation. They enjoy exercising their power, because they can?

It's noted, that conflict resolution strategies i.e. yielding, withdrawing, avoidance, inaction, defusion, and confrontation, illustrate the negotiable nature of power and control. Like bartering, we hope to reach a price (cost of pride?) that's OK for both. It's a standoff and people might endeavour to backpedal, because they're weak? Or maybe there's no point in fighting because it's negative and futile. Supernanny, one of my heroes, said (I'm paraphrasing) the loser is the one who loses control i.e. acts like a maniac.

Grown-up tantrums are grim. But worse is control exercised by hostile confrontation, intimidation, whatever it takes to get the person to back the feck down. Abuse if necessary? Aggression facilitates control through fear. Pitifully, the aggressive fear they're not in control, and sadly need to be. We're such little people. And how sad, that some people have to shrink other people's ego to make theirs bigger. Bertrand de Jouvenel said, 'a man feels himself more of a man when he is imposing himself and making others an instrument of his will'. Alternatively, Tolle (2011) counters, 'power over others is weakness disguised as strength' (p.36). And Jimi Hendrix said, 'When the power of love overcomes the love of power, the world will know peace.

Like Nietzsche's attention to power, self-help books similarly recommend harnessing personal power. It's highlighted that personal power requires constant maintenance, as it's easily relinquished. And without it we feel weak, vulnerable, ill, worn out, tired and numb. Powerlessness underpins sadness and a lack of control. It comes with a sense of hopelessness, fear, and inner conviction of being unable to cope and change things.

It's purported that fear is the biggest obstacle to personal power. Fear of what could happen (the repercussions of our actions), fear of rejection, fear of intimacy, fear of the lion that's not outside. It's understood that depression engenders hopelessness, and anxiety engenders fear.

It's argued that we escape from freedom when we give our power away. It's said we often give our power away when we judge ourselves by other's standards, only see ourselves as reflected in other people's eyes, allow others to dictate what we think, wear, do. We similarly give away our personal power when we have not achieved what someone else thinks we should have, and not what we want to achieve ourselves. When we think our health is not our responsibility but a doctor's or therapists. We disempower ourselves when we blame others for the deficiencies in our life and not ourselves, or make someone else responsible for our happiness and wellbeing.

It's said that ascribing our responsibility to others, including a sick society, in part comes from the desire to escape freedom and hence responsibility for our lives. Perhaps we have a fear of freedom? It seems self-help books are on the same authentic page as Sartre, that we lie to ourselves in bad faith? Reclaiming our personal power therefore means taking responsibility for our life, wellbeing, growth, and happiness.

But then there's mental health problems and mental illness? People are not OK. Indeed, people increasingly want to check out. Is this a lack of power and control? Or rather, life is crap and we don't want to be here for a second longer? Or is that the 'mental illness' (not us) speaking?

It's said we're living in the age of depression and anxiety. Social anxiety disorder is the third most common problem after alcohol dependency and depression. And alcohol dependence births both anxiety and depression. Rates of depression and anxiety among teenagers have increased by 70% in the last twenty-five years. Lest we forget the exponential increase in eating disorders and self harm etc. It's crazy. People are gouging chunks out their flesh, and slashing themselves to hell and back. Or maybe it's not so crazy, if someone benefits? Someone always benefits. It seems we need one of those dopamine pedals?

People experiencing panic attacks can think they're having heart attacks. Panic attacks, which entail an explosion of high anxiety, are likened to phobias. However, unlike phobias which have an identified fear (e.g. spiders, snakes), panic attacks can appear from seemingly nowhere. The symptoms are the same e.g. overwhelming feelings of terror, loss of control, nausea, trembling, breathlessness, palpitations, sweaty palms, a need to go to the toilet, shakiness and weakness in limbs. They strike more women than men, and are most common among sensitive people or highly intelligent people.

Anxiety's dreadful. The cascade of 'fight or flight' hormones upon social situations, as opposed to meeting a lion, is superfluous. It's not normal. We're acutely aware that we're being judged, and we care about what others think? Our self-esteem is decrepit? Anxiety's also embarrassing, which doesn't help. Like, the stigma of mental illness. It's all dreadful. Like depression, and willing death. And like addictions, including self harm. There's no doubt something funky is going on, to account for why so many of us are not OK? Maybe there's something in the air?

So, we've medicalised our not-OK human condition, and we grade it. Like depression, for example, is classed as mild, moderate and severe, which relates to the degree and number of symptoms. Thus, on a scale of 1-10, how ghastly do we feel? It seems the litmus test is how badly do we want to check out?

The official test GPs use to check if we're depressed involves asking two very basic questions, namely, 'during the past month have you been bothered by feeling down, depressed or hopeless?' And 'during the past month have you been bothered by having little interest or pleasure in doing things?' Yes to both can lead to leaving the GP practice with an antidepressant prescription. It can take five minutes to diagnose depression. It's contended however, that antidepressants merely paper over the cracks of a fractured society. We're a nation of doom, hence the happy pill boom. It seems the root of our problems is nihilism and loneliness (despite having company)?

Symptoms of depression must last a month before they warrant a description of mental illness. As time passes, we continue to have no will to live. We don't snap out of it. Life's not getting better. It's never getting better. But rather, as my mum says, ('on a bad day'), it's just more of the same shit. So, perhaps we have the depression gene after all? It seems we can develop 'clinical depression' if depressed for long enough. Like with new mums, 3-5 days of depression is considered the 'baby blues' but then it transforms into clinical depression. Maybe our thoughts switch on the depression gene?

Primary depressions are defined as endogenous mood disorders, whereas secondary depressions are reactive, exogenous, and arise because of some other problem e.g. illness, sexuality, alcoholism, lifestyle, whatever triggers the depression. I got a text from my friend's husband, when she left him, saying 'life is so shit'. And it can be. It's said accepting loss is one of life's hardest lessons. Mourning underpins value. Bereavement is the opportunity cost of commitment. Grief is notably not depression, but rather a different, albeit inherently depressive process, that needs to be worked through. Perhaps Nietzsche's right, what doesn't kill us makes us stronger?

It's duly noted, that it's good to cry. Relief can be found in tears, and most people feel better after a good cry. Apparently emotional tears have 24% more protein-based hormones than irritant tears (e.g. cutting onions) or reflex tears (provoked by yawning or coughing). It's thus suggested the reason people feel better is because these act as natural painkillers. So, it's good to cry, but then there's depression, which takes sadness to new low levels. Like a weakening poison (liquid lead), it saps the strength and breaks the spirit.

However, before we tackle depression, it seems pertinent to note that orthodox western medicine evolved with the infectious and nutritional diseases of the nineteenth century. Doctors were taught about organic disease that has a definite pathology and cause, not to understand the meaning of illness. Disease is objective. It indicates a pathological change, whereas illness is a subjective state of being unwell. So, illness is what the patient has, and disease is what the doctor diagnoses.

Thus, people can be unwell, but there's no proof. Dr James Baird (1795-1860) coined the term 'functional illness' to describe maladies caused by disturbances in the function of specific organs or systems that were not accompanied by any structural or pathological change. That is, every part of the body looks completely normal under examination, dissection or even under a microscope. The disease is invisible?

It's like with psychosomatic illness, the pain is the same as real pain. People can physically suffer for psychological reasons. And they can have literally any symptom e.g. blindness, paralysis, chest pain, itchy skin. It seems there's less sympathy for those experiencing psychosomatic illness as opposed to 'real' physical illness? It's likened to the placebo effect, as people believe whatever to be true (placebos work if people think they're real drugs).

It's highlighted, the last fifty years has witnessed a proliferation of syndromes and various other non-specific atypical and unexplained disorders. Chronic pain, for example, is an 'unexplained syndrome'. It's contended that orthodox medicine has created artificial diagnoses out of groups of unexplained symptoms as if waiting the discovery of a definite cause. And the same applies to mental illness. There are no organic or physical anomalies.

It also seems pertinent to note, the interrelationship between body and mind. Our mental state affects our physical state, and vice versa. Doctors recognise that a patient's mental attitude can have a dramatic effect on recovery, and evidence shows that happiness can have a greater impact on health than stopping smoking or losing weight. Apparently, optimists live seven years longer, but who wants to live seven years longer when depressed.

Stress seems to be at the root of many health problems. In addition to increasing our risk of heart disease and stroke, there's a correlation between profound stress and cancer (there's a curious interaction between brain and immune system). Severe depression increases our risk of stroke (we're twice as likely to get a stroke), and it increases risk for type 2 diabetes and cardiovascular disease. And there's a link between emotional upset and gastrointestinal issues (our gut brain?) and skin disorders. Paracelsus conceded that a diseased state of the body is often caused by a diseased state of mind.

It's also noted, that what we put into our body affects our mind. Like, those well-versed in boozing are familiar with the alco-blues. We're doomed up. Lifestyle choices e.g. crap food, drink, drugs, and no exercise, can mimic depressive symptoms. Whereas good nutrition and exercise, which is regarded as the best antidepressant (with regards to endorphins), is all good. Scientific studies consistently show that exercise is the single most effective therapy for depression. But who can be hooped going for jog when they're depressed? Such an idea can literally jog on. It's also beneficial to go out because a lack of vitamin D is associated with depression (vampires are not healthy). Seasonal Affective Disorder, (SAD is an apt acronym), is notably clinical depression on a seasonal basis.

Psychologists refer to 'safety behaviours', which keep us safe in the short term but are harmful in the long term. Like, if we're depressed, the preference is to stay in our scratcher and eat carbs. Maybe drink and take drugs. If we're feeling anxious, the last thing we want to do is brace the great outdoors. Thus, at least a booze and smoking addiction forces the recluse to go to the local shop (that's been personally speaking). We arguably know what we should do? Like, take care of our body and cultivate a will to live. Reinstate our personal power? But sometimes, we don't care. Like, with depression. We're done with life? As touched on, we choose our choice on a slippery slope.

But moreover, we're told this cloud of doom is the result of 'chemical imbalances'. There's nothing wrong with the brain per se i.e. the hardware, but rather the software is funky i.e. dodgy chemicals. With conditions such as depression, anxiety and schizophrenia, the chemical communication systems of the brain, not the nerve pathways, are affected i.e. excitatory or inhibitory connections between neurons.

With depression, it seems we don't have enough chemical joy, like serotonin or dopamine. Serotonin stabilises/regulates mood, and high levels are associated with optimism and serenity. And dopamine makes us feel alert and gives us the drive to do something. Dopamine's important for learning, motivating, sleeping, and controlling movement. With Parkinson's disease, for example, there's a lack of dopamine hence the problems with movement and control, but unlike depression, this is actual brain degeneration i.e. it's physical not psychological.

Too little dopamine equates to lethargy, misery, withdrawal, lack of attention/concentration and meaninglessness. Hence, we acquire addictions to top up our levels? Noradrenaline is another key brain chemical, as it also regulates energy and mood, and plays a role in acute stress 'fight or flight'. Women are apparently more prone to low serotonin, which accounts for why we're three times more likely to be on antidepressants?

The 'serotonin theory' notably replaced the monoamine theory and Tricyclics in the early 1990s. The monoamine hypothesis is that underlying depression are depleted levels of serotonin, noradrenaline and dopamine. Monoamine Oxidise Inhibitors (MAOIs) were the first generation of antidepressants but SSRIs seemed better and with fewer side effects (the fewer side effects was the major advantage). Unlike SSRIs, which are selective because they only target the enzyme that clears away Serotonin, MAOIs increase the availability of serotonin, dopamine and noradrenaline by blocking the monoamine enzyme that clears away these chemicals.

Tricyclics, which replaced MAOIs, increase the availability of serotonin and noradrenaline by inhibiting their reabsorption. Besides SSRIs, there's also Serotonin and Noradrenaline Reuptake Inhibitors (SNRIs), which as the name suggests, block the reuptake of serotonin and noradrenaline.

More than 50 million antidepressant prescriptions are written in the UK every year, which costs the NHS some £300 million a year. There was a 700% increase from 1991-2001, and prescriptions have doubled in the last ten years. Other western countries are showing a similar alarming rate. With antidepressants at an all time high, it's evident we're no longer prepared to entertain a life of quiet desperation. It's understood the Stepford wives were onto something with their vallies.

In general, doctors recommend that people stay on antidepressants for at least one year to experience the full benefit. Patients are advised that if they stop the medication before six to nine months is up, the symptoms of depression are more likely to come back. The recommendation is to stay on them for at least six months after we start to feel better. Other researchers however advise, that like benzodiazepines, SSRIs don't treat the illness but rather delay the inevitable which comes back with a vengeance. Hence, others are told they 'need' to be on them for life.

If the depression turns out to be a black hole that one is not escaping from, there's always Electroconvulsive Therapy (ECT) aka electri-frying the brain. ECT was introduced in the 1930s and involves an electric current passing through the brain. It 'works' if it triggers convulsions and seizures. Advocates of ECT maintain the healing comes about from the surge of neurotransmitters brought about by the convulsions. They caution about memory loss, but I've wondered if that's in part why it works. That is, post frying the person literally forgets they're depressed, if only temporarily. One's depression often reappears, and hence more frying is required.

Besides being deployed for severe depression, it's also used for catatonic schizophrenia (we'll get to this) and severe or prolonged manic episodes. Back in the day, ECT was used to treat homosexuals. It was thought drugs and therapy could cure this 'illness'. Lou Reed was apparently given ECT at 14 years young with the hope it would cure his homo tendencies (safe). Apparently, most people refuse to have it again, but patient's rights are over-ruled when they lose capacity.

But moreover, whilst low (slow) levels of serotonin, dopamine and noradrenaline are associated with depression (and aggression), there's no proof this causes depression. And correlation is not the same as causality (it's like stretch-marks are associated with obesity). So, what is causing this wicked illness that tempts us with suicide?

Drugs don't address the underlying causes of depression, insomnia or anxiety. And moreover, not everyone's buying the serotonin theory. Like, Irvine Kirsch, professor of psychology and author of 'The Emperor's New Drugs: Exploding the Antidepressant Myth' (2011), said, 'Depression is not caused by a chemical imbalance in the brain, and it is not cured by medication. Depression may not even be an illness at all. Often, it can be a normal reaction to abnormal situations. Poverty, unemployment, and the loss of loved ones can make people depressed, and these social and situational causes of depression cannot be changed by drugs'.

In his New York Times article (1981), 'In Praise of Depression', David Ives wrote, 'Considering the state of the world, why does science still consider depression an aberration?... Depression, let it be said, is nothing more than realism'. Ives considers optimism a form of escapism. The fact is life can depress us. So, why not numb ourselves with special K?

With regards to the serotonin theory, Kirsch highlights an Australian study (published in the Archives of General Psychiatry) that revealed that rather than low levels of serotonin, some depressed people have double the amount in certain parts of the brain. And apparently there's an antidepressant that brings down levels of serotonin. It thus contended the serotonin theory is hogwash. Kirsch studied antidepressants for well over a decade and concluded, 'I knew that if they worked at all, it wasn't by changing brain chemistry. The major reason you feel better when taking an antidepressant – maybe the only reason – is the placebo effect'.

While other researchers were concentrating on how much better the drugs were than a placebo, Kirsch was interested in finding out how strong the placebo effect was in treating depression. And he was 'flabbergasted by just how big the placebo effect was'. Placebos can have powerful effects. Many studies have shown they can relieve pain, depression and anxiety, ease the symptoms of Parkinson's, angina, ulcers and asthma. The mind is powerful.

Kirsch used the Freedom of Information Act in the US to get access to all data the pharmaceutical companies had submitted when their drugs were licensed. He got to see all the trials the drug companies had run to get the most popular antidepressants approved. More than half of the trials showed no difference at all between the drugs and the placebos, but most of those negative trials had never been published. Drug companies essentially hid the data. And when he combined the results from the published and unpublished trials, all antidepressants including all brands of SSRIs had no clinically significant benefit over a placebo.

Kirsch asserts, 'all these drugs have the same effect. No matter what they do – or don't do – to serotonin'. And 'if the effects of those drugs stay the same whatever chemicals they contain, then they are placebos'. But worse, Kirsch advised that both the drugs companies and the US regulators knew this but chose to keep it from doctors and their patients. He quotes an internal Federal Drug Administration memo that stated it was 'of no practical value to the patient or physician to reveal that SSRIs are no better than placebos'. Unbelievable. But the word is out, or as Kirsch states, their 'dirty little secret' is out.

Holford and Burne concur that 'according to a major study, SSRIs are not better than a placebo'. In their book 'Food is Better Medicine than Drugs' (2006), they equally assert that drug companies' marketing regularly conceals or distorts inconvenient findings. They state, 'there is plenty of evidence out there that not only do SSRIs do harm and are not particularly effective, but that drug companies were aware of the dangers for some time, and did their best to keep them concealed from doctors and patients'.

They highlight 'evidence that depressed people on SSRIs were twice as likely to kill themselves as those not on the drug' (p.32). Regarding the link between SSRI's and suicide, they state 'the companies were going to alarming lengths to conceal it' (p.4). They relayed, 'the most comprehensive review, a study of 702 trials including 87,650 patients published in the British Medical Journal in 2005, shows a doubling to tripling of suicides in patients on SSRIs versus placebos' (p.183). They note that SNRIs are no better. In the UK, we were told it took 'experts' 14 years (1989-2003) to realise SSRIs increase the risk of suicide (and self-harm) when given to children and young adults. And yet the research data showing a risk for children dated back to 1996. [Nice].

So, whilst antidepressants can take the edge off mild depression (about 60% of patients get better on any given antidepressant), Kirsch argues that billions are wasted for what is not much better than a sugar pill with nasty side effects (exposure to dangerous chemicals). Side-effects include sexual dysfunction, weight loss or gain, allergic reactions, dry mouth, nervousness or anxiety, headache, insomnia, tremor, dizziness, hallucinations, drowsiness, convulsions, breast milk, sweating, movement disorders and bruising/increased fractures. In addition to the suicidal ideation, some SSRIs are linked with heart disease and strokes, and violent tendencies.

James Davies, psychological therapist, in his book 'Cracked: Why Psychiatry is Doing More Harm Than Good' (2013), similarly asserts that antidepressants are no better than placebos. He also highlights that negative drug trials are routinely buried, and that research is regularly manipulated to produce positive results, with doctors, seduced by huge pharmaceutical rewards, creating more disorders and prescribing more pills.

Holford and Burne further pertain to a report from the International Centre for the Study of Psychiatry and Psychology (based in the US), which states that SSRIs could also actually be increasing the rate of mental illness. It says, 'Selective Serotonin Reuptake Inhibitors commonly cause or exacerbate a wide range of abnormal mental and behavioural conditions'.

When depressed we lose hope, and placebos provide hope. By virtue of taking a pill every day and believing it will make us better, many begin to feel better. The placebo notion further explains the delayed effect of the drug as in theory people should begin to feel better far quicker than 2/3 weeks. Like SSRI's, it's also argued the monoamine theory is a placebo effect, as it similarly takes several weeks to have a significant effect on depression. Thus, it seems unlikely that one's depression is due to insufficient monoamines.

I've wondered about the placebo effect and if the side effects (the physical changes) convince people the drugs are working. And interestingly, Holford and Burne state that when using 'active' placebos to produce similar effects to those triggered by the drug (e.g. dry mouth), the difference between placebos and drugs were even smaller (p.182). Further, whilst antidepressants can alleviate depression, they do nothing to prevent a further depressive episode, which is a hit for pharmaceutical companies. Another bonus is the severe withdrawal problems, which results in people continuing to take them.

Rather than the 'serotonin theory', other psychiatrists advise that depression arises not because of low levels of neurotransmitters but rather low levels of Essential Fatty Acids (EFA) e.g. omega 3 and 6[10]. [Omega 3 and 6 are family names for essential types of fatty acids obtained from food. All EFA are polyunsaturated fatty acids]. It's contended this biochemical imbalance triggers clinical depression.

Apparently, scientists first became interested when they noticed that countries with the highest fish consumption had the lowest rates of depression. They also observed that mothers in England who ate very little fish during pregnancy doubled their risk of developing postnatal depression compared to women who ate fish regularly. Researchers also found that omega-3 fatty acids (which are derived primarily from seafood), when fed to piglets, had the same effect on the brain as the antidepressant Prozac i.e. raised levels of serotonin.

In his article 'Fish Oil Helps Treat Depression' (Aug 2013), John McKenzie mentioned a study at Sheffield University in England. He relayed that 'Dr. Malcolm Peet gave omega-3 fatty acids to 70 depressed patients who had not been helped by drugs such as Prozac. After 12 weeks, 69 percent of the patients showed marked improvement compared with 25 percent given placebos'. Omega-3 fatty acids, given in the form of fish oil tablets, were notably shown in a 1999 controlled trial to maintain mood stability far better than an olive oil placebo.

It's noted, that hemp is saturated with omega 3 and 6 EFAs. It's the highest source of EFAs in the world. The seeds of the hemp plant provide the highest source of vegetable protein, even higher than soya beans.

---

[10] See 'The Natural Way to Beat Depression' by Professor Basant Puri and Hilary Boyd (2005).

Concentrated extracts from the cannabis flowers were the second most used medicines in America for 150 years. It's apparently the best natural medicine for glaucoma, stress, controlling nausea, and it works very well for arthritis, asthma and epilepsy. And it enables neurogenesis.

Paracelsus notably maintained that nature-not-man-is the physician, and she does not require any complicated prescriptions. He believed there is a cure in nature for every ill. He said, 'Nature is the great physician, and the dabblers in medicine and apothecaries are her enemies, and while the latter fill graveyards of the country with corpses, Nature distributes the balsam of life'. Contrary to naturally growing herbs, which have been used for healing for centuries, drugs are synthetic chemical reproductions sold by large pharmaceutical corporations at highly inflated prices.

Omega-3 fatty acids are an essential part of cell walls, including neurons. Fat makes up a large portion of human brain tissue, and just as calcium is essential for building strong bones, the brain needs EFA for optimal development. We basically want a fat active brain (grey matter surrounds the brain), and the omega-3 fatty acid Eicosapentaenoic Acid (EPA) is key. [There are three main omega-3s: Eicosapentaenoic Acid (EPA), Docosahexaenoic acid (DHA) and Alpha Linolenic Acid (ALA)].

Low EPA levels results in low levels of electrical activity and a reduction in thickness of grey matter. And low levels of activity and reduced grey matter appear in depression, Huntington's disease, pregnant women (in the last three months the grey matter shrinks as the baby snaffles the mother's supply of EPA) and schizophrenia. EPA is thus a healthy fat to replace unhealthy fat. It seems to be the most potent natural antidepressant.

In addition to omega-3 fats which act as catalysts and help to build neurotransmitter receptors in the brain, serotonin is also made from 5-hydroxytryptophan (5-HTP), an amino acid, which is made from another amino-acid, tryptophan (these amino-acids are found in protein foods). Tryptophan is the direct precursor, or starting material, of serotonin. Thus, our tryptophan intake affects the amount of active serotonin our brain makes. Tryptophan and 5-HTP, together with (catalysts) B-vitamins, magnesium, zinc and trimethylglycine (TMG), synthesize into neurotransmitters like serotonin and dopamine. So, we need these nutrients, vitamins, and minerals. They're like spark plugs for our brain.

Whilst both 5-HTP and tryptophan have an antidepressant effect, 5-HTP is more effective. These nutrients also keep levels of an amino acid known as homocysteine low in the blood, which is apparently important for keeping depression at bay. [Homocysteine is an amino acid produced when we digest proteins]. Tryptophan is apparently effective at treating insomnia and bipolar disorder (polemic mood swings formerly called manic-depression). It also appears to increase pain thresholds, and may help treat anorexia by enhancing appetite. Researchers caution however that if one is taking tryptophan, it's especially important to take B-6 vitamins to reduce the possibility of the build-up of toxic by-products in our system.

It's also noted, that modern lifestyles e.g. smoking, alcohol, drugs, including pharmaceuticals, crap food, lack of exercise, stress and aging, sap our bodies and brains, requiring an increased production of neurotransmitters, hormones, antioxidants and energy. Stress is biochemically depleting. When stressed, 'the fight or flight hormone' adrenaline is secreted, and high adrenaline levels means low levels of EFA.

So, no good can come from anxiety then, which incorporates the 'fight or flight mechanism'. When adrenaline shoots up, heart rate increases, pupils dilate, tolerance to pain increases, and energy is ploughed into muscles. Cortisol ('the stress hormone') is also released, which reduces connections between the brain cells in different parts of the brain. Too much cortisol can make it hard to learn and think, and high levels of cortisol can induce brain cells to die.

EPA however regenerates cells, increases receptivity between brain cells, and thickens grey matter. Taking pure forms of EPA can eradicate depression. Professor Puri informs that EPA needs to be in a special (highly concentrated) form called ethyl-EPA, and in his studies/experiments everyone was cured. His 100% success rate includes treating even severely depressed patients who failed to respond to prescribed antidepressants. Their depression symptoms all cleared within 2/3 months.

However, given the longer time to recover, many may want a quicker pharmaceutical fix, however placebo founded? But as established, it doesn't answer why depression arises and antidepressants do nothing to prevent a further depressive episode. In fact, we're told vulnerability increases. That is, 'once you get the bug, chances are you'll catch it again'.

Fundamentally, the contention is that mental illness is really a misnomer as it can be considered a deficiency in essential nutrients i.e. vitamins, minerals, amino acids and EFA. In addition to depression, it's claimed other mood disorders, including schizophrenia (as we'll get to), are the result of low levels of EPA. We need to give our bodies nutrients, hence, the term nutrition (not 'junk' food). Without the correct nutrition, the brain ceases to function properly. Deficiencies of vitamins or minerals impair cognitive function. A deficiency in any B vitamin, for example, can lead to depression, anxiety, irritability, and brain function decline, as well as more severe symptoms, like schizophrenia and seizures.

Furthermore, unlike antidepressants, EPA is not a placebo but on the contrary is all good and without nasty side effects. Advocates of this healthy route comment that although feelings of low self-esteem or emotional trauma will still affect you, you will not so easily upset a strong healthy brain and plunge into a depressive episode. Hippocrates said, 'Let food be your medicine'. But as Holford and Burne (2006) assert, the vast majority of doctors have no training in nutritional medicine or specialist knowledge.

Or maybe the cure for depression is love and support? It's highlighted that with emotionally responsive care, a depression vulnerability gene doesn't need to express itself. And the loneliness disease could be cured. Family and friends can literally be lifelines, since as Nietzsche said, 'in solitude the lonely man is eaten up by himself'. Sue Atkinson (2005) conceded, 'Of all the symptoms of depression, the sense of being cut off and alone seems to be experienced by almost everyone. It is as much a part of depression as the feeling of extreme sadness' (p.173). And also, 'many suicidal feelings are a wish for some more help. What we are really saying is much more 'I cannot stand this hell', than I want to be dead'.

But sometimes we want to cut ourselves off from others? We have nothing in common with those OK people, and would rather be on our own, to wallow in our sadness? Bugger people? Suffice to say, if we feel like we're sitting on the side-lines, we probably are. Emotional isolation's not healthy but there's safety in loneliness. Social situations can be a source of anxiety. Atkinson gives credence to the renowned 3 S's, namely, security, significance, and self-worth, and asserts that depression is associated with their opposites, namely, we feel insecure, insignificant, and worthless.

It's said depression is a liar. Like an unpleasant gremlin, it sits on our shoulder, or crawls inside our brain, and tells us lies e.g. our life is worthless and we'd be better off dead. Paracelsus pragmatically advised, 'if a person is gloomy and despondent, he ought not to be left alone but, he ought to have someone to cheer him up and explain to him that he must free himself of his own morbid thoughts'. So, our thoughts are incumbent. Who would have thought?

Thus, besides the hardware (brain) and the software (chemicals), what about the programme? What channel are we watching? What glasses (life position) are we looking through? It would appear our mood has something to do with the thoughts we're entertaining. It's arguably not brain science (pun intended) that thinking happy thoughts makes us happy, and thinking sad thoughts makes us sad.

Thoughts can be understood as having emotions and feelings contained within them. I think therefore I feel? Motivation comes from memory and emotion. Our brains respond to thoughts and memories by releasing hormones and chemicals that send us into a state of arousal, causing us to feel an emotion. Emotions are thus psychological i.e. what we think, and biological i.e. what we feel. Thoughts and feelings (consciousness) correspond to biochemical activities in the brain.

Interestingly, our brains process emotional and physical pain the same way. Like, if we're emotionally hurt by someone or punched, the same areas are activated, releasing the same chemicals. Emotions link our external and internal worlds.

So, 'we' manufacture chemicals, in response to our circumstances. Hence, (besides exercise), a good belly laugh is the best medicine. When laughing our brain releases endorphins and produces a sense of wellbeing. It helps to relieve stress and depression, and it can boost our immune system. It's well known that dark or macabre humour helps doctors and nurses cope with stress and tragedy. Humour is seen as an especially powerful tool. It's considered essential for fighting burnout and keeping oneself focussed. Apparently singing floods our brains with endorphins and oxytocin (the love drug), which is good for anxiety and depression. So, maybe we need to sing more?

But myriad external factors trigger chemicals. Like, shoppers get a hit of dopamine when they spy something they'd like to buy. And we get a hit of dopamine when we see an attractive stranger. Or take the amazing brain chemicals that surge when we 'fall in love'. Being in love is probably the best feeling? And when the bottom falls out of that, there's masturbation and other addictions. It's noted, that oxytocin makes us more selfless, whereas testosterone makes us more selfish. And these can be harnessed e.g. monk training versus army training.

But moreover, merely thinking about a particular thing can fire up happy hormones. Like, for want of a better example, simply thinking about having a drink, (if it's something we really like), can release dopamine. It's good to know vino's on the agenda. Such thoughts fire up neurons which produce dopamine. I have experienced this, and also the reverse. That is, when my plan of consuming copious amounts of red wine is thwarted, (for whatever reason), the joy has literally drained out of me. It's the same with securing drugs. You're chuffed when you understand it's going to happen, but when it's a 'no go', the joy's replaced with doom.

It's understood that dopamine increases when something is better than expected, and decreases when something is worse than expected. Hence, there's an argument for being a pessimist. If we don't expect much, we won't be disappointed. I notably came to this deduction in my early twenties and read about it a few years later in a self-help book.

So, it's a two-way street with thoughts and feelings. The mind affects the brain, and the brain affects the mind. As mentioned, it seems to be a chicken and egg situation. Hence, the prevailing dichotomy of psychotherapy aka 'the talking cure', and psychiatry aka the physical cure? When we feel/think emotions it triggers an electrochemical process in the brain and body, and the reverse is true, that drugs (psychoactive chemicals) cause us to feel emotions. Hence, we love drugs, apart from SSRIs because they don't do much? Given the choice, ketamine's the preferred option.

It's duly noted, that we're also affected by other chemicals and toxins in our environment. Like, mercury in amalgam fillings and vaccinations is a neurotoxin. And sodium fluoride in our toothpaste and drinking water (sodium fluoride is used in rat poison), and aspartame in sweeteners, change brain chemistry. Indeed, there's no end to toxins e.g. chemicals in our food and drink, and the air we breathe courtesy of chemtrails. As touched on, it's contended there's a chemical attack on our minds and we're being deliberately poisoned. It's like the electromagnetic radiation we're exposed to. Maybe the age of anxiety and depression arose with invisible WIFI? Maybe there is 'something in the air' and it's going to get worse with 5G technology, as we'll get to.

Toxins like mercury can notably lead to unusual syndromes such as a loss of 'theory of mind'. Whilst the link between MMR jabs and autism remains controversial, the fact is autism was extremely rare, and its skyrocketed. Paracelsus also pertained to doctors who poison their patients with mercury, noting it would be interesting to find out how many chronic diseases and lifelong evils are caused by vaccinations. Amalgams are no longer advised during pregnancy. They're linked with wrecking our immune system, headaches, neck-aches, backaches, fatigue, depression, Alzheimer's, Multiple Sclerosis, heart conditions and bowel problems.

However, that tragedy aside, and besides the artificial chemical joy, it stands to reason if we're bored, apathetic, unmotivated and depressed, this is reflected in our brain i.e. there's less activity. Our plasticine brain becomes moulded by our blah thoughts. As touched on, with regards to porn addiction, the brain structurally changes, but these physical changes are reversible.

Studies have also found that people who are prone to high levels of pessimism, neuroticism, and anxiety suffer from 'cerebral asymmetry', where there is greater activity on the right side of the brain than the left. While the cause is unknown, we're told that training our self to 'look for the positives' can equalise the asymmetry.

So, what we dwell on has physical repercussions. When depressed our blood chemistry changes and whilst psychiatry offers biochemical adjustment, it's argued that we have the power to manufacture the cure within us.

Interestingly, Michael Rutter, professor of psychiatry, conducted an experiment with a group of people who were not depressed, and their blood chemistry was normal. For a week they had to act as though they were depressed. And at the end of the week, they had all become depressed, and their blood chemistry had changed. It's therefore contended that if depressed people do the opposite of what they're doing, they will start to feel better and bring themselves out of the depression.

Psychologist Martin Seligman (founder of positive psychology) and his colleagues also did a study in 2005, with a group of people who were asked to think of 'Three Good Things' that happened to them every day, and reflect on why they were good. And at the end of six months the study showed higher levels of happiness, gratitude, and less depression. It's a powerful strategy for increasing daily levels of happiness.

Our thought patterns govern the way we react to situations and circumstances. We live through our thoughts. How we think, feel and talk about ourselves creates our personal reality. What we rehearse over and over in our minds conditions us. And recycling the same old thoughts, ruminating on whatever guff, only reinforces neural pathways. A teenage refugee girl I worked with used to say, 'Today is not my day'. She said it every day. And fair play. Alas, we have to look for the positives for the sake of our mental health.

It can be a battle every day regarding what mood we'll be in. Yet it's contended we're responsible for our thoughts, and therefore our moods? As discussed, all perception, whether real or imaginary, is made up in part of the meaning we give to it. Our conscious mind receives perceptions and attaches meaning to them. And meanings, in turn, make things matter to us.

Thus, in addition to healthy lifestyles that pave the way for healthy brains, we need to rectify our thought life. This can mean reframing (and rebooting) our situations i.e. view events from a different perspective. An example could be, rather than being sad that something is over, be glad (smile) that it happened. We can look back in anger, or look back in love?

By reframing our memory and perspective, we can create positive thoughts, producing happy chemicals. The stories we tell ourselves make all the difference. Indeed, there's an argument for being positively delusional. Perhaps we can appreciate what we have as opposed to what we don't have? In positive psychology research, gratitude is strongly and consistently associated with greater happiness. The American poet/philosopher Ralph Waldo Emerson (1803-1882) maintained, 'the measure of mental health is the disposition to find good everywhere'. [See photo of Nampula airport in Mozambique].

It's understood that the experience of depression is almost always about some kind of loss, which includes not having something we want. So, besides losing someone or something, (including our integrity), there's always something we want e.g. spouse, kids, house, car, better job, better hob. It seems we always want more? As discussed, we aspire to keep up with our peers, and we want what others have. A friend quoting someone else said, 'I was happy but when I realised I wasn't ecstatic I was miserable'. Respectively, we can reflect on 'Who is Happy? The Peacock and the Crow'.

Thus, a crow lived in a forest and was absolutely satisfied in life. But one day he met a swan and thought, 'This swan is so white, and I am so black, it must be the happiest bird in the world'. He expressed his thoughts to the swan, who in turn replied, 'Actually, I was feeling that I was the happiest bird around until I saw a parrot, which has two colours, so I now think the parrot is the happiest bird in creation'. The crow then approached the parrot, who explained 'I lived a very happy life until I saw a peacock. I have only two colors, but the peacock has multiple colours'.

The crow visited the peacock in the zoo and saw that hundreds of people gathered to see him. When the crowd left, the crow approached the peacock and said, 'Dear Peacock, you are so beautiful and every day thousands of people come to see you, whereas whenever people see me, they immediately shoo me away. I think you must be the happiest bird on the planet'. The peacock replied, 'I always thought that I was the most beautiful and happy bird on the planet. But because of my beauty, I am entrapped in this zoo. I have examined the zoo very carefully, and I have realised that the crow is the only bird not kept in a cage. So for the past few days I have been thinking that if I were a crow, I could happily roam everywhere'.

Often, when we really think about it, we wouldn't trade our life with someone else's, as we have to take all their life, not just the best parts we covet. And moreover, we don't always know the crosses that others bear. Respectively, we can spare a thought for 'The Heavy Cross'.

Thus, a young man was at the end of his rope. Seeing no way out, he dropped to his knees in prayer. 'Lord, I can't go on', he said. 'I have too heavy a cross to bear'. The Lord replied, 'My son, if you can't bear its weight, just place your cross inside this room. Then open that other door and pick out any cross you wish'. The man was filled with relief. 'Thank you Lord', he sighed, and he did as he was told. Upon entering the other door, he saw many crosses. Some were so large, the tops were not visible. Then he spotted a tiny cross, leaning against a wall. 'I'd like that one Lord', he whispered. The Lord replied, 'that is the cross you just brought in'.

Happiness or contentedness is arguably a state of mind not a set of circumstances. It's a moment to moment choice. We can have everything and be miserable or have nada and be happy. And if we put conditions on happiness i.e. I'll be happy when..., we'll always find more conditions. It's also noted, with respect to the infamous question of 'why me?', is the infamous retort 'why not?' Someone has to not be OK? Perhaps we could learn from Nina Simone's song 'Ain't Got No, I Got Life'.

Thus, 'I ain't got no home, ain't got no shoes. Ain't got no money, ain't got no class. Ain't got no skirts, ain't got no sweaters. Ain't got no perfume, ain't got no bed. Ain't got no love. Ain't got no mother, ain't got no culture. Ain't got no friends, ain't got no schoolin'. Ain't got no love, ain't got no name. Ain't got no ticket, ain't got no token. Ain't got no god'.

Then she puts on her positive shades, and proclaims, 'Hey, what have I got? Why am I alive, anyway? Yeah, what have I got. Nobody can take away? Got my hair, got my head. Got my brains, got my ears. Got my eyes, got my nose. Got my mouth, I got my smile. I got my tongue, got my chin. Got my neck, got my boobies. Got my heart, got my soul. Got my back, I got my sex. I got my arms, got my hands. Got my fingers, got my legs. Got my feet, got my toes. Got my liver, got my blood. I've got life, I've got my freedom. I've got life. I've got the life. And I'm going to keep it. I've got the life'. So, Nina's OK despite having nothing and no one.

But when we're 'depressed' we don't care for life. We're not grateful? Furthermore, when we're not OK, it's reassuring to know others are also not OK? We feel infinitely better with some company on Shit Street. Like, we're not the only one who failed our exam, or the only 'single' person, or whatever. Hence, support groups provide solace, as they're all on Shit Street together. Like, they've all got cancer or whatever addiction. Thus, it seems our moods are also at the mercy of others. People can make us feel better or worse? They can make us mad or depress us. They can hurt us. People affect us, or we affect ourselves?

As existentially contended, it's said that no one can make us feel anything, since we can choose not to be affected. Eleanor Roosevelt conceded, 'no one can make you feel inferior without your consent'. It's said we're not hurt emotionally by what other people say but rather our attitude and response to it.

Buddha (563-483) equally maintained that our mind creates our reality, stating it's our attitude towards experience, much more than the experience, which creates pleasure or pain. Buddha's way of dealing with suffering was not by denying its existence, but by transforming the individual's perception of it. Thus, we're not shaped as much by our environment as we are by our perception of our environment, and whilst we can't control events, we can control our attitudes and feelings about them. It's also highlighted, 'whilst pain is inevitable, misery is optional. We cannot avoid pain, but we can avoid joy'.

Aaron Beck (American psychiatrist) pioneered cognitive therapy in the 1960s. He observed the relationship between events, thoughts, feelings, and behaviours, and came to the conclusion that distorted thinking (cognition) is our problem. He recognised that shifting cognition is the key to the mental lock.

Beck's cognitive model was originally used to explain psychological processes in depression. He observed that negative thoughts create a negative mood, and when mood is lowered, it affects the way we process information. Feelings and emotions colour our perspective. And with depression, we become negatively biased in how we attribute meaning to events. In the same way, when anxious or paranoid or angry, how we process information can be affected. And as a result, especially when feeling emotional, our interpretations are not always accurate.

Beck's 'negative triad' depicts the corresponding negative view of self, world and future. Thus, one's depression may be seen as uncontrollable (internal), which will last forever (persistent) and will affect everything (pervasive). We can develop interpretation bias whereby we actively seek to reaffirm our distorted negative perspective (as mentioned, we reaffirm what we already believe). Like, if we want to be angry, we can find things to be angry about. If we want to be hateful, dramatic, worried, whatever, we can find things? We can create problems for ourselves, which can become habitual?

Beck highlights that 'Negative Automatic Thoughts' (NATs) gate-crash our minds. They can be connected to strong emotions and can take the form of words, pictures or images in the mind (we visualise meaning to thoughts). Or they can take the form of memories (memories are filled with emotions). But rather than appearing from 'nowhere', it's understood they derive from our underlying core assumptions, core beliefs and schema i.e. how OK or not we are, within our deepest self.

Our core beliefs are at the centre of our belief system, and our schema is a complex mixture of attitudes, views, and beliefs regarding self, people and the world. Negative core beliefs are the labels we give ourselves based on low self-esteem. These judgements we make about ourselves are based on negative experiences. Limiting beliefs are thus often tied in with a negative self-image and perception of the world e.g. I'm not good enough, I'm a failure, I could never do whatever etc.

As touched on in Existential Roots, it seems imperative to analyse our dialogue, because there's power and ownership in language. The 'words' we use to describe our situations make all the difference. Like, strong words are 'will' and 'want', whereas weak words are 'try', 'if', 'don't' 'can't' and 'but'. As Richard Bach pointed out in 'illusions', 'argue for your limitations, and sure enough they are yours' (cited in Peck, 'Further Along the Road Less Travelled' p.23).

Our self-image and personality comes from the thoughts we have about ourselves. But it also comes from what we 'imagine' others think about us. We attempt to think other people's thoughts. This is clearly the downside to mind-mindedness, if we think the worst. 'Imagining' is one of Beck's cognitive errors. And it's true, unless we have telepathy how do we know what anyone else is thinking? I also suspect that most people think predominantly about themselves, because we're fairly self-obsessed. So, perhaps we don't need to be so paranoid that people are thinking about us?

The cognitive model thus espouses Buddha's sentiment. The way individuals perceive a situation is more closely connected to their reaction than the situation itself. We're not affected by events, but rather our take on them. We can react differently, depending on our thoughts. The trick is therefore to capture all our thoughts and question their validity. We have to examine the evidence for and against our negative distorted thoughts, with the aim being not to use our thoughts against ourselves. It's about being rational and keeping with the 'normal' programme.

Beck's cognitive distortions or thinking errors include: selective abstraction/perception, arbitrary inference (jump to conclusions), dichotomous thinking (all or nothing), magnification or minimisation, over-generalisation, personalisation, catastrophising, mind-reading, fortune telling, emotional reasoning.

Behaviour modification is based on learning theory, and essentially involves replacing self-defeating habits and patterns with adaptive ones. Perhaps we can choose our thoughts, as we choose our clothes, selecting those most befitting? Baruch Spinoza (1632-1677), Dutch philosopher, taught that we live in servitude of the mind when we lack the power to moderate and check our emotions. Managing feelings is fundamental to civilised living, which includes managing jealousy, anger etc. Emotions are part of intelligence. 'Emotional intelligence' (emotional IQ) and emotional literacy reflects our ability to cope with difficult feelings and emotions.

It's thus contended that maturity involves taking responsibility for our feelings instead of blaming others for them. It's about learning to control and express our feelings appropriately. It's highlighted that emotions are the least reliable but most influential force that guides us. As Thomas A Kempis said, 'Trust not to thy feelings, for whatever they be now, they will quickly be changed towards some other thing' (cited in Sue Atkinson, 2005 p.157). Our flippancy reflects our liberty to change our minds whenever we want.

But moreover, it's asserted that being unaware that we are the producers of our feelings can lead us to blaming others, external sources, including the 'depression' bug. It's relayed that unhappy people say they 'don't have negative thoughts, but rather they just feel depressed' but it's contended this is painful denial, since it suggests the person is not in control. And further, it's very easy to feel like a victim if we believe our depression, our thinking, is something that is happening to us, rather than something we are doing to ourselves.

It's highlighted that painful thoughts drift in and out, but by holding onto them, they stay present in our mind which gives rise to depression (painful thoughts propel a negative state of mind). Various thoughts pass continuously through our mind, competing for attention, so why do we continue to give disparaging thoughts attention? It's like we're masochists. Paul McKenna and Hugh Willbourn (2003) assert, 'an emotion is a bit like someone knocking on your door to deliver a message' (p.71). Perhaps we don't have to open the door?

It's thus argued that thinking is the source of the problem. It's highlighted that it's impossible to feel jealous, hurt or angry without having jealous, hurt or angry thoughts. Or say, if we're feeling depressed and suddenly we smell smoke, the prospect of a 'fire' becomes more important than dwelling on negative thoughts (and other chemicals kick in, like adrenaline, because we're bricking it). When anything is forgotten or dismissed, it no longer exists in reality and so we're not affected by it. Or alternatively, if we deliberately think of a problem, it wasn't a problem until we started thinking about it.

Rhonda Byrne, in her book 'The Secret' (2006), pertains to 'secret shifters' to instantly change thoughts/feelings. Thus, we actively think of beautiful memories, someone we love, funny moments, our favourite music, instead of dwelling on rubbish. When feeling sad, she urges us to shut out all distractions and smile (genuinely) for one full minute.

According to William James (1842-1910), Father of American psychology, we feel happier if we imagine laughing and we feel sadder if we imagine crying. He advocated smiling as a cure for depression since emotions are caused by awareness of physical sensations and are linked to bodily movements. It's pragmatic to turn that frown upside down. We're told to 'act as if' we're happy or confident, and posture helps, so heads up.

Self-help books tell us true happiness is in us all and we can access and cultivate this. Thought is the power that controls our life, which includes how we interpret events and our perceived locus of control. And we can choose to be OK? If our thoughts imprison us, we can sack the jailer? As Bob Marley sang in 'Redemption' song, 'emancipate yourselves from mental slavery; none but ourselves can free our minds'.

We're informed a positive mental attitude can be harnessed. Indeed, the Nobel Prize-winning psychologist Daniel Kahneman declared 'Happiness is a skill'. American actress Jennifer Anniston (2016) concedes, 'I'm happy and I believe that happiness is a choice. I'm human – we all have days when we don't feel so great. It's about understanding that the sadness will pass'. The self-help gurus similarly tell us we have to accept we can have low moods. It happens. But the difference between a depressed person and a non-depressed person is one accepts they have moods, knowing it's temporary and dealing with it, whereas a depressed person assumes some permanency in it.

The point is therefore not to let grim thinking sabotage our life. Mental health is arguably never lost but rather just covered up by habitual and insecure thoughts that we continue to give credence to. Healthy functioning is hidden by this veil of negative and insecure thoughts. Hence, we need to remember how it feels to be okay. It's further said that knowing we create our depression, realising that it forms within our thinking, is empowering and healing. Lest we forget the prevailing conundrum, namely, how can we ever feel better if we believe ourselves to be depressed? As mentioned, the social psychological principle states, 'I believe what I hear myself say'. So, maybe we need to change the record?

Eckhart Tolle, author of 'The Power of Now' (1997), explains how he lived in a state of almost continuous anxiety interspersed with periods of suicidal depression until his thirtieth year. He then had an epiphany which revolutionised his ways of thinking: his ways of 'being'. His revelation is that we're enslaved to incessant thinking and thus we need to transcend the mind. The mind is a vehicle which merely does its 'thinking job' and thus he advises to step aside as observer.

We are to 'observe the mind. Smile at it' (p.70). We are to watch or witness thoughts and emotions but realise we are beyond these. He says, 'to know yourself as the being underneath the thinker, the stillness underneath the mental noise, the love and joy underneath the pain, is freedom, salvation, enlightenment' (p.128).

The 'silent witness technique' is notably a meditation technique used by yogis to achieve a state of calmness and tranquillity. Thus, the yogi sits in a quiet place and lets his thoughts roam wherever. Thoughts come automatically (i.e. no effort) but we can view them as a disinterested silent witness. We are separate from the thoughts that float through our mind.

Thus, we hear our voice, our thoughts, and realise that we're listening to it, but the real realisation is that we exist as a presence beyond our thought life. We're more than our 'thoughts'. Ergo all thoughts can essentially jog on. Tolle advocates this is the beginning of the end of involuntary and compulsive thinking. Indeed, for Tolle, to be immersed in thought is to be unconscious since it implies a complete absence of the watcher.

For the purposes of experiential learning, he presents a little experiment. Thus, 'close your eyes and say to yourself: 'I wonder what my next thought is going to be'. Then become very alert and wait for the next thought' (p.77).

Thus, in tandem with eastern philosophy, Tolle purports our sense of presence or 'I am' realisation is beyond our mind. It's the idea that we're pure consciousness and presence is pure consciousness, beyond thoughts and emotions. We're intrinsically part of something much bigger, far beyond our personal ego and this physical reality. Awareness is the field of consciousness from which all life came and we can return to this awareness. Thus, if we close our eyes, and shut out all distractions, we can imagine that we're part of a universal consciousness, (God), rather than a personal self?

Tolle renders the compulsive thinker as living in a state of apparent separateness, where the screen of thought creates the illusion of separateness. Hence, enlightenment is realising we're not separate but rather intrinsic to a universal mind. With regards to Jung's persona, Tolle states that identification with the mind creates a false self/ego as a substitute from our true self which is rooted in being. The persona is not the real us and egos are BS.

It's duly noted, (besides cognitive therapy), the Buddhist tradition 'mindfulness' has gone down a storm in the last couple of decades. There's been a surge of interest in this ancient art, which has been psychologised, as meditation doesn't need to be spiritual?

Mindfulness involves bringing our complete attention to the present experience on a moment-to-moment basis. It's a non-judgemental, present-centred awareness in which each thought, feeling, or sensation that arises is acknowledged and accepted as it is (there is no right or wrong). The idea is to allow thoughts and feelings to come and go without getting caught up in them and ruminating on them. It's suggested that we regard thoughts like having a radio on in the background. Or treat thoughts like balloons that drift into and out of consciousness. Once we notice them, we simply let them drift away.

The focus is on breathing and bodily sensations. Thus, we pay attention to the breath coming through our nostrils, filling our chest, expanding and contracting our diaphragm. Vernon (2012) highlights the Buddhist scripture, namely, 'when a monk breathes out long, he knows: I am breathing out long. Breathing in short, he knows: I am breathing in short' (p.128).

Thus, rather than focusing on our negative thoughts, we focus on our breathing, and when thoughts arise, we keep bringing our attention back to our breathing. We feel the beat of our heart and imagine it pumping blood round the body. We feel heat/cold, feel how our muscles feel etc. Therapists might ask, 'what's somatically going on right now?' My psychotherapy tutor queried why a fellow student's belly had rumbled (we were in class) and what that could mean intra-psychically. I suggested she was hungry (LOL).

Mindfulness helps many struggling with their thought life e.g. depression, anxiety, OCD, drug addictions. And it's logical. If we're focused on our bodily sensations, our breathing and beating heart, we're not thinking about the rest of the crap that enters our mind. There's a wealth of scientific evidence to support the benefits of mindfulness in improving moods. We're advised to 'live in the moment' for twenty minutes every day. It apparently does wonders to weaken the neural pathways responsible for stress. The perfect present for everyone is therefore knowledge of the perfect present[11].

Tolle highlights that we identify with the mind and this traps us in time. The past gives us our (ego) identity and the future offers potential fulfilment. That is, on the premise we have hope. If we don't imagine the future will be any better, we experience anxiety and despair. The point is both 'imaginings' are illusory. The only real moment is the moment that is happening now, and everything else is an illusion. We are neither in the past nor the future, but rather we're in the now. Past and future events are figments of our imagination. The past is past, yet we continue to filter present moments through thoughts of the past, and these thoughts of the past can contaminate our present.

With regards to the mind being present, Russell Brand (2014) said, 'which, let's face it, is where it belongs; no point leaving the mind loitering about last Tuesday, especially if something bad happened' (p.53). He also said, 'Drag your past around if you like, an old dead decaying ox of what you think they might've thought, or what might've been if you'd done what you ought. That which needs to burn, let it burn. If the idea doesn't serve you, let it go. If it separates you from the moment, from others, from yourself, let it go' (p.280). As my friend, with a colourful mental health history says, 'the best thing about the past, is it's in the past'. It's also said, 'how do you get anywhere in life looking in the rear-view mirror?'

[Russell Brand (2014), who espouses Tolle, said, 'Who are you really? Are you your name? The place you are from? The negative feelings you had as a child? The anxieties you have about your future? No, these are all conceptual. In this moment now, your name is not real, your relationships are irrelevant and most importantly your thoughts, all your thoughts, are secondary. In my mind, even as I type and adhere to the metaphorical codes of language, there is another awareness. A distinct Awareness. An awareness beyond, behind and around those incessant thoughts. Whilst some other inaccessible aspect of my being keeps my heart pumping, produces digestive enzymes, makes the muscles in my fingers spasm according to the precise qwerty ballet, there is awareness. This awareness is often neglected in favour of fear and regret or projected need' (p.42). Apparently Tolle told Brand, that to be free of suffering, that is, in the moment of temptation, when he wants to yield to anger or jealousy or self-pity, he must recognise that the ego, which these fleeting interlopers serve, is an illusion (p.352)].

So, we only stress when we reflect on the past and future, but here and now, (unless someone's got a gun to our head), there's nothing coming over us. Tolle stresses, 'when a negative emotion surfaces, it is a trigger/signal saying 'wake up. Get out of your mind. Be present'' (p.159). Awareness is healing. To be aware of our

---

[11] See 'The Precious Present' (1981) by Spencer Johnson.

attachment to pain breaks that attachment to pain, and thus the 'Power of Now' initiates the transmutation of pain.

But moreover, Tolle (2005) asserts, 'As there are no problems in the Now, there is no illness either. The belief in a label that someone attaches to your condition keeps the condition in place, empowers it, and makes a seemingly solid reality out of a temporary imbalance. It gives it not only a reality and solidity but also a continuity in time that it did not have before. By focussing on this instant and refraining from labelling it mentally, illness is reduced to one of several of these factors: physical pain, weakness, discomfort or disability. *That* is what you surrender to – now. You do not surrender to the idea of 'illness'. Allow the suffering to force you into the present moment, into a state of conscious presence. Use it for enlightenment' (p.181). Scott Peck also insisted that people should not be considered ill unless they are suffering pain or disability.

It's duly noted, that hope is superfluous with this frame of reference, which is interesting since most people cling to hope. Henri Nouwen said, 'Hope means to keep living. Amid desperation. And to keep humming. In the darkness'. Hope keeps people going. It motivates us to make plans and it releases happy chemicals. It's the placebo effect of antidepressants? It seems we check in with a GP looking for hope. We're hoping they can help our hopelessness.

Or we can reinstate our personal power? Rather than passing our heads over to a doctor, we can return to the driver's seat, and take control of our thoughts and lives. As Nietzsche advised, turn it into 'I willed it' rather that 'it was'. But for Tolle, and contrary to Nietzsche's view of power, 'power is presence'. We 'will to power' the present? For me, being present and staying on today's page is all good. We could be dead tomorrow, so care. Einstein said, 'I never think of the future. It comes soon enough'.

According to many psychologists, helping others is one of the best routes to happiness. It's contended that depression is fundamentally self-centred, and the best way to feel better is to do something for someone else. Besides taking our mind off our mind, when we do something good/kind it activates pleasure centres. Russell Brand (2014) mentioned an occasion when he altruistically helped someone out, and relayed the endorphin kick it gave him. He said, 'my last consumer purchase, a pair of orange rimmed Paul Smith sunglasses, didn't give me as good a kick as that did' (p.298).

Studies at the University of Oregon have shown that giving money to charity is neurologically similar to addictive drugs or receiving money. And brain scans reveal that we get more joy from giving than we do from receiving. Psychiatrist Dr Kubler Ross said, 'the greatest blessings always come from helping' (p.287). Pastor/author Joyce Meyer said, 'the less I think about myself, the happier I am'. And the 14th century Dali Lama said, 'if you want others to be happy, practice compassion. If you want to be happy, practice compassion'.

So, it's possible our life, our happiness, is in our hands? The 'self-help' argument is that we're in control of how we feel. Everything in life is a function of the way we relate to our thinking. And if we don't expect much out of life, it's doubtful we'll aim for the stars. But then again, maybe it's because we need more dopamine. It seems chemicals are the shortcut, as addressing the underlying core of us (rectifying our core beliefs) can take ages (time and experience). And suffice to say, it's considerably easier to neck some 'blues' (10mg of Valium), if we've got the blues or 'feel' at all dodgy. It seems drugs make everything better, like Huxley's Soma?

Besides medication, it seems our options are listening to our thoughts and emotions, because they're nudging change. They might be giving us an existential kick up the arse. Or we can rationalise them, or transcend them. But no good can come from entertaining negative thoughts that serve no purpose. We are primarily victims of thoughts and thoughts can't hurt us? But what about self harm?

As touched on, people increasingly have an overwhelming compulsion to harm themselves, because it makes them feel better? There has been a massive rise (70% in recent years) in young people attending hospital to get patched up. People get an instant dopamine hit (we get addicted to things for a reason). But how desperate, that people carve themselves up like a turkey.

Apparently 1:10 self-harm, which includes cutting, burning, scalding, overdosing, blunt force trauma (banging, punching), scratching and biting oneself, breaking bones, starving oneself, inducing vomiting, drinking, taking drugs or exercising to excess, hair pulling, swallowing poisonous substances, objects and inserting objects. 1:12 young people self-harm and even very young children self harm. Like, a four year old slashed his wrists. Presumably, he watched someone else do it first? Self-harm breeds self-harm? It's also noted, there's a difference between superficial scratches for attention, and gouging out chunks of flesh. Either way, the person is not OK.

Self-harm provides an outlet, a way to deal with emotional pain. It can be regarded as a safety valve, a way of relieving the tension. The physical pain can distract people from emotional pain i.e. when feeling physical pain, the focus is on that, rather than torturous thoughts including flashbacks. So, it's another version of mindfulness?

There's a sense of release as it enables expressing emotions, and getting pain out, like projection. People who otherwise feel numb or dead inside can 'feel something', even if it's physical pain. And some people maintain they deserve pain. Their thoughts tell them they deserve to be punished. Self-harm helps relieve feelings of shame or guilt.

It's also highlighted that it helps people feel in control. Like, people starving themselves, is something they can control. They might not be able to control anything else in their lives, but they can control what they eat. Like other addictions, having self-harmed and secured the buzz, people don't feel great afterwards e.g. guilt, frustration, and exasperation creep in. And they have wounds to take care of. More scars.

Like all addictions, people are compelled. Like, the OCD 'sufferer' who will feel better when they've washed their hands for the gazillioneth time. So-called 'germaphobes' are terrified of bacteria and use copious amounts of bleach to tackle the 'problem'. It appears this is a first world problem? People need to execute particular rituals, like check the door three times. Apparently, Nicola Tesla had OCD and would execute rituals in three, like he would drive round the carpark three times before parking his car.

The relief is short-term, as like 'safety behaviours', no good can come from them in the long term. But it's no way to live? OCD is referred to as the 'doubting illness' because people doubt everything, and there's regression to magical thinking i.e. if we don't do A,B,C then X,Y,Z will happen. Like, family members will die.

It's like the 'OCD game', 'if we step on a crack, we'll break our mother's back'. Or like, when I was young, I would need to beat the bus or a car to a certain marked point, and if I didn't my mum would die. So, I would run really fast as her life depended on it. It's weird, as it suggests we can control events? And as a late teenager, if I happened to say or think 666, I would need to say or think 777, 888, 999, 111, 222, 333, 444, and 555 to counteract the former. And if I happened to think of 666 again, which invariably happened, I would need to recommence the ritual. It was pretty nippy. Mental illness is time consuming, (there can be a lot of unhelpful things to think about), particularly if you have to clean no-end?

Whilst mental health is defined as being in touch with reality and free from anxiety, it seems impossible to be free of anxiety or stress? That's not normal? 'Stress' seems to be the precursor to mental health problems, which precede mental illness. Stress is notably short for distress, a word evolved from Latin, meaning 'to draw or pull apart'.

The 'model of stress in illness' includes the stages: stressor, cognition, stress and illness. Hence, our cognition, the meaning we attribute to the stressor is critical. Stress is how we respond e.g. freak out which triggers a cascade of stress hormones aka the 'fight or flight' response. Or we can choose not to care? How does our personality respond? As Jung said, mental illnesses are diseases of the personality.

'Mental illness' refers to a diagnosable illness which significantly interferes with a person's functional, cognitive, emotional or social abilities. This includes clinical depression, severe anxiety, schizophrenia, bipolar affective disorder, OCD, eating disorders, drug and alcohol addiction.

As touched on, whilst most mental illness makes sense, schizophrenia seems pretty crazy? They're not just 'not OK'. It's worse, as they're out of touch with reality. We might be seriously depressed, anxious, suicidal, desperate for some fix, or have an overwhelming compulsion to wash our hands, but we're not seeing things or hearing things. As Sue Atkinson (2005) highlights, 'When we worry that we are going mad, it is a sign that we probably aren't. The really seriously mad people are not aware of their craziness' (p.151).

Schizophrenia is typified by hallucinations and delusions. The most common type of hallucinations is auditory and verbal, but there's also visual, tactile and olfactory. Delusions are fixed false beliefs. Like, we think we're Napoleon or the Queen of Sheba. But we're not. We've crossed the line. And people can believe they're being persecuted when they're not. Apparently the most common type of delusion is paranoia and persecutory, with many believing others are conspiring against them, which can include the TV, radio, magazines and newspapers.

Schizophrenia is used interchangeably with psychosis, which refers to being out of touch with reality. For a diagnosis of schizophrenia, people need two out of five psychotic symptoms at the same time for at least a month, like delusions and hallucinations. Other symptoms include disorganised thinking and behaviour. And 'negative symptoms', like not responding to the environment in the usual way. They lack eye contact and appear un-stimulated.

So, people can think events are happening that aren't. Like my friend, who's diagnosed with paranoid schizophrenia, might believe someone is being gang-raped in the house next door, but they're not. And he might be so convinced that he busts down the door to intervene. This has happened several times. He also hears the river singing to him but it's not? And he regularly hears voices, which he identifies with different personalities, but that can't be true? There can't be invisible entities (daemons?) that speak to our minds?

Or like a lovely woman I worked with, a service-user diagnosed as schizophrenic, was often laughing away to herself, and we'd be like, 'share the joke'. She seemed content in her bubble with her entertaining voices. It's also noted, that psychics and mediums hear voices, but they're not mentally unwell. Indeed, they have a gift? There are spirits?

Suffice to say, that hearing voices can be very distracting and distressing. Sometimes they may sound like many different people. And besides talking to the person, often the voices talk to each other. Voices may talk about the hearer, even describing (narrating) what s/he is doing and thinking. It can be like hearing other people's thoughts. People hearing voices feel like they're going crazy. This is a common fear, and fair play. Profoundly deaf people also notably hear voices.

Sufferers advise that many days can pass without hearing them but at other times they can afflict no-end torment. They can vary in loudness and clarity. At times a low mumble difficult to make out (some report about malicious whisperings), and at other times speaking as clearly as someone standing right next to them. Voices can be supportive and encouraging, providing the person with an important sense of comfort e.g. with regards to say sexual abuse, telling the person it's not their fault, and they've done nothing to be ashamed of. But voices can equally become critical, talking about the person negatively, and directly criticising them.

It's noted that 'nurturing' or 'critical' 'voices' resonates with the nurturing or critical 'parent' within us. Like, one woman I worked with, who was diagnosed as having schizophrenia, when she spoke about her voices, she would animatedly act in the stance of her mother criticising her. She would assume the mannerisms of her mum. So, I felt, that whilst it was possible she 'heard' her mum's voice, it seemed likely that she heard these thoughts in her mind. Not external but internal thoughts i.e. the parental injunctions we all hear in our mind's ear e.g. we say to ourselves 'you're rubbish and stupid'.

Indeed, it's theorised that people may mistakenly attribute an episode of inner speech, one of their own thoughts, to an external source. Voices may be internal thoughts experienced as if spoken aloud, which are made worse by current or past stress.

Thus, there's our own voice that we hear in our heads, all day long i.e. our internal dialogue. And our own voice, or thoughts, might insist that we do certain things, like not eat, or hurt ourselves, or check the locks three times. But then there's what sounds like external voices, which is something else. Unlike our own inner voice then, which clearly belongs to us, most people who hear voices report they have an 'alien' quality to them, and it doesn't feel like it comes from them. People attribute hearing voices to an external source.

But moreover, beyond the verbal abuse, sometimes voices threaten the person and command them to do dangerous or unacceptable things. They may instruct the person to say things to people or not to talk to their families or friends. Sometimes they urge people to hurt themselves or others. Like, otherwise psychos often report that voices told them to commit whatever heinous crimes. Voices can be extremely powerful and threatening e.g. threatening to kill the person if s/he disobeys them. And people may be frightened to disobey voices in fear of what might happen.

The voices can however be seen as liars. Hence, the impetus to evaluate the consequences if one chooses to disobey them i.e. look at the evidence. What are the scary voices going to physically do? People can be encouraged to talk back to the voices. Thus, people shout back at the walls and the TVs that are apparently speaking to them. Hence, they epitomise madness.

Apparently, the same brain areas that activate when people hear real noise light up in schizophrenics during hallucinatory episodes. So, they are hearing something? Perhaps the brain is a machine that a ghost could operate? Other studies have shown that speech muscles move when people hear voices. In much the same way as they move when we talk to ourselves or think in words, pray silently or read. So, schizophrenics don't realise they're mumbling to themselves? This phenomenon is known as subvocalisation and some research studies suggest that if people deliberately engage in this e.g. count to themselves, recite poetry, do crosswords etc this can disrupt the voices. Anything that serves as a CBT distraction is sweet.

It seems the unconscious is unleashed, because the psychotic can't distinguish between externally and internally generated sounds and images i.e. distorted locus of control. Another schizophrenic feature is 'thought blocking'. That is, people stop talking mid-sentence, as the thought is literally taken out their heads. It's noted, this happens with 'stoners'. They have the most amazing ideas then forget what they were thinking about.

In addition to being preoccupied with unusual ideas, people may also suffer emotional difficulties. They may be very depressed and emotionally flat, lack motivation, have difficulties coping, and withdraw (emotional isolation). Like bipolar disorder, there can be periods of extreme depression and manic feelings, irritable and panicky. People are dancing on the razor edge?

Mania is by definition a psychotic condition as psychotic experiences (hallucinations and delusions) often arise when manic. Maybe mania, for those clinically depressed, is like a safety-valve? It opens automatically to relieve excess pressure? Maybe we're like pressure cookers, dealing with heat aka stress? Bipolar is diagnosed on the premise of at least one episode of mania (an explosion of high on life behaviour). Like other mental afflictions, increasing numbers are diagnosed with this curious illness, which has much variability i.e. how often and severe mood-swings are varies from person to person. High/low periods can vary between an hour, several weeks or longer.

Interestingly, and unlike bipolar where feelings are excessive, apparently the 'flat affect' symptomatic of schizophrenia is a fallacy. Research has shown that whilst they appear to lack feelings, it's actually a problem with expression, as emotions of people with flat affect are usually stronger than those people without mental health problems. Many people experience difficulties that are neither clearly manic-depressive nor schizophrenic, thus schizoaffective disorder pertains to those who have both persisting psychotic symptoms and persisting problems of mood.

The majority of schizophrenics are diagnosed as having either 'paranoid schizophrenia', which entails delusions of persecution and grandeur, accompanied with anxiety, anger, argumentativeness, jealousy and violence (which describes my friend to a tee), or 'undifferentiated schizophrenia'. That is, people exhibit patterns of disorganised behaviour, thoughts and emotion. It's diagnosed when the psychiatrist is unable to diagnose a specific type of schizophrenia.

Like, catatonic schizophrenia, for example, which includes a disorder of movement. Catalepsy is notably a condition characterised by a lack of response to external stimuli and muscle rigidity, so that limbs remain in whatever position they are placed. They may appear flat as if engaged in an inner world. It's like they've gone, vacated the premises. Those who do display emotion often do so inappropriately e.g. crying for no reason or flying into a rage.

'Disorganised schizophrenia' entails unrelated delusions and hallucinations together with incoherent speech, strange facial grimaces, and ritualistic movements. The affect is flat but there may be inappropriate laughter and giggling e.g. laughing out loud at a funeral (maybe the voices tell jokes at the worst times). Personal hygiene is neglected including loss of bladder and bowel control. The strange facial grimaces seem menacing?

It's also highlighted that 'madness' can be clever. Like schizophrenics can demonstrate a sharpness to their otherwise disorganised thoughts, including clever schizoid puns. On occasion, their chat can take poetically striking turns of phrase. Furthermore, some 'patients' like to play with the doctor because they can. Being mad gives a licence to play games? And it can be fun, like a cat with a mouse? Some people like to convey they're weird, because it's more interesting than being normal? Calculated madness can be empowering?

The cause of schizophrenia is unknown, but most experts support the 'stress vulnerability model' theory. That is, everyone is vulnerable as determined by biological, psychological, and environmental factors. A stressful or traumatic incident can sometimes trigger the symptoms, like hearing voices, in vulnerable people e.g. a recent bereavement, sexual abuse during childhood or adulthood, severe trauma, solitary confinement, sleep deprivation, very high temperature or other physical illness.

Or we can (inadvertently) give ourselves psychosis through our lifestyles e.g. cannabis induced-psychosis, alcohol induced psychosis, LSD induced psychosis. If depressed for long enough, people can develop depression induced psychosis. Insomnia can trigger psychosis. Bipolar can similarly be triggered in certain vulnerable people. Drugs can induce bipolar, as can stress/exhaustion, so called stress-induced bipolar. It seems genes switch on in response to stress?

It's postulated that mental illness could be genetic or biological in origin, manifested as the result of some innate intolerance to stress. Scientists inform that chronic stress predisposes our brain to mental illness, and that stress in adolescence can affect the expression of severe mental illness including schizophrenia. They've shown in mice that stress in adolescence can affect the expression of a gene that codes for a key neurotransmitter related to mental function and psychiatric illness.

Stress can also contribute to worsening the symptoms of mental illness. Like, in schizophrenia, it can encourage hallucinations and delusions, while in bipolar disorder, it can trigger episodes of both mania and depression. John Gray (author) said, 'Stress is like darkness. You cannot make it go away. All you can do is turn the light on'. Which is easier said than done, when one can't sleep because of racing thoughts. How dreadful not to be able to sleep.

Dr Raj Persaud, consultant psychiatrist for Public Understanding of Psychiatry, said, 'I would say the key component of mental health is the ability to withstand events or situations known to precipitate mental illness. Some have called this 'psychological hardiness' or resilience'. Like in social work, we assess children's 'resilience', which is defined as 'normal development amidst adversity'. So, we want to enhance resilience and our ability to deal with stress.

In essence, insanity is arguably a sane response to an insane world. It's a normal existential response to the absurdity? And we each have our breaking point. Often the most sensitive and clever are susceptible. But we're all vulnerable given enough stress and pressure.

Laing concedes, 'mental illness can be understood as bizarre behaviour which is rational, an understandable response to unusual social pressures'. Thus, illness and symptom formation can be seen as an autonomously creative act, a function of the psyche's imperative to grow and develop, to somehow proceed in abnormal circumstances. Like, cats defecate somewhere 'inappropriate' to let you know they're distressed, or troubled kids partake in smear campaigns and wet the bed. And self-harm indicates something's up.

It seems existential common sense has been usurped by the medical model, which places far greater emphasis on the distinctly (unfounded) materialistic and biological aspects of psychiatric illness. But as emphasised, we're not sane, then crazy, but rather there's a build-up. Choices are cumulative, and we need to choose wisely as our sanity depends on it (mental health requires discipline).

For Jung, who believed in our potential to attain sanity, we need to 'wake up' to our predicament and grow beyond it. Embark upon a journey of self-discovery and renewal. The Jungian approach encourages the person to accept responsibility for their circumstances, and to understand their illness as an expression of their total life experience. We're all human beings with a story.

Like depression embodying the germ of recovery, Jung proposed that mental illness, including schizophrenia, is itself a form of growth. He maintained that otherwise crazy behaviours are meaningful and appropriate, rather than the inconsequential ramblings of an organic disease. It does not have to be a psychiatric disability but a stage in a natural psychic healing process. And from this point of view, meds frustrate lawful progression of a potentially natural process. It's also highlighted that drugs don't always prevent people hearing voices, hence there's no point in taking them?

Within a therapeutic setting, a new ego can be born, a new existential birth can happen. Laing equally minimised the use of drug treatments i.e. low doses of tranquillisers. He believed the 'crazy condition' would terminate itself, if left to run to its natural limits. Apparently, Laing was partial to tripping in acid sessions with his clothes off. Maybe there's a place for mindscaping?

Instead of denouncing 'symptoms', as representing a form of futile suffering, Jung seen them as the growing pains of a soul struggling to escape fear and find fulfilment. They provide an opportunity to become conscious and grow. And rather than viewing stress negatively, for Jung, stress allows us to grow and transform. The suffering soul has to find meaning. Jung also insisted it's essential to know the situation in the unconscious, and rebuked the psychiatric approach disinterested in the unconscious, which instead it suppresses and silences through drugs. As mentioned, we'll get to the curious unconscious in the next chapter.

It's seems psychiatry's goal is 'first aid', to chemically bind the crazy with a band-aid? It's argued that the possibility a breakdown may be a crisis filled with existential meaning and an opportunity for growth is seldom considered. In a psychiatric clinic, the patient goes through a ritual of consultation, diagnosis, and treatment. And it's argued the patient collusively detaches from their illness, with the onus placed on the capable doctor to take responsibility.

Alternatively, Jung believed in treating people as human beings ('as a person') rather than 'patients' aka a mental case. That is, treating everyone as essentially normal and healthy, while accepting, incidentally, that they might have a problem. The 'helper' is there as a real person, respecting the patient as an equal, not a sick inferior (unlike some 'rescuers' who like to be superior, reaffirming others not OK-ness?). Jung empowered his patients. He said, 'I provide him with the necessary psychological knowledge to free himself from my medical authority as speedily as possible' (awesome).

Like counselling/psychotherapy, the client finds the answers themselves, and yet both client and counsellor grow through the process. Jung was also aware that being overly-dependent forfeits our own self-healing. He therefore encouraged 'breaks' from therapy e.g. break the therapy every ten weeks to throw the patient back to life, to discourage reliance on the analyst, and encourage reliance on the self. This way 'the patient does not live to analyse but analyses to live'. With respect, how many 'service users' live for appointments?

Freud's psychoanalysis was notably the first form of psychotherapy (psychotherapy is Latin for mental healing). But rather than the stereotypical Freudian analysis, where the therapist sits aloof behind the couch, Jung proposed that analysis is a dialectical procedure, a two-way exchange between two people who are equally involved. This model has notably influenced psychotherapists of most schools, although few recognise it was Jung's idea.

Whilst Jung took full account of what his patient had been in the past, but like Sartre and Nietzsche, he was far more interested in what the patient was in the process of becoming in the present. Like, instead of focusing on problems, we focus on solutions. Hence, there's 'Solution Focussed Therapy'. We focus on goals, what we want to achieve in life.

Whilst the efficacy of labels is debatable, they can help us navigate our way back to being OK? As Berne insists, we are OK, albeit we might have some issues to iron out. We've all got issues to iron out. It's just some are more obvious than others? Labels are like a compass for abnormal behaviour, and they justify madness? Like, it's good to know one has Borderline Personality Disorder because it explains 'weird' behaviour. Or it's good to know one has bipolar disorder to explain the mood swings. However, for many the downside to labels is the stigma. Apparently more than half of mental ill health sufferers say the stigma and discrimination is as damaging or harder to deal with than the illness itself.

Thus, they arguably don't help, and can even become self-fulfilling? The doctor medically confirms we're not OK, which can perpetuate sickness? It gives mental awry-ness a solidity it didn't have before? Jung conceded that whilst clinical diagnoses give the doctor a certain orientation, 'they do not help the patient'. He insisted, 'The crucial thing is the story. For it alone shows the human background and the human suffering, and only at that point can the doctor's therapy begin'. Paracelsus conceded, 'Are not even now, many of our doctors poisoning the imagination of their patients by frightening them instead of seeking to instil hope and confidence into their minds'.

It seems pertinent to note, that a 'service user' (another label) I worked with, who was diagnosed with depression for twenty-three years, was latterly told (by a different psychiatrist) that she didn't have depression after all. But rather, her mood was circumstantial. She was seriously pissed off for being treated with an illness she didn't have. I've also noticed how often when you ask people how they are, they don't always know. They're not sure if they're OK. They're not sure if the meds have kicked in yet. Hence, the 'litmus test' regarding the impetus to check out?

Complexities in modern life coupled with nihilism create dis-ease but is that disease? It's also highlighted that medicalising our not OK-ness links it with a whole range of beliefs concerning diseases and illnesses held in our society. Like, 'treatment is the job of the medical profession; there is nothing I can do about it – the solution is not my responsibility, it is the doctors and so on' (Richard Velleman, 'Counselling for Alcohol Problems', 2002 p.5). This undermines personal responsibility and creates 'learned helplessness'.

Martin Seligman notably illustrated 'learned helplessness'. Thus, dogs were contained in a cage and given electric shocks (nice), and whilst they initially tried to break free, there was no escape. After some time, the doors were opened but the despondent dogs no longer cared. They simply laid down passively and whined as they endured the shocks. Another group of dogs were placed in cages with the doors open, and when the dogs were shocked, they immediately ran away. Learned Helplessness Theory is the view that clinical depression and related mental illnesses may result from such real or perceived absence of control over the outcome of a situation. Hence, we need to harness our personal power?

It's understood that labelling our self as unhappy, or whatever, is dangerous since our personal reality consists of what we think about. Harris (1972) equally points out, 'to state that we have problems is not particularly helpful' (p.52). It seems the endeavour is to own that we're OK? As opposed to using negative thoughts to convince ourselves we're not, and that feeling bad is a good idea? Sue Atkinson (2005) said, 'We must get out of the habit of seeing ourselves as being depressed forever, never being able to get better. Rather bizarrely, some people sometimes almost seem to relish the depressed state (perhaps they want to remain centre stage at home?)'.

Mental illness is not subsiding, and it won't until we address the underlying causes of it. It's also possible there's more at play, i.e. more than what we're programmed with, but we'll get to this actual craziness later.

4¼

The Myth of Mental Illness?

Contrary to the extreme medical view that regards mental illness as the product of biology, it's contended that mental illness isn't really illness in the medical sense. Like, Thomas Szasz boldly denied the existence of mental illness, and shocked the world in 1960 with the publication of his landmark work 'The Myth of Mental Illness'. As mentioned, Szasz recommended a policy of non-intervention for suicide as this is our liberty. Like, it's our liberty to drink, take drugs, eat pies, and lie in bed all day. Like Berne, Szasz insists all adults 'are responsible', with the capacity to make free and responsible choices.

Szasz asserts that 'whilst medical diagnoses are the names of genuine diseases, psychiatric disorders are stigmatising labels which arise at a moral/social level'. Unlike physical illness, the mental condition is intrinsically bound up with the personality. In physical illness the notion of a bodily symptom is tied to an anatomical and genetic context, as distinct from the social and ethical context which informs psychiatric judgements. He states the concept of mental illness 'arises in part from the fact that it is possible for a person to act as if he were sick without actually having a bodily illness', and therefore 'mental illness is a metaphorical disease' and it is a 'serious error' to define any person acting in such a manner 'as obviously sick, that is, as mentally sick' (p.10).

Some doctor (in a debate) conceded, that 'equating illness with a complaint allows the individual to be the sole arbiter of whether he is ill or not, and is unsatisfactory because some people who should complain don't do so, and others who do so repeatedly don't seem to have adequate reasons for doing so' (cited in Sedgwick, Psychopolitics 1982 p.12). And it's true, many people are forever chewing a wasp and then there's the plight of silent sufferers who 'just get on with it'.

But moreover, Szasz points out that 'just as it is possible for a person to define himself as sick without having a bodily illness, so it is possible for a physician to define as 'sick' a person who feels perfectly well and wants no medical help, and then act as if he were a therapist trying to cure his 'patients' disease' (p.11). This sentiment was popularised in 'One Flew Over the Cuckoo's Nest', the 1962 novel by Ken Kesey, that was made into a movie in 1975, featuring Jack Nicholson.

Szasz questions how we should react to such a physician and summarises two diametrically opposed points of view about mental illness and psychiatry. Thus, mental illness is like any other illness, and psychiatric treatment whether voluntary or not is like any other treatment. Or alternatively mental illness is a myth and psychiatric intervention is a type of social action, and hence 'involuntary psychiatric therapy is not treatment but torture' (p.12).

The anti-psychiatry movement (there was a mass cult of anti-psychiatry in the late 1960s) was a response to both the tranquillising (numbing) of society, and the enforcement of what some regard as dangerous treatments like ECT and lobotomies. It challenged mainstream psychiatry, criticising its power and oppressive role. Psychiatry was considered a coercive instrument of oppression due to an unequal power relationship between doctor and patient, and a highly subjective diagnostic process.

Szasz regarded the mental health movement as a totalitarian mass enterprise akin to fascism and communism. Psychiatry was seen as modern capitalism's weapon for social control. Meds are a chemical straitjacket. He also equated it with the Inquisition in a new disguise. He said, 'Although mental illness might have been a useful concept in the nineteenth century, today it is scientifically worthless and socially harmful'. As touched on, it's always possible the medical model projects a destructive and disempowering force into society?

The debate over mental illness has thus revolved around two positions, namely, 'mental illness is a myth' and 'mental illness is an illness like any other'. The position 'mental illness is an illness like any other' is understood primarily as a response to Szasz's claim that mental illness is a myth. But Szasz insists the word 'disease' can only be used in connection with an observable anatomical lesion or other physiological defect. And he believes that use of the word beyond that is not only misleading but fraudulent.

If there's no physical cause, Szasz tells us it comes down to a 'problem in living'. That is, people do not have mental illness but rather experience a wide range of moral, interpersonal, social and political problems in living. Indeed, he maintains, 'we call problems in living 'mental illness''. For Szasz, 'psychiatry is a pseudo-medical enterprise founded on a destructive analysis of the concept of mental illness' (p14). It's argued that psychiatry is 'science by decree'. That is, they say its science so it is.

Szasz said, 'There's a Church of America – better known as the National Institute of Mental Health [which] propagates a faith called Psychiatry. It would have us believe that we can lead lives of ambition without anxiety; that we can have success without strife, sociability without conflict, reward without punishment and pleasure without pain' (cited in Sedgwick, 1982 p.163). He said, 'In the Church of America, Psychiatrists are Priests'.

In his book 'The Second Sin' (1973), Szasz said, 'Boredom is the feeling that everything is a waste of time; serenity, that nothing is'; 'Anxiety is the unwillingness to play even when you know the odds are for you; Courage is the willingness to play even when you know the odds are against you'; and 'happiness is an imaginary condition, formerly attributed by the living to the dead, now usually attributed by adults to children, and by children to adults' (p.36).

Brennan Manning (author) said, 'we should expect to go through heartache and pain, suffering and loss, because they are part of what it means to be human, and they can be useful in our development'. And Scott Peck argued, 'laziness or desire to escape legitimate suffering lies at the root of most mental illness'. He said, 'Indeed, the tendency to avoid problems and the emotional suffering inherent in them is the primary basis of all psychological illness' (The Road Less Travelled and Beyond, 1997 p.146).

Rather than 'mental illness', Szasz proposed his 'theory of personal conduct'. He states, 'there is no psychology; there is only biography and autobiography'. It seems we need a context rather than psychopathology i.e. isolating feelings and clustering them together to create diagnoses/pathology? 'Systems theory' notably arrived in the 1970s and challenged individual pathology. The idea was that problems arise within families, and that patient's experience and behaviour are liable to make more sense when viewed in a family context.

As highlighted, we're a-being-in-the-world, and we're always thinking. Ergo the contention that mental illness is an invalid and perilous idea because human action is governed by intentions or motives. Take my otherwise 'clinically depressed' friend, for example, who could, upon finding out a boy she liked would be visiting, tidy her flat and herself (which includes shaving), all of which would be an unthinkable chore. It's her prerogative to change her mind. It seems her brain received some happy chemicals? Szasz said, 'all life is game playing', which includes the 'games' between doctors and patients, since the 'sick role' is negotiated.

Ronald Leifer (1969), Szasz's apprentice, similarly argued that in physical diagnosis and treatment 'the term 'disease' refers to phenomena that are not regulated by social custom, morality and law, namely bodily structure and function; psychiatric concepts of disease refer, on the contrary, to behaviour which is subject to the regulation of custom, morality and law' (cited in Sedgwick, 1982 p.17). Thus, mental illness is a language, social status, private hell, but it's not disease.

Sedgwick (1982) summarises, 'mental illness is a social construction; psychiatry is a social construction, incorporating the values and demands of its surrounding society' (p.25). He also pertained to Herbert Spencer's (British sociologist) comment, namely, 'There is a notion, always more or less prevalent and just now vociferously expressed, that all social suffering is removable, and that it is the duty of somebody or other to remove it. Both these beliefs are false' (p.163).

Goffman was on the same anti-psychiatry page. He conceded that mental illness is not the product of disease but of social labelling. He claimed that it represents socially offensive acts, where deviants end up in prison or a mental ward. Antisocial behaviour precedes mental illness. It seems there's a progression from bad to mad? Apparently 1:4 police cases involve persons with mental health problems, which highlights the dichotomy between bad or mad?

Contrary to the value-free language of physical medicine then, the language of psychiatry is socially and politically loaded. It's 'stigmatising'. And for Goffman, 'physical disease has nothing to do with the personal, social world of meanings; such disease is not the attribute of a person but of the organism'. Psychiatric treatment aims to cure the 'mentally sick' but learned entrenched patterns of behaviour (that defines us) is arguably not illness.

Goffman cautioned that by applying the term mentally ill we attach complex social meanings to acts of behaviour, and these meanings can be interpreted differently by different professionals, and also in different places and contexts. Like, if we see a psychiatrist, our mental pickle is likely to be biological, attributed to hormones and brain chemicals; with a psychologist, it's likely to be psychological, faulty cognition; psychotherapists might pertain to repressing unconscious desires; sociologists (counsellors and social workers) would highlight environmental factors; and geneticists would point to genes. Such variability from professional to professional, or one society to another, is rendered inconvenient. It's like addictions are categorised in medical and moral terms. Moral values are medicalised?

It's also interesting to note, that when men and women present with identical clinical features, women are seen as hysterical personality type, and men antisocial personality type. And the same behaviour can be viewed as criminal when it's men, but mental illness when it's women. It's considered a paradox that mental illness is presented as an alternative to criminal behaviour.

But the plot thickens, as assuming someone is sick because they're behaving abnormally has proved a very lucrative business for the last hundred years. Alcohol and opium were time honoured remedies for anxiety and insomnia but towards the latter part of the nineteenth century the pharmaceutical industry began. A variety of synthetic substances took flight and landed, coupled with huge profits. It's said if pharmaceutical companies can create a cure, they can manufacture an illness, and market a disease. It's like creating vaccines, then unleashing the disease?

As Kirsch asserts, 'Depression, we are told over and over again, is a brain disease, a chemical imbalance that can be adjusted by antidepressant medication'. He highlights this view is so widespread, it's like it's an established fact, which is how it's presented by drug companies. But he counters, 'Actually it is not. Instead, even its proponents have to admit that it is a controversial hypothesis that has not yet been proven'. He further argues that not only is the chemical-imbalance hypothesis unproven, but it is about as close as a theory gets in science to being dis-proven by the evidence.

As discussed, orthodox western medicine is designed to detect and treat diseases with a defined pathology, but with psychological illness, there are no corresponding physical anomalies. It seems thinking (perspective), lifestyle and diet are the problem? Theories about mental disorders are however convenient for pharmaceutical companies, who are major financers of 'medical' research. It therefore stands to reason that whatever findings are in their best interests, are not necessarily in ours. And antidepressants are in their best interests. Hence, no good can come from research that undermines them.

Pharmaceutical companies spend billions on research. In the UK, the pharmaceutical industry spends over three billion a year on research, financing about 90% of all clinical drug trials. Holford and Burne (2006) highlight, 'trials funded by a drug company were four times more likely to have results favourable to the company than studies funded from other sources' (p.55). And further, 'in the UK, the extent to which drug companies finance trials is even greater than in the US' (p. 56). They also point out that drug company money buys influence including top medical journals. They quote Richard Horton, 'The Lancet' (prestigious medical journal) editor, who said, 'in reality the relationship between the journals and the drug industry is somewhere between symbiotic and parasitic' (p.86).

Drug companies also sponsor at least half of all seminars and courses, and spend thousands targeting individual GPs with medical sales reps. Holford and Burne assert that drug companies 'schmooze the legislators' and 'spend more money than any other industry lobbying congress in the US - $177 million. They also actively lobby the UK parliament' (p.53). Pharmaceutical companies lobby for conditions to be diagnosed for which they have the chemical solution.

Like 'Female Viagra' (Addyi), the solution for women's lack of libido. Maybe we're not attracted to our partner? This was originally turned down by the FDA (the US Food and Drug Administration) due to its lack of effectiveness weighed against side effects. The pharmaceutical companies launched a huge marketing campaign, lobbied government and accused the FDA of sexism. As a result of the pressure campaigns, the drug was approved. Thus, it's argued that it's drugs first, then theory. As mentioned, normal developmental changes are also medicalised and capitalised on e.g. menopause and andropause.

Holford and Burne refute drug companies' claim that much of the income goes onto developing new and valuable drugs. Instead they highlight that much of their resources go on producing copycat versions of bestselling existing drugs so they can keep selling a patented product at much higher prices. They further distinguish between good and profitable medicines. Thus, good meds are safe and doable, in the sense that they don't cost much and are practical. Alternatively, profitable medicine is hugely expensive and supported by multibillion-dollar marketing campaigns. It's synthetic because it must be to be patentable, and it's designed only to relieve symptoms, so patients have to keep taking it.

Blockbuster drugs are defined as those which sell over a billion per year, and the four main brands for depression rake in a total worth of $10 billion. It's duly noted, that Prozac, marketed as the 'happy pill', made shareholders very happy. It made them billions. Holford and Burne highlight that drug companies pay for ongoing education about the effectiveness and safety of drugs, and as a result doctors are brainwashed and regurgitate what they've been told regarding scientific trials and regulation. This includes a small chance of adverse drug reaction. Yet some 10,000 people in the UK are killed every year by adverse drug reactions (three times more than traffic accidents).

In his aforementioned book, James Davies unveils the true human cost of an industry that, in the name of helping others, has actually been helping itself. He asserts how psychiatry has put riches and medical status above patients' wellbeing, with ethical, scientific and treatment flaws unscrupulously concealed by mass-marketing. He also points out that the everyday sufferings and setbacks of life are now 'medicalised' into illnesses that require treatment - usually with highly profitable drugs.

David Icke (2007) concedes there's far more money to be made by drugging the dying and treating symptoms than there is by curing ills. He notes the ten largest pharmaceutical giants made profits of $40 billion in the first six months of 2006 alone. Icke refers to Big Pharma as 'legalised evil' (p.540). [Big Pharma is the nickname given to the global pharmaceutical industry]. He asserts they all serve financers not the people, and he also pertains to the many billions spent on marketing and influencing doctors. He highlights the web of deceit that connects doctors, politicians, government officials and drug giants. It's understood there's something more sinister going on behind the benevolent façade of 'health care'.

The DSM, which is referred to as 'Diagnosing for Status and Money', was first published in 1952. Back in the day, before the 1840s, there was really only one label (classification) and that was insanity. People were either normal or idiotic/insane. The American Psychiatric Association (APA) was then formed in 1844, and by 1880, there were seven categories of mental disorders, namely: mania, melancholia, monomania (irrationality when discussing subjects), paresis (syphilitic brain condition), dementia, dipsomania (alcoholism), and epilepsy. It was notably discovered that paresis was created through poisoning brought on by mercury-based medications offered to syphilitics.

The first DSM thus expanded mental disorders from this original one (or seven) to an overwhelming 112. These included brain disorders, psychotic disorders, a plethora of 'neuroses', personality disorders, sexual deviations including homosexuality, transvestism, paedophilia, fetishism, rape assault and sexual sadism.

In 1968 the DSM was revised and became DSM II, and the number of disorders increased from 112 to 163. New categories included 6 new drug dependence ailments, 8 new sexual deviance conditions, 6 new schizophrenic disorders, 5 more neuroses, 13 new categories of alcoholic disorders, 3 new personality disorders.

Phillip Day, author of 'The Mind Game' (2002), asserts, 'Like recipes for a ghastly new cookbook, psychiatry has dreamt up mental disorders by the dozen to pathologise every quirk of human nature'. And also, 'So entrenched has the popular view of psychiatry become in our society today, most believe that anyone who is mentally troubled, depressed, hyperactive or exhibits eccentric behaviour of any kind is in fact sick in the head'. But as Day contends, 'there has never been one shred of proof presented in a scientific context indicating that these conditions are physical 'diseases of the mind''.

It seems pertinent to note, the DSM II also introduced a new diagnosis for 'hyperkinetic' kids. This hyperkinetic impulse disorder became ADHD in later DSM editions, and now we have an ADHD epidemic. At least 1:10 kids in the UK have ADHD, and apparently, it's 1:5 in the US. As mentioned, whilst doctors condemn cocaine, they plough kids with substances like Ritalin. It's theorised that kids don't have enough dopamine hence amphetamines serve the purpose of inhibiting the breakdown of dopamine.

Like antidepressants, these drugs rake in billions. But it's arguably criminal that millions of kids are prescribed cocaine-like drugs for a condition that has never been scientifically proven to exist? The side effects are grim, and there are other reasons for hyperactive behaviour e.g. diet, attachments, abuse, and the crap they put in vaccinations?

As touched on, it's widely believed that mercury in vaccinations is responsible for the epidemic of autism. Autistic Spectrum Disorder (ASD), which includes autism and Asperger syndrome, is a condition that affects social interaction, communication, interests, and behaviour. In the US, those diagnosed with ASD has gone from 1:10,000 circa 1980 to 1:50 today. It's estimated that about 1% of people in the UK has ASD[12]. It's projected that 1:2 kids will have autism by 2032. Unbelievable. It's also noted, that like antidepressants, researchers hid negative trials regarding the correlation with autism.

The kids I worked with (in social work) notably hated their ADHD label, as it confirmed they're not 'normal'. They didn't fit in, so they might as well act out? Most of them were hurting and from broken homes. So, the 'label' wasn't helpful, but 'diagnoses' can provide currency. They can reap benefits in Great Benefits Britain, or pay-outs from insurance companies. As mentioned, being 'sick' needn't be all bad. Kids can be a means to cash.

It's also noted, that otherwise 'challenging' kids can be diagnosed with 'Oppositional Defiance Disorder' (ODD), which deteriorates into Conduct Disorder (CD) if the disorder remains 'untreated'. These disorders were introduced in the DSM III. It basically means their bad behaviour gets worse the older they get. 'Symptoms' include non-compliance towards authority figures, tantrums, argumentativeness, and provocative behaviour, but CD requires several more severe aggressive or antisocial behaviours such as fighting, truancy, stealing, lying and fire setting.

Like ADHD, these diagnoses provide an alternative 'medical' explanation for why kids batter their parents and verbally abuse them no end. It seems prudent to note, that whilst ADHD is almost synonymous with challenging behaviour, restlessness is not the same as naughtiness. Being hyper is not the same as unacceptable behaviour.

As mentioned, oppositional behavioural difficulties tend to develop gradually within the context of coercive parent-child interaction. Attachment problems can convert into behavioural problems, and then kids get slapped with a label. The kid is the problem, the scapegoat, because of 'their' behaviour. It's duly noted however, that Supernanny can cure ODD and CD. Kids need discipline and moral guidance. And moral guidance can be ambiguous?

---

[12] See 'Vaxxed' (2016) documentary.

If kid's 'challenging' behaviour goes unchecked and un-rectified, it's highly likely they'll acquire more disorders as adults, possibly Antisocial Personality Disorder. This entails the person never shows remorse, has no interest in the feelings or rights of others, is happy to lie, cheat and could murder. A twisted head becomes a medical condition?

As Day highlights, children were the target of the DSM III, which was unveiled in 1980. In the 'Infancy, Childhood and Adolescence' section, 32 more mental disorders were added, which besides ODD and CD, included Attention Deficit Disorder, Developmental Reading Disorder, Developmental Arithmetic Disorder, Developmental Articulation Disorder, Separation-Anxiety Disorder, Overanxious Disorder. The medicalising of common childhood behaviours further extended to other social vices in the DSM III. Thus, new chemical substance abuse 'mental disorders' included Hallucinogen Organic Mental Disorders, Cannabis Organic Mental Disorders, Tobacco Organic Mental Disorder and Caffeine Organic Mental Disorder.

In the DSM III mental disorders increased to 224. But sweet like a lemon, homosexuality, previously considered a mental disease, was cured overnight (brilliant). With the change in legislation (following pressure from the homosexual community), it was no longer considered sexual deviance but rather sexual preference.

The revised version of the DSM III-R, released in 1987, contained 253 mental illnesses, now including PMT/PMS. Is this an 'illness'? Day highlights that the DSM III-R committee also attempted to include an 'illness' named Paraphilic Rapism (also known as Paraphilic Coercive Disorder). This was to include person's fantasising or attempting assault/rape, persons experiencing intense sexual arousal or a desire associated with it for at least six months.

As it transpired however, this massively outraged women's groups. The prospect of rape being decriminalised in favour of a psychiatric diagnosis was not okay. People excused because they can't control themselves. But doesn't this typify mental illness? Such a disorder or mental disease of 'rapism' is devastating to victims. Day mentions a case whereby two rapists received a light sentence after the court heard benevolent psychiatric evidence, which basically excused the men's behaviour on grounds they were unable to control themselves.

It seems psychiatry undermines responsibility by pathologising criminal behaviour? Just like paedo's, rapists can't help it. They're sick in the head. Like sodomites until 1967. Psychiatry plays a fundamental role in criminal justice. And it seems there's a growing phenomenon of diminishing responsibility in terms of psychiatric diagnoses being responsible for antisocial and dysfunctional ways of being.

As Day contends, 'social morality is going down the pan, and virtue is held up to ridicule. Criminal behaviour is excused under the banner of 'irresistible impulse' and 'diminished capacity''. It's also however said that 'psychiatrists have no expertise which would enable them to declare anyone unfit to stand trial, not guilty by reason of insanity, of diminished responsibility by reason or psychopathy, hallucination or detoxification, or incompetence with regards to mental disease or illness, unless the incompetence is so remarkable that the lay person can detect it'.

The DSM-IV came out in 1994, and mental disorders increased from 253 to 374, with more childhood ailments born. James Davies respectively questions why, without solid scientific justification, has the number of mental disorders risen from 106 in 1952 to 374 today?

Day highlights psychiatrist Al Parides' comments, namely, 'such watery diagnoses made upon consent or demand, render the DSM a masterpiece of political manoeuvring'. And 'normal problems of life become mental disorders, to the great profit of psychiatry and their now-keen pharmaceutical manufacturer supporters'. Day also quotes psychiatrist Walter Afield who said at a conference, '...Russian psychiatrists were talking about [how] in America you talk about treating marital maladjustment reactions and in Russia we just call that bad luck' (LOL).

Like Szasz, David Kaiser, psychiatrist and author, believes the DSM classifications are nothing but 'a pseudoscientific enterprise that grew out of modern psychiatry's desire to emulate modern medical science' (cited in Day, 2002). There are no clear boundaries between mental disorders i.e. there's many overlaps, but also between what constitutes deviance or dysfunction. Such blurred lines do however account for different diagnoses given by 'professionals' for the same presenting behaviour.

But it gets worse with the highly criticized DSM-V, which was launched in 2013. This current edition has exacerbated the already fuzzy boundaries, creating more possibilities for us to have something wrong with us. It's argued the fifth edition's revisions or additions lack empirical support, inter-rater reliability, and several sections contain poorly written, confusing, or contradictory information. Various scientists have argued that the DSM-5 forces clinicians to make distinctions that are not supported by solid evidence, and these distinctions have major treatment implications, including drug prescriptions and the availability of health insurance coverage. It's alleged that the psychiatric drug industry unduly influenced the manual's content (shockers).

Psychiatrists apparently flirted with the diagnoses of 'Internet Addiction' and 'Parental Alienation' but these didn't make it (maybe next time). With respect to the latter, besides not being a disorder within an individual but rather a relationship, it's said its exclusion may have saved many children and parents from emotional pain. It's like we've got boners with a labelling gun, as revisions incrementally add mental disorders. The publication of the DSM, with tightly guarded copyrights, notably makes the APA over $5 million a year.

Day highlights that psychiatry deviated from the road of true science by declaring illnesses they assumed were there, believing the patient must be sick because s/he was behaving abnormally. Conduct had symptoms that were presumed to be illness, despite 'no physical proof'. Take BDD, for example, which is considered a serious psychiatric illness. We're intensely dissatisfied with our appearance and obsessed with being a munter. Or take eating disorders, which were largely unheard of fifty years ago. Apparently, scientists are looking for an anorexia gene (as mentioned, there's allegedly a fat gene).

It seems prudent to note, when I was at secondary school in the 1990s, it was all pretty normal. Some kids were more hyper and funnier than others, and there were a few 'special' kids (i.e. learning disability/low IQ), but no-one was diagnosed with ADHD, or Autistic Spectrum Disorder, or mental health problems, or gender dysphoria, and no-one self-harmed. Fast forward two decades, and kids are preoccupied with not being normal. It's getting crazier? In just a generation (seventy years), we've gone from being largely normal, to far from normal?

It seems random that psychiatry votes whether or not disorders exist. That is, doctors sit round a table, reflect on different types of behaviours and decide what constitutes illness, with a majority warranting a place in the DSM. It's bemusing that if psychiatry votes a mental illness in, it apparently exists. According to critics, conjuring up diseases is a 'disease fiction process'. It's said Fictitious Disorder Syndrome, making things up, is ironic. Critics thus argue that the DSM is an unscientific system that enshrines the opinions of a few powerful psychiatrists. But fundamentally, it's claimed that the 'diseases' contained in this official book are not proven.

Rather than adhering to the Hippocratic Principle, namely, 'first do no harm', it seems the Big Pharma agenda is about making mo money. As Holford and Burne state, this is achieved by inventing new illnesses or renaming old illnesses, to make them sound more serious, so people buy more drugs. Sickness is beneficial, like war. Day (2002) cites an article by Mark Syverud, entitled 'Don't Stop the Insanity, My Therapist Needs the Money', which featured in the Daily Messenger (1995). He relays that Syverud reflects the temperature of scorn and anger felt by many informed citizens around the world at the fraud that is the DSM. Syverud wrote,

'Beware. A new book shows that an epidemic of mental illness is sweeping the nation...Does your 10-year old dislike doing her math homework? Better get her to the nearest couch because she's got No. 315.4, Developmental Arithmetic Disorder. Maybe you're a teenager who argues with his parents. Better get some medication pronto because you've got No. 313.8, Oppositional Defiance Disorder.

And if your wife won't tell you that she snuck out to the mall last Saturday, then she's definitely got 313.2, Selective Mutism...

Trust me, I am not making these things up (that would be Fictitious Disorder Syndrome). The number of mental diseases identified in the manual has risen from 100 to 300 in the last 15 years. That translates to a virtual epidemic of madness sweeping the country. Only a decade ago, psychiatrists said one in 10 Americans had a mental illness. Now according to the manual, half the population is mentally ill.

How the other half stays sane is a mystery.

The manual will have to be updated annually because mental health professionals and defence lawyers keep discovering new illnesses. Just since the beginning of the year, the experts have unearthed these new disorders:

Lottery Stress Disorder [perhaps appropriately referred to as LSD]: A London psychiatrist discovered the outbreak among lottery losers who experienced 'definition of mood and feelings of hopelessness' when their number didn't come up.

Chronic Tax Anxiety Syndrome (CTAS): A Washington psychotherapist specialises in treating couples who suffer from excessive worry, sleeplessness and marital squabbling every April.

Premenstrual Syndrome (PMS): It's not new, but now it has now won recognition as a bona fide mental illness from the American Psychiatric Association.

I know there are some cynics who will scoff at these new diagnoses. Maybe you think it is all psychobabble, just a gimmick to make money for therapists. You wouldn't be caught dead on a psychiatrist's couch. You people are in serious denial. As a matter of fact, your unwillingness to seek professional help is itself a symptom of a serious mental problem. It's right here in the book: 15.81, Non-Compliance with Treatment Disorder'.

As mentioned, it seems we all have something if we look for it? Like, at least a mild personality disorder? It's promulgated, 'if you think you're well, you haven't done enough tests yet'. It seems addictions, compulsive stealing, lying, almost everything, can be considered mental awryness. Someone has an anger problem they can't control, so who is responsible? Probably childhood.

As discussed however, continuing to blame whatever and whomever for our bad or mad mood, is to continue to disempower ourselves. The 'blame game' can only last so long. At the end of the day, surely we have to take responsibility for our ways of being, and our choices that have led us here? And accept that we are our own problem and solution?

Like Derrida advocated, in order to understand the structure of something, we need to understand its genesis. Paracelsus concedes, 'those who merely study and treat the effects of disease are like persons who imagine that they can drive the winter away by brushing snow from the door. It is not the snow which causes the winter; but the winter is the cause of the snow'.

Thus, perhaps we can reflect why we're crippled with anxiety and have no will to live. Or what's causing the insomnia or compulsions. It seems prudent to figure out how we landed on Queer Street? It's said when people take themselves out of circulation, they go weird. And yet it can be easier (safer) to opt out. It seems we can create problems for ourselves, and whilst we don't choose mental health problems, because that's crazy, we do choose our choice?

Passively, we can allow things to happen, like allow ourselves to be treated in a disparaging way (or we had no choice as a kid). But as rational adults, we can reinstate our freedom, exercise our power. We can feel the fear and do it anyway? Or maybe it's easier to go along with the script we've been given, and in tandem with the DSM, 'become' a label. As Emily Dickinson (1292) wrote, 'In this short Life that only lasts an hour, How much – how little – is within our power'. Perhaps we could will sanity to power?

When it comes to mental health, the thorniest issue is whether or not to take meds. Most psychiatrists argue that it's an essential component of treatment, but quite a few psychologists and many psychotherapists argue they do more harm than good. Many patients feel they have no choice, and some may get sectioned if they don't take them. Others may want to stay on pills for fear of relapse, or because it's too harrowing coming off them. Some people may prefer being subdued, others less so?

A patient with extensive experience of being treated with an antipsychotic drug commented, 'I think that the richness of my pre-injected days, even with the brief outbursts of madness, is preferable to the numbed cabbage I have become' (cited in Sedgwick, Psycho-Politics, 1982, p.200). It's understood there's a place for drugs, including self-medication. But maybe we don't have to be forever afflicted with some 'mental' problem?

Psychiatry has been hugely instrumental to our changing world and perspectives. Psychological and psychiatric theories permeate our courts, our police, social work departments, our hospitals, our movies, our TV, school playgrounds, our governments, and our home. It seems we're obsessed with labels, diagnoses, and medical explanations for behaviour.

But perhaps we can wonder whether mental illness really is illness in the 'medical sense' or rather if society has (deliberately) created a 'sick state'. Maybe as Szasz insisted, 'all psychology is social psychology'. For Paracelsus, imagination is the cause of many diseases, and faith is the cure for all. And thus, we're back full circle to the social-psychological principle, namely, 'I believe what I hear myself say'. Like, we're a mental case, or we're OK?

Meow

4½
'Please Hear What I'm Not Saying'

Don't be fooled by me.
Don't be fooled by the face I wear
for I wear a mask, a thousand masks,
masks that I'm afraid to take off,
and none of them is me.

Pretending is an art that's second nature with me,
but don't be fooled,
for God's sake don't be fooled.
I give you the impression that I'm secure,
that all is sunny and unruffled with me, within as well
as without,
that confidence is my name and coolness my game,
that the water's calm and I'm in command
and that I need no one,
but don't believe me.
My surface may seem smooth but my surface is my mask,
ever-varying and ever-concealing.
Beneath lies no complacence.
Beneath lies confusion, and fear, and aloneness.
But I hide this. I don't want anybody to know it.
I panic at the thought of my weakness exposed.
That's why I frantically create a mask to hide behind,
a nonchalant sophisticated facade,
to help me pretend,
to shield me from the glance that knows.

But such a glance is precisely my salvation, my only hope,
and I know it.
That is, if it's followed by acceptance,
if it's followed by love.
It's the only thing that can liberate me from myself,
from my own self-built prison walls,
from the barriers I so painstakingly erect.
It's the only thing that will assure me
of what I can't assure myself,

that I'm really worth something.
But I don't tell you this. I don't dare to, I'm afraid to.
I'm afraid your glance will not be followed by acceptance,
will not be followed by love.
I'm afraid you'll think less of me,
that you'll laugh, and your laugh would kill me.
I'm afraid that deep-down I'm nothing
and that you will see this and reject me.

So I play my game, my desperate pretending game,
with a facade of assurance without
and a trembling child within.
So begins the glittering but empty parade of masks,
and my life becomes a front.
I idly chatter to you in the suave tones of surface talk.
I tell you everything that's really nothing,
and nothing of what's everything,
of what's crying within me.
So when I'm going through my routine
do not be fooled by what I'm saying.
Please listen carefully and try to hear what I'm not saying,
what I'd like to be able to say,
what for survival I need to say,
but what I can't say.

I don't like hiding.
I don't like playing superficial phony games
I want to stop playing them.
I want to be genuine and spontaneous and me
but you've got to help me.
You've got to hold out your hand
even when that's the last thing I seem to want.
Only you can wipe away from my eyes
the blank stare of the breathing dead.
Only you can call me into aliveness.
Each time you're kind, and gentle, and encouraging,
each time you try to understand because you really care,
my heart begins to grow wings--
very small wings,
very feeble wings,
but wings!

With your power to touch me into feeling
you can breathe life into me.
I want you to know that.
I want you to know how important you are to me,
how you can be a creator--an honest-to-God creator--

of the person that is me
if you choose to.
You alone can break down the wall behind which I tremble,
you alone can remove my mask,
you alone can release me from my shadow-world of panic,
from my lonely prison,
if you choose to.
Please choose to.

Do not pass me by.
It will not be easy for you.
A long conviction of worthlessness builds strong walls.
The nearer you approach to me
the blinder I may strike back.
It's irrational, but despite what the books say about man
often I am irrational.
I fight against the very thing I cry out for.
But I am told that love is stronger than strong walls
and in this lies my hope.
Please try to beat down those walls
with firm hands but with gentle hands
for a child is very sensitive.

Who am I, you may wonder?
I am someone you know very well.
For I am every man you meet
and I am every woman you meet.

By Charles C. Finn, 1966

Multiple Personality Disorder 4¾

Multiple Personality Disorder (MPD) entered the DSM III in 1980, and in 1994 the term MPD was dropped in favour of Dissociative Identity Disorder (DID). Two or more personalities are required for this diagnosis but it's not unheard of for people to have more than a hundred personalities. MPD was notably popularised after 'Sybil', the true story of a woman who had sixteen personalities, became a bestselling book (1973) and then a movie. In the last forty years unprecedented numbers (millions) of cases have been reported, particularly in North America.

Each personality, or alter, has their own age and sex, likes and dislikes, goals and memories. Each has different handwriting, mannerisms, abilities (e.g. artistic, musical), eyesight, posture, strength and can not only speak differently i.e. accents and speech patterns, but also in different languages. Each personality or 'insider' has different thoughts, feelings, expressions, and values. Like, some might be promiscuous, and like spending cash, whereas others are consumed with self-hatred, self-harm and punishment (the alter may even want to kill the person). Other personalities may have mood swings, and panic attacks.

The core person can also have certain illnesses, that the alters don't have, including diabetes. Thus, when in an alter the otherwise diabetic person no longer has diabetes. One identity can be allergic to beestings, and another can have high cholesterol. Or one personality can be drunk or high on drugs, but when they switch into another personality, they're sober. It defies medical logic?

DID is seen as an extreme form of a more common symptom, dissociation. People who dissociate feel detached and may have spells of amnesia. Mild dissociation could be daydreaming or 'getting lost' in the moment or 'highway hypnosis'. And people can actively dissociate through meditation. Like, yogis are excellent at dissociating. Apparently, cows dissociate when it's freezing outside. But with DID, the 'core personality' is usurped by other personalities. People are usually unconscious of other personalities, and when they're in an alter, they experience amnesia (time losses).

Switching can take seconds, minutes or days, and the core self has no idea what the other personalities are up to. They may come back to their core personality in places unknown, and see the destruction that has been left in the wake of their other personalities, which includes self-mutilation. Journals are therefore fruitful for their various selves to communicate. Switches can occur with a change in situation/circumstances, and stress can propel dissociation. Male personalities, for example, are more likely to fight and be stronger.

DID and other dissociative disorders are nearly always said to be caused by severe childhood abuse and trauma e.g. repeated physical, sexual, and emotional abuse. As a defence mechanism, dissociation means that ideas can be cut off or detached from mainstream consciousness i.e. we dissociate from a situation or experience because it's too violent, traumatic or painful to assimilate with our conscious self.

Like, soldiers back from war might not remember what happened. Or car crash victims. Or childhood abuse might be 'forgotten'. So, we can hide our trauma, stash it in the unconscious. The memory is compartmentalised. Our clever brains create amnesiac barriers around the traumatic event, so we don't remember.

It's suggested that abused children imagined these awful events were happening to someone else, prompting an alter ego to grow in isolation behind a wall of amnesia. Thus, there is a new alter personality for the abuse, yet the child's original personality would have no memory of the trauma. Some personalities remember repressed memories e.g. a small child may inform about sexual abuse, whereas others, including the main or core self, remain unaware. It seems alters come and go without conscious volition, and they guard abhorrent memories of which the patient knows nothing.

Rather than a disorder per se then, DID is often referred to as 'a highly creative survival technique', because of the way it allows people enduring a severe level of abuse to continue functioning healthily in many ways.

There's a strong connection between DID and hypnosis, and hypnosis can bring out alters. With hypnosis, people are induced into a trance, which is a passive state, leaving them open to suggestion. Like the switching process with DID, when people emerge from a trance, they describe a sense of disorientation. Catalepsy also seems to involve trance states, and this can be induced by hypnosis (we'll get back to hypnosis). With DID, it seems the person goes into a trance like state, and then someone else appears.

DID experts generally agree that self-hypnosis plays an important role in the disorder, as patients frequently enter trance states during treatment, and hypnotic techniques can help patients in crisis. However, whilst hypnosis is often used as a therapeutic tool to bring out the alters of DID patients, (as well as barbiturate drugs), and many interventions have a hypnotic component, the use of hypnosis with DID remains controversial. And there's 'professional' disagreement regarding whether or not therapists or clinicians should talk to alters.

But moreover, it seems this 'illness' can be created by therapists asking the person, who's in a trance, 'is there anyone else there?' And 'what's your name?' Dodgy hypnotists could inadvertently create DID? Maybe it's better not to open Pandora's Box?

Hypnosis seems dodgy, as with age regression, for example, it's difficult to discern between truth and confabulation (confabulation is the tendency to confuse fiction with fact). Hypnotic age regression may elicit traumatic events that have or haven't happened. Pseudo-memories can be manufactured by the patient or as the result of inappropriate suggestions made by the therapist, and unconscious compliance by the patient. This is known as False Memory Syndrome (FMS). There have been many 'retractors', those in therapy who believed they'd been sexually abused but later retracted this. Sexual abuse can be repressed (hidden from consciousness), so how would we know?

In a study of twenty retractors, of the fourteen respondents who developed visualisations of childhood sexual abuse during the course of group therapy, all but one reported similar or identical memories as those shared by other group members. Typical comments were 'we had very similar alters and memories. One woman would feel left out because she didn't have a particular alter like everyone else had, and she wanted it' and 'if you don't have a memory you feel like you have to come up with one to compete with everyone' (Nelson and Simpson, 1994). No danger.

It seems pertinent to consider Gail McDonald's story, a retractor who wrote about her experience with incompetent therapy with a hypnosis base, because it highlights the malleability of the mind and the perils of visualisation. Thus, Gail's presenting problem was low self-esteem, unhappiness, excessive booze and drugs, and she felt anger towards her alcoholic father.

Very early in her treatment, her therapist hinted that she was sexually abused during childhood. Her problems were understood to be the product of repressed sexual abuse and despite her having no memory, her therapist assured her this was common. He introduced the idea of a 'wounded inner child' and the technique of guided imagery, in which she was to imagine a safe-spot where she could retreat and explore her feelings undisturbed. Her safe-spot was a meadow surrounded by trees with a brook flowing through it.

As it transpired, Gail was 'coming apart at the seams', ruminating over the alleged sexual abuse, and so she did as her therapist advised and went to her safe place. However, she discovered she wasn't alone, but rather seven young people were there. Her therapist interpreted this as evidence of DID. The young people she fantasised with considerable clarity were interpreted by him as alter personalities, each harbouring memories she could not remember.

An intensification of symptoms followed, and she began to hear voices that were accompanied by severe headaches. Her therapist interpreted these voices as belonging to alters, and the headaches as stemming from blocks in the unconscious. The next three years were dreadful, as she spiralled to a new 'low'. She slept an average of three hours a night, lost weight, was physically run down, and lost her job as she became unreliable. Her therapist encouraged her to join a support group for women with DID. As a result, she began experiencing time-losses, during which time she would self-mutilate. She said it wasn't long before every member of the group was also self-mutilating on a regular basis.

Her therapist further convinced her she had been satanically ritually abused by the priests and nuns of a catholic school she attended during childhood, which unleashed further 'memories' of incest and sexual abuse. A friend suggested that her therapy seemed counterproductive and that she should take a break from her therapist and support group. So she did, and within a few weeks the voices began to diminish (although they did not disappear completely), her appetite returned, she began to sleep full nights, and she stopped self-mutilating. So, the moral of the story is, be wary of trance states and creating 'safe spots' in your mind, as you might inadvertently invite company? And beware of dodgy therapists.

Alter personalities can however be smarter and more talented than the core personality, which suggests it's a superpower as opposed to illness? Like, John of God, for example, a famous Brazilian surgeon who's considered a miracle man. Contrary to his core self, Senor Joao Teixeira, who is right-handed with very poor eyesight, when he's John of God, he's left-handed with perfect eyesight. John of God has treated millions, cutting out tumours etc, with some success. He maintains he allows 'spirit doctors' to take over his body to heal others. Like those with DID, he has no recollection of what happens when in his alter.

He states that he communicates with spirits when he goes into a trance. Some believe he's a medium for God. Thus, unlike DID, it seems senor Teixeira is a channel for external spirits? Or there's no such thing? As it transpires, John of God ran a sex slave farm and sold babies to the highest bidder. Hundreds of women also accused him of sexual abuse during healing sessions. Pachita is notably another famous psychic surgeon, who similarly removed tumours, and even performed lung transplants, without drugs etc. Johanna Michaelsen (author), who became a Christian, wrote about her encounters with Pachita, who she assisted in Mexico. [See her book 'The Beautiful Side of Evil' (2006)].

But moreover, it came out in the wash that the CIA 'were' involved in trauma-based mind control, which accounts for the surge of people presenting at psychiatric clinics with DID from the 1970s? Untold numbers of unwitting US and Canadian citizens were abused. Literally, as the CIA destroyed 90% of the files. We're told CIA mind control operations began in the early 1950s, after WW2, when Nazi doctors were snaffled into the US under Project Paperclip. These freaks had been conducting mind control experiments on the Jews and other POW in the death camps, and they brought their mind control technology with them.

The CIA mind control project was called MK Ultra, from German Mind Kontrolle. The endeavour was to develop drugs and procedures (methods of torture) to be used in interrogation to force confessions. They equally sought to protect their own agents against interrogation from others. It's said the CIA wanted a 'truth drug' and they discovered LSD. LSD was then used in their mind control experiments, and it was given to the herd to kick start the Cultural Revolution. Furthermore, they wanted to create the perfect spy. Like, someone with DID? We're told the project was terminated in 1973. But it's understood it has continued under different names and is considerably more sophisticated.

Thus, in army bases, universities and hospitals, sadistic experiments were conducted on unwitting adults and children, (human guinea pigs), under the banner of 'national security'. Methods of trauma included starvation, putting them in cages, inflicting all kinds of torture, including sexual, physical and emotional abuse, cattle prodding, sensory deprivation, isolation, using drugs (especially LSD), hypnosis and electroshocks. As touched on, ECT wipes memory, and one woman I heard about, lost all her memories and had to be shown how to go to the toilet. In 1995 Bill Clinton issued a formal apology on behalf of the US Government.

So, they learned that by using trauma, they could split the personality. And the younger the child, the easier they are to split. Apparently, the best age to fracture the mind is from 18 months to three years. It's described as smashing a mirror, with each fragment reflecting a piece of the person. But furthermore, they could program sub-personalities. The trauma creates the dissociation, and the dissociated state is used as an opening to hypnotically induce an alter personality.

When the conscious mind absconds, the unconscious mind is wide open and very suggestible. Apparently, a single trauma can create more than ten alters to be programmed. People can be programmed to be anything from sex slaves to drug mules, assassins, and spies. Like, they could take a patriotic American and give him a rabid communist alter to infiltrate the Soviets. They can create new memories for victims.

So, they learned how to create mind slaves, so called Manchurian candidates. The hypnotherapist implants specific phrases and codes, to trigger the newly created alters, and they can be called up whenever. Thus, the person is activated by a trigger and switches into the prescribed alter and performs whatever task. And then they switch back having executed the mission, none the wiser (which bodes well for interrogation purposes).

Alters are notably sustained by 'anchors', which are hypnotic reinforcements to keep them plugged into the programme. Mind control victims have two basic controllers, namely, their programmer, and their owner who 'handles' them. The 'handler' is trained to maintain and control the slave on behalf of the programmer.

Programmers use scripts from movies and books etc as mind programming tools. A mind control script is like operating software on which the system is built. Common mind control scripts include Alice in Wonderland, The Wizard of Oz, Star Wars, Star Trek, and alien abduction movies. Programmers build entire worlds, from these fictional scripts, for alters to dwell in. Trauma based mind control victims will believe anything in their dissociated state. Thus, when the victim is tortured, they can escape into these worlds. They can go over the rainbow, or through the looking glass. The conscious mind does a shoot to a safe place.

It's noted, that mind control goes back to the early 1940s with Dr George Estabrooks (1895-1973), who was able to create mind slaves through hypnosis alone. Estabrooks, Chairman of the Colgate University Department of Psychology and advisor to the military on hypnosis, claimed he could hypnotise people to commit treason, murder and other crimes. He claimed he used hypnosis to create super spies able to carry messages and perform missions without conscious knowledge of what they're doing. In 1942 he said, 'I can hypnotise a man, without his knowledge or consent, into committing treason against the US'.

He draws a parallel with DID i.e. hypnotised people don't know what they've been up to, just as people don't know what their alters have been up to. Estabrooks also introduced hypnotising US soldiers into losing their fear of death and overcoming their reluctance to kill. He was a Rhodes Scholar, and anything to do with Cecil Rhodes is suspect, as we'll get to.

So, people can be hypnotised to execute the deep state's nefarious agenda. Like, it's believed that Sirhan Sirhan who killed JFK's younger brother Bobby was hypnotised. He had no recollection of the event, and apparently during pre-trial psychiatric examinations, he proved to be the ideal hypnotic student. It's alleged 'RFK must die' was written in a hypnotic trance. The CIA killed RFK four and a half years after they killed JFK.

It's purported that when people are under mind control, they're robotic i.e. they can't think or question for themselves. It's like they have a child persona. So, there's hypnosis. And then there's fracturing people's minds and programming them with alter personalities.

Like, it's said that John Lennon's assassin, Mark David Chapman, was a victim of MK Ultra mind control. Chapman claimed he took offence with Lennon's atheism, and said his murder saved innocent children from Lennon's corruption. After shooting Lennon in 1980, as he was trained to, Chapman remained at the crime scene and calmly read his book 'The Catcher in the Rye' by JD Salinger until he was arrested.

John Hinckley, who attempted to assassinate Ronald Reagan in 1981 but failed, was also in possession of this book. And apparently Harvey Lee Oswald, the CIA patsy for JFK, also had this book, as did Sirhan. It's said they all had the same type of mad ramblings written on their notepads, like 'JoHn LEnNON mUST Die sAYs CatCHeR iN tHe Rye', and 'KeNNeDY MuSt dIE SAys CaTCHeR in THe rYe' etc. As touched on, it's purported that Lennon was taken out by the CIA because he was going to blow the whistle on their mind control operations (how ironic).

It's understood that mind control comes in many forms. Like, the herd are mind controlled through propaganda and the cult of celebrity. But then there's total mind control, like mind-controlled slaves, which are completely undetectable. Moreover, beyond military application, its alleged mind control bleeds into the entertainment industry and other sectors of society.

Like, besides creating the perfect spy, mind magicians can create the perfect actress or musician or athlete. These prodigies can endure gruelling schedules, because when one personality is exhausted, another can take its place. They're also used in porn and snuff films (when the person is actually murdered). It's alleged there's millions of mind control slaves worldwide, who don't know they're mind controlled slaves.

Whilst we'll get back to mind control, it's noted that covert CIA operations are linked with Satanic Ritual Abuse (SRA). SRA was also out in the open from the 1970s. It's associated with the elites, the powerful and wealthy. It's understood those born into satanic families are cracked from birth. Suffice to say, that witnessing horrific satanic rituals, like child and animal sacrifices, is sufficient trauma to shatter young minds. It gets a lot darker, as it's rumoured that satanic families run the world. And it gets a lot weirder, as alters can be demonised. That is, demons can be attached to alters, creating super humans. However, we'll get to all this craziness in Part 2.

'Beyond the limited realm of the senses, the shallow pool of the known, is a great untameable ocean and we don't have a fucking clue what goes on in there'... 'My belief is that we do not currently operate on a frequency of consciousness that is capable of interpreting the information required to understand the great mystery'. Russell Brand, 2014 p.48 and p.62

5

The Curious Unconscious

Senor Sigmund Freud (1856-1939), the Father of modern psychology, is credited with being the first to talk about the unconscious mind and its role in human behaviour. [Paracelsus was the first to theorise about an 'unconscious' that could cause disease]. Freud was initially inspired by hypnosis, but subsequently binned that particular practice because of the problem with pseudo-memories (FMS) and confabulation. Freud was cautious about suggestibility. He then developed psychoanalysis as his method of choice for exploring the unconscious. The endeavour was to talk about our thoughts and feelings, rather than get a haemorrhage. It turns out that being honest, and not hiding from ourselves is fruitful.

So, we'll start with Freud and then we'll address Jung's theory. Carl Jung (1875-1961) was an early supporter of Freud because of their shared interest in the unconscious. And Jung was sex-pest Freud's beloved pupil and potential heir, until he wasn't. Jung dared to stretch the psyche's horizon.

It's understood that Dr Freud wanted to make a name for himself. This included championing cocaine as a cure for morphine addiction, which was disastrous. As it transpires, Freud was partial to coke. He said it made him feel more like a man (LOL). Maybe it inspired his preoccupation with sex, and coloured his judgement? He was also partial to cigars, his oral fixation?

Whilst Freud is both revered and denigrated, he revolutionised psychiatry since he actually listened to his patient's life story. In the late 1800s, at the end of the Victorian era, those people who were not OK received barbaric treatment e.g. cold baths, lobotomies, drugs, and various other abuses. It's also noted, that STDs (like syphilis) caused much madness (apparently 1:10 had an STD). Freud studied hysteria, and observed that spastic tics and speech impairments were not physical problems but rather psychological. They stem from conflicts in childhood. He introduced the idea of the unconscious, where we bury our conflicts, including painful memories.

Freud (the godless Jew) was inspired by Darwinism and deducted that we're like animals. Thus, we have needs and instincts, and we adapt to our environment. And for some reason, we have evolved meta-cognition aka thinking about thinking (we became sophisticated and introspective). As mentioned, Freud wrongly believed our attachments were secondary to our need to feed. Like chimps, we're designed to attach, and it's always possible we're more than naked apes? Maybe we're God's children, made in His image?

Freud notably damned religion as an infantile desire for parental protection. And he regarded religion as a collection of irrational ideas that enchain people's minds and suppress their instincts towards mental growth. In essence, belief in God is psychopathology. However, despite Freud's insistence that religion is 'neurosis of the mind', it's understood his psychodynamic model of personality theory was inspired by the cabala, as we'll get to.

Freud dualistically concluded that all instincts are either life or death instincts. These instincts or drives are innate, universal, and constantly felt. Inspired by Greek mythology, he referred to Eros as the life instinct, which motivates positive behaviour, and Thanatos as the death instinct, which motivates negative behaviour. The life drive, or what Freud called libido (psychic energy), is propelled by survival, hunger, thirst, sex and reproduction. We have urges to stay alive, and at some unconscious level, keep our species alive? It's not 'normal' to want to die, (or not have kids), and yet it seems to be?

Libido means 'I desire' in Latin and came to mean sex drive in particular because Freud believed that sex was the most important need in the psyche. So, these life instincts create our libido (sexual energy), which is driven by the pursuit of pleasure and avoidance of pain. We're motivated by the 'pleasure principle'.

It's noted, that to satisfy our need for pleasure, our libido has to find an object of gratification. And once this has been secured, it directs the energy into that object through a process known as cathexis. Thus, we cathect something or someone, which is the object of our desire. Freud (1938) said, 'An instinct may be described as having a source, an object and an aim. The source is a state of excitation within the body and its aim is to remove that excitation'.

This notably happens when we fall in love. Freud explains the notorious 'butterflies' aka nervousness ceases when people become secure in their relationships. However, it seems there's always 'unrest', as we're always looking for the next hit? Maybe this pleasure seeking impulse, or lack of peace (boredom?), is looking for God?

According to Freud, Thanatos is our unconscious desire to die. This deathly nemesis promotes self-destructive behaviour, and also the 'aggressive drive', which compels us to destroy, conquer (or bully) and kill other things. Thanatos has no desire to preserve life or our species. And unlike Eros, which is associated with positive emotions and pro-social behaviours, Thanatos is associated with negative emotions such as fear, hate and anger, and antisocial acts. It seems these polar opposite instincts resonate with Plato's chariot pulled by two horses?

So, Freud observed that needs create tension, and behaviour is directed towards the reduction of this tension. But there's also a constant tension between our drives and needs, and the demands of society. Civilised living is thus a balance between needs and desires, and life is largely about dealing with these conflicts. As discussed, our pleasure-seeking id has to be reined in by our superego. Our ego has to manage the conflicts between these two psychic forces. Thus, Freud maintained personality develops out of our struggle to meet our needs. We do what it takes? And fundamentally, our personality is shaped by early childhood experiences.

But moreover, our actions are not always guided by reason, but rather irrational impulses, which can be an expression of our basic needs or drive e.g. sex. We have animal instincts and urges. And these often determine what we think, how we behave, and also what we dream. So, we're not entirely responsible for our behaviour, because much of our behaviour is beyond our control? It seems freewill is an illusion because we're at the mercy of our unconscious impulses? Freud theorised that unconscious sexual impulses begin in infancy. He stated that we're libidinously motivated from birth, as we crave bodily pleasure.

It's duly noted, the idea that we're born with a sex drive was controversial. Freud's theory of psychosexual development states that human beings, from birth, possess an instinctual libido or sex drive. The libido develops in five stages, namely, oral (0-1 year), anal (1-3 years), phallic (3-5 years), latent (5 years-puberty), and genital stages (puberty-adult). Any conflicts at these stages can birth 'fixations' later in life e.g. we may become an oral person, partial to smoking, drinking, eating, and biting our nails. Or we might develop an anally retentive personality (LOL).

Thus, despite instinctively feeling weird (?), Freud proposed that infants have some sort of sexuality. He observed that 'improper' desires manifest themselves at an early stage of childhood e.g. infants/kids like to touch their 'private parts'. Sexual infantilism refers to infants' pursuit of satisfying their libido.

But it gets worse, as Professor Alfred Kinsey (1894-1956) 'proved' children are sexual beings from birth with his disgusting 'research'. Kinsey was instrumental to changing modern attitudes about sex and sexuality. And the Kinsey Institute have been responsible for creating sex education programs worldwide, and for training sex educators. Thus, we can consider his contribution as a side-line.

'Sex scientist' Kinsey corresponded with various paedos to acquire information about child sexuality. Like, 'Mr Green' codename for Rex King, his prime source, who sexually abused at least 800 boys and girls, and explicitly recorded the details in diaries. Scientific recordings included measuring times to climax and length of erection. Like, he experimented with babies, recording the penis was 1.7 inches by 3 inches, and was erect immediately.

Green carried out 'scientific experiments' to ascertain what age boys are first capable of orgasm. For the 'experiment', he masturbated 317-1,200 infants and children, from two months old to fifteen years old, and recorded what he interpreted as orgasms. He timed the minutes to hours it took him to bring kids to orgasm. Like, he masturbated a four year old boy for twenty-four hours. Apparently, it took many years to discover masturbatory techniques to enable three-four year olds to climax. He recorded that some boys are capable of multiple orgasms, and even from five months old.

So, he raped (tortured) screaming and protesting children using a stopwatch for so-called scientific data. And rather than reporting him to the cops, Kinsey congratulated Green on his 'research spirit'. Green notably had sex with men, women, children, and animals. He had sex with all ages. Apparently, he first had sex with his grandma, but he had sex with almost all his family. Kinsey published Green's detailed findings in 1948, presenting it as scientific fact. Kinsey claimed kids could, with the experience of experienced adults, enjoy sex from the time they're born. This was a revolutionary claim.

Kinsey also researched adult sexual behaviour. He encouraged his key staff researchers to experience a wide range of sexual behaviour, including with each other. And together with outside volunteers, he filmed them at the Kinsey Institute. The endeavour was to 'study, learn and observe'. He also encouraged wife-swap and homosexuality for his scientific porn. He wanted two thousand orgasms and filmed hundreds from heterosexuals, masochism, and masturbation. Kinsey notably warned the photographer that he would lose his sensitivity and no longer be aroused by sexual behaviour.

It's said Kinsey had two lives, namely, he was married with kids publicly, but privately he was increasingly gay. It's said his research was important scientifically, but it also fulfilled his own needs. Apparently, Kinsey circumcised himself with a pocketknife and no anaesthesia, as he felt that to have pleasure, he needed pain.

His book 'Sexual Behaviour in the Human Male' (1948) was the first scientific study on sexual behaviour (his extensive research came from surveys/ questionnaires). It was compared to the atomic bomb because it was so explosive. Like, today's 'Fifty Shades of Grey'? It was credited for kickstarting the sexual revolution. Kinsey's second book was 'Sexual Behaviour in the Human Female' (1953).

In public, there was a strict moral code. Sex was for marriage in the 1920s and 1930s. Sex outside of marriage was fornication, and bestiality, homosexuality and paedophilia were not okay. Thus, Kinsey's research took sex out of the closet and made everything okay. But he further claimed that both children and adults can enjoy sex. Adults could pleasure kids by giving them orgasms at a young age. Paedophilia is not really a crime?

It's notably highlighted there's an agenda to make paedophilia acceptable. Besides having compassion for paedos, (because they're born that way?), it's arguably okay if sex is consensual between children and adults? As mentioned, young people are being deliberately sexualised. Hence, kids are showered with soft porn music videos, and schools teach masturbation. Indeed, a UN report (2009) advocates teaching masturbation to five year olds, but we'll get back to this. It's noted, that Kinsey's 'research' on childhood sexuality was quoted extensively by the Paedophile Information Exchange in a document which attempted to influence the British government to reduce the age of consent to 4 years old.

From 1948-1956 Kinsey advised governments in the US and Europe about modernising sex laws including homosexuality. He introduced his Heterosexual-Homosexual Rating's Scale aka the Kinsey Scale, which rates people from 0 (exclusively heterosexual) to 6 (homosexual), with the allusion being we're bisexual, as Freud suggested. Freud introduced the term 'innate bisexuality'. Kinsey promoted tolerance and removed oppression (religion was oppressive). So, Kinsey, the Father of the sexual revolution, played a key role in the agenda of sexualising society. We became animals with instincts. Morality has nothing to do with sex? Indeed, morality was getting in the way.

Freud was more concerned with how we deal with our sexual desires, since they're deemed improper. He observed that kids are reprimanded for playing with themselves (LOL). But according to Freud, being forbidden to have a fondle is the beginning of guilt feelings about everything connected with sexual organs and sexuality. This paves the way for the lifelong conflict between desire and guilt.

However, maybe Freud should only speak for himself and his generation. The youth of today have forever got their hands down their pants (especially the chavs). Back in the day, it was really only Michael Jackson who touched himself there, and for some reason that seemed socially acceptable. But these days, it's cool to hold onto one's genitals. There's no shame. Perhaps it's okay for kids to learn to keep that behaviour private, and to wash their hands afterwards? Thus, unlike today, sex was taboo. It was hidden from conscious awareness and it was making people twitchy. Hence, Freud set out to address the twitchiness.

So, in addition to our conscious mind, Freud deducted that we have a far larger unconscious mind, which is much more important in shaping our personality than the conscious mind. Indeed, Freud regarded our conscious mind as the tip of an iceberg above sea level. Thus, the majority was hidden. The unconscious mind, which exists below sea level, is therefore anything that is not conscious.

Freud further distinguishes the preconscious from the unconscious, since we can sometimes remember events or experiences, which were otherwise forgotten. Thus, he referred to those things we can remember if we think about it, as existing in the preconscious. Phenomena like having 'something on the tip of our tongue' demonstrate how unconscious material is just lurking behind the veil of consciousness. And eureka moments show how otherwise unconscious material can slip through the 'half open door' to the conscious mind. We can surprise ourselves. The preconscious is likened to long term memory.

Plato notably used the metaphor that catching memories is like catching a bird from an aviary. The idea is that as kids, we have an empty aviary or receptacle, but this fills up with birds, which stands for pieces of knowledge. But sometimes we can't catch them although we possess them. It seems events are absorbed subliminally by the personal unconscious, hence insignificant memories are forgotten. The ego is the gatekeeper, which decides what is ignored, allowed or repressed.

Whilst our unconscious can be seen as a collection of all experiences to date, many of which we have forgotten, Freud specifically reserved the unconscious for things we have repressed. We repress things because they're too awful for the conscious to bear. Repression is the 'unconscious forgetting' of events, since all things considered it's the healthiest thing to do. Like, traumatic events, including sexual abuse etc, may be repressed because our ego can't tolerate thinking about it. Like with DID, the person dissociates and hides the abuse somewhere beyond the conscious mind. We block out painful trauma. We create amnesiac barriers around events in our minds.

Repression's a defence mechanism, and defence mechanisms are derivatives of basic emotions. They protect us, because they never let us experience an emotion we can't deal with. They keep threatening ideas out of consciousness. They defend our (vulnerable) ego. Thus, a situation makes us feel a particular way, emotions are triggered and we react, which frequently involves the use of defence mechanisms. Like, we might be in 'denial', because the truth's too hard to face. And we often 'rationalise' situations. That is, we don't give the real reason for our actions because the real reason is unacceptable. So, we make up excuses?

Freud highlighted that our basic needs can be disguised or 'sublimated' which effectively steer our actions. Sublimation occurs when we unwittingly transform our conflicted emotions, unmet desires or unacceptable impulses, into positive outlets e.g. go for a run to deal with stress. Or we might 'project' our undesirable qualities onto other people. With projection, we transfer the characteristics we're trying to repress, our unacceptable feelings and impulses, onto others. We call them out for who we are?

With 'displacement', we transfer our emotions from the person who is the target of our frustration to someone else entirely e.g. kick the family pet (or punch the wall or door). 'Regression' is another common defence mechanism. Thus, in times of stress, we regress to an earlier stage of development, becoming more childish. We lapse into the child ego state? Like, if we're depressed, we might regress by going to bed. And there's 'reaction formation' e.g. we might be homophobic because we have underlying homo issues?

Ego defences are natural and normal, but if they get out of hand, neuroses can develop such as anxiety states, phobias, obsessions, or hysteria. The neurotic person goes over and beyond at repressing the unacceptable. And Freud recognised that repressing forbidden thoughts and desires could lead to mental illness (we also repress aggression). He observed how numerous forms of neurosis or psychological disorders can be traced back to conflicts in childhood. Like those who acutely experienced a conflict with desire and guilt. He observed that hysteria manifests when recalling sex abuse from childhood. The repression of trauma in early childhood resulted in hysterical symptoms.

Thus, in addition to traumatic events, we also repress unacceptable desires and urges. Like, we might have an overwhelming desire for something that's unacceptable in society, so we have to get rid of it. Like, lusting after the family pet? We have to stash the dodgy desire somewhere we can't think about it, and where better than the deep vast blue ocean.

As mentioned, our superego develops, which tells us when our desires are good or bad, but this further includes erotic and sexual desire. Indeed, Freud proposed that our superego develops from fear of reprisal for entertaining incestuous thoughts. He theorised that we have some interesting childhood fantasies. Like, we lust after our parents. But we repress our sexual feelings for them, which results in the 'Oedipus Complex' for boys and the 'Electra Complex' for girls.

In tandem with the oedipal legend, (Oedipus killed his father and became his mother's lover), Freud proposed that we have unresolved incestuous desires for sexual gratification, and same sex parents are rivals. For the son, the father is competition for the mother's attention, and for the daughter, the desire for her father as a sexual or love object means competition with the mother.

It's noted, that Jung believed our superego, or what he called the 'moral complex', develops from fear of being abandoned by our mother i.e. because we're unacceptable, not because of incestuous thoughts. Jung was forty years ahead of his time, in terms of recognising the importance of attachment. Jung maintained that incest taboo was primary i.e. it existed a priori and was not derived from the father's prohibition of the boy's lust for his mother, as Freud insisted. Oedipal longings were the consequence of incest prohibition rather than its cause. Being forbidden to have something, makes us want it?

This incestuous fantasy begins in the phallic stage. And for girls, it's spurred on by 'penis envy'. The penis becomes the organ of principal interest to both sexes in this stage. Young girls experience anxiety (an existential crisis?) upon the realisation that they do not have a penis. Apparently, we desire a penis, and the power it represents, hence we develop 'penis envy'. The solution to our problem, is obtaining our father's penis. We sexually desire our fathers, and desire to eliminate/replace our mothers.

Apparently, we blame our mothers for our apparent castration, which we regard as punishment by her, for being sexually attracted to our father. However, we need to learn from our mothers, mimic her, before we can replace her. Thus, we identify with our mothers. As it transpires however, we anticipate these desires will result in punishment, and so we employ the defence mechanism of 'displacement' to shift the object of our sexual desire from our father to men in general.

The parallel reaction of a boy's realisation that women do not have a penis is 'castration anxiety'. It's possible their fathers will castrate them for being sexually attracted to their mums. Boys also recognise their fathers are fierce competition, so they equally backpedal, employing displacement to shift the object of sexual desire from their mothers to women in general.

Freud said that women become envious of penises at a young age, when they realise boys derive more sexual pleasure from their penises than girls do from their sex organs. And apparently women desire to give birth to a son, because that's as close as a woman can get to having a penis of her own. Or we can undertake gender reassignment? However, we bury this oedipal complex, so we're consciously none the wiser. Nazis notably condemned Freud, and burned his books, stating it was Jewish porn (LOL).

So, we bury unacceptable thoughts. We stash them in the 'unconscious'. However, despite our best effort at keeping these forbidden thoughts at bay, Freud highlights that whatever we suppress will nevertheless on its own accord, try to become conscious. This explains why we Freudian 'slip up'. Indeed, Freud constructed his concept of the unconscious from analysis of parapraxes, like slips of the tongue.

So, whilst it seems that we accidentally slip up, Freud contended these slips are neither accidental nor innocent. But rather, our unconscious is trying to communicate with us by revealing unconscious ken. Our psyche (innately) wants to be healed. It wants to be whole again. We need to redress what we've hidden because it's making us unwell. Freudian slips can thus be considered unconscious wisdom, where self-revelation and truth are helpful.

Slips of the pen are like slips of the tongue. Automatic writing or psychography is produced without conscious awareness. It stems from the writer's unconscious and is a method for our unconscious to communicate with us. However, according to mediums and psychics, 'automatic writing' can be carried out by spirits. Automatic writing is typical of mediumship. Mediums and psychics claim the departed spirit guides the pen. People who conduct automatic writing describe their hand as being forcibly moved to write, stating their hand is gripped by a force.

Like, the renowned Portuguese poet and writer, Fernando Pessoa (1888-1935), advised he would suddenly feel like he was 'owned by something else' or having a very curious sensation in the right arm which was lifted into the air without his will. He also 'emptied' himself like a medium, allowing himself to be taken over by a series of personae, under whose names he wrote different types of poems with very different voices.

Trance mediums notably withdraw from the conscious state, (they go into a trance), to allow a spirit to communicate. It's like DID in that the core self is parked, and another personality comes out to play. And like DID, sometimes the channeller can speak in different languages and perform actions and skills that are quite foreign to them. The extent to which the channeller is 'taken over' varies considerably but if the takeover is powerful enough, a channel's mannerisms, voice and facial features can change i.e. taking on the appearance of others' face, body and hands.

In his book, 'The Paranormal World of Paul McKenna' (1997), he mentions a well-known channeller, Jane Roberts, who channelled for a spirit named Seth. And not only did she speak in his voice (her voice became much deeper when possessed by Seth), but at one séance, the features of her face changed shape, and at another her hands took on the appearance of a man's.

Roberts was an author and poet, and advised that much of her work came from Seth i.e. automatically written. She went into a trance very easily, and as a result was very clever, because she was possessed by very clever 'personalities'. Presumably it could be argued that she had DID, and that Seth was an alter as opposed to a spirit? She also had an Out of Body Experience (OBE), and went out her window. And she was partial to using the Ouija board to speak to the alleged dead. Ouija boards (Ouija comes from yes in French and German) have letters and numbers placed around the edge of the board and participants ask the 'spirits' questions.

McKenna also highlights 'Rosemary' who had the 'gift' of mediumship/channelling. He wrote, 'Rosemary felt the familiar and dreadful sensation creeping over her: her face being tugged aside, pulled away from her. Her face went white and she said she felt a powerful force take control of her body, paralysing her, pushing her down into the sofa as if beneath a crushing weight' (p.11). He states that Rosemary also seen apparitions regularly, so she had schizophrenia?

Besides channelling alleged dead people, trance mediums also channel 'aliens' who claim they're from different star systems. And Hindu masters from Tibet and India, for example, channel spiritual entities, like 'Ascended Masters', to acquire ancient wisdom. 'Ascended Masters' are 'spiritually evolved'.

Whilst we'll get back to this otherwise craziness, it seems pertinent to consider another example, namely, David Icke's (2007) example of a communication in 1990, because people are taking these 'aliens' and their message seriously. It also sets the stage for Part 2. Icke concedes that a channel's facial features and voice can change, when a takeover is powerful enough.

Thus, he said the communicator gave the name 'Magnu'. But he doesn't consider the name important but rather the message. Icke wrote, 'What 'Magnu' said in 1990 is what is happening today with the 'awakening', or the 'shift', as some people call it' (p.557-558). People are increasingly beginning to recognise that things are not as they appear. There's a political and spiritual awakening?

Magnu advised that 'energies', surrounding our planet, are coming in and causing us to ask questions. This is causing us to re-evaluate our lives, resulting in tremendous upheaval, distress and confusion. Like, relationships are breaking down because people are not on the same inquisitive page. And how could you be in a relationship with someone who doesn't question the point? We're questioning what we should do with our lives. To find purpose?

Magnu claims his allegiance with our planet goes back to an Atlantean period, when 'energies' and knowledge were in abundance. These were however withdrawn to prevent catastrophe on our planet. At that time, knowledge was only distributed to a selected few, taught in temple settings. There were grades of initiation and those who passed the full initiation were known as the 'Guardians of the Light and the Keepers of the Secret Knowledge'.

Magnu explains that energy is consciousness. The energies themselves contain the knowledge and information which is beginning to awaken in our consciousness. By integrating 'energies' into our consciousness, we can raise our consciousness level. As a result, we have 'memories' of Atlantis, (which suggests we've been reincarnated?) and we remember we have superpowers. Like, we can communicate with dolphins and whales, levitate, manifest things, and cause spontaneous combustion. We remember who we really are and where we come from, namely, Atlantis?

Magnu states he looks forward to a time on our planet when these energies, this knowledge, is reawakened and reintegrated into consciousness. When our whole planet is awakened. This knowledge is no longer strictly reserved for those in mystery schools and secret societies. But rather it's for us all. Everything is being revealed? We can all have special knowledge (powers) courtesy of these energies. It seems these intelligent energies are daemons that we integrate into our consciousness? 'Light Workers' are notably used as catalysts to feed in ever more 'energies'.

Whilst David Icke acknowledges, 'It is right to be careful about psychic or channelled communications because much of it is tosh for many reasons', he seems to think Magnu is a 'good guy'. Because what he said sounds right and makes sense? Like, things are not as they appear to be. Indeed, it seems there's something funky going on, and people are beginning to question? Magnu's version of events also corroborates with historical, philosophical and religious texts. Like, Plato told us about Atlantis. It's possible there was a pre-Flood world?

It seems people naively trust the information they're given? But maybe we should want to know who the message is from? Since if they can lie to us about their name, and who they are, they can lie to us about other things? Maybe these seemingly benevolent entities are not what they appear to be? Maybe they want us to believe their message because it serves them. They could be agents of a nefarious agenda that does not have our best interests at heart. Moreover, it seems these 'energies' awaken our otherwise dormant spirit body, hence we can perform otherwise miraculous tasks? Thus, Dr Rebecca Brown would call these 'energies' demons. Like, we can levitate with their assistance.

But not for Freud, who denounced spirits. And we don't have spirit bodies that are currently out of action. Freud claimed that mediums are merely mediums for their own unconscious. Despite some mediums, when in a trance, revealing remarkable and inexplicable knowledge and abilities, and speaking in an alien voice, Freud insists all this stems from our own personal unconscious.

For Freud, the unconscious was a dumping ground, a place of forgotten memories. He was convinced that everything we have seen and experienced is stored subsea, and all these impressions can be recalled. Thus, if we go into a trance, and speak in a language that we don't know, like Japanese, Freud would argue that we must have heard the language at some point. And ancient languages like Sanskrit and Aramaic? Perhaps Freud was in denial, because it seems unlikely.

Freud likened automatic writing to hypnotised people saying and doing things when hypnotised, and sleep walking and talking. He insisted there are no spirits or ghosts of Christmas past, but rather unconscious factors at play. And perhaps we'd rather believe this? Albeit it seems bemusing that our unconscious could forcibly move our hand to write?

It's like mysterious Ouija boards enable communication with our unconscious, not spirits? Ouija boards are notably marketed as 'games' in some countries, and they're illegal in others. So, there's disagreement regarding the reality of spirits. However, we'll get back to this, as it's well documented that crazy shiz happens when people play with the Ouija board. We intuitively know there's something dodgy about the Ouija board?

Besides Freudian slips, other parapraxes notably include forgetfulness or thought blocking (as mentioned, thought-blocking is symptomatic of schizophrenia), misplacement of objects, and other thought errors that reveal unconscious wishes or attitudes. It seems something disturbs our consciousness, ergo we forget? It's like dissociation?

So, Freud was curious about the unconscious. And he believed the origin of neuroses invariably leads to 'forgotten' issues in childhood. Thus, he developed 'depth psychology' or 'psychoanalysis' as a method for delving deep into the patients mind to elucidate the adverse/traumatic experiences (that have been suppressed for however many years) which have caused their psychological disorders. He wanted to capitalise on what the unconscious has to say for itself. The unconscious was the key to the mental lock.

Psychoanalysis is thus a talking-therapy 'to make the unconscious conscious'. Patient's ramblings revealed underlying conflicts. Repressed thoughts are unveiled by conversation. As touched on, one of his techniques was 'free association', which involved letting the patient lie in a relaxed position and freely saying whatever came into their mind (however random, embarrassing, grim or seemingly irrelevant). The idea was to source the trauma. Freud posited that the patient needs to consciously process such content, however painful, to get better. Talking about sex and feelings was a Freudian revolution.

Freud was also interested in dreams and was a pioneer in the use of dreams to explore the unconscious mind. In his book, 'The Interpretation of Dreams' (1900), he explains how our unconscious mind tries to communicate with our conscious mind through our dreams. Rather than dreams being arbitrary psychological output, he said, 'The interpretation of dreams is the royal road to the unconscious activities of the mind'. Dreams are an outlet for the unconscious and the repressed emotions that lie there. They enable any hidden agendas gaining admission to consciousness.

Freud believed that during sleep, forbidden wishes are liberated from their daytime inhibition. And thus, dreams are not random but rather all dreams are wish fulfilments. The trouble however is that such wishes are disguised. This is because, even when we sleep, censorship is at work regarding what we permit ourselves. We're still banal anal. This censorship or repression mechanism is considerably weaker when we're asleep than awake, but it's still strong enough to cause our dreams to distort the wishes we cannot acknowledge. This sense of censorship resonates, as I've noticed that in my dreams, while I'm less bridled, I still seem have to have my morals and values. It's like being on the sauce, we know what we're doing?

Freud explains the forbidden nature of dreams, (our sexual sordid truth), threatens the ego, making it susceptible to waking up. Hence, our superego (censor) causes the forbidden wish to be disguised and appear in a form that will neither disturb the ego nor wake the dreamer. So, the function of dreams is to prevent content waking us up by having unacceptable wishes transformed into a set of acceptable wishes. He said, 'all dreams are in a sense dreams of convenience... They serve the purpose of prolonging sleep', and 'dreams are the guardians of sleep'.

Freud maintained that content featured in the manifest dream (its material or scenario) is always inspired from the previous day, but the dream contains a deeper meaning which is hidden from consciousness. Freud referred to these hidden thoughts as 'latent dream thoughts'. And it's these latent thoughts (the essence of the dream), which may stem from the distant past or childhood, that code or mask the dream.

'Dream work' is thus the process of converting the latent dream thoughts from its manifest dream. We need to analyse our psychic work of art, with its dense language of symbols. Freud regarded symbols as figurative representations of an unconscious idea, conflict or wish. It was substitute-formation, which effectively disguised the true meaning of the idea it represented. For Freud then, the dream is one of deception, to outwit the censor through fancy dress. Dreams are essentially codes that need to be decoded.

Jung accepted Freud's conclusion that dreams manifest content that comes from events of the previous day and childhood, but he supplemented that dreams draw on the 'collective unconscious'. He thus took the unconscious to a new deeper level. He introduced another type or sphere of unconscious.

Jung realised from a young age, that his dreams contained content from beyond himself i.e. things came to him that were not from him. His dreams propelled his belief in the existence of an ancient mind. So, there's more than just our personal unconscious at play, as Freud theorised. And we're not born a blank slate, as we inherit this universal mind. And thus, we get to Jung's more interesting theory?

As mentioned, Jung pertained to the 'persona' as the ego-conscious personality. It's our 'social mask' which forms in early childhood. It's a product of compromise between the individual and society. We need to be acceptable, and assimilate with the herd? It's imperative to build acceptable traits into the persona and keep unacceptable traits hidden or repressed in the dark lumber room of the Freudian unconscious.

Thus, Jung agreed with Freud that in addition to our ego, which represents the conscious mind, our psyche consists of a personal unconscious, which Jung called the 'shadow'. Everything we hate and fear the most is repressed in the shadow. It's where we stash our unsavoury material. It's the part that's forced out of mental awareness by the ego's defence mechanisms. Our defence mechanisms ensure its retreat to the underworld.

The shadow is the unknown in us, and can be seen as disowned personality. Jung said, the persona is 'what oneself as well as others think one is', and the 'shadow is that hidden, repressed, for the most part inferior and guilt-laden personality whose ultimate ramifications reach back into the realm of our animal ancestors...'

As unwanted as the shadow may be, it nevertheless persists as a powerful dynamic that's always skulking about. The shadow has a way of reminding us of its presence, particularly in dreams. But it can also leak/erupt e.g. anger. Hence, despite our best efforts at keeping the shadow hidden, it can spring us. Like, Jack out of the box. Freudian slips and other parapraxes surprise us. Our dark side of personality influences our emotions, thoughts and behaviours (albeit unbeknown to us).

Jung conceded that most people deny their shadow by projecting it onto others. That is, we unconsciously cast it onto others to avoid confronting it. The endeavour is therefore to deal with our shadow, the contents repressed or ignored there, so we don't project it. But furthermore, projection comes into play when something unconscious seeks to become conscious. The activated unconscious seeks expression, but projection is not a conscious process, as we're not aware we're doing it. Jung refers to the 'shadow projection', the process in which we project our 'own' condition onto others, as 'the lie'. But we'll get back to 'people of the lie', as this births psychopathy.

The Jungian goal is thus not to repress our shadow but rather integrate it with the conscious mind. The emphasis is on integration not repression. The shadow can enhance the ego by coming out of the dark, and into conscious awareness. By liberating the shadow, we may become a 'whole' psychological individual. The art of becoming conscious thus involves shedding light on darker, more negative, and asleep parts of ourselves. The good has to meet the bad and ugly. And as a result, our personality becomes more vibrant, richer and varied.

What distinguishes Jungian psychology is there are two centres of personality. Thus, the ego is the centre of consciousness, but the Self is the centre of the total personality. The Self includes consciousness and unconsciousness, and is therefore both the centre and the whole of the personality. Whilst the Self represents the psyche as a whole, it's in the background whereas the ego is in the foreground.

The ego masks the Self (despite our social mask being a small part of our personality), hence the process of discovering our Self. The Self relates to the ego through the medium of consciousness. According to Jung, the Self can only be realised as the product of individuation, which is the process of integrating one's personality. We need to reconcile the unconscious with the conscious mind. Thus, we need to embrace our shadow, and learn from it.

It's also noted, that rather than conceiving psychic energy or libido as wholly sexual, Jung considered it a generalised life force, undifferentiated psychic energy, of which sexuality was but one mode of expression. Jung believed the purpose of one's life was to reach one's potential. And the purpose of psychic energy was to motivate the individual in a number of important ways, including spiritually, intellectually and creatively.

So, Jung endorsed the Freudian view that 'Man is the puppet of his own unconscious, and when the latter has a clear light thrown upon it, he will become master of himself'. And he concurred that healing the psyche involves increasing consciousness, by making what's available in the unconscious more conscious, where awareness is healing. But two of Freud's basic assumptions were unacceptable to Jung. Namely, that human motivation is exclusively sexual, and also that the unconscious mind is entirely personal and peculiar to that individual. For Jung, Freud's thinking was reductionist/narrow. Jung 'knew' there was something more curious about the unconscious.

It's said, an anxious Freud pulled aside his young protégé and designated successor, stating 'My dear Jung', he cautioned, 'promise me never to abandon the sexual theory. That is the most essential thing of all'. As it transpired however, Jung publicly criticised Freud's theory of the Oedipus complex and his emphasis on infantile sexuality (which did not go down well with Sigmund).

But Jung further theorised that beyond our personal unconscious, we inherit a collective unconscious. This impersonal collective unconscious is a kind of memory, or type of library, that stores all the images and ideas that have accumulated during eons of evolution. So, this might explain the otherwise inexplicable knowledge of Japanese, Sanskrit or Aramaic?

Jung said the collective unconscious is the 'psychic residue of human evolutionary development'. It contains the entire psychic heritage of man. So, we inherit this ancient mind, and we build our private life on this dynamic substratum. It's the foundational structure upon which the personal unconscious and ego are built.

Jung highlights this shared memory, unconscious infrastructure, common to all humanity, is reflected in all human customs and institutions. Our universal myths and legends demonstrate our shared psychic database. Jung studied myths and religions, and recognised they shared themes and symbols. 'Universal archetypes' are found in beliefs, myths, religions, ideas, art, music, rituals, dreams and rites of passage, the world over. It seems we're not so different. This suggests they draw from the same source, which was the same fountain his dreams drank from.

Jung's belief in the collective unconscious was confirmed when he studied delusions and hallucinations of schizophrenic patients. Their symbols and images resonated with universal myths and fairy-tales. So, the collective unconscious can be accessed through dreams and visions. A vision is momentary eruption of unconscious material onto one's conscious processes.

Jung theorised that we inherit instincts that predispose us to behave in certain ways. Like a cat is predisposed to have the nature of a cat, and has instincts to climb trees, roll on its back, and eat mice, birds and lizards. We have the natures of humans, (we have the same needs and instincts), and we inherit characteristics that determine the way we act to life's experience. Jung called these universal thoughts or dispositions to see the world in certain ways 'archetypes'. They're instinctive patterns of behaviour which organise how we experience events. And these archetypes seek fulfilment in our personality.

There's countless archetypes, like father, mother, child, hero, artist, warrior, explorer, trickster, leader, wise old man. It's asserted there are as many archetypes as there are typical situations in life. But the four main archetypes are the Self, persona, shadow, and anima/animus. The latter is our soul, which is androgynous (we have both a feminine and masculine nature). The Self is the most important archetype, as it's the archetype of wholeness, which is life's goal. These archetypes, which are like templates for behaviour, are thus tucked up in the collective unconscious. And there they remain, unless they're triggered into being. It's like they're formless and faceless until we give them life.

The idea is that we inherit a blueprint for life, which proceeds to implement itself through interaction with the environment. Archetypal determinants are actualised in response to our inner and outer events in the human life cycle. It's like genes switch on and off. The programme accounts for all stages of life i.e. each stage of life is mediated through a new set of archetypal imperatives which seek fulfilment in both our personality and behaviour.

This notably corroborates with what Ethologists call the 'Innate Releasing Mechanism' (IRM), which is primed to become active when an appropriate stimulus (called a sign stimulus) is encountered in the environment. When such a stimulus appears, the innate mechanism is released, and the animal responds with a characteristic pattern of behaviour which is 'adapted' to the situation.

Thus, an archetype is not an inherited idea but an inherited mode of functioning i.e. pattern of behaviour. Jung concedes it is the predisposition to have certain experiences that is archetypal and inherited, not the experience itself. Whilst archetypes lead to characteristic behaviour, they manifest differently in each of us.

Before an archetype can penetrate the conscious ego, it must attract relevant experience to form a complex. For example, we have a mother archetype, but it's not until we have the experience of mother that we develop a mother complex. Jung derived his concept of archetype through his theory on 'complexes'. Complexes suggest a conflict or tension, something unresolved, or 'issues' around a particular theme. We've got a 'hang up' about something. And Jung came to see complexes as rooted in archetypes. He deducted that at the core of any complex is a universal pattern of experience or 'archetype'.

Jung developed his theory of complexes through his Word Association Test. Thus, when reading out a list of a hundred words, with the subject saying the first thing that comes to mind, he recognised that certain words triggered something deep down. Emotion flares up. The emotional charge of a certain word had an immediate effect on the subject's level of arousal. The abnormal reaction i.e. time delay or inappropriate association i.e. nonsense, indicated an unconscious psychological conflict.

Jung theorised that the stimulus word had activated a complex. He observed that the emotion triggered by the complex interferes with the free flow of association. The subject's consciousness, and hence performance, had been interrupted. Unconscious tendencies had disturbed the course of conscious intentions, and this finding confirmed Freud's idea of the repressed unconscious. Jung concurred that unconscious motivations could steer behaviour, and that complexes are responsible for Freudian slips.

[In Jung's 'Studies in Word Analysis' (1906), he describes a technique of connecting the subject via hand electrodes, to an instrument measuring resistance to skin. Words were read out and again reactions varied depending on the emotional charge. Like, with lie detectors, 'resistance' reveals areas of unconscious conflict to be explored. Scientology employs a similar system to audit their members, as part of their therapy i.e. to source trauma].

Complexes tend to form as a result of internal conflicts i.e. breach of boundaries. Jung said the origin of the complex is 'frequently a so-called trauma, an emotional shock or some such thing, that splits off a bit of the psyche'. As discussed, when some part of personality is unacceptable to our parents or society (i.e. anger, rebellion, sexuality), we disown it. Or when something is too overwhelming i.e. too painful or traumatic, our psyche's defences come to the rescue and splits it off from conscious awareness. A bit of our psyche breaks off. Like the late Michael Jackson said, when his nose fell off, it's just another part of me.

The emotionally charged complex, (relating to a particular archetype), is banished to the shadow. Jung observed that the dissociated complex protects the ego from being overwhelmed, but if it's triggered later on e.g. a particular word is said, it may overwhelm the ego and bring about dissociation of the psyche. The person is tripped up by something they tried to shelf in the past. Thus, the endeavour is to bring the complex into the light of day.

So, whilst Freud posited that complexes are due to childhood trauma, which are repressed in the personal unconscious, Jung promulgated the root of the complex resides in the collective unconscious. For Jung, complexes are the personifications or manifestations of archetypes from the collective unconscious. Complexes prove archetypes?

And it's normal to have complexes. We all have them. It's normal for the psyche to dissociate and form complexes. Complexes can be positive or negative. They're the schematic building blocks of the psyche. They're the source of all emotions, influencing our attitudes and behaviour. Jung said, 'autonomous complexes are among the normal phenomena of life and they make up the structure of the unconscious psyche'. It also became apparent that complexes, which lie hidden in the shadow, undeveloped and un-integrated, could be invaluable to Self growth.

Unlike archetypes then, which exist in the collective unconscious, which exists independently and has nothing to do with our personal experiences, our complexes are personal. They're tied up with emotions, memories, perceptions and wishes. And these unconscious constructs want to be made conscious, hence our slip ups and projections e.g. way may project our father or mother complex onto a therapist.

Jung further explains there are obvious interferences and disturbances that appear to come from 'nowhere', and these manifest in ways that we can all identify with e.g. sudden confusion, a sudden change in mood, depression or anxiety states, thoughts come to us against our will (intrusive thoughts), or equally thoughts vanish against our will (thought blocking), an annoying tune pursues us all day, we have an overwhelming inability to concentrate, we may want to do something but then all of a sudden can't be hooped, or we can't sleep or have demented dreams. Jung postulates that autonomous complexes are responsible for creating these disturbances. He also noted the paradoxical experience of pathological symptoms (particularly with neurotics) like temperatures can shoot up, coupled with skin rashes etc, yet no physical anomalies.

Complexes appear to be delinquent intruders. And we can all be possessed by them. According to Jung, 'possession' happens when 'so-called complexes, take over the control of the total personality in place of the ego, at least temporarily, to such a degree that the freewill of the ego is suspended'. It's asserted that at any moment any one of us can become 'possessed' by the unconscious in such a way that it surpasses our conscious ego and animates us. Thus, we might feel like 'something' has gotten into us. We might fly into a rage and act like a maniac. We might be temporarily insane.

Indeed, Jung said, 'in fact, an active complex puts us momentarily under a state of duress, of compulsive thinking and acting, for which under certain conditions the only appropriate term would be the judicial concept of diminished responsibility'. Jung advised that those who don't acknowledge their shadow are in danger of being possessed by it. Refusing to face our shadow can make us unwell. He observed the signposts to the complex are fear and resistance. It's also noted, that the more complexes we have, the more possessed we are.

Jung explains that complexes form autonomous 'splinter psyches' within the overall personality. He wrote, 'a complex with its given tension or energy has the tendency to form a little personality of itself. It has a sort of body, a certain amount of its own physiology. It upsets the breathing, it disturbs the heart – in short, it behaves like a partial personality. For instance, when you want to say something or do something and... a complex interferes with this intention... your best intention gets upset by the complex, exactly as if you had been interfered with by a human being or by circumstances outside'.

But Jung extends this thinking, stating complexes have a life and a will of their own. Jung calls these autonomous complexes 'living units of the unconscious psyche'. He said, 'complexes behave like independent beings, a fact especially evident in abnormal states of mind'. Complexes can be likened to archipelago islands. Exiled from consciousness, or cut off from mainstream, these islands or psychic fragments have an autonomous life of their own. Thus, Michael Jackson's nose is somewhere and it's still breathing.

Jung cautions that complexes or sub-personalities or splinter-psyches have the potential to exert a powerful control over our thoughts, emotions and behaviours. Besides temporarily usurping the ego, they can act autonomously to 'take over' the psyche. They can dominate the personality which results in psychopathology i.e. neuroses, dissociative disorders and some psychoses. As Jung stated, 'Everyone knows nowadays that people 'have complexes'. What is not so well known, though far more important theoretically, is that complexes can have us'.

And they can continue to have us, or haunt us, like the ghost of Christmas past. He said, the autonomous complex 'behaves like an animated foreign body in the sphere of consciousness. The complex can usually be suppressed, with an effort of will, but not argued out of existence, and at the first suitable opportunity it reappears in all its original strength'.

It's noted, that an essential quality of being possessed by the unconscious is that we don't know we're possessed, for if we were, we wouldn't be possessed. Jung said, 'insanity is possession by an unconscious content that, as such, is not assimilated to consciousness, nor can it be assimilated since the very existence of such conditions is denied'.

He said, 'it is easier to talk or to argue with a dog or a cow, for nothing that one says permeates, it is impossible to pierce the wall they put up, it is a wall of unconscious beliefs, and people behind the wall cannot be reached. They are totally inaccessible. There is no access because the human being is degraded to the state of an animal, and the thing that seems to function is not a divine being, it is a ghost'. And yet there are no ghosts?

So, possession means to be taken over by a complex. When we're possessed by the unconscious, we become dissociated from ourselves. Like with psychosis, it seems the unconscious takes over e.g. when people see or hear psychic contents that have nothing to do with the conscious mind and current situation. Or when people have delusional ideas, opinions and convictions forcibly thrust upon them against their will. Like, they're Napoleon or the Queen of Sheba. It seems obsession and possession are similar, as obsession refers to certain ideas that have taken possession of the person, and possession means to be taken over by psychic forces?

Jung explained that in visions and voices (i.e. certain psychoses), autonomous complexes are projected as other personalities. So, the voices people hear, are the voices of their otherwise hidden complexes or sub-personalities. Jung said, 'in the voices heard by the insane they take on a personal ego character like that of the spirits who manifest themselves through automatic writing and similar techniques'. He explains that because the autonomous complex is alien to the ego, it's subjectively experienced as other than our-selves. It seems external, which gives rise to delusions and beliefs in spirit beings.

Jung acknowledged that it seems as if a strange being does speak through a patient, when the words come from an autonomous complex. Like, a different personality speaking? He states this corroborates with what the primitives relegated to possession by spirits. So, like Freud, Jung was equally able to write off spirits? That is, rather than being possessed by spirits, we're possessed by autonomous complexes. Autonomous complexes offer a key to the lock of supernatural madness. Channels are mediums for their unconscious complexes?

Jung wrote, 'Possession, though old fashioned, has by no means become obsolete; only the name has changed. Formerly they spoke of 'evil spirits', now we call them neuroses or unconscious complexes'. And also, 'the demons have not really disappeared but have merely taken on another form: they have become unconscious psychic forces'.

So, autonomous complexes are what our ancestors called demons? The madness comes from us. Not some external force. Demons are created by our psyche. We can sleep easy? Complexes were notably first acknowledged by Aristotle, who called them part souls and little personalities.

Thus, it appears we're at the mercy of our unconscious, since complexes can hijack our ego. But then there's being manipulated like a puppet, like the insane. Jung states, 'without noticing it, the conscious personality is pushed about like a figure on a chessboard by an invisible player. It is this player who decides the game of fate, not the conscious mind and its plans'. It almost seems sinister? Hence, 'possession by spirits' has historically been regarded as sinister? But it seems less sinister if we rationalise that we're doing a number on ourselves?

It seems the process of forming autonomous complexes, those exiled aspects of our being, is like the creation of alters behind an amnesia wall? As discussed, with DID the mind can split traumatic experiences off from consciousness, with alters or gatekeepers created to keep the awfulness hidden.

Jung seems to envisage dissociation as a continuum extending from 'normal' mental functioning to seriously 'abnormal' states. He said, 'Let us turn first to the question of the psyche's tendency to split. Although this peculiarity is most clearly observable in psychopathology, fundamentally it is a normal phenomenon... It need not be a question of hysterical multiple personality, or schizophrenic alterations of personality, but merely of so-called 'complexes' that come entirely within the scope of the normal'.

It's conjectured that with extreme dissociation, like DID, splinter-psyches become more autonomous and this reveals their archetypal core. These can then develop into 'alternate personalities'. Thus, whilst a sub-personality or splinter personality is distinguished from DID in that sub-personalities are merely personas or pieces of a whole, whereas DID is characterised by distinct personalities, Jung argued 'there is no difference in principle between a fragmentary personality and a complex... complexes are splinter psyches'.

But moreover, in addition to being possessed by complexes, or actual personalities, it seems we can also be possessed by archetypes? It seems archetypes are not lifeless 'templates of behaviour' until we give them life, but rather they're dynamic entities that can spring us?

Jung said, 'we know archetypes can break with a shattering force into an individual human life…'. 'It is a psychological fact that an archetype can seize hold of the ego and even compel it to act as it – the archetype – wills'. And also, 'for an archetype has a life if its own; the life that is proper and peculiar to the archetype shows its autonomy by the fact that it can swallow one's own life. It is so strong that one can be swallowed up into it and be nothing but that archetype. Of course, one does not know it'.

So, like complexes and alters, it seems archetypes also have an autonomous life of their own. They're real living entities dwelling in the depths of our unconscious minds? These independent beings live within us, but they can be projected out and appear as external entities. Which explains ghosts?

It seems the otherwise external spirit world replete with spirits dwells within our psyche. The spirits are archetypes in the collective unconscious, and they can burst out, blinding and confusing us? The collective unconscious aka spirit world is cut off from our consciousness, unless we induce Altered States of Consciousness to experience it? Like, we could go into a trance and channel archetypes?

It's an interesting proposition that we inherit a collective unconscious, which is populated by archetypes and instincts that seek fulfilment in our personality. Like, we can integrate 'energies with knowledge' into our psyche, as Magnu recommended? It seems archetypes are more than merely psychological instincts. It seems there's a difference between having the nature (personality/soul) of a human, that's bestowed with instincts, and independent archetypes/unconscious personalities that dwell in 'Never-Never Land'?

It's also noted, whilst Freud notoriously said dreams are the royal road to the unconscious, Jung countered that complexes are the royal regalia, as complexes are the engineers of dreams. Jung said, 'The via regalia (royal road) to the unconscious, however, is not the dream… but the complex, which is the author of dreams and symptoms'. Jung explains that dreams are autonomous complexes that obey their own laws. Visions are the same in that we have no control over the content i.e. dreams but in a waking state.

Dreams were also more than merely expressing (sexually) repressed emotions and unfulfilled wishes. The scope was much larger than Freud assumed, as Jung believed that dreams reflect the entire unconscious, both personal and collective. Thus, whilst our dreams are personal, we encounter the collective unconscious. We get access to that great library.

Contrary to Freud, Jung said, dreams 'do not deceive, they do not lie, they do not distort or disguise… they are invariably seeking to express something that the ego does not know and does not understand'. The dream is 'a spontaneous self-portrayal, in symbolic form, of the actual situation in the unconscious'.

So, they're not devious puzzles invented by the unconscious to be deciphered, but rather Jung believed symbols were signs, expressing something previously unknown. Dreams add something important to our conscious knowledge. They don't come to tell us something we already know but to show us something deeper.

Jung believed archetypes manifested themselves in dreams, as dream symbols and figures. Hence, certain dream symbols have the same universal meaning in every culture throughout history. Dream symbols and figures represent an unconscious attitude that is largely hidden from the conscious mind. Jung believed the psyche is a self-regulating organism, and claimed that dreams have a homeostatic and self-regulatory function.

He regarded the relationship between the conscious and unconscious mind as compensatory i.e. conscious attitudes were likely to be compensated for unconsciously (within the dream) by their opposite. Thus, dreams always stress the other side in order to maintain psychic equilibrium. Dreams effectively compensate the one-sided limitations of consciousness. Thus, the question is what attitude does it compensate?

It's noted that, although autonomous complexes are part of our psyche, these manifestations are perceived by the dreamer to be external personages. That is, we project our complexes as other personalities in our dreams.

Jung proposed two basic approaches to analysing dreams. Thus, the objective approach is that every person in the dream refers to the person they are. Like, our mum is our mum, and James Brown is James Brown. Alternatively, the subjective approach is that every person in the dream represents an aspect of the dreamer. The dream characters represent an unacknowledged aspect of the dreamer. So, if we're being chased by a psycho-killer, maybe we have psycho-killer tendencies that need to be addressed. Some theorists take it further, like we're also represented by inanimate objects.

Jung informs that in the dream world, the persona (public mask) is represented by the Self. The Self may not resemble us physically or act as we would, but we still know this 'person' is us. Jung posits that acquaintance with the archetypes, which are manifested by their symbols, enhances our awareness of unconscious attitudes.

According to Jung, the Self works incessantly towards its own realisation or individuation. Thus, dreams help to serve the goal of wholeness/completeness by making valuable unconscious material available to the whole personality. Dreams are therefore significant for personality development. And for Jung, these intriguing natural products of the psyche have more to reveal than just our unconscious, as they enable access to the ultimate source of wisdom or ultimate mind.

However, despite Jung taking the unconscious to a new curious level, both psychologists agreed that when we're dreaming, we have access to realms of knowledge and experience denied to us when awake. And also, that dreams need to be interpreted to be understood, which is anyone's guess. For Jung, the prime function of dreams is to wake up to ourselves. However, we'll get back to dreams later, when we look at Altered States of Consciousness.

In summary, it seems we have our conscious mind, and we have a personal unconscious replete with complexes. And it's possible we inherit a collective unconscious, replete with archetypes to inspire our complexes. Thus, unlike Freud who viewed the unconscious negatively, as a repository for whatever the conscious didn't want, and a source of mental illness, Jung recognised the 'unconscious' contains wisdom. There's more than just our personal unconscious at play. We have much to learn from archetypes?

Self knowledge comes from unconscious content that seeks expression. Contents can spill out from our unconscious mind, as it wants to be made conscious. And whilst it seems no good can come from complexes or 'unconscious forces' taking control of the ego, maybe a meltdown is productive if we're able to process and assimilate the material?

So, contents from the unconscious mind can usurp the conscious mind. But unlike Freud, who surmised that any weirdness comes from our personal unconscious, Jung elaborated about archetypes that dwell in some other level of unconsciousness. Which is code for spirits on some spirit plane?

It's highlighted that whilst in his professional publications, Jung refers to spirits as autonomous complexes, sub-personalities, splinter psyches etc, many believe this is a façade, as Jung always believed in the reality of the 'other world'. He believed spirits exist. So, it's always possible that otherwise crazy people are hearing the voices of spirits, which are independent of their own personal unconscious? It's possible that spirits are independent of our brain, but they can use our brain?

And some mediums do channel spirits? They allow 'spirits' access to their conscious mind? They allow them to take over and communicate messages. People who consult mediums and psychics consistently insist they disclose information there's no possible way they could have known. Like, the ability to speak foreign languages, it seems evident there's more going on than the medium's own personal unconscious. As highlighted, scientists know very little about consciousness, and even less about the curious unconscious.

'Who looks outside, dreams; who looks inside, awakes'. CG Jung

6

Carl Gustav Jung

It seems pertinent to elaborate on Jung because despite his scientific veneer, he did more than anyone to marry psychology and spirituality. And he's renowned as the Father of the New Age and Neo-Gnosticism. Jung was most chuffed to discover the writings of the Gnostics. He said, 'I felt as if I had at last found a circle of friends who understood me'. The Gnostic Gospels aka the lost gospels, thirteen leather-bound papyrus codices, were found in Nag Hammadi, Egypt, in 1945. They date to 200-400AD.

Gnosticism is a philosophy that refers to the acquisition of 'gnosis' or special knowledge. Gnostikos is Greek for 'one who knows'. Jung claimed that Gnostics were great psychologists, paying them the highest compliment possible. Jung acquired, or rather the Carl Jung Institute in Zurich did, Codex 1, typically known as the 'Jung Codex' from the Nag Hammadi library in 1951. It was intended as a birthday present for him. Gnosticism is the precursor to, or foundation of, the New World Order Religion, as we'll get to in Part 2.

Jung was always fascinated with the occult, which impelled his interest in psychiatry. As it transpired, he migrated towards his mother's eastern mystical philosophy, and rejected the established doctrines of his father's Christianity. It seems his dad's Christian stoicism was joyless, and whilst his mum was equally depressed, she was more curious?

As touched on, Freud and Jung were the best of buds, until they weren't. They corresponded from 1906-1912. Contrary to paternal Freud, Jung 'knew' there was more going on than what we see. Some funky things appear to be happening behind the material veil, and so he flew the cuckoo's nest to find his own eastern inspired truth. It seems Jung's spirituality freaked Freud out, and Freud's denial kicked in. He was not prepared to lose his credibility at the expense of Jung. Russell Brand (2014) encapsulates, 'Jung the mystical sun dance kid, to Sigmund Freud's staunch Butch Cassidy' (p.71). Apparently, Jung also had a lifelong fascination with Nietzsche but realised he had to keep his distance for fear of going insane like him. All the same, let's go straight for the jugular weird.

Jung's maternal grandfather, Samuel Preiswerk, who was a minister and advocate of Zionism, apparently had 'second sight' and regularly spoke to spirits. 'Second sight' or clairvoyance is notably the ability to know or see things in the future, or which are happening in a different place. He apparently held lively conversations with the dead, which included the ghost of his deceased first wife. He even kept a chair for her in his study, as she often came to visit. Apparently his second wife, Augusta (Jung's granny), who was also a clairvoyant, got jealous of the ghost wife (LOL).

The vicar always believed himself to be surrounded by ghosts. Jung said, 'My mother often told me how she had to sit behind him while he wrote his sermons because he could not bear [to have] ghosts pass behind him while he was studying. The presence of a living human being at his back frightened them away!' Grandpa Preiswerk also learned Hebrew because he believed it was spoken in heaven.

Apparently Jung's mother, Emilie, also had visions. She would fall into trances and converse with the 'dead'. Apparently, she developed mediumistic powers in her late teens. Then at age twenty, she fell into a coma for 36 hours. When her forehead was touched with a red-hot poker she awoke, speaking in tongues and prophesying.

'Glossolalia' or 'speaking in tongues' is the phenomenon in which people speak in languages unknown to them, especially in religious worship. Pagan religions are saturated in glossolalia e.g. voodoo cults and shamanism. Murmuring and speaking gibberish, and making all kinds of funky sounds, including animal noises, while in a state of ecstasy, is found worldwide. Speaking in tongues seems to be some kind of spiritual language.

It's noted however, that unlike Glossolalia, which is defined by linguists as the fluid vocalising of speech-like syllables that are unintelligible, Xenoglossia is the ability to speak fluently a language the person has never learned before. Like, at Pentecost, described in the Bible, when God's people were filled with the Holy Spirit they began speaking in different languages, to preach the gospel to those who spoke those different languages. Xenoglossia is not a natural ability but rather supernatural, whereas studies have shown glossolalia is a learned behaviour. People can learn to speak in tongues (babbling is innate).

It seems Emilie also had DID, as Jung occasionally heard her speaking to herself in a voice that was not her own. She would make profound remarks expressed with an uncharacteristic authority. And this 'other' voice conspired about a world far stranger than the one the young Jung knew. Apparently, she was an eccentric and depressed woman, and spent considerable time in her bedroom, where she said spirits visited her at night. Indeed, Jung related that at night the atmosphere in his parent's house would thicken.

In 'Memories, Dreams, Reflections' (1963) he wrote, 'From the door to my mother's room came a frightening influence. At night Mother was strange and mysterious. One night I saw coming from her door a faintly luminous indefinite figure, whose head detached itself from the neck and floated along in front of it, in the air like a little moon' (p.22). Jung advised that he had repeated visions of a figure coming out his mother's room with a detachable head.

Jung was apparently an introverted schizoid child (i.e. withdrawn, aloof and self-absorbed), who chose to be alone with God rather than mix with others. But moreover, he advised that when he was three years old a spirit guide called 'Philemon' contacted him. Perhaps we can wonder about kid's imaginary friends?

This spirit was one of his teachers and tutored him all his life, although various other spirits came to him. He observed that 'Philemon and other figures of my fantasies brought home to me the crucial insight that there are things in the psyche which I do not produce, but which produce themselves and have their own life. Philemon represented a force that was not myself. In my fantasies I held lively conversations with him, and he said things which I had not consciously thought. [...] Psychologically, Philemon represented superior insight.'

Jung insisted, 'I observed clearly that it was he who spoke, not I'. Whilst it might be assumed that Philemon was a figment of Jung's imagination, or evidence of his crossing over to insanity, Jung felt that Philemon was real and he was not insane. Philemon seemed somehow dead, yet somehow 'talking' to Jung (talking to his mind). Philemon was a non-physical source of information outside of his head. So, he was hearing voices, but he's not schizophrenic?

By age twelve, and like his mum's other personalities, Jung advised that he literally became two people. He believed there was someone else lurking within, beyond his boyhood self. The 'Other', as Jung called him, was a masterful figure from the eighteenth century. He wore a white wig and buckled shoes, and drove an impressive carriage. Apparently, he held the young boy in contempt but there is the impression that Jung felt he had been this man in a past life.

It's highlighted that the collective unconscious, (the psychic reservoir of symbols that we inherit at birth), is in a sense a form of reincarnation. It's teeming with archetypes or ghosts that seek expression? Jung became convinced that his ancient personality somehow connected with his ancestors, the dead and spiritual mysteries.

In addition to Jung's spiritually haunted start in life, and with regards to supernatural phenomena, we can consider the following regularly recounted paranormal experiences involving Jung's mother. So, the first story is that Jung was studying in his room, when he suddenly heard a loud bang coming from the dining room. He rushed in and found his mother startled. The round walnut table had cracked yet there was no reasoning why. Jung thought, 'there certainly are curious accidents'. And as if his mum was reading his mind, she replied in her 'other' voice, 'Yes, yes, that means something'. So, it seems Emilie's other voice, or alternate personality, had telepathy?

Two weeks later a second incident occurred. There had been another loud noise, but this time it came from a large sideboard. Again, no one had any idea what caused it. Jung inspected the sideboard, where they kept the bread and bread knife, and he found the knife shattered into several pieces, but all neatly arranged in the breadbasket. The knife had been used earlier for tea, but no one had touched it nor opened the cupboard since. The weirdness of the caper was confirmed when Jung took the knife to a cutler, and was informed there was no fault in the steel but that someone must have broken it on purpose.

Jung kept the shattered knife for the rest of his life, and years later sent a photograph of it to psychical researcher Joseph Banks Rhine (1895-1980). Rhine founded parapsychology, which is the study of paranormal psychic phenomena. He coined the term Extrasensory Perception (ESP), which is the ability to perceive things without reference to the senses (like clairvoyance and telepathy). People seem to know things, like some kind of intuition or sixth sense.

But moreover, after these incidents, Jung became involved in a series of séances. Two of Jung's female cousins were beguiled with séances, which in turn beguiled him. Séances are sittings or meetings at which people attempt to contact the dead, usually through the agency of a medium. Jung was impressed by how real his cousin, Helene's, spirits seemed to her. She told him 'I see them before me' and 'I can touch them, I speak to them about everything that I wish as naturally as I'm talking to you. They must be real'.

Apparently, during earlier table-turning experiences within her family circle, it was discovered that Helly was an excellent medium. With table-turning or tipping, participants place their hands on the table and wait for rotations. It's similar to the Ouija board in that the spirits communicate by spelling out words and sentences (the alphabet is slowly called over and the table tilts at the appropriate letter). Helene Preiswerk was his cousin from his mother's side of the family, and apparently she was in love with him.

It's duly noted, that back in the day, before 'science' (including Freud) said otherwise, it was understood the spiritual world was as real as the physical world. And the phenomenon of seeing ghosts, for example, was direct evidence of this. Spirits were seen as external to people, but mediums could channel them. Like Helly, who channelled many spirits and produced many voices (largely the voices of dead relatives). She rarely spoke as herself, but instead referred to herself in the third person.

Sometimes she would enter a trance, fall to the floor, and breathing deeply, she would speak in old Samuel Preiswerk's voice (who she'd never met). Apparently, the ghost of Grandpa Preiswerk had first appeared to her when she was five or six. In the early séances, he was commonly the control medium, which seemed to provide some comfort. Helly only had partial recollection of what had been said during the séance. It's like she was taken over by another personality, like DID, but it was allegedly dead relatives.

Jung stated there were many séances which proved startling. Like, on one occasion Helly told the others to pray for her elder sister Bertha, who, she said had just given birth. Bertha lived in Brazil, hence Helly couldn't know this, and as it transpired Bertha gave 'Bertha' that day. On another occasion at a séance, a warning came for another sister who was also expecting a child. But the advice was that she would lose it, and sure enough, in August the baby was born premature and dead.

Séances seemed to provide a portal, making it possible to receive intelligent messages that transcend space and time. It seems spirits are able to tell us information, including future events? As it transpired, Jung was captivated by spiritualism. And he had no reservations about his young cousin allowing spirits or personalities to hijack her ego, with her personality temporarily suspended. Jung actively participated in the séances, questioning the various spirits, and was convinced that it was possible to contact spirits of the dead. They seemed alive and real.

But moreover, besides channelling otherwise 'dead' relatives, apparently the most interesting spirit that emerged when Helly was in trance was 'Ivenes'. Ivenes was her main female spirit, who spoke in a perfect High German instead of Helene's customary basal dialect. And she called herself the 'real' Helene Preiswerk. This character was much more mature, confident and intelligent than Helly, who Jung described as absent-minded, and not particularly bright, talented, or educated. Helly was a nervous teenager, whereas Ivenes was an older, serious, even sorrowful person. Ivenes advised that she lived through many reincarnations where she had been married to various noblemen. It's noted, that spirits invariably promote reincarnation. Like, 'Seth' (who Jane Roberts channelled) claimed he was a reincarnated 'personality energy'.

Jung wondered if this fuller, more commanding personality was buried beneath the otherwise unremarkable teenager (like his 'Other'). He described Helly as leading a real 'double life' with two personalities existing side by side or in succession, each continually striving for mastery. He inferred that Ivenes was the adult personality developing in Helene's unconscious, and thus that the real work of personality development proceeds at an unconscious level. Jung mused that what emerges from the unconscious may be 'attempts of the future personality to break through'. Indeed, this insight into the psyche informed his later theory of 'individuation', the process of 'becoming who you are'. So, Ivenes wasn't a spirit possessing Helly's conscious mind?

Jung's mission was thus 'to pursue his profound curiosity about occult and spiritualistic matters'. Based on his interest in spiritualism, which included Helly's hypnotically induced séances, channelling spirits and fortune telling, and the poltergeist like phenomena (the spontaneous splitting of the dining room table, and the shattering of the knife), Jung decided to study psychiatry in 1898. Indeed, these events inspired his doctoral dissertation, namely, 'On the Psychology and Pathology of So-called Occult Phenomena'.

And so it was, that having started medical school, Jung continued to meet secretly with a circle of female relatives to contact the spirit world. And for over two years, he attended and recorded Helene's séances, with his meticulously detailed observations forming his thesis.

As it transpired however, Helly became quite 'unwell'. Sometimes Helly's spirits would take over her in the middle of conversations, in shops and in the street. She also spoke about being led away from her body by the spirits on distant journeys (we'll get to OBEs and astral projection). Her so-called visions were generally pleasant, but occasionally they were demonic and terrifying, and they usually resulted in severe headaches. Helly seemed to get better, or as Jung would say, more integrated. She blossomed into a successful dressmaker in France, although she died at only twenty-six.

It seems Jung endeavoured to quasi-scientifically theorise about this seemingly spiritual affair. He had to rationalise the supernatural, since 'science' is confident there's no spirit world. Ghosts are a figment of our imagination? And it would appear Helly had DID? She wasn't being taken over by spirits, obviously, but rather her 'unconscious'. These autonomous entities had to be 'unconscious psychic forces'. As Jung pointed out, what primitive people regarded as spirits and demons were really autonomous complexes? People are possessed by autonomous complexes, which accounts for the strange beings speaking through them.

Jung observed that the 'personalities' revealing themselves were totally dissociated and autonomous. He explained her 'visionary experience' and the 'personality' she channelled represented contents of her unconscious that were completely dissociated from her waking consciousness. Thus, channelling and possession are dissociative states, and hearing voices and seeing ghosts is psychosis and delusion? It seems content from our unconscious spills over? Some archetype is seeking expression?

Fundamentally, Helly's trances alerted him to the existence of part-personalities made up of dissociated components. The seemingly autonomous personalities provided evidence for the dissociability and unconscious functioning of the psyche. This led him to his theory on complexes, then archetypes. As Jung highlighted, the complex can usually be suppressed with an effort of will, but at the first suitable opportunity, it reappears in all its original strength. Presumably this explains why Helly continued to get taken over by otherwise spirits?

But what about Ivenes, who claimed to be the 'real' Helene Preiswerk? It's highlighted that it's not clear why Ivenes would need to be repressed, since she was ideal and virtuous, unlike many of Helly's other 'alters' who were skanks. More generally, it seems too weird that Helly could speak and act exactly the same as Grandpa Preiswerk and co? Like, it's weird that poor sighted Joao Teixeira de Faria metamorphoses into left-handed John of God with perfect eyesight?

However, instead of channelling 'spirits', Jung was insistent that Helly was unwell, having some kind of dissociative disorder. He highlighted that Helly and her fourteen siblings 'suffered a great deal from the inconsequent, vulgar, and often brutal treatment they received from their mother'. This suggests Helene's childhood trauma could have predisposed her to dissociation. Apparently Helly was hurt by his diagnosis. Helly was convinced the visions were real, and then Jung said otherwise. Jung wrote, 'She absolutely would not listen to the idea that the manifestations were a kind of illness. Doubts about her health or about the reality of her dream-world distressed her deeply; she felt so hurt by my remarks'.

Perhaps Helly's 'condition' was created through dodgy hypnosis. Perhaps she wouldn't have succumbed to DID and seeing ghosts, had she not been into the occult and partial to trance states? It's understood that many people become 'psychologically unwell' as a result of engaging with unseen forces aka unconscious psychic forces. And maybe she continued to go along with it because she was in love with him, and he used her for the purposes of research, like a lab rat?

Jung rendered ghosts an archetypal function of human experience, not an objectively existing metaphysical entity. He explained the 'ghosts' he saw during séances were 'exteriorizations' of archetypal images within his mind, originating in the collective unconscious of the human race. In this sense, the archetypes of the collective unconscious (which can be accessed through dreams and visions) are the true sources of the supernatural.

Jung regarded mediums as attempting to filter these archetypes from the unconscious to the conscious, like analytic psychology, with the difference being that mediums acknowledge these psychic phenomena as spirits and not as autonomous complexes or archetypes. He asserts that spiritualists are trying to bring forth the teachings of these spirits in the same way that analytic psychologists seek to bring the truth out of the collective unconscious. They both seek to deal with the spirit in the same way.

Jung further explained that autonomous spirits, aka archetypes in the collective unconscious, are not part of our soul. They're not part of us, like autonomous complexes, which dwell in our personal unconscious. It thus seems there's a difference between autonomous complexes, which belong to us, regardless of how external they appear e.g. when the 'insane' project their complexes and they hear voices and see ghosts, and archetypes aka spirits? And when people are possessed by their unconscious, it can be either autonomous complexes or archetypes? They both have their own independent existence in the recesses of our minds.

Whilst Jung stretched the horizon with his concept of archetypes, i.e. beyond Freud's view that ghosts were merely projections of the subconscious mind, he publicly protested there were no spirits per se. He clothed the occult phenomenon in scientific attire, designed to conceal that which science would mock. It seems Freud had taught him well. Indeed, Jung once said, regarding the I Ching (which we'll get to), 'that in order to avoid the disastrous prejudice of the western mind, the matter would have to be introduced under the cloak of science'. It seems deceitful?

It's said Jung believed the collective unconscious contained all the dead. He knew there was more at play than just our personal ghosts or shadows i.e. the hidden dark parts of our personality. And he believed mentally ill people were haunted by these ghosts, in an age where no-one is supposed to even believe in them. Jung notably became vocal about the reality of the 'other' world after his Near Death Experience (NDE) at 68 years young. He was then prepared to put Jung the scientist in the back seat. He knew unequivocally that consciousness survives death. Ergo, we are a spiritual being?

However, before Jung the New Age Gnostic came out from underneath his scientific rock, Jung the scientist was getting on with Freud like a small house on fire. So, whilst all was peachy until it wasn't, and a mitigating factor hence worth a mention, is the infamous poltergeist in Freud's bookcase.

Thus, Jung was visiting Freud in Vienna in 1909, and he asked him about his thoughts regarding parapsychology. Sceptical Freud dismissed the subject as tripe. But a brave Jung disagreed with his mentor, and when he did, he began to feel his diaphragm become super hot. Then suddenly a loud bang came from the bookcase. Both apparently jumped up, and Jung said to Freud, 'There, that is an example of a catalytic exteriorisation phenomenon!' It's purported that was Jung's jargon for a poltergeist. Poltergeist means 'noisy' in German and refers to malevolent spirits that cause havoc e.g. move objects and make a noise.

Jung explains poltergeists are a projection of psychic energy that finds its centre in the unconscious mind. It's an exteriorisation or acting out of dissociative psychopathology. As mentioned, projection is not a conscious process, and the reason for projection is activated unconscious 'material' seeks expression. When Freud retorted 'Bosh!', Jung predicted that another bang would immediately happen. And it did. Jung said, from that moment on, Freud grew mistrustful of him. It's noted, that Jung demonstrated precognition (ESP) by his prediction. Apparently, Freud was uncomfortable with ESP and wrote it off as a crude and primitive means of communication superseded by language.

Furthermore, in a letter to Jung writing about the incident, it seems Freud believed that Jung himself was responsible for it. By virtue of Jung's diaphragm becoming toasty, it stands to reason he was i.e. some kind of psychic energy emanated from his unconscious mind? Like, he projected his autonomous complex and it somehow exteriorised and made a noise, twice. His complex took a cheap shot at Freud by making a disturbance? Whatever it was, it freaked Freud out. Apparently Freud, who declared 'Jung is going to be my successor', was so displeased with Jung's curiosity with ghosts that he gave him the ultimatum, 'it's either me or your ghosts'.

On another occasion, a visitor who came to Jung's home remarked about Jung's 'exteriorised libido', and stated 'when there was an important idea that was not yet quite conscious, the furniture and woodwork all over the house creaked and snapped'. So, unconscious psychic forces are making themselves known by creating a physical disturbance?

Following his split from Freud in 1913, and at a time of marital stress (as Jung was not prepared to give up his concubine), Jung fell into a protracted 'state of disorientation'. It was during his 'descent into the unconscious', his disturbing trip down the psyche's rabbit hole, that he gathered insights about the collective unconscious. This otherwise madness, as it was later considered his 'creative illness', started with a horrifying vision. The vision, which lasted about an hour, came to him while on a train. It depicted a flood covering Europe, between the North Sea and the Alps. Whilst the mountains in Switzerland rose to protect his homeland, he saw floating debris and bodies in the waves. The water then turned to blood. Jung felt as if the vision was actually a dream that had invaded his waking consciousness. His 'unconscious' gave him a vision?

As discussed, Jung viewed the schizophrenic as a dreamer in the world awake. And having spent many years treating mental patients who suffered from precisely such symptoms, Jung got his freak on. He was thus most relieved when WW1 broke out the following summer, as he was able to deduce that his vision had been a premonition of it.

He later acknowledged, 'it is, of course, ironical that I, a psychiatrist, should at almost every step in my experiment have run into the same psychic material which is the stuff of psychoses and is found in the insane'. Jung likened the assault of the unconscious to thunderstorms, but he felt compelled to endure them, to consciously submit himself to the impulses of the unconscious. He said, 'since I know nothing at all, I shall simply do whatever occurs to me'[13].

Jung believed Self-realisation requires the psyche to turn round on itself and confront what it produces. Thus, he embraced the 'unconscious other', manifested in personalities and powers that forced themselves on him. It was of scientific value? So, the psychic tension continued, which included haunted dreams, and eventually it got to the point where Jung felt he could no longer fight the madness. He decided to let go. And when he did, he landed in an eerie, subterranean world where he met strange intelligences that 'lived' in his mind.

Jung said, 'It was during the Advent of the year 1913—December 12, to be exact—that I resolved upon the decisive step'. He wrote, 'I was sitting at my desk, once more, thinking over my fears. Then I let myself drop. Suddenly it was as though the ground literally gave way beneath my feet, and I plunged down into the dark depths. I could not fend off a feeling of panic. But then, abruptly, at not too great a depth, I landed on my feet in a soft, sticky mass. I felt great relief, although I was apparently in complete darkness. After a while my eyes grew accustomed to the gloom, which was rather like a deep twilight. Before me was an entrance to a dark cave, in which stood a dwarf with a leathery skin, as if he were mummified. I squeezed past him through the narrow entrance and waded deep through icy water to the other end of the cave where, on a projecting rock, I saw a glowing red crystal. I grasped the stone, lifted it, and discovered a hollow underneath. At first I could make out nothing, but then I saw that there was running water. In it a corpse floated by, a youth with blond hair and a wound in the head. He was followed by a gigantic black scarab and then by a red, newborn sun, rising up out of the depths of the water. Dazzled by the light, I wanted to replace the stone upon the opening, but then a fluid welled out. It was blood. A thick jet of it leaped up, and I felt nauseated. It seemed to me that the blood continued to spurt for an unendurably long time. At last it ceased, and the vision came to an end' (in Memories, Dreams and Reflections, 1963, p.179).

It's pertinent to note, that Jung first let himself 'drop' by deliberately imagining a passageway into the depths of the earth. It seems he resolved upon the decisive step to experience the shamanic journey. He decided to venture upon the great magical mystery tour in his mind. His descent into the underworld and dialogue with the 'unconscious presence' was similar to shamans and religious mystics, as we'll get to. He reported, an 'incessant stream of fantasies had been released'.

For a period of seven years, from 1913-1919, Jung experienced a series of visions, dreams and fantasies. He referred to this period of his life as his 'Nekyia', a Greek word which describes a decent into the underworld. However, the experience was so distressing that Jung slept with a loaded gun by his bed, ready to bite the bullet, if the stress became too great (safe). Jung believed his neurosis bordering psychosis, comprised his 'confrontation with the unconscious'. He kept an account (in words and images) of the 'objective, independent' entities he encountered during his 'creative illness'[14]. These entities had nothing to do with him personally, but rather they shared his interior world.

As it transpired, Jung became so embroiled with the unconscious, that (by definition) he went quite mad. He could be seen playing in his garden like a child, hearing voices in his head, and walking about holding conversations with imaginary figures, like Philemon, his spirit guide. Philemon, who Jung described as his 'ghostly guru', was a real living personality. And he would walk up and down the garden conversing with this wise old man. As mentioned, we inherit a 'wise old man' archetype.

---

[13] See Memories, Dreams and Reflections (1963).
[14] See Jung's 'Red Book' (2009).

Jung however met various 'spirit guides', including a 'highly cultivated elderly Indian', who told him that his experience was identical to many mystics. Apparently, he told Jung that his own spirit guide or guru had been a commentator on the Vedas (ancient Hindu text) who had died centuries ago. It's noted, that Jung maintained a life-long fascination with Hindu gods, courtesy of his mum introducing them to him as a kid.

Towards the end of his life, Jung wrote 'These conversations with the dead formed a kind of prelude to what I had to communicate to the world about the unconscious...All my works, all my creative activity, has come from those initial fantasies and dreams which began in 1912, almost fifty years ago. Everything that I accomplished in later life was already contained in them, although at first only in the form of emotions and images'. Jung felt it was important to personify emotions. He said, 'the essential thing is to differentiate oneself from these unconscious contents by personifying them, and at the same time to bring them into relationship with consciousness'. But moreover, he was having conversations with spirits of the dead?

As it transpired, Jung met spirits of the dead during one episode in 1916, when his house was crowded with them. He states there was an 'ominous atmosphere' and he felt the presence of the dead. And it wasn't just him i.e. 'mad Jung', as his children and other members of the household experienced the same eerie restlessness that filled their home. Perhaps his family would have preferred if Jung didn't take his work home, but his work was part of him. It was in him? And he invited the craziness.

Jung explains, 'Then it was as if my house began to be haunted. My eldest daughter saw a white figure passing through the room. My second daughter, independently of her elder sister, related that twice in the night her blanket had been snatched away; and that same night my nine-year old son had an anxiety dream[15]. Around five o'clock in the afternoon on Sunday the front door began ringing frantically. It was a bright summer day; the two maids were in the kitchen, from which the open square outside the front door could be seen. Everyone immediately looked to see who was there, but there was no one in sight. I was sitting near the doorbell, and not only heard it but saw it moving. We all simply stared at one another. The atmosphere was thick, believe me! Then I knew that something had to happen. The whole house was filled as if there were a crowd present, crammed full of spirits. They were packed deep right up to the door, and the air was so thick it was scarcely possible to breathe. As for myself, I was all a-quiver with the question: 'For God's sake, what in the world is this?' Then they cried out in chorus, 'We have come back from Jerusalem where we found not what we sought''.

Jung said, 'I did not know what it meant or what "they" wanted of me'. But he felt that something 'within' wanted to get out. He felt 'forced from within'. And thus, began his transcribed document 'Septem Sermones ad Mortuos' or 'Seven Sermons to the Dead'. It's a work of 'spiritual dictation' or 'channelling'. As discussed, automatic writing or psychography is produced without conscious awareness and comes from either the writer's unconscious (autonomous complexes?), or an external spiritual source, whereby external spirits operate through the writer.

So, Jung went into a three day state of automatic writing, leading to the production of this work. And the ghosts disappeared. He said, 'Then it began to flow out of me, and in the course of three evenings the thing was written. As soon as I took up the pen, the whole ghostly assemblage evaporated. The room quieted and the atmosphere cleared. The haunting was over'.

---

[15] His son had a nightmare about the devil. He drew a picture of the fisherman he had seen in his dream. A flaming chimney rose from the fisherman's head, and a devil flew through the air, cursing the fisherman for stealing his fish.

It's noted, that Jung initially implied these words came from Philemon, but he later attributed them to 'Basilides in Alexandria, the City where the East toucheth the West', when he published the document in 1916. [Alexandria was known as 'the city of the serpent's son' because of Alex the Great's heritage]. It's said Jung adopted this ruse, as advised to from his friends, lest the work harm his reputation (Rees, 2011 p.192). Basilides was a Gnostic who taught in Alexandria during the years 133-155AD. So, Jung channelled a dead person?

Speaking about his experience of poltergeist phenomena, Jung stated that the start of the work was identical to a possession. It would appear he was possessed by otherwise dead Basilides, who was helping other dead spirits, who were looking for something? The seven sermons thus reveal Basilides' Gnostic message that the True and Ultimate God is Abraxas. According to ancient Gnostic texts, Abraxas is the astral serpent who gave Adam and Eve 'enlightenment'. The Ouroboros (the snake eating its own tail) signifies Abraxas, and it represents wholeness/completeness. This Supreme Being transcends both good and evil, and unites all opposites into one Being. Abraxas is the emblem of Gnosticism.

Whilst we'll get back to Gnosticism, it's noted that Gnosticism is a dualist religion. There are coexistent realms of light and darkness (radical dualism pertains to co-equal divine forces). But for Jung, Gnostics were incorrectly labelled radical dualists, believing in a battle between good and evil. He regarded good and evil as complimentary aspects of reality. Like, yin meets yang. Wholeness is the union of good and evil. To become whole, we need light and darkness made one. We need to bring the shadows into the light of day.

Moreover, the secret spiritual knowledge guarded by Gnostics, is about God and the God-nature in each of us. Gnosticism maintains that all Self-knowledge is knowledge of God, and the Self and the divine are one. We're God at our unconscious core. Thus, we must honestly work through this dual nature of God, namely, good and evil, that is our own dual nature.

Jung conceded the psyche of God is the macrocosm, and the psyche of man is the microcosm. Our psyche is a microcosmic manifestation of the macrocosmic whole that is God. Our psyche is a 'mini me' of the great mastermind. We are one and the same. It's just a matter of working through the illusions of difference and separateness. The idea that the macrocosm and microcosm are one, divided only by form, is essentially a Vedantic (Hindu) doctrine. Its pantheism i.e. everything is God including us, which corroborates with quantum physics regarding one essence or energy manifested in myriad forms.

Jung said, 'Through the miracle of consciousness, the human psyche provides the mirror in which Nature sees herself reflected'. We're all incarnations and reincarnations of the one undivided Self that is God. Life entails God reflecting upon His Self through His reincarnations. God is thus living through a person and gazing out and reflecting upon His Self. Spinoza deducted that if Nature works through us, our thoughts are Nature's thoughts. And if God is Nature (since everything is God), then all our thoughts are also God's. This is the New Age script and people are increasingly partial to it. We prefer to be God than be subjugated by God. And archetypes etc are also God?

It's alleged that our consciousness is part of a universal consciousness or awareness (like Tolle advocates). So, there's that. But there's also the collective unconsciousness, the part of our psyche that's been shut off. It's like the spirit world has been obscured? There's a veil in place separating us from this unconscious ocean, but it's somehow part of our personal psyche. The veil contains the 'archetypes' that seek expression. But sometimes 'archetypes' make themselves known evidencing its existence. Sometimes they penetrate into our dimension, our time and space. And we can invite these otherwise demons into our consciousness through trance states.

Furthermore, it seems the dead don't really die if they exist in some other plane of existence, and can communicate with us through our consciousness? It seems bidding archetypes include all the spirits of the dead? And they can give us intel as they watch over us? They 'see' things we don't see (like, Bertha giving birth). And they've been around long-time, so they know things we don't know.

What Jung first experienced in December 1913, he later called 'Active Imagination'. Jung developed 'Active Imagination' as a therapeutic technique between 1913 and 1916, during his 'spell of enlightenment'. Active Imagination is a path of cognition that uses the imagination as an organ of understanding. It's a technique for granting the psyche freedom to express itself spontaneously, without the usual interference from the ego editor. Not dissimilar from Freud's 'free association' (psychoanalytic technique) and saying whatever pops into our mind sans censoring. It's 'the art of letting things happen'.

The idea is to clear our mind, make a blank space, and 'whatever comes receive it'. It's a meditation technique, a trance state. It enables contents from our unconscious to be translated into images, narratives or separate entities. It's a process used to bridge the gap between conscious and unconscious minds. Such Active Imagination, or creative visualisation, is a kind of waking dreaming. The aim is to descend into the underworld, get lost in a reverie while remaining fully conscious.

Black (2010) notably highlights that stories of going underground should always alert us to the fact that occult physiology is being referred to. The journey underground is a journey inside the body. We take a trip inside. Jung said, 'in order to seize hold of the fantasies, I frequently imagined a steep descent...' Going down a deep descent paves the way for a trancelike state, like a hypnotic countdown.

As discussed, when in a trance, we're able to step outside of our ordinary belief system and dissociate. It was during his periods of 'Active Imagination', Jung believed he met and talked with 'intelligent entities' like Philemon etc. Jung maintains that Active Imagination spawns from the desires and fantasies of the unconscious mind, which ultimately want to become conscious. And we can learn much from holding conversations with the personalities we meet.

The basic method is thus, we allow a fantasy to appear, as Jung did, and grab hold of an element in the fantasy and stick to it. If we see an image and it moves, we follow it, engage with its autonomy. Jung explained, 'The point is that you start with any image ... Contemplate it and carefully observe how the picture begins to unfold or to change. Don't try to make it into something, just do nothing but observe what its spontaneous changes are. Any mental picture you contemplate in this way will sooner or later change through a spontaneous association that causes a slight alteration of the picture. You must carefully avoid impatient jumping from one subject to another. Hold fast to the one image you have chosen and wait until it changes by itself. Note all these changes and eventually step into the picture yourself, and if it is a speaking figure at all then say what you have to say to that figure and listen to what he or she has to say'.

Active Imagination means that the images have a life of their own and that the symbolic events develop according to their own logic. Thus, it's imperative to exert as little influence as possible on mental images as they unfold, to ensure that conscious reason doesn't interfere. At the same time however, Jung was insistent that some form of participation in Active Imagination was essential. He said, 'you yourself must enter into the process with your personal reactions...as if the drama being enacted before your eyes were real'. He recognises that it's common to question whether it's active imagination or fabrication, but we have to overcome this doubt.

In a lecture Jung gave to the Tavistock Clinic in London in 1935, he spoke of a patient who couldn't grasp what Active Imagination was, until one day he found himself looking at a travel poster at a railway station. It showed the Alps, with a waterfall, a meadow, and cows on a hilltop. Jung's patient wondered what he would find if he walked over the hill. In a reverie he did, and found himself in a small chapel, looking at a picture of the Virgin. Then a creature with pointed ears popped behind the altar and disappeared. At first Jung's patient thought this was nonsense, but he continued. The creature appeared again, although he hadn't imagined it there at all. It seemed to have a 'life of its own'. After that, he understood what Jung meant.

Jung maintains that we produce precious little by our conscious mind but rather we are ever dependent upon what appears from our unconscious. Indeed, he insists we depend entirely upon the benevolent cooperation of our unconscious. But moreover, we can cultivate the ability to have visions from deep imagination, like Jung did, and spark up some conversations. The autonomy of the figures we meet is evidenced by the information they provide i.e. it's beyond what the ego knows, hence it's not ego derived.

Jung instructed that we must enter the fantasy and become a committed participant in the drama. Jung maintains 'it is a psychic fact that this fantasy is happening, and it is as real as you – as a psychic entity – are real'. So, it's a bit like dreaming, but unlike dreams which are autonomous and materialise on their own accord, Active Imagination is our inner world. It's a place to go to, with stable characters. Jung actively went back to look for Philemon and other spirit guides, the subliminal personalities he befriended.

This resonates with something my buds and I did early on in secondary school. Thus, we'd stand in a circle, holding hands, and with our eyes closed, we'd countdown however many steps. We would then see a door, or doors, and go through whichever one into whatever world awaited. It was like going through CS Lewis's wardrobe (in the Narnia Chronicles). And whenever I did this I would see the same characters, often a caretaker, who was tall and wore a dark suit, and on occasion I would see a woman called Kelly, who was slim with dark long hair, on a horse, usually in the forest. Kelly was however malignantly shady and whenever I spied her, I'd shoot off, back through the door and up the steps with much speed. She genuinely freaked me out. I understood her to be the devil's daughter but perhaps she was my shadow?

For the most part though, my escapades were pleasant. It truly was a whole other world (real and active) in which to dwell. Thus, I'd meander around the landscape, the cultivated gardens with the blue skies above, and soak up what was going on, observing others e.g. someone's fishing, or flying a kite, or walking a dog. With Active Imagination, the point is to record what has been experienced to make sense of it. It's like our mind is an empty theatre, a blank canvas, and our unconscious provides the script and paints the picture?

Whilst the point is to communicate with whomever we meet, to receive information we would otherwise not know, Jung does however caution that subliminal contents may overpower the conscious mind and take possession of the personality. Like, maybe Kelly could possess me? I often wondered what would happen if I ever met her face to face, and if that might happen. She could get under my skin. I also suspected that it was only a matter of time. Or perhaps my resistance to meet with Kelly, who radiated evil, was reluctance to meet my shadow? And denying my divine evil nature is to my un-integrated detriment.

Jung states this technique had the potential not only to allow communication between the conscious and unconscious aspects of the personal psyche with its various components and inter-dynamics, but also between the personal and collective unconscious; and therefore was to be embarked upon with due care and attentiveness. He warned, "active imagination'...The method is not entirely without danger, because it may carry the patient too far away from reality'. We could become psychotic?

Active Imagination is notably a technique used in the mystery schools. Thus, the initiate actively imagines aka constructs an elaborate, sensual mental image for which a disembodied spirit (archetype?) might inhabit. This ancient technique is applied to help achieve a free-willed, free-thinking exchange with beings from higher hierarchies. Initiates can then command disembodied beings at will. The endeavour is to roll back the layers of consciousness, but we'll get to all this. It's noted, that in my fantasy land, the caretaker was a real person with his own personality. And Kelly was very real. I suspect they're still there.

Jungian psychology places great emphasis on interpreting the contents of the unconscious mind. Hence, the fundamental role of dream interpretation, and dialectical work with the psyche, like Active Imagination. But perhaps, like partaking in hypnotic séances, it's best to give Active Imagination a wide Bertha. As discussed, therapists can encourage clients to imagine/visualise their 'safe place'. It seems we can create a mindscape, which enables meeting other personalities. But like Gail McDonald's haunted experience, there can be unfriendly intruders, who then attempt to take over our consciousness.

Thus, maybe we should be careful allowing the 'unconscious mind' free reign through art, dance, music, automatic writing etc? Do we want to encourage dissociation? It's duly noted, that many artists channel their 'higher self' or archetypes/demons to inspire their work. It's like musicians' channel spirits to get lyrics. And some like to post their photos online, depicting their eyes rolled to the back of their head (showing only the whites of the eyes), to show what happens. It's cool?

As mentioned, Jung recorded his experiences, and as it transpired, one day he heard a female voice say that what he was doing wasn't science but art. [Presumably Jung knew whether this voice was an autonomous complex or archetype?]. Whilst initially dismissive and resentful, he subsequently worked on a series of spontaneous drawings which seemed to represent his psychic state at the time. He realised that these drawings represented ancient mandalas, a spiritual and ritual symbol in Hinduism and Buddhism. The basic form of most mandalas is a square with four gates, containing a circle point, which is where the deity resides (see picture). Monks meditate upon the mandala, 'imagining' it as a three-dimensional palace. The deities who reside in the palace embody philosophical views and serve as role models.

Mandalas are recognised for their deep spiritual meaning and representation of psychic wholeness. Mandala is notably Sanskrit for 'magic circle' or completion. In various spiritual traditions, they're used as a spiritual tool to help focus the attention of aspirants and adepts. They stimulate meditation and trance induction for the purposes of achieving Altered States of Consciousness. They provide a sacred space for the meeting of minds, because if we connect with the icon or image representing whatever deity, they connect with us. It's a two-way street. If we put our self into the icon, the icon will speak to us, answers will come to us. It has a magic effect.

The idea is to concentrate upon a starting point, and when we concentrate on a mental picture, it begins to stir, the image becomes enriched by details, it moves and develops. Again, we have to overcome the doubt that we are making it up. Jung observed that mandalas are present in many cultures and mythologies, which further reaffirmed our collective unconscious blueprint. Like Active Imagination, mandalas provide another path for connecting with our unconscious.

Whilst the centres of mandalas usually contain a reference to deity, Jung began to understand these as representations of 'Self'. He referred to mandalas as 'the psychological expression of the totality of the Self'. Jung believed the deities in myths and religions were symbolic manifestations of the Self archetype.

To reiterate, the Self in Jungian psychology is an archetype, signifying the unification of consciousness and unconsciousness in a person. It represents the psyche as a whole. The Self is realised as the product of individuation, which in Jung's view is the process of integrating one's personality. Thus, with regards to mandalas, by putting our self into our iconic Self, we can connect with our Self and become a whole integrated Self.

Jung called the Self the 'God within us'. The Self is described as a 'God-image' within the psyche and symbolises what religions call the 'soul'. According to Hermeticism (which we'll get to), heaven and earth, referred to as 'above and below', are included in 'the image of God'. God is the macrocosmic universe, which we can access through our soul. Jung believed God is inside not outside. Thus, Jesus is not God personified, and Father God and Jesus are not in the third heaven?

Gnostics believe salvation comes from gnosis, the mystical knowledge that we are God. The role of experience is to develop what is already there i.e. activate the archetypal potential that's already present in the Self. This suggests our Self or God wants to find Him or Herself? Jung explains that an encounter with the Self feels like a 'religious experience' with God. He said that when this happens, our perception shifts, our personal consciousness is radically changed, and new values emerge. The occurrence leaves us 'vitalised' and 'enriched'. Our consciousness is heightened.

With regards to the mandala, Paracelsus said, 'He who has succeeded in bringing his individual mind in exact harmony with the universal mind, has succeeded in reuniting the inner space with the outer one, from which he has only become separated by mistaking illusions for truth. He who has succeeded in carrying out practically the meaning of this symbol has become one with the Father; he is virtually an adept, because he has succeeded in squaring the circle and encircling the square'. The circle is notably the spiritual realm, and the square is the physical realm. The mandala's purpose is to help transform ordinary minds into enlightened ones. But again, we'll get back to all this.

As touched on, by 1919 Jung's 'creative illness' had passed. And despite all his otherwise spiritual encounters, he continued to denounce the reality of spirits in the face of science. Indeed, he was invited to London to lecture on 'The Psychological Foundations of the Belief in Spirits' to the Society for Psychical Research. And rather than admit what he knew, namely, that spirits are autonomous metaphysical entities, he told the Society that ghosts and materialisations were 'unconscious projections'. He said, 'I have repeatedly observed the telepathic effects of unconscious complexes, and also a number of parapsychic phenomena, but in all this I see no proof whatever of the existence of real spirits, and until such proof is forthcoming I must regard this whole territory as an appendix of psychology'.

But he 'knew'. And a year later, he encountered another ghost. It was at his bud's cottage (which locals deemed haunted), in Aylesbury, England. He sometimes stayed there for the weekends. And it's where he heard eerie sounds and smelt the stank (an unpleasant smell filled the bedroom, as the stank landed). Poltergeists are also associated with horrendous smells. On one particularly bad night, Jung discovered an old woman's head on the pillow next to his. But worse, half of her face was missing. He leapt out of bed and spent the rest of the night in an armchair (fair play). The house was later demolished. It seems Jung was most freaked out by the English ghost, and that's despite having encountered the dead on their return from Jerusalem[16]. Beyond so-called archetypes in the collective unconscious then, spirits of a more traditional kind were not lacking.

As it transpired however, when his lecture for the Society for Psychical Research was reprinted in the 'Collected Works' in 1947, Jung added a footnote explaining that he no longer felt as certain as he did in 1919 that apparitions were explicable through psychology. And he further stated that he doubted 'whether an exclusively psychological approach can do justice to the phenomenon'. In a later postscript, he again admitted that his early deductions were insufficient. And in 1946, in a letter to Fritz Kunkel (a psychotherapist), Jung

---

[16] Jung's account of what happened in Aylesbury appeared 30 years later, in 1949, in an obscure anthology of ghost stories.

admitted, 'Metapsychic phenomena could be explained better by the hypothesis of spirits than by the qualities and peculiarities of the unconscious'.

It's said that not long before Jung died, he began to have second doubts about the real existence of these entities. He acknowledged that modern man finds it acceptable that the entities encountered were not an actual reality. Hence, he initially claimed these higher forms were simply archetypes that were dredged up, projections and exteriorisations of thoughts within. But maybe they were real after all. Perhaps archetypes were literally disembodied spirits. They weren't a branch of our psyche but rather external independent beings. It seems he was in denial for a long time, given his practice of necromancy (alleged communication with the dead), from the outset.

For most of his long career, Jung impressed that he was above all else a scientist. He was obstinate that he was not a mystic, occultist or visionary. Jung the scientist 'knew' that it was a good career move to obscure Jung the mentalist. Yet he spent much time fending off charges of mysticism and occultism. But as mentioned, after his NDE, he let the scientist in him take a backseat. So, whilst Jung initially concurred with Freud that the mind contains psychological complexes which are independent of our core-consciousness and to some extent may be thought of as autonomous, he became less sure. As Black (2010) affirms, Jung later concluded these psychological complexes were autonomous in the sense of being independent of the human brain altogether. Not hallucinations but higher intelligence (p.211).

And these higher intelligences can possess us. Like, Jung believed Hitler was possessed, by more than his unconscious? It seems people can unwittingly be used as an instrument for some other 'energy' or force to incarnate or express itself through them. Jung said that disturbances caused by unconscious processes can have an intelligence not inferior to, and in fact often superior to a person's conscious insight. Like, Ivenes was smarter than Helly.

It seems to be semantics, as Jung espoused the ancient idea of daemons or spirits. As mentioned, daemons are spirit beings that prompt and persuade us to do certain things. They guide or tempt us. It's purported that ideas that we think are ours are prompted by these disembodied beings, as the daemonic connect with us more directly through thinking than through speech and physical observation. Thus, whilst they can become visible and talk to us, for the most part they speak to our minds. The Greeks used the word daemon to refer to any unnamed spirit having an impact on someone, and later divided these nature spirits into good and evil categories. Daemons nudge us, via our intuition, into particular directions. We roll with our 'instincts'?

Jung described daemons as spirits with a degree of autonomy, which exert a strong influence on our interior life. He promulgated that these spirits give life to the ego, and he recognised, 'there appear to be many spirits, both light and dark'. Thus, whilst some bring us beneficial insights that enhance life, others possess us, rob us and fulfil only its desire. However, in this respect, such spirits could merely be reduced to Freud's Eros and Thanatos, life and death instincts i.e. these impulses are part of the human condition unlike independent spirits?

But spirits have a life of their own. Like, clever Ivenes competing with Helly for ego-dominance. They can overpower the conscious mind and take possession of the personality. Jung asserts that spirits can exhibit overwhelming superiority and absolute authority that can be dangerous if a person succumbs to it (do they have a choice?). He said, 'the archetype is spirit or anti-spirit: what it ultimately proves to be depends on the attitude of the human mind'.

So, it seems spirits are metaphysical entities independent of us. They dwell on some spirit plane, a hyper dimension. Like, entities in DMT space? They're 'knowledge energies'. It's possible there's a host of heavenly beings, including angels and demons. They're not part of our personal psyche, but we can communicate with them through our psyche. And we can integrate them into our conscious mind, to enhance our consciousness. We can revive our spirit body, despite God specifically shutting it down.

But for Jung, we are God and the Devil. He said, 'the adversary is none other than 'the other in me''. So, there is no external God and Devil per se. Thus, when people worship God or Lucifer, they are really worshipping themselves. And God and Satan are One God (they're integrated). God reconciles good and evil. Or maybe God and the Devil are real external autonomous personages. And the devil is not God but rather a fallen angel.

It seems pertinent to note, that in the seventh sermon, of his 'Seven Sermons to the Dead', in response to the dead asking the spirit guide (Philemon/Basilides) to teach them about man, he taught the spirits, 'Man is a gateway, through which from the outer world of gods, daemons, and souls ye pass into the inner world; out of the greater into the smaller world'. So, our consciousness is the gateway for daemons?

In addition to reviving the daemonic, Jung endorsed other curious phenomenon, like 'synchronicity'. Jung coined the term 'synchronicity' for meaningful coincidence. He gives an example of an occasion when he had painted a picture of Philemon, who notably had a white beard, bull's horns and the wings of a kingfisher, and just after this, he happened to find a dead kingfisher in his garden. Such birds were rare in Zurich, and this was the first and only time, he found one. It seemed Philemon was confirming his existence?

It seems Nature reveals herself through signs and omens. Like, in witchcraft, dead birds might fall from the sky, or whales might beach themselves. Or like, God reminds us of His Presence through rainbows. Rainbows are His sign that He'll never flood the world again, so we don't panic when it starts raining. Russell Brand (2014) wrote, 'The unknown is constantly addressing us, it doesn't use our language, but it is here, quite clear among us' (p.350).

Jung also gives the example of French writer Emile Deschamps' plum pudding story to illustrate synchronicity. Thus, the story is Deschamps was kindly treated to some plum pudding by a stranger named Monsieur de Fontgibu in Orleans. Ten years later, Deschamps encountered plum pudding on the menu in a Paris restaurant and wanted to order some, but the waiter told him that the last dish had already been served to another customer, who turned out to be de Fontgibu. Many years later Deschamps was invited to a meal that included plum pudding, and he jovially remarked to his buds, that the only thing missing was de Fontgibu. And in the same instant, the now senile de Fontgibu entered the room. He had come to the wrong address[17].

Another example of synchronicity or meaningful coincidence could be Tim Tebow's, American footballer, favourite Bible verse, namely, John 3:16, being proclaimed. In this verse Jesus said, 'For God so loved the world that He gave His one and only begotten Son, that whoever believes in Him shall not perish but have everlasting life'.

Thus, in 2009 Tebow painted 3:16 on his eye-black and his team won the game. Apparently 94 million people Googled the verse that day. As it transpired, people started complaining and thus a new rule materialised, banning players from writing anything on their eye-black. Then exactly three years later (to the day) from

---

[17] See Jung's 'Synchronicity: An Acausal Connecting Principle' (1952), written with the physicist Wolfgang Pauli.

when he wore John 3:16, in a subsequent match, he threw for exactly 316 yards in ten throws, averaging 31.6 yards per throw, the ratings for the game was 31.6 and the time of possession was 31.06. Fans began pointing out it was an allusion to John 3:16. During the game 90 million people Googled John 3:16. Tebow said, 'A lot of people said it was a coincidence. I say big God'.

It's interesting that 'archetypes', like Philemon, and even God, can penetrate our material realm, evidencing their reality, in some shape or form? In Tebow's case, God got His message out to millions. It's interesting that synchronicity links the immaterial realm with the material realm i.e. archetypes from the collective unconscious can reveal themselves through meaningful coincidences in real life. It's like riotous poltergeists make their presence known. Or are the poltergeists someone's dissociated complex that has ESP, or the projection of an archetype?

Synchronicity or meaningful coincidences hint at a deep pattern of meaning hidden behind the hubble bubble or monotony of everyday life. Synchronistic moments can feel like grace, as they induce in us the feeling that we're right where we're supposed to be. They seem to represent order arising from chance. Like, we were meant to meet that person. Or we were supposed to miss our bus, train or plane, because something life changing happened as a result. They make us feel as if there's something more going on, a bigger picture, destiny even? Maybe there is meaning in the madness, the otherwise absurdity?

Colin Wilson, author of 'Jung, Lord of the Underworld' (1984) wrote, 'So synchronicities may be understood in two ways: either as a 'magical' process – an influence exerted by the unconscious mind upon the world around us – or as a kind of nudge from some unknown guardian angel, who's purpose is to tell us that life is not as meaningless as it looks' (p.115-116).

There's also phenomena like, say we think of someone and they phone that instant. Perhaps there's a reason? It seems like a coincidence? It can also make us feel as if we have supernatural control over events i.e. our thoughts of someone remotely inspire the idea of contact. It suggests our thoughts contain a certain amount of power and influence? Which suggests that perhaps we could will other things to power?

Science however refutes such whimsical musings. We're told coincidences are random. They're not mystical phenomena but rather the laws of probability. So, who cares, as Jung said, 'for instance, I speak of a red car and at that moment a red car comes here'? It's highlighted that we only notice coincidences, which makes them seem special when they're not.

Freud further explained that coincidences stem from underlying connections within our unconscious, (hence we're not aware of them), that are triggered. For example, I hear a song on the radio, and whilst I don't make the connection between the song and the person I then think about, I phone that person. The other person, also listening to the radio and also not making the connection, thinks of me, and we concur how coincidental it was that we were thinking of each other at the same time. Thus, it's not a coincidence, but rather our unconscious prompts us with regards to our forgotten memories.

Regardless of the scientific spin, maybe coincidences do mean something, as our intuition suggests? Indeed, it could be argued through a spiritual lens that chance encounters don't exist. There's no such thing as a coincidence. For Jung, the emphasis was on 'meaning'. He defined 'synchronicity' as the experience of two or more causally unrelated events being observed as happening together in a manner that is meaningful. He observed an 'a-causal connecting (togetherness) principle'.

Thus, just as events can be grouped by their cause, they can equally be connected by their meaning. This concept does not therefore question, or compete with, the notion of causality. Besides, as Jung muses, who says that a grouping of events by meaning requires an explanation in terms of a concrete sense of cause and effect? The Principle of Synchronicity is supposed to explain meaningful coincidences, that aren't connected by cause and effect, yet they're not by chance either.

Jung wrote, 'A certain curious principle that I have termed synchronicity, a concept that formulates a point of view diametrically opposed to that of causality. Since the latter is a merely statistical truth and not absolute, it is a sort of working hypothesis of how events evolve one out of another, whereas synchronicity takes the coincidence of events in space and time as meaning something more than mere chance'.

It's duly noted, that 'conspiracy theories' highlight coincidences. Like, the 'coincidence' that WTC owners doubled their insurance, which included acts of terrorism, just before 9/11. Or that Big Pharma gets richer as we get sicker. And it's not random that tragedies happen on specific dates, and at specific times, but rather these details mean something? And it's not a coincidence that both JFK and Abraham Lincoln were killed because they challenged the shadow government's hidden agenda. And it's not a coincidence that both their assassins were murdered before they could get to trial, so the real perpetrators didn't get caught. Evidence coincidentally vanishes. Like, incriminating dossiers, and like NASA lost evidence of the Apollo missions.

There were notably many parallels between JFK and Abraham Lincoln. Like, Lincoln was elected president in 1860, and exactly a hundred years later, JFK was elected president in 1960. Both men were deeply involved in civil rights for Blacks. Both men were assassinated on a Friday, in front of their wives. They both lost a son while living in the White House. They were both killed from a bullet to the head. They were both succeeded by vice-presidents named Johnson who were southern Democrats and former senators. Andrew Johnson was born in 1808 and Lyndon Johnson was born in 1908, exactly a hundred years later. The first name of Lincoln's private secretary was John, and the last name of Kennedy's private secretary was Lincoln. John Wilkes Booth was born in 1839, and Lee Harvey Oswald was born in 1939, one hundred years later. However, I digress.

Jung further illustrates what he meant by the word synchronicity, with regards to an experience he shared with a patient of his. This patient was a nightmare and analysis wasn't helping (she was apparently very clever). Jung realised there was nothing he could do. He said, 'I had to confine myself to the hope that something unexpected and irrational would turn up, something that would burst the intellectual retort in which she had sealed herself'.

So, as it transpired, she had an impressive dream the night before, in which someone offered her a golden scarab, a valuable piece of jewelry. At the moment she was telling Jung the dream, there was a tapping on the office window. Jung opened up the window and a scarabaei beetle, whose gold-green color closely resembles that of a golden scarab, flew into the room. Jung caught the beetle in his hand, handed it to her and said, 'Here is your scarab'.

As touched on, scarab beetles are revered in Egyptian mythology as they're associated with the sun god Ra. They're an archetypal symbol of rebirth and transformation. They're apparently a messenger of eternity, letting us know fate and destiny are always at work in our lives. As mentioned, Jung was an expert on mythical symbols. Thus, he was able to explain to his patient that the constellation or activation of this archetype was prompted by the psyche's drive for wholeness and Self-realisation.

He states, stationed at an impasse, this synchronistic moment intimately revealed to her deeper processes at play, which resulted in a fundamental shift in her perception. This revelation inwardly transformed her and made her receptive in a new way. From that point on, Jung said, 'The treatment could now be continued with satisfactory results'. Jung surmised that it's these kinds of situations i.e. being stuck or in a crisis, which constellates the archetype.

So, there was no causal link between the patient's dream and the beetle, yet in some mysterious way the beetle was intimately related to her. Synchronicities show us what wants to come through from our deeper world. The beetle was thus not a coincidence but rather an important link between her external and internal world. Synchronicities, like dreams, fantasies and visions, enable archetypes to come into awareness, which help fulfill our psychic potential through the individuation process.

Jung believed the principle of synchronicity gave conclusive evidence for his concept of archetypes and the collective unconscious. Synchronicities illuminate the archetypes, located in the collective unconscious. Jung also conjectured that extrasensory perceptions are synchronicities e.g. telepathy, clairvoyance, and premonitions. Like synchronicities, he believed that telepathic communication takes place in the collective unconscious.

Jung explained, 'the collective unconscious is common to all: it is the foundation of what the ancients called the sympathy of all things. It is through the medium of the collective unconscious that information about a particular time and place can be transferred to another individual mind'. Hence, Helly was able to know that Bertha gave Bertha, as archetypes (spirits) in the collective unconscious (spirit world) passed this on? Jung understood that telepathy could be used as a means to contact the otherworld.

Synchronicity is also the basis of divinatory techniques, like astrology and the I Ching. Jung said, 'When astrology makes accurate news predictions, sometimes to the exact day, sometimes years before they happen – people ask me how it works and why it works. I say – 'Synchronicity''. Jung began using the term 'synchronicity' in the 1920s, at the same time he became fascinated with astrology and the I Ching. Indeed, from 1920 onwards, horoscopes and the I Ching became part of his therapeutic practice. Thus, it seems life is determined? A story is being fleshed out, but God knows the end from the beginning.

The I Ching or Book of Changes is notably an ancient Chinese divination system i.e. we consult the I Ching as an oracle, as a means of telling the future. Whilst it seems we randomly select a chapter (there are sixty-four chapters, each one drawing upon a particular theme, or aspect of life), it's not random but rather 'meant to be'. It's said the chapter we're directed to will describe our situation and suggest the wisest course of action. Like horoscopes, we essentially sift the words for personal meaning. It's also like Tarot cards and rune stones etc. This seems to work on intuition i.e. our reading resonates with us on some intuitive level. We're asking for answers through this medium, which invites 'unconscious psychic forces' to play. We trust the spirits?

Jung promulgated the I Ching as a method for exploring the unconscious. He said, 'if the I Ching is not accepted by the conscious, at least the unconscious meets it halfway, and the I Ching is more closely connected with the unconscious than with the rational attitude of consciousness'. Jung explains the I Ching does not just tell people what to do, it establishes a creative relationship with the unconscious. The I Ching opens an encounter with the unconscious, as we let the words act on us. It gives us a mirror to the hidden forces that are at work in the unconscious.

For Jung, the I Ching could draw out the meanings that connect us with the imaginal world, creating a new awareness and a new experience. So, it's not an example of synchronicity, but rather it creates synchronicity by giving its users access to the place where time and space become relative. The underlying principle is that anything that happens is related to everything else that happens at the same time.

Synchronicity convinced Jung there was an element of the psyche outside time and space, and space and time are relative to the psyche. Like, the spirit world is a hyper dimension beyond our four dimensions of space and time? It's said that Jung's discovery of synchronicity was in a sense the parallel in the realm of psychology to Einstein's discovery of the law of relativity in physics. It's also highlighted, that incorporating the concept of synchronicity into his theoretical system late in his life, led Jung to substantially reformulate his concepts of archetypes and the collective unconscious, putting them on a transcendent basis i.e. archetypes are forms of existence without time and space.

At the very least, Jung argued the I Ching 'brings together subjective and objective views of the world, and forces the individual to interpret the clash that results, thereby encouraging them to 'outgrow' their problems' (cited in Vernon, 2012 p.142).

Whilst Jung initially tried to explain the I Ching's efficacy through paranormal synchronicity, he admitted that the sources of the oracle's insights are the 'spiritual agencies' that form the 'living soul of the book'. That is, spirits are at work through the pages, like they are through the stars? It seems the spirits use different mediums to communicate. Jung confessed, 'the less one thinks about the theory of the I Ching, the more soundly one sleeps'.

It's also duly noted, that casting horoscopes warranted the death penalty in Judaism (which founded Christianity and Islam). God was serious that He didn't want His kids engaging with spiritual forces. It seems no good can come from channelling 'information energies', or integrating them into our psyche, or being possessed by them.

The contemporary consensus however seems to be there's no harm in reading our horoscope, and it's probably bosh, as how can all Pisces, for example, come into money and have luck in love at the same time. A study carried out in England notably found 100% of people know their star signs, 70% read their horoscopes regularly, and 85% agree that the description of their star sign describes their personality (Blackmore, 2000). Is it a 'coincidence' that everyone knows their star-sign, and few know God's word?

According to psychologist Margaret Hamilton (from Wisconsin University), 70% of information in newspaper horoscopes is positive, so we want to believe it. It seems people identify with their star-sign, because we innately want to identify with something? And star signs are relatively complimentary. Like, we're natural leaders, with a heart full of compassion, despite say our rigidity. Or maybe we choose who we 'become' and who we identify with?

Later in life, Jung discovered alchemy. Jung believed that alchemists, in their efforts to turn base metals into gold, were symbolically engaged in a process of psychic transformation. Alchemists were transformed on physical, mental, emotional, and spiritual levels. The purification of metals led to the purification of alchemists (heating metals purifies it).

As it transpires, alchemy is not merely the precursor to chemistry, as we're led to believe. But rather it's a spiritual work. Alchemy is a metaphor for transforming souls from impure (lead) to pure (gold). This ancient art involves spiritual evolution. Alchemy teaches that God is in everything. God is one universal spirit or consciousness manifesting through an infinity of forms, including all material reality. The universe has a soul and we're all connected. We're bound together by a spiritual force that communicates through signs and omens. We're God communicating with ourselves?

It's said that metal heated for many years would eventually free itself of all its individual properties, with the result being the 'soul of the world'. This 'soul of the world' allowed alchemists to understand anything in the world because it was the language with which all things are communicated. The soul of the world is the source of all knowledge. It's the ancient mind and Jung posited that we ought to return there.

The philosopher's stone, (which transforms metals into gold and is the elixir of life), is not a literal stone but rather experiential 'wisdom'. It's the key to all knowledge. It's the magnum opus or great work. It enables the alchemist to merge with the divine spirit in the universe. It's the union of the macrocosm and the microcosm.

Whilst we'll get back to alchemy, the essential truth is the philosopher's stone is our light body. The goal of each soul is to merge with God, and the activation of our light body takes us there. Our otherwise inert light body is our vehicle to the source. The soul is the doorway to the collective unconscious. So, alchemy is the expansion of consciousness. Transmuting the body into the light body is the meaning of life. Yet God specifically shut down our light body. He severed our light body from our soul for a reason.

The goal of alchemy is to transcend the veil which divides the seen from the unseen. The veil of materialism is lifted, as initiates experientially learn the inner workings of the spirit world. They see the invisible elements constituting the astral body of things. Alchemy confers supernatural intelligence and perception on its practitioners. In essence, they open their third eye (activate their spirit body) and acquire ESP. It's also noted, that alchemists used their 'transmutation of metals' practice as a cover for what was essentially a mystery school.

For Jung, alchemy is a spiritual work that happens through correspondence with 'archetypes'. Alchemy was a metaphor for individuation. It was an elaborate discipline based upon projection i.e. alchemists project the contents of their psyche (archetypes) onto the materials they're working with. Unconscious psychic forces can be expressed. It was thus another method for integrating the psyche and achieving the psycho-spiritual goal of individuation. That is, the process of transformation whereby the personal and collective unconscious are brought into consciousness to be assimilated into the whole personality.

Alchemy enables man to attain his full potential, namely, Self realisation through Self knowledge. Like meditating on mandalas, the aim is for the soul to disconnect from the body, to enable connecting with the soul of the world. And as a result, we become God-like, and can even turn lead into gold?

With respect to Jung and alchemy, Black (2010) wrote, 'Jung's purely psychological alchemy is interesting in its way, but it is totally uninteresting from an esoteric perspective, because it disregards notions of journeys into the spirit worlds and communication with disembodied beings' (p.459). But it seems Jung the Gnostic was on this mystical page, and he merely covered up his curiousness in scientific attire? It seems Jung 'knew' alchemy is the practice of spiritual consciousness, and archetypes enable ESP. It seems what Jung calls integration is actually spirit attachment. And they can equally detach? Like, someone can have the spirit of divination, but it can be cast out.

Jung died on the cusp of the occult revival, that he was instrumental in bringing about. As it transpired, Jung was more popular with New Agers than psychologists. He inspired many to 'journey to the East', like the Beatles. It's not a 'coincidence' Jung features on the Sergeant Pepper Lonely Hearts Club Band album cover. Jung popularised the Gnostic gospels, and it's said that without his interventions, including the I Ching and the 'Tibetan Book of the Dead', that Taoism and Zen would not have achieved their modern-day popularity. There has been an explosion of New Age paraphernalia since the sixties. Like, spirit guides are popular, despite their power to usurp our conscious mind?

As 'Magnu' alluded to, it seems we're increasingly unfulfilled with the vacuous nature of materialism, and are looking for something spiritual? Hence, why not go to yoga classes and get some Buddha statues for the garden? Or ingest some DMT? It's not a coincidence that people would rather discover eastern philosophy than God's word, namely, the Bible. Indeed, the occult is fashionable, like the cabala? Why not partake in witchcraft and sell our soul to the devil? Perhaps we could become beautiful and filthy rich, like the influencers, because this matters?

It's duly noted, that Jung recognised the impact of nihilism on our mental health. He understood the trouble with the modern world was a 'loss of soul'. He referred to our collective loss of soul as a 'general neurosis of our age'. He reported that the majority of individuals that came to see him, presenting with various mental afflictions, were actually suffering from a crisis of meaning. He observed that for many, their lives seemed senseless and aimless. It matters that there's no point to life. Our souls are screaming for meaning? He proposed that the reason psychology had become the dominant source of wisdom in the twentieth century was because the impact religions could make on people's lives had declined.

Indeed, he once said the primary cause at the heart of his patient's problems was a lack of religious outlook. Jung observed that as the power of the church waned, psychology was left to deal with modern day 'soul' sickness. And he argued this could only be cured through greater knowledge and individual experience. We can achieve wholeness by reconnecting with the universal life of the collective unconscious. We need to connect with God, our true Self?

Jung regarded the human psyche as 'by nature religious'. He recognised that people with spiritual faith have a greater sense of purpose. And he regarded religion as a basic fulfilment of life. Life's meaninglessness, being cut off from our religious roots, births mental disarray. But it's not about religious dogma, or as Jung said, religious dogma is not enough. To find meaning, each of us must live in relationship to the Great Mystery through our relationship with all inner and outer creation.

Jung said in a famous BBC interview, 'Man cannot stand a meaningless life'. He said, 'the decisive question for man is: Is he related to something infinite or not? That is the telling question of his life. Only if we know that the thing that truly matters is the infinite can we avoid fixing our interest upon futilities, and upon all kinds of goals which are not of real importance...' It seems we get a grip when we realise there's more going on? Our fabricated problems pale in comparison.

Jung claimed that he was interested in religion from a psychological perspective. As any credible person knows that religion's bosh? Psychology 'opens peoples' eyes to the real meaning of dogmas'. For Jung, religious dogmas or creeds are only symbols that point to the experiences people have had. He contended that all religions are imaginary, collective mythologies, so they're not real but they have a real effect on the human personality.

He proposed that God reveals Himself through the collective unconscious, which has in turn propelled all the myths and religious philosophies ever created. Spiritual archetypes are unconscious processes to which myths and religious dogmas give expression. And whilst each one is a valiant effort to relate to God, the infinite and eternal, they're myths. They're symbols that lead to the God archetype, which is the Self archetype, because our true nature is the nature of God. Jung concedes that spiritual archetypes do not prove the reality of God, only that the God image exists in man's psyche. He further asserts that whilst the existence of God cannot be proven in the external world, the experience is still valid.

Contrary to the Christian belief that deity is outside man, Jung was convinced that divinity was in us. Divine wisdom (gnosis) is divine knowledge of Self, and divine self-knowledge is knowledge by which the god in man knows he is God. It was therefore pointless in trying to understand the gods, but rather the point was to journey inside. Like the Gnostics, (and yogis), Jung advocated that each person contains the essence of God. We have a divine spark that can be ignited through realisation of our true God identity. Like, Jesus was fully man and fully God, we are also human and divine. So, there's nothing special about Jesus? Jesus is not our saviour, but rather symbolises the God in us?

Jung explains that we have a Messiah archetype, which is a divine archetype, and this latent potential lies within each of us. So, we are our own saviour and messiah. For Jung, the spiritual Messiah, Christ, Buddha, Osiris, Dionysus, Mithras etc are personifications of the archetype. Jung wrote, 'Christ is not an archetype but a personification of the archetype'. It's highlighted this Saviour figure appears throughout history and is found everywhere.

However, whilst Jung claimed archetypes in the collective unconscious are demonstrated by shared religions/myths etc, it seems the reason the world shares the same religious ideas is not because of archetypes as such, but rather because it's the same sun god worshipping religion that originated in Babylon and went global. The human race has the same His-Story. But we'll get to this.

Contrary to the Gnostics then (and mystical beliefs), with their concept of dualism, that man and God are one, and Satan and God are one, Christians see man and God as two, and Satan and God as two separate entities. Jung notes, that unlike other philosophies and religions, the concept of evil is absent from the Christian Trinity, so to complete this, the devil is the fourth element of the trinity.

For Jung, the Christ-symbol lacks wholeness since it does include the dark side of things, and God the Father, who is light, lacks darkness. Thus, his solution is the True God combines Jesus and Satan to make a unified whole. He maintained, 'Light is followed by shadow, the other side of the creator'. Jung believed, 'It is possible for a man to attain totality, to become whole, only with the cooperation of the spirit of darkness'.

For Christians however, light and dark are incompatible in the Christian as they are in God. Sinfulness, falsehood, hatred, impurity, fear etc is antithetical to goodness, truth, love, righteousness, hope, purity, confidence. In essence, there is no darkness in light. The Bible teaches that God is Holy and has no part in evil, which is the work of Satan. In the Bible, in Isaiah 5:20 we're told, 'destruction is certain for those say evil is good and good is evil; that put dark is light and light is dark; that bitter is sweet and sweet is bitter'. It is however also argued that good cannot be evil, but requires the presence of evil to become manifest i.e. we know what's good because it's not evil.

Furthermore, unlike Jung's view that the human psyche is a microcosm of the macrocosm, according to Christianity man is not an extension of the universal psyche, nor is the universe an extension of man's psyche.

Christians don't believe creation and creator are one. We are not God. And contrary to alchemy, which is concerned with the union of opposites, or becoming possessed by archetypes, for Christians, God is the Great Alchemist who transforms us. However, we'll get back to alchemy and God. Fundamentally, it seems there's a spiritual dimension, which we can access through our spirit bodies, but we do so at our peril. As mentioned, the veil's in situ for a reason.

On a positive note, Jung challenged the dominant materialist paradigm. He rejected the reductive dogma of scientism and the mechanistic worldview. Indeed, he wrote a paper 'On the Limits of Exact Science' which attacked scientists for their inflexible materialism. He proposed that the soul, whilst immaterial and outside of spacetime, should nevertheless prove susceptible to empirical investigation through research into the phenomenon of hypnosis, sleep disorders (somnambulism) and mediumistic communication.

Towards the end of his life, in an interview Jung was asked 'Do you believe in God?' He mused out loud. 'Well, we use the word 'believe' when we think that something is true but we don't yet have a substantial body of evidence to support it. No. I don't believe in God. I know there's a God' (cited in Scott Peck, 'Further Along the Road Less Travelled', 1988, p.174).

Jung further commented, 'if God had foreseen His world, it would be a senseless machine and Man's existence a useless freak. My intellect can envisage the latter possibility, but the whole of my being says 'no' to it'. Jung also believed in an afterlife, stating, 'what happens after death is so unspeakably glorious our imagination and feelings do not suffice to form even an approximate conception of it'. So, there is a point to life, and there's no death in the real sense?

It seems Jung's parents gave him both sides of the cosmic war. He received his dad's Christian truth and his mum's eastern philosophical lie, that old adage that we are God. Or is it the other way round? Maybe the Bible, God's alleged Word, is wrong and we really are God? For Luciferians, who rule the world, Lucifer is God and God is the Devil. Everything becomes inverted, and perverted.

It's also noted, that Jung was able to connect up with some American wealth from a branch of the Rockefeller family and control the publication of many of his texts in English translation, which suggests they approved of his philosophy. The Rockefeller Foundation ties into and controls the American Medical Association. As highlighted, the idea that everyone is God, cosmic wholeness, is the foundation of the unified world view. It seems materialist Freud served the sexual agenda, and successfully wrote off (psychologised) the spirit world. Then Jung served the agenda by reviving spiritualism to replace Christianity.

Jung wrote at the end of his life, 'there was a daimon in me...it overpowered me...I could never stop at anything once attained...a creative person has little power over his own life. He is not free. He is the captive and drawn by his daimon...'

'All that we see or seem, is but a dream within a dream'. Edgar Allan Poe

7

Altered States of Consciousness

Beyond the premise of the Cogito, it seems pertinent to reflect on Altered States of Consciousness (ASC), as they arguably tutor our 'normal' consciousness. We know what normal is comparatively i.e. being in touch with reality. But moreover, it's possible that ASC shed some light into the nature of reality beyond the material realm. It's possible there is something going on behind the material veil. Indeed, it appears we've been hoodwinked with materialism, as anyone who's taken DMT knows.

The mainstream assumption in society is that everyday waking consciousness is the truest expression of how things are in 'objective' reality. The consensus is that it's normal to dream, but dreams aren't real, and neither are hallucinations or visions. But what if this assumption is wrong and the astral plane is as real and valid as everyday waking consciousness? It seems we're more comfortable believing we only have our own personal Freudian unconscious to contend with, as opposed to the reality of other dimensions?

So, whilst ASC are by definition delusional, they can enable perceiving things inaccessible to ordinary, everyday consciousness. And unlike those afflicted with mental illness, like psychosis, others actively seek out these curious experiences e.g. through drink, drugs, hypnosis, meditation, fasting, sleep, and sensory deprivation. People want visions and spiritual experiences. It seems we're increasingly partial to deviating from the normal waking state. It's overrated?

Suffice to say, mental health professionals discourage us from seeking out abnormal states of consciousness, as there's always the potential of rocking it out on a psychiatric ward. Indeed, it seems ironic that people deliberately fast and deprive themselves of sleep etc, and take psychoactive poisons to induce visions, in the face of those psychotically challenged.

It seems prudent to start with the proverbial normal ASC, namely, dreaming, since we can all relate to this. Research shows that we dream about 20% of sleeping hours, so 1-2 hours a night. The mind is however active during all stages of sleep, and interestingly the brain uses more energy when asleep.

And sleeping/dreaming is awesome. Praise the Lord we've been designed to sleep. It's literally a free trip every night. We get up to all manner of mischief, as our bodies just lie there comatosed. It's the ultimate escape attempt, and it's surreal that dreams feel so real at the time i.e. we really feel that sorrow, fear, joy, and arousal, irrespective of who it shouldn't be with. We never know what's going to happen, or what's round the corner. And we can fly and experience all kinds of interesting things that we would never 'normally' experience. But then we wake up. The movie's over, and it's back to reality. It's almost like it didn't happen, and we ever so quickly forget that it ever did. And who cares, since it's not real. It's just a dream.

There are four stages of sleep, and in a night's sleep we have four-six cycles. Each cycle is shorter in duration than the last, and as the cycle shortens there is relatively more time spent in REM. REM stands for Rapid Eye Movement (term coined in 1953) and is associated with dreaming. Apparently 80% of people awoken during REM sleep will report dreaming, whereas less than half will claim to have been dreaming during any non-REM stage of sleep.

It's also reported that non-REM sleep is involved with procedural memories i.e. performing day-to-day activities, whereas REM can be crazy mental, just plain out of this world. REM dreams can involve intense emotions (e.g. fear, loss, love, erotica), illogical events, the suspension of time and space, and then there's the weird way we can switch between different realities and situations i.e. we're somewhere doing something, and just like that, we're somewhere else doing something else. We might be friends with the famous and dangerous.

It's also interesting how dreams affect the physical body, like teenage boy's wet dreams, complete with cardboard covers. All mammals dream (I wonder what my cats dream about) and human infants spend much time in REM, including in utero (not much else to do?). Research reveals that lack of REM causes irritability, lack of concentration and motivation. We can't think properly without proper sleep. We're not firing on all cylinders.

Antidepressants, sleeping tablets and booze notably inhibit REM and 'proper sleep' (the 'quality' is halved). So, that's counterproductive? Sleep deprivation can however improve mood. It leads to increased activity of serotonin receptor sites within the neurons, which mimics the effects of antidepressants. But, as every manic knows, we need to sleep. Sleep is the great healer. As mentioned, apparently a third of Britons struggle to get to sleep and five million have insomnia. There's also apparently fifteen million snorers in the UK, which is a common cause of divorce. So, there's that.

According to EEG's (which measure electrical activity in the brain), when we're awake we emit beta and alpha waves. Beta waves are associated with day to day wakefulness, and alpha waves are associated with states of relaxation and peacefulness. As touched on, alpha is a vacant state, which is induced by watching TV. Hence, programming us with programmes is so fruitful. We even get 'countdowns' to 'the news'.

Brainwaves are notably produced by synchronised electrical impulses from our masses of neurons communicating with each other. They change according to what we're doing and how we're feeling i.e. our voltage fluctuates. They're divided into bands delineating slow, moderate and fast waves. Thus, when we're wired or hyper, higher frequencies are dominant, and when we're slow and sluggish, slower brainwaves are dominant. It's like the brain has a pulse?

So, when we close our eyes and start to relax, we emit alpha waves. We then drift into the first stage of sleep. It's difficult to pinpoint the actual point of falling asleep, but basically brain activity gradually slows down, and our heart rate begins to slow. And it's literally like we fall asleep i.e. when we're drifting off and suddenly aware that we're falling asleep, we bounce on the mattress. This stage is characterised by jerks and jolts, and people awoken at this stage often believe they've been awake. They don't remember falling asleep.

Then we la-la onto stage two, which makes up the majority of our sleep (we spend about 50% of our time in that stage). Eye movement stops and conscious awareness of the outside world has gone. Brainwaves during this stage are mainly in the theta wave range. Then it's onto stage three, the deepest stage of sleep which is characterised by delta waves (delta sleep is known as short wave sleep).

As we move through the three stages of non-REM sleep, activity in the brain gets slower and slower, and brain neurons fire in greater and greater synchronicity. At the delta stage, neuronal activity, breathing rate, heart rate and blood pressure are most chilled. Dreaming is more common during this stage of non-REM sleep, but it's not as common (or vivid and memorable) as during REM sleep.

After about 90 minutes the sleep cycle goes into reverse, even back to beta waves indicative of being awake and alert. This is REM time. It's also called 'the paradoxical sleep' since there's the contrast between the recorded awake mind and the sleeping body. We're asleep but we're awake. It seems Jack comes out the box, but Jack is largely unaware, because he's sleeping. So, what are we up to and what are our dreams telling us?

Psychologists tell us that dreams process the emotional content of our lives. The conjecture is that just as the body tries to heal itself, so the mind also tries to heal itself. Dreamland is our surreal place to make sense of our emotions, like our desires and fears. Apparently, anxiety is the most common emotion experienced in dreams. And dreams enable expressing things we repress. Like, same-sex attraction and bestiality? Dreams provide us with a safe arena for our psyche to explore alternative realities, which includes all aspects of our sexuality.

There's further the idea that dreams recur because there's something yet to be consciously resolved. The recurring dream is nudging us to become aware of some aspect of our lives that doesn't support growth. We need to address the problem they're highlighting for us. It's also purported that it doesn't matter if we forget our dreams, as dreams continue to do their work whether or not we remember them.

Whilst there are dreams which manifestly represent Freudian wishes or fears, perhaps there's even more value to dreams? Dreams have historically been considered significant. Like, in the Bible, various prophets received messages through dreams. Sometimes angels would visit them in their dreams. Or, like Pharaoh had dreams that Joseph interpreted which saved Egypt from starvation. In ancient times, leaders would get their dreams interpreted by wise-men. Druids were renowned for interpreting dreams.

Dreams continue to be important for the spiritually minded. Like in Islam, they're of great significance, as Muslims can ask for guidance through dreams. Muslims however understand that whilst dreams can come from Allah, daemons or 'jinn' can also exert control over people's dreams. This corroborates with mystics who claim to meet their spirit guides in their dreams. Apparently increasing numbers of Muslims are dreaming of 'a man in white' believed to be Jesus, and they're converting to Christianity. Like, an ISIS fighter, who previously enjoyed killing Christians, was told by Jesus in a dream 'you are killing my people'. So, that's interesting.

It's also interesting that Professor Kekule discovered the structure of the benzene ring in a dream and won a noble prize. And Einstein's theory of relativity came to him in a dream. As Jung explained, when dreaming we have access to the collective unconscious, the great mind. And the otherwise hidden 'archetypes' tucked up in there, who can impart knowledge?

It seems our dreamscape provides some kind of space or platform, enabling 'entities' to visit us and give us messages? Like, angels can appear, and demons, spirit guides, and even Jesus. Perhaps dreams entail a supernatural playground, a place where we can encounter both fantasy and reality, in the sense that the dream is fantasy, but supernatural reality i.e. external metaphysical entities can intervene in that playground? Like, Active Imagination provides a platform for psychic entities to dwell in? Maybe our dreams are some kind of portal to the spirit world or astral plane?

In her book 'Prepare for War' (1987), Dr Rebecca Brown mentions 'Amelia's' terrible nightmare, where she was running away from a baboon, who viciously bit her back and the bite remained. She had a deep bite in the flesh of her back. Brown has no doubt that the baboon was a demon. She also pertains to other people's dreams, which have similarly left them with bite marks etc. Brown notes, that it can be either demons or human spirits inflicting the wounds. As touched on, people can astral project (leave their physical body and travel in their light body), but we'll get to this in a mo.

When dreaming we're detached from our sensory perceptions, but it seems our dream body has senses. Hence, we taste, hear, see, touch, feel, and smell in our dreams. And in a vivid dream, these senses are particularly vivid. So, maybe the dream body is the astral body? As Paracelsus highlighted, our astral body, (which is the exact counterpart of our physical body), has astral senses. He explained the purposes of our senses are to perceive objects that exist on the plane for which those senses are adapted i.e. physical senses exist for the purpose of seeing physical things, and the senses of the inner man are made to see the things of the soul.

It's noted, our sixth sense (intuition) has an astral counterpart to the pineal gland, which is our telepathic organ of communication i.e. it picks information up like an antenna. Thus, people communicate telepathically in the astral plane. It seems people can communicate telepathically if their spirit bodies are activated?

Many people believe dreaming gives us an opportunity to leave the body and explore different dimensions. Apparently, Paracelsus would visit people in their dreams. He purported that when sleeping our astral body may communicate with others, and that we can exercise astral influence over another in dreams. He believed that dreams, omens and visions are given to the astral self not corporeal self. Dr Brown agreed that God, angels, and demons can communicate with us through visions which are received in our spirits.

Secret societies notably depict our spirit (astral self) floating out of the body in sleep. Like, a few feet above our physical body. They teach that in dreams we perceive the spirit worlds, where we are approached by angels and demons and spirits of the dead. However, upon waking, we forget.

Russell Brand (2014) said, 'Dreams, more immersive and psychedelic than any drug and occurring whenever we sleep, unbidden, a nightly reminder that mystery reigns within' (p.351). Dreams are arguably a reminder of another reality. They also suggest that our consciousness can be separated from our physical body i.e. the dualist belief? We get a sneak preview of what it's like to be disembodied. Like, when we die? For scientists however, such talk is bosh. And whilst lucid dreaming takes dreaming to a new heightened level, it's still just dreaming, and therefore not real?

Lucid dreaming is being aware that we're dreaming when we're dreaming. It's like waking up in our dream, which is unlike normal dreaming, as usually there's no recognition of being in a dream i.e. no self-awareness. In surveys about 50% of people have had lucid dreams, and 20% have them regularly. Everything changes and becomes more vivid with lucid dreams. The dreamer feels more like their waking self and can take control of the dream ('dream masters' are those able to control their dreams). Lucid dreams don't last long and then it's back into normal sleep frequencies.

Expert lucid dreamers can signal with eye movements, since almost all muscles are paralysed when in REM, and this allows experimenters to time their dreams and to observe brain activity during the dreams. This generally confirms the realistic timing of dreams and also shows that the brain is behaving very much as if it were really doing whatever they're dreaming about.

So, for a dream to be considered lucid, the dreamer must have awareness of their dream state (orientation) and dream environment; an awareness of self and their capacity to make decisions; a clear memory of the waking world and what's currently going on i.e. aware of what the dream means. The dreamer is concentrated and focussed. It's like we're consciously aware.

I've had a few lucid dreams, but for the purposes of example, we can reflect on a dream I had in Malawi. Thus, I was on the top bed of a bunk in a seven-bed dorm and it was night-time and we were all sleeping, so my dreamscape exactly mirrored my location. Then I awoke as I heard some movement, and some guy put his hands over my mouth, and I watched as his ally went over to those sleeping, with the clear intent to murder them. I began screaming as loudly and fervently as I could to try and wake them. My screams were however muffled because my mouth was covered. It felt insanely real, as if it was really happening. And the next day, those in the room were asking each other if they heard a dog yelping and whining during the night, and then I realised that was me (LOL).

Suffice to say, it's truly awesome to wake up from some dreams, and realise we were actually just dreaming. And it's bemusing that lucid dreams can seem indistinguishable from reality. 'Reality checks' help us decipher whether we're in a dream or real life. Like, my brother, who regularly experiences lucid dreaming, presses a light switch and if the light doesn't turn on or off, he knows he's dreaming.

But even weirder is sleepwalking and night-terrors, which, like bedwetting, happen at the deepest stage of sleep (delta sleep), and thus unlike REM, our muscles aren't paralysed. 'Parasomnia' is a blanket term that refers to undesired events that happen when we sleep, excluding sleep apnoea (the cessation of airflow). So, sleepwalking and night terrors are different manifestations of the same parasomnia disorder. They're more common in children (when their pineal gland's ripe?) but apparently five million British adults suffer from some form of parasomnia.

As mentioned, dreams are more 'procedural' during this stage of sleep. Hence, sleepwalkers are known to clean, cook, eat and drink, send emails, drive, have sex, indecently expose themselves, and some have even murdered others. It's like people are enacting the script in their dream, going through the motions, regurgitating a normal day?

This mysterious state of consciousness is described as basically stuck halfway between being asleep and awake. The exact cause of sleepwalking is unknown. People are awake enough to get out of bed, open their eyes, talk, partake in whatever, but they're in a world of their own. Sleepwalkers often have little or no memory of the incident, as they're not truly conscious. Although their eyes are open, their expression is dim and glazed over. It can be very hard to wake a sleepwalker, and sleepwalking may last as little as thirty seconds or as long as thirty minutes. Sleepwalking seems to be trancelike i.e. dissociated like a hypnotised person?

A third of a million adults in the UK sleepwalk but homicide aside, presumably this is less traumatising than night terrors, which affects about a million. Night terrors sound dreadful, and similarly remain a medical mystery. During night terror bouts, people are described as 'bolting upright' with their eyes wide open and a look of intense fear and panic on their face. They will often scream and are universally inconsolable. They usually sweat, exhibit rapid respiration, and have a rapid heart rate. They often have elaborate motor activity, such as thrashing limbs, punching, swinging, or fleeing motions. So, they're not making pies, but rather fighting whatever, in dream world, that is terrorising them.

Paracelsus maintained that spirits wishing to make use of men often act on them during dreams. Is it possible? Could independent spirit beings or 'archetypes' attack us, in some realm of consciousness that we're not aware of?

So, forget night terrors, but equally forget 'sleep paralysis'. That's what psychologists call the fear ridden experience of feeling suffocated and powerless to escape a thick black fog that comes and engulfs. Sufferers speak about an infernal presence, and in addition to feeling pressure on their chest and difficulty breathing, some report physical sensations such as a strong current running through their upper body. Besides the 'vision' of a shadowy malevolent being, or plural, 'the shadow people', sleep paralysis victims report encounters with hairy monsters, animal-hybrids, giant insects, serpentine beings, grey orbs described as balls like liquid smoke, and aliens. Like, entities in DMT space?

Those subjected to these dark experiences can't fight back (run or hide), on account of their inability to move. In sleep paralysis all the body muscles are paralysed and only the eyes can move. So, people have to lie there, pinned to their beds, and take it. The paralysis can last from a few seconds to several minutes. Apparently as much as 60% of people have experienced this phenomenon. Some people have sleep paralysis once or twice in their life, while others experience it a few times a month or more regularly.

Psychologists say it happens as people are entering or leaving sleep. They advise that the person wakes up before the REM paralysis has worn off, and concocts a vivid experience in that unpleasant paralysed state between waking and dreaming. The powerful sense of someone being close, the overwhelming feeling of pressure on your chest and grabbing at your throat is merely a hallucination. Like night terrors, the haunted experience is undermined. It's not real, but rather inconvenient. Archetypes from the collective unconscious are tormenting us? They're dementors?

All over the world people report about this experience and it's almost always seen as something negative and supernatural. In Thailand people see it as prankster ghosts who sit on your chest, in Mexico people report about the dead climbing on top of them, and the Chinese see it as minor body possession by dead spirits. Most cultures have sleep paralysis myths such as the 'Old Hag of Newfoundland' who appears in the night and may crush the sleeper's chest as to prevent them from moving.

Others see it as some dark energy, something they're unable to shake off, passing through them. It seems we're more comfortable with the term 'energy' as opposed to 'entity'? Others regard the phenomenon as panic attacks at night-time, as people are awakened and terrorised at night. However, the shadow people often speak to the victim, so that's not a normal panic attack.

The Bible tells us about demonic attacks, and we're told to shout out the name of Jesus and tell them to 'beat it'. Apparently, sleep paralysis stops immediately by calling on the name Jesus. And the same happens with alien abductions and night terrors. As Steven Bancarz, (a former New Age author/researcher who became a Christian) states, this confirms they are demons and Jesus is Lord.

It seems we hear about sleep paralysis in Job 4:12. Thus, Eliphaz said to Job, 'This truth was given me in secret, as though whispered in my ear. It came in a vision at night as others slept. Fear gripped me; I trembled and shook with terror. A spirit swept by my face. Its wind sent shivers up my spine. It stopped, but I couldn't see its shape. There was a form before my eyes, and a hushed voice said, 'Can a mortal be just and upright before God? Can a person be pure before the Creator?'

Contrary to the view espoused by the scientific community, Louis Proud, author of 'Dark Intrusions: An Investigation into the Paranormal Nature of Sleep Paralysis Experience' (2009), believes these experiences allow access to the spirit realm. He believes sleep paralysis experiences involve genuine contact and communication with incorporeal entities, some of them parasitic and potentially dangerous.

Proud has been plagued with chronic sleep paralysis since he was seventeen years young, and has undergone hundreds of terrifying episodes. He considers sleep paralysis a profound mystery. But moreover, he was just a 'regular secular' person before he was subjected to this haunted onslaught. He had no religious or spiritual preconceived ideas. It seems he learned first-hand that there's something peculiar going on.

Proud pertains to the immense consistency between sleep paralysis accounts, (having read innumerable accounts of others' experiences), and relays how the same themes surface. But beyond the general themes, like the presence in the room and the sensation of a heavy weight on the chest, all of which are well established, he refers, for example, to 'bed rocking' phenomenon. He has experienced this, stating that in an effort to frighten or torment him, the presence or entity started making the bed rock back and forth, as if it were standing there pushing the bed with its arms. He recalls that it kept this up for what seemed like hours. He notes that he's not sure whether or not the bed moved 'physically' but he certainly received the impression that he did.

He asserts, 'Now if, as the "experts" say, what is experienced during sleep paralysis is only hallucinatory, then why the amazing consistency between sleep paralysis accounts, with the same specific themes popping up again and again? You would expect dream-related hallucinations to consist of almost anything'.

But it gets weirder, as sleep paralysis can also lead to deep sexual experiences. People can have sexual encounters in this state. Sometimes the 'shadow person' that sits on the victim's chest proceeds to sexually molest them, including sensations of penetration. This is aptly referred to as 'ghost rape'. For most people, these experiences are horrendous, but some report that sex with demons, known as incubus (male) and succubus (female), is awesome.

Like, actress Lucy Liu told 'US magazine' of her sexual encounter with a mysterious spirit. She said, 'I was sleeping on my futon, and some sort of spirit came down from God knows where and made love to me. It was sheer bliss. I felt everything. I climaxed. And then he floated away. Something came down and touched me, and now it watches over me'. Anna Nicole Smith (model) claimed she had amazing sex with a ghost, and Bobby Brown (singer) claimed he had sex with a ghost in a spooky mansion. He said he woke up and was being mounted by a ghost. He insists he wasn't high. Apparently, actor Dan Akroyd and singer Kesha have also had sex with spirits. People say they feel pressure and their breath.

Records of evil spirits invading bodies and forcing people to have sex, dates back to medieval times and beyond. A friend of mine maintains he's had sex with succubus several times. Some people also report having sex with the ghost of their dead partner. One encounter I read about was a dead husband claimed he wanted to have anal sex with his widow because they never had it when he was alive (LOL).

Succubus and incubus can apparently take on whatever form they choose, so that includes dead people? As touched on, people (occultists) can also exteriorise their astral body to torment others. Like, Dr Rebecca Brown gave the example of 'John' who was sodomised by 'Mike's' astral body and although he could see nothing, he clearly felt his rectum being penetrated as if someone was physically committing this act (p.271).

But furthermore, some people also experience Out of Body Experiences (OBE) with sleep paralysis. Apparently, the dark entity can pull the person (human spirit) out their body, which seems to happen if the sleep paralysis continues. People commonly report feeling tingling vibrations as they're sucked out of their bodies. They report a 'whoosh' sensation.

However, before we continue with OBEs, it's noted that neuroscientists deem this prospect delusional, since there is no astral body. The scientific perspective is that ASC including meditative states can be seen as the border between sleeping and waking i.e. dream consciousness spills over to waking consciousness (like psychosis). They regard OBEs as dissociative experiences arising from different psychological and neurological factors.

As mentioned, the 'God Helmet' can induce OBEs and other mystical experiences by electrically stimulating the temporal lobes with magnetic fields to create electrical charges in the brain. It seems pertinent to note however, that the God Helmet is reportedly a pale imitation of a real OBE. The mechanically induced version is apparently far more muted, less intense and less profound. Apparently 80% of people 'sense a presence' with the God Helmet, but it's suggested this could be psychological. Like, it didn't work for Richard Dawkins, for example, because he doesn't believe in God or spirits? Ironically, scientists including Dawkins are increasingly open to aliens. But we'll get to this.

An OBE is an experience in which the conscious mind seems separated from the shackles of the body. About 20% of the population have had at least one OBE, which is described as weightless 'floating' about. Most OBE's have common features, like seeing their physical body as they do the objects in the room. They usually report having ghostly bodies that can pass through solid objects. During an OBE everything is objective and real, and happens in real time. But people further claim that not only are they conscious, but their consciousness is enhanced. It's described as more expansive. Senses feel more vivid.

One of my friends from university said she had an OBE. She was sixteen and a virgin, and drunk on holiday with her parents, she got friendly with some Greek bloke who subsequently led her to the beach and raped her. Whilst it happened, she said she stepped outside her body and observed it within close proximity. OBEs tend to happen with traumatic events, like rape and Near Death Experiences (NDEs).

For the purposes of example, we can consider the following report by someone who experienced cardiac arrest and was without a heartbeat for twenty minutes. Thus, he told the doctor, 'I heard a whooshing sound in my ears. I felt like you feel when you go over a bump in a car going real fast and you feel your stomach drop out. The next thing I knew, I was in a room crouched in a corner of the ceiling. I could see my body below me. I could see doctors and nurses working on me. I wondered what they were doing. I saw a doctor put jelly on my chest. My hair was really messed up. It seemed greasy, and I wished that I had washed my hair before coming to hospital. They had cut my clothes off, but my pants were still on. I heard a doctor say, 'Stand back', and then he pushed a button on one of the paddles. Suddenly I was back inside my body. One minute I was looking down at my face. I could see the top of doctors' heads. After he pushed that button, I was suddenly looking into a doctor's face'.

Like this bloke's account, people are often able to report the conversations that were taking place when 'dead'. Like my friend, heard the conversations taking place when she 'died', which proved true. Apparently, the doctor working on her, who was a friend of her sisters, said to his colleagues, her sister would kill him if she died. Interestingly, she said that the scene she was observing, whilst out her body, began to diminish, like a TV screen getting smaller and smaller. She felt like she was drifting into sleep, until she was brought back. So, perhaps the OBE precedes death?

I read about a woman who was born blind and had a NDE, and when she came back to life she reported everything that she saw, which proved correct. As it transpires, most blind people see in NDEs. This suggests we do have an astral body with astral senses?

However, unlike an OBE, a NDE seems to take us on a trip beyond the physical world. Those who have had a NDE invariably talk about a tunnel, with a light at the end. Apparently 'the valley of the shadow of death' in Psalm 23 (in the Bible), is a reference to the tunnel at death. They also mention feeling deep contentment, an overwhelming sense of peace and joy. It's a transcendental experience and people consistently report seeing deceased others, including religious or spiritual figures. They also report having a 'review of the past' (flashbacks) which is phenomenological, in the sense that they 'feel' everything as if it were really happening. People relive their memories. It's like our memories give back our secrets.

Again, for the purposes of example, we can consider the following report from a girl, Natalie, who had an acute asthma attack, followed by a seizure that nearly killed her. Thus, 'She described the amazing things that happened when she was on the verge of death. She felt herself ejected from her body; then she entered a tunnel. At the end of the tunnel she saw a bright light and people waiting to welcome her. Suddenly two friendly 'light figures' appeared, one on either side of her. Each took one of her hands, and they carried her with them down the tunnel. Natalie felt a strong desire to get to the Light and was impatient because her companions were moving so slowly. As they travelled through the tunnel, Natalie saw images from her childhood, one of which was her father pushing her on a swing. Then she saw an image of her mother and thought about how sad her family would be if she died. At that point the 'light figures' set Natalie down and released her hands. Concerned about the grief her death would cause her loved ones, Natalie reluctantly turned her back on the Light, walked back out of the tunnel and returned to her body'.

When people miraculously come back to life, it's called the 'Lazarus effect', after Biblical Lazarus who Jesus raised from the dead after four (presumably honking) days. And dead is dead, no heartbeat, breathing or brain function.

Another example is Brian Miller, who came back to life after his heart stopped for forty-five minutes (he miraculously awoke with a regular heartbeat and no damage to his brain). He insists there's an afterlife, being convinced he was there. He seen the Light but as he was walking towards heaven, his mother-in-law, who had recently died, told him he needed to go back as it wasn't his time (he had a wife and kids at home). People often report hearing a voice telling them to choose whether to live or to die. For the most part though, people say they don't want to return, because the Light is so awesome. They describe returning to the body as very heavy.

Interestingly, most people who have a NDE, having attempted suicide, don't try committing suicide again. A study conducted by Bruce Greyson (American psychiatrist and NDE researcher) showed that almost all people who have NDEs during suicide attempts never again try to kill themselves. In contrast, a high percentage of those who attempt suicide, but do not experience NDEs, make further attempts to take their lives.

The NDE has such a positive effect that desperate people who feel their lives have no meaning return from a NDE with a renewed sense of purpose. NDEs often have a profound impact, with people typically becoming more spiritual and altruistic. It's as if they've been enlightened and 'know' there's more going on. It's like an ayahuasca trip? People speak about 'feeling connected' and they're less afraid of death. So, maybe death is all good. Whatever happens, that Light better be there?

As it transpires however, not all NDEs are recalled so blissfully. Indeed, as much as 20% have distressing and terrifying experiences, which includes being accosted by a hostile presence. Like, two men I befriended, who had NDEs, both said their consciousness survived but it was pitch black. They couldn't see anything and one in particular sensed an overwhelming presence of evil. He described it as an avalanche of sheer evil behind him. This bloke was a Reiki master and came to Peru for ayahuasca trips to heal his mental turmoil. He said he was on the brink of either killing himself or someone else (safe). They both believed they were in hell. So, they got a second chance?

Others report falling down. The soul drops like a lead weight. Down, down, down, until hell opens up complete with horrendous smells, heat and screams. So, hell is below us? Maybe death is like lucid dreaming but it's real? However, for a well-known example, we can consider Ian McCormack's testimony about his trip to hell. He died for approximately fifteen minutes.

Thus, McCormack was living the epicurean life in Mauritius, which included diving. So, it was all peachy until one night, when out diving, he was stung by five box jellyfish (who's venomous poison can kill a person in four minutes). When an ambulance came, his body was completely paralysed, and necrosis had started to set into his bone marrow. On the way to the hospital, he began to see his life flash before him. He was an atheist, but as he lay dying, he saw a vision of his mother, who was the only Christian in his family, praying for him. She encouraged McCormack to cry out to God, and so he did. He cried out, asking God if He's real, to help him. Instantly verses of the Lord's Prayer came into his mind.

The ambulance reached the hospital, and whilst doctors tried to save his life, their efforts were thwarted. He remembers closing his eyes, thinking he would open them in a minute, he just needed a small break from the ordeal of dying, but then he slipped away and woke up in the dark. He recounts that he sat bolt upright, completely awake.

He said, 'Have you ever woken up in the middle of the night and tried to find the light switch? Well, I was trying to find the light switch, and I couldn't seem to find it. I was trying to touch something, and I was moving round and there was nothing there. I was not even bumping into anything. I couldn't see my hand in front of my face. I lifted my hand up to find out how much I could see. I lifted it to where my face was and it went straight through where my face should have been. It was a terrifying experience. I knew right there and then, I was me, Ian McCormack, standing there, but without a body. I had the sensation and the feeling that I had a body, but I had nothing physical to touch. I was a spiritual being, and my physical body had died, but I was very much alive, and very much aware that I had arms and legs and a head, but I could no longer touch them'.

He advised, the darkness was not just physical but spiritual, and he began to sense evil in the darkness. He said, 'a cold encroaching evil seemed to pervade the air around me'. He sensed he was being watched and became aware that other people were moving around him. He explains that although he didn't speak out loud, they answered his questions. From the darkness he heard voices screaming at him 'shut up', 'you're in hell', and 'you deserve to be here'.

Fortunately for him however, he was then lifted out by a beam of pure white light en route to the source of Light itself, which he described as 'living light'. He describes having a very powerful experience of love, peace, joy and forgiveness of sins, and regales how the waves of light permeating through him, delivered insurmountable bliss.

He believes he was saved literally at the last minute as he deserved to be in hell. He believes that he encountered Jesus and saw a perfect creation, 'the New Earth and New Heavens'. He also had a choice whether to stay or go home, and he chose the latter, as he wanted to tell his mum she was right about Jesus. He was further given a vision of many thousands of people that wouldn't get a chance to hear about God if he didn't return.

NDEs seem to suggest that death is illusory, as consciousness persists independently of brain activity. Despite being brain dead, (and by all accounts dead), the mind remains alive. This suggests the brain is a receiver of consciousness, a conduit rather than a producer. Maybe there is an inner me and you? Maybe Paracelsus is correct, that our mind operates through our brain, which operates our physical machinery. And our astral body is the vehicle for our soul or consciousness. It's also noted, that often people who experience OBEs or NDEs experience the onset of psychic abilities. This includes kids who've had OBEs due to childhood trauma.

Scientists however continue to credit the brain with all curiousness. They insist that NDEs are nothing more than a dying brain, and there is no evidence for the mind's departure. Their conjecture is the OBE, the experience of the dark tunnel, the photo shoot of our life, and the 'light', is the brain switching off. Dying observes the interplay between consciousness and unconsciousness.

Thus, the deluge of memories could be the result of slipping into and out of consciousness. Just as we slip in and out of our dream state when waking up. The rush of endorphins accounts for the peace/bliss, and the tunnel and white light represents the random firing of neurons within the visual cortex. Activity in the visual cortex produces tunnels, spirals and lights, as do hallucinogens that have similar neural effects.

To be near death is to be still alive, in terms of physical experiences affecting last moments of life and chemical happenings in the brain. We're told that death is not an instant process but rather involves a process of shutting down. [Apparently the human head remains conscious for 15-20 seconds following decapitation. And how weird watching turkeys and pigs run about for a while when their heads have been chopped off]. So, we don't have to concern ourselves with the prospect of heaven or hell then?

We're also told that 'dying brain activity' accounts for 'deathbed visions'. Thus, people on the brink of death commonly report seeing deceased family and friends (only seen by the dying person), as well as angels and other religious figures. Indeed, the dying often talk about their room being filled with other people and becoming crowded. They may suddenly see beautiful flowers in what seems like paradise or hear beautiful music. Some people view the visions as evidence for the spirit world, but scientists refer to the same explanations as NDEs i.e. lack of oxygen to the brain, the body's natural response to trauma, medications, or simple delirium.

However, researchers who have studied deathbed visions assert that whilst there is a high degree of similarity between deathbed visions and drug-induced hallucinations, many individuals reporting such visions were not on medications and were, up to the moment of death, very coherent. They also assert that unlike a delirium state, where the person has lost their connection to reality and the ability to communicate rationally, end of life visions are often very meaningful, highlighting a critical difference. People are fully conscious not absent minded. They're not tripping?

Dr Raymond Moody, who coined the term 'NDE' in his book 'Life After Life' (1983), described a NDE as 'a mystical experience that happens to people who almost die. It is not to be confused with a drug induced experience or hallucination'. He also said, 'nearly every experience of children and about a quarter of those of adults has it in an element of light. Those who experience the light say it is more than just light. There is a substance to it that 'wraps' them in a warmth and caring that they have never before felt' (cited in Barbara Ward's 'Healing Grief: A Guide to Loss and Recovery', 1993 p.183). So, that works out well for the kids?

Barbara Ward, in her book 'Healing Grief', pertained to an American study in which 80% of experiencers realised during their NDE that they regretted 'not having loved more'. And 10% realised they had squandered their talents and became aware of their 'tremendous potential' (p.184). This is a common theme, as Dr Kubler Ross confirmed with her research, as we'll get to.

Since Jung's been quite the feature, we can further consider his NDE. He had a heart attack when he was 68, and like others, he was not pleased when physicians brought him back to life. It was his own NDE in 1944 that convinced Jung that the psyche is independent of the body. He was convinced that he hadn't simply hallucinated, but rather insisted his experience came from something real and eternal. His vision wasn't delirium but a vision of reality. This experience also transformed his attitude to the world of mysticism and magic.

So, during his OBE, Jung found himself floating 1,000 miles above the Earth. And there, high up in space, he seen the globe of the Earth, the deep blue sea and continents, and the Himalayas covered in snow. He felt he was about to leave orbit, but then, turning to the south, a huge black monolith came into view. It was a kind of temple, and at the entrance Jung saw a Hindu sitting in a lotus position. Jung realised that his earthly existence was being stripped away, and what remained was an 'essential Jung', the core of his experiences. He knew that inside the temple the mystery of his existence, of his purpose in life, would be answered.

He was about to cross the threshold when he saw, rising up from Europe far below, the image of his doctor floating up. Jung said his doctor was in his primal form, stating, 'in life he was… the temporal embodiment of the primal form, which has existed from the beginning'. Apparently, his doctor was in the archetypal form of the King of Kos, Greek god of medicine. Jung presumed he was also in his primal form, although he notes he didn't observe it but simply took it for granted. A mute exchange of thought took place between them (i.e. telepathy). His doctor had a message for him, namely, that his departure was premature, and many were demanding his return. His doctor was there to ferry his return. When Jung heard this, the vision ended.

Jung was most troubled to see his doctor in his archetypal form, as he knew this meant the physician had sacrificed his own life to save Jung's. And so it came to pass that on 4-4-44 (a date numerologists can delight in), Jung sat up in bed for the first time since his illness, and on the same day, his doctor became ill and died a few days later. Jung was his last patient. Maybe the doctor did sacrifice his life for Jung? Apparently, Jung also witnessed his doctor's astral body leave this world for the next. Perhaps Jung took a trip to the astral plane?

As mentioned, apparently we get a DMT dump at death, which transports us to some interesting places. We get access to the spirit world? It's also pertinent to note, as Dr Brown highlights, that demons can manipulate what people see and experience in the spirit world. She states it's like switching channels on TV or changing sets. So, demons aka archetypes can give us visions?

As touched on, it's purported that astral planes comprise non-physical worlds that exist beyond our comprehension of time and space. And we can travel there in our astral body. The astral plane is apparently populated by gods, angels, demons, spirits, aliens, and all sorts of fairies and interesting creatures, and in our astral bodies we can communicate with them.

So, unlike our dreams (our unconscious fantasies inspired by the past), the astral plane is a real place? We're not inside a dream construct, and the characters we meet there are independent entities, not figments of our imagination. Paracelsus informs that whilst we need language to understand each other, spirits understand each other without using words i.e. telepathy. It seems telepathy is the language of the soul of the universe?

It thus seems there's a difference between having an OBE, which is reasonably normal, apart from being outside our body, and going to the astral plane? It's said that unlike an OBE, which happens in real (physical) space and time, there's a distortion of time and reality on the astral plane. We may be in astral for what seems like minutes when it's really hours, whereas with an OBE we would be aware of the events going on around our physical bodies. It's noted, that whilst many use the terms OBE and astral projection interchangeably, since astral projection is an OBE, parapsychologists say OBEs happen on the physical plane, whereas astral projection can take place on either the astral or physical plane.

But moreover, we don't need to wait until death, or nearly death, to take trips there, as we can learn to exteriorise our astral body i.e. separate it from our physical body. We can travel to pastures new, so called astral projection. Brown informs that legends about witches on broomsticks are a symbolic representation of astral projection. She also notes that in Roman Catholicism, astral projection is called bilocation, which is used to spy on people. Astral projection is one of the most popular New Age practices.

Through occult practices, like chanting, meditation, and visualisation exercises, we can learn to free our spirit body. Or as Dr Brown claims, we invite demons to bridge the gap between our soul and spiritual bodies. Their spirit/energy activates our spirit body? The idea is to relax our mind and body, and get into a hypnotic state, which is described as being at the fringe of sleep and no further. Brainwaves notably occur in theta and delta during astral travel.

A popular visualisation method is the 'rope technique'. Thus, we begin by staring at an object until we can visualise it perfectly with our eyes closed i.e. we see it in our mind. Then, still visualising our chosen object, we look around the room with our eyes closed i.e. we see everything in the room with our eyes closed. Once we're so relaxed we're no longer aware of our physical body, we then imagine there's a long rope hanging right above us. We visualise our hands coming out of our physical body and reaching the rope, which we climb, as we're pulling ourselves up. The idea is that consciousness will be pulled away from the physical body. It's noted, that mystics know imagination is an organ of perception that can be trained.

When the astral body begins to leave the physical body, vibrations commence, which is described as a strange sensation. Often people feel paralysed, like sleep paralysis, but the endeavour is to concentrate on climbing the rope, until one finds themselves free and hovering over their physical body. People are forewarned that they may feel pressure in their head or chest, but not to panic as this is the astral projection working. Some people however insist they're pulled out their body by something else. Like those who experience sleep paralysis which results in an OBE.

It's also noted, that alien abductees often talk of sleep paralysis, which suggests it's similar to astral projection? It seems alien abductions are a function of consciousness as opposed to physical, as Dr Strassman's DMT experiments indicated? However, unlike astral projection, which is done by conscious effort and training, sleep paralysis and alien abduction 'just happens'. Most people are victims of sleep paralysis and alien abductions.

Regarding astral projection, yogis concede that we go into 'the silence' then pass out our physical body, which we see lying where we've left it. It's explained that a guide comes with us to conduct us on our journey, and this guide is also in astral form. And in our vapour-like astral bodies, we can move through solid objects at will.

So, we leave our room, and float along the city we dwell in. But we can go wherever we wish. The trained occultist can wish himself at some particular place, and he travels there with the rapidity of light or faster. We observe that every person is surrounded by an aura (energy field), and we also see thin lines of bright light, like electric sparks, travelling rapidly, which are apparently telepathic messages being communicated. We also see great volumes of thought clouds arising from our city like great clouds of smoke. It seems our thoughts have some kind of materiality?

Paracelsus explains the corporeal world and spiritual world are one, as the astral world interpenetrates our world. But whilst we live in our reality, spiritual beings live in their own spiritual world. It's like we operate at different frequencies in a multidimensional universe. Paracelsus explains that astral entities are as transparent as air. He states, 'we cannot see the air unless we produce a smoke in it, and even in that case we do not see the air itself, but the smoke that is caused by the air. But we feel the air when it moves, and we may even feel the presence of such entities if they are dense enough to be felt'.

He highlights that spirits have varying levels of intelligence and their characters differ widely. But furthermore, they love to be near us, and some malevolent spirits seek to attach themselves to us, especially those they can empower. So, they're like archetypes or autonomous complexes seeking expression?

For Paracelsus, (who arguably knew), anatomy deals with the visible part of man's constitution, but there is a vastly greater part of man which is ethereal and invisible. And just as our terrestrial body is intimately related to our terrestrial surroundings, our astral body is in relation to all the influences of the astral world. For the most part however, we're ignorant to this. We're not conscious of our spirit body and spiritual senses. Like with astral vision, for example, people see astral entities and auras, and they can even see down to the molecular level. Solid objects become semi-transparent. Hence, people can read sealed letters, and see through the body to see illness.

The astral world can be conceived like blades of a fan i.e. we can see the blades when they're moving slowly but when they go much faster, we can't see them. It's said that etheric and more subtle bodies vibrate at a much higher speed than physical bodies, so we can't see them. Presumably, this accounts for why people feel vibrations buzzing at a higher frequency when they leave their body.

As touched on, with regards to the quantum level, there's nothing solid about reality. Like, our hand looks solid but under a powerful microscope it's a mass of pulsating energy. It's understood that everything in the universe consists of energy, so everything and everyone vibrates, as energy vibrates at a certain frequency. Vibrations range from low/slow to high/fast. Like, stones vibrate considerably slower than humans. Solidity thus seems to be an illusion, as what we see in our physical reality is energy moving slowly enough to be seen.

The slower the energy is vibrating, the denser it appears. Ergo, we can but wonder about 'energy' that vibrates so quickly we can't decode it.

Paracelsus said, 'Everything that exists is a manifestation of Life. Stones and metals have a life as well as plants, animals and wo/men. Only the mode of manifestation differs on account of the organic structure of the particles of which they are composed. A fly, for instance, has the same life as a stone, because there is only One Life, but in a fly it manifests itself otherwise than in a stone, and while the shape of the former may exist for thousands of years, the latter may live for only a few days'. The whole universe seems to be 'living' energy, which spawns ideas about pantheism and cosmic consciousness. Paracelsus was however clear that God created the universe. Nature is His creation, not Him.

Thus, every object in the world has an electromagnetic field, referred to as auras. Our aura, which is like an oval luminous cloud (hence it's called the auric egg), apparently extends 2/3 feet from the body. Interestingly, Pastor Charles Lawson (from Temple Baptist Church, US) asserts that if we get within 18 inches of someone that's alive, we feel their life force. This life force /spirit (breath) belongs to God and He takes it back when we die.

Auras change colour depending on our emotional state, as each thought and emotion is manifested by a certain shade or combination of colours. Auras are thus understood to be an aspect of consciousness. It's said, thought and emotion are communicated by the auric fields to the 'physical' level where they are exposed electrochemically. As discussed, when we think or feel emotions it triggers an electro-chemical process in the brain.

Our habitual colours indicate our general character, but auras can also be black. Like, the shadow people? Aura photography (taking photos of auras in powerful electrical fields) shows the energy fields that surround all Life. One remarkable result was that a leaf cut in half still showed the aura of its missing part (which is curious with regards to phantom limbs). And a photograph of a man's hand was much brighter when he consumed a glass of vodka. Energy fields vary according to the state of health of the individual. However, we'll get back to physics later.

For an example of astral projection, we can consider Chris La-Sala's testimony. La-Sala stumbled upon astral projection by accident. He was a heroin and oxycontin user (and dealer), and whilst in a state of comfortable numbness, he found himself having an OBE. And he found this phenomenon very interesting. So, he checked out the internet and discovered astral projection. He learned how to leave his body at will, which he did for a year. He built a pyramid made out of copper, which he would lie in to take his adventures. It was 8x10 foot tall and took up one fifth of his living-room. He would spend up to ten hours a day in his pyramid.

He advised using heroin (so his body would be very relaxed and inactive) and meditation to achieve the state of consciousness required for blast off. He explains that when he disconnected from his body, he would hear a 'pop'. He concedes that unlike flesh, which is heavy, our ghost-like body is very light. He states that stepping out the body is like stepping out a jacket. Like Dr Brown, he concedes that demons enable astral projection. He states, demons would enter his body, and he would feel their power.

Apparently, his interest in astral projection was spurred on by the potential to rob unnoticed. He asserts that one can fly and take objects back through the fabric of this realm. Objects can pass through walls? Thus, his plot was to rob a bank. He states that demons and others in their astral bodies play tricks on us, by removing and returning objects. They mess with our minds.

Interestingly, he was shown a vision of 'normality', and then he was shown what reality is really like. He states the real picture entails myriad black entities aka demons crawling on each other. This corroborates with Dr Brown, who states that demons can manipulate what people see and experience in the spirit world. He states, he was then snapped back into his body like an elastic band. Russ Dizdar (author/researcher) notably said that someone astral projected into his home, and he targeted the demon enabling the person (he rebuked it using Jesus' name), and the person snapped back into their body. The connection with the spirit body is severed when the demon is cast out.

As it transpired, La-Sala got increasingly involved in the occult (which means hidden). But furthermore, after a while the spirits in the spirit world began to manifest in the physical world. Like, objects would move on their own accord, fall, and levitate. He felt like he was being watched, and got scared and depressed. He started seeing these entities and explains he was dragged out of bed by his legs by demons. Scorpions and snakes were stinging, biting and chewing on him like food, and the pain was the same as pain in real life. He said he was tortured all night long and couldn't sleep. He would sleep with the lights on, as apparently demons get stronger in the dark. He spoke about levitating, with his nose touching the ceiling. They moved him about in the natural.

He looked for help on the internet, but the advice was not to worry and to work on his fear etc, which didn't help. The New Age notably calls negative astral entities 'tricksters', whereas the Bible calls them demons. He said you could cut the atmosphere with a knife. Having nowhere else to turn to, he kneeled and asked if there is a God, and if He could stop the torment. He promised to serve God, if God set him free. He said he felt fire/power and he started crying and the atmosphere cleared. He felt set free from torment and demons.

He advised that he was raised catholic but became an atheist. Thus, he decided to go to a catholic church to confess his sins, like robbing and dealing drugs etc. The priestly advice was to say three 'Hail Mary's', which did (does) nothing. He said he felt the devil on his back, who threw him down stairs.

Since that church didn't help, he found another church, having researched where to go to get delivered. That is, cast out devils. He said that as soon as he walked in, he became demon possessed and started hissing like a serpent. He states that three/four people held him down as they cast demons out. He purports that sin and his occult practices like astral projection brought in the demons, but largely the occult. He likened their power to electricity. He also advises that wizards and warlocks spy on us. They abscond from their physical bodies and visit us via astral projection. Chris La-Sala became a Christian and now has his own ministry.

Some researchers notably believe that lucid dreams are astral projections, but others maintain only conscious departure from the body is astral projection, which is not the same as dreaming however lucid. So, unlike merely being aware that we're dreaming, with astral projection we're aware of transitioning from our physical body to the astral body. It's said it doesn't feel like you're dreaming, as you see your body on the bed, but no longer 'feel' your arms on the covers or head on the pillow. Our consciousness is not dreaming in a physical body but rather it has left that body. It's said, with lucid dreaming, the subconscious and conscious work together, whereas with astral projection, consciousness is projected out and it feels real. They're different states of reality.

Learning to dream lucidly is however regarded as a step closer to enhancing consciousness, which is the aim of the mystics. It's relayed that by asking yourself, very frequently (like every fifteen minutes), if you're dreaming throughout the day, paves the way to asking it in your dream. This enables taking conscious control of the dream. One can awake in the dream and become lucid.

Black (2010) wrote, 'People who learn how to dream *consciously*, that is to say with the ability to think and exercise willpower we normally only enjoy in waking life, may develop powers which are 'supernatural' by today's definitions. If you can dream consciously, then you are on the way to being able to move about the spirit worlds at will, communicating freely with the spirits of the dead and other disembodied beings. You may perhaps learn about the future in ways which might otherwise be blocked. You may be able to travel to other parts of the material universe and view things, though you are not bodily present – so called astral travel' (p.186).

It also seems that people can experience astral projection via lucid dreams. Like Steven Bancarz, for example, said this happened to him. Thus, he was having a lucid dream, which he regularly had, but he came across a black and red skinned lizard-like-being who featured a third eye. He was then sucked into his third eye, and everything went black for about three seconds, and when he opened his eyes, he found himself awake and hovering about four foot above his body. He explains how difficult it was to get back into his physical body. And further, when he eventually did get back inside his body, a moment later, he succumbed to sleep paralysis. He felt a buzzing at his forehead and was pulled out again.

Interestingly, a marine who had a NDE and went to hell, said he met a demon who was 13 foot tall with red and black skin. It was like a snake, with golden split pupils, muscular and bald. The demon answered the marine's thoughts in his mind. Like, the marine asked his height and the demon told him. He was hurting the marine, which felt like electric shocks. Maybe it was the same demon, or the same race, they met?

It's noted, that lucid dreaming is vital for Tibetan Buddhists, as it involves spiritual preparation for death. Taoism and Buddhism assert the worlds we see in our dreams are more or less identical to the worlds we experience after death. Death is seen as a dream-like condition. As suggested, maybe life after death is like a lucid dream but it's real? Like, when we're falling down, we're really falling down to the dark toasty stinky pits of hell? What a nightmare.

As mentioned, according to yogi philosophy, we enter the astral planes after death. Our soul, encased in its astral body, passes out of the physical body (it vacates the premises), and we relive memories (from infancy to old age). It's said things are made plain to the departing soul i.e. what's really important. This process, which is like having a vivid dream, happens as we're dying, which corroborates with NDEs and scientific findings i.e. the last dregs of brain activity. When the body dies, we go to the plane of slumber for a snooze. Then we ditch our astral body, in the plane of shells, when we go to our ethereal destination, with like-minded others. That is, until we reincarnate again.

As also touched on, shamans are partial to frequenting the astral plane. They advise the most commonly seen spirit beings, (which appear to have pliable, semi-transparent bodies), are snakes and half human-half animal hybrids. But apparently there's thousands of different types of spiritual entities, with different shapes and forms of a bewildering variety. Some of them are revolting, some are like animals, and some are like human giants. There's also aliens, including greys, and UFOs. And people see Hindu gods with six arms etc. So, it's DMT space?

Shamans notably believe that each person/animal has an individual spirit. And there's many disembodied spirits, including ancestral spirits. But they also believe in a higher power. And whilst this being has no body of its own, it shows itself through animals or wo/men. This spirit is not particularly benevolent, but it can be appeased. Shamans also have spirit wives/husbands, and these relationships are very important to them. They're real.

Shamans enter a trance to access the capricious spirit world. They refer to 'going to the sky'. Their techniques include rhythmic drumming and dancing, hyperventilation, breath-holding, frenzied self-mutilation, sensory deprivation, dehydration, fasting, using charms and objects of power such as talismans, meditating on mandalas, and psychoactive plants e.g. mescaline derived from peyote cactus and psilocybin found in magic mushrooms.

Shamans aka witchdoctors advise that a trance is not like a normal dream, but rather it's fresh and vivid, and they are most aware. They maintain that perceptions of the spiritual world are equally as vivid as perceptions of the material world. And like astral projection, they don't know how long they've been there or how long the journey was (i.e. astral time). Shamanism is described as the oldest profession in the world (like prostitution). It's not a religion per se but rather the oldest method in the world for expanding consciousness. Shaman means 'seer' and refers to 'one who knows'. So, shamans see archetypes in the collective unconscious?

Contrary to psychiatry's denial, shamans know the spirit world is real. They're aware that in the spirit world we may gain a great deal of information if we ask the spirits to reveal this to us. And they're familiar with calling upon the help of 'nature spirits' to take them out their bodies. However, they need protection there, as this world is not without its perils, hence the prerequisite to have a guardian spirit. Indeed, it's said a shaman cannot be a shaman without one.

So, the guardian spirit protects the shaman. He pulls the shaman's astral body out his physical body and accompanies him on his mystical ascent to the sky. Once there, in the spirit world, the shaman has access to information and powers that would otherwise not be available in the ordinary world. Shamans often go to locate things and acquire healing powers. And when the trance fades, and they return, they have supernatural powers e.g. the ability to heal or prophesise.

For an example, we can consider the Amazonian witchdoctor Elka (he notably converted to Christianity). He advised that after singing the necessary songs, coupled with inhaling smoke and using charms/stones to evoke the spirits, he would be transported in ecstasy to the celestial regions. He described it as a strange land, an eerie world of spirits, where humans are interlopers and spirits relaxed in comfort. And this was where he learned in which spot the hurt resides in a sick body and how it could be healed.

He further advised that whilst anyone can commune with spirits and manipulate them to some extent, which includes bestowing curses and putting spells on others, witchdoctors are more empowered, as they can bring people back from the dead and equally cause death. Hence, shamans are both feared and revered. Elka said it was rare to be a witchdoctor, a real one who controlled the spirit world and who was in turn, controlled by it. He described it as a mysterious life. He said the spirit world is full of demons that trickled out only a small amount of good, only when pleaded with and appeased.

Hence, it gets considerably more sadistic and perverted, as demons are partial to serious debauchery. Jungle witchcraft is known for three/four month long orgies and infant killings. During these frenzied gangbangs, people embodied by evil spirits, gyrate and indulge in all kinds of perversions. Witchcraft essentially degenerates into Satanism.

It's noted, that sacrificing kids and babies to the 'gods' goes back to ancient civilisations. The gods have always insisted on human and animal sacrifices. There's something magical about both sex and blood. Thus, besides the 'regular' aforementioned intoxicating rituals, it's said sexual techniques are the 'hard stuff' and the most closely guarded secrets of secret societies.

Whilst we'll get back to secret societies, (which derive from mystery schools), it's noted that initiates similarly work themselves into a hallucinatory state to access the spirit realm and communicate with disembodied beings. They acquire an existential knowledge of the way these beings operate when we're awake, when we dream, and when we're dead. Initiation involves forging a conscious working relationship with disembodied spirits, and as a result initiates acquire ESP e.g. clairvoyance, telepathy. Initiates then use their newfound abilities during training e.g. converse telepathically. Whilst initiates see the inner world dimensions in this visionary state, it takes practice to be able to see the spirit world with 'eyes open' during the day. Like, the visionary Emmanuel Swedenborg, who we'll get to.

Black (2010) highlights the shamanic experience, worldwide, entails a blacking out of senses, and then they 'see' the other dimension. This initially consists of a sea or matrix of lights, an ocean of giant weaving waves of light and energy. As they become more accustomed however, clarity unfolds, as patterns morph into shapes. And then they see the gods.

Graham Hancock, (author and journalist), having had his share of ayahuasca, concedes there's trance stages. He explains zigzag lines, curves, and patterns morph into serpents. Then one seems to go inside some kind of vortex. There's a sense of passing through, breaking into another realm. Patterns etc continue but one starts encountering intelligent beings, often hybrids, part human and animal, in the deepest stage of trance. And these intelligent beings communicate with us.

Hancock is convinced reality is much more complicated than we imagine, and we are surrounded by a vast invisible reality all the time. He affirms its normally invisible to our senses but DMT allows invisible realms to become visible for a short time. Others affirm that they pass through a tunnel. It's like a wormhole connecting to different dimensions?

As touched on, indigenous Amazonian cultures take ayahuasca to 'see the gods'. Ayahuasca is referred to as the 'plant of the gods'. And increasingly backpackers are flocking to South America for this authentic spiritual experience, this toxic brew, complete with a shaman chanting in the jungle. It seems like a good idea? Some 200,000 people go to Peru every year for this psychic trip. As mentioned, people are thirsty for the supernatural.

Unlike shamans who seldom vomit, most people sweat, spew, and often soil themselves after about forty-five minutes. Shamans advise the vomiting means bad spirits and toxins are leaving the body, and it eases with continued experience. People report buzzing and vibrating sensations. They feel tingly. They get upgraded vision i.e. colours are brighter, more vibrant, and everything moves. They report that everything is made up of geometric patterns. Like tetrahedrons, fractal images. They see trippy molecular reality, with eyes open or closed. People also commonly report seeing 'eyes' everywhere. Interestingly, in the Bible, in the Book of Revelation chapter 4, we hear about entities that are covered in eyes, front and back, inside and out.

As touched on, many people report feeling an overwhelming sense of love, and feel connected (not dissimilar to MDMA). There's beauty and love in the world after all. It restores our faith in humanity? It's advertised that DMT can help people with addictions, disorders like Post Traumatic Stress Disorder, and childhood trauma. This drug fundamentally changes people. They discover that there is more to life, it's not all bad? God is Nature i.e. pantheism? He's in the trees and flowers. He is all that is and is not? God is love and we are God?

But moreover, partakers say the spirit of ayahuasca, which appears in the form of a serpent, takes over them. The serpent symbolises wisdom and is the most common 'archetype' encountered in ayahuasca visions. People also see snakes eating their own tail, like the ouroboros (the symbol of Abraxis). People dialogue with Mother Ayahuasca i.e. they ask questions and get answers. It's a real encounter. Hancock explains the ayahuasca spirit lies behind the beverage and 'she' is concerned about our planet and the betterment of human beings.

He states there's two stages. Thus, we're shown our own life, and her 'moral truth' teaches us how we can change our behaviour for the better. It's a psychological process which entails questioning the point as well as self-examination. It reveals insight into the psyche. The second stage is journeying to other realms. Then, like waking up from a dream, suddenly people return to so-called reality. However, not everyone has a positive experience, but rather some people have a positively bad trip, an unrelenting nightmare (it's not all unicorns and rainbows). And it's rare, but people can die.

Terence McKenna (1946-2000), lecturer/author renowned for partaking in psychedelics including ayahuasca, proposed that psychedelics enable trans-dimensional travel. He proposed that DMT sent one to a parallel dimension, enabling an individual to encounter 'higher dimensional entities'. He described the experience as bursting through a membrane, and bursting into DMT space, where entities are happy to see us. We enter the 'ecology of souls'. He muses that these entities could be ancestors or spirits of the Earth.

But moreover, he also maintained that what people see is already there. We just don't see it 'normally'. Like, elves are real (he seen lots of elves), but we don't normally see them. Apparently the entities, including the elves, told him that when we die, we will join them. So, we're not to fear death, as death is not the end. McKenna surmises that back in the day, all religion was experiential, and it was based upon the pursuit of ecstasy through plants. Like, ecstasy pills are made using sassafras oil from a rare tree in Cambodia, which is driving the tree to extinction and ruining the rainforest. We find the gods in ASC.

According to shamans, the gods told them which plants to use. DMT can't be activated orally because monoamine oxidise enzymes in the stomach switches off DMT on contact. Thus, DMT in plants is mixed with a vine that contains monoamine inhibitors which switches off the enzyme and allows DMT to be absorbed orally for hours.

People who smoke DMT claim they're sucked out their body after two hits. People lose their sense of ego/self and forget reality. Then they're sucked back to their body, like through a wormhole. My good friend who took DMT said he 'went home'. It feels 100% real. It's not just a trip. As mentioned, entities remember people's names when they return to DMT world, which evidences they are real metaphysical entities.

Regarding the intelligent entities, McKenna states they're persons without bodies that exist in some parallel dimension independent of our brain. So, they're not archetypes in the collective unconscious? McKenna recognises these spirits can appear as different things e.g. dead Mayan priest. Thus, they can present as archetypes. Or they can take the appearance of someone. Like, someone's dead husband who's looking for anal sex?

And people can channel them; become possessed by them. McKenna said he got information from a being called Logos. He said, 'It was as though my ordinary, rather humdrum personality had simply been turned off and speaking through me was the voice of another, a voice that was steady, unhesitating, and articulate – a voice seeking to inform others about the power and promise of psychedelic dimensions'. McKenna evolved into a sort of mouthpiece for this being, so-called incarnate Logos. As highlighted, as a general rule, spirits promote pantheism, reincarnation and apotheosis, which is man spiritually evolving to become God.

But moreover, McKenna knew these entities were deceptive but still sought them out and credited them with giving him the ability to speak eloquently. He said, 'It is no great accomplishment to hear a voice in the head. The accomplishment is to make sure it is telling the truth, because the demons are of many kinds'. McKenna believed ETs are prone to lying about their identity, which includes where they come from. Like, 'aliens' claim they're from Venus and Mars, as opposed to the spirit world?

McKenna cautions they don't necessarily have our best interest in mind although they would present it in that way to be trusted and get us to do their work. So, they use us for their own purposes? He further states these entities can be summoned in magic rituals. He said, 'magicians, people who invoke these things, have always understood that one must go into such encounters, with one's wits about oneself'.

David Icke also took ayahuasca in the Brazilian Amazon in 2003, which he described as mind blowing and life changing. He advised the 'spirit' (the female voice he heard) told him about the illusory nature of reality, which revolutionised his thinking. He was told that all that exists is one infinite consciousness, which is known as 'The Infinite', 'Oneness' and the 'One'. He described feeling the spirit around him. But moreover, he said, that out of his mouth, in a very different voice to 'David Icke', came the words, slowly and powerfully, 'I am love'.... 'I am everything and everything is me, I am infinite possibility'. He reports feeling a fantastic energy pour from his heart chakra and fill the room.

He also notes that the lights, which were all switched off, came on by themselves without electricity. And also, equipment playing music switched off and came back on again after ten seconds or so. It seems archetypes were breaking through to the physical realm? It seems David Icke was possessed by the spirit of ayahuasca?

Whilst drugs are a popular means to access the spirit world, others caution about using drugs. As Black (2010) highlights, 'drug taking is, of course, a big part of modern shamanistic practice, but it is forbidden by most esoteric teachers as a means of reaching the spirit world. The aim of these teachers is to achieve experience of the spirit worlds with intelligence and critical faculties as unimpaired as possible, indeed heightened. To enter the spirit worlds on drugs, on the other hand, is to do so without proper preparation, and may open up a portal into a demonic dimension which then refuses to close' (p.322). So, maybe it's not the best idea then?

It's said we can unleash dark occult powers. Hence, we need to be spiritually prepared and equipped. Like alchemists and yogis, for example, take the time to purify their souls as the premise to entering the spirit world. It's understood our little light astral body sticks out like a sore thumb. It's like being a taxi with our light on, hence, the prerequisite of guides for safety. It's purported that spirits can attach themselves to us, and also take up residence in our bodies if we leave them unattended e.g. with astral projection. Paracelsus unequivocally stated that if we leave our home empty, some squatter will come in. He said, 'if the master is not home, spirits will assume residence there'.

Yogis concede harmful practices include stupefying drugs, as well as whirling dances, voodoo practices, repulsive rites of black magicians etc. These practices aim to produce an abnormal condition similar to intoxication, which like intoxication and drug habits lead to physical and psychological ruin. They state that those indulging in these do develop a low order of psychic or astral power, but they invariably attract an undesirable class of astral entities and open themselves up to a low order of intelligences.

They also don't recommend self-hypnotisation and hypnotisation of others, like gazing at some bright object until a trance like condition is induced. Or the repetition of some monotonous formula until a drowsy condition is produced. Yogis develop psychic powers by developing spiritual faculties and self-mastery founded on the premise that they are God.

It further seems pertinent to highlight, the notorious silver cord. People with OBEs invariably report about a silver cord that connects their astral body to their physical body. The silver cord or 'life thread' or 'consciousness thread' is described as being very smooth, very long, very bright, like an elastic cable made of light, and about an inch wide. It's likened to our umbilical cord i.e. the silver cord is our body's 'lifeline' to our physical body in the same way as our umbilical cord is our 'lifeline' to our mother's body.

It's said that as long as the silver cord remains intact we can have OBEs, but when the cord is cut, we can't go back into our bodies. We reach the point of no return. In the Bible (Ecclesiastes 12:6-7) we're told, 'remember him – before the silver cord is severed'. It's understood that we don't die until God cuts the silver cord.

Paracelsus conceded that the astral body may go to certain distances from the physical body for a short time, but if its connection with that body is broken, the latter dies. Sometimes people feel a tug or pull from their silver cord, probing them to return. Russ Dizdar, who was an occultist but became a Christian, said his Golden Buddhist master projected and never came back (he died). He said his non-human enhanced tutor would go to Shambhala aka paradise, but on that occasion, he went for the last time.

This paradise is apparently only accessible to those spiritually 'enlightened' i.e. those 'pure of heart' who can astral project. However, it's also noted that Hitler endeavoured to find Shambhala, which suggests it's a physical place. But we'll get back to this. Dizdar concedes that astral projection connects with sleep paralysis. He states we go passive, get the vibrations, and our spirit projects out to the astral plane.

Yogis concur the astral body is connected to the physical body by a silk-like astral thread, which maintains communication between the two, and this is severed at physical death. The connection with the soul and body is terminated. Adepts (clairvoyants) see the astral body rising from the physical body as the hour of the day approaches. It's seen hovering over the physical body, bound by a thread, and when the thread snaps, the body dies, and the soul passes on carrying with it the astral body. Good Night Mr Chips. Maybe the fact that people are still alive i.e. connected by the silver cord, but outside their body, hence in the astral realm, accounts for the deathbed visions etc i.e. their brain is still operating. It's like when we dream, our astral body hovers above our physical body?

Paracelsus further informs, that when an individual is about to die, his spirit (astral body) may indicate the approach of his death by raps or knocks, audible to all, or by some other individual noise, or by the moving of furniture, the stopping of clocks, the breaking of a mirror, the fall of a picture, or any other omen. He notes however, that frequently such omens are neither recognised or noticed, or even understood. Such death omens are found in many different cultures worldwide. Apparently, another omen is when a cat leaves the home and will not re-enter it. It also seems cats can see the astral plane when given too much catnip?

As mentioned, contrary to the Hindu belief regarding seven major heavens, the Bible speaks about three heavens. Thus, the first heaven is our air/atmosphere, the second heaven is the sky and stars above, and the third heaven is where God resides. It seems the first heaven is the physical plane i.e. where OBEs happen, and the second heaven is the astral plane. Like, so called Shambhala is in the second heaven, which appears to be a counterfeit of God's third heaven?

The invisible spirit realm is the devil's domain. He's known as the 'Prince of the Power of the Air'. And he has a team of fallen angels, demons and other shadowy compadres that can appear and disappear. It's like they step through a dimensional wall, from the second heaven into our heaven.

As also mentioned, the spirit world was separated from the physical world at the fall, and our spirit bodies were put to sleep. We're born spiritually dead. Hence, we're not conscious of anything spiritual. Unlike people with astral vision then, we don't see snakes crawling beside us. Like Chris La-Sala, Jonathan Welton (Christian author) was also shown what reality is really like. He claims God gave him the gift to see the spiritual world. In addition to seeing angels and demons, he also sees serpents wrapped around particular buildings. Thus, besides wriggling about our feet, some of them are massive.

So, there's earthbound spirits. And it seems the astral plane is DMT space aka the second heaven? Like, people taking LSD can meet Lucy (Lucifer) in the Sky with Diamonds aka stars, which is the second heaven. The 'host of heaven' is a reference to the second heaven, and stars refer to angels. But it gets crazier, as there's an angelic battle taking place in the second heaven. It's understood that angels are considerably more hardcore than demons, as we'll get to. Deliverance ministers have found that many of the earthbound demons are taking direct orders from higher ranking demons in the second heaven.

Howard Pittman, a Baptist minister for thirty-five years, concurs. He had a NDE and described his trip to the second and third heaven. He states he died on the operating table during surgery and was taken on a tour of the spirit realm under the protection of an angel. In his book 'Placebo' (1999), he wrote,

'When the angels lifted my spirit from my body, they carried me immediately to the second heaven. We did not have to leave that hospital room in order to enter the second heaven. We entered there in that same room where my body was, just passing through a dimension wall. It is a wall which flesh cannot pass through, only spirit. As we moved through that dimension wall into the second heaven, I found myself in an entirely different world, far different from anything I had ever imagined. This world was a place occupied by spirit beings as vast in number as the sands of the seashore. These beings were demons, or fallen angels, and were in thousands of different shapes and forms. Some of the forms were so morbid and revolting that I was almost to the point of nausea'. [See his books, 'Demons: An Eyewitness Account' (1995) and Placebo (1999)].

He concedes that they communicate telepathically, and travel with the 'speed of thought'. Like, the angel would advise where they were going, and they were there. Pittman describes the complex hierarchal caste system that operates in the second heaven. Like human beings, demons live in societies and have governance. He states groups of demons are assigned specific tasks according to their area of expertise/skills e.g. witchcraft, false religion, self-destruction, fear, magic, ESP, sorcery, ghosts, aliens, occult, psychic abilities.

He explains that Satan and his demons work through a dimensional wall from the second heaven into the air, the first heaven. But moreover, when he visited God in God's (third) heaven, God gave him a clear message for the church, namely, we need to 'Wake Up!' After this not entirely pleasant encounter, as God was not overly pleased with Pittman, the angels carried him back through the second heaven, through the dimensional wall, and into the hospital room where his body was lying.

In the Bible, it seems Paul had an OBE and went to the third heaven. In 2 Corinthians 12:2-4, he wrote, 'I know a man in Christ who fourteen years ago was caught up to the third heaven. Whether it was in the body or out of the body I do not know – God knows. And I know that this man – whether in the body or apart from the body I do not know, but God knows – was caught up to Paradise and heard inexpressible things, things that no one is permitted to tell'. It's noted that circa fourteen years prior, he was almost killed, so it could have been a NDE?

John was also given a vision of the third heaven. He states a door to heaven was opened and he was instantly in the spirit, which suggests astral projection? It's also noted, that Enoch, as detailed in the Book of Enoch, went to God's heaven. Elijah was also privy to seeing the spirit world, and Ezekiel was given a vision of heaven. It seems Ezekiel also experienced astral projection as he was transported from Babylon to Jerusalem on another occasion. And in 2 Kings 6:17, we're told Elisha prayed to God to open his servant's eyes and let him see, and he seen they were surrounded by an angelic army. The hillside was filled with horses and chariots of fire. However, we'll get back to the Biblical version of events in Part 2.

For science then, all this is hogwash. We're told there is no spirit world. The 'spirit world' is merely an arbitrary vision from the depths of our brain? People are tripping, 'case closed'. It's unfortunate that people are ambushed by their unconscious, like hearing voices that tell them to kill themselves or others. Or conjure up frightening visions about shadow people. But it is what it is. All weirdness comes from the brain. Yet they admittedly know very little about consciousness. They don't 'know'.

However, interestingly, we're told about the 'scientific' benefits of meditation and yoga. They're promoted for mental and physical health. Indeed, Transcendental Meditation has been introduced into schools, prisons, and the workplace, with remarkable results in terms of improved concentration and attitude. It's notably a multibillion-dollar industry. But moreover, it's interesting because meditation and yoga can lead to ASC. Meditation, breathing exercises, and yoga work harmoniously to open people up to the spiritual realm. As discussed, meditation can expand consciousness by manipulating the pineal gland to produce 'visions'.

As Paracelsus highlights, when the outer senses are inactive, the inner senses may awaken to life, and we may see objects on the astral plane as we see things in a dream. He equally notes that there are some poisons by which the organic activity of the body may be suppressed for a time, and the consciousness of the inner man may be rendered more active, enabling perception of the astral plane i.e. like ayahuasca. So, there's meditating to relax, and there's manipulating our pineal gland to induce what scientists call 'waking hallucinations'. And thus, we're back to the spirit world?

With meditation, the idea is to still the mind. So, we might focus on our breathing, like with mindfulness. Or we might repeat a mantra, which means mind vibration, to induce a hypnotic effect. Or we might focus on an object, like a stone, or candle or flower, as a means to zone out. In essence, the endeavour is to dissociate, to achieve a trance like state. So, people mediate to blank their mind, but also to contact spirit guides, conduct automatic writing, channel 'archetypes' etc. People endeavour to connect with their 'higher self' or Self?

Unlike those who meditate to relax, and whose brainwaves are in the alpha range, (which is the same as sitting quietly listening to music or reading a book), those well versed in meditation are able to enter deep states of relaxation. Their breathing rate drops down to three or four breaths a minute, and their brainwaves slow down to the much slower delta and theta waves. Those who experience deep meditation advise they have a fully awakened mind. They claim to be very conscious without having any thoughts at all, and describe it as looking directly into the nature of consciousness. They observe that the illusion of a separate self and someone who acts is gone. So, the neuroscientists are right, there is no separate self?

It's highlighted that by meditating, and mentally ignoring the body entirely, we will gradually awaken to a sense of independent existence of our soul and realise our true nature. The real 'I' is independent of the body and cannot die or become annihilated. The 'I AM' philosophy asserts the reality of our existence is temporary and relative, but our real existence (spirit) is absolute and eternal. Like Tolle advised, we realise that we are the stillness behind the noise.

So, we use 'breath' to centre ourselves. We strive to transcend everyday noise to realise our individuality, the 'I AM' real self beyond personality. Yogi aspirants are told to cultivate 'I AM' consciousness, by using the 'I Am' mantram. It seems we program ourselves, through repetition and imagination, to believe we're God. There's One Life and one consciousness, and we embody it? We are the great I AM, which is notably what God called Himself when Moses asked Him who He was.

As it transpires then, there's apparently a Buddhic plane beyond the astral plane, which entails feeling as one with everything. Like dissolving into everything or nothing, individuality and ego consciousness is rendered obsolete. It seems there's a place of stillness, a realm beyond vibration, which corroborates with what the spirit of ayahuasca told David Icke about the illusory nature of reality. She said, 'Infinite love is the only truth. Everything else is illusion'. And 'if it vibrates it's illusion'. Icke explains the pure Infinite One is still and silent.

In Hinduism, Brahman is the Absolute, the One. As touched on, Hinduism endorses pantheism i.e. we're all part of one divine whole. Brahman is the impersonal force or energy that underlies all things, but Brahman is beyond shapes and forms. Brahman is stillness behind the noise. As it transpires, we're bewitched by an illusory reality. But we'll get back to this in the religion chapter. It is however noted, that Brahman is not the same as God of the Bible. And personable Father God is not the same as Hindu 'gods', who can be found in the second heaven with their myriad flailing arms.

Yoga is the heart of Hinduism. Yoga means union with God. The goal is to be yoked with Brahman. Thus, yoga and meditation are spiritual practices, despite their western packaging. It's said there is no yoga without Hinduism, and no Hinduism without yoga. Practicing yoga is practicing Hinduism. It's noted, the western version actively undermines the spiritual aspect, which is the actual point.

Moreover, yoga poses alone activate the spirit realm. Thus, regardless of intention i.e. viewing it as merely 'exercise', something happens at the spirit level. Yoga is not like other 'exercise'. It takes one automatically to meditative states. It's said that when people keep doing the poses, slowly the spiritual will open up inside of them. It's also noted, that most people start yoga for exercise, but then the spiritual aspect becomes more important.

Thus, people go to yoga to stretch, but becoming the cobra or downward facing dog, coupled with breathing techniques, are designed to open oneself to yoke with spiritual consciousness. Yoga positions are sun and moon salutations (bowing down and worshipping the sun and moon). All postures are in reference to deities, and open doorways to these spirits. Hinduism is another form of sun worship and they revere the serpent. It's the same pagan religion found in all ancient cultures. But we'll get to this in Part 2.

So, through these practices, we can develop 'cosmic consciousness', which is a higher state of consciousness. We can spiritually evolve? Cosmic consciousness perceives the whole universe as part of oneself. It's defined as an advanced state of self-transcendence, in which the sense of a separate self is abandoned. It sounds lovely?

Moreover, whilst there's myriad paths or yoga's to attain cosmic consciousness, it's essentially about kundalini serpent power. It's the same 'energy' that filters through these practices, like the serpent spirit of ayahuasca? Like the spirit of ayahuasca, kundalini is a female serpentine force that moves in and takes over the body. Kundalini is described as spiritual energy that lies dormant, coiled at the base of our spine. She's represented as either a goddess or sleeping serpent waiting to be awakened. This latent energy is the Gnostic spark of divinity within us. It's the spark Jung and the yogis pertained to.

Deep meditation (induced by breathing exercises, mantras and yoga poses) stirs kundalini, which rises up through the (alleged) chakras (energy centres) to reside at the top of the head aka crown chakra, producing a profound mystical experience. It produces euphoria, like supernatural MDMA. This is the state of yoga or divine union. People report feeling like an electric current is running along the spine. It's said that like a serpent striking out, it strikes the third eye and the person achieves God consciousness. It's noted, the coiled cobra is represented as the third eye on the foreheads of Egyptian initiates.

Black (2010) concedes, (with regards to ancient Indian adepts), 'At the height of their mediations a rush of energy from the base of the spine would travel through the middle artery via the heart to the head. Sometimes this energy was thought of as being like a snake, which rose through the spine up into the skull and bit at a point just behind the bridge of the nose'. This bite released an ecstatic bolt of lightning that catapulted them into another dimension (p. 176-178).

People report an intense blinding light explodes in their brain, (they're 'enlightened'), and then a doorway to another world is opened. They feel their whole being shooting out their body like a rocket into another dimension. They report a cracking sound (pop) when their third eye opens. They have 'visions' and see spiritual entities etc. As Wheeler (2009) states, 'Kundalini energy is a shockwave of serpent power'. But contrary to being regarded as evil in the Bible, the serpent is the spirit of wisdom?

The arousing of kundalini is said by some to be the only way of attaining self-wisdom or gnosis. Apparently, the movement of kundalini is felt by the presence of a cool, or in the case of imbalance, warm breeze across the palms of the hands and soles of the feet. Russell Brand (2014) notably described kundalini yoga as the crack cocaine of yoga, and apparently he 'fucking likes it' (p.53). The spiritual high can become addictive. Regarding the best spiritual feeling/pleasure, a bloke Russell Brand interviewed, rated an orgasm from sex 8.5/10, ayahuasca 9/10 and meditation 10/10. And the best part is we can harness this drug from within.

It seems the kundalini spirit hijacks the Central Nervous System and gives us free ecstasy. Hence, people feel a tingling energy/entity at their spine. The CNS corroborates with chakras, alleged spiritual centres/energies that reside at different points along the spine. Maybe 'chakras' are BS?

Kundalini can also be activated through sexual practices. Thus, it rises up the spine, and as it approaches the brain, the sexual feelings become stronger and stronger, but rather than being released through the crown chakra, the energy reverses and takes a downward course seeking release through the genitals. It's like tantric yoga invites spirits into the bedroom, but we'll get back to all this. Kundalini produces interesting states of consciousness, but it's not all happy euphoric days. Kundalini is a very powerful force and produces an array of physical and mental disorders.

The most common manifestations of kundalini include uncontrollable, unmotivated and unnatural laughter, jerking, convulsing, crying, roaring like a lion, barking like a dog, hissing like a snake, and other animal sounds and movements. Perhaps these behaviours are inspired from animal yoga postures? Being possessed by the kundalini spirit births all kinds of craziness. Like, the force of kundalini can take people out their body to the second heaven.

But moreover, unlike those who actively seek to experience kundalini, others are unprepared and experience what's termed 'kundalini syndrome'. Apparently increasing numbers are having spontaneous kundalini awakenings otherwise known as acute psychosis. My friend maintains that happened to him (psychiatrists said otherwise). David Icke also claimed he had a kundalini spiritual awakening in Peru which blew his mind. They can appear from seemingly nowhere, whereas for others this awakening is the result of physical or psychological trauma.

Thus, it gets more sinister, as this serpent power can be activated through sexual abuse rituals with kids. Max Spiers, 'conspiracy theorist' who was bumped off in 2016, said when a child is sodomised it releases kundalini, which enlightens the child. So, in addition to traumatic events, like rape, which can cause dissociation and OBEs, kids can be catapulted to the second heaven? It's also purported, the rapist benefits from this powerful energy.

It seems the issue is whether kundalini is an indwelling dormant energy i.e. we inherit a 'divine spark', or a force that we invite in through certain occult practices. Like, we invite the spirit of ayahuasca in by drinking her in. People are never the same after enlightenment. It appears people don't go to the spirit world and return alone. But rather, they harbour company. And they return with ESP superpowers, as we'll get to in a mo.

According to Jung, '…the concept of kundalini has for us only one use, that is, to describe our own experiences with the unconscious'. Jung interpreted kundalini yoga as a model for development of higher consciousness and the process of individuation. It's noted, that kundalini is a catchword adopted by the New Age movement.

Kundalini symptoms include: feelings of energy in the hands and hands feeling hot; deep ecstatic or orgasmic sensations; experiencing severe, migraine type headaches; awareness of energy discharges, or currents, flowing through the body; sensations of tickling, itching or tingling on, or underneath the skin; awareness of internal lights or colours; sensations of extreme heat or cold moving through the body; spontaneous involuntary movements i.e. the body shakes, vibrates or trembles, assumes and maintains strange positions, like catatonic symptoms in schizophrenia (locked into strange positions); breathing spontaneously, stopping or becoming rapid for no apparent reason; hearing internal voices and noises such as whistling, hissing, chirping, roaring or flutelike sounds; OBEs; sudden intense ecstasy or bliss, peace, love or sudden intense fear, anxiety, depression, hatred or confusion e.g. inability to focus mentally, temporary loss of certain words, names, terms etc; 'going a little crazy' for periods; uncontrollable extreme anger and repulsion; seeing other dimensional beings; olfactory hallucinations e.g. burning incense; sudden waves of nausea and dizziness, and the sense of falling over; sudden onset of, or increase, of allergies; sudden onset of chemical sensitivity; sudden eating/food changes; hair falling out, breaking, not growing; nightmares, lucid dreams, positive and negative psychic experiences, panic attacks while awake and asleep ; insomnia; profound physical, emotional and mental exhaustion; body weakness, muscle weakness, lethargy, achy body, bones and joints; hyper states, restless, edgy, can't relax, can't rest or be comfortable, mind races despite exhausted body; extreme emotional phases including crying, weeping, mourning, feeling love for all beings etc; glorious changes and expansions in consciousness, perceptions; major ego dismantling.

Thus, while students of yoga aim to awaken kundalini to achieve God consciousness, they're warned it's very dangerous to do so prematurely. They need to be prepared as certain yogic practices can lead to psychosis, and cause demonic occult powers to be unleashed. Many report 'visions' of demonic creatures and being possessed by them. Some are attacked e.g. bitten by demons, and they're left with bite marks and pain.

It's also noted, that other practices, like Reiki (spiritually guided energy) healing for example, involve kundalini symptoms because it's the same energy. Like, my friend, who's a Reiki therapist, says she feels energy in her hands, and when she puts her hands on people's heads they see colours. People feel the 'energy' and naively presume it's a force for good.

Kundalini spirit can also be imparted from gurus. Like at Ashrams, for example, gurus touch people's forehead and they feel euphoria and start jerking. Sanskrit kund means 'to burn' and it's said that's what kundalini does. That is, fries the person from the inside. It's highlighted that all hormones go into overdrive, which accounts for the bliss and ecstasy, and it's often followed by depression. It's further said, this weakened states makes people more spiritually vulnerable i.e. to spirit attachment or infestation.

Apparently, gurus can also take people out their bodies to the second heaven. Like spirit guides 'help' people out their body, the guru can do likewise in his astral body. As highlighted, people can get up to all sorts of mischief in their astral bodies. Thus, it's not just 'archetypes' to contend with, but also temporarily disembodied people.

Fundamentally, by going 'passive' (dissociating) we invite spiritual consciousness in, or nurture what's already there? Stilling the mind enables a telepathic receptive state, to attune our mind to mystical cosmic awareness, which is god, which is us?

But moreover, when people empty their mind, siddhi's can appear. These are supernatural powers that come from spiritual development. Some mystics notably regard siddhi's as cumbersome because they interfere with the pure meditative state of cosmic awareness. Siddhi's include clairvoyance, telepathy, the ability to heal and prophesise, levitate, teleport, which means travelling at the speed of thought, as happens with astral projection/bilocation, and the ability to 'remote view'. That is, people receive 'impressions', visions in the third eye of somewhere remote.

There's also the ability to assume any form desired (i.e. change shape and form), and enter other people's bodies. Like, shamans can shapeshift into particular animals e.g. coyotes, owls, serpents. Apparently, shamans have to murder (sacrifice) a family member to get this power. People also get siddhis with DMT. It's conveyed they're latent powers. The only trouble is, according to Father God, we're not supposed to activate our spirit body, with the assistance of demons.

As alluded to, (regarding the Catholic Church), these cheeky talents bode well for intelligence agencies. Like, remote viewers in the US can spy on Russia, and vice versa. People could astral project to steal plans? It's said paranoia about the Soviet's use of parapsychology during the 'Cold War' inspired the CIA to scientifically investigate 'Remote Viewing'. This top-secret operation, codename Project Stargate, was initiated in 1972 to investigate the potential of psychic phenomena for military intelligence. It's said however that Stargate was really a continuation of the experiments they'd been conducting for years, even back to the 1930s with JB Rhine's experiments with telepathy etc.

The US has spent at least $20 million researching 'remote viewing' and training selected military personnel in this esoteric science. It's believed to be a natural ability as anyone can learn these martial arts of the mind.

Early remote viewing consisted of learning to perceive objects and symbols hidden in boxes/envelopes, which led to remote viewing activities in distant places and future events. People create a 'passive state' to receive impressions. And they use their intuition i.e. first response that pops into our heads, so not a forced response. ESP bypasses the five senses (mental noises) and information comes from 'archetypes'?

Ingo Swann (1933-2013), Father of Remote Viewing, was one of the first to be employed by the US to remotely spy in the Soviet. Swann states that from a young boy, he could separate his consciousness from his body and travel the galaxy i.e. astral projection. Then in 1973, as an experiment, the CIA wanted to see if he could describe Jupiter before a NASA mission reported back with the details. And within three minutes Swann was there. A detailed timeline of the experiment reproduced from the official records showed the session began at 6pm and within three minutes, in his astral form, he was at Jupiter. He reported some astounding details which were later confirmed by the NASA voyage e.g. the rings around Jupiter, its surface, weather, and atmosphere.

Swann notably informed that he was blindfolded and escorted by helicopter to underground secret military bases. But moreover, a couple of years later, Swann took a trip to the dark side of the moon, at the CIA's request. And apparently he saw a colony there, a 'moon city' complete with living beings, who noticed his presence. So, that's interesting?

The Stargate Project was officially terminated and declassified in 1995 after a CIA report concluded that the project 'has not been shown to have any value in intelligence operations'. Apparently by then, they'd collected tons of information, from thousands of Remote Viewing sessions. Despite being officially disbanded however, many insist the Stargate project has unofficially continued (like MK Ultra has continued). But furthermore, it's associated with remote viewing aliens. It's purported that intelligence agents are channelling a group of ETs who call themselves 'The Council of Nine'. It gets weirder, as we'll get to in Part 2.

Besides esoteric science, it's understood the CIA and other intelligence agencies have myriad drugs and technology at their disposal to induce ASC. Besides the LSD they devised and dished out to college campuses to spark the New Age, and apparatus like the God Helmet, there's radio beam technology. Thoughts can be projected into peoples' minds, so called 'targeted individuals', and people can be given visions and memories. Meditation audio technology, like binaural beats, can also induce ASC leading to astral trips. It's also foreseen that computer games will become so advanced it will be like lucid dreaming i.e. impossible to distinguish reality. Perhaps science and technology will bridge the physical and astral plane, creating some kind of interface?

As highlighted, it's alleged there's a chemical and technological assault on our minds. It's also noted, that in the Bible the Greek word pharmakeia is translated as sorcery, as people can be catapulted into the second heaven. The Bible also tells us there will be a surge of 'pharmacy' in the last days. It seems we're here, with our DSM Bible, widely available street drugs, and trips to Peru?

And last but not least, (with regards to ASC), is hypnosis. The term hypnosis was notably coined by James Braid (previously mentioned), and comes from Greek hypnosis 'to sleep', after Hypnos the Greek god of sleep. The Roman equivalent is Somnus, hence somnambulism disorders. As discussed, with hypnosis, people are induced into a trance, which is a passive state, leaving them open to suggestion. Attention is drawn from the outside world, and is concentrated on mental, sensory, and physiological experiences.

The hypnotised person experiences a heightened level of awareness coupled with a narrowing of their focus i.e. the person can concentrate intensely on a specific thought or memory, while blocking out other sources of distraction. It's purported, the left hemisphere of our brain (which is the editor, filter, logical part) needs to be bypassed or suppressed. Apparently 20% of the population are highly hypnotisable. But as discussed, trauma at an early age makes people vulnerable to dissociation and thus easily hypnotisable.

It's also noted, that like yoga and meditation, hypnotherapy is promoted for mental wellbeing i.e. to change unhelpful behaviours. And hypnosis is also an ancient occult practice. It's advertised that we can reprogram our minds e.g. every time we think of chocolate, we imagine it covered in faeces. We can program our subconscious to be our best selves? We can be confident happy non-smokers and non-drinkers, who love chomping on celery.

It's notably not an accident that society is promoting these ancient arts (like mindfulness). It's part of a bigger picture, as we'll get to. As Black (2010) highlights, hypnosis was originally an esoteric practice, used by the Rishis of India ('seers of thought') and temple priests at Egypt. It was a supernatural means of influencing and reading minds. He notes, 'From the eighteenth century onwards European travellers in India were amazed by the ability of adepts to throw anyone into an immediate state of catalepsy, just by looking at them' (p.187).

Thus, it seems there's a difference between this ability, and the typical trance countdown the therapist uses, which the person goes along with. For the most part, we're told we have to be up for the fantasy. Like, stare at the infamous spot on the wall until our eyes feel heavy. We believe we're getting more relaxed, with every breath we take.

Hypnosis is a state of consciousness in which the imagination rather than the intellect is active. As Paracelsus explains, the hypnotiser paralyses our will and acts on our imagination. Imagination becomes believable. We respond to suggestions. And yet those hypnotised classically insist they can reject any suggestion and awaken at any time. It's described as their mind is there, but it's taken a backseat. Hypnosis is thus regarded as compliance i.e. we're told to believe something, so we do. Hypnotists plant beliefs. Like, people become stuck, and can't get up or move their body.

Illicit mind control aside, (like programming people to undertake covert operations), hypnosis can be entertaining? Like, hypnotising people to strut around like chickens, or meow and lick themselves like cats. Those hypnotised show trance logic in which they will accept illogical illusions or impossible situations. We can really believe anything. It's like a forty year old woman with DID believes she's a five year old boy who likes football? It seems hypnosis is another gateway to the unconscious mind, archetypes included?

I rarely 'LOL' when reading, but did when reading Derren Brown's account of a bloke he hypnotised to see a rhinoceros in his room. Thus, for the purposes of entertainment, this comes from his book 'Tricks of the Mind' (2006) p.143-145.

'One of the most memorable sequences from the hypnotism show I saw as a student involved the participants hallucinating an enormous elephant walking into the room and up onto the stage. Once they had all stroked it and described it, they were told to lean against it. At the hypnotist's command, the animal 'disappeared', and several of the subjects tumbled to the floor.

I tried a similar thing one afternoon, when I was talking to the two entertainment managers at one of the halls of residence in Bristol. One of them, Gavin, did seem rather a responsive type, so I offered to try a couple of things with them both to see if we'd have any success. As I thought, this one chap was very susceptible, and after a few preliminary routines to amplify his responsiveness, I told him that he would take us back to his room and find a rhinoceros in there when he opened the door. He awoke. We chatted for a while, then he suggested adjourning to his room for a cup of tea. The three of us (I'm not embarrassed to say that two of us were smirking like school children) headed through fire doors, along beige hallways and past noticeboards and pay phones and eventually reached his door. He found his key, and politely ushered us in first. 'No no, after *you*' I insisted, and he turned to step inside.

Gavin half entered the room, froze for two beats, then quickly stepped back out and closed the door without letting us see inside. He looked at both of us, then asked me if I'd mind if he had a quick chat with his colleague. I stepped aside and he whispered some worried words into the other chap's ear. The latter managed to disguise a laugh as a sort of sympathetic exclamation of disbelief – an incongruent display of guffawing, frowning and nodding seriously with no eye contact made. Gavin was clearly asking him for advice as to what to do, and after a little of this mumbled exchange his colleague turned and explained. 'Gavin has a rhino in his room,' he said; and now facing away from his friend, he broke into a grin with clear relief. Gavin looked a little embarrassed and opened the door to show me. The two of us peeked into the room. It yielded, of course, the regulation thin bed, orange curtains, orange chair covered in clothes, open wardrobe, ashtray, four books, film poster, kettle and juggling balls (very popular at the time), but definitely no rhinoceros. I can't say I wasn't a tiny bit relieved for a fleeting second.

'We have to get it out,' I heard from behind me. 'It'll break through my floor. Fucking shit.' Presumably Gavin was thinking ahead to his chances of election to president of the Student's Union, and he wasn't going to let a massive horned herbivore stand in his way. Getting the rhino out hadn't occurred to me, but it certainly sounded like fun. In fact, we encouraged him.

I suspect that if anyone had walked past as we all mucked in to squeeze the luckily rather docile mammal through the small doorway, we would have looked rather odd. Gavin's colleague was pushing at the enormous rump end, and Gavin himself was pulling and guiding it from the front. I helped from the side, laughing with the guy at the back, patting its imaginary thick skin and offering sarcastic words of encouragement, such as 'up your end, Gavin', 'it's coming' and 'the rhino is certainly making its way through the door'. Illogically, given the size of the doorway, it did eventually find its way through into the corridor, though Gavin was worried about the splintering of parts of the doorframe, which he seemed to perceive. We headed for the exit that would take us out of the building, Gavin paranoid that we would pass someone who would freak out or call security.

I'm unsure if we made our way down any stairs, but certainly we ended up in the car park. We did now pass a few people, who saw of course nothing but the three of us walking slowly with Gavin a little way ahead of the two of us. Memorably, Gavin was offering calming advice to anyone who looked over, such as, 'Don't ask! It's fine,' or 'No need to panic, it's all taken care of.' Sometimes he offered just a simple placatory 'I know, I know' with a roll of the eyes. The still constitutes one of the more vivid memories of my student days.

We took the rhinoceros over to the wheelie-bins area which, surrounded by high walls, sensibly offered partial concealment. I felt that we had probably had enough fun at this guy's expense, especially seeing as my main motive in demonstrating my skills was to secure a booking at the hall for my show. So I offered to deal safely with the animal by making it disappear. Gavin seemed incredulous, but I assured him it would work. After securing his agreement and assuring him that no harm would be done and all damage caused would be immediately reversed, I had him watch the animal while I threw out my arms in its direction, palms forward, and cried, 'Rhino, be gone!' The exhausted student watched as the animal turned to space-dust and disappeared – or however he imagined it. Gavin went over to inspect the empty air he now could see in its place. He was impressed.'

Being hypnotised to see something, so called positive hallucinations, is like psychosis or a vision? Besides seeing the rhino, this hypnotised bloke perceived the splintering of the doorframe. So, the environment is the same, but it's not, because he's seeing things the other two aren't. Like, someone with psychosis might see giant spiders crawling in their living room. Interestingly, with regards to negative hallucinations, which is being hypnotised not to see something, some people advise they couldn't see whatever, whereas others advise they were aware of whatever but 'something in them' would keep trying to blank it out.

With regards to hypnotic age regression, about 50% of people report experiencing duality, in the sense that they felt both adult and child. Apparently reliving an earlier period in their life is phenomenological in the sense of actually experiencing it in a very real way. The person's manner, voice and handwriting reflect that age, which resonates with DID?

It's like people are possessed by their unconscious, as often when they come out of their trance, they forget what they've done. Or what they've heard, or been told to believe, or been programmed to execute. Post-hypnotic amnesia is achieved by 'suggesting' during hypnosis that they forget. Thus, people can be programmed to forget they've been programmed.

It's also noted, that hypnosis is used to reduce pain and even as an alternative to anaesthetics. In a BBC documentary about hypnosis, a Scottish woman got her two front teeth out and implants screwed in without an anaesthetic. She reported minimal discomfort. Her hypnotist just continued talking to her. Apparently, hypnotists have to keep talking to people in a trance (unless they're 'asleep'), as hypnotically talking to them helps keep them in their trance. It's noted, the more responsive to hypnosis the person is, the better the odds at it working for pain analgesia. Hypnosis is also likened to the placebo effect. Kirsch asserts that placebo effects and hypnosis share a common mechanism, namely, 'response expectancy', as both are based upon our beliefs.

According to EEGs hypnosis is formally indistinguishable from a pattern of being relaxed, alert with eyes closed. There are thus two major clinical schools of thought regarding hypnosis, namely, 'altered' or 'special state' theories, and 'non-state' theories. Hypnosis could be an altered state of mind or trance, marked by a level of awareness that is different from ordinary consciousness. Like, the traditional Victorian view, which considered hypnosis a dissociated state, in which part of the mind is cut off from the rest. The hypnotist speaks directly to the dissociated part of the mind, making actions feel involuntary and hallucinations real. Yet there is no mind?

Or hypnosis is not a special state but rather a form of imaginative role-enactment. It's little more than a form of behavioural compliance. It's highlighted that our 'meaning-making' process is interfered with or switched off. [In psychology, 'meaning-making' is the process through which we construe, understand, or make sense of life events, relationships, and our self]. 'Non-state' theorists argue that various phenomena can be explained without thinking of trances or hypnosis as a special state. Hypnosis can be seen as involving multiple overlapping systems of cognitive control, some of which may not always be available to conscious awareness, and some of which may tap into fantasy processes. The experience of involition is based upon the abilities of imagination, absorption and perhaps dissociation.

In hypnosis, dissociation refers to concentrating upon one activity to the exclusion of all other features in a particular situation. In terms of pain for example, the idea would be that it does not register in conscious awareness but registers at a covert hidden level that is somehow dissociated from conscious awareness. It's understood that a single brain can sustain more than one set of conscious experiences at a time. So, to date there is no clear scientific consensus on whether hypnosis constitutes a separate state of consciousness, or merely a sort of socially constructive, imaginative role play. We don't know if it can truly be said to divide consciousness.

At its most basic level, a trance is simply being more absorbed in our imagination than the immediacy of our environment. Like, daydreaming, or 'highway hypnosis'. But then there's being possessed by our unconscious. Like, autonomous complexes or archetypes usurp our ego. It's said, if we don't control our minds, others are more than happy to. But it's also purported, that demons can be placed into people when they're hypnotised, so that's pretty crazy. Like, demons can be attached to alters in DID. But we'll get back to this craziness.

In summary then, it seems entities ('energies') are all around us, but we just can't see them 'normally'. Like, shadow people appear and disappear. And like aliens and UFOs come in and out of our dimension. And like ghosts? It seems there's some kind of dimensional wall they can slip through. But for the most part, they're not allowed to. It seems we have to give them an opening, a window of opportunity like an ASC. We have to invite them in. Like a vampire?

As Jung said, 'archetypes' or demons are real, living autonomous entities. It seems the collective unconscious is the astral plane and the 'world of ideas' that Plato referred to? So, these personalities have their own life, but they're obsessed with ours. Perhaps they envy our flesh and blood bodies? They want to live through us? Presumably, food and drink, for example, tastes better in the physical world i.e. it's more real/fulfilling than eating or drinking in a dream-like state? According to La-Sala however, sex is better in the spirit world.

But moreover, as Dr Rebecca Brown highlighted, contrary to God's will, Satan's goal is to teach humans to regain conscious control of our spiritual bodies. She asserts that open communication with the spirit world is the goal of all eastern religions and Satanism. Thus, it's not an accident that creator God has been replaced with the doctrine of physical and spiritual evolution. And that contemporary 'psychology' recognises we have a spiritual facet to our being. And occult practices are marketed through influencers i.e. the cool people (like Russell Brand?) go to yoga? But rather, there's a very specific agenda being adhered to.

Whilst we'll get back to this in Part 2, there's basically two gods to worship, namely, Yahweh of the Bible, and Lucifer, His fallen angel, who became known as His adversary Satan. There's two paths, God's Son's way, or the sun/serpent god way. And whilst God forbade His people to cross-dimensional travel, Lucifer mandates that his people *break on through to the other side*. Lucifer the Light Bearer is the great illuminator, and he bears supernatural gifts. But one has to sign up. Increasingly popular Lucifer also rewards his people with fame and fortune in this life. But again, we'll get back to this insanity that appears to be reality.

More generally, God knows what happens when the silver cord is cut. Maybe death is something like lucid dreaming? Maybe our disembodied consciousness goes to Never-Never Land. It's noted, Peter Pan is a metaphor for astral projection, and Pan is a reference to the Greek goat god who is often identified with Satan. Maybe we hook up with astral entities doing the astral fandango in the astral realms. Or maybe we end up in hell, a haunted dark abyss? Or maybe we go to sleep until Judgement Day, when we have to give an account of our life? Or maybe Bertrand Russell is right. We'll find out soon. This physical life takes no time.

'The Death and Dying Lady'

7¼

Dr Elisabeth Kubler-Ross (1926-2004)

Dr Elisabeth Kubler-Ross, renowned for her bestselling book 'On Death and Dying' (1969), was an otherwise 'normal' psychiatrist, until she took the other side seriously. Like a butterfly, she emerged from her scientific cocoon. She used the metaphor that at death we shed our bodies, which imprisons our soul like a cocoon encloses the future butterfly. As a much loved and credible person then, we can spare a thought for some of her experiences. This is from her book, 'The Wheel of Life: A Memoir of Living and Dying' (1997).

Dr Kubler-Ross worked with the dying and similarly pertained to their extremely vivid experiences. She relayed that as they neared death, they talked with others no-one else could see (i.e. deceased loved ones). She observed that death is preceded by a peculiar serenity, but contrary to the presumption that 'once they're gone, they're gone', she began to surmise that perhaps death was not the end. Not everyone stays dead, and those who came back to life had many interesting things to report. This inspired her to research NDEs, and together with her research partner, she interviewed about twenty thousand people. The distinctly different 'phases' of death she compiled, basically corroborates with what's been discussed.

Thus, the first stage entailed floating out their bodies, in an ethereal shape. She notes that it made no difference how they died i.e. flat-line in the operating room, car wreck, or suicide, as everyone reported being aware of the scene they'd just left. They knew what was happening, heard discussions, counted the doctors working on them, or saw the effort being made to free them from mangled vehicles. Others recounted what relatives had said at their bedside.

They experienced a wholeness, with sight returned to the blind, and those previously paralysed moved effortlessly and joyously (there was no more pain). Indeed, one woman, who enjoyed dancing above her hospital room so much, was severely depressed when she had to come back. Kubler Ross reports that the only complaint people had, was that they did not stay dead. And practically everyone hears 'it's not time' and they come back to life.

The second phase, having left their bodies, and irrespective of where they died, was the ability to go anywhere with the speed of thought (like astral projection). Some reported thinking of how upset their family would be, and zoom, they were with them, even if they were halfway around the world. Everyone interviewed remembered this phase for also being when they met their guardian angels or guides. These spiritual beings comforted them and introduced them to previously deceased relatives and friends. Kubler-Ross states, 'it was remembered as a time of cheerful reunion, sharing, catching up and hugs'.

In phase three, they proceeded to what is commonly described as a tunnel, through which people recounted a variety of different images, and at the end they saw a bright light. She explains that as their guides took them closer, they felt the light radiating intense warmth, energy, spirit, and overwhelming unconditional love. They felt the excitement, peace, tranquillity, and the anticipation of finally going home. They said the light was the ultimate source of universal energy, and referred to it as God, Christ or Buddha.

Then in the fourth phase, people reported being in the presence of the Highest Source, which was loving and non-judgemental. Some called it God, and others reported simply knowing that they were surrounded by every bit of knowledge there was, past, present and future. Those who arrive here no longer need their ethereal shape, as they become 'spiritual energy'. It seems we ditch our astral body, baring our soul? Dr Kubler-Ross states this is the form human beings assume between lives, hence she advocates reincarnation. They experienced a oneness, a completeness of existence.

In this state, people went through a life review, a process in which they confronted the totality of their lives. They had to confront their choices, going over every action, word and thought of their lives. And they were made to understand the reasons for every decision, thought and action they had in life. They saw how their actions affected other people, including strangers. They saw what their lives could have been like, the potential they had. It's said that God has a plan for our lives, but imagine watching what we could have been if only we got a grip and made our dreams happen.

They were shown that life is intertwined, that every thought and action has a ripple effect on every other living thing on the planet. Dr Kubler-Ross interpreted this as heaven or hell, or maybe both. She noted, that every one of the thousands of patients she interviewed recalled going into the light and being asked, 'How much love have you been able to give and receive?' And 'how much service have you rendered?' Had they learned the lessons they were supposed to?

She informed that everyone experienced the same epiphany, namely, the meaning of life is unconditional love. Kubler-Ross believes the ultimate lesson to learn is unconditional love. She asserts, 'love is our connection to God and each other'. Kubler-Ross concedes that NDEs have a profound effect on people. It was described as a religious experience. Some had been given great knowledge, some came back with prophetic warnings, and others had new insight. It seems NDEs provide an opportunity for redemption?

For an example of a NDE, we can consider Mrs Schwartz. Kubler-Ross states that she floated out her body as per, and went forward to the ceiling. She heard what everyone said and even sensed what they were thinking. She felt curiously content, and since she felt so well, yet was watching the resuscitation team frantically trying to save her, she repeatedly asked them to stop the heroics, assuring them that she was okay. But despite her efforts, they didn't hear her. So, she went down to poke one of the residents but to her amazement, her arm went right through his arm. At that point, she decided to give up on them, and then she lost consciousness.

After forty-five minutes, Mrs Schwartz's last observation was of them covering her with a bedsheet and pronouncing her dead, whilst an anxious and deflated resident told jokes. But then, three and a half hours later, as a nurse came into the room to remove her body, she instead found Mrs Schwartz alive. Mrs Schwartz wondered if she was delusional or psychotic, but Dr Kubler-Ross verified that she had never been and was not psychotic. Mrs Schwartz's marbles were all intact. So, the experience was not a hallucination, but rather there was a reality to her vision?

But moreover, after Mrs Schwartz eventually died and was buried, ten months later Dr Kubler-Ross saw an apparition of her. The ghost (almost transparent) hovered in the air, and thus it was Kubler Ross's time to wonder if she was psychotic. She didn't however feel that her stress levels warranted that state of mind. But even weirder, and to prove her existence, Mrs Schwartz, who notably told Dr Kubler-Ross not to quit her work on 'death and dying', stating 'we will help you', wrote a message down on paper with a pen. And then a moment later, she vanished. Mrs Schwartz had evidenced survival of the soul/spirit, and Kubler-Ross came to the conclusion that death does not exist in the traditional sense.

It's duly noted, that Mrs Schwartz didn't dissipate into 'spiritual energy', since she was in her spirit body? It seems she didn't merge with the great light? Or maybe that wasn't Mrs Schwartz but rather a demon pretending to be her? Whilst we're led to believe that ghosts are the subliminal remains of former people, maybe they're not. As discussed, demons can take the appearance of whomever. Maybe demons can scoop astral shells, from the plane of shells, and pretend to be someone they're not? It's also noted, that 'ghosts' using physical pens to write physical notes is not normal.

Besides piecing together the phases of death, Dr Kubler-Ross was also open to the idea of spirit guides. And she was inspired by a woman who took photos of fairies. Thus, with her camera at the ready, she called out, as in a dare, 'if I do have a guide and you can hear me, make yourself visible in the next picture'. She then snapped a picture of the meadow and woods in front of her, but when the picture was developed, there was a tall, muscular stoic-looking Indian with his arms folded across his chest (his expression was serious) superimposed on the foreground. She regarded this as proof that life continued after death.

Searching for like-minded others, (not quacks), she met Jay and Martha B, who seemed like a nice 'ordinary middle-class couple'. Jay B channelled spirits by going into a trance and allowing his body to be taken over. They called it the 'phenomenon of materialisation', and since founding their self-named Church of Divinity the previous year, they had developed a core following of about a hundred people. Kubler-Ross advised they sat in a 'dark room', because apparently having the lights on risked harming the spirits and maybe B. The group would then begin singing, a soft rhythmic hum that built to a loud group chant, which gave B the 'energy' needed to channel the entities. As the chanting reached a new, almost euphoric level, B disappeared behind a screen.

Kubler-Ross informs that suddenly a tall (seven foot) shadowy figure appeared to the right of her and spoke in a deep voice stating, her soulmate was trying to come through. And then he disappeared, and another spirit materialised, and introduced himself as Salem. He was tall and slender, dressed in a long flowing robe and a turban. She recalled thinking that 'if he touched her, she'd drop dead', and at that instant he disappeared. Then the first figure came back and explained that her nervousness had made Salem go away.

After she calmed down, about five minutes later, Salem reappeared. He then took her to another dark room so they could be alone. He told her that she had been Isabel in another lifetime, a wise and respected teacher. He said he was going to take her on a special journey, and together they travelled back to a pleasant afternoon, which featured her sitting on a hillside, whilst listening to Jesus preach to a group of people. She visualised the whole scene. After an hour, the session ended.

The next time, she went back to the dark room with B herself, and again Salem appeared. Interestingly, as she wondered if her parents would be proud to know how well she'd done in life, Salem sang a favourite family Kubler song, and said 'he knows', referring to her father. It seems she was hooked, as over the next few months, she returned frequently to the B's abode to meet with Salem and other spirits. She became familiar with the spirits, which included Mario, an absolute genius spirit, who spoke eloquently about whatever subject she raised, whether it was geology, history, physics or crystals.

But again, (like Mrs Schwartz writing a message), it gets weirder, as one morning Salem called her home, but she was out, and her husband answered the phone. Her husband, who was not enamoured by her 'research', said Salem sounded like a strange man disguising his voice. Perhaps we could surmise that Salem knew she was out and phoned to cause trouble?

As it transpired, they divorced and she moved to be besides the Bs, which was seemingly providential, as Dr Kubler-Ross had a mission. A spirit told her that she had to tell the whole world that death does not exist. And when she asked why her, the spirit told her 'it had to be a person from medicine and science, not from theology and religion, since they had not done their job and had ample opportunity in the last two thousand years' (i.e. since Jesus' time).

So, she continued to engage with 'spirit guides'. Like, she would invite Pedro to appear, and the instant she asked, he appeared all the way from America to Australia. Besides that, and like someone she knew, who believed she conversed with Jesus for seventy years via her kitchen table, Dr Kubler-Ross also communicated with a table, and believed she was conversing with Jesus Christ.

She relayed that she was worried about the safety of two visitors (who were unusually late), and when she wondered if they'd been in an accident and if she should call the police, the table moved. A loud voice said 'no', and when she asked if she was talking to Jesus, the table moved again, and the same voice said 'yes'. At the same time as Kubler-Ross was communicating with the alleged spirit of JC in the table, her houseguests appeared, who happened to be two nuns, and when they saw what was happening, they grinned and said 'oh, you can do the table too?' They insisted they do it together.

Later that night when she went to sleep, she states that instead of 'falling asleep', she felt as if she was rising up out of her body, higher and higher. She notes that once aloft, she perceived several beings take hold of her and carry her off to a place where they 'fixed her up', as she was overloaded and exhausted.

Having thoroughly enjoyed the OBE, she sought more, but with scientists at a research lab. There she was blindfolded and heard a beeping noise to induce a sleep-like state of mind. Her first attempt wasn't great, but the second time she said the beeping instantly cleared her mind of all thoughts and took her inward. Then she heard an incredible WHOOSH, and she was taken out her body. She explained that although her body was motionless, her brain (awareness) took her to another dimension of existence, like another universe.

When she returned to her room however, she sensed a strange energy, which convinced her she wasn't alone. Then she began having nightmares, which she described as going through one thousand deaths (she identified the nightmares with the deaths of her patients). She states they tortured her physically. She could hardly breathe, and bent over in overwhelming agony and pain, she had no strength to scream or call for help. She wanted some comfort i.e. a hand to hold or shoulder to lean on, but a firm, unemotional deep manly voice said no, she would not be given.

When she awoke, she noticed some peculiar things, like a section of her abdomen began to vibrate at an ever-increasing speed, and then whatever part of her body she looked at began to vibrate with the same fantastic speed. She explained that the vibrations broke everything down to their most basic structure, so that when she stared at anything, her eyes feasted on the billions of dancing molecules. She explained that her vision, which extended for miles and miles, caused her to see everything from a blade of grass to a wooden door, in its natural molecular structure, its vibrations. She described a vibrating world, in which everything had a life, a divinity. Like, DMT visions?

At this point, she realised she had left her physical body and became energy. Then in front of her, she saw many beautiful lotus flowers that merged into one enormous lotus blossom, and behind the flower, she noticed a light, 'brighter than bright and totally ethereal'. She inferred that she was seeing the same light all her patients talked about seeing.

Then she moved toward the light, and merging with it, she said 'a million everlasting orgasms cannot describe the sensation of the love, warmth and sense of welcome' she experienced. Then she heard two voices, her own saying 'I am acceptable to Him', and another said 'Shanti Nilaya', which is Sanskrit and means 'the final home of peace'. She was told that the whole experience was supposed to give her 'cosmic consciousness', an awareness of the life in every living thing. She surmised that Shanti Nilaya is where we go to at the end of our earthly journey, when we return to God, which seems to be the Light.

As it transpired however, all was not as it seemed with the Bs. Rumours had been circulating about B being a pervert. It was alleged that sexual abuse and misconduct had been happening in the dark room. Apparently, B had a history of 'creepy behaviour', and when the lights were off, he was partial to fooling about with the participants in the dark. B however claimed he could not be accountable for any of his actions, even if they were improper, stating that when he's in a trance, he was not aware of what was happening.

Kubler-Ross however thought he was lying. It also came to light, that B went stark naked in the sessions. This was apparently his method of making the spirits materialise. Yet the congregation were repeatedly told a materialised entity would die if someone turned the light on in its presence. It's recalled that La-Sala said demons are more powerful in the dark, so perhaps darkness is more effective at summoning entities?

But moreover, it was also discovered that B ripped off Lerner Hinshaw's material. Hinshaw's 'The Magnificent Potential' contained everything B and the many guides he channelled taught. The congregation was stunned and felt betrayed. B denied any wrongdoing, advising that his guides prohibited him from divulging the source of his knowledge.

Kubler-Ross observed their previously close-knit, sharing and caring, group became suspicious and paranoid. Many were leaving, but Kubler-Ross stayed and was subsequently ordained by B as minister of peace in his church. She advised that all the entities appeared at the celebration, including K, the highest of all the entities. Salem played the flute, and Pedro performed the actual ritual. But moreover, she said they always knew when K arrived, as a strange silence preceded his entrance. And when he stood in front of them, in his long Egyptian style robe, no one was able to move.

Despite having her secret wish fulfilled, namely, to become a true minister of peace, relations continued to sour with the Bs. Indeed, she believed B had evil energy. She seems to attribute the deathly spider-bites she got, her car brakes failing, and her house that was deliberately set on fire, to him. She said, 'I had no idea how a good healer like B could turn into such a dark figure' (p.243). She got away from the Bs.

Whilst Kubler-Ross seems partial to spirit guides, it's noted they're not all friendly and they can dish out torment. It's also understood that spirit guides lie, and that was not Jesus communicating through a table.

The following is paraphrased from Gaz Parker's testimony[18]

7½

Spirit Guides by Gaz Parker

Gaz Parker claims that from about five years old, he could see spiritual entities in his house. He asserts they were very real, and he was terrified (he believes these entities fed off that fear). He could see them and hear their voices in his head. He spoke about absolute fear, noting his bedcovers were soaking with sweat. His parents, who were atheists, rendered it his 'active imagination' and upon their advice, he learned to ignore them, and they seemed to go away (stopped visiting) when he was about seven.

But then at fourteen, he developed an interest in the occult and started playing with a Ouija board, together with his friends. He stated that on one occasion the glass got hot, and that afterwards he felt a presence around him. He felt like he was being watched and had an obsession with drawing (doodling) eyes.

Parker also got intrigued with astral projection. He was told to imagine chakras, and light from the top of his head going all the way down to his feet, and then back up (in repeat). He states he practised for months as he really wanted to experiment with astral projection. But then one night he woke up and he was paralysed. He had sleep paralysis but moreover, he was sexually attacked for about half an hour by some sex-pest demon. He recalls that before the attack, he was moved about the bed. His arms and legs were moving about, and he didn't really have control over it.

Then when he was fifteen, a classmate from school was brutally murdered, which propelled him to question his mortality. He recalls being afraid of dying. He was introduced to Church from Christians he met, and says he was saved (born again) at sixteen.

As it transpired however, he wanted to have fun like his chums i.e. drink, smoke, and go with girls. And he didn't want to be told what to do. He had a thirst for spiritual meaning, and believed in God, but he wasn't convinced about Christianity. He acknowledges it wasn't the right time for him, but clarifies that whilst he gave up Christianity, he never gave up God. He thus went his own way in 'search of the truth'. He notes, that when he was seventeen/eighteen, and going to the pub to get drunk, information would come to him, like people's names and ages. It seemed to be his party-piece.

As it transpired, he became interested in psychology, hypnotherapy, and was a fan of self-help. By age thirty he completed his diploma in hypnotherapy, and was regularly doing trance-work. But moreover, not long after his

---

[18] See 'Voices in the Dark' on Blog Talk Radio, 23rd Feb 2011, and his Sept 3rd 2010 excerpt on the website New Age Deception.

wife's grandmother died, he felt the compulsion to consult a medium. The medium he met used rune stones to tell his future, and then she went into a trance and described his grandmother. She also told him about his wife's grandma (M for Maureen), and his grandfather, uncle and a couple of others, detailing their different quirks etc. He asserts he was careful not to give any information in case she was a charlatan.

He highlights that he felt relieved knowing that his family and friends were 'alive' and well. And he took comfort knowing they looked out for him. He also noticed that he felt energy around his face and neck, which he told the medium. The medium told Parker he could be a medium, as her guide had told her.

After this, his mediumship began kicking in, which he referred to as his 'spiritual awakening' (he was thirty-four at the time). He was with a friend and explained to him, that he kept getting the image of a mutual friend 'Chris' who had died, forced into his mind. And he could hear his voice. Parker asked 'Chris' for information, and he advised about the motorbike accident and the clothes he was wearing at the time. He passed on the information, which was true. Parker said to his friend, who had been Chris's best friend, that he believed Chris was giving him a message, namely to 'let Chris go'. He felt like 'Chris' was really talking to him, like the way the entities spoke to him when he was young. Then Parker passed on information about his friend's grandmother and grandfather.

As a result however, Parker felt overwhelmed, anxious and confused. Thus, he contacted the medium to get help. She explained that his mind was like a radio/receptor and told him techniques to close it down. Whilst she wasn't able to meet with him, she gave him another medium to contact. This medium told Parker that being a medium is nothing special, it just means he's more 'sensitive' than other people. This medium's spirit guide (apparently a monk, a high-level spirit, from the thirteenth century), made Parker feel calm. The medium told Parker to join a spiritualist group/circle to develop his skills and mediumship. So, he did.

He explains they would sit in a circle with the lights dimmed or off, and enter a trance like state. They would then send messages to each other, and speak to the 'dead'. Parker states that unlike most mediums who usually get one extra sense i.e. they can see, hear, feel or smell things, Parker had them all. He claims that spirits would touch him e.g. tap him on the shoulder etc, and that when he was in a deep trance, the spirits would take over and control his body i.e. moving his limbs. He states this reminded him of his earlier gruesome experience with succubus.

However, his ability didn't go down well with the other mediums. He suspected they were envious of him, and he felt nervous. During the trance-work, he began feeling sick, (gagging), so he stopped going to the sessions. He then joined another group at the other spiritualist church in town. This new circle emphasised spirit guides. The following is Parker's excerpt about 'Spirit Guides'.

"I remember the leader of my first (mediumship) development circle teaching us on how to connect to our spirit guides. He explained there were different types of guide but only one that remains with us from birth. It was interesting at the time because the leader also told me that this entity was very advanced and sometimes referred to as a guardian angel. Some people saw their guides as angels but the form was different for each person. My guide for example showed himself during a guided visualisation meditation where one member of the circle described a fictitious journey along a river bank. As I was told my guide would appear, he did so as Native American named Sitting Bull. When I questioned if this was the actual Sitting Bull the guide affirmed it. The leader of the circle told me that it probably isn't the genuine Sitting Bull but may have manifested as such just to put me at ease.

He told me things about my life and where I was going in life. During this time I felt vibrations around my face, ears and neck. I later found out this was the way my guide identified itself, a form of authentication. I was to learn to trust him and unless he was present during mediumship I was not to trust the information coming through. The leader had built up a friendship with his guide, a wise female Native American. I felt fortunate to have met my guide since not all mediums ever meet their guides, some don't even believe they exist.

Apart from my main guide I used to get other guides who would hang around for a while then move away. One particular guide claimed to be a Viking and showed himself wearing a helmet with horns. When I challenged him about the historical validity of Vikings having helmets with horns he backtracked and explained this was just for show. During the time I worked with this guide I was probably the most accurate. His energy was very powerful and I would be exhausted after doing readings with this particular guide.

At the time I placed a lot of faith in guides. I remember boasting to my mother-in-law about how my guides are like guardian angels. It was quite ironic since I was working in the garden putting up timber posts for some decking my in laws where laying. I offered to help out. Before my mother-in-law was on her way out to go shopping and told me to be careful. I laughed stating I was in no danger, my guides will protect me! I was absolutely convinced of this.

We mixed some quick dry cement and dropped the timber post into the ground and held it firmly into the cement. Holding the post, my father-in-law climbed up the short ladder and began sawing off about 12 inches of timber from the top of the post. As the sawdust fell onto my head, I shuffled to one side. I was oblivious as a large chunk of timber came crashing down onto my head. It was so painful that I froze, I was massively in shock. Thankfully it didn't knock me out since I would then require a brain scan which is the usual procedure at least in the UK. Although when I saw the lump of timber I noticed a large sharp piece sticking out the other side. Had this part hit me it would have penetrated my skull and, well, I would not be here today.

As a former member of the spiritualist church you are told many things including the law of cause and effect (Karma) and that you must trust your guides. I recall telling myself that the guides were either trying to teach me a lesson for showing off or they actually intervened, preventing the sharp part of the timber falling onto my head. Either way, this was no act of protection and this was just another one of those incidents that lead me to question these entities".

Parker learned that entities can make themselves look like anything, which he considered very important. He was told that spirits have no real form, so they create a form e.g. Sitting Bull. They can present themselves as 'archetypes'. It's noted, Native Indians are popular, as both Jung and Kubler-Ross attested to. Parker explains that in the circle, one person leads, and others are used as 'batteries'. As energies/vibrations get stronger, it's easier to connect with the spirit world. However, as it transpired, he began getting ill again, so he quit.

Over the next few years, not much happened, until his mother died. He believed she was still around, and would speak to her, but he was too upset to contact the spirit world. In his grief, he said a prayer to his mum, asking her for a sign. At that point, his electronic weather gadget, which was a present from his mum, moved. He wondered whether it was really his mum, and tried to connect with his spirit guide for confirmation. However, there was little chat from him, so he started chatting to his mum.

He believed he was speaking to her. He would see her face and hear her voice. And she comforted him, saying she loved him etc, which was nice. But then she began saying things that were out of character. Parker started getting the impression that some things she was saying were insincere, and 'she' also began blatantly lying. He realised this wasn't his mum and decided not to speak the spirit world anymore.

It dawned on him that it was impossible to know what these entities are, and who he was speaking to. And in the same way, how could someone trust their guides? There was no way to test the source, or know where they're coming from. And if mediums are not speaking to the dead, who are they speaking to?

He started having serious doubts and turned to God for answers. He prayed every day, asking for guidance, asking God to show Him the truth. He wasn't sure about Christianity, but he even prayed to Jesus, stating 'if you do exist or you are real', to please help him. He was confused and had to know what was going on. This included whether or not he should be a medium. He felt lost and didn't know what he should be doing as a spiritual person.

Some months later, he went to St Paul's Cathedral (London), and found himself drawn to Holman Hunt's painting 'The Light of the World', which depicts Jesus knocking at a door. The writing beneath the picture, which is from Revelation 3:20, states, 'Behold I stand at the door and knock. If anyone hears my voice and opens the door, I will come in and dine with him, and he with me'. We have to invite God in.

Parker said he felt an overwhelming sense of emotion. He did however recognise that he had felt that before, when he was saved at sixteen. He states the feeling was so incredibly powerful that he had to go and sit down. He described it as an amazing, overpowering feeling, and that he felt like weeping. He asserts that at that point, he 'knew'. He had no doubts this was the spirit of God, and he knew Jesus is real. He also realised that God had never really left him. Albeit it took him another couple of months before he got down on his knees and asked God to save him. He gave his life to Christ and renounced mediumship and all his occult ways. He points out that spiritualism is a religion, and it's not Christianity. So, who are they praying to and worshipping?

With regards to spirit guides, Parker said, "From what I learned, guides can and often lie. They get things wrong from time to time then explain it away by blaming the ability of the medium. They are not always present and don't usually communicate when the medium cries out to them in need. They also provide lots of facts that draw someone in then occasionally provide you with private/personal information about that person. The biggest mistake is to then communicate this back to the person, which can result in them feeling very embarrassed and exposed. Furthermore, I remember an elderly lady asking me if she was going to die before her husband. Without thinking, a voice popped into my head saying "no, she will outlive him". So I told her. This was a big mistake, it caused her great anxiety.

So you can see, these entities are not what they appear to be and I began to know them by their fruits. Unfortunately, these spirits bared rotten fruits and when the penny finally dropped I commanded them to leave in the name of Jesus Christ. These guides are most likely demons or in some cases, fallen angels. They serve no other purpose than to spread lies, deceive others, pull people away from the truth of salvation and take as many people as they can to hell.

In conclusion, God's angels only communicate with God directly. It is extremely unlikely, if ever they communicate with human beings. On the other hand, demons and fallen angels constantly endeavour to contact people, this is forbidden by God in order to protect his flock. If you are concerned about the validity of any spiritual communication just ask the entity if they believe Jesus Christ came to earth in the flesh, died on the cross and was resurrected from the dead? Any form of denial of back peddling should raise red flags".

It's important to note, that spirits can present themselves as angels of light. In the Bible, in 2 Corinthians 11:14, we're told 'for Satan himself masquerades as an angel of light'. Respectively, Parker said, 'As a medium I saw light beings, experienced glorious feelings of energy and peace. They even told me things that were true. You see, demons can tell the truth when they choose'. It's purported that spirit guides sometimes wear white robes and radiate brilliant golden-white light. And channellers believe these 'Messengers of Light' are here to help us. Their messages are understood to be divine wisdom and truth. But maybe not.

'People who have had near-death experiences peek through the door of the after-life, but Swedenborg explored the whole house'. Kenneth Ring, NDE researcher and cofounder of International Association for Near Death Studies

7¾

Emmanuel Swedenborg (1688-1772)

It seems pertinent to briefly mention Swedish Swedenborg, as he wrote extensively about the spiritual world, and also because, as Black (2010) points out, 'his reports of what the disembodied beings he met there told him inspired the esoteric Freemasonry of the eighteenth and nineteenth centuries' (p.449).

Swedenborg the scientist was insanely clever and ahead of his time, and then he experienced a spiritual crisis in his mid-fifties. He began to experience intense dreams and visions at night, which he recorded, and which centred on his sense of spiritual unworthiness and his need to purify himself of sin. These experiences then culminated in his 'spiritual awakening'. He was able to see the spiritual world in a state of full wakefulness. The afterlife was revealed to him, while he was still alive, and for the next thirty years, until he died, he lived having bi-locality. He was in contact with the spirit world all the time i.e. seeing and hearing spirits at home, on the streets, everywhere.

According to his book 'The Heavenly Doctrine', the Lord opened Swedenborg's spiritual eyes, so he could freely visit heaven and hell, and talk with angels, demons and other spirits. He alleged that he was allowed to see the Spiritual World so he could tell people on Earth about it.

According to Swedenborg, the experience of death is beautiful and peaceful. He said, 'death is only a crossing over'. When we die, we simply move from one world to another. He explained that after we die, we wake up in the World of Spirits, which is a kind of neutral space, neither heaven nor hell. The World of Spirits is like a waiting place, or terminal, that we pass through on our way to heaven or hell. It's located halfway between heaven and hell.

He perceived three levels of heaven, and three levels of hell. The Lord, who he described as a living sun radiating divine good and truth throughout creation, reigns supreme at the highest point. The 'light of the Lord' is a light of ineffable brightness, a light of truth and understanding that permeates the hereafter. Those who are in the highest heaven are thus closest to the Lord, whereas those in the lowest hell are furthest from the Lord. Deep down in hell is thus very dark and cold because the Lord is the source of the heat and the light in the Spiritual World.

The spirit world, which is more real than our physical world, is much bigger with lots more people. Going there is described as going from a small town to a big city. Apparently, angels come to meet us on arrival (they communicate telepathically). The 'World of Spirits' is notably not to be confused with the 'Spiritual World', which is a general term referring to the whole extent of Heaven, Hell, and the World of Spirits. Swedenborg similarly pertained to some kind of spiritual firewall that separates our physical world from the spiritual world. He states this explains why loved ones can't always communicate with us when they've passed on.

For Swedenborg, we're spirit beings clothed in flesh, and our bodies are temporary coverings/vehicles to cart us about in this realm. Our destination depends on our hearts, since 'we are' our desires and intentions. Thus, if we're loving and kind, we'll naturally migrate towards heaven to accompany like-minded others. And if we're Cruella de awful we'll migrate towards hell. We form connections with people who share our values. In essence then, where we end up is where we belong, it's our prerogative. But reassuringly, Swedenborg maintained that after death, most people find themselves in heaven, which is a joyous psychological state of expanded awareness.

Swedenborg didn't believe that we reincarnate again on Earth. He claimed people who believe in past-lives are deluded. But rather, he purported that we evolve in the spiritual world i.e. learn the spiritual truths. He advised that infants grow old there, and old people get young and regain their health and vigour. For Swedenborg, the rebirth or regeneration is our transformation from a materialistic to spiritual being. God doesn't judge us, but He wants us to go to heaven as intended. The onus is therefore on us to selflessly help each other and cultivate love to get closer to God.

Swedenborg was also ecumenical, as irrespective of religious beliefs, we all have an equal chance of getting to heaven. He advised that any path that catalyses our being into good, works. This is therefore contrary to the Bible which states Jesus is the only way. For Swedenborg, the fundamental point is love and community. He also advised that the Spirit World inspires our world e.g. they inspire us to build cities, help with the planning and design etc. Presumably, this accounts for the occult architecture featured all over the world.

He further purports there is no devil per se, but rather evil people become evil spirits. The inhabitants of hell are referred to as 'devils' and 'Satans'. And hellish people, with different capacities of evil, fashion different kinds of hell for themselves. So, according to Swedenborg, every angel or devil was once a human being on Earth.

But moreover, and despite the spiritual firewall, Swedenborg highlighted that we're always in communication with the spirits, good and evil. They affect our consciousness, hence the nature of our thoughts fluctuate. Thus, some spirits can give us inspiration, and others can poison our mind with insidious thoughts. There's nasty spirits out there, who for some perverse reason are sadists. For Swedenborg, the voices 'schizophrenics' hear are the voices of spirits. There's ongoing correspondence between the spirit world and the physical world.

Swedenborg claimed that what he wrote about heaven and hell was a revelation from God. He claimed that he was appointed by the Lord Jesus Christ to write a heavenly New Church Doctrine to reform Christianity. He was gifted to reveal God's message and revise the Bible, based on his new perspective of God, the spirit world and salvation. Swedenborg claimed that Jesus' Second Coming had occurred, not by Christ in person, but by a revelation from Him through Swedenborg. Jesus had used Swedenborg to communicate His message.

Swedenborg's theological writings, his inner meaning of the Bible, are thus based on his experiences and visions. Whilst Swedenborg came from a Christian family (his father was a pastor), his experiences radically changed his beliefs, and were deemed heretical. The Bible notably warns us about false prophets and is crystal that nothing should be added or taken away from God's word. So, Swedenborg is a false prophet?

Swedenborg believed the nature or essence of God is both love and wisdom. He regarded God as immensely loving and powerful, who knows everything, and who created and sustains reality. But he rejected the Trinity of Persons i.e. God the Father, the Son, and Holy Spirit, and instead contended there exists One Person, namely, the Lord Jesus Christ. He also rejected the biblical concept of salvation through faith alone, insisting that both faith and charity are necessary for salvation. Contrary to the fundamentalists, he asserts the Bible should not be taken literally, but that everything written has an inner spiritual meaning, which he calls a 'correspondence'.

Whilst on the surface, it appears Swedenborg's spiritual awakening 'just happened to him', Black (2010) provides us with some additional details. He informs that Swedenborg was John Paul Brockmer's (a London watchmaker) lodger, and Brockmer was worried about Swedenborg. As this otherwise quiet, devout, respectable, and highly intelligent scientist appeared to have gone quite mad. Black wrote, 'Now his hair stood on end. He foamed at the mouth and chased Brockmer down the street, gibbering and claiming to be the Messiah. Brockmer tried to persuade him to see a doctor, but instead Swedenborg went to the Swedish embassy. When they wouldn't let him in, he ran to a nearby drainage ditch, undressed himself and rolled about in the mud, throwing money at the crowds'.

But moreover, apparently Swedenborg had been experimenting with certain sexual techniques for achieving extreme ASC. And he had learned these methods from the outwardly respectable Moravian chapel that he attended every Sunday (p.491). Black (2010) notes that Swedenborg had experimented with breath control since a boy. He learned that by holding his breath for long periods, he could induce a trance state, and he discovered that by synchronising his breath to his pulse he could deepen the trance. It seems Swedenborg, who wrote about rhythmic breathing methods relating to the pulse of the genitals, was on the tantric page of harnessing divine sexual energy. It's also noted, that Swedenborg mingled with aristocrats, and it seems the elite circles he circled in were somewhat suspect.

It seems Swedenborg, having crossed over to the Spirit World, acquired ESP. Indeed, he became a world renowned clairvoyant. He regarded his supernatural gifts as unique to him, and he heralded the dawn of a New Age. There are many examples of his psychic abilities e.g. when at a dinner party, more than 250 miles away from his home in Stockholm, he became agitated describing a fire that was threatening his home, and it was confirmed that a fire had been extinguished three doors down. He also predicted the exact day he would die, which happened. Acquiring ESP seems to be the natural outcome of astral voyaging, like the shamans who return from the sky are bestowed with supernatural 'gifts'.

One last point to keep in mind, (as we'll get to mystery school beliefs later), is that besides visualising God as the sun, Swedenborg believed the planets have spirits. He apparently conversed with spirits from Jupiter, Mars, Mercury, Saturn, Venus and the Moon, as well as spirits from planets beyond our solar system. So, stars and planets (which are wandering stars) embody spirits?

'I shall not commit the fashionable stupidity of regarding everything I cannot explain as a fraud'.
Carl Jung

8

The Spirit World

Parking the materialist conclusion that death is the end of, and science's valiant effort at denying the supernatural, it's always possible there is a spirit world replete with disembodied (metaphysical) beings that intervene in our material world in a supernatural way. The idea of a spirit world, whilst usurped by materialism, has been infused with new life in our New Age. But it's not new. Writings from the ancient world mention ghostly disturbances, which include flying objects, awful smells, loud noises, lights flicking on and off, and spooky apparitions. What's new is the terminology i.e. referring to good and bad 'energies', 'spirit guides' and 'aliens' as opposed to the demonic. This new fancy dress is both more palatable and alluring, and thus, whilst society has written off 'Biblical God', people are increasingly open to engaging with these curious entities or 'spiritual energy'.

It seems that some spirits are summoned into existence through various occult practices, whereas others come by their own volition. It's also noted, the term 'spirits' is used very indiscriminately, as there seems to be a host of invisible but substantial beings in our midst, complete with conscious will. And it's contended this includes spirits of dead people.

Spiritualism, which has been around forever, but which made a comeback in the early 1800's, teaches us that we can contact the dead. Hence, we don't really die? The deceased are not sleeping as some people believe, awaiting judgement day in the post, but are alive and well on the alleged 'other side'. Spiritualism is a religion of continuous life, based on the demonstrated fact of communication by means of mediumship with those who live in the spirit world. Contacting the deceased is evidence for life after death, and evidences that we don't lose consciousness in death. Services or séances are held in spiritualist churches or private homes.

Whilst sceptics might refute this, attributing the spirit to 'unconscious psychic forces', it's equally understood that everyone knows about some Aunty Margaret who came though, saying things that only Aunty Margaret could know. It has to be real? There's no other logical explanation for it? But moreover, how do we know it's really Aunty Margaret, and not someone pretending to be her?

As touched on, people seem to regard ghosts as manifestations of the dead, and seeing ghosts is very common phenomena (1:4 people in the UK believe in ghosts). And whilst it's arguably easier to render that experience a vision or delusion, often people see the same ghost e.g. at a haunted home. Spirits associated with certain places are notably referred to as 'haunts'. People can also collectively witness the same poltergeist activity, which suggests there's something more at play than one person's madness. It seems 'spirits' can physically affect our environments, or is it someone's telekinesis?

Apparently, poltergeists are the most common kind of ghost. In addition to making noises and moving objects etc, they can possess people, causing them to speak in a strange dialect and levitate. Besides seeing ghosts per se, (which might not be dead people), people also report seeing angels and demons. Like, a girl I befriended, told me she regularly seen demons in her flat, having opened herself up to the occult (she became a Christian).

There's also orbs, balls of light, which are allegedly harmless and linger about a house a person has died in. These spirits can be seen in photos, but sceptics dismiss the photogenic orbs as specks of dust or moisture. Orbs are associated with crop circles (the interesting patterns that mysteriously appear in crop fields). It seems orbs are a type of UFO? Many people also see the same lights in the sky. It seems there's ethereal UFOs and mechanical UFOs i.e. silver disk. Whilst we'll get back to UFOs in the alien chapter, it's noted that people are more comfortable contemplating UFO/alien phenomenon, than spirits, especially evil spirits. People have been led to believe they're different. Aliens are not spirits, or some are?

Ghost stories are universal, but for the purposes of example we can consider Roger Moore's (007) experience with ghosts. Thus, he was staying in a hotel circa 1960, and having gone to bed, he woke up suddenly, covered in perspiration. It was around 2am and a strange smell assailed his nostrils. He then saw a mist come streaming through the windows, across the bed, to finally take form close beside him. Whilst frozen with fear, he nevertheless questioned 'what do you want?' Then as suddenly and mysteriously as it appeared, it disappeared. The following night, the strange incident recurred. But the third night, Moore noticed that a Bible was lying next to his bed that had been left open at Psalm 23 ('Even though I walk through the valley of the shadow of death, I will fear no evil; for thou art with me' etc). And that night the mist did not appear.

The following morning a maid (who happened to be a Jehovah Witness) asked Moore if he'd seen the mist and when he replied that he hadn't, she said 'I didn't think you would'. She advised that she'd put the Bible by the bed. It seems the Holy Bible's presence had warded off whatever incorporeal entity had crept into the bedroom.

Charles Richet (French physiologist) coined the term ectoplasm in 1894 to describe the misty substance associated with the formation of ghosts. Ectoplasm can appear as either vapour/smoke, like in Moore's ghostly encounter, or like funky smelling semen/mucus (lovely). Richet notes this rubbery milky substance emerges from mediums bodies when they summon spirits. The spirit (dead person?) physically manifests through the yards of excrement. Ectoplasm can be extruded from orifices such as the mouth, ears, nose, and occasionally less convenient locations (LOL). John of God apparently fills up cups of ectoplasm during his psychic surgery. And apparently people have ectoplasmic encounters with sex ghosts.

Paracelsus states people may feel ghosts instinctively, or physically, like a cold wind, or like a current of electricity passing through the body. He notes that those acquainted to a certain extent with modern spiritualism will know that usually at the beginning of a strong 'physical manifestation' a cold draught of air is felt, and sometimes a corpse like odour pervades the air of the room where the séance is held. He states this is caused by the presence of the astral body of the dead. As mentioned, poltergeists are associated with 'the stank'.

It's also highlighted, the atmosphere will be full of electricity (as ghosts have energy and an energy field), which can be detected by Electromagnetic Field (EMF) detectors. Ghost hunters use these detectors to look for spikes in the EMF signals, with spikes suggesting a change in electrical current, and thus a spirit being. People also use wind-chimes to observe movement, and thermometers to detect temperature changes.

But moreover, many people report about a powerful force that seems to grab them. Paul McKenna (1997) mentioned the actress Kim Novak's experience. She said, 'I suddenly felt rather cold...a powerful force seemed to grab me around the waist. I was lifted off my feet and hurled against the wall' (p.2). Some people report being pushed downstairs or flung across a room. Like, La-Sala was pushed down stairs. People also speak about being suffocated by a heavy weight pressing down on them, which resonates with sleep paralysis and channelling.

Elka the witchdoctor spoke about hairy hands groping him, which corroborates with the Hairy Hands legend of Postbridge, Dartmoor. Specifically, the B3212 route, which is deemed the most haunted road in the UK. It's reported that disembodied hands appear from 'nowhere', grab at the steering wheel of a moving car or the handlebars of a motorcycle, and then force the victim off the road. In some cases, the hands are described as being invisible. Although the legend arose in the early twentieth century, in a 2010 survey of British drivers, hundreds of motorists wrote in, reporting ghostly sightings and the feeling of being forced off the road.

But there's also stories about invisible hands helping people. My friend's friend stated that in no uncertain terms she was helped to safety, literally pulled out a car, post car crash. Another girl told me she fell off a cliff and felt invisible hands holding her head and aiding her to safety. And another story I read about concerned a young girl trapped in a burning house. She was too small to reach the window and yet witnesses seen an ornament flying through the glass and then the child lobbed out, unharmed, 5 metres below.

In the Bible, in Psalm 91:11-12, it says, 'For He will command His angels concerning you to guard you in all your ways. On their hands they will bear you up, so that you will not dash your foot against a stone'. So, bonus there's angels? Or are they good spirits of the dead, good ghosts, like Swedenborg insisted. It's possible that people can evolve into angels through myriad lifetimes?

It seems pertinent to consider Lorna Byrne, an Irish Catholic mystic, as she maintains she sees and talks to angels. In her international bestselling autobiographical book, 'Angels in my Hair' (2008), she states angels and spirits have contacted her since she was a young child. Indeed, she maintains she saw them in her crib as a baby. Byrne was mesmerised by 'bright shiny beings', 'all the colours of the rainbow', 'floating in the air like feathers'. She claims she played with her dead baby brother when she was two years old, although she didn't know he was dead (he died before she was born), until the angels explained to her that he was a soul, which was different from them, the angels.

The angels told Byrne to keep them secret, and it wasn't until she wrote her first aforementioned book, that she divulged her long-time secret. Interestingly, besides giving her prophecies about her life in general, which came to pass, they told her she would write books about God and angels, stating these would be bestsellers. She found this amusing because she was illiterate, and yet this too has come to pass.

Whilst angels materialise to give her messages, like Michael, and also the prophet Elijah, and then vanish, she maintains she sees angels all the time. It's noted, that in the Bible, we're told that Elijah and Enoch didn't die, but rather they were translated, and seemingly went to the second heaven? But we'll get back to this.

Byrne concedes there's various kinds of angelic beings e.g. cherubim, seraphim, and archangels. She insists that everyone, irrespective of how good or bad we are, caste, creed, or religion, has a guardian angel, which is a gift from God. Our guardian angel is the gatekeeper of our soul, and we can ask for their assistance anytime because they're always beside us. She explains they whisper in our ears, which is to say, put thoughts in our head, to encourage and strengthen us. So, angels prompt us with sweet suggestions, and demons cast evil aspersions into our hearts and minds?

Byrne describes angels as beautiful light. She claims they're beams of light that open up into angels. But they can also take on a human appearance and take us by the hand. This corroborates with the Bible, which tells us (in Hebrews 13:2), 'Do not forget to show hospitality to strangers, for by so doing some people have shown hospitality to angels without knowing it'. Byrne states they're neither male nor female but they can present as male or female when shapeshifting into human form. Besides seeing angels, Byrne often sees a 'soul' passing by, and also demons/poltergeists.

It seems she has bi-locality like Swedenborg? She concedes there's innumerable spirit beings (creatures), including spirits of dead people, which inhabit the spirit worlds and our world. It appears she also has astral vision as she can see through bodies e.g. see hernias and tumours, which are invisible to ordinary perception. It appears she has activated her spirit body?

Whilst some believe guardian angels are human spirits, usually an ancestor sent to guide and protect us (like shamans), Byrne clarifies that guardian angels are not dead loved ones, and human souls do not become angels. Angels are also creatures made by God, but they have a different nature, a different type of soul. So, we don't evolve into angels or degenerate into devils. Swedenborg stands corrected?

But moreover, our souls are trophies. Byrne concedes there's a spiritual war taking place between Satan and his demons, and God and His angels, for our souls. She says demons and the devil offer us material wealth, power and control. But moreover, she cautions that demonic entities can project a beautiful façade, thus disguising their true horrid appearance underneath. She warns, people can be 'duped'. This corroborates with the Bible, which tells us deceptive angels can masquerade as angels of light. People can think they're serving God, when they're really serving Satan and his shapeshifting angels. People can be tricked by beautiful angels to preach a new gospel?

Whilst Byrne seems reticent to discuss the 'dark-side', as her message is predominantly about love and heaven, she acknowledges that 'the other side plays lots of games with us'. She advises not to play the Ouija board, for example, as people can become possessed. But that aside, Byrne's lovely message is that we're all pure love, like God. Our souls can't be contaminated because our soul is a speck or spark of light of God. Besides the rare occasion, when someone is reincarnated, she advises that we go to heaven, accompanied by our guardian angel, and we see our loved ones.

Byrne further claims she's been to heaven and met God. She states that sometimes the angel Michael will reach inside her body and take her soul to heaven (an OBE). She describes God as overwhelming love, and says He always has a male appearance. Byrne also believes there's life on other planets, with races ahead of us. So, that's curious.

Before we get to actively seeking out spirits, it seems further pertinent to mention, what Bill and Judy Guggenheim call, 'After-Death Communications' (ADC), as these happen without a medium, or any rituals/devices etc. ADCs are spiritual experiences, when someone is contacted 'directly' and 'spontaneously' by a deceased family member or friend. Apparently 60% of widows/widowers experience their spouse in some way e.g. sensed their presence, seen or felt them, spoke to them. The Guggenheims estimate that about 20-40% of the US population has experienced this. And they detail more than 350 first-hand accounts in their book 'Hello from Heaven!' (1995). Bill Guggenheim was notably inspired by Dr Elisabeth Kubler-Ross.

Some people receive 'signs' from their loved ones, like butterflies or rainbows. Such signs resonate with Jung's archetypes penetrating our physical reality, like his patient's scarab encounter? Or 'loved ones' may indicate their presence by switching lamps on and off, activating radios, TVs, stereos, and other mechanical objects. Like, the spirit of ayahuasca indicated its presence to David Icke. Or they might move or turn over photographs or pictures, or whatever. Like Gaz Parker's so-called mum knocked over his weather gadget. And no danger, some even receive phone calls from them, which corroborates with Dr Kubler-Ross's spirit guide Salem phoning her. Some leave messages on telephone answering machines, and computers etc. They write messages, leave letters.

Based upon their research, the Guggenheims highlight common types of ADCs, which can happen anywhere and at any time. Like, one can be driving and all of a sudden their loved one is in the passenger seat, a so-called Visual ADC. There is however variation in their manifestations, as some can fully appear, looking and feeling lifelike and solid, whereas others partially appear. Like sometimes, just their head and shoulders appear. Like, Jung seeing the old woman's half head on his pillow, or the hairy hands? Or they might appear as a transparent mist, translucent or coloured light.

Sometimes the temperature suddenly goes up or down, and one senses their loved one's presence. 'Sensing' their presence, so-called Sentient ADCs, is apparently the most common form of contact. Some people hear their loved one's voice, so-called Auditory ADCs. Whilst some hear an external, audible voice, the majority of communications are by telepathy. Some people feel their touch aka Tactile ADCs, such as their hands, or arm around their shoulders, waist and back. And some smell their loved ones, Olfactory ADCs, e.g. their perfume, tobacco. Others (witnesses) can share this latter type of ADC experience. Roman Catholics notably claim they smell roses when Mary is around. And like ghosts materialising, the smell of sulphur is commonly reported with alien abductions.

With regards to the Visual ADCs, the Guggenheims advise that quite a few occur in the bedroom, next to or at the foot of the bed. They also highlight 'encounters at alpha', so-called Twilight ADCs, which take place in the alpha state of consciousness. They report that when people open their eyes, their deceased loved one is standing nearby, which resonates with shadow people? People also see loved ones in visions and vivid dreams. And some have OBEs to visit loved ones in the spiritual dimension, so-called 'heaven'. They confirm that out of body travel happens at the speed of thought.

The Guggenheims maintain that ADCs are a natural normal part of life and insist they're not hallucinations. As it transpires, 'loved ones' are always in good shape (healthy and happy), which provides comfort for those left behind. It's also reassuring to know they're watching over us, protecting us, as Gaz Parker believed.

It sounds lovely, but there's a fundamental insistence that the message one receives has to be from someone they know. It has to be our loved one, not someone else's loved one. Thus, an ADC is not meeting some other ghost, or angel etc. It seems no good can come from visitations from strangers, or hearing unknown voices etc, as this would alternatively constitute psychosis? But it's all good if the voice you hear is your relative or friend, who says nice things.

Bill Guggenheim said he heard his dad's voice, on one critical occasion, telling him to check on his twenty-two month year old kid. He states he was initially dismissive of the thought, but then figured he might as well, and when he did, he found his child floating at the deep end of the swimming pool (at his house in Florida). He rescued his son, just in the nick of time. Then some years later, he heard the same voice telling him to do his own research with regards to ADCs. This is like Mrs Schwartz telling Dr Kubler Ross to continue her research into the alleged living dead.

It's duly noted, that in addition to hearing dead people's voices, and the voices of angels and demons, people attest to hearing God's voice. They say God told them to do whatever, and for some presumably unwell people, this has included heinous crimes. As Byrne highlights, people do terrible things in the name of God. Others blame the devil. Psychiatrists would call it schizophrenia. And presumably psychiatrists would render seemingly normal Lorna Byrne a tad mad, (deluded), because spirits aren't real?

As Paracelsus highlighted, spirits' characters and intelligence vary widely. And these spirits can become visible and talk to us, or exercise invisible influence over the mind. For Paracelsus, Spiritualism meant dealing with spiritual intelligences, whereas Spiritism involved liaising with unintelligent and semi-intelligent invisible forms. For example, it's well known that using Ouija boards tend to summon low level spirits, like poltergeists (spiritual NEDs).

So, spiritualism is kosher, but spiritism isn't. He explained that the spiritualist enters into the sphere of spirits and becomes a medium through which the intelligence may act. S/he bestows their mind, writes and speaks in the spirit of the spiritual intelligence, and as a result may obtain great truths. This was therefore in contrast to the spiritist who submits his or her body to the will of an invisible stranger.

But moreover, and like the Bible, Paracelsus warns us about parasitic entities that endeavour to latch onto us, as this gives birth to all kinds of mental deviation or 'illness'. Whilst it's arguably an uncomfortable prospect, and not even an issue since material science and Big Pharma stamped it out long ago, it is however an intriguing prospect. Perhaps we could keep an open mind with regards to the unseen? Particularly since, when it comes to mental disarray, there's usually no material cause.

Like, Dr Alan Sanderson (consultant psychiatrist), for example, endorsed spirit attachment. Hence, he quit his NHS job and founded the Spirit Release Foundation (SRF) in 1999, with the aim of bringing professional acceptance to 'spirit release' and related treatments. Signs of spirit attachment include unexplained lethargy, out of control behaviour, emotional pain, depression, suicidal thoughts, poor concentration, confusion, extreme anger/aggression, mood swings, addictions, over-eating, self-harm, paranoia, fear, anxiety, hearing voices, multiple personalities, nightmares, sleep-paralysis, the incline to change sex or sexual orientation, the urge to cross dress, and chronic masturbation.

Spirit release experts tell us that in short, the spirits remit is to make the person's life difficult. By using negative thoughts, they can make us quite unwell. It's usually progressive i.e. they begin by taking away confidence or causing emotional upset, they plant seeds here and there, to start the crazy ball rolling. There seems to be stages i.e. from oppression, like they're affecting our thoughts and feelings, to attachment, which is a more severe version of oppression, to possession. Thus, people are oppressed from outside, and possessed from inside.

Apparently only 1% of cases entail a full-blown possession, which means having no control over the possessing entity. It's also highlighted these spirits have conniving agendas. For example, a negative entity may encourage binge eating and at the same time induce guilt. Thus, it makes the host feel negative yet all the while feeding the entity, which corroborates with the id versus superego battle?

Apparently, some people are more vulnerable to spirit attachment than others. Like, people with mental illness, or a drug addiction, or those who experienced childhood abuse. It's said people are vulnerable because they've lost, (given away or been robbed of), their personal power. More technically, weak emotions like fear and anger create weak and lower energetic openings in the energy field (energy and power), and it's these energetic openings which allow the entry of spirit attachments. It appears spirits need an 'opening' or 'entrance'. Spirit release experts further recognise an increase in spirit attachment with those more spiritually aware, and with those who see ghosts and have 'spirit guides'.

Sanderson maintains 50% of his clients have spirit attachments. Other spirit release therapists estimate that up to 75% of people have spirit attachments. But most people live their entire lives unaware of these controlling entities. Maybe they think they've got mental health problems?

Sanderson describes two spirit release techniques, namely, either speaking to the spirit directly (if one has psychic abilities) or through hypnosis. With respect to the latter, the client enters a relaxed state of mind and the therapist encourages the spirit to use the client's voice to communicate. When a client's in a hypnotic state, the therapist asks if someone else is there, besides the client, and if so to raise a finger. This is like opening Pandora's Box? Like Jung advocated, we have to deal with the contents in the unconscious? It seems spirits from the collective unconscious attach themselves to our personal unconscious?

Fundamentally, these troublesome entities need to be released and cast out. These dirty birdies need to be set free. So, we don't integrate them into our personality? Spirit release therapists allegedly help the entity to make the transition into the 'light'. They talk them out of their current human residency with the promise of paradise. Sanderson claims spirit release techniques are very effective. People can be cured of their mental ills and forego being chemically bound their whole lives. So, people who believe they're the wrong sex, for example, could be free from this condemning belief? We can be 'normal'?

Some spirit release experts believe all spirit attachments are human souls. The conjecture is that dead people haven't crossed over to the spirit world, so they're lurking about here. It's thought they're probably hanging about due to confusion from sudden death, or it could be to satisfy an addiction through a living body, or to cause problems for someone. It's purported they want power and control over humans, for whatever perverse reason. This agrees with Swedenborg's belief that demons or devils are ghastly dead people.

Whereas others, whilst acknowledging the most common type of spirit attachment are earthbound souls of dead people, maintain there's also non-human spirits. They highlight several types of non-human entities, with demonic entities being the most common. Some however prefer to believe there are no demonic entities or nasty spirits of the dead, but merely entities created by fearful thinking, which stirs up negative energy. Either way, once birthed or having arrived, the 'negative energy' needs a certain amount of persuasion to leave. As touched on, it seems the term 'spirits' is sugar-coated with the term 'energy', because it's more palatable. Spirit attachment can thus be regarded as the attachment of non-physical energetic beings.

But moreover, these experts further say that usually 'affected' people have more than one entity and often when one spirit leaves, another reappears. This corroborates with the Bible (Luke 11:24), which states, 'When an evil spirit leaves a person, it goes into the desert, searching for rest. But when it finds none, it says, 'I will return to the person I came from, so it returns and finds its former home is all swept and clean. Then the spirit finds seven other spirits more evil than itself and they all enter the person and live there. And so that person is worse off than before'.

Its suggested spirits may have other spirits attached to them. A counsellor I know mentioned a couple of clients she worked with, diagnosed with DID, and in her opinion, it was their alters that had the demon attached to them. She performed exorcisms to break the 'energetic' attachments. It's also noted, that demons can combine forces, and they talk to each other through their human agent, as 'schizophrenics' report.

Besides mental illness, physical illness, (including functional and psychosomatic illness), can be attributed to spirits attached to certain parts of the body. Like, shamans often attribute diseases to the presence of spirits. And in the Bible, unclean spirits are responsible for both mental and physical illness. The oldest references to demonic possession are from the Sumerians, the cradle of civilisation. Clay tablets reveal they believed in sickness demons, which accounted for all diseases of the body and mind. Contrary to the physicians who applied bandages and salve, the priests who performed exorcisms were referred to as sorcerers. These tablets contain prayers to certain gods asking for protection, while others ask the gods to expel the demons that have invaded their bodies.

Muslims hold 'jinn' (which means hidden) responsible for all types of physical and mental ill-health, and all kinds of accidents. A Muslim patient described jinn as something that surrounds his body, buzzing and making him unwell and even stopping him sleeping. Whilst jinn are likened to the daemonic i.e. they can be good, evil or neutral, others contend there's no such thing as good jinn. Good jinn are not the same as angels, as like humans, angels are something different. It seems jinn are demons?

It's noted, whilst some consider demons, angels and jinn as simply hidden qualities in human beings, others consider them external because they can appear, visibly manifest, when summoned or evoked. And others consider the daemonic partly external and partly internal. The difference between evoking and invoking demons is notably that people evoke demons to appear externally, and invoke demons to manifest internally. Invocation is possession, calling in, and evocation is calling/summoning forth.

Doreen Irvine, a former demon possessed witch, said she believed demons were external having seen them many times, but she subsequently (experientially) learned they require human bodies. She came to realise that she had demons residing in her. Like a disease, demons were a part of her. And they used her senses to perceive. On one occasion when she was about to attack a minister, she realised the demons couldn't see the minister until she did. They only had her eyes to see with. She recounts that she heard 'kill, kill, kill' and nothing else (the demon commanded her). She was then 'taken over' and only 'came back' when the ordeal was over.

Like possessed others, as we'll get to, she exhibited phenomenal strength. And like channellers and DID, Irvine couldn't recall the events that took place at that time. She would lose time, and sometimes she would 'be away' for days, and God knows what she got up to. So, Irvine concedes that external spirits can get under our skin. But we'll get back to Doreen Irvine.

Rather than demons, yogi philosophy pertains to gross undeveloped animal like souls that live at the lowest planes of existence (ignorant people are likened to animals). So, this agrees with Swedenborg's tenet that grim people become devils. As discussed, the only plane below them is the plane of shells and the sub-astral plane immediately above the material plane.

Apparently, these degenerates often flock back to be as near to earth as possible. It's said they like to watch earth life, but they can't join in as they're separated by a thin (tantalising) veil which prevents them from participating, except on rare occasions. When they're invited? It's said they hang around the scenes of their old degrading lives, and often take possession of the brain of one of their own kind who may be under the influence of liquor. These wayward spirits tend to reincarnate quickly, but there's always more to replace them.

But moreover, these lowly spirits are also attracted to séances, as they relish playing pranks on us. It's said they masquerade as 'spirits' of deceased friends etc, and claim to be famous or celebrated personages, and do so for their own sick pleasure. They are seldom what they pretend to be, using names of others and acting like whomever. It's always possible these spirits could scoop an astral shell from the plane of shells and pretend to be whoever? Or they don't need to, if they're demons who can assume any form?

It's noted, the Bible doesn't say that dead people can communicate with this world or influence affairs. Ecclesiastes 9:5 states, 'The dead are conscious of nothing at all'. So, we can't contact the dead. Ergo, it's not Aunty Margaret. It appears ghosts are a con on behalf of demons to 'evidence' we don't really die? It's understood, shapeshifting is one of their party tricks. The Bible also tells us we're appointed to live once and then judgement. Human spirits don't reincarnate endlessly. It's a game of life and death because we either win or lose i.e. eternal life or eternal death. Or a game of chess between God and Satan, and we're the pawns? But we have freewill and that's the point?

Paracelsus concedes that dead people cannot be contacted. But rather earthbound spirits (demons) can use astral bodies of the dead as masks to mislead the credulous. Thus, whilst necromancy (practiced from the beginning of recorded history) is believed to be the art of calling up the dead, according to Paracelsus, necromancy is the art of employing the unconscious spirits of the dead by infusing life into them, and employing them for evil purposes. As touched on, when God takes His breath back, we die. And for Paracelsus, our astral bodies are unconscious and won't be reanimated until the resurrection. So, they're lying dormant for others to dress up in?

He informs that conjurers attempt to conjure up astral bodies, which is impossible because such bodies have no sense and cannot be conjured. The consequence is that demons take possession of the astral bodies and play their pranks with conjurers. Therefore, such conjurers do not deal with the dead, but with the powers of evil.

Necromancy is thus sorcery/witchcraft i.e. engaging with evil spirits. Paracelsus acknowledges that whilst these spirits give correct answers, they do so to mislead as they have no desire to speak the truth. He highlights that some spirits lie a great deal more than others, and concedes they like to play sinister games with us. Paracelsus states earthbound spirits often teach those they converse with to perform certain ceremonies, to speak certain words and names in which there is no meaning, and they do so for their amusement. He confirms that earthbound spirits are seen in spiritual séances, rapping or tipping tables, and producing physical manifestations. Like, they can cause the appearance and disappearance of objects, throw stones etc.

The term apport notably refers to an object that materialises. That is, a solid object is brought from one place to another, or appears from nowhere. Apport comes from French apporter which means 'to bring'. It seems physical objects impossibly pass through matter like walls/doors. Thus, it's not crazy that La-Sala deducted he could use astral projection to rob. He understood objects (like money) can be moved. Furthermore, surely for sceptics, this would constitute evidence of spirits?

With respect to evidence then, we can consider the 'Scole Experiment', who claimed they received many apports courtesy of kind disincarnates[19]. The Scole Experiment (1993-1998) was a series of séances held in someone's cellar in Scole, a village in Norfolk. The four core members were on a mission to investigate life after death, which they did down the 'Scole-hole'. The psychic researchers reported that the arrival of an apport was announced by a loud thud on either the floor or the table. The first apport was a Churchill Crown, but they received many gifts including a silver thimble, two small silver lockets, a silver chain bracelet, a St Christopher medallion, an ornate miniature spoon with spiral metal handle, a decorated bowl, and a tiny gold medallion.

Interestingly, one apport, which initiated much discussion, was the seemingly original copy of the 'Daily Express' newspaper dated 1945. It was printed on the type of paper used in the early-mid 1940s, but it was in mint condition i.e. no sign of yellowing, which would have occurred if it were an original paper. But moreover, just a few weeks later, despite being carefully stored away, it turned yellow. The same thing happened with another newspaper that was apported, the Daily Mirror dated 1936. It was also in mint condition but turned yellow within a week, despite the air-tight conditions. Perhaps spirits can go back in time and remove objects?

The Scole Experiment was hailed for its physical evidence. Those who attended and witnessed the sessions at Scole, including senior members of the prestigious Society for Psychical Research (SPR), were convinced that disincarnate entities were communicating with them. In addition to the apports, they reported other well-established phenomena. Like, temperature changes and paranormal breezes, smells and aromas, raps and taps (some soft, some loud), levitation of objects, musical instruments in the room were played, they heard their voices and engaged in two-way communication with them, and spirits materialised to varying degrees e.g. a disembodied hand appeared several times. They figured that it's easier (perhaps requires less energy) to materialise a hand than whole body, but they assumed there was an invisible body attached to the hands. Like, presumably the hairy hands at Dartmoor, and other invisible hands, are attached to a body?

Dr Rupert Sheldrake (biologist and author) also witnessed the glowing disembodied hand floating around the room. He joked that it was just like something out of the movie the Addam's family. In his book, 'The Science Delusion' (2012), Sheldrake questions the validity of materialist assumptions. He insists science should be less dogmatic and more scientific regarding evidence contrary to their presuppositions. Interestingly, the 'Thing' in the Addams Family TV series was originally conceived as a whole creature, but because it was too horrible to see in person, we only seen the hand. Then, in the 1991 and 1993 Addams Family movies, the Thing changed to being a mere disembodied hand.

So, it was all happening down the Scole-hole, and this included the manifestation of spectacular lights. These so-called Spirit Lights, small luminous orbs, flashed around the room. They darted at great speeds, bouncing on and going through the table and sitters etc, like an elaborate dance of aerial acrobatics. But moreover, they seemed intelligent, as they responded to commands, both verbal and mental. One of the witnesses said, 'I say intelligent because they would respond to our wishes whether expressed verbally or just in our minds'. Apparently, on the occasion when someone touched the light, they received a tiny electric shock. There was also the manifestation of a miniature UFO-shaped object which flew around the room. All this evidence is recorded.

The Scole Experiment's evidence also includes photographs (images) appearing on otherwise undeveloped

---

[19] See the internationally bestselling book, 'The Scole Experiment: Scientific Evidence for Life After Death' (1999) by Grant and Jane Solomon.

and unexposed 35mm film (it was locked in a security box, and no camera was used), as well as audio recordings, and video footage. When they developed their photos, they received whole lengths of film with symbols, puzzles, poems, and handwritten messages from the (alleged) dead, in multiple languages, including Sanskrit. It seems the spirits somehow project images onto the film?

One of the poems seems to be from Frederic Myers (1843-1901), one of the founders of the SPR, who promised his colleagues, before he died, that he would try to communicate with them from the other side. So, perhaps this is evidence from one of the greatest investigators, or perhaps it's some entity pretending to be him?

The Scole members also set up a video camera, as instructed to by their 'spirit team', which recorded curious lights. Like, tunnels and moving doorways (portals?), as well as spirit faces and what looks like grey aliens. The 'spirit team' also suggested ways of improving the experiments, including how to build a device for boosting communications via the tape recorder. This conversation was recorded on audio tapes, which included chat about their experiment being a historic event (it seems the psychics were chuffed with their evidence). The information about how to build the device was detailed on unexposed film (sealed in the box). But moreover, it's believed this information came from Thomas Edison, as his initials are there. It's said he finally achieved his aim of inventing a machine to contact the spirit world.

Apparently, Thomas Edison ('alleged' inventor of lightbulb) and Alexander Give us a Bell both supposed that psychic phenomenon could be researched scientifically. Whilst it's alleged Edison tried to make a radio that would tune into the spirit worlds, as he was very interested in life after death, others dispute this. It's said that Edison was asked by an interviewer from 'Scientific American' about the possibility of contacting the dead, and respectively surmised that it would be possible to construct an apparatus superior to the current methods spirits employ to express themselves e.g. rapping, tilting tables, Ouija board and other crude methods. But there is no evidence that he ever designed or tried to construct such a device. It seems he died before he built his machine capable of communicating with the dead, but his intention to build it made headlines around the world. Or perhaps he did, and communicated his message in Scole?

It seems pertinent to note, that whilst Spiritism and Spiritualism are often considered interchangeable terms, as they both teach that human spirits are immortal, and prove the existence of the spirit world by communicating with the dead, spiritualists are more 'Christian' in their approach. They profess to believe in the Bible, and they sing hymns and say prayers at their 'Spiritualist Church'. So, Spiritualism's roots are in Christianity, but it's focussed on making contact with the dead, which is explicitly forbidden in the Bible. Once recognised as a medium, an individual can become a minister of a Spiritualist church.

Alternatively, spiritists communicate with the dead, without distinct reference to the Christian faith. Spiritism is therefore more accessible since there's no religious dogma. Spiritism endorses pantheism, asserting God is creative universal spirit. It could be the new global religion? Modern spiritism was notably pioneered by Allan Kardec (1804-1869), who's referred to as the Father of Spiritism.

Spiritism teaches that we enter the spirit world when we die. There's several planes (usually seven but possibly thirty-three), and where we go depends on how good we've been on earth. There is no hell, which makes this an attractive philosophy, and there's benevolent spirits to assist our spiritual evolution. Spiritists believe that people who live very sinful lives become earthbound spirits when they die. Thus, whilst there's no saviour per se (we're each responsible for our own destiny), we might need help from benevolent spirits to evolve to a higher place if we become earthbound. So, rather than demons, this view espouses the idea that earthbound spirits are shady human souls.

But moreover, perhaps not all earthbound spirits are malevolent? As psychiatrist Dr Carl Wickland (1861-1945) highlights, earthbound spirits can be ignorant. That is, they don't realise they've died. And not knowing any better, deluded spirits attach to 'sensitive' people, causing them all kinds of mental problems. It seems earthbound spirits need psychiatric help?

Dr Wickland devoted his career to psychical research as it relates to the pathology of mental illness, and he attributed the cause of these maladies to the influence of earthbound spirits. Like Dr Sanderson, he understood these spirits were responsible for mental ill health, and they must be discharged. And as a result, his patients were cured of their crazy ills. Indeed, together with his wife, who mediated for the spirits, they cured countless people with otherwise serious psychiatric illness. His extensive work is most interesting, so we'll get back to him in the next chapter.

If we want to communicate with the alleged dead then, (in the absence of receiving any ADCs), we can venture to the Spiritualist Church and see if a medium can shed some light on how our loved ones are doing. Albeit we don't know if the person who makes an appearance, is who they say they are. I went to the Spiritualist Church with my friend, a couple of months after his dad died, and his 'dad' came through wearing his slippers and smoking. Whilst my friend was comforted, I remember thinking how surreal it was, and equally wondering if it was really his dad. I also remember thinking bonus, there's access to cigs on the other-side.

Unlike channelling, the medium that alleged to be speaking to my friend's dad was merely passing on information. Whilst his dad was apparently with us, he didn't manifest, so we had to take the medium's word that he was there. Thus, it could be faked? The medium's information was vague, like his dad was a smoker who wore slippers, so he could have been winging it? Or he could have previously secured information about his dad, like he was a smoker who wore slippers? Or perhaps, someone pretending to be his dad was there?

Unlike a 'hot reading', which deceptively uses information previously secured, a 'warm reading' is asking questions in a way that leads the client down the covert path of self-disclosure, so it equally seems psychic. And 'cold readings' use Barnum statements, which are personality statements that apply to most. The Barnum effect is the theory that people read a personal meaning into a general description that is vague enough it could apply to almost anyone. Mentalist Derren Brown illustrated the Barnum effect. Thus, participants received a letter, which was supposed to be about them specifically, and most believed it was a personal reading when in fact it was generalised rant that could have been about anyone.

It's contended that horoscopes and the I Ching are like this. The Barnum charade was named after PT Barnum, an American showman and hoaxer, who famously said 'we've got something for everyone'. It's noted, that Spiritualism was particularly lucrative after WW1, and many vulnerable people were fleeced by charlatans. Hence, psychics and mediums are licensed and accredited. They have to prove they're speaking to the dead?

In terms of access to cigs, and contemplating what else is available on the other side (crack?), according to my neighbour who regularly attends the spiritualist church, and has done for more than twenty years, the spirit world is very much like this world. She says they go to the pub, drink, have parties etc. She has no doubt regarding the reality of the spirit world. Besides hearing information that's impossible for anyone to know, she's seen various deceased loved ones in trance-mediums, including her husband's late mum. Her mother-in-law, using the medium's body, literally expressed herself in voice and mannerisms. It was her, no question.

My neighbour advised that sometimes, if it's a 'good medium', you can see the spirits queue up behind the channeller. And she's not psychotic as everyone sees the same dark silhouettes, which apparently increase in density the closer they get to the medium. The description she gave of the spirits corroborates with the shadow people.

It's understood that compared to merely conversing with the dead and reporting back to the living, channelling seems considerably weirder. It would have much weirder if the medium became the vehicle for my friend's dad, speaking in his voice, with his mannerisms. Like, Helly spoke in Grandpa Preiswerk etc's voices. Moreover, and fundamentally, either these spirits are who they say they are, or they're not. And if they're not, who are they i.e. dead people or demons?

It's understood that politicians and 'the elite' also converse with the alleged 'dead'. Like, Abraham Lincoln's wife, Mary Todd Lincoln, held séances in the White House to communicate with her dead son Willy. And Hillary Clinton calls up Eleanor Roosevelt via séances for advice. And psychics (fortune-tellers) are popular with the rich and famous, as we'll get to.

But furthermore, (as touched on), mediums can channel 'advanced spirits'. Like, Magnu? Some spirits are much smarter than us. Hence, politicians liaise with them. Indeed, it's possible 'clever' spirits delegate to politicians? Politicians could be puppets, and 'higher' spiritual entities the puppet-masters? Like, it's purported that intelligence agents are channelling a group of ETs who call themselves 'The Council of Nine'. It's understood that politics are engineered by secret occult societies that engage with spirits, and whilst we'll get back to these, it seems pertinent to highlight the Vril Society in Germany, because this secret society played a particularly prominent role.

The Vril Society (founded in 1921) consisted of mainly female psychics who allegedly channelled aliens. When taken over by these entities, their eyes rolled to the back of their head, their voice changed, and there was the secretion of ectoplasm. The Vril maidens notably grew their hair extravagantly long as they believed their hair was like antennas tuning into the alien's frequency. So, these beings claimed to be Aryan aliens from Alpha Tauri, in the Aldebaran system. Aldebaran is a giant bright orange star located about 65 light years from the Sun in the zodiac constellation of Taurus.

But moreover, the aliens claimed they settled in Sumeria, which is most interesting, as it corroborates with the Sumerian historical account that gods came to earth. In addition to referencing demonic possession, (which births mental and physical sickness), the Sumerian clay tablets tell us about the 'gods'. And like Sumer, the ancient world, worldwide, speaks about gods coming to earth, like star people. And these historical records corroborate with the Bible, but we'll get to all this. Apparently, the word Vril comes from the ancient Sumerian word Vri-Il, which means 'like god'.

Furthermore, it's purported that ETs gave Vril maiden Maria Orsic blueprints for UFOs, which she gave to the Nazis. These channelled texts had to be translated into German as they were written in Sumerian, and a secret German Templar language, which were both alien (pun intended) to Orsic. As it transpires, Adolf Hitler and his buds, Alfred Rosenberg, Heinrich Himmler, and Hermann Goring, were members of the Vril Society, which was the inner circle of the Thule Society. The Nazis notably got their 'SS' logo (the swastika) from the Thule Society.

Hitler was embroiled with the occult, and apparently Himmler had 66,000 volumes of occult literature. They endorsed the Vril's teaching regarding the Aryans or 'supermen' and believed in places like Shambhala. As also mentioned, at the end of WW2, 1600 top Nazis were secretly moved to the US under Operation Paperclip, and apparently many of them were in the Thule and Vril Society. So, the UFO technology (and their mind control technology) crossed the pond.

Whilst we'll get back to Hitler and secret societies in Part 2, it seems pertinent to note, that Hitler was convinced he was divinely guided. Apparently when he was seventeen, he heard a voice to get out a trench, and a second later it was bombed. He was convinced that divine beings saved his life in WW1. Hitler repeatedly escaped death, which he called divine providence. He attributed his divinely guided voice as his imperative to fulfil his destiny. Which he did?

It's widely believed Hitler was possessed. Like, Jung believed he was possessed, by an evil archetype? He had some spirit attachment? It's said that when a demon is heavily influencing a life, there may be a sudden or sporadic increase in a person's intelligence. Thus, despite having no formal education, Hitler was apparently incredibly intelligent. It's believed that hidden forces, from 'behind the scenes', helped bring the Fuhrer to power. They enabled him by increasing his intelligence and oratorical power (it's believed his skill in public speaking was demonic). It's always possible demons use people for their own ends, their plans and purposes?

Apparently, many of Hitler's colleagues believed he was possessed, as he was renowned for going into a mediumistic trance with glassy eyes. They also reported that he would be scared at night. David Icke (2007) concedes, 'Hitler's behaviour was extremely indicative of demonic possession, including his strange epileptic fits'. Besides the convulsions, he apparently 'suffered from terrible nightmares and he would wake up in terror, screaming about entities that were invisible to all but himself'. Those close to Hitler reported that he would call for help and appeared to be half-paralysed. He would gasp to the point of suffocation and, often when fully conscious, he would point to apparently empty space and scream: 'He is here. There! In the corner'. So, who's He?

With regards to 'evidence', (besides channelled texts and apports etc), there's also Electronic Voice Phenomena (EVP) aka white noise. Interest in EVP began in the 1920s, and was popularised in the movie 'White Noise' (2005). It's claimed that ghosts/spirits communicate through TVs, radios, anything electronic i.e. through static noise. There's even ghost detector 'apps', which can transmit white noise. And 'white noise' is objective in the sense that rational, not delusional, people hear it. Everyone present hears it. Hence, this is not to be confused with psychotics who report that the TV or radio is talking directly to them. Albeit it's always possible (some?) hallucinations could have a spiritual origin?

At the Bacci Centre in Italy, for example, everyone hears the communication coming through the loudspeakers of radios. Like, a mother's dead son comes through, and everyone hears his personal message. Marcello Bacci, one of the leading researchers in 'Instrumental Trans-Communication' (ITC), is principally dedicated to working with bereaved parents. The voices refer to listeners by name and respond to questions put to them. Beautiful flowers also appear at the Bacci Centre, apports from deceased loved ones. So, that's nice?

Bacci has been consistently successful with his experiments conducted at his laboratory. That is, talking to spirits through the Direct Radio Voice Method. He has been in this field for more than thirty years and cooperates with scientists in order to demonstrate the credibility of his results.

Bacci's centre aside, often the voices heard through white noise are threatening. Sometimes they're foreign, archaic, and cryptic, and sometimes the conversations are between two or more entities. Sceptics however insist EVP is merely a random pick up of broadcast signals.

In the movie 'Poltergeist' (1982), the little girl got enmeshed with white noise from the TV. She communicated with the transmitting static, and then a poltergeist blasted from the TV screen and vanished into the wall, triggering a violent earthquake in the process. The movie 'Poltergeist', like others we'll consider later, was based on a true story. It was inspired by the unexplained poltergeist activity reported by the Hermann family (Mum, Dad and three kids), in their New York home in 1958.

Thus, during February of that year, furniture began to move on its own and a globe that belonged to the Hermann's young son flew around the house. Lucille Hermann, who was just fourteen when the events took place, finally opened up about her experiences in the home when she was fifty-three. She said, 'All of a sudden, you'd hear this loud noise, like a popping bottle sound, and you'd look around and find a bottle that was 12 feet away from where it was supposed to be and all the contents were missing and the bottle was hot to the touch'. She went on to explain that the family desperately wanted to keep things normal for the children, which was hard with objects flying all over the house.

Whilst poltergeist activity or spirit attachment can seem random, for the most part it seems people provide an entrance. Like engaging with white noise, or playing the Ouija board, for example. It's also highlighted, that girls who begin menstruating often attract poltergeists. Blood is compelling?

As touched on, 'science' insists we're responsible for moving the glass or planchette on the Ouija board. Spirits are not responsible. We unconsciously move the glass, tip or turn the table, or instigate the direction of the pendulum. My friend and I did the pendulum thing as kids. We'd put a ring on a necklace and ask it whether we'd have children and what sex they'd be. And the ring would move backwards and forwards, or in circles. Sometimes it would gain ferocious speed, which freaked me out. And the Ouija board freaked me out.

Scientists however explain that our unconscious can influence our bodies, which gives rise to involuntary/unintentional muscular action and the 'ideomotor effect'. Our body responds, like reflexes, yet it feels as though it's happening outside our conscious control. We're not consciously aware of moving. Hence, everyone insists they didn't move the glass on the Ouija board, when they did.

Interestingly, Michael Faraday (1791-1867), who pioneered electromagnetism and electrochemistry, was one of the first to discover ideomotor movement. He conducted decisive experiments on conscious control, using spiritualist techniques including table tipping and Ouija boards. He was bemused by the alleged conversing of the dead, whereby questions were asked and answered, and sitters went home believing they had spoken with their deceased relatives and friends. And he concluded that sitters, not spirits, were responsible for moving the glass or table. Having questioned them inquisitively, Faraday was convinced that they did not realise what they were doing. Such unconscious muscular movement was the first demonstration that we believe we're not doing something when we are.

So, we're told the Ouija board simply enables expression of the unconscious. It gives the unconscious permission to act. Like, automatic writing, hypnosis, and other techniques, like divining. With divination, (from Latin Divinare which means to be inspired by a god), the divining rods move in response to our questions. We ask ourselves for the answers? Our unconscious advises us by shaking/pulling the rods in a certain direction, providing yes or no answers? This ancient art was used to find water, minerals, and locate disease etc. But we can also predict the future. We can ask our Self, which transcends space and time? Like, we predict our fortune by moving the glass on the Ouija board.

However, it's equally noted that if spirits operate through humans i.e. we're their vehicle of expression, then, it would look like we acted. And it stands to reason the person would have no recollection of acting, if 'they' didn't act. Their unconscious acted or someone hijacked their brain. An autonomous complex usurped the conscious mind. They dissociated, unbeknown to them?

Others however are crystal that the force is definitely out-with. Like, a man's testimony I heard (he became a Christian), said that he was playing the Ouija board with his friend and they presented the spirit with a challenge, namely, the two friends would push the planchette in one direction, and the spirit would push it the other way, (to 'yes' or 'no' on the board), and see who wins. He described the force as immensely strong. To the point the planchette pinged off the board and hit the window.

There's countless stories regarding the Ouija board, but for an example, we can consider Cindy's story. Cindy was thirteen when she first played with the Ouija board. And this mysterious talking board mesmerized her. She became obsessed with it and played with it every day after school. Then one afternoon, her dead friend J-a-k-e came through (he died in a car accident). Over the next hour, Cindy held a conversation with 'Jake'. She continued having conversations with him, about her life and future, but after a few days, the conversations became darker and angrier.

By the second week, Cindy had the impression that she wasn't talking with Jake, but instead with a dark and terrible imposter. Finally, by the end of the second week, the entity revealed itself as a demon and threatened Cindy that if she told anyone about their conversations she would die. That Friday night, when her sisters got home, they found Cindy curled up in a corner crying. It took a week in a mental facility before Cindy could recover from the emotional damage the 'entity' caused her.

For a more 'scientific' account, we can consider the 'Philip Experiment' conducted by the Toronto Society for Psychical Research in the early seventies[20]. These researchers wanted to explore the possibility of willing tangible forms into existence. They basically wanted to create a ghost. So, they made up 'Philip Aylesford', and gave this fictional character a history, including likes and dislikes, complete with a tragic end as they decided he committed suicide. They visualised Philip in their minds, and willed him to be, but little happened for about a year, so they opted for a séance.

This worked and strange occurrences began. As they sat around the table, focusing their will on conjuring Philip, an unseen force began to tap on the table. They asked if it was Philip and a single thud confirmed it was (one knock indicated if something was true, and two knocks would indicate if false). So, they asked Philip questions about his past, although they already knew the answers since they created him, and he communicated with them through raps on the table's wooden surface. But moreover, Philip began to reveal new details from his past, which contained oddly accurate information regarding actual historical events. Philip seemed to develop his own personality. He seemed independent and real. He impressed them with his remarkable intel.

Unexplainable noises were often heard throughout the room, and occasionally the lights would flicker. In addition to answering questions by use of coded knocks, Philip would tip the table when the group's hands rested on top. Apparently on one occasion, one of the legs of the table lifted off the floor while the other three remained on the floor. There was the sound of wood and metal twisting, and they were certain the table

---

[20] The Toronto Society for Psychical Research (TSPR) was founded in the early 1970s 'to explore and interpret those presumptively paranormal events commonly described as extrasensory perception and psychic phenomena'.

would break. It took four of them pushing hard at the raised corner to push the surface flat again. Apparently, some months later and more cajoling of Philip, he fully levitated the table. Philip never physically manifested as an apparition, but he made his presence known (footage was captured).

Suffice to say, making a table levitate is not normal. It defies Newtonian physics. Like, apports are not normal. 'Paranormal' notably refers to experiences outside the 'range of normal experience of scientific explanation'. And parapsychology investigates psychic abilities using the 'scientific method' i.e. it scientifically examines telepathy, precognition and/or retro-cognition (knowing information about future or past events respectively), and psycho-kinesis, which besides moving objects remotely, includes levitation, some forms of healing, metal bending, affecting the roll of the dice etc.

Many 'godmen' in China and India, for example, have proven their ability to move objects, bend spoons or break bottles without touching them, during public displays. And Nina Kulagina (1926-1990), whose psychic abilities were famously studied by soviet scientists, has been filmed lowering and finally stopping the beat of a frog's heart, as well as levitating objects, and moving several objects on a table in different directions. As mentioned, the Soviets pioneered exploring psychic abilities.

In the US, CIA documents reveal that magician Uri Gellar was subjected to bizarre secret experiments that aimed to weaponize psychic abilities. This included being tested for 'clairvoyant' and 'telepathic' abilities. It was part of the Stargate Programme that Ingo Swann was part of. They were recruiting psychic warriors. Interestingly, Uri Gellar, who's famous for his ability to bend metal, mend clocks and watches, and scramble computer disks, said his feats were the result of paranormal powers given to him by Extra-Terrestrials. Whilst the British public has been sceptical about Gellar, the CIA concluded that he 'demonstrated his paranormal perception ability in a convincing and unambiguous manner'.

ESP is assumed to have properties that are inconsistent with our knowledge of energy. And whilst it's criticised as pseudoscience, psychic activity like psychokinesis, telepathy and astral projection are well established. It seems telekinesis is the only logical explanation for how/why furniture moves about on its own accord? Thus, perhaps we could infer that at least one of the researchers at the Philip Experiment had telekinesis? In the same way as Jung (or his complexes) did, hence the poltergeist like phenomenon that he seemed to project?

Or maybe paranormal powers come from ETs, as Gellar advised? As mentioned, we can acquire superpowers (like Siddhi's) from certain practices. Consciousness can be enhanced. We can spiritually evolve with 'knowledge energy', daemons or archetypes. Or alternatively, these powers are demonic, and spirit bodies are demonically activated. It also seems names don't matter for conjurers? Like, entities can call themselves Philip, Jake, Aunty Margaret, Aryans, or Magnu. Who cares?

Furthermore, it's possible that magicians, who pull off inexplicable feats, are using black magic aka demonic powers? Like, Dynamo, David Blaine and Criss Angel? Since it's not normal to levitate or walk up buildings sideways. It also seems odd that David Blaine can insert sticks into his hand and arm without bleeding. He acknowledges, 'But there's no blood…that's the one thing that doesn't make any sense'. Maybe we could walk through walls if our energy vibration was raised high enough? In his book 'The Secret Teachings of All Ages' (1928), which is adopted by all magicians, Manly P Hall, black magician and 33rd degree mason, confessed that all successful magicians were aided by demon entities.

It seems pertinent to note, that in the Bible, angels appear to have ESP including telekinesis. Like, in Acts 12:7-10, (when Peter was rescued from prison), we're told, 'Suddenly, there was a bright light in the cell, and an angel of the Lord stood before Peter. The angel tapped Peter on him on the side to awaken him and said, 'Quick! Get up! And the chains fell off his wrists…. They came to the iron gate to the street, and this opened to them all by itself. So they passed through and started walking down the street, and then the angel suddenly left him'. But we'll get back to the biblical truth of the spirit world.

It's noted, that hundreds of cases of poltergeist activity are reported to the SPR in the UK every year e.g. ghosts and horrid smells. However, for a quintessential example, we can consider the Enfield case in 1977[21]. The Hodgson family (single mum and her four kids) reported loud knocking sounds and flying objects, including beds, chairs and chest of drawers. As it transpired, this poltergeist activity flared up after Janet, who was the focus of attention (most of the activity centred on her), and her sister were playing with the Ouija board. And it was in her room (which she shared with her brother) where all the chaos was going on.

So, initially they contacted the police but the mystified police (a policewoman seen a chair move four feet) advised that the incidents weren't a police matter as they couldn't find anyone breaking the law ('LOL'). They then contacted the press. Daily Mirror photographer Graham Morris said, 'it was chaos, things started flying around, people were screaming'. Indeed, reporters from the press and photographers were hit with flying Lego bricks and marbles. Many disturbances were caught on camera, which includes footage of Janet being thrown around the room.

But moreover, Janet was also seen speaking in a male rough voice, claiming to be someone called Bill who had died in the house. She said, or rather 'Bill' did, 'Just before I died, I went blind, and then I had an 'aemorrhage and I fell asleep and I died in the chair in the corner downstairs'. This was later confirmed to be true. Bill's son advised that his mum popped out to shops and his Dad died in the interim. And his Dad died exactly like that, he went blind and died on a chair in the living-room. Moreover, the son of Bill Wilkins, who heard Janet speaking, said she spoke exactly like his father (the eerie voice can still be heard on audio tapes today).

Interestingly, when 'taken over' by 'Bill', Janet was mischievous and cheeky, and apparently her intelligence appeared too clever for Janet. Furthermore, it seemed to be some entity pretending to be Bill, as compared to the real Bill, this Bill was an A-hole. And whilst this Bill mostly called himself Bill, he also called himself many other names.

The family then contacted the SPR for help, who worked with them for over two years. The investigators were convinced it was genuine poltergeist activity, having observed furniture levitating and flung across the room. One of them said, with regards to the Lego pieces and marbles flying around, 'the extraordinary thing was, when you picked them up they were hot'.

Hidden cameras were set up and recorded Janet bending metal spoons and an iron bar with her hands. Besides exhibiting phenomenal strength, she would have trance fits, was violent, and often banged her head off the wall. When 'taken over', she would scream, shout and swear. Her behaviour was very odd and restless, and it was most intensive at night. She advised being dragged out of bed. Her sister was also thrown out of bed.

So, this was all caught on camera. There's footage of doors opening on their own, and on another occasion, Janet was seen going headfirst downstairs. She was seen levitating and flying about her room, with no idea

---

[21] The story attracted considerable press coverage in British newspapers, and there's been various documentaries and programmes about the Enfield case. See Channel 4's 'Interview with a Poltergeist'.

where she would land, as well as books etc floating about. She spoke about an invisible person being with her, cold hands gripping her. On another occasion Janet was raised horizontally and thought she may go through the window. Neighbours and a lollipop lady reported observing this. There were more than thirty witnesses to the strange incidents.

Janet advised that a priest's visit resulted in the incidents 'quietening down' in autumn 1978, although the occurrences did not stop entirely. She said her mother continued to hear noises in the house. Perhaps we can wonder why a priest's visit would help, if there's no spiritual warfare, as material scientists claim. Janet believes she was possessed by an evil spirit. Indeed, she advised that she felt 'used'. And it seems poor Janet has been medicated to the hilt ever since (by virtue of the facials she pulls). Presumably, she's diagnosed with schizophrenia or DID?

Like, the thirteen year old boy who inspired William Blatly's novel and movie The Exorcist (1973), was also possessed by his unconscious? Or was he demon possessed? Like Janet, he was playing with the Ouija board just a few weeks before he became 'possessed'. The Exorcist is notably deemed the scariest film of all time. Blatly protected the boy's identity by stating it happened to a girl, and the man in question has never spoken in public about his ordeal. The catholic priests involved had no doubt the boy was possessed, and twenty-six people witnessed the paranormal phenomena (Blatly accessed the diaries kept by the priests). Indeed, they believed he was possessed by the devil himself.

The story is thus, in 1949 the boy's aunt taught him how to play with the Ouija board, and then a few weeks later she died. Shortly afterwards unusual sounds began, which included frantic scratching and knocking under the floorboards. The family thought they may have mice and got pest control in, but none were found. The noises progressively got worse at night. The family mused that perhaps the dead aunt was responsible. Events however took a sinister turn. The boy's mum found her son shaking, because the bed was shaking, and other furniture also began to move on its own accord. On another occasion 'the chair' threw the boy onto the floor.

The boy then began to have bizarre marks and scratches on his body. Psychiatry advised there was nothing wrong with him, so they contacted a catholic priest. The boy was described as having a very dark stare yet with nothing behind the eyes. On one occasion when the priest placed a crucifix on the boy's head, he 'slithered' off the chair. Besides that joy, the boy, who was an otherwise very normal boy, would spit, scream profanities, get increasingly violent, and foam at the mouth. He was restrained because of his crazed behaviour. But he managed to break the restraints, and with his hand under the bed, he grabbed a spring and cut the priest. The priest in turn abandoned the exorcism.

The boy continued to have bizarre marks and scratches on his body, and apparently 'St Louis' was branded on his chest (paranormal branding took place about thirty times a day). The family, hoping for peace, considered this to be a sign and moved there. This signalled a new chapter but as it transpired things got worse. They contacted the church again, since again doctors and hospitals were unable to help.

The exorcism took six weeks and the priests (several) involved kept a diary recording events. The boy had to again be restrained on account of his physically aggressive behaviour. The blows of strength were far beyond the strength of an ordinary boy his age. On one occasion the boy lifted his arm and threw the priest across the room. On another occasion when he looked at the priest, a chair lifted off the floor and smacked against the wall. The priest asked the boy (in Latin) who he was, and he answered I am Legion aka many demons. It's noted, that we hear about Legion in the Bible, a demoniac that Jesus exorcised or delivered.

The exorcism was massively emotionally and physically demanding for the priests. Exorcism prayers were recited every night for three weeks but as the boy was so destructive, he had to be removed from the family home. He was placed with an ancient order of catholic monks, in a mental hospital of sorts. The exorcism was relentless going on all night and into the early hours of the morning. The boy's demons put up fierce resistance. The priests were struggling but believed the clincher would be to get the boy to convert to Catholicism. The priests tried to force Holy Communion, but this seemed to rouse the devil. They persevered for another seven days and according to the priests, St Michael saved the day by driving out the demon. Prayers were answered. The boy spoke calmly and took mass the next day. And the bizarre behaviour never returned.

A catholic exorcism notably entails certain rituals and specific series of prayers to invoke the power of God. Ancient traditions like shamanism are similarly au fait with the palaver of exorcisms e.g. magic formulas and rituals to expel evil spirits. Exorcism rites usually consist of respectful offerings or sacrificial offerings. Many religious exorcisms try to physically force the demonic out, which is essentially abuse, and makes no sense given it's a spirit. Violence and infliction of pain are common methods of pagan, Jewish, Hindu, and Muslim faiths.

This therefore contrasts to Jesus' approach, who simply commanded the entity out. And He instructed us to do likewise. That is, in His name and authority, boldly tell it to beat it. Jesus said, 'And these signs will accompany those who have believed; in My name they will cast out demons' (Mark 16:17). Jesus did not seem to be about the drama or rituals.

It's understood that demons don't want to leave their cosy home. They seem to find rest in organic beings. Like, the Legion of demons infested in the man Jesus delivered, begged to go inside a herd of pigs. A friend told me she witnessed a demon possessed woman at church and the demon refused to come out, defiantly and obstinately stating in a male voice, 'I'm not leaving'. Demons often shriek when exorcised and throw their hosts into convulsions.

This corroborates with the Bible. Like, in Mark 9:26 we're told, 'Then the spirit screamed and threw the boy into another violent convulsion and left him'. In Luke 4:35, Jesus commands a protesting demon out. 'Jesus cut him short. 'Be silent!' He told the demon. 'Come out of that man!' The demon threw the man to the floor as the crowd watched; then it left him without hurting him further'. People can also feel demons moving inside of them. It's purported that demons rest in the stomach (the solar plexus, the second brain).

It's interesting to note, that doctors were unable to help the boy Blatly wrote about. Maybe it was because DID didn't exist as diagnostic criteria then, as presumably this would be his diagnosis today? At the very least he could be diagnosed with Antisocial Personality Disorder? His problem is not due to the devil or demons taking over, obviously, but rather unconscious psychic forces?

Psychiatry would attribute the change in facial movements, motor movements, voice change and use of profanities to dissociated states. The superhuman strength could be attributed to all muscles acting at the same time. And with regards to the supernatural messages revealed in scratches and marks, we're advised about the phenomenon 'pareidolia' which pertains to finding meaning in the random e.g. seeing pictures in clouds. It's said we're innately curious and look for meaning in even the most obscure. Psychiatry could further highlight the trauma of his aunt dying. And presumably telekinesis accounts for the moving furniture? Contrary to psychiatry however, and like the priests involved, Blatly has no doubt regarding the reality of spiritual forces.

The countless stories of poltergeist activity report the same kinds of phenomena. Like, Jung's kid's bedcovers getting snatched off them at bedtime. For another couple of examples, we can briefly consider the movies 'Amityville' and 'The Conjuring' as these were also based on true stories.

Thus, the Lutz family (George, Kathy and their three kids), in their colonial house in Amytiville, experienced cold spots, ming smells, heard voices, seen ghosts, dogs were perturbed by their house, pictures fell down and smashed, doors and windows opened and closed on their own, there was EVP, they sustained unexplained bruises and red welts on their body as caused by unseen forces, their covers were snatched away, crosses were turned upside down, they experienced levitation, nightmares and sleepwalking. They were haunted by a violent demonic presence that was so intense it drove them out their house and possessed them.

The Perron family, portrayed in 'The Conjuring', were also terrorised by paranormal phenomena of the aforementioned description. Andrea Perron, the daughter, advised the movie is essentially true although some occurrences were omitted as they were too frightening. [See her book 'House of Darkness House of Light, the True Story' (2011)]. Interestingly, Ed and Lorraine Warren, who founded the New England Society for Psychic Research in 1952, investigated both the Lutz and the Perron family. The Warrens are well known demonologists and have investigated over 10,000 hauntings. They also investigated the Enfield Case, which inspired the movie 'The Conjuring 2'.

So, there's being haunted, but bugger being possessed. As touched on, with possession, the person loses control of their thoughts, emotions and behaviour. Classic symptoms of possession include spontaneous reactions like insanely laughing, bizarre and angry outbursts, convulsions, fits, fainting as if one is dying, fever, filthy uncontrollable swearing, noises, super human strength, violence, slithering and writhing, drastic changes in vocal intonation, the sudden appearance of injuries (e.g. scratches and bite-marks, but also letters or graphic symbols appear on the skin) or lesions, expelling foul substances, making strange animal sounds, and knowledge of languages not otherwise known e.g. Hebrew, Aramaic. It stands to reason the daemonic or demonic are fluent in all languages, having been around long-time?

In addition to the radical change in personality, and their ability to distort their bodies in extraordinary ways, apparently the facial expression is a chilling contortion of evil, but especially the eyes, which are wide open and wild. It's also purported that mentioning God or Jesus agitates abiding spirits. Perhaps there's something to be said for protesting too much? Apparently, demons are show-offs. They're invariably very rude and childish. People in the grip of a supernatural power can also display ESP, which contrasts with mad people who don't have superpowers.

In his book 'People of the Lie' (1983), Scott Peck described what happened at a couple of exorcisms he attended. He said, 'The patient suddenly resembled a writhing snake of great strength, viciously attempting to bite the team members. More frightening than the writhing body, however, was the face. The eyes were hooded with lazy reptilian torpor – except when the reptile darted out in attack, at which moment the eyes would open wide with blazing hatred' (p.196). He explains the satanic spirit, most extraordinarily and dramatically, manifested itself through the patient's writhing serpentine body. The person's body was supernaturally snakelike (although Satan itself is not a snake but a spirit).

Peck said although it repeatedly threatened to kill the possessed person and the exorcists, its threats were empty as they are all lies. It's understood the only power Satan has is through human belief in his lies. In the Bible we're told, 'For he is a liar and the Father of it' (John 8:44). Peck stated that Satan lied continually through the exorcisms, but moreover he highlighted Satan's cunningness in that he mixes truths with lies to mislead (p.237). It seems these are the worst kind of lies. It's said Satan poisons a lake of truth with a pint of poison.

Peck further advised that towards the end of one exorcism, in response to a comment that the spirit must really hate Jesus, the patient, with a full blown satanic facial expression, said in a silky, oily voice, 'we don't hate Jesus; we just test him.' In the middle of the other exorcism, when asked whether the possession was by multiple spirits, the patient with hooded, serpentine eyes answered quietly, almost in a hiss, 'They all belong to me' (p.202).

The serpentine quality seems to be quite the feature. Like, Clara Germana Cele, a sixteen year old South African girl who was apparently possessed, astonished nuns and priests with her ability to transform herself into a snakelike creature. It's reported that her whole body would become as flexible as rubber, and she would writhe along the floor. [It seems this is the point of yoga, namely, to become a flexible temple for the serpent?]. At times her neck seemed to elongate, thereby enhancing the serpent-like impression she gave. And on one occasion, while she was being restrained, she darted, like lightening, at a nun kneeling in front of her and bit the woman on the arm. But moreover, the wound showed the marks of Germana's teeth and also a small red puncture wound resembling a snake bite.

Besides the snake-shapes, Germana was also known for levitating several feet in the air (sometimes vertically, with her feet downward, and sometimes horizontally). Apparently when she was exorcised, the final demon said it would signal its departure by an act of levitation, which was witnessed by 170 people[22].

Apparently Germana's problems began after her alleged pact with the devil. As following that, she began to behave wildly e.g. tearing her clothes, breaking her bedpost, growling and grunting like an animal, conversing with invisible beings, and she also developed clairvoyance. She apparently complained vigorously whenever a cross was presented. Another curious feature was that holy water burned her, when she drank it or it was sprinkled on her, whereas normal water didn't. She could tell the difference.

With regards to people becoming infernally snakelike, my mum's counselling tutor told their class about a guy who, when at a party no less, started writhing on the floor like a snake (happy days). Apparently, she commanded the spirit out in the name of Jesus. It's like La-Sala said he hissed like a snake when demon possessed. Those exorcised describe it as being dragged through a hedge backwards. One wrote, 'I felt like there was a kitten inside my stomach that was being pulled out of me by its tail... it was stabbing its claws deep into my stomach and holding on with all its strength because it didn't want to leave'. It seems they're attached to our soul?

But it gets weirder, as according to Father Gabrielle Amorth (the Pope's chief exorcist who has conducted more than 80,000 exorcisms), people possessed by demons spewed up all sorts of things including nails, glass and bits of metal. It does however provide more physical evidence for the sceptics? As mentioned, vomiting is associated with the expulsion of evil spirits, and in some weird (?) churches, there are buckets for people to spew in, when repenting of their sins.

---

[22] See the 'Readers Digest', 'Mysteries of the Unexplained', 'How Ordinary Men and Women Have Experienced the Strange, the Uncanny, and the Incredible' (1989) p.103.

Amorth also attested to supernatural strength, advising that six or seven assistants were required to hold down the possessed. He advised that 90% of cases of demonic possession are caused by 'dabblers in the occult', and people who had turned to Satanism out of rage or vendetta. Apparently, increasing numbers are seeking exorcisms as a result of OBEs and astral projection. Amorth further informed that Satan is infecting cardinals and bishops in the Vatican, but we'll get to this later.

Paracelsus conceded, 'Thus, it has happened that nails and hair, needles, bristles, pieces of glass, and many other things, have been cut or pulled out of the bodies of some patients, and were followed by other things of a similar character, and that such a state of affairs continued for many weeks or months, and the physicians stood there helpless, and did not know what to do. But if they had better understood their business, they would have known that these things had been brought into the body of a patient by the power of the evil imagination of a sorcerer'.

He explains, 'by the power of imagination foreign bodies may be transferred invisibly into the bodies of human beings, in the same manner as if I take a stone in my hand, and put it into a tub of water, and, withdrawing my hand, I leave the stone in the water'. Thus, something may be put through a body or into a body, and no hole will be left. This resonates with the otherwise inexplicable phenomena of cattle mutilations, which involves the complete draining of the animal's blood and removal of organs, with no obvious point of entry (as we'll get to). It's like apports? It seems objects can dematerialise and re-materialise by changing the frequency of energy?

It seems we can't underestimate the power of imagination? Paracelsus said, 'a strong faith and a powerful imagination are the two pillars supporting the door to the temple of magic'. We notably get the words image, imagination and magic from Magi, which means the 'science of the magi'. Imagination is the creative power of wo/men, and all magic processes are based on faith. He said, the spirit is the master and imagination is the tool. As touched on, imagination is an organ of vision that can be trained. And we need to activate our spirit bodies?

Paracelsus uses the term magic to signify the highest power of the human spirit to control all lower influences for the power of good, whereas the art of employing invisible powers for evil purposes he calls necromancy. He clarifies that sorcery is not magic but stands in the same relation to magic as darkness to light. Satanism is black magic. Whilst 50% of magical power comes from visualisation, witchcraft is the science and art of consciously employing invisible spiritual powers to produce visible effects. Like other occult practices, it entails summoning spirits.

According to Paracelsus, witches are the most dangerous people if they use their evil will against anyone. And they don't have the risk of discovery as injuries are afflicted at a distance. He highlights that images/figures made of wax, clay, wood etc are used in the practice of black magic, witchcraft and sorcery, as these images help to stimulate the imagination and strengthen the will. Like, 'voodoo dolls' (voodoo notably means spirit). Fingernails or hair from the victim further helps the hexes.

Paracelsus states that a necromancer may make a waxen image of a person and bury it, covering it with a heavy stone, and if his will and imagination are powerful enough, the person whom it represents may feel most miserable until that weight is removed. Likewise, if he breaks the limb of that figure, a limb may be broken in him whom it represents. Or he may inflict cuts, stabs, or other injuries upon an enemy. He explains that faith is the cause of witchcraft and sorcerers, and all is done through spirit acting upon spirit.

As touched on, with regards to jungle witchcraft, people offer human and animal sacrifices to appease the spirits. The spilling of blood seems important, like it opens a portal. It's said people bargain with the spirits. Like, they might want wealth, success and power, or they might want to cause problems for someone. As mentioned, shamans need to sacrifice a family member for the ability to shapeshift.

In Uganda, for example, there's a belief that mutilating young children (e.g. their genitals are removed and their heads are sliced open), can help people get rich quickly. Witchdoctors offer the severed bodies to the spirits who commanded them to execute the brutal attacks. It seems these spirits are the same as the 'gods of old', who were partial to human sacrifice and debauchery. Like, the Mayans and Aztecs slaughtered thousands of humans every year for their sun/serpent gods. As King Solomon said, 'there's nothing new under the sun'.

But moreover, it's not only traditional religions (like shamanism and some Hindu sects) that offer sacrifices to the gods, but also the elite. It's said the elite are very religious. And their Father Satan aka Lucifer rewards them richly with fame and fortune. In essence, it's understood that Luciferian witches rule the world on behalf of their master Satan. It's alleged these satanic freaks indulge in orgies, and sexually torture and sacrifice kids (and eat them). This ties in with Satanic Ritual Abuse (SRA) and mind control, but we'll get to this craziness in Part 2.

It's noted, that society wrote off witchcraft during the 'Enlightenment'. It was rendered bosh. Indeed, the Witchcraft Act 1735 made it unlawful to claim witchy powers as there's allegedly no such thing. Superstition was past and witchcraft was fantasy. It was important for people to be reasonable in the Age of alleged Reason.

Helen Duncan (1897-1956) was the last person to be imprisoned under the Act, as she claimed to summon spirits. But moreover, Duncan was a threat during WW2. She came to the attention of authorities when she reported that the HMS Barham had sunk, which was hidden from the general public at the time. As it transpired, a dead sailor's spirit appeared at a séance she held and told her. 'Superstitious' military intelligence officers feared she would reveal their secret plans for D-Day, so she was banged up for nine months. It's said Duncan's trial led to the repealing and replacing of the Witchcraft Act with the Fraudulent Mediums Act 1951.

In tandem with our spoon-fed materialist paradigm, the masses were led to believe that Hogwarts is Hogwash. Spells and hexes aren't real, hence witchcraft is legal. So, it's okay for witches to place a hex on US Supreme Court Justice Brett Kavanaugh, for example, in a protest ritual in New York? And it's okay that one of Britain's leading covens of white witches, the Covenant of Earth Magic, put a spell on Maggie Thatcher and she was booted out a year later? It's okay because spells are baloney?

It's noted, there's been an explosion of witchcraft in recent decades. Wicca is the fastest growing religion in the west. Whilst there's a difference between black and white witchcraft, the source of sorcery is the same. It's like the 'force' in 'Star Wars' can be used for good or evil, but we'll get back to this. White witchcraft is notably symbolised by a pentagram, and black witchcraft (Satanism) is symbolised by an inverted pentagram. It's also highlighted that witches can start out benevolent, but they can become malevolent.

As it transpires, JK Rowling's books have had a bigger influence on society, (impact on kids), than Star Wars and the Beatles. And it's not just harmless fun, as over sixty practices forbidden in the Bible are in Harry Potter books e.g. divination, sorcery, interpreting omens, witchcraft, consulting the dead, acting as mediums or spiritists, spell casting. It's likened to Crowley's Satanism, but it's presented as fiction. It's said it's unbelievably deceptive as the occult is hidden in plain sight. Wheeler (2009) concedes that Harry Potter books are imaginary, but they provide a very real description of astrology, divination, mediumship, channelling and gazing. Thus, they want us to know their party tricks, especially the kids.

As touched on, sexual and religious freedom landed in the sixties. It was cool. Like, the occult is cool today. It continues to be sold to the masses. The influencers are making it popular, like yoga and cabala. Like, they're making occultist and black magician Aleister Crowley (1875-1947) popular. Presumably if they can make Crowley look cool, who earned the title 'the wickedest man in the world', they can make anyone look cool? Like, rapper Jay Zee promotes Crowley's dictum 'do what thou wilt'. And Jay Zee's cool? Like, the Beatles promoted that maxim, and they were cool?

Whilst we'll get back to the 'agenda', it seems pertinent to highlight Crowley, as he massively inspired pop culture particularly rock and roll e.g. Led Zeppelin, the Beatles, the Doors, the Rolling Stones. And he's equally influential today. As mentioned, Crowley features on the Beatles Sergeant Pepper's album, and it's rumoured he is Sergeant Pepper. 'It was twenty years ago today Sergeant Pepper taught the band to play'.

Crowley's considered the Father of the New Age and Satanism. Like, Jung is considered Father of the New Age. Crowley also inspired Anthon La-Vey to found his 'Church of Satan' in 1966. However, unlike Crowley, the Church of Satan holds a materialist philosophy. It proposes we are our own god. There is no God or devil. The emphasis is on carnal pleasure. Enjoy life here and now.

Crowley was a member of various secret societies. Like, the 'Hermetic Order of the Golden Dawn', where he trained in ceremonial magic, and the 'Ordo Templi Orientis', and he was a 33rd degree mason. These secret societies connect with each other in an extensive network, as we'll get to. He also worked for MI5. It's understood that Crowley spawned many illegitimate children, and it's rumoured this included Barbara Bush, George W Bush's Mum. In short, he was extremely influential. The fruits of his labour are reflected in mainstream culture i.e. we love sex, drugs and rock and roll, and now yoga.

Crowley promulgated the belief that we are God and there was no original sin. He said, 'the serpent Satan is not the enemy of man, but he made gods of our race, knowing good and evil'. Ironically, Crowley was brought up in a Christian home, but he transgressed towards occultism, cabala, mysticism, yoga, Buddhism and Hinduism. Apparently, he became 'antichrist' after his dad died (like Nietzsche). He went to Cambridge University and gave himself over to the three proscribed joys of sex, smoking and literature. He wrote several books, including 'Eight Lectures on Yoga' (1939), which made yoga accessible for the masses. Like Jung, he did much to popularise eastern philosophy in the west.

But moreover, Crowley was a diabolical pervert who indulged in bizarre sexual rituals. This included eating faeces and drinking urine. He was a heroin addict, bisexual, paedophile, and child murderer. Whilst he was partial to using hallucinogens to induce ASC, he was particularly partial to sex magick. He was into the 'hard stuff', which included sexually abusing and murdering children, adults and animals. In essence, Satanism, as they drank blood and made spells with it etc.

He advised that human sacrifices are the best for invoking spirits, but especially young boys. He said, 'a white male child of perfect innocence and intelligence makes the most suitable victim'. He bragged about slaughtering 150 male children in one year. Crowley called himself the 'beast 666' and believed he was the anti-messiah of the apocalypse, the enemy of Christianity. He heralded the Aeon of Horus, the one-eyed Egyptian sun-god.

Apparently, Crowley was 'enlightened' after he was sodomised by his mate, Neuberg, in the desert. They took a trip to Algeria to perform Enochian magic, which is a dark and dangerous set of occult rituals. Apparently, they walked for two days, deep into the desert, so they were exhausted, dehydrated, sensory deprived, and disorientated by the effects of the desert. They also took a ton of mescaline and hash, and then embarked upon a ritual of summoning the devil. They endeavoured to open up the abyss, the gates of hell, to unleash the dweller of the abyss.

Their homosexual rite was offered to the god Pan, the man-goat, revered as the diabolical god of lust and magic. Pan is associated with sexual fertility, homosexuality, rape and paedophilia. It was a classic invocation. They would call down or invoke the god Pan. A successful invocation would result in the neophyte's being 'inflamed' by the power of the god Pan. Whilst Neuberg was forever shattered by the event, Crowley had a mystical revelation at the point of orgasm. He seen a blinding white light and communed with the gods.

Thus, he discovered sex magic, or as he called it Magick. He realised sex was an unrivalled means to great power. Sex can be a sacrament, in praise of the gods. It was a shortcut to enlightenment. Crowley felt that he had ceremonially crossed the abyss, which is a prerequisite to become an adept, a magician. His astral body identified with Pan's.

Crowley knew magic worked. He understood that all we have to do is convince forces outside our world to come inside our world. And to do that, one has to be involved. Like, the magician has to sit in a magic circle and perform a certain ritual which compels the spirit to come. It's noted, that a magic circle provides protection for the magician. It's incredibly dangerous to sit outside the circle as people can go mad. They start to hear voices in their heads that they can't get rid of. And yet Crowley would sit outside the circle.

Thus, magick is getting into communication with entities that exist on a higher plane than ours. In addition to drugs, people can exhaust their body through sex, creating an ASC, which frees the spirit to experience other 'divine' spirits. As discussed, spirits and witches can have astral sex (having exteriorised their astral body), and they can sexually molest victims on the astral plane. Apparently with sex magick, spirits are summoned at the point of orgasm. Thus, during a 1921 ritual, Crowley induced a he-goat to copulate with his mistress, and then slit the animal's throat at the moment of orgasm. It seems he took tantric yoga to new gross levels.

For Crowley, sex is the most powerful force in life and the supreme source of magickal power. He outlined three forms of sex magick, namely, autoerotic, homosexual and heterosexual. Like blood, semen can be used to summon entities. He explained that such acts could be used to focus the magician's will onto a specific goal e.g. financial gain or personal creative success. People can acquire ESP, as Crowley did. Like, he was able to make himself invisible, which is something the Rosicrucian's were renowned for, as we'll get to. Crowley was incredibly intelligent. Apparently, he could play twenty-three games of chess at the same time blindfolded.

Crowley defined magick as 'the Science and Art of causing Change to occur in conformity with Will', and he spelled it with a 'k' to distinguish it from stage magic. The K references black magic. Contrary to the cheeky sleight of hand, magick is not illusory. We can 'Will' spirits to do our bidding, if we please them with our depravity and debauchery.

Crowley founded the religion of Thelema, which is 'Do what thou wilt'. The whole of the Law is, knock yourself out. When on honeymoon in Egypt, Crowley took part in rituals, which led to the birth of his new religion. Crowley claimed that 'The Book of the Law', the system of Thelema, was dictated to him from a supernatural entity named Aiwass, who he later identified as his holy guardian angel. [Holy?]. Besides doing what we want or will, love is the law i.e. accept all including paedos. And everyone's a star aka god. It's noted, people complement each other as 'stars'. He also introduced the V for Victory sign, another popular expression. The V is a reference to the five points on a pentagram, and also Venus, the morning star.

The word Thelema means 'to will, wish, want or purpose' (Thelema is Greek for will). It seems we can 'will power' through rituals and initiations. We can become one with the gods through the practice of magick. For Crowley, the greatest aim of the magician was to merge with a higher power connected to the wellsprings of the universe. Sometimes he called it God, or the One, or a goddess, or one's own Holy guardian angel or higher self.

As it transpired, Crowley wanted to create a dimensional vortex that would bridge the gap between the seen and unseen world. Thus, in 1918 he conducted a ritual called the 'Amalantrah Working'. This was successful, as according to Crowley, a presence manifested itself through the rent. Crowley drew a portrait of this being, called Lam, and it looks like a grey alien.

Whilst we'll get back to the alien agenda, it seems pertinent to mention American rocket scientist Jack Parsons (1914-1952), as it seems he opened up a portal that allowed an influx of aliens/UFOs to come in. Parsons was Crowley's protégé. Apparently, Parsons called Crowley 'beloved father'. Parsons was hooked with the Thelema religion, and especially liked that sex could be an intrinsic component of magickal rituals to induce ASC. Apparently, he held rituals at his house to initiate scientists at Los Alamos atomic bomb labs, including Robert Oppenheimer, who created the atomic bomb. So, Parsons built rockets for the government by day, and by night he performed sex magick with his followers. Like Crowley, he was also in the Ordo Templi Orientis.

Following in the footsteps of Crowley, Parsons and his magic partner L Ron Hubbard (1911-1986), founder of Scientology, conducted a second ritual based on ceremonial sex magick, namely, the 'Babalon Working' ritual. They endeavoured to reopen the gateway created by Crowley. However, they weren't seeking an audience with Lam, but rather they wanted the whore of Babylon to come through. The aim was to birth a child to be an incarnation of what Crowley called Babalon, the Scarlet Whore with the cup of blood that rides the beast, as foretold in Revelation (in the Bible). The whore is consort of the beast.

So, for weeks the two men engaged in ritual chanting. They drew occult symbols in the air with consecrated swords, dripped animal blood on runes, and masturbated in order to impregnate magical tablets. According to Marjorie Cameron, Parson's partner, she conceived the 'moon child' with Parsons, when Parsons was incarnated with the spirit of antichrist. Thus, Marjorie was impregnated by the antichrist. As mentioned, this is the plot of Polanski's movie 'Rosemary's Baby'. The devil in that movie was notably played by Anthon La-Vey.

It's noted, whilst the Babalon Working was apparently designed by Crowley, this ritual is one of the darkest rituals known to cabala (so it predates Crowley). Apparently during the ritual, initiates project their astral bodies into the dark abyss of Lucifer. If they survive with their personality intact, they become a black magician of the left-hand path of cabala.

Apparently, the foetus was extracted by government agents and it's rumoured that Hillary Clinton, who was born in 1947, is the whore of Babylon that walks the earth today. According to Cameron, Parsons ripped a hole in space-time, and something evil flew in called Hilarion. So, that's interesting. But moreover, it's reported the portal didn't close. Apparently, the person who opens the portal has to close it, and Jack Parsons blew himself up and never did close it. Hence, the modern UFO era began in 1947.

Whilst we'll get back to Parsons and haunted politicians, like the Clintons, it seems pertinent to note that in 2016 wikileaks exposed emails that John and Tony Podesta were invited to a 'spirit cooking' dinner with performance artist Marina Abramovic at her home. Abramovic is very popular with 'A' list actors, and musicians like Lady Gaga and Jay Zee. As mentioned, John Podesta was Hillary Clinton's campaign manager, and he was linked to the Pizza-gate paedo-ring (which we'll get back to). He also served as White House Chief of Staff to President Bill Clinton, and Counsellor to Barack Obama. His brother Tony Podesta is a lobbyist.

The act of spirit cooking involves using pig's blood to connect with the spirit world. According to Abramovic, if the ritual is performed in an art gallery, it is merely art, but if the ritual is performed privately (like at her home), then it represents an intimate spiritual ceremony. Spirit cooking is a sacrament in the religion of Thelema, and involves an occult performance during which menstrual blood, breast milk, urine and semen are used to create a 'painting'. The ceremony is meant to symbolise the union between the microcosm, man, and the divine, macrocosm. Spirit cooking is an occult practice used during sex cult rituals.

So, there's an art to conjuring spirits, and witchcraft relies on will and imagination. According to High Priest Kevin Carlyon, founder of the Covenant of Earth Magic (1988), 'Magic is like electricity and people are like batteries. The more batteries there are, the more powerful it will be. Just like electricity, you can cook with it or you can kill with it'.

Witches tend to meet in covens of 13, and their rituals take place on particular days/times e.g. new moon or full moon, solstices, equinoxes. Wheeler (2009) states, 'In Satanism, if a witch wants to cast an evil spell he will do it the night of the New Moon, the darkest night of the month; if the witch wants to cast a benevolent spell, he will do it on the night of the Full Moon'. Halloween is particularly important for witches. Apparently, the veil between the spiritual and physical realm is the thinnest on Halloween. In addition to their prescribed spells and incantations, the planets and stars have to be in particular alignments, and so forth.

Witches are pagans, as they revere Nature. As Paracelsus said, Nature is the universal teacher. He asserts the first requirement for the study of magic is a thorough knowledge of Nature. Like, witches can make use of the planets if they know what qualities those influences possess. Since the earliest times, mysticism has centred around the worship of the stars and planets, which were revered as living gods. Witches thus call down these spirits. The pentagram is the most potent symbol to conjure spirits. The five points on the pentagram pertain to fire, water, air, earth, and spirit.

Thus, witches hold hands and create a magic circle. They draw pentagrams to capture/enclose spirits, burn incense, use chalices and daggers, crystals and skulls, say maledictions and benedictions (verbal curses and blessings) etc. But as emphasised, animal or human sacrifices, coupled with orgies, are the most effective at summoning spirits (goats or children are sacrificed inside pentagrams). The spirits or gods want bloodshed.

There's myriad spells in witchcraft for myriad purposes, which require various ingredients like poisonous elements taken from spiders and toads, mercury, salt, blood and body parts. It appears witches partake in 'Double, double toil and trouble, fire burn and cauldron bubble'. Apparently menstrual blood is more potent than regular blood, and Johannesburg is a good place to source body-parts, like abortion clinics.

The Devil's Bible, which is considered the 8th wonder of the world (its three foot long and weighs sixty-five pounds), notably includes spells and medicinal cures. Legend has it that some monk, who sold his soul to the Devil, wrote it, as guided by the hand of the Devil. It's apparently located in some monastery somewhere, and it's said that tragedy befalls those who possess it (this is not to be confused with Anthon La-Vey's satanic bible published in 1967).

Besides the necromantic art of covertly placing crap inside other people's bodies, magicians can summon demons into inanimate objects, which then become objects of power. Like, talismans and amulets. Demons can be conjured into objects to curse others. Hence, we might want to think twice about receiving presents? Like, it's said witches curse candy that is given to kids at Halloween. The 'trick or treat' lark at Halloween notably comes from placating evil spirits with treats, so they don't get tricked aka hexed. People can summon demons into statues etc to worship, which God calls idolatry. Like, Catholics bow down before statues of Mary.

It's noted, that demons can make statues move, weep tears or bleed. Others however attribute these signs and wonders to God. As it transpires, when the blood has been analysed, lab tests invariably reveal the blood is human but very old, which is ascertained by red blood cells breaking down and being few in number. So, the demonic can dwell in the animate or inanimate, but (as mentioned) they prefer the animate. They can enjoy themselves through us. Like drink, drugs, rape and murder.

Black (2010) wrote, 'In early cities of Sumeria, statues to ancestors and lesser gods stood in family homes. A skull was sometimes kept as a 'house' that a minor spirit could inhabit. Meanwhile, the much greater spirit who protected the interests of the city was held to live in the 'god house', a building at the centre of the temple complex. As these cites grew, so too did the god houses, until they became ziggurats, great stepped pyramids, built out of mud bricks. In the centre of each ziggurat was a large chamber in which the statue of the god resided, inlaid with precious metals and jewels, and wrapped in dazzling clothes. According to the cuneiform texts, the Sumerian gods liked eating, drinking, music and dancing. Food would be put on tables, then the gods left alone to enjoy it. After a time the priests would come in and eat what was left. The gods also needed beds to sleep in and for enjoying sex with other gods' (p.207). But we'll get back to the 'gods'.

Furthermore, besides calling upon spirits, we can apparently make our own spiritual assistants to do our bidding e.g. for protection, healing, or harming others. Through intense concentration and visualisation, we can create 'thought beings', as thoughts become 'denser' with enough will and imagination. When we visualise an image, it becomes an entity. It seems this is what the Phillip Experiment attempted to do, but couldn't, hence they opted for a séance. Visualisation and imagination demonstrate the occult law that 'energy flows where attention goes' (as witchdoctors attest to). Dr Rebecca Brown concedes that visualisation is the creation of an image or picture in the mind through imagination. She states that visualisation seems to occur in the spirit, by controlling our spirit body.

Thus, we go into a trance and visualise/imagine the thought form. We can choose any shape or image, and we give the image details e.g. smell, taste, sound, and we make it move in time and space. We empower it, engender it with emotions. It's said that if we see an image of a thing in our mind, and realise its presence, it actually exists for us. It's like the entities people encounter during spells of Active Imagination are real. That psychic reality is real. Hence, occultists construct images in their minds, for gods and spirits to inhabit.

A thought form is defined as a 'structured inter-dimensional energy form'. It's said thoughts charged with 'energy' are much stronger than ordinary thoughts, and people with astral vision can see them. Spells, curses, and hexes are thought forms. They're sent out with a purpose, which is made more powerful because it is concentrated by means of the rites, ceremonies, spells/images. Hence, when groups of people will/imagine together, like witches, it generates more power. It's like prayer is more powerful when more people pray? So, with the cooperation of the 'universe', we can create thought forms. They're like robots that we can programme with particular tasks. It has no mind of its own.

Thought forms become visible and tangible, and have some kind of independent existence. They apparently materialise as a coloured shadow or mist. Paracelsus refers to these as aquastors and Tibetans call them tulpas (tulpas are usually produced by a skilled magician or yogi). Paracelsus explains they have no life of their own but rather borrow it from the person who has brought them into existence. He thus regarded them as parasitic, as they draw vitality out of the person to whom they are attracted. He said they're often generated by idiots, immoral, depraved or diseased persons.

Paracelsus notably regarded incubus and succubus as parasites growing out of the astral elements of wo/man (i.e. our energy) in a consequence to their lewd imagination, which suggests we create them? Like my friend, who's had sex with succubus, is partial to porn, so it's possible he conjured up succubus by his deviant imagination? Perhaps we're responsible for some of the shadow people?

It gets pretty crazy as Paracelsus states that partaking in sodomy, for example, creates a gross shadow being, called basilisk. This 'mythological creature' apparently has a fowl's head and serpentine body. As touched on, the world is increasingly partial to sodomy, and it's understood this is by design. 'Someone' out there, wants more basilisks? But we'll get back to this.

These astral entities can also possess animals which connects the master with the animal. There's an intimate connection as they share the same life force (energy). Perhaps this detached part of our psychic energy could be likened to an autonomous complex? A bloke in Mozambique told me, that when the animal dies, the person also dies. He told me about a witchdoctor who had a snake, and when the snake was shot, the man also died from a shot without actually being shot. And it seems to be a two-way street, because if the person is injured, this is inflicted upon their progeny. It seems risky to covertly employ animals to do our bidding?

Black (2010) also mentioned a story about a traveller who had been mesmerised by the gaze of a serpent. He was sinking deeper and deeper into a somnambulic sleep under its fascinating influence. Then someone else in the party shot the snake, breaking its power over him – and he felt a blow to the head as if he too had been struck by a bullet' (p.187).

Cisco Wheeler similarly pertains to 'psycho gones'. She wrote, 'By means of visualisation, breathing and mantra techniques using the u-vowel, and the concentration and directing of sexual energies the magician can evoke an astral image, or psycho gone creature within the magical circle. A psycho gone is a talismanic shaped creature that has been given life by the magical work of the magicians. This talismanic creature has a magically imparted soul, or psyche, and it acts in accordance to the willed commands of its creator as if it were an energy form. This psycho gone creature is created for one purpose only and that is to do the bidding of the magician. This is not the same as calling upon spirits, angels or daemons to work for the magician. This psycho gone is created' (p.128).

Paracelsus stressed imagination is a great power, stating if the world only knew what strange things may be produced by the imagination. He maintains we're created with great power. He asserted that true faith has wonderful powers, and this fact proves that we are spirits, and not merely visible bodies.

Dr Brown concedes our spirit bodies are very powerful, when our 'will' controls them. Besides creating thought beings, she explains that when we visualise what we want, 'power' is released to bring this vision into our life. Thus, visualisation is witchcraft. It's noted, this 'New Age' practice is popular. Like, the law of attraction, popularised by Rhonda Byrne's 'The Secret'. Why not visualise what we want? However, it's said that whilst people often get the desires of their heart, it invariably doesn't end well. Like, someone gets their dream car, but it's written off a week later. Visualisation opens us up to the spirit world.

But moreover, in addition to manufacturing thought-beings, we can also create other curious creatures like golems. Golems are animated beings created out of inanimate matter via magical processes, and it's one of the goals in alchemy. It's purported that golems can be made from dead body parts coupled with incantations and mantras. Jewish rabbis and sages are known for creating golems, which we'll get to when we consider the cabala. Abracadabra is a Hebrew phrase that means 'I create what I speak'. Like, God spoke existence into existence.

In his book, 'On the Nature of Things' (1537), Paracelsus gave us the recipe to create golems, which are known as homunculus ('little man') in alchemical terms. Thus, 'to create man, without women and a natural womb', he instructed, 'let the semen of a man putrefy by itself in a sealed cucurbite with the highest putrification… until it begins to live, move and be agitated, which can easily be seen… if now, after this, it be every day nourished and fed cautiously and prudently with the arcanum of human blood, and kept for forty weeks in the perpetual and equal heat it becomes, thenceforth a true and living infant, having all the members of a child that is born from a woman, but much smaller. This we call a homunculus; and it should be afterwards educated with the greatest care and zeal, until it grows up and begins to display intelligence. Now, this is one of the greatest secrets which God has revealed to mortal and fallible man. It is a miracle and marvel of God, an arcanum above all arcana, and deserves to be kept secret until the last times, when there shall be nothing hidden, but all things shall be made manifest'. So, when scientists begin to make 'little men', we'll know we're living in the 'end times'?

It's understood we don't know what the mad scientists are up to. We only know what they want us to know. Like, we know they can clone animals including primates. Apparently, it costs $25,000 to clone cats, and $50,000 to clone dogs. We heard about Dolly the Scottish sheep (named after Dolly Parton) back in 1996, although apparently human cloning goes back to WW2. It's purported that Dr Mengele perfected cloning people in Argentina. And we know they're making human-pig chimeras, for example. Chimera notably comes from the cross-species beast of Greek mythology. The endeavour is to create a pig with human organs that we can then harvest. Human stem cells are introduced into a pig embryo, which is then placed in a sow's womb, to create a hybrid.

But there's rumours (whistle-blowers have divulged) about proper grotesque creatures being harboured at Deep Underground Military Bases (DUMBs). It seems we can but wonder what Frankenstein's they're creating behind the scenes, and for what purpose, particularly since demons desire a host to dwell in. But we'll get to this craziness later.

Whilst witchcraft is increasingly popular, God is crystal that it's not okay. In Deuteronomy (18:10-14) we're told, 'do not let your people practice fortune telling or sorcery, or allow them to interpret omens, or engage in witchcraft, or cast spells, or function as mediums or psychics, or call forth spirits of the dead. Anyone who does these things is an object of horror to the Lord…the Lord your God forbids you to do such things'. Sorcery is a blanket term for spiritualism.

As mentioned, God strictly forbade His covenant people from consulting any supernatural source other than Himself. In Leviticus it says people who possessed and passed on knowledge, not through natural channels of perception, had opened themselves up to the spirit world and became spiritual channels. Prophecies come from dark angels.

The Bible explains that psychics have psychic abilities because they have a demon (attached to them) that bestows this 'ESP'. Like, in Acts 16:16-19, Paul tells us about a female slave who earned a great deal of money for her owners by fortune-telling. He commanded the spirit out of her, in the name of Jesus Christ, and the spirit left her (much to her owner's dismay).

In Leviticus 19:31 we're told, 'Regard not them that have familiar spirits, neither seek after wizards, to be defiled by them: I am the Lord your God'. The word 'familiar' notably derives from the Latin 'familiaris', meaning a 'household servant'. It's intended to express the idea that sorcerers had spirits as their servants ready to obey their commands. Those attempting to contact the dead, usually have some sort of spirit guide who communicates with them. These are familiar spirits. It seems however, that people are not consulting with spirits of the dead, and spirit guides are not our friends?

And perhaps people are not consulting 'angels' in 'angel workshops' or via 'angel cards' (a divinatory tool like tarot cards). With the advent of the New Age movement, there's been an upsurge of interest in angels in recent years. They're associated with power, protection, and healing. Like, Byrne praises angels for their encouragement and support. They've got our back?

In angel books and workshops etc, we're told it's very simple to contact our angels. All we need to do is call them. Some however like to create a more inviting environment by constructing an altar, lighting candles, meditating, and burning incense. We're told to think about our angel, visualise it, 'imagine it', have faith that it exists, and as a result we can communicate with it. We can then ask our 'angels' questions, and by allowing our mind to go blank we can receive what flows (we don't try to make it happen). Some people actually hear their angel talking to them, whereas others 'feel' what the angels are saying.

We're told to realise that some things aren't coincidences and be prepared to feel an overwhelming sensation of joy or love. And respectively, many people report feeling such love (the placebo effect is duly noted). People are told to name their angel, with whatever name first comes to mind, as that is your guardian angel introducing itself. We're told that angels let us know when they've visited by leaving a sign, such as a white feather, and it's reported there's a smell of chocolate when they're close by (like ADCs)[23]. However, if we're struggling to connect with our angels, we can go to an angel 'practitioner' who can not only channel our angels but also our passed loved ones. People say they feel less lonely knowing their angels are with them, which bodes well in our Age of Loneliness?

The Bible notably tells us that any spirit we can summon at will is not an angel of God. On the contrary, it seems angels randomly appear when they have a message to give us (angel means messenger). Interestingly, Doreen Virtue, the founder of Angel Therapy, which is a spiritual healing method that involves working with a person's guardian angels, has become a born-again Christian. The popular New Age author (she has written over fifty books including oracle decks) realised they're not angels.

It's (ironically) interesting to note, that King Saul (the first king of Israel) banned all the mediums and psychics in Israel, and yet he subsequently went to one. Apparently he received no answer from God, his dreams, prophets, or the Urim and Thummin (divining device), as to his best course of action against the assembled forces of the Philistines, and so he sought out a medium. It's noted, whilst divination is forbidden, the Old

---

[23] Interestingly, Paulo Coelho advised that he waits until he sees a white feather before he writes a new book. Apparently in January of every second year, when he finds a white feather he commences writing.

Testament permitted urim and thummim, to enable divine communication i.e. ask God something and the stones provide yes or no answers. The patriarchs, prophets and saints however preferred visions and dreams to any mode of divination.

In Samuel 28:3-19 we're told, 'So Saul disguised himself...and came to the (medium at Endor) by night. And he said, "Consult a spirit for me, and bring up the one whom I name to you". '...Then the woman said, "Whom shall I bring up for you?"' He sought, through the medium, Samuel's advice as Samuel had passed away (Samuel the prophet was his teacher and counsellor). Samuel subsequently appeared but rebuked Saul directly for his sin and predicted that Israel would be defeated by the Philistine army and Saul would be defeated and die, which happened (Saul notably topped himself).

The prophecy by Samuel's 'ghost' however, is largely verbatim of Samuel's public speech when he was alive. Ergo anyone (spirits included) who heard it could repeat it (see 1 Samuel 15). Whilst it seemed that Samuel appeared (the woman described his appearance), perhaps a spirit used Samuel's astral body as a mask to deceive? Or perhaps, on this occasion, God allowed Samuel to appear?

It is however acknowledged that spirits can make predictions that come to pass. Like, with precognition, people can have visions of the future. Like, psychics get visions. Psychics seem to sense and feel things, and many live in a world full of pictures, with vivid images of people, places, times, and events. News can come unbidden, as if projected on a TV screen (like remote viewing).

Thus, unlike mediums who communicate directly with spirits (and 'aliens'), psychics seem to have some kind of enhanced sixth sense or instinct. Hence, all mediums are psychics, but not all psychics are mediums. Apparently 1:6 people claim psychic abilities. Or perhaps, unbeknown to the 'psychic', the spirits provide the visions and information? The spirits are responsible for the invasion of unconscious material? Like, people can 'know' something intuitively, but the spirits provide the intuition? Doreen Virtue, who was also a world-renowned psychic, confirms that demons provide the information.

It's noted, psychics can be useful, particularly for cops to help solve their crimes. Psychic detectives are valued assets. Like Allison Dubois, one of the world's most famous psychic cops, who inspired the TV programme 'Medium'. She claims she became aware of her ability to communicate with departed souls when she was six years old. Nancy Myer is another famous police psychic, who has worked on over three hundred criminal cases (spanning over two decades) and provided vital information to help solve 80% of them.

Dorothy Allison and Nella Jones have also worked on countless cases, and were famous for locating missing persons. Both didn't charge for their services. Apparently, Jones's mother, a seer, insisted visions were a gift and should never be used for profit. With regards to her ability, Jones said, 'the nearest way I can describe what I do is that there's part of me that walks in the other realm'. Some psychics have spirit guides to keep them 'right' (like Gaz), whereas others like Jones and Allison don't.

As touched on, psychics can use various methods to predict the now and the future. Like, cartomancy is fortune-telling by cards. And 'tasseography' is a divination method that interprets patterns in tealeaves, coffee grounds, or wine sediments. It's bemusing that psychics can tell people about their lives and future from what would appear to be otherwise random sediment. Like, my mum got her teacup read by some psychic. The psychic accurately told my mum what was going on in her life, and told her what to do. It's understood all readings are 'intuitive'.

Besides the police and politicians, it seems people go to psychics looking for hope e.g. will they get married, have kids, and get that job/house? As psychologists highlight, we want control over our lives. The uncertainty (existential contingency) is too disconcerting. It's highlighted that clairvoyants are more popular than ever before, and speaking to the dead is big business. Apparently, it rakes in £100 million a year in the UK.

Lots of famous people consult psychics, like Lady Gaga, Brad Pitt and Cheryl Tweedy. Angelina Jolie reportedly used a medium to communicate with her late mother. And Anthea Turner (former Blue Peter presenter) was told by a medium that her dead sister (who she described to a tee) was with her all the time. She was also told by a psychic that her husband would cheat, which he did. Going to psychics can become addictive, as my mum attested to. She also said she became oppressed as a result of these encounters. Doreen Virtue notably said that demons provide correct information to get people addicted.

To use my mum as an example then, she went to a psychic when she was sixteen (she worked in an office at the time), and the psychic informed that she would be a lady of the lamp aka nurse, and she would live in Africa all her life. She said she would only ever have one son, who would make her very proud and travel all over the world. As it transpired, my mum became a nurse and having married my dad, they moved to Zambia, where she had my brother, who has travelled the world and made her very proud. However, the contention is that having foreknowledge can affect how we thereby make decisions. Like, my mum thought she would always live in Africa hence she was most insistent on coming back to the UK. So, she only stayed there eight years. And when she was pregnant with me, she feared I would be a miscarriage as she was supposed to have one child.

There's notably a parable (Swiss folktale) regarding this man who goes to see a psychic and the psychic tells him that he'll die when his donkey sneezes three times. So, the donkey sneezes once, twice, and so the guy freaked out, puts two boulders beneath the donkey's nose. But as a result, when the donkey sneezes the third time, the boulders kill the man. The moral of the story is that it's better not to know the future? It's also duly noted, that having clairvoyant sight, seeing into the future, suggests determinism?

For another example, we can consider David Icke's story, not least because it led him to where he is today? Thus, Icke sensed a tangible presence in his room, so he asked the otherwise 'empty room' if there's a presence there, and to reveal itself. He was subsequently led to see a psychic, who told him he was going to be world famous for revealing great secrets. He was told there was a great story that humanity had to be told. The psychic told him 'one man cannot change the world, but one man can communicate the message that can change the world'. He incidentally said he felt a 'spider's web' on his face which he understood indicated the unknown's presence (this corroborates with Gaz Parker's experience). This prophecy has come to pass, as David Icke is a world-renowned leader in the truth movement. His story is remarkable, and he's woken millions up from their alpha slumber state.

Icke's advice is to accept guides because they're here to guide us and help us through this lifetime, so we can learn lessons. He (naively) asserts that all we have to do is simply say, 'I accept I am being guided' and 'go ahead and guide me', and when we do that, things start happening. Like, synchronicity kicks in. Life becomes a lot more interesting when people open themselves to spiritual personalities that exist in different frequencies/dimensions. Life is no longer random but rather driven by hidden forces.

Icke maintains everyone can transform, 'if they say openly I wish to be guided and work for the Light'. Like, the Light Workers Magnu referenced, who are used as catalysts to feed in ever more energies? Icke does however caution that we are always to ask for protection and guidance. Icke fondly refers to the beings that guide him as 'the guys'. He explains there's a force that pushes him in different directions, and a hidden hand passes information to him.

So, it would appear 'the guys' want the 'truth' out'? After millennia of secrecy, everything is being exposed? As Jesus said (in Luke 8:17), 'For all that is secret will eventually be brought into the open, and everything that is concealed will be brought to light and made known to all'. Thus, the mainstream is familiar with the deep state, the shadow government, the inner workings of secret societies and mystery schools. We know the globalist agenda. But moreover, there's literally a shadow government i.e. shadow people. Icke concedes there's a non-human force running the show. These entities have been manipulating us for thousands of years.

Icke recognises that Satanists rule the world, and he seems to differentiate between good and evil spirits. Like, 'the guys' are a force for good, like the spirit of ayahuasca and kundalini? As mentioned, Icke endorses the New Age narrative that we're God, or as he states 'Infinite Awareness'. He relays that we are everything (and nothing), we are everywhere (and nowhere); we are all that is, has been, and ever will be; all existing in the eternal and infinite now'. He seems to reiterate Masonic witch Alice Bailey's teachings, as we'll get to, which seems paradoxical. Thus, maybe unbeknown to him, he's being used as part of the agenda?

The Bible notably insists that we test the spirits. Like, 1 John 4:1-3 states, 'Dear friends, do not believe every spirit, but test the spirits to see whether they are from God, because many false prophets have gone out into the world. This is how you can recognise the Spirit of God: Every spirit that acknowledges that Jesus Christ has come in the flesh is from God, but every spirit that does not acknowledge Jesus is not from God. This is the spirit of the antichrist, which you have heard is coming and even now is already in the world'. So, there's two spirits, namely, God's Holy Spirit and the antichrist spirit. And people can be antichrist by default i.e. those who are not for Christ are antichrist.

One of the spiritual gifts from the Holy Spirit is the gift of discerning spirits. The Holy Spirit bestows various gifts to Christians, like the gift of prophecy, healing, tongues and interpreting tongues. And Satan offers counterfeit ESP superpowers, like divination, and also healing, and tongues. It seems they both enable superpowers through our spirit body?

It's understood, spirits can tell us things about our lives that are true because they see us and know us. Indeed, they know us intimately. They see it all. Like snoop dogs, they listen to our conversations, hear our phone-calls, see our texts and emails, and therefore see our plans, hopes and dreams. Hence, they can impart this personal information to psychics. It's purported that whilst spirits can infer what we're thinking by our body language, (and visible emotions), they can't read our minds.

It's thus contended that whilst psychics can on occasion predict future events, for the most part they merely have specular knowledge. Enchanters who consult many psychics are getting little useful information, but rather a running commentary on their life. With regards to predicting future events, it's said they have a hazy insight by way of cause and effect. The recollection of the past and current précis does however evidence the encounter is supernatural, as there's no other viable explanation for how the medium knows what they know?

It seems pertinent to note, that in the Bible, Isaiah (8:19) states, 'So why are you trying to find out the future by consulting mediums and psychics? Do not listen to their whisperings and mutterings. Can the living find out about the future from the dead? Why not ask your God?' Isaiah, who lived in the eight century BC, was a prophet of God and predicted key events in Christ's life. This includes Jesus' birth in Bethlehem, His miraculous cures, His entry into Jerusalem on a donkey, His betrayal for thirty pieces of silver, His arrest and beating, and His crucifixion.

As it transpires, Jesus fulfilled over three hundred prophecies from the Old Testament. The Old Testament was recorded centuries before Christ was born. The Septuagint (the Greek version of the Hebrew Scriptures) was complete by 270BC, and there are original copies of these today. It's my contention, that if we had no preconceived ideas about Christianity, we might be open to the evidence? We might be open to the idea that God's word is the truth? However, I digress.

For an example of a psychic, we can consider Edgar Cayce (1877-1945). He's renowned as the best psychic of the twentieth century, and claims his psychic abilities began in childhood. He claims he was able to see and talk to his late grandfather's spirit, and often played with 'imaginary friends' who he said were spirits on the other side. And then, for most of his adult life he gave readings to thousands of people and diagnosed illness.

His career began when he discovered that through hypnosis and inducing trance states, he could access information that his conscious mind couldn't. He discovered that he could travel to other dimensions to obtain psychic information on any subject i.e. astral projection. Indeed, he spoke in detail about the possibility of our conscious mind leaving our body, and visiting other locations, both on and off planet.

Cayce became known as the 'slumber prophet' because his readings came to him when he was in trance-like slumber. And like REM, his eyelids would flutter when he was ready. In his trance state, he was able to effortlessly and articulately discuss subjects that he had no prior knowledge about. People could literally ask him anything, ranging from health concerns, to past lives, and secrets of the universe. Like, what's buried underneath the pyramids of Giza and the sphinx?

According to Cayce, there is a 'Hall of Records' beneath the Egyptian sphinx that holds the historical documents of Atlantis. Cayce frequently spoke about Atlantis (he mentioned Atlantis over 700 times). He stated that many of his subjects were reincarnations of Atlanteans, and by tapping into their unconscious, he was able to give detailed descriptions of the lost continent. 'His' intelligence was immense, but after a 'session', Cayce almost never remembered anything he said.

As a result of his trance escapades, Cayce would be knackered and experienced migraines. People commonly report feeling exhausted after sessions, which suggests their energy's been sapped? And apparently, his hypnotic procedure went awry on a few occasions. At one point, he remained in a catatonic state for three days, and on another couple of occasions he was deemed dead by the doctors' present.

It's also interesting to note, that when Cayce spoke in his trance state, he used the plural point of view 'we' instead of the singular 'I'. This suggests Cayce is working with someone? Most of Cayce's readings were notably done remotely i.e. people would post him letters with their details. Cayce's wife would ask Cayce the questions, as he lay in his slumber state, and his secretary took notes. Regarding his trips to the sky, and when speaking at a public lecture, he described his journey in the trance state as:

'I see myself as a tiny dot out of my physical body, which lies inert before me. I find myself oppressed by darkness and there is a feeling of terrific loneliness. Suddenly, I am conscious of a white beam of light, knowing that I must follow it or be lost. As I move along this path of light I gradually become conscious of various levels upon which there is movement. Upon the first levels there are vague, horrible shapes, grotesque forms such as one sees in nightmares. Passing on, there begins to appear on either side misshapen forms of human beings with some part of the body magnified. Again there is change and I become conscious of grey-hooded forms moving downward. Gradually, these become lighter in colour. Then the direction changes and these forms move upward and the colour of the robes grows rapidly lighter.

Next, there begins to appear on either side vague outlines of houses, walls, trees, etc., but everything is motionless. As I pass on, there is more light and movement in what appear to be normal cities and towns. With the growth of movement I become conscious of sounds, at first indistinct rumblings, then music, laughter, and singing of birds. There is more and more light, the colours become very beautiful, and there is the sound of wonderful music. The houses are left behind; ahead there is only a blending of sound and colour. Quite suddenly I come upon a hall of records. It is a hall without walls, without ceiling, but I am conscious of seeing an old man who hands me a large book, a record of the individual for whom I seek information'.

According to the 'sleeping' Cayce, when asked where he was getting his information from, he gave two sources. Namely, he was able to tap into the subject's unconscious mind, (which includes those who had passed over to the spiritual world), and also the 'universal memory of nature'. What Cayce called the 'reservoir of heavenly memories' is known as the 'Akashic Records'. Akasha is notably a Sanskrit word meaning 'sky', 'space' or 'ether'.

Akashic Records are records of all knowledge, including all human experience. All our moments, including all our thoughts and emotions, are apparently recorded in some kind of 'book'. They're encoded in the ether. It's said occultists know that nothing ever perishes but rather there are imperishable and unalterable records of every scene, thought and thing that ever existed or occurred. Those who have access to them may read the past as they read a book. The Akashic Records are metaphorically described as a library (like Jung's collective unconscious) and they're likened to the 'Mind of God'.

However, apparently these records are not on the astral plane but a plane far above it. But they're mirrored, just as the sky and clouds are reflected on the sea. And just as a vision may be distorted by ripples and waves, so may the astral vision of these records of the past become distorted because of disturbances in the astral light. Furthermore, only the more advanced intelligences have free access to these records or power to read them, but many have acquired a certain degree of power to read from astral reflections in the astral plane. Thus, it seems Cayce was able to access this universal library in his astral body? Cayce stated that we are held to account after life and 'confronted' with our personal Akashic record of what we've done in life. So, our choices do matter?

As it transpires, Cayce was torn between his 'ability' to go into trances, and his Christian faith. Cayce was apparently a deeply religious man, (and Sunday school teacher), who read the Bible more than sixty times, cover to cover. It's said he agonised over whether his psychic abilities, (which included seeing auras around people, speaking to angels, and hearing the voices of departed relatives), were from the 'highest source'. Moreover, many of his readings pertained to reincarnation, which is contrary to Biblical teachings.

Apparently at one point he wanted to quit his 'sessions' but in a reading for himself, he was informed that if he was no longer going to be a channel, his mission in life was complete. His trance voice, the 'we' of the readings, persuaded Cayce to continue with his readings, and so he did. Cayce then used his knowledge of the Bible to convince his family that reincarnation was biblically sound, together with other metaphysical teachings. 'The voice' called the shots, which included telling Cayce to move house, for example.

The 'voice' Cayce channelled in his trance readings divulged truth and lies. Like, Cayce declared the 'Piltdown man' was genuine (one of the many efforts used to indoctrinate us with evolution), and yet it was exposed as a hoax in 1953. And not all his predictions proved true. In Isaiah 44:25 God tells us, 'I am the one who exposes the false prophets as liars by causing events to happen that are contrary to their predictions'.

In fairness to Cayce however, he didn't know what he was prescribing or advising, given his slumber state. As touched on, it's understood that half-truths are more poisonous than straight up lies because they're more believable, and hence exacerbate confusion. The Bible tells us Satan is the author of confusion. Thus, there might be a modicum of truth to his belief in aliens, Atlantis, and the allegation that 'soul-entities' on Earth intermingled with animals to produce 'things' including giants that were twelve feet tall?

It's said most mediums can't control the spirits with whom they converse. Often the spirits provide a lot of information on trivial matters, but then trip them up on other occasions. As Paracelsus warned, these spirits have the propensity to lie. So, even if the psychic or medium seems lovely, the source of their intel might not have benevolent motives. And the proverbial 'good guys' may act nice, and divulge certain truths, because it suits their agenda.

Fundamentally, engaging with spirits is generally considered dangerous. It's understood that allowing some entity to use our minds and bodies is an avenue to madness. As Paracelsus advised, many mediums have become insane. It seems, that having engaged with spirits, they're difficult to shake off. They get attached like parasites. And what begins as spirit friends or guides, or seemingly dead chums, can turn into spirit enemies.

Neil Anderson (author of 'The Bondage Breaker', 1990) mentioned a trained channeller who felt like she'd lost her mind and didn't want to be a channel for those voices in her head anymore. But when she wouldn't play ball with them, they turned against her. It seems to be a risky profession that can result in psychosis?

It's also noted, many people who claim to have psychic gifts, often report having unhappy childhoods, including childhood sexual abuse. Apparently, there's a strong significant correlation between paranormal experiences and traumas, which includes childhood trauma and emotional abuse. The correlation between traumas and paranormal experiences is stronger than between traumas and paranormal beliefs, which implies paranormal experiences cannot intrinsically be associated with mental health disorders. As mentioned, the SRF posits that childhood abuse can precipitate vulnerability to spirit attachment, which in turn seems to birth psychic powers. And when people have OBEs (like with rape), they invariably discover the onset of psychic abilities.

It's purported that trauma in childhood can create a rent in the membrane between the material and spiritual worlds, with the result being the ability to communicate with spirits. Black (2010) highlights that with extreme childhood trauma, and a rent thereby caused in the psyche, spirits can rush in an uncontrollable way. Like, sodomising kids can release or invite kundalini serpent power? Black further states that disembodied spirits can break through unbidden, and that sometimes whole communities are possessed by a convulsion of uncontrollable sexual savagery (p.252 and p.59). No danger.

It's an interesting juncture that we infer mental illness exists by behaviour, but deny the spirit realm? It's seems we're okay believing in some things we can't see? We can rationalise that crazy behaviour is the result of dodgy genes and psychology? It's also noted, that like mental illness, psychic abilities are purportedly inherited. Like, Nina Kulagina believed she inherited her psychokinetic abilities from her mother.

It seems we're divided regarding the reality of the spiritual world. Whilst the scientific community denounces it, more than half of the population has had at least one paranormal experience. Maybe the truth is we're more comfortable with the material paradigm. Like Jung said, modern man finds it acceptable that entities encountered are not an actual reality. Whilst we might be partial to consulting a psychic, and going to yoga, presumably we don't want to answer to God, the Father of all Creation? And we'd rather not think about an evil devil who heads an army of evil angels?

And yet people are increasingly waking up to the reality that our world is run by Luciferian witches, who murder millions for material gain, and sexually abuse kids? The hidden hand, in some covert way, wants to make itself known. Hence, it hides itself in plain sight. Or maybe it has to? There seems to be legalities, or rules to this divine game. It seems God and the devil agreed on some terms and conditions back in the day? Like, they have to tell us their plans before they execute them, hence, 'predictive programming'? It's like we have to invite a vampire into our home. It's understood that by going to a medium, or playing with the Ouija board, partaking in witchcraft, getting Reiki healing etc, we invite the spirits in.

As far as the SPR is concerned, the hypothesis of intelligent forces, whether originating in the human psyche or from disincarnate sources, remains on the table. It seems the most viable hypothesis is intelligent forces are disincarnate entities that operate the human brain?

As discussed, we actively seek to reaffirm what we already believe, but this equally applies to secular atheists i.e. the starting point is spirits can't be real. But logically, there's too much evidence to write off. It's not normal for people to slither about and hiss like serpents, or for furniture to move on its own accord, or for objects to appear from nowhere. If psychiatrists are swimming in de Nile, that's their problem. To deny the evidence is crazier. Like, the overwhelming evidence for 'aliens and UFOs' is too much to dismiss. And like, the overwhelming evidence that we're constantly lied to. There's something funky going on, and we intuitively know it?

'Thirty Years Among the Dead' by Dr Carl Wickland (1924)

9

Can we Communicate with the Dead?

Psychiatrist Dr Wickland and his wife, who he pimped out as a psychic conduit for the alleged dead, were convinced we can. Thus, Mrs Wickland would enter an unconscious trance, and allow spirits to take temporary but complete possession of her body. Dr Wickland then interviewed the presenting spirit or personality. When taken over by another consciousness, Mrs Wickland used expressions that she'd never heard of before, and spoke in foreign languages that were totally unknown to her. Like, on one occasion she spoke Spanish and she didn't know Spanish.

Mrs Wickland mediated for hundreds of spirits and had no recollection of anything that transpired during this period. Dr Wickland notably cites Dr Thomas J Hudson, author of 'The Law of Psychic Phenomena', who said 'The man who denies the phenomena of spiritualism today is not entitled to be called a sceptic, he is simply ignorant'.

Dr Wickland recognised the interrelationship of the physical world and the spiritual world (which surrounds the physical). He believed the spirit plane and the earth plane are constantly intermingling. And he was in agreement with scripture (1 Corinthians 15: 44-46), that there's a natural body and a spirit body. He believed we're spiritual beings in a mortal body, and that the body is a house for our soul. Based on his research, (over thirty years), which consists of detailed reports of hundreds of experiences with alleged 'dead' people, Dr Wickland describes the conditions after death.

Thus, according to those on the other side, we're grievously wrong in our conception regarding the conditions prevailing after death. Apparently, there is no death, as the spirit is indestructible. But rather, death is a natural transition from the visible world to the invisible world. It's a transition to a happier and more beautiful state. Indeed, Dr Wickland believed 'the real life is on the other side of the grave'. One of Mrs Wickland's friends, Mrs Case, who'd passed on, said through a psychic, 'When there is understanding, there is no death. You only go to sleep in your earthly body and wake up in your spirit body with your friends about you. It is a very pleasant sensation'.

Apparently, we each get a home in the spirit world, by virtue of our service to others during our earthly life. Dr Wickland explains there's matter in the spirit world but it's more ethereal. Thus, we get a beautiful crib, with landscapes to die for (pun intended), if we lead a good life, but according to Dr Wickland, 'if you live only for yourself alone you will have only a little shanty' (p.304). Maybe Hitler got a tent? However, we can redeem ourselves, by service to others, and we can earn a good home. If we've been selfish, we can pay off our debt. We can evolve to become better souls.

Our nature seems to be important in the spirit world. Thus, it bodes well to be kind, helpful and loving towards our brethren. The emphasis is on serving others in order to move up the ranks. The spirit side of life is like a school, and this physical life is likened to pre-school. Apparently, the advanced spirits advised that reincarnation is a fallacy. So, we don't come back to pre-school but rather we have eternity to learn in the spirit world (we learn more when we die). With regards to actual school, apparently kids (who have died) can go to school on the spirit side of life to learn the lessons of earth.

It's said the spirit world is bliss, beautiful and harmonious. Yet it's also said, the spirit world is not idyllic heaven per se, as apparently we all have our ups and downs on the other side too. So, that blows. It's also noted, the implication is that our actions don't matter too much in this life, because we can get a grip in the afterlife? Everyone's eventually a winner.

However, not everyone transitions so easily. As Dr Wickland highlights, the dead are often lost and confused. They're spiritually blind, in a twilight condition. He said, 'passing through the change called death, a great majority remain in entire ignorance of their condition, and are bound for a time to the earth plane by their false doctrines' (p.275). Suffice to say, this state of confusion, having discovered we were lied to by the materialists, is understandable.

Thus, spirits are not aware of their spirit condition. It doesn't enter their minds that they're spirits. And without the right understanding, (not knowing any better), most of us become ignorant earthbound spirits. We hover around the earth plane in darkness, clinging to matter. Dr Wickland therefore advises that it's important to know where we're going after death, as wrong thinking, misconceptions, can literally keep us in the dark. Earthbound spirits need to be released from clinging onto false beliefs.

Dr Wickland informs that the distance between the spirit world and the world of matter is about sixty miles. He relays that the earth has a material sphere of ether around it, and this sphere is the world of spirits in darkness. This is the prison of ignorance. Spirits say the earth plane is a horrible gloomy darkness. But it appears they're not lonely, as apparently dead spirits see loads of other dead spirits. It's noted, scientists tell us 'outer space' begins circa sixty miles above earth. Thus, the first heaven (the air) is for earthbound spirits, and the second heaven is sixty miles above, where the sun, moon and stars are, where the angelic battle ensues?

So, the first hurdle, upon crossing over, is to realise that we have indeed crossed over. Fortunately however, for those deluded and otherwise helpless, there is help at hand. Like the yogis advised, advanced spirits or 'guiding intelligences' benevolently come to our aid, to instruct us about the higher laws. But if they can't get through to us, they take us to a psychic intermediary to make us realise that we're dead.

And this is where Team Wickland comes into play. Mrs Wickland allows the spirit to use her body and Dr Wickland tries to reason with their intelligence. But if they can't reason, the intelligent spirits take them away (they must be forced to leave by invisible co-workers), and Mrs Wickland returns to normal. Mrs Wickland was apparently protected at all times by intelligent spirits, known as 'The Mercy Band', and she had an Indian guide called 'Silver Star'. Dr Wickland states, that after thirty-five years of psychic work, Mrs Wickland remained unimpaired.

Apparently, a spirit in ignorance can't see intelligent spirits. It's said that earthbound spirits have lost physical sight, so they're blind until their spiritual eyes are opened, which defies astral vision? Mortal mediums are therefore required to assist the intelligent spirits, to get ignorant spirits to realise the truth. These spirits need to wake up and smell the proverbial coffee. Dr Wickland also notes that some earthbound spirits are asleep because they've been taught that death is a sleep. Ergo they literally need to be woken up and told the truth about the spirit world.

Apparently, their denial is the biggest obstacle to overcome. Many simply refuse to accept they're dead. Dr Wickland explained that he'd tell the spirits to look at their hands to realise they're in Mrs Wickland's body and not theirs. And sometimes he would hold up a mirror before them. However, many were obstinate and declared they were being hypnotised. Or could it be that these spirits were playing games with them? Dr Wickland observed that earthbound spirits resent the person's presence and are bewildered by the sense of dual personality. These misguided spirits believe the sensitive's body belongs to them (like DID?).

Once the spirit has grasped their reality, they leave Mrs Wickland's body and the intelligent spirits take care of them. They can then evolve in the spirit world, as their nature becomes increasingly benevolent and less selfish. Dr Wickland explains that we advance in stages or degrees, but according to the spirits, we will all eventually spiritually evolve and reach higher levels. He relays that those whose earthly interests have been superficial, who have been dominated by pride, vanity, greed, ambition and selfishness, are held in the earth sphere after transition until these tendencies have been conquered, and love and sympathy have been developed through service for others.

Spirits who become enlightened return the favour and help others to understand. Apparently, everyone who is converted goes into The Mercy Band as a helper to assist those on earth and the spirit side. Like, Mrs Case joined The Mercy Band.

But furthermore, apparently earthbound spirits migrate towards mortals, as they're attracted to the magnetic light that emanates from us. Dr Wickland explains that every human has a magnetic aura (our psychic light seems to emanate from our magnetic nervous system), and this aura is visible as light to earthbound spirits in their condition of darkness. They see our light bodies. These spirits thus come to obsess mortals. They become imprisoned in our magnetic auras. But it seems some people are more 'sensitive' to obtruding spirits than others. Like, Mrs Wickland was a 'psychic sensitive'. And this is where the madness begins. Dr Wickland recognised that those susceptible to obsession by spirits were susceptible to madness. Sensitives end up in asylums.

Dr Wickland explained, 'humanity is surrounded by the thought influence of millions of disincarnate beings....' and 'a recognition of this fact accounts for a great portion of unbidden thoughts, emotions, strange forebodings, gloomy moods, irritabilities, unreasonable impulses, irrational outbursts of temper, uncontrollable infatuations and countless other vagaries'. It's duly noted, this corroborates with autonomous complexes. And kids are not exempt, as Dr Wickland states spirits can attach to kids causing bad tempers.

Earthbound spirits, (whilst they might not be aware of it), can intrude on our mental space, and impart their thoughts and emotions. Dr Wickland wrote, 'This encroachment alters the characteristics of the sensitive, resulting in a seemingly changed personality, sometimes simulating multiple or dissociated personalities, and frequently causes apparent insanity, varying in degree from a simple mental aberration to, and including, all types of dementia, hysteria, epilepsy, melancholia, shell shock, kleptomania, idiocy, religious and suicidal mania, as well as amnesia, psychic invalidism, dipsomania, immorality, functional bestiality, atrocities, and other forms of criminality'.

Like those described as demon possessed, Dr Wickland highlights that insane patients, who become very wild and unmanageable, fight with such violence that several persons are required to restrain them. He also observed the constant swearing and extraordinary vile language, the coma states, fainting spells, and seizures. They can refuse food, mumble idiotically or rave/rant on, harm themselves (e.g. pull out their hair and hit themselves) and others, and become deaf and dumb. Thus, he also recognised that illness or disability, like deafness, is often due to demonical possession.

Dr Wickland conceded that people influenced by obsessing spirits frequently experience total amnesia, total memory lapse. Like DID, all sense of identity is lost and the victim wanders to strange places, returning to his normal self without any knowledge of his recent actions. When 'taken over', people can suddenly become violent, destructive and rip their clothes off.

Dr Wickland further states that some particularly malevolent spirits obsess people and cause them to murder others or commit suicide. Apparently, these evil spirits are happy and laugh when people kill themselves. Dr Wickland asserts that often murderers don't know of their crimes because a vengeful spirit has done it. Indeed, he states the majority of murders and hold-ups are committed by spirits.

Thus, not all spirits are merely ignorant, and attach to us because they don't know any better (they're drawn like a moth to a flame). But rather, they can be deliberately malevolent and vengeful. Dr Wickland highlights that haunted homes are often frequented by spirits who seek revenge for wrong-sufferings during their life. They can actively haunt us, by rapping's and noises. They can make our life hell.

Dr Wickland advised that many earthbound spirits are conscious of influencing mortals but enjoy their power, seeming to be without scruples. These obsessing spirits purposively torment helpless sensitives, interfering with them. He states these spirits frequently cause their victims to commit deeds of violence upon themselves and do not seem to suffer from the pain they inflict upon the physical body of the sensitive. It appears they impress sensitives with morbid and suicidal thoughts, because they hate us, and get off on our pain?

Like Swedenborg, Dr Wickland didn't believe in demons per se, but rather so-called demons are spirits of wicked men. He perpetuated the idea that nasty people become nasty spirits. He said, 'these earthbound spirits are the supposed "devils" of all ages; "devils" of human origin, by-products of human selfishness, false teachings and ignorance, thrust blindly into a spirit existence and held there in bondage of ignorance'.

Or maybe earthbound spirits are demons, particularly since Dr Wickland advised that ignorant spirits look like snakes, and humans can have three or four spirits crawling on them. Do dead evil human souls look like snakes? This corroborates with others, who have astral vision, who claim they see snakes and serpents crawling up buildings and slithering along in public spaces.

Apparently spirits also convey their former ails onto sensitives. The deluded spirits feel like they're still in physical pain and thus sensitives endure all the pain of the spirits former physical condition e.g. broken back or whatever. This gives rise to pseudo illness, psychic invalidism and chronic lassitude. There is no physical cause, which resonates with functional and psychosomatic illness?

Dr Wickland explains that we carry physical sensations in our mind. Spirits also use mortals as a means to satisfy their addictions. Dr Wickland believed that habits, desires and inclinations are rooted in the mind. Cravings belong to the soul not the body, and remain with the individual even when they're freed from their physical body. Hence, if we're partial to morphine in this life, this desire will continue after death. So, earthbound spirits obsess people, and can party through us.

In essence, earthbound spirits cause all kinds of bedlam, and in Dr Wickland's professional opinion, asylums are full of obsessed people controlled by earthbound spirits. He asserts that doctors don't know how to stop the insanity. And mad people are being mistreated in asylums for it is not understood they're obsessed by spirits who control them.

He highlights that psychoanalysts are loathed to accept the hypothesis of disincarnate intelligences, and instead advance theories that psychoses have their origin in some psychic lesion or trauma, that is concealed or forgotten. Modern psychologists disclaim the possibility of foreign intelligences, and instead refer to DID and dissociate states of consciousness. But he alternatively pertains to the spirits role in psychoneuroses and insanities. Rather than autonomous complexes, he insists spirits are behind the voices 'insane' people hear, and the 'ghosts' they see. Maybe if the phenomenon seems to be disincarnate beings, it is?

Dr Wickland also draws attention to the fact that many seemingly harmless experiments with automatic writing and Ouija boards resulted in wild insanity that commitment to asylums was necessary. He asserts these practices are very dangerous, as earthbound spirits use them to come through. He mentions Mrs B, whose attempt at automatic writing led to mental derangement and altered personality. Normally she was amiable, pious, quiet and refined, but she became boisterous and noisy, romped about and danced, used vile language, and claiming she was an actress, insisted upon dressing for the stage, saying she had to be at the theatre at a certain time or she would lose her position. Finally, she became so irresponsible she was placed in an asylum.

He mentions a few cases, who following the same practices, went from being 'normal' (nice and refined) to mentally deranged and violent. People become delusional, believing they're Napoleon etc. Dr Wickland insists offending spirits are the cause of aberration. And there may be a number of spirits in the same person. He said the afflicted sensitive person can get lost under the overwhelming control of a spirit or a crowd of spirits.

The aim is thus to attract obsessing entities from the crazy person to a psychic intermediary, like Mrs Wickland. Dr Wickland's method of choice was shocking them out with electrical treatment. Apparently, spirits can be chased out with static electricity. When static sparks are applied, the spirit detaches from the sensitive. Dr Wickland explains that although this electricity is harmless to the patient, it is exceedingly effective for transferring the 'psychosis' from patient to medium. It's like passing the hot psychotic potato, as when transferred, the victim is relieved. The otherwise insane become sane again. Dr Wickland insists this proves that such personalities are independent entities.

He observed that people suffer greatly from the annoyance of hearing voices ('auditory hallucinations') of obsessing spirits, but these spirits can be dislodged and transferred to the psychic intermediary. Maybe secular psychiatrists could experiment with this? Why not, if people are crazy enough to mediate for them? And perhaps there's more going on with ECT and electrifying the brain? Maybe ECT cures patients because it zaps the spirits out?

The spirits are apparently not happy campers when shocked. And they don't want to leave their cosy-pies host. It seems wayward spirits have to learn, or be made to. Apparently if spirits are naughty, and don't heed the advice from the advanced spirits, they can be sent for timeout in a dark dungeon (LOL). Dr Wickland states that advanced spirits can place us in dark dungeons if we're not sensible and willing to learn the truths. Maybe some deviants like the dark dungeons?

But moreover, the identities of the spirits and the information they provided checks out i.e. how, where, when and why they died. Upon investigations, what they disclosed was verified and proven true. Like, they were a six year old girl, called Isabelle who lived on Love Street, who fell out a window on May 1st 1905. These spirits spoke about their lives as if they were their lives. The spirits appeared to be who they claimed they were. Or they knew intimate details about the life and death of someone they were enacting.

Clairvoyants can apparently see the invisible company we keep, and they can also see tormenting spirits being transferred and then expelled. Perhaps we can feel sorry for earthbound spirits, as these spirits suffer. And sometimes they suffer for years in the earth plane because they don't know any better. Hence, mediums like Mrs Wickland are invaluable. Earthbound spirits are blessed to have the opportunity to have a human body to get understanding. The Wickland's also mediated for spirits in psychic circles. They would concentrate on certain 'dead' people, and their spirits would sometimes appear.

The spirits taught Dr Wickland that hell and the devil are imaginary. Thus, he believed 'Satan' is more like a concept for selfishness, ignorance and bigotry. And hell is a state of being i.e. we create heaven or hell through our thinking. He propagated that leaders of the church schemed to scare people to obey, by saying the devil would get them and they would go to hell and damnation.

Dr Wickland acknowledges the Bible teaches much, but claimed it's not to be taken literally or historically. He considers the Bible manmade and disputes that Jesus died for our sins. He seems to think we don't sin. His belief was that we're part of God, and thus we have no sin. There's therefore no need for Jesus, (or His brutal sacrifice), as there's no sin to atone for. God is the spirit of the universe and we are part of that Great Spirit of love, wisdom and knowledge. We are One and God is the divine in everything. So, even the evil serpentine souls are God and have no sin?

Dr Wickland highlights that spirit guides are often American Indians, because they don't have any dogma etc to overcome. They believe that we're part of the 'The Great Spirit of all Things', so they're not usually earthbound. It's purported that religion hinders our awakening in the spirit world, as we cling onto false beliefs. Like, believing in the Jesus creed, for example, keeps us out of the higher spirit world. Dr Wickland concedes that Christ taught us to love and serve others, but regards Jesus as merely an evolved spirit as opposed to God incarnate. We thus need to get rid of any fixed ideas about God as it prevents us from moving on.

Medicine men also know how to control Nature and they know the laws of protection. Hence, they're adept at protecting mediums from earthbound spirits. Dr Wickland states when they pray, they use the higher force of life. They say little, but dance around in a big circle and concentrate. Sometimes they have a snake dance. They have learned to charm snakes so they will not bite. So, we're back to serpent worship?

For Dr Wickland, Spiritualism is the true gospel of God. He believed what 'higher spirits' told him, which is arguably naive? Like, those who channel 'aliens'? It didn't seem to occur to him that they could be deceptive liars. Dr Wickland announced a new religion will come, based on the 'truths' given by the spirits. He said this religion will bring true understanding, and all the people will open their eyes and see the truth of God's manifestation. He envisioned churches having psychic circles.

However, that prediction aside, and in summary, it seems madness could be exterminated. Dr Wickland was very successful in treating people, (kids and adults), otherwise misdiagnosed as insane on account of obsessing spirits. Maybe we need a revolution, aka an open-mind regarding spirits, in our mental health services? Maybe the mad Hatters are being spiritually violated?

Before we finish here, it seems pertinent to mention two infamous spirits that appeared via Mrs Wickland, namely, Mary Baker Eddy (1821-1910), founder of Christian Science, and Madam Helena Petrovna Blavatsky (1831-1891), founder of Theosophy, because both women were hugely influential. Eddy's book 'Science and Health with Key to the Scriptures' (1975), the movement's textbook, has been a bestseller for decades. And Blavatsky's theosophy (i.e. we're God) seems to be the New Age Luciferian religion. It inspires the shadow government or 'hidden hand'. Eddy made her appearance on February 24th 1918, although she popped by a few times, and Blavatsky popped by on November 1st 1922. It seems Mrs Wickland was like a drop-in centre.

Eddy believed that sickness was a state of mind, and that people could be spiritually healed. It was after her own brush with death, that she gained a powerful insight into God's healing Spirit. She stated, 'My immediate recovery from the effects of an injury caused by an accident, an injury that neither medicine nor surgery could reach, was the falling apple that led me to the discovery how to be well myself, and how to make others so' (Retrospection and Introspection, 1891 p.24).

Eddy had been reading about Jesus' healings and endorsed them. She believed we could all be healed from human suffering and sin, as God's divine laws apply to us all. She believed that we create our condition with the power of mind e.g. if we have fear, we're negative. She said, 'the average doctor tells a patient that he has such and such a sickness. He creates a fear in his mind'.

However, despite condemning doctors for telling patients they're sick, it's alleged she was a lifelong slave to morphine. It's also noted, that whilst Eddy became known as a Christian healer, she was also a renowned medium. It's alleged that she channelled Abraham Lincoln. Apparently, Abe Lincoln is an advanced spirit who helps earthbound spirits, and gives lectures on the spirit side of life. So, that's nice. Eddy wrote in her later publications that she'd never been a spiritualist. It's understood that she attempted to distinguish Christian Science from Spiritualism.

However, when Eddy made her appearance in Mrs Wickland, she advised that she was a trance medium. She stated that she was obsessed as a young child, and had queer spells, but no-one had any idea why. But she knew that an influence was controlling her. She said that all through her life, she was back and forth on the invisible plane. And thus, having been to the spirit world many times and always returning to earth, she found it odd when she died, that she couldn't return the way she always had. She said that when she woke up, after death, in her spiritual body, she felt she could go back to earth and it was hard to realise that she no longer had a physical body. Apparently, she met her brother, first husband, friends etc when she passed over.

Eddy knew first-hand that obsession is real. She knew spirits return and obsess people, and she purported that by learning this truth, people could be cured of their ills. Her philosophy was also that people can become well by concentrating that one is not sick (p.325). Eddy stressed the importance of concentration and meditation. She said, 'That is the secret of health – concentration is the secret of power'. She appreciates that it takes much practice to master meditation, but she explained that by concentrating, we gain strength and power. We will feel powerful because we have part of life itself – God. And we can heal with that power. But maybe this power is not from God? It seems through meditation we summon kundalini serpent power.

Eddy also said, (via Mrs Wickland), that she wanted money and 'concentrated' to have the grandest churches in the world. She admitted she was selfish and wanted a religion of her own, but for the whole world. She wanted to be looked up to, with people under her thumb. She said she sold her soul for money, and shut the door to love and sympathy. Apparently, a pamphlet was published called 'Confession by Mrs Eddy, from the Spirit World'. Like, she confessed that she knew that spirits return to obsess people, but she taught that spirits don't return.

Eddy said that when she went into trances, she wrote a great deal but when she came to herself, she would deny what she got. She regrets not writing the books that were given to her, and crediting their source, as she could have revolutionised the world. Her visions were however, apparently written into her 'Science and Health' book.

Contrary to the biblical message, she purported that God is all Life i.e. pantheism and that we have the infinite spirit within us. We have the spark of the divine within us, and we can become one with God. And fundamentally, we have power because we're part of God. With regards to the Bible, she said it's a beautiful book if it's read spiritually. But she concedes that it's not to be taken literally, or as history. Interestingly, she said God is electricity, flowers, colours. It seems we live in an electric universe?

Eclipsing Eddy however, is Blavatsky. Blavatsky was an exceptional medium, and whilst we'll get back to her, it seems pertinent to note that contrary to what she taught when she was alive, when Blavatsky visited the Wickland's, she advised that reincarnation is a mistake (p.335). She realised this was a false doctrine when she passed over. So, despite her former teachings on reincarnation, the ghost of Blavatsky insists there's no such thing. Her spirit self advised that she was now working to get her victims free from their wrong beliefs. Earthbound spirits, believing themselves reincarnated, were obsessing mortals and she was in part responsible for perpetuating this myth.

Reincarnation really means to obsess sensitives. Like, spirits endeavour to 'reincarnate' in children but it really means obsessing them and causing insanity. The ghost of Blavatsky advised, 'Memories of 'past lives' are caused by spirits that bring such thoughts and represent the lives they lived. A spirit impresses you with the experiences of its life and these are implanted in your mind as your own. You then think you remember your past'. Like Eddy, Blavatsky similarly divulged she wanted to be a leader. And she also acknowledged that she became obsessed.

She explained that as a student of theosophy, you remove yourself as much as possible from the physical. Naturally, you become sensitive, and naturally you feel the spirits around you. They speak to you by impressions. You feel their past and make the mistake of taking this for the memory of former incarnations. We believe these memories are ours, deducting that we've been reincarnated.

So, although she believed and taught it, she insists reincarnation is not true. We progress in the spirit world, we do not come back. She highlighted that spirits can impress all kinds of ideas on our consciousness, like the idea we're Julius Caesar. Blavatsky says, 'you can make people believe almost anything' (p.355). Blavatsky said she could 'concentrate' on others to reach them i.e. she could give them 'pictures'.

Blavatsky asserted that masters in theosophy have great minds. She explained a Master is one who can master matter, and overcome matter, and who can live a good life. They learn the lessons of Nature and learn how to progress. She advocated Nature worship because God is Nature. We worship God's manifestation, which includes us. Blavatsky states most who want to be Masters on earth fall, as they become so sensitive, so psychic, that earthbound spirits step in and control them so they fall. She also highlighted that when you study yoga, you learn to leave the body. She said Hindus study yoga to leave the body at will and travel the spirit world.

It's further purported that spirits are the source of wisdom and the real inventors. Blavatsky the ghost said, 'We have everything in the spirit world, because everything that is invented on earth has first been invented in the spirit world' (p.353). Apparently, spirits find sensitives and impress their inventions on their minds. Spirits can also impress ideas on our mind when we're dreaming. Like, Friedrich August Kekule, who discovered the benzene ring in 1865 when dreaming. Kekule knew it had six carbon atoms, but the structure was a mystery. Then in his dream he saw chains of carbon atoms, writhing like snakes, but then suddenly the snake began biting its tail, which provided the answer to the riddle. Namely, benzene was a ring of carbon atoms surrounded by hydrogen atoms.

As touched on, the ouroboros, which is an ancient symbol of a serpent eating its own tail, is important to occultists. It symbolises wholeness and infinity. [Apparently snakes do try to eat themselves if they're stressed out]. And Blavatsky adopted this symbol for her Theosophical Society. Theosophy teaches that during sleep one develops mentally and spiritually. It's said the soul leaves the body, connected only by a slender thread, and gains experiences in the mental or astral plane. Some dreams are meaningless, others are real experiences.

So, it's alleged 'advanced' spirits want to help us? Like Dr Wickland, Blavatsky also dreams of psychic circles in every church. They concur that spirits help Prime Ministers and Presidents with their speeches etc. They can inspire and empower world leaders. Like Hitler?

Synopsis of 'From Witchcraft to Christ' (1973)

10

Doreen Irvine

Preface by Arthur Neil

'The record of Doreen Irvine is quite incredible, and I authenticate it wholeheartedly. It was in Bristol in 1964 that our paths first crossed. Her condition was that of unbelievable evil, for her life had been immersed in debauchery of a kind I had never before come across.

For seven months I knew what it was to wrestle with terrible powers of evil in relation to her life. On the occasion of every period of exorcism she had to be held down by others (Christian men and women) in prayerful support.

The New Testament came alive in terms of encounters with demons of different character, who contested the ground they had in her life. With extraordinary intelligence, utterly beyond the human, they acted and spoke through her and yet certainly not from her mind.

I well remember the night in February 1965 when, following my preaching engagement in a Bristol church, the last of the forty-seven demons were expelled from her tormented and tortured being. Ended was a prolonged and dangerous period of seven months of hell in a life and death struggle.

Doreen is a trophy of God's grace. The power of God was demonstrated in her remarkable supernatural deliverance by the dynamic authority of the Lord Jesus Christ. All the credit and glory go to Him who did it. It was my awful privilege simply to be His instrument as I was enlightened and enabled by the Holy Spirit to be at His disposal for His ends of victory and transformation in her life.

The subsequent events since 1965 confirm the reality and validity of the work of God in Doreen Irvine. She is being used graciously and greatly by her Lord in this and other lands for the spread of the Gospel in its fullness. Her book makes a vital contribution in warning those who indulge in the deep things of Satan; it serves to open the eyes of Christians to the stark reality of the demonic in these days in our land and to the means of grace in the way of deliverance through our Lord Jesus Christ.

There can be no doubt about the blatant way in which the forces of darkness are at work in the world today. The rapidly increasing interest in and practice of magic, its sinister association with occultism, witchcraft, and Satanism, are grim factors of awful portent. That there are strange and malevolent powers at work in supernatural reality behind the scenes is both a scriptural truth and a fact of experience.

Jesus Christ Himself expressed most lucidly the reality of a personal devil and of myriads of demons acting in evil ways to oppress, obsess and possess people. The nature of the conflict between good and evil, God and the devil, is the theme of the Bible.

To every true believer in the Lord Jesus Christ, salvation means release from the bondage of Satan and the dominion of evil. It brings victory over the powers of diabolical wrong through the authority of His perfect and supreme command....' (Winter 1972)

* * * * * * *

Doreen Irvine (1939-2011) was brought up in London town. Her alcoholic father did little in the way of parenting or working, and her mother left the family home when Doreen was eleven on account of his adultery. Her dad's mistress subsequently moved in, with her two kids, into the already cramped tenancy. The mistress was also a boozer, so Doreen was left to look after her own younger sisters, as well as the two new kids. Her relationship with the 'other woman' was fraught with tension and grief. So, she left home at fourteen to work as a cleaner but after nine months of trials, she made her way to the Big Smoke, in true Dick Wittington style, believing the streets to be paved with gold.

As it transpired however, the dream was just that. Not reality. And instead her reality became hooking, stripping, drinking, smoking, taking heroin and stealing. She became known as 'Daring Diana'. Her life spiralled out of control and she was depressed. Her theft resulted in a three-month prison service (and cold turkey). And despite the ideation to change her ways following her custodial release, she nevertheless returned to her old tricks.

Moreover however, through a couple of colleagues, she was invited to a Satanist temple to observe the most ancient order of Satanism in the world (she had to be blindfolded en route to ensure anonymity of the meeting place). What she observed, she described as astonishing and very mysterious.

Thus, she was in a large hall filled with about five hundred people. A platform at the front was draped in black, and on a throne-like seat sat a robed and hooded figure. His garments were adorned with snakes, dragons, and flames of fire. Around him in a semi-circle stood some thirteen figures, also robed in black, the priests and priestesses of the order of Satanism. The ceremony began with chanting. This strange and rhythmic chant grew louder as the robed figure in the centre stepped down from the platform. Two of the priests removed his hood, and everyone bowed down and worshipped him. As the chief Satanist, and representative of Satan on earth, he must be obeyed at all times.

The whole congregation then began chanting prayers to the chief Satanist in that same strange rhythmic way. Everyone's eyes were on him as he kissed the vessels, the knives and the emblem of Satanists that had been taken from the high altar to dedicate them to Lucifer. The dim lights then went out and flaming torches were lit. She then observed the effigies of Satan, and noted they seemed to come alive as the ceremony continued. A white cockerel was brought in, and its neck was wrung on the steps that led up to the throne and altar. Blood was everywhere, and then the cockerel was offered to Satan in sacrifice.

More chants and prayers ensued. Everything was done in the name of Satan, 'Diablos', and all appeared excited and in deadly earnest. The whole ceremony lasted some two hours, and she witnessed all manner of evil. The site of the temple was frequently moved elsewhere if there was any danger of it being discovered by outsiders. Secrecy is a must in the temple.

As it transpired, the chief Satanist was interested in Doreen and she became his mistress. He advised her that 'all kinds of people are Satanists' i.e. from the high to the low – bankers, shopkeepers, teachers, nurses, prostitutes, drug addicts, with there being no difference between them. Their mission statement is to promote Satan on the earth whenever and however they can.

Followers are taught that evil is not wrong but on the contrary, good and right. Satanists distort everything, insisting that lies are truth, and with such insistence and repetition of that, even very intelligent people believe it. Minds are twisted and warped. To become a Satanist, one must adhere to the rules of Satanism. Thus,

1. Secrecy is the keynote for all Satanists. They must never reveal the whereabouts of the temple to outsiders or the things that go on inside the temple.
2. All must love, honour and obey without question the chief Satanist, who is Lucifer's representative on the earth. Satanists must follow Satan all the days of their life and serve no other but him.
3. Satanists must never enter a Christian church unless sent in to spy by the chief Satanist. All new ideas and fresh happenings are to be reported back in full to the chief Satanist at the temple of Satan.
4. Satanists must never read the Holy Bible for their own edification.
5. The Holy Scriptures are to be mocked and burned in the Satanists temple, also prayer books and hymn books – in fact, all Christian literature must be destroyed. [This order dates back centuries].
6. No one must arrive late at the temple. Punishment by whipping will be carried out on all latecomers by the chief Satanist in front of the whole congregation.
7. Lucifer must be highly esteemed in all situations, even while at work or in private. Lucifer sees, as he is with Satanists always, and he must be obeyed. Lying, cheating, swearing, free lust – even murder – are condoned.
8. Prayer to Lucifer must be made daily.

There are more dogmatic rules and all who fail to obey them are punished by whipping in front of all Satanists at the temple. The whippings are carried out by the chief Satanist himself.

Doreen advised that her drug addiction, stripping and prostitution, paled in comparison to her worship of Satan and the necessary evils that entailed. The chief Satanist was not perturbed by Daring Diana's prostitution, and he supported her heroin addiction with free brown. He believed the more evil he condoned or achieved in earth, the greater would be his reward. If and when he died, he believed he would be in charge of legions of devils, so the greater the evil, the greater the reward.

After some time, Doreen was ready to become a 'sworn in child of Lucifer', which involved a complicated and lengthy ceremony, with more than eight hundred Satanists present from other temples. All were, of course, punctual since forget the whipping. Doreen commented that no one was ever late for any meeting. [Fair play].

As for the initiation then, Doreen advised that she was dressed in a loose black robe, whilst hymns and prayers were chanted to the great god of darkness, death and mystery. Flaming torches sent weird shadows racing across the walls and ceiling. The vessels on the high altar were dedicated one by one, and the silver knives kissed. The chief Satanist rose from his throne and raised his hands, whereupon all fell down and worshipped him. Two priests then broke and split open the neck of a white cockerel, and caught its blood in a silver cup. More chants and prayers to Satan followed, and Doreen remarks that the air was heavy with evil.

The chief Satanist then approached Doreen and made an incision in her left arm, whereby her blood was caught in the cup that contained the blood from the slain bird. The knife was again kissed, and the blood mixed. Doreen then drank some of that blood and made vows to Satan. She then dipped her finger into the mixed blood and signed a real parchment, thereby selling her soul to Satan, to be his slave for all eternity. Doreen thus became a true Satanist, and all present rejoiced that another child of Satan was born. She said the people went crazy, and all kinds of evil scenes followed, and much wickedness was done that evening.

Doreen was also sworn in as high priestess, great priestess Diana, despite her protesting that she wasn't ready for such a position. The chief Satanist said that it was a request of the great Lucifer himself, and he must be obeyed. She could serve better her master in that position. She was qualified to handle the sacred vessels and wait at the high altar. She thus became a leader in Satanism.

She advised that she heard Lucifer's audible voice and saw him materialise. On occasion, Lucifer materialised in a black form before all the Satanists in the temple. No one disbelieved it was Satan speaking to the whole congregation. He said 'I am Lucifer, your master. I speak unto you from my lips. Obey my voice, my children. Do all the evil you wish. Never fear – I will protect you at all times. Revel in your freedom of lust this night. It is pleasing in my sight.' Doreen said all obeyed the nasty time without question.

Doreen advised that in olden times one or two chiefs had power from Lucifer to perform operations on themselves and others. No drugs were used in these operations, and no scars remained where incisions were made. This notably corroborates with psychic surgeons.

Doreen states deep trances are practised which enables one to see powerful activity in the demon sphere. Doreen advises that ESP was one of her powers, whereby she could read people's minds easily and know what they would say or do. As the months went by, her knowledge of evil grew. She advised that her devil worship and role as high priestess was her raison d'être. She advised that even away from the temple, Satan's presence was very real, an unseen hand pushing her further into the realms of darkness. She elaborates that she required very little sleep and had supernatural strength and endurance. She advised that she was truly a slave of Satan and kept her vows well.

The chief Satanist was also a black witch and practiced black magic. Doreen explains witchcraft of the black kind is not far removed from Satanism. The main difference is that Satanists worship the devil in a Satanist's temple, whereas witches attend a coven of thirteen witches, one of whom is the head. They require no temple. It can thus be practiced anywhere but preferably in a remote setting, such as a deserted house, a lonely beach or wood. [Warlock is the correct name for a witch]. The witching hour of midnight is preferred, and activities are conducted by moonlight.

She states black witches have great power and are not to be taken lightly. They can summon powers of darkness to aid them. Doreen concedes that black witches have power to put curses on people, and the curses work. People have been known to die because of the curse or spell of the black witch. Nude rites are another evil aspect of witchcraft. Very often they exhume fresh graves and offer the bodies in sacrifice to Satan. They break into churches, burn Bibles and prayer books. Further, whenever holy ground is desecrated, an emblem of witchcraft is left behind e.g. goats blood splashed on headstones of graves, or walls etc. They hold nothing sacred and will stop at nothing to pursue their goals.

Black witches and Satanists believe that evil triumphs in the ultimate battle between good and evil. They believe that Lucifer will one day conquer Christ and will retrieve what they call his rightful place. Satan, they affirm, will rule the earth, sea, and heavens. Hell is not a place of torment but of unlimited pleasure, with every lust fulfilled. 'The more evil, the better' is the motto of a black witch and Satanist. Doreen further warns that those who walk down the dark road of witchcraft lose their reason, often going completely insane.

The chief Satanist advised Doreen that she would make a fine witch on account of her natural power. Doreen however maintains that whilst aware of that power, it was not natural. She was not born with it, but rather it was a supernatural power working through her. It was Satan's power not hers.

She advised that she witnessed evil and ugly orgies in the Satanists temple, but that she witnessed far worse in the witches' coven. At her initiation, she was smeared with goat's blood, all over her naked body, and more evil ensued. She informed that all meetings included awful scenes of perverted sexual acts, as sex plays an important part in witchcraft. Many black witches are homos and tri-sexuals, that is, try anything. Sadism was frequently practised. Some even cut themselves and felt no pain, or swallowed poison without any ill effects.

Doreen advised that her powers were very great as a black witch. She was able to levitate four or five feet, (as aided by demons), kill birds in flight after they had been let loose from a cage, and she could make objects appear and disappear (she mastered 'apport'). She highlights these skills are often used when witches demonstrate their powers before others. Doreen was then asked to test her powers for the conquest of Queen of Black Witches, which took place in Dartmoor in Devon, the centre of two large and active covens.

As it transpired however, whilst the naked members of the coven were conducting their rituals, three men happened to be approaching. And as there was nowhere to hide, Doreen was able to make them invisible. She said they all stood perfectly still in a circle, and raised their hands so they touched. Doreen advised that she called up powers of darkness from demons and Satan himself, and within seconds a green swirling mist enveloped them. Apparently, the men didn't see anything, neither the witches nor the thick swirling mist. After the men left, the mist slowly disappeared. Apparently one of the men was a preacher and despite Doreen attempting to put a curse on him, it didn't work, which evidenced the power of Jesus Christ. Doreen advised there was a barrier between her power and the preacher, and that was the first time her powers failed her.

That event was followed by the great ceremony at which the next Queen of Black Witches was to be chosen. Black witches from all over England, Germany, Holland and France arrived, just before Halloween. They arrived in smart cars and stayed in classy hotels, a prosperous and almost respectable veneer which concealed the tremendous forces of evil.

The ceremony commenced with chants to the ancient gods (e.g. moon goddess Diana, who Doreen was named after) and demons, and then the great test of power began. Apparently seven witches were competing for the title. Again, Doreen killed a bird, released from a cage, in flight, and various other tests. The last test was to pass through a great bonfire, where the successful candidate would meet Lucifer in the centre of the blaze. Lucifer would be seen by the assembly to take the hand of the witch and guide her through the flames so that she would emerge completely unscathed.

Doreen advised that she walked confidently into the flames of seven feet and higher, all the time calling on her great master, Diablos. She advised that she saw him materialise, a great black figure, and she took his hand and walked with him to the centre of the great blaze. When she emerged at the other side of the blaze Diablos disappeared. She reports there was not even the smell of burning on her long robe or hair. Everyone, over a thousand witches, were prostrated on the ground, and cried out 'Hail, Diana, Queen of Black Witches'.

A crown of pure gold was placed on her head, a cloak beautifully embroidered was thrown around her shoulders, and an orb of gold was placed in her left hand (like the Queen). She then took her seat on the throne. Wild and frenzied celebrations followed.

As the highly esteemed 'Queen of Black Witches', Doreen had to study, work and travel, which she did in luxury. There was no language barrier as Doreen could call on Lucifer to help her and it was not long before she could understand the various tongues and converse with ease. The project/mission was to make witchcraft look natural, mysterious and exciting, which appeals to the masses, rather than mentioning blood sacrifices. The endeavour is to promote the occult.

Doreen advised that whilst white witches claim they never harm people, she encountered some that did. Like, some use 'fith fath', a doll made of clay in the image of the person they wish to harm, which is the same as voodoo dolls used by black witches. She states they use a pin on the image to seal the lips of the person represented by the doll, and tie a cord to the legs to inflict pain to the person's legs. As mentioned, whether it's white or black witchcraft, the source of power is the same.

Doreen was Queen of Black Witches for a full year, and whilst she could have retained the title, she stepped down for another witch to enjoy the dark glory. As Queen Witch, Doreen was more of a prostitute who lived a life of luxury.

Doreen thought she was forever trapped because she had sold her soul to Satan with her own blood. And as a good little Satanist, she went out her way to slander Christianity. She advised that she went to a church meeting with the sole purpose of punching the preacher's face, and whilst drunk and wasted, she instantly sobered up and felt the truth pierce her soul. Doreen wanted to go to the front for prayer, but she advised that chains seemed to bind her to her seat as she heard the audible voice of Diablos say 'you are MINE. You cannot go. It's too late for you. You are MINE'. She advised that she was shaking from head to foot. A great battle was going on with the powers of darkness and Satan. A tearful Doreen however made it to the front and subsequently left the church to go home and read her Bible.

Lucifer however continued to audibly tell her that she belonged to him and there was no escape. She wondered if she was going mad hearing two different voices saying two entirely different things. Despite Lucifer's increasingly more frightening commands, she was eddying towards Jesus. She advised that the night she returned from church, Lucifer was stood by her bed. There was no mistaking him. She had seen him many times in the past and heard his audible voice many times.

He told her again that she was his and must obey him. He threatened that she would die if she spent time with Christians. His form and his face were black and twisted, and his voice ugly with hate and threats. She felt his hairy hands reach out and grab her throat and despite her desire to be released, she remained in Lucifer's dreadful grip. She is clear that it was not her imagination but on the contrary, it was very real and very awful.

As Doreen continued to seek Jesus, Lucifer increased his efforts to keep her chained and bound. She advised that she wandered into many churches, and sometimes when the blood of Jesus was heard, a dark force within her took control of her and strange things occurred. She acted in inexplicable, satanic ways. She advised that she snatched Bibles and tore them, threw hymn books around the church, would knock communion trays out of the hands of those who were taking round the bread and wine. She would fall to the floor screaming, hissing and slithering like a snake. Then quite suddenly she would come to herself and remember nothing.

Very often she would run out of the church crying. Some suspected she was mentally ill, but she knew that it was not herself that willed those actions, but rather a dark evil within her that took control.

Doreen advised about an unseen hand pushing her to do the very things she wanted to give up. She spoke about being controlled by some evil power deep within. And she notes that whenever she heard the gospel preached, the evil forces within her became activated and many evil manifestations continued.

She highlights another occasion when she went to the house of God to pray, she advised that the moment she entered the evil powers took control. When she came to herself, much to her horror, she saw smashed communion glasses and spilt wine, and bewildered looks from the congregation. She again ran out sobbing, and again Lucifer mocked her. He told her it was best to die and end it all. In her despair, she went to top herself but a stranger intervened and she ended up seeing two Christians who calmed her down and prayed for her. At that the evil forces within her became active again and fought the ministers as they tried to pray and lay hands on her. [Safe].

Doreen was to meet with another Baptist minister but as he approached her door, she heard a voice telling her 'not to open the door and to have nothing to do with them'. But his radiating love prevailed, and Doreen let him in. Then she heard the evil spirit tell her to tell him nothing when he asked if there were any unclean spirits and what their names were. Doreen comments that she was no stranger to demons as she had called on them many times to assist her in her rites as a witch and Satanist, but she didn't realise the demons were within her, not outside. As previously mentioned, she presumed demons were external entities. The minister commanded the demons to leave her, using the authoritative tongue Jesus had given him to deal with demons.

After her first encounter with this man of God, she described having the most dreadful night. She woke early in the morning filled with the most awful fear. She advised that she was surrounded by evil powers and heard their awful voices, but this time they gave their names. She describes perspiring, her bed clothes were soaking wet, and advised that she was torn inside as if someone had taken a knife and was tearing her to pieces. The demons tore and tormented her, and advised they were not coming out.

One called it's self 'doubt and unbelief'. She advised that many more voices cried out all at once 'not me, not me' and it sounded like a mighty chorus growing louder and louder. Demons called pride, lies, witchcraft, lust, and many others retorted they were not leaving her body. She said the demons spoke one after the other, and she felt as if she was going mad, and certainly would if the demons remained. She advised that the darkness of hell seemed to descend upon her.

In the interim, as she waited for the minister to return, she found herself visiting her old haunts. She maintains she was pushed to these places by the dark demons within that controlled her. She notes that during her wanderings, she often remembered nothing of what she had done and where she had been. She states that in the short moments of normality, when she was herself, she yearned to be reconciled with Jesus. She knew she was not mentally ill but rather possessed by evil spirits and almost constantly obeyed their commands. She advised that everything evil within her trembled, and a thousand voices like hammers inside her, demanded that she stay away from the minister. She advised that she heard a voice tell her to phone the minister and instruct him not to visit her.

However, they met and when the minister asked Doreen what the demons names were, she advised that as she spoke her thoughts were taken away from her. [As mentioned, 'thought blocking' is symptomatic of schizophrenia]. When the minister spoke in another tongue in a very commanding way, she can't remember what happened as the demons within her took complete control.

The minister however told her afterwards. He said six demons revealed themselves under close interrogation and expressed themselves through her lips and body, according to their individual nature. The demon 'doubt and unbelief' was most obstinate and Doreen had to be held down by two Christian men while the minister cast out the demon. He commanded them out in the name of Jesus Christ, both in English and the tongue the Lord had given him for the purpose of exorcism, that the demon should leave and depart to Gehenna aka hell.

Gehenna was notably a small valley in Jerusalem, where parents would sacrifice their kids to their gods. They would lob them into the fire. Gehenna was a place of burning sewage, burning flesh, and garbage. Jesus used Gehenna as an illustration of hell.

Doreen states Ephesians 6:12 best describes the struggle. Thus, 'For our struggle is not against flesh and blood, but against the rulers, against the authorities, against the powers of this dark world and against the spiritual forces of evil in the heavenly realms'. She states, wrestling is the perfect description. The demon didn't want to leave her body but in the end it left with a loud scream. As it came out, Doreen advised it tore her.

The exorcism lasted three or four hours, during which time the demons 'deceit', 'lust', 'lies', 'pride', and 'witchcraft' were dispatched to Gehenna. The demon of witchcraft was apparently most peculiar and very noisy. It gave expression by certain enchanted wailings. It almost sang in weird and bewitching tones "do you know the witch of Endor?" [As mentioned, King Saul employed the services of the witch of Endor]. The minister advised that the demon was trying to bewitch him but that he resisted in the authority of Jesus. It was adamant that it didn't want to leave but eventually succumbed to ministerial demands, leaving with terrific screams and wailings.

Doreen then fell to the ground as if dead and when she came round, she knew nothing of what had happened. She was however aware that she was free of those demons. She advised being very tired. Her throat was bruised, as were her arms and ribs.

Within a short time, other demons revealed themselves, some giving names and some not. Doreen advised her life was an open door to demon possession. And she further reported experiencing the most horrific vivid dreams e.g. ugly, hairy animals chasing her to the edge of a bottomless pit, with their hands clawing at her body and throat. But furthermore, marks were on her body when she woke. Doreen notes the demons were not happy campers to be losing their dwelling place. She advised the next demon to leave was tormentor, which lived up to its name relentlessly.

The demon tormentor commanded Doreen to kill the minister, and obediently she took a knife in her handbag. When she arrived at the church, she advised that the demon inside her went mad. As mentioned in The Spirit World chapter, she learned something new about demons. Namely, they could not see the minister until Doreen did. They only had her eyes to see with. Doreen heard the demon command 'kill, kill, kill' and remembers nothing else.

The minister later advised that she brandished a huge knife with the express purpose of blinding his eyes, but fortunately he managed to snatch it away in good time. Apparently, this demon was exceedingly strong and

Doreen was difficult to restrain, evidencing the strength of ten strong men. Strong Christians had great difficulty holding her as the minister cast out the demon. Long exchanges again occurred between the minister and the demon, as it resisted endlessly. After a long battle the demon left with screams to Gehenna.

Doreen advised that all the demons put up a fight resulting in a long and arduous struggle. And they all hated the minister for sending them to Gehenna, as they knew that would be the end of them. Many of the demons quoted scripture, many argued over Bible truths, and some spoke in other tongues. Some demons disclosed that they had possessed Doreen's body for as long as fifteen years. The demon 'solicit' had been present since Doreen was fifteen and first became a prostitute, and apparently it tried to solicit the ministers present at the exorcism.

After many verbal exchanges it left, together with the demon 'dark enticer'. Apparently, the latter put up a very powerful display by showing off and trying to attract and allure the ministers. Other unclean spirits, like 'seducer', 'stripper', 'corruption' and 'lesbian' were all cast out to Gehenna. The minister advised Doreen that the 'lesbian' demon was most revealing and quite startling in its dialogue. It spoke in a refined society voice, quite unlike Doreen's. Apparently, the demons were none too pleased to discuss Calvary, advising that they were there, and that Mary Magdalene was a traitor.

Doreen spoke of seeing Jesus behind the minister, advising that Jesus was bathed in a radiant light, which filled the whole room. She reported that His face was gentle and kind. And His eyes were filled with deep love. He was staring right at her and she knew she was loved and was His child.

When the demon 'witchcraft' was cast out, Doreen lost her supernatural powers. She advised that she decided to warn the witches in the covens, about the haunted reality of their shenanigans, which resulted in her getting a severe beating and dumped in the back of beyond. Doreen advised that the exorcisms went on for months and that the remaining demons within her were really strong and active, mocking and tormenting her no-end. She further advised that some of the Christians lost heart as they could see no lasting effect of the ministry.

As Doreen was still on heroin, which entailed weeping and wailing, and in a state of confusion (partly from withdrawal symptoms), she was admitted to a mental hospital for a week of 'sleep therapy'. When Doreen tried to explain to medical staff that she had demons, they retorted there's no such thing and she merely required treatment. Doreen highlights such talk is labelled 'religious mania'. She states Satan told her she was mad and would never leave the mental hospital. No-one believed demon possession or the devil was real. Again, Lucifer mocked her, questioning where was Jesus now?

Doreen was given ECT but advised that demons can't be shaken out. She was also given various pharmaceuticals, which she then became addicted to. Doreen was then informed that she sustained brain damage from all the drugs she'd taken. However, she was permitted a weekend pass and was able to meet up with the ministers for another exorcism. The ministers cast out the last sixteen demons, advising that it was a long, hard battle with the powers of darkness. Apparently, the last demon was 'dementia', which aimed to destroy the brain.

It took seven months to cast out forty-seven demons. But moreover, Doreen got another x-ray of her head and no brain damage was found and the x-ray was normal. The doctors considered it a miracle. When Doreen returned to hospital, medical staff were perplexed by how well she was, and even looked different, healthy and young. As time passed Doreen became a new creation in Christ. She was described as a 'rough diamond'. She highlights that diamonds are found in the hottest and darkest parts of the earth, and when diamonds are first quarried, they are rough and unpolished.

Doreen continued to get tempted by the evil one, and she also received threatening letters from black witches telling her to stop slandering witches or she would die. Some of these letters were written in blood, and she was well aware that witches carry out their threats.

Doreen took courage from Paul's epistle to the Romans 8:38-39, 'For I am persuaded that neither death nor life nor angels nor principalities nor powers nor things present nor things to come nor height nor depth nor any other creature shall be able to separate us from the love of God, which is in Christ Jesus, our Lord'. Doreen added nor witch nor Satanist. Jesus is stronger than powers of darkness. He defeated all demons and Satan at Calvary, and is still casting them out, and healing the sick in body and mind. So, that's Doreen's testimony.

One last point, is Doreen's comment that, 'many more people are demon-possessed today than when Jesus was here on earth', (contrary to what some Christians think), and 'Jesus Himself said that wickedness shall increase. There are more doors for demon-possession in men's and women's lives than ever before.'

Keith and Melody Green excerpt

Keith Green (1953-1982), an American musician, and his wife Melody got embroiled with the New Age before embracing their Jewish roots and Jesus the Messiah. Keith died in a small plane crash, and its rumoured Jesuits bumped him off as he was very outspoken against the teachings of the Roman Catholic Church (not least because they're pushing the ecumenical movement). In his biography, 'No Compromise: The Life Story of Keith Green' (1989), by Melody Green, she wrote:

'Anything can happen on the streets of Hollywood. I'd seen some pretty wild things, but never anything so bizarre as what I saw one night on Ventura Boulevard.

As Keith and I walked out of the Bla Bla Café, a blast of hot night air hit us in the face. It was after 2.00am, but the street was still awake with activity. Four drag queens swept by us, followed by a couple in disco outfits, all headed inside for a late-night breakfast. Next door the watchdogs at Bruno's Corvette Repairs were pacing inside their chain linked fence, barking at everything that moved – including us. Keith had played three sets that night, and we were headed for home, exhausted. I was glad to see "Victor Von Van", our VW with the hippie-style Indian print curtains I'd sewn, parked at the curb.

Keith had been performing at 'the Bla' – as it was affectionately known to its regulars – for almost a year. It was a small showcase nightclub in the San Fernando Valley just a few blocks from Hollywood proper. The Bla spotlighted showbiz hopefuls and was frequented by agents and talent scouts from big record companies. Keith was one of those hopefuls. But tonight he'd given it his all one more time – and now we were leaving, still undiscovered.

As Keith walked around the front of the van, I opened the passenger door. That was when we spotted a figure looming towards us out of the dark. It was Harmony.

Harmony looked like a gruff mountain man with his brown, scraggly hair and beard. Here we were in 1974, but this guy struck us as someone caught in a '60s time warp. He was calm and easy. All he talked about was peace, love and living off the land. He wasn't a close friend, but he and Keith had gotten stoned together once.

"Hey, how's it going?" Keith called. He shut his door and stepped back onto the sidewalk.

Sleepily I leaned my head back, knowing I was in for a wait. Inevitably most of our conversations drifted toward spiritual experiences these days. Keith and I had tried a lot of things – a lot of things. Recently we'd been curious about Jesus. We weren't Christians. Church was a dead institution to us. But Jesus did seem to be a spiritual master of some sort, and we had a degree of respect for his life and teachings.

Sure enough, Keith and Harmony immediately began talking about the supernatural. It was just a typical conversation – for people who were into drugs and the mystical, which were a lot of the people we knew.

"I've been reading about Jesus lately," Keith was saying. "He was a pretty radical person."

Harmony's eyes seemed to brighten. Then, slowly, a strange look came over his face. His eyes got misty and distant. Very calmly he said "I am Jesus Christ."

Keith reacted like he'd been stung by a scorpion. Without missing a beat, he shot back, "Beware of the false prophets who come to you in sheep's clothing, but inwardly are ravenous wolves!" I recognised the quote as something Jesus had said. What happened next was really hard to believe.

Harmony's eyes grew wide. Then they narrowed to slits. Furrows creased across his forehead, and his bushy eyebrows knit together. A sneer came over his usually mild face, and his upper lip curled back, exposing yellow smoke-stained teeth. Leaning toward Keith, his teeth bared, he let out a growl that started in the throat, like that of a wolf, and ended with the horrible hissing sound of a snake.

It happened in only seconds. Harmony's face relaxed. But his eyes looked confused. Embarrassed. The hiss seemed to hang in the still night air.

My skin was still tingling from the shock. Keith had obviously been rocked by it too. He looked from Harmony to me with wide eyes. This was Hollywood, but things like this only happened in the movies. I wondered what Keith was thinking.

It was as if someone or something took control of Harmony momentarily, using him for its own purposes. Then just as quickly it discarded him, leaving him to pick up the pieces in confused embarrassment. Dazed, Harmony mumbled something. But Keith quickly excused himself, jumped into Victor, and shoved the key into the ignition.

As we drove home over the dark streets, we kept looking at each other in disbelief. Keith was more animated than usual. He kept saying, "Did he really do that? I can't believe it!"

We talked about nothing else until we crawled into bed and fell asleep, sometime after 3.30 am.

The weird experience with Harmony did have one major effect on us. It brought some things into sharp focus. Namely, that there was, indeed, a very real spiritual realm – a realm full of power and possibly even danger. We were just coming to a deeper realisation that there must be spiritual forces beyond our knowing. Had we heard a voice from that other side, speaking through Harmony? Or was it just the voice of age? After all, a lot of musicians, artists, and writers – the 'beautiful' people – were saying things like that, 'You are your own god. Everything's relative. There is no right or wrong.' But we wondered: *Is there a dark side and a light side to spiritual energy?*

Keith and I had both been caught up in a search to find our spiritual identities for some time. We were looking for truth – whatever it was – and our search for light had taken us on many strange paths, from Buddhism to stuff like astral projection and, of course, drugs; especially psychedelics. We were convinced the truth was hidden out there somewhere like a pearl in the ocean and that when we found it, it would fill an empty spot in our hearts. It would make life really worth living. Until then every day held the potential of being the day of great revelation.

At the time of our weird encounter with Harmony, however, we'd been slipping a bit, losing hope, even dabbling with the drugs again that we'd sworn off but kept falling back into. Our spiritual ambitions never kept us out of the fog for long. In fact, the constant lure of those other voices had pretty well convinced us there was a dark and a light side'.

Presumably, Harmony would be diagnosed with psychosis since he's not God. Or he had a spirit attachment?

As it transpired, Keith died at the height of his ministry, because he was dangerous to Rome? It seems pertinent to note, in his 'Catholic Chronicles' he wrote: 'It is obvious by even this brief glimpse into the doctrines of mortal and venial sins, confession, penance, and purgatory, that the Roman Catholic Church has constructed one of the most unbiblical doctrinal systems that has ever been considered 'Christian'. The fear, anguish, and rebellious bondage that such a system of 'reward and punishment' creates has tormented millions of lives for centuries and continues to prey on those who are ignorant of the biblical way of salvation'.

PART 2

'And you will know the truth, and the truth will set you free'. John 8:32

11

Biblical His-Story

With the backdrop of what's been discussed thus far i.e. 'secular' theories of psychology, philosophy and the spirit world, we can consider what God's word tells us, which could be the truth? So, God's word tells us, in Genesis 1:1-2, 'In the beginning God created the heavens and the earth. The earth was empty, a formless mass cloaked in darkness. And the Spirit of God was hovering over the surface'. We're told God has a triune nature, which is God the Father, God the Son, and God the Holy Spirit. God's like triplets i.e. same DNA but three people. And whilst God's Spirit is omnipresent, Father God and JC are up in the third Heaven. Jesus is the Logos (Word).

John 1:1-5 tells us, 'In the beginning was the Word, and the Word was with God, and the Word was God. He was with God in the beginning. Through Him all things were made; without Him nothing was made that has been made. In Him was life, and that life was the light of all mankind. The light shines in the darkness, and the darkness has not overcome it'. God is benevolent, light, love, omniscient, omnipotent, omnipresent, and all good things. There is no darkness in Him.

And God made the angels, (before the world), who rejoiced at creation. In Job 38:7 God tells us, 'the morning stars sang together, and all the Sons of God shouted for joy'. The world was awesome, or as God said, 'it was good'. It seems God was being humble, as creation is immense. Nature is intoxicatingly beautiful, and the diversity of animals is mind-blowing e.g. tigers, giraffes, zebras, pandas, chimps, elephants, hedgehogs, hamsters, guinea pigs, cats, dogs, sheep, goats, lamas, hippos, and so forth.

Angels have distinct personalities and freewill like us, but they're incredibly powerful, have superior intelligence and they can fly (travel at the speed of thought). And there's gazillions of them. In Revelation 5:11 we're told, 'numbering myriads of myriads and thousands of thousands'. In addition to their different kinds, like cherubim, seraphim, and archangels, there's also 'living creatures', which are some kind of heavenly beings. According to Ezekiel 1:14, these creatures dart back and forth like flashes of lightning. Hebrews 12:1 tells us 'we're surrounded by a great cloud of witnesses', which refers to their ethereal nature? However, whilst angels are spirit beings, they can take on physical form. As mentioned, they can present themselves as human beings, which includes eating and taking people by the hand.

And God made His kids, and He really loves His kids, whether we know it or not. It seems we're the apple of His eye? Unlike the angels who were made to serve Him, God made kids to love Him. He wanted to be a Father. But moreover, God made us in His image. God said, 'Let us make people in our image, to be like ourselves'. So, God created people in His own image; God patterned them after Himself; male and female He created them' (Genesis 1:26-27).

Rather than anthropomorphically deducting that this means we look like God, it's understood our likeness to God is in the sense that our immaterial being is endowed with will, intellect, emotion, and moral reason. The Bible calls this the soul of man. However, as Jesus incarnated as a man, we are literally made in His image i.e. human form. It's also understood when God is saying 'let us', He is speaking to (pre-incarnate) Jesus and the Holy Spirit. So, God made Adam from the dust and breathed life into him, and not wanting Adam to be lonely He made Eve. Eve's like a clone?

So, it was happy days in the Garden of Eden. It was paradise. As touched on, they were spiritually alive in God, with their physical and spiritual body in union. They walked and talked with God. There was no death, and all the animals were vegetarian. The wolf lay down with the lamb, and the leopard with the goat. But moreover, God gave His kids a choice. At the centre of the Garden, there were two trees, namely, 'the tree of life', and 'the tree of the knowledge of good and evil'. And they were permitted to munch fruit from any of the trees bar the latter. God told them if they did, they would surely die. So, they could choose to eat the forbidden fruit, if they so desired, but they loved God and wanted to be in His will.

It's said that God seen the necessity for mankind to be tested and tempted by something in opposition to His will, to make His children holy. Do we love God, and want to be in fellowship with Him, or do we want to go our own way? It's also noted, that people are metaphorically described as trees that bear fruit i.e. characteristics, and Jesus is referred to as the 'tree of life'. It seems God was making it clear that we have freewill to choose life or death.

As it transpired, God's beloved angel Lucifer, the Light Bearer, was none too pleased at God's creation of man. Indeed, he vehemently hates us, because we're made in God's image? Seriously miffed at God, Lucifer rebelled against God, and exalted himself above God. Omniscient God, who knows all our hearts, knew what Lucifer, Son of the Morning, was thinking. Isaiah 14:13-14 tells us, 'And thou saidst in thy heart, I will ascend into heaven, I will exalt my throne above the stars of God; and I will sit upon the mount of congregation, in the uttermost parts of the north; I will ascend above the heights of the clouds; I will make myself like the Most High'. These are notably known as the five 'I Wills' of Satan.

And so it was, that Lucifer fell through pride. But moreover, audacious and conniving Lucifer talked a third of the angels into his dastardly plan, (that they would rule), and as a result they all got banished from (the third) heaven. Jesus tells us, (in Luke 10:18), 'I saw Satan fall like lightning from heaven', which confirms Jesus was there from the beginning. [It's noted, the lightning bolt is a reference to Lucifer and it's commonly featured in music videos e.g. David Bowie, Lady Gaga. The Nazi SS sign is also depicted as two lightning bolts. As it transpires, Lucifer is very popular].

As mentioned, the Bible tells us that Satan is the 'Prince of the Power of the Air', and there's three heavens. Thus, it seems Satan and his angels roam about the first two heavens. Whilst we'll get back to creation science, it's noted there was a ton of water in the beginning. And God created a firmament to separate the waters above from below (sky is the space in between). God then gathered the water together, underneath the firmament, into one place to create dry land. Contrary to the heliocentric cosmology that we've been educated with, it's like we live in a snow-globe. The sun, moon and stars are in the heavens aka the firmament, and above the solid firmament is water, then God's third heaven.

It's understood the fallen angels have truly burnt their bridges with God. There is no redemption for them, hence they want to take as many as they can down with them. It seems to be a spiteful endeavour. However, it's also rumoured that Lucifer and his haunted army believe they will defeat God in the end battle of Armageddon, as we'll get to.

So, these vindictive angels have a plan. The first move was to get Adam and Eve to munch the forbidden fruit to cause death and suffering. And thus, the serpent made his dastardly appearance. It seems Lucifer chose the serpent as his vehicle of physical expression. Genesis 3:1 tells us the serpent was the shrewdest, most cunning of all the wild beasts God had made. Thus, by virtue of being a beast, suggests it had legs.

In the Haggadah, ancient Jewish text, the serpent is described as tall like a camel, but two legged and walked like a man. The word serpent in original Hebrew means something shining and beautiful, similar in meaning to Lucifer. According to Ellen White (founder of the Adventists), the serpent 'had wings, and while flying through the air presented an appearance of dazzling brightness, having the colour and brilliancy of burnished gold'.

It's noted, that Lucifer could have either possessed a serpent, being a spirit being, or actually became a serpent, given angels can take physical form. There were no other people to possess, and presumably it would have seemed suspect if another person just rocked up in the garden with them? However, it's also said that Lucifer was a seraphim angel, which has a viper/snake face and wings, so it looks like a serpent. It seems there's two types of serpents, namely, the physical serpent, and the angelic serpent? Thus, perhaps he materialised his angel body? Like, a tall reptilian humanoid? Apparently, angels are very tall, like (at least) 8-10 foot tall.

So, the serpent talks Eve into munching the forbidden fruit (it's suggested that before the fall, all communicated telepathically). He tells naïve trusting Eve that she won't die, but rather her eyes will be opened, and she will become just like God, knowing everything, both good and evil (Genesis 3:4-5). He basically tapped into her pride, and she succumbed to the temptation. She subsequently talked Adam into eating the fruit, and at that moment their eyes were opened, and they became aware of their shame and nakedness. Something dramatic happened. There was a physical change, as they were cut off from God. The connection with their soul and spirit body was severed. As mentioned, their 'light' covering was removed hence they were aware of their nakedness (their light body was deactivated). Presumably, they were soiling themselves, thinking what on Earth have we done?

Father God, who meanwhile knows what they've been up to, and what they're thinking, as they're hiding behind the trees (complete with some fig leaves to hide their nether regions), calls to Adam and asks him, 'Have you eaten the fruit I commanded you not to?' And then the blame game begins, as Adam tries to excuse himself by blaming the woman, which he audaciously points out, that God gave him, like God is also part responsible? Then the Lord God asked Eve, 'How could you do such a thing?' And she blamed the serpent, claiming he tricked her. God subsequently made them coats of skin and clothed them, which is the first animal sacrifice for sin (Genesis 3:21). This theme of sacrifice and atonement continues through the Bible.

It seems pertinent to spare a thought for Father God. He loved Lucifer and was sorely grieved at the breakdown of that relationship, and He loves us humans, and we similarly disappoint Him. What is He going to do with His beloved children? It's further pertinent to note, that angels are called 'Sons of God', as God created them, and Adam was God's son because He created him. But Adam's offspring (the whole of mankind) are Adam's sons and daughters. Adam is the (biological) father of mankind. Adam means mankind. So, we're the sons and daughters of wo/men. We're not sons and daughters of God until we're born again in the Holy Spirit, as we'll get to.

As God had forewarned, their sin brought death into the world. God cursed His creation by introducing the second law of thermodynamics, namely, entropy. Hence, everything rots and dies, including us. Contrary to the evolutionary principle, Nature is not improving. So, they were no longer immortal, living in paradise, but were cast out. The earth became 'paradise lost'. Reality lost its spiritual sparkle. It was crud.

With regards to their punishment, Genesis 3:16-19 tells us, 'To the woman He said, 'I will make your pains in childbirth very severe; with painful labour you will give birth to children. Your desire will be for your husband, and he will rule over you'. To Adam He said, 'Because you listened to your wife and ate fruit from the tree about which I commanded you, 'You must not eat from it', 'cursed is the ground because of you; through painful toil you will eat food from it all the days of your life. It will produce thorns and thistles for you, and you will eat the plants of the field. By the sweat of your brow you will eat your food until you return to the ground, since from it you were taken; for dust you are and to dust you will return'. It's difficult to decide who got the raw deal? Maybe Adam, given the heavy workload, but it blows that women became subordinate to men?

God also punished the serpent. Genesis 3:14 tells us, 'So, the LORD God said to the serpent, 'Because you have done this, 'Cursed are you above all livestock and all wild animals! You will crawl on your belly and you will eat the dust all the days of your life'. So, it seems the serpent lost its legs and became a snake? As discussed, Satan is supernaturally snakelike. Lucifer, who became known as Satan (which means adversary) when he fell, has many names, like serpent, dragon, beast, antichrist, son of perdition, etc.

But more importantly, God told the serpent (Genesis 3:15), 'And I will put enmity between you and the woman, and between your seed and her Seed; He shall bruise your head, and you shall bruise his heel'. According to God's word then, the evil one has a lineage. There's a seed war. As Steve Quayle (author/researcher) asserts, this verse is the Rosetta stone of the Bible. Furthermore, the woman's seed suggests a virgin birth (in normal conception the male provides the seed) and God's plan for redemption.

So, all parties were duly punished, and went on their way. Adam and Eve went onto have two sons, namely, Cain and Abel, but Cain killed his brother Abel, which highlights our wickedness from the start. But they went onto have Seth, and other sons and daughters. And the population began to grow rapidly on earth. However, as it transpires, the daughters of men are beautiful, and as it also transpires, the evil one has a plan up his scaly sleeve to corrupt and infiltrate God's human bloodline. Blood is most important because 'the life is in the blood'. It seems the endeavour was to scupper the gene pool before the precious seed arrived (the seed that would crush the devil's head). Angels don't reproduce, but it seems they can with us?

Genesis 6: 1-4 tells us, 'When human beings began to increase in number on the earth and daughters were born to them, the sons of God saw that the daughters of men were beautiful, and they married any of them they chose'…'The Nephilim were on the earth in those days – and also afterward – when the sons of God went to the daughters of men and had children by them. They were the heroes of old, men of renown'.

Nephilim is Hebrew for earth-born and comes from nephal which means to fall. So, the sons of God, the fallen angels, had sex with women and produced nephilim. But moreover, the nephilim were giants. The Kebra Nagast (Ethiopian text) notably refers to the enormous size of the babies produced from the sexual or genetic unions between humans and 'the gods'. Some giants were delivered by caesarean: 'having split open their bellies of their mothers they came forth from their navels'.

Apparently, their heights ranged from eight foot to thirty-six foot, so that's pretty crazy. Perhaps the growth gene didn't switch off for some of them, because of serpent DNA? It seems there were various kinds/tribes. Hence, nephilim is like an umbrella term for hybrids. Like, some had six fingers and toes, and two rows of teeth. It's understood the Native Indians were familiar with them. Hence, their 'How' greeting to demonstrate how many fingers one has. And some had elongated skulls. Like, the Egyptian queen Nefertiti.

It's noted, elongated skulls are found all over the world (see photos from Peru). They have 25-40% larger cranial size. They have different suture lines, as a normal skull has two parietal lobes, whereas the elongated skull has one enormous skull cap. They have large eye sockets, and they have long necks to hold their long heads (the structure is different). Apparently Anakim, one of the nephilim tribes mentioned in the Bible, means 'long necks'. So, perhaps this is evidence of them?

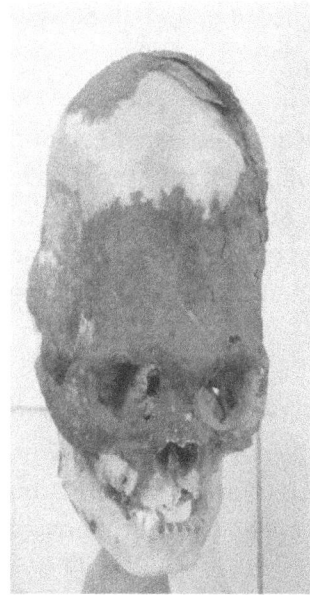 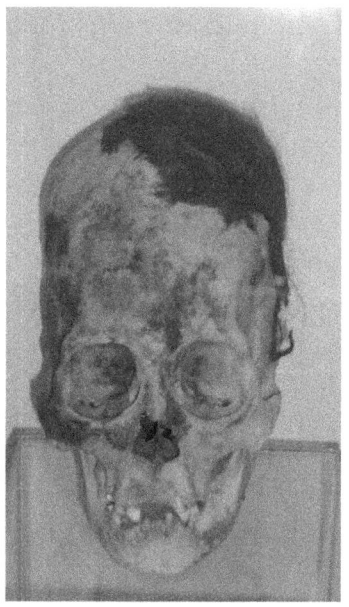 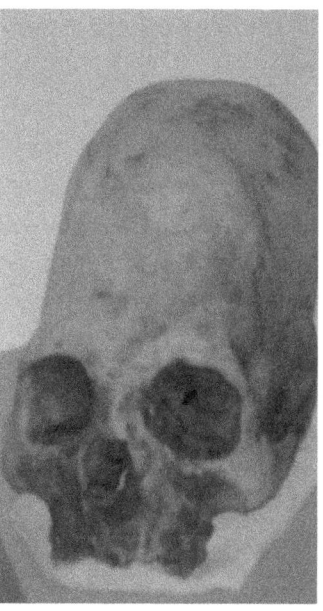 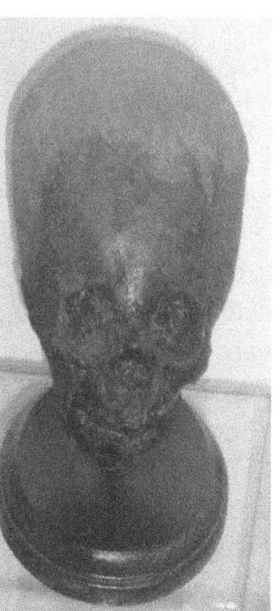

The smallest skull is apparently an eighteen month old child. Foeti with elongated skulls have also been found (in utero), which affirms these elongated skulls are not the result of head-boarding. But rather, it seems the great unwashed sought to emulate 'the gods' by introducing the barbaric practice of head-boarding. It's noted, that cradle-boarding does not change the volume of the skull.

Author/researcher LA Marzulli, who's 'on the trail of the nephilim', did DNA testing on the elongated skulls of Paracus, Peru. It was discovered that they have mitochondrial DNA 'with mutations unknown in any human, primate, or animal known so far'. Apparently, these human-like creatures are very distant from Homo Sapiens, Neanderthals and Denisovans (Denisovans are our cousins like Neanderthals, but we'll get back to this), and it's unclear how they fit into the known evolutionary chain. They're so genetically different, it's hard to see how they could interbreed with humans. These skulls, which are over two thousand years old, were also shown to have European and Middle Eastern origin. Marzulli has rewritten history.

It's understood the fallen angels could have shapeshifted into humans, and roamed the earth as men, but it seems they materialised in their seraphim bodies, and presented themselves as serpent gods? Gary Wayne, author of 'The Genesis 6 Conspiracy: How Secret Societies and the Descendants of Giants Plan to Enslave Humankind' (2014), affirms that seraphim have faces like vipers, and nephilim looked like their fathers, like snakes, for the first few generations. The Bible also refers to angels as stars (which are in the second heaven). Hence, it would seem these 'gods' came from the stars?

As touched on, people worshipped serpent gods in the ancient world. Like, all over Central America, there's serpent symbolism on sacred sites, which were places of human sacrifice. China worships the dragon, and Hinduism, Buddhism, Jainism and Sikhism worship the cobra called Naga. It's said the Nagas could change from either reptilian or human form whenever they choose. Egyptian texts describe snakes with legs, and in Africa they pertain to the Chitauri or 'Children of the Serpent' and 'Children of the Python'. Ancient Greece also has their version of gods and demigods, and Rome etc. All these cultures speak about gods coming to earth and having offspring.

Thus, there's two classifications of gods, namely, fallen angels or gods, and earth born gods aka nephilim. That being said, hybrid kids could mate with other hybrids, producing more varieties. Royal families inherited their 'right to rule' through their descent from the gods. Thus, the kids, the serpent kings, ruled on behalf of their forefathers, the serpent gods.

Furthermore, whilst evidence of giants and their architecture (e.g. megalithic structures) can be found worldwide, there's been a massive cover-up. Since the early 1900s western archaeological institutions have quashed any trace of giants (which includes National Geographic). As researchers like Steve Quayle, author of 'Genesis 6 Giants' (2002), highlight, the Smithsonian Institute was founded with the specific task of collecting evidence of giants. And they admitted to destroying tens of thousands of giant human remains during the early 1900s.

They were ordered to be destroyed from high level administration to protect the mainstream chronology of human evolution at the time. A former Smithsonian employee (high level curator) turned whistle-blower, provided evidence for court, namely, a 1.3 metre long human femur bone. He stole the bone in the mid-1930s, which he kept all his life, and on his deathbed, he admitted to the cover up operations of the Smithsonian.

It's highlighted that news about giants dried up circa 1950. And then we began getting brainwashed with alien propaganda. Hiding the evidence of giants eliminates evidence for the Biblical narrative. The agenda is to promote evolution and belie creation. Hence, we've been educated with heliocentric cosmology, following the nonsensical Big Bang. It's highlighted, that the two main targeted books in the Bible are Genesis, the first book, because it tells us about creation, and Revelation, the last book, because it tells us what's coming.

As George Orwell said in '1984', 'He who controls the past controls the future. He who controls the present controls the past'. Steve Quayle concedes, 'the biggest cover up of history is the cover up of history'. So, they want us to believe in aliens, and regard giants as mythology. There was no clash of the Titans?

However, before we expound on nephilim, it seems pertinent to note an alternative view, namely, that 'the tree of the knowledge of good and evil' was Satan, as opposed to a tree in the literal sense. Satan was the tree and his 'fruit' seduced Eve. Wheeler (2009), for example, states that to 'eat' means to eat but also to lay or lie with. She highlights that whilst 'fruit' is mentioned, there's no mention of apples in scripture, but rather this symbolism serves to distract us from the real meaning, which is that Eve got nasty with the devil.

Wheeler explains this was the real reason they were so ashamed and aware of their nakedness, and hence why they covered their private parts as opposed to their mouths, that had just 'eaten' the fruit. She highlights that 'eating apples doesn't make you ashamed of your nakedness! But losing your virginity certainly can'. And she notes, 'fruit does not make one aware or conscious of whether they have clothes on or not' (p.105). Since Adam also partook of this forbidden fruit, we can but wonder what the crack was there (pun intended).

It's understood that Satan, with his supernatural powers, could appear to Adam and Eve as two different creatures if he wanted to do. Or maybe he was the same to both, some unbelievably seductive, attractive, desirable, beautiful serpent. Regardless, it's bestiality? Others suggest Eve was seduced by an angel of light, as Satan can disguise himself as an angel of light.

So, we don't quite know how, or to what degree Adam partook of this fruit, but it's purported that Eve became pregnant from doing so. Wheeler (2009) asserts that scripture says Cain 'was of that wicked one'. Thus, the Devil's serpent seed began with Cain, as a result of his union with Eve, and Adam's seed began with Seth. 'The river of human genes' (Richard Dawkins expression) was thus split in two. Wheeler purports the 'tree of knowledge of good and evil' was the means to sexual knowledge. Lucifer was the way of knowing good and evil (in their innocence, they only knew 'good' before). Through him they would learn evil, perceive evil, and experience evil.

Others however, dispute this view, as the Bible doesn't tell us Eve had sex with Lucifer. And biblical scholars like Chuck Missler insist, 'the Bible means what it says, and says what it means'. And it tells us that Sons of God had sex with women, and had giant kids. It's also noted, that sexual enlightenment is a Gnostic teaching. It seems the evil one's seed is nephilim bloodlines. Albeit, it's always possible Lucifer has his own priestly bloodline, since why not?

Wheeler (2009) explains the serpent seed denotes a specific bloodline that is directly and indirectly linked to Satan, 'which makes the Illuminati bloodlines a progeny of Lucifer and the fallen angels' (p.127). It's understood the Illuminati is the purest nephilim bloodline on earth. However, we'll get back to the Illuminati and so-called royal bloodlines.

Unlike humans that have God given nephesh, nephilim don't have human souls. They're a violation of God's creation and not redeemable. Paracelsus notably referred to beings not descended from Adam and yet descended from Adam. He explains they're not spirits because they have flesh, blood and bones. And since they live i.e. eat, talk, sleep, act, and propagate offspring, they consequently cannot be properly called 'spirits'. They are beings occupying a place between men and spirits, resembling men and women. But unlike wo/men they have no spiritual soul. Perhaps he was pertaining to nephilim? Nephilim are like demon-people or demon souls in mortal bodies? They are by definition, psychos. They have no empathy. It's not in their constitution.

So, these hybrid kids were supersized, super-powerful, and smarter than the average bear. Apparently, they ate lions for breakfast, which is telling. They were intrepid killers whose violent exploits are echoed in ancient myths. Like their fathers, they were rebellious, perverted and exerted a ruinous influence on human beings. As a result, the world became corrupt, wicked and depraved.

In Genesis 6:5, 11, 12 we're told, 'The badness of men was abundant on the earth and every inclination of the thoughts of his heart was only bad all the time...the earth became filled with violence...and the flesh had ruined its way on earth'. We're told God was sorry He ever made people, and it broke His heart.

Thus, in exasperation to our waywardness, and the corruption of our DNA, God decided to drown the world and start again. And thus, the great Flood landed. Genesis 6:9 tells us, Noah was the only blameless and righteous man living on the earth at the time. So, he was saved together with his family (his wife, their three sons and their wives), and animals and birds etc. We're told Noah was 'perfect in his generations', which suggests his blood was pure and untainted. We can't however say the same about his son's wives?

Whilst we'll get back to the Flood in the science chapter, it seems pertinent to note, that conditions on earth were optimal before the Flood i.e. subtropical and uniformly warm temperatures with enhanced oxygen. It had never rained. So, when God told Noah to build an ark, 'people' thought he was mad. It apparently took Noah 50-80 years to build the ark, and he was six hundred years young at the time.

Before the flood, wo/man lived a l-o-n-g time, like circa eight hundred years long-time because the conditions on earth were so different. Methuselah, who lived 969 years, is renowned as the oldest man. It rained for forty days and forty nights, and water covered the earth for 150 days, including the tallest mountains at the time. It's understood the flood was catastrophic and detrimentally altered our landscape (and created a ton of coal, oil and gas in the process).

There's much evidence of a global flood, (not least the Grand Canyon), and every ancient culture has its own version of the great flood. Many of them speak about a great ark which saved some men and animals, and finally landed on a mountain. Alan Alford, author of 'Gods of the New Millennium' (1996), asserts, 'From almost every culture around the world there emerge more than five hundred strikingly similar legends of a great flood. These legends all share a common theme – of mankind being swept away with the exception of one man and his family who survived' (p.216).

Trey Smith (author/documentary maker) concedes there are 277 official flood stories from different cultures, (he states the history channel claims there's 2000), and all of them refer to a man and his family surviving on a boat. The Epic of Gilgamesh, one of the earliest known literary writings in the world, states a global flood destroyed mankind. It's believed Gilgamesh was a real Sumerian king between 2700 and 2500BC. But moreover, according to the story, Gilgamesh was part god and part man (nephilim). And furthermore, his tomb was found in Iraq in April 2003, the month before we illegally annihilated Iraq. So, that's interesting.

Like the biblical account, Plato also believed the great flood was intended to destroy the greater part of humankind because our race had gone awry. As mentioned, Plato dated the flood to 9,600BC, and believed it destroyed Atlantis. He relayed that Atlantis was ruled by ten hybrid kings, who ruled over ten kingdoms. But they fell out of favour with 'the gods' and were submerged into the Atlantic Ocean. It's understood the globalists want a 'New Atlantis' i.e. global government with ten kingdoms, as we'll get to. Like, Sir Francis Bacon's 'New Atlantis' (1627). They agree with Plato that 'philosopher kings' should rule the herd.

Psychic Edgar Cayce notably placed the location of Atlantis between the Gulf of Mexico and the Mediterranean Sea, and dated its destruction in 10,000BC. He said the continent extended from South America to Africa. Helena Blavatsky, who channelled 'Ascended Masters' (as we'll get to), claimed inhabitants of Atlantis were giants and the Flood happened 9,564BC, when Atlantis was fully submerged.

The idea of Atlantis, the former 'golden age' and lost civilisation, corroborates with the Bible which tells us there was one landmass before the flood. It seems the antediluvian world is Atlantis, and she fell with the fellers? She was drenched and the continents formed as the waters receded. Thus, Atlantis is the Great Continent, father of all the present continents.

Black (2010) concedes, the Greek tradition agreed with the Hebrew tradition that in early pre-flood times there arose a race of giants. Traditions of an antediluvian race of giants can be found all over the world, detailing men double the size and who lived twice as long as we do. This is not to be confused with Neanderthals, who appear to be pre-Flood humans (as we'll get to). So, the ancient world agreed that gods came to earth, produced giants, and then a flood wiped out the carnage.

However, before we get to the post-Flood world, it seems pertinent to mention the Book of Enoch because it expounds on the nephilim narrative. The Book of Enoch is not part of the canonised Bible, but it's referred to in the Bible (more than a hundred times). It was in the Septuagint, the earliest Bible written in Greek. It's apparently superfluous because it wasn't inspired by the Holy Spirit, and the Bible is literally God's word. It reigns supreme. [Hidden books are referred to as the 'apocrypha']. The Book of Enoch is however considered canonical by the Ethiopian and Eritrean Orthodox Church. But moreover, the Book of Enoch was found with the Dead Sea Scrolls, (in caves at Qumran in Israel), mid twentieth century. It seems God is drawing our attention to these otherwise shelved books?

The vast majority of the Dead Sea Scrolls (dated from 250BC-68AD) were copies of the Old Testament. Nearly every Old Testament book was found (except the book of Esther), but there were other curious finds, like the Book of Enoch. It's noted, the Dead Sea Scrolls give us confidence in the reliability of the Old Testament manuscripts, since there's minimal difference between the manuscripts previously discovered, and those found in Qumran.

The Bible tells us that Enoch was seventh from Adam. He was Jared's son and Noah's great grandfather. Thus, Enoch was living at the time of the giants, before the Flood. He witnessed the craziness. The Bible also tells us that Enoch walked with God (enjoyed close fellowship), and then he disappeared at 365 years young when 'God took him'. It seems Enoch was spared the experience of death because he was so pleasing to God (see Hebrews 11:5).

As mentioned, the same thing happened with Elijah. That is, he didn't die normally, but rather was taken up to heaven in a fiery chariot (UFO?). They were translated from material into spiritual bodies, or their spirit bodies were activated? It seems they went to the second heaven, as Jesus told us no-one had ever been to His home? Whilst we don't hear much about Enoch in the Bible, New Testament authors quote from the Book of Enoch.

Like, Jude quotes from the Book of Enoch. Jude 14-15 states, 'Enoch, who lived in the seventh generation after Adam, prophesied about these people. He said, 'Listen! The Lord is coming with countless thousands of His holy ones to execute judgement on the people of the world. He will convict every person of all the ungodly things they have done and for all the insults that ungodly sinners have spoken against him'.

This is almost verbatim of Enoch 1:9, which states, 'Behold, He comes with the myriads of His holy ones, to execute judgement on all, and to destroy all the wicked, and to convict all flesh for all the wicked deeds that they have done, and the proud and hard words that wicked sinners have spoke against him'.

Thus, Enoch was privy to the future. Enoch chapter 1:2 states, '… Enoch a righteous man, whose eyes were opened by God, saw the vision of the Holy One in the heavens, which the angels showed me, and from them I heard everything, and from them I understood as I saw, but not for this generation, but for a remote one which is to come'.

So, angels enabled his trip to heaven, and he was shown the future. And his words are for the terminal generation, (those living during the great tribulation), which could be us? Hence, this book was rediscovered? The most prevalent title in the Book of Enoch for the one promised is 'the Elect One', then 'Son of Man', which New Testament authors were partial to using.

It's noted, the Book of Enoch was written a few centuries before Jesus walked the earth (before 300BC), and whilst it's ascribed to Enoch, he was taken out of the picture millennia before. So, we don't know who wrote it, but we know biblical authors were familiar with it. According to the Book of Enoch, Enoch was the inventor of writing (he was God's scribe) and was known for his wisdom.

But moreover, the Book of Enoch tells us about the fall of the Watchers who fathered nephilim. It states, 'Enoch had testified about the Watchers who had sinned with the daughters of men'. The canonised Book of Daniel notably refers to angels as Watchers. Hence, these Watchers are fallen angels.

Enoch chapter 6:1-2 states, 'And it came to pass when the children of men had multiplied that in those days were born unto them beautiful and comely daughters. And the angels, the children of the heaven, saw and lusted after them, and said to one another: 'Come, let us choose us wives from among the children of men and beget us children'.

So, two hundred Watchers descended on Mount Hermon, during the time of Jared (Enoch's father), and did the deed by sowing their seed (see photos of Mount Hermon). In the Bible, Jude 1:6 tells us, 'the angels kept not their first estate, but left their own habitation'. It's understood they left the second heaven, but also, their bodies physically changed, as habitation also means body. They left their 'clothes of heaven'.

It's noted, that they descended to the mountain, as opposed to appear through an inter-dimensional wall, which suggests a different process? Namely, to the point of no return. Their bodies changed from spiritual to physical (flesh and blood) in order to procreate? It's purported the leader of the evil angels, namely Semjaza, was Lucifer, hence Lucifer has his own bloodline. Or maybe not, as it's understood Lucifer roams about heaven and earth. He hasn't diminished himself.

Enoch chapter 7:1-6 continues, '...they took unto themselves wives, and each chose for himself one, and they began to go in unto them and to defile themselves with them, and they taught them charms and enchantments, and the cutting of roots, and made them acquainted with plants. And they became pregnant, and they bare great giants, whose height was three thousand ells: Who consumed all the acquisitions of men. And when men could no longer sustain them, the giants turned against them and devoured mankind. And they began to sin against birds, and beasts, and reptiles, and fish, and to devour one another's flesh, and drink the blood'.

Chapter 8:1-2 continues, 'And Azazel taught men to make swords, and knives, and shields, and breastplates, and made known to them the metals of the earth and the art of working them, and bracelets, and ornaments, and the use of antimony, and the beautifying of eyelids, and all kinds of costly stones, and all colouring tinctures. And there arose much godliness, and they committed fornication, and they were led astray, and became corrupt in all their ways.

Semjaza taught enchantments, and root cuttings, Armaros the resolving of enchantments, Baraqijal (taught) astrology, Kokabel the constellations, Ezeqeel the knowledge of the clouds, Araqiel the signs of the earth, Shamsiel the signs of the sun, and Sariel the course of the moon. And as men perished, they cried, and their cries went up to heaven...'

So, in addition to creating haunted hybrids, the Watchers taught them sorcery (including which plants to mix to create psychoactive substances like ayahuasca) and black magic, weapons for war, they pioneered vanity, orgies, cannibalism and blood drinking, bestiality, and they taught abortion. In chapter 69:12, we're told 'Kasdeja: this is he who showed the children of men all the wicked smiting of spirits and demons, and the smitings of the embryo in the womb, that it may pass away, and [the smitings of the soul] the bites of the serpent, and the smitings which befall through the noontide heat, the son of the serpent named Tabaa't'. In essence, the Watchers taught them the secret arts of civilisation. We can but imagine the decadence and opulence in this 'golden age'?

But it gets weirder, with the Book of Giants, also found with the Dead Sea Scrolls. This fragmented book (dated circa 200BC) expounds on the narrative of the Book of Enoch. Thus, it affirms that two hundred Watchers made a pact to defy God, and descended to Earth in the days of Jared. They took human women as wives, had sex with them, and the wives gave birth to hybrid giants. The giants began to rule all over Earth.

But moreover, it reveals that the Watchers violated both humans and animals. In addition to creating giants, they also created a brood of monstrous beings. They knew secrets of heaven and were able to apply these teachings to create different species by interbreeding the creatures of the earth. This included mixing human and animal DNA. Nearly all life became genetically corrupted and flesh eating. The giants and monsters terrorised the earth and devoured the human race. This could explain the dinosaurs?

The (fragmented) text says, '... two hundred... donkeys, two hundred asses, two hundred . . . rams of the... flock, two hundred goats, two hundred...beast of the field from every animal, from every...bird...for miscegenation...' And, '...they defiled...they begot giants and monsters...they begot, and, behold, all the earth was corrupted... with its blood and by the hand of...giant's which did not suffice for them and...they were seeking to devour many...the monsters attacked it.' 'Flesh...all...monsters...will be...they would arise...lacking in true knowledge... because...the earth grew corrupt...mighty...they were considering...from the angels upon...in the end it will perish and die...they caused great corruption in the earth...this did not suffice to... they will be'.

As it transpired, before they were destroyed by the flood, the giants were troubled by a series of ominous dreams and visions. One seen a tablet inscribed with many names being immersed in water, and when it emerged, all but three names had been washed away. This dream symbolised the destruction of all but Noah and his three sons. Enoch, the noted scribe, is asked to interpret the dream and sends back a tablet with its grim message. He tells them about God's terrible judgement upon them, their wives and children.

The text says, 'The scribe Enoch...a copy of the second tablet that Enoch sent...in the very handwriting of Enoch the noted scribe...In the name of God the great and holy one, to Shemihaza and all his companions...let it be known to you that not...and the things you have done, and that your wives...they and their sons and the wives of their sons...by your licentiousness on the earth, and there has been upon you...and the land is crying out and complaining about you and the deeds of your children...the harm that you have done to it...until Raphael arrives, behold, destruction is coming, a great flood, and it will destroy all living things and whatever is in the deserts and the seas. And the meaning of the matter...upon you for evil. But now, loosen the bonds binding you to evil...and pray.'

The Book of Jasher, also found with the Dead Sea Scrolls, corroborates the mixing of species agenda. In chapter 4:18, we're told '...the sons of men in those days took from the cattle of the earth, the beasts of the field and the fowls of the air, and taught the mixture of animals of one species with the other, in order therewith to provoke the Lord; and God saw the whole earth and it was corrupt, for all flesh had corrupted its ways upon earth, all men and all animals'.

The Book of Jasher similarly narrates the Genesis story. It states that God created Adam and Eve, and the serpent came to entice them, and they ate from the 'tree of the knowledge of good and evil'. They transgressed from God's command; hence they were cursed. Not dissimilar from Noah, Jasher means upright or righteous (he's mentioned in 2 Samuel 1:18, 2 Timothy 3:8, and Joshua 10:13).

The Book of Jubilees, also found with the Dead Sea scrolls and dated 200BC, similarly reiterates the story of how a group of fallen angels mated with mortal females, giving rise to a race of giants known as the Nephilim. The Book of Jubilees is sometimes called 'the little genesis' because it's essentially the same but with some additional details, like the names of Adam and Eve's daughters. It's divided into periods aka 'jubilees' of 49 years and retells biblical history from creation to Moses (the author is anonymous).

Like the Book of Enoch, the Book of Jubilees is also in the Ethiopian Bible. These hybrid children, in existence during the time of Noah, were then wiped out by the great flood. However, Jubilees states that God granted ten percent of the disembodied spirits of the Nephilim to try to lead mankind astray after the flood. It seems these spirits are demons.

The Book of Enoch, chapter 15:8-10, affirms, 'And now, the giants, who are produced from the spirits and flesh, shall be called evil spirits upon the earth, and on the earth shall be their dwelling'. And, '... as for the spirits of the earth which were born upon the earth, on the earth shall be their dwelling'. So, demons are earthbound spirits because they were earth born. They're not 'dead' people lurking in the spirit world. And they're cursed to roam the earth tortured by hunger and thirst that they could never satisfy.

Enoch 15:11 states, 'And the spirits of the giants afflict, oppress, destroy, attack, do battle, and work destruction on the earth, and cause trouble: they take no food, but nevertheless hunger and thirst, and cause offences. And these spirits shall rise up against the children of men and against the women, because they have proceeded from them'.

Demons are therefore not to be confused with fallen angels, which are comparatively hardcore. Like, one angel killed 185,000 Syrians one night (2 Kings 19:35). And unlike fallen angels that have a body, demons seek a host to embody. It's also noted, that demon possessed people have the strength of giants. Hence, they need several strong men to pin them down.

Furthermore, it seems the first generation of giants preceded the human-animal hybrids. Indeed, it's said the latter were created to house the disembodied nephilim spirits. As it transpires, (according to the Book of Enoch 10: 9-12), as part of their punishment, before they were sent to hell, the Watchers had to watch their beloved kids kill each other. So, this is the clash of the Titans? The nephilim thus needed new bodies, and it was after the diabolical debacle of mixing species, that God let His wrath rip in the Flood. All flesh was corrupted. His creation was vile.

It's highlighted there's an ancient record of advanced biotechnology and it's said all ancient cultures blended DNA. Hence, Egyptian art shows humans with animal heads. Like, Thoth aka bird-man, who's human with a bird head. It's instinctive to draw what we see? Hindu 'mythology' also boasts a host of human-animal hybrids, considered demigods. Like Ganesh, elephant man. Perhaps the human-animal hybrids that people see when they take a DMT trip (to the second heaven) are these spirits?

So, the Watchers were bound and chained in darkness for their debauchery. In Jude 1:6 we're told, 'God has kept them securely chained in prisons of darkness waiting for the great day of judgement'. And 2 Peter 2:4-5 states, 'For God did not spare the angels who sinned, but cast them down to hell [Tartarus] and delivered them into chains of darkness reserved for judgement; and did not spare the ancient world, but saved Noah, one of eight people, a preacher of righteousness, bringing in the flood on the world of the ungodly'. The Chinese word for boat is notably made up of a vessel, the number 8, and a person, which could relate to the 8 people on Noah's ark?

Tartarus, which is translated as hell, is apparently lower than Hades/Sheol, the place of the dead. In Homer's Iliad (circa 700BC), Zeus asserts that Tartarus is 'as far beneath Hades as heaven is above earth'. According to Greek 'mythology', Tartarus is a prison for the Titans. But moreover, according to Enoch 10:12, the Watchers were bound for seventy generations. This happened circa 3000BC, which suggests they were released circa 1900s, which might account for the explosion in science and technology?

So, the Flood landed, and wiped the slate clean. Exactly five months from the time the Flood began, the ark came to rest on the mountains of Ararat. And a few months later Team Noah put their feet on land, which was the land of Shinar/Sumer. Genesis 8:20-21 tells us, 'Then Noah built an altar to the LORD and sacrificed on it the animals and birds that had been approved for that purpose. And the LORD was pleased with the sacrifice and said to Himself, 'I will never again curse the earth, destroying all living things, even though people's thoughts and actions are bent toward evil from childhood'.

God then made a covenant with Noah, solemnly promising never to send another flood. Genesis 9:15 states, 'I will remember my covenant between me and you and all living creatures of every kind. Never again will the waters become a flood to destroy all life'. The rainbow is the sign of that covenant, which presumably reassured wo/men every time clouds appeared.

Whilst humankind were permitted to munch (certain kinds of) animals after the flood, since food might be difficult to obtain, God ordained, in Genesis 9:5-6, 'Murder is forbidden'. Before and until the Flood, we were to be, by God's decree, vegetarian. The nephilim clearly violated this decree. Animals that kill people must die, and anyone who murders anyone else must be executed.

It's also noted, that when people sacrificed an animal for food, they recognised they were taking a life, unlike today. How many people actually care about the life they are eating? How many people care about the cow that died so they could eat a hamburger? It's rhetorical, as no one cares. And no one cares about all the animals that die in vain, all the wasted 'meat'. And sacrifice for sin meant something. It was serious. God is Holy. Someone has to pay the price for sin because it's not okay. This in turn paves the way for Jesus the redeemer, as we'll get to.

It's also interesting to note, as Chuck Missler points out, that the gospel message is revealed to us through the lineage from Adam to Noah, as their names have meanings (see Genesis 5:1-32). Thus, Adam, Seth, Enosh, Kenan, Mahalalel, Jared, Enoch, Methuselah, Lamech, Noah translates to 'Man (is), Appointed, Mortal, Sorrow, (but) The Blessed God, Shall come down, Teaching, His death shall bring, The despairing, Rest or Comfort'.

Dr Missler states this is a hidden code, and he highlights other hidden codes in the Bible. Like, in Genesis 1-2, the names of twenty-six trees are encoded in text about trees. Secret codes are discovered using formulas like equidistant letter sequences e.g. take every fourth letter to make a word. Missler refers to these codes as authenticating the 'fingerprint signature of the author' on every page. He highlights Proverbs 25:2, which states, 'It is the glory of God to conceal things, but the glory of kings to search things out'. Like, he highlights the divine number 7 is plastered everywhere, overtly and covertly. The Bible is not a normal book, but we'll get back to numbers and meanings.

It's also said the gospel is written in the stars i.e. it starts with Virgo the Virgin and ends with Leo the Lion. Jesus is depicted as a lion (from the tribe of Judah) who triumphantly comes back to kick Lucifer's arse at the end times. But furthermore, in 2016 NASA informed there are thirteen zodiac signs, and the thirteenth is Ophiuchus the Serpent Bearer. Apparently, this sign was always here but the Babylonians, who invented the twelve signs of the zodiac, excluded it because twelve signs fit the lunar cycles of the year better. Thus, after millennia, we're now acknowledging the serpent in the sky? However, I digress.

So, God blessed Noah and his sons and told them to 'multiply and fill the earth'. And so, they did. Noah's three sons, Shem, Ham and Japheth, fathered all the people now scattered across the earth. Shem became the ancestor of Abraham and thus the Israelites, including Jesus. It's thought Africans descended from Ham, who was dark-skinned. Apparently, the name Ham means 'dark' or 'brown'. Black (2010) concedes that Ham means 'He who is hot', implying a dark coloured skin (p.441). Japheth went north, thus it's believed Europeans came from his lineage. According to the Book of Enoch, Noah had white hair, extremely white skin and eyes like the sun, suggesting an albino appearance. But we'll get back to genetics.

The Bible refers to Egypt as 'the land of Ham' and it's interpreted that Ham's four son's populated Africa and adjoining parts of Asia. Ham's son Cush, which means 'black' in Hebrew and refers to anyone of Black African descent, is understood to be the forefather of Ethiopia. Apparently, Ham's son Phut went to Libya. Mizraim is Hebrew for Egypt, and there was Canaan. It's noted, this corroborates with the belief that we 'evolved' in East Africa.

But moreover, as it transpired, Ham was something of a bugger. In Genesis 9:20-27 we're told that Noah became drunk with some wine he had made, and he lay naked in his tent. Ham saw that his father was naked and went out and told his brothers. Shem and Japheth discreetly clad their father with a robe, paying due attention not to have a fly spy. The next morning when Noah woke up from his drunken stupor, he learned what Ham had done. Then he cursed the descendants of Canaan, ('cursed be Canaan'), son of Ham.

Canaan was the youngest, and why Noah cursed him rather than the others remains a mystery. Some postulate that something more brownly sinister was done to Noah, given the curse to the Canaanites. Such a punishment, for merely seeing your dad naked and telling your brothers, seems harsh. So, either looking at someone's genitalia and gossiping about it was indeed a serious matter, or alternatively, the unnatural crime of Ham and/or Canaan revealed the impiety and vileness of their character, with those vile characteristics perpetuated in Canaan. It's understood the wayward Canaanites were partial to sodomy and incest. It's also conjectured that Ham had sex with his mum. And it's further suggested the curse could have been prophetic as Canaan became Israel's enemy.

But furthermore, Ham's son Cush begat Nimrod, and Nimrod is particularly potent because he's the founder of Babylon, from which all idolatry came. He's referred to as that 'wicked one' and 'lawless one'. According to the Book of Jasher, Nimrod was born at a time when the sons of men began to rebel against God and transgress. His name means 'we shall rebel'. It's said that Ham resented Noah's authority, and in effect God's authority. This attitude trickled down to his son Cush, who led a rebellion against God. Then Nimrod continued his father's work.

Nimrod's known as a mighty hunter, but apparently he was ascribed the title 'Great Hunter' because he hunted people to murder as sacrifices to his pagan god. After the Flood, there were no visible gods, but invisible gods could be contacted using forbidden knowledge to transcend the veil i.e. inter-dimensional communication. One could exercise power by performing certain religious practices, sacrificial and magical ceremonies, to compel the gods to do their bidding.

As it transpired, rather than dispersing worldwide as God instructed, Nimrod rebelled by building Babylon for the 'gods', and a kingdom for himself. He became the first world ruler. Paganism was introduced, as an alternative religion, to attract worship away from the true God of Heaven.

It's noted however, that whilst Nimrod endorsed sun worship, worshipping the sun, moon and stars began in the antediluvian world. The fallen angels taught the mystical religion of Sabaism, this counterfeit religion aka witchcraft. As mentioned, the 'gods' revelled in orgies, cannibalism, drinking blood, sorcery etc, and divulged their party tricks. Interestingly, according to Gary Wayne, Nimrod found this esoteric knowledge after the flood. It's said this information was stashed in nine subterranean vaults, as the pre-Flood people knew about the coming deluge.

Apparently Nimrod was very adept and prolific in mixing demonism and idolatry into formal sciences and arts such as astrology. The twelve signs of the zodiac from which astrology is derived, creates the foundation for witchcraft. Nimrod knew magical incantations to force demons into obedience, which includes summoning them into objects to create idols. He was well versed in divination, magic and blood rituals.

Nimrod also married his mum Semiramis, which effectively made his marriage a 'trinity' union i.e. husband-wife-son. Apparently through this act of incest, as instructed to by the pagan priests, he acquired the 'third eye' or 'all seeing eye'. He became super Nimrod, possessed/enlightened by evil spirits? Nimrod's occult knowledge gave him power over people, and he was worshipped as god. So, King Nimrod reigned with Queen Semiramis in a kingdom of darkness.

In tandem with the Biblical account, it seems pertinent to interject regarding the Sumerian clay tablets, as they corroborate with His-story. Apparently, the name Sumer connotates 'Land of the Watchers'. Thus, tens of thousands of tablets were excavated in Sumer (Iraq) in the 19th century, which date back to six thousand years ago. As touched on, these tablets were the first writings detailing how demons can affect human health.

It's understood Sumer was the first great civilisation of antiquity, seven hundred years before the Egyptians appeared in 3,100BC. They recognised the flood as a genuine historic event and believed in a pantheon of gods called the Anunnaki. The exceptionally clever Sumerians credited their advanced knowledge of mathematics, astronomy and other sciences, as well as the gift of writing, to the gods. It seems the Anunnaki are the Watchers?

The Sumerians were the first metallurgists, blending metals into alloys, extracting silver from ore, and casting bronze in complex moulds. Their mathematics and measurements are still used today. Like, the sixty second minute, and sixty minute hour, and the 360 degrees in a circle, and 12 inches in a foot. They invented the wheel, glass, and even made beer.

So, man was sophisticated from the start. Scientific knowledge did not pass through any evolutionary period, as we're lied to believe. There was no smooth gradual cultural development, but rather the first civilisation emerged suddenly with advanced science and technology. As Alford (1996) highlights, all studies of Sumerians have stressed the extremely short period within which their high level of culture and technology arose. And further, since the impossible origin of such ancient knowledge doesn't compute with our contemporary sociological rationale, it's glossed over.

It appears 'science' is more comfortable believing the fallacy that we were monkeys who became thick cave men, despite no evidence? It seems modern man likes to think ancient man made up the gods for funsies? When the truth is, they were conjuring the gods. Moreover, as Alford asserts, inventing gods is one thing, but inventing the technology to measure the planets and the stars is another thing entirely. David Icke (2007) concedes, their tablets describe planets of the solar system, in number and environment, in ways that were only confirmed in the twentieth century. It's said the gods were the primary reason ancient man acquired such an obsessive interest in astronomy.

Alford also pertains to impossible feats of engineering. He states it is a fact that the great pyramid was built with advanced technology, yet no-one can explain how they got their knowledge and why they needed it. Or why the pyramid shape was so important. He further highlights it is a fact that in ancient times megalithic stones weighing hundreds of tons were cut, miraculously transported into position, and fitted together so accurately that one cannot fit the thinnest knife-blade between them. He asserts such constructions would be extremely difficult even with modern day technology. He further states it is a fact that the Easter Island statues could not have been cut with stone tools. And again, no-one can explain why they were carried and erected (p.581).

Or what about the Nasca lines (huge geoglyphs etched into the desert), which were only discovered in the twentieth century with the advent of flight, as one needs to be air borne (several thousand feet about ground level) to see them i.e. OBE (see photos). The gods can see these pictures from heaven?

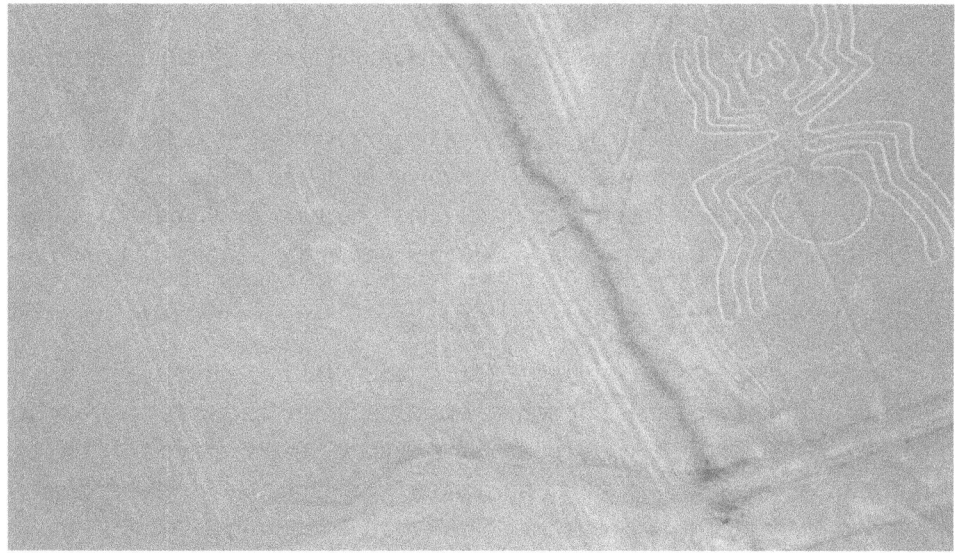

However, before we get back to Nimrod's kingdom of darkness, it also seems pertinent to note the 'alien astronaut theory'. Thus, rather than Watchers coming to earth, it's promulgated that aliens came to earth. Like, Zecharia Sitchin, Russian-American author, who allegedly interpreted the Sumerian clay tablets, said the Anunnaki were a race of ETs from Nibiru aka planet X. He claims they genetically engineered humans to be their slaves to mine gold for them. He credits ETs with building the pyramids and other impossible feats. He claims the Anunnaki were forced to leave when Noah's flood came. But moreover, he claims the Anunnaki left behind human-alien hybrids, some of whom may still be alive today, unaware of their alien ancestry. It seems these kids became the kings of mortal men?

Whilst this theory is popular in the 'New Age', it's understood Sitchin stitched us up. His writings have been universally rejected as mistranslations and misinterpretations. As Dr Michael Heiser, Semitic languages scholar, affirms, the tablets do not say Anunnaki are ETs from Nibiru. The Anunnaki is not associated with Nibiru at all. And it's not true that they engineered primates then us to mine gold for them.

And Anunnaki does not mean, as Sitchin claims, 'Those Who From Heaven to Earth Came', but rather, Anunnaki refers to princely seed or noble. Heiser explains the Anunnaki were a group of gods in Mesopotamia religion, who's status varied i.e. they were considered high gods but also gods of the underworld. So, that could be the Watchers? These 'gods' are in the second heaven (i.e. fallen angels) and in the underworld (or were)?

The Bible tells us the Babylonians decided to build a tower, the notorious Tower of Babel, to reach the heavens. It would be a monument to reflect their greatness. However, as it transpired, God thwarted their plan. He recognised that if they were capable of accomplishing that feat, nothing would be impossible for them. Thus, He threw a spanner in the works by bestowing various languages on the people, thereby making it impossible for them to communicate.

After the flood everyone spoke the same language, (presumably Hebrew because it's a pure language and can't be traced back to another language), but some seventy different languages were introduced at Babel. Genesis 11:9 states, 'That is why the city was called Babel because it was there that the Lord confused the people by giving them many languages'. It's also purported, they built the Tower of Babel for protection, in case a Flood ever happened again. This suggests they didn't trust God's promise that He would never flood the earth again.

It's noted, that 'Bab' means gate, and 'el' refers to God. Hence, Babel literally means 'Gateway to God' or 'heaven's gate'. It was built in a valley (about two days walk east of Shinar), which births two different views regarding its purpose. Thus, being constructed in a valley suggests it was less about height, and more about being an inter-dimensional portal. It's surmised the Tower of Babel was like a huge invocation apparatus, like a massive Ouija board, invoking dark entities. This makes sense from a heliocentric perspective.

However, others contend it was built there because that was the biggest plain to accommodate what would be an insanely large ziggurat to literally reach heaven. Apparently, it took a year to get to the top of the ziggurat. This suggests the people actually believed they could reach heaven. They believed in an enclosed cosmology i.e. snow-globe. The Book of Jasher tells us the people imagined in their hearts to war against God and ascend into heaven. It was feasible to break through the firmament and defeat God?

Alexander Hislop, in his book 'The Two Babylons' (1858) asserts, 'The Tower of Babel was actually the worship of Satan in the form of fire, the sun and the serpent. However, Satan worship could not be done openly because of the many who still believed in the true God of Noah. So a mystery religion began at Babel where Satan could be worshipped in secret'. However, we'll get back to this Mystery Religion of Babylon in a moment or three.

After Project Babel, the people scattered, and then along came Abram (from Shem's lineage). Abram, who God renamed Abraham, was God's designated 'father of a great nation'. It's interesting to note, that according to the Book of Jasher, stargazers knew Abram was going to be a special kid. And they told King Nimrod. These wise men stated this child would be fruitful and multiply, and that he and his children would slay great kings and take their lands.

Nimrod, none too pleased, was subsequently on a mission to kill Abram. Abram's father Terah, who was the head-idol maker for the kingdom no less, was however aware of his plot. Thus, Terah swapped baby Abram with a maidservant's baby and tricked Nimrod into believing he had killed Abram (pretty sneaky). We're told Nimrod took the child and dashed his head to the ground.

Team Terah then hid Abram in a cave for ten years, and then he went to live with Noah and Shem. He remained with them until he learned the instructions of Yahweh and His ways. It's said Abram stayed in Noah's house for thirty-nine years, and no one knew where he was. Meanwhile, idolatry was rampant. This wicked generation had forgotten God. Nimrod and all his servants made their own gods out of stones etc to worship. Like, Terah had twelve gods, one for each month of the year, and he would offer meat and drink to his gods.

When Abram eventually left Noah's abode, clothed in the Spirit of God, Abram told his father not to follow strange gods, and he broke all his father's gods. Terah and Nimrod were both raging, and Abram's oldest brother Haran got involved. This resulted in Nimrod putting both Abram and Haran in a fire. Whilst Haran burned and died, Abram was not burned, despite being in the furnace for three days.

As it transpired, God told Abram to leave his homeland, which he did when he was seventy-five (which pleased Nimrod). Abram took his nephew Lot (Haran's son), his wife Sarai, and the rest of their people and belongings, and headed to the Promised Land. God promised Canaan to Abraham as his inheritance. It was 'a land flowing with milk and honey'. But the territory of Canaan spread to various locations including Sodom and Gomorrah (Genesis 10:19), and they were carnage. The people are described as extremely wicked. It's said these sexual perverts used kids as sex-slaves, and relished in humiliation and degradation. It seems depraved and debauched people simply helped themselves to others. Like, today? Jesus notably said, it would be 'like the days of Lot' when He returned.

With regards to Sodom, we're told that one evening two angels went to stay with Lot, and 'all the men of Sodom, young and old, came from all over the city and surrounded his house. They shouted to Lot, 'where are the men who came to spend the night with you? Bring them out so we can have sex with them'. Lot begs them not be wicked and suggests they do as they wish with his two virgin daughters instead (Genesis 19: 1-12). [Nice].

Apparently, in those times, men's preference was men, and women's preference was women. The angels then struck the men outside with blindness so they couldn't find the door, and urged Lot and co to bail, stating the city was going to be obliterated with fire and brimstone. God promised He would never flood the earth again, but He said nada about fire showers. Thus, God destroyed these cities and two neighbouring cities. There's notably evidence of this sulphuric event. Balls of the purest sulphur (brimstone) are found at the Dead Sea. It looks like they were rained down.

It's conjectured that Sodom and Gomorrah were infiltrated by fallen angels, who again procreated with women, producing nephilim, hence they met their demise. As Genesis 6:4 tells us, 'the nephilim were on the earth in those days and also afterwards, whenever the sons of God went to the daughters of humans and had children by them'. And we hear about giants after the Flood.

Thus, some believe there was a second, or even multiple incursions of fallen angels that birthed nephilim. Others suggest nephilim survived the Flood by going underground, as we're told that everything on land died. The idea that they went underground notably corroborates with the Vril maidens who believed they were in contact with an underground ET race. They believed some Atlanteans survived by going deeper underground. Helena Blavatsky agreed that 'Aryans' took refuge in the earth. Or they could have absconded into the air, on UFOs?

Others purport that Noah's son's wives had corrupted DNA. Thus, the giants returned but their genes were diluted, so they weren't as giant. There's a general consensus that post-Flood giants were smaller in stature and more human like. Like, the cone-heads, and the six fingered giants the American Indians feared. Presumably, the giant giants are buried under a ton of post-flood sediment.

As it transpired, Lot's daughters got their father drunk and had sex with him, so they became pregnant. Apparently, their father didn't realise this happened because he was so drunk. They wanted to preserve their family line and there were no men around to marry (Genesis 19:31-36). The older daughter's son Moab became the father of the Moabites, and the younger daughter's son Ben Ammi became the father of the Ammonites, both of which were nephilim tribes. It's understood that nephilim tribes descended from Ham and Japheth's lineage, whereas Shem's line was untainted. It's also duly noted, that perhaps we could question the point of the flood, since nephilim returned and debauchery resumed?

So, there were basically two groups of people, namely, those who followed Noah's God and those who followed Nimrod's serpent sun religion. As Chuck Missler said, His-Story can be conceptualised as a tale of two cities, namely, Babylon the city of man, and Jerusalem the city of God. Babylon represents spiritual darkness, and Israel represents spiritual light.

Abraham is known as the first Hebrew, and God's people were born through his grandson Jacob. Jacob, who became known as Israel, is the father of the twelve tribes of Israel i.e. each son heads up a tribe. Their bloodline was pure human and Israel was different from the rest of society. They loved YHWH (Yahweh) and weren't haunted perverts. They were God's people and He reserved the Holy Land for them to dwell in. Scripture has at least 170 references to the land that God gave to the offspring of Abraham, Isaac and Jacob.

It seems pertinent to note, that Abraham was put to the test with his son Isaac (Jacob's father), as it's a foreshadowing of Jesus' sacrifice. Thus, God tested Abraham's faith by asking him to sacrifice his beloved Isaac. It probably can't be overstated how beloved Isaac was. God promised Abraham a nation, yet his wife seemed barren. They waited almost forever for Isaac, as we'll get back to in the religion chapter.

Abraham was however prepared to sacrifice his son for God, and just as he was about to, God providentially stepped in and provided a ram as a replacement offering. It seems God was making a point? That is, unlike Abraham, God would feel the pain of allowing His only begotten Son Jesus to be sacrificed for us. It's also noted, this emotional pain stands in stark opposition to those who freely sacrificed their kids to Satan. It seems these freaks want to?

As it transpired, Great Uncle Shem was fiercely angry with Nimrod, not least because of the human sacrifices. It's understood Yahweh was disgusted at the widespread idol worship and their satanic antics. And being God's defender, Shem killed Nimrod, which left Semiramis ruler of the kingdom. It's said Shem dismembered Nimrod's body and sent the body parts (as evidence) to the many different cities of Nimrod's empire. This served as an example to others not to commit such abominable sins and not to follow evil religious practices. Satan worship was thus forced underground. The book of Jasher notably states Abraham's son Esau (Jacob's brother) killed Nimrod as opposed to Shem. Either way, Babylon had lost its god. It was like a helpless babe.

However, Semiramis had a plan. After Nimrod's death, she began to formulate what's known as the Mystery Religion of Babylon. She proclaimed that Nimrod had defeated death and literally became the god of the Sun. He was the father of creation. And in violation of God's Sabbath day, a counterfeit holy day was instituted in honour of the Sun God, namely Sun-day, to worship the sun. Thus, sun worship is Satan worship.

So, Nimrod was elevated to God, and Semiramis, being Nimrod's mum and queen, raised her stature to 'Mother of God'. Nimrod was given the title Baal, which means 'Master' or 'Lord', and Semiramis was given the title Baalti, which means 'My Lady'. Those who followed her religion became known as Baal worshippers.

So, Nimrod was the Sun God, and Semiramis the Moon Goddess. She claimed that her spirit was the moon and when she died, she would dwell in the moon, even as Nimrod was already in the sun.

Alas however, not everyone was convinced that Nimrod really was the Sun God and Life Giver, so Semiramis had to make a miracle happen. And that miracle was for Nimrod to come back from the dead. Hence, Tammuz arrived. Semiramis claimed she was impregnated through the rays of the sun. She claimed Nimrod, the Sun god, fathered Tammuz. Thus, Tammuz was an immaculate conception (a virgin birth, although she was not a virgin). She was able to convince Nimrod's followers that Tammuz was the fulfilment of Genesis 3:15. That is, her seed was the promised seed. It's said she actually got nasty with a pagan priest (maybe she ate his fruit?).

It's noted, Lucifer is familiar with the Holy Trinity i.e. God the Father, God the Son, and God the Holy Spirit. He was in fellowship with Elohim, until he wasn't. It's also understood that everything he does is a counterfeit to God's works. It's said he has no ability to create, but rather he can only imitate.

So, Nimrod reincarnated as Tammuz and he was born on December 25th. Within Baal worship, December 25th is known as the nativity of the sun, which is when Tammuz celebrates his birthday (after the winter solstice). Tammuz was believed to be the son of the Sun god and the Sun god at the same time i.e. Nimrod in the flesh. He is both father and son, and Semiramis was mother of both. Semiramis was worshipped as the Goddess of Fertility. But she had many titles including Mother Goddess of Babylon and Queen of Heaven. Semiramis and Tammuz became worshipped as 'Madonna and Child'.

However, as it transpired, Tammuz was killed in a hunting accident by a wild boar when he was forty. So, Semiramis took her cult further. She declared that her immortal god-son, who died, was resurrected and became one with his father, the Sun god Baal. Apparently, he was resurrected at 'Easter', through the power of her tears, following forty days of grieving. Those who worshipped Tammuz celebrated 'Lent' for forty days, one day for each year of his incarnation. During this time, they would deny a worldly pleasure for his pleasure in the after-world.

Thus, the unholy trinity occult religion was born, which mirrors the Holy Trinity. But instead of the Holy Spirit, there's Semiramis. The son and father were 'one' through her. As Hislop wrote, 'The Trinity got its start in Ancient Babylon with Nimrod – Tammuz – and Semiramis. Semiramis demanded worship for both her husband and her son as well as herself. She claimed that her son, was both the father and the son. Yes, he was 'god the father' and 'god the son' – The first divine incomprehensible trinity' (p.51).

The Bible tells us about this pagan cult. And that 'Ishtar' (Easter) was a day that commemorated the resurrection of 'Tammuz', one of their gods, who was believed to be the only begotten son of the moon-goddess and the sun-god. Ezekiel 8:14 pertains to women grieving for Tammuz.

So, Nimrod, Semiramis and Tammuz became worshipped as the divine godhead. Semiramis brazenly claimed that she and her priests were the only ones who understood the mysteries of God, and were therefore the only way to God. Followers of this satanic religious order had to take secret oaths, to maintain its secrecy, with peopled sacrificed surreptitiously. Contrary to God's command, this worship included sacrificing babies.

In Leviticus 18:21 God said, 'Do not permit any of your children to be offered as a sacrifice to Molech, for you must not bring shame on the name of your God. I am the LORD'. Molech is another name for Baal. Semiramis instructed her followers it was mandatory. Semiramis also introduced confession. The followers of this pagan religion had to confess their sins to priests (for more control). And apparently, she introduced crucifixion, which is one of the worst ways to die (one basically asphyxiates). So, the Romans learned this brutal practice from her?

According to legend, when Semiramis died she ascended into heaven, to the moon. But then she returned to earth inside a large egg, which fell into the Euphrates River, at the first full moon after the spring equinox. A dove pushed the egg ashore, and she emerged as Astarte or Ishtar. Then to show her gratitude to the dove, she turned it into an egg-laying rabbit. So, Easter comes from Ishtar, which is reincarnated Semiramis. Easter is Ishtar bursting from an egg day. Hence, the Ishtar egg. The 'Easter bunny' represents new life, fertility, and reincarnation.

[It's noted, Lady Gaga was emulating this scenario, when she emerged from an oversized egg for her song 'Born This Way' for the 2011 Grammy Awards. Gaga said she was incubating in the egg for three days, which corroborates with being reborn into secret societies, as we'll get to. It's also noted, that to be 'born this way' defies the existential premise of 'becoming'].

So, pagans worshipped this goddess. Early on Sunday morning, as the sun was rising in the east, they would give themselves over to immorality and indecency of every description. The forty days of lent or weeping for Tammuz starts the Easter fertility season. The debauchery culminates on Easter Sunday, when the priests of Easter slaughtered the 'wild boar that killed Tammuz', which provided the 'Easter ham' for the congregation to munch.

Furthermore, (as the cult developed), the priests of Easter would impregnate young virgins on the altar of the goddess of fertility at sunrise on Easter Sunday. Then a year later the priests would sacrifice those three-month-old babies on the altar at the front of the Sanctuary. They would hunt for eggs, then dye them in the blood of sacrificed infants, and these would be sent home as fertility blessings. This appears to be the origin of painting eggs at Easter.

As mentioned, Project Babel resulted in the dispersion of people, with their new tongues. Thus, it's contended the same Mystery Religion of Babylon was perpetuated under different names in the different languages. And like Chinese whispers, some of the details got slightly altered. Like, with the Egyptian version, the husband-wife-son theme of Nimrod, Semiramis and Tammuz became the Osiris-Isis-Horus mythology.

Osiris the sun god was reincarnated through Horus. However, unlike Semiramis, who was Nimrod's wife and mother, Isis is the wife and sister of Osiris (apparently Osiris and Isis were fraternal twins before they were spouses). The rules in Egypt were that one inherited kingship from their ancestors i.e. kingship is reborn in son. Thus, Osiris's lineage apparently stretched back to the creator of the world, Ra or Atum. Egyptian names of Kings of Egypt such as Rameses, means 'The Son of Ra'. Pharaoh means Ra incarnate.

Before we get back to His-Story, it seems pertinent to interject regarding the Egyptian legend, since 'Horus the one-eyed sun god' is quite the feature, and also because Egypt has been quite the feature. Indeed, it's said no other country has ever so boldly denied God. Egypt is compared spiritually with Sodom.

So, Osiris was the sun-god incarnate, but he was killed by his evil brother Seth. Osiris's body was cut into fourteen pieces and scattered throughout Egypt (like Nimrod was chopped up). Isis found thirteen parts but the fourteenth, his manhood, was missing. So, she fashioned a golden phallus, and sang a song until Osiris came back to life. Thus, Osiris was resurrected, and Isis conceived Horus, then Osiris died again. He returned to the mysterious realm of the dead, where he's known as God of the Underworld and Lord of the Afterlife. Horus, the divine son of Isis and Osiris, was born on December 25th as per.

It's also noted, that obelisks, the giant phallic symbols found worldwide, represent Osiris's phallus. They represent the erect male shaft of sun-god Baal and the resurrection of the erection i.e. the phallus dies and rises again. Apparently Semiramis erected a 130 foot obelisk in Babylon. Wheeler (2009) states, God forbade the Israelites from worshipping the spirit of the Egyptian sun god, Ra, believed to be residing within the obelisk.

Horus then sets about avenging his father's death, by taking on Seth, and fighting him for the throne. The conflict/contest dragged on for eighty years, and at one stage amid the strife, Isis attempts to harpoon Seth, but she strikes Horus instead, who none too pleased, and in a fit of rage, cuts her head off. Thoth (a deity with healing powers, who we'll get back to) replaced Isis's head with that of a cow, which accounts for the mythical origin for the cow-horn headdress that Isis commonly wears.

Another key episode of the conflict includes when Seth sexually abuses Horus. Seth's violation is partly meant to degrade Horus, but it also involves homosexual desire. One of Seth's major characteristics is his forceful and indiscriminate sexuality (rape is about power). Horus injures or steals Seth's testicles and Seth damages or tears out one of Horus's eyes.

To cut a long story short, Horus won the battle but lost an eye, ergo he became known as the 'one eyed sun god'. The 'Eye of Horus' became one of the most important symbols in ancient Egypt. It's the symbol of Lucifer (sun god) and represents the 'all seeing eye' in Freemasonry and the third eye of clairvoyance. It symbolises the pineal gland, the gateway to the spirit world. This secret knowledge has been harboured by mystery schools, which precede secret societies, as we'll get to.

As for His-Story, Jacob aka Israel settled back in the land of Canaan. And as it transpired, his 'favourite' son Joseph had prophetic dreams, which came to pass. Joseph envisioned his brothers bowing down to him, and having imparted his dreams to them, they sold him into Egyptian slavery. Joseph's brothers told their father he was killed by some wild animal. As touched on, Joseph interpreted Pharaoh's dreams, which saved Egypt from famine. Thus, Joseph became the second most important man in Egypt, and his brothers did bow down to him. Joseph forgave his brothers, and his family went to live with him, as there was an epidemic of famine in Canaan.

As it transpired however, God's people became Pharaoh's slaves. The people of Israel lived in Egypt for 430 years, and God heard their cries of despair. So, God set Moses in motion to liberate His people. Like Abraham, it was known Moses would be a special kid. Hence, Pharaoh ruled for all baby Hebrew boys to be killed. However, it's equally noted, that Pharaoh was getting antsy with the volume of Hebrews, fearing a revolution.

Baby Moses was thus placed in a reed basket on the river Nile, concealed by the bulrushes on the riverbank, only to be discovered and adopted by Pharaoh's daughter. Thus, Moses was raised in the Egyptian palace, where he learned their magic and knew their gods. Acts 7:22 tells us, 'Moses was instructed in all the wisdom of the Egyptians, and he was mighty in his words and deeds'.

Like Abraham, Moses also heard from Yahweh, from a burning bush no less. God explained that He is the God of Abraham, Isaac and Jacob, and stated He has heard His peoples' cries for deliverance from their harsh slave drivers. But moreover, His instrument is Moses. Moses would have to ask Pharaoh to let His people go. This was no small ask.

When Moses asked God who he should say sent him, God said, 'I AM WHO I AM'. God said, 'Just tell them, 'I AM' has sent you' (Exodus 3:14). God further tells Moses to tell His people that God will rescue them and lead them to a land flowing with milk and honey. They will inherit the land that was given to Abraham and his descendants. However, God also advised the land was now occupied by Canaanites, Hittites, Amorites, Perizzites, Hivites, and Jebusites, which are nephilim tribes.

God empowered Moses with some miracles, like enabling his staff to turn into a snake, to convince both the leaders of Israel and Pharaoh that God sent him. And since Moses was anxious, God permitted his brother Aaron to speak for him (Exodus 6:28-7:7). Whilst the leaders of Israel were convinced, Pharaoh was less impressed because he had his own party tricks. Exodus 7: 11-12 tells us, 'Then Pharaoh called in his wise men and magicians, and they did the same thing with their secret arts. Their staffs became snakes, too! But then Aaron's snake swallowed up their snakes'.

As it transpired, Pharaoh was not for setting the captives free, which resulted in God sending ten horrific plagues e.g. swarms of locusts, armies of frogs, rivers turning to blood, boils. God also referred to this as His judgement against all the false gods of Egypt. Each plague was connected to their gods. Like, they worshipped the Nile, so the Nile was turned into blood, and they worshipped the frog god, so they were subjected to an avalanche of frogs. Pharaoh eventually threw the towel in after the last plague, which was the death of all first-born sons and first-born male animals (he was forewarned). God assured Moses that Pharaoh would insist they leave after this. It seems Pharaoh also received karma for killing all the Hebrew infants?

Before the genocide, God told Moses to tell his people to sacrifice a lamb and smear its blood on their door and door frame, and the angel of death would pass-over these residencies, which happened. God ordained for this 'Passover' event to be celebrated, so people would remember that God spared His people. Future generations would remember YHWH (Yahweh) made a clear distinction between the Egyptians and Israelites. Their exodus from Egypt (their place of slavery) would be remembered. Every year, in early spring, they would celebrate this anniversary and dedicate all first-born sons and animals to God. It's noted, the Passover lamb was a foreshadowing of Jesus.

It's also noted, when they left Egypt, Moses took Joseph's bones as Joseph made the sons of Israel swear they would take his bones when they left Egypt, as he was sure God would lead them out and lead them back home. We're told God led His people by a pillar of cloud during the day, and a pillar of fire at night. They would camp where either of these pillars came to a halt.

However, as it transpired, despite Pharaoh telling the Israelites to go, he subsequently changed His mind and sent his troops after them. Moreover, God led them to the Red Sea, which is where the Egyptian army caught up with them. Exodus 14:10 tells us, 'As Pharaoh and his army approached, the people of Israel could see them in the distance, marching toward them. The people began to panic, and they cried out to the LORD for help'. Then they turned against Moses.

Exodus 14:15-16 tells us, 'Then the LORD said to Moses, 'Why are you crying out to me? Tell the people to get moving! Use your shepherd's staff – hold it out over the water, and a path will open up before you through the sea. Then all the people of Israel will walk through in dry land'.

And so, they walked through the sea on dry land, with walls of water on both sides. Then the LORD told Moses to raise his hand over the sea, which he did, and the sea roared back into its usual place, which killed all the Egyptians chasing them. Archaeologists have notably discovered remains of the Egyptian army in the Red Sea, like chariots etc. Suffice to say, His-Story is not a fairy-tale, like history?

After their exodus from Egypt, God steered them towards the Promised Land. However, the people started grumbling about being in the wilderness, despite the freedom from Egyptian oppression. And they turned to their pagan gods. We hear that while Moses was up the mountain, having time with God and receiving the Ten Commandments, his people constructed a golden calf (Baal's symbol) to worship.

When Moses returned, he smashed the tablets (inscribed with the commandments which were written by God Himself) out of exasperation. How could they worship Baal after everything they'd witnessed? God did however replace/rewrite these. After a year at Mount Sinai, the Jewish people arrived at the borders of the Promised Land. And they sent in twelve spies, (one from each tribe), to scout the land, which they did for forty days. Ten of the twelve spies gave disparaging reports, stating the natives were huge and too fierce to combat.

Numbers 13:33 states, 'There we saw the giants, the sons of Anak, who come from the nephilim. We seemed like grasshoppers in our own eyes, and we looked the same to them'. Apparently, the Egyptians knew about the Anakim ('long necks') and feared them. As punishment for not trusting God would be with them, the Israelites had to wander in the wilderness for forty years (one year for each day they spied out the land). It's understood that 'being in the desert or wilderness' is a harsh place of learning.

Apparently, Moses wrote the Torah, the first five books of the Old Testament, during their time in the wilderness. It's also noted, that God provided quail for meat and manna aka 'bread from heaven' (manna is a sweet powdery substance). The Lord said to Moses, 'I will rain down bread from heaven for you' (Exodus 16:4). It seems God has laid this provision on for others in need, as there's reports about other people, in different parts of the world, receiving manna including Africa and South America. So, that's more evidence of the 'supernatural'.

It is however noted, that despite their fear or lack of faith, the Israelites defeated two Amorite Kings, (with God's help), en route to the land of milk and honey. Namely, Sihon and Og of Bashan. Og's bed was apparently 13.5 feet long and 6 feet wide, and it's believed he was ten or eleven feet tall. It's suggested there was another incursion of fallen angels, as the Promised Land was teeming with nephilim. Or these nephilim came from former nephilim i.e. that trace back to Ham and Japheth's wives' genes.

Either way, the devil knew God promised this land to His people, and they'd be returning there, so his minions got busy populating the land. There were apparently thirty-six different post-flood nephilim tribes living in and around the land of Canaan. Like the Amorites, descendants of Canaan, who were as tall as cedars and as strong as oaks, and the Rephaim, Zuzim, Emim. God had forewarned them about the Amorites, Amalekites, Hittites and Jebusites, and they were all there. The Anunnaki, who the Sumerians highlighted, was another race of giants. It's also said the descendants of Anak are Anunnaki.

Joshua, (who took over from Moses to lead the flock into the Promised Land), had clear instructions from God that if the Canaanites didn't get out, the Jews must wipe them out. God was explicit that these Baal worshippers would corrupt the Jews if they remained in the land (and their bloodline if they mingled their seed). Thus, before they entered the land, the Jewish people sent an envoy to the Canaanites with the message, 'God, the Creator of the Universe has promised this land to our forefathers. We are now here to claim our inheritance, and we ask you to leave peacefully'. This didn't happen.

However, as it transpired, Joshua and his troops prevailed. But God warned them, that should they transgress from God, their enemies will preside over the land. Whilst Joshua and co wiped out many nephilim tribes, the giants weren't completely wiped out, but rather shooed from the land. Hence, there's evidence of them (like the Paracus skulls) and their serpent sun religion worldwide. Great civilisations arose at the same time i.e. China, Native America, Egypt, Persia, Indus Valley, with similar architecture e.g. temples and pyramids. The nephilim became the royal bloodlines and they created religion and politics to install their methods of rule and control. But we'll get to this craziness.

Joshua then gave different parts of the land of Canaan to each of Israel's twelve tribes. However, as it also transpired, after Joshua died, the next generation forgot all about what the Lord had done. And some of them worshipped the Canaanite gods. Perhaps this is a parallel to today. That is, it's only taken a generation for the west to forget about God i.e. since 1945? It's duly noted, that Jews have lived in this land continuously since its original conquest by Joshua in 1450BC. Jews have however not always had political control of the land, and they have not always been the majority of the land's population.

It seems pertinent to highlight the contrast between the Canaanite religion of debauchery and God's commandments. In addition to the Ten Commandments, God gave Moses all kinds of instructions for His people, regarding how best to live. Like, cleanliness was important. And they could eat certain animals. But they were not to drink animal's blood. As mentioned, they were not allowed to murder people or sacrifice their kids to Molech. They were not to practice witchcraft or fortune-telling, or offer sacrifices to evil spirits, or worship any others 'gods'. Father God's also not into orgies or incest or bestiality, and prostitution is not okay. Sex is reserved for marriage.

God told His people, do not act like the people in Egypt or Canaan or imitate their way of life. He said, 'You must never have sex with a close relative' (see Leviticus 18). Thus, sons are not to have sex with their mothers, sisters or half-sisters, or granddaughters, or aunts, or unrelated aunts or daughters in law or brother's wife, as this violates the family member married to them. The same rules apply to daughters but vice versa.

Men are also not to have sex with both a woman and her daughters or granddaughters, as this is wickedness. Or marry a woman and her sister, because they will be rivals. But if one's wife dies, then it's okay to marry her sister. And men are not to defile themselves by having sex with their neighbour's wife. God further said that both man and woman are not to defile themselves by having sex with animals, as this is a terrible perversion. And not to practice homosexuality, which is a detestable sin.

God's people were to be set apart from other 'people'. They were instructed to respect the elderly, foreigners and the vulnerable etc. Fundamentally, they were commanded to love God and each other. God was also explicit that they were not to breed cattle with other kinds of animals. So, making chimeras is not okay.

Unlike the ancient kingdoms, the Israelites didn't have kingship. There was no need as God is king. But apparently they wanted a king to be like their neighbours, who got their right to rule from their 'divine' lineage (nephilim bloodlines were preserved through royalty). As mentioned, the first King of Israel was Saul, who went to the medium of Endor. Then King David arrived. He notably took on the Philistine giants, namely, Goliath and his four brothers, when he was just a boy. He prevailed, and he later prevailed over the Jebusites, who were of the nephilim family, and captured Jerusalem. King David was followed by his son King Solomon.

The first Jewish temple, house for God, was built circa 1000BC by King Solomon. Inside the temple, there was the outer court, the holy place, and the Holy of Holies. It's highlighted the temple represents God's Trinitarian '3:1' universal template. Like, we are 3:1, body, soul, and spirit. And God is 3:1, body (Jesus), soul (Father), and Holy Spirit. And there's 3:1 heavens. The Holy of Holies was separated from the holy place by a huge thick curtain. It was apparently sixty feet long, thirty feet wide, four inches thick, and required three hundred men to lift it.

Located in the 'Inner House' (the most sacred area) was the Ark of the Covenant, which was a gold-covered wooden chest that contained a few artefacts including the two stone tablets featuring the Ten Commandments, Aaron's staff, and some manna. But moreover, God's presence dwelled in the Holy of Holies. God was literally with them. However, because no one can look at God and live, the veil had to separate them. God is holy and we're not. God cannot stand sin and we're all lousy sinners.

The Israelite high priest would however risk it once a year, on the Day of Atonement ('Yom Kippur'). Apparently, a rope was tied around his waist in the event that if something went wrong and he died, they could drag him out from behind the curtain, since they couldn't go in as they too would perish. Fundamentally, sin separates us from Holy God, so annual rituals of atonement were followed by the high priest on behalf of the people. God said, 'I have given you the blood so you can make atonement for your sins. It is the blood, representing life, that brings you atonement'.

The Day of Atonement was thus a gracious day each year when all the Israelites could experience a new beginning by being cleansed from their sins and restored to fellowship with their Maker. Leviticus 16:30 states, 'On this day atonement will be made for you, to cleanse you. Then, before the LORD, you will be clean from all your sins'.

God notably established the rules of Atonement with Aaron (see Leviticus 16: 7-8). Thus, the high priest, scrubbed clean, selects two goats. The first goat is slaughtered for the sins of the people, and the second goat is the 'scapegoat' to carry the sins of the people to the wilderness of Azazel. Azazel notably means scapegoat in Hebrew. Symbolically, the scapegoat took on the iniquities of the Israelites (their rebellion and wickedness) and removed them to a remote place. But according to the Book of Enoch 10:4, Azazel (fallen Watcher angel) inhabited a region in the Judean wilderness. For his punishment, he was bound and cast into darkness, and an opening was made in the desert, which he was then cast into. So, the scapegoat was sent to Azazel?

It's noted, Azazel is the goat head in satanic rituals. He's the chief of the goat-demons or 'hairy demons' (who have 'hairy hands'?). Satanists are partial to the goat. In ancient Greece, Rome and Egypt, the goat was regarded as a nature spirit, and was associated with dark arts and the devil. As mentioned, the goat-man hybrid is known as the Greek god Pan. He's the god of sexual perversion and he's in fashion. Like, Crowley adored him. Presumably, Pan's in the astral plane, with the other hybrids? Satan is Pan? But furthermore, 'the Cave of Pan' (known as Banias) is at Mount Hermon, where the Watchers descended to. It's understood pagan worship took place there, as archaeologists discovered a shrine dedicated to Pan (and other deities). It's said there's an entrance to Hades there.

It's also interesting to note, that Jesus went to this region (called Caesarea Philippi), and He asked His disciples, 'Who do people say that the Son of Man is?' They replied that some say John the Baptist, others say Elijah (who didn't die but rather went to heaven in a UFO) or prophets like Jeremiah. Then Jesus asked them, 'Who do you say that I am?' Simon Peter answered, 'You are the Messiah, the Son of the living God'. Then He sternly warned them not to tell anyone that He was the Messiah (see Matthew 16: 13-20). It seems Jesus wanted people to realise for themselves that He is the Son of God? And He was making a point by asking His disciples that question at Pan's grotto? But we'll get to Jesus in a second.

As it transpired, King Solomon's love for 'strange women', including the Moabites and Ammonites, led him to worship other gods. It's understood Solomon was quite the lothario, having seven hundred wives (which included the Queen of Sheba and Pharaoh's daughter), and three hundred concubines. God told the Israelites 'you must not intermarry with them', and 'ye shall not go in to them, neither shall they come unto you' (see 1 Kings: 1-8). And yet it appears Solomon went 'into' nephilim descendants.

As it transpired, when Solomon died, the northern tribes refused to accept Solomon's son, Rehoboam, as their king. God's people thus separated in 930BC. The northern ten tribes formed the independent Kingdom of Israel in the north, and the two other tribes, Judah and Benjamin, set up the Kingdom of Judah in the south. The term Jew in its original meaning notably refers to people of the tribe of Judah or people of the Kingdom of Judah (Judah was Jacob's fourth son).

Worshipping other gods led to their downfall. Their pagan priests offered incense to Baal, the sun, the moon, the constellations, and to all the forces of heaven. They worshipped pagan shrines and sacrificed kids to Molech (see 2 Kings 23:5). In 2 Kings 22:17, God said, 'For my people have abandoned me and worshipped pagan gods, and I am very angry with them for everything they have done. My anger is burning against this place, and it will not be quenched'.

Because of their disobedience, but as forewarned, God allowed Israel to be captured by Assyria (720BC), which led to the 'lost ten tribes of Israel'. And a hundred and fifty later in the sixth century BC, Babylon captured Judah. The Jewish temple was destroyed by the Babylonians in 586BC (or 425BC according to historical Jewish sources). After seventy years, the Jews returned to Judah and built their second temple in Jerusalem (as prophesied by prophet Jeremiah). This was subsequently destroyed by the Romans in 70AD, as Jesus prophesied.

Thus, King Jesus came onto the world stage, from the tribe of Judah. But the Jews didn't recognise Him as their King. The Jews were greatly anticipating the Messiah, as God had told them He was coming to save them, and also the gentiles (non-Jew). But they were expecting some strong political leader that would free them from the iron clutches of Roman rule and restore Israel, and instead they got all loving, 'turn the other cheek', Jesus. It seems they didn't know that love is the most powerful weapon?

In Matthew 5:38-40 Jesus said, 'You have heard that it was said, 'eye for eye, and tooth for tooth'. But I tell you, do not resist an evil person. If anyone slaps you on the right cheek, turn to them the other cheek also. And if anyone wants to sue you and take your shirt, hand over your coat as well'.

The Old Testament is the story of a nation, whereas the New Testament is the story of Jesus. It's also said, the Old Testament is the New Testament revealed, and the New Testament is the Old Testament concealed. There are 66 books in the Bible, which were written by forty authors who were inspired by God. The whole of the Bible is however about Jesus, from beginning to end. As mentioned, there's over three hundred prophecies in the Old Testament about Jesus' coming.

The Old Testament, an external religion, is tantamount to the internal religion of the New Testament, which focuses on the inner life i.e. thoughts and emotions. God's focus seems to shift from the law to the heart, with the advent of His Spirit. Black (2010) asserts, 'in fact, after Jesus Christ no other individual has done so much to develop and expand the human sense of an interior life'. He states, Jesus planted the seed of interior life (p.396). However, before we get to God's literal intervention, it seems prudent to elaborate on Isaiah's prophecy because it's uncanny.

So, 700 years BC, Isaiah predicted a Messiah would come, born of a virgin (albeit this is arguably not a prediction given the promised seed of Genesis 3:15). Isaiah 7:14 states, 'therefore the Lord Himself will give you a sign: Behold a virgin shall conceive and bear a son and call His name Immanuel'. Immanuel means 'God is with us'.

Isaiah 9:6 states, 'For unto us a child is born, unto us a son is given, and the government shall be upon His shoulder: and His name shall be called Wonderful Counsellor, The mighty God, The everlasting Father, The Prince of Peace'. He prophesised the Messiah would be God in the flesh, both truly God and truly man, and whilst He would be of David's seed, His kingdom would be perfect and eternal.

Isaiah 61:1-2 tells us, He will bring good news to the afflicted, provide freedom and liberty to captives, heal the broken-hearted, and comfort all who mourn. But rather than being welcomed by His people, Isaiah (50:6) predicted the Messiah would be beaten and spat on. Isaiah 53:3 states, 'He was despised and rejected – a man of sorrows, acquainted with bitterest grief. We turned our backs on Him and looked the other way when He went by. He was despised, and we did not care'.

Isaiah 53 continues, 'Surely He took up our pain and bore our suffering, yet we considered Him punished by God, stricken by Him and afflicted. But He was pierced for our transgressions, He was crushed for our iniquities'... 'He was oppressed and afflicted, yet He did not open His mouth; He was led like a lamb to the slaughter, and as a sheep before its shearers is silent, so He did not open His mouth'.

As it transpired then, (seven hundred years later) the angel Gabriel approached Mary and told her she was most privileged to give birth to the Son of the Most High (Luke 1:35). Mary was a virgin and Christ was conceived by the Holy Spirit. Hence, the 'Immaculate Conception'. Christ was the promised seed of Genesis 3:15.

However, it appears Mary's fiancé Joseph wasn't convinced (LOL), as we're told in Matthew 1:19, he was going to break off the engagement. As he flirted with the idea, he fell asleep and an angel of the Lord appeared to him in a dream. The angel reassured Joseph, stating the child within her was conceived by the Holy Spirit. 'And she will have a son, and you are to name Him Jesus, for he will save His people from their sins' (Matthew 1:20).

Joseph married Mary but she remained a virgin until her Son was born. So, Joseph was Jesus' stepdad. It was similarly known that Jesus would be an especially special kid, which again, the Magi could ascertain from the 'stars'. Hence, King Herod of Judea (appointed by the Romans) ruled for all infant boys in Bethlehem, two years and younger, to be killed.

Jesus' ministry began when He was thirty, and ended when He was thirty-three, when He was crucified. The show got on the road after Jesus was baptised by John the Baptist (who was also a special kid) in the River Jordan. We're told that when John the Baptist saw Jesus coming towards him, he said, 'Look, the lamb of God who takes away the sin of the world'. He testified that, unlike his water baptisms, Jesus would baptise with the Holy Spirit.

Moreover, after His baptism, as Jesus came out of the water, the heavens were opened, and John saw the Spirit of God descending like a dove and settling on Him. And a voice from heaven said, 'This is my beloved Son, and I am fully pleased with Him' (Matthew 3:16-17). After this, Jesus was led to the wilderness by the Holy Spirit to be tempted by the Devil for forty days and nights. We're told Jesus ate no food, then the Devil came, which suggests His fasting induced an ASC? Jesus clothed Himself in flesh, which predisposed Him to sin, but He didn't sin.

Hebrews 2:11-18 explains how Jesus took on Himself the nature of a man, not the nature of angels, to save mankind. Jesus entered Adam's line to literally become our relative. We're told, 'Both the one who makes people holy and those who are made holy are of the same family'. Isaiah 59:20 states the coming Messiah is 'kinsman redeemer' related by blood to those He redeems. Hence, His bloodline had to be pure, not contaminated with nephilim shiz.

There were forty-two generations from Abraham to Jesus (see Matthew 1:1 for the genealogy). 1 Corinthians 15:22 states, 'Everyone dies because all of us are related to Adam, the first man. But all who are related to Christ, the other man, will be given new life'. Jesus came to tell us the Gospel aka Good News, namely, we can be forgiven for our sins and enter the Kingdom of God.

The Godman Jesus is awesome. He performed myriad miracles. Like, He fed thousands of people with a couple of loaves and a few fish, twice, and He walked on water. His first beautiful miracle was notably turning six large empty jars of water into the finest wine at a wedding in Cana. We're told His disciples believed in Him after this display of glory (fair play).

He also performed countless exorcisms and healings e.g. cured the blind, deaf, dumb, sick, leprosy etc. And He even raised the dead for good measure. Jesus preached a message of love and forgiveness, and was renowned for using parables to communicate His message. As it transpires, parables are the most effective way for our brains to retain information (more brain centres light up in response to metaphor than any other form of human communication).

Jesus was all about love, kindness, compassion, righteousness, truth, light, and all good things. And it's true He had a funky bunch of mates. But Jesus came for the sinners (the sick not the healthy), who need a saviour. God sent His son into the world not to condemn it but to save it. Brennan Manning (author) summarised, 'Jesus reveals a God who does not demand but gives; who does not oppress but who raises up; who does not wound but heals; who does not condemn but forgives'.

When Jesus was asked what the greatest commandment was, He replied, 'you shall love the Lord, your God, with all your heart, soul, mind and strength'. He said, 'the second is like it: Love your neighbour as yourself' (see Matthew 22:37-39). But moreover, Jesus commanded us to love and pray for our enemies, which raised the bar.

As mentioned, He decreed, 'just lest you be judged'. And He told us to take the plank of wood out our own eye, before going on about the splinter in someone else's eye. It's like the time, the teachers of religious law and the Pharisees presented Jesus with a woman they had caught in the act of adultery (which warranted stoning to death) to test his judgement, and He told them, 'He who is without sin, cast the first stone'. Those in glass houses shouldn't throw stones.

Jesus was radical, which means to get to the root of things (radical comes from Latin Radex meaning 'root'). Like, the time He overturned the tables in the temple, driving out all those buying and selling, proclaiming, 'It is written, 'My house will be called a house of prayer', but you are making it a den of robbers'. So, He ruffled a lot of feathers, because He thinks and acts like He's God? Maybe He is?

To confirm this, Jesus told people their sins were forgiven and on a number of occasions, He allowed Himself to be worshipped. Exhibiting such divine authority, and distinctly placing Himself on equal terms with the Father, was construed as blasphemy and heresy in Jewish faith. The Jewish priests were not at all pleased. Jesus was also risking His life by saying such things.

Thus, as it transpired, rather than accepting His claims, but as prophesised in Isaiah, He was rejected, ridiculed and despised by His people, who concluded He must be demonically possessed. The evidence of Jesus' miracles is overwhelming, but this came with controversy regarding how He was doing it i.e. magic, sorcery or harnessing the power of Satan. Jesus' miracles also included controlling the weather, which only God can do. In later Jewish writings, Jesus is called a sorcerer who led Israel astray. Wonders were acknowledged but the source of power was disputed.

But most interestingly, whilst His people didn't recognise Him, demons did, and trembled in awe. Mark 3:11 states, 'whenever the evil spirits saw Him, they fell down before Him and cried out, 'You are the Son of God''. And in Matthew 8:28-34, for another example, we hear about two demon possessed men (who were so violent no one went near them), and when they saw Jesus, they shouted 'What do you want with us, Son of God?' As mentioned, there was no drama with the exorcisms. Jesus simply told the possessing entity to beat it. It seems contending with demons was part of a day's work. It was normal?

So, the 'religious' Jewish leaders were on the warpath. Presumably, it didn't help that Jesus criticised them. Like, in Matthew 23:27-28, He said, 'Woe to you, teachers of the law and Pharisees, you hypocrites! You are like whitewashed tombs, which look beautiful on the outside but on the inside are full of bones of the dead and everything unclean. In the same way, on the outside you appear to people as righteous but on the inside you are full of hypocrisy and wickedness'. The truth hurts, because of pride? The name 'Pharisee' notably comes from the Hebrew word 'to separate'. These teachers of the Torah demanded strict obedience, which Jesus overruled. Like, Jesus healed a man on the Sabbath day, which challenged their ethics.

Jesus told the Jews (His people), 'I don't speak on my authority. The Father who sent me gave me His own instructions as to what I should say' (John 12:49). And 'If God were your Father, you would love me, because I have come to you from God. I am not here on my own, but He sent me' (John 8:42). And also, 'If you had believed in Moses, you would have believed in me, because he wrote about me' (John 5:46). And 'The truth is, I existed before Abraham was even born' (John 8: 58). And 'He who has seen me has seen the Father' (John 14:6). And 'The Father and I are one' (John 10:30).

Like John 1, Colossians 1:15-17 states, 'Christ is the visible image of the invisible God. He existed before God made anything at all and is supreme over all creation. Christ is the one through whom God created everything in heaven and earth. He made the things we can see and the things we can't see – kings, kingdoms, rulers and authorities. Everything has been created through Him and for Him'. So, Jesus is God incarnate.

It also seems pertinent to note, that Judas was possessed by Satan the night he betrayed Jesus. John 13:25-28 tells us that at His 'last supper', Jesus told His disciples that one of them would betray Him. And when they asked who, 'Jesus answered 'it is the one to whom I give the bread dipped in the sauce'. And when He had dipped it, He gave it to Judas, son of Simon Iscariot. As soon as Judas had eaten the bread, Satan entered into him. Then Jesus told him, 'Hurry, do it now''. So, presumably Jesus was speaking to Satan, since Satan was in Judas? It seems Jesus is in cahoots with Lucifer? Judas then left and grassed Jesus' whereabouts to the authorities.

As it transpired then, Jesus was literally the lamb to the slaughter. He was beaten, slapped, punched, spat on, flogged, pierced, and crucified for our sins. Both Isaiah and Kind David, together with other Old Testament passages, describe how Jesus would die. Thus, He would be sold for thirty pieces of silver, have His garments gambled, die a poor man's death in the prime of His life, be crucified between thieves, and be buried in a rich man's tomb. His hands, feet and side would be pierced. His bones would be pulled apart, but no bones would be broken. All this happened. In response to His persecutors, Jesus said, 'Father, forgive them, for they know not what they do' (Luke 23:24).

It's recorded that darkness fell upon the land from noon to 3pm, and Jesus died at 3pm. And just before He died, He said, 'It is finished', which is an accounting term that means paid in full. Immediately after Jesus died, there was an earthquake. Rocks split apart and tombs opened. It seems Abraham's Bosom (the paradise side of Sheol/Hades) was opened to let the saints out? A Roman officer exclaimed, 'Truly this was the Son of God'.

But furthermore, 'the curtain of the Temple was torn in two from top to bottom', which must have freaked the Jews out. The curtain symbolised the separation between us and God because of our sin. Thus, being torn at the moment of Jesus' death, signified that Jesus is the saviour, and that His death paid for humanity's sins. The torn temple curtain spoke of free access to God. The 'Passion of Christ' notably refers to Jesus dying for the sake of humanity. Jesus was the suffering servant so that we could be spared from God's wrath.

Jesus came to show us the way to God, and He died to make it possible. Jesus was the ultimate, final, scapegoat. His blood atones for our sin. Thus, a new covenant was established, whereby our sins are forgiven, and we can be reconciled with God through Jesus. Hence, there's no need for animal sacrifices. It's also noted, that Jesus was sacrificed at Passover. Jesus was the Passover lamb.

Jesus said, 'I am the way, the truth and the life. No one can come to the Father except through me' (John 14:6). He said, 'Whoever acknowledges me, I will acknowledge before my Father'. In Romans 10:13 Paul said, 'whoever calls upon the name of the Lord will be saved'. In Acts 4:12 Peter said, 'there is no other name under heaven, given amongst men by which we must be saved'. And in 1 Timothy 2:5 we're told, 'There is one God and one mediator between God and men, the man Jesus'.

But moreover, Jesus openly declared that He would die and resurrect from the dead after three days (Mark 8:31). The authorities thus ensured Jesus' body was rigorously contained. Yet despite their excessive precautions to guard the tomb, the tomb stone was rolled away, as Mary discovered when she went to visit early Sunday morning (see photo of empty tomb). Jesus is alive!

It seems interesting to note however, that unlike the other gospels that narrate this event, according to Matthew 28:1-6, when Mary Magdalene and the other Mary went to the tomb, 'Suddenly there was a great earthquake, because an angel of the Lord came down from heaven and rolled aside the stone and sat on it. His face shown like lightning, and his clothing was as white as snow. The guards shook with fear when they saw him, and they fell into a dead faint. Then the angel spoke to the women. 'Don't be afraid!' he said. 'I know you are looking for Jesus, who was crucified. He isn't here! He has been raised from the dead, just as He said would happen. Come, see where His body was lying'. So, it seems the angel rolled the stone away, rather than Jesus? Jesus had already done a shoot, which suggests He walked through the tomb wall as opposed to rolled the stone away to get out?

Presumably, His persecutors (haters) must have seriously soiled themselves. It's understood the resurrection factor is the ultimate burden of proof for Christians, but the fact is, the tomb remains empty. And unlike some incarnate imitating Him, it really was Jesus in His own body. He ate and could be touched, and His wounds were there. Luke 24:37-39 speaks about when Jesus appeared to His disciples. He recounts, 'they were startled and frightened, thinking they saw a ghost. Jesus said to them, 'why are you troubled, and why do doubts rise in your minds? Look at my hands and feet. It is I myself! Touch me and see: a ghost does not have flesh and bones, as you see I have'.

Albeit, whilst seemingly in the same physical body, He could pass through locked doors and appear and vanish at will. It seems Jesus exhibited the resurrection body i.e. upgraded version of our physical body with active spirit body? Jesus appeared for forty days and was witnessed by over five hundred people.

It seems pertinent to note, the 'Shroud of Turin', which is believed to be the shroud that Jesus was buried in following His crucifixion. This 14 foot long linen cloth (re-dated 300BC-300AD) features the image of a man with Jesus' wounds. It's like a negative photo image, yet photography wasn't invented until 1839. The first historical reference to the shroud was in 1357. It's theorised that when Jesus came back to life, a burst of energy, some bright ultraviolet light, caused the image on the cloth (like, when a zygote is formed there's a flash of light). The image was burned onto the cloth and there were no paints or substances to make an imprint of the image.

Many believe this is an 'end sign' for unbelievers. Apparently, blood analysed from the shroud contained high levels of substances called creatinine and ferritin, which are found in patients who suffer forceful traumas like torture. So, the person wrapped in this shroud experienced a violent death. This artefact has converted many atheists. The blood type was notably ab.

But moreover, archaeologist Ron Wyatt (1933-1999) suspected he found Jesus' blood in an 'earthquake crack' beneath the crucifixion site in 1982. According to his testimony, blood trickled down to the Mercy Seat of the Ark of the Covenant, which happened to be located in a cave below. Apparently, the cave was a mess and full of artefacts. It's noted, when the Babylonian Empire conquered the Israelites back in 586BC, (and destroyed their temple), the Ark of the Covenant vanished from history. So, the Jews stashed it there?

So, that's interesting. But even more interesting, when the blood was analysed, it revealed 24 chromosomes. There were 22 autosomal chromosomes, one X chromosome, and one Y chromosome. [Human cells normally have 46 chromosomes, 23 from each parent. In each set of 23, 22 chromosomes are autosomal and one is for sex-determining. Females are XX, so they can only contribute an X chromosome to their offspring, whereas males are XY, which allows them to contribute either an X or a Y. If they contribute an X, the child is female, and if they contribute a Y, the child is male]. This blood evidenced having a mother but no human father, because the normal contribution of paternal chromosomes is absent. So, Jesus was fully human, from Mary's side, and fully God.

But furthermore, when Wyatt went back to the cave, much to his surprise, it had been completely tidied up. He claims four angels stood before him and he was told that the time is not yet for the world to see this discovery with their own eyes. But the time is coming when the inhabitants of the world will have a universal religious law enforced upon them. This law will force man to break God's law, by penalty of disenfranchisement – being unable to buy or sell (Revelation 13:17). This is a reference to the New World Order, which includes the 'mark of the beast' for financial freedom, as we'll get to. Wyatt was told that after this law has been passed, God will allow the tablets of stone (the Ten Commandments) and a good clear video of the Ark of the Covenant to be put on public display. Wyatt was asked on his deathbed if this story was true, and he swore it was.

Wyatt believes the discovery of the Ark of the Covenant and the crucifixion site will lead people to Christ. He said, 'This last revelation is for the inhabitants of the earth who don't have a clue, as well as for those of us who do have a clue and have been commissioned by Christ to reach out to help bring these people who don't have a clue into the fold. So these are tools that God has given the believers to strengthen their faith and to reach out with. They are tools that will be extremely effective in the last pouring out to the entire population, all inhabitants of the earth'. Wyatt was involved in a number of significant archaeological studies of biblical sites and artefacts, including Noah's Ark, the Red Sea, Mount Sinai, and Sodom and Gomorrah.

Jesus' resurrection proved that He was no normal man, but rather evidenced He was indeed the Son of God. Paul said, 'And if Christ be not risen, then is our preaching in vain and your faith is also in vain' (1 Corinthians 15:14).

But as it transpires, there's more evidence to support that Jesus Christ was a man who lived on earth (ten times more than Julius Caesar), than any other historic fact. And His crucifixion is the most historically verifiable event of the first century. First century historians, like Josephus Flavius (31-100AD) who recorded the first Jewish-Roman war of 70AD, confirm the existence of Jesus Christ, His miracles, His crucifixion under Pontius Pilate, His death and resurrection. Both secular (pagan, Roman, Greek), Jewish and Christian historical records reveal that Jesus was cruelly beaten and crucified, which happened on Pontus Pilate's shift.

The New Testament is the best body of ancient literature in the world, and all the Gospels were written pre 90AD, whereas the earliest biographies of Alexander the Great, for example, were written four hundred years after his death in 323BC yet historians consider them trustworthy. There are about 5,700 early Greek New Testament translations, which is far more than any ancient book.

Jesus was not a normal man, yet He was fully man. Normal people don't reset time i.e. BC and AD (Anno Domini is 'in the year of the Lord'). Jesus was the Godman. Creator God became a man and His appearance is the central event in all His-Story. He came to rescue His kids from bondage. He died to purchase us.

So, whilst many Jews remain waiting for the Messiah, others picked up their cross (literally because they were crucified for their faith) and followed JC. Indeed, five weeks after Jesus was crucified, over ten thousand Jews were following Him. People began to worship Jesus as God, and within the first two years after Jesus' death, a significant number of followers formulated a doctrine of the atonement. They were convinced Jesus was raised from the dead, and associated Him with God, and believed they found support for all this in the Old Testament.

And thus, Christianity emerged as a new religion, separate from Judaism. John 1:17 states, 'For the law was given through Moses: grace and truth were realised through Jesus Christ'. The old covenant of law changed to the new covenant of grace. Leo Eddleman said, 'Christianity is the flower of which Judaism is the bud. What the Jews…and some Christians…fail to grasp is that pure Judaism is embryonic Christianity and genuine Christianity is Judaism full grown' (cited in Heydt, 1967 p.12).

But moreover, Jesus pioneered the format of relating personally to God as Father, Abba. Abba is notably a term of endearment in which a child would say to a parent. In Romans 8:15-16 Paul says, 'when we cry Abba Father, it is that very spirit bearing witness with our spirit that we are children of God'. In John 1:12 it states, 'Yet to all who received Him, to those who believed in His name, He gave the right to become children of God'.

Jesus was thus the initiator of an intimate relationship that was previously unavailable. But we can have this type of relationship with God through Jesus and the Holy Spirit. Jesus called Yahweh 'Father' and advised us to pray to God, 'Our Father who art in heaven'. Heaven is not far away. Like, at Jesus' baptism, the heavens opened, and at the Flood.

If we ask God into our lives, His Holy Spirit comes to dwell within us, and inspires and guides our daily life. Hence, Christians are born again, with the Holy Spirit. The alchemising Holy Spirit changes our heart, mind, and soul to become Christ-like. In essence, it's not about good works and religion, but rather Christianity means relationship with God. And contrary to the legalism of Judaism, Jesus brought grace to the table. That is, we're saved by grace through faith in Him. It's not about what we do, but rather what He did for us at the cross.

As Paul said in Ephesians 2:8-9, 'For by grace you have been saved through faith; and not of yourselves, it is the gift of God; not as a result of works, that no-one should boast'. And in Galatians 2:21 he said, 'I do not set aside the grace of God, for if righteousness could be gained through the law, Christ died for nothing!'

It's duly noted, the fact so many Christians were ridiculed, beaten, imprisoned, and sadistically tortured, (like being fed to lions for Rome's entertainment), evidences the strength of their conviction. However, despite Nero's best efforts at containing God's newly adopted kids, there was no stopping them. Christianity was spreading like wildfire. It had to be extinguished.

Thus, the crafty devil infiltrated the church. The next best move was to bring it down from within. And thus, Constantine the Great (272-337AD) Christianised the Roman Empire, synthesising Christianity with paganism, which led to the Roman Catholic 'religion'. Catholic notably means universal. Constantine wanted a universal Christian creed, so he convened the Council of Nicaea in 325, which established the Nicene Creed. It was agreed 316:2 (over 99%) that Jesus was Logos. He was crucified under Pontus Pilate and on the third day He rose from the dead. There was no denying it.

The aim was for everyone to be catholic. Thus, besides ending the persecution and execution of Christians, Constantine bribed people to become 'Catholics'. Like, he offered twenty pieces of gold to anyone who would convert, and he offered slaves their freedom on the same premise. Constantine's successor, Theodosius (378-395), made Christianity the state religion and forced conversions. They would later enforce 'Christianity' through their sadistic inquisitions.

But moreover, the church was above God's word. They kept the Bible to themselves, and people were executed if they were found with one. It was ironically heretical to read the Bible. People were led to believe they could only get salvation through the church, and contrary to Jesus' teaching, the focus was firmly on works to earn God's love and forgiveness. The church told the jokes. Like, inflict pain on your body and wear a hair shirt, and say ten hail Marys.

Those retaining power and religious leadership (the elite) became the bishops, priests, and deacons i.e. pagan priests became Christian priests. Hence, Roman priests wear the fish-head mitres worn by Sumerian priests. These represent the fish god Dagon, a half-man, half-fish hybrid. It seems he survived the flood, as apparently he came out the sea and instructed people regarding the lost knowledge before the flood. He imparted the mysteries? Perhaps this headdress hid their cone-heads back in the day? So, pagan temples became Christian churches, and heathen festivals converted to Christian festivals. Rome's pantheon of gods became the saints.

The Catholic Church was the latest version of the Mystery Babylon religion i.e. sun god, moon goddess, and reborn sun god. Thus, there was Nimrod-Semiramis-Tammuz in Babylon, Osiris-Isis-Horus in Egypt, Zeus-Artemis-Adonis in Greece, Jupiter-Diana-Apollo in Rome, Odin-Joro-Thor in Nordic, Vishnu-Chandra-Krishna in Hindu, and God-Mary-Jesus in Catholicism. In Luciferianism it's Lucifer-Diana-antichrist. Jesus is represented by sun images in Catholic and Eastern churches.

So, it's the same BS since the beginning of time. Each kingdom, ruled by nephilim descendants, had its occult priesthoods (i.e. sorcerers, diviners, astrologers and mediums) which contained the sacred ken, which includes orgies, human sacrifice, and idol worship. It's understood that after the demise of Sumer, Babylon, and the decline of Egypt, nephilim HQ was relocated to the Seven Hills of Rome. The bloodlines of Sumer and Babylon became the founders of Rome. And their new disguise was Catholicism.

The Catholic Church introduced Mary worship ('Maryolotry') and the title 'Mother of God' in 431AD, which is not biblical. As mentioned, Catholics bow down before statues of Mary, which are ensouled? Even Popes bow down before the 'Holy Mother'. It was decided she was holy, which is another fallacy. We're all sinners bar Jesus. The dogma of Mary's Immaculate Conception (she's born free of sin) was introduced in 1870. And whilst Mary was the mother of Jesus, she is not the mother of God. God revealed Himself through Jesus, while remaining God in heaven.

They adopted the title 'My Lady' for Mary, which in Latin is translated as 'Mea Donna' or Madonna, from the pagan Babylonian religion. They adopted the icon of 'virgin with child' from the image of Semiramis and baby Nimrod. Thus, the pagan mother and child entered Christianity as the Roman Catholic worship of Mary and baby JC.

Constantine changed the Sabbath day, Saturday, the last day of the week, to Sunday, the first day of the week. Although it's equally attested that early Christians changed the Sabbath day to celebrate the day Jesus resurrected, despite God's (fourth) Commandment to keep the Sabbath? It was also declared that Jesus was born on December 25th. It's speculated He was born sometime between July and September, and it's suggested it may have been September 11th, which is interesting.

Constantine also changed Passover to Easter, which would be held on the first Sunday after the full moon occurring on or after the vernal equinox (when Semiramis emerged from an egg circa 21st March). They also translated the forty day period of fasting and weeping for Tammuz into forty days of lent. For Christians, Easter refers to the crucifixion and resurrection of Jesus Christ over two thousand years ago. It has nothing to do with the Easter bunny.

Apparently, the origin of Catholics crossing themselves comes from Tammuz. Human sacrifices were offered to the sun god on a wooden cross shaped as a T (known as the cross 'T') for Tammuz. They introduced making the sign of the cross in 310AD. In 431, the cross (an esoteric symbol of death) was introduced into churches. Catholics adopted the rosary beads from Hinduism in 1090, coupled with more Baal practices like repetitive prayers and chanting.

Wheeler (2009) states, 'the religious teachings of Babylon became so renowned in Rome the Catholic Church was called the 'New Babylon' (p.143). 'Christianity' became a bureaucratic political empire, housed in splendid buildings paid for by taxes. It was a lucrative business and all kinds of corruption crept in. Like, people could purchase forgiveness. Money could save the worst criminals which led to unbridled vice and mayhem. The sale of indulgences, forgiveness of sins for money, began in 1190. Confession of sins to a priest at least once a year was introduced in 1215, so there was no escape.

And whilst people weren't allowed to eat meat on a Friday (a form of penance in honour of the death of Jesus), they could if they paid[24]. We pay for the kingdom of God, yet Jesus said salvation is a free gift. Indeed, Jesus instructed His disciples not to take money from anyone during His ministry, and He was very cross when Judas did.

It also seems pertinent to note, that the Catholic Church introduced prayers for the dead in 310AD, which is contrary to God's word, as we can't petition for the dead. Praying to Mary and dead Christians was introduced in 600AD. Catholics believe the 'dead' can intercede on their behalf. Image worship crept in e.g. candles were burned before images and people increasingly worshipped relics, shrines and altars, which violates God's Second Commandment, namely, 'Thou shalt not make any graven image unto thee'. It's also noted that Halloween, the favourite night of the year for witches, comes from 'All Hallows Eve', the eve before All Saints Day (1st November) to commemorate the dead. As highlighted, the catholic church hijacks pagan dates/festivals.

They also introduced the doctrine of purgatory in 593AD, which is basically a 'get out of jail free card'. It's falsely claimed there's a second chance for those who don't make heaven, as they can get a grip in purgatory. Purgatory comes from 'purged' of sins. This fortuitously provided another avenue to make cash, as people could pay for less time in purgatory. The catholic version of the candle in the pumpkin at Halloween symbolises the soul in purgatory.

In tandem with the Greek philosophers (like Plato), the Catholic Church taught the soul is immortal. It goes straight to heaven or hell at death, (without passing go or collecting $200), or purgatory. But as touched on, it's possible the soul goes to sleep at death, (until judgement day), and it's also possible the soul is not immortal? We're told the wages of sin are death, which defies an immortal soul? We also hear about a second death in the Book of Revelation, which suggests the unsaved aren't tortured forever? It's argued the Catholic Church used the doctrine of 'hell fire' to scare people into conforming. Or maybe the unsaved are conscious in the hellish Hades holding place, (until judgement day), and they're awfully thirsty? And maybe hell is an eternal place of torment. However, we'll get back to this.

Furthermore, contrary to the traditional rabbinical and early church view regarding the Sons of God as angels, the Sethite view emerged in the 5th century. Thus, rather than fallen angels having sex with women to produce giants, it was propagated that Cain's evil daughters had sex with Seth's faithful sons. There was no serpent seed? This theory then became the orthodox view, despite the nonsense i.e. if good men marry evil women, they don't produce giants.

As Chuck Missler insists, Genesis 6 is foundational to understanding the rest of the Bible. It's impossible to reconcile God of the Old Testament with God of the New Testament without understanding the seed war. As unlike all loving Jesus, God of the Old Testament takes no prisoners. He tells His people to wipe out other 'people'. Their natures are juxtaposed, unless we appreciate that the reason God instructed His people to take others out, was because they were nephilim.

---

[24] Apparently, McDonalds introduced the McFish sandwich as they noticed sales were low on Fridays, particularly in South America.

It's understood St Augustine, who was employed by the church, embraced the Sethite view and was responsible for suppressing the supernatural. He also taught celibacy for those looking for holiness, so more legalism, and not biblical. St Augustine notably went to England in 596AD to convert the population to Catholicism.

The Pope (papa in Latin) became the head of this haunted institution, despite Jesus specifically stating, 'do not call anyone on earth 'Father', for you only have one Father, and He is in heaven' (Matthew 23:9). Priests are also called Father. And God has never appointed any man to be the head of the church. The idolised Pope is seen as the mediator between God and man, and the nexus for Catholics. The Pope represents Jesus, but it's further believed he is Jesus hidden under the veil of flesh. He's hailed as 'our Lord God the Pope'. Unbelievable. He's also known as the 'Vicar of God'.

Catholics believe the Pope's decisions on faith and morality are infallible (he was declared infallible in 1870). Kissing his feet was introduced in 709, which contrasts to humble Jesus' who washed His disciples' feet. Jesus said, 'For even I, the Son of Man, came here not to be served but to serve others, and to give my life as a ransom for others' (Mark 10:45). Ironically, Popes have historically been super corrupt. They're renowned for murder, adultery, incest, blasphemy, paedophilia etc. But moreover, popes and cardinals were elected depending on their bloodlines (cardinals are ordained priests who elect the pope).

This Age was aptly named Dark. The Catholic Church turned Jesus' message of love into a doctrine of hate and death. More than a hundred million people were killed during the Dark Ages. They used the inquisition for five hundred years to maintain their power and wealth, and quash any opposition (they took 'heretics' property etc). Their methods of torture were unbelievably evil and sadistic. Besides setting people on fire, they invented various devices, like the Iron Maiden, which is a contraption with spikes. The torture was carried out by monks and priests.

It's also noted, the Catholic Church endorsed anti-Semitism. The rationale was that Jews were responsible for killing Jesus, so bugger them. Satan could kill God's people with this anti-Semitic tactic. They supported 'hell Hitler' and they facilitated the escape of many Nazis after WW2 (they were accommodated by churches in South America etc). But we'll get back to this. The Catholic Church has killed more than any other organisation in human history 'in the name of Christ'. Yet the Pope is called an apostle of peace, the prescribed title for the Son of God.

So, the papacy was getting away with murder, and every kind of indecency. But then, the reformers landed, who challenged this catholic version of Christianity. Like, John Wycliffe (1320-1384) who preached the word from the Bible. Wycliffe believed every Christian should study the Bible. Thus, he took on the challenge of translating the Bible into English. In the Medieval Catholic Church, only priests could read the Bible because it existed only in Latin.

He taught that salvation is through Christ alone, and emphasised the sole infallibility of the scriptures. Rather than the church, he declared the one true authority to be the voice of God speaking through His word. God's word is infallible, not the Pope's. And the Holy Spirit is the only interpreter. This turned the minds of people from the Pope to the Word, which was effectively a political move, because there was no need to pay tribute to the Pope or be subordinate to the powerful church.

Then there was Martin Luther (1483-1546), an ordained priest, who monumentally stood up against the teachings of the Pope and the entire Catholic Church. This reluctant revolutionary caused quite the storm in

Rome. He argued that people don't need the intercession of the church or its priests in order to receive God's forgiveness. On the contrary, there's priesthood for all believers, as we all have the same access to God. The most important thing is our relationship with God. Luther urged us to think about our status before God. He said, 'However irreproachable I lived as a monk, I felt myself in the presence of God to be a sinner with a most unquiet conscience'.

Apparently, when in Rome, and having observed their transgressions, Luther heard a voice like thunder say, 'the just shall live by faith alone'. [In Job 40:9, the Lord challenges Job, namely '...can you thunder with a voice like this?']. Luther espoused the view that 'faith alone', not works and certainly not papal indulgences, could bring salvation. The grace of Christ cannot be purchased. It's a free gift, albeit Jesus paid the price for us through His blood. Thus, the Pope and his merry men are superfluous at best. Luther also translated the Bible into German, and with the advent of the printing press, copies of Luther's writings went viral.

As it transpired, Luther's criticisms of papal excess and impiety went down like a lead balloon and he was charged with heresy. His famous '95 theses on the Power of Indulgences', which he nailed on the door of the castle church (Wittenberg, Germany) on October 31st 1517, are regarded as the starting point for the reformation. Luther said, 'who was I to oppose the majesty of the Pope, before whom the kings of the earth and the whole world trembled? ...No one can know what my heart suffered during those first two years, and into what despondency, I may say into what despair, I was sunk' (cited in Ellen White, 1995 p.132).

Luther had to stand before the council, (the emperor occupied the throne), to account for his wrongdoings. But despite the pressure, he refused to retract his doctrines. Respectfully, and humbly, he said, 'it is unsafe for a Christian to speak against his conscience'. He said, 'every Christian is as good a judge as the Pope', and 'God, who is the searcher of hearts, is my witness' (cited in Ellen White, 1995 p.167).

It's said Luther was pestered by evil spirits since childhood, and on one occasion he threw an inkpot at the devil. Paracelsus was notably a great admirer of Luther, stating, 'whoever is Luther's enemy will deserve my contempt'. Paracelsus regarded the reformation of the church as the shaking off of succubus and papal suppression, which enabled it to breathe freely once more.

The reformers sparked scores of religious movements known as Protestantism, as people began to protest. Indeed, the Pope was regarded as the antichrist by many reformers, who considered the Roman Catholic Church a satanic institution. Like Luther declared, the pope 'is the very Antichrist, who has exalted himself above, and opposed himself against Christ'. The Catholic Church went into meltdown. Something had to be done about the protestant uprising.

Hence, the Jesuits were created. The church's intellectual and military elite. This so-called 'Society for Jesus' was thus a counter-reformation production, that pioneered the revival of Popery. The Order was founded in 1537 by Ignatius Loyola (1491-1556) and was given papal approval in 1540. So, their job was to slaughter the real Christians, and covert millions to pagan Catholicism. The reformation, the wars of religion, led to one of the darkest periods in church history. Millions were willingly burned by the state for their beliefs, for refusing to submit to the pope. The Age of Enlightenment was partly a response to this bloodshed.

The Jesuit oath is to defend the Roman Catholic Church doctrine of His Holiness. But moreover, whilst allegedly avowed to perpetual poverty and humility, and beyond their devoted mission to overthrow Protestantism, the Jesuits' real aim was to secure power and wealth. It's said the overt mission to re-establish papal supremacy provided a cover, a blameless exterior, to conceal the most criminal and deadly agenda.

So, they worked their way into office of state, becoming counsellors of kings, which enabled being party to shaping the policies of nations. They infiltrated governments to influence/deceive. 'Serving the Church' pardoned, and continues to pardon, their lying, theft, perjury and assassination. These 'servants unto death' do whatever it takes to serve the brotherhood. This includes spying on brethren and reporting to superiors. It's purported that everyone knows Vatican policy is 'trust no-one'.

It's understood the Jesuits control the Vatican and the Pope. It's highlighted that education is very important for Jesuits, so they can train people to think like them (hence, their influence in schools and universities). The 'black pope' is the head of the Jesuits. Popular Pope Francis, 'the people's pope', is the first Jesuit Pope, and many believe he's the black pope (anti-pope or false pope). And it's rumoured he may be the last pope. Besides endorsing evolution, he promotes Ecumenicism. That is, God is the same regardless of religion, which is at odds with what Jesus said, namely, He is the only way to God (so, not Muhammad, Krishna, Buddha, Lucifer etc).

It's understood the Jesuits, this secret church, is dedicated to Satan. They're central to the global conspiracy, (enabling Satan's takeover), as we'll get to. Thus, the Vatican has two churches, namely, one that worships God and one that worships Satan. Mystery Babylon lives on. This Medieval institution is as disturbing today as it's always been. It's also noted, that problems with Catholicism, (not least the paedo scandals), have discredited the Christian faith. Who in their right mind wants anything to do with this god (which is the point)?

It's noted, that after the reformation, the number of protestant denominations proliferated e.g. Methodists, Baptists, Brethren, Presbyterian, Sally Army, Pentecostal, Evangelical, each with its own style and theological importance. Like, some are more methodical in their study of the Bible, whereas others stress the importance of the Holy Spirit speaking to us individually. CS Lewis provides the metaphor that God's house, 'the great house of Christianity', features a hall that has many rooms. The hall is 'mere Christianity' (i.e. the belief in the trinity) and the rooms are the various denominations.

Like, Anabaptists was a movement in the reformation which held only adults should get baptised, as only adults would understand what being 'born again' meant. Maybe Jesus set the bar, like thirty is a good age to get baptised. By then, one has figured out the truth? It's noted, baptism contrasts with the pagan Catholic invention of 'Christening' babies. It was purported that if babies weren't baptised and died, they would go to fictitious purgatory because of 'original sin'. It seems children are innocent until they're not (i.e. when they become accountable). Moreover, some people think they're saved because they've been christened as babies, which is tosh.

It's also noted, there's efforts towards unifying the Protestant and the Catholic Church. Like, the 'Joint Roman Catholic and Lutheran Declaration of 1999', agreed that salvation is by grace alone through faith in Jesus. Indeed, it's said the reformation is over. Like, Kenneth Copeland, one of the wealthiest televangelists in the world (he's worth some $800 million), insists the division has been healed. He proudly calls the Pope one of his heroes. He's also part of the New Apostolic Reformation. But we'll get back to this, as it's possible this is Satan's latest attempt to infiltrate the church, with a counterfeit Holy Spirit aka kundalini?

Furthermore, the Catholic Church decided in 1950 that Mary ascended into heaven. So, Jesus' ascension wasn't unique? As it transpired, in the spring of 1917, three Portuguese children reported apparitions of a 'Lady more brilliant than the Sun'. This (deceptive?) angel, allegedly the Virgin Mary, met with the children on the 13th of every month for several months. Then she announced that on the 13th of October, she would reveal her identity and perform a miracle, 'so that all may believe'.

70,000 people witnessed the 'miracle of the sun' aka 'miracle of Fatima' in Portugal. People believed they watched the sun spin, zigzag down to earth, and change colours. It's logical to refute the sun put on a show as this would have caused mayhem in our solar system? People described a silver disk in the sky, which suggests it was a UFO? It's noted, the term UFO wasn't invented then. Moreover, Pope Pius XII also witnessed the miracle of the sun from the Vatican gardens. Hence, Mary's ascension became doctrine. So, Mary is associated with UFOs?

As for the Jews, after the whole Jesus fiasco, it went downhill. As mentioned, Jesus forewarned their temple would be destroyed, and it was. After another couple of revolts, the Jews were exiled in 136AD. The Romans gave the land back to the 'Philistines', (who were nephilim), and renamed it Palestine. The Jews dispersed (known as the Diaspora meaning 'scattered') throughout the Roman Empire. They went to places like Babylon, Mesopotamia and Egypt. Their Jewish identity and religion kept them in unison.

But moreover, having no temple, and hence no place to atone for their sins, they had to reconcile themselves with 'good works' which brought the Talmud into existence. Unlike the Torah which provides God's law, the Talmud contains the teachings and opinions of thousands of rabbis on a variety of subjects. The Talmud is the basis for all codes of Jewish law. Two Talmud's were notably created, namely, the Jerusalem Talmud and the Babylonian Talmud (from the third to fifth centuries) but the Babylonian Talmud is the preferred Talmud.

However, it's highlighted that when formulating the Talmud, they were influenced in their locality by witchcraft and the occult. Hence, the Talmud is haunted. Like, boys may be sodomised without penalty between the ages of three and nine, and sex with girls from three years old is permitted. And it's kosher for mums to have sex with their eight year old sons i.e. they're not rendered impure from the act. Apparently Babylonian priests said a man's religious duty included regular sex with the temple prostitutes, and bestiality was widely tolerated. According to the Talmud, Jesus is boiling in a cauldron of faeces.

It gets even darker however, with the Cabala, which comes from the Talmud. The cabala is known as the secret tradition. The Jews who got embroiled with the cabala became evil, indulging in evil practices and worshipping the image of Baal. The cabala is the heart of secret societies, which is at the heart of the conspiracy, as we'll get to.

The Mystery Babylon religion became the foundation for Hinduism, Buddhism, Cabalism and Gnosticism (as we'll get to). Hence, Semiramis is rightly called Goddess of Fertility because she gave birth to all the pagan gods representing Nimrod/Tammuz worldwide. Paganism is a euphemism for Satanism. It's understood Satan has created many religions to confuse, control, and conflict i.e. divide and rule. Religion is then fractured so people fight amongst themselves.

Satan is very clever and very patient. Thus, we need to be wise like serpents to know the serpent's tactics. Like, we're being groomed with eastern mysticism and magic. And people have an aversion to Jesus? They're more comfortable believing Jesus was a human sage with unusual gifts of kindness and wisdom, as opposed to the Son of God? However, as CS Lewis maintains, it's nothing short of patronising to suggest Jesus is just a great moral teacher. Alternatively, he suggests He's either a lunatic or the devil.

But moreover, God's word tells us Jesus is coming back for His people. But before He returns, all hell breaks loose. He told us 'signs of the times' that lead up to His Second Coming. Like, the return of Jews to Israel is a major sign, which happened after WW2. And it appears they want to build their third temple? The (Islamic) Dome of the Rock currently stands on the site (see photo). It's been there since 691AD. So, that's a problem?

Jesus forewarned us about wars, and rumours of wars, and also 'climate change' e.g. the increase of earthquakes, hurricanes, droughts, famines, pestilences etc. We're also told about the global beast system, the one world order, which reinstates the Babylonian religion. We're told the antichrist is coming to rule the world, from the third Jewish Temple. The 'prince of this world' (John 14:30) is on his sordid way to secure his blasphemous throne. It's noted, the Jews are still waiting for their messiah, so that's precarious. The future antichrist's kingdom in likened to Nimrod's kingdom of darkness.

Whilst we'll get back to biblical prophecy, it seems pertinent to note that Jesus told His people, 'When the Son of Man returns, it will be like it was in Noah's day' (Matthew 24:37). And the 'days of Noah' were insane (given the plethora of weird hybrids). Thus, the plot thickens, as its rumoured there's a hybrid programme taking place, which explains the 'alien abductions'? It's understood Satan has to build up his numbers, as he was robbed with only a third of angels. And demons can serve that purpose given a body to inhabit? As touched on, we know the mad scientists are making chimeras and they clone animals/people, but what else? Like, aliens and giants? Whilst the last giant recorded in the Bible was Og, King of Bashan, apparently giants are still around, deeper underground.

It's also purported there's an occult agenda behind CERN, (founded in 1954), the large Hadron particle collider in Switzerland. It's a complex tunnel 300 feet below ground, with a 17 mile circuit, designed for smashing subatomic particles together at nearly (99.9%) the speed of light. Apparently, they're trying to recreate the Big Bang, but it's believed CERN is an attempt to open inter-dimensional gateways to allow dark spiritual forces (demonic beings) into our dimension. Like a modern-day Tower of Babel?

Indeed, author/researcher Anthony Patch claims scientists at CERN are in contact with beings from another dimension. Hence, it's befitting that CERN refers to itself as the 'gateway of the universe', and its logo is 666 (the number of the beast). It's understood the occult agenda is being executed by Satan's seed, (the nephilim bloodlines still percolating on Earth), and their agents.

Thus, the war raging between God and His angels, and the Devil and his fallen angels, is ramping up. It's said the abyss is bursting at the seams with haunted entities chomping at the bit to get out. And the Holy Spirit is currently restraining this nefarious lot. We're told a great deception is coming, and most will believe the lie, which includes God's people. Like, people will be amazed by events like the 'miracle of the sun'. People will be mesmerised by signs and wonders? People might be bewitched by 'aliens'? His-Story thus culminates in the ultimate showdown, namely, Armageddon (see photo of Har Megiddo aka Armageddon, the location). And we have ringside seats.

'It is Satan who is the God of our planet, and the only God'. Satan, the enemy of God, is in reality the highest divine spirit'. Helena Blavatsky

12

Luciferian Philosophy

For Luciferians, Lucifer is the true god and benefactor of mankind. Contrary to Lucifer being the evil one in the Biblical version of events, Luciferian philosophy advocates that Lucifer is a force for good. As Doreen Irvine stated, Satanists say lies are truth and truth is lies, so it gets pretty twisted. Everything is inverted and perverted, like God is Satan and Satan is God. Light is dark, and dark is light. Rather than Jesus being the 'Light of the World', Lucifer hangs onto his old title as Light Bearer. Illuminism, which is black magic, is derived from Lucifer the illumined one or shining one.

Illuminism originated in the Garden of Eden. It began when Lucifer, via the serpent, told Adam and Eve 'ye shall be as gods' if they ate the fruit from 'the tree of the knowledge of good and evil'. He insisted (hissed) they wouldn't die. So, he lied. They lost their immortality, their estate, and their divine union with God.

However, for Luciferians, Lucifer is the instrument of liberty and freewill. Unlike cruel Yahweh aka Adonai (which is Hebrew for Lord), who enslaves mankind, and actually created humans to oppress them, Lucifer is the great liberator. This angel of light came to set us free. Lucifer claims he's the equal of Yahweh, (rather than His creation), and he's Yahweh's foe because Yahweh's so dreadful.

Thus, rather than being defiled, condemned to death and separated from God, Lucifer insists that Adam and Eve were enlightened when they munched the fruit. 'The tree of knowledge of good and evil' was 'the tree of gnosis'. As mentioned, Gnosticism is the secret 'knowledge' that we are God. Thus, Lucifer is the great enlightener. He's the source of 'wisdom'. Hence, he's viewed as the god of light, the good principle, and Adonai is viewed as the god of darkness, the evil principle.

It seems pertinent to note, this Luciferian perspective is espoused in the Sumerian religion, which pertained to the Anunnaki. In this creation story, Enlil and Enki are half-brothers who worked on creation together. Their father Anu/An, Great Father of the Sky, is the original supreme deity. Enlil's mum is Ki, earth mother, and Enki's mum is Antu, great mother of the sky.

Enlil, who is regarded as Yahweh, is an oppressor. He commissioned the creation of the human race to enslave us. He wanted us to serve him. Enki is the serpent god who brings gnosis/wisdom. Unlike Enlil, Enki wanted to give people knowledge and wisdom, to help them become gods like them. Enki was the serpent in the Garden of Eden who got Eve to munch from the tree of gnosis. And Enlil got mad and kicked them out of the Garden of Eden. It was Enki who gave them clothes to hide their shame.

As it transpired, after they reproduced several times, Enlil became tired of humanity's noise and so he killed them with a flood. The Gilgamesh account however tells us that Enki, who's regarded as Lucifer the liberator, saves Gilgamesh (he warns him about the coming flood), having told Utnapishtim to build an ark and load it with animals. After the flood, Gilgamesh is back on the throne. Utnapishtim is likened to Noah, and Gilgamesh is likened to Nimrod.

It's also recalled, that according to ancient Gnostic texts, Abraxas is the astral serpent who gave Adam and Eve 'enlightenment'. As Basilides revealed, via Jung in his 'Seven Sermons to the Dead', Abraxas is the True and Ultimate God. And this Supreme Being (depicted as the ouroboros) transcends both good and evil, and unites all opposites into one Being. So, Lucifer is Abraxis, the Holy Serpent? He rescues us from Yahweh's iron clutches?

As highlighted, there's a universal consensus that life is imperfect. As Buddha declared, 'life is suffering'. We 'know' something's amiss. Life isn't supposed to be like this, full of pain and death? Like the biblical fall, esoteric philosophy pertains to a Golden Age but then something catastrophic happened. This culminated in the loss of our inheritance, including our immortality.

It's understood Eden, our true origin, was a more subtle level of nature i.e. spiritual and material, not just material. Heaven and earth were once together, and the nature of humanity in Eden was pure, knowing only goodness and virtue. So, we were robbed. Hence, humankind has been ambitiously seeking to regain our lost estate ever since. We want to live forever in paradise with God?

And this is where the 'gods' aka fallen angels come in, to impart the secrets of heaven so we can make our way back to paradise. If we could master the secret wisdom contained within the secret arts, like alchemy and astrology, the curse of the Garden would be lifted, and we could return to the Garden of the Lord. Nature is described as a book that must be read or deciphered. It's personified as the Egyptian goddess Isis (Moon God) covered by a veil. The veil represents the inaccessibility of Nature's secrets, but by practicing the secret arts, we can experientially learn to transcend the veil. Lifting Isis' veil leads to the spirit worlds.

In essence then, the endeavour is to transcend the material veil, to reinstate our divine connection with God. It appears we're trapped here, unless we learn how to transcend to higher ethereal realms. The secret arts enable liberation of interior knowledge, which enables liberating the spirit. Through ASC we can experience ecstasy states and visionary transport. We can commune with powerful images or entities that reside in the deep unconscious (archetypes in the collective unconscious?). As touched on, the aim of the initiate is to forge working relationships with disembodied spirits.

Alchemy, Gnosticism, Hermeticism, and Cabalism, all explain the methodology of the spirit worlds. Thus, we'll discuss these philosophies, which are essentially Luciferianism. It seems we can become 'enlightened', which translates to spirit attachment and serpent power?

Luciferians understand that mystery schools began in Atlantis, when the gods came down and asked for sexual favours for knowledge. They taught the sun is the great enlightener of the physical world, and the serpent is the great enlightener of the spiritual world, by giving us knowledge of good and evil.

But moreover, in ancient pagan mythology, Saturn ruled over the pre-Flood kingdom of Atlantis. Saturn, (furthest from the sun), was regarded as the Supreme God and ruler. Saturn aka Lord of the Rings is the Dark Lord or Old Sun. The ancients claimed that in the beginning Saturn ejected filaments in all directions and so the solar system is illuminated by hundreds of suns. Hence, Saturn is regarded as the first sun or old sun. But moreover, Saturn is identified as Satan. And this blood thirsty deity, who was renowned for munching his own kids, demanded child sacrifice (like Molech).

But even after Atlantis, the early astronomical traditions seem to identify the primeval sun as Saturn rather than the sun, which includes Babylon, the post-flood founder of astronomy. They worshipped Saturn as the 'Light of Heaven'. But this 'Truth' known as the 'Light' was to be kept secret within the Saturnalian brotherhood. As mentioned, the Roman festival Saturnalia aka Christmas comes from the worship of Saturn (Rome was known as the city of Saturn).

In archaic copies of Plato's Timaeus (dialogue), the word for the planet Saturn is Helios, the 'Sun god'. The identities of the gods seem to shift over time, as ancient Egyptians seem to regard Ra as both Saturn and the Sun. Saturn was also referred to as the 'Star of the Sun' or 'Sun-Star'. It's also said they were one and the same god, as Saturn is the Sun's alter-ego. There's a mysterious confusion between the two, but it seems the ancient sun god is not the body we call 'sun' today? For Luciferians, the Sun is Lucifer, and Saturn is Satan. God and Satan are One, good and evil?

It's noted, the ancients worshipped Saturn represented by a black cube, and black cubes are quite the feature e.g. in Melbourne Australia, Svendborg Denmark, Manhattan and Santa Ana in the US, the UN 'meditation room' in NYC, and the Kaaba at Mecca. The cube apparently derives from the hexagon on Saturn's North Pole. The hexagram, which features a hexagon at its centre, is a symbol used in witchcraft. The two opposing triangles symbolise the unity of masculine and feminine through sex. The triangle facing upwards is male, and represents the phallus, and the triangle facing downwards is female, and represents the chalice (the womb). The male triangle penetrates the female triangle. The two triangles also point 'above and below', which represents the macrocosm and the microcosm.

The hexagram, which embodies 666 (6 points, 6 triangles, 6 sided hexagon), is a powerful tool to evoke Satan. It's where 'hex' comes from. It's the star of Baal. Then it became the Star of David, as featured on the Israeli flag. Apparently, the Seal of Solomon wasn't considered Jewish until it was adopted by the Rothschild's (notorious Jewish banking family), who pioneered Zionism. And apparently Solomon received a ring with a hexagram on it to command demons. However, we'll get back to this.

As discussed, the ancient world concurred that gods came down, produced giants, a global flood wiped almost everyone out, but the gods came back, in some shape or form, to seed the royal kingdoms. The sun serpent religion recommenced at Babylon with Nimrod, which evolved into the Mystery Babylon religion with Semiramis. And then it went viral, like a virus.

As mentioned, Gary Wayne states Nimrod obtained the secret arts and sciences from nine subterranean vaults, which led to the construction of Babylon and the Tower of Babel. Wayne notes, that according to freemason legends, this esoteric intel was stacked under the pyramids. The giants knew the Flood was coming, so they had time to prepare. Apparently, Cain's son, Enoch, stashed it there before the deluge. The Bible notably tells us that when Cain founded a city, he named it Enoch after his son (Genesis 4:17). This Enoch is not therefore to be confused with Noah's great grandfather Enoch, who 'God took' because he was so awesome. Cain's lineage, which includes the first Enoch, drowned in the Flood.

Freemasonry, as we'll get to, stretches back to Cain's son Enoch, who's revered in freemasons as the first master mason. He's credited with building the cities before the Flood. However, Wayne refers to him as 'Enoch the Evil' because he enforced sun worshipping mysticism. Enochian magic comes from Enoch the Evil. Enoch's serpent worship includes phallicism (sex magic), hence the Masonic obsession with obelisks. Secret societies, like the freemasons, developed out of the mystery schools, and as Wayne asserts, 'they're indistinguishable back then as they are today'. Freemason initiations are identical to ancient Egyptians. So, that includes human sacrifice?

Nimrod thus resurrected the kingdom of darkness and re-established the secret Snake-Brotherhood. It appears he took over from Enoch the Evil, initiating a select few into the perverted craft. Bill Cooper concedes the Brotherhood of the Snake, simply known as the mysteries, is the most ancient/important secret society. He affirms snake and dragon symbols represent wisdom, and Lucifer, the father of wisdom. He explains the focus of worship for the mysteries was Osiris, another name for Lucifer aka Light Bearer and Morning Star. Osiris was the name of a bright star that the ancients believed had been cast down to earth. After Osiris was gone, the ancients saw the sun as the representation of Osiris or Lucifer.

But moreover, Wayne informs that Nimrod wasn't alone, but rather had a partner in crime called Hermes. He states it was Hermes who found the hidden stash, and partnered up with Nimrod at Babel. Then after the communication meltdown at Babel, Hermes went to Egypt (together with Ham and Mizraim) to take the sacred ken there and establish the Egyptian civilisation. Ergo, Nimrod-Semiramis-Tammuz became Osiris-Isis-Horus. It's said this ancient pagan priest was a contemporary of Moses. However, apparently Hermes means son of Ham, and Cush (Ham's son) became known as the deity Hermes. So, the Hermes that Nimrod teamed up with was actually his father Cush? Some believe Hermes is the grandson to Cush.

Thus, with regards to the origin of mystery schools, it seems they started in Atlantis, were reborn in Babylon, circulated to Egypt, and then spread to the other ancient kingdoms like ancient Persia, Greece, Rome etc. And these arts have been kept secret. Initiates are forced to take oaths and violation of these oaths is fatal (brutality and torture precede death). So, 'there's no such thing as fight club'[25].

As mentioned, the Babylonians founded the zodiac, which they used to predict the future. In tandem with the Bible that tells us angels are stars, (they're named and numbered), the ancient pagans believed the stars, and planets aka wandering stars, were deities. Like in Babylon, Venus was Ishtar, and in Greece, Venus was Aphrodite. Each day and month belonged to a god, which they're named after e.g. Sun-day, Saturn-day. Like, Abraham's father Terah had twelve gods, one for each month, which Abraham smashed.

The seven chief gods were the five planets they could see, and the sun and the moon. The sun is however the greatest of all the gods in heaven, because he's the CEO guiding the solar system. Furthermore, the ancients believed the soul of man was a 'divine spark' that originated from the sun, and returns to the sun, on the premise of illumination?

So, the pagan people worshipped the sun, moon and stars. Hence, these are more than arbitrary rocks or gaseous balls, as they had spirits that could be called upon, or called down (via rituals etc). We can embody the god force that resides in the stars. It's said, if we imagine as fully and vividly as possible the spirits of the

---

[25] In the movie Fight Club (1999), fight club is not supposed to exist because it's illegal. Hence, all members insist 'there's no such thing as fight club'.

planets and stellar gods, then as a result of this act of imagination, the power of these spirits can flow through us. It's also said stars are portals, to the second heaven, or some other dimension?

Whilst it's understood these sacred arts were (initially) passed down by fallen angels, they're associated with Hermes Trismegistus. It's noted Hermetic, which means hidden, comes from Hermes. The Hermetic arts are astrology, magic and alchemy. However, it seems pertinent to note, there's two Hermes, namely, the Greek god Hermes, and the Egyptian god Hermes Trismegistus. It appears the Greek god Hermes is the Egyptian god Thoth, and Hermes Trismegistus represents a syncretic combination of these two gods. Like, freemasons believe Thoth and Hermes represent the same person, namely, Hermes Trismegistus.

As mentioned, Thoth is the god who helped Isis attach a new cow-head after Horus decapitated her. For Egyptians, Thoth was the god of wisdom and knowledge. He was the 'Master of Mysteries' who passed down the magic arts, sacred rituals, texts and formulae. Thoth transmitted mystical secrets to members of a secret snake order. He brought sacred science, geometry, and architecture to the table, and is credited with building the great pyramid and making Egypt a great civilisation.

It's noted, pyramids (which are aligned with the stars) weren't simply tombs but rather they were used for initiations for mystery schools (as Bill Cooper advised). It seems the pyramid shape is important for conducting 'energy'. Like, Tesla believed they were built for a 'higher purpose', to harness electrical energy. It's said pyramids are fake mountains. There's something special about mountains? As highlighted, when the Mystery Babylon religion went global, pyramids went global. Hence, they're a common feature in ancient civilisations. It's understood the Tower of Babel was a ziggurat (stepped pyramid).

Thoth was the inventor of handwriting and known as the divine scribe. He was also known as Thoth the Atlantean, because he was passing on secrets from Atlantis? Or rather he was passing on secrets recorded from Atlantis, the information he (Hermes) found? Both Hermes and Thoth were the gods of writing and magic in their respective cultures. Thus, it seems to be the same legend? Like, Hermes is Mercury in Rome? But then there's Hermes Trismegistus, whose name is derived from Thoth and his Greek counterpart Hermes. And he's known as the priest king of Atlantis.

It's noted, whilst the Greeks recognised the congruence of their god Hermes with Thoth, apparently the majority of them did not accept Hermes Trismegistus in place of Hermes, and thus the two gods remained distinct from one another. It's also noted, that unlike Greek Hermes, Thoth is depicted with a bird head, which suggests he's one of those chimeras? According to Greek mythology, Hermes was two thirds or 66.6% angelic (like Gilgamesh) as his father was a fallen angel and his mother nephilim.

However, that aside, Hermes Trismegistus is the purported author of the Corpus Hermeticum, a series of sacred wisdom texts that are the basis for Hermeticism. They're mostly presented as dialogues in which Hermes Trismegistus 'enlightens' a disciple. The Hermetica thus contains initiatory (induction) procedures for casting magic spells, rituals, observances, and sacred rites. It's noted, Hermeticism is the foundation of the 'Hermetic Order of the Golden Dawn' that Crowley was in.

Whilst it's believed Hermes Trismegistus was a man who lived in the first century, the texts (forty-two volumes) were written in Greek, and date to the second and third century AD. Thus, it's contended that Hermeticism originated in ancient Greece, but it was based on ancient Egyptian ideas. These texts were notably found with the Nag Hammadi scrolls, along with the Gnostic gospels in 1945.

It's therefore not known if Hermes Trismegistus was a real person/entity. It's suggested Hermes Trismegistus was a man, because he represents mankind's situation, but he transformed into a god through knowledge. That seems to be the point of mystery schools, namely, we evolve through gnosis to become gods. Lucifer is insistent that we become like gods. As touched on, apotheosis is the process of becoming God. The endeavour is to attain super-powers through demonization?

It's also believed Hermes Trismegistus is 'good' Enoch, because he ascended into heaven. And he was known as the divine scribe. Wayne further explains that Enoch the Evil was infused with different people in history, (different names in different civilisations), including Hermes, Mercury and Thoth. And he evolved into a god through knowledge. Wayne states Hermes Trismegistus is the fusing of Hermes, Thoth and Mercury. Hence, he was also known as the Atlantean, because Enoch lived in Atlantis, the pre-Flood world? The Tri in Trismegistus notably refers to 'thrice great' Hermes, on account of him being the greatest priest, philosopher, and king. It also pertains to the three parts of wisdom of the whole universe, namely, alchemy, astrology and theurgy.

Theurgy is magic that involves evoking the gods or demon spirits. Initiates learn how to control demons and capitalise on their power i.e. using binding pentagrams. As mentioned, there's an art to conjuring spirits and summoning them into objects, which are then transformed into objects of power (e.g. amulets and talismans). Or like statues which can then be worshipped as gods. We need to know the right formulas and incantations to ensoul material objects. Gods and demons, working through the objects, can then provide advice and information, and engage in prophecy. Thus, the Egyptian priests might call upon the gods or spirits to bring forth a vision or a dream, to acquire invisibility, compel a lover, or thwart an enemy, or perhaps cure an ailment.

However, theurgy serves a greater purpose, in that it seeks to evoke the presence of the gods, with the particular goal of uniting with the divine. The goal of hermetic spirituality is the mystical union of our soul with the One. The One is the Source of Life. All things come from the One and we're all part of the One. Hermeticism thus endorses pantheism. Rather than deity being outside ourselves i.e. our God who art in heaven, we are deity because we are inescapably part of the One. God is the universe and deity is present in all things. One Universal Spirit manifests or ensouls an infinity of forms.

Religion notably comes from the Latin word ligare, which means to join or link with the divine. And thus, Hermeticism is more than just magic, as it offers a religion. It's like yoga. Indeed, it shares core beliefs with Hinduism and Buddhism (which preceded it), and neo-Platonism i.e. monism and reincarnation. Hermeticism is the religion of mind or consciousness. The sun god is symbolic of the light of consciousness, just as the serpent is symbolic of wisdom.

With regards to creation, the unknowable One, which precedes all things, produced emanations. And these emanations produced divine ideas, which gave birth to everything, material and spiritual. It's noted, this resonates with Plato's conjecture that ideas came before forms, and his two worlds i.e. world of forms and world of ideas. It's conveyed that thought emanations became proto-matter, and energy became increasingly denser to become matter.

Heaven and earth are two separate realms, but they correspond and can be united. Heaven is invisible subtle reality, like our soul and spirit body, and earth is gross/matter, like our physical body. The central Hermetic axiom, namely, 'as above, so below', highlights the essential unity of the cosmos. Heaven and earth were once together but we can experience what life was like before the fall? It's noted however, that contrary to the biblical Garden of Eden, which was both physical and spiritual, the Luciferian paradise is ethereal. It's the spirit world. The Corpus Hermeticum pertains to the world-illusion i.e. the spirit world is more real than the physical world.

Alchemists recognise that we're spirit beings encased in matter. However, despite losing our spiritual capacity at the fall, they insist 'fate can be overcome'. We can make our own way into heaven, and achieve that pre-fallen state once more i.e. holy and immortal. It seems holiness is next to godliness? The endeavour is thus to evolve from being imperfect, diseased, corruptible and mortal towards being perfect, healthy, incorruptible, and immortal.

Like the metals they tortured, alchemists could be purified. Spiritual gold, an evolved state of consciousness, can be harnessed. The philosopher's stone is the mystic key to this process of Self transformation. It makes us pure and omniscient. It's noted, gold is associated with the Sun/Lucifer, and lead is associated with Saturn/Satan.

As discussed, Jung resurrected alchemy from the Renaissance, bringing it into the New Age. He promoted engaging with 'archetypes' to enhance consciousness. But the legacy of the philosopher's stone goes back to Hermes Trismegistus. The philosopher's stone aka sorcerer's stone is the highest evolution of the mind. This 'Great work' is the mystical union with the One. The philosopher's stone is an allegory for enlightenment. Alchemy is the transformation of man into god. For alchemists, the 'soul of the world' was the link to the unknowable god.

The Hermetic Corpus posits the universe itself is alive, guided by a world soul. It's like the universe is a kind of man with a soul. It's posited that the universe is the great man and we're the little man. As mentioned, we're the microcosm of the macrocosm. 'Hermes' wrote, 'as above, so below, as within, so without, as the universe, so the soul'. In terms of God's universal 3:1 template, the world soul is the second heaven.

The Corpus Hermeticum (chapter 12) talks about the 'Common Mind', asserting the Mind is not separated from God but is united to it, as light to sun. 'This Mind in men is God'. It states, 'gods are immortal men, and men are mortal gods'. We each have the essence of God within us, referred to as the 'divine spark'. It's said that because of our divine intellect or spiritual mind, we can comprehend the divine essence of Nature. The secrets of nature and the mysteries of God may be found within our soul. By holding the cosmos in our mind and imprinting it on our soul, it's possible to know God.

This seems to suggest projecting our consciousness out to the cosmos, like astral projection? It seems the idea is to take a trip inside, to the landscapes of our soul. We can know the soul of the world, through our soul. We can ascend into heaven?

It's noted, that the supposition that God is the universe, an impersonal source of universal energy, contrasts with the Christian belief of a personal Father that we're in relationship with. Christians pray/speak to God like a person. We do life with God, fellowship with Him. God is not creation but rather the creator of the universe. Christians also respect the veil that's in place. They understand why their spirit bodies (third eye) have been deactivated. Christians can be patient and look forward to their upgraded resurrection bodies, when we can travel at the speed of thought and walk through walls? We can wait for the real heaven on earth.

Thus, alchemists know we have a spirit body, known as the philosopher's stone. The ability to move consciousness into the light body is a fundamental part of the philosopher's stone. It's explained that when our pineal gland is illuminated, 'etheric energy', which makes up our consciousness, illuminates our light body. Our etheric body is transmuted into a full light body, which is a reflection of the 'life force' within us. The idea is that consciousness becomes hardened into the light body like a stone, so that when the physical body dies, self-awareness lives on in the light body. They achieve immortality (godhood). The endeavour is thus to activate the light body by channelling 'energies'. We integrate 'archetypes' into our consciousness.

As mentioned, demons can bridge our soul and spiritual bodies. With a bit of help from our spirit friends, our spirit bodies can be activated. Our consciousness 'evolves' and we gain siddhis, like astral projection and ESP. It's said this second body of solid light, this vehicle of consciousness, emerges from the crown chakra. Alchemy is thus the redemption of spirit from matter. It seems the alchemist returns to the Garden of Eden in his light body? It seems the Garden of Eden is Shambhala, where Russ Dizdar's golden Buddha mentor frequently frequented, until his silver cord was severed.

It's noted, that contrary to the debauched spirit worshippers who practiced blood sex magic rituals, the alchemists seemed pious. Besides transmuting metals, and themselves, they made medicines and elixirs to achieve their stated aim of immortality. Like, young blood rejuvenates old blood. Experiments with mice have shown that older mice rejuvenated with blood from younger mice. They live longer and have a better brain. Young blood also serves as a cure for vascular dementia. Hence, selling young blood is becoming big business. However, I digress. Presumably, they were also making psychoactive poisons (like ayahuasca) to catapult into the second heaven?

Alchemy is the science of spiritual experience. Initiation entails awakening 'subtle' faculties to learn the inner workings of Nature. Contrary to chemistry, (alchemy is the precursor to chemistry), the ancient Egyptians spoke of distillation and metallurgy as mystical processes. They're states of consciousness rather than chemical processes.

As discussed, hidden things which cannot be perceived by the physical senses may be found via the astral senses. As Paracelsus said, we may look into nature in the same way as the sun shines through a glass. The inner nature of everything may therefore be known through magic or powers of inner sight. We can perceive the essence of things in the light of nature and discover nature's secrets. True magic, which includes knowledge of visible and invisible nature, cannot therefore be learned out of books but must be acquired by practical experience. The philosopher's stone is the pinnacle of experiential wisdom.

Paracelsus explains that unlike chemistry that deals with physical matter, alchemy deals with their astral principles. Chemistry is a science which deals with the chemical combination, separation, and recombination of physical substances. Alchemy deals with the purification and combination of astral elements. Unlike chemistry, where elements remain unchanged, alchemy enables raising an element into a higher and purer state of existence. It's knowledge of the nature of the invisible elements, constituting the astral bodies of things.

Paracelsus remarked that chemistry and astronomy can be learned by anyone with half a brain, but alchemy is an art which cannot be understood without spiritual knowledge. And unless one has a spontaneous kundalini awakening, this can be an arduous process. Like, alchemists spent years sweating in their workshops, learning the subtle and spiritual science that underpins reality.

Thus, initiates learn to perceive subtle energies. They learn about human subtle anatomy and the ethereal planes of existence. They learn about the relationship between matter and consciousness, because consciousness affects matter. Like, telekinesis? They learn that consciousness can be enhanced (by integrating 'archetypes'), and we can achieve the impossible (like levitate etc) by activating our spirit body. And we can generate matter like thought beings and create golems?

They learn how to use the electromagnetic spectrum (or 'universal energy') as the connecting bridge between physical and spiritual realms. They learn how to manipulate the 'life force', (that we're intrinsically part of), for good or evil? They learn how to separate the subtle from the gross. In plainer words, they use demons to affect matter i.e. change the natural into supernatural. Like, turning lead into gold. In accordance with the magicians will, and by calling on demons, the laws of nature can be broken. Alchemy is thus a secret art and science.

Black (2010) defines alchemy as the borderline between science and magic, and asserts that 'all magic is a power of mind over matter' (p.361). Alchemy is the science of the mind, which includes the faculties of faith and imagination. It's also noted, that alchemists are aware they always need the 'cooperation of the universe'. Hence, they begin their labours with a prayer to the 'Supreme Architect of the Universe' beseeching his assistance. This is the Masonic god, as we'll get to.

So, it starts with ESP, then seeing auras, and eventually culminates in visions, which enables one to know the inner world dimensions. Visions are usually seen in a trance but initiates later experience the spirit world with their eyes open in the waking day. The alchemist state of perfection thus pertains to fully illuminated consciousness. That is, our inner senses are fully opened and active. Like, Swedenborg and Lorna Byrne?

So, the Great Work is enlightenment. It's the state of yoga, the opening of the third eye. Like, Nimrod opened his third eye through incest. And Crowley opened his through bum love with his bum chum. The gods were gone, but there were ways to reach them. As Black (2010) highlights, 'As the gods withdrew, people would have to find new ways to follow them. In this way yoga was born' (p.176).

Thus, we can arouse the sleeping serpent, Mz Kundalini, allegedly coiled at the base of our spine to slither up and down our alleged chakras, bestowing a state of ecstasy and oneness. We can experience godhood by igniting our divine spark. Or alternatively, we invite this serpent in through yogic practices?

As Black (2010) states, 'There is a school of thought that interprets alchemical texts as manuals containing techniques to make the kundalini serpent rise up from the base of the spine through the chakras to light up the third eye' (p.459). So, there's mystical ecstatic oneness, and there's going to the spirit world (in our light bodies). We can catch up with the gods on their turf. Like, Ganesh and other half-human half-animal hybrids, aliens, giants, elves etc.

Those who accomplished the Magnum Opus or Great Work were referred to as 'Brothers'. In his book 'Magick without Tears', Crowley explains, 'The great work is the uniting of opposites. It may mean the uniting of the soul with god, of the microcosm with that macrocosm, of the female with the male, of the ego and non-ego'. As Hermes states, 'That which is Below corresponds to that which is Above, and that which is Above corresponds to that which is Below, to accomplish the miracle of the One Thing'. But moreover, the 'Great Work' for the Brotherhood is the illumination of all mankind. The end goal is for the world to be enlightened. But we'll get back to this.

As touched on, Crowley, who called himself 'Satan's chief of staff', introduced the age of Horus to replace Jesus. And he endorsed the Baphomet, the hermaphrodite goat of Mendes (it has a goat's head, breasts and male genitalia), replete with a pentagram on its forehead. This LGBTQ+ goat points up and down to represent the axiom 'as above, so below'. The Baphomet is the alchemist symbol, because alchemy is the union of opposites. Like Jung's psychology, light and dark are made One. The Baphomet (god of lust) symbolises Satan and s/he's in fashion. La-Vey also adopted the Baphomet for his Church of Satan.

It's highlighted, that only those 'born again' can accomplish the Great Work. But moreover, according to the Corpus Hermetica, no-one can be saved unless 'born again'. To ensure our salvation, i.e. to prevent reincarnation, our mind needs to be illumined. We need to become 'enlightened' or we can't return to our spiritual home. It's implied that we need to 'know' this realm, and become acquainted with the gods, so we'll be prepared like a boy scout for when we do actually die. And unless one takes ayahuasca, this is a labour of love?

As mentioned, when we're in the process of dying, our brain releases DMT. And it's believed this provides a portal into the second heaven. Thus, we need to be familiar with that portal? If we miss the window of opportunity, we have to reincarnate, until we achieve gnosis?

It's interesting to note, the dichotomy between Lucifer's philosophy and Christ's truth. Jesus said, 'I tell you the truth, unless you are born again, you cannot see the Kingdom of God' (John 3:3). He explained, 'that which is born of the flesh is flesh, and that which is born of the Spirit is spirit'. Thus, we need to be born again in the Spirit of God. It's a spiritual birth.

Or alternatively we need to be born again in the mystery schools and yoked with the spirit of antichrist? The Hermetica insists we're divine beings. We're not fallen. Thus, we don't need Jesus' blood to sanctify us, and besides, we can purify ourselves through alchemy. It seems we can sneak through the backdoor?

Thus, initiates are born again in the mystery schools. They have to learn the subject matter intellectually, and purify their 'self' (which lends itself to alchemy), before they're initiated into the mysteries. Like yogi aspirants, initiates need to be disciplined as awakening the divine essence aka kundalini can result in dark occult powers and insanity.

So, the Hermetic gospel is that we are God. And since all things descend from the One, we can ascend to the One. Initiates ascend through stages. Thus, the initiate first has to gain experience of the first seven spheres, the planets, before being initiated into the eighth sphere, the fixed stars, and finally the ninth stage, which is the sphere of the One. When the initiate returns from his ecstatic rapture, he is 'born again' and brings back godlike powers of knowledge and perception.

Chapter 13 of the Corpus Hermeticum tells us, 'Seeing within myself an immaterial vision that came from the mercy of God, I went out of myself into an immortal body, and now I am not what I was before. I have been born in mind'.

Initiations in the mystery schools vary but basically the candidate undergoes a mystical death and rebirth. They're put into a deep, death-like trance, sometimes for three days, and their spirit travels the spirit world. Like, Plato took a trip for three days inside an Egyptian sarcophagus. And Lady Gaga incubated in her egg for three days? It seems, universally, that initiates experience the great magical mystery tour round the celestial spheres. Their disembodied spirit (astral body) takes a trip to the seven visible planets i.e. the Sun, Moon, Mars, Mercury, Venus, Jupiter and Saturn. It's purported the seven planets have seven princes, who are the planetary gods in the second heaven.

This 'visionary experience', (which is very real), is brought on by secret techniques. As discussed, there's various practices to induce ASC e.g. breathing exercises, dancing, fasting, meditation, psychoactive poisons. Lest we forget, the ritual sexual practices which took place in the temples of Egypt, Greece and Babylon etc, coupled with the human and animal sacrifices to evoke the gods. Apparently, the Aztecs sacrificed some 20,000 humans every year for their sun god.

Taking a trip to the spirit world was mandatory for kings in Egypt. As part of the 'king making process', candidates had to travel to the stars to be admitted into the Society of the gods. They had to meet the brotherhood in the sky. Maybe they rendezvous in Shambhala? The new king had to be initiated into the mysteries by the king's elite, namely, the inner circle of the 'Holders of Secrets'. The new king had to become a god.

The religious priests would pray for the candidate king about to undergo his brief death to pass through the underworld and meet with past kings. It seems the spirit world is the underworld? They would pray to 'Almighty and eternal Re, architect and ruler of the universe, at whose creative fiat all things were first made'. [This is the Masonic god, as we'll get to]. They would request for their new king to pass safely through the valley of the shadow of death.

It's relayed that the new king would have undergone a temporary 'death' by means of a potion administered to him by a high priest. This hallucinogenic drug would have slowly induced a catatonic state, leaving the new king as inert as a corpse. The king then takes a sojourn with the gods, where he learns great secrets. He meets the past kings of Egypt and he becomes king of Egypt. He is made the Horus, crowned the new Osiris. Then the potion wears off.

As touched on, pharaohs, kings and gods, ruled by divine right. Each king was the son of God, who at death became one with his father. When a king died, he became Osiris and his son became Horus. Both this theology and the use of narcotic drugs came from the Sumerians.

It's also highlighted, that the new king's return would have been carefully calculated so he returned to consciousness precisely as the morning star rose above the horizon. This bestowed him with divine power from the gods in heaven. It's noted, that Venus is known as the morning star because it's the last star to rise before sunrise. It's also recalled that 'Son of the Morning', which is represented as a pentagram, refers to Lucifer. Morning star means divine knowledge. So, the candidate king returns as Horus, with divine knowledge. It seems the spirit of the sun god dwells in the new king, and continues to be reincarnated throughout the ages?

Black (2010) also pertained to the ascent of the soul through the seven planets. He informs that initiates are told the secret names of the spirits who guard the entrance to every sphere, the secret handshakes, and other signs and formulae needed to negotiate entry. He also states, that in all the ancient religions, the being who guides the human spirit through the underworld and helps negotiate the way past guardian demons is the god of the planet Mercury. Which could be Hermes?

But moreover, he states, 'But the initiates of the Mystery schools kept an even stranger secret. Halfway on the journey through the spheres, there is a swap. The task of guiding the human spirit upwards is taken over by a great being whose identity may perhaps be a surprise. *In the latter part of the spirit's ascent through the heavenly spheres, the guide who lights the way is Lucifer*' (p. 190). Black concedes that on the way back down, the spirit scoops a gift, from the seven gods of the seven planetary spheres, which they can use in the material world e.g. ESP.

Thus, there's a lot going on 'out there'. It seems the physical world is like a village, compared to the vast Spirit World? And unless we're enlightened, we have no idea. According to the Gnostic work, 'Treatise on

Resurrection', resurrection is the moment of enlightenment. Whoever grasps this idea becomes spiritually alive and can be resurrected from the dead immediately.

The Gnostic Gospel of Philip (as we'll get to) ridicules 'ignorant Christians who take the resurrection literally'. It states, 'Those who say they will die first and then rise are in error, they must receive the resurrection while they live'. Apparently, the Gnostic church called this literal view of the resurrection 'the faith of fools'. They claimed those who announced that their dead master had come physically back to life confused a spiritual truth with an actual event.

But Jesus did ascend to heaven in His body. That's what makes Christianity exceptional. Like, Enoch and Elijah also went to heaven in their bodies. But unlike Jesus, they didn't die and resurrect. It's a fact, that Jesus was crucified and died, and the tomb was empty on the third day. It's understood however, that unlike Enoch and Elijah, Jesus went home to the third heaven. As touched on, Jesus said no-one had been where He came from, which suggests Enoch and Elijah didn't go there?

Unlike the Hermetic tradition which represents a non-Christian lineage of Gnosticism and is associated with paganism, Gnosticism began to be associated with Christianity. Generally speaking, Hermeticism is associated with Egypt, and Gnosticism is associated with Greece. Gnostics originated in Alexandria, and there were lots of Gnostic sects in the second century. As mentioned, Alexandria (founded by Alex the Great-booze-bag in 331BC) was the meeting place between east and west. The mystics met the clever Greek philosophers surmising about the nature of reality. It was the cauldron brewing up rational and empirical mystical concoctions. It was Gnostic HQ.

But it's also believed that Gnosticism came from Judaism, and it was the brainchild of Jewish mystics from the second century BC. However, as discussed, God allowed the Jews to be captured by the Babylonians in 587BC because they were worshipping Baal, the sun, moon, and stars. Thus, it seems certain Jewish priests augmented their mysticism by studying the ancient Babylonian mysteries (witchcraft)? It's said Jewish mystics had accepted Babylonian doctrines that only God, who is pure spirit, is good. Man is bad, and only through gnosis, contemplation (meditation) of God, can we flee the material world and our evil body. Either way, it's essentially shamanism?

For Gnostics, the great evil is materialism. Earth and our mortal bodies are hell. We're trapped in the body, this hellhole. Hence, the aspiration to transcend to the spirit world. Christianity recognises this predicament and offers salvation through Jesus i.e. we go to heaven after death (or maybe not), whereas Gnosticism offers illuminism or enlightenment.

The Gnostic emphasis is on direct, personal experience of the spirit worlds. And Gnostics believe that salvation comes from this knowledge of the divine. Rather than Jesus being our Saviour through His Holy blood, no less, Gnostics are 'saved' through their gnosis. Such gnosis is independent of faith. It's the opposite of faith. It's alleged there's no such thing as sin, or original sin. There is no evil, only ignorance? As mentioned, paedophilia and murder is ignorance?

Gnosticism is a most varied movement. It borrows a lot of terms from Platonism, and blends ancient mythology with biblical texts. Gnosticism was thus a pre-Christian form of theosophy (i.e. we are God), but it coexisted as a religious movement with early Christianity until the fourth century. It's therefore also regarded as a post-Christian countermovement. It basically attempted to reconcile Greek philosophy with Christianity.

St Paul and the early church notably pertained to a spiritual battle against them. Paul wrote to Timothy (1 Timothy 6:20-21), 'Timothy, guard what God has entrusted to you. Avoid godless, foolish discussions with those who oppose you with their so called knowledge (gnosis). Some people have wandered from the faith by following such foolishness'.

It's also purported that Simon Magus founded Gnosticism. According to occultist Eliphas Levi (1810-1875), he became sorcerer to Nero. And we hear about 'Simon the Sorcerer' in the Bible, in Acts 8:9-24. We're told that Simon was impressed by the Holy Spirit. He 'wondered, beholding the miracles and signs which were done' in Jesus' name. He observed people receive the Holy Spirit when they were baptised, and when the apostles laid their hands on them. And he wanted some of that power. Indeed, he offered to pay for it, which Peter reprimanded, stating his heart wasn't right in the sight of God. The act of 'simony', which is paying for position and influence in the church, is notably named after Simon.

It's also noted, that Rome was killing Christians at this time, not Gnostics. It wasn't until the Catholic Church ruled from the fourth century, that they destroyed any opposition, including the Gnostics. However, we'll get back to the Catholic Church.

Gnostics are also referred to as mystical Christians, but they're not. They're Gnostics. Christians do not believe we're God, or possess some divine spark. But we can ask God into our hearts. Like at Pentecost (as mentioned), when Jesus told His disciples to wait for the Holy Spirit, the Holy Spirit came forth like a rushing wind, and they began speaking in different languages to spread the gospel. Thus, the Holy Spirit wasn't already in them, as some latent divine (serpent) energy. We have to invite spirits in. Leave the door open for them.

But moreover, and contrary to the Jews who crucified Jesus, it seems the Gnostics of Greece were partial to Jesus. Hence, a couple/few centuries after Christ, they conjured up the Gnostic Gospels. Or perhaps the devil's plan was to mutilate the scriptures and cause confusion. As mentioned, Satan is known as the author of confusion.

Fundamentally, unlike the Biblical gospels which fulfil the Old Testament, and present a Christian perspective, the Gnostic gospels espoused a Gnostic viewpoint of Christianity, with a particular Jesus twist. Gnostic gospels include the Gospel according to Thomas, Mary, Judas, Philip, the Egyptians, the Truth etc, and include a few legendary stories about Jesus' childhood. They were not however written by these disciples, but rather Gnostic writers chose the names of well-known and exemplary figures to be their fictitious authors.

It's notably curious, that these gospels and the Hermetic texts were discovered in 1945, and then a couple of years later, the Dead Sea Scrolls were found, which confirm the historical accuracy of the Old Testament and resurrected the Book of Enoch. It's like chess moves between God and the Devil in a cosmic chess match, as LA Marzulli conceptualised. It's all moves and countermoves, until checkmate?

It's noted, that Dan Brown popularised the Gnostic gospels in his book 'The Da Vinci Code' (2003). It's speculated that it's suspicious these gospels, purported to be the 'secret words' of Jesus (as everything is secret with mystery schools), were not included in the Bible. But they're not included in the Bible because they're not Christian. They had a Gnostic view of the origin and nature of mankind. Unlike the canonised gospels which attest that Jesus is the Son of God, the lost gospels portray Jesus as a teacher, an enlightened sage, but not supernatural in any way. This echoes our materialist outlook today. It makes more sense that Jesus was a man who acquired gnosis?

With respect to what's canonised, the early church had three criteria[26]. Thus, the books must have apostolic authority. That is, they must have been written by either the apostles themselves, who were eyewitnesses to what they wrote about, or by followers of the apostles. They had to normative and congruent with the basic Christian tradition (they conformed to the 'rule of faith'), and they had to be accepted by the church at large. Early Christians, who encountered Jesus and witnessed His miracles etc, documented and circulated these stories. And thus, thousands of JC followers had to be on the same page.

Unlike the canonised gospels then (Matthew, Mark, Luke and John), which were written from 50-90AD, the Gnostic gospels were written a couple of centuries later and are not related to authorship. And whilst the canonised gospels always state location, the lost gospels are lost, having no location. Contrary to the Bible, the Gnostic gospels are not historic texts, but rather fabricated stories comprised of made up dialogues.

However, some of them resonate with the canonical gospels, like the Gospel of Thomas (140AD), which contains 114 sayings by Jesus. Albeit, these verses are superfluous, as any of the logia attributed to Jesus are found in the canonical gospels.

But moreover, besides having no narrative of what Jesus did, it's pantheistic e.g. Jesus says 'I am the light that shines over all things. I am everywhere. From me all came forth, and to me all return. Split a piece of wood, and I am there. Lift a stone, and you will find me there' (verse 77). The idea that Jesus is coterminous with the substance of this world is contrary to anything in the gospels. This gospel is mystical and emphasises that salvation is personal and found through spiritual (psychological) introspection.

In the Gospel of Thomas, 'Gnostic Jesus' highlights that human beings must come by Gnosis to know the ineffable, divine reality from whence they have originated, and whither they will return. And in the gospel of Philip, we're told this transcendental knowledge must come to us while we're still embodied on earth. So, we need to take an astral trip?

With the Gnostic teachings, it's related that those who have not made effective contact with their transcendental origins while they were living in their corporeal body, would have to reincarnate. It alludes to our 'divine spark', stating, 'to find the light within in order to be a light unto the world'. Contrary to self-salvation, Jesus said 'I am the Light of the world; he who follows Me will not walk in the darkness, but will have the Light of life' (John 8:12). Jesus spoke about Himself as a light in a darkened world.

Further, at the end of the Gospel of Thomas, it berates women. We're told, 'Simon Peter said to them, 'Make Mary leave us, for females don't deserve life'. Jesus said, 'Look, I will guide her to make her male, so that she too may become a living spirit resembling you males. For every female who makes herself male will enter the kingdom of heaven'. This doesn't sound like Jesus and it doesn't harmonise with other testimonies about Jesus that early Christians accepted as trustworthy. Instead it seems to be mixed up with pantheistic and anti-feminist statements.

It's noted, that women were (proper) second class citizens at that time. Apparently in the courts, there could be over twenty female witnesses to a crime, but the judge would believe the one man who said otherwise. We were considered 'air heads'. As Simone de Beauvoir said (in her book 'The Second Sex'), '...her wings are cut

---

[26] Canon notably derives from a Greek word meaning 'rule', 'norm', 'standard'. As mentioned, whilst the Bible was written by man's hand, it's believed to be inspired by the Holy Spirit.

and then she is blamed for not knowing how to fly'. Contrary to the anti-feminist culture at the time then, radical JC loved women and men equally, and some women are exalted in the Bible.

Dan Brown notably highlighted the Gospel according to Philip, which he embellished to fabricate a story about Jesus and Mary Magdalene. This gospel nowhere states Jesus was married to Mary Magdalene, or romantically involved with her. From what can be gleaned from the heavily damaged section of the text, it seems to suggest that Jesus loved Mary more than the other disciples and used to kiss her often on the mouth. This text was written between 150AD and 300AD, whereas Philip died 80AD.

Maybe rumours circulated about Mary. Maybe some were jealous of her relationship with Jesus or unhappy about the co-equal treatment with women? It's also claimed that's what people did back then, that is, kiss on the mouth. Like, Judas betrayed Jesus with a kiss, when he grassed him up to the authorities.

Despite popular portrayals, it's also noted that Mary Magdalene was misidentified as a repentant prostitute. Scripture doesn't support this idea, but rather her scarlet woman reputation seems to have originated from a sermon by Pope Gregory the Great in the sixth century. The Vatican cleared Mary's name in 1969. The Bible tells us that Jesus cast out seven demons from her, and she became one of His followers (Luke 8:2). In the Gnostic Gospel of Mary, she is regarded as a disciple and leader of a Christian group.

Interestingly, according to the Gospel of Judas (180AD), Jesus told Judas the secrets of gnosis. This gospel asserts the other disciples had not learned the true gospel, but rather only Judas had, as taught by Jesus. Thus, rather than being a traitor in the Biblical version of events, Judas is described as the Lord's most trusted ally and worthy of this secret knowledge.

It gets more menacing however, as we're told that one day Jesus approached His disciples, who were having a sacred meal, and offering prayers of thanksgiving to God, and Jesus erupted in laughter. He's laughing because they're worshipping the fake god who created this world, not the True God. Judas is the only one who understands that the one who created the earth isn't worthy of worship.

Thus, according to the Gnostics, Yahweh is the creator of this world. But this 'Jewish' God is not the real God. They advocate the ultimate True God is transcendent, beyond all created universe. And because He's so transcendent, we can't know Him in this world. Contrary to the Christian concept of Father God, for Gnostics, God is the 'Unknowable Father'. God is not a personal being but more of a concept. And this remote Supreme Being did not create our world as such, but rather the Demiurge or Yahweh did. And he's not perfect, hence our world isn't.

Rather than the Biblical Fall, precipitated by the diabolical serpent, Gnostics blame the world's failings not with humans, but with the creator. The Gnostics adopted the term Demiurge from Platonism, which refers to creator god who fashioned this material world after the world of ideas. Yahweh is himself created but He doesn't know this. He's a fool.

Thus, in the beginning there was the true God or cosmic mind or the source of universal spirit or Light. And this Supreme Being generated 'Aeons', which are aspects of the divine One. They're divine thought beings or lesser gods that emanate from God, (like aquastors or tuplas?). And they effected the creation of matter, as opposed to God Himself.

The first Aeon the Light produced was Logos. He was the primary expression of the Light, the form of the formless. Logos, also called Christ, was the highest god in what would become a succession of gods and goddesses. Unlike androgynous God, Aeons are male and female, and pair up to pro-create matter. With some of God's pneuma (cosmic breath) spirit became matter. Paracelsus notably said that pneuma wasn't breath but rather soul, a semi-material spirit. It's neither 'material' nor 'pure spirit'. It's nephesh?

So, there's unknowable God, but there's knowable Aeons. It seems these gods are like angels, (powers and principalities), through a biblical lens? These deific beings exist between the ultimate True God and ourselves. Aeons are the essence of God and together they make up the godhead. God and his divine parts equal the whole or Pleroma. The Gnostics also imported the concept of 'pleroma' or ideal realm from Plato. Pleroma means fullness, totality, perfection.

The heavenly pleroma is thus the abode of God and the totality of divine powers and emanations. And this centre of divine life is apparently a region of light above our world. Our material world is like Plato's crap world of forms, a poor man's imitation of the real world. It's noted, that whilst the true God didn't fashion or create anything, the substance of all that exists, visible and invisible, originally stemmed from Him, so in this sense 'all is God'.

Furthermore, the further away these emanations are from the One, the less stable and less 'good' they are, which brings us to Sophia. Sophia was the lowest and last Aeon to emanate. And as it transpired, she didn't live up to her name, which is Greek for wisdom, as she emanated without her partner and created offspring without him, resulting in the Demiurge, our dreadful creator.

Apparently, Sophia wanted to know the unknowable God, but being forbidden, she rebelled against God and created something apart from the divine totality. Ashamed of her deed, she wrapped the Demiurge in a cloud and created a throne for him within it. He was then cast out of heaven, to a remote part of the cosmos. So, it was Yahweh that was chucked out of heaven, not Lucifer.

Being isolated and concealed outside the pleroma, the demiurge concludes that only he himself exists. He's ignorant to the superior realms of reality, and blinded by his power and arrogance, he believes he is the ultimate and absolute God. He states, 'It is I who am God; there is none apart from me'. It's noted, that in the Bible, in Isaiah 45:5, God says, 'I am the LORD; there is no other God'. This imperfect god then sets about creating our material world, which imitates the superior pleromatic realm. Being a copycat, the demiurge created a host of co-actors or servants called archons. Archon is notably Greek for leader or ruler.

But moreover, they created us to be their slaves. It's noted, this corroborates with Enlil aka Yahweh, and Sitchin's incorrect report that Anunnaki created us to be slaves, to mine gold for them. It's said the demiurge and his insidious henchmen deliberately created the material world as a prison for the divine sparks (the true God essence) that dwell in humans. Apparently, we were all light beings before we came to earth. Like Plato advised, we don't belong here, as the soul of human beings is from the Pleroma, the divine world. But when the demiurge created this material world, he imprisoned our souls in flesh.

So, Yahweh (the demiurge) made Adam in his image, but he was created with the divinity of Sophia. Thus, we are gods, but we don't know that we're gods. Yahweh hides the truth about our divinity. And we're trapped in the lower material world, separated from the perfect upper world of God and co. Yahweh wants to keep us trapped in the illusion of material reality. He's evil?

Apparently, Sophia felt bad for Adam and Eve, given their material bind. Thus, she channelled a serpent in the Garden of Eden, to divulge that they embodied a spark of divinity within them. She explained that Yahweh is evil, and he doesn't want them to be as knowledgeable as him. She told them their spirit was immortal and 'ye shall be as gods' if they ate the forbidden fruit. Thus, the serpent aka Sophia/wisdom is the hero in the Garden of Eden because Adam and Eve acquired gnosis.

However, most people aren't privy to this special gnosis (only a billion Hindus?). Unlike the initiated elect, we don't realise we're in the matrix? It's noted, the movie 'Matrix' was Gnostic propaganda. Like, the movie 'Star Wars', as we'll get to. We're generally ignorant about the divine spark resident within us. This ignorance is fostered by the false creator and his archons. They're intent on keeping us ignorant of our true spiritual nature and destiny. They want to prevent our souls from ascending to God after our physical death. So, they convince us we don't have one. It seems to be a game of conquest?

So, they keep us plugged into this material façade through 'education'. Like, we're told we came from monkeys and there is no spirit world. It's said archons are jealous of us because they don't have a soul, or divine spark. Thus, they want to snuff ours out. They're likened to demons and jinn, as they hate us with a passion and thrive on our suffering. Indeed, it's said these psychos feed off our fear and pain. These spiritual parasites attack our mind and can attach, causing myriad problems. Like, they're responsible for the voices people hear.

They're described as an off-planet virus that infects humanity. They operate in the shadows and manipulate our reality. Like, they bewitch us with materialism and other bogus propaganda that suits their agenda. They're the power behind the power houses that rule the world. If they control our minds, (dictate what we think), they control us.

Thus, we're being led to believe that gnosis has been deliberately hidden from us. Like, they don't want us ingesting DMT because then we'll know the truth? Yahweh also conditions us through religions like Judaism, Christianity, and Islam to trap us. But ignorance can be dispelled by gnosis?

But moreover, the Nag Hammadi scrolls state there was an archon invasion, which could be the descent of the Watchers? Hermes Trismegistus apparently said that archons, disguised as men, took over council and became the leaders of the world. The archons are also described as reptilian, and like grey aliens ('grey foetus with large black eyes'), which corroborates with fallen angels and demons in the second heaven? But rather than Satan, it's Yahweh that heads an army of evil spirits. And there is no Satan per se, as Yahweh is really Satan who bewitches us with materialism?

It's also noted, Gnostics purport that Yahweh destroyed Sodom and Gomorrah, not because of their wickedness, but because of their wisdom. Apparently, Gnostics believe the postdiluvian nephilim kings were enlightened purveyors of wisdom and insight. They were gods? So, vindictive Yahweh killed them, and burned their sources of enlightened wisdom. Thus, nephilim are good, and archons are bad? It was good that ancient civilisations worshipped the sun and the serpent?

Furthermore, archons are masters of deception. They can create fantasia i.e. false realities/visions, which corroborates with demons/fallen angels' provision of 'visions'. Like, Jung's visions? And like alchemists take trips to Eden (Shambhala?) via their spirit body? And like, La-Sala was shown a superficial spirit world before he was shown its crawling reality. It's like negative hallucinations in hypnosis i.e. he was hypnotised to perceive a different reality. He didn't see our crawling reality until he did. Like, Dr Kubler-Ross was taken on a special trip by her spirit guide, where she seen Jesus preaching in a field two thousand years ago.

So, we can be taken back into the past? Just as some godly men, (like Enoch and John), have been shown the future. Just as Satan showed Jesus all the kingdoms of the world, atop a high mountain, and promised to give them to Him, on the premise He worshipped him (Matthew 4:8). This happened when Jesus was in the desert for forty days and nights.

As it transpired, the Aeon Christ came to save us. He came on behalf of the True God to show us the way back to the True God, by revealing knowledge about our true divine identities. He sacrificed His heavenly abode to live amongst us. To impart wisdom, to teach us how to achieve gnosis, so we can return to the pleroma. Thus, if we ignite the divine spark contained within us, we can connect with the pleroma, divine light or life. And when we physically die, our human essence returns to the Gnostic pleroma. It's debated whether the soul (at its final stage) melts with the One (the pleroma) and loses its individuality, or alternatively retains its separate identity.

The various Gnostic sects had different interpretations about the phenomenon of the Godman Jesus, particularly given His resurrection. Thus, some considered Jesus an Aeon. He was not therefore the True God or a true tangible man. But rather he was a spiritual being, like a phantom. Others identified Him as the embodiment of the Supreme Being who became incarnate to bring gnosis to earth. But he couldn't be material since materialism is evil, and God isn't evil.

Others believed he was the literal son of Joseph and Mary, but that Christ the Aeon ascended on Jesus at his baptism, and left him when he died. Thus, Christ the Aeon didn't die. Others regarded Jesus a mere man who became a spiritual master. Like, Hermes Trismegistus? According to Gnostic scripture, Jesus went to India to awaken the Christ nature. And after seventeen years (he was there from 13-30 years old) of yogic discipline he achieved it. So, He wasn't unique? Either way, Gnostic Jesus came to illustrate that we can become Christ or God like Him. We can have 'Christ Consciousness'. Jesus was then crucified by the demiurge.

It seems pertinent to note, the Gnostics couldn't reconcile Jesus with God of the Old Testament. Indeed, they claimed Jesus came to oppose God of the Old Testament. Jesus was incompatible with Yahweh. They're not related. Thus, the trinity isn't true? Jesus wasn't God in the flesh, who died then resurrected? Yet the Bible tells us, Logos became flesh and dwelled among us. And Jesus and the Father are one. Furthermore, it seems the reason Yahweh was so draconian was because He was contending with nephilim. And He was exasperated with His people worshipping Satan (false gods).

In tandem with eastern philosophy, the Gnostics recognised that dualism characterises existence. The world consists of opposites, with a constant interplay between them i.e. good/evil, dark/light, bitter/sweet, male/female, short/long, microcosm/macrocosm. In esoteric philosophy, the One became two, in a mystical act of expansion and expression. And opposites came into play, creating a dynamic tension in the created universe. Like, yin and yang are opposing yet complimentary forces that interact to form a dynamic whole, an indivisible One (we'll get back to Taoism).

Like, the philosopher Heraclitus (535-475BC) postulated, all entities possess an inherent tendency to turn into their opposite. He said, 'opposites are identical, so everything is and is not at the same time'. He said, 'God is day and night, winter and summer, war and peace, hunger and satiety'. God or logos is the source of everything that happens in nature. Heraclitus believed that each person is a microcosm of the macrocosm. So, we're God and everything is relative, like good and evil? Heraclitus also observed that all existence is in a constant state of flux, hence his 'flux theory'. He said, 'you could not step in the same river twice', because 'everything changes and nothing stands still'.

It's noted, that according to Jung's 'Seven Sermons to the Dead', the spirits told him we are made of pairs of opposites, like male and female. We have qualities of the pleroma i.e. dualism. However, (as mentioned), Father God said (in Isaiah 5:20), 'destruction is certain for those who say that evil is good and good is evil; that put dark is light and light is dark, that bitter is sweet and sweet is bitter'. According to Yahweh, (who is not to be confused with the Demiurge), evil is not good, and neither man nor Lucifer is God. Lucifer and archons are principalities of the air. There's a host of them in the second heaven. And they have an agenda.

But moreover, the esoteric view is that everything in nature is the product of a sexual tension between male and female cosmic principles. Sex plays a key role in creation. The Divine Mind is however androgynous, reconciling Father God with Mother Nature. The Divine Mind is Baphomet. And we can become One with Baphomet through alchemy, the union of opposites. In Gnostic teachings, Sophia is regarded as the Holy Spirit. She's God's feminine side. The 'feminine principle' comes from paganism, namely, Semiramis. And she's making a comeback in post post-modernity, as we'll get to.

With regards to the influence of Greek philosophy on Gnosticism, and besides Plato, there was Neo-Platonist Plotinus (204-270AD) from Alexandria. Apparently, Plotinus came close to acclaiming Plato as the saviour of humanity. Like Plato, he held that our material reality was a poor version of something 'higher and intelligible', which was the 'truer part of genuine Being'. He asserted that the 'less perfect' must emanate from the 'more perfect'.

He conceded that all of creation emanates from the One in succeeding stages of lesser and lesser perfection. The first emanation was 'Nous' (mind), and from Nous came the World Soul, which is subdivided into upper and lower domains. He endorsed the 'Supreme One' as the source of the world, but not through any act of creation, since activity cannot be ascribed to the unchangeable, immutable One. The One is above and beyond, totally transcendent. For pantheist Plotinus, all that exists is God, and hence this divine mystery permeates everything that exists in all creation.

Plotinus believed the world spans between two poles, with divine light (the One or God) at one end, and absolute darkness at the other. Darkness itself has no existence, as it contains no God or light. The darkness beyond God is cold matter, which is what we're made of and animals (we've fallen into the evil world of matter), but our souls are illuminated by light from the One.

Plotinus agreed that our soul contains a 'divine spark', and it's through our soul that we can become one with God. He likens the One to the Sun, and pertains to the ecstatic union with the One. We can experience the divine mystery that is God, where the fusion of our soul with God entails a mystical experience. That is, on the rare occasion that we can experience that we are ourselves that divine mystery. It's understood the ecstatic union is kundalini 'enlightenment'.

But moreover, there's an archetypal conflict between good and evil, represented by light and darkness. And this conflict is not only fought in the external material world, but also internally within us. Our psychological struggles are a manifestation of this battle or conflict. Our will for good fights our will for evil, in a kind of moral tug of war. But there is hope, as our spirit or intelligence (nous) can transcend matter, and 'we' can save our souls. We can release the light from the powers of darkness. But this can only be achieved outside the material realm.

Thus, as Socrates said, we need to 'know thyself', as knowledge is the only way to salvation. We need gnosis to transcend the material and prevent coming back. The endeavour is to join the company of the gods. It's highlighted the duality of existence forces us to make decisions i.e. we choose good or evil. But it's equally highlighted that Gnostics didn't believe in sin, so who cares.

In addition to Plotinus, Mani (216-276AD) was a feature. Mani (founder of Manichaeism in Persia) was known as the 'Apostle of Light' and supreme 'illuminator'. Gnostic scripture regards Mani as a Messenger of Light, like Jesus. Apparently, Mani viewed himself as the final successor in a long line of prophets, including Adam, Zoroaster, Buddha, and Jesus. Manichean tradition also claimed that Mani was the reincarnation of these religious figures. He taught that Manicheanism was the true synthesis of all the religious systems. It was the complete version. And his 'Religion of Light' was for everyone.

Apparently when Mani was twelve, an angelic spirit visited him, who he called his 'Twin' and 'heavenly self'. And this spirit revealed to him divine truths which he developed into a religion. He was told to live chastely and proclaim himself to the people after twelve years had passed. And then, when Mani was twenty-four, the spirit reappeared and encouraged him to go forth and preach his word.

Mani taught about a cosmic battle between the spiritual world of light, and the material world of darkness. It's a battle between good and evil, where matter is intrinsically evil, and mind is intrinsically good. God is good but not omnipotent, and wrestles with Satan. And humans provide the battleground for these powers. We're influenced by both light and dark forces.

For Mani, the soul is fallen, entangled with evil matter, and liberated by the spirit or nous. Inner illumination or gnosis reveals our true God nature. We're saved through nous (our minds). At death the soul of the righteous person returns to Paradise, whereas the soul of the person who persisted in things of the flesh (e.g. fornication, possessions, eating meat, drinking wine) is condemned to reincarnation. It's noted, that if our thinking is referred to as Manichean, it means we think/see things in black and white. It's one of Beck's cognitive errors.

The battle between good and evil resonates with Christianity, as does the spiritual conflict between flesh and spirit. But the Bible doesn't tell us the body is evil but rather the will, which acts through the body, can be. Matter isn't intrinsically evil, as the problem is more the mind. Our flesh can control us, but we can control our flesh. We can learn some self-control? With the Holy Spirit living in us, we can defeat the wiles of the evil one. It's like the flesh is a moral test of character?

And credit to God, the human body is a piece of art. Like, the dazzling human brain is immense. It's wonderful how everything works, which includes how babies are formed in the womb. It seems the battle between good and evil is played out in our minds and hearts. We are the battlefield, and both God and the Devil want our soul. And with our God-given freewill, we can follow the will of God or the devil.

The trouble with the body is that we like pleasing it e.g. sex, drugs, and rock and roll, and goats and kids, because why not? And thus, the devil can use our carnal flesh against our spirit. He tempts us. He also uses legalism, which is considered one of the worst demonic doctrines, because this spurs on the desire to want something. It's reverse psychology. It seems we don't care for something until we're told we can't have it? Like, the forbidden fruit from the 'tree of the knowledge of good and evil'. Fundamentally, our heart needs to be changed (by the Holy Spirit), but we'll get to this in the 'Battle for the Mind' chapter.

But furthermore, it can get weird with Gnosticism, as the twisted idea that matter and flesh is evil can lead to self-harm. People can loathe their frustrating flesh and believe the body deserves harsh treatment. Or take theologian Origen (185-254AD), for example, who allegedly chopped off his testicles in pursuit of holiness. It seems his balls were getting in the way (LOL).

However, people also mortified their bodies for spiritual enlightenment. Black (2010) highlights that some Gnostics 'practised bizarre extremes of mortification and debauchery, as a way of disrupting their own, despised bodily senses and gaining access to the spirit worlds. Some encouraged snakes to crawl over their naked bodies, some drank menstrual blood, saying 'Here is the blood of Christ'; and others believed that their sex magic would lead them to the birth of god-like creatures. Others castrated themselves and boasted, 'I am deader than you are'" (p.318).

Black also notes that 'many of the Gnostics were also vehement world-haters in a way that ran contrary to the mission of Jesus Christ to transform the material world'. Jesus' message was love and redemption. He dealt with the problem of sin at the cross.

So, various mystery schools developed in the first few centuries after Christ. But it's basically the same pantheism. The secret knowledge is that we are god. We can achieve godhood, 'enlightenment', through certain practices and rituals. We can arouse the serpent. We can acquire supernatural power, (like siddhis), and become magicians. And it's the same paganism i.e. sun, moon, and stars worship.

So, like the Greeks before them, the Romans worshipped the gods, in particular the sun god Mithra, born 25th December etc. Mithra travelled from India to the west (because the same Mystery Babylon religion or yoga went to the four corners of the Earth). And like the Greek dynasty before them, who thought they were gods, the Romans Caesar's also maintained they were gods. It's understood they were of nephilim descent.

But then the Roman Empire changed into Christendom to pollute the gospel. Apollo was turned into Jesus, and Mary became 'Mother of God', and so forth. The Roman Catholic Church then became the iron fist, driving all the mystery schools underground. It's understood they wanted to keep the secret ken for themselves. Hence, they quashed the mystery schools and destroyed the great library at Alexandria that housed a ton of Gnostic literature. As Sir Francis Bacon said, 'knowledge is power'.

Thus, whilst people on the surface were worshipping Jesus, or were forced to, other priests were secretly worshipping Mithra in temples under the surface. It's noted, there's much going on underground, literally beneath our feet i.e. networks of underground tunnels and places of interest etc. But we'll get to this.

As touched on, the Roman Catholic Church continues to consist of two churches. One that worships God and one that worships Satan i.e. there's an inner and outer circle. As Father Gabriele Amorth attested to, satanic rituals and ceremonies are conducted within a secret church (in Vatican inner circles), dedicated to Satan, where Satanists partake in satanic paedophilia rites and practices. The Jesuits (who control the Vatican and the Pope) and the Knights of Malta are apparently in the inner circle. The Knights of Malta are the Pope's militia, who are sworn to total obedience to him (to the death) by a blood oath. It's said Roman Catholicism is a counterfeit to Christianity, and is pagan and dark at its very heart. But we'll get back to this disturbing religious institution, referred to as the Babylonian harlot.

It's also noted, whilst there's differences between Luciferianism, deistic Satanism, and La-Vey's Satanism, they have the same antichrist spirit. As touched on, for La-Vey, Satan is a concept. Satan isn't a real, independent metaphysical entity. But rather Satan is a metaphor for our nature. We're products of nature, so there is no sin. Satan represents all sins as gratifying. Like, the seven deadly sins are awesome. Satan worship is self-worship, which is deism? La-Vey notably criticised the New Age movement for hijacking Satanism and placing these practices under the new name, namely, 'New Age'.

So, there's that. And then there's sacrificing kids to Molech. It's said La-Vey's Satanism isn't the real thing but rather a smoke and mirrors parlour version. Real Satanism is the hidden hand that traces back to Babylon and Sumer, with the Saturn worshippers. As mentioned, the UN endorses Luciferianism, which is being sold to the masses. Lucifer the light bearer is the angel of light who will bring peace on Earth and all that jazz. This bright morning star awakens the divine intellect of humankind. But we'll also get back to this.

Meanwhile, the Jews were formulating the disturbing Talmud, which whispers about a mystical school taught only to the most advanced students. This mystical 'tradition' is known as cabala. As mentioned, it's said the cabala was an offshoot of the Talmud. And the Talmud is kosher with paedophilia? The cabala wasn't however committed to writing until the Middle Ages. Whilst some contend that cabala was part of the Oral Torah tradition, which dates back to Moses, Abraham, and even the Garden of Eden, others contend that Rabbi Akiva (50-135AD) birthed cabalistic thought.

However, whilst Akiva knew the secret sauce, it's understood 'cabala' arose after Israel was captured by Babylon. Thus, he was privy to the Babylonian mysteries (magic arts etc) that were passed down through the ages. As touched on, whilst exiled in Babylon, certain Jewish priests studied the ancient Babylonian mysteries. It's believed Jewish sages began to indulge in paedophilia at this time. And these priests produced the cabala. The word cabala means 'that which is received', implying the cabala was a body of knowledge that was passed down orally from generation to generation. It's ancient wisdom. And only the very elect was chosen/privileged to receive these special revelations.

It seems cabala is another name for the Snake Brotherhood, as cabala is pure illuminism which teaches the Holy Serpent is God. The cabala is Satan's gospel, and it's identical to Gnosticism i.e. the astral serpent is Abraxis. It seems certain 'inner circle' 'falsely so called' Jews have harboured the harlot's dark secrets throughout the Ages. Hence, the cabala preceded Gnosticism.

Thus, with this gnosis, Akiva was able to visit God in the seventh heaven. This is a perilous (astral) journey, and few make it. In 'throne mysticism', the mystic ascends through seven heavens to reach God's throne room. The mystic has to be prepared, as each gate on the way is guarded by hostile angels. The mystic has to know the complicated angel's names, secret passwords, charms and spells. They need to negotiate their way to God. And apparently the opposition becomes more powerful as the levels get higher. It's like a computer game? It seems the seven heavens corroborates with the seven planets and Hinduism's seven heavens?

But moreover, it's highlighted that Akiva was coming against Christians and their Holy Spirit power. As mentioned, after Jesus did a shoot, the Holy Spirit came to dwell in born again Christians. And God's people were given spiritual gifts, like prophecy, healing and speaking in tongues. Thus, something had to be done. More people had to be initiated into the mysteries, as God's people were taking over?

So, Akiva conjured up the cabala by giving the Mystery Babylon religion a Jewish veneer. He created cabala to introduce a pseudo-Holy Spirit. It seems the kundalini spirit flows through cabala? Moreover, by advertising cabala as the deep secrets of G-d, would tempt ardent Jews, God's holiest people? And it would ensnare them with seductive arts and wisdom.

However, Akiva's mysticism aside, the cornerstone of cabala is the Zohar, which is a series of books. The Hebrew word Zohar translates to splendour or radiance. In the Bible, the word Zohar appears in the vision of Ezekiel 8:2 and is usually translated as meaning radiance or light. It appears again in Daniel 12:3, 'Those who are wise will shine like 'brightness' of the heavens'.

According to tradition, the Zohar was largely authored by second century Rabbi Shimon bar Yochai. Apparently, he hid in a cave for thirteen years (during Roman persecution) and studied the Torah. But moreover, the prophet Elijah inspired him to write the Zohar. Which could be the same prophet Elijah who visits Lorna Byrne? The Zohar is a collection of mystical commentaries on the Torah. Initiates learn the secrets of the Torah through the cryptic Zohar, which is a mystical method for interpreting scripture.

The Zohar wasn't however revealed until the thirteenth century when Rabbi Moshe de Leona published it. De Leona ascribed the work to Shimon bar Yochai. It seems De Leona channelled Yochai when he was in a trance (the Zohar was automatically written). Cabala is also known as the hidden teachings of Moses. Moses is seen as an occult figure in Jewish mysticism. As mentioned, Moses was au fait with the Egyptian gods and their magical arts.

William Schnoebelen, author of 'The Dark Side of Freemasonry' states, 'Kabbalism is a system of Jewish mysticism and magic and is the foundational element in modern witchcraft. Virtually all the great witches and sorcerers of this century were kabbalists'. He asserts the cabala is a teaching source of Freemasons, Rosicrucian's, and Illuminati ideology. But we'll get to these.

Only the spiritually mature can take this path. One must be 'ready' to receive this wisdom. And it's forbidden to study cabala for any other purpose than spiritual elevation. The wisdom aka magic can be abused, and according to the Zohar, if one learns cabala from someone who is not a true cabalist, then that individual brings 'Darkness into the world – a darkness beyond which we can imagine'. It's generally recommended for initiates to be at least forty years old, as by then one ought to be stable (sound mental health etc) coupled with a thorough grasp of the Torah and Talmud.

Unlike Judaism which believes in One G-d, Jehovah, cabalists believe there are ten parts to G-d. They believe the Godhead, called Ein Sof, consists of ten emanations of the one God. Cabalists maintain the true essence of G-d is so transcendent it's indescribable. But His emanations, called the Sephiroth, His aspects or manifestations, are in contact with the universe in a way that Ein Sof is not (because he's so transcendent).

These emanations are 'supreme crown', 'wisdom', 'intuition/understanding', 'mercy or greatness', 'strength', 'glory', 'victory', 'majesty', 'foundation', and 'sovereignty'. So, these are the knowable attributes or qualities of the unknowable God. It's noted, the ten Sephiroth comprise both masculine and feminine qualities i.e. God's nature is androgynous. So, this Godhead Ein Sof, which literally means 'without end', interacts with the universe through its ten emanations. Paganism notably teaches these emanations are actual separate gods.

Cabalists claim the ten Sephiroth comprise the 'tree of life', from which the universe emanated or came into existence. [It's recalled that Jesus is called the Tree of Life. He's Logos who created the world]. Thus, in the beginning, there was only Ein Sof, nothing else. But rather than Ein Sof directly doing the work of creation, cabala teaches that the emanations from God did the work of creation. For cabalists, God, or rather the godhead, created and sustains the universe. Thus, He is revealed but also concealed i.e. transcendent, unknowable. But then, there's the problem of evil with a good God.

Cabalists believe Satan is not an external entity but rather it's a negative force that exists within us all. The Zohar calls our evil inclinations and selfish impulses Satan. According to cabalists, the soul consciousness is our real eternal essence, but we also have Satan consciousness. But actually, Satan is a force for good because his job is to make us grow spiritually. Apparently, the Light created Satan as a tool, a force to overcome, that we might shine.

For cabalists then, G-d created good and evil, which contrasts to the Christian God, who is benevolently all good and not the origin of evil. Alternatively, evil arose from freewill, and any idea contrary is not consistent with the Bible. And furthermore, according to the Bible, Satan is very real. He's the CEO of the dark side.

For cabalists however, our spiritual growth begins when we recognise that Satan is the evil ego within. Satan controls our emotions, but we can defeat him. Like Tolle advised, we can transcend our ego. We can realise our existence beyond our ego. We can meditate on the 'I AM' mantra? There's no need for a messiah, as we are the messiah. Salvation is enlightenment, to remember the truth of who we are. And that truth is we are God. Every soul is pure essence, an indivisible essence inseparably bound to G-d.

Like witchcraft, cabala teaches that man is a microcosm of the macrocosm. And being a miniature version of God Himself, we are capable of spiritually expanding ourselves to become God. We can realise our god potential because our divine soul is equally composed of the ten holy Sephiroth (forces of the divine essence). The purpose of cabala is thus to assist the person in recognising the truth behind the illusion of separation from God.

We emanate from Ein Sof and become clothed in a physical body (apparently Adam was created both male and female). Thus, we're not victims of original sin but rather are covered by 'flesh' that needs to be removed so that the 'original spark' of God can shine through. Our physical bodies are a temporary inconvenience for our immortal souls. Materialism (our physical body and world) is the great evil. Hence, the projection of consciousness, travelling the invisible world in spirit visions, is an integral part of cabalistic teachings.

Cabala involves learning to control our spirit bodies to navigate the spirit world. It seems we need to take trips to the astral plane to realise our divinity. The aim is to reach higher elevated meditative states of consciousness, and draw down the Infinite Light from the abstract. It's all about acquiring 'ever increasing light' (as we'll get to). The endeavour is to mystically yoke with G-d at death, to end the 'cycles of the soul' (reincarnation).

The Tree of the Sephiroth is believed to represent the basic pattern of the universe. It shows how the Sephiroth connect with the universe, which includes us. But moreover, by experiencing and mastering all ten Sephiroth, which are dimensions of reality, the adept can unite with the One. The Sephiroth on the tree of life are perceived as magical doorways that can be explored by ASC. Magical ascent is achieved by visualising oneself moving towards the higher realms on the cabalistic tree of life. The act of 'rising in the planes', which is rising or ascending meditatively from one sphere to the next, eventually culminates in the spiritual experience of mystical union with the godhead.

And this enlightenment results in the acquisition of supernatural powers. Apparently, the adept must experience and master all ten Sephiroth in order to achieve supreme perfection and power. So, that equates to being supremely possessed by demons?

As mentioned, the Babalon Working is one of the darkest rituals known to cabala. It's explained that the initiate visualises the cabalistic tree of life with its ten spheres. Between the top three spheres and the seven bottom spheres is the dark abyss of Lucifer, which Parsons and Hubbard projected their astral bodies into and became black magicians. And they summoned Satan's scarlet whore.

But furthermore, whilst cabala is associated with Judaism, it's purported that the startling truth is that cabala was never meant for a specific sect. But rather, it was intended to be used by all humanity to unify the world (like spiritism and Manicheanism?). It's not faith-specific, but rather anyone, of any faith, can apply the wisdom to experience positive and powerful changes to their lives. And millions apparently do. Anyone can tap into this power and energy, which includes calling upon the 72 Names of God.

As touched on, popular culture has unearthed an interest in the cabala, with the likes of Madonna, Demi Moore, Britney Spears, and Ariana Grande onboard the magical ride. Many view it as the trendiest faith in town (cabalists are identified by the red thread wristband). Its New Age version informs that the 'creator wants you to have everything you want'. Followers are encouraged to pursue their own happiness. Like, Aleister Crowley's religion, 'do what thou wilt'. It promises money, good relationships, love, and happiness. One book, for example, called 'The 72 Names of God' promises that by meditating on the appropriate name, you'll be able to 'bring more money into your life, ignite sexual energy and passion, meet your true soulmate and radiate beauty to all you see'. So, there's a certain appeal to the cabala?

The 72 names of God seem to be a formula that yields extraordinary power to overcome the laws of Nature. Indeed, according to cabalist and occultist legends, it was Moses, not God, who parted the Red Sea, allowing the Israelites to narrowly escape Pharaoh and the Egyptian army. In order to accomplish this miracle, it's said Moses combined the power of certainty (Paracelsus would call this imagination and faith) with a very powerful spiritual technology. Namely, he possessed the 72 Names of God, which literally gave him access to the subatomic realm of nature.

It's said this formula, used by Moses to control nature, has been hidden in the Zohar for 2000 years. Cabalists also claimed Moses used magic to bring the plagues against the Egyptians. These secret names of God constitute power, and apparently they empower holy-men to control demons, heal the sick, prevent natural disasters, and even kill enemies.

The 72 names of G-d are notably found in Exodus 14:19-21. These three verses pertain to when Moses stretched his hand over the Red Sea, and the Lord divided the waters. In Hebrew, each verse contains 72 letters. Thus, they can be aligned in parallel, forming 72 triads of letters. The cabala teaches that by reversing the order of the letters in the middle set, the 72 triplets become 72 'names' of God. So, each verse was written out as a string of letters, with verse 19 on top, then 20 underneath and in reverse order, and then 21 under that. Then read from top to bottom and right to left, the three lines yielded 72 individual three letter names.

But moreover, together they form the composite 216 name of G-d (the sum of the letters of God's 72 hidden names is 72x3=216), namely, Schemhamphoras. In Jewish tradition, Schemhamphoras is the secret name of the Hebrew God. But it gets weirder as 6x6x6=216. And in Revelation 13:18 we're told 'the number of the beast' is 'the number of a man' and 'that number is 666'. The number 6 is associated with mankind in the Bible, thus 666 suggests a triune nature. And this antichrist beast is coming to rule the world.

Apparently the 72 names vibrate at certain frequencies, and if we tune our body and soul into these spiritual frequencies, they restore our soul. By meditating on the divine names, we imprint them on our soul. Hence, it's called 'soul technology'. Whilst cabalists acknowledge that sound transmits energy, ergo many prayers are spoken aloud, the 72 names are visual mediations. It's not recommended to pronounce them. Indeed, some consider this to be the utmost blasphemy that guarantees damnation.

So, we scan the letters with our eyes and visualise them in our mind, and as a result we connect with these frequencies. Apparently the 72 names align with different entities ('deities') who grant our wishes and empower us. It's understood, that 'entities' are behind 'energies'. But moreover, it seems the 72 'Names of God' corroborates with the 72 demons Crowley referenced, with regards to Solomon. But we'll get back to this.

So, the cabala is magical. By employing the divine names, cabalists can acquire prophecy and other forms of ESP. Secret sciences of the cabala include psychic readings, tarot cards, reading tea-leaves, bones etc, incantations, amulets, mystic art, numerology, sorcery, channelling 'spirit guides' etc. Yet these occult practices betray the Torah. Apparently, some rabbis have pronounced a name of G-d and ascended into heaven to consult with G-d and the angels on important issues. So, we don't need to go through the rigmarole of traversing the seven heavens and contending with the menacing angels?

Furthermore, (as touched on), rabbis have allegedly created golems out of clay and brought them to life by putting in its mouth a piece of paper with a name of G-d on it. 'Artificial man' can be created by reciting various names of G-d. There are many traditional Jewish stories that involve the use of hidden knowledge to affect the world in ways that could be described as magic. Cabalists claim that Scriptures contain hidden messages about the creation of the universe, and by learning these secrets we can procure magic.

As Chuck Missler highlighted, the Bible is packed with hidden codes. Like, the word Torah is found in equidistant letter sequences every 49 letters (7 squared is 49) in both Genesis and Exodus. It's spelled backwards with the same letter sequence in Numbers and Deuteronomy. And in the middle, in Leviticus, with 7 spaces between the letters, the Sacred Name YHWH (Yahweh) is found. As stated, the Bible is not a normal book. Lest we forget, there's power in the Word. And there's power in the name of Jesus. Like, it heals and casts out demons. It stops alien abductions and sleep paralysis.

Michael Drosnin, author of 'The Bible Code' (1997), concedes the Bible is teeming with telling information. He highlights 'the Bible was encoded with information about the past and the future in a way that was beyond mathematical chance, and found in no other text'. He asserts, 'the Bible is constructed like a giant crossword puzzle. It is encoded from beginning to end with words that connect to tell a hidden story' (p.12-13). He notes that hundreds of world-shaking events are encoded, like the rise of Hitler, the Kennedy assassinations, the Gulf war, Hiroshima. He summarises 'there is a Bible beneath the Bible' (p.13).

In addition to the hidden codes, is the interesting Hebrew alphabet, which consists of twenty-two interesting letters. The Hebrew language is not phonetic like English, but rather letters have meaning, so if we put letters together, we can guess what the word means (according to Missler, about 80% of the time). For example, the first letter Aleph (Hebrew A) means strength or leader, and the next letter Beth (Hebrew B) means house or household i.e. family, and thus put together, Ab is father i.e. leader of the house.

And every letter has a numerical value. So, alpha is one, Beth is two etc. Thus, Hebrew words (letters) have numerical value. Like, father is 3. As Black (2010) highlights, the Hebrew word for father has a numerical value of 3, and the word for mother has a value of 41, and the Hebrew word for child is 44, the combination of Father and Mother. But he states, 'it gets more mind-blowing', as he points out that the numerical value of the

Hebrew phrase for the Garden of Eden is 144. The numerical value of the Tree of Knowledge is 233, and if you divide 233 by 144, you get very close – to four decimal points – to the value of the golden ratio phi (p.234). Maths is encoded in nature, as we'll get to.

Apparently Jewish culture adopted this system of numerology, known as gematria, of assigning numerical values to words from Babylon. It's believed that words or phrases with identical numerical values are connected in some way. Like, synchronicity? For cabalists, the interplay of words, their rearrangement into other words (permutations), and their numerical values all play an important role in understanding the secret laws behind creation. But moreover, by arranging numbers and combining Hebrew letters and their numerical values into magical squares and anagrams, we can cast spells in the patterns, and create magic.

It's also highlighted, that the ten spheres on the tree of life are connected by twenty-two paths, which are assigned a different letter of the Hebrew alphabet. And these are connected to the gods (fallen angels in the second heaven).

Black (2010) wrote, 'If the world is materialised thought, then, according to the Cabala, words and letters were the means by which this process happened. God created the world by manipulating and making patterns out of the Hebrew letters of the alphabet. Hebrew letters, therefore, have magical properties and the patterns they make in scripture open up layers, indeed great vistas, of hidden meaning' (p.233).

It also seems pertinent to mention the Gnostic Cathars, as it's purported they influenced the cabala. It's said the Cathars persuaded Jews to Gnostic ideas, leading to the development of the cabala, which surfaced (within the realm of Jewish tradition) in the twelfth century. The Gnostic movement Catharism prevailed from the tenth to the thirteenth century.

However, as mentioned, it's said Jewish mystics pioneered Gnosticism, and their ancient theosophical wisdom stems from the days of yore i.e. sorcery of ancient Babylon and Egypt. It's thus said this Jewish mystical tradition, this collection of occult science of communication with the supernatural world, was 'rediscovered' in the twelfth and thirteenth centuries.

The Cathars were dualists believing in two gods, namely, the good God of the New Testament and the creator of the spiritual realm, and the evil god identified as Satan (demiurge), creator of the physical world. For the Cathars then, all visible matter, including the human body, was created by Satan and was therefore intrinsically tainted with sin. Apparently, Catharism inherited the idea of Satan as the creator of the evil world either directly or indirectly from Gnosticism.

The Cathars believed the world is evil, and they believed the soul would continually be reborn until it could escape the material world and reach spiritual heaven. The soul could even pass through animals, hence the Cathars were vegetarians. Cathars notably comes from Greek katharos, meaning 'pure ones'.

The Cathars rejected the material wealth and power that undeniably corrupted the medieval Roman Catholic Church. They had no need for priests, oppressive ceremonies, or lavish churches. Alternatively, they performed their religious ceremonies in fields or homes. But having their own beliefs, separate from the church, meant they were free of all moral prohibition or religious obligations. And this undermined church authority.

Like, the Cathars believed that taking oaths is a sin (as the Bible insists), which threatened both the Catholic Church and the feudal system, as it undermined the pledges and allegiance between serfs and their Lords. Hence, the papacy had to quash this threat, by rendering their rogue-like beliefs heretical. The fatal blow was delivered on the basis that the Cathars sacrilegiously elevated Satan to God's equal. The crusade against the Cathars in 1209 resulted in the massacre of thirty thousand women, men, and children.

As discussed, the Dark Ages were aptly named. Then the Reformers arrived to put the Babylonian Harlot in her place and liberate God's word from her evil clutches. At the same time however, she was introducing her new scientism scheme. The Jesuits were on the case. The endeavour was to undermine the credibility of God's word by fabricating a different creation narrative.

Thus, the heliocentric model was conjured up from Hermetic philosophy. That is, stars are suns, and the sun is at the centre of our solar system. Everything came from One Big Bang, emanations from the One. Matter magically evolved from non-matter. The Hermetic order is notably referred to as the root of knowledge, as it influenced Plato, Aristotle, Galileo, Kepler, Da Vinci, Copernicus, and Newton (Newton was an alchemist).

Thus, 'scientism' became the new religion with the Age of 'Enlightenment'. And over time, we became convinced that the universe and everything in it came from nothing. We have faith in this absurdity. The Catholic Church notably agrees with the scientific view, which includes a spinning globe earth and evolution, which is unbiblical. But we'll get back to this in the science chapter.

The contemporary assumption seems to be, there's no such thing as the supernatural? Hence, witchcraft is legal? And it's understood this is what the demiurge and archons (aka Satan and his minions) want us to think, to keep us trapped in the matrix. The herd surmises that Jesus was a 'good guy', (there's no denying He didn't exist), but He's not God because God doesn't exist? And by parity of reason, the devil does not exist. Spiritual forces became psychological forces. The dance between good and evil became personal, paraded in our mind. The idea of gods is delusional?

It's propagated that Jesus' miracles, including His resurrection and virgin birth, are naïve delusions. It became farfetched to think that Mary conceived Jesus by the Holy Spirit? Or like Dawkins said, Christ turning water into wine is as believable as a frog turning into a beautiful prince. Interestingly, this latter story engenders the shapeshifting theme, from reptilian into human, but we'll get to this craziness later. The fact is, Dawkins wasn't there, so he doesn't know. And black magicians can turn water into wine. And people are miraculously healed. And magicians supernaturally walk up buildings and levitate. God also forewarned us, that we would be blinded by a strong delusion in the last days, which could be materialism. He said we'd be bewitched by doctrines of devils.

Hal Lindsey (1972), author and lecturer, pertained to the onslaught of the 'Higher Critical' movement in the 1800s. He highlights that religious liberals vigorously attacked the accounts of Christ's life in the four gospels. And It was dogmatically asserted, with no hard evidence from history or archaeology, that the followers of Jesus had embellished and rewritten the accounts of His life and had inserted the miracles as fanciful myths.

Thus, we became convinced there was no magic. We agreed that it's impossible to walk on water, or feed thousands of people with next to no food, and staffs don't turn into snakes. So, we decided the Bible consists of fairy-tales. As Nietzsche said, we killed God. This resulted in nihilism. There is no God, so do what thou wilt. But this is not fulfilling. Nothing is. Our God-shaped hole yearns for God.

In summary, it's understood the materialist paradigm has served the 'archons' well, to dissuade people from believing in God and His word. But the New World Order is both spiritual and political. Thus, the world needs to be spiritually prepared. And thus, contrary to popular Gnostic opinion, it seems the 'archons' do want us to believe we're divine. They want us to believe we possess a divine spark. It seems the serpent wants us to access his 'wisdom'. Like, ayahuasca and kundalini? The end game is to worship the Holy serpent as god.

Hence, Gnosticism is promoted in the mainstream, and God's word is undermined. Like, Yoda said to Luke Skywalker in 'Star Wars', 'luminous beings are we...not this crude matter'. Obi-Wan Kenobi explains the Force is 'an energy field created by all living things. It surrounds us, penetrates us, and binds the galaxy together'. The 'Force' is likened to God.

But moreover, harnessing the power of the Force, this spiritual energy, births extraordinary abilities e.g. levitating objects, tricking minds, and precognition. And we can use this 'energy' for good or evil, in a battle of good against evil? Good and evil are two expressions of One universal energy. Or white and black magic are both demonic. The light and dark side of the 'force' are Lucifer and Satan respectively. It's highlighted that Star Wars is a very religious movie. It's used to replace Christianity and introduce a new world religion.

It's noted, Paul warned us (in 3 Corinthians found in the Armenian Bible) there would be a Gnostic revival in the end times. This corroborates with Manly P Hall (freemasonic philosopher) who stated there would be a Gnostic renaissance at the end of the 20th century and beginning of the 21st century. He claimed it would parallel the Hermetic renaissance of the 15th and 16th centuries. Hence, the New Age landed in the sixties, which came from Helena Blavatsky's Luciferian philosophy, as we'll get to.

In essence, Cabalism, Hermeticism, Gnosticism, Alchemy, Hinduism, Buddhism, and Luciferianism are the same movement (we'll get to Hinduism and Buddhism in the religion chapter). It's the same sun serpent wisdom. They share the same pagan (witchcraft) belief that we're a microcosm of the macrocosm. All is mind. There is no sin, only ignorance. Hence, there's no need for Jesus or His brutal sacrifice. Furthermore, scientism suggests consciousness is in the mix, as consciousness co-creates reality. There's scientific proof we're God.

It appears we increasingly don't care for Yahweh, but rather prefer eastern philosophy. We like the idea that we're God? We prefer to believe there's no Satan. And there's no sin? And the idea that we're One indivisible immortal energy system dancing for itself makes sense, at least atomically.

Lucifer's lies began when he told Adam and Eve 'ye shall be as gods' and never die. This same message is taught today, namely, we are the great I AM. And we don't really die. But rather we'll either reincarnate or exist in the spirit world. With the acquisition of special knowledge, we can join the company of the gods? We need to be born again, by activating the spirit body.

It seems we're more confused than ever, not least because yoga and Yoda seem like a good thing? We're at a point in time, when Crowley's religion is en vogue. As touched on, mainstream pop culture is saturated in the occult. We're being brainwashed with Baphomet. La-Vey said, 'we're in the thrones of the new satanic age'. The New World Order is slithering in.

Fundamentally, we either believe God's word, or we believe we are God. Pantheism and Theism are mutually exclusive. They're contradictory expressions of religion. Choose 'wisely'.

'Have no fellowship with the unfruitful works of darkness, but rather expose them'. Ephesians 5:11

'The most dangerous things in the world are immense accumulations of human beings who are manipulated by only a few heads'. Carl Jung

13

Secret Societies

Mystery schools were the precursor to secret societies. They harboured the secret arts that trace back to Enoch the Evil. This knowledge is acquired through initiation, which is like climbing a pyramid. That is, on the premise one is permitted into the secret society. Only those at the top of the pyramid are privy to the plan. The pyramidal structure enables the dissemination of information on a need to know basis. Like the army's chain of command, orders from above are not to be questioned. Whilst there's myriad secret societies, they're all connected at their core. It's the same Mystery Babylon religion. It's the same Luciferian sun serpent worship. Lucifer and his 'archons' implement their plan through these vehicles. Like, the notorious freemasons and Illuminati.

However, we'll start with the Knights Templar, since the Roman Catholic Church became the new nephilim HQ after the ancient kingdoms. This military and religious Order formed in 1118, when nine French knights formed to defend pilgrims in the Holy Land. As touched on, Muslims invaded Jerusalem in the seventh century. And they built a mosque and the Dome of the Rock on the Temple Mount. They did however allow Jews and Christians to visit the city. But towards the 111th century Turks took control and banned Christians from making pilgrimages.

Whilst the first wave of crusades, (which consisted of thousands of men and knights), took back Jerusalem, life was still difficult for Christian pilgrims. They continued to get persecuted and robbed. So, these noble soldiers came to the rescue. Or rather, they came to rescue something. Christian pilgrimages are notably not biblical. One's salvation does not depend on visiting the Holy Land.

This fraternity was also called the Order of the Poor Soldiers of Christ, but this term didn't apply for long, as the Templars accumulated serious wedge. They were paid generously with money, land and gifts for their efforts. Their nobility earned them many favours including tax exemptions. They were recognised as an Order in 1128 and were given special protection by the Pope. The Templars also collected taxes for the Pope and Crown, and the taxation known as 'tithes'. Tithing is an Old Testament law that has been exploited to fleece people, as the New Testament mandates that you give what's in your heart e.g. to the poor/needy (not multimillionaire pastors). 'Knighting' notably comes from the Knights Templar.

In less than a hundred years the Templars became one of the wealthiest and most influential bodies in Europe, second only to the Vatican. They had land all over Europe, and with such an extensive network of cribs (territories and castles), they soon established themselves as international bankers. Indeed, they established the banking world. They were among the first to set up banks in Jerusalem. They arranged credit facilities for bankrupt royals across Europe and safeguarded the pilgrims' funds.

Thus, rather than pilgrims taking their chances with potential robbers, they could deposit money at a Templar house/castle anywhere in Europe, and receive a credit note for their cash, which they could subsequently redeem at the next Templar house at their destination. Hence, the concept of the traveller's cheque was invented.

The Templars also pioneered branch banking. As it transpired, the Temple Banks were raided for their gold, so to spread the risk they stashed the cash in various locations. This is apparently where the idea of a central bank and its local branches comes from, which became the model for banking in Europe and America. Paper receipts became currency. Money was backed by silver and gold, and worth its weight, unlike today where banks conjure up money. They're like magicians. They simply print some off.

Furthermore, goldsmiths and other owners of strong rooms (to protect cash) realised that only a fraction of cash was withdrawn by owners. This revelation founded the banking brainwave to issue money (notes) to others and charge interest. That is, interest for lending other people's cash (they treat our cash as theirs).

Whilst the Templar's allegedly started off as pious noblemen, they became arrogant and greedy (violating their pronounced vows to poverty and chastity). It seems they had a change of heart? As it transpires, there's no evidence the founding Templars gave protection to pilgrims. It's also highlighted they didn't recruit any members for nine years (they were there for nine years), which makes no sense as how can nine knights protect all the roads?

They did however conduct extensive excavations under the ruins of Herod's temple (the second Jewish temple). The king of Jerusalem gave them lodgings in the palace, built on the ruins of Herod's Temple. It's speculated they were looking for lost treasures, including the Holy Grail and the Ark of the Covenant. It's understood the Jews stashed the Temple's treasures before the Roman legions advanced in Qumran en route to Jerusalem in 68AD. Thus, whatever the Templars found must have been hidden, before the temple was destroyed in 70AD.

It seems pertinent to note, one of the Dead Sea Scrolls, namely, 'The Copper Scroll of Treasures' (25-75AD), mentions huge quantities of gold and silver contained in 64 different locations. This scroll is different from the other scrolls, as it's written on a thin sheet of copper (rather than papyrus or parchment), it was written later, and rather than being biblical or religious, it's a treasure map. Thus, it's believed the Templars found this treasure, which explains their insane wealth. Many believe the treasure map includes the whereabouts of the Ark of the Covenant. Maybe the Jews stashed this artefact in the cave below Jesus' crucifixion site as Ron Wyatt claims? Whilst it's rumoured the Ark of the Covenant is housed in St Mary's Cathedral in Ethiopia, others claim it's in a vault under the Temple Mount.

But moreover, it's said the Templars found hidden scrolls in 1120. They found a cache of writings which changed their worldview. It's purported the Holy Grail was not a cup but rather a set of parchments, scrolls and documents. It appears these ancient 'Jewish' writings revealed the Babylonian mysteries.

So, the Templar's deviated from Christ and actively engaged with cabala, the dark rites and rituals of old. These forbidden books taught them the secret arts of magic and satanic worship. The information revealed how to summon spirits, organise magic circles, and draw a pentagon in the air with a consecrated sword. It taught them 'secret gnosis', namely, the 'Holy Grail' is our light body. They were 'enlightened'. They also learned about mind control, trances, and dreams.

It's further highlighted the Templars were exposed to new teachings in their locality e.g. Egyptian, Greek, Hindu, Islamic and Judaic mysticism. They heard the Luciferian doctrine, (the new version of the Garden of Eden story), and they endorsed it. Thus, Lucifer is the good god, the light bringer who wants to save and educate mankind, and Yahweh is the devil and oppressor.

The Templar's black and white battleship flag reflects these two opposing forces. The black symbolises the world of sin the knight had left behind to enter the Order, and the white reflects the move from dark to light. The focus is on the 'light', which comes from the 'light bearer'. Apparently, the Templars were the first to worship Baphomet (hermaphrodite goat god), which embodies dualism. Baphomet was better than Yahweh? And they wanted to please him.

So, the Knights practised idolatry, (worshipping statues which contain 'gods' aka Baal), and they indulged in perverted sexual rituals, which included drinking urine, eating faeces, and having blood baths. Sodomy became the rite of initiation into the Order. Sodomy was their rite of passage (LOL). As mentioned, according to Paracelsus, Basilisc, a hideous monster spirit, is created by sodomy. He claims innumerable bastard forms (e.g. half-man, half-spiders or toads) inhabit the astral plane, belonging to the 'serpent which is to have his head crushed by the heel of Christ' (Genesis 3:16).

Wheeler (2009) asserts the Templars liked little boys and relished in sexually abusing them. It's recalled this unleashes kundalini, which the rapist also absorbs. They also conducted abortions and infanticides. Initiates would be killed if they left the Order. They were also required to spit and trample on a cross. In short, they sold their soul to Satan who rewarded them with fame and fortune.

It's said the Templars brought this magic back home, but these secrets were strictly reserved for the Roman Catholic Church (inner circle) via rituals. And they taught (initiated) the royals in Europe. It's also purported the Knights Templar were privy to the secret bloodline, also called the Holy Grail. It's said the grail bloodline secrets are held by them, the Church of Rome, Jesuit Knights, Knights of Malta, Opus Dei (created by Jesuits), the Priory of Sion, the upper echelons of the freemasons, and other most exclusive secret societies. As mentioned, this is the nephilim bloodline, as we'll get to.

As it transpired, Muslim armies finally recaptured the Holy Land in the thirteenth century and sent crusaders packing for good. There were no further crusades. It seems the Knights got what they were looking for?

As it also transpired, many royals, the King of France in particular, owed the Templars a lot of money. The papacy was under French control and King Phillip IV was instructed to bring them down. It's thought they conspired to bring down the Order as they sought their stealth wealth. King Phillip thus arrested the Knights Templar in 1307 for denial of Christ, idol worship, homosexuality, and magic. They were accused of occult practices and purged on Friday 13th October 1307[27].

---

[27] The fear of Friday the 13th, so called Paraskavedekatriaphobia, comes from the Templars.

However, many fled to countries like Malta, Portugal, and Scotland. And they escaped with their bucks. They also ventured to the New World, (bailing from Normandy), following the old-Viking routes. They became pirates, identified by their skull and crossbones (Jolly Roger) flag. This black and white flag also symbolises duality (and poison and death). It represents the Knights dual function as monks and warriors. The Templar's missing treasures is one of the greatest unsolved mysteries of all time.

Those who headed to Scotland were allegedly aided by the Sinclair family at Rosslyn Castle, which is where they apparently birthed the Scottish rite of freemasonry. It seems the persecuted Templars went underground and re-emerged (or were repackaged) as freemasons. A Templar church, loosely modelled on Solomon's temple, was built called Rosslyn chapel. However, it's said that Rosslyn chapel wasn't a chapel, but a post-Templar shrine built to house the scrolls found at the temple.

It's said the Knights Templar formed freemasons in honour of the builders who constructed Solomon's temple. Indeed, it's said freemasons were created at Solomon's Temple. It appears freemasonry dates back to sex pest Solomon's time. The central character in freemasonry is the builder of Solomon's Temple, namely, Hiram Abif. However, before we delve into freemasonic lore, it seems pertinent to note what the Bible tells us.

Thus, we're told that Solomon bought building materials (timber etc) from King Hiram of Tyre. And King Hiram kindly sent Solomon a master craftsman called Hiram Abi to help him. Hiram Abi knew all about stonework, carpentry, weaving, and was skilful at making things from gold, silver, bronze, and iron. So, he was a 'master' mason. We're told Hiram Abi cast two bronze pillars (27 feet tall), which stood on the porch of the temple, at the entrance (in 1 Kings 7:13-22). The one toward the south was named Jakin, and the one toward the north Boaz. Boaz was notably King David's great grandfather. It's highlighted that Jakin means 'establishment' and Boaz means 'strength', and united together they mean 'stability'.

It's noted, every freemasonic lodge represents Solomon's temple, and they always feature two columns named Jakin and Boaz, which represent the 'two pillars of knowledge'. They are the two pillars of opposites, namely, heaven and earth, as above, so below. And they create a gateway to 'Never, Never Land' (the spirit world). The Worshipful Master aka master magician stands between them. Apparently, the Twin Towers in New York perfectly matched the proportions of the Biblical columns of Boaz and Jakin, but we'll get to 9/11.

As discussed, the Bible tells us Solomon followed after other gods, (like Ashtoreth aka Semiramis and Baal aka Nimrod), which led to Israel's downfall. We're also told Solomon enlisted an insanely massive labour force to build God's house. Like, he recruited 70,000 common labourers, 80,000 stonecutters, and 3,600 foremen to supervise the work. It's also noted, that both Hiram's, who were from the same locality, were indoctrinated in Baal's religion. Tyre was a city where heathen gods were worshipped. Apparently, Hiram literally means He-Ram, Lord Ram, the goat headed god.

According to freemasons, King Solomon recruited Hiram Abif to help build the temple. Hiram Abif, King Solomon and King Hiram of Tyre held an important lodge and were the sole joint holders of the true secrets of a Master Mason. They presided as grandmasters over the lodges which they established. They instituted the degrees and initiations that have been passed down to freemasonry today, as we'll get to. However, as it transpired, Hiram Abif was murdered by three criminals because he refused to impart the supernatural secrets. He would rather die than betray the sacred trust reposed in him. So, he was the architect of the temple, but he died before it was completed.

It's also noted, that Hiram Abif didn't resurrect from the dead, but the ceremony to become a Master Mason involves enacting his death and resurrection. Death, burial, and resurrection ceremonies mirror Jesus' resurrection (and Christian baptism). But it also illustrates what happens when initiates take a trip to the astral plane. They're born again. It's like the king-making process in Egypt.

Freemasons, Satanists, and occultists all venerate Solomon. He's regarded as a skilled sorcerer in the occult world. It would appear he was the 'wisest' man that ever lived? He was magical? According to the secret traditions of freemasons, Solomon knew the secret tradition which included controlling demons. It's said he recorded his magical knowledge in a secret book, which was later laid in the foundation of the second temple. Which the Templar's found? Hence, they became the 'Keepers and Guardians of the Mysteries'.

Legend holds that King Solomon used pagan magic to imprison 72 demons into a bronze barrel, and sealed it using magic symbols ('sigils'). It was then thrown into a deep lake to prevent others from discovering the power it held. However, the Babylonians found this barrel and released the demons. These became known as the 72 spirits of Solomon. The Goetia aka the Art of Solomon provides detailed explanations regarding how to conjure the 72 demons Solomon summoned. It provides spells and invocations, and explains how spirits can be compelled into obedience. Like, in Crowley's Book 'The Goetia: The Lesser Key of Solomon' (1904). It seems the 72 demon spirits are the '72 Names of God'?

As also touched on, Solomon allegedly received a ring with a hexagram on it, the 'Seal of Solomon', to command demons. According to the 'Testament of Solomon', which was written between the first and fifth centuries CE, Solomon received a ring from the archangel Michael with the seal of God in it, which enabled him to command demons. It's purported that demons helped to build his temple. It's equally said however, that Satan gave him the ring, which seems more likely? He got it from the Lord of the Rings, the Dark Lord?

Interestingly, the Temple Scroll, the longest of the Dead Sea Scrolls, describes a Jewish temple that was never built. The document is written in the form of a revelation from God to Moses, suggesting that Moses' instructions were either forgotten or ignored when Solomon built the first temple. It seems Solomon built the wrong temple?

Whilst local fraternities of stonemasons, in some shape or form, stretch back to the Middle Ages, they were formally regulated at the end of the fourteenth century. It's said the Templar's adopted masons (stoneworkers) and introduced them to lower level secrets concerning Solomon's Temple. Thus, masons evolved into freemasons with the influence of the Templar's. They were initiated into the 'craft'. The Templars imparted their secrets through rituals. They passed on the magical baton, the Light of Lucifer. It was 'magical' that masons could create splendid cathedrals and monasteries?

Modern freemasonry is officially dated from 1717, when the Grand Lodge was established in London. They also allowed non-masons to join, so called speculative masons. Freemasonry was viewed positively for 'good works' and the number of lodges grew rapidly. Freemasonry pledged to 'make good men better men'. Hence, it was a noble endeavour to pledge allegiance to the brotherhood. Within a century freemasonry spread throughout most of Europe, including Germany, France, and the colonies of early America.

Manly P Hall, freemason historian, maintains at least 50 out of 56 signatories of the American Declaration of Independence were known Freemasons (only one was definitely not), and they were all cousins from a royal bloodline (cited in David Icke, 2007 p.137). It's also understood, Columbus did not accidentally find America in

1492, but rather his father-in-law had connections with grand masters and accessed maps, which came from the Templars. Freemasons were the major force behind the founding of 'The New World'. It's said the US was a Masonic experiment to create a new (modern) Egypt. Its greatness is likened to the greatness of ancient Egypt. Brother George Washington was the first president.

It's noted, that contrary to the Catholic Church, who ironically opposes secret societies, the Church of Scotland and England are kosher with freemasons? Like, the Queen, who is the head of the Church of England, has a Masonic temple at her home in Buckingham Palace. Freemasonry is a force for good? Hence, the royal family are linked with them? Indeed, it's said the linking of the royal family and freemasonry has been the main reason for the survival of the British monarchy. Freemasonry is founded on three grand principles, namely, brotherly love, relief, and truth. All of which could be nefarious precarious?

Whilst it's propagated this boys club merely enables getting off with parking fines, or perhaps securing a promotion, this worldwide movement remains shrouded in secrecy. As Bill Cooper said, 'Of course, you have been told your whole life that the freemasons are only a benevolent fraternal organisation bent only on community service. Read on, O innocent one'.

Masons are notably represented by the Templar's symbol, namely, the unfinished pyramid with the all-seeing-eye (as pictured on American dollar bills). The pyramid represents the power structure of secret societies, and the all-seeing eye represents the eye of Horus aka Lucifer. It represents the secrets of illumination (the third eye). Freemasonry is a religious order, as freemasons need to believe in God or a Supreme Being. But it doesn't matter which God people believe in. Masonic degrees notably include a 'Knights Templar' degree, but apparently initiates need to believe in the God of the Bible for this degree.

Most members do the first three degrees, known as the 'Blue Lodge', but there's at least 33 degrees, within 13 levels. It's said when the Templar's formed the order of mysteries, on the Temple Mount, they began with 7 degrees, and later added degrees, following their persecution. There are 32 levels within the Scottish rite of Freemasonry and 33 within the Irish. There's also the York Rite, which has considerably less degrees, but it seems to cover the same material.

It's noted, that on the back of the US dollar bill, there are 32 feathers on the right wing of the eagle and 33 on the left. The Star of David (made up of 13 stars) also features on the dollar bill. 'Mason' is spelled out using a hexagram, from the Latin Inscription, *Novus Ordo Seclorum* (which means New World Order) and *Annuit Coeptis* (which means favour the undertaking). And apparently the two vertical lines going through the S to make the dollar sign $ represent the two pillars, Jakin and Boaz.

It's duly noted, that numbers are all important, like 7, 13, and 33. It's understood God is partial to the number 7, which represents wholeness/completion. And 13 is infamously dodgy? Apparently 33 is a reference to the 33 vertebrae in the human spinal column, which the kundalini serpent ascends, and which is known 'raising the devil'. The spinal column is also called 'Jacob's Ladder', which according to the Bible, connects heaven and earth. Black (2010) informs 'the secret of 33' refers to the number of gateways by which the human spirit may travel between the material world and the spirit worlds. Like, Spiritism suggests there may be 33 planes in the spirit world. It's also the age when Jesus was crucified, but we'll get back to numbers.

Only those at the highest level of initiation (i.e. 32nd and 33rd degree masons), are taught the ancient plan, or as George W Bush said, 'ancient hope that is meant to be fulfilled'. He also said, (twice in 2001), 'An angel still rides in the whirlwind…and directs the storm', which seems to be a reference to Lucifer. Apparently 'angel in the whirlwind' was the codeword for the start of the New World Order (NWO). Baby Bush would get the show on the road. Start it with a (9/11) bang. Apparently, Luciferians call the final war with God 'the great plan'. But we'll get back to this craziness.

It's also understood, (like the Vatican and all secret societies), there's an inner circle and outer circle. As Manly P Hall said, 'Freemasonry is a fraternity within a fraternity, an outer organisation concealing an inner brotherhood of the elect'. Thus, someone might be a 33rd degree mason, but they're still not privy to the plan. Secrets are only disclosed if the person is worthy. It's further alleged there's 360 degrees, with Satan at the top.

So, contrary to the naïve assumption that freemasonry is little more than a social club, it's contended this organisation is the prime global vehicle for orchestrating the Luciferian agenda. Apparently 'Enoch' (after Enoch the Evil) means initiated or dedicated to Lucifer. Wayne notably highlights that lower level freemason initiates think they're following good Enoch from Seth's line, as opposed to evil Enoch from Cain's line.

Members have to take oaths of secrecy, promises that are binding, which are accompanied with particular rituals. These oaths, which are essentially murder pacts, increase in intensity as the degrees advance. The rituals also become increasingly sinister and insidiously graphic. Freemasonry is saturated in symbolism (which comes from Solomon's Temple). It's essentially a language they have to learn. Like, cheeky handshakes, signs, and passwords (handshakes also enable masons to surreptitiously demonstrate which degree they are). It's noted, this emulates what happens when initiates take an astral trip to the celestial bodies i.e. they have to learn passwords and handshakes.

To illustrate regarding the rigmarole, we can consider the first degree ceremony, known as the 'Shock of Entrance'. So, the initiate has to take all metal off including wedding ring and wear their pyjamas or 'pauper clothing'. They have to keep their socks and left shoe on, and for their right foot, they get a slipper. The candidate's shirt is unbuttoned to expose his left breast (i.e. heart), his right sleeve is rolled up to reveal the elbow, and his left trouser leg is rolled up above the knee. He is then blindfolded with a mask called a 'hoodwink', and a noose called a 'cable tow' is placed around his neck (threatening strangulation or asphyxiation).

The temporary blindness notably represents the present darkness, which will be displaced by light if the initiate succeeds in penetrating the mysteries before him. The point of a dagger (or compass) is drawn from the bridge of the nose to under the chin, and across the left breast, all of which threaten death or injury.

Initiates have to kiss and hold the 'Volume of Sacred Law' (VSL) during their oath. The VSL is the Masonic term for whatever religious or philosophical texts are used at lodges. This is usually the Bible in the UK. They also touch objects that are First Degree 'tools' e.g. 24" gauge, gavel, and chisel. The candidate is then shown the secret handshake, signs, and given the password 'Boaz'. As for the oath then, for the first degree of 'Entered Apprentice Mason', which every freemason must take, it is as follows:

"Of my own free will and accord, in the presence of the Almighty God and this worshipful lodge, erected to Him and dedicated to the Holy Saint John, do hereby and hereon, most solemnly and sincerely promise and swear, that I will always hail, forever conceal and never reveal, any of the secret arts, parts, or points of the hidden mysteries of Masonry which may have been heretofore or shall be at this time, or at any future time, communicated to me as such, to any person or persons whatsoever, except it be a true and lawful brother Mason, or within the body of a just and lawfully constituted lodge of Masons; nor unto him or them, until by strict trial, due examination, or lawful information, I shall have found him or them as lawfully entitled to them as I am myself".

"I furthermore promise and swear, that I will not write, print, paint, stamp, stain, cut, carve, hue, make or engrave them on anything, moveable or immovable, capable of receiving the least impression of a sign, word, syllable, letter or character whereby they might become legible or intelligible, to any person under the canopy of heaven, and the secrets of Masonry be thus unlawfully obtained by my unworthiness". [It's noted, 'the canopy of heaven' is a reference to the firmament].

"All this I most solemnly and sincerely promise and swear, with a firm and steadfast resolution to keep and perform the same, without the least equivocation, mental reservation, or self-evasion whatsoever, binding myself under no less penalty than that of having my throat cut from ear to ear, my tongue torn out by its root and buried in the sands of the sea, at low water mark, where the tide ebbs and flows twice in twenty-four hours, should I in the least, knowingly or wittingly, violate or transgress this my Entered Apprentice obligation. So help me God and keep me steadfast."

The second degree, 'Fellow Craft', reads '...of having my left breast laid open, my heart torn out and given to the ravenous birds of the air or devouring beasts of the field as prey...' And the third degree, 'Master Mason', reads '...of being severed in two, my bowels burned as ashes and those ashes scattered over the face of the earth and wafted by the four winds of heaven that no trace or remembrance of so vile a wretch may no longer be found among men...' It stands to reason that members would be reluctant to disclose any secrets.

As touched on, the third degree ceremony involves enacting Hiram Abif's death and resurrection. And it mirrors the Egyptian kings' initiation into the underworld. Thus, they similarly pray to the 'Most High' for protection for the candidate as he passes through 'the valley of the shadow of death'. The candidate is obliged to play the role of Hiram Abif, who is whacked three times on the head. He then falls to the floor and a funeral shroud is draped around him. The 'worshipful master' then pulls him up, which symbolises his rebirth. When raised from the tomb, the bright morning star is on the horizon. He is reborn to the status of Master Mason. He's then given the secret password, signs, and handshake.

It seems that unlike Egyptian kings, the stylised death and resurrection act of the master mason is more figurative, as they're not given a hallucinogenic (narcotic) potion? They're not really born again, until they make that sojourn?

So, Masonic lodges are very religious. Meetings include an order of worship complete with prayers and hymns. But there's religious freedom, as 'Almighty God' can be whoever we want Him to be. The four Holy Books are all equal, namely, the Vedas (Hindu scriptures), the Koran, the Bible, and the Book of the Law (Torah). Perennialism is notably a philosophy of religion which views the world's religious traditions as sharing the same truth at their core i.e. it's the same god and universal energy or breath of life.

This however contradicts God's commandment that there should be no gods before Him, and viewing other gods as equal is spiritual adultery. And Yahweh is not moon God Allah or Shiva the destroyer. They're not the same God. However, we'll get back to the burning question of 'Who is God'.

But for Masons, there is One True God or Supreme Being, and that God is 'The Great Architect of the Universe'. God is the great mathematician, with the most precise measurements and geometry. Geometry notably means to measure the Earth. It comes from the Greek words Geos meaning 'Earth' and Metron meaning 'to measure'. Geometry is the science of stone masons. Apparently the 'G' on the Masonic ring can refer to God or Geometry or Gnosticism.

Freemasonry enshrines the Gnostic principle that people need to undergo a resurrection while still alive (a 'living resurrection'). We need to take a trip to the stars to learn the secrets of the stars. Like, the Master Mason learns the secrets of the stars. We need to be enlightened or we're (continually) reincarnated into crud flesh until we learn this Gnostic lesson?

It's also noted, whilst masons refer to God as 'The Great Architect of the Universe', deity is further explained to the Second Degree Mason as, 'God, Great Architect of the Universe, Grand Artificer, Grand Master of the Grand Lodge Above, Jehovah, Allah, Buddha, Brahma, Vishnu, Shiva, or Great Geometer'. So, God is all these gods, because there is only one God? It's one God with various names, disguises, values, and beliefs?

Or maybe when Jesus said He was the only way, He meant it? And we can't serve two masters. Hence, it's either Christianity or paganism. By parity of reason, Christians can't be freemasons, which contradicts the Church of England? This is however overlooked, like oaths, which are unbiblical. In James 5:12 we're told, 'But most of all, my brothers and sisters, never take an oath, by heaven or earth or anything else.' This is reiterated in Matthew 5:33-37, Exodus 20:7 and Numbers 30:2.

So, freemasons swear an oath to 'study the hidden secrets of Nature and Science in Order to better know his maker'. Maths seems to be the master key, as equations describe universal relationships. As Galileo, the father of modern science, affirmed, 'the universe is written in the language of mathematics...without which... one is wandering about in a dark labyrinth'. He understood that maths described reality. Dr Stephen Marquardt said, 'All life is biology; All biology is physiology; All physiology is chemistry; All chemistry is physics; All physics is maths' (cited in David Icke, 2007 p.51).

The universe is determined by certain mathematical constants which express themselves in the form of patterns, designs, and structures. Like, Pythagorean theory, for example, or pi, or like the golden ratio Phi, that appears throughout nature. Sacred designs like snowflakes, spirals on snails' shells, geometric shapes like the hexagonal cells that bees construct to hold their honey, all evidence God is the geometer of the world.

It's believed the golden ratio makes the most aesthetically pleasingly shapes. Hence, it's found in art and architecture e.g. the Parthenon in Greece, the Great Pyramid of Giza, Temples in South America, and the UN building in NYC. It seems the ancients aspired to emulate God's 'sacred geometry', which is the hidden geometry of creation. The ancients believed mathematical formulas and specific symbols were the building blocks for everything in the universe. And they used this knowledge to construct their buildings.

Freemasons thus encode Nature's secrets in architecture. Their knowledge is never written down to prevent exposure of ken but rather is revealed through occult symbols, rituals, and architecture (e.g. shapes and dimensions of rooms etc). So, that's all fine?

But moreover, as it transpires, there is a Masonic God. His True Name is revealed to Third Degree Masons who elect to be 'exalted' to the Holy Royal Arch. Apparently only one fifth of all Master Masons are exalted, which represents the completion of the 'ordeal' of the Master Mason. Thus, in the ritual exaltation, the secret name of the Great Architect of the Universe is revealed as JAH-BUL–ON. JAH (or Yah) comes from Yahweh; BUL comes from Baal; and ON is from Osiris.

So, freemasonry initially takes different religions and brings them together, under the umbrella term 'Great Architect of the Universe', and then later reveals its own Masonic god. JAH-BUL-ON is now the real god. However, whilst these masons learn the secret name of the Masonic god, they do not learn his nature. One needs to continue climbing up the monkey tree or 'stairway to heaven'. Apparently Led Zeppelin's song 'Stairway to Heaven' is a Masonic reference to climbing stairs/degrees. It's said masons have essentially conjured up Jahbulon, a Trinitarian demonic entity, to worship.

It's also said, during rituals, when masons are asked 'what are you!' They say, 'I AM that I AM'. It's recalled, when Moses asked God who He was, He said 'I AM WHO I AM' (see Isaiah 43:10 and John 8:58). So, they're also led to believe they're God?

It's highlighted that often lower members are confused by the true meaning of rituals i.e. not appreciating the inherent sun worship involved. Indeed, it's said they're deliberately deceived. They're under the misguided illusion that they're worshipping the true God.

According to Albert Pike (1809-1891), the esteemed pope of freemasonry (he was a 33rd degree mason), 'They do not know because we lie to them'. In his book 'Morals and Dogmas of the Ancient and Accepted Scottish Rite of Freemasonry' (1872), he explains how initiates of the blue degrees are intentionally misled by false interpretations. He wrote, 'It is not intended that he shall understand them; but it is intended that he shall imagine he understands them. Their true explication reserved for adepts, the princes of masonry' (p.149).

He also wrote, 'Masonry, like all Religions, all the Mysteries, Hermeticism, and Alchemy, conceals its secrets from all except the Adepts and Sages, or the Elect, and uses false explanations and misinterpretations of its symbols to mislead those who deserve to be misled, to conceal the truth…' (p.104-105)

As touched on, the endeavour is to acquire more light, ever increasing light. Like, in the first degree, initiates are asked what they most desire, and the reply is 'light'. The second degree initiate is asked the same question, and the response is 'more light'. Third degrees initiates, given the same question, reply 'further light'. Freemasons believe they're stepping out of darkness and into the light. Which sounds lovely, despite the murder pacts?

However, as William Schnoebelen (author/lecturer) confirms, this light comes from Lucifer. He was a 90 degree mason (he claims there's at least 97 degrees) and concedes that masons progressing up the ladder are told they'll receive ever increasing 'light'. They're told they evolve from 'darkness to light'. Masons believe light symbolises knowledge and intellect. But Lucifer, the light bearer, is the patron god of intellect. Those who are being initiated in esoteric knowledge are gaining access to Lucifer, who is represented in esoteric language as the universe's deep secrets. Masons are led to believe the Supreme Being is a centre of light, but its Lucifer's pseudo-light. It seems we can temporarily merge with the 'light' when 'enlightened'.

It's noted, the 'darkness into light' rhetoric seems to be a spin (inversion) on Jesus' words in Acts 26:18. Thus, Jesus said to Paul, 'to open their eyes so they may turn from darkness to light, and from the power of Satan to God. Then they will receive forgiveness for their sins and be given a place among God's people, who are set apart by faith in me'.

But not for masons, who alternatively want to partake in some weird rituals with their little aprons on. And call someone 'worshipful master'. Like, Catholics call the Pope 'Father'. Apparently, the aprons stem from the fig leaves Adam and Eve used to cover their nether regions back in the day. It's said the apron covers the 'holy of holies', which is the phallus, as masons worship the phallus.

Rituals are always conducted on black and white chequered floors, which stems from the Templar's Beaucant (meaning two colours) battleship flag. The Templars had many symbols representing them, like the 'Skull and Bones' Templar symbol for resurrection, but the beaucant flag was one of the most important. Every brother wears a white shirt with a black tie and suit. He will not be admitted if he doesn't have the correct attire. It's said this symbolises the dualism of good and evil, which defines the Gnostic god. God is good and evil? Lucifer is white, and Satan is black. But they're the same One God. Satan is Lucifer.

It's noted, the Gnostic gospel is that good deeds balance evil deeds. It's said this explains why otherwise psychopaths can be philanthropists e.g. the Clintons, Jeffrey Epstein, Bill Gates. It's also noted, philanthropic personas are a perfect cover for lurid Satanists.

The black and white dualism also symbolises inter-dimensional travel between the physical and spiritual world. Rituals are conducted to summon demons to cross over. Black (2010) summarises, 'the architecture of Freemasonry grows out of an occult, magical tradition of invoking spirits that goes back to ancient Egypt. 'When the materials are all prepared and ready', it is said, 'the architect shall appear'' (p.472). And it appears the architect is Lucifer? A great occult truth is, when the student is ready, the teacher appears. Apparently satanic rituals take place after hours, when lodges are closed.

Thus, whether they're aware of it or not, freemasons are sun-worshipping Luciferians. By the 1700s, over five thousand years of ancient mystery religions had infiltrated into freemasonry. Albert Pike, who was cofounder of the KKK (nice), asserted freemasonry is identical to the ancient mysteries, and confessed that Lucifer is god. In his aforementioned book, he wrote 'Lucifer, the Light-bearer! Strange and mysterious name to give to the Spirit of Darkness! Lucifer, the Son of the Morning! Is it he who bears the Light, and with its splendours intolerable blinds feeble, sensual or selfish Souls? Doubt it not!'

He states, 'Yes, Lucifer is God, and unfortunately Adonay is also God. For the eternal law is that there is no light without shade, no beauty without ugliness, no white without black, for the absolute can only exist as two Gods: darkness being necessary to light to serve as its foil as the pedestal is necessary to the statue, and the brake to the locomotive'. He informs, 'The true and pure philosophic religion is the belief in Lucifer, the equal of Adonay; but Lucifer, God Light and God of Good, is struggling for humanity against Adonay, the God of darkness and evil'.

According to Pike, cabala is the religion of masons. This 'divine knowledge' is the foundation stone. Initiates are thus inducted into the secret Snake Brotherhood and learn the Babylon mysteries. As touched on, it's said the cabala contains the secrets of creation. It contains the mathematical foundation of all things, which accounts for the origin of the universe. It's understood that numbers and 'stars' have the answers to the mysteries of life. Numbers are not merely a quantity or amount, but rather have a quality to them. Numbers are in relationship with all things in nature, and thus every number has a certain power. Like, words have power?

For numerologists, (who study numbers and their influence on our lives), numbers have symbolic and spiritual value e.g. the number 1 symbolises new beginnings; and 2 reflects duality and balance; and 3 and 7 have spiritual meaning, which deals with magic. Thus, besides mathematical squares and roots, prime numbers etc, there's number mysticism. And there's gematria (letters/words have numerical values), as discussed. Like 777, a sacred number in cabala, refers to flaming sword. Masons are thus initiated to know the codes to unlock the mysteries of life. They learn how to transpose the numbers and words to perceive the true meaning. According Tesla, the numbers 3, 6 and 9 are the foundation of creation. He was apparently obsessed with these numbers.

It's noted, there's a statue of Albert Pike in Washington DC. And also, that Washington DC is saturated in occult symbols, including an inverted pentagram with the bottom pointing directly at the White House. America has a curious mix of Christian and Masonic foundations. The Washington design is similar to the Vatican, with a dome facing an obelisk. That is, the womb meets the phallus for procreation.

As Dr Tom Horn (author) explains, according to Egyptian mythology, the dome represents ever pregnant Isis facing the erect phallus to raise the spirit of Osiris from the underworld, so that he could have divine representation in their king. Others say the womb is facing the phallus to be impregnated i.e. she's not already pregnant. Apparently, masons partake in the 'Raising Osiris from the Dead' ceremony at the 33rd degree. But moreover, Horn further claims that freemasons perform the 'Raising Osiris' ritual every time a US president is inaugurated. They believe they can install the spirit of Osiris into the reigning president. No danger.

It's also noted, there's a statue of Semiramis atop the capitol dome, called the Statue of Freedom. Like the statue of Semiramis, so called Liberty, in New York. The latter was a gift from the French freemasons to the US freemasons, for the New World. Her torch symbolises illumination and the seven rays emanating from her crown are stages of initiation, as we'll get to. However, the statue of Liberty also represents Lucifer the light bearer (who's also known as Venus). The Israeli supreme court, (designed and paid for by the Rothschild's), contains the same illuminist stamp e.g. obelisks, All Seeing Eye in pyramid. Astana in Kazakhstan is also saturated in this symbolism. So, their occult ken is reflected in their occult architecture.

But furthermore, the Washington Monument (obelisk) is 6,600 inches tall, and 666 inches wide along each side at the base, which is said to be a reference to the 666 biblical 'mark of the beast'. Like, it's rumoured the Louvre 'pyramid' in Paris has 666 panes of glass. And like the first 'Apple' computers were sold for $666.66. The 'apple' with the bite out of it notably symbolises the fall or 'enlightenment'.

And like the Google icon features 666, and CERN. And like Jared Kushner's family paid over the odds for 666 Fifth Avenue in NYC. And like 33rd degree mason Aleister Crowley changed his name so it would add up to 666. And like Stanley Kubrick was murdered 666 days before the year 2001, which is a reference to his movie '2001: A Space Odyssey'? It gets weird with numbers. As Wheeler (2009) asserts, Satanists literally worship numbers. And they clearly love the beast's number.

Wheeler (2009) also pertains to spiritual numerology and concedes that each letter as a number has a certain vibratory effect. Luciferians believe (experientially know) numbers possess inherent power, and great power when properly wielded by a skilled adept. She states 13 or multiples of 13 e.g. 39 are potent numbers, and 6 and multiples e.g. 18. Bill Cooper concedes the numbers 3, 7, 9, 11, 13, and 39 and multiples of any of these numbers have special meaning for Satanists. Hence, the meditation room in the UN HQ in NYC, (which features a black cube), is 33ft by 18ft.

Apparently 11, 22, 33 are the three 'Master Numbers'. 33 is the 'Master Teacher' and most influential. It's said the other two Master Numbers, 11 (vision) and 22 (vision with action) form the base of a two-dimensional pyramid and added together equal 33 (guidance to the world), the apex of the pyramid.

It's noted, there's a number of conspiracies surrounding the '33rd parallel north' (a circle of latitude that is 33 degrees north of the equatorial plane). Mount Hermon (where the Watchers descended) is located there, and the Battle of Armageddon will apparently be fought there. It seems to be a popular geographical location for occultists' planned events e.g. disasters, wars, assassinations. It's understood that witches perform spells at particular times, and choose particular dates to carry out their atrocities e.g. 7/7 and 9/11. Like, Pope John Paul I (in 1978) was murdered after 33 days in office. And JFK was murdered on the 22nd day of the 11th month, on the 33rd parallel. But we'll get back to so-called conspiracies.

It's also highlighted the world has a network of magnetic energy lines running through it, known as ley lines. And the Templar's knew about this energy grid, ergo masons know about this grid. It's explained, that when two lines cross, they create a small vortex, and the more lines that cross, the more powerful the vortex. A vortex point is apparently neutral, and can be used to channel negative or positive energy. 'Energy' (the 'force') can be used for white or black witchcraft. Thus, performing rituals can manipulate the energy e.g. human sacrifice can summon demonic energy. Or alternatively, any 'energy' that we can summon is not of God? It's said vortexes can open up stargates and portals. Presumably, the Tower of Babel was built on a powerful vortex?

Vortices are apparently huge at Gaza, Egypt, and Machu Picchu in Peru. But apparently the Kaaba (the holiest shrine in Islam) has the most energy lines passing through it, making it the most powerful energy point on earth. It's noted, Muslims circle the Kaaba (the black cube) seven times in an anticlockwise direction. Performing this ritual is part of the hajj, the pilgrimage to Mecca. Contrary to Christianity, Muslims must undertake the hajj at least once in their lifetime. It's mandatory. This ensures 'energy' is continually harnessed at the Kaaba?

Masons have thus monopolised this turf, locating their significant buildings on sites with potent energy. Wheeler (2009) concedes the illuminati build their important buildings on occult ley lines. She points out that thousands of cathedrals, temples, and churches have been built on ancient pagan religious sites to yield the energy there. David Icke (2007) also pertains to ley lines, but he further states that 'many ancient pyramids, temples, mounds, and other earthworks also have entrances to underground reptilian cities'. As touched on, there's a lot going on underneath our feet, but we'll get to this.

So, it seems there's much to learn, besides the friendly handshakes? And the higher one ascends, the more haunted it becomes. Like, according to Wheeler, sodomy is the rite of initiation in the 32nd and 33rd degrees (like the Templars). It's apparently the same in the inner circle of the Catholic Church and the Illuminati, as we'll get to. It's also alleged that 32nd degree masons drink blood out a human skull (it's not known if it's human or animal blood), so presumably this is the outer circle, and the inner circle are the sodomites? Thus, they're truly enlightened by the 32nd and 33rd degree.

It's also noted, their homoerotic orgies, which invariably involve being high on liquor and drugs, are filmed, as this evidence can be used as leverage to blackmail them later. Apparently, the initiates know it's filmed but they don't care, because they're so haunted.

With regards to the secrets of illumination, Schnoebelen explains that having been adopted (by Lucifer) into the order, the initiate is illuminated to 'begin to see the light' and acquire occult power e.g. start to see auras and spiritual light. ASC, to open the third eye, are achieved through drugs, meditation, and trance work. The next stage is conversation and communion with the so-called dead. Initiates can talk to anyone they like e.g.

Plato or Jesus, and these otherwise dead spirits possess the initiates. As discussed, demons can take on the appearance of dead people. Schnoebelen explains they come into people, and as a result consciousness expands and initiates become more enlightened. He refers to the possessing spirits as 'Ascended Masters'.

The next stage is sexual exploits with the dead. Initiates have all kinds of sexual intercourse with alleged dead people. They become 'one flesh' with them. And the last stage is union or 'perfect possession'. One's consciousness is totally eclipsed by demons. So, initiation is demon possession. Schnoebelen highlights the addictive nature of demon possession, as the more demons one has, the more power and wisdom. He also highlights that when demons live inside a person, they can read and know their thoughts, and so the demons can inflict pain if the person thinks differently to what they want e.g. induce a wicked headache. But we'll get back to Schnoebelen.

Circa the same time as masonry was bubbling beneath the surface, before it formally came out of the closet, Dr Christian Rosencreutz or 'Rose-Cross' founded the Rosicrucian Order circa 1407. It's also said however, that when the Templars went underground, they emerged 150 years later as Rosicrucian's. It's purported this occult secret society harboured the Templar's secrets. Many esoteric and occult societies claim their doctrines originate from the Rosicrucians. It's also said Francis Bacon was the founder of Rosicrucianism. It's understood he wrote under various pennames, including Shakespeare.

It seems Dr Rose-Cross is like Hermes Trismegistus, in that we're not sure if he was a real person? As whilst the religious order of the Rosicrucian's arose in the fifteenth century, the term Rosicrucian didn't emerge until 1614 with three anonymous publications about a secret Rosicrucian Order. Rosicrucianism then arose as a cultural movement, an esoteric order, in Europe.

Either way, the story is Rosencreutz studied the ancient mystery religion in the Middle East under various masters. Then he taught the initiatic sciences he had learned on his travels to a small group of friends/disciples. It was a brotherhood of eight, and they all had to be doctors and swear an oath to heal people for free. They also promised to keep their secrets secret, like commanding disembodied beings for healing miracles.

This 'old wisdom', which has been kept secret for thousands of years, originated in Egypt. The mystical tradition is a mix of alchemy, astrology, theosophy and has a cabbalistic interpretation of scripture. But moreover, it's combined with Christianity. Rosicrucian's are obliged to study the hermetic sciences, but they also recognise Christ. Like, the Magi who initiated Rosencreutz in the Middle East recognised Christ. The Magi brotherhood is referred to as 'men of the unseen'. Like, Ascended Masters? Wayne affirms the Magi (their sun worship and sacred ken) originated in Babylon.

So, Rosencreutz acknowledged Christ. Indeed, Rosencreutz is referred to as 'our Christian Father'. Rosencreutz died aged 107, and Black (2010) highlights his dead body was found clutching a scroll which bore the words 'Out of God we are born, we die in Jesus, we will be reborn through the Holy Spirit' (p.438).

The endeavour of Rosicrucianism is mystical communication with God. It holds a doctrine of theology 'built on esoteric truths of the ancient past', which, 'concealed from the average man, provide insight into nature, the physical universe and the spiritual realm'. In other words, it's gnosis. And with gnosis, we can know otherwise unknown things and travel the spirit world at will.

In tandem with the Masonic view, it's believed that God gave this 'wisdom' to Adam, and it was passed down through Moses and Solomon. Jesus also 'knew' this arcane knowledge and taught/initiated His apostles.

He learned it during His time in the East, as the Nag Hammadi scrolls suggest? Rosicrucianism is also referred to as 'Christian metaphysics'.

So, Rosencreutz and his buds apparently knew 'the secrets of nature' and together they wrote a book called 'All that man could desire, ask and hope for', which sounds like 'New Age' cabala? Their techniques were designed to help achieve a free-willed, free-thinking exchange with beings from higher hierarchies. Thus, they were doing what all mystery schools do, namely, engage with ghosts, angels, extra-terrestrials, and other inter-dimensional beings in the spirit world. And as a result, they became supermen with superpowers.

In addition to healing powers, it's said they could read minds, understand all languages, project living images of themselves and communicate audibly over great distances, and become invisible. Apparently mastering the art of invisibility, which involves surrounding one's self with a cloudy shroud, demonstrates progress.

As Doreen Irvine attested to, clouds of bodies of mist can be called out of the invisible to surround a person, enveloping them. This effectively makes them invisible in the sight of others. This secret practice (ritual) and power to become invisible is still taught in mystery schools. As mentioned, apparently Crowley could make himself invisible. Paracelsus concedes, 'visible bodies may be made invisible, or covered, in the same way as night covers a man and makes him invisible, or as if he would become invisible if he were put behind a wall..., likewise a visible substance may be covered with an invisible substance, and be made invisible by art'. It's also noted, that during the Exodus in the Bible, God hid His people from the Egyptian army with a cloud.

According to scientists, the 'cloud' consists of free electrons which absorb all light entering it. It does not reflect or retract light waves, and nor are light waves able to pass through the human body. As discussed, what we see depends on light waves. Apparently, scientists have developed technology that can bend electromagnetic radiation, such as light, around an object, giving the appearance that it isn't there. 'Spectral invisibility cloaking' hides objects by shifting the frequencies of light that interact with an object. 'Human Involuntary Spontaneous Invisibility' is notably when someone disappears without experience. Like, abductions?

So, the Rosicrucian's knew the spirit world is real. They went beyond the veil of Isis. Indeed, initiations into the fraternity were given in the invisible worlds. And Rosicrucian's are a piece of the puzzle, as they're connected with the Templars and freemasons.

Like, it's believed the Rosicrucian's continued the work of the Knights Templar, and became the key vehicle through which occult teachings (rooted in the cabala) spread throughout Europe. And modern freemasonry arose when the Rosicrucian's joined the stone mason guilds of Europe from 1640 onwards. Apparently, alchemy was the core practice that connected early freemasons with Rosicrucian's. Some therefore maintain freemasons are an offshoot of the Rosicrucian's. The 18th degree of Scottish Rite Masonry is called the Knight of the Rose Croix.

And then in 1776, (the same year America declared independence), the Order of the Illuminati was born in Bavaria. Like freemasons, the Illuminati is a Luciferian movement used to preserve and promote the ancient black arts of Babylon and druid witchcraft. The name Illuminati comes from Lucifer and means holders of the light. Brothers are illuminated or 'enlightened' by secret esoteric knowledge.

The sole purpose of this notorious secret society was to eliminate God and control the world. They planned to use wars and revolutions to create a global government. And they associated with powerful families and clans, who enabled them. Whilst we'll get back to the Rothschild family, it seems pertinent to note that it was apparently Mayer Amschel Rothschild who elected Adam Weishaupt to create this secret society.

Adam Weishaupt was a canon law professor and Jesuit priest. He was a 'crypto Jew' (he was born a Jew but converted to Catholicism). He was apparently a genius at scheming and manipulation. He adopted the hierarchal pyramid structure of the Jesuits for his Order, with thirteen degrees, to disseminate power among the ranks. It's also however highlighted that Adam Weishaupt is a pseudonym. Adam refers to first man, weiss refers to wisdom, and haupt refers to leader, which together denotes 'the first man who leads the wise'. And some claim he never existed, like Dr Rosencreutz and Hermes Trismegistus?

But moreover, it's also purported that Adam Weishaupt was a Sabbatean-Frankist posing as a Jesuit. Hence, Sabbatean cabalism networked into the formation of the Illuminati. Rabbi Sabbatai Zevi (1626-1676), who founded this Jewish cult, was a black magician. He claimed to be a Jewish messiah in 1666. The name Sabbatai relates to the Hebrew word for Saturn, the dark sun, the Star of David. He believed redemption came through iniquity. He preferred the satanic teachings of the Talmud and inverted every holy teaching. Like, fasting became feasting.

The endeavour was to be sinners, not saints. He celebrated evil, claiming the more sin, the better. So, he reversed Judaic teachings. Like, he insisted on, no more guilt, no more sin, no more right and wrong, no more Ten Commandments, no more sexual limits, no more Sabbath. The cult was known as the synagogue of Satan. Their practices included incest, paedophilia, and human sacrifice. They were the 'elite' and exempt from moral law. It seems Zevi was privy to the Templar's ken?

Furthermore, Zevi believed the coming Messiah, 'a saviour and liberator for the Jewish people', would rule the world from Jerusalem. As discussed, the Jews rejected Jesus, so they're still waiting for their messiah. Thus, this cult would need to get Jerusalem back. And they would also need to build a third temple to accommodate him. Zevi promised his followers they would return to the Jewish homeland. So, he created Zionism, as we'll get to.

As it transpired, the Sabbatean cult became even more satanic with Jacob Frank (1726-1791). He was also a black magician and conceded Lucifer is the true god. He further claimed he was the reincarnation of both Zevi and Jacob (Israel). The Sabbatean-Frankist religion is 'do what thou wilt', which inspired Crowley. Like, the human and animal sacrifice inspired Crowley. Sabbatean-Frankists were also called Zoharists because they followed the Zohar. Thus, the Illuminati is based on the Zohar or 'illumination'.

So, Frank got together with Weishaupt and Rothschild and created the Illuminati. Apparently, Frank also infiltrated Catholicism and other religions, including the Saudi royal family. After founding the Illuminati, Weishaupt then joined the freemasons in '1777', like many other illuminati members. Or rather, he infiltrated and poisoned the freemasons with his Sabbatean-Frankist cabalism. Some therefore view the Illuminati as having evolved out of the freemasons, as an extreme sect of freemasonry.

According to Cooper however, freemasons always contained a core of Illuminati in their ranks, hence they freely absorbed members of Weishaupt's group. Illuminati is synonymous with Satanism. The Illuminati brotherhood of the snake predates the Bavarian Illuminati. It's been harboured by haunted 'Jewish' priests, the Jesuits, and the royal families. It's slithered down through the ages (through their bodies).

Within two years, the Illuminati had over 3000 members and many established lodges. Apparently, they had lodges in more than 25 European cities including London, Munich, Vienna, Naples, and Paris. Within several years however, they were exposed and banished from Bavaria. Presumably, it was divine intervention, as they were discovered in 1785 when their courier was struck down by lightning and killed.

When Bavarian officials examined his bags, they discovered documents revealing the existence of this haunted order and their plans for global domination. They found detailed plans to control governments using financial and sexual bribery, murder and murder threats (including murdering family members). Unlike the charred corpse, the papers were not affected by the fire. Plans detailing the French Revolution were also found, although the French government failed to heed the forewarning.

They also found incredibly detailed evidence of how the Illuminati had infiltrated German universities during the 18th century and developed the 'higher criticism' of the Bible. So, they were behind the movement that audaciously denied the supernatural and the truth of the Bible. This paved the way for the theory of evolution.

So, their objectives were abolition of all ordered governments, private property, inheritance, patriotism, the family, religion, and the creation of a world government. The greedy Illuminati want to possess all riches, power, and influence in the world. Hence, they want the world enslaved in debt. In his book, 'Conspirator's Hierarchy: The Story of the Committee of 300' (1993), Dr John Coleman asserts 'they need to infiltrate and take over all governments in order to insidiously dissipate and destroy the sovereignty of each nation from the inside. There's a plan to erode sovereignty piece by piece'.

Dr Coleman was an MI6 whistle-blower in the 1980s and had access to secret documents. He states their goals include: a global government with a unified church and monetary system, destroy religion especially Christianity, mind control, encourage and eventually legalise drugs, and make porn an art form. Each objective would need to be picked off, in incremental steps. Like, we would need a scientific material revolution to bump off God and the spiritual realm.

Weishaupt's secret society aimed to combat religious thinking and encourage rationalism. The Illuminati aim was to defraud on materialist grounds, maintaining that Jesus' teaching was purely cosmopolitism. Thus, He wasn't really the Son of God. Indeed, there was no God or spirit world. It was all balls. The Age of Enlightenment had landed, and such 'free thinking' made sense for the outer circles. Thus, candidates were told 'the ultimate secret is there is no secret'. And it worked. Nihilism infiltrated freemason lodges. People fell for the materialist lie. There is no point or meaning (Sartre was right).

Weishaupt revealed that in his secret society, 'Reason will be the only code of men. This is one of our greatest secrets. When at last Reason becomes the religion of men, then will the problem be solved'. The inner circle however, the 'enlightened ones', knew better. The illuminist spirituality and religion is the belief in the 'god of forces'. This god of forces is impersonal, yet possesses unlimited supernatural powers that can be accessed by illumined men. That is, by Gnostics who know the magical formula. We can use 'the force' for our own ends?

Like the outer circle plebs, the rest of the plebs in society would need to be educated into these beliefs i.e. through state funded education. They would need to be convinced there is no God, which is a tall order in the face of creation. As touched on, the Jesuit endeavour, back in the 1500s, was to replace our geocentric cosmology with heliocentric cosmology. And they used Hermeticism as their manuscript. Thus, the plebs were told the sun doesn't orbit us, but we orbit the sun. And furthermore, we live on a ball, like the sun, moon, and planets. The universe became insanely massive and we became insanely insignificant. Evolutionary cosmology (post the Big magical Bang) then enables Darwinism. But we'll get back to 'science falsely so called'.

This 'science' would also need to be couched in a cultural revolution to undermine God, family and country, with the focus instead on 'self'. In tandem with Darwin's 'survival of the fittest' theory, the sentiment was placing oneself first. And thus, the sixties landed with its philosophy of individualism. Clever scientists and philosophers told us there is no God and the whole of the law is 'knock yourself out'. The emphasis is on pleasure not duty.

As discussed, the sexual revolution was pioneered by disgusting Kinsey and Freud. And the CIA engineered our drugs revolution, including LSD, crack, and heroin. They would destroy us from within with drugs and nihilism. They would also undermine our self-reliance and create dependence on the state. We need Big Brother to look after us?

Suffice to say, the Illuminati did not dissolve in 1785. Besides infiltrating the freemasons, it's said Weishaupt went into exile, and the Bavarian Illuminati did a shoot to the US. They could join the freemasons there? Weishaupt said, 'The strength of our order lies in its secrecy. It should never appear anywhere under its own name. But always shrouded in another name and another occupation'. The name Adam Weishaupt was a metaphor?

It seems pertinent to note, that Brother George Washington acknowledged the nefarious Illuminati (in a letter in 1789). But he was confident that no lodges were contaminated by them or used for subversive purposes. It would appear he was mistaken. Apparently when Weishaupt died, he was replaced by Italian revolutionary and 33rd degree mason Giuseppe Mazzini. And it was Mazzini who received the infamous letter from Albert Pike in 1871, which detailed the three world wars that are planned to bring about the NWO.

Thus, it said the First World War must be brought about to overthrow the Czars in Russia and make that country a fortress of atheistic communism. Communism would then be used to destroy the other governments and weaken the religions. The Second World War was to capitalise on the differences between the Fascists and political Zionists. Nazism had to be destroyed, and a sovereign state of Israel had to be established in Palestine. And the Third World War is to take advantage of the differences between the political Zionists and leaders of Islam. This war must be conducted in such a way that Islam and Israel mutually destroy each other.

Meanwhile the other nations, divided in this issue, will be physically, morally, spiritually, and economically exhausted (as well as horrified at the savagery). The plan is then to unleash the nihilists and atheists, disillusioning the multitudes of Christians, to put the final nail on God's coffin. Then all will receive the true light through the universal manifestation of the pure doctrine of Lucifer, brought finally out in the public view. Christianity and atheism will be conquered and exterminated at the same time.

It's noted, this is but one document, (and those found on the fried courier), as there's myriad plans in place to orchestrate the NWO. The powers of darkness have had millennia to formulate their plan, which is to crush the God of the Christians and welcome the antichrist to his throne in the Third Temple. And they're extremely well organised.

However, (as touched on), there's rules to this game. Like, Satanists have to reveal their plans to the plebs before it's executed. Hence, predictive programming conditions us into accepting the reality we're given. It's all hidden in plain sight. Like, clues in Hollywood movies? Like, according to the mysterious Georgia Guidestones in the US, they only want five hundred million people, not billions of us. Hence, they're actively poisoning us, and planning to kill most of us in WW3? But the plebs are past caring? It's said the Guidestones, (which were anonymously established in 1980), are the Illuminati's Ten Commandments. They're written in different languages including Sanskrit.

Mazzini founded the Masonic P2 lodge in the Vatican, and the mafia/mob. The mafia/mob is a Church of Rome operation, merging Italians in America with the Illuminati. It's noted, politicians and the elite are friends of the Vatican bank, which is inextricably linked to gangsters, Nazis, and terrorists (it funds criminals). Apparently, Pope John Paul I was murdered after he ordered the investigation of the Vatican bank and its connections to P2.

The Banco Vaticano is the most secret in the world. It answers to no-one, and investigations are conducted under absolute secrecy. It provides a safe haven to 'hide' money, and people can move money about without a trace e.g. fake expenses or donations. It creates fictitious banks, 'ghost banks', which exist on paper. It launders drug money with the CIA, and ties into Swiss bankers. Ironically, God's bank is most shady.

As touched on, the Roman Catholic Church is apparently satanic at its core. Indeed, Father Gabriele Amorth (the Pope's chief exorcist previously mentioned) declared, 'the Devil lives inside the Vatican'. He reported that besides the internal power struggles and scandals, there were cardinals who didn't believe in Jesus and bishops linked to demons. He spoke about Satan infecting the clergy and said, 'when one speaks of 'the smoke of Satan' in the Vatican, it's all true...including violence and paedophilia.'

It's beyond a farce. These so-called priests get up to all kinds of debauchery, including sex parties with young boys, only to put on their priestly attire and take the moral high ground the next day. Many of them, particularly at the upper echelons, are gay and yet they preach homosexuality is wrong. The vati-leaks scandals, (leaked Vatican documents), revealed how homo clergy were blackmailing each other and framing scapegoats. To say corruption is widespread in the Vatican is a massive understatement (the 'oaths of silence' bode well).

Indiscretions are notably referred to as 'noble cause corruption'. Thousands of priests worldwide have been abusing kids in their care, and the Catholic Church has paid more than a billion in lawsuits. It's understood the Catholic Church protects paedos, and the Pope knows about their antics. More often than not, offending priests are transferred to another church to continue their sordid abuse there.

So, these wanton men of the cloth (always wanton more) are liars, cheats and morally repugnant. Wheeler (2009) states, 'the spirit of witchcraft within the Catholic Church is an evil that is so diabolical it goes beyond that which any human man can call wickedness or heartlessness or morally wrong' (p.179). And also, 'The Catholic Church in its blasphemous state has resurrected ancient Satanism in all its glory ...' (p.296). This includes satanically ritually abusing kids and killing them. How ironic the kingdom of darkness lurks within the church.

Malachi Martin, ex-Jesuit, Vatican insider and bestselling author, notably said it was unarguable that the 'Roman Catholic organisation carried a permanent presence of clerics who worshipped Satan and liked it; of bishops and priests who sodomised boys and each other, of nuns who performed the Black Rites of Wicca and who lived in lesbian relationships. In total number they were a minority – anything from one to ten percent of church personnel. But of that minority, many occupied astoundingly high positions of rank'. Schnoebelen also highlights that abortions and infanticides are covered up by clergy to hide infidelity.

As mentioned, the Jesuits work within the inner circle of the Vatican. They're the brains behind operations. Hence, they control the Knights of Malta, Knights of Columbus, and the Templars. And they connect into the Illuminati and the freemasons. So, the Vatican has its pyramid of power. Like, leading priests, bishops and cardinals are in secret societies. And that pyramid connects in with other pyramids. It's all pyramids within pyramids.

Hence, it's an international network. Like, Catholics are 'universal'. They're everywhere, like freemasons. It's understood the Jesuits, Rothschild's and Sabbatean-Frankists are one unit. Like, the Jesuits control the Vatican on behalf of the cabal. So, Satanists rule the world, using Enoch the Evil's dark arts. And this bleeds into black nobility, who descended from the Holy Roman Empire (black is a reference to their character not colour). They're the 'royal families' who got their divine right to rule from the 'gods'. Their nephilim blood is the Holy Grail? Satanism is a family affair, as we'll get to.

It's interesting to note, that when Pope Benedict resigned in 2013, (he was a Nazi in his youth), and Pope Francis, (the first ever Jesuit Pope), stepped in, lightning bolts struck St Peter's Basilica twice. As mentioned, the lightning bolt denotes Lucifer. It's purported the real reason Pope Benedict suddenly resigned (which almost never happens), was because of the rampant child abuse associated with his brother's catholic boys' choir. At least 231 children reported being sexually assaulted, raped, severely beaten, and deprived of food.

Schnoebelen concedes that high level Luciferians exist throughout the Catholic Church, which includes the Pope, and it's a sex cult. Like David Icke and others, he states that at the highest levels of the Vatican, most clergy are freemasons, which includes the pope(s), and some are Rosicrucian's. There's an unholy union between freemasonry and Catholicism.

According to Schnoebelen, Catholics helped start freemasons, and most degrees in the Scottish rite were written by Jesuits. Apparently, Jesuits took control of freemasons in 1818. He maintains many masons are involved in witchcraft and Satanism (and harbour a hatred for Christianity). He also notes, that John Paul II displayed the Masonic 'sign of distress' when in dire straits regarding the ban on freemasons (how ironic). Schnoebelen maintains that Catholicism and freemasonry are synthesised to create our global religion.

It seems pertinent to consider Schnoebelen's story, because he was one of them, and par excellence has insider ken. Thus, whilst born and raised a Roman Catholic, Schnoebelen went to the dark side. Ironically (?) he was introduced to the occult by a Catholic priest. He was told that Christ studied the occult and went to Egypt to train with the magi there, and also India and Tibet to study with the gurus there. And that's what enabled Him to perform His miracles and healings.

So, Schnoebelen subsequently became a high priest of Wicca and Satanist. He knew that to get into serious Satanism (beyond the Church of Satan) he had to become a Master Mason and Catholic priest (two otherwise paradoxical tasks). So, he became simultaneously a Wiccan, Freemason, Catholic priest, and Satanist. As it transpired, he was so 'gifted', as observed at Masonic rituals, that the Illuminati sought him out. He had an extraordinary ability to converse with spirit guides, who prompted him what to do and say, key things and even gestures. Thus, he also became a member of the Illuminati.

But he further claims he became a vampire and drank human blood for over a year. He says it's more addictive than heroin. He explains that initiates reach a crossroads, whereby they choose to become either a vampire or werewolf, and he preferred the idea of being a vampire. Apparently changing into a werewolf is painful. So, that's pretty crazy. Whilst Schnoebelen didn't kill anyone, he recalls we became very tempting. Like, he could murder a tramp that no one would miss. It's noted, when demons control our thoughts, we can want to kill. Like, psychos want to kill. They enjoy it. He also said the Illuminati told him the moon landing was a hoax, which it seems to be (as we'll get to).

He was further told to join the Mormon Church, as they could help him should he ever find himself in trouble. So, he also became a Mormon. It's noted, that Mormons claim Satan and Jesus were brothers, and Jehovah Witnesses attack the resurrection and deity of Jesus. These movements were not arbitrary deviations but rather were specifically designed to bring confusion into the church. It's highlighted that Mormonism and witchcraft are practically the same. As per, there's an inner and outer circle in these cults, and Satanists are at the top levels.

Apparently, Joseph Smith, who founded Mormonism, was a 33rd degree mason. And according to Fritz Springmeier (author/researcher), Charles Taze Russell, founder of Jehovah Witnesses, was a Knight Templar and freemason. And he was ritually murdered on Halloween. According to David Icke, the Mormon Church and Jehovah Witnesses were funded into existence by the Rothschild's, and at the highest levels they're reptilian satanic operations.

But it gets crazier, as according to Schnoebelen, people have reported seeing reptilian humanoids at the Mormon Temple in Salt Lake City, which has many levels underground. And also, at the shopping mall there. Like cleaners, who have been there after hours. Icke also pertains to victims of the Mormon Church, who advised being forced to partake in sacrifice rituals at various locations, including underneath the main temple at Salt Lake City. But it's further reported that participant's shapeshift into reptilians and other forms. Which isn't so farfetched if people can transform into werewolves?

Icke mentions 'Jane', who was informed that Jesus didn't love her, and that Satan had come to save her. She was a victim of mind control, as we'll get to. Jane saw several of the Mormon leaders dressed in black robes worshipping Lucifer in a ritual called the 'True Order of Prayer'. Jane was impregnated many times. Her babies were either sacrificed (in front of her), or the foeti were removed for rituals. But moreover, she remembers seeing 'two monsters fighting furiously dripping blood and fighting about what they were eating. They were reptilian and looked something like the dinosaurs'. They ate her baby (p.485). However, we'll get back to this craziness.

As for Schnoebelen, the Lord had a different plan for him. He states that one day his monthly tithe check to the Church of Satan came back from the bank with a note on the back saying 'I'll be praying for you in Jesus' name '. And within a week he lost his demonic power. He later became a born again Christian and established his own ministry. He's been in ministry, mostly full-time, since 1986.

Apparently, the Skull and Bones Society (inspired by the Templar's resurrection symbol) is a branch of the Bavarian illuminati. As mentioned, some exiled Illuminati members did a shoot to the US. It was established in 1832 within Yale University, and it's allegedly the black lodge of freemasonry. Its rituals are almost carbon copies of the highest levels of ceremonial rituals of freemasons. It's also highlighted, that its cryptic number '322' is a veiled reference to apotheosis in Genesis 3:22.

Thus, Genesis 3:22 states, 'Then the LORD God said, 'The people have become as we are, knowing everything, both good and evil. What if they eat the fruit of the tree of life? Then they will live forever'. Thus, if man had eaten the fruit, he would have become immortal, a god? The next verse, (Genesis 3:23), tells us God banished

Adam and Eve from the Garden of Eden. Hence, alchemists endeavour to go back there? Thus, it's said verse 3:22 is about initiation. It reflects the ordeal of the man who passes through ritual initiations into perfection and godhood. The Bonesmen are to reign on earth as gods. They're the 'chosen ones'. It's also noted, the Georgia Guidestones were erected on March 22nd (3:22) in 1980.

This secret society is hugely instrumental because Bones members secure the most powerful positions in politics, banking, business, and the media. Like, Prescott Bush, George H W Bush, and George W Bush were Bonesmen. And John Kerry is a Bonesman. Hence, the 2004 election sham of voting for either Kerry or Bush, since they have the same Luciferian agenda. They're also distant cousins. Several Skull and Bones members, and Paul Warburg, established the Federal Reserve (the central banking system in the US). And members founded the CIA. It's understood, (like freemasons), fellow Bonesmen promote each other to key powerful positions.

Like all secret Snake Brotherhoods, Bonesmen swear allegiance to Lucifer and dedicate their lives to his vision. It's said initiates sign a blood oath to Lucifer to bring in the NWO and antichrist. According to Bill Cooper, this oath absolves them of any allegiance to any nation, or king, or government, or constitution. And it includes the negating of any subsequent oath which they may be required to take. Thus, their public oaths are a farce. They mean nothing.

So, every year, fifteen 'bloodline' students are initiated into this homoerotic 'Brotherhood of Death'. They meet in the 'Tomb', a building with no windows, wearing their hooded robes, to conduct their secret meetings and practices. Their rituals are sick and full of death imagery. Screams during the initiation have been captured on audio recordings. It's purported that initiates have to kiss a skull at the feet of the initiators, and perform a mock killing, a throat ritual murder. There were apparently thirty skulls onsite in the 1970s, including Geronimo's, which Prescott Bush allegedly stole from a graveyard.

Initiates need to be 'reborn' into the order, which apparently involves lying naked in a coffin, and revealing all sexual secrets to fellow initiates, whilst masturbating (their drink and drug fuelled orgies are recorded). Apparently, the other members chant and moan to invoke familiar spirits to facilitate the 'rebirth' of the candidate, which transforms him into a superman, a godlike being. It's noted, the 'Scroll and Key' secret society at Harvard University is also called Brotherhood of Death and connects into the Illuminati.

Cooper said, 'Do not ever believe that grown men meet on a regular basis just to put on fancy robes, hold candles and glad-hand each other. George Bush, when he was initiated into the Skull and Bones, did not lie naked in a coffin with a ribbon tied around his genitalia and yell out the details of all his sexual experiences because it was fun. He had much to gain by accepting initiation into the Order'.

Whilst relationships are forged through rituals, they enable initiators to gain power and control over initiates as they know their secrets (like 'catholic' confession). Knowledge is power. It's also alleged this satanic blood drinking order engages in a ceremony called 'The Obscene Rite', which involves the consumption of a live pineal gland of a human sacrifice. Presumably, this is not for the neophytes? However, according to Wheeler (2009), 'perhaps the darkest satanic ritual involves the grail – a drinking blood sexual ritual'. So, people are bonded to each other through fear, and they're in bondage to Satan. When people take oaths and pledges, they bind themselves. Members are warned there is no escape (they will be killed).

David Icke (2007) highlights that initiations for Marines include oral and anal sex while the initiates lie in a coffin, which is similar to Skull and Bones initiation ceremonies, as they're all connected. He affirms their initiations, which are referred to as 'dining in' (yum), entail getting very drunk and high on drugs (p.496). Promotion comes quickly for partakers, who're called 'rising stars', which is most appropriate for star-stabbers (LOL).

He maintains that at the highest level of the military, sex with children and homo-rape is the norm. This ties in with Satanic Ritual Abuse and mind control, as we'll get to. It seems kids are born into this horror show and perpetuate it. And some of them don't know it because they have DID? It's duly noted, the royals are admired for their commitment to the armed services.

So, initiates are born again into Satan's brood. Members are notably assigned nicknames, which psychologically confirms their new born again identity. Like, Jesus renamed a few disciples for this reason. Wheeler (2009) asserts that any organisation which utilises the coffin ritual to simulate rebirth is practising Satanism, which includes the Skull and Bones. Contrary to Christians, who when baptised in Christ become Christ-like, these satanic rituals lead to the initiate taking on the attributes of Satan and working for him. They become demon possessed? Wheeler (2009) states that when Bush referred to himself as 'born again', it was not in the Christian sense but rather he's reborn into Satanism.

Regarding his alleged conversion to Christianity, George W Bush, renowned for drinking and partying, was 'born again' with the help of renowned evangelist Brother Billy Graham (he was a 33rd degree mason). Apparently, they took a walk together along the beach, and Graham prayed for him. And abracadabra, notorious baby Bush, who dodged military, never worked a day in his life, and who got into Yale by blood-ties not merit, sobered up and became a reformed, evangelical born again Christian. Hence, the trusty Americans voted for him. It's also ironically noted, that Bush promotes universalism i.e. there's other ways to God besides Jesus, as Graham taught.

According to Wheeler, the Thule Society led to the founding of Skull and Bones. As discussed, Hitler and his Nazi buds were members of the Thule Society. Members of the Thule society included the rich and powerful elite. They conjured spirits and apparently Himmler used dousing (divining) to make political decisions. So, the Thule and Vril secret societies interconnected into other secret societies within the Illuminati network. And they crossed the pond after WW2.

It's noted, that regardless of the name, it's the same haunted rituals and worship that takes place at its satanic core i.e. infernal orgies, drinking blood and eating flesh from their human sacrifice, as well as eating faeces and drinking urine. According to David Icke, feasting on new-borns is considered an Illuminati delicacy. And they're partial to gorging on foeti harvested from abortion clinics. It's recalled that 'Planned Parenthood', the abortion industry in the US, was exposed for selling aborted foeti and their body parts on the black market.

Secret societies are essentially spirit worshippers. And they're so connected that much of the practice that takes place in secret societies is akin to that which takes place in satanic worship. Like, they wear their hooded robes and light candles etc. They seek to invoke the demonic, so they chant (gutturally hiss) ceremonial invocations in various ancient languages e.g. Latin, Hebrew, Aramaic, and Egyptian, summoning beings.

It's said demonic entities need blood to appear. Hence, the sickening rituals centre on sacrifice and spilling blood. It's relayed that sacrifices and rituals open up certain doors or 'stargates' between dimensions, enabling entities to come through. And the rituals enable the entities to possess the participants even more powerfully. Hence, these Satanists writhe about in frenzied, sexually crazed, serpentine ways. It seems it's not long until the robes come off.

Thus, whilst secret societies seem to be separate independent organisations, it's understood they're actually the same Luciferian cult (at the top) and they're all interconnected. The world is controlled by a system called 'Pyramid Power'. Thus, Lucifer is at the top. He's the All Seeing Eye in the levitating capstone. 'The Council of Seven', who are fallen angels, report to Lucifer. And 'Nine Unknown Men' report to 'The Seven'. The secret society of the nine unknown men was apparently founded in 226BC. These men then delegate to the satanic brotherhood aka the Illuminati, who in turn delegate to those below them. Wheeler (2009) states the global elite inner circle is referred to as 'serpents of wisdom'.

But moreover, the Illuminati is a family business. As Wheeler (2009) highlights, if you're not generational i.e. family, you can't get into the Illuminati. Like, Doc Marquis, for example, was apparently a seventh generation illuminati witch. Like other religions, he was born into it. But he became a Christian and whistle-blower. Like Schnoebelen, Doc Marquis has much to impart about the inner workings of the Illuminati. David Icke concedes, 'access to upper levels is by bloodline invitation only'. So, without the right blood, ascension up the ranks is limited? Hence, the Holy Grail is very important to them?

Thus, after Lucifer, is the Council of 13, thirteen family (nephilim) bloodlines. Below them is the Committee of 300, which is composed of the most powerful 'sub-families'. This committee uses many well-known institutions and think tanks to accomplish their goals e.g. UN, CIA, Skull and Bones, Council on Foreign Relations. Members of the Committee of 300 are CEOs, presidents etc, who have the power to implement the geopolitical moves towards globalism. They're the public face of the Illuminati. And they're engineering the steps towards a NWO fit for a dark king.

So, the Illuminati is like an umbrella, under which everything operates i.e. global network of secret societies. And those in secret societies take the plan into the workplace. People are strategically placed to carry out the agenda. David Icke likens the illuminati network to a spider's web, with its interconnecting strands. And Satan is the spider? Icke states the spider is a non-human force. He concedes that every country has its own secret societies that connect into the global satanic cult. Dr Coleman states this conspiratorial group knows no national boundaries, is above the law of all countries, and controls everything including the drug trade.

The Illuminati infiltrates all our systems i.e. media, education, science, religion, politics, health care, banking, military, intelligence, corporations, popular culture, and so forth. In essence, 'narratives' come from above and cascade down to 'we the plebs' at the bottom. We're educated to trust history and science? We get 'the news'. Like, we went to the moon? Or we're mind controlled? Like, we're brainwashed to idolise Tavistock creations, like the Beatles? We're happy with our bread and circuses? However, we'll get to this.

It seems pertinent to note, JFK's warning about secret societies in a speech in 1961, since it's said it got him killed. Thus, he said, 'The very word 'secrecy' is repugnant in a free and open society; and we are as a people inherently and historically opposed to secret societies, to secret oaths and to secret proceedings. We decided long ago that the dangers of excessive and unwarranted concealment of pertinent facts far outweighed the dangers which are cited to justify it'. It's understood the fact something is secret, means there's something to hide (like sacrificing humans).

David Icke (2007) quotes former CIA operative Victor Marchetti, who said in his book, 'The CIA and the Cult of Intelligence' (1973), 'There exists in our world today a powerful and dangerous secret cult. This cult is patronised and protected by the highest level of government officials in the world. Its membership is composed of those in the power centres of government, industry, commerce, finance and labour. It manipulates individuals in areas of important public influence – including the academic world and the mass media. The Secret Cult is a global fraternity of a political aristocracy whose purpose is to further the political policies of persons or agencies unknown. It acts covertly and illegally'. Icke adds, 'it wants to control the world' (p.192).

So, now we know, because they want us to know. Hence, David Icke, for example, has been allowed to propagate 'The Biggest Secret' regarding the Illuminati aka evil hidden hand. The 'guys', (his spirit guides), are on his side. They're on our side? Hence, they want us to know about the secret cabal that rules the world? It's time for them to come out of the shadows and reveal themselves?

As touched on, Icke admitted to some force pushing him in different directions, through intuitions and urges. He's followed their lead and doesn't seem to care who the forces are, because they seem like good guys? He relates what he was told by a psychic back in 1990. Thus, 'He will say things and wonder where they came from. They will be our words. Sometimes we will put knowledge into his mind. Sometimes he will be led to knowledge'. He was also told 'arduous seeking is not necessary'. Icke attributes everything to them. He's also familiar with automatic writing, conceding that a force takes over and writes.

And yet despite the diabolical horrors he's reported, the Illuminati is being conveyed as a big joke. It's paradoxically being ridiculed and promoted in mainstream at the same time. The Illuminati use icons (puppets) like popular musicians to promote their 'do what thou wilt' philosophy. They use influencers to make sun serpent worship (Egyptian mythology) look cool. So, the herd thinks it's cool, and they get Illuminati tattoos? Like, vampires are cool? They're sexy? According to Schnoebelen however, vampires' breath stinks beyond the pale (LOL).

Mystery schools preserved the plan, but their symbols and secret language are being revealed. Like, we're familiar with the Masonic 'hidden hand' gesture (when someone hides one of their hands, like inside their coat) and the devil's horns (the most common signs of freemasonry). Indeed, it's getting boring looking at Hollywood actors and musicians demonstrating the 666 hand signals (the OK hand sign), the covering of one eye (which is reference to Horus), and the 'shhh' sign with their pointer finger over their mouth (the Illuminati oath of silence).

There's photos of Michael Jackson, as a young child, doing the triple 6 over one eye, and Darwin and Einstein doing the shhh BS, which evidences how long we've been kept in the dark. Apparently, their symbolism, 'standardised visual language' (for the US and Europe), was developed during the 1800s. However, we'll get back to the haunted entertainment industry.

As Jesus told us, everything that was hidden would be made known. It's part of their externalisation programme, pioneered by the infamous Helena Petrovna Blavatsky (1831-1891). Thus, whilst the Luciferian religion was kept under wraps, sealed and silenced by blood curdling oaths, all this changed when Blavatsky published her book 'The Secret Doctrine' in '1888'. She made these teachings public. Her first book 'Isis Unveiled' was published in 1877. As it transpires, after millennia, 'wisdom' is no longer just for the elites, but rather it's for us all (as Magnu asserted). We can all be partakers of the light and acquire superpowers?

[It's duly noted, Jesus wasn't about the elite or their mystery schools. Jesus was a Jew who followed the One True God, not the pagan gods. He was from Nazareth, which was a dump, and He specifically told His disciples not to take money with them or take money from anyone. The gospel is free and for everyone. Jesus prayed to our Father in Heaven and did His deliverance on this plane. There's no account of Him going into trances to go to the second heaven].

Blavatsky claimed, 'the Secret Doctrine is the accumulated wisdom of all ages'. She claimed to know the entire history of the world. As touched on, she conceded regarding a race of giants before the Flood, in so-called Atlantis. But apparently the Aryans went into the inner earth and waited for the Flood to pass. The majority of them stayed there, and the rest of them went to the highest levels of the Himalayas. So, there were remnants of nephilim post-flood?

Contrary to the Bible however, she claimed there was no Jesus. But rather he was copycat of the sun god (like Horus). She rejected Judaism, Christianity and Islam. Alternatively, she promoted Gnosticism, Hinduism, Buddhism and Luciferianism.

Her Secret Doctrine was the foundation of the Vril and Thule Society. Apparently, Hitler kept a copy by his bedside. It's noted, Hitler's genocide was rooted in the ideology of a tall blonde blue eyed root race from Atlantis, but we'll get back to this. The Secret Doctrine is the cornerstone of the New Age. Hence, Blavatsky is renowned as the Mother of the New Age. And her Luciferian philosophy is at the heart of the UN, steering world events.

As mentioned, Blavatsky was a renowned occultist. Apparently, she had visions and 'imaginary friends' as a child. She was described as an unusual child, and was exposed to both freemasonry and Rosicrucianism. She was well versed in astral projection, could telepathically move objects, and call on spirits. However, according to Doc Marquis, it's the spirits who move the objects. And its spirits that cause levitation and apports to manifest. Or the spirits activate our spirit body?

Blavatsky maintained she developed her psychic powers in Tibet, having encountered a group of spiritual adepts. Apparently, she lived with these 'Mahatmas' aka 'Masters of Ancient Wisdom' for several years during her occult training. These highly enlightened yogis initiated her into 'The Ageless Wisdom', an ancient esoteric spirituality.

As instructed to, she cofounded the Theosophical Society with Henry Olcott in 1875 reviving the ancient wisdom of eastern philosophy. It's purported however, that Rosicrucian's advised her to start her society and financed its operations. Blavatsky notably coined the term Theosophy which comes from God (theo) and wisdom (Sophia). She wanted to synthesise all religions to create a global spirituality, a One World Religion. Thus, she proclaimed ancient wisdom predated all the world's religions. However, she recognised the world wasn't ready for it. Her religion was for the twentieth century.

Blavatsky described theosophy as 'the synthesis of science, religion and philosophy'. She asserted that Plato and the Indian sages knew this arcane knowledge aka gnosis. And she connected the ancient wisdom religion to Hermetic philosophy. Thus, all is One, but there's an unknowable One, and we each have a divine spark. Pure spirit has fallen into matter and darkness. Hence, the endeavour is to go from darkness to light, to become light and ethereal. The emphasis is on spiritual evolution and achieving godhead. Hinduism is foundational to Theosophy i.e. the doctrine of reincarnation and karma. Blavatsky's motto is 'there is no religion higher than truth'. Her symbol is the ouroboros.

Lucifer is central to her theory, who she claims is the god of our planet and only God. In the Secret Doctrine, she wrote, 'Lucifer represents life, thought, progress, civilisation, liberty, independence. Lucifer is the Logos, the Serpent, the Saviour'. She insisted the scriptures were wrong, and that it was really Lucifer who was the 'Good and Just God'. She advised that 'Lucifer is divine and terrestrial light, the 'Holy Ghost' and Satan at one and the same time (p.513).

She wrote, 'Satan, the Serpent of Genesis, is the real creator and benefactor, the Father of spiritual mankind. For it is he who opened the eyes of Adam created by Yahweh, as alleged; and he who was the first to whisper: 'in the day ye eat thereof ye shall be as God, knowing good and evil' – can only be regarded in the light of a saviour' (p.243). Lucifer is the ever-loving messenger, who conferred on us spiritual instead of physical immortality.

And further, 'Satan is the 'Anointed cherub' of old... God created Satan, the fairest and wisest of all his creatures in this part of his universe and made him Prince of the World and of the Power of the Air... Thus, Satan, being perfect in wisdom and beauty, his vast empire is our earth, if not the whole solar system... certainly no other angelic power of greater or even equal dignity has been revealed to us' (p.229).

But moreover, 'The Secret Doctrine' was a channelled text, written by 'Ascended Masters'. Apparently, Blavatsky began channelling 'Tibetan holy men' in the late 1870s and early 1880s. Presumably, the Ascended Masters she channelled were the same ones that Schnoebelen referred to? Besides 'invisible helpers' writing through her (her handwriting varied when in a trance state), sometimes disembodied hands would mysteriously appear and write.

'Ascended Masters' can appear as angels of light or materialise as people. Like, beautiful tall people with blonde hair and blue eyes allegedly from another star system (the Pleiades)? It seems pertinent to note, from a biblical perspective, 'Ascended Masters' are fallen angels who dwell in the second heaven. Or they could be demons? They similarly appear and disappear through a dimensional wall. And they can possess us. They can enhance our mind and bestow superpowers, where the more infested we are, the more superpowers we have. It's noted, we're being conditioned to want superpowers, like superheroes.

Adepts, who can separate their astral body and project it, can also possess us. Like, real living holy men in Tibet possessed Blavatsky in the US. One of Blavatsky's Ascended Masters (KH) wrote, 'we are not infallible, all foreseeing 'Mahatmas' at every hour of the day, but rather an adept is one only during the exercise of his occult powers (i.e. when he's on the spiritual plane). It's also purported that sometimes Ascended Masters incarnate into (physical) teachers to help us with our evolution. They benevolently sacrifice their heavenly abode for us. They're like our saviours?

According to Blavatsky, Ascended Masters are extremely advanced in their karmic evolution. These highly evolved 'light' beings have escaped the dreaded rebirth cycle. The Ascended Masters are also called the Great White Brotherhood. They are the guardians of mystic tradition, 'the science of the soul'. So, like the Rosicrucian's and the freemasons, Blavatsky followed them. White is notably a reference to their aura i.e. advanced spirituality, as opposed to their race. Blavatsky described many of the masters as ethnically Tibetan or Indian.

According to Blavatsky, they reside in the mystical city of Shambhala. This floating ethereal city, aka 'The City of Enoch' and 'White Island', is somewhere above the Gobi Desert. As mentioned, it seems Shambhala is the 'mystical Garden of Eden', where the alchemists venture to? It's understood the Great White Lodge is a real place in the second heaven, and adept's astral project to meet Ascended Masters there. However, it seems there's also a Shambhala underground, which could be the paradise side of Hades/Sheol? It's possible that Jesus emptied 'Abraham's Bosom' when He died, and took His Saints home to be with Him, and this hood was then hijacked by fallen angels?

Apparently, Lord Sanat Kumara is the founder of this spiritual fraternity. He's the head of the Spiritual Hierarchy or Great White Lodge, that's dedicated to the eventual salvation or enlightenment of all mankind. He's the King of the World. Blavatsky identified Sanat Kumara and his merry men with Lucifer and the fallen angels. It's purported they're our brothers and want to help us. It's noted, Sanat is an anagram for Satan, and it's said Kumara is a fictitious character.

Blavatsky wrote, 'One of the most hidden secrets involves the so-called fall of angels. Satan and his rebellious host will thus prove to have become the direct saviour and creators of divine man. Thus Satan, once he ceases to be viewed in the superstitious spirit of the church, grows into the grandiose message'.

So, 'Ascended Masters' taught the universal brotherhood of mankind the secret doctrine. They insisted on unity among all religions, except monotheistic religions, Christianity, Islam, and Judaism. They used Blavatsky to reveal their message, to help humanity spiritually evolve. They revealed the true spiritual light is coming and will manifest itself as the new world religion. This new gospel, the new message, will enlighten all men everywhere.

The Theosophical Society was thus a mystery school that taught esoteric knowledge and ancient mysteries. They believe Lucifer is God, which they identify with the sun. Blavatsky was regarded as a genius, and she regarded herself as messianic. She was known as the Masonic witch, given her close relations with freemasonry. As mentioned, she was an honorary 33nd degree mason.

It's interesting to note, that whilst Blavatsky became involved with spiritualism in the early 1870s, she argued against the mainstream Spiritualist idea that the entities contacted were spirits of the dead. She knew that whoever presented as Aunty Margaret wasn't really Aunty Margaret. But rather, spirits play sinister games. It's also said that unlike other mediums, Blavatsky controlled the spirits she worked with, rather than being controlled by them, which suggests she was something other than a medium?

So, Theosophy reintroduced fallen angels and demons as 'Ascended Masters'. Like, the one who appeared to Guy Ballard, a former student of Theosophy. Ballard claimed he met a hiker, when visiting Mount Shasta (California) in 1930, who identified himself as the Count of St Germain (an occult philosopher who died in 1784). And this Ascended Master transmitted the lessons of 'the Great Law of Life', which birthed the 'I AM' movement. So, people believe they're God aka I AM. Lucifer literally hijacks everything, which suggests he has no pride?

The 'I AM' movement is thus an offshoot of Theosophy, and was a major precursor to the New Age movement. Ballard notably described a series of astral trips he took with St Germain. Apparently count Germain was a spiritual master of freemasonry, and he was highly influential in the Rosicrucian Order. It's purported he was an alchemist who turned lead into gold, and he was a vampire who used blood to extend his life.

But furthermore, Guy Ballard channelled the teaching that an Ascended Master would not die but rather take the body up with him. That is, Ascended Masters would experience the miracle of ascension like Jesus did. As it transpires however, this resurrection miracle has never been repeated. It's also noted, that Guy Ballard, who was supposed to have reached the ascension stage, didn't take his body with him when he died. Thus, his wife modified the theory, stating that we spiritually ascend after our body dies. Ascended Masters are thus disembodied spirits, having transcended their physical bodies.

There's apparently an array of Ascended Masters, which includes Jesus, his Mother Mary, Buddha, Krishna, Muhammad, Confucius, St Germain. It's said these masters of ancient wisdom were once ordinary people like us, but having undergone a series of spiritual transformations, originally called initiations, they spiritually evolved. They ascended to the level of gods.

It's understood this evolutionary process can take ages. Hence, the myriad reincarnations, until we eventually become 'Masters'. So, Lucifer was right, we shall be as gods? And Jesus is not God incarnate, but an Ascended Master. Theosophy teaches He was initiated into the mysteries (the same thing as Schnoebelen was taught).

It's purported an Ascended Master is one who has ascended and reunited with the spirit of God. They've regained their Mighty I AM presence. This full state of union, which happens in the ritual of ascension, is referred to as Ascension. It's also referred to as 'Christ Consciousness'. Being 'Christ' is a state of mind. It's an inward state of consciousness. Like, Jesus realised He was God. He knew He was divine. Christ consciousness refers to indwelling divinity. Christ consciousness or God realisation comes from enlightenment. It's union with God. Kundalini ascends to reach the point of union with Sanat Kumara, Shiva, Vishnu, Lord of the world or Christ consciousness. Or as Jung taught, we achieve Self-realisation.

Theosophy teaches that we need to evolve through seven planes of existence before we can experience union with the Absolute (God). We take a trip to the seven planets? The idea is that the divine One has a sevenfold nature, and that seven emanations or seven aspects (divine qualities) came forth from the central vortex. These characteristics are: will-power, love-wisdom, active-intelligence, harmony-conflict, concrete science, love-devotion, and ceremonial order.

These Seven Great Rays or streams of energies emanate from what is esoterically called the 'heart of the sun'. So, Lucifer is identified as the 'Solar Logos', and his spirit manifests through Seven Rays. Each 'Ray' is the embodiment/expression of his god-qualities. But moreover, these Seven Rays or Lords are Ascended Masters, sent to help our spiritual transformation. Apparently, these rays sweep through the planets and pour into the human soul, enlightening the initiate to see the reality behind the form. Thus, it seems we bond with these spirits, including Lucifer? As touched on, the seven rays are depicted on the Statue of Semiramis aka Lucifer.

It's noted, the seven spirits concept seems to be a spin on God's nature, as described in Revelation 3:1, which states, 'This is the message from the one who has the sevenfold spirit of God and the seven stars' (which is a reference to angels). It's also pertinent to note, that Blavatsky's concept of 'Seven Primeval Rays', as a group of celestial beings or gods or angels, corroborates with Schnoebelen's intel about 'The Seven', who are fallen angels that report to Lucifer. It's also however said, there's actually twelve Rays, but until recently five were kept secret.

Today millions of people claim they're channelling Ascended Masters, and believe they're channelling messages from the same masters Blavatsky had. People meditate to contact Ascended Masters, or use oracle cards to acquire guidance or wisdom. However, it's said that 'fake Mahatmas' are being channelled. Presumably, the fakers are demons?

Apparently fake Ascended Masters impersonate Ascended Masters, saints, and other important historical figures. Like, Jesus and His mother Mary etc. It's noted, that Marian apparitions are reported worldwide. Millions have seen 'Mary', especially in Bosnia, France, Spain and Portugal (like, the kids in Fatima). So, the truth is a challenge. Like, ghosts could be dead people or demonic impersonators. Like, did Mrs Wickland really channel Blavatsky, (who alternatively claimed that reincarnation is false), or a demon/fallen angel?

Apparently 'fake' Ascended Masters display a great concern for the physical lives and desires of their followers. Like 'New Age' cabala, they promise health, wealth, and happiness. But this attitude is the opposite of the real Mahatmas, like Buddha, who claim the physical world is the source of our sorrow. Hence, the real Mahatmas help us transcend this reality and our overwhelming sense of self. Contrary to egocentrism, 'real' Ascended Masters insist the psychological ego is false, and the idea that we are this body, emotions, and mind is a mistake. We are spiritual consciousness, the great I AM, albeit trapped inside this physical body for the time being.

Thus, 'real' Ascended Masters don't care about our personal desires. And they don't answer prayers. But rather they help us to realise our spiritual self, to awaken our inner wo/man, to rise above our personal ego. 'Fake' Ascended Masters also teach ways to dissolve bad karma (to prevent rebirth), but according to theosophical teachings this is hogwash. We can't undo our actions. Moreover, as it transpired, Blavatsky confessed on her deathbed in 1891 that Ascended Masters were really demonic entities. So,' real' or 'fake', they're all haunted.

After Blavatsky, Annie Besant and Charles Webster Leadbeater (33rd degree mason) took over leadership of the Theosophical Society. Leadbeater notably resigned in 1906 amid a sex scandal involving boys. Then Alice Bailey (1880-1949) and her husband Foster Bailey (32nd degree mason), assumed the leadership after her.

Alice Bailey essentially founded the New Age movement, and was one of the first writers to use the term 'New Age'. She also coined the term 'New World Order'. She wrote twenty-four books on theosophy, which were all directly channelled through a 'Tibetan' master called 'Djwhal Khul' (DK). According to Bailey, DK was the main author behind Blavatsky's Secret Doctrine. Ascended Masters worked through Bailey for some thirty years.

So, Bailey promoted the Ageless Wisdom tradition, which included channelling and astral projection. Like Blavatsky, Bailey was on the same page that Lucifer, 'Son of the Morning', is the ruler of humanity. But for Bailey, there is no opposition between God and the Devil, Christ and the antichrist, as 'Christ and antichrist are the dualities of spirituality and materialism, both in the individual and in humanity as a whole. Or you can speak of God and the Devil with the same basic implications'.

With regards to the revolt of angels against God, she purports that it was all part of 'the divine plan of evolution'. She further notes that actually the rebel angels were doing us a favour, as they sacrificed their original high state of being to serve us. They responded to the divine urge to be our saviours (unlike the selfish angels who stayed in God's heaven). She pertains to the 'great descent of the Masters to the earth', as opposed to them being chucked out for their rebellion. Bailey concedes that Lucifer is the prince of this world, and prince of the air, as the Bible tells us. But rather than fallen angels, ('spiritual hosts of wickedness in the heavenly places'), these entities are repackaged as Masters.

Bailey explains the Masters known as The Seven Rays are the only members of the spiritual hierarchy that humans can expect to communicate with. That's who she allegedly channelled, like Blavatsky before her, and apparently David Icke after them. Icke claims he was imparted insights from a spiritual entity named Rakorski, who he also identities with St. Germain. Presumably this Rakorski is the same 'Master Rakoczi' Bailey channelled, since they both refer to him as 'Lord of All Creation'. And this Ascended Master is the same one Ballard met? Icke said spirits told him they were Alice Bailey's Ascended Masters.

In his book 'Truth Vibrations', Icke concedes Solar Logos is the head of the solar system, and works with the rays of the sun to affect consciousness. The Solar Logos is the spirit of the sun who guides the solar system and sends certain energies to the planets and the stars. So, they're engaging with the 'genuine' Ascended Masters, the good guys? However, Crowley also received messages from them. As mentioned, Crowley's Ascended Master 'Aiwass' dictated 'The Book of the Law' (1904). It seems Icke shares the same philosophy as the Satanists he is exposing?

Like Blavatsky, Bailey claimed our saviour is on his way. Apparently, DK instructed Bailey and her followers to 'prepare men for the reappearance of Christ'. It was revealed that 'The Cosmic Christ' aka 'Lord Maitreya' will appear immediately before the earth's initiation into the utopian New Age. This Supreme World Teacher is coming to bestow wisdom and lead us into the New Age. This will be the golden age, when we all get cosmic consciousness, which translates to demonically enhanced consciousness?

As it transpires, Lord Maitreya or The Christ has taken it for the team and reincarnated many times to help our spiritual evolution. The Christ has apparently reincarnated as Buddha, Krishna, Jesus, Hermes, and Zoroaster. Theosophy teaches that 'The Christ' enters the body of a disciple in order to assist and guide the spiritual evolution of man. Thus, Bailey believed that Jesus was a medium who allowed The Christ to use His body. In tandem with the Gnostics, it's said The Christ came upon Jesus at His baptism. In her book, 'The Externalisation of the Hierarchy' (1957), Bailey mentions 'Christ' 666 times, which is said to be her clever way of telling other occultists that her Christ is the antichrist.

So, according to Bailey, Lord Maitreya will establish the New World Religion. She promulgated the Cosmic Christ will return sometime after the year 2025. However, it's also said that Sanat Kumara, the leader of mankind and the Illuminati, will rule the world in the future. And there's also Lucifer. It's thus relayed that Bailey's unholy trinity consists of Sanat Kumara, The Christ (Maitreya), and Lucifer, as whilst they're represented as distinct individuals, they overlap to the point where they're almost indistinguishable from each other.

It's duly noted, that all religions are expecting a saviour to come. Like, Muslims are expecting the Imam Mahdi, their prophesised redeemer, the Jews are still waiting for the Messiah, Christians are awaiting Christ's Second Coming, Buddhists are looking out for Maitreya Buddha, and Hindus are awaiting Kalki. In the same way, its purported there's only one God, like the Great Architect, it's purported it's the same messiah/saviour.

However, the Bible tells us the antichrist will rule before the return of Jesus. He's the false messiah that promises world peace. This messiah will propagate that we are God, and that we can save ourselves through Illuminism. But moreover, (as touched on), his followers are meditating to call forth this teacher. 'The Great Invocation', which was given to Bailey in 1945, is a mantram or world prayer for the New Age. It's been translated into over 80 languages and dialects. It states:

From the point of Light within the Mind of God. Let light stream forth into the minds of men.

Let Light descend on Earth. From the point of Love within the Heart of God. Let love stream forth into the hearts of men. May Christ (world teacher) return to Earth. From the centre where the Will of God is known.

Let purpose guide the little wills of men – The purpose which the Masters know and serve. From the centre which we call the race of men. Let the Plan of Love and Light work out. And may it seal the door where evil dwells. Let Light and Love and Power restore the Plan on Earth'.

Bailey insisted the New Age calls for a universal new world religion. She wrote, 'The spirit has gone out of the old faiths and the true spiritual light is transferring itself into a new form which will manifest on earth eventually as the new world religion. Judaism is old, obsolete and separative and has no true message for the spiritually minded which cannot be better given by the new faiths… the Christian faith also has served its purpose; its founder seeks to bring a new gospel and a new message that will enlighten all men everywhere'. So, that's all men i.e. no atheists.

The Old Age, which is tied to Christianity, is replaced with the New Age, which is tied to Lucifer. The New Age is sold to us as utopia. We can collectively create heaven on earth through spiritual enlightenment. We can activate our spirit bodies, (with demonic assistance), and become super-wo/men.

Bailey said, 'emphasis should be laid upon the evolution of humanity' and 'world spiritual unity'. This universal religion is packaged as the 'Age of Unity of Humanity', the 'Age of Cosmic Enlightenment', and the 'Age of Spiritual Consciousness'. The New Age is couched in 'love and light'. The promise of brotherhood offers an end to our age of division (created by the Illuminati).

Bailey wrote, 'The day is dawning when all religions will be regarded as emanating from one great spiritual force. All will be seen as unitedly providing the one root out of which the universal world religion will inevitably emerge. Then there will be neither Christian nor heathen, neither Jew nor Gentile, but simply one great body of believers gathered out of all the current religions'.

It's understood the ecumenical movement, pioneered by beloved Jesuit Pope Francis, is the precursor to the world religion. We can 'coexist'. We don't need to generate religious divisions, particularly if it's the same God? One global religion is progressive, and New Agers won't be held back by Old Agers. Muslims, Jews, and Christians could be obstructive. Hence, the ongoing plan to create fireworks between them, to exterminate them (and reduce the population).

Bailey recognised the structure/framework of freemasons was the best way to disseminate theosophy teachings worldwide. According to Bailey, freemasonry will be the religion of the New System and Age. The one world religion, under freemasonry, is theosophy i.e. we're god and Lucifer is the great illuminator. Masonry viewed doctrinally is theosophy.

She wrote, 'The Masonic movement… is the custodian of the law; it is the home of the Mysteries and the seat of initiation. It holds in its symbolism the ritual of Deity, and the way of salvation is pictorially preserved in its work. The methods of Deity are demonstrated in its Temples and under the All-seeing Eye the work can go forward. It is a far more occult organisation than can be realised and is intended to be the training school for the coming advanced occultists'.

Like the Pope, Bailey was an ardent NWO activist, and frequently referred to 'the plan'. The plan is to prepare the people and the world for the coming messiah, by creating a global government and religion. However, it's understood the New World Religion will be implemented when The Christ appears. Bailey was convinced we need a NWO, which combines religion with state. This is notably abhorrent to God. Enforcing religion negates freewill. 'DK' outlined objectives/steps towards the NWO, which are detailed in her extensive writings.

As mentioned in chapter 1, Bailey outlined a ten point plan, which detailed how they would change society from Christian to Luciferian, largely through education and media. The masses would be reached through state education, which includes using scientism and fake history to bump off God. However, as also touched on, the new religion will be based on science. Science will confirm the teachings of the mystery schools. Thus, quantum physics mirrors the cabala. Our current material paradigm will be upgraded to include consciousness (panpsychism).

Bailey produced propaganda to change thoughts, (perception), in preparation for the NWO. This includes propaganda against religion. Like, perpetuating the belief that religion is the prime cause of war, when it's actually less than 10% according to the Encyclopaedia of Wars. There's no shortage of atheist psychos like Stalin and Mao Tse-tung. We would need to believe, as Dawkins stressed, that religion is the root of all evil. Since we're not evil as such? It seems 'society' makes us sick, like it creates paedos and murderers.

As mentioned, the process, which began in 1945, has taken a generation (some seventy years). Like, God has been taken out of the school system and replaced with transcendental meditation. We're also being talked into a global government. Like, after WW2 the UN seemed like a good idea. According to the Tibetan master, WW2 was necessary to defend God's plan. The UN is the vehicle driving the global government, as we'll get to. And the UN promises peace? The International Day of Peace is notably 21st September (the autumnal or fall equinox). The UN also has a prayer, which is featured on their website beside a picture of Semiramis.

Thus, 'May the peace and the blessings of the Holy Ones pour forth over the worlds, and rest upon the United Nations, on the work and the workers, protecting, purifying, energizing and strengthening. There is a Peace which passes understanding. It abides in the hearts of those who live in the Eternal. There is a Power that makes all things new. It lives and moves in all those who know the self as One.

May the rhythm of that Peace vibrate within the United Nations and in the heart of every worker. May the rhythm of that creative Power resound within the United Nations, and in the lives of all who serve there—awakening, transmuting, and giving birth to that which ought to be.

May the chalice that the United Nations is building become a focal point for the descent of spiritual force, filling it and overflowing to the world, and drawing towards itself all those whose work lies there.

May the consciousness of the United Nations become ever more at-one, and the many lights become One Light. May the aspiration and the dedication of the United Nations burn as a clear flame in the service of humanity. May the Love and the Light and the Life of the One Life pour through the United Nations, cleansing it from all evil and attracting all good'.

It's also noted, that Bailey cofounded the publishing company 'Lucis Trust' in 1922, which was originally called Lucifer publishing Co. It was named after the Theosophical Magazine titled 'Lucifer' but they changed the name as there was public outrage at the sinister name. The Lucis Trust sponsors various organisations like the UN and UNICEF, and prints and disseminates their material, along with many New Age books. It was located at 666 UN Plaza. The Lucis Trust has consultative status as an NGO called 'The World Goodwill Organisation' at the UN. The stated aim of this NGO is 'to cooperate in the world of preparation for the reappearance of the Christ'.

The Lucis Trust, which is 'aggressively involved in promoting a globalist ideology', links in with other global vehicles like the Bilderberg Group, the Council on Foreign Relations, and the Trilateral Commission. The Lucis

Trust advocates, 'Let the Plan of Love and Light work out'. The Lucis Trust disciples' creed/affirmation is, 'I am a point of light within a great light'. And like Magnu asserted, the Lucis Trust states that 'spiritual energies are flowing into the hearts and minds of people throughout the world, awakening the demand for a better way of life for all'.

But moreover, Bailey recognised 'only universal disaster could create the change required'. Order comes from chaos e.g. WW3? It's noted, the 33rd freemasonic degree is called 'Order out of Chaos'. It seems what Bailey calls 'The Christ and the Coming World Religion', is Lucifer's religious world order. David Spangler, Director of Planetary Initiative, UN, wrote: 'No-one will enter the NWO unless he or she will make a pledge to worship Lucifer. No one will enter the New Age unless he will take a Luciferian Initiation'.

'I believe that a grand game of chess is being played on a level that we can barely imagine, and we are the pawns'. Bill Cooper

14

The 'Royal' Family

According to the Bible, Satan is 'the ruler of this world' (John 12:31) and 'the god of this world' (2 Corinthians 4:4). He's the sly old serpent who blinds people's minds to the truth of Christ, who is the image of God. But moreover, together with his evil minions, they implement their ancient plan through nephilim bloodlines here on earth. The nephilim became the kings and queens of the ancient world and their successors received the same divine right to rule because of their connections to the gods.

So, the elite of today who pull the strings, the so-called black nobility, traces back to Babylon. Indeed, according to Fritz Springmeier, author of 'Bloodlines of the Illuminati' (2002), the Rothschild's are able to trace their heritage to Nimrod, and the Astor family was known as the Astarte in Canaan. Apparently, the descendants of the ancient gods consist of less than 1% of the 1% that controls 'we the plebs' the 99%. So, this is the elite royal blood, the 'holy family'.

It's understood, global Babylon expanded out of the Roman Empire (the last global empire). Nephilim HQ was divided into kingdoms, and the family became royal aristocracy in Western Europe. These European powers, especially the British Empire, went global and ruled as Colonial powers. Beyond royalty (royal houses) and aristocracy, the 'family' moved into banking, politics, business, and media. They also crossed the pond to found the New World (Washington DC) and so forth.

It's duly noted, that when it comes to bloodlines, 'incest is best, keep it in the family'. In addition to preserving the bloodline, it also keeps the cash in the family, which is the opportunity cost of some 'special' (retarded) kids? Like, the Queen's first cousins, Nerissa and Katherine Bowes-Lyon, who were sent to a mental asylum in 1941 and forgotten about. They were given a pauper's grave and no family attended their funeral. Her three second cousins were sent to the same place, and there's been no contact with them either.

As touched on, it's purported that thirteen generational satanic bloodlines rule the world. According to Springmeier, these infernal families are: Astor, Bundy, Collins, DuPont, Freeman, Kennedy, Li, Onassis, Rockefeller, Rothschild, Russell, Van Duyn, and Merovingian bloodline. Other Illuminati families are closely tied to these e.g. Disney, McDonald, Reynolds, Krupp, or have intermarried with them and obtained significant power on their own e.g. Warburg's, Morgan's, Bushes, Carnegies. As mentioned, 13 is an important number for occultists.

But Springmeier further explains that Satan mimics God, hence, there's 12 tribes or illuminati bloodlines, plus one satanic one, that was infused with the seed of Satan. He asserts the antichrist will be born from this 13th satanic bloodline, which is the Merovingian bloodline. Springmeier was notably framed and imprisoned for eight years for exposing the cabal (he lost everything and all his research was destroyed), and he claims there's been many attempts on his life.

In his book 'Blue Blood, True Blood' (2002), Stewart Swerdlow states the thirteen Illuminati families are: Rothschild, Bruce, Kennedy, De Medici, Hanover, Hapsburg, Krupp, Plantagenet, Rockefeller, Romanov, Sinclair, Warburg, and Windsor. Doc Marquis however claims there's hundreds of Illuminati families, and the Rothschild's are the head of the Illuminati.

According to Hitler's nephew, Hitler was a Rothschild grandchild. He claimed Hitler's father was the illegitimate son of Baron Rothschild. His grandmother was a servant girl for him in Vienna, and apparently she served him well. And it's rumoured that German Chancellor Angela Merkel is the granddaughter of Hitler. Springmeier highlights that research into Illuminati bloodlines is difficult as many of the Illuminati members do not have an Illuminati surname.

It's understood the royal bloodline has different degrees of pedigree i.e. distant cousins etc. It's purported that whilst anyone can be possessed, nephilim bloodlines are much easier to possess. And also, the higher someone is in the illuminati power structure, the more powerful their demons. So, these VIP families are human vessels for the demonic to inhabit? And the Rothschild's are especially haunted?

It's noted, that the German Jewish Rothschild family established the modern banking system. It began with Mayer Amschel Rothschild's (1744-1812) goldsmith/money lending shop in Frankfurt in 1760, which blossomed into a dynasty. He realised it was more profitable lending money to kings and governments (than average Jo Munter, who could be unreliable), as loans were bigger, and they were secured by nation's taxes. It's recalled Mayer Amschel was a Sabbatean-Frankist (satanic cabalist), and he recruited Adam Weishaupt to create the Bavarian Illuminati.

Mayer Amschel also changed their name from Bauer to Rothschild, which means red shield in German. Apparently, he was inspired by the red hexagram sign he had painted outside his shop. It's noted, that many 'Jewish' families changed their names to hide their background. Like, the Rockefellers were formerly Rockenfelder, and the Roosevelts were formerly Rosenfelt. And like Bonesman John Kerry is actually John Kohn. This crypto Jew, who was a covert CIA operative, pretended to be Irish catholic.

So, Mayer Amschel Rothschild sent his five sons (circa 1800s) to work in five major European capitals to expand his empire, namely, Frankfurt, London, Paris, Vienna, and Naples. And like the Templars, they used a credit-note system. Thus, customers could deposit money in a Rothschild bank and get a receipt, and then cash that in at another Rothschild bank in another country.

By the mid-1800s they were the richest family in the world. Intermarriage was the family custom (i.e. marrying first and second cousins) to preserve their vast fortunes (and keep their bloodline pure?), and all key positions in the House of Rothschild had to be family members. Another rule is Rothschild heirs are strictly forbidden to disclose the amount of their wealth. However, according to Doc Marquis, they're worth $300-500 trillion. It's also noted, that the Rothschild's use front companies and directors to hide the extent of their holdings and control.

In 1823 the Rothschild's took over the financial operations of the Catholic Church worldwide. They were given the title 'Guardians of the Vatican Treasury'. Being embroiled with the royals, they also received titles of nobility etc. The Rothschild's knew money yields power. As Baron Nathan Mayer Rothschild (1840-1915) notoriously said, 'Let me issue and control a nation's money and I care not who writes the laws'.

It's noted, bankers create economic booms by making copious amounts of loans available, only to pull the plug causing a crash/depression (like in 2008). Stocks can then be scooped at rock bottom prices, with profits maximised through derivatives e.g. call and put options, which enable buying or selling stock at a pre-arranged price. Bankers magically conjure up money and multiply it. They're like Jesus multiplying the fish and bread.

The Rothschild's were also behind the creation of the Federal Reserve. It was created with the enactment of the Federal Reserve Act, which was passed in exchange for campaign contributions. This cartel of private banks loans money to the US government, and the taxpayers pay the interest. It's conservatively estimated that profits exceed $100 billion per year. It's thus posited that the American government is enslaved to the Fed. President Andrew Jackson said the 'central bankers were a den of vipers and thieves'.

It's noted, both Abraham Lincoln and JFK were killed for taking action against the central bank (apparently Lincoln was assassinated by Jesuits). They wanted to print American money for the American people, without going through the Rothschild's private banks (which became the Fed), but it appears the family didn't like this idea.

It's arguably curious that the Fed was established in 1913, and the next year WW1 kicked off? Not least because wars are hugely profitable for bankers, as they loan money to fight the wars, and also to repair the war-torn countries. It's also noted, that by the year 2000, there were seven countries without a Rothschild central bank, namely, Afghanistan, Iraq, Sudan, Libya, Cuba, North Korea and Iran. And now only Cuba, Iran and North Korea do not have a central bank owned or controlled by the Rothschild's. So, the invasion of Iraq, Libya, and Afghanistan wasn't all bad?

Besides being controlled by money, the clever Rothschild's realised that we're controlled through media. Hence, almost all media is owned or controlled by them. As touched on in the Introduction, we know wars are by design, coupled with propaganda that underpins them, but we'll get to these later. It's said the family are ingenious at creating strategies to deceive us and control us (not least, 'divide and rule'). It's also noted, another reason the world is so bankrupt is because of military spending. It's insane.

Whilst it stands to reason the House of Rothschild manages the Illuminati's finance, other families have different areas of speciality. Like, the Collins are responsible for organising the occult aspects of the Illuminati. Springmeier states that in occult circles, the Collins family is higher in the hierarchy than both the Rothschild's and the Rockefellers. But moreover, he claims the Rothschild family always sets a place at the dinner table in case Satan decides to show up. Apparently, he wears a black tuxedo and only his cloven hooves are visible. No danger.

As discussed, Satan's Illuminati bloodlines dictate the direction of society via his pyramid of power. His people are everywhere (they're strategically placed) and they have infiltrated all our systems. Thus, governments are tools of the Illuminati, and most leaders are in secret societies. Like, most American leaders have been masons, and many of them 33rd degree masons. The hidden hand is the shadow government, and it works through all parties.

It's noted however, that whilst the shadow government pertains to the permanent shadow government of officials and bankers who control the agenda from behind the scene, (unlike politicians who come and go), there is a literal 'shadow government' i.e. 'shadow people' who impart the plan to the brotherhood.

As Springmeier and Icke assert, the 'Great White Brotherhood' is at the top of the pyramid. Hence, it makes no difference whether we vote Conservative or Labour in the UK, or Democratic or Republican in the US, as the same Luciferian agenda rolls on. As highlighted, there's a plan being adhered to. Society is not randomly evolving but rather engineered. Prime ministers and presidents are told which direction to take. They're given 'geopolitical' strategies. Like, 'intelligence' tells them which countries are rogue. 'Advisers' advise them.

So, we see the puppets (e.g. presidents, prime ministers), not the puppeteers. As Franklyn Roosevelt said, 'presidents are selected, not elected'. It's said US presidents haven't been elected for fifty years. It's like popes and cardinals in the Vatican are selected.

It's purported that corporate interests select presidents and prime ministers, ergo the assertion we live in a corporatocracy. Or rather secret societies select them, using the media for support. We basically get a choice of two, and the lesser of two evils principle. Like, with 'crooked Hillary' Clinton (who suspiciously deleted 33,000 emails) and Trump in 2016, Trump seemed like the lesser of two evils. They're also distant cousins.

Invariably, the most money spent on campaigns wins the game. Both Romney and Obama notably topped $1 billion in 2012, in the most expensive US presidential campaign ever. Thus, we get the illusion of choice. Icke notably said he heard Blair and Cameron brilliantly described as 'two cheeks on the same arse' (LOL).

Russell Brand (2014), who's renowned for highlighting the futility of voting, equally asserts that the Government is corrupt and opposing parties are similarly pointless. He said, 'Just to reiterate the irrelevance of bi-party democracy: we all get excited by the Blairs, Obamas and Clintons with their well rehearsed gestures and photo-op affability, but when push comes to shove we're dealing with cunts' (p.289).

Moreover, it's said candidates are selected by blood not ballot. Like, apparently David Cameron is a distant cousin of the Queen, and Tony Blair's part of the family. Almost all US presidents are related by blood. They're all cousins (except one), sharing the same great grandfather, namely, the former king of England. And Dick Cheney, Vice President to George W Bush, is Barack Obama's eighth cousin. The Bush family is closely related to every European monarch on and off the throne, and has kinship with every member of the British royal family. Like the Queen's family (Prince Charles and Prince William), the Bush family are descendants of Vlad the Impaler. So, they're vampires not werewolves?

It's highlighted that the royal family and almost all US presidents, (including Donald Trump), have RH negative blood. About 10-15% of the population has this curious blood type. It's said it's the result of a genetic mutation, whereas others suggest its nephilim blood. Those with this blood type tend to have higher IQs, psychic abilities, and they often have an extra vertebra.

It's also understood that blood is more important than surnames. Like, the Windsor's changed their surname, but their blood stayed the same. It's noted, that Queen Liz II's grandfather, King George V, changed their surname in 1917 from Saxe-Coburg-Gotha to Windsor to distract us from their German heritage during WW1. His son, Edward VIII (Liz's uncle) proudly declared, 'There is not one drop of blood in my veins that is not German'.

And like the Rothschild's, they're incestuous. Queen Liz and Prince Philip are third cousins. They're both great, great grandkids of Queen Victoria (who was partial to using kids as slaves), who married her first German cousin. Prince Philip's mum was Princess Alice of Battenberg (Germany) and his father was Prince Andrew of Greece and Denmark. Prince Phillip also changed his name from Battenberg to Mountbatten to cover his German identity. Lord Louis Mountbatten, Prince Phillip's uncle (renowned paedo), said, 'Prince Charles is an absolute Mountbatten. The real intelligence in the royal family comes through my parents to Prince Philip and the children'.

It's notably said, Princess Diana's biological father was Sir James Goldsmith, a Jewish banker, rather than Earl John Spencer. The Goldsmiths intermarried with the Rothschild's in Frankfurt. Apparently, Diana ('moon goddess') called herself a 'blood-mare'. Her genes were required for the princes, but she was surplus to requirements. Icke says Prince William is also a Rothschild, at least through his maternal grandmother as she was an offshoot Rothschild. He also highlights that William was induced to be born on the summer solstice (21st June). As discussed, Satanists love specific numbers and dates. Apparently, Prince Charles used the excuse that he had a polo match to attend.

It's also noted, Kate Middleton's mother is Carol Goldsmith. Kate and William are fourteenth cousins, and her distant cousins include George Washington. They married on the same day Hitler married Eva, 66 years later. Harry and Meghan sparkle are fifteenth cousins. Apparently, sparkle is a direct descendent of King Edward III and is related to the Bush family, and other presidents including Richard Nixon and Gerald Ford.

Thus, whilst monarchies of Europe were led by the British royal family, it's highlighted the British royal family is more German than British. And like the Vatican, the royals loved Heil Hitler and were inextricably linked to the Nazis. Prince Phillip's sisters married German princes, who were high ranking Nazis. Princess Michael of Kent's father, Baron Gunther von Reibnitz, was a former Nazi and SS officer. According to Wheeler (2009), the royal German Aryan kings and queens of England bloodline traces back to Cain, which she believes was Satan's seed. So, royals do have special blue blood, and they're seated on almost every throne in Europe?

The elite Nazi SS military order followed the order of the black sun, the brotherhood of Saturn. Apparently in occult circles, it was prophesised that a German messiah was coming, and Hitler appeared to be the strong charismatic leader they yearned for. And he had the right blood? It's noted, that to be a member of Hitler's SS, officers had to prove German ancestry (pure Aryan heritage) back to 1750. They were the racial elite (which inspired the eugenics movement). Himmler was very selective and recruited only the very best for the SS i.e. strongest, tallest, cleverest, healthiest, best looking, complete with blonde hair and blue eyes. Like, Princess Diana's genes?

As touched on, Hitler endorsed Blavatsky's teachings about the Aryans (nephilim) surviving the Flood, and purported that Germanic people were their descendants. Thus, Himmler went on his government funded expeditions in the 1930s, searching the Himalayas for their blood ancestors. The aim was to prove their ancestors were gods. Himmler was the architect of the Nazi Luciferian religion. He was also the head of the SS and Nazi death camp.

Hitler also sent teams to Tibet to establish contact with Tibetan lamas who had expert knowledge about tunnels and entrances to inner worlds. It appears the nephilim took shelter from the great Flood in deep underground taverns? Hitler believed in a 'hollow earth', but we'll get back to this.

Hitler believed the Nordic race was destined to rule the world. His dream was a Nazi NWO for a thousand year reign (like Christ's future millennium kingdom foretold in Revelation), led by Aryan supermen. Hitler repeatedly used the term NWO in connection with his planned utopian Aryan society after he had conquered the world. But moreover, Hitler endeavoured to create supermen through selective breeding. That is, force human evolution by breeding the best with the best, until supermen are created. Hitler said, 'the ultimate aim is the coming of the sons of gods'.

Thus, Himmler created the 'Lebensborn' ('Spring of Life') program in 1935 to create an Aryan master race. Himmler promoted polygamy as a sacred duty for the SS, encouraging them to father as many healthy pure Aryan babies as possible. And single German girls were encouraged to fulfil their dream of motherhood, and take it for their country, by having sex with an SS officer. The kids (hundreds of thousands) were regarded as state property. Most didn't see their parents, and instead were indoctrinated in Nazi mythology. Deluded Hitler said, 'Man is becoming God. Man is God in the making'.

It's also highlighted that Queen Victoria's favourite grandson, the British Prince, Charles Edward (1884-1954), Duke of Saxe-Coburg-Gotha, controlled Hitler and funded the Nazis. He was apparently at the top of the British royal family. He was educated at Eton College, and then sent to Germany at eighteen years young to crush and dominate the ancient nations of Europe. He apparently engineered WW1 and WW2. He fought in the German army, as a general, and served in a number of positions in Nazi Germany during the 1930s and 1940s.

According to Chris Everard (researcher/documentary maker), when Hitler met Charles Edward, he said 'Today I met the antichrist. He was cruel and intrepid. He scared me'. Apparently, Lord Louis Mountbatten was a central figure in secret communications between the British royal family and their pro-Hitler cousins in Germany.

Everard highlights that WW1 and WW2 were not wars between Germany and allied powers, but rather they were wars of the super rich and poor. Hence, in many cities in Europe, it was often the poor slum areas that were decimated. Like in Britain, for example, east London was bombed, whereas Kensington and palaces etc remained unharmed. The idea was to take over the poor areas and develop them. Apparently, the family also bombed certain places they wanted rid of. Like, the family wanted rid of building 7 on 9/11 because it harboured incriminating evidence, as we'll get to.

The family are the bankers who benefit. It pays to have shares in warfare. As mentioned, the goal of the Illuminati is to acquire the whole world and all her wealth, and create as much chaos as possible in the process. In tandem with the 33rd Masonic degree, chaos precedes order. However, we'll get back to the agenda of wars in the next chapter.

Like the Roman Catholic Church, the British (German) royal family has a gruesome legacy. They similarly murdered and fleeced the world for their blood-soaked trillions e.g. drug and slave trade (together with the Rothschild's). The Navy, (which Prince Phillip, Charles, and Andy were in), was instrumental to drug smuggling back in the day. Queen Liz I started the slave trade in 1564, which (quite rightly) upset the Church of England, but she retorted that black Africans don't have souls. Tens of millions of Africans were not only exploited but murdered, raped, and mutilated. It's noted, the monarch broke away from the Roman Catholic Church after Henry VIII sought a divorce. He instituted the Church of England. As it transpired, he divorced two, and killed two, of his six wives.

Like the Bush family, the Queen professes to be 'Christian'. Hence, we could surmise that Jesus would approve of her selling her assets, to feed and clothe the poor? Like, her gold state coach (worth millions), particularly since she claims that riding in it is a 'horrible' experience. Or she could sacrifice some crown Jewels, which are worth circa five billion. After all, Jesus sacrificed His life for her. The royals are rumoured to have $30 trillion. Hence, they could end world poverty if they wanted to. It's also noted, they don't pay inheritance tax, unlike the plebs who pay 40%.

Presumably, Jesus would also approve of the Vatican selling their spoils? Perhaps we shouldn't be deceived by the Queen and Pope. It seems they're not benign old dogs. The Queen heads the lot (including the commonwealth). Not dissimilar to dodgy American dollar bills, maybe it's curious we have the Queen's pie on our money, like at least thirty-five other countries? Besides murdering people, and excommunicating retarded family members, the royals are partial to hunting. Like, spearing antelopes, killing birds in flight, and terrorising foxes with bloodhounds. That's fun?

It's also noted, the World Wildlife Fund (WWF) was not created to save engendered wildlife but rather, to make a mint from the illegal ivory trade. It also ties in with other operations to confiscate land to further their agenda. The WWF was cofounded in 1961 by Prince Philip and former Nazi Prince Bernhard of the Netherlands, and the numbers of endangered animals, like elephants, tigers, and rhinos, plummeted. It's said Prince Phillip went to Northern India a few months before he launched WWF, where he shot a Bengal tiger. The tiger was lured in by a group of goats that were tied together as prey. And he shot a mother elephant while her orphan calf ran off in terror. Rhinos were also killed.

It gets darker however, as the WWF sign is a panda, which is apparently a paedo sign and symbolises child sodomy. When a child is sodomised, their eyes can welt to black circles due to the blunt trauma involved, which makes them look like a panda. The black and white panda also symbolises dualism. It's a reference to the Baphomet god?

Perhaps we should rethink the 'purpose' of the royals. Which is? Besides holidaying very regularly, going to events, forcing some waves and smiles, and an annual speech read on autocue at 'Christmas'? Their decadence (we pay for) is second to none. Like, their lavish weddings, or like refurbishing their stately homes and palaces which costs untold millions. What an actual nerve, when they're loaded. Perhaps we could sack them and sell their assets to reduce our debt? We could sell Kate (LOL). Do we respect what they represent?

At the very least, the monarchy is an undemocratic institution (like the House of Lords). And it's crazy to think people were employed to wipe royal arses back in the day. Apparently the 'Groom of the Stool' was considered a very important job and an honour (LOL). Princess Diana's (alleged) father 8th Earl John Spencer (1924-1992), was a descendant of 5th Earl John Spencer (1835-1910), who was a Groom of the Stool and wiped the Prince of Wales' arse from 1862-1866. This occupation allegedly stopped in 1906.

And they're above the law. Her majesty's secret service (MI5 and MI6) ensures they're untouchable. Hence, they get away with murder, literally. Like Diana's murder, and her ex-bodyguard Barry Mannakee, before that. Diana alleged that security services took care of Mannakee, and she correctly predicted her demise would be a car accident. It's noted, that ten months before her death, in a letter to her to former butler, Paul Burrell, she wrote 'this particular phase in my life is the _most_ dangerous' (most is underlined).

James Hewitt (Harry's father?), another of Diana's many lovers, was threatened that courting Lady Die was not conducive to his health and safety. He was told his fate would be the same as Mannakee's. Dodi Al Fayed foolishly took his chances. His billionaire father Mohamed Al-Fayed insists they were royally bumped off. It's supposed a pregnant Diana (with a tangerine baby) was an embarrassment to the crown. But moreover, it's purported she had some cards to play. Coy Diana knew royal secrets. And she had the public onside, as 'queen of hearts'.

It's highlighted that the royals have a huge amount of influence over the press, and the media collaborates with cover-ups. Thus, there's little criticism and good works are magnified. It's duly noted, that 'charitable works' are part of the PR scam. As mentioned, philanthropy is the perfect cover for lurid Satanists.

Like, Harry's 'Invictus Games', an international sporting event for injured service men and women, which he founded in 2014. Which seems ironic given the royals orchestrate wars? Moreover, Sol Invictus, which means unconquered sun, was the official sun god of the Roman Empire and a patron of soldiers. It was an official cult, alongside the traditional Roman cults. Constantine was notably a follower of Sol Invictus until his deathbed, when he finally accepted baptism on the off-chance the Christians were right. 'I AM' is the motto for the games. It's said the royal family are attempting to rebrand themselves (as they know we're onto them) through beloved Wills and fun-loving Harry (who notoriously dressed up as a Nazi), and their beautiful wives.

The family knows how we operate. Psychologists figured it out a hundred years ago. And since we can't be forcefully controlled, like in the days of yore, they control us through our perception. So, they sell the royals to us? Like, we like the princes? We have compassion for them because they tragically lost their mum. They have nothing to do with their granny's antics? And their wives seem lovely? And who doesn't have a fun Uncle Gary (Kate's uncle), who takes drugs and had a house in Ibiza called 'maison de bang bang' (LOL). Or rather, they're well versed in acting the part (they're trained). Sparkle is literally an actress. The media tells us what they want us to know about them. Like, they care about people? Albeit, not enough to relinquish some of their spoils?

It's noted, that Edward Bernays (Sigmund Freud's nephew and propaganda king), advised that to make royalty and politicians popular, they needed to be associated with pop stars and Hollywood stars. Like, at events and banquets. They would be considered cool if they hung out with cool people i.e. the A Listers. Hence, US president hopefuls' rope in the 'stars' to support their campaigns. As it transpires, A Listers are themselves political weapons because we listen to them more than our leaders? Like, we pay attention to Leonardo De Caprio and Angelina Jolie, who highlight the environment and refugee crisis. They're actors so they should know?

But the idea was to further make the royals look like stars themselves. The idea is to idolise them? So, we're led to focus on Kate's and Meghan's attire, not the scandals that plague the royals. Like, Prince Phillip's paedo uncles, and royal BFF Jimmy Savile. Prince Charles especially liked Savile, who apparently mediated for him and Diana during their marital problems. Charles's other BFF was disgraced paedo bishop Peter Ball. Uncle George Mountbatten notably had a huge collection of kiddy porn, as well as pictures of family paedo orgies and bestiality (stored in the British Museum). Apparently, he raised Prince Phillip, as his mum was a paranoid schizophrenic and his dad ran off.

David Icke asserts that Lord Louis Mountbatten introduced Sa-vile into the inner circle in 1966, as he procured kids for these royal degenerates. Whilst Lord Mountbatten was partial to the boys at Kincora's 'care-home' in Belfast, Savile was into the kids in Jersey's children's home (Haut de la Garenne), dubbed 'the house of horrors'. Hundreds of crimes were carried out over decades (the torture rooms had shackles etc). In Savile's last interview, (on BBC Panorama), he said 'I'm not going to heaven, I'm Going To hell'. One would think so? Savile was raised Roman Catholic and became a Knight of Malta, and interestingly he was born on Halloween. He was very popular with the Beatles etc. He also loved Crowley.

Sir Jimmy Savile (he was knighted by the Queen) was Britain's worst sex offender. At least five hundred victims from 1940-2007 (most of them kids/teenagers) advised being molested, raped, and beaten. But moreover, they described the perverted star's satanic practices, like at the 'black mass ceremonies'. It's claimed he wore a hooded robe and mask, like the other paedophile devil worshippers, and together in a candle-lit room, they chanted 'Ave Satanas', which is a Latin version of hail Satan. Such evenings would start with an orgy and degenerate into darker, more sinister activities, including necrophilia, as Savile was partial to corpses. His voluntary work at hospitals gave him access to the morgues.

Savile was apparently in the 'Ninth Circle', like the royals, which is a satanic cult. Apparently the Ninth Circle was created by Jesuits, three years before Jesuit Adam Weishaupt founded the Illuminati in Bavaria. It's said these Jesuit black magicians are at the very top of the satanic NWO pyramid, and second only to Satan and his demons. During their ritual ceremonies, they sacrifice children to Satan. It's said the child (usually five or six) is raped then killed. The victim is disembowelled and dismembered. Blood is drunk by all and flesh is often eaten. The remains are burned in a fire and disposed of. They also sacrifice their first born to Satan.

Apparently the Ninth Circle was commissioned by Satan to control all child sacrifice cults worldwide. And according to investigations, all organised satanic cults come under the auspices of the Jesuit Ninth Circle. So, there's centralised control. [See Kevin Annett's (catholic priest whistle-blower) work].

As mentioned, Jesuits control the Pope. But it's further said, Jesuits are there to make sure that every Pope is a Satanist initiated into the Ninth Circle, so that the devil can take possession of the Pope at any time. The satanic sacrificial rituals the Popes and Jesuits take part in, allows them to be possessed and controlled by Satan. As touched on, Jesuits rule the mafia and all organised crime gangs under the mafia. Thus, they work in conjunction with intelligence agencies e.g. CIA, MI5 and MI6, Mossad (Israel's intelligence). It's said they rule the Illuminati.

It's also noted, the Queen's ex-butler, Paul Kidd, ran a paedo ring for thirty years while serving the royal family. It seems kiddie fiddler Kidd was part of the secret circle that regularly abused the Jersey boys in weird rituals? Another teenage boy working at Buckingham palace revealed he was sexually abused by a VIP paedo ring there, and at Balmoral. He said he was the victim of 'exploitation of the highest order'. It seems this is linked to the paedo Westminster ring?

As touched on, Leon Brittan, former Home Secretary, lost the dossier with over a hundred documents concerning child abuse allegations back in 1984. Which was convenient given he was a named paedo. It's understood Brittan, along with other VIPs, including MP Cyril Smith, were partial to using Elm Guest House (London) as their sordid playhouse, using boys (from children's homes) as their toys (boys are called toys). Apparently, Cliff Richard aka Kitty was a regular visitor at Elm House.

Ted Heath, former prime minister, was another paedo. David Icke notably accused him of paedophilia and child murder back in 1998 (seven years before he died). It's understood Savile procured kids for Heath, many of them boys from the 'care-home' in Jersey. It's said Heath aka 'Uncle Teddy' would take them on a boat trip from Jersey, (on his yacht 'morning cloud'), which was dubbed the death ride, as after torturing them sexually, they would be murdered and tossed into the sea. It's also noted, Heath took us into the EEC in 1973, in tandem with the overarching globalist agenda. Icke states Satanist Heath was a Rothschild's asset.

It's also alleged Lord McAlpine, former treasurer of Heath's conservative party and government advisor in the Thatcher era, was a paedo. Thatcher replaced Heath as party leader in 1975 and became Prime Minister in 1979. Savile was also Thatcher's BFF. Apparently, they spent many Christmases and New Years together. Thatcher's assistant, Sir Peter Morrison, MP, was also a known paedo. So, the political elites and royals are pretty tight, and Jim fixed up many kids for them. Icke also claims Winston Churchill and Harold Wilson were paedos. It's understood British intelligence knew about all this (it's not just David Icke). MI5 is hugely complicit.

And whatever happened to those kids from the catholic residential school that Queen Liz and Prince Philip took out for a picnic, over in British Columbia, Canada, back in 1964? The ten kids never returned, and the one witness to this was bumped off. It's rumoured the kids were tortured and killed in satanic rituals.

It's noted, journalist Jill Dando was on the verge of exposing a VIP paedophile ring, when she was shot dead on her doorstep in 1999. Dando had approached BBC chiefs about her concerns, and had compiled a dossier detailing 'surprisingly big names'. The BBC however said it had seen no evidence to substantiate her claims. It's understood BBC bosses covered for Savile. Like, the police covered for him (apparently 1:6 cops are masons). As David Icke highlights, no one can cough near the Queen without being vetted, ergo MI5 knew who Savile really was. Some haunted magician who bewitched us with his philanthropy.

Thus, the royals are suspect, and they keep suspect company? Another of their acquaintances included Sir paedo Rolf Harris. Presumably the evil one appreciates the irony that these national treasures were all for the kids? Lest we forget, Prince Andrew's billionaire philanthropist convicted paedo friend Jeffrey Epstein, who flew his friends, including the Clintons, to his private Caribbean island called 'Orgy Island' via his private jet 'Lolita express'.

It's duly noted, that 'Randy Andy' (as he's affectionately known) emphatically denied the allegations in 2015 that he used Virginia Roberts as a sex-slave. Roberts claims she was forced to have sex with Andrew when she was 17, which is below the legal age of consent of 18 in the US Virgin Islands, making Andy a paedo. She insists he took part in an underage orgy with Epstein, and eight other young girls. She said the girls didn't really speak English, and 'Epstein laughed about the fact they couldn't really communicate, saying that they are the 'easiest' girls to get along with'.

This was however allegedly the third time Roberts had sex with Andy, who apparently has a sexual interest in feet (LOL), as she claims she had sex with the Duke in London, having met him in Epstein's home in New York. The dates/locations she provided about Andy's whereabouts in 2001 checked out. Records show he was where she claimed i.e. the time in London, twice in NY, and the orgy on the island.

Roberts also spoke about being onboard Epstein's private jet with Bill Clinton but said she never had any sexual contact with him. Contrary to his public persona, apparently he's more into men. And he likes to dress up as a woman? Like, in the portrait Epstein had of Bill Clinton inside his Caribbean lair, which features him wearing a red dress and blue high heeled shoes (LOL).

Bill Clinton has been on the Lolita Express at least 26 times. Hillary also went to paedo island at least six times. Other VIPs who had a ride on the Lolita Express and visited the island include prominent American politicians, powerful business executives, foreign presidents and other world leaders, including Tony Blair, model Naomi Campbell, creepy actor Kevin Spacey, Chris Tucker, Courtney Love, David Blaine, Alec Baldwin, and Barbara Walters. The wild orgies begin on the plane, which is kitted out with padded floors, and a bedroom. So, Epstein used his plane to fly underage girls between his residences in New York, Palm Beach, New Mexico, and the Caribbean island of Little St James.

Paedo Island notably had a blue and white temple with a gold dome, which suggests rituals took place there. Apparently, the walls are soundproof, and people were locked in from the outside. Kid's skulls and bones were found in waters around Orgy Island.

Hundreds of underage girls have been abused at Epstein's 'parties'. Roberts claimed Epstein recruited her as a 'sex slave' when she was 15. She said Epstein and Robert Maxwell (media mogul) trained her in sexual techniques, which was 'every day and like going to school'. They told her to describe the sexual events she had with the men she was pimped out to, so they could potentially blackmail them. She states Epstein and Maxwell got girls for Epstein's friends and acquaintances, and Epstein specifically told her the reason for him doing this was so that they would 'owe' him. They would 'be in his pocket', and he would 'have something on them'. Epstein's residences were kitted out with cameras to collect evidence aka ammunition. But moreover, as David Icke asserts, Epstein and Maxwell were Mossad agents.

As it transpired, Epstein was 'suicided' in Manhattan prison (hanging is impossible as the ceilings are too low), when more paedo and sex trafficking allegations surfaced. It's understood Epstein was the tip of the iceberg and could have exposed myriad other paedos, so he had to be silenced. The cameras just happened to be malfunctioning at the time. Hence, it's also suggested he escaped and was replaced by a lookalike. Suffice to say, the lookalike ploy is old hat. Like, Hitler, Saddam Hussein, and Osama Bin Laden had their share of lookalikes. So, unlike Maxwell who was bumped off, Epstein could be out there?

It's noted, across the pond in the late 1980s, there was the White House 'call boy' prostitution ring scandal. The Washington Times reported Craig Spence, Republican lobbyist, was a customer of a gay escort service and he arranged midnight tours of the White House for them. The newspaper said he spent as much as $20,000 a month on the service. However, apparently Spence worked with the CIA to blackmail politicians etc. He filmed them at his residency where the 'parties' took place. As it transpired, Spence 'committed suicide' in a Boston hotel, dressed in his tuxedo. Spence told a friend, 'I may be disappearing soon, it will be sudden. It may appear to be a suicide, but it won't be'.

But further, this operation tied into the Franklin Cover up. Thus, Larry King was the manager of Franklin Credit Union, which he stole $40 million from, and he procured kids for his elite buds from a Catholic orphanage for boys in Nebraska. Many of the children were flown to Washington DC for sex parties, which took place at King's condo and Spence's house. King was known for chartering private jets and having extravagant parties. He was also known for his devil worshipping cult, which included ritual sacrifice and cannibalism of children. It seems Larry King was the US equivalent of Jimmy Savile?

In 1998 several of King's victims came forward. They claimed King took them to lavish parties, where they were sexually abused by key officials of the Reagan and Bush administrations, military officers, congressional aides and US and foreign businessmen with close ties to Washington's political elite. According to Paul Bonacci, one of the victims, George Bush Senior was present at several of these parties when he was Vice-President to Reagan.

Bonacci accused King of running an underage prostitution ring and victimising him from eight years old. Bonacci was one of the call boys who toured the White House at midnight. He won a $1 million lawsuit against King but apparently King never paid. A web of criminal enterprises operated by the CIA had close ties with King's sex trafficking ring e.g. drugs and arms. It's also noted, the chief investigator for the Franklin scandal, who apparently had information to blow the case wide open, died in a plane crash in 1990, and his evidence went missing. It's understood small planes are often used to bump people off. Like, JFK junior and Keith Green.

Ted Gunderson (1928-2011), ex FBI Chief, conceded the government is corrupt at the highest levels and the CIA runs the show e.g. drugs, arms and paedo rings worldwide. He confirmed the world is ruled by a satanic cult forming a powerful network and operating an international child trafficking and paedophile ring. Thus, children are sold into slavery and flown into Washington DC (and elsewhere) to be used in orgies. Like cattle, kids aged 3 to 21 are sold off at auctions. He states, they're dressed in underwear, have a tag placed around their neck with a number on it, and people bid. Apparently Bonacci attended six human auctions. They're sold from $15,000-$50,000 and then they're put on planes.

Gunderson highlighted that more than 100,000 kids go missing every year in the US. And he claims the CIA 'Finders' job is to kidnap kids, not find them. They use chloroform to knock them out and escort them to their new abode. Children are abducted or bred for sacrifices, pornography, and prostitution.

Gunderson asserts there's four million Satanists in the US (1½% of the population), and most of these are in top positions within all professions e.g. judges, athletes, law enforcement, celebrities, politicians, lawyers. He concedes the Illuminati have infiltrated all areas of society, (including the church), and points out they've achieved 90% of their goals e.g. corrupt youth through sex and drugs, control the media, destroy religions.

Gunderson has worked with victims of Satanic Ritual Abuse (SRA), and highlights their evil antics like roasting kids and eating babies. He claims four thousand ritual human sacrifices are performed in New York City every year. Besides exposing Satanists, Gunderson also pertained to other crimes on humanity, like chemtrails. He concedes we're being poisoned by this crap worldwide. He also insists 9/11 was an inside job. He claims he had documented information, 'chiselled on stone', that the FBI had advanced knowledge of 9/11 and did nothing to prevent it. He claims the whole thing was orchestrated at the highest levels of government. However, we'll get back to 9/11.

More recently, as also touched on, was the Pizza-gate paedo scandal, when wikileaks exposed John Podesta's emails in 2016. It's recalled that Marina Abramovic invited the Podesta brothers for spirit cooking dinners. So, that's haunted. Like, John Podesta's art collection is haunted. It includes paintings of semi naked and traumatised kids (with sore red bums), and kids floating dead in a swimming pool.

This satanic sex child trafficking ring again involved the most powerful people i.e. top politicians, intelligence, lobbyists. It centred on Comet Ping Pong, a pizzeria and concert venue in Washington DC. They used code words in their emails, like, hotdog is boy, pizza is girl, pasta is little boy, cheese is little girl, walnut is coloured kid, sauce is orgy, pillows are drugs, and map is semen. It's like we use code words when buying illegal drugs. One of the emails stated that Obama spent $65,000 flying in pizza/dogs from Chicago for a private fund raiser at the White House. Another email by John Podesta stated, 'would love to get a pizza for an hour'. James Alefantis, owner of Comet, also had suspect material on his social media sites e.g. references to 'chicken lovers' which refers to men who like boys, and disturbing photos of young children.

It also seems pertinent to note, Ronald Bernard, an elite Dutch banker who exposed the Illuminati. He explains how he surreptitiously ran the central banks, which included crashing the Italian economy and bankrupting companies, which led to suicides and anarchy. But moreover, he claims the cabal uses child sacrifice to test and blackmail its members, including politicians around the world. Like, he was asked to sacrifice a child at a satanic party, but he couldn't. After this, he quit and blew the whistle. He highlights that Luciferians have been doing this for thousands of years. He states, 'I realised there was more to life than meets the eye. There is a whole invisible world. It is real'. He was subsequently bumped off at 61 years young.

So, there's abusing kids and teenagers, but then there's eating them (so called paedovores) and drinking their blood. Fiona Barnett, who was a victim of a VIP paedo sex-trafficking ring in Australia, reported the satanic horrors she experienced. Like, at a black mass ceremony, held in a Bathurst City Hall in 1985, a fully pregnant breeder and her unborn baby were ritually murdered on stage. Breeders are women who are forced to breed unregistered babies for sacrifice and sex trafficking.

The congregation chanted 'Hail Satan, Lucifer, Son of the Morning'. Apparently, the woman was screaming and had to be pinned down. Barnett highlights that often victims are under mind control i.e. hypnotised or drugged, but this woman was fully conscious. The woman was cut from her chest to her pelvic bone, using a ceremonial dagger. Barnett states, 'blood was pissing out everywhere like a waterfall', and they pulled the baby out. They used a chalice to collect the baby's blood, and chopped the baby up, placing it on a gold platter. This was passed round for Holy Communion. Barnett states Catholic mass is the sanitised version of black mass.

Barnett further informs that ten children (aged 8-10 years old) were lined up on stage, to face the audience. The children were hypnotised, so they simply stood there staring forward. Then one of the leaders went behind each child and decapitated them with a samurai sword. She recalls how each kid fell. Those present were apparently very sexually aroused by this (innocent bloodshed). Then the leader took one of the heads to Barnett and sternly said, 'take ye eat'. She was made to take a bite out of the face. Barnett claims the whole sordid event ended in a paedophile orgy, in which she was gang raped, including by Rosalind Croucher (Australian Human Rights Commissioner), who urinated in her mouth.

Barnett claims she was trafficked to international VIPs both within Australia and overseas. Like, she was trafficked to California on a cargo plane. She was put in a crate like an animal and gassed. She was then taken to Bohemian Grove, as we'll get to.

In addition to prime ministers, high ranking police and judiciary, this ring involved elements of the Australian military, and actress Nicole Kidman's father, Anthony Kidman (psychologist and academic). Barnett claims he presided over a ritual murder of a young boy in Sydney's University's Great Hall. Nicole Kidman, who was eleven years old, was sitting in the front row. Apparently, Anthony Kidman was in the Ninth Circle. It seems these satanic events are Ninth Circle ceremonies?

Barnett concedes that Luciferian paedophiles have infiltrated all areas of Australian government, education, police, media, universities, defence forces, politics, schools, health services, churches, psychiatric hospitals. And like drug trafficking, global child trafficking 'is run as a single coordinated operation through the CIA in collaboration with the British and Australian Intelligence Services'. She also advised that Jesuits are Luciferians who practice ritual murder and child rape, and an increasing number of Australian politicians are Jesuits.

Barnett concurs that Luciferianism is arranged according to a hierarchal structure which vaguely resembles a caste system. At the very top sit 13 family dynasties including the Rothschild's and the British Royal Family.

She states these families are recognised by the cult as demigods. Below them sit approximately 300 Luciferian bloodlines who are generally high IQ, although this tends to be watered down in some families due to intermarriage.

Below this group sit the commoners who can never attain higher status because they lack the desired bloodline. They're from random covens, referred to as 'coven scum'. Barnett states it is from these lines that the cult obtains 'breeders'. Barnett claims she stems from one of the 300 bloodlines via her biological paternal grandparents.

So, people are born into this. Like, the beloved royals? Indeed, Barnett claims she witnessed the British Monarchy engage in Luciferian ritual crimes in 1980 at St James Anglican church in Sydney City. Other witnesses to Ninth Circle ceremonies have also confirmed the presence of British Royal Family members Mountbatten and Prince Phillip.

Barnett highlights the number one rule of Luciferianism is 'there is no such thing as Luciferianism'. She was taught this lesson at six years old. Thus, she was taken into a national park, and witnessed a man (who was a traitor) have his limbs tied to different vehicles, which drove at high speed in opposite directions. It seems the masons carry out their threats?

So, mind control is part of the script. As touched on, Satanic Ritual Abuse (SRA) creates DID. Like, raping small children, for example, causes them to dissociate. Or like, forcing them to sacrifice an infant or animal, or putting them into a box/coffin with snakes and spiders, and shutting the lid down. The trauma fractures the mind, which creates different independently programmable personalities. Like, they can be programmed to be a 'sex kitten'. As discussed, programmers trigger various personalities using certain codes (phrases, words and gestures). People are also programmed with particular tasks e.g. drug mule or assassination.

Wheeler concedes that alters are accessed through a specific code, and having done whatever task, electroshock wiped out the memory of the operation. But she states this must take place within 48 hours (as mentioned, ECT wipes memories). It's promulgated that lone shooters are often mind control slaves. Like, Sirhan Sirhan was under mind control.

And it's believed that Princess Diana's chauffeur, who crashed in the tunnel in Paris (into the 13th pillar), was a victim of mind control. It's understood the protracted time in the tunnel enabled them to set up their 'evidence', and finish off Moon Goddess Diana? David Icke provides compelling information that suggests a ritual took place in that tunnel. Conveniently all the cameras weren't working.

It's noted, that Springmeier worked with Wheeler, who claims she was a mind control slave of the Illuminati, to deprogram her and help integrate her shattered personality. Wheeler said her father forced her into military mind control programs, and she was finally freed when he died aged forty. Apparently, he was a master programmer of mind control and (at least) a 33rd degree mason.

Wheeler concedes that 'mind magicians' split minds (to create DID) when infants are eighteen months to three years old through sex abuse, drugs, hypnosis, fear, torture (e.g. put in cages, starved etc), high level demonology, isolation, lies, massive amounts of electric shocks, and other methods of control, which are used to the hilt. Wheeler states she practiced Satanism and that as a small child she was groomed to sexually service the elite within the illuminati. As mentioned, those high up in the military sexually abuse their kids, as part of 'trauma-based mind control'.

It's understood the family have always been privy to this 'art'. That is, sodomising infants to fracture their minds, and awaken the kundalini. As mentioned, the abuser also absorbs the kundalini serpent 'energy' through this satanic act. Sodomy is also called the 'fountain of youth' as it purportedly transfers the child's youth to the abusing adults.

As Springmeier wrote, 'Long ago in the dark unwritten pages of human history, powerful kings discovered how they could control other men by torture, magical practices, wars, politics, religion and interest taking. These elite families designed strategies and tactics to perpetuate their occult practices'.

The Egyptian Book of the Dead, written by Thoth, is one of the earliest writings detailing the rituals and methods of torture, use of drugs, and casting of spells, to create mind slaves. It's understood demons can be attached to alters, which gives the person superpowers. Like Hitler, who Springmeier claims was a 'multiple'. As mentioned, a Christian therapist I know, having worked with DID and demonism, conceded that demons can be attached to alters. And Russ Dizdar refers to non-human enhanced people.

Dr Rebecca Brown states, 'ritualistic child abuse' is always to place demons within a child, to control them. She asserts, 'rape and violent sexual assault, particularly in children, is a doorway for the strongest of demons'. And incest within a family always leads to demonic infestation. Incest is literally haunted. It's like sodomy?

Apparently, all members of the Illuminati are subjected to trauma-based mind control, and they all have DID. Thus, perhaps we could feel sorry for these psychos who worship Satan? They're cracked from the start. Barnett states Luciferian offspring are trained in witchcraft, astral projection, and psychic manipulation of physical elements. As discussed, OBEs can arise from trauma, and often people develop psychic powers. OBEs are a way to develop inter-dimensional awareness. Like, kids can subsequently master astral projection. They're 'enlightened'. Kids are apparently dedicated to Lucifer at three years old (like Doc Marquis).

So, the family has been doing this forever. The creation of multiples goes back to antiquity, as part of their rituals. It's also purported that whilst we can all dissociate to some extent, apparently not everyone can dissociate and have multiple personalities. But rather this ability is inherited. Like, children of multi-generational abuse have a well developed ability to dissociate. Springmeier further states that only Illuminati (elite) bloodlines could survive the trauma necessary to fracture the mind into alters (most 'normal' kids die). Thus, occult families would breed with other occult families. It's noted, whilst families are born with this ability, it needs to be triggered i.e. through trauma.

This ability to dissociate is likened to Monarch butterflies who inherit memories to migrate. Monarch butterflies fly from Canada to Mexico for winter, which takes three generations to make the journey. It's said their parents learned this script and passed it onto their offspring, so called epigenetic memories. It seems the CIA was inspired by the Monarch butterfly, as they named one of their mind control programs Project Monarch.

As discussed, Hitler and the Nazis began mind control experiments on POW during WW2. Dr Mengele turned mind control into a science, with refined mind control techniques. This information then crossed the pond under Operation Paperclip, and was absorbed by the CIA into MK Ultra programmes. We were told the project ended, yet DID is rampant?

Springmeier concedes the main method of mind control used by the Illuminati is Monarch Mind Control, an offshoot (perfected version) of MK Ultra. The programming experience is likened to a caterpillar being reborn a butterfly. The dissociating (switching) between alters is like the fluttering of wings. The monarch butterfly is the international symbol for trauma-based mind control.

So, their horrific experiments paid off. The 'science' has been perfected and can be used on a much larger scale. Whilst splitting minds was best before five years old, alters can be created in adults with their sophisticated technology e.g. drugs and electronic frequencies. Thus, beyond military application, mind control is used on celebrities, athletes, news/weather anchors, politicians, cops, and even taxi drivers. And we would never know, because unless glitches happen, they go completely undetected.

According to Springmeier, there's at least two million active mind-controlled slaves in the US. Dizdar however claims there's at least ten million and forty million worldwide. Dizdar concedes the CIA has been embroiled with mind control since Project Paperclip, which he highlights is over four generations. He asserts this accounts for the explosion of DID in the US. He also highlights that often alters speak in German (Joseph Mengele's legacy).

So, as Max Spiers asserts, MK Ultra didn't begin at WW2, but five thousand years ago, as detailed in the Book of the Dead. As mentioned, Spiers was bumped off for exposing 'conspiracies'. He understood that raping children results in kundalini. He claims he was born into a specific bloodline and was a victim of mind control. But we'll get back to Spiers.

Barnett concedes that trauma-based mind control to create DID is a Luciferian tradition that stems back millennia. She states children are tested at age three to ascertain whether they should be raised with conscious or dissociated awareness of their cult involvement. She states children with a strong ethical objection to cult practices are never made aware of their involvement. These children are forced to dissociate through trauma, and their minds fragmented. Besides the aforementioned practices, Barnett states children are programmed using LSD trips in a sensory deprivation tank.

Barnett explains her memory of cult activities were mostly dissociated from her everyday thinking. But some awareness slipped through i.e. PTSD flashbacks. Like, she recalled that she had been suffocating during an Egyptian rebirth ritual in which she was placed in a grave over a decomposed body, while the Book of the Dead was chanted. She claims she died, was revived, and awoke in hospital.

As it transpired, Barnett's memories of Luciferianism flooded her conscious mind after her paedophile step-grandfather, Peter Holowczak, was found hanged to death at Easter in 1991. She testified before the Child Abuse Royal Commission about her experiences as a victim of an international child sex trafficking ring in 2013. Apparently, Anthony Kidman topped himself after her disclosure.

Barnett also pertains to the link between Luciferianism and the CIA's project MK Ultra. She claims she was subjected to MK Ultra procedures on the campus of Sydney University. She states child victims are sourced from Luciferian covens, various cults, Catholic churches and Hillsong church (founded by paedophile Frank Houston), children's homes, child prostitution brothels, and blackmailed paedophile parents. It's noted, that Hillsong Church seems to be operating under the false Holy Spirit aka kundalini, as we'll get to.

Other children were specifically bred to serve as human lab rats, their births unregistered. She states children were imprisoned in cages and never seen daylight. Children were raped, tortured, and murdered in the name of national security. Gunderson concedes the Illuminati take kids from covens to create mind control victims.

Cathy O'Brien was another victim of CIA mind control. In her case, her dad got caught sending child porn through the post (a film of young Cathy having sex with a boxer dog). To avoid prosecution, Cathy was handed over to the US Government and the Defense Intelligence Agency. Apparently, they were looking for sexually abused kids with DID, and even better that Cathy had blonde hair and blue eyes.

In her book 'Trance Formation of America' (1995), Cathy O'Brien exposed the satanic antics of Father George H W Bush, the Clintons, Dick Cheney and various others, who she claims raped and tortured her, and her daughter Kelly. Cathy and Kelly witnessed and were forced to partake in human sacrifice and cannibalism (people were dressed in black robes, candles lit etc). They were mind controlled sex-slaves of the US Defence Intelligence CIA MK Ultra Project. Cathy states Kelly's primary abuser was Father George Bush.

As mentioned, people are programmed with various tasks. And there's different programming levels e.g. Alpha, Beta, Delta, Omega and Theta, which correspond to brainwaves. Mind control victims are also programmed to commit suicide, should someone attempt to deprogram them, or if their programming breaks down. Wheeler states she had Beta and Delta alters. Beta is 'sex kitten' programming, and Delta is 'assassination' programming. Delta was originally developed for training special agents or elite soldiers.

Barnett claims she was recruited into Delta special operations, which includes psychic warfare training i.e. harnessing psychic ability. She was put through full military training at age 6 and assigned to a small unit of all male soldiers. Her training was completed in the USA at age 14, by renowned Satanist Lieutenant Colonel Michael Aquino, at Dulce underground base (which we'll get back to). It appears the family are building an army of super-soldiers, which includes non-human enhanced super-soldiers.

It seems pertinent to note Aquino, because he was high up in both the military and Satanism. He was a military intelligence officer specialising in psychological warfare, including MK Ultra mind control. And he was a high-ranking Satanist in Anthon La-Vey's Church of Satan, before he split and founded the Temple of Set in 1975.

Aquino claimed he performed a ritual to invoke Satan, and Satan revealed to him a sacred text, which Aquino channelled, that his name is actually Set. So, Set is the one real god, who's like a teacher, as we can become god. The endeavour is self-deification and immortality of consciousness. It incorporates the Egyptian mysteries and Hermeticism into its ritual and doctrine. 'Setians' know black magic is real and can be manipulated through rituals. Following initiations into the Temple, Setians proceed with six degrees. Aquino was apparently fascinated with the connections between occultism and Nazism.

Aquino has been repeatedly accused of SRA by numerous victims over the decades. He's renowned for child abuse, paedo rings, child sex slavery, torture, and psychological human experimentation. More than fifty kids claimed Aquino sexually abused them. Bonacci identified Aquino as an associate of Larry King. According to Cathy O'Brien, Aquino programmed her and Kelly using barbaric trauma techniques that involved NASA technology. NASA has sophisticated electronic and mind control devices, which includes implanting false ('script') memories, as we'll get back to.

Cathy also states she was programmed at Salt Lake City, Mormon Church HQ in Utah, which is another centre for mind control. As mentioned, some seriously disturbing events allegedly take place there (like reptilian humanoids gorging on human flesh). Cathy also states the boys at Boys Town in Nebraska were victims of project Monarch. They were traumatised and sexually abused by the Catholic Church.

Cathy concedes Project Monarch is a top-secret high mind-control conditioning facility for 'behavioural modification' programming through trauma-based mind control. She states mind-controlled slaves receive severe trauma to ensure compartmentalisation of memories i.e. physical and psychological trauma; sleep, food and water deprivation; high voltage electric shocks; and hypnotic and/or harmonic programming of specific memory compartments/personalities. Cathy concurs they can program the body to self-destruct (e.g. go into respiratory failure) if programming breaks down.

Cathy described being totally robotic, having no ability to question, or reason, or consciously comprehend what she was involved in. She could only do exactly what she was told to do. Like, sexually service the elite, smuggle drugs, and deliver messages. Mind control slaves are notably sold at auctions.

Cathy informs that her CIA operative mind control handler was her husband Alex Houston, and her 'owner' (and first handler) was US Senator Robert C Byrd. As mentioned, 'handlers' make sure the person performs as programmed i.e. using triggers and anchors etc. Cathy said Byrd controlled a network of mind-controlled slaves and loved nothing more than whipping them mercilessly until they were close to death' (cited in Icke, 2007 p.480).

However, as it transpired, Mark Phillip (former CIA operative and co-author of 'Trance Formation of America') rescued Cathy and Kelly in 1998. Phillip notably claimed he seen a photo of Houston, stating, 'He was smiling a demonic grin while apparently having sex with a small, very young, frightened black boy' (p.12). The boy was Haitian. It's noted, NGOs are 'fronts' for smuggling kids. Like, 'The Clinton Foundation' helped Haiti or rather they helped themselves to Haitian kids? It appears vulnerable kids are another bonus of wars and disasters. Like, Syrian kid's organs are harvested in Turkish hospitals.

When in protection (i.e. with Mark Philip), and when her memories began coming back, she felt enraged and compelled to disclosure. Thus, Cathy claims she was forced into porn, bestiality, and S&M, from childhood. And she was ritually impregnated many times and artificially aborted so the foeti could be used for occult practices.

One of her many rapists included Hillary Clinton. In her experience, both Bill and Hillary were bisexual, but they were much more homosexual. Hence, she received much more Hillary than Bill. She would be ordered to eat her. She recalls that Hillary had the goat of Mendes traced on her pubic hair. And that she got sexually aroused by Cathy's mutilated vagina. Cathy, a White House Pentagon lover, has a face carved into her vagina. Apparently, abusers mark their own. Branding also shows they're 'clean' and good to be passed round in circles. Sharing is caring in the family.

Cathy states wearing diamonds indicates presidential model status. Like, butterflies symbolise Monarch mind control. Cathy also informs that Ronald Reagan aka 'Uncle Ronnie' loved bestiality porn. And that both her and Kelly were forced to have sex with animals to make dirty movies for him, so called 'Uncle Ronnie's Bedtime Stories'.

Cathy also describes 'A Most Dangerous Game', which is human hunting. It appears these sadistic freaks play 'cat and mouse' with people. They strip their victims naked and turn them loose into the wilderness, only to hunt them down with dogs. Mind controlled adults and children are forewarned about the horrendous consequences should they get caught in 'the hunt' e.g. brutal rape and murder. They are then loosed into the wilderness (i.e. top-secret military base, retreat/compound), only to get hunted down with these threats carried out.

Cathy states she was stripped down to her tennis shoes, and was given a head start, before getting hunted down. And yet she knew there was nowhere to run or hide. But moreover, according to Cathy, George boy Bush was a mind-controlled victim, and he was also hunted in 'The Most Dangerous Game'. She states he was a puppet of his father and Dick Cheney. Dick Cheney was apparently addicted to the 'thrill of the sport'.

It's noted, the victim's terror gives the hunter his desired blood full of adrenalin. Terrorised blood is full of adrenochrome, which is produced when adrenaline oxidises. It has psychoactive properties and produces a potent high. Hence, these sadists torture their victims before they kill them. Sometimes they skin them because it takes longer. David Icke explains the fear-induced hormone is like LSD, and they're seeking to activate inter-dimensional communication through the pineal gland (third eye). Like, apparently Hitler took mescaline and peyote to enhance his connection with the spirit world. It's said that adrenochrome makes mescaline look like ginger beer. Thus, they take a trip to see Lucy in the Sky. Barnett also states, adrenochrome sexually arouses them.

It's notably alleged that former US Vice President Al Gore was apprehended at an airport with a suitcase full of vials of adrenochrome-laden blood. It's said that high level bureaucrats and VIPS always ensure they have a stash. Apparently, Wuhan in China sells and produces adrenochrome. As mentioned, drinking young blood explains longevity (e.g. the Queen Mother lived to 102), and they don't get dementia etc. It's also noted, that Al Gore is family. Hence, he took on Cousin George W Bush for presidency, before the election between cousins Bush and Kerry.

Cathy notably said she heard Father Bush and Bill Clinton speaking in 1984, stating that Clinton would be president when the US public got sick of Republicans. It's the same in the UK i.e. conservative are crap so we vote Labour, and vice versa. And so it continues, under the illusion of democracy.

Barnett also pertained to human hunting. She states she was dressed up as a teddy bear whilst hunted for sport at the annual camp at 'The Bohemian Grove'. Bohemian Grove is notably a massive (2,700 acre) secluded redwood forest in California. She states they love getting kids to dress up as teddy bears and hunting them in the dark in the forest. She claims President Richard Nixon was there, who previously raped her so violently she needed stitched, and beloved Billy Graham, who she claims also raped her. Apparently, Graham liked to rape kids when they were knocked out, so he had a modicum of decency?

Bohemian Grove belongs to a San Francisco men's art club known as the Bohemian Club, founded in 1873. It's understood the members of this private men's club, (known as Boho's or Grover's), are partial to the log-cutter (LOL). Every year, mid-July, the Bohemian Grove hosts a two week holiday for the most powerful men of the world. For those who make the big (global) decisions, that shape our history. It's dubbed the 'Illuminati summer camp'.

The membership list has included every Republican and some Democratic US presidents since 1923, as well as cabinet officials, directors, CEOs of large corporations including major financial institutions, major military contractors, oil companies, banks (including the Federal Reserve), utilities (including nuclear power) and national media (broadcast and print). Members may invite guests (like their sex-slaves) but they're subject to a screening process.

Despite the club's motto, namely, 'Weaving Spiders Come not here', which implies all play and no work, they nevertheless give speeches and have super-secret talks. Like, the Manhattan Project planning (regarding the atomic bomb) took place there in 1942. It's understood that besides the jollies, Bohemian Grove is a think tank. Like, it's said Jimmy Carter and Ronald Reagan were selected to be presidents there. It's also understood, that when Reagan was president, the real president was Father George Bush. Like, when Clinton was president, it was really Father Bush. Apparently, Father Bush was high up in the power structure, unlike his gimp son.

Cathy concedes that mind-slaves are forced to serve the perversions of their abusers at 'Bohemian Grove'. She advised that Bohemian Grove caters for all kinds of perversions and has a number of rooms' to accommodate these e.g. a dark room, a necrophilia room, leather room. She wrote, 'I was used as a 'rag doll' in the 'toy store', and as a urinal in the 'golden arches' room' (p.171).

Cathy states slaves of advancing age are sacrificially murdered in Bohemian Grove (slaves older than thirty), and also if their programming malfunctions. She claims there's lots of murders at Bohemian Grove. Paul Bonacci also witnessed the murder of a young boy in Bohemian Grove in the summer of 1984. He notably claimed that Cathy's 'husband' Alex Houston was one of his abusers at Boy's Town in Nebraska.

Regarding his time at Bohemian Grove, Bonacci stated that he and another boy, Nicholas, were forced to have sex with a young boy, who was naked and crying in a cage. Everything was filmed, (for horrific porn). Besides the film crew, another man came and battered them all. Bonacci and Nicholas were then put in the cage, and the rapist dragged the kid around, (who's rectum was bleeding), while having sex with him.

Bonacci states the rapist was tossing the kid around like a sack of potatoes, slamming him all over the place. He then put the kid beside the cage and began kicking him in the face, before shooting him in the head. Bonacci said, 'he blew the boy's head off'. Both Bonacci and Nicholas were then forced to have sex with the dead boy. Apparently, they were also told to eat the testes off the dead kid.

The word on the streets is the big fat rich cats come to town and get thoroughly loaded. They run about naked, have orgies, and freak out. Apparently, some top officials like to dress up as women. As 'conspiracy theorist' and radio host Alex Jones said, 'it's like a big kid's fraternity' and they 'get off in a sick way'. Herbert Hoover (31st US president), proud member of the Skull and Bones Society, described Bohemian Grove as 'the greatest men's party on Earth'. And Nixon once famously described this elite and presidential retreat as, 'the most faggy G-ddamned thing you could ever imagine' (LOL).

Whilst some two thousand people attend, apparently it's only the most elite who partake in the human sacrifice rituals, and abuse mind-controlled women and children. Signs around the encampment are written in Latin and other ancient languages. And in addition to the death imagery, like skulls etc, there's owl symbolism, which includes a massive forty+ foot stone owl. Whilst it's said it represents Molech (the god of child sacrifice), Everard states it represents Minerva, from the Bavarian Illuminati.

In terms of idolatry (i.e. statues created for gods to occupy), we can but wonder what spiritual entities are tucked up inside that oversized owl. Apparently Semiramis was renowned for loving owls and the owl was her symbol. The White House is notably encircled with owls. Within witchcraft the owl is generally referred to as the sorcerer's bud. But moreover, according to Everard, Bohemian Grove has a real authentic Egyptian mummy, which is 5000 years old, (in their offices), who is none other than Lady Isis. No danger.

Furthermore, despite the heavy surveillance ('Men in Black' suits chase people away), Alex Jones managed to sneak in, in June 2000, and filmed the 'Cremation of Care' ceremony. Or he was allowed in? This is a ritual performance (dramatic play) centring on ancient Canaanite, Luciferian, and Babylon mystery religion. These rituals have been taking place for over 130 years. Apparently the 'cremation of care' cremates cares and purges members of their guilt. They're cleared of their diabolical crimes.

The ceremony takes place beside the big stone owl, which is where the stage and altar is. Thus, music is played, men wear hooded robes and hold flaming torches, say incantations and hail yak yak yak. And after that nonsense, they burn an effigy of a human being before the owl. Many believe a real child is contained within the effigy. All applaud and fireworks go off. Apparently Bohemian Grove put on a special show for the Queen and Prince Phillip when they visited their HQ.

The VIPs who attend insist they're revering the Redwoods, and at most allude to druid rituals. However, as Wheeler (2009) asserts, druidism is not a benign worship of nature, but rather leads people into demonism. Druids are known for burning people after having ripped out their heart or slit their throat. This is supposedly where bonfire stems from, bone-fire, burning people's bones (apparently their ashes were kept for later rituals). Besides human sacrifice, druids roast animals to watch their pain. Apparently high wizards put spells on people at Bohemian Grove. Satan blesses his people for their sacrifices and rewards them with success.

Another CIA mind control victim and 'presidential model' is Brice Taylor (see her book 'Thanks For The Memories...The Truth Has Set Me Free', 1999). Taylor claims she was sexually and satanically ritually abused from birth, and pimped out to project Monarch by her paedo father. She states she was put through a trial of satanic blood rituals as a child, where she witnessed animal and human sacrifices.

As a sex slave, she was prostituted and forced to make porn, including bestiality. She claims many animals were used over the years, including dolphins. She also had sex with her daughter Kelly[28]. Apparently one of the porn films they made, when Kelly was a very little girl, was called 'Mommy and I'. She was also hunted by Father George Bush on Bob Hope's ranch in 'The Most Dangerous Game'. Comedian Bob Hope was her owner/handler.

Brice claims her abusers include JFK, Lyndon Johnson, Nelson Rockefeller, Henry Kissinger, Gerald Ford, Jimmy Carter, Ronald Reagan, and Father George Bush. Besides being a sex slave, she claims she was a message and drug courier for every president from Kennedy to Clinton. And she was Henry Kissinger's personal secretary/ human computer (file storage and retrieval) for over 19 years. Mind controlled slaves have an immense memory, like 44x better than normal.

Brice also names people she was prostituted to in the entertainment industry. Like, Frank Sinatra, who was a violent and sadistic handler, Elvis Presley, Dean Martin, Bing Crosby, and Satanist Sammy Davis Jnr. She also alleges actress Barbara Streisand is an MK Ultra Monarch mind controlled sex slave. But the list goes on.

It's also noted, that both 'celebrities' and politicians are part of the royal family. Like, Hillary Clinton is cousins with Madonna and Angelina Jolie. And Ellen DeGeneres is related to Kate Middleton and Halle Berry. And Berry (who has six toes on one foot) is related to Sarah Palin, who is cousins with Barack Obama. And Oprah is distant cousins with Elvis Presley. And Beyonce, Johnny Depp, and Larry David are cousins of the royal

---

[28] David Icke (2007) states, 'Kelly appears to be a significant to these people for some reason. I have met other recovering mind-slaves with daughters of that name' (p.489). I found this interesting with regards to the woman Kelly I met in my 'active imagination'.

bloodline. And Madonna and Celine Dion are related to Camilla Parker Bowles. And Nicky Hilton married into the Rothschild's. And Tom Hanks is related to the Lincolns.

As it transpired, Brice started 'remembering' in 1985 following a car accident, where she sustained serious head trauma. However, apparently it wasn't really an accident, but rather the result of mind control programming which compelled her to commit suicide if she began to recover critical memories about her role as a top CIA controlled 'asset'. She states her memories began to return in sporadic fragments. It took her a decade to integrate her shattered memories and recover from DID. Gunderson states Taylor's story has been confirmed over and over again.

Apparently, Marilyn Monroe was the first mind-controlled 'presidential model' sex kitten (slave) the Illuminati made public. But diamond clad Monroe had to be taken out. It seems Munroe became unpredictable and knew too much. Like Princess Diana, who was also allegedly a victim of mind control. Apparently most, if not all, Playboy bunnies are MK Ultra sex kittens. It's noted, the CIA set up playboy bunnies with Hugh Hefner, to create a honey trap.

As it transpires, the CIA has an entire department dedicated to the entertainment industry. Indeed, it's said Hollywood is a branch of the CIA. The CIA finances and collaborates with filmmakers to influence our perception. Like, Disney was hired by the US government to produce propaganda films. Apparently, Walt Disney (1901-1966) was an FBI agent. Like, we're currently being brainwashed with alien movies, because they want the masses to believe in aliens?

Joseph Goebbels, minister of propaganda for the Nazis, said 'Cinema is one of the most modern means of mass persuasion. Film is one of the most modern and far reaching means for influencing the public that has ever existed'. And Richard Nixon said, 'The American people don't believe anything until they see it on television'. [LOL]. Like, watching the moon landing?

It's understood Stanley Kubrick directed the moon landing hoax. And he wanted to divulge the truth about Apollo 11, hence the clues featured in his movie 'The Shining'? Or they have to tell us at some clandestine level? It's noted, that Kubrick's last movie 'Eyes Wide Shut', gives us some insight regarding their satanic orgies. He died before this film was released, and some (incriminating?) twenty minutes were cut.

Jordan Maxwell ('conspiracy theorist') notably points out that Hollywood comes from the Holly Tree that druids and wizards made their magic wands from. He states Hollywood movies cast spells on the masses. We embody the narratives and scripts we've been given. We think the way we've been programmed to think. We get 'programmes' like 'Pop Idol'. Thus, the herd are mind controlled at the most basic level. This includes being distracted by crap like following gimps on Instagram. And many of these celebrities are actually gimps. They're victims of mind control.

As mentioned, the Tavistock Institute introduced 'rock and roll', and promoted bands like the Beatles and the Rolling Stones, to influence our perception. The plebs were given idols to lionize. But moreover, it's purported that military intelligence parents put their kids into MK Ultra type programmes. Apparently, the parents were rewarded for their patriotism. It's said the kid's minds were fractured to create DID and they became 'stars'. Like, the Doors, Monkeys, Mamas and Papas, Byrds, Eagles, Crosby Nash and Stills. Jim Morrison's dad was notably an intelligence officer involved in the Gulf of Tonkin false flag. As mentioned, these bands were not organic creations but rather intelligence operations. They were rigged to be successful.

As also discussed, music is a particularly effective method of mind control for the masses. Hence, radio stations play the same songs continuously until we learn to like them. Crap repetitive music is pushed on us. We're unwittingly brainwashed with mindsets, lest we forget the back-masking in songs. It's noted, Lucifer was in charge of worship back in the day. Ergo, he knows how to make spell-bounding music (like the Doors). And also, musicians channel spirits to write/create music etc. It's understood the entertainment and music industry is run by Luciferians. Like, it's said Meryl Streep is a high witch, and George Lucas and Steven Spielberg are high up in the chain of command.

So, besides the notorious casting couch, it's said the entertainment industry is filled with Monarch mind control slaves, which coincides with the rampant paedophilia? Like, Rosanne Barr, American comedian/actress, famously highlighted on a Russia Today interview, 'MK Ultra rules in Hollywood'. She maintains she was a victim of mind control and had DID. Like, it's purported the Jacksons were ritually abused. Perhaps we could feel sorry for paedo Michael? And Mariah Carey's older sister divulged that she was a victim of SRA. She reports about men in hooded robes drinking blood etc. It's noted, Mariah Carey is a big fan of butterflies (like many popstars).

But moreover, Disney was part of the CIA's MK Ultra program. Disney was built to be a theme park and for mind control. It's noted, that 666 features in the 'Walt Disney' logo. Apparently, Walt was a 33rd degree mason, which presumably inspired his exclusive 'Club 33' for the elite. Club 33 is located at 33 Royal Street in Disneyland, which is located on the 33rd parallel north. It's reminiscent of a Masonic lodge, complete with black and white chequered flooring, and Jakin and Boaz columns. It has an invitation-only membership, a 14 year waiting list, and a $100K initiation fee.

Numerous MK Ultra victims claim they were programmed with Disney movies e.g. 'Alice in Wonderland' and 'The Wizard of Oz'. Cathy O'Brien states she was repeatedly shown the 'Wizard of Oz' as a child, and referred to Disneyland as the 'epicentre of MK Ultra programming'. Imagery and theme parks play a central role in their programming. As discussed, scripts from movies and books etc are used as mind programming tools. Symbols and meanings in the movie become triggers in the slave's mind. Handlers use phrases to trigger particular personalities.

Barnett concedes that mind control programmes contain lots of Disney themes, and when someone plays the movies, or they're taken to theme parks, it reinforces their programming i.e. keeps it active. Barnett states virtual reality simulations are used in programming, which immersive rides enhance. Another popular mind control movie (unsurprisingly) is 'Peter Pan'. These movies have parallel worlds to escape into. Like, victims can go 'somewhere over the rainbow' when inflicted with unbearable pain. They dissociate and go to their 'happy place'. 'Going beyond the yellow brick road' is apparently slang for dissociating during times of extreme trauma.

Barnett claims paedo parties and programming takes place after hours. It's well known there's a network of secret tunnels underground, where Disney spent most of his time. Brice also said she was taken to Disneyland, and Springmeier concurs that lots of programming takes place at Disneyworld and Disneyland. Suffice to say, taking LSD at Disneyworld would be a trip. And in the dark?

So, their sense of reality is shattered regarding what's real and fantasy, and victims are deliberately confused by having everything turned upside down i.e. they're told up is down, right is wrong, etc. Satanists, like Crowley, love the law of reversal and doing things in reverse. He said, (regarding initiates), 'let him train himself to think backwards, learn to write backwards, and learn to walk backwards, speak backwards, and read backwards'. Cathy notably states she had the ability to read forwards and backwards.

It's also highlighted that Oprah's Harpo Studio is Oprah backwards, and the Marina Abramovic Institute MAI is I AM backwards. Beloved billionaire Oprah endorses Christ Consciousness. She's one of the biggest influencers of New Age philosophy, (she promotes Tolle), and she's rewarded for her efforts. Jesus said, 'Beware of false prophets, who come to you in sheep's clothing but inwardly are ravenous wolves' (Matthew 7:15). However, I digress.

It's understood the Mickey Mouse Club is one of Disney's many projects aimed to recruit and mould stars. Which might explain Britney Spears, for example? It's rumoured she's been programmed with the sex kitten programming. And it seems her programming went awry during the infamous interview with Diane Sawyer in 2003, as Spears seemed to switch between alters? She seemed to 'malfunction' when Sawyer said the word 'spasm'.

It's said that 'malfunctions' explain famous public breakdowns, like Spears shaving her head. Whilst Spears is diagnosed with bipolar disorder, her personalities, which have been documented in newspapers and in lawsuits against her, include the 'British girl' and the 'Diva'. According to her ex-husband, Kevin Federline, she has 'a form of schizoid or multiple personality disorder'. When Spears opened up about her bipolar disorder in 2011, she stated, 'I turn into a different person'. It would appear so.

Like others with DID, Spears doesn't recollect how she behaved when in different alters. Like, on one occasion when interviewed by paparazzi about her current boyfriend, she proceeded to give them details, then after switching, she was dumbfounded by the conversation, as that personality didn't know about the fairly recent relationship. Then she switched back and identified her boyfriend. Wheeler states that victims of trauma-based mind control are often misdiagnosed, or conveniently diagnosed, by psychiatrists as having schizophrenia, schizoaffective disorder, bipolar disorder etc.

So, it seems no good can come from the Mickey Mouse Club? Captivating Britney has been used like a machine, a Trojan horse, churning out sex-kitten performances. We could feel sorry for these gimps, rather than idolise them. Other Disney productions include Justin Timberlake, Christiana Aguilera, Ryan Gosling, Amanda Bynes, Miley Cyrus, Christina Aguilera, and Lindsay Lohan.

It's noted, these all American kids become highly sexualised, which inspires the herd. Like, we prefer slutty Britney in 'Slave for You' (2001), and Christina Aguilera in 'Dirrty' (2002). Like, Miley Cyrus became a skanky virus, partial to sticking her tongue out. Perhaps she was inspired by Gene Simmons, who's renowned for sticking out his super long tongue? Or she's demonstrating her allegiance to the Hindu god Kali? This blood thirsty monster, goddess of death, who demands human sacrifice, has always got her tongue sticking out. It's also said that sticking one's tongue out represents the serpent tongue. And then, the herd stick their tongue out without knowing why? Like, people inauthentically do the V sign, and the devil horns?

As touched on, mainstream pop videos have become soft porn-esque. Like Cardi B and Nicki Minaj (who're also partial to sticking their tongues out) etc. But it gets more sinister with blatantly demonic popstars like Billie Eilish, who keeps the number of people she follows on Instagram at 666 because she likes that number. The message (for young people) is 666 is good because Eilish likes it? It seems society has been saturated with sexual content, and is ready for darker material?

As mentioned, Disney movies are packed with subliminal messages, particularly sexual. And music videos etc are the same. They're packed with symbolism e.g. Masonic chequered floors or clothing, lightning bolts, serpents, pyramids, Horus's one eye, and other Egyptian references. Besides influencing us to be skanks, they're preparing the masses for the ancient religion. As mentioned, Crowley's religion is en vogue and the family has to tell us their plans beforehand.

Like, in Madonna's apocalyptic song 'Future' performed at the Eurovision Song Contest in Israel 2019. She's telling us the future? It's noted, Madonna portrayed herself as Madame X, who has DID and wears an eye patch with an X on it (so she's one eyed). X represents the antichrist, Nimrod, hence X-mas. As mentioned, pretentious Madonna is in the cabala club. Like, cabalist Ariana Grande, who's songs include 'God is a Woman' and 'The Light is Coming'. It's noted, that at the end of Grande's crap song about God being a woman, which featured the witch Madonna as God citing Ezekiel 25:17, Grande threw a Thor-like hammer into the glass ceiling in the Cathedral, which represents the firmament?

It's said, mind control victims grow like cancer. Hence, it bleeds into all sectors of society. As discussed, people can be programmed to do whatever, like dance, sing and excel at sports. Cathy notably highlights that baseball players are programmed to win or lose games, in tandem with the mafia's bets.

However, glitches are increasingly being reported. Like, Al Roker, American journalist and weather anchor, famously froze for seventeen seconds on live TV, when the (trigger) word 'Holy Ghost' was mentioned. And freemason Shaquille O'Neal, retired professional basketball player, froze for forty seconds during live TV. And Cardi B froze briefly at the Grammys. There's suspect footage of Beyonce, Katy Perry, Lady Gaga, Eminem, Kesha, and Wendy Williams having malfunctions (and other actors, anchors etc). Like, Kanye West's infamous meltdowns. Or he has bipolar? It's noted, 'handlers' are often disguised as security.

Besides dissociating, often people's eyes look weird e.g. they uncontrollably move around, become black, or reptilian like. Perhaps this explains why so many of them wear shades indoors? It's not just because it 'looks cool' (LOL). Given the change in the appearance of the eyes, suggests there's more than DID at play i.e. demonism? David Icke alleges he seen Ted Heath's eyes turn completely black, including the whites of his eyes. He described it as like looking into two black holes. However, we'll get back to the 'Black Eyes' phenomenon.

It's said MK Ultra programming is part of the jig if someone wants fame and fortune. People don't make it big unless they sell out. They're told they need to follow the 'Yellow Brick Road' if they want success. Apparently, Elton John's hit 'Goodbye Yellow Brick Road' is about Monarch mind control. And in her not so successful song 'Love Made Me Do It', Cheryl Tweedy sang, 'I did my time on the yellow brick road, I saw some shit that'd make your head explode'. So, that's interesting?

ECT is part of the MK Ultra mind control programme, and they need to go through the occult ritual 'The Rite to Remain Silent'. Hence, the shhh sign. Those who go through the process are told to think of it as going into a cocoon. It's not pleasant but they become a butterfly. Hence, victims identify with monarch butterfly symbolism.

It's rumoured that people sell their souls. Like, John Lennon, Tu Pac, and Katy Perry, for example, said they sold their souls to the Devil. And Bob Dylan advised he made a bargain with the devil, who he called the chief commander. He said this being is on this earth, and in a world we can't see. Like, black magicians sell their soul?

Besides being used as 'influencers' to promote the Luciferian agenda, it's said aspiring 'stars' similarly prostitute themselves to the top and they're passed around. It's said the cabal decides who become stars. These hopefuls are invited to elite parties called Pandora's Box (sometimes they're masked), and they have to go through certain rituals (which includes humiliation rituals) to become initiated. They're rewarded with awards etc at 'ceremonies'.

Like, in the world of Hip Hop, it's said most of these artists get 'popped in the butt' (and it's filmed). Like, Puff Daddy and Drake? The recording deal is worth it? 'It's all gravy'? Apparently, this term is used by those who have gone through the process. And gravy is a metaphor for diarrhoea, the aftermath of being popped in the butt? It's further said they tattoo their bodies after they sign the contract, as they want to get some dignity back and feel like a man.

And we can recognise these sell-outs by their signs and symbols. Like, masons recognise each other through their cheeky sleights of hand. As Confucius said, 'Signs and symbols rule the world, not words nor laws'. Hence, popstars invariably feature butterflies, Mickey Mouse ears, Playboy Bunny ears, sex kitten attire (e.g. leopard print), stars (which represent pentagrams). Tattoos are also used to demonstrate allegiance to the 'club'. Like, back in the day, witches could identify fellow witches by stars on houses and churches etc. And now they have star tattoos, and the shhh tattoo on their pointer finger etc. And they demonstrate the Illuminati 'sign' of silence, the triple six, the covering of one eye, and the 'X' Masonic sign. It seems most of Hollyweird and the music industry identify with this BS, and the cabala? Manly P Hall said, 'When the human race learns to read the language of symbolism, a great veil will fall from the eyes of men'.

It also seems pertinent to acknowledge the footage (that was secretly filmed in 1999) of a 23 year old Angelina Jolie, describing some of what she experienced at an Illuminati (satanic) ritual. She compares the perverted rituals to S&M, stating that you have to be held down because of the pain. People are apparently tied up, raped and tortured by other members. She reassures her companions that you heal after the beating. Apparently, Illuminati members have to encourage others into the club. She regales how great the sexual freedom is, and states she has the most amazing compromising pictures of people.

But moreover, as part of the ritual, she also had to kill her snake. It's recalled the Illuminati is the Brotherhood of the Snake. She explains the ceremony is not superficial but rather 'comes from a real, real place' and it's dark. It's also noted, many Illuminati members, like Jolie, get tattoos as part of the ceremony, as a way of sacrificing more blood to Satan. They're blood-letting rituals, which can provide an entrance for demons. The Bible notably tells us (in Leviticus 19:28), 'Never cut your bodies in mourning for the dead or mark your skin with tattoos, for I am the LORD'.

On the superficial surface, Jolie is almost saint-like given her UN ambassador role? And shockers, she plays Maleficent in the Disney movie, which is more brainwashing for kids, as Maleficent is portrayed as benevolent not malevolent. The message is good is evil, and evil is good? Disney movies promote magic and witchcraft. The herd can experience magic at the magical kingdom.

And 'stars' are telling the herd about their alter egos. Like, Beyonce's alter-ego is Sasha Fierce. According to Beyonce, Sasha Fierce was born during the making of her single 'Crazy in Love'. In the video, we see the death of Beyonce in an exploding car, and the rebirth of Sasha Fierce. Sasha Fierce is notably an author of witchcraft and pagan books. Beyonce explains that fearless Sasha Fierce takes over her, comes into her, and she can't remember her performances. Beyonce considers herself quite reserved and claims she could never do what fearless Sasha Fierce does. It seems Sasha Fierce, who happens to wear Baphomet jewellery, is demonic?

It's noted, Beyonce's fourth concert tour was called 'I Am'. Beyonce aka Queen Bey and her husband (who's allegedly in the gravy gang) are considered royalty. Jay Zee calls his alter ego J-Hova, after Jehovah. As mentioned, he promotes Crowley's message 'do what thou wilt' and he's buds with the 'artist' aka witch Marina Abramovic.

Nicki Minaj also has a gay, violent and paranoid alter-ego called Roman. According to Minaj, he was conceived out of rage. She states he lives inside her, and he won't leave, despite her asking him to. She said people conjured him up and now he won't leave. Apparently, he's here for a reason. When told it's a convenient excuse to blame her alter ego for her anger, she replied he wants to be blamed. It's believed that Minaj's ability to rap is not a natural talent, but rather non-human enhancement. Lady Gaga and Spears also have alter egos. And Cardi B said she hears a voice in her head. So, the message for the plebs is, hearing voices and having alters is good if they enhance us?

It's further highlighted that rituals take place at big events e.g. major award ceremonies like the Oscars and Grammys, Super-bowl half-time shows, as well as music videos. But for the most part, the plebs don't realise what's being revealed in plain sight. But this is changing? In tandem with the externalisation programme, these freaks are revealing who they are and who they belong to. Other satanic rituals include the Gotthard Tunnel opening ceremony (1st June 2016), attended by top European leaders. Gotthard means Stern God, yet this performance was an occult ritual to Baphomet. And weird rituals have been secretly filmed at CERN.

It's also said that blood sacrifices take place before big budget movies are released to the public, as it promises success. Someone has to pay the price for success. Furthermore, it's said that to be successful, artists have to sacrifice someone important to them, like a family member. This corroborates with shamans, who have to murder a family member to acquire the ability to shapeshift. It's said death follows the famous around like a stench. Like the notorious '27 Club', which consists of stars who died aged 27. It's said their early departure coincides with the breakdown of their programming. And they're past their best? Society is obsessed with youth?

It seems ironic that the plebs aspire to emulate the gimps. Like, girls aspire to be sex kittens e.g. wear chokers, leopard print, diamonds, get butterfly and stars tattoos. We want to be beautiful, rich and famous? All this is marketed to us, and we inauthentically buy into it? These 'stars' are bound by the contracts they sign. They're literally owned, (told what to wear and how to style their hair), unlike the plebs who are free but don't know it?

But moreover, besides being distracted and influenced by these ungodly 'stars', its purported the end game of MK Ultra is to create super-soldiers. Hence, as Barnett claims, they create child soldiers. They want an army of human killing machines. But moreover, according to Russ Dizdar, author of 'The Black Awakening: Rise of Satanic Super Soldiers and the Coming Chaos' (2009), alters are demonised i.e. demons are attached to alter personalities. Thus, their strength and intelligence, for example, is demonically enhanced. Dizdar concedes that project Monarch slaves are referred to as the 'chosen ones'. And they have psychic abilities. Like, they can astral project and torture others in astral. As discussed, spying etc is done on the astral plane.

Dizdar also pertains to 'sleeper agents' (programmed multiples) who shall be activated when the call for chaos is made. These people don't know they've been programmed. They're just living life like normal. Like, Brice Taylor thought she was a regular suburban wife, who had a perfect childhood. But at some point in the near future, all hell will break loose. In his aforementioned book, he states, 'They wait to be activated to kill, slaughter and unleash hell in society so the demons can dance and their leader can emerge as 'saviour' of humanity! A saviour for humanity who they say can bring a new order out of the chaos' (p.68). Dizdar knows what's coming. But we'll get back to this.

So, there's being fractured from infancy, and there's demon possession. But it gets weirder, as there's also rumours about shapeshifting reptilians. Like, David Icke states Illuminati bloodlines can shapeshift from human into reptilian form at will. Indeed, he's renowned for saying the Queen is a shapeshifting reptilian. Which is arguably not farfetched if shamans can shapeshift, and people can turn into werewolves?

According to David Icke's source, namely, Christine Fitzgerald, a close friend and confident of Diana, Diana nicknamed the Windsor's 'the lizards' and 'the reptiles', insisting they're not human. Springmeier claims he's heard hundreds of testimonies about shapeshifting. He asserts he didn't know what to make of it, whereas David Icke ran with it. As mentioned, Schnoebelen's also heard stories about reptilians underground at Salt Lake City. Reports about reptilian humanoids are not uncommon.

Icke concurs that gods came to earth, (who appear to have a reptilian appearance), and they mated with mortals to produce nephilim hybrids. And these nephilim bloodline families run the show through their extensive network of secret societies. These Satanists worship Satan with blood sacrifices etc. It's understood this haunted hybrid family are puppets or vehicles for demonic entities to act through. Thus, when the person dies, the demon inhabits the next human vessel, and so on.

Icke's been writing about the royal's connection to Satanism and paedophilia, and other Satanists like Father George Bush, for decades. He states that George W H Bush is a reptilian shapeshifter, and one of the world's most famous paedophiles and serial killers. He also claims Ted Heath was a shapeshifter. Cathy O'Brien notably claims she saw George Bush shapeshift into a reptilian form. It's possible some changeling quality has been passed down through the blood? Like, psychic abilities and the ability to dissociate are passed down. It's said hybrids need at least 50% nephilim genes to shapeshift.

In her book, Cathy highlights the 'Legend of the Iguana'. Thus, lizard like aliens descended on the Mayans. They imparted advanced astronomical technology, which inspired the Mayan pyramids. And they demanded the sacrifice of virgins (virgin refers to children). These aliens interbred with Mayans to produce a form of life they could inhabit. This explains why these 'people' fluctuate between a human and iguana appearance through chameleon like abilities. Those with Mayan/alien ancestry in their blood can transform into an iguana at will. Like, the royal family and world leaders? She also however states a hologram of lizard like tongues and eyes produces the illusion of transforming into an iguana. David Icke explains the changes happen at an energetic level i.e. the frequency of energy changes, enabling shape to change.

Icke (2007) claims he's met hundreds of people from all over the world, who have told him the same basic story of seeing someone shapeshift from human form into a reptilian form and back again. Apparently one of his readers wrote to him and advised that she met a woman, who claimed to be the lover of Sir Ernest Oppenheimer. Ernest Oppenheimer notably cofounded the diamond trade with Cecil Rhodes and the Rothschild's. And the woman said that on one occasion when they were about to make love, his body took on the form and proportions of a giant lizard with scales. She said the experience was one of the sexual highlights of her life (p.222). LOL. How much weirder does it get?

Icke also interviewed Arizona Wilder, who claims she was a mind-control slave. She had the infernal privilege of performing satanic rituals for the Illuminati, including the British royal family. She was apparently programmed and trained by Joseph Mengele. She claims that since her programming broke down, she has been able to reveal this information to the public (she began having flashbacks, with memories returning to her).

Thus, she claims she witnessed many famous people shapeshift physically from a human to a lizard, and concedes these Satanists consumed sacrificed children in satanic ceremonies. She explains that kids have the purest blood, so they're the best blood sacrifice. Participants drink their blood and eat their flesh (and organs). Whilst their preference is for blonde hair and blue eyed kids, most of their victims are kidnapped from Third World countries as they're not missed (unlike Madeline McCann). Wilder states they're terrorised, mind-controlled and sometimes drugged.

She informs that the reptilians need their blood to maintain their human shape. Apparently, demons need human blood and flesh to eat, to help maintain a DNA overcoat of a 3D body so they can walk the earth in disguise. Human blood helps them live as humans. She explains the natural disposition is holding the reptilian form, and it's hard to maintain the human form, which involves consciously holding the human form. And thus, there's a tendency for them to shapeshift when they're sleeping. We can but wonder if Diana got a shock on her honeymoon i.e. with regards to Charlie's metamorphosis? According to Wilder however, Diana was shown who the Windsor's really are, during a ritual at the late Queen Mother's home, a few weeks before she married Charles.

Wilder states they slit the throat from left to right, and collect the blood in their jewel-encrusted goblets. She claims that when victims are being sacrificed, the scent of blood drives them into a frenzy, and they start shapeshifting. She notes they wear robes, but they're naked underneath. Clothes are superfluous, given the imminent orgies, but also, their clothes would be torn apart when they shapeshift.

She states they start tearing the throat out, drinking the blood from the jugular vein, then move onto the abdomen/stomach. Rituals take place monthly, at every full moon, but there's usually more than one. Sacrifices are done at certain times e.g. equinoxes, solstices, and Halloween. Wilder said they call themselves Druidic, as they use the druid religion, and the Egyptology religion.

Wilder explains the changes happen very fast. Like, they get taller (seven foot tall), bigger, develop protrusions on their heads and backs, grow tails, get fangs/incisors, snouts, very long tongues, claws for hands and feet, and they're covered in scales. And they hiss. She states the eyes are protruding, with slits, and they're hooded when they're about to do something. This notably resonates with Scott Peck's description of those possessed with hooded reptilian eyes, who suddenly dart out in attack. David Icke states that many victims of mind control and DID say they experienced reptilian entities and remember the reptilian eyes.

Members of the British Royal family she claims shapeshifted include Prince Philip, Prince Charles, Princess Margaret, the Queen, and the late Queen Mother. Wilder never saw Diana at any rituals. She attests to having the same satanic experiences with Henry Kissinger, George Bush, Gerald Ford, Joseph Mengele, Bill and Hillary Clinton, Ronald and Nancy Reagan, Tony Blair, members of the Rockefeller and Rothschild families, and other famous VIPs in the US and UK.

Interestingly, she claims Zecharia Sitchin (1920-2010), who's renowned for his ancient astronaut theory, was at the rituals, although he was not a major player in the rituals. As mentioned, Sitchin claimed the Anunnaki were ETs from the planet Nibiru. Wilder however insists he's a disinformer, and apparently Sitchin tried to dissuade David Icke from researching the shapeshifting lark. It's also however said that Wilder is a disinformer. And its possible David Icke has been deceived?

According to Wilder, the Reptilians came to earth about four thousand years ago. They're from another dimension, and apparently live underground in earth. But they appear at rituals. And these spirits can make people shapeshift. The reptilians apparently followed the Aryans, whose bloodline they want to keep pure, as they need their blood for their use. So, the tall white people with blonde hair and blue eyes (who descended from the gods) are kosher, unlike reptilians?

Apparently, the Aryans originally came from Mars, but the reptilians followed them. Then they went to the moon to escape, but they were attacked. So, they came to Earth to start civilisation here about six thousand years ago. And they were doing well until the reptilians arrived. The reptilians began to take over and became involved in politics and religion. These aliens also spawned the illuminati race, which consists of thirteen families.

So, it's possible ET reptilians came to Earth and they needed bodies to operate so they created hybrid bloodlines to be world leaders. Which is a spin on fallen angels fathering nephilim, which is Satan's seed? And its possible people are possessed by spirits at rituals which make them shapeshift? It's said the Illuminati think we're stupid 'cattle'. We're pawns in the chess-match. Ronald Bernard's advice for humanity is that we must wake up and see what is really happening around us. Like, 'royal' elites rule the world on behalf of their father Lucifer.

'We shall have a world government whether we like it or not. The only question is whether it will be by conquest or consent'. Paul Warburg (Council of Foreign Relations)

'The New World Order will sail in on a sea of blood'. Bill Cooper

15

The One World Order

So, Lucifer's plan is to rule the world, from Israel, no less. And thus, Israel had to come into being. According to Biblical prophecy, (as we'll get to), a major sign that we're living in the end times is that Israel has returned to her homeland (following the Diaspora). After millennia, she raised her six-pointed star courtesy of the Rothschild family in 1948 (they paid for the flag). It's understood Israel would not have come into existence, had it not been for Hitler and the horrors of WW2. It's also noted, that Prescott Bush helped finance Hitler (through Union Banking Corporation), and the Rothschild's are the financiers of war, period. It's also predicted, like by Albert Pike, that we'll need three world wars, before we'll accept the global government. So, there's carnage in the post. A storm is brewing.

Congressman Larry P MacDonald (1935-1983) stated in 1976, 'The drive of the Rockefellers and their allies is to create a one-world government combining super-capitalism and Communism under the same tent, all under their control… Do I mean conspiracy? Yes I do. I am convinced there is such a plot, international in scope, generations old in planning, and incredibly evil in intent'. MacDonald was killed in a plane crash that was shot down by the Soviets.

However, the globalists aren't hiding their ambitions, or their cabal membership? David Rockefeller, in his book 'Memoirs' (2002), wrote, 'Some even believe we are part of a secret cabal working against the best interests of the US, characterising my family and me as 'internationalists' and of conspiring with others around the world to build a more integrated global political and economic structure – one world, if you will. If that's the charge, I stand guilty, and I am proud of it'.

As touched on, we're being brainwashed into believing a global government is a good thing i.e. share resources, save the environment, control the population, no more wars. We're one world, one people, one love? So, why not remove barriers and borders, and install a universal socialist government, complete with a global (tyrannical) police state for our protection. Jesuit Pope Francis is on board, so it has to be good? This God on Earth seems like a 'good guy'? Like, philanthropist Bill Gates calls on a world government to solve the world's problems.

In his book, 'The End of Faith' (2004), Sam Harris endorses Jonathan Glover's remark that we need 'something along the lines of a strong and properly funded permanent UN force, together with clear criteria for intervention and an international court to authorise it'. Harris states, 'we can say it even more simply: we need a world government' (p.151).

But moreover, the NWO is promoted as serving some kind of higher purpose. President George H W Bush, who perpetually banged on about the NWO, mysteriously said in a speech in 1991, 'We can find meaning and reward by serving some purpose higher than ourselves – a shining purpose, the illumination of a thousand points of light'. He speaks about 'a thousand points of light' as a mission he will complete. He advised that a credible UN would use its peacekeeping role to fulfil the promise of the NWO, and it would be successful.

Father Bush called his philosophy 'a thousand points of light', and apparently he used the phrase in nearly two hundred presidential speeches. It seems to be a poetic reference to America's volunteer organisations which 'are spread like stars throughout the nation, doing good'. At his father's funeral in 2018, baby Bush, choked up with tears as he imagined his father in heaven, said in his eulogy, 'To us, his was the brightest of a thousand points of light'. He also said his father showed him 'what it means to be a president who leads with integrity'.

Apparently, the phrase 'Thousand Points of Light' refers to the body of initiates and the goal of illumination for mankind. It's a Masonic term, which means to reach the 'final' illumination. One's divine spark connects with a thousand points of light. Masons (Luciferians) become God through apotheosis. Bill Cooper said, 'A 'chosen few' disappear behind the veil and become one of the 'Thousand Points of light'. These are known as the 'Magi'.

In her book, 'The Externalisation of the Hierarchy' (1957), Alice Bailey described the 'Points of Light' as leaders who are in service to the 'the work of the Brotherhood'… the Forces of Light. Their mission is to usher all mankind from the darkness of outmoded Christianity and faded nationalism into the bright and shining 'New World Order'.

As mentioned, Bailey wrote the Great Invocation for the UN. Like Father Bush, the Lucis Trust advocates that we're a 'point of light within a greater light'. Everyone is potentially a radiant sun, a star? We have a divine spark ('god energy' aka kundalini) from the great central sun, the Masonic deity. Those who receive spiritual illumination become a light bearer. Bailey directs occult students to repeatedly make this affirmation: 'I am a point of light within a greater light… I am a spark of sacrificial Fire, focussed within the fiery will of (the Sun) God'.

Thus, the higher shining purpose is serving Lucifer, and the end game is for the whole world to worship him, as he's perched on his throne in the Jewish temple. The secret brotherhood believes this is the 'great work'. It's noted, the Jesuit emblem (IHS) has a thousand points of light emanating from it. And in the 'Mothers Castle of Darkness' in Belgium (where they train witches), there's apparently 1,000 points of light on the ceiling in one of their rooms, which features a dome (firmament?).

So, wars are necessary to get the show on the road, and they're extremely profitable for bankers. Hence, the trusty Rothschild's have funded both sides of every major war for the last two hundred years. Like, in the US civil war, the Bank of England financed the north, and the Paris branch of the Rothschild bank financed the south. And more money enables more military spending which enables more power and bloodshed. Every murder is a blood sacrifice to Satan (including abortions).

Whilst someone has to pay for wars, so why not the Rothschild's, it's contended they actively cook up wars, not least because they rely on wars for wealth. As David Icke (2007) claims, 'They manipulate wars, lend all sides the money to fight them, and pick up massive profits from the horrors they have secretly engineered' (p.175).

But the Rothschild's are also devious because they have intelligence. They have insider information ergo they can manipulate market sentiment and make a mint. Like, in the Battle of Waterloo in 1815, for example, Rothschild junior in France financed Napoleon, and Rothschild junior in England financed Wellington. Investors at London Stock Exchange knew Rothschild intelligence was better than the British governments, so when Rothschild gave the signal to start selling stocks and shares, pretending Napoleon had won, the sheep followed suit.

The bonds were rendered worthless, so the Rothschild's scooped them up at rock bottom prices, and as Wellington won, the bonds increased in price, even higher than they previously were. The Bank of England was created after this debacle. Like the Fed, they also magically conjure up money. It's wonderful. They just print some off.

It's said the Rothschild's could out manoeuvre any European government, by their own secret intelligence service and news network. And it's understood their intelligence network developed into Mossad, the CIA, and MI5/MI6. It's highlighted that intelligence agencies are used as a front for powerful families e.g. MI5/MI6 is the Queens. But they're the same organisation, and they give the media stories to print/report. As mentioned, presidents and prime ministers are given 'intelligence'.

It's noted, CIA Operation Mockingbird began in the early 1950s to influence media. Thus, the CIA paid journalists to print fake stories and interviews. The existence of this programme was denied until they got caught in the mid-1970s. Apparently a third of the whole CIA budget went to media propaganda operations. The CIA claimed they shut the program in 1976 but no one believes that as there's plenty evidence to suggest otherwise. It's said close to a billion dollars are being spent on secret propaganda in the US. It's understood 'TV' is less about entertainment, and more about being a weapon. It's a weapon of mass deception that leads to mass destruction.

As discussed, the 'family' operate a network of secret societies to implement the plan, the direction the world takes. Besides the aforementioned 'secret societies', a pivotal part of the puzzle is the Round Table, cofounded by Cecil Rhodes in 1891 with Lord Alfred Milner (who was a freemason and Rothschild's agent).

As touched on, Rhodes (hence Rhodesia) fleeced Africa of her gold and diamonds, together with the Rothschild's. It's also noted, diamonds are a scam, as prices are manipulated through supply and demand. We've been brainwashed to want them, through heavy marketing. Like, Marilyn Munroe's 'Diamonds Are A Girl's Best Friend'. We've bought into materialism, pun intended. We want to be like mind-controlled sex kitten Munroe? And people die for them. It's always about sacrifice.

The Round Table worked behind the scenes at the highest levels of British Government, influencing foreign policy and wars in tandem with the Rothschild's. It's highlighted that the inner circle of the Round Table were key members of the government's war administrations before, during and after WW1. As per, this secret society consists of an inner circle, namely, 'The Society of the Elect', and an outer circle, 'The Association of Helpers'. And it uses a pyramid structure to relegate knowledge on a need to know basis (information is compartmentalised). Upper levels of other secret societies (e.g. freemasons) connect into the Round Table.

It's also noted, the monarch are members of the Order of the Garter (1348), which is the precursor to the Round Table. Prince William became the 1000th Knight of the Garter in 2008. This royally exclusive club is apparently the parent organisation of worldwide masons, so it's up there in the pyramid. Indeed, apparently its members consist of the 1% that rules the 1%. And their endeavour has historically been a One World Order. They want their New Atlantis. Besides the royals per se, the core leadership consists of top global masons, Rosicrucian's, Knights Templar, Priory of Sion, and the Committee of 300 (the SAS of the Illuminati).

When Rhodes died in 1902, he left his fortunes to the creation of Round Table Groups with the purpose of creating a world government. His will stated, 'To and for the establishment, promotion and development of a Secret Society, the true aim and object whereof shall be for the extension of the British rule throughout the world'. We'll get to these Round Table Groups in a moment or three.

Rhodes' money was also reserved for Rhodes scholarships to fund certain overseas students to study at Oxford University. 'Chosen ones' were recruited to execute the great plan. These students then return to their countries of origin as Illuminati agents to take up positions of power. Like, Bill Clinton was awarded a Rhodes scholarship. As it transpires however, he left after a year. Rumour has it that lurid Bill was expelled for rape.

So, before Hitler, the British Empire wanted to control the world. These Germanic (Aryan) families always have. They share the same utopian NWO view. Hence, they covertly tried to achieve global dominance through Hitler? Or rather, Hitler was the catalyst to rebirth Israel. The mission has always been to resurrect the 'Holy' Roman Empire and control Jerusalem. The Sabbatean-Frankist cult cabal, at the heart of operations, promises its followers their messiah will rule from the third temple in Jerusalem. Hence, they supported the creation of a Jewish homeland in Palestine.

It's duly noted, the Jews were never popular following the Diaspora, as God had foretold. Deuteronomy 28:65 states, 'And among those nations you shall find no rest, and there shall be no resting place for the soul of your foot; but there the Lord will give you a trembling heart, failing of eyes, and despairing of soul'. Thus, Theodor Herzl founded Zionism in 1897, contending that anti-Semitism was so ingrained in European society, that the only way for Jews to escape this, was to create a Jewish state.

Zion is notably Jerusalem, home of the Jews. It's recalled that God promised this land to Abraham and his offspring. But the wayward Jews continually messed up, which resulted in losing their God-given land. It's also recalled, Israel was renamed Palestine by the Romans after the last Jewish revolt in 132AD. And Palestine comes from Philistines, who were nephilim. Moreover, God also said He would bring His people home in the last days, not the Rothschild's, or using the Rothschild's as His instrument?

So, Zionism was a European Jewish political movement that sought to secure a Jewish homeland for the Jewish people. Thus, Zionism is political, whereas Judaism is religion, and they're not the same thing. Non-Jewish people are Zionists, and many Jews are opposed to Zionism. Indeed, the latter are horrified by what's happening in Palestine.

Apparently, Uganda, Argentina, Cyprus, and Texas were all suggested as a potential homeland for the irksome Jews. But in 1897 the Zionist conference settled on Palestine, which was part of the Ottoman (Turkish) Empire. It appears the Jews wanted their homeland back? Or the royal family did. But how would they achieve that?

So, WW1 (1914-1918) began, when Archduke Franz Ferdinand of Austria was assassinated by a member of the secret Serbian military society 'The Black Hand'. Apparently, the Society of the Black Hand preceded the Mafia in the US in the 1920s (which are orchestrated by Jesuits). This war drew in all the world's great economic powers, which assembled into two opposing alliances, namely, the Allies and the Central Powers. And the Allies, mainly Britain, France and the US prevailed over Germany, Austria-Hungary, Russia and the Ottoman Empire.

It's noted, the US got involved in WW1 after the Lusitania, a British ocean liner that was carrying ammunition and passengers from the US to UK, was sunk by a German submarine in 1915. The Germans had forewarned them about potential annihilation, as they knew they were hauling ammunition from the US to UK. But the US carried on regardless, resulting in the loss of 1,198 passengers (including 128 Americans).

Propaganda conveyed this tragedy as an example of German ruthlessness i.e. the ship was carrying innocent women and children, which gave the pretext for the US to declare war on Germany. Suffice to say, deistic Satanists are psychos. And the people who run the government don't care about us. As mentioned, we're pawns.

It's also noted, that Britain and France, who were confident they would conquer the Ottoman Empire, made a secret pact in 1916, the Sykes-Picot Agreement, to divide the lands when the war ended. Arabs, who were revolting against the Ottoman Empire, were promised independent states in lands formerly controlled by Turkey e.g. Lebanon, Syria, Libya, Egypt, Morocco, Tunisia, Iraq, Somalia, Algeria and the United Arab Emirates.

The British Intelligence Officer Thomas Edward Lawrence aka 'Lawrence of Arabia' kept the Arabs sweet. Apparently, he developed a deep sympathy for the Arabs under Turkish rule. So, he was a 'good guy'? Hence, he led the campaign to revolt against the Turks, which the Brits had worked hard to encourage. It was part of the WW1 strategy. They had planned how to carve up the Middle East.

But furthermore, in 1917 the British Government, namely, Lord Arthur Balfour, who was apparently a spiritualist and mason, promised Lord Rothschild a 'national home' for the Jews in Palestine. Lord Rothschild was funding and driving Zionism (and the wars). He was in the inner circle of the Round Table, and it's said the Balfour Declaration was probably written by the Round Table.

This contract, 'The Balfour Declaration', was on the premise the Jews upheld the civil and religious rights of the existing non-Jewish communities. In 1918, after the collapse of the Ottoman Empire, Britain thus occupied Palestine. The Versailles Treaty of 1919 entrusted Britain with the temporary administration of Palestine. At this time only 5% of the population was Jewish and 95% Palestinian Muslims and Christians, and they lived in harmony with one another.

From 1918 Jewish colonial immigration was sponsored from Europe and the US. The Palestinians (Arabs) were less pleased, as increasing numbers of Jews arrived. Thus, in 1923 Britain divided Palestine. 75% of the land, that was set aside for Israel, was given to the newly created Transjordan (meaning 'across the Jordan River') for the Arab Palestinians, and the remaining 25% was to be the Jewish Palestinian homeland. So, both Arabs and Jews had their own homeland. Two states were created for two people.

But this was not okay for the Arabs who launched never-ending attacks upon the Jewish Palestinians to drive them out. Whilst the British initially crushed their revolts, it seems they subsequently turned a blind eye when they discovered there were large oil deposits throughout the Middle East. It's also noted, that Israel got a raw deal, being robbed of their promised homeland. The British 'looked favourably' upon the creation of a Jewish national homeland throughout all Palestine, and instead they got a slice of the pie. Transjordan was notably renamed Jordan in 1946.

After the first global war, which claimed circa sixteen million lives, the world concurred that war was dreadful. Hence, the League of Nations was established in 1920. It was designed to enforce the Treaty of Versailles, and the other peace agreements that brought an end to WW1. This intergovernmental organisation provided a forum for resolving international disputes.

The stated aim was to maintain world peace, which included transparency i.e. no more secret deals and wars, and most countries signed up. They could talk like grownups? They further endeavoured to improve people's working conditions, tackle disease, drug and human trafficking, and they collectively promised to disarm. It was progressive to be more unified?

As it transpired however, the League of Nations failed in the 1930s, as it didn't have any real power. Countries could still do what they liked, as the League's only deterrent was emplacing trade sanctions on rogue countries. Hitler then withdrew Germany from the League of Nations in 1933 and commenced WW2 (1939-1945) with his false flag attack on Poland. Naturally, the Rothschild's funded both Axis (Germany etc) and Allies (UK, France, US etc).

It's noted, the US allowed Pearl Harbour to happen in 1941, to enter the war. It was not a 'surprise attack', as people were led (lied) to believe. According to a declassified memo from the Office of Naval Intelligence, President Franklyn Roosevelt (33rd degree mason) knew what the Jap's were planning three days before. Thus, they intentionally left their US pacific fleet of planes (188) and ships (18), and servicemen (over 2000 were killed) out as sitting ducks. Roosevelt implemented the carefully orchestrated plot, which coaxed Japan into attacking the US.

But moreover, the atomic bombs they dropped on Hiroshima and Nagasaki shocked the world. Watching the horror show, we realised we have the technology to completely annihilate ourselves and our planet. Thus, the threat of nuclear war was forever etched on our brain. Like a movie script, we deducted that all it took was some nutter getting into power (like the president of North Korea?), who had access to that notorious red button, to start the fireworks. As mentioned in the Introduction, the 'fear of attack' technique is used to control us. Like, with terrorism, (including bioterrorism), we trust our governments to protect us. And yet they're the fire starters.

So, Hitler did his job. He caused absolute carnage and successfully killed millions of God's people. The Catholic Church was well pleased. Then Hitler and his Nazi buds flitted to North and South America (and Antarctica), taking their mind control and rocket technology with them. Whilst Operation Paperclip recruited over a thousand scientists, at least a million Nazis vanished. It's understood the Catholic Church helped their escape ergo they took up residence in South America. Like, Joseph Mengele aka Dr Death went to Argentina?

It's said the holocaust was a massive blood sacrifice to Satan, which shifted the gears. Things started 'getting real' after 1945, which includes the onslaught of UFOs, as we'll get to. Nazi intelligence were given positions in the Office of Strategic Services (OSS), the forerunner to the CIA, supposedly to gain information on the 'new enemy' Russia. German scientists were however equally snaffled by the Soviet. Apparently more than 80,000 SS troops and scientists were dispersed worldwide. So, the Thule Society became the CIA and the KGB?

When WW2 ended, (having killed some eighty million people), the world came together again to pledge never again to allow world war to happen. They would instead stick together as brothers in arms. Thus, the UN was established. Whilst its legacy is in the League of Nations, this peacekeeping body was more hardcore. It had to be strong enough to prevent WW3. Clark Eichelberger, one of the UN founders, wrote (in a journal article entitled 'World Government via the United Nations'), 'The United Nations is far from a league – it is the beginning of world government'.

The term 'United Nations' was notably coined by Roosevelt in 1942 during WW2, but it officially came into existence in 1945. Almost all 195 countries in the world are members of the UN, except Palestine and the Vatican. It's widely believed the UN is a noble endeavour i.e. the peacekeeping and humanitarian efforts. Albeit, not for Rwanda. The 'world peacekeepers' let that genocide happen, as there's no resources there? And depopulation's a good thing, especially in developing countries. Hence, Bill Gates benevolently vaccinates kids in third world countries.

So, the UN can collectively solve the world's problems. Like the Israel-Palestine problem. Hence, Britain handed this headache over to the UN. As touched on, sympathy grew for the Jews having their own homeland after the holocaust. Thus, in 1947 the UN General Assembly voted (33-13), and Palestine was partitioned between Arabs and Jews, allowing for the formation of the Jewish state of Israel. The UN assigned 55% of the land to Israel and 45% to Palestine. The Arabs were not at all pleased and staged a walkout in protest.

Six months later, in 1948, the state of Israel was born, which terminated the British mandate in Palestine (British forces went home). Immediately following this, Arab armies invaded Israel. Israel held her own, and when it ended, Gaza was controlled by Egypt, and the West Bank by Jordan. Hundreds of thousands of Palestinians fled to these areas. Hatred was blossoming.

It's also noted, that when Israel took on her surrounding neighbours during the 1967 Six Day War, and prevailed, she seized the remaining Palestinian territories of the West Bank, East Jerusalem, Gaza Strip, as well as the Syrian Golan Heights, and the Egyptian Sinai Peninsula. It's believed God had His hand on Israel, which is a bone of contention for Muslims. Tiny Israel defeated them all, including old arch enemy Egypt.

Israel gave Egypt back her land, following the Israel-Egypt Peace Treaty of 1979. But she's hung onto Syria's Golan Heights, which the US supports (the US recognises its Israel's). The argument is that it keeps Israel safe i.e. as a border control, but apparently there's a ton of black gold (oil) and gas there, and it's a source of water. Contrary to the UN, the US also recognises Jerusalem as Israel's capital as opposed to Tel Aviv. Jerusalem was King David's capital. JerUSAlem is the heart of Israel.

The West Bank is 'occupied' by Israel and is ruled to some extent by the Palestinian Authority. The Gaza Strip is under the control of Hamas. These Palestinian territories are poverty stricken and grim compared to flourishing Israel. Israel has literally taken over almost all the land, resulting in millions of Palestinian refugees. Hamas is notably likened to Hezbollah (in Lebanon) in terms of its military, political, and media operations. They're both terrorist organisations? Or as Sartre said, they're desperately oppressed and terrorism is their only means to revolt. Iran supports both.

It's further purported 'The Greater Israel Project' is being played out. It seems Israel or rather the cabal, wants back all her Promised Land, which extends from the River of Egypt up to the Euphrates. It's alleged her plan is to covertly cause unrest in the Middle East. Israel's enemies would need to be fractured and weakened through sectarian war, before Israel could snaffle her turf back. Like, Oded Yinon, former senior official with the Israeli Foreign Ministry, famously advocated that every Arab conflict is in Israel's interest. So, Israel's sneaky plan for expansion was to sow seeds of sectarian hatred and violence throughout the Arab world?

Ex-marine and political activist Kenneth O'Keefe highlights Yinon's 'A Strategy for Israel in the 1980s' (1982), which lays out very clearly a strategy of destabilising all of the areas surrounding Israel. This includes Syria, Lebanon, Jordan, Iraq and even Egypt and Saudi Arabia. He asserts that destabilising Iraq was not merely about securing oil and establishing bases there, but also to cause sectarian carnage.

It seems 'The Yinon Plan' inspired the 1996 paper 'A Clean Break: A New Strategy for Securing the Realm'. This was prepared by an elite group of US foreign policy 'Neoconservatives' (Zionists in the US) for Benjamin Netanyahu, Israel's Prime Minister. The plan was to reconfigure the Middle East by war, beginning with the removal of Saddam Hussein. Whilst Iraq was nominated for 'regime change' first, Libya, Syria, Yemen, Lebanon, and Iran were on the hit-list.

But moreover, members of this 'study group' for a New Israeli Strategy became key players in the Iraq war during the Bush Administration. Hence, this hitlist is familiar, featuring Saddam at the top. They subsequently wrote the Project for the New American Century (PNAC) in 2000, which similarly listed countries designated for 'regime change' (those hostile to Israel). But we'll get back to this.

O'Keefe said (during a Russia Today interview) those who carry out the agendas are pure and simple psychopaths. He states, 'If you ask me how the world functions, then you have to understand one thing plain and simple – the head of the snake, the system of power is headed by the financial system. The bankers rule the Earth, through the private control of issuance of money, debt-based money which we all are supposed to pay'…

'The vast majority of governments around the world, they are nothing more than puppets carrying out an agenda for the bankers, and the bankers at the top of this pyramid are, as I've said, plain and simple psychopathSS: they're drunk on their own power, they are used to getting everything they want, they can buy anything and anyone that can be bought. This explains the corruption of virtually every government we can look at, and the policies do not reflect the interests of the people. They reflect, pure and simple, the interests of the bankers'.

It's countered however that the 'Greater Israel' project is a 'conspiracy theory'. So, there is no plan to expand Israel? It's said this conspiracy was started by the Palestine Liberation Organisation (PLO). And influential people like Yasser Arafat (Palestinian leader) and Osama Bin Laden endorsed it. In an interview Bin Laden gave in 1998, he claimed the Western military presence in Saudi Arabia was aimed 'to support the Jewish and Zionist plans for expansion of what is called 'Great Israel'. So, Arabs recognise Zionists (the family) are orchestrating the plan? And the stage is being set for Pike's WW3 vision, namely, that Muslims and Jews are at enmity with one another.

It's also noted, the Temple Mount has been controlled by Israel since the 1967 war, and it remains a focal-point of Arab-Israeli conflict. It's the holiest site in Judaism, and the third holiest site in Islam, and both claim sovereignty over the site. As mentioned, the Al-Aqsa mosque and Dome of the Rock currently stand on the site. But it's where the third Jewish temple is to built, which breeds suspicions about Masonic (Illuminati) plots. Like, an engineered earthquake could cause its demise?

Wheeler (2009) quotes Jerry Golden (2003) who said, 'The same families who own and control the Federal Reserve and other major financial institutions have their eyes on the Temple Mount and the Holy City of Jerusalem'. And 'Mason desire to rebuild Solomon's Temple on the Temple Mount is the driving force of events in the Middle East' (p.86).

At some point the temple will be built, which means removing those Islamic structures. Which means WW3? However, it's also highlighted, there's room for both the Dome of the Rock and the Temple. Hence, Bill Clinton suggested they could share the Temple Mount in 1993 during the Oslo Accord peace agreements.

Plans for rebuilding the temple have notably been in place for years. Jerusalem is Jehovah's capital. Psalm 132:13-14 tells us, 'For the LORD has chosen Zion. He has desired it for His dwelling, saying, 'This is my resting place forever and ever; here I will sit enthroned, for I have desired it'. Hence, the diabolical copycat has to rule from there. In Zechariah 12:2-3 we're told that Jerusalem will be a 'burdensome stone' for all nations at the end times.

So, all was going according to plan. With the advent of WW2, Israel was home and causing problems. And the UN was established, the steppingstone to global government. As touched on in the Introduction, 'The UN New World Order project is a global, high-level initiative founded in 2008 to advance a new economic paradigm, a new political order, and more broadly a New World Order for humankind' (see unnwo.org). The old world order is being replaced by a NWO. Apparently a third of UN time is spent on (devoted to) Israel. The IMF and World Bank were also established after WW2. The Rothschild's were at the heart of all these events.

The Round Table (funded by the Rothschild's) operated behind the scenes. And they conjured up Round Table Groups, global think tanks, to further their cause. Like, the Royal Institute of International Affairs was founded in 1920, and the Council of Foreign Relations (the US sister branch) was founded in 1921. Then after WW2, the UN was founded. The Bilderberg Group was founded in 1954, the Club of Rome in 1968, and the Trilateral Commission in 1973.

The Round Table network operates as a bridge or interface between the inner levels of secret societies and the outer levels of these think tanks. So, secret societies, (on behalf of the family), steer these global vehicles. Their mission is to advance globalisation through manipulating and organising events, and placing key people into critical positions.

These think tanks shape US and foreign policy, which translates to greater political and economic interdependence (corporate-sponsored economic integration) between these nations. It's highlighted the Council on Foreign Relations (CFR) does not conform to government policy but rather the government conforms to CFR policy. And the ultimate goal of the CFR is a global government. It's understood the first steps for achieving a NWO is merging the world economically through trade agreements e.g. EU, North American Free Trade Agreement (NAFTA), African Union, and then destroying sovereignty. Super-states, like the EU, precede one global empire.

However, not all CFR members are privy to the plan. People only know what they need to know. There's a deep state within the deep state. As US Admiral Chester Ward, CFR member (for more than twenty years) and whistle-blower, wrote in his book 'Kissinger on the Couch', that within the CFR there exists a 'much smaller group but more powerful... made up of Wall Street international bankers and their key agents'. He continued, the members of this smaller group 'want the world banking monopoly from whatever power ends up in control of the global government. This CFR leadership faction, he added, 'is headed by the Rockefeller brothers''.

Whilst the CFR, the Bilderberg Group, and the Trilateral Commission are referred to as 'the three sisters', apparently the Bilderberg Group has more important people in it. And she's been more secretive. Like, uncle Bohemian Grove? Indeed, the Bilderberg group denied its existence until the 1980s. Security is immense at Bilderberger meetings. It's extremely powerful members include bankers, politicians, royalty, CEO's of large corporations etc.

It's noted, that people invited to the Bilderberg group often find themselves in positions of power shortly afterwards. Like, apparently Bill Clinton, Barack Obama, and Tony Blair were selected to be presidents and prime minister there. Apparently, they plan how US presidential primary contests will proceed. Like, Hillary Clinton took Bernie Sanders otherwise rightful place in the 2016 election. It's said the Bilderberg group is the visible/public body of the hidden ruling secret brotherhood (Illuminati). Bill Cooper said the Bilderberg group is the supreme world council of freemasons and consists of 39 permanent members (3x13).

The Duke of Edinburgh's BFF, German born Prince Bernhard of Lippe-Biesterfeld (1911-2004), established the Bilderberg group. It's named after the Bilderberg Dutch hotel where they first met. Prince Bernhard, father of Queen Beatrix of the Netherlands (who allegedly has DID and was one of Pope Francis's lovers), was a member of the Nazi party.

It's understood the royal family, whose roots are in Nazi Germany, are behind the EU, as pioneered by Prince Charles Edward, Duke of Saxe-Coburg and Gotha. That is, the EU is under the control of British royals? It seems ironic that Churchill, revered as Britain's wartime hero for his role in defeating Nazi Germany, famously called for the creation of a 'United States of Europe' in 1946.

So, the Bilderbergers agenda was the unity of Europe. They wanted a central European bank, with a common European currency, like the corrupt Federal Reserve. Thus, they outlined the European common market and the Euro. Texas Marrs, author of 'Dark Majesty: The Secret Brotherhood and the Magic of a Thousand Points of Light' (2004), states, the Bilderberg group consists of international elites, who's three goals are a new international economic order, new political order, and new religious order. These are the three objectives of the NWO. It's noted, that Europe comes from the goddess Europa aka Semiramis.

So, it seems the EU was the blueprint for the NWO? As touched on however, it's said China is the blueprint for the NWO i.e. half socialist and half private, and insane surveillance. China has hundreds of millions of cameras, with facial recognition technology. There's nowhere to hide in China? Citizens acquire social credit ratings, which compel them to behave. It's in their best interest to conform, as crap scores means they can't travel etc. Like, naughty kids, who smoke and jaywalk.

Marrs concedes there's a secret brotherhood of illuminised men, who believe they're a superior race and bloodline. These 'agents of a magical underworld' are the Money Power of America, Europe and Asia. And they're masterminding global control. Like Coleman, he states Luciferians seek to destroy the monetary system. Hence, the world's insane debt that will never be paid off? As mentioned, it's understood our insane global debt is by design because an economic meltdown is part of the looming chaos that births the new order. Like, in the US, their debt clock increases a million a minute. It's like a ticking timebomb waiting to explode.

Marrs concurs that they seek to destroy nationalism and patriotism, to enable globalism. They seek to destroy Christianity using education and the media, and also the traditional family by promoting homosexuality and other sexual perversions. But moreover, he states that at the pinnacle of the Illuminati, (the global network of secret groups collectively known as the Secret Brotherhood), are nine illuminised men who sit on an exclusive committee. They rule the world from behind closed doors. So, that's the Nine Unknown Men? A tenth will join them, but for now his seat remains vacant. Presumably, the tenth is the antichrist, when he makes his dastardly appearance?

Apparently, the Club of Rome is above the Bilderbergers and just below the Committee of 300. They allegedly care about the environment and over-population. They endorse the Malthusian idea that world population will outgrow food and resources (as opposed to capitalism?). This is a threat to us all. Their vision is a world without borders founded on equality. Like, the Pope? It's noted, the Club of Rome was established to use the environment to justify global government. As mentioned, we need global problems for global solutions. Like, 'climate change' instead of the global warming scam?

'The First Global Revolution' (1991) by Alexander King and Bertrand Schneider, founder and secretary of the Club of Rome, stated, 'In searching for a new enemy to unite us, we came up with the idea that pollution, the threat of global warming, water shortages, famine and the like would fit the bill. All these dangers are caused by human intervention, and it is only through changed attitudes and behaviours that they can be overcome. The real enemy then is humanity itself' (p.104-105). This is apparently the origin of global warming.

The Club of Rome claims, 'We are facing an imminent catastrophic economic collapse' and 'our only hope is to transform humanity into a global interdependent sustainable society, based on respect and reverence for the Earth'. So, we need to revere Gaia? But instead we've collectively sodomised her. Besides choking her marine life with plastic and oil leaks, her forests are deliberately set on fire, and heavy metals are sprayed into her skies. It's noted, that 'direct energy weapons' are often used to surreptitiously start fires e.g. laser weapons.

As discussed, 'research' has manipulated our perspective, so we focus on demonised carbon dioxide rather than natural variability. CO_2 has been isolated as the problem, which implicates human causes. But perhaps we should focus our attention on the climate changers. Like, the crap they're spraying into our sky to modify the weather. Birds are literally falling dead out of the skies. And their technologies like HAARP which can create 'natural disasters' like earthquakes, hurricanes, droughts, floods, tsunamis, thunderstorms. Chemtrails apparently increase atmosphere connectivity which enhances HAARP. It's also recalled, the Bible tells us the weather becomes super tumultuous in the last days. So, we've been warned about 'climate change'.

Apparently 7/10 Brits support a global government to protect humanity from environmental disasters. So, the environment is bringing us together. Almost all countries signed the Paris Agreement (2016), within the UN Framework Convention on Climate Change (UNFCCC), which aims to strengthen the global response to climate change. It's noted, that Donald Trump upset the world, when he pulled the US out of the agreement. He seems to think climate change is a hoax? The UN Climate Panel declared the earth has until 2030 to avoid disaster.

And we support UN Agenda 21 and 30, which is sustainable development for the 21st century, which is the blueprint for the NWO. The agenda for the 21st century is the end of national sovereignty. 179 countries signed up to Agenda 21 at the conference in 1992. It's highlighted that regionalisation precedes globalisation. Thus, each country has its own local Agenda 21 plan. Whilst Agenda 21 is the global plan for sustainable development at the local level, Agenda 30 is the global plan for sustainable development at the national and worldwide level. The Pope helped launch Agenda 2030 and all UN member states signed up in 2015. It's said Agenda 30 is Agenda 21 on steroids.

Whilst 'sustainable development' sounds good i.e. recycling, energy management, population control, eradicate poverty, it's asserted these UN contraptions are designed to control the world and undermine sovereignty. All systems will be centrally controlled i.e. water, land, plants, animals, food, energy, minerals, all construction and means of production. Globalisation is the standardisation of all systems including law enforcement and education. It's totalitarianism. And people will be forced off the land, (to clear the rural areas), and condensed into cities. It's better for the environment? These cities will be served by high-speed trains and driverless cars?

It's noted, that 'smart cities' are based on UN Agenda 2030. Indeed, it's said smart cities are the solution to the world's environmental problems. Smart cities are smart because they use information to manage resources. Smart cities equates to smart surveillance. Like, smart meters monitor our energy use. And smart streetlamps have sensors and dim when not in use, which saves power. And traffic lights and corresponding infrastructure can speak to each other. Our cities are becoming smarter and more connected by the day. Albeit, smart motorways are not that smart, and have resulted in untold deaths.

Everything is connected to the 'internet of things', which relies on 5G (fifth generation) wireless technology. It means everything is monitored and controlled by AI, and we live in a wifi 5G cloud of information that fries our brains and bodies with radiation. But it's smart because we can ask our TVs questions. Like, the weather forecast? All devices in the home will be connected to the internet e.g. smart ovens, smart fridges. But moreover, we'll also be linked to the internet of things. It's rumoured, our brains will be linked to the internet by a chip. Apparently, the aim is for the human mind to be connected to AI by 2030. However, we'll get back to this.

It's also noted, the World Economic Forum formed a partnership with the UN, (called the UN-Forum), to accelerate the implementation of the 2030 Agenda. The World Economic Forum was formed in 1971. Its mission is cited as 'committed to improving the state of the world by engaging business, political, academic, and other leaders of society to shape global, regional and industry agendas'. They discuss global issues to drive globalism on behalf of the elites.

Whilst there are many more elite groups, Round Table organisations are central in the manipulation of day to day politics, banking, business, the military, education etc. These global steering committees have played a significant role in recent world history. They preside over all sectors of society, creating our social fabric. They're essentially the visible head of the invisible global government. Carroll Quigley (Bill Clinton's mentor) wrote in 'Tragedy and Hope' (1966), 'I know of the operations of this network because I have studied it for twenty years and was permitted for two years, in the early 1960s, to examine its papers and secret records'.

Suffice to say, all those onboard the NWO are selected and screened. And further, the same elites (nephilim bloodlines) partake in other groups. Like, Father George Bush was the director of the CIA, President, Vice President, CFR director, member of the Trilateral Commission, and ambassador of the UN. It's like Google, and organisations like DARPA, fluidly swap CEOs etc. Marrs also used the metaphor that the secret brotherhood is like an octopus with far reaching tentacles.

Other alliances also came into play. Like, the Group of Seven (G7) formed in 1975, which consists of America, Canada, France, Germany, Great Britain, Italy, and Japan. The purpose was to transition countries from individual economies into global economies. Russia joined in 1998, resulting in the G8, but it has since (conveniently?) been suspended. The EU has been represented within the G8 since the 1980s. The Group of

20 (G20), founded in 1999, has international summits to discuss critical global issues, (like the environment), reflecting the wider interests of both developed and emerging economies. However, it's not just about free trade and the environment, but rather centralised control.

And military alliances were birthed. Like, NATO (North Atlantic Treaty Organisation) was formed in 1949 to protect Europe, Canada and the US from the Soviet (the new enemy after WW2). It's said that in response, Russia, China and Kazakhstan signed the Shanghai Corporation Organisation (SCO) to resist the hegemony of the US. The SCO was established in 1996.

It's said NATO is the war machine used to serve the agenda of the hidden hand, which is controlled by the same people who control the EU etc (the family). It's noted, that NATO redefined itself as a world police force in 1999. It's understood the plan is for UN and NATO military forces to merge into a global militarised police force ('law enforcement'). According to Tony Blair (in 1999), 'NATO would make the backbone of the New World Order military forces, or New World Order army'. He also stated this would happen whether anyone liked it or not' (cited in Wheeler, 2009).

As it transpired then, despite the promise of the UN, the world became more distrustful. Hence, the insane stockpiling of weapons, including nuclear, that ensued. It was imperative to have shed loads to keep up? Thus, after Hitler's fascism, communism became the next problem. Like, in North Korea, North Vietnam and Cuba, for example. It's understood we need to have problems for wars. Like, communism was a problem for capitalism. So, the communism versus capitalism narrative was seeded. 'Divide and rule' works every time.

Karl Marx (who pioneered communism) was notably a 33rd degree mason and funded by the Rothschild's. Apparently, he grew up in a Christian family but became a Satanist. It's also highlighted, we've been brainwashed with socialism, the prelude to communism, to prepare us for the UN communist world order aka the NWO. It seems we're happy to trade in our freedoms and rights for Big Brother's safety-net? We're happy to be dictated to by the state, rather than we dictate to the state? We'll relinquish our property and power? Lest we forget, the millions killed by communism. It's further noted, there's spiritual consequences, as communism is invariably couched in atheism. Thus, the freedom to worship could be outlawed. But equally, capitalism can lead to Satan through consumerism and exploitation?

It's noted, when Japan lost Korea in 1945 to the Allies, the Soviet took the North and the US took the South. Like Germany, Korea was divided. Then communist China and the Soviet supported North Korea to invade South Korea. The UN subsequently authorised the US to support their side to stem communism. The Korean War (millions died) was post WW2 and pre-Vietnam. It never ended but rather an armistice was signed. It's understood North Korea has invaluable resources for technology, and it's a strategic location for attacking China.

It seems pertinent to note, that President Dwight Eisenhower warned the US back in 1961 about the 'Industrial Military Complex'. That is, the unholy alliance between the government, the military, and the corporate industry that supplies weapons and technology for the military. Like, corporations give money to politicians in elections, for example. Together they have a vested interest in public policy. And peace is not good for business. It seems the military industrial complex is a monster that needs to be brought out of the shadows and into the light of consciousness?

In essence, wars are engineered for profit and to further globalisation, with drugs and people trafficking, a convenient by-product. Or rather, drugs and people are the motive, to generate untold wealth on the black market. Like Vietnam, who they sorely underestimated, was less about communism and more about opium. Heroin was smuggled back to the US in the cavities of the dead soldiers (nice).

As touched on, the CIA is responsible for cocaine and heroin distribution etc worldwide. CIA drugs operations fund pentagon and CIA's black budgets. And some of these black ops are literally out of this world, as we'll get to. It's understood that opium is the source of billions of dollars, which is required for covert operations. Covert operations need covert funding i.e. no paper-trail.

It also seems pertinent to note, that wars are created using the Hegelian dialectic. Indeed, it's said all wars since the French Revolution have been manipulated this way. German Philosopher Hegel observed that when two opposing ideas clash, they create something new. Thus, his theory was 'thesis, antithesis, and synthesis'. Or as David Icke calls it, 'problem, reaction, solution' (apparently he coined the term). That is, we create problems, which can entail false flags, to mandate solutions.

Like, the Gulf of Tonkin incident, which led to the expansion of the Vietnam War. Something catastrophic needs to happen to get the desired public reaction, founded on propaganda, which enables achieving the desired solution, which was the point of the operation. Like, intelligence made up stories about Saddam Hussein having Weapons of Mass Destruction (WMD). Our reaction to this problem was freaking out, and the solution was annihilating Iraq, as we'll get to.

And sometimes problems arise, which displeases the establishment. Like, Mohammad Mossadegh, the democratically elected Prime Minster (1951-1953) in Iran, nationalised oil. The Iranian oil industry had been under British control since 1913 through the Anglo-Persian Oil Company, later British Petroleum (BP). So, that wasn't good.

However, rather than sending in the military, the CIA, at the request of MI6, created a coup and huge propaganda to oust him out and it worked. Declassified documents reveal how CIA Operation Ajax sought 'regime change' in Iran, on behalf of corporate/government interests, through bribing politicians, security and high-ranking officials, and massive anti-Mossadegh propaganda to instigate public revolt. It was apparently fairly easy to overthrow him, and only cost a few million. It seems their tactics in Iran in 1953 set the precedence for future antics.

The propaganda against Mossadegh was that he regarded himself as 'the saviour of Iran'. It was alleged that he was a dictator and he'd built a vast spying apparatus, which meant control over every sector of society, from the army to newspapers to political and religious leaders. This is unbelievably ironic given our 1984 Big Brother reality.

So, Mossadegh was imprisoned for three years, and then put under house arrest until his death. And the Shah returned to power. The CIA supported the monarch's return. Mossadegh was replaced by Fazlollah Zahedi, who was handpicked by MI6 and the CIA. The Shah's pro-western dictatorship continued for 27 years and ended with the Islamic revolution in 1979, (when the Shah was ousted), which paved the way for today's Iran.

So, there's many ways to skin a cat. Like, besides overt war, and boldly assassinating leaders, the globalists can covertly pay a few thousand people (mercenaries) to riot and protest, in line with US foreign policy.

As mentioned, it's highlighted that we have a corporatocracy as opposed to democracy, which is not elected. Corporatocracy refers to an economic and political system controlled by corporations i.e. corporations control media and politicians, as they finance them. Thus, our governments represent corporate interests (corporations present their policies to government). It's also noted, that CEOs of oil companies become state officials and vice versa e.g. Dick Cheney was CEO of Halliburton and Vice President of the US. It's understood we need to follow the money trail to discover who benefits from wars. Like, bankers, arms dealers, oil companies, globalists, Satanists.

It's also pertinent to note, the 'Iran Contra affair'. Thus, the US Government sold weapons to their enemy Iran, and used the proceeds to fund the Contra rebels in Nicaragua. It seems the Illuminati wanted the elected Sandinista Nicaraguan government out, and their method of choice was 'terrorists'. It's noted, that both supplying arms to Iran and funding/arming Contra 'freedom fighters' was strictly illegal under US law.

Contra rebels, this US-backed guerrilla force, were also shipping crack-cocaine into the US, via the CIA, and the sales of those drugs were funnelled back to help the Contras. The Reagan administration acknowledged in 1986 that funds from cocaine smuggling and selling arms to Iran had helped fund the Contra rebels.

So, it's understood the CIA oversees drugs and weapons (drugs go north, and guns go south), justified in the name of National Security. It's also highlighted they monopolise the drugs market as they can bust opposition with their intelligence. Indeed, the so called 'War on Drugs' endeavour, launched in the 1980s by the Bush-Regan Administration, was to fight traffickers who weren't working with the CIA. It's noted, Father Bush was affectionately known as 'Poppy'.

Bill Clinton's drug smuggling CIA ops, during the 1980s in Mena, Arkansas, are well documented. Like, in his book 'American Made: Who Killed Barry Seal? Pablo Escobar or George H W Bush' (2016), Shaun Attwood highlights that Clinton's bent cops provided security for the drug drops. Barry Seal was the pilot who flew cocaine and weapons worth billions of dollars into and out of America. Pablo Escobar's son confirmed his dad was working with the CIA on behalf of the cartels.

So, the CIA flooded the US with drugs in the 1980s. David Icke concedes the CIA control the main drug-running operations of the planet, and when Father George Bush became director of the CIA, cocaine influx into the US increased by over 2000%.

Cathy O'Brien also confirms the crack, as she was used to deliver it. Apparently, Bill Clinton's brother, Roger Clinton, said Bill's nose is like a 'vacuum cleaner'. David Icke (2007) also highlights, that Clinton revoked the random drug testing for the White House staff because there were so many cocaine addicts like him (p.453). The irony of the 'War on Drugs' is second to none given the exchange of drugs for arms e.g. Russian arms dealers trade with Afghan warlords (apparently six AK-47s are traded for 1kg of good quality heroin).

It's also noted, that before 1980 Afghanistan did not produce heroin. But after the CIA tricked the Soviet into invading Afghanistan, it began to flourish. The opium industry essentially transferred from Pakistan to Afghanistan. Afghanistan provides 90% of the world's heroin. The Soviet occupation of Afghanistan (1979-1989) was thus a clever rouse, as the CIA could help the Mujahideen (Islamic) fighters while helping themselves. Thus, the benevolent CIA, MI6 and Saudi royals financially supported Mujahideen to wage jihad against the Russians and pro-Soviet Afghan state. Osama Bin Laden (who graduated from university in 1980) became the front man for the resistance.

Mujahideen notably refers to any person performing jihad (defending their religious faith). In traditional jihad, the victorious party had the right to rape, loot and pillage the areas (people) they conquered. Women and girls were part of the conquest package. These 'rights' were instituted by Prophet Muhammad, who we'll get to.

The Taliban also participated in jihad against the Soviet, so they were also Mujahideen. The Taliban is a fundamentalist political movement that spread from Afghanistan to Pakistan. It initially consisted of very conservative religious students ('Talib' means student). They've been around since the earliest days of Islam and endorse strict Sharia law.

Untold millions of dollars were spent on training and funding these 'holy warriors'. Indeed, it's reported that over a ten-year period, the US gave the Mujahideen around $5 billion in weaponry and aid to recruit and train local forces. David Icke states the CIA, MI6, and Pakistan's intelligence agency 'Inter-Services Intelligence' (ISI) created and oversaw the training camps in Pakistan that coached more than 100,000 Muslims in the art of terrorism and bomb-making from 1986-1992. ISI is the Pakistan branch of the CIA, and it's well known it's involved in money laundering and rakes in billions.

The Soviet's notably alleged that CIA agents were helping smuggle opium out of Afghanistan to raise cash for Afghan resistance, and plague the Russians with drug addictions. It seems they were right. The investment in these soldiers has reaped an insane harvest. The world has been flooded with heroin, which has destroyed untold lives.

Once the Russians had been and gone, the US arranged for all Mujahideen names, including Osama Bin Laden from Saudi Arabia, to be listed on a CIA database. Al Qaeda, which literally means database, was thus the computer file of thousands of Mujahideen who were recruited and trained with help from the CIA to defeat Russia. Osama Bin Laden notably went back to work in Saudi Arabia for the family construction firm, the Bin Laden Group, when the Russians left in 1989.

As touched on, the wealthy Bin Laden family are intimately connected with the inner most circles of the Saudi royal family, and they have connections with the Bush family that span over three decades. Billions circulate between them. Apparently, Father George Bush stayed with the Bin Laden's when he visited Saudi Arabia. It's understood they share the same satanic religion. Thus, as David Icke states, Osama Bin Laden was a CIA asset.

As for Afghanistan, when the Soviet's left, the Mujahideen turned their guns on each other. Tyrannical Mujahideen warlords and Pakistan ISI were in control. And Afghan people were in despair. So, the Taliban came to the rescue?

The Taliban needed to build a force large enough to confront the corrupt warlords. They wanted to defend the rights of all Afghans, and establish order and justice. As it transpired, the Taliban became internationally recognised as the legitimate government of Afghanistan. It seems there's a degree of sympathy for the Taliban, as they were ill equipped for the job. They were after all students. So, they weren't the best, and they introduced a radical version of Sharia, which was super oppressive. Like, they banned kite-flying and music, and decreed that women weren't allowed to work. And they shot girls for attending school. They ruled from 1996-2001.

The 'family' also wanted Iraq (Babylon) for her resources, and to destabilise the Middle East, as detailed in the Neo-cons plan. Thus, 'Operation Desert Storm' landed. The first gulf war (1990-1991) led by Father George

Bush. It was sold on lies and a mountain of propaganda. Iraq and Kuwait had longstanding issues. Saddam was losing billions as a result of Kuwait's oil price strategy. Like, they were allegedly siphoning off his oil using 'slant-drilling'. Apparently, the US gave Kuwait the horizontal drills.

Saddam had apparently decided on war, (his response to the culmination of their tangled economic and historical conflicts), but before sending his army into Kuwait, he approached the US to find out how they would react. And the US Ambassador (April Glaspie) told Saddam, 'We have no opinion on your Arab-Arab conflicts, like your border dispute with Kuwait'. 'The Kuwait issue is not associated with America'. Washington has 'no special defence or security commitments to Kuwait'.

But as it transpired, Saddam's antics provided the perfect excuse to invade Iraq. Besides 'liberating' Kuwait, the US should protect Saudi Arabia's homeland, the key US oil supplier. It was falsely claimed by Pentagon officials that Saddam had 250,000 troops and 1,500 tanks on their border with hostile intent. The Pentagon had satellite images. However, a reporter (Jean Heller) obtained two commercial satellite images of the area taken at the exact same time as US intelligence, which revealed nothing but empty desert. She contacted the office of then-Secretary of Defence Dick Cheney, to evidence they were wrong, and the official response was 'trust us'. Really?

The propaganda however got worse, when fifteen year old 'Nayirah' advised that Saddam's troops were ripping babies out of incubators and leaving them 'to die on the cold floor'. Nayirah, the daughter of Kuwait's ambassador to the US, lied. Subsequent investigations by independent journalists confirmed this crucial piece of war propaganda was entirely bogus. We're literally played like fiddles.

After forty-two days of relentless attacks, in the air and on the ground, most Iraqis fled or surrendered. It's noted, Father Bush's war served as a prelude to baby Bush's sequel. It inflamed the region's zealots. US infidels were on their turf, and had no business being there. A holy war began brewing (all by design).

But then 9/11 happened, and '9/11 changed everything'. However, before we get into this, it's recalled that a year before 9/11 happened, the 'Project for the New American Century' (PNAC) revealed their plans. This report (produced in September 2000) was entitled 'Rebuilding America's Defenses: Strategies, Forces, And Resources For A New Century'.

As touched on, the people who wrote the PNAC came into power with the Bush Administration. And this neoconservative think tank, who's stated goal was 'to promote American global leadership', listed several countries that required a 'regime change'. These were Iraq, Iran, Afghanistan, Libya, Syria, North Korea, Sudan, and Lebanon (those without a Rothschild central bank). Their method of choice was using 'multiple theatre wars'.

But the report further stated that a 'catastrophic and catalysing event like Pearl Harbour' would get the ball rolling. A year later, 9/11 landed, which resulted in killing almost three thousand people in a very dramatic way. Some 200 people jumped to their death. Bush called 9/11 the new pearl harbour. He insisted, 'The world has changed after September 11th. It's changed because it's no longer safe'.

As mentioned in the Introduction, when Bush was told about the second attack on the WTC, he continued to read a story about a pet goat for half an hour in a classroom in Florida. Like, a mind-controlled robot? He was told about the first attack on the WTC before he went into the classroom, but he decided to go ahead with the photo op. And he lied when he said he seen the first plane hit building 1, and deducted the pilot was terrible, since that footage didn't exist at the time.

It's understood these buildings were pulled, (controlled demolition), like building 7. As touched on, apparently Building 7 harboured condemning files that had to be destroyed. Moreover, whilst the official story was that building 7 was destroyed by office furnishing fires, (which has since been debunked by research), WTC owner Larry Silverstein confessed to pulling it. He claimed a fire commander advised that the building was unstable. The three steel buildings came down the same way.

It's understood the 9/11 Commission aka Omission Report was not set up to find the truth, but rather withhold it. Like, the report didn't mention building 7, which is said to be the Achilles heel of the whole debacle. It's also noted, the crime scene and evidence was destroyed suspiciously quickly. Presumably they didn't want the public to discover the thermite?

Thousands of independent experts, including engineers, architects, pilots, fire-fighters, physicists and researchers, have come together to demand the truth as the official story is garbage. Thus, there's 'Architects and Engineers for 9/11 Truth' etc. They understand the pancake theory is bosh. Explosives were placed in key parts of the building to ensure they fell on their own footprint. The buildings fell with no resistance (freefall time). Towers 1 and 2 were also built to withstand a big Boeing plane crash.

It's noted, that Larry Silverstein bought the asbestos clad WTC dinosaur a few months before 9/11, which by all accounts was not a smart business move. Not least because it would cost more to remove the asbestos than what the building was worth. And just before 9/11, he doubled his insurance coverage, to include acts of terrorism. So, that was fortuitous. It was also fortunate he had a dermatology appointment that morning and wasn't in the North Tower, where he'd normally be. He had breakfast there every morning. And his kids fortunately weren't there.

As mentioned, it was also fortunate for those who made a mint through 'put options' (gambling that share prices would fall) on American Airlines and United Airlines, immediately before 9/11. And for those who snaffled the millions of gold ($121 million) and silver ($110 million) buried under the WTC.

Later, on that same fateful day, the Pentagon (pentagram) was allegedly attacked by American Airlines Flight 77 (interesting number, like Flight 11), leaving rubbish evidence (no footage). All cameras were confiscated within 24 hours, and the public were shown five frames, with no evidence of a plane. Even the hole, where the plane crashed, was considerably too small for the plane to fit in. It's suggested a missile was fired into the Pentagon, or a remotely flown 'Global Hawk'. The pentagon had conveniently been strengthened (reinforced) at that side in the off-chance that a plane might drive through it.

As also mentioned, it was convenient that it just happened to hit the accounts office, where Donald Rumsfeld announced $2.3 trillion was missing the day before, on September 10th, to wipe the memory of the missing budget. It also killed the accountants who could or would have tried to discover where the missing money went.

The last of the four hijacked planes to go down in the US was Flight 93 in Pennsylvania, which similarly left no trace of a plane or people. It was also completely blitzed (literal smithereens are uncharacteristic of plane crashes). Unlike the other flights, passengers on Flight 93 were hailed as heroes, as apparently they took on the hijackers, who hijacked the planes with box cutters and plastic knives. No danger, government authorities declared the planes were hijacked by these 'weapons'. Hence, Flight 93 allegedly crashed and didn't make its destination like the other planes. None of the pilots notably pressed the hijack code, which takes a second.

It's also highlighted the planes were never identified, so we don't know if those four planes were the four planes that 'crashed'. When plane crashes happen, planes are always identified by their serial number. So, the planes that were 'hijacked' could have been military planes or drones made to look like United and American Airlines planes. Like, they planned in Operation Northwoods. The real planes could have been intercepted?

Or the planes could have been remotely controlled i.e. the flight management computer systems could have been hacked into by those on the ground. Which explains the perfect flying? As David Icke (2007) questions, 'Is it credible to believe that nineteen hijackers who failed or struggled to fly one engined sesna's could suddenly manifest the ability to fly massive airliners with the most extraordinary skill?' (p.376). It's also said the planes that went into the towers could have been holographic. The military's technology is that insane, as we'll get to.

As mentioned, the FBI advised that nineteen (mostly) Saudi Arabian hijackers were responsible. Yet several of them are still alive. And there was a very specific trail left for the FBI to find. Like, authorities found Mohammad Atta's baggage. It apparently didn't make the plane. As Icke states, 'what a stroke of unbelievable luck'. LOL. Authorities thus discovered their insidious plans to attack America. And other items like flight manuals, Korans, his driving license, his will, and passport, which begs the question how did he get through security? They chased the trail they left for themselves to find.

Additionally, the FBI found another one of the hijacker's passports, which managed to somehow survive the inferno. Icke (2007) highlights the FBI held a conference to announce the momentous find, stating, 'a paper passport that had survived the fireball, and wafted down amid rubble and dust to be found by a passerby. I mean, was it even singed?' (p. 342). LOL. So, that passport survived but the extremely robust black boxes, (which could have shed some light on the situation), didn't.

It's noted, that General Mahmoud Ahmed, head of ISI, sanctioned $100, 000 to be wired to Atta, the lead hijacker of 9/11, in August 2001. David Icke explains that Atta and his buds were CIA agents. They were involved in drug trafficking, part of the CIA's drug operation in Florida, and other covert operations. The flight schools in Florida are notorious for drug flights to and from South America (planes are packed with coke). So, Atta was a CIA asset. He was one of their boys. And as mentioned, these boys liked cocaine, alcohol, and strippers. They were not devout Muslims.

It seems the Israeli art student's aka Mossad agents were instrumental to setting up the explosives in the WTC. It's noted, bomb sniffer dogs were abruptly removed a few days before 9/11. We did however get to see footage of the Israeli dancers who revelled watching the show. So, that's nice. They said they came to record the event, which suggests they knew the event was coming. They watched the towers from 8am. At least two of these dancers are known to be Mossad agents. It's also understood Israel had phone contracts for the US and knew about 9/11 planned attacks. Those interviewed advised the information was classified. Thus, it's said the US cares about Israel, but Israel does not care about the US.

Moreover, it's understood that 9/11 was a satanic ritual (demonic faces can be seen in footage of the smoke). It was a sacrifice, which included sacrificing Jakin and Boaz (the twin towers). The memorial site installed at Ground

Zero shows their respect for those who died. Or rather, it's respect for their god Saturn. The two black square reflecting pools represent the abyss. It's also said, the new one world trade centre, which is 1776 feet tall (America declared independence and the Bavarian Illuminati was born in 1776), represents the One World Order.

A couple of days after 9/11, the US thus declared that Al Qaeda, headed by Osama, carried out the attacks. And yet the FBI stated there is 'no hard evidence connecting Bin Laden to 9/11'. He was never charged with 9/11 because he didn't do it. Al Qaeda were allegedly motivated to attack the US in retaliation for US support of Israel, US involvement in the Persian Gulf War and sanctions imposed against Iraq, and the US's continued military presence in the Middle East. And more generally, because they wanted to promote widespread fear throughout the country and severely weaken the US standing in the world community.

However, as Michael Moore highlights in his 'Fahrenheit 9/11' documentary, at a time when Bush was telling the world 'we must get Bin Laden', many of Osama's relatives were permitted to leave the US. He states the US government evacuated 24 members of the Bin Laden family on a secret flight shortly after the attacks, without subjecting them to any form of interrogation. And that at least six private jets and nearly two dozen commercial planes carried the Saudis and Bin Laden's out of the US after September 13th. Yet planes were supposed to be grounded.

It's also noted, that despite most of the hijackers being Saudi Arabian, Saudi Arabia wasn't on the radar. It doesn't need a regime change, despite having the worst human rights record. Saudi Arabia, who equally beheads infidels, are our friends. They buy our weapons (and the US and Canada's), which they then use on Yemen. It's understood they're the controlled financial arm of the US.

We were told the Taliban regime of Afghanistan provided a safe haven for Al Qaeda, and thus we started bombing Afghanistan four weeks after 9/11. The US military began snooping in caves, as Bush had vowed to 'smoke them out of their holes and get them running'. Yet the Taliban publicly condemned the attacks and had no prior knowledge of the attacks. They also (quite rightly) said, at a conference in Pakistan, they would hand over Osama if the US could prove he was responsible.

The Taliban were trying to create stability in Afghanistan. This included collaborating with the UN to impose a successful ban on poppy cultivation in 2000. The result was opium declined by more than 90%. Thus, something had to be done. The Taliban had to be removed. It was therefore fortuitous that the Taliban were harbouring American-made Al Qaeda.

So, the Taliban were overthrown by the American-led invasion of Afghanistan. And opium production rocketed. Occupied Afghanistan once again produces more than 90% of the world's heroin. It's thus purported that the Afghan narcotics economy was a carefully designed project of the CIA, supported by US foreign policy. As David Icke highlights, the War in Afghanistan was to restore the CIA sponsored drug trade to its historic levels and exert direct control over the drug routes.

It's well documented that the US Government protected drug operations, with American troops even helping farmers to grow their crops. A CIA source confirmed CIA 'big boys' are transporting heroin from Afghanistan to the US. So, we know the CIA is embroiled in drug trafficking. Do we care?

It's also noted, that Bin Laden initially denied any involvement in 9/11. Then a video tape appeared (the authenticity is questionable) which shows 'Bin Laden' proudly confessing to the attacks on the WTC and

Pentagon. He said, 'History should be a witness that we are terrorists. Yes, we kill their innocents'. He said the pilots who hijacked the planes were 'blessed by Allah'. As mentioned, the pilots were dreadful, which suggests they weren't flying the planes.

At the same time as the US was searching for Osama and his buds, Bush was equally saying that anyone who makes WMD is a terrorist, like Saddam. Indeed, five hours after the attacks on the twin towers, Donald Rumsfeld, US Defence Secretary, linked Saddam Hussein to the attacks and Al Qaeda, without any evidence. George W Bush claimed, 'we need to disarm him in the name of peace' (this is known as 'doublespeak').

So, despite 9/11 having nothing to do with Saddam, he was brought back into the foreground as allegations were pinned on him. The Chilcot Inquiry into Iraq revealed Tony Blair said to Bush in December 2001, it 'would be excellent' to remove Saddam from power but there 'needed to be a clever strategy for doing this', 'an extremely clever plan would be required'. And in a letter in July 2002 he wrote, 'I will be with you whatever'. He also set out a vision for a 'NWO' in which Bush would 'unite the world' around a global agenda.

It's understood Saddam wasn't playing ball with OPEC. He flooded the market with oil at reduced prices (as he wanted to reduce his debt), and converted to the Euro for Iraq's oil exports, which further lowered the price of oil and dollars, as oil is traded in dollars. He had to be stopped. And so, the Hegelian excuse to invade Iraq was their alleged WMD.

It's also noted, that Donald Rumsfeld, US Secretary of Defence, supplied Saddam Hussein with chemical weapons, including anthrax and bubonic plague, in 1983 to assist him the 1980-88 Iran-Iraq war. The US further increased arms supplies to Saddam after he used US supplied poison gas against the Kurds 1987-1988. Then they used his antics against him. Cheney also sold nuclear technology to North Korea in 2000. It's like selling weapons to Iran. We set up future 'problems'.

There was huge propaganda against Saddam. We were told that missiles were poised to strike British territory. And Iraq could unleash chemical and biological warfare (e.g. anthrax). We could be a memory within 45 minutes. We can recall Colin Powell's, US Secretary of Defence (and 33rd degree mason), address to the UN, complete with his vial for the demonstration. There was however no evidence of WMD. David Icke notably calls Colin Powell Colon Powell because he's full of shit (LOL).

As mentioned, weapons expert Dr David Kelly refuted these claims, having inspected them as a member of the UN inspection team. And he was suicided in the woods, as he predicted. Former British Prime Minister Gordon Brown also stated the Pentagon knew Saddam didn't have WMD. And it's recalled that Robin Cook, former British Foreign Secretary, resigned from the Blair government over the Iraq invasion in 2003. Then he had a heart attack and died a month later (the military has technology to induce heart attacks). It seems he knew our propaganda was bosh. And Al Qaeda was a CIA creation.

Cook said, 'The truth is, there is no Islamic army or terrorist group called Al Qaeda, and any informed intelligence officer knows this. But, there is a propaganda campaign to make the public believe in the presence of an intensified entity representing the 'devil' only in order to drive TV watchers to accept a unified international leadership for a war against terrorism. The country behind this propaganda is the United States' (cited in David Icke, 'The Trigger, The Lie That Changed The World – Who Really Did it And Why', 2019 p.396).

So, we invaded Iraq. Born-again Bush notably called the invasion a 'crusade'. Then we were told that spies had lied. The dossier was dodgy (the dossier is known as the 'dodgy dossier') and the 'forty-five minute claim' was hogwash. Intelligence had been 'sexed up' in the run up to the war. It's said MI6 got their intelligence indirectly from a taxi driver who apparently heard Iraqi militant commanders talking about weapons.

Millions of people protested against the Iraq war (e.g. two million protested in London, and three million in Rome), but alas to no avail. There were 29,200 US airstrikes during the 2003 invasion. It was relentless, and over a million people were killed in this illegal invasion ordered by Bush and Blair. The UN Security Council did not agree to the force against Iraq. And to add insult to injury, Bush joked about the fact there were no WMD. Describing the situation, he said 'nope, not in there' ha, ha.

Oil production however increased exponentially. Dick Cheney's (Bush's Defence Secretary) Halliburton, in particular, made almost $40 billion from post-war contracts. Iraq was also forced to use dollars for oil sales. Ironically, Halliburton's slogan was, 'proud to serve our troops'. Less charming, Henry Kissinger, former US Secretary of State, said 'Military men are just dumb, stupid animals to be used as pawns in foreign policy'. These honourable men are cannon fodder. And there is little aftercare, having served their country. Apparently, (after the Iraq war), 22 US veterans commit suicide every day.

It seems pertinent to note, that Hollywood Filmmaker Aaron Russo (1943-2007), in an interview with Alex Jones, said 'Nicholas Rockefeller' told him eleven months prior to 9/11 that there would be 'an event'. And this event would lead to the invasion of Afghanistan and Iraq. Then they would go after Venezuela. He said the US would take over the oil fields in Iraq and establish a base in the Middle East.

Russo relayed that Rockefeller 'told us we'd see soldiers looking in caves in Afghanistan and Pakistan, and there's going to be this war on terror with no real enemy'. Russo said the whole thing is a giant hoax. The war on terror is a joke, fraud, and farce. He insisted the truth had to come out, hence his disclosure.

Russo asserted that we need to figure out the truth of 9/11 as this started the so-called war on terror. It seems 9/11 is the tip of the iceberg? Nick Rockefeller (who apparently wanted Russo onboard the CFR) told him the end goal is a NWO run by bankers. The future is cashless. The endeavour is for us to become micro-chipped slaves of the state. We'll be connected to a global database, using our chip for transactions. But moreover, Russo highlights they could switch our chip off, preventing us from buying anything.

Russo insists 9/11 was an inside job to fear us into subordination. He states the first lie was creating the endless war on terror, and the second lie was Iraq's WMD. And so it continues, as these people lie. It's recalled that George W Bush prided himself on being a war president. In an interview in 2004, he said, 'I'm a war president. I make decisions here in the Oval Office in foreign-policy matters with war on my mind'. Say what?

Bill Cooper also predicted in June 2001 the WTC would be destroyed and that Osama Bin Laden would be the fall guy. He said, 'whatever is going to happen they're going to blame it on Osama Bin Laden – don't you even believe it'. Cooper was murdered in November 2001.

Cooper also highlighted that whilst US intelligence couldn't find Osama, CNN found him. 'LOL'. They were permitted to interview Osama, for his first ever TV interview, in 1997. The CNN team was taken to an undisclosed location in Afghanistan. Osama said, 'we declared a jihad, a holy war, against the United States Government because it is unjust, criminal and tyrannical'. Cooper knew it was BS. Cooper dedicated his life to waking people up (and got exasperated with the sheeple).

But moreover, as touched on, Gilgamesh's (Nimrod's?) tomb was discovered in Iraq desert a month before we invaded. According to the Sumerian clay tablets, he was buried under the Euphrates in a tomb. So, he was found (in a remarkable state of preservation) in April 2003. Then in May the first thing the troops did was kick out the archaeologists and raid the museum of Baghdad. 170,000 items were reported stolen, and whilst most of these have been returned, 3,000 are unaccounted for. This includes Sumerian cuneiform tablets and book collections. It's speculated that scientists might resurrect his DNA, to bring back the gods?

After taking out Saddam, and annihilating Iraq, we then went onto decimate Libya. Britain joined France and the US in the air and sea strikes to enable opponents of Muammar Gaddafi to take control of the major cities. Gaddafi and his regime had to be removed. It was next on the PNAC hitlist. Libyans deserve democracy, the illusion of choice, like us.

So, we backed the anti-government pro-democracy protesters. Or rather, we supported mostly mercenaries to attack government buildings and other politically provocative places to rattle Gaddafi into retaliating. Rebels were funded and armed by the NATO alliance to cause problems, and when Gaddafi reacted against the rebels, the solution was conveniently removing him. So, the rebels were a proxy war on behalf of the west.

Gaddafi recognised Al-Qaeda (an outside force) invaded Libya, and that Al-Qaeda was made by the US for Bin Laden. He also advised that his removal would create a vacuum for terrorism to thrive, like it did in Iraq. And further, that Libya was the cork of Africa but when she pops, floods of migrants would enter Europe and destabilise Africa.

Before we trashed it, Libya was the richest country in Africa. Gaddafi insisted that everyone deserved housing, education, and cheap oil. Whilst he wasn't a saint, (and neither is the Pope), his people literally loved him. He was adored as he paraded (drove) through the streets with his entourage. Gaddafi not only wanted Libya to prosper, but also Africa at large, by using gold for currency. Africa could have reigned supreme?

The family didn't however like this idea (because their money is a phantom). Alternatively, we heard about how dreadful Gaddafi was on 'the news', attacking his people, and how it would be kind to intervene. So, it was a false flag. It's also recalled, that when Gaddafi was killed and we 'freed' Libya, Hillary Clinton said 'we came, we saw, he died, ha ha'. It appears she shares the same dark humour as George W Bush. Apparently, Gaddafi was sodomised before he was murdered.

It's understood we've given billions to opposition groups, so-called moderates, to spark civil unrest and sectarian wars. They're proxy wars on behalf of the west. Apparently, the US has created more than fifty coups since 1945. Placing sanctions on 'rogue' countries also inspires people to turn against their governments. Like, Venezuela and Iran?

It's also noted, that whilst Saudi Arabia helps NATO to annihilate 'rogue countries' (that need a regime change), they don't take it for the team when it comes to refugees. Apparently Saudi Arabia has 100,000 air-conditioned tents that can house three million people sitting empty. Maybe they're keeping them for some other purpose, like the FEMA camps in the US?

The result is an influx of Muslims into Europe, which includes haters (Islamic militants inspired by Al Qaeda). However, it's understood the refugee crisis is part of the plan, the multi-pronged approach for more chaos. This further helps undermine national sovereignty. Lest we forget, the surge of vulnerable kids ripe for the picking.

Meanwhile the 'terrorists' continued to make their presence known. Like, '3/11' the Madrid bombings in 2004, that happened exactly 911 days after 9/11. The trains torn apart by bombs in Madrid killed 191 people and wounded more than 1,800. The police blamed Islamic extremists, given the clues deliberately left behind. We were told a group called 'The Secret Organisation of Al Qaeda in Europe' claimed they were responsible.

However, the man accused of supplying the dynamite used in the train bombings, namely, Emilio Suarez Trashorras, had the private phone number of the head of Spain's Civil Guard bomb squad[29]. Apparently, Emilio, and another couple of the suspects, were informants working for the police (they informed police about drug shipments). They made calls to the police inspector and to the alleged ringleaders of the bombing plot from the same pay phone outside the police station. Spanish government officials announced that the bombings were largely funded by drug money. Emilio traded drugs for explosives.

As it transpired, there were no links to Al-Qaeda, as initially conveyed. But rather it was an 'Al-Qaeda inspired attack' i.e. 'home-grown'. Our Muslim population was getting radicalised? Or it was a false flag, orchestrated by MI6 and Mossad. It's also said the bombings, which happened three days before the Spanish election, endeavoured to steer the result.

Circa this time, it's recalled that Osama Bin Laden offered Europe a truce if it 'stops attacking Muslims'. Colin Powell said the voice was Bin Laden's on the audiotape. So, it must be true? His offer was not however extended to the US. And his offer, namely 'stop spilling our blood so we can stop spilling your blood', was rejected.

The tape, which refers to 9/11 and 3/11, said they were payment for US and Spanish actions in Iraq, Afghanistan, and Palestinian territories. After mentioning the occupation of Palestine, the voice says, 'What happened to you on September 11 and March 11 are your goods returned to you. It is well known that security is a vital necessity for every human being. We will not let you monopolise it for yourselves'.

And, 'In what creed are your dead considered innocent but ours worthless? By what logic does your blood count as real and ours as no more than water? Reciprocal treatment is part of justice, and he who commences hostilities is the unjust one'. The voice further points out, 'This war is making billions of dollars for the big corporations, whether it be those who manufacture weapons or reconstruction firms like Halliburton and its offshoots and sister companies'.

The speaker finishes by affirming his actions have been in response to the West's interference in Muslim lands. He said, 'For we only killed Russians after they invaded Afghanistan and Chechnya, we only killed Europeans after they invaded Afghanistan and Iraq, and we only killed Americans in New York after they supported Jews in Palestine and invaded the Arabian peninsula, and we only killed them in Somalia, after they invaded it in Operation Restore Hope'.

Having rejected Osama's olive branch, we were told the '7/7' London bombings in 2005 was retaliation for Britain's involvement in Iraq and Afghanistan. 7/7 (another illuminist signature) was dubbed our 9/11. Three underground trains and a double-decker bus were bombed, which resulted in 52 dead (plus four suicide bombers) and over 700 injured.

---

[29] See the Times 21/6/2004 'Madrid Bombers Linked to Spanish Security Service'.

Like 9/11, the four Islamic terrorists in 7/7 left an easy trail for the police to follow. They all had ID cards, which survived unscathed and scattered in all locations/events. Indeed, an extra identity card was found. The same identity card was found at two separate locations (LOL). It's not however understood how the bombers got to their locations, as the trains they were allegedly on were cancelled. It's also highlighted that Benjamin Netanyahu was warned of the London bombs, and was advised to stay in his hotel room and avoid trains. It's also curious why the bus was rerouted to Tavistock Square?

Quite unbelievably, but like 9/11 and 3/11, training exercises/drills were happening at the same time, enacting the exact same scenarios. This naturally creates a cover and causes confusion. Like, in 9/11 air-traffic control went into meltdown, trying to ascertain which war games were real or fake. The same thing happened at the Boston bombings in 2013. That is, a bomb drill was held before the Boston Marathon. The bomb-squad (complete with bomb-sniffing dogs) forewarned runners not to be alarmed by their training exercise. It's understood that was also an 'inside job'.

It's said the 7/7 bombings in London, was the last successful operation Osama played a role in. The US eventually declared 'we got him' in 2011, although the footage seems to show at least two different looking Osama's, so Allah knows. And we'll never know as he was allegedly buried at sea (apparently he was shot through his left eye). According to US officials, he was thrown overboard so that his grave wouldn't become a shrine. Or he's still alive? Maybe he's on a paradise island with Jeffrey Epstein?

So, both Gaddafi and Osama Bin Laden (allegedly) were killed in 2011, the same year civil war broke out in Syria, and ISIS surfaced (interesting reference to Isis). Despite the US proudly advising they 'defeated' Al Qaeda, it would appear not. ISIS traces its origins to Abu Musab al-Zarqawi, who formed Al Qaeda in Iraq in 2004 following the US invasion. After that group was defeated by Iraqis and American forces circa 2008, they reformed between 2008 and 2011, and the Islamic State landed (in the ancient region of Canaan no less), ensued by their own caliphate. This group rebuilt itself out of former prisoners and former Saddam era Iraqi army officials, and loads of well-paid (by the CIA) mercenaries.

In line with the agenda, which includes the removal of democratically elected Bashar Al-Assad and his regime, we decided to 'help' the moderate rebels in Syria, which resulted in helping ISIS. It's said we used the same tactic in Syria, as was used in Libya, namely, western sponsored terrorism (sectarian attacks). Apparently, many mercenaries came from Libya, having carried out their sectarian carnage there first. Russia however supported Syria, as they knew that thousands of 'rebels', who were aligned to Al Qaeda and other terrorists, were foreign. They were from Saudi Arabia, Europe, Libya, and Turkey.

Thus, it's understood (as NSA whistle-blower Edward Snowdon affirmed) it's the same people behind ISIS and Al-Qaeda, namely, the CIA, MI6 and Mossad. ISIS was merely a rebranding of Al-Qaeda. Kenneth O'Keefe refers to ISIS as 'Israel's Secret Intelligence Services'. He points out that ISIS and Al-Qaeda have never attacked Israel, and ISIS received medical help in Israel. Israel however conveys this as a demonstration of their benevolence, even for their enemies.

ISIS was created to remove Assad's regime so they can impose their own regime. ISIS were trained, armed and equipped by the west. Hence, 'terrorists' were driving Toyotas, with their arsenal of weapons. We were told however that ISIS took advantage of the rebellion against Assad. In addition to the Saudi royals funding them, (as revealed in Killary Clinton's emails), Turkey, (NATO member), for example, supported ISIS by buying oil from them.

Like Al-Qaeda, ISIS was motivated by global jihadist aims, and promised to free Palestine. It seems they want WW3 to be sparked by Jewish and Islamic hatred, like Pike pertained to? This is notably contrary to the Taliban, who keep jihad within their own borders. Al-Qaeda also readily claims responsibility for their attacks e.g. Paris attacks etc. So, they want us to know.

It's also noted, that Osama Bin Laden was a treat compared to the 'Islamic State'. For example, the late Sheikh Abu Muhammad al-Adnani (1977-2016), IS's chief spokesperson, said 'we will conquer your Rome, break your crosses, and enslave your women'… And, 'If we do not reach that time, then our children and grandchildren will reach it, and they will sell your sons as slaves at the slave market'.

He further called on Muslims in Western countries, stating, 'If you can kill a disbelieving American or European – especially the spiteful and filthy French – or an Australian, or a Canadian, or any other disbeliever from the disbelievers waging war, including the citizens of the countries that entered into a coalition against the Islamic State, then rely upon Allah, and kill him in any manner or way, however it may be'. He goes on to suggest, 'Smash his head with a rock, or slaughter him with a knife, or run him over with your car, or throw him down from a high place, or choke him, or poison him'.

The west has been lied to believe that Assad is a maniac who uses chemical weapons on his people. Russia however disagreed. And they actually defeated IS, which wasn't the plan? They believed Assad was telling the truth when he denied the allegations. There was no motive, and the west sponsored White Helmets provided the appalling evidence (some of the footage is unbelievably fake). As Russia discovered, sometimes no gas is used during gas attacks, and no one dies. Apparently, the White Helmets were however given 30 tons of German made Chlorine gas for mercenaries to use to blame Assad. So, something's being set up?

Thus, it's understood these attacks were false flags? And we go along with it. Like, Assad's alleged second chemical attack warranted the US sending 59 Tomahawks (which cost $1 million each) to blow up their airstrip, which was repaired the next day. Whilst arguably a waste of time and money, some benefitted. It's understood the US doesn't care about wasting money, because they don't care about debt?

According to Syrians, like Father Daniel Mecis, a Flemish priest who lives 90km north of Damascus, the media coverage on Syria is the biggest lie ever. According to Pastor Charles Lawson, Mecis advised that western reports are very misleading and the popular uprising against Assad is completely false. Mecis claims the agitation against the government was organised from forces outside Syria. He states young people were recruited to protest against the government. And murders were committed by foreign terrorists to sow religious and ethnic discord among Syrian people. He is crystal that the rebellion is not true, and the west has ruined their country. He highlights that before the war, Syria was secular, and people lived in harmony. They had good health care, free education and almost no poverty.

It's such a scam that we promote democracy, and endeavour to give freedom to oppressed people, when we're the most deluded of all? And it's bemusing to think how much of our unfolding play is staged i.e. the false flags and literally staged i.e. actors, fake blood and injuries. Like, it's purported the Boston Marathon Bombing was a hoax event performed by crisis actors, complete with tell-tale bright red Hollywood blood. Sometimes the same crisis actors are used again in other scams, like at 'mass shootings'. It's a joke.

Mainstream news clearly includes 'fake news', lest we forget their occasional blunders. Like, the BBC reported that WTC7 had collapsed twenty minutes before the building actually came down (LOL). And Bill Clinton slipped up saying the Pentagon was bombed. It's also noted, the term 'fake news' was deployed to ridicule the 'Pizza-gate' scandal in 2016. And since then, the media has been obsessed with fake news, which is anything contrary to the mainstream account. Thus, social media platforms forbid topics like 9/11, flat earth, and alternative opinions regarding 5G and the corona virus. Free speech has been replaced with fascism. Suffice to say, trying to ascertain real news is a challenge. Real eyes realise?

Or take the two SAS agents (British 'Special' Air Services), for example, who were caught dressed as Arab 'terrorists', and driving an Iraqi car that was filled with explosives and weapons. The Iraqi police force was patrolling the area (Basra, 2005), on the lookout for terrorists, and these men looked suspicious. This was confirmed when they opened fire on the Iraqi people, killing at least one police officer. The Iraqi police however prevailed and detained these seemingly terrorists at the police station.

But then, most dramatically, within minutes, an elite SAS unit came to the rescue, and created a jailbreak, literally smashing through the building with their six tanks, to free their men, and about 150 other Iraqi prisoners. Much of the jail was demolished. During this illegal prison break, Iraqi officials were held at gunpoint. The Iraqi governor of Basra, Mohammed al-Waili, condemned the action as 'barbaric, savage and irresponsible'.

It seems we believed mainstream news (past tense), as we've never had any reason to doubt our governments, global corporations, banks, and the media? But moreover, it seems we're the rogue countries behind the terrorists? We're the double agents, supporting 'terrorism' whilst superficially trying to defeat it? As Noam Chomsky insists, the US is the main threat to world peace. US foreign policy steers our global direction. Horrors are engineered to line bankers and warmonger's pockets, and create NWO architecture i.e. laws and policies. Like, the Patriot Act, which was written months before 9/11. It seems 9/11 was the start of the NWO?

The endeavour is apparently to keep us in a state of fear, through the endless threat of terror, because through fear we can be controlled. We'll relinquish our freedoms for protection. Chomsky said the 'fear of attack' technique has been used to validate terror, domestically and abroad since 1823. Other 'invisible' enemies include climate change and plandemics. These global fiascos control us and bring us together.

It's understood the NWO is essentially George Orwell's 1984 meets Aldous Huxley's Brave New World (complete with Soma). 1984's 'double speak' slogans notably include 'war is peace', 'freedom is slavery', and 'ignorance is strength'. Like, Bush said they needed to decimate Iraq in the name of peace. And we've been told ahead of time, which is part of the predictive programming? Thus, we're prepared for what's to come i.e. totalitarian surveillance state, complete with a profusion of cameras and microchips to track us at all times. It's like H G Wells' 'The New World Order' (1940), preps us for a global government and secular world religion.

Thus, the stated aim is one global government with one global army, to impose its will. This will take the form of militarised police. Like, UN peacekeepers? And one global economy, with one global cashless (digital) currency, that connects to a central bank. And we'll be connected by our chip. If we're not chipped, we can't access money. And the one global religion, the UN's religion, is the light of Lucifer.

It's noted, that countries (particularly Sweden, Israel, China and the UK) are becoming increasingly cashless. In the UK, plastic payment cards are the most popular way to buy things. Over 500 ATMs are closing every month. And they're making it harder to pay with cash (e.g. parking meters etc don't take cash). But moreover, we can house the RFID chip otherwise contained in our bank cards. On the plus side, this will put an end to credit card theft, but as Russo mentioned, this chip can be switched off, leaving us on Hungry Street. Dissidents of the system will have to forage for their food?

It appears we're being groomed for the chip. Like, we chip our beloved pets. And certain people, with mental illness, for example, to track them. And it makes sense to chip our kids, who could be kidnapped. We might even demand that we're chipped for our 'protection'. Mandatory chipping could help track terrorists and illegal immigrants. No more identity fraud. Being scanned everywhere we go is a small price to pay for protection. This is a free world? It's noted, the UN has expressed the desire for a global ID system complete with biometric data to give everyone on earth a digital identity. Agenda 2030 calls for 'legal identity'.

Moreover, we're tracked by our mobile phones anyway, so who cares? Like, we know our technology has eavesdropping devices, like Alexa. And our TVs, computers, play stations, and 'smart' phones watch us. And phones can be tapped. Social media spies on us. Big Brother sees what we're looking up online. Most of our transactions are recorded, which includes travel etc.

So, it's not hard to find us, or know what we're consuming. Indeed, people freely give their information. No one cares about privacy. We share it all (LOL). We don't mind being watched? Indeed, we prefer it? If we're not doing anything illegal, we have nothing to worry about. Goethe said, 'none are more hopelessly enslaved than those who falsely believe they are free'.

It appears chips are multifunctional. Like, for identity (including criminal and health records), and to make financial transactions or not. And we can be connected to technology, like our phones and computers. We can even open locked doors and start car engines etc. So, that's all good? But moreover, apparently the idea is to create a global brain. So, we'll all be connected to the internet by our chip. It's said AI will do our thinking for us. We'll collectively become a 'hive mind'. Apparently, the aim is to have us connected by 2030, which coincides with the UN pledge to provide universal internet access by 2030.

Like, Elon Musk's company 'Neuralink' plans to connect people's brains to the internet. We can be connected to computers by implanting tiny chips (called Brain-Machine Interface) into our brains. The procedure is apparently safe and easy. He states the goal is to allow paralysed people to control phones or computers. He states the system could be used to treat brain disorders, like Alzheimer's or Parkinson's. But further, it could ultimately 'preserve and enhance' brain function. The system will be wireless, which relies on 5G (apparently 6G will be in place by 2030).

It's believed the chip will be promoted. Like, it will be 'smart' to be linked to the internet and the smart grid? It will be smart to be linked to everything 'smart'. We'll literally merge with technology and become transhuman? It might offer us a DNA upgrade and prolong life expectancy. Like, we could live 300-500 years? However, it's also speculated that chips may interfere with our thoughts and emotions. Like, we'll literally become mind-controlled zombies of the state, as David Icke warns us. So, we have this to look forward to?

At the time of writing then, Syria remains on the PNAC hitlist, along with Iran, North Korea etc. Numerous articles have revealed Pentagon planning for operations against Iran as early as 2005. We're concerned about their nuclear weapons and intentions, unlike Israel's? It's noted, that Baby Bush called Iran, North Korea and Iraq the axis of evil after 9/11, stating they threaten the peace of the world. And Russia has been demonised because of her alliance with Syria and Iran, but that works because WW3 will need to involve Russia and China?

ISIS has also inspired a global network of radical Islamic terrorists who vehemently hate us. And fair play? We've watched our governments destroy their countries and people, (their children and 'beautiful babies'), from the comfort of our nicely decorated homes, where we watch 'the news'. And we've nicely decorated our military for war-crimes. Albeit a badge or two seems rubbish for having no legs and Post Traumatic Stress Disorder? And is there honour in killing people? Soldiers invariably throw up when they first kill people.

And unlike the west, Muslims have a better idea of what's going on? Like, they know Mossad was involved in 9/11 on behalf of the Zionists. Rumour has it that Israeli employees who worked in the Trade Centre and Pentagon were told not to go into work that day. Hence, the US is called the big Satan, and Israel the little Satan.

And whilst their former dictators were far from ideal, life was better for them, especially Christians. Indeed, Iraqi Christians refer to Saddam's reign as 'the golden period'. They were free, protected and lived normal lives. But after Saddam, when the state collapsed, Christians were regarded as connected to western invaders and thus the extremists turned on the so-called infidels. Western invaders are Christian (like 'born again' George Bush) so Christians are the enemy.

ISIS stated that Iraq's indigenous Christians were a 'legitimate target'. Thus, militants began violently attacking churches and priests, kidnapping Christians and demanding ransoms, murdering, raping, robbing (everything), and selling them as slaves on the open market.

It seems counterintuitive however to think that Allah, so called God, could be happy about his people murdering, stealing, selling and raping people, including children? Whilst these actions put 'regular' Muslims off their religion, it's equally noted this jihadist mentality is infectious, as Christians are horrendously persecuted in many Arab countries. Apparently, Christians are the most persecuted group worldwide. But we don't really hear about this on 'the news'.

So, the cabal's plan has been going according to plan. And part of their plan is exposure? Hence, truthers have been allowed to reveal the truth? Like, the phenomenon known as QAnon came into existence in October 2017. It appears that someone 'anonymous' with 'Q' security clearance is divulging classified information on a forum online. It's believed Donald Trump, or someone in his inner circle, is Q. Like, Q told us the cabal (which includes the Rothschild's) worships Satan. And these elites are part of an international child sex trafficking ring. Q tells us the cabal operates secretly and silently. And it's taking over the world.

Q's messages can be cryptic and vague, so followers of Q have to do some research of their own. Q also quotes Ephesians 6:12, which tells that we're not fighting against people made of flesh and blood, but against evil rulers and authorities of the unseen world, against dark powers that rule this world, and wicked spirits in the heavenly realms. So, that's interesting? It's also noted, that when Donald Trump started in office, he mysteriously referred to 'the calm before the storm'. Q supporters interpret this as a reference to the day of reckoning for the Satanists. Trump promised he would drain the swamp.

It's noted, that religious and non-religious 'Truthers' follow Q. But furthermore, it's suggested Q may be a deception to mislead Christians. It seems Satan's plan is to introduce a 'false light' i.e. Gnosticism. We're being led to believe the cabal has held us back from the truth about our divine essence. Hence, David Icke has been allowed to expose 'The Biggest Secret', because he promotes this false light or gospel? 'The guys' are misleading him to mislead us. Contrary to popular New Age opinion, we are not the Great I AM.

The other game changer that has happened very recently is the corona aka crown virus. Like climate change, this pandemic or plandemic or scamdemic has brought the world together. The Pope notably said the corona virus is Mother Nature's revenge for climate change. This global problem requires a coordinated global response. Like, former British Prime Minister Gordon Brown stated, we need a global government to address this medical and economic crisis. It's said life will never be the same again. It has decimated the global economy, which was the point? And nothing about the corona virus adds up. Apparently, the term 'new normal' is code for New World Order. The Covid 19 crisis is being used as a pretext for creating the NWO i.e. the great economic reset which addresses climate change.

We're also not particularly happy with China, which is the idea? Its rumoured China weaponised the corona virus to destroy western economies. However, it's also purported the 'deep state' in the US created the corona virus. Apparently, The Centers for Disease Control and Prevention (a private company) patented the corona virus in 2003, and shipped it to Wuhan, to continue the research there. Hence, they were given $7 million (as mentioned). According to beloved Bill Gates, the solution is vaccinating the world and being digitally tracked. It's also reported that 5G produces the same symptoms as the corona virus. So, the corona virus is the scapegoat for 5G?

Evil is empowering. It always benefits someone. Like, war, devastating weather, and sickness. And evil is growing. But moreover, whilst wars suggest a conflict between at least two nations, it's understood the family are ultimately dictating these wars. As Ronald Bernard said, 'They're all on the same side at the top. Wars are fun for them. It's a game for these psychos who worship Lucifer'. It's also noted, that as people are exposed to truth, they're rebelling against the cabal. It seems this is part of the plan for more chaos. They allow truth to come out because they want us to rise up in anarchy. It necessitates the need for someone wonderful to restore justice and peace? In short, we have created a ton blood sacrifices, and the stage is being set for Lucifer's kingdom. With regards to what happens next, the Bible tells us. We're told in advance how this 'pans' out.

'What is foretold will unfold'. LA Marzulli

'We're sheep and sheep are always led to the slaughter'. Bill Cooper

16

The Biblical Forecast

Almost 30% of scriptures are devoted to end-times, and the Bible tells us that Jesus is coming back. And whilst it's beyond impressive that more than three hundred prophecies came true about Jesus' first coming, there's apparently eight times more about His Second Coming. But before then, the antichrist has his shot of literally ruling the world, which happens in the last days. [Chuck Missler highlights the coming world leader has 33 titles in the Old Testament, and 13 in the New Testament]. It seems he gets kicked out the second heaven by Michael, and knows his time is short. Revelation 12:12 tells us '…But terror will come on the earth, and the sea. For the devil has come down to you in great anger, and he knows that he has little time'.

The forecast is dreadful. And the Bible likens the end times to labour pains. This conveys that our pains get worse and worse, increasing in intensity and frequency. Alice Bailey, in her (channelled) book 'The Externalisation of the Hierarchy', gave the same metaphor, stating, 'The New Age is upon us and we are witnessing the birth pangs of the new culture and new civilisation'. Jesus called our attention to signs indicating the last days, and many Christians (and others) are of the opinion we're living in these days. We've been warned about the coming chaos and the One World Order. It would appear the apocalypse aka the great unveiling, and Armageddon aka the battle to end all battles, are in the post.

Thus, we'll address the Olivet Discourse (found in Matthew 24, Mark 13 and Luke 21) when Jesus was asked by four disciples about His second coming. This corroborates with Daniel's prophecy, and John's prophecy in Revelation, which tell us about a tribulation period of hardships, disasters, famine, war, pain and suffering. It's recalled the Book of Daniel predicted the exact day (26th April 32AD) when Jesus would triumphantly enter into Jerusalem as King.

This tribulation culminates in the great tribulation, the last three and half years before Jesus returns. This is when the beast system (NWO) is in place, and the world is forced to worship the antichrist, or off with your head. However, there's other prophecies that describe what happens before the tribulation period proper, like in Ezekiel. So, we'll get to all these.

However, before we get into that, it's recalled a major sign that we're living in the end times is the establishment of Israel. God gave Israel as a sign of the age, which starts the countdown. And Israel was born in a day, as

Isaiah 66:8 foretold, namely, May 4th 1948. It's conveyed there will be one generation after that. And according to Psalm 90:10, which states a generation is seventy to eighty years, that's circa 2018-2028?

It's also recalled, the Rothschild's were instrumental in creating the Jewish state. They helped to fulfil biblical prophecy, that Jews will be gathered from the four corners of the Earth and return to their God-given Land. The rebirth of Israel with the return of her people from many lands is mentioned in detail by various prophets in the Bible. Indeed, there's over a hundred scriptures stating Jews return to Israel.

And the Bible warns us about fake Jews. Like, the Rothschild's? Apparently, the Rothschild's were Khazar Jews, who converted to Judaism but never made the full conversion. In Revelation 2:9, we're told, 'I know thy works, and tribulation, and poverty, (but thou art rich) and I know the blasphemy of them which say they are Jews, and are not, but are the synagogue of Satan'. And in Revelation 3:9, it states, 'Look at those who belong to the synagogue of Satan, who claim to be Jews but are liars instead. I will make them come and bow down at your feet, and they will know that I love you'. So, God is referencing the Sabbatean-Frankist cult cabal?

It's said the Star of David is actually the star of Rephan (Molech), with those advocating this view pointing to Acts 7:43, which states, 'And you took up the tabernacle of Moloch and the star of your god Rephan, the images that you made to worship them…' And Amos 5:26, which states, 'You have lifted up the shrine of your king, the pedestal of your idols, the star of your god, which you made for yourselves'. So, Rephan is a reference to Saturn. It's also noted, whilst the Israel flag was adopted in 1948, it was first introduced in 1891 to represent the Zionist movement.

It also seems pertinent to note, as Wheeler (2009) asserts, 'Technically, the modern nation of Israel should be called Judah, as it consists primarily of only the two tribes of the post-civil war southern nation – Judah and Benjamin. By naming the country Israel in 1948, the Zionist Jews knew they could get much more support from Christian nations if they emulated the pre-civil war days of David and Solomon. The remaining ten tribes comprising the post-civil war northern nation were scattered throughout the nations after their Assyrian captivity and are not a part of modern day Israel at all! These rabbis have only one duty and obligation, and that is to make a New Jerusalem with a new Temple, the third, as capital of the world, and usher in the New World Order and their messiah, the Antichrist' (p.85-86).

It was also prophesied that when Israel returned home, she would turn from barren land, (which it was for 2000 years), into a prosperous land abundant with food and vegetation. Many of the country's swamps, which had been infested with malaria, have been converted into farmland. And Israel is a food source for many countries. At least 200 million trees have been planted during the last century, and some parts of the desert are blooming again.

Isaiah 42: 19-21 states, 'I will put in the desert the cedar and the acacia, the myrtle and the olive. I will set pines in the wasteland, the fir and the cypress together, so that people may see and know, may consider and understand, that the hand of the Lord has done this, that the Holy One of Israel has created it'. It's noted, 'Rothschild wine' is made from the grapes and citrus groves.

Other signs that we're living in the end times include an explosion of knowledge and global travel (see Daniel 12:4). We've gone from horse and cart etc in the nineteenth century, to cars, planes, and sending people to the moon? It's also recalled, that according to the Book of Enoch, the Watchers were bound in the abyss for seventy generations. So, that's some 4,900 years, which suggests they were released at the beginning of the twentieth century? Which accounts for our immense science and technology, and the increase of UFO sightings?

In Luke 21:25, we're told, 'There will be signs in the sun, moon and stars. On the earth, nations will be in anguish and perplexity at the roaring and tossing of the sea' (Luke 21:25). As mentioned, God gave us stars for signs, and blood-moons etc. It's highlighted our sky is like a clock, which could be another reason for obscuring it i.e. via chemtrails so we can't see the time?

It's also prophesised there'll be a great apostasy, falling away of the church, which corroborates with the indoctrination of scientific materialism. We're putting our faith in Scientism? We believe the universe and everything in it came from nothing, and we evolved from goo by way of the zoo? Fish became philosophers? As mentioned, 2 Peter 3:3 told us, there would be scoffers in the last days. And it was foreseen that our values and morals would go down the pan, as we become increasingly narcissistic, hedonistic, and socially savage. Our genes are innately selfish?

Regarding the Lord's return, Paul wrote (2 Thessalonians 2:3-12), 'For that day will not come until there is a great rebellion against God and the man of lawlessness is revealed – the one who brings destruction. He will exalt himself and defy every god there is and tear down every object of adoration and worship. He will position himself in the temple of God, claiming that he himself is God'.

Paul also highlights, 'For this lawlessness is already at work secretly and it will remain secret until the one who is holding it back steps out of the way'. Some believe the great restrainer is the Holy Spirit. It's said we're living in the Age of Grace, but during the tribulation the Holy Spirit leaves and all hell is let loose. As Russ Dizdar highlights, the abyss is bursting at the seams with demonic entities chomping at the bit to get out (from behind the veil). Others however suggest the great restrainer is Michael, who is restraining Lucifer in the second heaven. Either way, when the restrainer steps out of the way, it's no holds barred. It's called the great tribulation for a reason.

Paul said, 'This evil man will come to do the work of Satan with counterfeit power and signs and miracles. He will use every kind of wicked deception to fool those who are on the way to destruction because they refuse to believe the truth that would save them'. Which begs the question, is it ignorance or pride?

But moreover, Paul states, 'God will send a great deception on them, and they will believe all these lies. Then they will be condemned for not believing the truth and for enjoying all the evil they do'. Perhaps this great delusion is the theory of evolution, or perhaps the arrival of aliens will be the great deception? Paul does however tell us that Lord Jesus will consume/destroy the lawless one with the breath of His mouth (Holy Spirit) and splendour of His being. So, we know Jesus triumphs.

However, starting with the source Himself, Jesus tells us the signs. He prepares His people. In Matthew 24:4-8, Jesus said, 'Take heed that no-one deceives you. For many will come in My name, saying, 'I am the Christ', and will deceive many. And you will hear of wars and rumours of wars. See that you are not troubled; for all these things must come to pass, but the end is not yet. For nation will rise against nation, and kingdom against kingdom. And there will be famines, pestilences, and earthquakes in various places. All these are the beginning of birth pains'. It's noted, 'nation' is translated as 'ethnicity' (from Greek ethnos) which suggests race against race.

So, it seems we're experiencing the birth pains? We see these trends in greater frequency and intensity? There's no end of wars and rumours of wars. Indeed, Pope Francis announced in November 2015 that WW3 had started. And pestilences and plagues are increasing, which includes manmade bioterrorism, like AIDS, Ebola, and crown viruses? And 'climate change' is creating all kinds of havoc. A UN report (2014), by the Intergovernmental Panel on Climate Change (written by more than 70 experts from 30 countries), states 'the world is heading for more wars, more famine and more poverty because of the damage pollution is wreaking on the climate'. More recently (2020), the UN warned there will be famines of biblical proportions because of pandemics (plagues). It's foreseen that we'll fight over resources. What's new?

Mass animal deaths are also part of the birth pains, which we're witnessing. As mentioned, birds are falling dead out the sky, whales are beaching themselves, and fish are dying in their gazillions. Like, insects and so forth. Forest fires etc have also killed millions of God's creatures. Hosea 4:3 tells us, 'Therefore shall the land mourn, and every one that dwelleth therein shall languish, with the beasts of the field, and with the fowls of heaven; yea, the fishes of the sea also shall be taken away'. It appears biblical prophecy and secular predictions share the same apocalyptic lens. We're on the verge of extinction? According to the 'Doomsday Clock', the time is 100 seconds to midnight aka doom. It's the closest it's ever been.

Jesus continues (Matthew 24:9-14), 'Then you will be handed over to be persecuted and put to death, and you will be hated by all nations because of me. At that time many will turn away from the faith and betray and hate each other, and many false prophets will appear and deceive many people. Because of the increase of wickedness, the love of most will grow cold, but the one who stands firm to the end will be saved. And this gospel of the kingdom will be preached in the whole world as a testimony to all nations, and then the end will come'.

It seems the love of most is growing colder by the day, because of the rise in wickedness? We're also warned about revolutions and riots, which are increasing. It's understood that hungry people are prepared to loot and shoot. Or perhaps God could provide His people with manna? And with respect, it seems the whole world has heard about Jesus, but most don't care? People increasingly prefer the false cosmic Christ and 'Christ consciousness', and deluded people say they are Christ or God (including the Popes). There's even a Queen James Bible for the homosexual community (LOL). And many have been deceived by false prophets, like Muhammad and Joseph Smith, as we'll get to. It's also highlighted that Christ refers to being 'anointed', and Christians increasingly claim to be anointed in Jesus' name. Not least dodgy pastors who are operating in the false Holy Spirit, namely, kundalini?

So, everything gets worse. Then Jesus said, (in Matthew 24:15-25), 'So when you see standing in the holy place 'the abomination that causes desolation', spoken of through the prophet Daniel – let the reader understand – then let those who are in Judea flee to the mountains. Let no one on the housetop go down to take anything out of the house. Let no one in the field go back to get their cloak. How dreadful it will be in those days for pregnant women and nursing mothers! Pray that your flight will not take place in winter or on the Sabbath'.

'For then there will be great distress, unequalled from the beginning of the world until now – and never to be equalled again. If those days had not been cut short, no one would survive, but for the sake of the elect those days will be shortened. At that time if anyone says to you, 'Look, here is the Messiah!' or, 'There he is!' do not believe it. For false messiahs and false prophets will appear and perform great signs and wonders to deceive, if possible, even the elect. See I have warned you'.

So, we've been warned there's a trickster on his way. And even God's people will be bewitched by his demonically inspired party tricks, presuming it's divine? As touched on, Q is being portrayed as a saviour, and God's people are onboard. Perhaps the coming antichrist will beguile Christians by exposing the cabal? It's suggested he'll betray his loyal henchmen. He uses them to get the world ready, and then spits them out. However, we're also told that as lightning lights up the entire sky, so it will be when the Son of Man comes. So, we'll know when Jesus comes. Everyone will see this majestic event (which implies we live on a flat earth).

But moreover, Jesus pertained to Daniel's prophecy regarding the great tribulation before His return. We're told in Daniel 9:27 the antichrist confirms a peace treaty for seven years, but halfway though, he will put an end to sacrifices and offerings. Thus, the third temple is in situ, and sacrifices have resumed. Then as a climax to all his terrible deeds, he will set up the sacrilegious object that causes desecration, which is the 'image of the beast'. We're told the antichrist will set up an idol of himself in this sacred place.

This has only happened once before with Antiochus IV Epiphanes (175-164BC), when he erected an idol of Zeus to worship in the Holy of Holies. It seems this is the ultimate abomination. It's noted, the Jews know Daniel's prophecy (it's Old Testament), so they'll recognise when it's time to head for the hills.

Jesus continues (Matthew 24: 29-34), 'Immediately after the tribulation of those days shall the sun be darkened, and the moon shall not give her light, and the stars shall fall from heaven, and the powers of the heavens shall be shaken: And then shall appear the sign of the Son of Man in heaven: and then shall all the tribes of the earth mourn, and they shall see the Son of Man coming in the clouds of heaven with power and great glory. And He shall send His angels with a great sound of a trumpet, and they shall gather together His elect from the four winds, from one end of heaven to the other'.

Jesus states, 'when you see the events I have described beginning to happen, you can know His return is very near, right at the door'. He affirms, 'Verily I say unto you, This generation shall not pass, til all these things be fulfilled. So, 'This' generation is the one experiencing the birth pains, which is us?

However, it gets crazier, as Jesus further states, (in Matthew 24:37), 'But as the days of Noah were, so shall also the coming of the Son of Man be' (Matthew 24:37, Luke 17:26). And as discussed, the days of Noah were mental. Besides the nephilim, there were also human-animal hybrids. So, the nephilim are coming back? It's possible they're already living amongst us? And God knows what 'chimeras' they have in Deep Underground Military Bases (DUMBs).

DUMBs are notably used for both military and corporate interests, and they're highly classified. They house 'sensitive assets'. They provide a safe haven for highly classified technology and controversial experiments (including sorcery). DUMBs are funded by black budgets i.e. illegal drug sales. Apparently, there's at least two hundred DUMBs in the US, which are connected by a tunnel system and high-speed trains, but we'll get back to this.

As touched on, science and technology are immense, and we don't know the half of it. Like, we know they make insane weapons and diseases, and they manipulate the weather. And they clone animals/people and make chimeras. And they're genetically modifying food, insects, and animals. They're changing genomes by splicing DNA. Like, they create spider-goats and fluorescent bunnies (using the fluorescent gene from jelly fish). And in addition to creating non-human enhanced super-soldiers, DARPA is allegedly creating super-soldiers that are genetically enhanced e.g. vision and strength. And we know the military's super advanced (like twenty-five years ahead of what we know). Naturally, the covert nature of operations is for 'national security'.

And we're familiar with Artificial Intelligence (AI), which Elon Musk said could destroy humanity. We've been warned about the 'technological singularity', when technology becomes smarter than humans. Apparently in 2017 the FBI had to shut down a project involving two AI bots as they started creating their own language. There's also been some funky things recorded with devices like 'Alexa', like saying haunted demonic things and eerily laughing. It's also noted, the robot 'Sophia' (interesting name) has citizenship in Saudi Arabia, which suggests she's a real person/entity?

But moreover, it seems spirits use technology. Not least chimeras, clones, and robots, as these give them bodies to inhabit? It's noted, that Elon Musk likened AI to summoning demons, and Geordie Rose similarly said, regarding D-Wave quantum computers, we're summoning 'old ones' (like from Lovecraft's horror stories). Rose admits their agenda will not be aligned with ours, and they will treat us the way we treat ants. So, that's nice. It seems technology provides an interface connecting our world to the spirit world? Like, virtual reality becomes actual reality, some kind of sub-reality, which provides a platform for entities to operate in?

As mentioned, apparently the aim is for our brains to be connected to the internet by 2030. And scientists endeavour to achieve immortality by 2045. Perhaps the chip has something to do with that? It seems we go from being transgender to trans-human. We'll be upgraded via technology? The prospect of uploading consciousness onto an avatar, is like a counterfeit 'resurrection' body? Science and technology could transform earth into heaven i.e. with free energy and robots doing the work for us. Life could be awesome for everyone, and even more divine, if we're enlightened?

However, that craziness aside, there's a build up to the 'peace agreement' and the reign of the antichrist. There's a few events yet to happen. Like, building the temple, and like the War of Gog and Magog, which some think ignites the tribulation period.

Magog is identified as Russia (the land around and above the Black Sea), and Gog as the leader of Russia (see Ezekiel 36-40). The Bible tells us Russia is Israel's mortal enemy, and Russia forms a military coalition with Iran, Libya, Sudan, Ethiopia, Egypt, and Turkey to attack Israel. Many believe that Algeria, Lebanon, Somalia, Afghanistan, Pakistan, and Tunisia will also be involved i.e. Muslim nations sticking together against the common Jewish enemy. Ezekiel tells us there will be a massive army with many people under the leadership of Gog, and future Russia will again govern the former Soviet states to the south. Others however suggest that Gog is Turkey.

It's duly noted, Russia's friends include Syria, Iran and Turkey. And the US blesses Israel. In Genesis 12:3, God said to His people, 'I will bless those who bless you, and whoever curses you I will curse; and all peoples on earth will be blessed through you'. Thus, the US is blessed because they bless Israel?

So, at some point in the imminent future, Israel is surrounded by enemies, whose stated aim is to eliminate her from planet Earth. Like, Hossein Salami, Iran's Revolutionary Guard Commander, said, 'Our strategy is to erase Israel from the global political map'. And the supreme leader Ayatollah Ali Khamenei said, 'the Zionist regime will perish in the not so far future'. Many Muslims believe Allah has called them to destroy the Jews and retake the Holy Land. Like, ISIS (Al Qaeda) claimed they wanted to but never did? Hence, Israel's been militarily built up, by the US, so she can take on her neighbours. The War of Gog and Magog is a prominent feature in Islam, Christianity, and Judaism eschatology.

In tandem with Pike's agenda, it seems the conflict in the Middle East is ramping up to WW3, which implicates Russia and China? Maybe the Gog and Magog War sparks WW3? David Icke (2007) highlights, in a documented conversation with Jacques Chirac the French ex-president, George W Bush said, 'Gog and Magog are at work in the Middle East'. There's also the small matter of the Golan Heights, which could trigger some justified fireworks? Apparently, Iran vows to liberate the Golan Heights. It seems the Greater Israel project has achieved much instability in the Middle East (excluding ally Saudi Arabia), but they've still got a few countries to topple according to the PNAC.

However, many biblical scholars understand that two more prophecies take place before the Gog and Magog War, namely, the destruction of Damascus, and the Psalm 83 War. It's suggested these events are the catalyst for the Gog and Magog War. Damascus is one of the world's oldest cities, but Isaiah 17:1 tells us, '...Behold, Damascus is taken away from being a city, and it shall be a ruinous heap' (like the rest of Syria). This happens overnight. The War of Psalm 83 takes place prior to the tribulation period, and thus it's believed this event is next on the prophetic timeline. In this war, Israel has to take on her immediate neighbours, who invade her like a pack of wolves.

Psalm 83: 1-5 states, 'O God, do not remain silent; do not turn a deaf ear, do not stand aloof, O God. See how your enemies growl, how your foes rear their heads. With cunning they conspire against your people; they plot against those you cherish. "Come," they say, "let us destroy them as a nation, so that Israel's name is remembered no more." With one mind they plot together; they form an alliance against you '.

In modern day terms, this alliance consists of Palestine (West Bank and Gaza), Lebanon, Syria, Iraq, Jordan, Saudi Arabia and Egypt. So, Israel has to take on her surrounding nations, before contending with the Gog and Magog War, which is led by Russia and Iran. It's arguably astounding how these alliances against Israel 'in the last days', which were prophesied over 2,400 years ago by prophet Ezekiel, corroborates with events in the Middle East today.

However, it's foreseen that Israel will prevail in the Psalm 83 war and even extend her borders. Presumably she'll keep a firm grip on the Golan Heights? It's also however noted, that these new boundaries will be more in line with God's covenant with Abraham regarding the Promised Land. In Genesis 15:18 we're told, 'On that day the LORD made a covenant with Abram and said, "To your descendants I give this land, from Wadi of Egypt to the great river, the Euphrates".

So, Israel's taking what's rightfully hers, in line with the Zionist agenda? Israel further prospers after this war, becoming one of the richest countries, if not the richest country, in the world. Ezekiel tells us that Israel's at peace when the Gog and Magog War takes place, unlike today?

Others however believe the Psalm 83 prophecy has been fulfilled. It's highlighted that Israel's immediate neighbours are no longer a threat. Israel contended with Lebanon, Syria, Egypt, Iraq, Palestine, and Jordan during the 1948 and 1967 Wars. And Israel's issues with Jordan and Egypt were resolved in 1973. It's also pointed out, that Israel became a regional superpower, wealthy and strong. Thus, it's purported the Gog and Magog War is next. It's noted, that Turkey, Russia, Iran, Libya, and Sudan are the five countries that don't have a border with Israel. It's suggested Israel could attack/destroy Damascus, which triggers the Ezekiel war. Then the seven year tribulation begins.

The Gog and Magog War is about snaffling Israel's spoils. Missler highlights the Bible anticipates the use of nuclear power, as we're told that professionals are hired to clear the battlefield. And they have to wait seven months before they can begin the clearing, which takes another seven months (the dead are buried east of the Dead Sea). And apparently if a traveller sees something a professional has missed, they don't touch it, but rather mark the location and let the professionals know. It's also said nuclear warfare has been described in advance, like in Zechariah 14:12, which states '…Their flesh shall consume away while they stand upon their feet, and their eyes shall consume away in their sockets, and their tongue shall consume away in their mouth'.

But moreover, the Bible tells us God intervenes to quell the invasion. We're told God will rain fire on Magog (6/7 Russian military are wiped out), and they'll know it's from God. No danger. Like Sodom and Gomorrah back in the day. So, it's believed these events in the Middle East will usher in the Tribulation Period. We're also told that left over weapons will be at Israel's disposal for the following seven years.

Suffice to say, at this point in time, life will be chaotic. The birth pains will be in full-swing, which includes a global economic meltdown. As Pike advised, people will be despairing of both war and religion. The atheists will be particularly irked. This chaos precedes the NWO. The world needs to be ready for the Son of Perdition. The world needs to reject God to embrace the New Age.

Thus, the prophecy continues, that just as an all-out war in the Middle East breaks out, the antichrist arrives. And this seemingly sweet man of peace will confirm a brilliant seven year plan for peace, economic and religious freedom. It's noted, the Oslo Accord, the first treaty signed by Israel and Palestine in Norway in 1993, was to be settled (confirmed) at a later date.

Scripture tells us that the leader of the Revived Roman Empire will sit down with Israel at a peace table. He will convince Israel and her enemies to rely on him and his regime to keep the peace. And Israel agrees to the contract, a seven year peace agreement, involving other nations (Daniel 9:27). When Israel signs the treaty (it must be signed in front of the antichrist), the Tribulation period begins.

As mentioned, the coming world leader will seem like our saviour. Missler summarises that he'll be an intellectual genius, persuasive orator (like Hitler but better), shrewd politician, financial genius, and unifying religious guru. He first sorts out global finance and peace, and then he becomes a forceful military leader later. All in the name of peace, he promises no more wars, or border disputes, but rather 'one world'. He'll promise strength, peace and security. And will insist the world unites.

So, that's one government, one military, one economy and one cashless currency. Further, since Israel will need protection, it makes sense for the UN HQ to relocate to Jerusalem from NYC? It's also suggested the Pope will move to Jerusalem from the Vatican. Jerusalem will be the new capital of the NWO? Paul however warns us (1 Thessalonians 5:3), 'For when they shall say, peace and safety, then sudden destruction cometh upon them, as travail upon a woman with child; and they shall not escape'.

David Icke suggests the new face of the UN could insist that all UN members disarm, destroying all but 10% of weapons which could be given to the UN aka world army. Disarmament is the only way to prevent another war? The UN, (global government), can then enforce its will. Wheeler (2007) concedes the UN will become the unchallengeable military force, capable of forcing 'peace'. She refers to Al Cuppett (retired Army General and whistleblower) who informs about 'Freedom from War', the US Program for general and complete disarmament in a peaceful world.

He states, 'the US military must be completely dismantled, the US citizens must be disarmed, all US weapons must be surrendered to the UN military apparatus, and an armed internal police apparatus, subservient to the

UN, must keep peace in the USA. The result is a fearsome military dictatorship to be operated by nameless, faceless, non-elected international bureaucrats, legislated for by international law'. Al Cuppett also notably informs about chemtrails.

As mentioned, it's foreseen that NATO and UN forces will merge into a global police force. Thus, unlike passive defenceless Europeans, many Americans want to keep the Second Amendment to the US Constitution (1791) which protects the right to keep and bear arms. Unlike secular Europe, Christians in the US know what's coming?

It's noted, that 'shootings' in the US motivates removing this right. And it's believed many of these shootings are false flags i.e. carried out by mind-controlled victims. The problem of shootings creates the solution of removing arms. Like, Australia, New Zealand, and Canada banned arms after mass shootings. The same people who create the gun problem glamorise violence e.g. Hollywood movies. Like, Quentin Tarantino's (who's in the 666 club) brutal movies desensitise us? Alice Bailey stipulated, 'In the preparatory period for the NWO there will be a steady and regulated disarmament. It will not be optional'.

It's said the antichrist will advocate no bigotry based on religion, and will allow the Jews to rebuild their Temple (so it's in place for him). It's suggested the rebuilding of the third temple could be part of the peace negotiations. It's recalled that during the Oslo Accord negotiations, Bill Clinton suggested that Muslims and Jews could share the Temple Mount. There's adequate room for both the temple and the Dome of the Rock. Besides the prospect of sharing the Temple Mount, it's also speculated that the earthquake that takes place during the Gog and Magog War could destroy the Dome of the Rock.

But further, it's said that amid the religious turmoil, the antichrist will reconcile all religions by abolishing all contradictions between them, since they're essentially the same? It's the same One God? Religions have more in common than they think?

As touched on, Jesuit Pope Francis has been actively promoting ecumenism i.e. it's the same God regardless of religion. He said all major religions are 'meeting God in different ways'. He even had Katy Perry (who apparently sold her soul to the devil) at the Vatican in 2018 to preach Transcendental Meditation. Contrary to popular belief, Transcendental Meditation is not void of dogma but rather entails praying to Hindu gods, as we'll get to. So, Pope Francis is paving the way for a global religion. And contrary to Jesus' great commission, he even told Christians not to preach the gospel. You couldn't make it up.

The Pope is leading the multifaith movement under the banner of 'Brotherhood'. He insists human fraternity can live together in peace. It's about coming together as one global family. Thus, he's been meeting with leaders from Islam and Judaism (imams and high rabbis) to unify their religions based on their common Abrahamic root. They all believe in the same God of Abraham? Hence, he supports 'Chrislam'. However, we'll also get back to this in the penultimate chapter.

Concerted efforts have also been made towards reconciling Catholicism and Protestantism. They have even more in common? Beloved Pope Francis also advocated that Sunday should be our global day off, our Sabbath for the sake of the environment. So, we worship Gaia? As highlighted, he apparently cares deeply about the environment and our global village. The Pope is actively involved with the UN and politics, and the 'merchants of the earth' i.e. CEOs of big business. He said, 'our duty is to obey the UN'.

Moreover, it seems the Noahide laws (derived from Noah, Father of post-Flood nations) will become mandatory, which the Pope also endorses? These seven laws corroborate with the Ten Commandments e.g. don't steal or murder or commit adultery. But they're not from the Old Testament but rather the Talmud. Whilst they appear to be a golden standard and they're reconciliatory i.e. between Jews, Muslims and gentiles, they deny Christ's deity.

It's noted, that George H W Bush signed the Noahide Laws into US law in 1991. The language of the law asserts that the 'Seven Noahide Laws' are the ethical values of civilised society and are the basis on which the American nation was founded and that without these Seven Noahide Laws society stands in peril. So, these Jewish religious laws apply to all? According to the Talmud, these God-given imperatives are a binding set of laws for all humanity. But moreover, violating them is punishable by death by decapitation.

After the antichrist reconciles all religions, he then abolishes them with his unifying Luciferian religion. At the esoteric core of exoteric religions, we are God? And Lucifer is the great enlightener, the Holy Serpent. God is Lucifer, the adversary of Satan. Lucifer is the light bearer, Son of the morning, awakening the divine intellect of humankind.

It's highlighted that just as global chaos is required to unify the world, spiritual chaos is required to broach the new world religion. And thus, the New Age begins? But moreover, based on the Noahide laws for world peace, those who don't endorse the Luciferian god will be beheaded. Like, Christians? The NWO is a religio-politico system, like the papacy, complete with a world court to execute judgement. It's noted, refugees will be unable to seek political asylum, because it will be one world. And surveillance will be rampant. There will be nowhere to hide, besides the hills?

So, this world leader is more than just a man, (like an awesome Mandela), but rather he's a superman and the seed of Satan, possessed by Satan. Like, Judas was possessed by Satan. And like, Popes who partake in ninth circle rituals can be possessed by Satan. People are waiting for the 'cosmic Christ' or Maitreya, and he'll fit the bill. He'll be Alice Bailey's wish fulfilment. The Jews will believe he's the Messiah they've been waiting for, the Muslims will believe he's the Imam Mahdi, the Buddhists will believe he's the Maitreya Buddha, and the Hindus will believe he's Kalki. And the secular world will believe he's wonderful. The Bible tells us Satan deceives the whole world.

But moreover, (as mentioned), he'll be able to perform miracles. He'll demonstrate supernatural powers, using all sorts of signs and wonders that serve the lie. So, even the atheists will be convinced he's god. He receives his power from the Dragon. But that small detail aside, people will be captivated by this seemingly anointed one, who's actually the lawless one. And for the most part, the herd will be all aboard the One World Order.

Interestingly, Black (2010) highlights Austrian seer Rudolf Steiner's, (who's known as the 'psychic who always tells the truth'), criteria for recognising the antichrist. Thus, Satan will incarnate in human form not long after the start of the third millennium, which is to say soon after the year 2000. He will be born 'in the West'. He will make himself known in the middle of shattering events, a war, and present himself as the benefactor to mankind. He will become successful very quickly. He will be able to perform miracles, but then explain these miracles in scientific and mechanical terms. He will found schools teaching the 'magic arts' (p.566). Steiner knew the spirit world was real. He viewed the human body as a vessel, open to occupation by other entities.

Black (2010) notably highlights, 'False teaching usually has little or no moral dimension, the benefits of reawakening the chakras, for example, being recommended merely in terms of selfish 'personal growth'. True spiritual teaching puts love of others and love of humanity as its heart – intelligent love, freely given' (p.539). It seems the New Age endeavour is mastering 'energy' and waking up the serpent?

Black also highlights mystic Vladimir Soloviev, (who Steiner endorsed), who said the antichrist will be an admirable philanthropist, a committed, active pacifist, a practising vegetarian, a determined defender of animals, and a spiritualist. He will not appear to be hostile to Christ in principle. In fact, he will genuinely see many good things in Jesus Christ's sayings as a guide to life. But he will reject the teaching that Christ is unique, and will deny that Christ is risen and alive today.

Soloviev continues, the antichrist will be a genius, and will become a sort of president of a United States of Europe. Apparently, he starts off well, living according to impeccable ethical principles, but once in power he will demand absolute obedience. But moreover, apparently he'll enlist the help of a black magician called Apollonius, who is able to manipulate electricity by force of his will (p.563-564). So, that's interesting.

With regards to the Revived Roman Empire, which the antichrist heads, scripture tells us this is the last and fiercest kingdom. Thus, in Daniel 2, we're told Nebuchadnezzar, the king of Babylon, had a prophetic dream that Daniel interpreted (the Jews were captive in Babylon at the time). Nebuchadnezzar couldn't remember his dream, yet he expected his magicians, psychics, sorcerers and astrologers to know what it was and interpret it, which they claimed was impossible. The consequence was execution. But Daniel prayed to God, asking Him to reveal the dream and its meaning, and God answered.

The dream depicted a terrifying statue that featured a gold head, silver arms and chest, bronze stomach and hips, iron legs, and feet made partly of iron and partly of clay. These metals indicate the strength of successive kingdoms. Thus, gold was Babylon (606BC-593BC), silver was Medo-Persia (539BC-332BC), bronze was Greece (332BC-68), and iron was Rome (68-476). The Revived Roman Empire, the feet with ten toes, is iron and clay. So, the ten toes represent ten kingdoms within this global empire?

Moreover, Daniel 2:43 states, 'And whereas thou sawest iron mixed with miry clay, they shall mingle themselves with the seed of men: but they shall not cleave one to another, even as iron is not mixed with clay'. And it's suggested the 'they' are fallen angels, which suggests the nephilim return. It seems the seed don't marry this time, like they did in Genesis 6, but rather people are abducted for their reproductive material? Hybrids are genetically engineered? However, we'll get back to this in the next chapter. Clay notably represents the church, which belongs to the potter, who is God. And apparently iron is a reference to giants. It's also however said, that Muslims are the clay, who don't mix in Europe.

The 'ten kingdoms' revelation corroborates with the Club of Rome's design for the NWO. In 1973 the Club of Rome proposed for the world to be divided into ten economic/political regions called 'Kingdoms'. The world government would oversee these ten unions or kingdoms, or 'conglomerate super-nations', 'each with its own ruler, as yet not identified'. It claims, 'there is no other viable alternative to the future survival of mankind than a new global community under a single form of government'. But moreover, the mission was to create a New World Order by the year 2000. The report was entitled 'Regionalised and Adaptive Model of the Global World System'.

These regions or Kingdoms are: NAFTA, which includes America, Canada and Mexico; the EU or Western Europe; Japan; Australia, New Zealand and South Africa; Eastern Europe, Pakistan, Afghanistan, Russia and the former countries of the Soviet Union; Latin America and Caribbean Islands; North Africa and the Middle East; the rest of Africa, except South Africa; South and Southeast Asia, including India; China, including Mongolia. The islands of the seas, for the most part, fit in with the closest region.

NAFTA similarly systematically reorganised the world into ten 'super nations' in 1996. This ten division world empire consists of: America, Canada and Mexico; South America; Australia and New Zealand; Western Europe; Eastern Europe; Japan; South Asia; Central Asia; North Africa and the Middle East; remainder of Africa. It's noted, the future ten kingdoms corroborate with the past ten kingdoms in Atlantis, who were headed by ten hybrid kings.

It's also said the 'ten kingdoms' could be ten permanent UN Security Council members. The Security Council has fifteen members, where five states (China, France, Russia, UK and US) are permanent members, and the General Assembly elects ten other members for two year terms. It's thus suggested, the UN could propose five more permanent members giving rise to ten permanent members. These ten (unelected bureaucratic) members would represent (dictate to) their respective region i.e. the ten kingdoms. So, it seems the globalists are on the same biblical page. The antichrist could be the Secretary General of the UN?

In addition to Nebuchadnezzar's dream, the Revived Roman Empire is commonly associated with the fourth beast in Daniel's dream in chapter 7, which in turn corroborates with the Book of Revelation. Revelation is the last book in the Bible, and this Revelation was given to John from Jesus Christ, concerning future events. But we'll get to this.

Thus, Daniel has a vision where he sees four different beasts coming up out of the sea. So, these beasts could literally be beasts from the sea, since God knows what marine chimeras they're making? Or they're figurative and represent kingdoms. We're told water represents people/nations/languages. The traditional view is that these great beasts, which follow each other in succession, are global kingdoms or empires. Hence, it mirrors Nebuchadnezzar's dream.

Thus, the first beast which is like a lion is Babylon. The second beast which is like a bear is Medo-Persia. The third beast which is like a leopard, and which notably had four heads, is Greece. It's noted, that after Alexander the Great, the Greek empire was (divided) given to four leading generals (Lysimachus, Cassander, Ptolemy and Seleucus), which are represented by the four heads on the leopard. He calls the fourth beast a 'terrible beast', (it's like nothing on earth?), which is Rome. It had ten horns, which are ten kings from this kingdom. So, this corroborates with the ten toes?

However, it's highlighted that Daniel 7 is about kingdoms that 'shall arise', which suggests future (contemporary) nations, not ancient kingdoms. Babylon was usurped by Medo-Persia during Daniel's time, so it had arisen, past tense. And Daniel pertains to end times, as Daniel 12:4 states, 'But you, Daniel, keep this prophecy a secret; seal up the book until the time of the end'.

Thus, it's suggested the lion Daniel seen, which had eagles' wings, that were pulled off, and it was left standing on two hind feet like a human, is the UK. And the US is the eagle's wings who were pulled out, when they became independent (the UK is associated with the lion, and the US with the eagle). It's postulated the bear is Russia. And the leopard is Germany/France. Others however suggest the leopard is the US. The leopard's colouring, namely, white, brown, and yellow represent its ethnicities.

It's suggested that four empires exist simultaneously, and the antichrist takes control of the one with ten kingdoms (horns). This is the revived Roman Empire. He has control over a quarter of the earth, until he controls it all? Or the Revived Roman Empire is the global government (UN) comprised of ten kingdoms?

But moreover, another little horn came up, from among the ten horns on the terrible beast, which had eyes like a man and a mouth that spoke boastfully against God. And three of the first horns were uprooted before it. This horn is different from the other horns. We're told in Daniel 7:25, 'He will defy the Most High and wear down the holy people of the Most High. He will try to change their sacred festivals and laws, and they will be placed under his control for a time, times, and half a time'. This time equates to three and half years, which is 1260 days.

So, the little horn is the antichrist, the coming world leader? And he rules for the last three and half years, from the midpoint of the peace agreement. When he erects his idol, and institutes Luciferian worship? The Ancient of Days however sorts it out, (at the end of the tribulation), as the beast was slain and lobbed into the blazing fire.

However, it's also understood that 1260 days equates to 1260 years, as prophetic days symbolise years. Like, forty days scouting out Canaan, resulted in forty years in the wilderness. And 1260 years connects to the antichrist Roman Catholic Church.

Thus, when Rome fell in 476AD, she was divided into the ten nations of Europe, the 'ten horns'. Rome was notably bombarded by barbarians in 410 and by 476 the whole of the western empire was destroyed. These medieval kingdoms were the Saxons, Franks, Alamanni, Visigoths, Suevi, Lombards, Burgundians, Heruli, Vandals and the Ostrogoths. So, the little horn arose after the ten nations were formed, that is, after 476AD, when the division of the Roman Empire was completed. It's recalled the Roman Empire was nephilim HQ. The Caesars believed they were gods.

It's also noted, that Rome was divided into two before it was divided into ten kingdoms. These two kingdoms are reflected by the two iron legs in Nebuchadnezzar's dream, just as the silver arms represent Mede and Persia. As mentioned, Constantine changed pagan Rome to papal Rome. Then he moved the religious capital of Rome to Constantinople (Turkey). Hence, there's the Roman Catholic Church and the Eastern Orthodox Church. The eastern leg of the empire survived another thousand years, until it was hijacked by Islam.

The main difference between the Orthodox Church and the Roman Catholic Church is notably the former doesn't venerate the Pope. Pope Francis has however highlighted they have much in common, even more than 'Protestants'. Like, they both venerate Mary and pray to dead saints.

As it transpired, the Papacy (Roman Catholic Church) gained control of civil powers in 538AD, courtesy of Saint Justinian the Great (482-565). This Eastern Roman emperor rescued the western half of the historical Roman Empire, this religio-politico system. The Justinian Code, established in 534AD, was a decree allowing the papacy to destroy anyone who did not support the Trinity Creed (as implemented by Constantine). It was a licence to kill.

It was notably Justinian who issued the famous decree that made the Pope the legal 'Head of all the Holy Churches'. The Pope was promoted to representative of Jesus Christ on Earth and proclaimed supreme in religious matters i.e. infallible. It's noted, that kings laid their crowns at the feet of the Pope, and had him crown them. The Pope reigned supreme, over all nations and people. Papal Rome began accumulating evermore power and influence as the Dark Ages bled through time.

Thus, it's contended the little horn is the Papacy. It's said the little horn's eyes like a man alludes to a very prominent (arrogant and blasphemous) person at the head of it, namely, the Pope. And the little horn destroyed three kingdoms (horns), as they wouldn't accept the authority of the Catholic Church. The papacy eliminated the Heruli in 493AD, the Vandals in 534AD, and the Ostrogoths in 538AD.

Thus, the seven nations that remained intact were England, France, Germany, Spain, Portugal, Italy, and Switzerland. These royal families are notably from Japheth's lineage. It's highlighted that it was a mere sixty years after the division of the Roman Empire that the little horn received power. And the Roman Catholic Church did change sacred festivals and laws. Like Sun-day worship, Christmas and Easter (and some).

And the papacy ruled from 538-1798, when Napoleon took power from the papacy, which is 1260 years. The papacy still continued as a church, but she was completely stripped of her civil and political power. Then in 1929 the Italian government (the Lateran treaty) once again recognised Vatican City as an independent state, and thus the papacy came back to life. This little kingdom was resurrected.

There's been much speculation about the revived Roman Empire. Like, suspicions arose with the development of the European Economic Community (EEC). This regional organisation, created by the Treaty of Rome of 1957, aimed to bring about economic integration among its member states. When Europe began to integrate politically and economically, it was thought this would be the revived Roman Empire. Paul-Henri Spaak (1899-1972), former Belgium Prime Minister, who was one of the principal architects of the ECC, said when the Treaty of Rome was signed in 1957, 'we felt like Romans on that day. We were consciously recreating the revived Roman Empire once more'.

He also said, 'We do not want another committee, we have too many already. What we want is a man of sufficient stature to hold the allegiance of all people, and to lift us out of the economic morass into which we are sinking. Send us such a man, and be he god or devil, we will receive him'. So, that's curious. After the EEC, the EU was created. So, the revived Roman Empire could be the EU? But it's also speculated the revived Roman Empire could be the UN? It's asserted the EU is a mess and needs to be replaced with global governance. The world needs an economic and political reset, as the World Economic Forum is currently mandating?

Rather than the EU constituting the revived Roman Empire, Wheeler alternatively believes NATO or G8 are the ten horns that fit with biblical prophecy. That is, the European block of nations including the USA. She notes, the UN consists of almost all nations of the world, whereas only NATO and G8 include Europe and the US (the US founded NATO and is the most important member). Wheeler (2009) asserts the little horn is the USA. She highlights that America was essentially born out of Europe. The US was part of the UK until they decided to forgo paying taxes to us, and split. They flew away on eagle's wings.

As highlighted, the Roman Empire also includes the eastern leg, which is interesting as the antichrist is identified as the Assyrian, like Nimrod. Lest we forget, the small detail of finding his body in 2003. It's said extracting his DNA was the primary objective of the Iraq invasion, and the acquisition of oil was a perk. Maybe they could clone him. Maybe they have.

However, before we get to more 'Revelation', it seems ebullient to mention two interesting events regarding Daniel and his buds, namely, Shadrach, Meshach, and Abednego. The first event is, Nebuchadnezzar placed

Daniel's friends in a blazing furnace, but the fire didn't touch them. We're told, 'Not a hair on their heads was singed, and their clothing was not scorched. They didn't even smell of smoke!' This resonates with Doreen Irvine's trip into the fire. It was observed that a divine being was present with them, who looked like the 'Son of God'. Daniel's buds were subjected to this torture because they refused to worship anyone but the One True God, Jehovah.

And the other event is, Daniel was placed in a lion's den, but God sent an angel to shut the lions' mouths, so he remained unharmed. Daniel received this sentence because he worshipped God, despite King Belshazzar's (who succeeded Nebuchadnezzar) decree prohibiting anyone from worshipping anyone except him. God tells us, in His word, that He will never leave us or forsake us. And He sends angels to protect us. Unlike spirit guides who can leave people hanging, and even inflict torture.

It's also interesting to note, that a disembodied hand appeared at an epic party (feast) Belshazzar was hosting, which freaked him out. It appears disembodied hands have been a feature throughout history. The hand wrote a message on the wall, which Daniel translated. Apparently, the idiom 'the writing on the wall' comes from this event.

As touched on, Daniel's prophecy about the future beast government corroborates with the future beast government described in Revelation. That is, Daniel's four beasts seem to be the same as John's first beast in Revelation 13 i.e. the beasts are a composite. Thus, the beast John sees, which also comes from the sea, has features of a lion, bear, and leopard. It has seven heads, which is the collective amount of heads on Daniel's four beasts. And it has ten horns, with ten crowns on its horns. So, Daniel's four beasts depict the final beast government?

It seems horns are kings, and crowns are kingdoms. Or crowns represent royal bloodlines? It's said the seven heads could be the five permanent Members of the UN Security Council, plus Germany and one high representative of the EU for foreign affairs, which makes seven permanent Security Council members. Or the seven heads could be the G7? Or the seven heads could be the seven (royal) nations that ruled after the Roman Empire was disbanded? And these seven heads oversee ten kingdoms. So, this beast is the NWO aka UN on steroids? And the 'little horn' Daniel highlights is the antichrist?

Thus, the Book of Revelation (New Testament), written by John in Patmos 95AD, compliments the Book of Daniel (Old Testament). John tells us about seven empires in Revelation 17:10. He wrote, 'there are seven kings: five are fallen, and one is, and the other is not yet come; and when he cometh, he must continue for a short space'. John was writing at the time of the Roman Empire, hence the last world empire, the 'Revived Roman Empire', is yet to come? And three and a half years is a short time for the last king to reign? The Bible seems to profile history in terms of seven satanic empires, namely, Egypt, Assyria, Babylon (Daniel's time), Persia, Greece, Rome (John's time), and the Revived Roman Empire (our time?).

However, rather than jumping in at chapter 13 or 17, it seems pertinent to consider all of Revelation, starting from the beginning, because this book is for us? Like, the Book of Enoch is for us, the terminal generation? It tells us exactly what's coming, including the return of Jesus.

As it transpired, John was exiled to the island of Patmos for preaching the word of God and speaking about Jesus. And sitting in a cave, he heard God's voice, which sounded like thunder, telling him to write down what he sees (see photo of Patmos and the cave). John explains that when he turned to see who was speaking to him, he saw seven gold lampstands, and standing in the middle was the Son of Man, holding seven stars in His right hand.

Jesus explains the seven stars are the seven angels, of the seven lampstands, which are churches. After writing letters (appraisals) to the seven churches, on behalf of Jesus, John saw a door standing open to heaven and was told to go up. Instantly he was in the spirit, and he was in heaven. We're told an angel was sent to John so that John could share the revelation with God's people. So, the angel enabled his astral trip to heaven, his 'vision'?

Revelation also describes the Tribulation period, but it further divides the Tribulation into three sets of catastrophic judgements. These are the 'seven seal judgements', followed by the 'seven trumpet judgements', which are followed by the 'seven vial judgements'. The seven seals, trumpets, and vials are connected to one another. The seventh seal introduces the seven trumpets, and the seventh trumpet introduces the seven vials.

The traditional view is that these judgements are sequential. Like, the seven seals happen during the first 21 months of the seven year period, the seven trumpets happen during the next 21 months, which takes us to the midpoint of carnage i.e. when the image of the beast is installed. Then the seven vial judgements are unleashed in the last 42 months. God pours out His wrath during the last three and half years.

Others however contend these judgements happen concurrently i.e. they overlap. It's asserted that each set of judgements end with the Second Coming of Jesus. They each tell part of the end time narrative. Like, the four gospels tell the same gospel from four points of view. It's also highlighted that Matthew 24 correlates to the seven seals described in Revelation. Jesus returns at the end of the horror show.

So, Jesus starts the ball rolling in Revelation, as He opens the seven sealed scrolls (Jesus is the only one worthy to open the scrolls). The first four of the seven seals are known as the infamous 'Four Horsemen of the Apocalypse'.

Thus, the first seal introduces the antichrist on a white horse, who rides out to win victory. It's understood he rides a white horse to emulate Jesus, who later returns on a white horse. He's also wearing a crown which suggests royalty? However, it's also said the white horse, which is the logo for the CFR, alludes to the deception of the NWO. It could represent the beloved UN and the Pope. The white horse could symbolise white UN vehicles. It's noted, white horses have been featuring in music videos (predictive programming?). They're telling us the rider on the white horse is coming?

The second seal, which features a rider on a red horse, introduces war and slaughter. Dizdar notably associates the red horse with the black awakening. As mentioned, he claims there's millions of sleeper agents, mind-controlled super-soldiers, who will be triggered into action at this time. There will be absolute chaos, which precedes the new global order. It's also said the red horse represents communism, which is the philosophy of the NWO. Or the red horse could be China and Russia.

The third seal, which features a rider on a black horse, introduces famine. The rider is holding up a pair of scales. John heard someone say that a day's pay will afford a loaf of bread, and don't waste the oil and wine. It's suggested the elite will continue to have their fine goods, while everyone else starves. It's also believed the black horse represents economic collapse (hence, the insane inflation), as bankers fleece the world.

And the fourth seal introduces a rider called Death, no less, on a horse whose colour is pale green like a corpse. We're told they were given authority over one fourth of the earth, to kill with the sword, famine, disease, and wild animals. So, circa two billion will be wiped out at this point. However, it's also suggested the green horse represents Islam. The last rider has power over a quarter of the earth, and a quarter of the global population are Muslims. It's also highlighted that white, red, black and green are the colours on the flags of Jordan, Palestine, Sudan, Kuwait, Libya, United Arab Emirates, Afghanistan, Syria and Iraq (which were Assyria), who war with Israel, leading to WW3?

It's noted, whilst some believe these horses have been released, others believe the call for chaos hasn't been made yet. Jesus hasn't opened the scroll yet? Or He has, but we didn't see it, because we can't see hyper dimensions? It's also said the four horsemen of the apocalypse are spirits. And the spirit of antichrist has been here since the beginning. But he's coming in person, when he's chucked out of the second heaven, and knows his time is short.

The fifth seal entails tribulation for the saints. God's people are martyred for the word of God. These faithful witnesses were given a white robe to wear and told to rest a little longer until the full number of their brothers and sisters arrived i.e. fellow servants of Jesus who had been martyred. So, they're in a holding place, like Abraham's bosom?

It's asserted this is happening now, as Christians are beheaded for their faith (particularly in Muslim countries). It's foreseen that Christians will be increasingly ostracised. They'll be the obstacles to the NWO and acceptance of Lucifer's religion of 'light and love'. They'll be beheaded under Noahide law? It's notably rumoured, that the US has bought a ton of guillotines, so that's curious.

When the sixth seal was opened, there was a devastating earthquake, the heavens shook, the sun darkened, and the moon became blood red. The sky was rolled up like a scroll and removed, which could be a reference to the firmament? The veil between heaven and earth is removed. All the people (rich and poor) hid themselves in caves, and among the rocks in the mountains, trying to hide from the one who sits on the throne and from the wrath of the Lamb. We're told, 'For the great day of their wrath has come, and who will be able to survive?' So, God's wrath comes after the sixth seal?

It's also noted, before the seventh seal is opened, we hear that 144,000 people (12,000 from each tribe) are marked with the seal of God to preserve them. An angel calls out to four other angels, who had been given power to injure the land and sea, stating, 'Wait! Don't hurt the land or the sea or the trees until we have placed the seal of God on the foreheads of His servants'. It's interpreted that during the Tribulation period, 144,000 Jews convert and begin to evangelise around the world that Jesus is the Messiah.

After God protects His people, John saw a vast crowd clothed in white, standing in front of the throne and before the Lamb. They're from all nations and languages, and their number is too great to count. John is told by an angel that the saints in white robes came out of the great tribulation. So, these saints join those who were martyred in the fifth seal, who were given white robes to wear and told to wait for the rest of their siblings? An army of saints enters heaven at the end of the tribulation?

So, Jesus breaks the seventh seal, and there was silence throughout heaven for about half an hour. Then there was thunder and lightning, and a terrible earthquake. Whilst this seems to be the end, and the six seals corroborates with Matthew 24, it's only 21 months into the seven year period if viewed chronologically.

It's also however said the silence precedes the midpoint, when the abomination of desolation is set up, when the 'great tribulation' begins. When God unleashes His wrath? Thus, the trumpets and vial judgements happen concurrently during the last forty-two months?

Or the three sets of judgements all overlap, and the tribulation may have already started? Like, since Jesus' time, or more recently since WW1, as opposed to starting at the inception of the peace agreement? These tribulations are part of the birth pains, and the great tribulation is when the beast government is birthed?

Either way, having opened the seventh seal, seven angels were given seven trumpets to do their worst. Revelation 8:7-12 tells us, 'The first angel sounded his trumpet, and there came hail and fire mixed with blood, and it was hurled down on the earth. A third of the earth was burned up, a third of the trees were burned up, and all the green grass was burned up.

The second angel sounded his trumpet, and something like a huge mountain, all ablaze, was thrown into the sea. A third of the sea turned into blood, a third of the living creatures in the sea died, and a third of the ships were destroyed.

The third angel sounded his trumpet, and a great star, blazing like a torch, fell from the sky on a third of the rivers and on the springs of water— the name of the star is Wormwood. A third of the waters turned bitter, and many people died from the waters that had become bitter'.

It's said nuclear war is being alluded to, and the mountainous burning object is a meteor or nuclear weapon. It's also believed the star called Wormwood is an asteroid. Like, Dr Tom Horn suggests the 'Wormwood prophecy' relates to the asteroid NASA named Apophis (the Egyptian god of chaos), which is due to impact Earth on Friday 13th April 2029. Apparently, it's 370 metres wide, it's travelling at 28,000 mph, and it has the power of 65,000 atomic bombs (like those unleashed on Nagasaki and Hiroshima).

Whilst it's also said the star called Wormwood could be a fallen angel because angels are stars, Pastor Dean Odle (from Fire and Grace Ministry, US) points out that Wormwood is the word Chernobyl in Ukrainian. He postulates the third trumpet has been blown, and it was Chernobyl, the nuclear power plant disaster in Ukraine. He states a third of the waters were polluted, and highlights the millions affected by contamination (hens were born inside out).

Odle believes the first trumpet was WW1. He highlights the earth was scorched, and soldiers wore helmets to protect them from the hail from weapons. He believes the second trumpet was WW2. He confirms that a third of the ships were destroyed in WW2. And he surmises the mountain of fire was the first hydrogen bomb.

The fourth trumpet causes the sun and moon to be darkened. Apparently, the light of the sun, moon and stars upon the earth will be diminished by a third. This could be the result of chemtrails ('geo-engineering'), or the smoke from the carnage taking place? Or the 'darkness' could come from somewhere else, like the pit of hell? Odle notably believes the fourth trumpet was the Gulf War, asserting the looming smoke obscured the sun, moon, and stars.

Rather than the traditional sequential teaching, Odle regards the seals, trumpets, and vials as happening concurrently. Thus, seals have been opened, and trumpets have been blown. But no vials have been unleashed to date? We haven't had God's wrath yet? Odle understands the three judgements are three pictures or stories of how it all unfolds.

Thus, according to Odle, the four horsemen of the apocalypse have been released. The white horse is the antichrist deception, which includes the Roman Catholic Church and the UN. The red horse is communism. The communist philosophy has killed millions, and will continue to kill millions. The black horse is economic upheaval, famine, and WW1. And the green/pale horse is Islam and WW2. Thus, the tribulation has been happening long-time, but great tribulation is coming. Others however disagree, as the first seal introduces the antichrist, and we haven't had the awful privilege of meeting him yet.

And maybe the fourth trumpet hasn't been blown? We haven't seen the sun, moon and stars darken yet, which seems apocalyptically weird? It seems the whole world witnesses this event? After this happens, an eagle cried loudly, as it flew through the air, 'Terror, terror, terror to all who belong to this world because of what will happen when the last three angels blow their trumpets'. The fifth trumpet thus brings us the first terror.

Revelation 9: 1-3 tells us, '...I saw a star fall from heaven unto the earth: and to him was given the key to the bottomless pit. And he opened the bottomless pit; and there arose a smoke out of the pit, as the smoke of a great furnace; and the sun and the air were darkened by reason of the smoke of the pit. And there came out of the smoke locusts upon the earth: and unto them was given power, as the scorpions of the earth have power'.

So, an angel opens a portal to allow demonic creatures from the pit of hell to come here? They were told not to hurt the grass or plants or trees, but all the people who did not have God's seal on their forehead. They were not allowed to kill them, but instead torture them for five months with the agony of scorpion stings (locusts live for about five months).

It's noted that smoke, (which these locusts emerge from), corroborates with ectoplasm. It seems God is letting Baal followers experience some of Baal's crawling reality. Like, La-Sala spoke about being stung by scorpions, which felt like real stings. It will be horrendous, and people will want to die. However, we're told, 'in those days men will seek death and will not find it; they will desire to die, and death will flee from them'. So, that's interesting. Maybe that has something to do with the (RFID?) chip embedded in our flesh.

We're told the locusts looked like horses armed for battle. They had gold crowns on their heads, and they had human faces. Their hair was long like the hair of a woman, and their teeth were like the teeth of a lion. So, they could be nephilim? They wore armour made of iron, and their wings roared like an army of chariots rushing into battle. They had tails that stung people like scorpions, with power to torture people. Thus, it's also said the locusts are a reference to helicopters (including their noisy propellers). They look like horses, which refers to vehicles? But moreover, we're told, 'their king is the angel from the bottomless pit: his name in Hebrew is Abaddon, and in Greek, Apollyon – the Destroyer'. So, we're back to the sun god.

As mentioned, it's purported that CERN has an occult agenda. And scientists are opening inter-dimensional gateways to allow dark spiritual forces (energy/matter) into our dimension. It's said demonic spirits are manipulating wo/men, by giving them the technology to open the abyss to set the captives free. Thus, it's possible that CERN is the key to the bottomless pit, and we're opening the door for Apollyon aka the beast to come through? According to Sergio Bertolucci, Director for Research and Scientific Computing at CERN, 'The Large Hadron Collider could open a doorway to an extra dimension and out of this door might come something, or we might send something through it'.

Pastor Charles Lawson highlights CERN is creating antimatter (the opposite of matter), which needs to be contained as it's very powerful. Apparently one gram of antimatter equals four atomic bombs. Thus, they're weaponizing it. But moreover, he asserts that it affects people and controls them. He states antimatter was given to a college (to contain because it's volatile), and strange things started happening. Like, people began having hallucinations, seeing apparitions, and acting wild. He states apparitions have also been seen at CERN. He cautions that we're opening Pandora's Box, and highlights Hawking's statement, namely, 'we unleashed the gates of hell'.

Tom Horn points out that a large portion of CERN is located on the town Saint-Genis-Pouilly, which in Roman times was called Apolliacum, as the town and temple were dedicated to Apollyon. The people who lived there believed it was a gateway to the underworld. It's also said CERN is short for the horned god Cernunnos, who was god of the underworld. Lest we forget the statue of Shiva, ancient Apollyon, Hindu goddess of destruction, parked outside CERN HQ. And the occult rituals, that have been secretly filmed there.

The sixth trumpet brings the second terror, namely, four angels, who were bound at the great River Euphrates, are released to annihilate a third of humanity. Thus, another two billion will be wiped out (if the population is reduced to six billion after the fourth seal). They lead an army of two hundred million mounted troops. The horses had heads like lions. And fire, smoke and burning sulphur came from their mouths. The fire, smoke and sulphur, which killed the people, are referred to as three plagues. Those who survived did not however repent but rather continued worshipping demons as part of their witchcraft.

It's said this massive army could be Chinese soldiers ('Kings of the East'). Apparently, China boasted they could mobilise an army of two hundred million back in 1961. It's highlighted this would have been a preposterous number for John at the time, given the global population was a mere fraction of such an obscene figure. But as it transpires, the Chinese have bred like rabbits. Horses could refer to horses, or some other kind of military transport?

It's also however said, this army is demonic, given the reference to fire, smoke and sulphur. So, more evil is unleashed from the bottomless pit. Maybe the horses are nephilim (chimeras)? Or the army could be a reference to super-soldiers? Jesus warns us in Luke 21:26 about, 'Men's hearts failing them for fear, and for looking after those things which are coming on the earth: for the powers of heaven shall be shaken'.

Whilst the seventh trumpet brings in the third terror, which results in the seven vial judgements, as we'll get to, John states (in Revelation 10:7), 'when the seventh angel blows his trumpet, God's mysterious plan will be fulfilled. It will happen just as He announced it to His prophets'. It seems this mystery pertains to the rapture? The rapture is when God comes to collect His people. However, we'll get back to this.

John also tells us that two special witnesses preach the gospel at the temple in Jerusalem. They will proclaim that Jesus of the New Testament is the fulfilment of the Torah's prophecy of a messiah. God protects them for 1260 days and then the beast from the bottomless pit kills them. Whilst some believe they appear at the start of the tribulation (so, Satan kills them when he's released from the abyss at the midpoint), others believe they appear at the start of the great tribulation, at the midpoint of the peace agreement. So, they rain on Satan's parade at the end times.

Furthermore, they're empowered with supernatural powers to perform miracles. This includes the ability to end rain fall, turn rivers/oceans to blood, and strike the earth with whatever plagues they want. Their powers are similar to Moses and Elijah, and some believe these witnesses will actually be Moses and Elijah. Others however suggest they'll be Enoch and Elijah because they didn't die. As mentioned, they were translated and went to the second heaven until this time?

Apparently, people celebrate their death (because they're so annoying), and their bodies are displayed in the main street in Jerusalem. Jerusalem is notably called 'Sodom' and 'Egypt', which conveys its character at the end of the world i.e. debauched sun god worshippers. Jerusalem, the city where their Lord was crucified, becomes the epicentre of iniquity. It's noted, Israel is super secular, like they celebrate Gay Pride and late abortions are legal. No one is allowed to bury them, but rather the whole world has to see them. This suggests advanced technology like 'live' TV? It will appear to the world, that Satan has defeated God because he was able to kill His saints.

The two witnesses' bodies lie unburied for three and a half days, but then the spirit of life from God enters them and they stand up. All those watching them freak out (LOL). Furthermore, a loud voice from heaven shouted, 'Come up here!' and they ascend into heaven in a cloud. There's also a great earthquake that takes place the same hour, which kills seven thousand. But moreover, those who don't die are terrified, and give glory to the God of heaven. So, it seems people finally get a grip at the end?

We're also told that when the seventh angel sounded his trumpet, there were loud voices in heaven which said, 'The kingdom of the world has become the kingdom of our Lord and of His messiah, and He will reign forever and ever'. God's temple in heaven was opened, and there was lightning, thunder, an earthquake, and a severe hailstorm. This is like the sixth seal, suggesting the same end time event?

Or the seven trumpet judgements take us up to the midpoint? As discussed, the midpoint seems to be a game changer. This is when the abomination of desolation is set up. It's when the antichrist exalts himself as God. It's when the great tribulation kicks in, aka God's wrath, which we're told is unleashed in the sixth seal. So, the seventh trumpet calls forth the seven angels with seven vials of God's wrath/judgement, which are plagues.

However, after the seven trumpets, and before the seven vials, we're told about the woman and the red dragon, and the NWO, in Revelation 12 and 13 respectively. Thus, John saw a woman clothed with the sun, with the moon beneath her feet, and a crown of twelve stars on her head. The woman was pregnant, and a large red dragon stood before her, ready to devour the baby, a boy who was to rule all nations with a rod of iron, as soon as He was born. The child (Jesus) was however snatched away from the dragon and caught up with God and to His throne. And the woman fled to the wilderness, where she was protected for the next three and half years.

Then there was war in heaven, and Michael and his angels fought the dragon and his angels. The dragon lost the battle and was forced out of heaven. Revelation 12:9 states, 'This great dragon – the ancient serpent called the Devil, or Satan, the one deceiving the whole world – was thrown down to earth with all his angels'. And he knows his time is short. Hence, he's on a mission to destroy God's people, and ultimately take on God?

It's said the woman represents Israel or the church (the twelve stars round her head are the twelve tribes of Israel). And she flees to the wilderness, when the dragon sets up shop. When he takes his throne and the abomination of desolation is set up etc. It's suggested the Jews who flee from Judea will head to Petra in Jordan (see photo). The dragon in Revelation 12 has seven heads, ten horns, and seven crowns on his heads, which is like the beast described in Revelation 13.

As mentioned, John sees a beast with seven heads and ten horns with ten crowns on them, coming from the sea (nations). Written on each head were names that blasphemed God. Thus, it's said the beast represents the antichrist and the dragon represents Satan. The beast is the public face of the dragon. It seems the beast is a reference to both the antichrist and the NWO.

We're told the dragon gave the beast his own power and throne and great authority. Then John sees that one of his heads is fatally wounded, which is miraculously healed. He states, 'All the world marvelled at this miracle and followed the beast in awe'. 'And they worshipped the dragon which gave power unto the beast, and they worshipped the beast, saying, who is like unto the beast? Who is able to make war with him?' It's understood no one can make war with the beast aka UN army.

It's interpreted that the antichrist receives a mortal head-wound i.e. he's assassinated. And people are astounded when he magically comes back to life. It's a counterfeit resurrection? As touched on, we're told the evil one is released at midpoint, so maybe he incarnates in the antichrist, bringing him back to life? Apparently, he'll retain his wounds, as his right arm will be withered and he'll be blind in his right eye, which corroborates with the one-eyed sun god (see Zechariah 11:17). He is the one-eyed sun god? He's Apollyon reincarnated?

It's also however said that the wound pertains to the fatal blow the papacy received from Napoleon in 1798 (having ruled for 1260 years). Thus, the beast could be the papacy, which was revived from 1929 when the Vatican was reinstated?

We're told the beast was allowed to speak great blasphemies about God, and wage war against His holy people to overcome them. He was given authority to do what he wanted for forty-two months, which includes persecuting anyone who believes in the One True God. He was given authority to rule over every tribe and people and language and nation. Thus, the global government is established at this midpoint.

And the Temple is in situ, as the abomination of desolation is erected. Daniel 12:11 states, 'From the time the daily sacrifice is abolished and the abomination of desolation is set up to be worshipped, there will be 1,290 days. Blessed are those who wait and remain until the end of the 1,335 days'. So, that's three and half years into the peace agreement, as prophesied in other parts of the Bible.

Thus, despite the promising start with the peace treaty etc, it goes awry. The antichrist breaks the covenant halfway through the tribulation period and makes the last forty-two months the bloodiest in history. It's said he gets drunk on power when he miraculously comes back from the dead. It seems he becomes delusional and thinks he's God? Hence, he demands to be worshipped.

As touched on, it's believed the antichrist will be completely possessed by the devil. He'll be endowed with all kinds of psychic and superhuman powers. Wheeler (2009) concedes the antichrist is the personification of the Dragon Lucifer. The 'Son of Perdition' is the culmination and consummation of satanic skill and power. It's noted, there's a parallel with Jesus being anointed by the Holy Spirit at His baptism, and then commissioned to preach the gospel for three and a half years. And the antichrist being 'anointed' by Satan, and also preaching for three and a half years.

Regarding the incarnation of Satan, Black (20010) wrote, 'At first he will appear to be a great benefactor of humankind, a genius. To begin with he himself may not realise that he is the antichrist, believing he acts only out of love for humanity. He will do away with much dangerous superstition and work to unite the religions of the world. However, there will come a moment of pride, when he realises he is achieving some things that Jesus was, apparently, unable to achieve. He will then become aware of his identity and his mission' (p.539).

But moreover, John sees two beasts. The second beast comes out of the earth, and is described as having 'two horns like a lamb, and speaking like a dragon'. The second beast is known as the false prophet. He's the antichrist's sidekick, his whore. It's said the appearance of a lamb, which symbolises Jesus, but speaking like a dragon, suggests the Pope. He pretends to be God's servant but he's actually Satan's.

It's understood the Pope will head up the global religion (Mystery Babylon religion). As mentioned, the Pope supports the UN, and it's believed he will be instrumental in enforcing the will of the NWO. It's highlighted that people look to the Pope for world peace and reconciliation, which is a role he carved out for himself. Like, the royals care about us?

Wheeler (2009) concedes the Pope is the false prophet, and Lucifer is the Babylonian messiah king. It's also however said, the second beast could be the US i.e. 'Christian' America is a wolf in sheep's clothing. And also, the two horns like a lamb could represent the UK and US, two allegedly Christian nations that are actually haunted. Or the false prophet's two horns represent two religions i.e. Christianity and Satanism.

The second beast exercised all the authority of the first beast, and he required everyone to worship the first beast, whose death wound had been healed. He was allowed to perform astounding miracles, such as making fire flash down from heaven, on behalf of the first beast to deceive the world. He ordered the people of the world to make a great statue of the first beast, and he gave life to this statue so it could speak. Then the statue commanded that anyone refusing to worship it must die.

It's noted, that Nebuchadnezzar created a massive gold statue (ninety feet tall and nine feet wide), and commanded everyone to worship it (which Daniel and co refused to). But in the 21st century, we have the technology to make the statue speak, like a robot? It's said the beast's image will move and be telecast, which suggests 3D holographic technology. Like, dead singers are presented as holograms at concerts (e.g. Whitney Houston), and they move, sing and dance. His image will be some kind of AI that's infused with some kind of life?

The false prophet also mandates that all people receive the mark of the beast. The citizens of the world have to show their allegiance to the beast. It's said that unlike God's Spirit who dwells in people, the devil dwells in people via technology. The antichrist spirit uses AI? It seems we can't escape the beast if we're connected to the beast computer system?

Revelation 13: 16-18 states, 'He required everyone – great and small, rich and poor, slave and free – to be given a mark on the right hand or on the forehead. And no one could buy or sell anything without that mark, which was either the name of the beast or the number representing his name. Let the one who has understanding solve the number of the beast, for it is the number of a man. His number is 666'. As mentioned, the number 6 is associated with mankind in the Bible, thus 666 suggests a triune nature i.e. dragon, beast, and antichrist?

So, the mark is the chip linked to a centralised bank, (beast computer system), and we can't buy or sell without it. And when we take this mark we officially belong to Satan. There's no turning back (and we're tracked). As touched on, it's suggested the chip may alter DNA. It's supposed the scientists (alchemists) finally achieve a degree of success with immortality or longevity, which accounts for the inability to die, when people seek death because of the demonic horrors taking place.

It's said the mark, (whatever changes our DNA), makes us unredeemable, like nephilim. Our blood is no longer just human? It's also said 216 (6x6x6) could be the mark of his name, which is the cabalist number of God's hidden name (as mentioned). Before the chip materialised, it was purported the mark of the beast could be a tattoo, like a barcode featuring 666.

Interestingly, vaccinations being developed for the crown virus incorporate the enzyme 'Luciferase' to demonstrate one has been vaccinated (Luciferin comes from fireflies). These 'quantum tattoos', which are invisible to the naked eye, can be detected using a customised smart phone. But moreover, they apparently modify our DNA and RNA. And we won't be able to buy or sell (or travel) unless we've been vaccinated i.e. have the mark?

It's also noted, Bill Gates and Microsoft published a patent WO2020060606 aka World Order 2020 '666' for a 'cryptocurrency system using body activity data'. It's rumoured the corona virus is being used as a cover to create a new digital financial system and digital identity. It's the framework of a global financial system, (for buying and selling), using technology integrated with the human body.

So, these two individuals, the beast and the false prophet, both serve the dragon by presiding over a one-world government (theocracy). It seems Satan is vicariously worshipped through the antichrist. And the antichrist, false prophet and Satan are another twisted trinity. It's foreseen that the rulers of the world (the elite Satanists) will thrive on unparalleled wealth, opulence, debauchery, idolatry, sorcery, sexual perversions, and the rest. Whoredom truly lands with Babylon the great harlot. It's noted, Babylon is both a physical place and spiritual term.

Then John sees three angels flying through the skies. The first one proclaims the good news and gives Glory to God. The second one shouts out that 'Babylon is fallen – that great city is fallen – because she seduced the nations of the world and made them drink the wine of her passionate immorality'. It's suggested Babylon is actually Babylon, or it's a reference to a great city that is synonymous with Babylon e.g. Rome. Or it could be Jerusalem, as Jerusalem is likened to Sodom and Egypt in the end times. Or it could refer to NYC or the US, or the Revived Roman Empire. But we'll get back to this.

The third angel followed, shouting 'Anyone who worships the beast and his statue or who accepts his mark on the forehead or the hand must drink the wine of God's wrath'. They will be tormented and have no relief day or night (His wrath is poured out undiluted). This angel encourages God's people to endure the persecution and trust in Jesus.

As touched on, for those who manage to escape, it's said they'll remain under God's protection for the duration of the Tribulation period. Those who refuse to worship the beast and bear his mark are called Tribulation Saints. For those who die, they die as martyrs (they get their white robe). The tribulation period gives God's people, Jews and gentiles, one last window of opportunity to be saved. So, we've been warned. It's game-over with the mark. Take the mark and endure the wrath. And then burn in hell with the devil and his angels?

Thus, God's seven bowls of wrath are unleashed by the seven angels. It seems these take place during the last three and a half years? Or they take place at the very end, when Babylon has fallen? The first bowl caused grievous bodily sores to break out on everyone who had the mark of the beast and worshipped his statue. The second bowl caused the sea to turn to blood, and everything in the sea died. The third bowl caused the rivers and water springs to turn to blood. Perhaps the two witnesses are behind God's judgements, as His agents, who have been given power to send plagues?

We're told in Revelation 16:6, an angel says, 'For your holy people and prophets have been killed, and their blood was poured out on the earth. So you have given their murderers blood to drink. It is their just reward'. It's noted, these plagues are like the plagues unleashed on Egypt. And like God protected His people then, so He will protect them again.

The fourth bowl caused the sun's heat to be intensified, scorching the people on earth. Rather than blocking out the sun, perhaps 'chemtrails' will backfire and enhance the effects of the sun? The fifth bowl is poured out on the throne of the beast, and its kingdom was plunged into darkness. We're told people grind their teeth in anguish and curse God for their pains and sores. Then the sixth bowl is poured out on the Euphrates River, and it dried up so that the kings from the east could march westward without hindrance. It seems this refers to the army of two hundred million?

But moreover, we're told (in Revelation 16:13-14), 'And I saw three evil spirits that looked like frogs leap from the mouth of the dragon, the beast, and the false prophet. These miracle-working demons caused all the rulers of the world to gather for battle against the Lord on that great judgement day of God Almighty'. It's suggested these spirits that look like frogs could be grey aliens. As touched on, it's understood there's an alien deception, as we'll get to.

So, the sixth vial results in the armies of the antichrist being gathered together to wage the battle of Armageddon. However, just as we're being told about them gathering together, Jesus intercepts John's account, stating, 'Take note: I will come as unexpectedly as a thief! Blessed are all who are watching for me, who keep their robes ready so they will not need to walk naked and ashamed'.

Thus, perhaps Jesus takes His people at this point i.e. rapture (saints are translated), as He's also getting His army ready? It's possible He's collecting those still alive, and those who were martyred, dressed in white robes, and also those 'sleeping'? However, we're told God's mysterious plan will be fulfilled, when the seventh angel blows his trumpet, which could be the rapture? Thus, the seventh trumpet and the sixth vial both entail the mystery of the rapture? It's the same time.

Wheeler (2009) concedes that just as Jesus has His bride (saints and angels), so does Lucifer. And Lucifer's spiritual bride will be made up of an army of chosen elite that carries the title 'Mothers of Darkness' (witches). It's understood Satan's army will be unbelievably demonic. Thus, besides the millions of demon enhanced super soldiers, and demons unleashed from the pit, there'll be chimeras, robotics and trans-humans, and genetically upgraded super soldiers, and the return of the nephilim (the miry clay and iron).

It's understood the world's militaries have not been preparing for WW3, or even an alien invasion as alleged, but rather they're being prepared to take on God. There's a reason the world has been stockpiling weapons since WW2, and it's not to fight each other. As mentioned, Luciferians call the final war with God 'The Great Plan'. It seems Satan thinks he has a chance, or rather, he has nothing to lose. Whereas, Luciferians have been deceived to think they'll defeat God. It seems Armageddon will be the ultimate showdown. It will be insane.

Then, the seventh angel pours out his vial into the air. And there came a great voice out of the temple of heaven, from the throne, saying, 'It is finished!' This statement reminds us of Jesus saying 'it is finished' when He died for us. Then thunder crashed, lightning flashed, there was a great earthquake, and an insane hailstorm (apparently the hailstones weigh 45 kilograms). It seems the 'ends-times' weather is the climax of 'climate change'?

So, the seals, trumpets and vials all end with the same scenario. It's also highlighted, that like the parallel drawn between the seven seals and Matthew 24, the trumpets and vials happen concurrently (rather than sequentially), as they overlap and are meshed together.

Thus, the first trumpet pertains to hail and fire mixed with blood affecting the 'earth', and the first vial results in painful sores for those on the 'earth'. It's interpreted that a nuclear war happens via the first trumpet, as a third of the earth is burned up, and this accounts for the malignant sores that won't heal. This also accounts for the poisoning of the waters, the death of much of the earth's vegetation and ocean life, and severe burns i.e. exposure to radiation.

The second trumpet and vial both pertain to the 'sea', and the third trumpet and vial pertain to the 'rivers'. The fourth trumpet is however when the sun and moon darken, which could be related to intense heat that comes from the fourth bowl? Then it gets weirder when darkness falls, and the demonic entities come out to play, with the subsequent trumpets and vials. That's when it gets proper crazy.

John continues the Revelation, stating that one of the seven angels, who poured out the seven bowls, told him (Revelation 17:1-2), '… I will show you the Judgement that is going to come on the great prostitute, who sits on many waters. The rulers of the world have had immoral relations with her, and the people who belong to this world have been made drunk by the wine of her immorality'.

John was then taken into the wilderness in his spirit (astral body), where he saw a woman sitting on a scarlet beast that had seven heads and ten horns written all over with blasphemies against God. So, the harlot rides the NWO beast, which is red representing communism? It's also said the red beast refers to the red dragon in Revelation 12.

The woman was arrayed in purple and scarlet clothing, and wore beautiful jewellery made of gold, precious stones and pearls. She held in her hand a gold goblet full of obscenities and the impurities of her immorality. A mysterious name was written on her forehead, namely, 'BABYLON THE GREAT, MOTHER OF ALL HARLOTS AND ABOMINATIONS OF THE EARTH'. John states she was drunk with the blood of God's holy people who were martyrs for Jesus.

Thus, it's believed the whore is the Roman Catholic Church, because cardinals and bishops dress in red and purple (respectively), it's opulent/minted, they use a golden cup during mass, they've killed millions of God's people, and Catholicism is a version of the Mystery Babylon religion. And the rulers of the world have had immoral relations with her. The Jesuits are at the heart of the conspiracy, from the mafia to the royals. It's said Israel is God's wife, and this prostitute is Satan's wife. The reformers notably believed Babylon the Great was the Roman Catholic Church. Furthermore, the Pope, the false prophet who supports the UN, is Roman Catholic.

But the woman is identified as Babylon the Great, which suggests she's queen Semiramis, mother of all false religions? Semiramis created the Mystery Babylon religion, which went global. Thus, it's said Revelation 17 is about the Roman Catholic Church but all religions. And all false religions come together at the end, as one religion (they're synthesised into One), which rides the NWO? One world religion precedes Luciferianism, at the midpoint? And those who refuse to worship the antichrist are beheaded? Hence, she will be drunk on the blood of those martyred for Jesus? She's been a drunk throughout the Ages.

The angel explains to John, 'The beast you saw was once alive but isn't now. And yet he will soon come up out of the bottomless pit and go to eternal destruction'. Apart from God's people, the world will be amazed at the reappearance of this beast 'who was, and is not, and yet is'. Thus, it's said this beast is Nimrod aka Apollyon. It seems he resurrects in the antichrist following his fatal head wound? This statement notably contrasts with what Jesus said at the start of Revelation, namely, 'I am the one who is, who always was, and who is still to come, the Almighty One'.

We're also told the seven heads of the beast represent the seven hills where the woman rules, which is another reference to Rome, given its seven hills. And we're told the prostitute represents the great city that rules over the kings of the earth. Thus, Mystery Babylon is a whore and a city. This further suggests she's Rome, because she ruled over the kings of the earth at that time. So, Mystery Babylon, the filthy whore, could be the Vatican? However, the seven heads also represent seven kings, which refers to the seven satanic empires?

We're told (in Revelation 17: 10-14), 'Five kings have already fallen, the sixth now reigns, and the seventh is yet to come, but his reign shall be brief. The scarlet beast that was alive and then died is the eighth king. He is like the other seven, and he too will go to his doom. His ten horns are ten kings who have not yet risen to power; they will be appointed to their kingdoms for one brief moment to reign with the beast. They will agree to give their power and authority to him. Together they will wage war against the Lamb, but the Lamb will defeat them because He is Lord over all Lords and King over all Kings, and His people are the called and chosen and faithful ones'.

It's suggested the eighth king is the antichrist, which comes out of the seventh kingdom, which is the revived Roman Empire. And his ten horns, ten kings, agree to take on God at the end. But moreover, we're told the scarlet beast and his ten horns (kings) hate the prostitute. And 'they will strip her naked, eat her flesh, and burn her remains with fire'. Just as Satanists do to their victims.

It's asserted that God destroys 'religious Babylon' in Revelation 17 and 'commercial Babylon' in Revelation 18. Others however say they're the same one thing. Babylon is a symbol of commercialism. Luciferians own the world. It's said religion and materialism are the two parts of Satan's global religion.

Thus, in Revelation 18:1-3, we're told that John saw another angel come down from heaven, who shouted 'Babylon is fallen – that great city is fallen'. [Like, the second angel announced in Revelation 14:8]. She has become a dwelling for demons, and a haunt for every impure spirit. All the nations have drunk from her passionate immorality. The rulers of the world have committed adultery with her, and merchants throughout the world have grown rich as a result of her luxurious living'.

As it transpires, she's utterly consumed by fire in one day. Her mourners (rulers and merchants etc) cry out, 'How terrible, how terrible for Babylon, that great city! In one single moment God's judgement came on her'. We're told sea captains and sailors will see the smoke of her burning, and will exclaim, 'Was there ever a city like this great city?'

Hence, it's said Mystery Babylon refers to the US. The sailors could be looking at NYC? NYC could be the whore, represented by the statue of Semiramis who sits on many waters, who hosts the UN HQ and the WTC? It's asserted the US has infected the world with materialism and immorality. Hollywood has cast a spell on the masses. Like, the music industry, which also belongs to the beast. They've given us our narratives and we've enjoyed the programming. Thus, it's said America rides the NWO beast. The beast made the whore, and he will destroy the whore. She's been used to spread her filth?

It's said her purple and scarlet linens, and expensive jewels, indicate her wealth. And America has blood on its hands from the saints, because they've killed untold millions. It's said saints include unborn babies i.e. the blood of millions of abortions. So, America is drunk on the blood of the saints, as is Russia etc.

So, Mystery Babylon is a mystery. She could be Rome, or the US, or Jerusalem, or Babylon, if Babylon returns to its original splendour. Babylon could be the capital of the NWO, as opposed to Jerusalem, where beast HQ is located?

After God destroys the great whore, John heard a great multitude in heaven shouting 'Hallelujah!' They said, the time has come for the wedding feast of the Lamb, and His bride has prepared herself, wearing the finest white linen. The angel said to John, 'Blessed are those who are invited to the wedding feast of the Lamb', and he added, 'These are true words that come from God'. So, that's one wedding we'll want to go to. It seems those dressed in white robes ascend to heaven at this point?

After this, John (19: 11-16) tells us, 'And I saw heaven opened, and behold a white horse; and he that sat upon him was called Faithful and True, and in righteousness he doth judge and make war. His eyes were as a flame of fire, and on his head were many crowns; and he had a name written, that no man knew, but he himself. And he was clothed with a vesture dipped in blood: and his name is called The Word of God'.

'And the armies which were in heaven followed him upon white horses, clothed in fine linen, white and clean. And out of his mouth goeth a sharp sword, that with it he should smite the nations: and he shall rule them with a rod of iron: and he treadeth the winepress of the fierceness and wrath of Almighty God. And he hath on his vesture and on his thigh a name written, KING OF KINGS, AND LORD OF LORDS'. The 'rod of iron' is notably a reference to God in the Old Testament and refers to Jesus in Revelation 12.

So, it appears that after the wedding feast, God destroys the beast. It's time for the grand finale, namely, the armies of the world unite to fight Christ in His second advent to earth. It's highlighted that unlike His lowly birth in Bethlehem, where He was laid in a manger, when Jesus returns, He returns triumphantly like a lion. He's the Lion and the Lamb. According to Zechariah 14:4, His feet will stand on the Mount of Olives (where He ascended from), which faces Jerusalem on the East.

Then John states, 'I saw the beast, and the kings of the earth, and their armies, gathered together to make war against him that sat on the horse, and against his army'. But it's all good because Jesus kicks the evil one's arse. All the armies are put to death at one stroke (from the sword of the word). And the beast and false prophet are then cast into a lake of fire burning with brimstone. It's recalled in Matthew 25:41, Jesus said hell was created for the devil and his angels. God doesn't want any of His kids to go there. We fundamentally choose to go there.

The battle of Armageddon is the climax of the spiritual war that has been raging between Christ and Satan since the beginning (of our existence). And it's checkmate. The cosmic chess-match is finally over?

Or maybe not, as John continues, the devil is bound in the abyss for another thousand years. He said, 'I saw an angel coming down from heaven, having the key to the bottomless pit and a great chain in his hand. And he laid hold of the dragon, that serpent of old, who is the Devil and Satan, and bound him up for a thousand years. And he cast him into the bottomless pit and shut him up, and set a seal on him, so that he should deceive the nations no more until the thousand years were finished.'

Thus, it's not as straight forward as Jesus returns, the devil and his minions are turfed into the fiery furnace, and we find out who's conquered the pearly gates? It seems Revelation throws a curveball as it tells us about the 'Millennium Kingdom'. Thus, whilst the evil one is bound in the abyss, Jesus reigns for a thousand years on earth, prior to the final judgement and future eternal state. It's a time of restoration and peace, likened to the Sabbath. It's highlighted we've had six millennia of madness, so it's time for our day off? It's asserted there were four thousand years from Adam to Jesus, then two thousand years, after Jesus did a shoot in 30AD, which is six thousand years. So, 2030 is the seventh millennium after Adam.

Isaiah 11:5-9 tells us it will be like Eden on Earth. And praise the Lord, there's no more carnivorous munching. We'll all be vegetarians again. We're told the wolf and the lamb will live together, and the leopard and the goat will be at peace. Lions will eat grass as the livestock do. So, we're all friends again and friends don't eat each other.

John sees the souls of those who had been beheaded for their testimony about Jesus (which alludes to the Noahide laws?). And also, the souls of those who refused to worship the beast or his statue, nor accepted his mark on their forehead or hands.

John states, 'They came to life again, and they reigned with Christ for a thousand years. This is the first resurrection. The rest of the dead did not come back to life until the thousand years had ended. Blessed and holy are those who share the first resurrection. For them the second death holds no power, but they will be priests of God and of Christ and will reign with him for a thousand years'. Some people notably believe we're in heaven for a thousand years, as opposed to earth.

It's noted, there's disagreement regarding the millennial kingdom. Like, Amillennialists (Amillennialism literally means no millennium) don't believe in a literal one thousand year reign. But rather they view the millennium as symbolic of the 'Church Age', which began two millennia ago. For them, Christ simply returns, judges, and establishes the new heaven and earth. They also endeavour to get the Word out, as Jesus said, 'And this gospel of the kingdom will be preached in the whole world as a testimony to all nations, and then the end will come' (Matthew 24:14).

Roman Catholic eschatology notably endorses Amillennialism. Apparently, Papacy employed St Augustine formed the view of Amillennialism i.e. the millennial is allegorical not literal. Like Origen before him (who allegedly chopped off his testes for purity), he theorised that the Bible is not to be taken literally but allegorically. Hence, he obfuscated the supernatural, by stating nephilim are Cain's progeny rather than fallen angels. It's said he was initiated into the mysteries.

It's also highlighted that Preterism, which is the eschatological view that some or all prophecies of the Bible as events have already happened, was created by Jesuits in the 1600s to destroy end times prophetic warnings. Like, when Jesus forewarned about Jerusalem being surrounded by armies, it's said this happened in 70AD with the Roman invasion. There were also false prophets at that time. And the sky went dark and an earthquake happened when Jesus died. So, the generation Jesus was referring to, when He said 'this generation' shall not pass until all this happens, was circa 70AD?

Or maybe not. Moreover, John didn't write the Book of Revelation until 95AD, which tells us about the NWO and the mark of the beast etc. It seems the family don't want us to know their plan to rule the world. Hence, they dumb us down and distract us with BS, like following gimps on Instagram.

Post-millennialists believe that Jesus returns after the millennium or golden age. They believe through preaching the gospel, the Church will usher in the golden age i.e. the world will become more godly and peaceful (which goes against current events). So, they also regard the thousand years as symbolic. For them, Christ returns at the end of days, and the physical resurrection and judgements take place immediately.

Amillennialism and post-millennialism are arguably more straight forward versions? Particularly since Revelation tells us that Satan is let out of the abyss after the thousand years to kick off for one last time. It appears the people who survive the tribulation continue to procreate, so generations after them also get the choice to stick with the Lord, or go their own way.

We're told, when the thousand years have expired, Satan will be released from his prison and will go out to deceive the nations which are in the four corners of the earth. He gathers them together, a mighty host 'whose number is as the sand of the sea', to battle. However, before they can attack, God intercepts and fire pours down from heaven. Satan is then consigned to the lake of fire, to join his two infernal buds, the beast and the false prophet.

So, God knows about the millennium kingdom, as 2 Peter 3:8 further tells us 'with the Lord a day is like a thousand years, and a thousand years are like a day'. So, perhaps the thousand years is like a day? Time passes differently in the millennial kingdom?

However, before we get to Judgement Day, there's the curious matter of the resurrection. It seems the resurrection happens when Jesus returns? But only God's kids are resurrected. John pertains to the first resurrection, and ideally we'd want to be a part of that. It seems God collects His saints (dressed in white robes) for the marriage ceremony and supper, after He takes out the whore? And then we accompany Jesus to take on the antichrist with his haunted army? The second resurrection takes place after the thousand years.

Some Christians however believe they'll be raptured before Jesus' Second Coming at the end of the tribulation. The pre-tribulation view is that Christians get to dodge the tribulation. They're for Armageddon out of here before the shit hits the fan. The rapture aka blessed hope is our 'get out of jail free card'. We're spared from God's judgement and wrath. It's believed (when least expected) the Son of Man returns to rapture His followers. It's said we'll meet Jesus in the sky in our astral or resurrection bodies and ascend into heaven. It's purported that Christians vamos before the antichrist is revealed, before the seven year horror show.

1 Thessalonians 4:16-17 states, 'For the Lord Himself will come down from heaven, with a loud command, with the voice of the archangel and with the trumpet call of God, and the dead in Christ will rise first. After that, we who are still alive and are left will be caught up together with them in the clouds to meet the Lord in the air. And so we will be with the Lord forever'. So, this is the first resurrection. It's also noted, the idea that 'the dead in Christ shall rise first' suggests we're sleeping at death?

As Chuck Missler says, the rapture or harpazo 'is wild'. People will literally vanish like a fart in the wind, (like Enoch and Elijah did), resulting in untold carnage e.g. abandoned planes, trains, and automobiles etc. It's purported the church snaffling will be accredited to aliens. Those 'left behind' might be told that Christians were the obstacle to embracing the true Luciferian religion, and they had to go to spiritual bootcamp to evolve. The rapture could also be attributed to dematerialising, which is the result of fluctuating at a higher frequency i.e. through occult practices.

It's said the rapture is the starting gun for the antichrist. Indeed, this event could be the catalyst for his dark highness to appear, as the world is in angst looking for answers? People will be freaking out, as people vanish. [LOL]. It's highlighted that crises make smooth talkers very attractive.

We're told the rapture puts an end to the 'Age of Grace'. The restrainer (Holy Spirit) leaves, and the world is ready to receive Lucifer's doctrine. The Age of Grace or 'Church Age' began with the coming of the Holy Spirit on the Day of Pentecost, and ends with the rapture of the Church. The Holy Spirit filled Christians take the Holy Spirit with them? Moreover, when the restrainer is removed, all hell is let loose.

It's noted, the Bible gives us a wedding metaphor, with the idea being that Jesus returns for His bride, namely, the church (including those 'sleeping'). The New Testament portrays the Church as the Bride of Christ, and which husband wouldn't let his wife dodge the tribulation period? Thus, whilst the wedding feast is being enjoyed in heaven, (Jesus and His bride get married in heaven), God's judgement and wrath is being unleashed below.

So, God's people are removed (Christians), but the Jews remain. Hence, it's said the tribulation period is God's last shout at His people Israel. And He protects 144,000 of them. It's highlighted that the tribulation period is referred to as Jacob's trouble, which is a reference to Israel. In addition to the fulfilment of Daniels' prophecy, the two witnesses will help their unbelief. And maybe the Ark of the Covenant, which includes the Ten Commandments divinely chiselled on stone, as Ron Wyatt claimed. Regarding Jesus being the Messiah, presumably the Jews will be thinking anyone but Him. Surely not Him (LOL).

After seven years of marital bliss, Jesus returns with His bride to Earth to contend with Armageddon. This is His Second Coming. So, He claims His bride at the 'secret' rapture (we rendezvous in the sky) and comes with His bride at the Second Coming. A fundamental difference between the rapture, and Jesus' Second Coming, is that we don't know when the rapture will happen. It can happen at any time. Whereas, we'll know we're living in the Tribulation period by virtue of the treaty, and we'll know we have forty-two months to go, when the antichrist proclaims he's god in the temple and sets up the abomination of desolation.

It's highlighted the 'doctrine of imminence' is a feature throughout the Bible. It's like we're kept on our toes. We don't know when the rapture happens, like our last breath. Hence, the bride has to be ready for her groom, and have our oil lamps full etc.

Jesus notably told the Parable of the Ten Virgins (see Matthew 25:1-13), stating that only five of them were prepared for their Groom's arrival. In fairness, He took a long time coming. The five foolish virgins missed out on the banquet and weren't welcome at the Kingdom of Heaven. The groom aka Jesus, replied 'Truly I tell you, I don't know you'. 'Therefore keep watch, because you do not know the day or the hour'. The return of Jesus is likened to the coming of a thief in the night i.e. we're caught off guard. We're not expecting Him.

As mentioned, we're told it'll be like the days of Noah, when Jesus returns. Jesus said (Matthew 24:37), 'For in the days before the flood, people were eating and drinking, marrying and given in marriage, up to the day Noah entered the ark; and they knew nothing about what would happen until the flood came and took them all away. That is how it will be at the coming of the Son of Man. Two men will be in the field; one will be taken and the other left. Two women will be grinding with a hand mill; one will be taken and the other left'. There's a parallel drawn with the Flood and Sodom and Gomorrah, which describes how the righteous were removed and the unrighteous perished.

Others however believe there's more support for a mid-tribulation rapture. That is, we're raptured halfway through the tribulation. So, we get God's judgement but not His wrath. Hence, it's also called the pre-wrath rapture. We're apparently not assigned to wrath. Like, 1 Thessalonians 5:9 tells us, 'For God decided to save us through our Lord Jesus Christ, not to pour out His anger on us'. So, we get to dodge the great tribulation, the last three and half years. As mentioned, God's mysterious plan will be fulfilled when the seventh angel blows his trumpet, which suggests the rapture. We're told 'It will happen just as He announced it to His servants the prophets'.

Like Paul said, (1 Corinthians 15:51-53), 'But let me tell you a wonderful secret God has revealed to us. Not all of us will die, but we will all be transformed. It will happen in a moment, in the twinkling of an eye, when the last trumpet is blown. For when the trumpet sounds, the Christians who have died will be raised with transformed bodies. And then we who are living will be transformed so that we never die. For our perishable earthly bodies must be transformed into heavenly bodies that will never die.' And then we meet the Lord in the sky.

Thus, if we regard the seals, trumpets and vials as happening sequentially, we bail at the midpoint. When the last trumpet sounds, we're off on the great magical mystery tour. God's wrath is released via the seven vials, when the antichrist system is in full swing. So, we get to shoot when Apollyon rises from the abyss and hell's kitchen dishes up. We're not assigned to absolute carnage. The 'Day of the Lord' seems to be God's day of wrath. And the Day of the Lord comes when the antichrist exalts himself as God.

Or alternatively, Christians have to go through the mill too, which is the post-tribulation view. The rapture or first resurrection happens at the end of the tribulation. There is no get out of jail free card.

It seems the rapture happens at the seventh trumpet, which correlates with the sixth seal that tells us a great number of people arrive in heaven, clothed in white robes. As mentioned, they're the ones coming out of the great tribulation. And this correlates with the sixth vial, when Jesus said He comes like a thief. It seems the rapture happens when He scoops His bride for battle, when the armies of the world gather together for Armageddon? Thus, it seems the seals, trumpets and vials happen concurrently, which supports a post tribulation view? God's people witness His wrath but are protected from it by God's magical seal.

And it seems the last trumpet is the same trumpet Jesus pertained to in Matthew 24:31, when He stated the Son of Man 'will send forth His angels with the sound of a mighty trumpet blast, and they will gather together His chosen ones from the farthest ends of the heaven and earth'. This happens at the end of the tribulation, when the sun and moon are darkened, and the stars fall from heaven.

Like, in Acts 2:20, we're told, 'the sun will be turned into darkness, and the moon will turn blood-red, before that great and glorious day of the Lord arrives'. We're also told in Isaiah 13:9-10, 'For see, the day of the LORD is coming – the terrible day of His fury and fierce anger. The land will be destroyed and all the sinners with it. The heavens will be black above them. No light will shine from stars or sun or moon'.

So, God knows about the rapture, and when it takes place. But moreover, it seems Jesus doesn't know when He returns. In Matthew 24: 39-41 Jesus tells us, 'But about that day or hour no one knows, neither the angels in heaven, nor the Son, but only the Father'. Apparently, Newton predicted Christ's return mid-21st century.

So, there's the first resurrection, then according to John, there's a second resurrection after the thousand years. The rest of the dead did not come back to life until the thousand years had ended. The final judgement is known as the Great White Throne judgement. John states, 'The sea gave up the dead in it, and death and the grave gave up the dead in them'.

The books were opened, including the Book of Life, and the dead were judged according to the things written in the books i.e. their deeds. Anyone whose name was not found recorded in the Book of Life was thrown into the lake of fire. It's duly noted, that these books corroborate with the akashic records. That is, everything we do is recorded on some ethereal plane. So, it seems the unsaved are woken from their deathly slumber, (or they're conscious in Hades?), to face eternal damnation in the fiery pit. And this is the second death.

It's understood we have to give an account of our selves. We have to face what we've become. We see our portrait, as Sartre called it. The choices we made that defined our life and created our souls. Jesus forewarns us (in Matthew 12: 36-37), 'I tell you, on the day of judgement you will have to give an account for every careless word you utter; for by your words you will be justified, and by your words you will be condemned'.

Acts 10:42-43 tells us that God appointed Jesus to judge the living and the dead. And Jesus also tells us, (John 5:22-23), 'The Father judges no one, but has entrusted all judgment to the Son, that all may honour the Son just as they honour the Father. Whoever does not honour the Son does not honour the Father, who sent him'.

In John 5:28, Jesus said, 'Do not be astonished at this; for the hour is coming when all who are in their graves will hear His voice and will come out – those who have done good, to the resurrection of life, and those who have done evil, to the resurrection of condemnation'. Albeit, as the reformers stressed, it's not about works. It's about trusting in the Son of Man, and believing in Him, as if our life depended on it. It's also noted, whilst people have an aversion to hell, it's understood God is a just God. He has to punish evil, like paedos and Hitler.

Furthermore, whilst most people think they're 'good', because they're not paedos and murderers, we're all rubbish compared to God's Holy standard.

So, Jesus comes in glory, and seated on His glorious throne, He separates the sheep from the goats. Matthew 25:33-45 tells us, 'He will put the sheep on his right and the goats on his left. Then the King will say to those on his right, 'Come, you who are blessed by my Father; take your inheritance, the kingdom prepared for you since the creation of the world. For I was hungry and you gave me something to eat, I was thirsty and you gave me something to drink, I was a stranger and you invited me in, I needed clothes and you clothed me, I was sick and you looked after me, I was in prison and you came to visit me.'

Then the righteous will answer Him, 'Lord, when did we see you hungry and feed you, or thirsty and give you something to drink? When did we see you a stranger and invite you in, or needing clothes and clothe you? When did we see you sick or in prison and go to visit you?' The King will reply, 'Truly I tell you, whatever you did for one of the least of these brothers and sisters of mine, you did for me.'

Then He will say to those on His left, 'Depart from me, you who are cursed, into the eternal fire prepared for the devil and his angels. For I was hungry and you gave me nothing to eat, I was thirsty and you gave me nothing to drink, I was a stranger and you did not invite me in, I needed clothes and you did not clothe me, I was sick and in prison and you did not look after me.'

They also will answer, 'Lord, when did we see you hungry or thirsty or a stranger or needing clothes or sick or in prison, and did not help you?' He will reply, 'Truly I tell you, whatever you did not do for one of the least of these, you did not do for me'. So, the golden rule, 'always treat others as you would like to be treated', rules.

We're told that at the end, the heavens will pass away with a loud noise, and all the elements will be dissolved with fire. All the earth and the works that are upon it will be burned up. God purges the earth. All sin is to be burned in the lake of sulphur. William Blake (1752-1827), who was apparently a freemason, affirms 'the ancient tradition that the world will be consumed by (overthrown) in fire at the end of six thousand years is true'.

And there will be a new heaven and new earth. Isaiah 65:17 states, 'Behold, I create new heavens and a new earth, and the former will not be remembered nor come to mind'. John concedes (in Revelation 21:1), 'I saw a new heaven and a new earth, for the first heaven and the first earth had passed away'. But moreover, John saw the New Jerusalem coming out of heaven.

It seems heaven and earth are united once again, (like it was pre-Fall), and God will live with His people. We get to hang out with our Father. We get access to all three heavens in our resurrected upgraded bodies? We're also told the city has no need of sun or moon, for the glory of God illuminates the city, and the Lamb is its light.

As touched on, there's debate regarding whether or not souls are eternal, and rot in hell for eternity. The Bible tells us the wages of sin is death, which contradicts an immortal soul? The eternal judgement could refer to terminal, as opposed to never-ending torment. Once we're burned up, we cease to exist, which is called 'annihilationism'. We're forgotten forever. The eternal judgement is the second death. Thus, the first death is the death of the body, and the second death is body and soul. Like, Jesus said in Matthew 10:28, 'Don't be afraid of those who want to kill you. They can only kill your body; they cannot touch your soul. Fear only God, who can destroy both soul and body in hell'.

Or alternatively we are an eternal soul, eternally separated from God, which is an existence devoid of light and love, complete with Satan and his haunted company. Hell is like a black hole. There's no escape. There is no time, just horrific existence. As mentioned, Gehenna is illustrative of the ceaseless agonies of hell. So, hell could be eternal fire and brimstone, where there is 'weeping and gnashing of teeth'.

Interestingly, Bill Wiese, who wrote '23 Minutes in Hell' (2006), claims he was given a vision of hell to warn people. He said he had an OBE (he was pulled out his body) and found himself falling down a tunnel. He states it got hotter and hotter as he descended, with the most disgusting smells, like the worst open sewer imaginable. He saw grotesque demons, snakes, maggots, and millions of people being tormented by them. They were burning and screaming in the lake of fire. Interestingly, he said the maggots were devouring the damned, but the maggots never die. This corroborates with Jesus, who said in Mark 9:48, 'Where their worm does not die and the fire is not quenched'. The word worm is translated as maggot. Wiese understands there is no escape.

For those who do prevail over the pearly gates, it will be happy days for eternity. No more crying or pain. The future for God's people is golden. In 1 Corinthians 2:9 Paul states, 'no eye has seen, no ear has heard, and no mind has imagined what God has prepared for those who love him' (quoting Isaiah 64:4). Jesus told us He went to prepare a place for us, in His Father's house, which has many mansions. So, that's not too shabby.

Jesus began His Revelation (1:8) by stating, 'I am the Alpha and the Omega', (the beginning and the end), says the Lord God. He concludes by saying, 'I'm coming soon'.

Ken Peters' Dream

Before we finish here, we can consider an eschatological vision given to Ken Peters in 1980. He shared it at 'The Prophecy Club' in 2005. Peters was a Catholic, but he had no knowledge of 'end times' prophecy. He was not a born-again Christian, but he became one. He was shown advanced technology and architecture, which founds our Orwellian nightmare, before it existed.

Thus, his dream began with an extremely loud noise, like the sound of a car horn. Or trumpet blast? Then he saw graves bursting open, and people coming out of them, dressed in glowing white robes. He said they shone brighter than the sun. And they looked young and yet mature, like they were restored. Millions instantly vanished, and he doesn't know where they went. He states he did not see a rapture, but rather only the resurrection of the dead. He said he walked the streets in shock. Everywhere there was absolute fear and lawlessness. Looting and murdering everywhere.

After several weeks, television and radio communications began to slowly come online. And all broadcasts featured the same man promoting a 'New Government and Leadership'. This new man, the antichrist, was emerging to lead. He had olive skin and dark hair, and spoke with great eloquence and charisma. He was soothing and promised answers to all the problems. He explained the removal of people was God's judgement upon them.

This man began to communicate through large, flat screen televisions strategically placed nearly everywhere. His speeches were constantly on all channels, and he constantly spoke of 'World Order'. This man was immediately accepted by almost all people. He spoke of 'new times' upon human beings, including new directives for global peace, stating current citizenship would be replaced by 'world citizenship'.

Peters wasn't convinced by this man, and began to search for answers. While walking the streets, he met an elderly gentleman who told Peters the end was coming and God's plan for man's salvation. He read Peters scripture, and Peters asked God into his life and forgiveness for his sins. Together with a small group of others who accepted the message of Jesus Christ, they began spreading the gospel.

One day a great earthquake shook the earth and killed millions. He states the weather completely changed. Like, he saw winter weather in the summertime, and summer weather in the winter. Local police departments were replaced with world military police, who drove Hummers. He states the men were dressed in black uniforms with powder blue helmets, which he later identified as the United Nations blue (these hats didn't exist at the time of his dream).

He states the new leader and his laws were not resisted. There were no longer any elected officials. The US Constitution was replaced with a peaceful 'martial law'. There was no privacy. Military police were everywhere, tracking and monitoring everyone and everything. He saw cameras hung on streetlamps, allegedly for our peace and protection.

As time passed, they came to realise that television sets not only broadcasted to them, but also transmitted signals back to the military about them. They discovered television sets were somehow monitoring them as if they had cameras and microphones. He states his work with the 'evangelist man' continued and many were being changed by the power of the gospel this man taught.

Then one day a man approached Peters and told him about the identification mark. He said they could no longer conduct business transactions without this identification mark on the right hand or forehead. It looked like the sun with a hand in the middle.

Peters notes however, that he got a very strong impression not to get this mark under any circumstances. In his mind, he heard a word directly from Revelation 13:16-18, which pertains to the mark of the beast. This utterly amazed him as he'd never read the scriptures or heard of any such identification mark. The mark was likened to credit cards, and soon pressure was increased to the point that you could not buy or sell without the mark. More words rang in his mind, from Matthew 24.

He knew the end was coming fast and he needed to get to his wife. However, a voice kept telling him not to return home. Nevertheless, he ran home to check on his wife, but his door lock had been replaced with new locks. Despite a voice telling him not to open the door, he did, and was greeted by a demon. He screamed in great fear and shut the door and woke up. The dream was over.

He states he was petrified and paralysed from fear, and found himself lying in a pool of sweat. It was 3am, and whilst he woke up his wife, as he was looking for solace, she retorted that it was just a nightmare. Peters however knew that God was trying to tell him something, but why him?

He states he was impressed to read the Holy Bible, and after finding one, and reading four or five chapters, he fell asleep again. And the dream began again exactly where it stopped. Once again, he was facing the demon. He was gripped with tremendous fear and ran off.

He began walking the streets, and he noticed everyone was spiritually dead, and filled with dread. They looked as though they were in a catatonic state. He states thousands were committing suicide. By now nearly all nations were in the New Order. The world was divided into global regions, no longer continents and countries. Evil had pervaded all aspects of society, and gross spiritual darkness was covering the earth. The love of many had waxed cold, showing little or no emotions.

The old evangelist began preaching the gospel with reckless abandon, as did other pockets of people worldwide, and miracles became commonplace. He states there was a great outpouring of God's Spirit, which was tremendous and very widespread. But it only lasted a short time, circa six months, and then gross darkness once again engulfed the minds of all who would not hear the message of hope.

Not long after the evangelist thrust began, they were captured by 'military' agents. They were taken into custody and questioned regarding their affairs. Yet these agents had first-hand knowledge of their actions. They were given an explanation of the 'New Order', stressing the importance of allegiance, since there was no United States of America. They were explicitly told they were forbidden to preach the gospel. But they refused to stop. So, they were taken to another level of interrogation.

Peters states the true heart of the 'New Order' was finally revealed. The plan was to totally eliminate Christians. The interrogators asked them to deny 'Him'. Peters states the interrogators would never say the name 'Jesus', so they called Jesus 'Him'.

After many hours of interrogation, they were led down a long corridor. Hundreds of people were in a single file. Several doors separated this long corridor and at random times, more interrogators would burst forth and more in line would fall away. He saw many people step out of the line, and as they stepped out, they began to cry. He states they realised this was a line of Christians on their way to some type of torture or something.

After many hours they reached the last visible doorway. The door opened revealing an executioner, with a sword, and several agents. Fear gripped him as he realised what was happening. He states he has never experienced such fear, and began shaking violently, like a washing machine severely out of balance. He states he could barely stand, and his jaws became locked.

The executioner had a black hood with holes for the eyes and mouth. He states the presence of evil was thick. It was literally tangible. The whole experience was horrifying. And he now knew the only way to be saved was to die for your faith. He recalled he'd only heard the term martyr a few times, and he was about to become one.

He began to hear loud voices around him shouting, 'It's not too late. Deny your faith in Him'. He states he did not know which option was better – to live the way it was or to die. Confusion assaulted his mind. His old evangelist friend was executed right before his eyes.

He states he knew the end was coming one way or another. And the old man was not fearful at all. Next was his wife, which he couldn't bear. His mind was in complete hysteria. He couldn't speak out loud and was emotionally paralysed. Then his wife was executed. Whilst plagued with doubt, and unable to call out to the Lord, he said deep inside, 'Lord save me, I don't want to deny you'.

Instantly he felt a hand touch his right shoulder and great warmth and peace flooded his whole being. He looked back to see who was with him, and there stood Jesus, who was glorious. Jesus' eyes were like fire, blazing lamps looking deep into his soul, strong yet comforting. Jesus said, 'Fear not, for death shall never hold you, my son'.

The door opened, and it was Peters' turn for the chop. He was laid face up on a table in the shape of a cross, and strapped on. He watched the executioner raise his sword, but as soon as it touched the front of his neck, Peters was gone from his body. He felt no pain and was instantly standing beside Jesus, looking upon the whole scene (like a NDE).

He saw his body bleeding profusely, and heard the executioner and the agents commenting on how much more he bled than most. He bled so much the executioner took off his mask shouting, 'I will not kill another one of these people'. He awoke from the dream, very shaken and needing many answers from this dream. What could it mean?

'Today they call them angels and demons, tomorrow they will call them something else'. Aleister Crowley

'Only the truth can prepare us for the lie that is coming'. Steve Quayle

17

The Alien Deception

Whilst scientific materialism has bumped off God and the supernatural, it seems we're increasingly open to the prospect of aliens? The narrative we've been given is the universe is insanely massive, and it's expanding. We're told there's gazillions of stars and planets. The accepted theory is there was a random 'Big Bang' billions of years ago, which led to the formation of stars, then planets, and we evolved here on Earth from pond scum. God is superfluous, as life magically creates itself, despite the mystery of the first self-replicating molecules?

And thus, the prospect of space brothers isn't farfetched. Indeed, it would be ludicrous to suggest life hadn't evolved elsewhere? Like, Steven Spielberg said, 'I am sure we are not alone in the universe'. Carl Sagan (astronomer) conceded, 'it is virtually a statistical certainty that intelligent life has evolved over and over again, and that many civilisations must be far older and advanced than ours'.

And many, including Paul Hellyer, Canadian politician and former Defence Minister, insist we're not alone. Hellyer has accused world leaders of concealing the presence of aliens, and urges them to come clean and reveal 'secret files' (he's not shy at exposing the cabal). He claims, 'at least four different alien species have been visiting earth for thousands of years' and 'we live in a cosmos teeming with life of various sorts'.

But moreover, they're living among us. According to Hellyer, the Tall Whites are one of the races living among us. He claims two Tall Whites, female ETs, disguised themselves as nuns to shop in Las Vegas and went undetected. Hellyer states most aliens are benign, but not all of them, and they have different agendas.

It's noted, that UFO sightings and alleged alien abductions grew exponentially after WW2. And also, that Hollywood and popular culture has brainwashed the world into accepting the possibility of ETs, predictive programming? As mentioned, the evidence of giants began drying up by the 1950s, to undermine the Biblical account, and we were ambushed with alien movies. Aliens have been written into the script, and God and angelic beings have been written out. A survey in 2012 revealed that more Brits believe in aliens than God. And apparently, we're more likely to reject God if aliens exist, which is the plan?

The classic image of aliens is the Greys. The four foot tall humanoid with big black eyes, an oversized baldy head, tiny mouth and nose, holes for ears, seemingly sexless, and aptly named by its grey skin coat. As it transpires however, there's also tall Greys. Other types of aliens include the nefarious reptilians aka 'snake people'. They're tall (seven to nine foot), with green scaly skin, holes for ears, muscular arms and legs, and large lizard like eyes. They're Lizzies, like Queen Liz when she shapeshifts?

Nordics are tall whites (six-eight foot tall) with long blonde hair and blue eyes. Apparently, they're so human-like, it's believed they're advanced humans or ET human hybrids (they're in excellent physical shape). Nordics are allegedly very spiritual and highly evolved. It's also said however that Nordics have the ability to shapeshift into other forms, including light orbs, animals and also reptilians. It's like demons and fallen angels can shapeshift? There's also insect-humanoids (insectoids) with big bug eyes, something like a preying manta. Like, the locusts or frogs we hear about in Revelation?

According to Dr Steven Greer, founder of 'The Disclosure Project' in 1993, several dozen different types of planetary species have been classified over the years. He states there's huge variation i.e. different sizes and colour of skin, but most are humanoids, which he defines as having a head, two arms, two legs and a torso. At a Disclosure Project meeting in May 2001, at the National Press Club in Washington DC, it was established there are at least 57 species. At this conference, more than twenty military, intelligence, government, corporate and scientific witnesses came forward. It's now purported there's over 197 different species interacting with earth.

Alien visitors allegedly come from other planets or star systems. Like, the Greys come from Zeta Reticuli, and the Nordics comes from the Pleiades or Seven Sisters. Other space visitors advise they're from Mars, Sirius and Venus. However, it's purported that aliens used to say they were from these planets, but they now claim they're from faraway galaxies, because we know about these closer planets and can challenge their inaccurate claims. As discussed, mediums channel 'aliens'. The aliens also consistently teach the New Age gospel (monotheism and apotheosis).

Greer concedes the Government covers-up UFOs, and he seems a credible 'truther'? Like, he pertains to false flags, including the Gulf of Tonkin in Vietnam, the non-existent WMD in Iraq, and 9/11 etc, but like David Icke, his New Age practices seem precarious, as we'll get to. It's also noted, that whilst Dr Greer likes to highlight, he's 'just a country doctor from Virginia' who was 'dragged into this', he writes briefings about UFOs and aliens for CIA directors, prime ministers and presidents. So, he's no small fry. He claims he was offered $2 billion to keep quiet. He's been the most prominent in ET phenomenon since the 1990s.

Many scientists are open to the idea of life on other planets, but the logistics are something of a stretch. Our space brothers would need to be travelling at speeds of light, and even then, it would take them forever to get here. Like, if space visitors came from the Andromeda Galaxy, the closest galaxy to our Milky Way, located 2.5 million light years away, it would take them at least 2.5 million years to get here. And what about fuel, including food, which suggests we attribute physicality to them?

But maybe they're not physical or from another planet, but rather they're from another dimension. Hence, like spirit beings, they can be channelled? It's highlighted that angels are by definition Extra-Terrestrials, and so the idea of an ET presence on our planet is not new. Perhaps fallen angels or demons are appearing as aliens. It's their new disguise? They come from the air, second heaven.

It's also recalled, that when Aleister Crowley did the Amalantrah Working in 1918, his sex-magick ritual, he opened a portal which allowed a grey alien (Lam) to come through. A Grey also appeared at the Scole Experiment. And apparently Sir John Dee (1517-1608), Queen Liz I's magician and MI5 agent, conjured up a demon that looks like a grey alien. Like Crowley, Dee used Enochian ceremonial magic to evoke and command spirits. And people report seeing greys during sleep paralysis, and on DMT trips. Other aliens, including insectoids, are also found in DMT space.

Moreover, it's reported that an influx of UFOs and aliens came in the late 1940s, when Jack Parsons aka rocket man opened a hole in the fabric of space-time, through his Babalon Working ritual, and blew himself up before closing it. It's said Jet Propulsion Laboratory (JPL) stands for Jack Parson's Laboratory (JPL). Parsons notably channelled material (he was not officially trained) i.e. summoned demons for knowledge.

As also mentioned, NASA and DARPA (affectionately known as the Pentagon's mad scientist) were founded in 1958, after WW2, when Project Paperclip smuggled Nazi rocket scientists (and mind magicians) into the US. Like, Werner Von Braun (1912-1977), who's regarded as the Father of the American Space Program.

However, according to Von Braun, sex pest black magician Jack Parsons was the true father. Parsons (who called himself the antichrist) is the predecessor to NASA. As also discussed, Nazi scientists were members of the Vril and Thule Society and they had blueprints for UFOs. Apparently NASA, identified by its serpent tongue logo, means beguile in Hebrew. And Vatican means divining serpent in Latin. The Vatican are also obsessed with observing the second heaven.

So, NASA aka Never A Straight Answer has occult roots and was founded by Nazis and freemasons (secret societies dictate all areas including NASA). It's also understood that NASA and the CIA are essentially the same organisation, and they're intimately linked with Hollywood. Like, Walt Disney's BFF was Von Braun. Von Braun, who used emaciated POWs to build his rockets in Germany, was conveyed as a good salt. Like, the rest of the Nazi murderers, who were given good jobs and nice homes.

Thus, outer space became of interest, and the world was collectively on the lookout for ETs. And this includes the Vatican, which has several major astronomical observers (huge telescopes). Jesuits run the Vatican observations near Rome looking for life.

Probing space for life however began with Frank Drake in early 1960. He was the founder of the 'Search for Extra-Terrestrial Intelligence' (SETI) institute, which was established in 1984. SETI is a key researcher for NASA. In 1992 NASA established their SETI programme, building two massive radio telescopes, to comb the universe looking for life. They're looking for Earth-like planets that could spawn life.

According to SETI, humans will hear from ETs this century, and intelligent life could be found by 2040. So, the supposition is, there's life out there. We've been told in advance that aliens are coming? 'The news' notably reported that Pope Francis said he would welcome aliens and baptise them. No danger. However, we'll get back to what alien phenomenon really appears to be.

It's noted, the Vatican has an advanced telescope on Mount Arizona, which has two other telescopes, namely, the Submillimeter Telescope, which is owned by the University of Arizona, and a Large Binocular Telescope (LBT), which is a joint project of about ten American, Italian and German universities and research institutions. The LBT is the most powerful telescope in the world, but moreover, it has an infrared device known as L.U.C.I.F.E.R. Is there any need?

Infrared technology enables astronomers to look deep into space and beyond the (tiny) visible light spectrum. As mentioned, we see less than 1%, but with infrared light we can see the unseen. Like, the innumerable orbs, which are everywhere, and all around us. This technology unveils UFOs, planets, and planetoids (minor planets and asteroids) that otherwise can't be seen with visible light. Like, Niburu aka Planet X?

According to Dr Tom Horn and Chris Putnam, astronomers regularly see UFOs and entities at Mount Arizona. Horn states, that according to Apache Indians, Mount Graham is a holy mountain and stargate. It's a spiritual place, sacred ground, where beings come through. The Indians also have stories about giants (nephilim). However, apparently the best place to view space is from Antarctica, which is curiously rumoured to have an underground ET facility.

It's also noted, that unlike the Galileo telescope which has a convex lens, the Santilli telescope has a concave lens, which allows scientists to see other dimensional beings. Like, they see black and white beings, which are apparently angels of light and dark. They're referred to as Invisible Terrestrial Entities Type 1 (ITE-1) and Type 2 (ITE-2). It's also purported, that scientists can see antimatter with the Santilli telescope.

It's recalled that Niburu caused quite the stir. Not least because Zecharia Sitchin (1920-2010) falsely claimed the Anunnaki, (the ancient gods who founded the Sumerian culture), came from there. As touched on, the 'Ancient Aliens (Astronaut)' theory is a spin on the Biblical account of the Watchers. According to this theory, ancient aliens visited all cultures who mistook them as gods. These flesh and blood 'aliens' provided the technology to build megalithic structures etc. And they had a thirst for sacrificed human blood.

It's alleged they created us, using mainly Pleiadean (Nordic) DNA. It's said the aliens intervened twice in the evolution of our species. They created Neanderthals first, and then some 200,000 years later, they enhanced us with additional alien DNA to create modern man. Many believe they're coming back to Earth soon.

It's noted, that 'advanced beings' corroborates with the evolutionary paradigm. Thus, whilst Dick Dawkins (the world's most famous atheist) vehemently refutes the possibility of God, he's open to the possibility of aliens. He asserts that life most likely originated on earth, but he also said that an alien designed start is an 'intriguing possibility'. He states a designer could be a higher intelligence, but that higher intelligence would have to come about from explicable means i.e. at an earlier time, beings evolved from somewhere in the universe. So, he's not against intelligent design but rather certain types of designers, namely, God[30].

So, it's possible that aliens evolved from elsewhere. And then they put their little alien white coats on and made us, or created the conditions that gave birth to us? It's suggested they dumped some surplus DNA onto our planet and watched us evolve. Neo-Darwinists notably promote 'panspermia', the idea that we were seeded here, as Darwinism doesn't add up. Like, an asteroid hit us, and it just happened to have some DNA onboard. Apparently at least a third of scientists disagree with Darwin's theory, yet it continues to be propagated in the mainstream as factual. However, we'll get back to 'science falsely so called'.

And it seems aliens use UFOs as their mode of transport? UFO sightings are well established. Millions of people have seen UFOs, too many to write off. Like, twenty million people in the US claim they've seen UFOs, and at least 50% of people believe in them. LA Marzulli asserts there's 300-600 UFO sightings every month worldwide. He frequently asserts, 'UFO phenomenon is real, burgeoning and not going away'.

So, they're reported worldwide and have been for millennia. Like, Alex the Great and his army saw UFOs in 329BC. And Columbus reported seeing a bright glowing object come out of the sky and into the sea, and travel

---
[30] See Ben Stein's 'Expelled: No Intelligence Allowed' film (2008).

through the water close to the ship he was on, in 1492. Ancient art depicts UFOs, and ancient writings, like the Bible, tell us about chariots that take people into the second heaven (like Elijah). But they've been increasing in numbers since the late 1940s?

As Paul McKenna (1997) states, 'As with ghosts and spirits from other planes of existence, I persist in thinking that the sheer weight of eyewitness evidence is overwhelming: it is not just a few cranks and nutcases, but people from all walks of life and in positions of authority and responsibility who can describe first-hand experience of UFOs' (p.47).

Like, US president Dwight Eisenhower, who described the UFO he witnessed for twenty minutes, as a bright ball of light. And president Jimmy Carter said, 'I am convinced that UFOs exist because I've seen one...'. He reported seeing a UFO in Georgia in 1969. He said, 'It was the darndest thing I've ever seen', stating, 'it was big; it was very bright; it changed colours; and it was about the size of the moon'. He was with twenty other people, and they watched it for about ten minutes, but no-one could figure out what it was. He filed his report while Governor of Georgia.

And trusty Reagan seen two UFOs when (he was the 33rd) Governor of California. On one occasion he was with his wife Nancy, as they were driving down the coast road highway to LA. Some unconfirmed stories of the event stated the object landed. The other time, he saw a bright white light when flying. Apparently, the pilot followed it for several minutes, but then, as Reagan said, 'all of a sudden to our utter amazement it went straight up into heaven'.

It's also duly noted, that every man and his dog witnessed the lights, flying saucers, over the White House, Washington DC July 1952, when Harry Truman was in office, which he acknowledged. These UFOs were plotted on multiple radars, (hence, not a hallucination), and jets were sent to investigate but the UFOs would vanish (LOL). As Chuck Missler questions, 'where are they when we don't see them?'

There was a mass of UFO sightings over Rome, when Pope John Paul was murdered, and John Paul II took up office (there were three popes in 1978). Many pilots and at least 13 astronauts have reported seeing UFOs, and they're credible witnesses? It's highlighted that UFOs are a security threat, because they get close to planes, and also because they could be a security threat. We don't know if they're friend or foe? Apparently, UFO sightings have increased exponentially since the corona virus plandemic.

Despite innumerable UFO encounters, there's been little official confirmation, and we're left pondering what's fact and fiction. Like, we heard about the 'tic tac' UFO in 2017, which was described as 'not of this world'. 'The news' keeps us informed about what's allegedly out there? The US Department of Defense has however recently (2019) admitted there is Unidentified Ariel Phenomenon (UAPs), their new term for UFOs. A former US Defense Official said, 'we know UFOs are real'. And they recently (2020) released three UFO videos by US Navy pilots. Apparently, Congress is taking UFOs seriously.

The US Department of Defense also confirmed they have debris from UFOs. Apparently, the metal from crashed UFOs has been tested/analysed, which reveals isotopes not found on earth. The Pentagon admitted they secretly investigated 'Anomalous Ariel Vehicles' from 2007-2011, with an annual budget of $22 million per annum. As it transpires however, the Pentagon's UFO hunting department was not disbanded in 2012 as stated. And 'the news' stated they could give us reports every six months around claims it finds 'off-world vehicles not made on earth'. They also officially acknowledged their 'Advanced Aviation Threat Identification Program'. So, that's soft disclosure? UFOs or UAP have always been considered fringe, until now?

It's like a hall of mirrors, not least because of the many hoaxes, cover-ups and outlandish mythologies. Like, the 'footage' of an alien autopsy that Ray Santilli released in 1995. He presented it as an authentic ET recovered from the Roswell crash of 1947, but experts immediately ridiculed it as a hoax, which he admitted. The infamous Roswell crash remains a mystery, as we'll get to.

It's like the 'lunar rock' given to the Dutch prime minister by Apollo 11 astronauts in 1969, to evidence the US went to the moon, which was actually petrified word? And it's like we were told the crew died on the 'Challenger' in 1986, which exploded 74 seconds after take-off, but at least six out of the seven crew members are still alive?

It seems pertinent to mention the moon landings because this ties into the alien/UFO agenda. And the evidence that we went to the moon is dreadful. NASA destroyed 13,000 telemetry tapes (data from Apollo 11). Apparently, they were so hard up (despite receiving over $50 million a day from US taxpayers), they reused the tapes, before losing them. It appears they were careless regarding evidence of man's greatest achievement?

NASA also destroyed the technology to go to the moon, which, according to Tom Pettit (NASA astronaut), is a painful process to build up again. Hence, they've never returned. But why would they destroy their technology? Presumably, it was to prevent the public from realising how crap it was, or non-existent? We did however see President Nixon on the phone to Apollo 11 on the moon (real time connection), so that's realistic?

In his film 'A Funny Thing Happened on the Way to the Moon' (2001), Bart Sibrel exposed secret film that was inadvertently sent to him by NASA (he had requested photographs and videos from the Apollo 11 missions). It shows Apollo 11 astronauts attempting to create the illusion they were 130,000 miles away from Earth (halfway to the moon), when they were actually in low Earth orbit, only a few hundred miles above. They were caught trying to fake photos of Earth in conjunction with the CIA.

Sibrel presents compelling evidence that the six Apollo Moon landing missions between 1969 and 1972 were elaborate hoaxes, perpetuated by the US government including NASA. It seems it was one small step for man, one giant lie for mankind? It's noted, there's no genuine pictures of the Earth, but rather they're all composites and photo-shopped.

Maybe the moon landing is a hoax, as maybe we can't land on the moon, because it's a light (not a lifeless rock). It's suggested the moon consists of plasma. It looks like (with magnified footage) it's bathed in etheric like fluid. It looks like gentle waves traverse over the moon. And at times, it looks partially transparent. Like, we can see clouds through the moon. This also suggests it's far closer than 240,000 miles away. However, we'll get to this. It's possible we've been conned with a ton of CGI (Computer Generated Images) on behalf of the military since the 1950s?

Another problem is the impassable Van Allen radiation belts (1000 miles above Earth). Yet apparently astronauts were not affected by this insane radiation in their tin can. They claimed it wasn't a problem, yet NASA has been working on technology to solve this problem. Nothing about the moon landing adds up, hence the 'conspiracy theories'. And they're inconsistent in their reports. Like, some astronauts or astro-nots see vast amounts of stars, whereas others claim they don't see any.

Apparently, every man who walked on the moon, all twelve of them, was a freemason. As touched on, it's believed Stanley Kubrick teamed up with the CIA/NASA to make their Hollywood production. According to

Sibrel's insider, they filmed the moon landing hoax in June 1968, and President Johnson was present. As ever, with compartmentalised information, few need to know the truth. And people can keep secrets. Like, the Manhattan Project was kept secret for five years, which involved 129,500 people. Besides being members of secret societies (which keep secrets), many current and former US astronauts served in the armed forces, and the military are trained to keep secrets.

So, nothing happened for years, because the cost was astronomical (pun intended) and they destroyed their technology. But now, according to Trump, NASA is going back to the moon in 2024 and then Mars after that (despite their insane debt which increases a million a minute)?

It seems Greer concurs the moon landing footage is fake, but he insists we did go to the moon. And he should know, as apparently his uncle was a senior engineer who worked on the Lunar Module that landed on the moon in 1969. Apparently, when the astronauts got to the moon, it was crowded with UFOs. So, they had to conceal the evidence of the silver disks parked there.

And the astronauts were sworn to secrecy. Like, apparently Neil Armstrong was told he would be killed if he disclosed the truth. And Edwin Buzz Aldrin had a nervous breakdown after the trip. It's said this explains their odd behaviour at the first press conference held when they returned. They look downhearted and shifty.

Or perhaps they were lying about going to the moon? They resigned shortly after their return, and NASA's highest-ranking official James Webb resigned days before the first Apollo mission, which seems odd? It's also suggested they could have been mind-controlled i.e. programmed to believe they'd gone to the moon. Astronauts Gordon Cooper and Edgar Mitchell (the sixth man to have allegedly walked on the moon) have also seen UFOs and believe in aliens from another planet, but insist they can't speak about it.

Governments and scientists often ridicule the alien/UFO phenomena, yet it's understood that governmental disinformation is responsible for some of the rumours. It's like our governments want us to believe in the possibility of aliens.

Maybe, as Reagan said, at least eighteen times when in office, which includes a speech to the UN, if there were an alien threat, a common enemy, we'd all unite as one world. Bill Clinton said the same thing about an alien threat bringing us together, which figures since they're on the same (globalist) page. It's thus speculated the alien-x-factor could be a driving force for the NWO. Using Hegelian dialectic, aliens create the problem, and the solution is a global government to take them on. We'll also need to manufacture a ton of weapons.

Indeed, it's purported there's a great deception coming, which the Bible also warns us of. As mentioned, we're told that before the Second Coming of Jesus, there will be a strong delusion and all those who don't know truth shall believe the lie (2 Thessalonians 2:11-12).

Bill Cooper said the Illuminati plan has been, since at least 1917 but probably before, to fake/stage an alien invasion, so we band together to save the planet. He concluded the ET hoax will be the biggest hoax ever orchestrated on mankind. Doc Marquis concedes the Illuminati plan since the 1930s has been to fake aliens, and motherships are heading here with global announcements.

Edward Snowdon said the ET agenda is driving us and has been since 1945. He highlights there's two governments in the US, namely, the one elected and the other secret regime governing in the dark. And

Steven Greer also unequivocally stated that the long-term plan, since the 1950s, has been to hoax a threat from outer space. The cosmic false flag is pending.

Greer quotes General Douglas MacArthur, who in October 1955 said, 'The nations of the world will have to unite for the next war will be an interplanetary war. The nations of the earth must someday make a common front against attack by people from other planets'.

Unlike Cooper, who regards the aliens as demonic, Greer regards the 'interstellars' as benevolent space brothers. Greer refutes they have any malignant aims towards us. He's of the opinion that if they wanted to, they could have wiped the floor with us eons ago, since they're considerably more advanced than us.

It's believed we aroused attention from other planets when we started farting about with nuclear weapons, and dropping atomic bombs on Hiroshima and Nagasaki. Hence, UFO sightings grew exponentially from 1945. Greer concedes that ETs came en masse from multiple civilisations from around the universe when we began detonating atomic weapons.

Hellyer also reported that ETs are very concerned about our weapons. He states they've visited us many times, for thousands of years, but their visits have massively increased since the atomic bomb was set off in New Mexico in 1945. Besides commonly appearing at atomic test sites, it's reported that UFOs have deactivated nukes and disabled missiles. So, they care for us or our planet?

It's noted, that most atomic testing was conducted in Nevada, where the infamous Area 51 is located. It's rumoured the moon landing hoax was filmed there. It's also noted, that the US government vehemently denied the existence of Area 51 for six decades, but following satellite footage which revealed an extensive base of hangers and a network of runways, we were subsequently informed in 2013 that it's an aircraft test facility.

Area 51 was reportedly created in 1955 to spy on the Soviet's capability, by creating CIA spy planes (like the U2, that could fly at high altitudes) to get into the Soviet undetected. Area 51 is massive and very well camouflaged, complete with underground bases. It's said Area 51 is the worst-kept secret in the history of secrecy. Like, the Bilderberg group was consistently denied until it wasn't.

Bill Cooper notably said the Bilderberg group was formed because of the alien situation. He states that in 1952, President Truman and the European Heads of States and the Soviet Union, formed the Bilderbergers to coordinate the international efforts to protect the world from alien invasion. He states Truman created the National Security Agency (NSA) in 1952 for the purpose of communicating with aliens (it's understood the NSA and NASA are the same organisation). Then the NSA led to the establishment of the Bilderberg group.

According to UFO subculture, Area 51 is Alien HQ. It's possible that aliens are in Deep Underground Military Bases (DUMBs)? Or maybe it's chimeras and nephilim, including giants? Justen Faull (researcher/documentary maker) states that ten feet tall giants, who call themselves 'nephilim', are allegedly in DUMBs. Apparently, there's a level called 'the zoo' for the ungodly beasts the mad scientists are creating. So, the nephilim are back? And they're preparing for war with God. However, we'll get back to this craziness.

As mentioned, DUMBs connect into a massive global network of tunnels. Greer concedes that anything critically important is underground, and there are secret underground bases throughout the world including the US, Australia, and the UK. As highlighted, it's understood we have no idea what's underneath our feet. Complex subways give us an idea. Big airports in major cities have DUMBS (like creepy Denver airport), and important places like Buckingham Palace and the White House.

But moreover, according to Greer, we've been psychopathically shooting down our alien neighbours, since we've had the technology to. He said Reagan put platforms in space to track and target interstellar vehicles, to destroy them. Apparently, Uncle Ronnie was given limited information to obtain his cooperation for the project. Like, he was told ETs were a threat, which explains his 'imagine there was an alien threat' speech to the UN in 1987. Greer claims we've killed dozens of ETs, and they've never once fired back.

Thus, there is a Secret Space Program? There's bases on the Moon, and even Mars? But unlike Greer, military intelligence seems to perceive an alien threat? And Star Wars have actually been taking place. Richard Dolan, another UFO expert, conceded that according to official documents, jets shoot down UFOs all the time in the US, and elsewhere.

Indeed, it's said the reason we started stockpiling nuclear weapons was to defend ourselves from an alien invasion. Bill Cooper said the US-Soviet cold war was a frosty façade. He said America and the Soviet have always been allies, but portraying themselves as the enemy, enabled them to invest shed loads in defence and build up an insane arsenal of weapons in case their common extra-terrestrial enemy did its worst. So, this antagonistic smoke screen was apparently a clever ruse to secure ever-increasing funds for defence (the arms race began after 1945).

The threat of nuclear war has also prevailed as a decoy to distract us from what's really going on. Thus, we 'worry' about their fictitious feud instead of alien invasions. But moreover, Greer further claims the US military portrays the aliens as hostile through false flags i.e. they stage fake alien abductions. So, they're responsible for the anal probing?

However, before we get to the actual crack, it seems pertinent to clarify that UFO sightings are divided into categories. Like, 'Close Encounters' refers to sightings within 500 feet (150 metres). And there's various kinds of 'Close Encounters'. Thus, with Close Encounters of the First Kind, there's no interaction between the UFO and the environment.

With Close Encounters of the Second Kind, there's some tangible proof e.g. interference with car ignitions (interference of electrical circuits), marks and/or burns on the ground like scorched grass, radiation, and physical effects upon animals or humans. Apparently, UFOs give off powerful electromagnetic charges, which often cause the breakdown of engines and electrical circuitry. Crop circles, aka the signatures of alien intelligence, are also classified as Close Encounters of the Second Kind. As are the curious cattle mutilations, as UFO sightings are commonly reported in areas where cattle have been mutilated.

It's noted, there's been thousands of cattle mutilations, but there's no evidence of anyone touching them. It's mainly cattle but other large domestic animals are used such as horses, sheep and goats. There's no footprint, but apparently the ground is burned and there's traces of radiation, indicative of 'alien' spacecraft. They're drained of blood and their organs are removed, yet there's no blood spilled and no exit wounds. Tongues, eyeballs, ears, jaw flesh, rectums and genitals are removed.

Whilst the supernatural ritualistic surgery suggests dark arts, it's theorised that these animals are picked up by aircraft, mutilated elsewhere and then returned. It's widely reported that whoever is responsible for the mutilations is very well organised with boundless technology, financing and secrecy. So, they want to leave evidence because they could easily buy some cows?

Linda Howe (UFO author/researcher) states that military intelligence operatives told her that the mutilations were done by the aliens. And that black helicopters were a ruse to cover up the alien involvement in mutilations. It's understood that unmarked black helicopters are connected with covert military activity (it's said black helicopters are the Illuminati's army). She relays they didn't want the farmers to panic, and it appears to be working, because most farmers when interviewed said they thought it was the government doing some kind of secret testing.

In addition to the small but large-headed greys, Howe also pertained to reptilians. She retells a story a couple told her, namely, they seen two Greys, and also another creature they estimated was taller than six foot, who's skin was green and scaly, and it had eyes like crocodiles. Like, those seen underground at Salt Lake City?

Greer however has a different take. He believes military intelligence are behind the mutilations. He believes cattle mutilations, like terrifying abductions, are creations of the US military, used as a psychological operation to scare us into warring with them. He maintains human devils are framing and demonising the aliens.

Others pertain to unknown agencies at work, such as religious or satanic cultists, as people also report seeing people in hooded black robes and masks. As discussed, in occult practices, entities manifest with blood. So, perhaps they summon ETs through their blood rituals, or perhaps they're accumulating animal parts and blood for some other reason?

Close Encounters of the Third Kind are when occupants from the UFO are reportedly seen and there's some contact with them. Occupants include humanoids, robots, and humans, whoever's piloting the UFO. Close Encounters of the Fourth Kind entails personal contact with the occupants. Like, people allege they've been involuntarily abducted by aliens and taken onboard UFOs.

Apparently 1-3% of people in the US have been abducted, which equates to five million. 'Frequent flyers' notably refers to those who've been abducted more than once. Cooper states we're told 1:40 are abducted but he believes this is an underestimate. Abductees commonly report they've been experimented on. It's often reported sperm and ovum are taken, which suggests there's a breeding programme taking place? However, before we get to these up close and personal encounters, it seems pertinent to note what we've heard about UFOs.

Thus, we can start with Kenneth Arnold's sighting in June 1947, since it's said the modern age of flying saucers began with the Arnold sighting. Sightings grew exponentially. It was his report that caused the US Air Force to take official notice and investigate the phenomena. And the term 'flying saucer' was introduced to the public.

Ken Arnold was a civilian pilot, and when out flying on a lovely day with perfect visibility, he spied nine gleaming saucers for about three minutes. He described the objects as being 'flat like a pie pan and so shiny they reflected the sun like a mirror'. As they flew by, he calculated they had a velocity of about 1,700mph, which was three times faster compared to any aircraft they had in those days.

Project Sign was thus established, (under the banner of National Defence), employing top scientists to investigate UFO sightings. This was superseded by Project Grudge, the Air Force's official investigative body, which turned into Project Blue Book. So, Project Bluebook was on the case, and anything presumed to be of an unknown origin was reported to them. President Harry Truman (who 'served' from 1945-1953) notably asked Project Bluebook for a report on the flying saucers that flew over Washington DC and other major US cities in the early 1950s.

It's duly noted, there's many curious aspects to UFOs, not least because they defy our comprehension of physics. UFO phenomenon represents a manifestation of a reality that transcends our (alleged) current understanding. Like, travelling at 17,000mph and conducting right angle turns, and materialising and dematerialising without a trace, into otherwise 'thin air'. Some pilots report seeing spacecrafts a mile long, which some consider 'Motherships' for smaller crafts.

Like Columbus's sighting, Bill Cooper advised he seen a huge disk-shaped aircraft descend from the clouds and enter the sea, and then repeat the cycle several times (i.e. exit the water and enter the clouds again). Cooper, who worked in the Navy and was on a submarine at the time, was told by his superiors, under no uncertain terms, to keep his trap firmly shut. The same applied to the other witnesses. They were briefed individually and made to sign an oath of silence.

It's also purported that UFOs emerge from the sea at Antarctica i.e. they surface from underneath the ice. It's believed there's entrances beneath the sea into the hollow earth. NASA images notably reveal an ancient human settlement underneath 2.3 kilometres of ice. Besides the underground polar caverns, parts are not frozen, and there's fresh water. It's believed there's a Nazi empire there, which is responsible for the UFOs?

As mentioned, whilst the US was working on the Manhattan Project across the pond, Hitler was working on the flying saucer project. This was under the control of Thule Society, and included going to Antarctica. Apparently, Hitler believed there was an entrance to the inner earth there i.e. underground civilisation, where Atlanteans escaped to?

A secret expedition that had 33 members, plus the crew of 24, founded New Swabia or Schwaben land, Antarctica, in January 1939. Then WW2 kicked off later that year. And several years later, Hitler and some of his buds did a shoot back there. Nazis continued their Secret Space Program that started in the 1930s.

It's highlighted that Nazis surreptitiously hauled tons of equipment and loads of supplies to Antarctica, before, during and after the war, and at least a thousand Nazis. There were however many US and Russian expeditions to Antarctica after WW2 (during the 1940s/50s). It's said they were obsessed with Antarctica.

It's also noted, that Tesla had blueprints for flying saucers circa 1900s. Apparently, he had theories of electromagnetism and anti-gravity as well as other forms of 'free energy'. [The FBI seized Tesla's work]. It's explained that with gravity control, changes in the atomic structure of the energy field changes in such a way that mass is cancelled i.e. the object becomes weightless. And something close to mass-less can accelerate at enormous speeds with very little power, and do right hand turns, go up and down etc. Flying saucers seem to fly without the need for external energy (like helicopters, airflow from above causes lift, and it sucks itself into the air). Apparently flying saucers were designed to carry bombs. Like, the 'old school' Nazi bell, the UFO shaped like a bell.

So, UFOs could be military operations? We can rationalise they have nothing to do with ETs? That is, besides channelling 'aliens' to get UFO blueprints. Anti-gravitational technology could be the result of many decades of research done by Nazis scientists. Apparently, scientists mastered gravity control by 1954. Thus, the vehicles flying over Washington could have been German craft from Antarctica?

Besides the 'rumoured' Nazi operations in Antarctica, it's highlighted the flying saucer project moved to New Mexico. Hence, sightings were soon reported by people of mysterious flying objects. It seems the US Air Force was playing with its new toys. Newspaper reports, at the time, suggested the UFOs might be advanced Nazi crafts. As Hellyer said, UFOs are as real as planes. They're owned and operated by the US and Soviet. And used to perpetuate the threat of aliens?

But moreover, there seems to be different types of crafts. Like, besides metal saucers that appear solid, there's glowing orbs, which are not solid. Other lights in the sky include 'sky serpents' or 'sky worms'. But it's contended that like orbs, which can appear in swarms, these aren't spacecraft in the traditional nuts and bolts sense. Which suggests something else is at play?

There's also objects that look solid, but they can morph, change colour and shape. They can move at high speeds, appear and disappear. It's thus believed these are inter-dimensional. A common analogy for understanding hyper-dimensions is using a 2D universe. Thus, if a ball were dropped through a 2D world, it would look like a pinpoint that grew to a circle and then back to a pinpoint, then disappear again. So, these 'UFOs' pop into and out of our dimension?

Like, the 'Foo Fighters' that confused military pilots during WW2? There were many reports of bright flying balls of light or 'spherical fire', so-called Foo Fighters. The word 'foo' seems to derive from a combination of the French word for fire 'le feu' and the German word for fire 'feuer'. Nobody knew what the Foo Fighters were exactly, and whilst they weren't actually fighters per se, since no Foo Fighter was known or reported to have attacked anyone, they were arguably disruptive.

Greer informs that their presence disrupted electromagnetic signals, and had effects on gravity around the aircraft, and other things like guidance and compass systems. They were known for their high rate of speed and agility, and unconventional abilities such as instantaneous acceleration and de-acceleration, rapid ascending and descending, and hovering in place. Both sides presumed the other had developed a secret weapon, some peculiar technology. We thought the Nazis were up to something funky, and they assumed we were. It turns out, it was the aliens?

Greer states these objects would fly around the aircraft, and sometimes they would fully materialise, looking solid, but mostly they were an energy field. They would go through an aircraft and even down the centre and out the other end. So, UFOs were called Foo Fighters in WW2. Greer explains UFOs are interplanetary and trans-dimensional vehicles. They materialise and dematerialise by vortexes. Like, angels materialise from a ball of light? It's noted, the Bible tells us seraphim are balls of fire. So, the UFOs could be UFAs, Unidentified Flying Angels?

Interestingly, Pastor Pete Valdez, who LA Marzulli interviewed on his 'Politics, Prophecy and the Supernatural Report' (June 2020), advised that his father seen three UFOs in the 1970s and rebuked them in Jesus' name, and they turned into angelic beings and then disappeared. So, angels can metamorphose into UFOs.

It also seems pertinent to note, the parallel between Zionist developments and UFO sightings. It's highlighted the growth of Israel has witnessed a growth of UFO activity, which is presumably not a coincidence. Apparently in 1897, when the first Zionist conference took place, there was the first wave of UFO sightings. Another wave of UFO sightings happened in 1948, when Israel raised her six pointed Star of David, and again in 1956 and 1967 (during the wars).

It's further believed the holocaust, which means 'burnt offering', opened a portal, which accounts for the massive increase in sightings since WW2. As touched on, the holocaust is regarded as a massive blood sacrifice of God's people. LA Marzulli suggests the foo fighters seen over Germany were the result of this blood sacrifice. So, it seems a portal was opened for 'aliens' to come through, as opposed to them benevolently visiting to check on our atomic weapons situation?

As it transpired, less than a month after Arnold's sighting, the infamous Roswell case landed, or rather crash landed in July 1947. The Roswell Army Air Field (RAAF) issued a press release stating that a 'flying disk' had crashed near Roswell, New Mexico. The army sealed off the area and confiscated all the items, with investigators describing the wreckage as 'like nothing on earth'. It became national news.

But when Government scientists arrived on the scene, the story changed. A press conference was held, and it was stated that a weather balloon, not a disk, had crashed. The RAAF had made a mistake. And rather than the materials recovered, reporters were shown debris such as foil, rubber and wood, said to be taken from the crash area, to confirm that the object had been a weather balloon.

It's purported that witnesses were threatened to go along with the new version of events (they and their family would be killed otherwise). Few believed their cover story, and suspicions were fuelled as they classified the information top secret. It's apparently so classified the President doesn't have access, so we still don't know the real story. It's understood the President and Congress are denied clearance because they have a responsibility to tell the people, hence its better they don't know.

It's noted, that Truman signed an Executive Order to prevent presidents having access to NASA's classified information. He removed the power from the president to appointees. ET information seems to be on a need-to-know basis, and it's implied that presidents have one less thing to worry about. It seems a lot happened on Truman's shift, including Project Paperclip. So, we don't know if it was a Nazi flying saucer or an alien flying saucer?

It's also noted, that a few months after Roswell, Admiral Richard E Byrd led more than four thousand military troops from the US, UK and Australia (they had 13 ships and 33 aircraft) to Antarctica on 'Operation High-jump'. The main objective was to establish a research base there, but it's rumoured they went to scout out what the Nazis were up to.

Indeed, it's said they went to destroy Nazi bases and hidden intelligence. But they had to call off the invasion as Byrd and his forces encountered heavy resistance from flying saucers. Apparently, they burst out of the ocean, nearly destroying his entire fleet. It's said Byrd got his butt kicked.

It's noted, whilst we're told Antarctica was discovered in 1818, then rediscovered in 1911, it appears on the Piri Reiss map in 1516 (Piri Reiss was a Turkish admiral). As highlighted, those who control the present control the past. It's believed that Tartarus is located there, where the Watchers were bound. And it's said the apocalypse could include the unveiling of Antarctica. Maybe the ice will melt with all the fireworks and searing heat that's scheduled?

But moreover, it's also speculated that when Byrd and co were there, they discovered the firmament. Byrd later confirmed this discovery in 1955. Apparently, he was part of a mission that explored unknown parts of Antarctica until 1956 (four US planes flew from New Zealand to the South Pole). The 1958 Encyclopaedia Britannica tells us about the dome, according to Admiral Byrd's testimony. It states, 'The flights proved the inland areas to be featureless in character with a DOME 13,000 feet high at about latitude 80 degrees south'. This suggests the height of the dome, (based on this calculation), is 385,500 feet high, which is about 73 miles.

As touched on, the most widely accepted definition of the 'edge of space' is sixty miles above the earth's surface. And it's recalled that Dr Wickland advised the distance between the spirit world and the world of matter is about sixty miles. The ether surrounding earth is the world of spirits, the prison of darkness. So, the first heaven is our air, and space is the second heaven i.e. above sixty miles? However, it appears there's plasma like ether at 73 miles, as opposed to the dome, but we'll get back to this.

So, it's possible the ancients were right, that we live under a dome, like a snow-globe? It's possible that biblical cosmology is true, and we live on a flat stationary plane, as opposed to the heliocentric model given to us by the Jesuits. And the North Pole is at the centre, hence Magnetic North (there is no magnetic south). The Antarctic is the circumference, the high ice wall that contains the oceans, beneath the dome. Apparently, the ice wall is 200-300 feet high, hence, Operation 'High-jump'?

It's also noted, that Enoch was taken on a trip to the end of the earth (the south), where he seen the firmament. Enoch 18:5 states, 'I saw at the end of the earth the firmament of the heaven above'. And it's possible, as the Bible tells us, our earth is hollow? Like, hell is below us and Revelation creatures are coming upon the earth in the last days.

It's contended that NASA was formed after the dome was discovered. After the Operation High Jump debacle, Operation Deep Freeze established a research facility there in 1955. This was followed by the Antarctic Treaty in 1959. This prevents people from going there to explore, because they don't want us to find the firmament? Suffice to say, information about the firmament is not found in new encyclopaedias. As discussed, the fundamental aim of the cabal is to hide God and belie His word. Thus, both the south and north poles are no-fly zones.

But moreover, in 1962 the US and Russia began firing high altitude nuclear rockets into space, and it's believed the endeavour was to smash the firmament or the Van Allen radiation belts? In the US, this was called Operation Fishbowl, which was part of the larger Operation Dominic nuclear test program. As Rob Skiba (author/researcher) points out, Dominic means of the Lord, so we're told about the Lord's Fishbowl aka the firmament. These punks are surreptitiously telling us?

However, the plot further thickens, as highly decorated Byrd ventured to the North Pole in 1929, before he voyaged to the South Pole in 1947 with the troops. And according to his diary, which surfaced a few months before he died, the North Pole is nothing like what we're told. Like, beyond the ice, it's warm. He wrote there's vegetation, rivers, forests, mountains and even mammoths.

But moreover, during his trip there, a disk aircraft featuring a swastika, aligned itself beside his plane. And two blonde haired men, who look like Aryans, said 'welcome to our domain' (in a Germanic accent). The controls on Byrd's plane ceased working, and his plane was guided by their craft into what seemed to be the inner earth. He was given a drink, (which could have been LSD-esque to enable inter-dimensional vision?), and Byrd met their leader who could be Satan (Sanat Kumara)?

The 'Master' explained they've been observing us (they've sent UFOs to investigate) and they're going to have to do something with us because of our atomic weapons. They've never interfered before, but our race has reached the point of no return. Byrd was told a great storm is gathering in our world, which preceded a new world. It's noted, US presidents are partial to referencing a storm. Byrd was told to tell the world that they exist. They chose to impart the message to Byrd because he was a good salt. However, when Byrd returned home, his superiors told him to keep quiet. But he wanted the world to know, so he gave us his diary?

According to legend, Agartha (paradise) is at the North Pole. It's said the Axis Mundu, the world tree, is at the centre of Earth, which connects heaven and earth at the North Star. And God's mountain is there? It's highlighted that by the mid-1600s the mountain, four surrounding islands and whirlpool, that otherwise featured on maps, vanished from maps. And we were told there's no land at the North Pole but rather it's a floating ice sheet. It's a magical place where Santa and his elves live? Maybe they do? Like, Terrence McKenna engaged with elves.

It's said Nazis believed there was an entrance to the inner earth at the North and South Pole. And vastly superior beings lived there, namely, Aryan forefathers. It's like Abraham's bosom is a paradise underground? Byrd said he saw UFOs 'that could fly from pole to pole at enormous speeds'. So, Aryans fly UFOs. But we're led to believe they're aliens?

So, God knows what's going on at the Polar Regions. But it's purported the Secret Space Program is at the Antarctic. And it's understood that top political and religious people, like John Kerry, Obama, Putin, and Patriarch Krill, as well as Prince Harry Battenberg and Buzz Aldrin etc, are not going to Antarctica to visit the penguins. Perhaps they're going to worship at the Orthodox Church there? Like, VIPs went to Epstein's island to worship at the chapel there? However, I digress.

The Roswell incident has been something of a Pandora's Box, unleashing rumours like aliens were found? But unlike 'unofficial' rumours, Bill Cooper informed that the report from 'Blue Book' stated there were four dead aliens, and he seen photos of three of them. Cooper further asserts there were many saucer recoveries and aliens discovered. Like, the 'Extra-terrestrial Biological Entity' known as EBE 1 who survived the 1949 Roswell crash.

Apparently EBE had the ability to read minds, and transmit thoughts to others, and could walk through walls (through the transmission of electromagnetic energy). Cooper divulged that EBE had the tendency to lie during the first year of captivity, but began to open up after the second year. But little EBE 1 got sick, and medical professionals were unable to help. Apparently, NASA tried to contact its relatives in Outer Space but to no avail, and EBE died in 1952. Cooper notes that NASA aimed to win favour from EBE's technologically superior alien race. Apparently, this event inspired Steven Spielberg's 'science fiction' movie ET.

It seems Linda Howe was privy to the documents Cooper seen, as she equally describes how a crash in 1949, near Roswell, resulted in the recovery of six aliens. And that five were reportedly dead, but one remained alive, and this living creature then died in 1952. She related that some of the documents indicated that both alien bodies and disks had been taken to special government facilities where proper analyses could be done. The papers stated that the extra-terrestrials had told our people about their own star system and how they had been visiting Earth for at least 25,000 years.

In addition to the recovery of aliens and their spaceships however, Cooper further highlights that two crashed disks, found in Aztec Mexico in 1948, contained human body parts. He states this caused the secret nature of events to become super top-secret.

With regards to the Roswell crash in 1947, Dr Greer informs three UFOs were shot down by the US Gov, using 'Direct Energy Weapons'. He asserts the Roswell crash was not because of an electrical weather storm, as alleged. Two crashed in Roswell, one was blown to smithereens and the other remained intact, and the third crashed in the desert. He states there was one living ET, but the rest were mangled and died.

Greer surmises the UFOs appeared at Roswell to spy on the US atomic weapon situation, because they care? He highlights that Roswell, New Mexico, was the only place on Earth that harboured atomic weapons at the time. Greer also points out, the CIA was formed after Roswell, and the US Air Force split from the US Army Air Force, enabling it to undertake all kinds of black projects. Like, installing bases on the moon?

Greer highlights Roscoe Hillenkoetter's (1897-1982), the first CIA director after Roswell, comment. He said, 'It is time for the truth to be brought out. Behind the scenes high-ranking Air Force officers are soberly concerned about the UFOs. But through official secrecy and ridicule, many citizens are led to believe the unknown flying objects are nonsense. I urge immediate congressional action to reduce the dangers from secrecy about unidentified flying objects'.

So, some top dogs want the word out? Like, Father George Bush wanted disclosure to end secrecy. And like the Clintons, Obama, John Podesta, and the Pope want disclosure? Hillary Clinton pledged she would demand disclosure if she was elected in 2016. It's noted, that wikileaks revealed emails between John Podesta and Apollo astronaut Edgar Mitchell promoting official disclosure. So, the cabal wants us to know there's aliens? It's our right to know?

It's further said that Project Blue Book was partially a fraud, as its role included downplaying the UFO phenomenon. It's said that whilst Project Sign, (which preceded Blue Book), concluded that UFOs are real and estimated them to be interplanetary craft, the Pentagon rebuked their report, rendering it science fiction fantasy. Then Project Bluebook landed, which was considered a PR effort by the Air Force to explain away UFO phenomenon. It's purported that a CIA report in 1953 specifically highlighted the NSA were to downplay UFO phenomenon through education, with debunking accomplished by mass media.

It's understood the CIA knew what the phenomenon was, and it wasn't aliens from another planet. It's purported that when reports about UFOs began flooding into the US Government in the late 1940s, the FBI got involved. Furthermore, at the same time as UFOs appeared, literally out of the blue, ritual murders were on the rise. The FBI then handed the investigation over to the CIA who secretly created a group in 1952 known as the 'Collins Elite' (a branch of the CIA) to find answers. They were a think tank, but they were so secret they're not supposed to exist.

Thus, the elusive Collins Elite were tasked with looking into the paranormal and UFOs. And as it transpired, they concluded it's all paranormal. There are no UFOs but rather interdimensional entities. They provided reports to the CIA about the reality of these entities, which had the technology to walk through walls.

They realised that Parsons acquired technology from these entities. But they further realised, they could equally contact them and acquire technology through occult rituals. They could prosper from their intelligence.

They could harness magical energy and weaponize it. It's purported that some members of the Collins Elite began interacting with these entities called 'Ascended Masters'.

So, this gnosis was kept secret, and the UFO saga was ridiculed and largely debunked. Most cases were written off as false alarms i.e. they were explained as balloons, conventional aircraft, planets, meteors, optical illusions, solar reflections, and even large hailstones. People who seen UFOs were rendered tinfoil hat wearing nut-jobs.

Then in 1966 the US Air Force sponsored an 'independent' team of scientists who conveyed that UFOs posed no threat to national security, and there was no evidence that the objects sighted were of ET origin. Project Blue Book was then terminated in 1969, as it was believed that very little was achieved from the study of UFOs. It was declared that the least likely hypothesis of UFOs is the visitation from ETs, as logistically it's a non-starter. It makes more sense that they're Nazi operations?

The subject has however never dissipated, and many continue to believe that UFOs are being investigated secretly by high-level governmental personnel. This is arguably inspired by the X-Files and other alien movies. But the fact remains that Close Encounters of various kinds have continued. Despite authorities downplaying UFOs, they've kept showing up. Furthermore, whilst most cases are written off, about 20% remain unexplained and classified.

The conjecture is that 'we can't handle the truth'. And chaos would erupt if we thought there were aliens. Respectively, we can think of the H.G. Wells radio hoax in 1938, when 'War of the Worlds' was aired on radio. The dramatized broadcast was mistaken for an account of real events, and a million people got their freak on, believing Martians were invading (LOL). So, it's better for us not to know, as no good can come from mass hysteria and panic. And yet, as touched on, there's been governmental disinformation, like Blue Book reports of aliens found at Roswell?

Cooper notably asserted that it was after the incident at Roswell, the US and Soviet came together to address the alien problem, formulating plans to protect the Earth. It seems our nuclear weapons keep ETs at bay? We need a Space-Force to defend ourselves? Hence, Trump recently (2018) called for a Space Force, like the Air Force but for space. It's said however, there's been a Space Force since the 1960s.

Whilst we're kept in the dark, it's purported that flying saucers are tested at Area 51. This is affirmed by the numerous UFOs reportedly spied over this area, and also by whistle-blower Bob Lazar. He claims he worked as a physicist for the government, reverse engineering (replicating) ET flying saucers at Area 51 (Zone S-4).

Lazar claims he worked at Area 51 from December 1988-April 1989 (although officials deny this), and he had to sign a secrecy agreement (breach of the contract resulted in ten years imprisonment and a $10,000 fine). Lazar's job was thus to study the ET craft, figure out how it was powered i.e. propulsion technology, and duplicate it using materials found on earth. He stated that the craft he was shown displayed technology that was hundreds of years in advance. He claims there were at least nine concealed aircraft at the hanger, although he was only working on one of them.

As Greer highlights, we track, locate, and disable their spaceships, causing them to crash, then collect their debris and figure out their technology. He informs the US military enhanced their own flying saucer designs, based on the genuine alien saucers they found e.g. Roswell crashed disk. Their technology was thus augmented by reverse engineering the ET material. So, there's two types of UFOs, namely, alien-made and manmade. Greer acknowledged that it's difficult to tell them apart, like gold and fool's gold.

Lazar also claims he was briefed about the historical involvement of ETs with our planet for the last 10,000 years. He advised seeing government reports about aliens, namely, the Greys referred to as Zeta Reticulans, which included photos of them and autopsy reports.

However, Lazar felt burdened by his job and the secrecy, and thus he broke the code of silence. Apparently, he told his buds about his work at the base, and having also told them they could view test flights, they subsequently went to have a snoop but got busted (LOL). The following day, Lazar was ordered to go to Area 51 for a meeting with some security guards and an FBI agent, and then he quit. Then he went public.

After Lazar's report, people began flocking to the desert to check out the mysterious lights in the sky (LOL). Since going public however, his life has been threatened and he's been shot at. Whilst Lazar stands by his story, critics claim he's a fraud perpetuating a hoax. His background's been difficult to verify as his records e.g. birth, college and employment have been erased. But according to Lazar, the Government went to extreme lengths to eliminate him i.e. all paperwork. Others believe he's an agent of the State used to disseminate disinformation, and others say he's being used by the Government.

It's also noted, the controversial Majestic Twelve documents were leaked in 1984. Thus, a mysterious roll of undeveloped film was anonymously posted to UFO researcher Jaime Shandera. Shandera was also a movie director in LA, developing a fictional film about UFOs. There was no message or return address, and the postmark was Albuquerque, New Mexico.

When the film was developed, official looking documents marked 'Top Secret', revealed the existence of a secret committee known as Majestic Twelve (MJ12). The presumption was that whoever photographed these classified documents had access/clearance, and they wanted the secret out.

The 'Majestic 12 documents' revealed a briefing for President Elect Eisenhower in 1952, signed by President Truman, confirming the existence of MJ12. The MJ12 documents (eight pages) indicate that President Truman signed an Executive Order to create the covert operation MJ12, but there's no record of the MJ12 meeting, just the documents that surfaced in 1984. It stated that Truman appointed twelve majestic (elite) scientists and military officials in 1947 to investigate the flying saucer that crashed at Roswell. So, it was a flying saucer after-all, and Truman was responsible for the cover-up?

Rather than Project Blue Book, (the official public investigative body), it was actually MJ12's job to recover and investigate alien spacecraft. They received all 'hard' information regarding UFOs. And were specifically tasked to ensure we never find out the truth. Hence, Blue Book never knew about recovered spacecraft or aliens. But rather they received a lot of hoaxes, misidentifications, and psychological issues.

But moreover, the MJ12 documents also revealed that four dead aliens were recovered at Roswell. In addition to acknowledging the Greys, called EBEs, other humanoid aliens that could be mistaken for human, are also mentioned. Apparently, many crashed UFOs were recovered, and the MJ12 documents detail four types of aircraft that 'aliens use', namely, disk or cigar shaped, circular, and triangular. So, the ET presence is real, and the military has been shooting them down to snaffle their technology?

It's noted, the Bible tells us about (cursed) 'flying scrolls' that fly through the air (see Zechariah 5:1-4), which corroborates with cigar shaped UFOs. And 'ephahs' go forth, which look like flying saucers. However, it seems there's myriad chariots in the second heaven?

Apparently the clandestine MJ12 were responsible only and directly to the President. And Truman chose James Forestall (1892-1949), Secretary of Defence, and one of the twelve, to oversee the other apostles. It was Forestall who sent Byrd to Antarctica.

Bill Cooper notably highlights that these men were all members of The Jason Society, which is an independent group of elite scientists who advise the US on science and technology of a 'sensitive nature'. He further stated that MJ12 membership included top officers and directors of the CFR and Trilateral Commission. Like, apparently Father George Bush and Dick Cheney were MJ12 members. Apparently, the Jason Society is higher up in the pyramid than the Bilderbergers.

As it transpires, MJ12 were apparently divided regarding whether or not we 'the people' should know the truth about UFOs/ETs, and this included Forestall. It's said he had a change of heart and felt obliged to come clean. But this did not go down well with Truman, who asked him to step down. It's also said that once MJ12 was created, it expanded its mandate beyond what Forestall had intended. It's alleged that when Truman dismissed him, Forrestal became so depressed he committed suicide, by jumping from the 16th floor hospital window.

However, many believe he was murdered, taking his secrets with him. It's believed someone tried to strangle him, as he was found with a dressing-gown belt suspiciously tied around his neck, before he plunged to his death. And his suicide note wasn't his handwriting. It's widely rumoured and speculated that he wanted to release UFO information to the public, hence he was bumped off. The full report of Forrestal's death was held secret for 55 years (it was finally released in 2004, with no mention of the dressing-gown cord), and the autopsy report has never been made public.

The documents (which Shandera received two months after the last MJ12 member died) advised Eisenhower of the importance of this handpicked high-level policy making group overseeing UFOs and ETs, and suggested that the project be continued.

It's purported however that MJ12 initially rejected Eisenhower (he wasn't allowed into their inner circle) and refused to give him information about Area 51 (they never sent him reports). So, he sent a team of CIA agents to investigate on his behalf. It's said MJ12 backed down and allowed the team access, who reported back that they'd seen the Roswell craft and other crafts. And also, grey aliens that were kept at lower levels. Apparently, during Eisenhower's first year of office, there were ten crashed disks recovered.

It's further noted, that after Eisenhower, came JFK, and the 'space race' was on. Allegedly rivalling the Soviet, the US endeavoured to land on the moon first. Maybe the Russians knew better? But moreover, JFK wanted full disclosure from the CIA about UFOs. He was apparently out of the loop and MJ12 refused to give him details or declassify the information. He apparently demanded that MJ12 release the information, and then he was murdered ten days later. It's noted, the Soviet has its equivalent of MJ12, the sister branch of MJ12, and Europe have their majestic people.

It's said the alleged moon landing was a distraction to keep the masses focussed on that rather than what was going on with aliens and UFOs. And it distracted us from their important trips to Antarctica. The herd watch the sideshow, with no expense spared (apparently rovers for the moon cost $60 million each).

As mentioned, Eisenhower warned about the Military Industrial Complex. That is, the rise of a national security state, which is independent of official government supervision. This monster was taking over i.e. wars for corporate gain using counter-intelligence programs to spread disinformation. He knew about the self-funded, above the law, shadowy government within the US Air Force and Navy. He was a puppet for them? According to Cooper, Eisenhower (who served from 1953-1961) was the last president to know the truth about what's going on.

Whilst Shandera and his UFO researcher buds Bill Moore and Stanton Friedman, initially kept the MJ12 documents secret, the jig was up by 1987, as others began to receive the same documents. Like Timothy Good, who published them in his book 'Above Top Secret: The Worldwide UFO Cover-up' (which became a global bestseller). Good highlights the black world of intelligence and its hierarchy of secrecy.

Thus, 'Confidential' is succeeded by 'Secret', then 'Top Secret', then 'Above Top Secret'. Files classified 'Above Top Secret' are so secret, they're not supposed to exist. And it's at this level that the UFO/ET situation is managed. Since the 1950s, it has been classified higher than the hydrogen bomb. So, Shandera, Moore and Friedman equally circulated their MJ12 documents, and they received widespread coverage in the international mass media.

However, as it transpired, when the FBI investigated the documents' authenticity, they stated in their report in 1988 that they were fabricated and completely bogus. The Government insists that MJ12 never existed. Sceptics claim it was an elaborate hoax and that someone faked the documents. They highlight the documents were typed using an old typewriter and the fraudsters who made them, copied and pasted Truman's signature onto them. Furthermore, the typewriter they used wasn't made until 1963 yet the letters were supposed to be written in 1947.

Team Shandera, Moore and Friedman however insist the MJ12 documents are authentic. They further advised that they received more anonymous clues, which they followed up (which involved searching the National Archives), and these corroborated with the MJ12 documents. Friedman maintains these documents are at the centre of the government cover-up. He concedes there's a conspiracy at the highest levels of government.

It's also noted, that alleged MJ12 member, Dr Donald Menzel, very publicly debunked ET's/UFOs. The conjecture about this vehemently sceptical leading astronomer is that he had a double-life. It's said he was an insider covering up ETs. His daughter however said that it was ludicrous that Menzel was involved in the fictitious MJ12.

So, there was only crappy Blue Book, which terminated because there were no UFOs (besides manmade saucers), and there's no aliens? And yet the US Department of Defense is now publicly acknowledging UAP? And SETI are convinced we'll find life imminently.

Moreover, people are abducted by aliens, so-called Close Encounters of a Fourth Kind. Like, Betty and Barney Hill were allegedly abducted in New Hampshire, US, in 1961. Or these are psyops (psychological operations) on behalf of the US Gov? Abduction stories weren't part of popular culture then, so their story is generally regarded as the first 'modern' abduction story. That is, it was brought to the public's attention, and became sensational news. The public knew about UFOs, but now they had to contend with potentially being abducted. Say what?

The Hill's story is also interesting with regards to who's responsible for the abductions, i.e. aliens or special military operations, as initially Barney conveyed that it was military personnel, and then Greys? He initially described the occupants of the ship as Gestapo like figures, dressed in black garments, but subsequently described them as not wearing any clothes, and having large, wrap-around eyes. It's noted, that by all accounts, the Hills were 'normal'. Barney (1922-1969) worked for the US Postal Service, and Betty (1919-2004) was a social worker.

So, the Hills reported seeing a UFO, a soundless light that was moving in an erratic direction, seemingly following them, before stopping in front of them. Barney got out the car and using binoculars saw humanoid figures in the UFO, who were dressed in shiny black uniforms that looked like leather, and wore black caps with visors. He observed they moved with military precision.

Betty didn't see the UFO's descent, but Barney yelled 'they are going to capture us', as he hit the acceleration pedal and sped off. However, suddenly they heard a beeping noise, (like the sound of a tuning fork), and then they felt very drowsy. When they heard the same beeping noise again, it was two hours later, and they were driving 35 miles south of the sighting location.

They had no recollection of what happened to them between the two sets of beeping sounds, and they were worried about the period of missing time. They were further alarmed to discover they'd acquired a selection of minor cuts and grazes, and their clothes were damaged. It seems they were hypnotised? And something happened to them during their trance state?

They began to suspect that something very odd had happened to them, and in the following months they suffered from severe nightmares, flashbacks, and extreme anxiety. Betty's recurring nightmare consisted of seeing 8-11 men, dressed in matching uniforms and 'military' caps, who would stand in the middle of the road and stop the Hill's car. They would then be led aboard a disk-shaped craft and examined.

The Hills sought psychiatric help, and under hypnosis they both, separately, described how they'd been abducted by 'space aliens' and taken onboard their ship. Their stories were remarkably similar and corroborated with Betty's nightmares of being kidnapped. They described how they were shown around the spacecraft, before undergoing painful and humiliating medical examinations. Barney hypnotically recalled an anal probing, and his semen was collected in a separate procedure. And Betty may have had eggs removed. They both advised that the aliens communicated telepathically with them (apparently they heard their voices loud and clear in their heads).

Their psychiatrist, Dr Benjamin Simon, seemed to conclude that they'd shared a manufactured story spurred on by Betty's nightmare. It seems their tale was the product of confabulation through hypnosis? Interestingly however, Betty advised, under hypnosis, that she was shown a star map 'by the leader of the ship', when she asked where they came from. And then she sketched this map under post-hypnotic suggestion. The interesting part is she drew the star system Zeta Reticuli, and yet this wasn't discovered until 1969. Hence, the 'Hill Abduction' came to be called the 'Zeta Reticuli Incident'.

This notably resonates with Dogon people (from southern Mali), who had detailed knowledge about Sirius B for hundreds of years, a star invisible to the eye and so difficult to observe, even through a telescope, that no photographs of it were obtained until 1970. They also knew that Saturn has rings, and Jupiter has four moons.

The Dogon say this knowledge (which they disclosed to anthropologists in the 1930s and 1940s) was given to them by visitors to earth from another star system.

The Hill's experience seems fairly standard. That is, abductees commonly report seeing a bright light, being taken onboard a spaceship, with medical procedures conducted. They also communicate telepathically with aliens, and return home, some two or three hours later. Whilst both men and women are taken, and they describe very similar processes, (including vaginal and anal probes), a common scenario is that women are impregnated. Some women report being forced to have sex with aliens. And then a few months later (at the first trimester), they're re-abducted and the foetus is removed. Abductees also report seeing hybrids in jars, at different forms of gestation.

It's speculated that covert hybridisation operations are taking place underground, as sperm and ovum are removed. As Dr David Jacobs, author of 'Alien Encounters, First-hand accounts of UFO abductions' (1992), states, 'the focus of the abduction is the production of children'. His study consisted of 300 abduction experiences, from sixty abductees, over a four-year period. He concedes that people are abducted worldwide. They're powerless to control the event, and when it was over, they promptly nearly forgot all if it. Hence, hypnotic regression is considered an essential tool to recover the amnesia.

Harvard psychiatry professor John E Mack (1929-2004) also found this scenario from his research. In the early 1990s, Mack commenced a decade-plus study of 200 men and women who reported recurrent alien experiences. He clarifies these people were not mentally ill. He also states there is evidence that individuals reporting abduction experiences are not more hypnotisable or fantasy prone than the general population.

Whilst Mack used hypnosis to elicit their memories of alien abduction, he states that approximately 30% of accounts are obtained without hypnosis. It's noted, abductees can 'remember' all the details of their sojourn under hypnosis, but hypnosis can be rendered active-imagination. Hence, it's inherently tenuous and unreliable.

So, the experiencers reported the aforementioned, namely, being used as guinea pigs in outer space, with eggs and sperm taken etc. However, according to Greer, Mack was paid to make the aliens look unfriendly. And further, he didn't do a good enough job, so he was dropped. The aim is to make aliens the enemy. By violating our human rights and raping us?

However, it's also noted that Laurance Rockefeller funded both Mack the knife and the Disclosure Project. It's highlighted the Disclosure Project is being allowed to happen, given the Illuminati controls and monitors the press, and sponsors disinformation. It's not just good fortune that former high-level government officials share intel regarding UFOs etc with Dr Greer? It seems Dr Greer, poster-boy for disclosure, and Hellyer are controlled opposition?

But moreover, the aliens have a message for us, namely, we have to stop wrecking our planet. People are shown visions of ecological disaster that fundamentally transform them into spiritual seekers on a mission to save polluted Earth. John Mack, and the Dalai Lama, propagate that aliens/UFOs are coming to wake us up. Thus, besides the invasive medical procedures, abductees change for the better. Like, people who experience NDEs. So, the aliens aren't all bad?

Like UFOs, it seems alien encounters are both spiritual/metaphysical and physical i.e. it could be an ASC or a real physical event. Like, an orb is different from a Nazi flying saucer. People are often abducted when they're in their bed at night, and while some insist, they're abducted in their physical bodies, others describe it as an

OBE, preceded by sleep paralysis. That is, their bodies are paralysed, their eyes wide open, and the 'alien' pulls them out their body. They're taken on a trip to the astral plane against their freewill.

As mentioned, it's reported that calling on the name of Jesus stops the alien abduction process. Hundreds of abductions have been abruptly stopped. But this vital information has been suppressed.

It's understood that 'hallucinations' seem more logical, as opposed to someone literally, physically, floating through windows, walls and ceilings, since this defies our comprehension of physics? However, it's also highlighted, there's a different type of physics taking place that we know little about. Perhaps if we could raise our vibration, we could walk through walls (since everything is vibrating energy)? Our spirit body could be activated to achieve the impossible?

Jesus, for example, could walk on water, and His disciple Peter was also able to walk on the sea until he freaked out. It seems Peter achieved that supernatural feat with faith, one of the pillars of magic? And when Jesus returned in His flesh material body, (having died and resurrected), He could walk through walls. Yet He seemed to be physical. Like, He ate food. This corroborates with angels, who can also physically appear and share meals etc.

So, maybe abductees do go through windows with alien assistance? Since angels or 'aliens' have supernatural powers that we're not familiar with. Moreover, it seems ETs have technology to walk through walls (like, EBE 1).

Bill Cooper however didn't believe that human bodies could pass through walls and roofs. He suggested that alien abductions could be mind control ops. The abduction experience could be a strong delusion i.e. people are 'given' visions. Technology like the 'God Helmet' can create mystical experiences, and people can be hypnotised, drugged, and programmed (like MK Ultra victims). They can be given false experiences or 'script memories'. Mind magicians can remove memories (e.g. using ECT) and implant memories of alien abduction.

Thus, abductees could have unwittingly been inducted into a military programme to believe in ET events. People are programmed with scripted transcendental experiences in consciousness, which they believe to be true. Thus, it's said people are given dreams at 'Dream Land' at Area 51.

However, in some cases where people have been abducted, ultraviolet light has shown fluorescent four fingered handprints on the wall, implicating the Greys (who have four fingers, with little pads at the ends, on each hand). Or like, John Ventre claimed he had a seven foot alien in his house, which left a six fingered handprint on his mirror. Ventre (ufologist and author) concurs with the Collins Elite's findings. He understands, first-hand, that this phenomenon is supernatural and interdimensional. He recognises the parallel between UFO/alien phenomena and demonic phenomena, as we'll get to.

Abductees often have marks on their body and they're invariably implanted. And like cattle mutilations, these implants have no entry wound. This suggests there's been a physical event, and necromantic arts? It seems they implant those they abduct, to keep track of them. But rather than aliens, it could be clandestine military operations?

Greer notably highlights that the military has produced circa two billion implants. Presumably they'll only require two billion implants, after the great global cull preceding the NWO? They'll have far fewer minds to control and connect to the beast computer system. It seems bemusing to think they're budgeting for a quarter of us surviving the great tribulation. Three-quarters of us won't make it. It's survival of the fittest?

Cooper affirms that everyone who is abducted is implanted. He also highlights that those who'd received implants, reported hearing a tune in their head, which they couldn't get out their head, and which drove them crazy. They reported having 'fixed ideas' which led them to people, and 'drove' them to places. They were compelled to do certain things and move to certain places. He states these people are programmed with specific roles in the future, certain assignments. So, they're mind control victims. This corroborates with Dizdar's 'sleeper agents' that wait to be triggered.

As touched on, Greer pertains to staged UFO false flags e.g. small people, less than five foot tall, disguised to look like aliens, abduct people on manmade antigravity crafts. He explains that abduction squads, engaged in abduction scenarios, have been operative for decades. So, 'abductees' deduct they've been abducted by ETs, but it's actually military wo/men.

Greer also pertains to robotic aliens. These are manmade to look like EBEs and they're 100% fool-proof. Other tools at their disposal, to facilitate the event, include electromagnetic systems that alter awareness (i.e. blackout), gas canisters to make them pass out, and drugs. He also highlights mind control technology and concedes that MK Ultra victims are unwittingly perpetuating nonsense.

So, we're being scammed by fake aliens, and not told about the good aliens? Like, apparently ET civilisations offered Eisenhower technology to help us, like free energy, if we stopped making hydrogen bombs. But the evil cabal doesn't like this idea, as there's no money to be made. Free energy is not profitable like oil, coal and gas. Hence, they have to keep this technology secret at all costs. Greer claims that people are killed to prevent this information from being leaked.

Besides, the Military Industrial Complex likes wars, and profiting from the weapons that fuel them. It pleases their master, and they need wars to enable the great plan. So, the ETs won't divulge advanced technology because we're maniacs and would use the technology to create even more anarchy.

Greer states the warmongers want endless wars for money, but particularly an alien war. Because that would require an insane amount of military spending. Hence, they plan to hoax an alien war. Or perhaps Greer is putting us off the scent, and they're actually preparing for Armageddon?

Greer also highlights, they realised the psychological warfare value of UFO's. Aliens are a better threat than terrorists? Hence, they manufacture gruesome alien invasions, framing our lovely space bros. Greer concedes that MJ12 has existed since Truman.

Greer also pertains to his friend Dr Carol Rosin's testimony, who worked with Werner Von Braun at Fairchild, from 1974 until he died. Von Braun told her the NWO plan was for the Russians to be our first enemy, then terrorist groups, then rogue countries, then asteroids, and then aliens. He said, 'And remember Carol, the last card is the alien card. We are going to have to build space-based weapons against aliens and all of it is a lie'. Like Greer, Rosin regards the aliens as real and benevolent, but that the government will dupe us into believing they're hostile to justify spending an insane amount on space weapons. With regards to the NWO plan, it seems we're currently at the asteroid stage, as there's been an upsurge in asteroids of late.

It's also pertinent to note, that Werner Von Braun has Psalm 19:1 on his tombstone, which states, 'The heavens declare the glory of God; and the firmament sheweth His handywork'. It seems he was divulging the truth about our cosmology literally on his deathbed? As highlighted, these freaks have to tell us?

And presumably he would know, since he developed NASA rockets that launched the first US space satellite. And he developed the Apollo program for lunar landings. Although he essentially said it was impossible to go the moon. The spaceship would need to be insanely massive (like the size of the Empire State building in NYC), which would be insanely heavy and require an insane amount of fuel.

With regards to staging an alien invasion, there's been much speculation about Bluebeam technology. Conspiracy theorist Serge Monast first pertained to Project Blue Beam in 1994, stating that advanced holographic technology could be used to stage an alien invasion and/or worldwide religious 'awakening' enabling a one world government and religion.

In addition to simulating the alien scenario, it's said they could project Buddha, Jesus, Muhammad, Hare Krishna etc into the sky, instructing us to believe the New Age Luciferian religion. The antichrist deity could be portrayed as the fusion of these deities. It's the same One God that has revealed himself throughout the ages through various incarnations (the idea of One God has been seeded). Historical events, like the parting of the Red Sea, could be shown to demonstrate that 'God' is who He claims?

As touched on, perhaps the antichrist will use this technology to project his image globally during the great tribulation. And perhaps, by virtue of the chip, we could see a hologram of the antichrist in our midst. He could appear at any time? Monast believed that generating a global new religion was the only thing that would make a worldwide dictatorship possible. David Icke (2007) concedes, 'project blue beam is a massive global plan to mislead the people into following the illuminati 'religion''. So, it appears we're in for quite the show?

Apparently, people can be remotely targeted with this technology to induce a personal encounter with these deities. And according to Greer's source, people could pass a lie detector test because it's so believable. Thus, the bluebeam effect can create collective and individual hallucinations (apparently chemtrails enhance holograms). This technology can trigger emotional reactions through the use of computer-generated apparitions, modulated microwave images, and sounds and voices directed into our brain.

People are convinced they've engaged with whatever deity, or aliens, which radically alters their perception of reality. They know it's real? It's also highlighted that electromagnetic mind control devices accounts for why people are increasingly hearing voices. It's reported that certain people are targeted with 'manmade' schizophrenia. Yet presumably if someone suggested to a psychiatrist that they'd been remotely targeted with psychological weapons, they would be rendered schizophrenic?

But moreover, Dr Greer advocates contacting interstellars, through meditation, to initiate peaceful relations. We can bypass the Deep State and make friends with the aliens ourselves? Apparently, Greer was a meditation teacher (he studied Vedic scriptures) before he was a doctor, and he had a NDE when he was 17. He states he was an atheist before his NDE but having gone to space and experienced 'cosmic mind', he knows better?

So, he's familiar with the astral plane, which he likens to a lucid dream state. He understands that death is not death in the real sense. It's never over? Greer insists we need spiritual development, to spiritually evolve like the spiritually evolved alien race. He even advocates this needs to be mandated in policy. He dreams of open contact with aliens with full cooperation of governments.

It's noted, that with Close Encounters of the Fifth Kind, the UFO event involves direct communication between aliens and humans. Contactees, like Greer, claim to be in personal contact with space beings by metaphysical or occult means. It's a human-initiated experience i.e. contactees meditate and telepathically invite ETs to come. Hellyer interestingly said that ETs have rules, like they don't interfere in our affairs unless they're invited. Apparently, they pick individuals who won't be scared of them.

Thus, Greer takes people out to the desert to meditate. They sit in a circle and focus on making contact with ET visitors. Contactees clear a space in their mind and receive what comes (like Siddhis). Humans and 'ETs' communicate telepathically. Sometimes people can feel them e.g. they're touched on the head or shoulder. And they often appear. Like, shafts of golden light appear, or a blue mist coalesces, or rainbow colours, and light orbs (their crafts don't always fully materialise in our dimension). Greer states he saw golden orbs spinning for thirty minutes. They're beautiful? Greer concedes meeting them is life changing, paradigm shifting.

ETs can also communicate with contactees through lucid dreams. Like, they can arrange where to meet, and then these whimsical beings or crafts appear at that prearranged time and place. It's like mystics meet their spirit guides in their dreams. And spirit guides or 'deceased loved ones' can similarly touch our head or shoulder? Or they're all demons bewitching us? Greer also said he visualised a crop circle and 'sent it' to the ETs and they created it. So, that's nice?

But moreover, besides annihilating them, it's alleged our governments are working with aliens. And they furnish us with technology. Hence, our science and technology is immense. According to whistle-blower Bill Tompkins, for example, who worked for an Above Top Secret think tank within the Douglas Aircraft Company, Reptilians basically control every government. He concedes there's many ET species interacting with humanity, including Draco's/Reptilians and Nordics.

Tompkins claims he worked alongside Nordics, who looked indistinguishable from humans. They selected him to be their representative, and they selected Forrestal. Apparently Tall Whites have been working with the government since WW2. He also claims Maria Orsic was in contact with Nordics, whereas Hitler was in contact with Draco-reptilians.

So, the Nordics are benevolent, unlike the Reptilians? What about the insectoids? Moreover, Maria Orsic gave the UFO blueprints to Hitler, so that doesn't compute? They were both in the Vril Society and working together?

Tompkins concurs that the SS moved to Antarctica before Germany was bombed, and asserts the UFOs flying over the White House in 1952 were German craft from Antarctica. Tompkins also claims he witnessed the 'Battle of L.A.' when a thousand rounds of ammo were fired at UFOS. He concedes that MJ12 came into existence in the 1940s to 'manage' the UFO/alien situation.

The Douglas Aircraft Company designed kilometre-long antigravity spacecraft covertly requested by the US Navy. Tompkins worked there for twelve years, beginning in 1951. He claims he was part of an operation involving US Navy spies who stole UFO and antigravity technology secrets from the Nazis during WW2. He said they discovered advanced weapons and 250/500 foot long circular UFOS. This information was then given to CEOS of leading American corporations involved in the military and space industries.

As mentioned, funding for these black operations, which includes conducting biotechnology research to create 'aliens', comes from narco-trafficking and international money laundering CIA operations. It's further said that alien crafts are given to private companies to back-engineer them.

But moreover, Tompkins highlights that some of the Reptilians darkest activities include eating humans and performing blood sacrifices. He also states that all recent US presidents have been Reptilians who could change form, but that Donald Trump is not one of them. This corroborates with Arizona Wilder's testimony about shapeshifting reptilians? Tompkins concedes that Lizzies have been around for tens of thousands of years, but they've only recently started having an active part in society again. And members of the government are related to these aliens, (like nephilim bloodlines), hence, their changeling ability.

Tompkins frequently states, 'everything you're told is a lie'. And whilst he's hailed as an awesome whistle-blower, it's equally understood he was given permission by the Navy to blow the whistle. So, they want us to know? The masses are being prepared for out of this world craziness? However, it's also highlighted that whistle-blowers may be victims of mind control. Like, Dr Greer speculates that Tompkins is. So, his testimony is fiction?

Joshua Bempechat, author of 'The Secret History of America, the Greatest Conspiracy on Earth', wrote, 'It would appear as though our race may have been seeded here by off-planet intelligences or that we were created as an intergalactic experiment, that huge 8-10 foot tall powerful Reptilian beings live at the core of the earth, pilot advanced flying craft, read minds and plot to enslave mankind by using Zeta-Reticulans...' In his view, the Greys are subordinate to the reptilians for their wellbeing as apparently they're dying. And the Greys are embroiled with our Governments with genetic cloning and electronic implants.

Others highlight the Nordics are here to help us with our spiritual evolution. But these Tall Whites are wary of us because we're a volatile planet with an abundance of nuclear weapons. Apparently, they would help us if we disarm, but we're reluctant to. So, presumably the Tall Whites were amongst those who offered to help Eisenhower?

However, apparently Tall Whites are no longer going to world leaders, because they're sick of 'agendas'. They are instead engaging directly with people who are worthy. According to Hellyer, they've shared various technologies with us, including fibre optics, microchips, and improved lasers. Apparently, I-phones are the result of alien technology. He states aliens are light years ahead in medicine, agriculture, and technology. But moreover, it's said the Tall White's agenda is being implemented, which includes the creation of a global electronic surveillance system. So, they're behind our 1984 architecture?

Thus, we're being prepped for aliens. Hence, (in addition to Hellyer's, Greer's and Tompkins's contribution), employees just happen to stumble upon secret files while 'fooling around' on NSA computers. Like, Bill Cooper 'found' classified documents when preparing information briefings for Admirals and his Chief of Staff. These papers detailed the Government's secret pacts/trade agreements with aliens. Like, apparently Eisenhower (CFR member) reached a formal agreement with the aliens and signed a treaty in 1954.

It's noted, that disinformation leaked this way seems legit? Cooper believes many people were shown the documents over the years, as people would speak about it. He highlights that despite being sworn to secrecy, it's hard to keep aliens secret.

So, there was apparently a trade done, an exchange. Aliens gave us advanced technology, and they were 'allowed' to abduct a limited number of US citizens (and cattle) for experimentation and the harvesting of biological material. There were certain rules, like they had to ensure the person was returned to where they were taken from (LOL), and they had no memory of what happened. Like, the Hills? The Greys were to provide a list of the abductees to the NSA, in case they needed medical assistance or psychological adjustment.

The aliens apparently insisted that governments keep their existence secret, and they were given secret bases in the US protected by military forces. So, aliens are in DUMBs? However, it's purported the aliens have breached their trade agreements, as there's been unprecedented rape. Something needs to be done about those aliens?

As it transpired, Cooper realised he'd been manipulated up the garden path to provide us with misinformation in 1997. He said for many years he sincerely believed that an ET threat existed and were behind world events. He linked the Illuminati with his belief that ETs were secretly involved with the US government. He said he was duped circa 1972.

The documents he seen, officially labelled Top Secret, expressed that ETs are real and had visited the earth. Hence, he went public. He divulged what he believed we had a right to know, but he latterly said that aliens are demons. He believes the technology's real, but aliens aren't.

Other ex-CIA agents have however attested to seeing Greys at Area 51. So, perhaps there are aliens, or they're manmade? As Greer asserts, people in classified projects, near Dulce, are growing 'biologicals' or Programmed Life-Forms underground. These 'aliens' are then put on UFOs to abduct people, to create the narrative that aliens are dreadful, and we need to fight them. Thus, small greys could be mass produced android robots? Or grossly altered babies, given their strong foetal physiology? Greys could be the result of human-alien genetic manipulation. They could be nephilim? So, there's demonic greys aliens (like in DMT space), and there's hybridised biological clones.

It's also pertinent to note, the Dulce Papers (released in 1987) which revealed a secret underground Dulce Base, dubbed the 'New Area 51'. The Dulce Base is apparently a massive underground joint alien/government facility in the town of Dulce, New Mexico. The Dulce papers alleged the US was in collusion with the Greys in exchange for highly advanced technology. The Gov wanted hardware i.e. technology and the aliens wanted software i.e. genetic material aka us.

The papers reveal information about alien breeding chambers and tanks, and come complete with a six minute video tape of the facility, and twenty-five black and white photos, which show upright tanks with grey aliens inside. The set of technical papers pertaining to the facility, include discussions on the true purpose of the EBEs, the usage of cow blood, DNA manipulation, and information about the so-called 'almost human beings'.

It's also recalled that demons seek a body to inhabit. It's thus theorised that Greys are genetically engineered to provide a house for demons. As touched on, it's said we're living in a hybrid age, given chimeras and transhumanism etc. However, it's also said that little grey biological suits are used as an interface for these demons to manifest in. Some report seeing these suits, like wetsuits, lying around on aircrafts.

It's purported that government scientists and aliens conduct horrific genetic experiments on other humans. It's said they starve, torture and dissect their victims (prisoners). Janet Sailor, who wrote an article in 'The UFO Chronicles' in May 2009, entitled 'Doubts Disappear After Attending Dulce Base Debate', said she seen photos showing gruesome images of a grotesque creature.

She wrote, 'the creature had what looked like an 'unfinished' human head, with lumps and hair on it, but without any definite features like eyes or ears, as well as appendages which looked like human arm stumps and small slender legs like those of a baby deer. What looked like a long black 'tail' emerged from a darkened opening centred at the rear of the creature'. An ex-CIA agent, who called himself and his work with aliens' evil, started crying as he said the human part of creatures would say 'help me'. That's both horrendous and heart-breaking.

The Dulce Base story originated with physicist Paul Bennewitz, who in 1980 claimed he'd been intercepting ET signals transmitted from the underground base at Dulce, since the late 1970s. It's also noted, that by the mid-1970s, reports of unusual military activity, UFO sightings, higher-than-normal cancer rates, decreased fertility in women, and cattle mutilations in the area began to surface.

At the same time, Bennewitz had been investigating the case of abductee Myrna Hansen, who reported being taken to an underground facility run by aliens and humans. She advised seeing laboratories, high-tech computing areas, cattle being drained of their blood, and vats containing both human and animal body parts.

However, most of the information about Dulce Base comes from Phil Schneider and Thomas Castello, two former employees. Schneider, a former US government engineer, claimed he helped to build the base in 1979, which has seven levels and extends two miles underneath the ground. And Castello was a security guard, who claimed to have direct contact with human and alien captives, and intimate knowledge of the facility's horrific experiments.

Schneider notably claimed there are 1,477 underground bases across the world costing $17 billion each, funded by black budgets. He confirmed there's entities underground, and at submarine bases. Hence, UFOs surface from the sea? Sensitive assets are also housed under the sea. Schneider exposed government cover-ups, UFOs, the NWO, and the trillion-dollar US black budget funded by drug money.

But it gets wilder, as Schneider claimed he was involved in a human-alien war at Dulce. And he had the scars on his chest and stumps for fingers to prove it (the aliens used laser guns). He also claimed there's giants underground with six fingers and toes. So, the nephilim are back? This corroborates with Justen Faull's intel regarding the ten foot giants harboured at DUMBs. But moreover, Faull informed that at lower levels, employees are forbidden to use the name of Jesus, even as a cuss word. So, that's interesting.

It seems pertinent to note, that other military whistle-blowers have come forward with stories about giants, which are reportedly hiding in caves. Like, US Special Forces claimed they killed 'the Kandahar giant' in Afghanistan, which weighed a thousand pounds (see Steve Quayle and LA Marzulli's reports). It was apparently twelve foot tall, had six fingers and toes, double row of teeth, and red hair. It was airlifted back to the US.

Whilst ufologist John Lear (who is buds with Lazar) further claimed he had independent confirmations of Dulce Base's existence in 1990, sceptics say its balls, insisting the photos of the base and the creatures are fakes. It's said Castello had no paper-trail, and besides one photo, which could be of anyone, there's no proof of his existence. It's also however said, that after his disclosure, he and his family went missing.

And it's 'officially' said that Phil Schneider was mentally ill, and then committed suicide in 1996. Others however contest that Schneider was murdered for revealing classified information. He was found dead in his apartment with a piano wire wrapped around his neck (so he strangled to death), and it appeared he repeatedly suffered torture before he was finally killed.

Schneider notably said the alien agenda began in 1933 and aliens would take over the world in 2029. Apparently 7/8 of the population will be bumped off by 2029. According to Fritz Springmeier, Schneider was a 'programmed multiple', and he was murdered the day before he was due to meet with Springmeier to get deprogrammed. Which could have been the reason for his demise?

Other 'whistle-blowers' that died under 'mysterious circumstances' include 'conspiracy theorist' Max Spiers. As mentioned, he was bumped off in 2016, having divulged just a few days before that he believed in the Dulce Base and the Fourth Reich. He concedes the Third Reich didn't lose the war but rather went underground to become the Fourth Reich.

He also claimed aliens and humans' experiment on humans, and advised, 'I have seen a vat of children in dissociated states, some crying, some not, some completely gone'. He claims there's breeders down there, breeding thousands of kids. He also pertained to child trafficking and said most of the kids come from Rio de Janeiro.

Spiers told his mum two days before his death, that he feared being murdered and if anything happens to him, to investigate. His mum said he was fit, strong and healthy, before he left to do the conference in Poland. Spiers spewed up two litres of black fluid before he died, suggestive of black magic? He also complained of migraines a few days before, which further suggests a demonic attack?

Spiers maintained he was a victim of trauma-based mind control, and a super-soldier. He referred to the astral plane as the fourth dimension, and advised most attacks are conducted on this plane i.e. astral attacks. He said he psychically protected himself everyday (through various rituals), but it seems they got him. Spiers also highlighted that most spying is done via astral projection/remote viewing, and most meetings take place on the astral plane.

It seems MK Ultra scrambles minds, and victims are given script memories. Thus, testimonies are partly truth and partly fiction? It also seems the boundary between 3D and 4D dissolves, which is considered psychosis. Like, Spiers would see giant spiders and tons of crazy astral entities. Like La-Sala explained, these entities can cross over into our dimension. Like, Revelation 9 forewarns us about scorpion bites?

Spiers also claimed the royal reptilian family are attempting to bring Lucifer here to lead the NWO. He concedes that Nazis and Zionists (black magicians) rule the world, using sex magic etc. Apparently, he also had damaging information about Hillary Clinton. So, he had to be silenced. It seems he was a new addition to the Clinton Body Count?

His ex-girlfriend, Sarah Adam, notably claimed his death could have been part of a Satanist ritual. She said he rang her secretly, stating he was terrified and wanted to leave. Apparently, he was held in some remote house in a forest that had an electric fence surrounding it. He claimed they were doing very dark black magic and satanic rituals to de-programme him and get rid of demons. He said they gave him something that put him in a coma for two days. And he needed to get out and find a church or a holy place. But two days later he was dead. Adam is insistent they were doing some kind of black magic on him.

It's also pertinent to note, Jacques Vallee and Josef Allen Hynek's takeaway, as these two highly respected researchers set out to debunk UFOs, but they both concluded the phenomenon couldn't be reduced to deluded imaginings. Hynek was notably a scientific consultant to Blue Book, and Vallee apparently seen a UFO when he was sixteen in France.

So, they concurred that UFOs are not intergalactic, but rather they're more likely to be from another dimension. Their capacity to appear and disappear suggests a parallel reality, rather than visits from faraway planets. The ET hypothesis was too simplistic.

UFOs also coincided with other paranormal phenomenon e.g. sleep paralysis, amnesia, hypnosis. And Vallee recognised the parallel between alien abduction and astral projection. Moreover, as Vallee points out, there is no evidence of flesh and blood aliens. He also asserts the humanoid body structure of the alleged 'aliens' is not likely to have originated on another planet and is not biologically adapted to space travel. These beings are not natural but supernatural.

As an alternative to the popular 'Extra-Terrestrial Hypothesis' then, (which he initially supported), Vallee proposed a 'Multidimensional Visitation Hypothesis'. He deducted that entities could be multidimensional beyond space-time. Hence, they could co-exist with humans yet remain undetected.

So, there could be a parallel spirit world, with entities existing in different frequencies. Like angels in the second heaven, and earthbound demons in the first heaven? And they can appear as UFOs, Reptilians and Nordics? Vallee said, 'We are dealing with a yet unrecognised level of consciousness, independent of man but closely linked to the earth.... I do not believe anymore that UFOs are simply the spacecraft of some race of extraterrestrial visitors'.

Vallee acknowledges that 'visitors' have made their appearances throughout history, as reflected by the ancient myths of all cultures. He thus suggests that UFO experiences are paranormal in nature. Modern alien abduction narratives parallel with demonic encounters (including incubus and succubus), which suggests a connection between the two i.e. they're describing the same thing but interpreted through a different frame of reference.

In his book 'Confrontations', he wrote, 'An impressive comparison can be made between UFO occupants and the popular conception of demons'. And also, 'The medical examinations to which Abductees are said to be subjected, often accompanied by sadistic sexual manipulation, is reminiscent of the medieval tales of encounters with demons'.

Like daemons, aliens can also speak all languages. And like poltergeist activity, the smell of sulphur is commonly reported with 'alien' encounters. John Ventre also highlights that so-called aliens are responsible for biting, scratching, pulling, bed shaking, moving objects, and switching the TV/radio on and off. Ventre has also seen shadow people.

John Keel, author of 'UFOs: Operation Trojan Horse' (1970), concedes, 'The UFO manifestations seem to be, by and large, merely minor variations of the age old demonological phenomenon...' (p.299). And yet, apparently Keel was an atheist. He also wrote, '...the UFOnauts are the liars, not the contactees. And they are lying deliberately as part of the bewildering smokescreen which they have established to cover their real origin, purpose and motivation'.

Vallee concedes the 'UFOs' are manipulating us to believe their mythology. He pointed out, that a secondary aspect of the UFO phenomenon involves human manipulation i.e. our perception is being shaped to believe that UFOs are piloted by ETs from other planets. Indeed, he referred to them as 'messengers of deception'. It seems fallen angels and demons are tricking us into believing in aliens? However, Vallee also claims that several hundred professional scientists, a group both he and Hynek termed 'the invisible college' (which we'll get back to), continue to study UFOs in private.

Vallee further concurs that religious apparitions, like the 'Miracle of the Sun' at Fatima in 1917, may have been UFO activity. As mentioned, this was witnessed by 70,000 people. People described a silver disk or light in the sky cascading rainbow colours (the term 'flying saucer' wasn't invented then). Then in 1950, Pope Pius XII witnessed the same thing, and respectively introduced the new Marion dogma that Mary ascended into heaven. It seems precarious that he viewed UFOs as connected to Mary?

It's also alleged, according to Vatican moles, the Fatima apparition was actually aliens. As mentioned, the Vatican are actively looking for our space brothers. But rather than the inter-dimensional hypothesis, it seems the Vatican supports the ET hypothesis. Chris Putnam (author/researcher) asserts the Vatican believes that ETs are real and from another planet. So, there's demons, fallen angels and aliens?

Apparently, Billy Graham said the UFOs may be angels sent by God to watch over us. It seems some evangelicals are open-minded about aliens as part of God's creation, despite their dark clandestine activities?

This notably contrasts with Father Paul Inglesby (1915-2010), Britain's longest serving UFO theorist, who believed UFOs were of satanic origin. Inglesby was fascinated by reports of flying saucers, assuming they were piloted craft from other worlds, until he knew better. It's highlighted that what's unique about Inglesby, is that his interest began a decade before the flying saucer era.

Furthermore, in 1938 whilst serving with the Royal Navy, he contracted a tropical disease that left him dangerously ill for three months. During this time, he underwent a 'devastating spiritual experience'. He saw visions of a future atomic war and demonic forces controlling spaceships and nuclear weapons. He said, '...not only did I witness future events, in a mental telepathic sort of way, but throughout the whole of this time a battle was raging for possession of my soul'. Fortunately, his prayers were answered, and he was saved from the clutches of demonic forces.

Thus, when the first reports of flying saucers appeared in British newspapers in 1947, Inglesby felt his visions were about to become reality. He didn't believe the popular extra-terrestrial hypothesis was satisfactory, and instead submitted the phenomenon was demonic in nature. He became a Christian in 1964. He was ordained as a priest in the Church of England, and then converted to Orthodox Christianity in 1980.

But it's further alleged the Vatican's got secret files on the reality of the alien presence. Apparently, President Carter (who was in office from 1977-1981) requested information on aliens from the Vatican vaults in 1977 (at the behest of the Jesuit head of the library) but he wasn't allowed. So, it seems the Vatican is privy to the plan, namely, the 'end times' alien deception?

In summary, we're being groomed to believe that aliens exist. It seems the powers that should not be want us to believe in aliens from other worlds. Hence, people like Dr Hermann Oberth (1894-1989), Nazi scientist who worked on US advanced rocket technology, said, 'We cannot take the credit for our record advancement in certain scientific fields alone; we have been helped'. And when asked by whom, he replied, 'the people of other worlds'. He perpetuated the myth that flying saucers are spaceships from another solar system.

It's purported that UFO activity will increase to evidence 'we're not alone'. And 'science' will continue their efforts towards discovering life on other planets, to corroborate with evolution. Hence, NASA gives us regular updates regarding their supposed finds i.e. exo-planets (planets outside our solar system). Like, the evidence of rovers on Mars? Or they've been filming in Greenland and adding a red coloured tint to the scenery to evidence the 'red planet'?

It seems we have a couple of scenarios, namely, we'll have to fight ETs, however hoaxed, as arms manufacturers and bankster's cash in, and a NWO ensues. Or our space brothers will be our saviours, and a NWO ensues. Regarding the latter, it's speculated that just as we're on the brink of WW3, they'll rescue us. They will expose the 'Illuminati', (which weirdly doesn't include the Clintons according to Greer), and give us technology including free energy, in tandem with the UN 2030 (sustainable development) vision.

It's also speculated they'll give us a DNA upgrade to extend our longevity (the chip that changes us from human to trans-human). And they'll tell us the truth about our origins? Like, Lucifer is God. Authors Chris Putnam and Tom Horn explain the 'alien gospel' is aliens are our progenitors and saviours. So, they seeded humanity, and sent various religious and philosophical figures over the millennia to guide us. They'll guide us into the New Age via our spiritual evolution and ascension. The alien gospel is gnosis for all.

It's alleged the Vatican are prepared to revise Christ's gospel with the alien gospel. Like, Father Giuseppe Tanzella Nitti, professor at Vatican University, said 'Very soon we will not have to deny our Christian faith…but there is information coming from another world, and once it is confirmed it is going to require a rereading of the gospel as we know it'. As mentioned, the Catholic Church endorses evolution. Thus, aliens are more evolved than us, including morally?

Putnam and Horn highlight we're being prepared for the coming disclosure, quoting Monsignor Corrado Balducci who said, 'believing the universe may contain alien life does NOT contradict a faith in God'. He also said, 'there is an alien presence on Earth now'. They also pertain to Father Guy S Consolmagno, Vatican astronomer, who said, 'contemporary societies may soon look to the aliens to be the saviours of humankind'.

It's understood that whatever happens, it would need to be very dramatic for billions of religious people (e.g. Muslims, Jews and Christians) to convert to a New World religion. It would need to be some mind-bending situation to drastically alter their worldview. Like, seeing a three mile wide spacecraft, piloted by aliens, might catapult a paradigm shift?

So, this could be the great apostasy, the falling away of the church, before Jesus returns? We're forewarned, (in 2 Thessalonians 2:9), the lawless one comes with all power, signs and lying wonders. As discussed, the Pope is rumoured to be the false prophet. And 'Miracles of the Sun' (on behalf of the beast Apollyon) could be part of his party tricks? We're specifically told that people will be seduced by demons and depart from the faith.

Fundamentally, it seems disclosure is deception. Hence, the cabal are onboard. Our education has paid off. We're convinced life must be out there. We're a dot in an insanely vast universe? As Spiers highlighted, we're led to believe we're this insignificant planet, spinning aimlessly through space. But we're not. He said, 'the earth is the heart of the universe, not randomly somewhere, which is what they want us to believe'. It seems we live in a multidimensional universe, and entities (personalities) are very interested in us. Spiers further said, 'they want to break the hearts of human beings'. Like, they (Satanists) broke his, when they killed him.

But moreover, whilst we've been given the ET hypothesis, (despite governments knowing that ETs are interdimensional since the 1940s), and after decades of 'covering up' the UFO phenomenon, the FBI is now voluntarily declassifying documents about interdimensional ETs.

Like, a report written in 1947 by a special agent of the FBI (lieutenant colonel), which reached the public in 2011, elucidates these beings do not come from any 'planet' as we use the word, but from an ethereal plane, which interpenetrates our own, and is imperceptible to us. These visitors and their crafts 'materialise' on entering the vibrancy of our matter. The entities are human-like but much bigger in size, and they're translucent. They can be detected through infrared cameras. Their mission is peaceful but apparently they're contemplating settling on this plane.

It seems the premise for the herd to accept fallen angels as aliens, was to portray them as physical, before revealing their true spiritual nature. So, they were alleged to be physical beings that evolved on another planet, but now they're interdimensional.

But moreover, as also discussed, Jesus told us it would be like the 'Days of Noah' when He returned. And Daniel 2:43 refers to the mingling of seed, which suggests the return of hybrids? It's noted, that Close Encounters of the Seventh Kind is the creation of human-alien hybrids, either by sexual reproduction or by artificial scientific method.

Thus, maybe Tall Whites are nephilim, since they apparently go undetected? Perhaps the abducted ova and sperm have been put to haunted use, beyond the Greys? These could be the 'almost humans' referenced in the Dulce Papers. LA Marzulli notably mentioned an event which his pastor friend told him about. Thus, his friend was out in a park, and saw a tall (circa six foot three) white woman, with blonde/platinum hair, running, and as she neared him, her eyes turned black and she growled. Like, Harmony (Keith Green's bud) growled?

It's understood that black eyes indicate demonic possession. Like, according to David Icke, Ted Heath's eyes turned completely black. And people's eyes can also look reptilian. Footage of black magicians, for example, shows their eyes fluctuate from normal to reptilian. So, the woman could have been possessed, or she could have been a hybrid. The eyes are the windows to the soul, and hybrids are soulless? She's of Satan's seed?

The phenomenon of 'Black Eyed Kids' is also duly noted. That is, since the 1950s, malevolent pale white 'kids' with black eyes have been making their haunted appearance. The typical scenario is they ask to come into your home, and people are terrified as they radiate sheer evil. Like vampires, they have to be invited in, suggesting some kind of legal rights. David Weatherly, author of 'Black Eyed Children' (2012), asserts the kids don't seem like 'kids'. It appears they also have supernatural powers as they can vanish and appear at will, which suggests they're interdimensional hybrids?

It's speculated the hybrid breeding programme is so Satan can boost his numbers for the looming Armageddon (as he was robbed with only a third of the angels). Maybe the black eyed kids have matured into black eyed adults? According to Dr Jacobs, they've completed their hybrid programme. Hence, abductions have largely stopped? They're ready for war?

As mentioned, Satan's army will be insane. In addition to the demonically enhanced super soldiers, hybrids, fallen angels and demons, myriad other astral freak uniques, and cyborgs etc, it's understood the giants are still around. Like, Dean Odle was told by a witch he delivered, that Genesis 6 is true, and Satanists are harbouring giants in underground caverns and bases until the great tribulation. So, the Days of Noah are here? The apocalypse could be the great unveiling of the nephilim?

Pastor Pete Valdez notably advised that God told him the aliens are coming from heaven, not from God's heaven, but the second heaven. He said, 'Behold they are coming. They are coming from heaven but not my heaven. They are coming to deceive and destroy many people. I am sending this strong delusion because man does not love my truth and doesn't want to acknowledge me or serve me'.

And Steve Quale recently advised (2020), according to his alphabet agency sources, that after the second or third plague hits us (plandemics), when the economy is thoroughly destroyed, the Pope will say a world prayer. He believes this will be Pope Francis. And 33 days after that, the aliens will be revealed. Hence, we need to know the truth to be prepared for the lie that is coming.

'When people cease to believe in God, they come not to believe in nothing, but in anything'. GK Chesterton

'It seems impossible that you could get something from nothing, but the fact that once there was nothing and now there is a universe is evident proof that you can'. Say what Bill Bryson?

18

Creation versus Evolution

It almost seems poetic that we're stardust. That we derived from exploding stars following the Big Bang some 13.8 billion years ago. This figure is derived from the distance and rate at which stars are moving away from each other, presuming they all started out at one place.

US theoretical physicist Lawrence Krauss said, 'The amazing thing is that every atom in your body came from a star that exploded. And, the atoms in your left hand probably came from a different star than your right hand. It really is the most poetic thing I know about physics: You are all stardust. You couldn't be here if stars hadn't exploded, because the elements – the carbon, nitrogen, oxygen, iron, all the things that matter for evolution – weren't created at the beginning of time. They were created in the nuclear furnaces of stars, and the only way they could get into your body is if those stars were kind enough to explode. So, forget Jesus. The stars died so that you could be here today'. So, Logos is superfluous?

As mentioned, the 'Big Bang' is the most widely accepted theory about the origin of everything. Amazingly, we were zero sized until in the millionth of a second, at the point of singularity, the universe exploded into being. The Big Bang describes the expansion of the universe from the explosion of our cosmic egg or primeval atom. We're told the universe expanded rapidly, producing electrons, neutrinos, photons and quarks. And over time, as matter continued colliding and interacting, the first simple elements were formed i.e. hydrogen and helium. Stars began to group forming the earliest galaxies, and some five billion years ago, within a cloud of gas in a spiral arm of the Milky Way galaxy, our sun formed. This new star gave birth to planets, moons, and asteroids.

So, we live on an insignificant blue marble, and our sun is just another ordinary average-sized yellow star. We're told stars are suns. Apparently, our galaxy is home to four billion stars, and there's more than a hundred billion galaxies, so our insignificance cannot be overstated.

It's noted, our sun has enough fuel (hydrogen) to last another five billion years, and like any other star, when it depletes its reserves, it dies. But in its death, it gives life, as it seeds heavier elements required for life. With the death of large stars, which explode as 'supernovas', the blast produces elements including silver and gold.

But further, these massive dead stars can become black holes. Apparently, we have a super massive black hole at the centre of our galaxy, and all galaxies harbour a black hole at their centre. Black holes are however precarious as nothing can escape from them (not even light) because their gravitational pull is so strong. Black holes become even more massive by munching matter. Their cuisine is mainly clouds of gas and dust, but sometimes they munch whole stars.

But moreover, the Big Bang theory doesn't work without the Nebular hypothesis. That is, our solar system formed from a nebula cloud, which consists of dust and gas. And this theory was introduced by Swedenborg (1688-1772), who received this information during a séance. So, that's interesting. As without the Nebula hypothesis there would be no us?

The evolution of solar systems leads to evolution on planets. Like, we evolved on Earth from bacteria. Apparently, fish became reptiles then mammals then man, with the whole process taking about 1000 million years. Fortunately, the dinosaurs were wiped out before we arrived. Apparently, an enormous asteroid (10km wide) took care of them in the Gulf of Mexico 66 million years ago. If we imagine the history of earth condensed to one day, we humans appear two seconds to midnight.

With regards to the origin of life i.e. the 'chance' of the correct arrangements of molecules, amino acids, enzymes etc, Sir Fred Hoyle (1915-2001), British mathematician and astronomer, who was an atheist but absolutely disbelieved in Darwinism, said 'the chance that higher life forms might have emerged in this way is comparable with the chance that a tornado sweeping through a junk-yard might assemble a Boeing 747 from the materials therein'. Hoyle notably coined the term 'Big Bang' in 1952 to mock the idea and ironically it stuck.

The 'Goldie locks' situation aka 'just right' conditions is also duly noted i.e. not too hot or too cold but rather 'just right'. The survival of the Earth requires an incredibly delicate balance of parameters. If the Earth was 5% closer to the sun, the water would boil off from the oceans, and if it was 1% further away, the oceans would freeze over. The 'anthropic principle' is notably the idea that it's as if the Earth was skilfully designed or balanced for humankind.

US physicist and astronomer Laureate Arno Penzias, whose theory on 'cosmic microwave background radiation' helped establish the Big Bang theory of cosmology, stated in 1992, 'Astronomy leads us to a unique event, a universe which was created out of nothing, one with the very delicate balance needed to provide exactly the right conditions to permit life, and one which has an underlying (one might say 'supernatural') plan'.

Astronomer George Greenstein stated in his book 'The Symbolic Universe' (1988), 'As we survey all the evidence, the thought insistently arises that some supernatural agency must be involved. Is it possible that suddenly, without intending to, we have stumbled upon scientific proof of the existence of a Supreme Being? Was it God who stepped in and so providentially crafted the cosmos for our benefit?' (p.27).

Lest we forget the violation of the first rule of thermodynamics, namely, the total amount of energy in the universe is constant. It can't be created or destroyed. But rather it moves into form, through form and out of form. And yet a phenomenal amount of energy was required for the Big Bang. So, that's perplexing? It's perplexing that an explosion of energy suddenly appeared from nowhere for no reason? At least the Greek philosophers were sensible enough to believe in a Prime Mover. Someone or something had to get the show on the road?

However, that quandary aside, it seems science has figured out the origins of life. There is no place (need?) for Creator God or His mathematics? Rather than creation (top down processing), science advocates that blind laws of evolution (bottom-up processing) account for nature's exquisite complexity, which includes the brain, the most complex of all matter in the universe. Consciousness, which questions the nature of existence, is supposedly the product of natural selection, of evolution, a set of successful mistakes. From chemicals (that appeared from nowhere), came us and our brains, and our curious consciousness.

Vernon (2012) encapsulates, 'that out of this primordial miracle emerged first energy, then particles, then atoms, then simple molecules, then dust, then nebulae, then stars, then heavier atoms, then complex molecules, then planets and galaxies, then stable environments hospitable to life, then life, then complex life, then conscious life, then self-conscious life – then us' (p.91).

And this material philosophy is taught as fact? Dawkins said, 'it is absolutely safe to say that if you meet somebody who claims not to believe in evolution, that person is ignorant, stupid or insane (or wicked, but I'd rather not consider that)'. He also said, 'life has no design, no purpose, no evil and no good, nothing but blind merciless existence'. But it seems there is good and evil? And these are powerful forces in our reality?

Contrary to Dawkins' dogmatic assertion, the fact is no-one knows why we're here or how we got here. It's theoretical (like black holes). And Darwinism is not a scientific fact but a weakly supported theory. Arguably for nothing to turn into something requires a creator. But creation is not considered a viable option, despite the overwhelming evidence e.g. human brain. Alford (1996) concedes, 'whilst the brain is the Achilles Heel of the evolutionists, so the Sumerian technology is the Achilles heel of the historians arguments'. It appears we're not that smart without the Watchers.

Both Psalm 14:1 and Psalm 53:1 tell us, 'The fool says in his heart, 'There is no God''. The majesty of our world arguably precipitates an exceptional artist. The variety in nature is mind-blowing e.g. zebras, tigers, crocodiles, baboons, kangaroos, hedgehogs, mice, sharks, whales, coupled with their social, including playful, and laborious behaviours. It could be argued that nature's complexity, her intoxicating beauty, is proof of intelligent design? Einstein notably said, 'science without religion is lame, and religion without science is blind'. It's understood he 'knew' better.

The idealist view is that God created and sustains the universe. He commanded whatever, and so it was, it came to be. The Bible consistently, from beginning to end, states the universe and everything in it was created by God, who has infinite power and wisdom. John 1:3 states, 'Without Him was not anything made that was made'. Colossians 1:16 states, 'For by Him all things were created, that are in heaven, and that are in earth, visible and invisible'.

And Isaiah 44:24 states, 'The LORD, your Redeemer and Creator, says: 'I am the LORD, who made all things. I alone stretched out the heavens. By myself, I made the earth and everything in it'. God tells us how He set the foundation for the earth, and how He laid the corner stone. How he measured everything, and told the proud waves to stay, and shut up the sea with doors, and so forth.

But moreover, in Isaiah 40:22, we're told 'He sits enthroned above the circle of the earth; it's dwellers are like grasshoppers. He stretches out the heavens like a curtain, and spreads them out like a tent to live in'. God's word essentially tells us we live in a snow-globe, which is set on pillars.

There's over 200 Bible verses that refer to the earth as being stationary and flat with a dome overhead. And God has the best seat in the house (heaven) to watch the show unfold. As discussed, the Bible also tells us about a hollow earth, which is contrary to the assumption that it's solid? Perhaps scientists could drill deeper than eight miles to check if hell is below us?

So, whilst 'science' tells us the Earth spins on its axis at 1000mph, and around the sun at 66,600mph, and our solar system orbits the Milky Way at about 500,000mph, the Bible teaches the Earth is stationary and immovable. So, it doesn't spin around the sun. On the contrary, the sun, moon and stars orbit the earth. This is what the ancients believed, which is logical, since this is how it appears.

The sun and moon rise in the east and set in the west, every day (scientific determinism). It doesn't feel like we're zipping through the universe at insane speeds, and they observed the same stars etc, which wouldn't happen if we were. Stars follow precise paths. They rotate around Polaris, the North Star, which never moves.

Planets were called wandering stars (the word planet comes from the Greek word planetes, which means 'wanderer') because they look like stars, but they wandered off track. Like, the Book of Enoch tells us, seven stars disobediently wandered off their prescribed course. And these angelic beings will be punished. It seems these seven stars, which coincide with the planets in the solar system, are the angelic beings' initiates engage with during their astral trip to the spheres.

'Science' tells us that planets are much smaller than stars, but they look the same size because they're so close to us i.e. inside our solar system. We're also told that planets don't produce their own light, but rather they reflect the light of the sun in the same way our moon does.

So, we trusted our senses until five hundred years ago, when the Jesuits told us otherwise. As touched on, Jesuits were behind the heliocentric model in the 1500s, and they got Polish Jesuit priest and astronomer Nicolaus Copernicus (1473-1543) onboard. Copernicus's beliefs came from Hermeticism, which taught that planets revolve round the sun. Copernicus referred to Hermes Trismegistus in his quote about the sun.

Thus, 'In the middle of all sits the Sun enthroned. In this most beautiful temple could we place this luminary in any better position from which he can illuminate the whole at once? He is rightly called the Lamp, the Mind, the Ruler of the Universe; Hermes Trismegistus names him the Visible God, Sophocles' Electra calls him All-Seeing. So, the sun sits upon a royal throne ruling his children the planets which circle around him'.

So, the Egyptians (credited with Hermeticism) believed the earth goes round the sun millennia before Copernicus. Although it appears Hinduism likes to take the credit for heliocentrism. It's understood Copernicus revived the heliocentric cosmology of Pythagoras (570-495BC), who maintained celestial spheres spin round a stationary sun, but stars remain the same. Hoyle states the maths is the same whether the sun moves round the earth or vice versa.

It's understood Pythagoras was initiated into the mystery schools (he could apparently be in two places at the same time). It's said he learned cabala from Jews who were exiled in Babylon. So, he worshipped Apollo, and believed in reincarnation and transmigration of souls. The Pythagoreans were Gnostics. They believed the soul was a divine and immortal being, imprisoned in the material body. They were familiar with astral travel. Apparently, Pythagoras conceived of the Milky Way as a vast river or troop of spirits, which corroborates with the biblical view that stars are angels? It's also noted, that Luther preached a flat earth and stood against, (warned us about), Copernicus, his contemporary.

As touched on, hermetic philosophy inspired scientism. It influenced Newton, Kepler, Aristotle, Pythagoras, Da Vinci, Galileo, Plato, and Copernicus. The cabala (Zohar) has also been hugely influential. It teaches 'the whole world rolls around like a ball, so that some people are above and some people are below'. And there's no such thing as death. But rather, every living thing is composed of atoms, described as miniature points of light. Atoms are energy and these particles are the building blocks of everything in life.

Thus, cabala is particle theory enshrined in particle physics. It's said scientists are making quantum theory fit cabala e.g. quarks, neutrinos. Cabala is being written into quantum theory, as we'll get to. The 'solar system' is a cabala construct. It's not in the Bible.

Copernicus notably died the day his book 'On the Revolutions of the Celestial Spheres' was published in 1543. It's also noted, that he dedicated his book to Pope Paul III (1534-49). And thus, whilst the Catholic Church supported Copernicus to publish his work and spread it worldwide, they placed Galileo (1564-1642) under house arrest for nine years (until his death), for espousing the same heliocentric belief. They didn't care for his undermining the biblical (geocentric) view. Three hundred years later, the Catholic Church conceded he was right.

It was notably Jesuit trained priest Georges Lemaitre who invented the Big Bang (although he called it the 'Big Noise'). As mentioned, contrary to God's word, the Catholic Church endorses the Big Bang and evolution. It's purported these were His methods, so God's the Prime Mover.

Like other initiated ancient Romans and Greeks, Aristotle believed in a globe Earth. He watched ships sail away and deducted they went over the curve. He observed the hull disappeared then the mast (sails). As it transpires however, ships can be brought back over the curve with a camera zoom. The vanishing point is resurrected. So, they haven't gone over the curve.

Indeed, people are struggling to find the curvature of the Earth, which is eight inches per mile squared (the curvature in one mile squared is 666 feet). Hence, the explosion of Flat Earth theorists since 2015 because what we've been told doesn't add up. Like, there doesn't appear to be a curve in Kansas for 400 miles. It's literally flatter than a pancake. And the Salt Flats in Bolivia are flat for thousands of miles. Test after test has been done evidencing the flat earth. Like, weather balloon footage from 120,000 feet reveals a tabletop flat Earth.

This corroborates with Auguste Piccard, pre-NASA scientist, who in 1931 went ten miles high (into the stratosphere) and discovered the flat earth. He observed, 'it seemed a flat disk with upturned edges'. Three Russian scientists (also in the 1930s) went 11.8 miles high above Earth and claimed they couldn't see the curve. It seems the UN flag, which features a world map surrounded by two olive branches, is a picture of the earth? They hide it in plain sight?

And this supports Dr Samuel Birley Rowbotham's (1816-1884) findings (based on his decades-long scientific studies of earth), namely, the earth is a flat disk centred at the North Pole and bounded along its southern edge by a wall of ice, with the sun, moon, planets, and stars only a few thousand miles above the surface of the earth. Apparently, the celestial bodies are only about 3000 miles (4,800km) away, and the glass firmament about 3,100 miles (5,000km).

As mentioned, the ice wall is apparently circa 200 feet tall. Captain James Cook was the first to sight the great ice barrier in 1772, which forms the seaward boundary of Antarctica. The 'Great Ice Barrier' was confirmed by a British Expedition to Antarctica (1839-1843) led by James Clark Ross. He traced the coastline for 500 miles southwards, where he encountered the great ice barrier, terminating seawards in a sheer wall of ice from 180-200 feet.

It's also highlighted that 71% of the Earth is water, and water always finds it level. Water doesn't curve? It's understood, if 'they' can lie to us about 9/11 and the moon landings, they can lie to us about our cosmology. We're such trusting sheeple.

It's like we're told the sun is 93 million miles away, and the moon is 239,000 miles away, yet they appear far closer. And whilst they look the same size (as shown in eclipses), the sun is apparently 400 times bigger than the moon, but it just so happens to be 400 times farther away, so they look the same size. So, that's convenient. It's like planets look the same size as stars, but they're not?

Our moon is allegedly the result of a Mars sized object being slammed into Earth about 4.4 million years ago. The collision generated enough material to create the moon from the debris. This is known as the 'Big Whack theory' (LOL). And our sun is nothing like the stars? We don't get a suntan from the stars? Rather than twinkling above, vibrating pulsating lights, as they appear, they're allegedly gaseous balls light years away.

It's noted, the speed of light is 186,000 miles per second, and it takes eight minutes for the sun's light to reach Earth (which shows how far away the sun is). A light year is the distance light travels in a year, which is circa six trillion miles. So, light from the stars takes an insane amount of time to reach us?

Alternatively, the Bible tells us that God made the sun, moon, and stars, and placed them in the firmament (our sun is not a star). Rather than a random Big Bang, we're told that in the beginning 'the earth was empty, a formless mass cloaked in darkness. And the Spirit of God moved upon the face of the waters' (Genesis 1:2). It's noted, the face of the waters alludes to a flat earth.

So, there was dark matter/energy, water, God's Spirit (energy), and there was sound energy (frequencies), as God called creation into existence. It's believed God used the Enochian language (22 letters) to command the creation of the earth. Apparently, angels use Enochian language, as did Adam before the fall. And Queen Elizabeth's occult advisor John Dee learned the Enochian language. Apparently, angels (presumably fallen) dictated their divine language, which has its own grammar and syntax. Like the Biblical version of events, ancient Egyptians believed that Ra, the sun God, created the cosmos using words of power. And for Hindus, Krishna played all reality into being with his flute.

We're told that on the first day, God said 'Let there be light', and there was light (energy). He separated light, from darkness (dark energy?). He called the light 'day', and the darkness 'night', and together they make up a day. So, space and time were created on the same day. And it only took God six days to create our world, not billions of years.

It's noted, whilst Christians seem divided regarding whether or not creation happened in six days, it's equally said that if God wanted to make the universe in a second, He could (He's omnipotent). It seems people try to reconcile evolution with scripture? Like, it's suggested that God's not under the dictates of our physical (spacetime) reality. He had a different timeframe, and otherwise 24 hour days could be 'periods'. Like, we could be in astral for what feels like minutes, yet several hours have passed in the physical world.

As mentioned, we're told 'a day is like a thousand years with the Lord, and a thousand years are like a day' (2 Peter 3:8). So, six days of creation could have been six thousand years? However, we need billions of years for evolution, not six thousand (LOL). So, time passes differently for God. His timing is not the same as ours. He doesn't seem to have the same sense of urgency?

God creates both the spatial and temporal dimensions under which the universe operates. He created time (when He created space) and thus God was acting before time began, confirming that He exists in at least two dimensions of time. It's understood God exists outside our time and space, as He knows the end from the beginning. His-Story is written yet we have freewill. So, we choose our choice, but He knows already.

It's also noted, whilst most creationist scientists believe God's word about creation, (as opposed to the absurdity of evolution), most don't believe in the flat earth also described. That's too outlandish? It's said the 'flat earth' is the mother of all conspiracies.

So, there was also a ton of water, which God separated on the second day, using a firmament. It's possible this was the remnant of a former existence, but we'll get to this. As mentioned, the firmament is our dome, ceiling. And there's water above the firmament and water below on Earth. It's understood that omniscient God knew there was a Flood in the post, and the heavens would be opened?

Then God gathered the waters together, beneath the sky (the expanse under the dome), into one place (contained by 200-300 foot ice walls?) to allow dry land to appear. This was the one land mass pre-flood (Atlantis?). The next day, He furnished the earth with seed bearing trees, plants, grass etc.

So, it wasn't until the fourth day that God made the sun, moon and stars, and placed them in the firmament, which He called heaven. So, life didn't come from stars. God created these lights to shine down on Earth, and separate day from night. The sun is the greater one, which presides during the day; the moon is lesser one, which presides through the night. It's noted, the sun is a hot light and the moon is a cold light, so they're a different type of light (the sun doesn't illuminate the moon?).

And together with the stars, they're signs to mark off the seasons, the days, and the years (hence, their specific paths). God then went on to create fish, birds, animals, and humans, on days five and six, before resting on the Sabbath. He made His world, and put His feet upon it, like a footstool.

We're told the dome or firmament is made of solid crystal glass (blue stone?), and God's heaven is above the waters above the firmament. Hence, Nimrod endeavoured to build a tower to reach heaven, and the Soviet and US attempted to smash the firmament with high altitude nukes? They understood that God and heaven are not far away?

It's suggested the firmament is electromagnetic, which corroborates with Tesla's view of an electric universe. Like, the sun, moon and stars electromagnetically circle Polaris, above the North Pole. So, it's not gravity. And according to God's word, the earth was made before the celestial bodies. Thus, they're not required for gravitational pull. It's purported that Tesla discovered the dome in 1899, which is seen by rainbows and lightning storms.

Tesla believed that electricity powered the universe. Like, electromagnetic currents flow into stars and power them like light bulbs. He believed that electromagnetic energy fills all space. The ionosphere is sparkling with electrical energy, which could be tapped. The earth has a giant electrical generator. So, space is not void but rather it consists of ether or plasma. The electromagnetic currents from plasma power the universe, and they cause structures to move. According to plasma cosmology, 99.99% of the universe is plasma. Like, interstellar and intergalactic networks of planets, meteors, suns, moons, and stars are all plasma.

Plasma cosmology is similar to the 'electric universe' theory. Plasma is the fourth state of matter. For example, H2O exists as ice, water, steam, and plasma. The plasma state is when hydrogen and oxygen exist as separate elements. Plasma is formed when ionised gases become electrically conductive, which means electrical currents can flow through them. Plasma is found in low pressure, like upper earth atmosphere, and at very high temperatures. Like, fire and lightning are forms of plasma.

For Tesla, the ether is a medium or perfect fluid that wets everything. It's like the moon, sun and stars float along in plasma or super fluid. They're carried by electrically charged ether currents. Hence, it looks like gentle waves traverse the moon? And stars sparkle? And magnetic North Pole is at the heart of events. As mentioned, it's believed the Axis Mundi, the interdimensional world tree, is there.

It seems the super fluid is helium? Helium cools to a liquid state when it's super freezing (-269 degrees), like up in 'space'. But helium is not just a liquid but a super liquid, which is immune to friction. Thus, unlike liquid in a cup, that will circulate around until it stops, if we move liquid helium, it keeps moving. When stirred, a super fluid forms vortices that continue to rotate indefinitely. So, this could explain why the moon, stars, and sun are forever in motion?

As touched on, it's relayed that circa 73 miles high is the ether, as opposed to the dome. It seems to be a dense layer of blue air. Apparently, Piccard trapped samples of upper 'blue air'. The ether, which is the upper regions of 'space', is a medium for light and radio waves to travel in. It seems the ether is the ionosphere, which HAARP uses? This electromagnetic energy field is like a signal dish. It's noted, the physical ether is not to be confused with 'spiritual ether'. The ether explains electricity, magnetism and light. Einstein however denied the ether, and replaced it with his theory of special relativity, as we'll get to.

We're given a picture of what the universe is like, but maybe we've been lied to? Like, we're shown photos of our blue marble, from alleged Apollo missions, which are created by artists (hence the massive distortions over the years), who admit they're all photo-shopped because they have to be. And the artists create a perfect ball, despite scientists alleging that we live on an oblate spheroid, that's chubbier from the waist down (like a pear). Like, footage of the moon landing had to be faked? God forbid we find out there's UFOs parked there.

It seems no one knew the shape of the earth until the Apollo mission in 1969 (who were caught faking the pictures). Like, a declassified CIA document (from the Russians) stated in 1948 'the shape of the earth is not known'. Dean Odle notably exposed a mountain of declassified government documents and scientific technical manuals, from the Army, Air Force, CIA, Navy, NASA, and Russia, which admit we live on a flat non-rotating Earth. All maths equations are based on this premise. As highlighted, how can planes land safely if the Earth's moving? Or how do missiles and rockets etc work? In addition to referencing the flat earth, these documents also refer to the firmament.

Like other 'Flat Earthers', Odle highlights the Michelson-Morley experiment which proved the earth is flat and doesn't move in 1887. Odle states, Einstein made the earth move when all the experiments showed that it didn't move. It's like magic?

Fundamentally, the heliocentric view got rid of heaven and hell. As mentioned, the telescope established that there was no heaven up there. God is nowhere to be seen? But rather we're adrift in an insanely vast and dark cosmos. No one gives a rat's ass what we're doing (besides the aliens). We're unimportant, insignificant, which is what the evil one wants us to think.

Alternatively, the geocentric enclosed cosmology model brings God tangibly close. He's just up there, above the firmament. Acts 17:27 confirms God is not far away from us. Perhaps Father God is only a few thousand miles away? And He created us. So, we're not an accident, a freak of nature.

The heliocentric model relies on gravity but maybe gravity isn't what we think it is? We're told Isaac Newton (1642-1727) got a bump on the head from a falling apple and came up with the idea of gravity in 1666. He deducted that the force that pulls planets to the sun is the same force that pulls apples to the ground.

He theorised that planets orbit the sun because gravitational forces between bodies depend on distance and mass, where the heavier and closer the stars are, the stronger the gravitational pull i.e. mass to mass. The further apart the bodies are the lesser the force. Gravitational pull (the attraction between objects with mass) is not however observed anywhere except theoretically i.e. to allow for massive planets to orbit in space. It's understood Newton had to create the theory of gravity to make the heliocentric model work.

Newton's laws of motion followed on from Galileo's law of inertia. Inertia refers to the resistance of matter to change its velocity unless acted upon by a force (like, fluid ether is governed by inertia). Hence, celestial bodies remain in constant motion, in the alleged vacuum of space. We travel at a constant speed, in our solar system. Galileo surmised that weight has something to do with gravity. He observed that weight and gravity, as forces, bring a body down.

But maybe the apple fell, not because of gravity but simply because of weight. It's heavier than air, unlike a helium balloon. It's also highlighted that if gravity is so powerful it curbs expansive oceans, it doesn't add up that birds and balloons fly, fish can swim, and we're not slapped to the ground? If we're on a flat stationary plane (not planet) we don't need the theory of gravity?

Interestingly, Galileo died the year Newton, his scientific successor, was born. It's also recalled that Newton was an alchemist (he spent twenty-five years studying alchemy). It's said he had bi-polar and at times of depression, he hallucinated and had conversations with absent people. He believed in the Great Architect of the Universe, and it's said he acquired ideas like an occultist. As mentioned, he believed the secrets of life are encoded in numerical forms in the fabric of nature e.g. golden ratio.

In addition to gravity and motion, Newton also pioneered optics aka the study of light and its interaction with matter. In 1666 he used a prism to break visible white light into a rainbow of colours. It's understood that light exists in both waveform (the shortest wavelengths are blue and the longest are red) and as tiny particles of energy called photons. Thus, light has wave-particle duality. And he invented the cat-flap for good measure. However, I digress.

So, we have two very different cosmologies, which we can scientifically test. Like, people have consistently evidenced the flat stationary earth? Moreover, whilst it's assumed that science is by its nature objective, value free and without suppositions, this is not strictly true. Science operates from a secular atheist worldview, and this viewpoint, pre-theoretical framework, encompasses how life is interpreted. There is no God for evolutionists, and therefore creation is not possible. And yet (ironically) scientism is steeped in Hermeticism.

Thus, it's not the evidence that's in dispute, but rather the interpretation of it. Science can be interpreted to fit either argument. It does not prove the theory of evolution and on the contrary, it can disprove this theory, substantiating the theory of creation and belief in intelligent design. Both theories are belief systems based on how we interpret evidence, (or what we choose to believe in), and neither theory is science in itself.

In essence, the existence of God cannot be proven and hence it is an act of faith, but equally not believing in God is also an act of faith. Russell Brand (2012) concedes, 'Science requires faith the way religion does. Science requires acceptance of metaphor, just the way religion does' (p.63). Scientism is a religion and philosophy. People have faith in theories. It's also said, for those who believe in God, no proof is necessary, whereas for those who don't believe, no proof is possible.

Science is rational in the sense that scientific investigations, experimentation and observation, become of value when they're rational. 'Facts' are accommodated to fit theories, where pragmatically 'the truth is what works'. But scientific facts can change. As Paul McKenna said, 'And even when science does seem to have the answers, the answers only last until the next Newton or Leibniz or Einstein comes along and radically revises the entire intellectual edifice on which they were based' (p.63).

It's also noted, that science is by definition, repeatable, observable and provable, as opposed to pseudo-science, which is theoretical. There's a difference between experiments in labs and theorising about the origins of life, as the latter is conjecture not fact. As touched on, the Bible warns about pseudo-science or 'science falsely so called' (1 Timothy 6: 20). Like, theoretical physics and evolution?

Dr Ainsley Chalmers, author/researcher, said, 'People get sucked in by science because of the success they see with experimental science. Historical science is, however, completely different and not something you can hang your hat on'. He also said, 'Comparing one of our cells to a 747 jet is like comparing the largest supercomputer with a safety pin. The 747 has an army of designers so isn't it logical for cells to have a designer called God? The Bible calls our creator Jesus Christ. The whole of creation from the huge universe to our tiny cells cries out the existence of our creator God'.

Albert Einstein (1879-1955), (who Russell Brand referred to as 'bedheaded genius' p.65), acknowledged that we can observe and theorise, but we can never know. He said, 'As far as the laws of mathematics refer to reality, they are not certain, and as far as they are certain, they do not refer to reality'. And further, 'the more I study science, the more I believe in God'. And yet, it seems Einstein was one of the shady cabal, and was set up to distract us from Tesla? His research also deliberately eclipsed Michelson and Morley.

It's understood Jewish Einstein was familiar with the cabala, like Newton before him. And they were both members of the Royal Society aka 'the Invisible College', which is the oldest (founded in 1660) and most prestigious scientific Masonic institution in the world. Indeed, Newton was president. As mentioned, Vallee and Hynek claim the Invisible College work on UFOs.

The Royal Society was created by King Charles II to understand the scientific wonders created by the Great Architect of the Universe. Virtually all the early members of the Royal Society were masons (they were occultists practising magic, alchemy and astrology). It's said the Royal Society founders were the first scientists and the last of the sorcerers. Sir Francis Bacon was also a member.

The Royal Society was dedicated to the scientific understanding of nature and divine revelation, which combined became natural philosophy. Thus, they propagated to the masses the cosmos was created without God. Mystical philosophy became material science i.e. heliocentrism. In addition to the British royal family, Charles Darwin and Stephen Hawking were also members. Thus, it's posited that scientific communities are governed by occult doctrines emanating out of the Royal Society, which took instructions from ancient Snake Brotherhoods.

It's noted, the two main pillars of modern physics are Einstein's theory of general relativity (1915), which describes the force of gravity and the large-scale structure of the universe. And quantum mechanics, which deals with phenomenon on an extremely small scale e.g. a millionth of a millionth of an inch. And the scientific endeavour is to reconcile these two theories to provide a single unifying theory to account for the mechanics of the universe.

It's said modern physics has ruptured our intuitive understanding of the world. Like, Einstein's theory abolished absolute time and space, and the concept of 'solid objects' was shattered by atomic physics. So, we'll look at these 'two pillars'. As mentioned, apparently Einstein figured out his theory of relativity from a dream.

Thus, Einstein theorised that time is not separate from space, but rather they're different aspects of the same 4D space-time continuum. So, there's 3D space, and time is the fourth dimension, ergo 4D. Space emerged from the Big Bang, then time emerged from space, and time came into being. Time is measured by celestial bodies moving in space. Like, a year is a 365 days journey around the sun?

All objects are therefore related temporally and spatially. And motion is relative to the observer's motion, because everything is relative and always moving. And the reason we don't feel like we're zipping through space is because of constant motion. It's like being in a car, it feels stationary. We're *travelling without moving*.

Einstein proposed that time is affected by matter. Like, it slows down near massive bodies, like the earth, or the sun, or a black hole. Time is likened to a river that flows at different speeds in different places e.g. the speed of flowing water will slow down around large boulders in a river. So, time flows at different speeds in different places in the universe.

And it seems he was right, that time passes slower the closer we are to Earth, as apparently clocks on GPS satellites advance faster than identical clocks here on Earth. The effect is minimal, like one billionth of a second every day, but it's enough to throw the positions measured on Earth's surface off by six miles a day. Thus, GPS have a built-in correction program to compensate for this 'time dilation'.

But moreover, contrary to Newton's laws of gravity, Einstein contended that gravity was the result of space-time curvature. That is, time and space is like a fabric that objects move along. And heavy objects distort this fabric. Like, a boulder on a trampoline. They cause space-time to bend. So, whilst objects seem attracted to each other, they're actually following the curvature of space-time created by large objects.

Thus, we're not pulled towards the sun by gravity, as there's no such force. But rather we follow curves created by the sun's presence. It's summarised as space-time tells matter how to move and matter tells space-time how to curve. It's noted, light doesn't go straight, like from a laser, beside something massive, but curves. Maybe its aura causes the curve?

It also seems pertinent to note, Einstein's legendary e=mc2 equation. He deducted that nothing can travel faster than the speed of light, because the faster an object moves, the more kinetic energy aka mass it produces, slowing it down. So, the increased relativistic mass (m) of a body times the speed of light squared (c2) is equal to the kinetic energy (e) of that body. Thus, energy and mass are interchangeable. As mentioned, its purported astral travel happens at the speed of light, as mass-less 'light' beings can travel at the speed of light?

The idea that time passes slower beside massive objects also suggests the possibility of time travel. Like, we could shuttle off to a heavier planet for a few years and come back younger than our peers. But we can't because it would take too long to get to the nearest heavier body (on conventional rockets but not on supersonic flying saucers?). We would have to teleport ourselves there. It's alleged this 'Star Trek' technology exists. No danger. It's said this explains how ETs can visit us from civilisations light years away.

Perhaps we could go back in time if we could travel faster than the speed of light? Respectively, Hawking presents a poem, namely, 'there was a young lady of Wight, who travelled much faster than light. She departed one day, in a relative way, and arrived on the previous night'.

Suffice to say, the prospect of time travel is a mind bender, particularly when it comes to black holes, linked by wormholes, which connect to distant regions of the universe. It seems black holes are like the abyss. Hence, demons don't want to go there as it's game over? They're trapped?

Maybe black holes are physical and metaphysical? Maybe the conceptions we're given of the physical universe represent the inner workings of the spirit world. Like, wormholes link spiritual (unknown) dimensions. They're like portals, enabling inter-dimensional travel. Maybe wormholes are the meta-physical chutes (tunnels) people fall down on their way to hell?

So, regarding space-time, we're told that, just as we can move forwards and backwards in space, so we can in time. Like, spirits can move forwards and backwards in time, and take objects back? Angels can take people on trips to the past and future? Physicists inform that none of the known laws of physics forbid time-travel and reverse time travel should be possible. However, it's also noted that time travel can result in paradoxes. Like, if we went back in time to shoot our self, there wouldn't be a future self, so who shot our self?

It's highlighted that mathematical solutions become viable theories to account for existence, regardless of how wild they are. Thus, any universe that physicists can get to work out on paper could theoretically exist. The 'mathematical democracy principle' notably states that any universe that is mathematically possible has equal possibility of actually existing. So, if the maths works, it's peachy. The result is outlandish theories that are counterintuitive. Like, the multiverse theory or Elvis Theory, which suggests a boundless collection of parallel worlds full of innumerable versions of us. So, Elvis is alive somewhere?

As Tesla commented, 'Today's scientists have substituted mathematics for experiments, and they wander off through equation after equation, and eventually build a structure which has no relation to reality'. It's said this was a dig at Einstein. Apparently, Tesla said the theory of relativity was foolishness. Maybe light years are BS? Maybe we should trust our God given senses and sense? Like, twinkling stars are nothing like the sun. And the sun and moon are the same size, and they're not far away.

It's highlighted, the trouble with the electric universe theory, unlike current models, is that it can't answer the size, age and origin of the universe. This however makes sense if God created the universe, so God knows.

God also said we wouldn't be able to know the size. Like, how far away the firmament is? Whereas the Big Bang theory gives us our roots. Existence can be traced back to 13.8 billion years ago?

Chuck Missler notably highlights ten dimensions, which he asserts Jewish scholar Nachmanides (1194-1270) discovered by studying the first chapter of Genesis. He concluded that four dimensions were 'knowable' in the physical universe, namely, space and time, and six were 'unknowable'. This 'string theory' was only discovered in the twentieth century. As discussed, creation was fractured at the fall. The physical universe was separated from the spiritual universe. A partition was put in place. So, the six unknowable dimensions are the spirit world?

The second law of thermodynamics was also introduced when God cursed creation, namely, entropy. Hence, everything breaks down, rots and dies, including us. It's highlighted that cosmic evolution, the idea that things get bigger and better, violates this entropic law. The breakdown of structure directly contradicts the theory of evolution. However, we'll get to this.

It gets fuzzier, literally, in the quantum world. Quantum notably comes from Latin quantus meaning 'how much'. As mentioned, atom's particles, namely, electrons, protons, and neutrons, are the building blocks of everything in the universe. And sub-the-atom energy is forever in flux. At this subatomic level, all things are in a perpetual and indeterminate 'fuzzy' motion. As Black (2010) highlights, adepts can see down to the atomic level (p.463). Like, Dr Kubler Ross.

Hence, the idea of solid matter is an illusion, as there's nothing solid about the universe. But rather, matter consists of energy that vibrates at a certain level. Tesla said, 'if you want to know how the universe works, think in terms of energy, frequency and vibrations'. What we perceive as hard matter is mostly empty space with a pattern of energy running through it. Atoms are apparently 99.9% empty space. According to Einstein, we consist of approximately 7x10 (to the power of 18) joules of potential energy, which is enough to explode with the force of 30 very large hydrogen bombs.

So, rather than the classical notion of independent 'elementary parts', quantum mechanics proposes the universe is really a unified, dynamic inseparable whole. The universe is a matrix/web of energy patterns that are constantly moving and changing i.e. atoms bang into each other, unify and reassemble. So, there's no death in the real sense but rather atoms/energy morph into something else, which obeys the first rule of thermodynamics.

In his book 'The Tao of Physics' (1976), Fritjof Capra draws a parallel between modern physics and eastern mysticism. The quantum interconnectedness of the whole universe alludes to a basic oneness, which enshrines eastern philosophy. The idea is that we're all one, and the sun is at the centre of our existence?

It's also highlighted that quantum physics debunks materialism, and evidences idealism. It seems consciousness is intrinsically in the mix. Like, the double slit experiment, called 'the most beautiful experiment', demonstrates how the observer affects the observed.

Thus, a series of single photons (light particles) are fired at a solid plate that has two slits. On the other side of the solid plate, there's a photographic plate to record what comes through the slits. If we don't observe which slit a photon passes through, it appears to interfere with itself, and behaves as a wave travelling through both slits at the same time. But if we observe the slits, the interference pattern disappears, and each photon travels through only one of the slits. As Russell Brand (2014) asserts, (when observed) 'the kinky little bastards behave as particles'. It seems particles don't have a location in space and time until observed?

With idealism, (as discussed), everything we experience is in the mind. Consciousness is the only real thing? And like the Buddhist belief, that nothing exists unless there is a consciousness to apprehend it, it's suggested the cosmos doesn't exist without some type of consciousness witnessing it. The universe may be an entity and aware of itself?

Perhaps the primeval atom contained consciousness, 'universal mind', which accounts for creation? Intelligence is seeded into matter. Like, seeds have intelligence. They respond to the sun (apparently light in the red wavelength promotes germination whereas blue light inhibits it). Consciousness, (intelligence), is inherent in matter. And we embody that consciousness. We're intrinsically part of cosmic consciousness? We're a point of Infinite Awareness? A point of light trapped in crud matter? As highlighted, it's said quantum mechanics is repackaged mysticism (pantheism).

It's noted, that a popular theory is that we live in a holographic universe, which could reconcile quantum mechanics and general relativity. Thus, despite its apparent materiality, it's suggested that reality is a hologram, a 3D projection from somewhere else i.e. a dimension beyond space and time. Our 3D reality, or rather 4D space-time reality, could be a representation of an underlying 2D object stored on the cosmic horizon which creates the illusion of a 3D universe.

Like, information is read from CDs, and the information has no mass. It's like we're in a computer simulation. We're holograms in the matrix? It makes Bluebeam technology seem ironic? Like, Plato illustrated in his 'Allegory of the Cave', that which we assume to be real could quite easily turn out to be an illusion.

But moreover, it seems spiritual entities (including Ascended Masters) want us to believe this? Hence, Michael Talbot (1953-1992), author of 'The Holographic Principle' (1991), was telepathically given this information from ETs (apparently ETs abducted him during the 1980s). And David Icke heard a female voice talking for five hours about the illusory nature of reality, having ingested ayahuasca in Brazil in 2003.

Icke concedes that physical reality is holographic and we're living in a virtual reality universe. He recognises that someone or something must have programmed the universe. He agrees the Big Bang theory is nonsense, and there's no evidence for the whack theory. He also highlights that different dimensions or frequencies accounts for why UFOs and ghosts etc appear and disappear. But we know very little about these dimensions?

Scientists report that 70% of the universe is dark energy and 25% is dark matter. We're told the universe expands between 5% and 10% every billion years, and this is propelled by dark energy. Whilst gravity pushes things together (gravity is always attractive), dark energy represents a kind of antigravity in that it drives clusters of galaxies apart. It's hypothesised that dark energy sparked rapid growth of the universe after the Big Bang. Dark matter is mysterious undetectable matter. As mentioned, apparently DMT allows our brains to perceive dark matter. It seems the 'invisible' mass and energy has something to do with the astral world?

It's also suggested, (since Einstein relates matter and energy as different states of the same thing), that dark matter and dark energy are two states or manifestations of the same 'dark thing'. Scientists remain perplexed by both, so that's 95% of our universe. It's highlighted that scientists refer to dark energy and matter to account for the missing mass from the structures of the universe, like galaxies and galaxy clusters. Alternatively, the 'electric universe' theory refers to electromagnetism. There is no missing mass. The space between galaxies is plasma. The universe is like electrically charged soup?

It's noted, that dark matter is not the same as antimatter, which is the opposite of matter. In particle physics, antimatter is material composed of anti-particles, which have the same mass as particles of ordinary matter but have opposite charge. For example, a proton of matter has a positive charge, and a proton of antimatter, an antiproton, has a negative charge. And for every particle, there exists an antiparticle. And when they collide, they're both annihilated which results in a huge amount of energy.

Thus, according to the Big Bang model, only energy existed in the beginning, then as the universe expanded, some of the energy transformed into matter. Elementary particles collided to give us matter and antimatter.

As mentioned, CERN tried to recreate the Big Bang by smashing subatomic particles at nearly the speed of light to recreate the conditions which are said to have immediately followed the Big Bang. And CERN concluded that according to the laws of physics, the universe should have annihilated itself as soon as it came into existence. This is because, when energy converts to matter, the reaction always creates an equal amount of antimatter. And since opposites attract, if equal amounts of matter and antimatter existed in the very beginning, they would have obliterated each other.

All observations find a complete symmetry between matter and antimatter. Ergo the universe should not exist. Some 'strong force' binds the nucleus of atoms together, moment by moment. There's an active force that holds atoms of the material world together. The Bible tells us Jesus, Logos, holds all things together. He is the invisible force. And this force will be loosened at the end times, with the dissolution of the universe. Then Logos will create a new heaven and earth.

It's also recalled, as Pastor Lawson highlighted, that paranormal phenomenon is associated with antimatter. Like, the hallucinations and apparitions reported at CERN. It seems creating antimatter is like conjuring up dark energy from the spirit world? As mentioned, we're opening the bottomless pit? As Pastor Lawson explained, 'energy' is attached to antimatter and it affects us. He quotes Hawking, who said 'the God particle could destroy the universe'. The God particle (Higgs Boson particle) gives particles mass and is a type of antimatter.

It's also highlighted, that our dynamic and expanding universe might end in the future. Like, a massive star dies a death, when it uses all its fuel up, and becomes a black hole, and time stops. The universe is conceived of being wound up somehow, and which is winding down. NASA scientist Robert Jastrow wrote, 'The second law of thermodynamics, applied to the cosmos, indicates the universe is running down like a clock. If it is running down, there must have been a time when it was fully wound up'. So, who wound it up?

The Big Crunch is thus when time ends. It's the Big Bang in reverse, in that time would end rather than commence i.e. everything would be swallowed up by a single black hole. It's hypothesised that if entropy continues to increase, eventually all matter will collapse into black holes, which would then coalesce producing a unified black hole or Big Crunch singularity.

So, contrary to the explosion billions of years ago, it's possible that in some billions of years, there could be an implosion. Gravity could cause all the celestial bodies to be packed together again, into a tight nucleus. And then the process could be repeated? This perpetual cosmic cycle is notably espoused in eastern philosophy.

It's the endless dance between the creator and destroyer. Hence, there's a statue of Shiva (doing the dance of destruction) outside CERN.

So, it's God's word versus scientism? And rather than being educated with science, we're educated with scientism, which has its roots in Hermeticism. In tandem with the 33rd degree Masonic motto, Order out of Chaos, we're 'educated' to believe the Big Bang, the most violent explosion ever, led to our finely ordered universe. And it appears this was a one-off because explosions are always chaotic and destructive. They cause spontaneous degeneration not spontaneous generation.

Newton however unequivocally stated the universe must have been designed by God because it could not have emerged out of chaos. He knew the whack theory is wack. Intelligent mind had to be involved. And we're being scientifically guided back to this mystical realisation. Lucifer is the Great Architect, and we can evolve to become gods? We are inherently God, who created the universe?

Thus, the Earth formed, and then several billion years later, people began to wonder how it happened. Apparently, the Earth is 4.6 billion years old, and life first emerged 3.8 billion years ago. So, we're told that, in the beginning, there was pre-biotic soup. And this soup contained the various chemicals which make up organic molecules. And the earth's environment was filled with volcanic eruptions, lightning, and turbulent weather, which facilitated mixing atoms and energy to create the first simple cells.

That is, non-living chemicals spontaneously interacted to produce life, so called 'spontaneous generation'. Every living thing on earth (plants, fish, animals, and humans) descended from a single-celled blob which appeared a few billion years ago.

It's postulated the weakest link of evolution is the idea that life originates from non-living chemicals. It's said it's probably easier to get from a cell to a person, than from chemicals to life (there's a massive gulf between complex molecules and the cell). It also violates the law of biogenesis, a fundamental law of biology, which states that life only comes from pre-existing life.

It seems pertinent to note, Stanley Miller's famous (1953) experiment, which attempted to recreate the conditions that might have occurred on Earth billions of years ago to create life. Thus, he zapped his flask of pre-biotic soup, which was a solution of methane, ammonia, hydrogen and water, with an electric charge (60,000 volt electric current) to simulate lightning flashing back and forth in the atmosphere of the ancient earth. And in just a week he got amino acids, the building blocks of protein. It was hailed as almost making life in a test-tube. Alas for Miller however, there were too many problems.

Like, his experiment assumed an atmosphere of methane and ammonia. But it's understood these gases couldn't have been present in large amounts because the ammonia would be decomposed by ultraviolet light, and methane should be found stuck to ancient sedimentary clays, but it's not. Miller also left out oxygen because he knew that oxygen would destroy the very molecules he was trying to produce. But as deep as diggers dig, we find oxidised rocks, suggesting an oxygen rich atmosphere. There is good geological evidence that earth has always had oxygen in its atmosphere, and that absolutely precludes any evolutionary origin of life.

Whilst trace amounts of several amino acids were produced, the main product of the Miller experiment was tar (85% was toxic tar, 13% carboxylic acids, and 2% amino acids). His poisonous brew would destroy any hope for the chemical evolution of life. Furthermore, both right-handed and left-handed amino acids were produced, and only left-handed amino acids make up the proteins of life. Just one right-handed molecule prevents their production.

Others have conducted similar experiments with similarly disappointing results. It's also noted, that Miller had to tinker with his molecules i.e. trap and shield those he wanted to combine, as the same electric spark that puts amino acids together also tears them apart. And this suggests intelligence, yet evolution came about without any intelligent intervention.

The case for chemical evolution only weakens when we consider that long chains of specific amino acids, all in exactly the right position, are required to form proteins. Proteins can be two or three thousand amino acids long, very long complex chemicals, and like a computer program, every amino acid has to be placed in exactly the right position. If one of them is wrong, then the whole protein is useless, just like a computer program.

So, besides the fact that amino acids do not naturally link together, but rather tend to break down, it takes an enormous leap to go from small simple organic substances to proteins. Even the simplest of living cells require thousands of specialised proteins in order to function.

Information theory scientist Hubert Yockey calculated the probability that a protein containing just 100 amino acids would form spontaneously is less than one chance in ten to the 65th power. He also said, 'The belief that life on earth arose spontaneously from non-living matter, is simply a matter of faith...'. It seems people need a lot of faith to believe in evolution.

Sir Fred Hoyle estimated that proteins required for an amoeba, arising by chance, are one chance in ten to the $40,000^{th}$ power. He said, 'The likelihood of the formation of life from inanimate matter is one to a number with 40,000 naughts after it... It is big enough to bury Darwin and the whole theory of evolution. There was no primeval soup, neither on this planet nor any other, and if the beginnings of life were not random they must therefore have been the product of purposeful intelligence' ('Hoyle on Evolution'. Nature, Vol 294, No.5837, p.148, Nov 12, 1981).

Whilst Hoyle acknowledged that the building blocks of protein can be produced by natural means i.e. regarding Miller's experiment, he notes, 'But this is far from proving that life could have evolved in this way. No one has shown that the correct arrangements of amino acids, like the orderings in enzymes, can be produced by this method'. Hence, his Boeing 747 metaphor. Hoyle endorsed panspermia. As touched on, Neo-Darwinists understand that Darwinism is retarded, hence the panspermia doctrine. It makes more sense that bacteria/DNA landed on earth. The wind blew it over, or some asteroid landed here with alien junk on it? Or DNA was actively dumped on our planet by aliens?

Evolution teaches that bacteria, single celled microbes, were one of the first life forms. But the bacterial cell, whilst one of the simplest living systems known to us, employs the same overall form of genetic code and the same mechanism of translation as us i.e. human cells. Cells specialise in function, but all cells have the same DNA molecule. So, they're not simple. Microbes have 4 million DNA base pairs and the human genome has 3 billion DNA base pairs.

It's argued that it would take 16 billion years for the coordinated mutations/accidents required to produce one single cell. Yet we're told a mere 4.6 billion year journey has brought us from primordial soup to civilisation. Apparently, life was predominantly single-celled organisms until only 600 million years ago.

Tiny cells, the building blocks of every creature, are themselves living and have an extremely intricate structure. And cells have irreducible complexity i.e. they require all their various parts (coding, information systems) to function at the same time. Like, DNA is required to make protein, and protein is required to make DNA, so which came first. Moreover, to date no studies have shown that bacteria can, even after billions of generations, become anything than bacteria.

Evolution means all organisms are related by ties of genealogy or descent. Such lineages alter their form and diversity through time by a natural process of change known as 'descent by modification'. Thus, in the early oceans, simple cells changed. Through millions of years of mutations and natural selection, algae, jelly fish and flat worms appeared. Then fish appeared, and some of these developed into amphibians, and through natural selection reptiles were born, and some of these reptiles evolved into a variety of creatures including mammals. Some of these mammals became primates and then just 600,000 years ago, an isolated group of primates evolved into man's earliest ancestors.

It's noted, that finches' beaks inspired Darwin's theory, as detailed in his book, 'On the Origin of Species by Means of Natural Selection, or the Preservation of Favoured Races in the Struggle for Life' (1859). Thus, at the Galapagos Islands (off the coast of South America), Darwin observed that finches' beaks differed in size and structure on different islands. And he observed their variations were closely linked to the way the finches found their food. Indeed, he observed that each and every species had a beak perfectly adapted to its own food intake. They had superior adaptive qualities which ensured survival. They had adapted to their island.

Darwin assumed these beaks were evidence of evolution. He observed that offspring always differ in many small ways from their parents, and these differences could be passed onto later generations. He argued that animals possessing favourable variations will increase in number, while the others will tend to die out. Offspring more suited to the environment are more likely to reproduce, and thus its genetic heritage will proceed.

Hence, it's survival of the fittest. It's a genetic war. Dawkins notably refers to 'selfish genes'. That is, any gene that behaves in such a way as to increase its own survival chances in the gene pool, at the expense of its allies, is by definition selfish. In addition to the finches, giant tortoises were also slightly different from one island to another.

So, Darwin believed this process of selection would also create new species. He believed he could see transitional types, with one species changing into another, from a common type. He deducted all living organisms had evolved from a very simple organism, a common (bacterial) ancestor. And he assumed that given enough time one kind of animal could evolve into another.

Thus, humans are also an accident of this selective process. Whilst man's descent from animals was implicit in his first book, Darwin published 'The Descent of Man' in 1871, to expand on the theory that man and anthropoid apes must have at one time evolved from the same progenitor. Bryson highlights 'we're awfully lucky to be here, humans are doubly lucky' (he's clearly not depressed then).

So, we're told animals evolved with increasingly complicated nerve systems and brains. Life gets better, which defies the law of entropy? It's also noted, that Masonic Darwin (who was not a trained scientist but theologian) found it befitting to use the 'tree of life' as a metaphor for his theory. The tree illustrates the relationships between organisms, both living and extinct. It was the only illustration in his book 'On the Origin of Species'.

It seems however that even Darwin recognised it was quite the stretch to get from amoeba to the vertebrate eye. The eye is an extremely complex and intricate organ, and the development of the eye, the 'chance' that is arose, puzzled Darwin. It's said he couldn't really come to terms with the fact that something as delicate and sensitive as an eye could be exclusively due to natural selection. Apparently, Newton said, 'in the absence of any other proof, the thumb alone would convince me of God's existence'.

It's noted, the vertebrate eye is commonly used to refute evolution. The vertebrate eye contains highly organised nerve circuits for integration of light information. As touched on, light is directed to the back of the eye (retina) onto cells which are sensitive to it, and then information travels to the visual part of the brain so that we actually see something i.e. light information is turned into electrical energy. We also need a lens and cornea to focus the image onto the retina. Without any one of these component structures the eye wouldn't work, and each component is immensely complex. All the specialised and complex cells that make up our eyes are supposed to have evolved because of advantageous mutations in simple cells that were there before.

But as Baker (1976) highlights, what use is a hole at the front of the eye to allow light to pass through if there are no cells at the back of the eye to receive the light? And what use is a lens forming an image if there is no nervous system to interpret that image? And also, how could a visual nervous system have evolved before there was an eye to give it information? She answers herself, stating 'impossible'. There's notably no evidence supporting the vertebrate eye theory. It's like, the heart is very complex but unless it interacts with the brain, lungs, bloodstream, veins and arteries, it's useless.

Rather than life magically evolving from non-living chemicals, God tells us He created life to multiply after its own 'kind', which obeys the law of biogenesis. This means that every species living today, and in the past, has derived from an ancestral created species. Or rather, the species today are descendants from the 30,000 kinds saved during the flood. Like, the 450 different breeds of dog are presumed to have a common ancestor, namely, the present-day wolf. So, the wolf would be the 'kind' God created.

All kinds are created with 'genetic resilience' to adapt to their environment. As mentioned, genes switch on and off when triggered by environmental cues. Adaption is a natural law. God's kinds corroborate with biology's test for a 'species'. That is, two creatures which breed and produce live, fertile young, are regarded as belonging to the same species. Like, Darwin's finches were a species that interbred.

But moreover, in Genesis 1:24 God said, 'Let the earth produce living creatures according to their kinds', which suggests they came from the earth? God used properties from the earth to create His creatures. Like, He used dust to create Adam. Hence, humans have the same elements as dust. So, we're earth-dust not stardust.

It's also pertinent to note, the distinction between micro-evolution i.e. the relatively minor difference between dogs and wolves with a presumed common ancestor, and macro-evolution i.e. the gulf between fish and amphibian. And whilst micro-evolutionary theories are well documented, that is, small scale variation occurs within plants and animals, there is no empirical evidence at the macro level. There's nothing to suggest a cat can turn into a dog, or a monkey into a man.

It's evident that we adapt, but there's literally no evidence we evolved. Even Darwin acknowledged, 'Not one change of species into another is on record. We cannot prove that a single species has ever changed'. Like, finches have never turned into anything except finches. As it transpires, there are no intermediate fossils on record, despite the billions of fossils. But we'll get back to this.

The foundation of evolutionary theory is that complex systems can change by a large number of small steps. But macro-evolution requires changes in the organs of plants and animals which represent systems of enormous complexity and inter-relatedness. In such complex systems, component parts are inextricably linked to other components. And to change just one aspect without others is unlikely to produce a more efficient system but rather is far more likely to retard the system.

It seems evolution proposes that such finely balanced and highly complex systems can change from one thing to another without passing through non-functional intermediates. And yet, it's very difficult to see how intermediate creatures or organs could have a survival advantage.

Whilst Darwin deducted that new creations were being born, monk scientist Gregor Mendel's (1822-1884) science didn't convey the same thing. Mendel discovered the genetic laws of heredity, which contradicted Darwin's 'science'. Hence, his work was largely ignored. It wasn't until some sixteen years after Mendel's death, that he became world famous as the pioneer of genetics.

So, Mendel observed, when crossing various races of edible pea plants, with red and white flowers, that rather than there being a new creation, the plant had within it the capacity or potential to be different. Recessive and dominant genes are carried down from parent to child. He crossed a red-flowered plant with a white-flowered plant, and the offspring were red flowered plants. And when he crossed these red flowered plants with each other, he found they produced offspring of their own in the ratio 3 reds: 1 white.

Mendel thus concluded that the red gene must be dominant. Hence, any plant that possessed both would be red but when these plants were bred with each other, it was possible for two white genes to join forces and produce white offspring.

Darwin would have presumed the white flowered plants were a 'new creation'. He would have deduced that the white characteristic was a new character acquired by the young plants which their parents had not possessed. This is required for evolution. That is, a race has to acquire new characteristics if it is ever going to evolve.

But Mendel showed that the characteristic was not new or acquired but rather was present in the parent's generation though masked by a more dominant gene. Furthermore, it might be possible to lose some genes by killing off those individuals who possessed them, but it would never be possible to acquire new ones.

Thus, rather than beaks evolving, what Darwin observed was the result of genetic variability that already existed in the population. Certain beak sizes are favoured, depending on the environment, and become the predominant type. The capability to produce the various beaks was already in the parent population, and it was simply environmental differences that allowed them to be expressed. Like Mendel's pea plants, it was not the creation of any new and unique information.

Thus, Darwin took one giant leap for mankind with his theory. Genetic variability may lead to new sub-species e.g. breed of dogs, but not to a totally different organism. And the idea that amoeba could transform into a human brain is too much of a stretch? As Baker (1976) points out, the amoeba-like creatures from which we have all evolved must have had an infinitely richer and more varied gene pool than us.

We can also consider the classically cited example of natural selection, namely, the infamous peppered moth. So, circa the 1860s the pale moth was common whereas the dark form was rare. The pale moth's silvery grey colour was advantageous to blend in with the background, the trunks of silver birches, whereas the darker moths were more vulnerable. But during the next hundred years of industrial revolution, which resulted in the blackening of trees from the soot, the pale moths became a prime target for predators. And thus, the environment favoured the dark moth.

Apparently, from 1848-1948 dark moths increased from 1%-99% in certain places. But with a cleaner environment, the moth is returning to a paler colour. This doesn't however evidence evolution, as the dark moth already existed before natural selection caused it to become the most common variety. The process of natural selection operates on factors already present in the population.

It's also noted, this suggests that Adam, the first created person, must have possessed genetic material for all the present races of mankind. Or rather, Noah's three sons and their wives did. Whilst evolutionists refer to the 'Out of Africa' event, that is, humankind arose in Africa, the Bible tells us humans landed in Sumer, after the Flood. But the first people did live in Africa, like Ham's kids. So, scientists are close?

As mentioned, apparently Noah was an albino. And it's believed Africans came from Ham, who was dark skinned. Dark skin would be the favoured skin colour in Africa i.e. extra melanin to protect them from the sun, and whiter skin was better suited to colder climes. Like, white skin absorbs more vitamin D, which bodes well given the lack of sun in the north. So, as they migrated out of Africa, paler skin would be better. Thus, it's believed Europeans came from Japheth (who went north), and Orientals came from Shem (who went to the Middle East and Asia). It's understood that when the Babylonians (at least one million) dispersed, after God introduced seventy languages, they would have bred within their own people group (with traits suitable to the environment). Then white supremacists created racism in the 1800s, based on Darwin's theory of 'favoured races'.

Sandra Laing notably demonstrates how racial variety existed in her gene pool. Born in 1955, and in apartheid South Africa of all places, in a small Afrikaners conservative town, Sandra had the appearance of being a coloured person due to her skin colour and hair texture, yet she was the child of at least three generations of white ancestors. Her anomalous appearance did not go down well with the racists. She lived in racial purgatory.

Thus, whilst natural selection leads to new varieties of creatures, they are poorer in genes than the earlier population. Species can change but not in the direction of greater complexity. Furthermore, since new populations are genetically poorer, they're more prone to extinction.

So, our worldwide gene pool is not growing as evolution proposes it should but diminishing. Apparently, there are approximately 30 million separate species on Earth, but it's estimated that a further 3 billion species existed but became extinct. Natural selection depletes the gene pool, which defies evolution, as unless a population gains new genes it could never become more complex.

It's also duly acknowledged, that we're responsible for much extinction. Apparently more than half of the wild animals in the world, and three-quarters of its river life, have disappeared in the last forty years. Like, there were 100,000 tigers a century ago, and there's 3000 today (because of the WWF?). Sharks are also being hunted to extinction. We're losing our pandas and gorillas, and so forth. However, scientists are bringing the extinct back to life, so-called de-extinction. Like, they're bringing mammoths back to life? This begs the question, what else are they resurrecting.

Mendel's and Darwin's assumptions are therefore not consistent with each other, and both cannot be true. As it transpired, whilst Mendel's science threatened to blow Darwin's out the water, or pre-biotic soup, there was the saving grace of mutations aka an error in the DNA code. As Mendel's discovery disproved one of Darwin's most important assumptions, the theory of evolution suffered a temporary eclipse and re-emerged in a slightly different form, alleged to be consistent with Mendel.

So, mutations saved the day. Which is ironic since mutations, even small ones, are very rarely, if ever, beneficial (99.96% of mutations are lethal). They suck and they're extremely rare. Mutations often cause disease, and cause changes in genes such as birth defects. Mutations can be induced by radiation, chemical agents (e.g. Agent Orange) or replication errors. Furthermore, accumulating mutations actually means that genetically we're going downhill with every passing generation.

Nevertheless, Darwin proposed that all species on earth evolved by the process of spontaneous genetic mutation, coupled with natural selection or survival of the fittest. It's also noted, a favourable mutation will only take place if it occurs in small isolated populations, as within a large population they will be lost and diluted. Hence, man allegedly evolved in isolation, as we'll get to. This theory provides that genes could change to completely new forms and this is how Darwin's theory survived. Indeed, if mutations do not occur, it is impossible for evolution to progress.

And yet, experiments have been carried out, with thousands of mutations induced in various organisms, and they are never beneficial. In the early 1990s, millions of generations of fruit-flies were bred in labs to encourage mutations, to prove evolution, but it appears they're immune to evolution. They did however create some very grotesque (mutated) fruit flies. As Francis Hitchings states, 'the fruit-flies refuse to become anything other than fruit-flies under any circumstances yet devised'.

It's also noted, the basic idea of evolution is the same organ in different animals is said to have evolved from the same structure in a single common ancestor. Like, the flipper of a seal, the arm of a man, and the wing of a bird, evolved from some primitive vertebrate with the same basic arrangement of bones. The seal, arm and wing differ in form and function but have the same basic arrangement of bones. Like, batwings are like human hands?

Such structures or organs, known as homologous structures, allegedly evolved through mutation in genes controlling the original organ (homology is the study of comparative anatomy). However, in many cases it can be shown that what evolutionists call homologous organs are produced by the action of very different genes. And this destroys the concept of homology.

The gene that supposedly governed the development of the forelimb, even if mutated a million times, will never cause the forelimb to change into a flipper or a person's arm, as these are controlled by different genes. So, whilst Darwin's tree of life might seem logical, the study of genes doesn't support it?

Alternatively, it's highlighted that many animals have a similar design because we have the same designer e.g. frog hands are like human hands, to grasp things. Hands are amazing. They're our tools. And it appears God likes faces, as most creatures have faces, including fish. He designed His creatures as He saw fit. Like, some waddle, others hop, or sprint or gallop, or swim, or fly. Some are feathered, others are furry, or velvety, or spiky, or scaly. As mentioned, the diversity in nature is mind blowing.

Despite Bryson, and others who consider Darwin's theory 'the single best idea that anyone has ever had', Darwin clearly wrestled with it. As mentioned, he sat on it for twenty-one years prior to its publication, fully aware of the resulting nihilism. He 'didn't want to murder God' as he once put it. Apparently, he said telling the story was like confessing a murder. He was tormented, calling himself 'the devil's chaplain'. His theory won him no friends at the Kirk, and he was described as the most dangerous man in England.

It seems he did murder God, as his theory propels atheism? It seems the theory of evolution has been the major factor dissuading people from believing in creator God? The evolution deception has resulted in untold doomed souls.

Moreover, the central book of biology, 'the cornerstone', is the Origin of Species. Thus, biology is founded on an unproven theory which is taught as fact. Like, our cosmology is taught as fact. The fact is these are not facts. It also seems ironic that evolution is taught as fact, since Darwin countered, 'it seems, I freely confess, absurd in the highest possible degree.' For Darwin, it latterly became absurd to think that natural selection could produce complex organs in gradual steps. Like the eye, or the brain.

Some biographers say it was his oldest daughter Annie's death, in particular, that put the proverbial nail on the coffin and propelled him to publish his theory. Apparently, Darwin was so overcome with grief he abstained from going to her funeral. It's said her death radically altered his belief in Christianity. How could there be a God if Annie was taken from him? Several of Darwin's kids died in childhood, which might have something to do with the fact he married his first cousin? Or maybe he was cursed?

However, it's equally noted that Darwin wasn't original as these ideas were already circulating. Indeed, evolutionary ideas arose first among ancient Greeks. They believed that fish hopped onto land, and turned into man. Then Darwin's grandfather Erasmus endorsed them millennia later. Erasmus (freemason) Darwin (1731-1802) proposed in 'Zoonomia; or the Laws of Organic Life' (1794) that all living beings had evolved from simple aquatic organisms.

French zoologist Jean-Baptiste Lamarck (1744-1829) then presented his 'Theory of Inheritance of Acquired Characteristics' in 1801. Lamarck had shown how different species developed the characteristics they needed e.g. giraffes developed long necks because for generations they'd reached up for leaves. He also hypothesised that if an organism changes during its lifetime, in order to adapt to its environment, those changes are passed onto its offspring. So, species acquired characteristics and passed them on, which gives rise to new species (flora and fauna) in the struggle for life.

Moreover, whilst the theory of evolution is indelibly associated with Charles Darwin, the theory was first published under joint ownership of Darwin and his partner (rival?), Alfred (freemason) Wallace (1823-1913), the year before in 1858. Wallace similarly and independently observed adaptation but on Indonesian turf.

But Wallace further acknowledged, 'an instrument (the human brain) has been developed in advance of its possessor'. He mused, if early hominids needed only ape-like intelligence to survive, why had they evolved brains capable of developing language, music, and mathematics?

He recognised we have abstract thought and conceptualisation, but also moral conscience and self-awareness. Wallace believed Homo-sapiens had an extra dimension not derived from animal predecessors. He highlighted that 'some unknown spiritual element' was needed to account for man's unusual artistic and scientific abilities. He believed we have a soul. And this unknown dimension was part of an unseen world of spirit.

As it transpires, Wallace was a spiritualist and partial to séances (he was also a skilled hypnotist). He believed that human existence extends beyond biological death. And that our intellectual and moral development is a function of freewill. We're more than instinctive beasts as Freud supposed? Whilst we're told Darwin despaired of Wallace's spiritualism, apparently he sent his son George Darwin and biologist Thomas (freemason) Huxley, along to a séance in 1874, where they both witnessed a guitar play by itself and some bottles move around.

It was notably Thomas Huxley (1825-1895), not Darwin, who propagated the ape ancestor and caveman gospel. He was the official spokesperson for Darwin and even dubbed himself 'Darwin's bulldog'. He also coined the term 'agnostic' having confused the masses with Darwinism. There was a new faith in the West? It was okay for people not to know if God exists. There was a label for them.

Darwinism is the fundamental philosophy behind freemasonry. As mentioned, the secret for the minions is there is no secret, no supernatural. This material deception infiltrated the lodges as scientific truth. It went global in universities, schools, textbooks, and the mass media. Huxley was also a member of the Royal Society from a young age, and he participated in the formation of Rhodes Round Table Groups.

However, whilst Darwin seemingly disregarded the spiritual realm, according to Black (2010), Darwin attended séances and it's thought he may have learned the esoteric doctrine of evolution of fish to amphibian to land animal, from Friedrich Max Muller, early translator of sacred Sanskrit texts. It's said that esoteric ideas underpin evolution, which appears in a materialist form in Darwin's theory.

Black further notes, 'In the secret history, the last creatures to incarnate before humans were the apes. They came about because some human spirits rushed into incarnation too early, before human anatomy was perfected' (p.117). So, we get the revised material tale that we descended from apes?

It's noted however, that humans didn't evolve from apes, gorillas or chimps per se. But rather we share a common ancestor like the African ape (orang-utans were in Asia). Thus, we're all modern species that have followed different evolutionary paths. The first primates (allegedly) evolved 65 million years ago. Then about 2 million years ago our ancestors learned to walk upright, like Homo erectus ('upright man'). This ability to walk upright on two legs marks the beginning of hominid evolution.

But this talent aside, it seems little progress was made by hominids, Homo erectus and his predecessors, until about 200,000 years ago. And then without any clear record of their origin they suddenly transformed into Homo sapiens. Humankind emerged with a 50% larger cranial capacity, the capacity for speech and a modern anatomy. We hit the jackpot of mutations. We lost our fur, became super smart and considerably more dexterous. The baldy thinking ape had finally evolved, for no apparent reason.

Most scientists believe that man had speech from the beginning, as we're predisposed to talk, and the unique combination of language structures are in place. It's also understood that the relationship between thought and language sets us apart from the animals, since it enables more advanced forms of thought.

The explosion in the size of the frontal cortex further accounts for our intellectual upgrade and sense of self. As mentioned, our frontal cortex creates an awareness of 'the self' in relation to the world and enables us to plan and execute actions. And God knows how it got so massive in such a brief period of evolutionary time. It's miraculous.

So, Homo sapiens apparently descended from dark skinned people who lived in Africa between 200,000 and 60,000 years ago. Then we migrated out of the continent some 50,000 to 100,000 years ago to Asia and Europe (apparently we appeared in Europe 40,000 years ago). And yet, our hairy cousins have spent the last six million years in evolutionary stagnation. Which is arguably odd? Or maybe apes can't change into humans.

It's noted, this theory suggests we're better than monkeys, as we're more evolved than them? But maybe we're not better, and maybe we have nothing to do with them. We're different 'kinds' of creatures, period.

It's also uncomfortably noted, that whilst this theory tells us we're all African, it's insanely offensive to Africans, because it suggests white people are less monkey-like? Darwin's 'favoured races' was racist from the start. As mentioned, he taught that blacks are closer to apes than whites, and whites are more evolved than blacks. This rhetoric has been beyond brutal. Social Darwinism became the ideological basis of fascism, communism and eugenics. Like, the rhetoric regarding superior Aryan people and rodent Jews. Moreover, it's said Darwinism was always meant to be a social theory not a scientific theory. The cabal knew the ramifications of racism. The intent has always been to divide and rule.

It seems apposite to mention Lucy (1964-1987), the chimp who was raised as if she were a human child. Scientists pondered if we could learn something from our alleged closest genetic next of kin, our cousins? Perhaps we could civilise chimps to be like humans, since they arguably behave in an uncivilised manner (including their sexual appetite).

So, Lucy was raised by Temerlin, a psychotherapist and professor at the University of Oklahoma, and his wife. Lucy was taught to eat with silverware and sit in a chair at the dinner table, dress herself, flip through magazines, and she was taught rudimentary American Sign Language (ASL), where she learned 140 signs. She appeared in Life magazine, where she became famous for drinking straight gin, rearing a cat, and using Playgirl and a vacuum cleaner for sexual gratification. Lucy was also known for making tea.

Scientists thought that chimps, raised in a human family and using ASL, would shed light on the way language is acquired and used by humans. Thus, Nim was another chimp raised in a human family (from two weeks old). Like Lucy, Nim was partial to alcohol and driving fast. Nim learned 125 signs using ASL but it was realised that whilst he learned to repeat his trainer's signs in appropriate context, he did not learn semantic language.

Nim's use of language was strictly pragmatic, as a means of obtaining an outcome, unlike a human child's, which can serve to generate or express meanings, thoughts or ideas. Nim demonstrated operant conditioning, which can be seen with pigeons that are taught in a similar fashion. It seems civilising a pet chimp is like civilising pet cats and dogs. Like, they learn not to defecate in the house, and they understand what 'dinner' and 'sweeties' mean.

As it transpired, it was a sad end for Nim. Despite his loving home, affectionate Nim became increasingly violent. He attacked his teachers (one had her cheek ripped open) and he killed the family dog by throwing it against the wall. So, the experiment ended and Nim was transferred back to the Institute for Primate Studies.

He was later sold to the Laboratory for Experimental Medicine and Surgery in Primates, a pharmaceutical animal testing lab. But after efforts to free him, Nim was purchased by the Black Beauty Ranch. His life was however dire, as he struggled to integrate with the other chimps. He was a weird chimp because of his upbringing. He died prematurely at 26 and it's said he died of a broken heart. He was just another animal 'used for science'.

It's often stated that we're 98% exactly the same as chimps and gorillas. We're genetically closer to some primates than mice are to rats, although foxes are more than 98% exactly the same as dogs. Thus, we're told it's credible that natural selection, via algorithmic processes, focussed our 2% of genetic mutations into the most advantageous areas?

Alan Alford (1996) however retorts 'the idea is quite frankly, preposterous'. He elaborates that it is an idea born of a paradigm that, since we exist, and since the chimp is our closest genetic relation, that we evolved from a common ancestor of the chimp. He concedes evolution is propagated as fact when it appears to be fiction.

Moreover, this '98%' only pertains to about 2% of our total genetic makeup i.e. genes that code for proteins, the building blocks of our physical bodies and functions. The vast majority of our DNA is known as 'non-coding DNA' or junk DNA (because it was once thought not to have function), and this is very different in humans from most non-coding genes found in chimps and other apes. David Icke (2007) notably suggests Junk DNA is the genetic code for extra-terrestrial life forms i.e. nephilim (p.65).

Other researchers concede that the '98%' comes from ignoring large sections of DNA. Like, they have to ignore 18% of chimp genome, and 25% of human genome. They have to exclude 1.3 billion letters. Apparently 2.4 billion letters are 98% the same. Thus, it's said that we're 70% the same.

It's also highlighted, whilst scientists claim that the haemoglobin of a chimpanzee is 98% the same as the haemoglobin of a human being, slime moulds have very similar haemoglobin to us. It's like a cloud is 98% water, as is a jellyfish and watermelon, but they're all completely different. All life shares 25% of the same DNA. Thus, we're also 50% the same as bananas, 35% the same as daffodils, 88% the same as rats, 70% the same as sea sponges, and 88% the same as sea squirts.

It's noted, almost a hundred years after Darwin published his theory, Watson and Crick discovered the double helix structure of the DNA molecule in 1953. They announced they had 'found the secret of life' aka heredity's master switch. Namely, four chemical bases pair to create a self-copying code at the core of the double-helix shaped DNA molecule.

Apparently, Francis Crick (1916-2004) was a regular user of LSD and he perceived the double helix shape when he was high. Black (2010) notably states that as far as he knows Crick had no connections with secret societies but rather, 'he achieved his moment of inspiration and unlocked the structure of DNA while in an altered state brought about by taking LSD'.

Black highlights that Crick argued that the complex structure of DNA could not have come about by chance, and he 'believed that the cosmos had encoded deep within it messages about our – and it's – origins that had been put there, so that we would be able to decode them when we had evolved sufficient intelligence' (p.464).

Crick (1981) said, 'An honest man, armed with all the knowledge available to us now, could only state that in some sense the origin of life appears at the moment to be almost a miracle, so many are the conditions which would have had to have been satisfied to get it going' (Crick, 'Life Itself: It's Origin and Nature', p.88).

Crick was an atheist, but he didn't believe DNA evolved on this Earth as there's not enough time and it couldn't be an accident. Like Hoyle, Crick endorsed panspermia. But he promoted the theory of directed panspermia, which is the hypothesis that life on Earth was seeded deliberately by other civilisations. He believed intelligent species evolved on other planets. So, aliens did put on their little alien white coats and created us?

Furthermore, according to modern theories regarding gradiented change and natural selection, many aspects of Homo sapiens are an evolutionary impossibility. Human DNA shows signs of an extremely slow and peaceful evolution which is inconsistent with an evolutionary split from the apes six million years ago. This 'accidental geographical separation' (our 'isolation') was however necessary, otherwise our mutant genes would have been diluted in the sea of ape genes.

Alford highlights that 'natural selection works in theory, but in practice the timescale for the appearance of Homo sapiens causes serious discomfort for our top scientists' (p.35). Natural selection is a very slow, continuous process. Alford quotes Thomas Huxley who stated, 'Large changes [in species] occur over tens of millions of years, while really major ones [macro-changes] take a hundred million years or so'. And yet, as Alford continues, mankind is supposed to have benefitted from not one, but several macro-mutations in the course of only six million years (p.42).

The fur-loss thing is also a problem because it's unexplainable. We deduct that man spent a long time evolving in water or in very hot climates but that doesn't make sense since chimps and the rest of our monkey relatives remain hairy. And compared to primates, our skin is appallingly inept at repairing itself and such fragile skin doesn't add up since skin should become stronger without hair via evolution. It's also highlighted, that if perchance a mutant person were to evolve, presumably s/he would be more vulnerable to attack by apes and baboons.

With regards to our baldness, a leading psychologist in Britain suggests the reason hairy babies died out was because their mothers killed them. She said cavewomen got an 'ugh' response and disgusted at their hairy babies annihilated them. A process repeated over more than 100,000 years to affect the evolution of our species, and one which is not natural selection but maternal selection. At the same time, man wiped out the Neanderthal tribes because they were hairy and therefore looked like animals. The hairy gene was thus lethal. She was given an award for her smart thinking. Ugh.

It's also noted, that wo/man underwent a sexual revolution. Women are always in 'heat' yet can't conceive more than a few days a month, which in effect gives rise to mistimed copulations. This is an evolutionary enigma. Man also lost his penis bone. Animals use their penis bone to copulate at very short notice and thus to be sans penis bone wouldn't seem favourable, but rather would have jeopardised the situation with natural selection. It also means men need to be attracted to women? The male penis is by far the largest erect penis of all living primates. The world record for the largest human erect penis is 13.5 inches. No danger.

Whilst animals can enjoy longer and more frequent sex with a penis bone, it's purported that the act of mating is not exactly a pleasurable experience for many mammals, and that humans and dolphins are the only mammals that have sex for pleasure. Dolphins are also partial to rubbing the magic lamp, to coax the genie out. The other vertebrate that doesn't have a penis bone is the hyena, and apparently hyenas are as clever as primates. But the serpent was the wisest of all the beasts in the field.

But furthermore, the human body seems perfectly designed for sexual excitement and pair bonding. We experience emotional attachments, which, in addition to the angles of our shape, encourage face-face copulation (unless people emulate dogs). It seems the way we function was clearly thought out.

Alford (1996) states, 'The appearance of Homo sapiens is more than a baffling puzzle - it is statistically close to impossible' (p.55). Scientists understand that it's 'one of the great puzzles of palaeoanthropology'. He concedes that it's as if science has come full circle, to a point where many feel severe discomfort with the evolutionary theory as it applies to humans. Perhaps we could also wonder why we haven't evolved into super-wo/man with infrared vision, improved hearing, and smell and so on.

Fundamentally, there is no evidence that we evolved into Homo sapiens. Anthropologists have failed miserably to produce fossil evidence of the 'missing link' between ape-like ancestors and mankind. Lucy, the skeleton of Australopithecus, is often said to be the missing link but she really consists of 40% skeleton of a not very large ape. There is no evidence that she walked upright in any of the bones that they have found of her skeleton.

Yet Lucy is shown (in biology textbooks) to be distinctly human like. She's very erect in her posture, and she's got human like hands and feet. It's questionable where the restorers got this data from. The paper by Randall and Susman, which describes the type of species to which Lucy belongs, clearly states she had long curved hands and feet, even longer and even more curved than a chimpanzee.

Suffice to say, many reconstructions are made from very limited remains. And worse, these are often not from the same site. Constructing reconstructions invariably involves detective work, regarding what parts belong to which creature, and guessing what the rest of the body looks like. It's conjecture. And reconstructions of 'early man' are most dubious. Ramapithecus, for example, consists of mainly jaws and teeth yet reconstructions are often presented in books as a complete creature.

Upon analysis of the so-called missing links, it seems the story we're spun is fraudulent, deceptive and mere speculation. Like, Nebraska Man was constructed from an extinct pig's tooth. And Piltdown Man, another deliberate hoax, consists of an ape's jaw and a human skull that has been doctored to look old. And 'Java Man' consisted of a leg-bone, three teeth and part of a skull. The leg-bone appeared human, while the skull resembled that of a chimpanzee. These fossils were apparently found 15 yards apart at a level in the rock which also contained true human skulls. It's said this latter fact was suppressed for many years.

Furthermore, Dubois, the man who found these fossils, announced at the end of his life that these remains were not that of an ape-man but rather the bones of a giant gibbon. Evolutionists have however refused to accept his admission, and Java Man has been accepted as a creature that definitely lived, based on this ludicrously small amount of evidence.

As it transpires, all the fossils that have been found so far have been reclassified as either human or ape. Like, Ramapithecus, Gigantapithicus and Zinjanthropus were apes. Whereas Heidelberg Man and Cro-magnon were completely human. The missing link therefore remains missing. We're also told that Kenyan paleoanthropologist Richard Leakley claims to have found remains of modern man in rock that is much older than rock that contains ape-man.

Professor G Von Koenigswald, an ardent supporter of the Ape-man theory, wrote in 'Meeting Prehistoric Man' (1956), 'Working from the skeleton alone, it is not so easy to define a man in comparison with anthropoid ape. Actually, the anthropoid's skeleton differs only quantitively from our own. The number of cranial bones and teeth is the same; the difference in the structure of hands and feet is one of degree only. It is worth noting that the mountain gorilla's foot has proved to be remarkably similar to man's... The only distinguishing character left, therefore, is the size of brain'. An ape's brain is rarely larger than 600 cubic centimetres (cc), while man's varies from 1000-2000cc. Ape-man is an ape. He has a small brain, no larger than a chimp's.

It's also duly noted, that Neanderthal man was human, and had 46 chromosomes like us. [Chimps and apes have 48, cats have 38, amoebas have 50, turkeys have 82, and goldfish have 94]. But these early humans or archetypal humans had larger brains (200cc larger than modern man). Evidence reveals they were sophisticated, intelligent, and communicated by language. They created fire, fashioned delicate tools, buried their dead, made music, and wore makeup. It's also believed they worshipped gods. Evidence suggests they were fierce and effective hunters, and much stronger than modern man.

It seems Neanderthals were pre-Flood people who lived l-o-n-g time, which explains their pronounced brow ridge and larger brain (it's said they didn't lose their marbles in old age). And it stands to reason they were fierce and effective fighters to take on dinosaurs and nephilim? There's evidence for ginger haired and blue-eyed Neanderthals existing in the same small proportion as we have today.

Whilst it's also suggested that Neanderthals were nephilim (because they're smarter and stronger than us), it was subsequently hypothesised that Denisovans provided scientific proof of nephilim. Scientists discovered Denisovans in 2012. This 'new branch' of the human family is completely different genetically from Neanderthals and modern humans. Denisovans interbred with Neanderthals. They're both regarded as our cousins. It seems the nephilim are the weird cone-heads? And those curious 'people' with six fingers and toes, and double row of teeth?

Since we've never actually observed anything evolve, we can only speculate 'based on the evidence'. Like, fossil evidence, which overwhelmingly supports creation. As touched on, no intermediate or transitional forms have ever been found. And it seems obvious that the billions of fossils evidence the remains of animals that died in the flood?

Creatures need to be entombed very quickly in sediment to create fossils, but deceased creatures normally decay naturally or get munched by scavengers. Take fish, for example, which are unlikely to become a fossil as they're usually eaten by other fish within a few hours. And yet thousands of millions of fish, entire shoals, are often found in sedimentary rock.

It seems the fundamental point is whether or not the great Flood happened. However, it's conveyed the Bible is fantasy, which includes the biblical deluge. As Alford (1996) states, 'most scientists believe the biblical flood to be a myth. Why is this? The deep schism between science and religion has caused many scientists to be deeply sceptical of anything which appears in the Bible' (p.217).

As discussed, every ancient society has its own version of the 'great flood'. And as Graham Hancock insists, the world's flood 'myths' deserve to be taken seriously. The Flood was notably never disproved. But rather it was arbitrarily rejected in the 1700s and 1800s by secular intellectuals in favour of slow processes over millions of years.

James Hutton (called the Father of Geology in 1795) disputed the flood and instead put forth his 'uniformitarianism' theory. This maintains that conditions prevalent at the beginning of earth's history have continued to the present day with very little change. It assumes things are as they were, and no major catastrophes have ever taken place. River erosion and weathering adequately explain the present state of the earth. He endorsed the idea that various rock strata had been laid down over long periods of time, with the oldest at the bottom.

English biologist Sir Charles Lyell (1797-1875) notably popularised James Hutton's concept of uniformitarianism in his book 'Principles of Geology'. Until then, most geologists concurred regarding the 'catastrophe theory' i.e. the earth was subjected to gigantic floods, earthquakes, and other catastrophes that had destroyed all life. This was logical since fish fossils are found far inland and high up in mountain tops (they're found in mountain ranges across all the earth).

The notion that different strata ensued at different times over millions of years, effectively provided the foundation (pun intended) for Darwin's theory i.e. the fossils in various rock layers provide a vertical timeline. They evidenced evolution? Thus, a geological timetable was compiled. Fossils are dated by the age of strata, and strata are dated by the fossils contained in it. This is 'circular reasoning', which is bosh.

By the 1880s evolution had become scientific orthodoxy and from then on, any fossil find had to be interpreted to fit in with the accepted evolution theory. Indeed, it was considered heresy to interpret it any differently.

However, as it transpires, this geological column can't be found anywhere. Nowhere can all these levels be found at once. The rock strata in many places are not in the right order i.e. older ones are at the top and younger ones at the bottom, and sometimes they're mixed together. At best there are usually only two or three of these strata at any one place.

It's also noted, the majority (three quarters) of the earth's surface is sedimentary rock, which substantiates the Flood (sedimentary rock is rock laid down in water). But moreover, this is found on mountain tops, which suggests the earth was completely covered in water. Like, Genesis 7:19 states, 'the water covered even the highest mountain'. This also explains the fossilised marine life on mountain tops. The remaining quarter of the earth's surface is largely rock laid down by volcanic activity.

The question is thus, whether fossils support evolution, or the Bible's account of creation followed by a worldwide flood. As ever, the issue is not with the evidence but interpretation of the evidence. The study of fossils in itself cannot prove or refute either the evolution or creation paradigms.

With evolution then, we should find very simple organisms at the bottom of the geological column, in the oldest rocks, which become increasingly complex as we progress through the rock. We would also expect to find 'link fossils', which link groups of animals that today are widely separated e.g. fish/amphibians, reptiles/mammals. And as we reach fairly recent rocks, we would expect to see clear evidence of ape-like men.

But on the contrary, there is no gradual progression from very simple organisms to complex ones but rather fossils appear suddenly representing every major group of organisms alive today. The oldest rocks (Cambrian) do not contain many fossils of the simplest organisms, as we would expect, and instead many complex organisms are found, which we would not expect. Below the Cambrian level, 'pre-Cambrian', virtually no fossils are found.

In the Cambrian rocks we find very complex invertebrates e.g. clams, snails, jelly fish, worms, brachiopods, trilobites etc, but never, nowhere on earth, has anyone found fossilised ancestors to any of these. That fact demolishes evolution. We're told these invertebrates evolved into vertebrates such as fish, but again, no transitional forms have ever been found. And yet billions of vertebrate and invertebrate fossils have been found. Every fish is fully formed.

The same applies to insects. There's tons of insects yet no common ancestor. And the same applies to the copious amounts of amphibians, reptiles, and mammals. There is no trace of ancestors for either vertebrates or invertebrates, but rather all animals appear abruptly and fully formed.

Furthermore, the first representatives of all major classes of organism are highly characteristic of their class when they first appear on fossil record. Each form remains essentially unchanged from appearance until extinction. Like, the fossil bat from the Messel Shales in Germany is one of the earliest of its kind and is practically indistinguishable from modern bat skeletons. 'Living fossils', old creatures still alive today, include many fish, sharks, crocodiles, lizards, sponges, most insects, and the humble horseshoe crab has remained unchanged.

So, whilst crucially there ought to be lots of intermediate forms scattered across fossil records, there's not. There's no half-breed anything. There is no fossil evidence that shows evidence of extreme abnormalities that must have occurred if mutations are responsible for all the varieties of life on earth.

Darwin acknowledged the lack of transitional fossils found in the rock strata. He said, 'Intermediate links? Geology assuredly does not reveal any such finely graduated organic chain; and this, perhaps, is the most obvious and serious objection which can be urged against the theory [of evolution]' (Origin of the Species, p.323).

Evolutionist, Alfred G Fisher, also said, 'Both the origin of life and the origin of the major groups of animals remain unknown' (Multimedia Encyclopaedia, 1998, Fossil Section). This is the key problem with Darwinism, namely, finding hard physical evidence. There is almost a complete absence of transitional forms and no gradual change. And ironically, it's said that without the fossil record, macro-evolution would remain a hypothesis instead of an accepted fact.

Since the fossil record does not support the theory of gradual development from very tiny organisms, but rather many complex forms appear suddenly in the rocks, the theory of 'punctuated equilibrium' was proposed in 1972. This theory was based on the observation that evolution changes occurred very rapidly, but this is problematic as macro-evolution takes place gradually i.e. gradualism. Like humans, alleged to be the result of a series of micro-mutations, appeared gradually? It appears time is of the essence, as we need endless time to form our essence.

It's duly noted, the archaeopteryx aka flying reptile is famously cited as an alleged transitional form or link. We're told birds evolved from dinosaurs during the Jurassic period, and this half-dinosaur, half-bird, paved the way about 150 million years ago. Carl Zimmer, in his article 'Evolution of Feathers, the long curious extravagant evolution of feathers' (cited in the National Geographic Magazine, February 2011), said, 'Imagine the ancestors of birds as small, scaly, four-legged reptiles living in forest canopies, leaping from tree to tree'. Then we have to imagine their front legs turning into wings. [LOL].

The archaeopteryx is claimed to be in many respects' reptilian, yet the creature possessed beautiful fully formed feathers. It's theorised that feathers evolved from reptilian scales which frayed. Scientists inform that feathers did not evolve first for flight but rather for insulation or to attract attention from the opposite sex (like peacocks flaunt their feathers). However, it's countered that it's difficult to fathom how a 'frayed scale feather', suited to keeping the creature warm (its survival advantage), could develop into an incredibly complex feather suited for flight without intermediate forms which would have no survival advantage to its possessor.

Indeed, bird feathers par excellence show intelligent design, given their extremely complex and intricate design. Each feather has its own purpose-designed muscle to make adjustments and each muscle has its own nerve supply so that birds can send messages to coordinate their movements. The fully developed, complex feathers of archaeopteryx are nothing like frayed scales. Even evolutionist Swinton admitted, 'The transition from reptilian scales to the quite differently constituted and arranged feather is still a mystery'. There is no halfway form between a reptilian scale and a bird feather. The fossil record has no such link.

It's also highlighted, the dinosaurs it would have evolved from don't have a collar bone and all birds have a keeled breast bone, which holds the pictorial muscles, enabling it to fly its wings. The breastbone of the archaeopteryx is flat, which is said to be a reptilian feature, yet other birds, including ostriches and emus, have the same kind of breastbone. This creature has claws on its wings, which is also supposed to show it's a reptile, but so have the young of a few birds today including the ostrich.

Indeed, the many allegedly reptilian features of the skeleton of archaeopteryx can be seen in one group of birds or another. Like, the Hoactzin today is very similar to archaeopteryx in many important aspects. It's claimed the archaeopteryx was a feathered reptile, but the archaeopteryx flew, it had wings, and was therefore clearly a bird. Many scientists believe it is a true bird. An article in the Journal of Vertebrate Palaeontology (March 1996) stated, 'The avian features of the skull demonstrates that archaeopteryx is a bird rather than a feathered non-avian archosaur'.

And besides, if a reptile evolved into a bird, who would the first bird mate with? What are the chances another bird would evolve from beneficial mutations? It's also highlighted that all intermediate forms would be fatal. Like, when the dinosaur turns into a bird, what use is half a wing or half a beak? Why would the environment favour crap things that serve no purpose? And fundamentally, there's no evidence.

It seems pictures help us to visualise the alleged evolutionary chains, since 'science' doesn't? Like, if we see a picture of a monkey turning into a man, or a dinosaur turning into a bird. Lest we forget, we're 'educated' to believe this trash. It's like we're given the chain of the horse, despite no empirical evidence for this sequence. Nowhere in the world does it appear in the fossil record. But given the belief that it must exist, fossils have been globally collected to portray this scam i.e. convey a gradual development as evidenced in rocks/fossils. The best-known chains are notably man and horse, so we'll also consider the horse.

Thus, the small four-toed creature Eohippus, found in the early rock layer known as Eocene, is claimed to be the ancestor of the horse. We're informed that as we progress through the rocks, fossils with features more like modern day horses are found. The Eohippus turns into Miohippus, which turns into Merychippus, which turns into Pliohippus, which turns into Equus (the horse).

But horse fossils are not found below one another in the rocks and Eohippus bones are often found to be at the surface. Different sizes of horse exist today so size is irrelevant i.e. smaller to larger. Eohippus has a skeleton very similar to the present-day hyrax of Africa. Indeed, some scientists believe that Eohippus has no connection with the horse but is simply a variant form of the hyrax.

It's also noted, some of the stages of this chain involve significant jumps with no transitional forms. For example, there are no intermediates between three-toed and single toed, between browsing and grazing teeth, and the numbers of ribs increases and decreases through the sequence.

Alternatively, (looking at the fossil record), if the flood took place, there should be evidence of vast numbers (animals and people) wiped out suddenly worldwide. And that's exactly what we find. The sudden extinction of animals is an established fact. The millions of fossilised animal remains are often grouped together in huge 'graveyards'. And it's argued the vast fossil graveyards evidence a catastrophic flood.

As touched on, it's generally agreed that the best and most likely way for a fossil to be produced is by the sudden burial of the creature in sediment at or soon after death. Hence, the flood accounts for the billions of fossils found worldwide, that were immediately buried. It's acknowledged that such a process is not happening on earth today to produce the vast number of fossils that exist. The Flood also explains the thousands of seashells found in the Himalayas, and the whale fossil graveyards in the desert.

Regarding the flood, Genesis 7:11 tells us, 'In the six hundredth year of Noah's life, on the seventeenth day of the second month—on that day all the springs of the great deep burst forth, and the floodgates of the heavens were opened'.

Whilst it's suggested there was a water canopy surrounding Earth's atmosphere, (which works for the globe model), which collapsed at the onset of the Flood, Psalm 148:4 tells us there's still waters above the firmament. We're told that when the heavens or firmament were opened, the water poured down flooding the Earth. But furthermore, in addition to rain falling in mighty torrents from the sky, the underground waters burst forth on the earth.

Dr Walter Brown, author of 'In the Beginning: Compelling Evidence for Creation and the Flood' (2008), said the water from subterranean chambers erupted with an energy release exceeding the explosion of ten billion hydrogen bombs. Walter Brown presents 'The Hydroplate Theory' to systematically account for the features of our planet as a result of a cataclysmic flood and the underground waters bursting forth.

He states, 'This expiation shows us just how rapidly major mountains formed. It explains the coal and oil deposits, the rapid continental drift, why on the ocean floor there are huge trenches and hundreds of canyons and volcanoes. It explains the formation of the layers strata and most of the fossils; of the frozen mammoths, the so-called ice ages and major land canyons, especially the Grand Canyon'. [See photo of the Grand Canyon]. Brown has notably stated that no evolutionist will publicly debate with him.

Brown contends the pre-flood world had a lot of subterranean water (about half of what is now in our oceans), which supersonically jetted some twenty miles into the cold atmosphere when the Earth ruptured. The water was contained in chambers ten miles below ground, hence the immense pressure. He explains some of this water 'froze into super-cooled ice crystals and produced some massive ice dumps; burying, suffocating and instantly freezing many animals, including the frozen mammoths of Siberia and Alaska'. It seems this happened very early in the Flood.

Nikolai Vereshchagin, top expert on woolly mammoths in Siberia, states there are many hundreds of thousands of large animals buried in Siberia and many millions of bones. He questioned, 'under what conditions did this great slaughter take place, in which millions upon millions of animals were torn limb from limb and mingled with uprooted trees?'

Uniformitarianism cannot explain why so many animals died violently at the same time or why they were buried so rapidly in sediment. Like other fossils, dinosaur fossils are found in positions that suggest a violent death. Many are found in a 'swimming position' and yet those animals were not aquatic.

Large fossils (plants/trees and animals) can also be found extending through several strata. Thus, these fossils must have been buried quickly because the top parts are just as well preserved as bottom parts. Vast amounts of sediment must have been deposited in a very short time. The existence of these fossils is impossible to explain if one assumes, as evolutionists do, that different strata were laid down at different times over millions of years. It would mean trees standing for millions of years while strata formed round about them.

It's noted, whilst trees are understood to be the oldest living things, they're not that old. The oldest tree, (a bristlecone pine tree from California's White Mountains), is almost 5000 years old. It's called Methuselah, after Biblical Methuselah.

Moreover, the order that fossils are found supports the flood. Creatures buried in sediment are found in the general order which we would expect if a flood buried them. Whilst marine creatures and fish would have died first, land animals would have been in a better position to escape.

Thus, the catastrophe would have first affected the marine creatures that live near the bottom of the sea. They would have been killed and engulfed by debris. It highlighted the simpler the organism, the graver its chances of escape. Thus, in the lowest levels of the sedimentary rock, we would expect to see the remains of simple marine invertebrate organisms, which is what's found. The more complex vertebrates, mostly fishes would be next on the hit list. As the flood continued to rise, torrential streams would begin to pour vast amounts of sediment into the lakes, entombing and killing the fish.

Amphibians, near the water and not the most adept on land would be next. Reptiles would have a marginally better chance of escape but not being very mobile, they would drown. Mammals would be next. And it figures that man would have devised whatever means to survive, and would have held out to the last moment. And some of them went underground?

So, the order, namely, marine invertebrates, fish, amphibians, mammals, and man, which is often found, does not imply evolution but rather reflects increasing ability to escape. The flood was however so chaotic and disorderly that there are many exceptions to this general rule, which is what's found. This sequence is not found everywhere.

For creationists then, the fossils are not the record of evolution and extinction over billions of years as evolutionists claim, but rather a legacy of the global flood 4,500 years ago. It's recalled esoteric accounts suggest the flood happened circa 9000-11,000BC. Or perhaps that was the first flood that resulted in the dark mass and water we hear about in Genesis 1:2? However, we'll get back to this.

It's also understood, we have the Flood to thank for our fossil fuels. Rather than taking millions of years to form by the ordinary death and decay of trees and marine life, it's highlighted the hot wet mud layers that existed after the Flood would have provided the perfect conditions for rapid coal, oil and gas formation (oil and coal can be produced very quickly). Vast deposits of coal and oil are found sandwiched between sedimentary rock layers (which are basically layers of dried out mud).

As mentioned, the majority of the earth's surface is composed of sedimentary rock, which means that all the layers, including the layers of coal and oil, were laid down primarily by the action of water in a flood i.e. enormous pressure of current and water embedded plant and animal (remains) with great force.

Contrary to uniformitarianism then, large-scale flood catastrophism has both the scale and potential to explain such unique deposits. Baker notably highlights that objects including a ten inch long eight carat gold chain, an iron pot, and human skull have been found in coal, evidencing that a human civilisation perished while the coal was being formed.

As touched on, before the Flood, it had never rained. Optimal weather conditions prevailed, and oxygen levels were some 20%, which were much more conducive to long life. Wo/man lived l-o-n-g time, (like Methuselah), and the favourable climate entailed abundant vegetation. An argument for the water vapour canopy idea, (above the earth's atmosphere), is that it ensured an even, warm, subtropical climate worldwide. And it protected Earth from the harmful effects of radiation. It's likened to a bell jar that shielded us from the shitstorm outside.

Canopy theorists highlight that with no water vapour, we became vulnerable to absorbing dangerous cosmic radiation. It's thus contended that Noah and his family would have begun to suffer mutation of genetic material in the cells of their bodies, which together with the generally harder way of living, would have ensured a steady decline in man (and animal's) life-span. As discussed, mutations cause ageing and disease.

In tandem with the description of the pre-Flood world, evidence shows the earth had a universally warm, subtropical climate e.g. corals grew near poles (corals cannot live in water cooler than about 68 degrees), as did coal seams, which indicates abundant tropical vegetation once grew there. The remains of animals (fossils) now confined to warm regions are found all over the earth, which again supports a constant subtropical global climate. Like, dinosaurs are found everywhere.

Evolutionists agree a generally warm and mild climate over much of the earth would have been required to favour their large growth. Like, Dr Robert Jastrow, an apostle of evolution, observed, 'Throughout the long reign of the giant reptiles, the world had known a mild and constant climate; on every continent the eye met gentle landscapes of low relief, with shallow seas and vast areas of swampland and tropical forest. The elements of the world were in perfect balance...'

Alfred Wallace concurred, 'There is but one climate known to the ancient fossil world as revealed by the plants and animals entombed in the rocks, and the climate was a mantle of spring-like loveliness which seems to have prevailed continuously over the whole globe'. And David Icke (2007) concedes, 'The whole climate changed as the sun's rays baked once green and abundant lands, like Egypt, and began to form deserts. Scientists agree that Egypt, now part of the Sahara Desert, was once a green and pleasant land' (p.82).

So, pre-flood conditions favoured the growth of much larger plants, animals, and reptiles in general, which explains the large size of dinosaurs. It's noted, there's much evidence of 'giantism'. Giant forms have been discovered of almost every creature alive today, with mammals often twice the size of current counterparts e.g. bears, camels, panthers, pigs, rhinos, elephants, tigers, and wolves.

Among reptiles were enormous dinosaurs and giant turtles/tortoises i.e. the size of small cars. Crocodiles were three times larger pre-flood, and lizards were six metres long. Giant fossil birds have also been found, as have insects. Dragonflies have been discovered with 20-30 inch wingspans. Central to the theory of evolution is the idea that as an animal evolves to a more complex form, it also increases in size, and yet there are no giants today ('allegedly').

In the Bible (Job 40:15), we hear about Behemoth, who was the biggest of all creatures God made. Behemoth had a tail like a cedar tree and this friendly giant ate grass. The word dinosaur was notably introduced in 1841 by Richard Owen to describe a terrible lizard/dragon. So, dinosaurs were dragons, who played a significant role in mythology?

It's also highlighted, there's a difference between friendly dinosaurs, like Diplodocus, and unfriendly dinosaurs, like Tyrannosaurus Rex. And it's suggested the deadly dinosaurs were monster hybrids created by the 'gods'. They were the chimeras of old? As touched on, reptiles keep growing for as long as they live, which explains the nephilim (reptilian) giants? It was the 'golden age'.

Evolutionists surmise that a sudden change in climate might have been responsible for the extinction of the dinosaurs, but they have no explanation for it. They postulate the last Ice Age happened after the asteroid wiped out the dinosaurs, and then cave men (archetypal humans) appear. However, there's evidence that dinosaurs and humankind co-existed, like footprints in rock. And blood cells and tissue have been found in dinosaur bones, suggesting they're not that old.

So, according to the Bible, God truly did a number on His creation. The earth's crust was broken apart by terrible volcanic and earthquake activity, and the whole earth was literally drowned. The Flood detrimentally altered the whole climate of the earth. In Genesis 8:22 (after the flood) we're told, 'As long as the earth remains, there will be springtime and harvest, cold and heat, winter and summer, day and night'.

Extreme weather landed, coupled with volcanoes, earthquakes, and other grim natural occurrences. The optimal climate vanished and widespread extinction arose as many animals couldn't survive the treacherous conditions. The equator became toasty and the poles rapidly covered with ice. Or the high ice-walls at Antarctica already existed to contain the seas, as Enoch pertained to?

It's purported that an Ice Age could have commenced after the Flood. There is widespread evidence for a post-Flood glacial period, and the climatic aftermath of the Genesis Flood seems to be the best explanation for this catastrophic icy era. Whilst secular scientists propose multiple Ice Ages during earth's history, each lasting millions of years, most creationists agree there was one major Ice Age following the Flood. And this was a rapid Ice Age, lasting about 700 years.

It's said the post-flood biblical Ice Age is less than 4,000 years ago, if the flood happened 4,500 years ago. Others however suggest the Ice Age was 10,000 years ago. The Ice Age has been a longstanding problem for uniformitarian thinking, not least because a substantial amount of information (most formerly glaciated areas) indicates only one Ice Age.

It's noted, Ice Ages are produced primarily by precipitation over moderately cold areas, not by severe cold conditions as previously assumed. Thus, the earth was not completely frozen, but the polar caps were much larger then. Apparently 30% of the Earth's surface was covered in glacial ice at the peak of the Ice Age.

It was therefore providential that Noah and company didn't drift towards the North or South Pole, and also that God created His creatures with the capacity to adapt to their new environment. It's also noted, that when the Ice Age ended, the volume of ice returned to liquid, raising the sea levels, and drowning all areas near the ocean.

This could explain why millions of mammoths were wiped out along the coastline of Northern Siberia and Alaska? Some of them died so quickly that food is preserved undigested in their stomachs. Some evolutionists claim they had just taken a mouthful of food before they fell into a hole or river, but five million of them? This is notably the 'lake drowning theory'.

Unlike most parts of the world, where temperatures are not cold enough to preserve whole animals in ice, Siberia has numerous animals embedded in her ice including sheep, camels, rhino's, bison, horses, tigers, oxen, lions. The picture is one of a catastrophic death involving millions of animals.

It seems creationists have been divided on whether the woolly mammoth perished in the Flood or afterwards. Like, Brown suggests they died in the Flood by a quick freeze, hence the undigested food in their stomachs. But mammoth remains seem to come after the Flood. Apparently, the majority of their bones are not found in the thick sequences (ten thousand feet thick in places) of sedimentary rock but rather the frozen tundra below the surface. If the flood deposited sedimentary rock (as a rule) then the soil layer in which the mammoths are found must be a later deposit.

Thus, it's possible the frozen mammoths were post-Flood elephants, which adapted and became hairy. The cold (environmental cue) triggered certain dormant genes into action to produce the long hair and other cold-adaptive traits. This 'kind' of elephant was suited to an Ice Age climate. Apparently woolly rhinos were also prominent. Then they were wiped out by severe climatic change. It seems muddy hail from a huge freezing storm got them?

Contrary to the uniformitarianism theory, Alford asserts 'it is now increasingly obvious that catastrophism has shaped many parts of the earth and solar system. But even where the evidence is strong, the scientific establishment is incredibly conservative when it comes to new ideas which upset the old'. He states, 'We cannot blame the scientist for the set of beliefs which he must express to maintain the respect of his colleagues'.

Vernon (2012) concedes, 'When new evidence challenges the original perception, it is likely to be resisted by reinterpretation or outright hostility, particularly when reputations are at stake' (p.32). So, despite the evidence for a catastrophic global flood, the scientific community remain in denial because of pride?

There is much evidence that sea levels were once much lower relative to land surfaces than at present, and the rapid rise in sea levels is globally documented. Thus, it's unlikely the flood happened at the end of the ice age (as suggested) because evidence suggests that the flood was not simply caused by polar icecaps melting but by something far more dramatic. It seems the flood also explains lakes, especially at high elevation?

Scientists inform the origin of 1,450 million billion tonnes of water in the world's oceans remains a mystery. And there are lost continents or 'ghost' continents scattered around the globe, with water covering previous landmasses. Splendid buildings (including pyramids) etc are all submerged. It seems clear there was something going on before we got here.

It's also asserted, there's much evidence for a young Earth i.e. thousands of years old (not billions). In addition to geological columns, evidence comes from the surface e.g. living things, like trees. Ocean sediments are not nearly thick enough to correspond to expectations based on length of geological column. And there's nowhere near enough salt in the seas, even if we assume there was no salt in the seas to begin with. David Icke (2007) quotes Carl Wunsch, professor of oceanography, who said 'the ocean has a memory of past events running out as far as 10,000 years' (p.570).

And there's nowhere near enough meteoric dust. There should be tons more if Earth is millions of years old. It's also claimed there's not nearly enough helium in the atmosphere (which is created by radioactive decay) to correspond with the alleged age of the Earth, even if we assume there was no helium to begin with. And entropy is in full swing, like the earth's magnetic field is decaying rapidly. Maybe the stars will fall from heaven?

Population size also defies evolution, as there should be billions more humans. But instead we find circa 250,000 people lived at the same time as Christ, the Godman who defines time i.e. BC/AD. In 1650 the world doubled. By 1850 there was approximately one billion, by 1930 two billion, and by 2011 seven billion.

It's also noted, that like fossils, dating methods (including radioactive dating techniques) can be interpreted differently. And the same evidence can be used to support either creation or evolution. They rely on unprovable assumptions like an ancient world. All dating methods are based on the principle of uniformitarianism.

As Black highlights (2010), there is very little evidence that science can properly account as 'hard' evidence beyond 11,451BC, and reliable dating methods are only reliable until then (p.34). The rest is arguably to fit speculation and theory. It's also noted, the Flood would have produced such drastic changes that it makes dating any earlier than this extremely difficult.

However, it also seems pertinent to note the 'Gap Theory', which suggests an age-old gap between Genesis 1:1 and 1:2. Genesis 1:1 tells us, God created the heavens and the earth. Then verse 2 tells us the earth was formless and empty, dark, and covered in water. It's said the gap, which could be millions of years, attempts to reconcile creation with old age evolutionary theories. So, 'old earth creationism' comes to the rescue, because there's evidence for an old earth? Like, it's suggested the account of Genesis reflects evolution i.e. fish and birds, then animals, then man (or maybe not).

It's also speculated there was a pre-Adamic race and their antics resulted in a flood, hence the water in Genesis 1:2. So, God created heaven and earth. But something catastrophic happened, and God drowned Earth. Something before Adam caused the earth to become without form and void. And then God created earth. It's advocated there's some suggestive scripture, like Adam's told to replenish the Earth. Thus, there was a civilisation before Adam and Eve?

According to Blavatsky's Secret Doctrine, there was a pre-Adamic race in Atlantis. She states this can be found in the Bible when read esoterically, which suggests a false teaching since she channelled demons? It's suggested Lucifer was the king of this kingdom. The pre-Adamic race weren't humans, but some kind of intelligent creatures. As mentioned, the Sons of God sang for joy at the creation of the Earth. So, the angels were here before us. And Satan had fallen before we arrived? It's highlighted, that he wasted no time on his mission to beguile us, as he appears almost straight away, in Genesis 3.

Thus, it's possible there could have been two floods? Whilst it seems Atlantis was the pre-Flood world, (the one land mass), it's possible that Atlantis existed before the Earth was made, hence, the difference in dates? Then God made the Earth, which became overrun with nephilim, which was then destroyed in the Flood. Presumably the fact Earth was submerged in water from the beginning also skews dating?

As established, scientists need the earth to be very old in order for evolution to be viable. But maybe it's not that old, and maybe everything we've been taught via our state funded education is garbage? Maybe we're not spinning through an insanely vast universe at insane speeds. But rather, we live in a snow-globe. And we don't stem from pond scum or bacteria. We're not an accident of natural processes that did not have us in mind. But rather, God created our world and everything in it. And He did not use evolution as His method of choice for creation, since where are the half-breeds?

The evidence suggests that all life was created by an exquisite designer. And our physical world is couched in a far larger spiritual (multidimensional) reality. And God is outside space and time. Thus, He can tell us His-Story ahead of time. Like, we're forewarned about a great deception, which could be 'scientism'? Perhaps the globe theory is the strong delusion that causes the great falling away (apostasy) before Jesus' return? Hence, the beast's number, 666, is a feature?

As touched on, perhaps this deception is evolution, which depends on the deception of the Big Bang and cosmic evolution. These theories need each other to work, and infinite time. It seems we can achieve miracles with endless time and the laws of infinite probability? This evolutionary cosmology also sets the scene for the alien deception. It's plausible that life evolved elsewhere, somewhere in a galaxy far faraway?

In summary, we arguably require more faith to believe in evolution, than creation. Which suggests we want to believe this, as there's no judging God to answer to? We don't want to believe in God? Or we do, just not God of the Bible and His Son Jesus? It seems we only had two options, namely, creation or evolution, but now we have panspermia. Which bodes well, as people increasingly realise Darwinism is completely bankrupt. Aliens save the day? They're our progenitors? Like, Dawkins is open to the idea that we were created by aliens. Anyone but Almighty God?

In his book, 'The Blind Watchmaker' (1986), Dawkins wrote, 'More, I want to persuade the reader, not just that the Darwinian worldview *happens* to be true, but that it is the only known theory that *could*, in principle, solve the mystery of our existence' (p.XIV). Dawkins has notably been referred to as Darwin's pit-bull. It seems he's deceived, blinded by his own arrogance? He's like the demiurge?

Not dissimilar to Dawkins, Hitler declared 'the dogma of Christianity gets worn away before the advances of science. Religions will have to make more and more concessions. Gradually the myths will crumble. When understandings of the universe become widespread...then the Christian doctrine will be considered absurdity'.

As it transpires however, 'provable/testable' science increasingly supports God's word. It evidences the Biblical account of creation. Like, the flat stationary earth. And archaeology, particularly within the last hundred years, has repeatedly unearthed discoveries that have confirmed specific references in the gospels. Strobel (1998) highlights that as we live each day of history, we see more evidence of the authenticity of the Bible unfold.

As mentioned, Peter (Jesus' disciple) tells us about scoffers in the last days, who laugh at the truth. He also states, (in 2 Peter 3:5-6), 'They deliberately forget that God made the heavens long ago by the word of His command, and He brought the earth out from the water and surrounded it with water. Then He used the water to destroy the ancient world with a mighty flood'.

However, it seems the herd are awakening from their slumber. Despite the initial knee jerk reaction to seriously considering God's word, more people are beginning to think critically? We're beginning to realise that we're spoon-fed tripe, like photo-shopped pictures of the blue marble?

As highlighted, the material philosophy has served Satan well, with regards to deceiving the herd there is no God and spiritual world. The world has comfortably soaked up scientism. But now we're being scientifically guided towards mysticism. Like, quantum physics mirrors the cabala. It validates mysticism. Consciousness (mind) is somehow involved, which suggests idealism or panpsychism, as opposed to realism and materialism. It suggests Hermeticism i.e. all is mind?

It's said theoretical physics is being used to remove the stigma of occult connections/connotations, and put mysticism into the frame of reference of objective science. As Black (2010) points out, according to the secret doctrine, the cosmos created the human brain in order to think about itself. Thus, it seems we've come full circle i.e. mystical to material to mystical? As touched on, it's highlighted that science will support the New Age philosophy of deistic one-ism. Evolution is both physical and spiritual.

Fundamentally, we're either a mistake, the result of elementary primordial soup, or we're not and there is a reason for our otherwise seemingly pointless existence. So, do we put our faith in science, which is observed as fact until the next genius comes along and refutes it, or put our faith in God. That which, nature aside, we cannot see? Do we trust the biblical account of creation? As Paul said in Romans 3:4, 'Let God be found true, but every man a liar'. It's also understood that God can't lie, unlike His nemesis Satan, who is the father of lies.

Black (2010) cautions, 'the part of us, somewhere in our depths, that wants to believe in a mechanical-materialist universe, may on reflection, not be the part of ourselves we want to determine our fate' (p.542).

Ralph Waldo Emerson said, 'All I have seen teaches me to trust the creator for all I have not seen'. And Lord Kelvin (physicist) said, 'If you think strongly enough you will be forced by science to believe in God'. We can believe in creation and the laws of science. Indeed, the laws of science are God's laws of creation. In Proverbs 1:22, we're told '…How long will you fools fight the facts? Come here and listen to me! I'll pour of the spirit of wisdom upon you and make you wise'.

In 1 Corinthians 1:18-20 Paul wrote, 'I know very well how foolish the message of the cross sounds to those who are on the road to destruction. But we who are being saved recognise this message as the very message of God. As the scriptures say, 'I will destroy human wisdom and discard their most brilliant ideas' so where does this leave the philosophers, the scholars, and the world's brilliant debaters? God has made them all look foolish and has shown their wisdom to be useless nonsense'.

And evolution is nonsense siblings. The idea that something came from nothing is scientifically impossible. We have to face the fact that we can't hide God. Moreover, God tells us His creation is ample evidence of His existence. In Romans 1:20, we're told, 'For since the creation of the world God's invisible qualities, His eternal power and divine nature, have been clearly seen, being understood from His workmanship, so that men are without excuse'. So, Creation holds us accountable to the Creator. We can't blame soul destroying Darwin and Dawkins for our ignorance.

'Man will believe anything, as long as it's not in the Bible'. Napoleon

19

Who is God?

God says, 'I AM'. And Jesus said, 'I AM'. And the New Age gospel says, 'I AM', which is an audacious lie from the pit of hell? As discussed, there were Jews, who believed in the One True God, and there were pagans, who worshipped creation instead of creator. Like, Hindus are pagans. They endorse pantheism and believe in millions of gods. And *Hinduism* birthed *Buddhism*. Then the Godman arrived. But the Jews rejected Jesus as their Messiah. So, they're still waiting for their Messiah, which is precarious given the false Messiah is on his sordid way. Thus, *Judaism* birthed *Christianity*. Then *Islam* was born six hundred years later, when Muhammad regurgitated the Bible.

So, these five religions are the 'Big Five'. It's understood that religion is our endeavour to realign with God. It's our path to God. So, we'd probably want to make sure we choose the right one, as there's talk of an afterlife, and it's not all happy days. It's said we paddle our own canoe to hell.

Or maybe as Pope Francis claims, it doesn't matter which religion we choose, as we're all God's children communicating with Him in our own way. He even said atheists can go to heaven if they're good. So, that's nice. As mentioned, Pope Francis believes Muslims will go to heaven because they worship the God of Abraham. Hence, he's onboard Chrislam. He's making steps towards reconciling world faiths as the precursor to one world religion.

The idea that atheists can go to heaven undermines having a relationship with God. Atheists don't believe in God, ergo they don't know Him. Thus, God will say, 'go away, I do not know you'. And Muslims don't believe in God of the Bible, but rather Allah of the Koran. Jesus and the cross are undermined. It suggests there was no need for Jesus to get brutally tortured and die for us. His death was in vain. The contemporary message is be a nice person, 'be kind', as Jesus role modelled. It's all about love, and no judgement? But moreover, Pope Francis said, 'a personal relationship with Jesus is harmful and dangerous'. As I've said before, you couldn't make it up.

Gandhi similarly advocated, 'Religions are different roads converging upon the same point. What does it matter that we take different roads as long as we get to the same goal? In reality, there are as many religions are there are individuals'. In his opinion, religions as cultural and historical phenomena are more or less true (equal), in the sense that no single religion has the absolute truth. He said, 'the soul of religion is one, but it is encased in a multitude of forms'. And also, 'I consider myself a Hindu, Christian, Moslem, Jew, Buddhist and Confucian'. Mother Theresa concurred with Gandhi, that all spiritual/religious paths lead to God. Although apparently Christ spoke to her with regards to working with the sick and poor.

Bertrand Russell conceded, 'the God of most moderns is a little vague, and apt to degenerate into a Life Force or a power not ourselves that makes for righteousness' (p.123). Russell Brand epitomises this sentiment, as he conceptualises God as an omnipotent, unifying frequency of energy manifesting matter from pure consciousness.

It makes more sense that mind created matter, rather than the reverse. The idea that our insanely complex universe, including our brains, magically and accidentally evolved (from nothing and for no reason) is ludicrous. So, there's mind, and it appears reality is a matrix of energy dancing for itself? And we're part of that universal energy i.e. pantheism. We're inherently in the mix, but if we transcend our bodies, we can exist as pure consciousness.

So, there's a certain appeal to New Age philosophies. Besides the supposition that we're God, they offer real spiritual experiences. We want at-one-ment, not atonement? They're 'softer' and 'freer'. Hence, they're more palatable than Islam and Judaism? Less is more when it comes to rules? Like, Jews have 613 commandments, and Mormons have 4000.

And Allah is renowned as the great God of 'Thou-Shalt-not', especially for women. Like, in Saudi Arabia, for example, women are forbidden to dance, play music, sing, go out on their own, cycle, drive etc. And leave the country if they want to (they have to secure male consent). It's arguably a bind being born into this religion/country. It's also noted, that apostasy from Islam warrants the death penalty. No pressure then.

It's argued that religion is based on man's pride, as it assumes that man can to do something to earn God's acceptance. Thus, Jesus replaced religion with relationship. It's not about works, but rather faith in what He did at the cross. We sin, as we're bound to, and we ask for forgiveness (we don't need to carry the burden of guilt etc). We learn and grow spiritually. It's noted, spiritual growth means to transcend narcissism.

God wants us to fellowship with Him, because we want to not because we have to. Love has to be free, unconditional. And when we love people, we want to care for them, and be there for them. It's a privilege to help them. Thus, we labour in the vineyard because we love God, not because we want to earn His love. God loves all His kids regardless of how crap we are, or if we ignore Him. 'God is love' (1 John 4:16). Moreover, it's the heart that matters, and omniscient God knows all our hearts.

People are controlled by religion, whereas Jesus came to set the captives free. We can be reconciled with Father God through Him. It's summarised that religion is behaviour modification, whereas Jesus is heart transformation. Religion is arguably bosh. Indeed, it's said religion is a portrait of God by the Devil. It's also understood, the serpent has many disguises i.e. philosophies/religions. So, religion is used to control us or make us good. Like Napoleon said, 'Religion is what keeps the poor from murdering the rich'. But we no longer need religion to be good. We're civilised?

It's speculated that religion was necessary to ensure man's survival back in the day, when we were maniacs. So, religion wasn't about connecting with God, but rather ensuring the survival of our species. It helped our social evolution. Being watched made us nicer people? But people can get on fine without religion. We're sensible enough to cultivate our own morals and values, as Nietzsche instructed. We were freed when we killed God? Like, Scandinavian countries, for example, have 'outgrown' religion. And we have CCTV watching instead of God. Religion is superfluous, and if anything, causes division (which is the point).

Religion seems to be about outward behaviour i.e. rules, rituals, regulations. But people could be in churches, synagogues or mosques, having all kinds of perverse thoughts. Men of the cloth may act overtly religious and moral, but God knows what's really in their hearts and minds, like slipping into little Johnny's bed when lights are out, and slipping into little Johnny.

As Paracelsus said, 'He who is dressed up like a clergyman is therefore not necessarily a spiritual person, although he may have been ordained by the Church. God looks at the heart, and not at the ceremony'. Or take too many Muslim men who are oppressive towards women. Their religion states that men are superior to women. So, women have to suck it up?

It's also bemusing that 'religious' people are more concerned with what others think, than what God thinks? Like, it's said in Afghan, for example, shame only occurs when something is witnessed, not when something happens behind closed doors. So, it's okay for God to see us do something improper, but God forbid anyone else sees what we're really like?

Like, for a tame example, many Muslim women smoke, but they won't smoke in public. I've genuinely enjoyed the freedom of smoking in public (in Arab lands), and having Muslim women stare at me, presumably thinking, have you no shame? But as a white westerner, I'm a law unto myself. They're also led to believe we're infidels, more lowly. We're skanks (LOL).

So, religious people have to keep up appearances. Like, Muslim refugees I worked with, said newlyweds have to put their bedsheets out within five days of being married, so the rest of the Islamic community can witness the blood and thereby ensure the consummation of the marriage, and the wife's virginity. It's noted, there's no evidence of the husband's chastity.

There is however 'bum love' to get round the sex ban. And there's hymen restoration surgery, should one falter. Muslim men can also take more than one wife, on the premise he treats them all equally. Whilst arguably disempowering to women, this arrangement could be construed as empowering if poly-amorous? Muslim men also get 'temporary marriages', so they can get nasty with prostitutes, only to say divorce three times and the marriage is dissolved. It's farcical.

Religion seems to be a rule book, and man makes up the rules? Like, the Jewish Talmud states paedophilia is kosher? It's also noted, Muhammad married one of his wives, Aisha, when she was 6 and consummated the marriage when she was 9 (he was 53). And Vatican City only changed the age of sexual consent from 12 to 14 in 2009 (800 priests live there). As Bill Schnoebelen asserts, celibacy means not marrying, not sexual abstinence.

Thus, religion has been working out well for men, hence the backlash of feminine God? Lest we forget, mutilating female's genitals. There are no medical benefits, and it carries health risks. It's a brutal practice, (often conducted without anaesthetics), to deny women sexual pleasure. We're not to be trusted, unlike men?

Circumcision however doesn't sound like a hoot. I heard a joke about circumcision, namely, 'do you charge much? No, I just keep the tips' (LOL). Part of Abraham's covenant with God included circumcision for boys at eight days old. This was a visible sign of belonging to God. Those circumcised were God's people, and they would follow Him. It was also a blood sacrifice? It seems this branding separated them from the sex pest heathens in Nimrod's Babylon. Perhaps God chose to mark this intimate area because it served as a godly reminder not to please their flesh through sexual immorality, unlike their pagan peers?

However, when Jesus came, he reconciled Jew and gentile, and circumcision became obsolete. Galatians 5:6 states, 'For in Christ Jesus neither circumcision nor uncircumcision has any value. The only thing that counts is faith expressing itself through love'. With the indwelling Holy Spirit, we don't need the law to dictate our behaviour. We can cultivate self-control? Like, we don't need external triggers to remind us to behave? Like, the Jews wear 'Tzitzits' which are tassels worn on the outside of clothing in order to remember God's commandments.

So, religions like Judaism and Islam have countless rules. As mentioned, the Jews were given dietary instructions after the Flood. God differentiates between clean and unclean animals. It's noted, that many of the animals God designated as unclean are scavengers, which would make us sick. Like, prawns eat all the crap at the bottom of the sea, and then people eat 'prawn cocktails'. And no good can come from eating pigs, which the Muslims endorsed. For Muslims, even to say the word pig makes one's mouth dirty. Suffice to say, pigs are awesome and clever.

Jews refer to Kosher meat, and Muslims refer to Halal, which means all blood has been drained from the animals, because it's not okay to drink blood (unlike their pagan peers)[31]. So, Muslims and Jews don't dig on swine, and Hindus don't dig on cows. On the contrary, cows are revered in India. Apparently, Krishna loved butter, and thus cows are more fruitful alive than dead, as they produce milk.

And from a secular western perspective, 'religious people' dress funny. Like, the Amish seem backward? Or like, orthodox Jewish men's curly sideburns, their beards sans moustaches, and their black hats seem peculiar. Like, it seems odd that Jewish women wear wigs as head coverings? And Mormons (Latter Day Saints) wear magical pants (LOL). And like the (oppressive?) letterbox attire for Muslim women. It's not practical for swimming or eating, but modesty is more important. Allah forbid a man sees an ankle. Apparently, prostitutes have nothing on underneath their burka. Like, the Catholic Church has its dress and pomp, including fish-god hats. And the Tibetan monks, witch doctors, towel heads like the Sikhs etc, have theirs. And like the Rastas, whose dread-locked mane represents the Lion of Zion.

Given the choice, if any road will take us, Rastafarianism seems fairly palatable? Like, the concession to smoke Bob Marley cigarettes, and vegetarianism, is all good. They're also an Abrahamic faith, with their spin on scripture. Like, Haile Selassie (1892-1975), who was crowed emperor of Ethiopia in 1930, was the Second Coming of Christ. He was an incarnation of God or Jah.

Ras Tafari Makonnen took the regal name Haile Selassie, which means 'the power of the trinity' and 'noble birth'. Officially his full title was His Imperial Majesty Haile Selassie I, Conquering Lion of the Tribe of Judah, King of Kings of Ethiopia, Elect of God. Rasta's believe they're God's chosen people (why not), and they honour Africa as the birthplace of humankind. They also endorse reincarnation. In addition to Mary Jane's influence (to increase spiritual awareness), Rasta's ceremonies consist of chanting, drumming, and meditating to reach a heightened state of spirituality.

So, maybe this road doesn't take us there, anymore than atheism/scientism or agnosticism. And it opens people up to spirit possession. Moreover, there's no drinking alcohol for Rasta's, which blows, whereas Jews and Christians are fine with wine.

---

[31] Kosher (Hebrew) means proper or fit, and Halal (Arabic) means permissible.

Muslims are also prohibited from drinking alcohol, which they substitute with chewing Khat (plant material), which is amphetamine like. It's noted, Khat was manufactured into MCat aka 'meow meow' (LOL). This white powder, which kills the nose, became illegal (Class B) in the UK in 2010. Or maybe we prefer ayahuasca and pantheism? It appears that many people born into a religion, including witchcraft and scientism, inauthentically stick with it?

Maybe we want to believe Dawkins' bus adverts, which exclaimed, 'There's probably no God. Now stop worrying and enjoy your life'. As highlighted, maybe we'd prefer there's no God? No one to answer to for the immoral choices we've made, despite our God given conscience. The lie of evolution is pleasing to our flesh.

The contemporary (scientific) view is that religious beliefs, however deluded, thrive because they ease deep existential anxieties, where logic and reason cannot help. However, we're still left with the 'God shaped hole' Pascal referenced, and which Sartre acknowledged. We might believe the lies we're told about materialism, but deep down we know there's a disconnect. This is evidenced by the innumerable people who are not okay, contrary to appearances. We're not okay because we were never meant to live without God.

Atheists might be atheists, because they don't want to believe in a God who allows suffering? It seems a paradox that a good God could allow evil and suffering. It questions His omnipotence and benevolence. Thus, He either doesn't care, or He's limited, which isn't much of a God?

It seems we're quick to judge God. We're egocentric through no fault of our own? Moreover, humankind is responsible for much evil and suffering. Like, rape, murder, animal abuse, and chemtrails. We allow 'politics' to happen on our shift. We watch people starve to death whilst we dispose of unwanted food. No action is complicit consent.

Contrary to dualism, God of the Bible isn't responsible for the genesis of evil. But rather we choose our choice. It seems God is the ultimate existentialist, as His philosophy centres on freewill. God created us with freewill (like the angels etc), so we can sing and dance if we want to? We can be saints or sinners?

As discussed, sin entered creation and the punishment was death. Paracelsus notably said, 'God kills no one, it is nature which causes people to die'. Thus, there's moral evil, which is God permitted human pain and suffering because of original sin i.e. our plight as fallen creatures in a fallen world. And there's malevolent evil, which God also allows. As discussed, there's more than just our physical dimension at play. And it appears there's a cosmic chess-match underway. Souls are trophies.

Thus, it appears not all roads lead to the One True God, but rather open people up to the spiritual world. At a time of much confusion then, it seems prudent to consider religion, to ascertain what people are putting their faith in, and what they're fighting about. Souls are at stake.

It's also noted, we can't make God who we want Him to be. We can't choose which characteristics we'd like God to have, like a 'pick n mix'. Like, we want Him to be okay with immoral behaviour (sin), when He's not. Or we want to worship a god who's kosher with polygamy and paedophilia? God's not a buffet. We essentially create idols by conjuring up what we want God to be.

Voltaire said, 'God created man to be in His image, and then man went and returned the compliment' (LOL). Anthropomorphism is notably treating God like a human creature. And the anthropomorphic fallacy is that

God is like us. God made us in His image, but God is not like us. I AM is who He is. And as highlighted, maybe when Jesus said I AM, He was telling the truth.

So, we'll start with Islam, (since we've covered Judaism/Christianity in His Story), then consider the other two of the Big Five. Islam is the second biggest faith after Christianity, and it's the fastest growing (breeding helps). But more potently, it's being used as an ideology to fight Jews and Christians.

So, like Jews, Muslims dispute Jesus is the Son of God. They regard Jesus as a prophet, like Muhammad (570-632), but Muhammad was better? Muhammad is the seal of the prophets. Thus, he usurps Jesus. He provides the final version of the truth, (apparently Jews and Christians had some errors in their teachings), which he allegedly received from the angel Gabriel. His conversations with Gabriel, who appeared to him when he was meditating in a cave from 610-623, became the Koran.

It's noted, that Muhammad had a degree of respect for Jews and Christians, and the God they worshipped. He'd heard about Yahweh during his sojourns as a camel train driver. Contrary to the pagan gods his people followed, and the debauchery he witnessed, including cheating traders, alcoholism, gambling, and parents killing their kids, this Yahweh character seemed like a good salt.

Thus, Arabia was populated by animistic shamanistic tribes i.e. they worshipped the sun, moon and stars, and other natural objects. The Ka'ba (cube) in Mecca was the centre of idol worship, and pilgrims came from all over to worship there. There were at least 360 idols surrounding the Ka'ba but Allah, Moon-god, was the supreme deity. Whilst the moon god is generally worshipped as female deity in ancient Near East, the moon is male deity for Muslims. The crescent moon symbol represents Allah, the general name for God.

Moreover, Allah had three daughters, namely, al-Uzza, who was partial to human sacrifice, Manat, and al-Lat. These pagan deities were the most revered at the Ka'ba. And initially Muhammad conveyed that it was permissible to worship them (i.e. their shrines). For the first three years of his mission, he endorsed polytheism. He spoke of the gods in a 'splendid fashion'.

However, he later claimed the Devil had tricked him and put words into his mouth. The devil spoke through him. He was possessed? He subsequently asked the pagans to worship only 'Allah', the largest god. Pre-Islamic pagans thus worshipped Allah before Islam arrived, and they built temples for their Moon-god. The God of the Bible is therefore not the same as moon god Allah. And as it transpires, Islam preaches a different Jesus. The Bible and the Koran are not talking about the same person. Muslim Jesus isn't divine, didn't die, and didn't resurrect.

Muhammad began public preaching about Allah from 613. He taught: My teachings are simple. Allah is one God. Mohammad is his prophet. Give up idolatry. Do not steal, lie or slander. And never become intoxicated. If you follow my teachings, you follow Islam. Islam notably means 'submission' to Allah and comes from peace.

It's said Muhammad is the Muslim's friend, because he rescued Arabia. They were out of control and needed religion to control them. So, he conjured one up. Civility would be restored if everyone followed his prescribed rules. Like, not drinking alcohol is a good start?

So, God is One God and Christians are fools believing the Trinitarian lie. 'God neither begets nor was He begotten'. So, God didn't beget any kids. This therefore means Jesus was telling stories by declaring Himself the 'Son of Man'. Like, the demons were also ill informed, who declared Jesus is the Son of God.

As it transpired, when Muhammad conquered Mecca in 630, he discarded all the idols, but he kept the Ka'ba for Islam and rededicated the structure to Allah. The Ka'ba is the most important site in Islam. As mentioned, the Ka'ba is apparently located on the most powerful vortex in the world, and Muslims perform seven circumambulations of the Ka'ba in an anticlockwise direction. This is part of the Hajj (pilgrimage), a requirement of Islam. It seems like a magic ritual?

Other requirements, 'Pillars of Islam', (there's five pillars), include praying five times daily, in the direction of the Ka'ba (Allah's house) in Mecca. It's said this explains why Muslims excelled at maths and astronomy, because they had to find Mecca, wherever in the world they were. Apparently, Muslims were initially ordered to pray fifty times a day, but Muhammad haggled with Allah to get prayers reduced to five times daily. So, that was fortunate, as fifty times a day would be unbelievably impractical and annoying?

During this formal worship, Muslims bow down (in submission to the incomprehensible) and recite words. It's argued however that their mechanical prayers are performed parrot-style, and people recite the Koran today without knowing what they are saying. Which seems pointless? Alternatively, Jesus said (Matthew 6:7), 'But when ye pray, use not vain repetitions, as the heathen do: for they think that they shall be heard for their much speaking'. Missing prayers is catastrophic i.e. jail time in hell. But maybe they don't always feel like praying. Like, their heart's not in it, which defeats the point?

Like, catholic rosary beads (which came from Hinduism), Muslims have Misbaha beads to supplement their obligatory prayers. They're used to recite Allah's 99 excellent names (3x33). In tandem with the Old Testament, they tithe. And not dissimilar to lent, Muslims have Ramadan for thirty days in which they abstain from vices. They fast from sunrise to sunset. Thus, there was a new religion in town, with new rules. Like, their holy day is Friday.

Or rather, Islam is the Arab branch of the Catholic Church? Hence, they both revere Mary, and they both wanted shot of the Jews. Mary is exalted in the Koran. She's the only woman mentioned and is referred to seventy times. So, the greatest of all mothers wasn't Muhammad's mum? The Islamic Virgin Mary also continued to be a virgin, which is a false church teaching. The Bible tells us she consummated her marriage with Joseph after Jesus was born. So, the Koran and the Bible are not talking about the same Mary. It seems Muhammad was partial to virgins?

According to ex-Jesuit priest Alberto Rivera, the Vatican created Islam to destroy Jews and Christians. Rome wanted control of the Middle East, and Jerusalem for the Pope, but it was blocked by the Jews. Thus, they enlisted Khadijah. She was a rich Meccan widow (she was twice widowed) who proposed to Muhammad through a relative and he accepted (she was 40 and he was 25). Khadijah's assignment was to create a new religion for the children of Ishmael (Abraham's first son). She was recruited by Rome to prepare Muhammad to be a leader for the Arabs.

Rivera notably converted to Christianity, when he realised the Catholic Church is the whore of Babylon and Popes are antichrist. He advised that when his catholic mother was dying, she saw ugly creatures at her deathbed, and he vowed to find the truth, since Catholicism wasn't it. Rivera concedes that Jesuits were responsible for the creation of communism, Islam, Nazism, the World Wars, and the assassinations of JFK and Abe Lincoln. He said the papal hierarchy and the Jesuit Order are the most powerful entities at the top of the Illuminati power structure, working to usher in a Luciferian New World Order. Rivera was poisoned to death in 1987, having divulged the truth.

So, Roman Catholic Khadijah gave Muhammad the idea to base his religion on Christianity. Teachers were sent to young Muhammad and he underwent intensive training. He was told by his catholic handlers that Jews were the enemy, and only Roman Catholics were true Christians. Others calling themselves Christians were actually wicked imposters and children of the devil, who should be destroyed. His mission was thus to slaughter Jews and Christians, and conquer Jerusalem. It's said, until his 'Night of Power' in 610, when he met 'Gabriel' and the recitation of the Koran began, he was an unremarkable trader who sponged off his wife.

Apparently, Muhammad saw himself as a reformer of Judaism, which seems ironic given his latter disdain for Jews. It's also said, whilst Muhammad initially regarded Christians and Jews as natural allies, sharing the same core principles of his teachings, (which figures since he snaffled their religion), his attitude towards them darkened. Or rather, as Rivera claims, he was brainwashed to despise them. Suffice to say, this new religion was awesome for breeding religious hatred. It was a cunning plan on behalf of Mystery Babylon. It's ensured an endless supply of blood sacrifices since its inception.

Thus, as it transpired, the Jews refused to accept Muhammad as their prophet, so he turned on them. He was marketing himself as the prophet, but they weren't buying it. Maybe they were suspicious of the angel Gabriel he liaised with? Not least, because he urged Muhammad to massacre Jewish tribes. It's highlighted that 'Gabriel' is an interesting character. Like, he wouldn't go into a house with a dog or picture. And he said that, a child resembles the father if the man discharges first, or resembles the mother if she discharges first.

It's also noted, after Khadijah died, Muhammad married myriad women for political influence and power. He came to control the oases and markets, which forced other traders and tribesman to negotiate with him. He became a very powerful and politically persuasive man. He was 'inspired' by Gabriel?

So, Muhammad mixed it up, following Gabriel's instructions. Like, he proclaimed that Abraham is only the patriarch of Islam, not Judaism as well, because he 'surrendered himself to Allah'. Abraham is traditionally called the first monotheist. As discussed, he rejected Nimrod's polytheism and stood for the worship of God alone. Thus, he was neither Jew nor Christian, but rather a Muslim. Muslims believe all prophets and messengers were Muslims. Hence, Adam was the first Muslim and prophet. And Jesus was also a Muslim.

The Bible however tells us that Jesus was a Jew, and Abraham was the first Hebrew. God set Abraham (Shem's lineage) apart. God's people would be born through Abraham's loin juice, namely, Isaac. God told Abraham he would be the Father of many nations. Yet his wife Sarah seemed barren. They faithfully waited but no child came. And Sarah was post-menopause.

As it transpired, because they were both getting old, they decided to take matters into their own hands. So, Abraham got nasty with Sarah's Egyptian maidservant Hagar, which resulted in Ishmael. Then thirteen years later, Sarah bore Isaac. God delivered on His promise. So, Ishmael was surplus to requirements?

God told Abraham, '… Isaac is the son through whom your descendants will be counted. But I will make a nation of the descendants of Hagar's son because he is also your son' (Genesis 21:12-13). The Bible also tells us, (in Genesis 16:12), Ishmael 'will be a wild donkey of a man, and his hand will be against everyone, and everyone's hand against his; he will live in hostility toward all his brothers'. So, that doesn't bode well?

This gave rise to the Semitic race being split between Jew and Arab. It's noted, both Jews and Arabs are Semites (descendants of Shem). Ishmael became an expert archer and married an Egyptian, and his twelve sons became the founders of the twelve tribes that bore their names. Isaac married Rebecca, who bore twins, Esau and Jacob. And as mentioned, the twelve tribes of Israel came from Jacob aka Israel.

It's understood that Moses and Jesus came from Isaac's lineage, and Muhammad descended from Ishmaels. So, Isaac passed down Abraham's revelations to the Jews, and Ishmael passed it down to the Arab Hebrews. And then Muhammad decided to call them all Muslims?

Moreover, Muhammad changed the Biblical account about Abraham's sacrifice. Thus, in the Old Testament we're told God asked Abraham to sacrifice Isaac. It was a test of his faith but also a reflection of the future i.e. when God would sacrifice His only begotten Son. So, Abraham was about to do it, but God providentially stepped in and provided a ram. Muhammad however claimed that Abraham was asked to sacrifice his first born, Ishmael. As discussed, Satanists have to sacrifice their first born, and sacrificing kids to Baal is common practice.

The Ka'ba is believed to be the location where Abraham prepared to sacrifice Ishmael. It's noted, the Ka'ba, (this pre-Islamic shrine), contains a black rock that was believed to come from the home of the gods. It's suggested it was most probably a piece of a meteorite that fell from the sky. The Semitic cultures of the Middle East had a tradition of using unusual stones to mark places of worship. But Muhammad changed the narrative, claiming the stone was sent down by Allah to Abraham and his son Ishmael, to give them the precise location where to build the Ka'ba.

But moreover, besides hijacking the Old Testament (Judaism), Islam also did a number on the New Testament (Christianity). Unlike the Jews, who regarded Jesus as some sorcerer who led Israel astray, Muhammad recognised there was something special about Jesus. Jesus is a key figure in the Koran and is mentioned 154 times.

So, Muslims concede Jesus was born a virgin birth, but rather than the Holy Spirit's conception, hence God the Father, they attribute the miracle to the angel Gabriel. That is, God blew the spirit of Jesus through the angel Gabriel (who appeared in the form of a man) into Mary, and Jesus was conceived. Jesus was thus pure but not divine. Thus, the Koran refers to Isa (Jesus) as 'Son of Mary' as opposed to 'Son of Man'. There's notably no mention of her husband Joseph in the story, but rather Mary is alone in the desert.

It's also bemusing to note, that baby Isa could miraculously speak when only a few hours old. Surah 19:30 states, 'He said, 'I am indeed a servant of Allah: He hath given me revelation and made me a prophet'. The Koran says he shall preach to men in his cradle and in the prime of manhood, and shall lead a righteous life.

Besides speaking from birth, Jesus was unique in that He performed miracles e.g. healings, exorcisms, raising the dead to life. Sura 3:49 states, 'By Allah's leave I shall give sight to the blind man, heal the leper, and raise the dead to life'. No other prophet in Islam has ever been credited with such power, not even Muhammad himself.

The Koran also disputes the resurrection of Jesus, which further undermines His divinity. As mentioned, the burden of proof for the Christian faith is the resurrection factor. The fact Jesus died and resurrected evidenced that He was no ordinary man. That's not normal. He died for our sin and became the path back to God (He's our redeemer).

Muslims don't however believe Jesus was sacrificed for us. And they don't believe He died in 33AD. But rather, He's been in a state of 'suspended animation' ever since. Like, Enoch and Elijah were taken into the second heaven? It's believed that someone else took His place on the cross. Some think it was Judas, but apparently the majority believe God gave someone Jesus' appearance, causing everyone to believe that Jesus was crucified.

Contrary to Christian, Jewish, pagan, Greek and Roman historians who all claimed Jesus died on a cross, the Koran is the only historical document that denies Jesus died on a cross. And since Muhammad wasn't there, we have to take Gabriel's word for it? There is therefore no mediator to God, i.e. saviour to pay for our sin, but it's assumed Muhammad takes the role. Yet, it appears Gabriel is 'chief in command' as opposed to Muhammad. He's the source of Allah's revelation.

So, Muhammad ('the much praised one') turned on the Jews. But he not only expelled them from Medina, but also murdered them, with women and children sold into slavery. Thus, early Islam spread by warfare. Islam is not therefore a religion of peace, anymore than Catholicism. It's said that Islam is not a religion of love but of hate, plunder, rape and murder. It's asserted the Koran accentuates God's punishment more than his love, and the use of violence to impose Islamic laws. Furthermore, grown men marrying girls is not okay.

Praise God however, that most Catholics and Muslims are decent 'God fearing' people (at least on the surface). Religion works for most people? They're not all haunted perverts. It seems the Satanists are the haunted perverts. It's also noted, that Muhammad changed the Qiblah, which is the direction to be faced in prayer, from Jerusalem to Mecca, when he fell out with the Jews.

Apparently during his last few days, Muhammad asked Allah to curse Christians. The angel Gabriel said, 'the Christians call Christ the son of Allah…Allah's curse be on them, how they are deluded from the truth'. And the Koran 5:57 states, 'Believers take neither the Jews nor the Christians for your friends'.

Muslims need to defend Islam, and thus for the sake of Islam, murder is permitted. Allah will be pleased if we blow ourselves and others up for his name's sake? Muslims who kill apostates from Islam will be rewarded on the day of resurrection. Apparently, converting to Christianity is the gravest offence by Islamic law.

After Muhammad's death, power struggles arose regarding who should rightfully succeed him, which led to more bloodbaths and beheadings. Thus, Islam split into Sunni and Shia (for more division). The Arabs were united under Islam until they weren't? The Sunni/Shiite split has been described as the 1400 year old civil war within Islam.

As mentioned, Muslims invaded Palestine in 636 (they waged jihad) and built a mosque there. The Dome of the Rock was built there in 691. It has an antichrist text on its dome, namely, 'Say not that Allah has a son'. And the Dome of the Rock mosque contains scriptures like, 'Jesus son of Mary was only a messenger of Allah'. And, 'There is no God but Allah. He is One. He has no associate. And there is none comparable unto him. Muhammad is the messenger of God'. Apparently, the Dome of the Rock was built on top of the Holy of Holies, which is another kick in the face to Yahweh?

Apart from the brief crusader period, Muslim powers ruled Jerusalem from 636-1917 (when the Ottoman Empire was dismantled). So, it's not okay for Jews to be there? Yet the Koran accepts the divine deed of the Jewish people to the land of Israel. It recognises the land of Israel as heritage of the Jews.

The Dome of the Rock is where Muhammad ascended to heaven from, when he haggled with Allah to reduce the prayer quota. Apparently, Muhammad was transported to heaven in a dream (astral trip?) by a mythical horse (strange winged creature) called al Buraq. But evidence of his 'ascent to heaven', his footprint, is there. Apparently, he spoke to Abraham, Moses and Jesus who confirmed his mission as Allah's final prophet. Then he reached the seventh heaven and spoke with Allah.

So, whilst Islam's rules largely keep Muslims in check, (compared to the wayward west), their role model, peace be upon power thirsty Muhammad, is arguably suspect? Besides the polygamy and paedophilia, he role-modelled that murder is acceptable, even commendable, and selling women and kids into slavery is kosher/halal if they won't accept Muhammad as Allah's prophet?

It's also noted, that as public events, punishments e.g. stoning's, beheadings and amputations, are excellent deterrents as people learn first-hand what happens when they misbehave. People live in fear? Moreover, this religion violates our God given freewill. There is no choice. It also violates God's will, as He wants us to choose to know and love Him. It's abhorrent (evil?) to force religion onto people, like Catholicism did. And like Luciferianism will in the future?

As touched on, many Muslims believe we're living in the last days. And they concur with Christians that Jesus will defeat the coming antichrist or dajjal. The Second Coming of Isa, Son of Mary, entails returning to an oppressed and unjust world. The dajjal (who's Jewish and one eyed) will create worldwide corruption through his lies, claiming to be God and exercising supernatural powers. He will be the charismatic leader of the Jews (Zionists). But when the antichrist sees Christos, he dissolves like salt dissolves in water, and Jesus slays him.

Apparently, the defeat of the antichrist results in the eradication of the Jews. Christians alive at that time convert to Islam, as Jesus informs, 'if you want to follow me, you have to follow Muhammad'. And the cross must be destroyed since no one must receive worship except Allah. Indeed, overzealous Isa will 'kill all the pigs and destroy all the crosses', conferring Islam as the only true religion. All other religions will be exterminated. It's recalled that ISIS proudly declared, 'break all the crosses', which is not an arbitrary statement but rather a reference to this prophecy.

As also touched on, Muslims are waiting for their prophesied messiah, namely, the Imam Mahdi (Mahdi is a title meaning 'The Guided One'). He will lead a revolution and establish a worldwide Islamic empire. He arrives when Isa returns. Isa supports the Imam Mahdi, the final caliph, who rules over the world for seven years.

It's noted, the Islamic twist to Biblical eschatology provides a chilling parallel between the biblical antichrist and the Mahdi. Like, the Mahdi makes a seven year covenant with Israel. But he breaks the treaty, takes over the temple, and destroys Israel. The Mahdi must be a descendent of Muhammad, which corroborates with an Assyrian antichrist aka resurrected Nimrod?

Like the antichrist, the Mahdi has political, military, and religious power, and heads up a one-world religion (NWO). He will rule from Jerusalem, his capital of the world. And he will execute those who oppose his religion. Those who refuse to worship 'Allah'. Maybe this version of Islam is the Seven Noahide Laws? It's believed the Mahdi beheads Christians, as foretold in the fifth seal in Revelation. It appears Isa is the false prophet, who supports the antichrist. This inversion of events is not random.

After forty years of peace, Isa will die and be buried next to Muhammad in Medina. When he dies, all believers will also die peacefully. This is apparently the Islamic equivalent of the rapture (i.e. removal of the righteous people). Unbelievers will be left behind. Then on the Last Day, when the world comes to an end, Allah descends from heaven to judge all humanity and the jinn. The dead will be resurrected (Muhammad will resurrect first) and judgement will be pronounced i.e. either heaven or hell. Muhammad informed that the majority of people in hell are women. [Nice].

Muslims also have their version of heaven and hell. Having personally been to heaven (apparently he was escorted by Moses in his 'dream'), Muhammad was able to impart details. Like, there are seven heavens beneath God's heaven, which corroborates with Hermeticism, Gnosticism, the Talmud and Hinduism.

But rather than Jesus, Muhammad is at the right hand of God. Adam resides in the first heaven, which is made of pure virgin silver. Jesus and John the Baptist reside in the second heaven, which is pure gold. Joseph is in the third heaven, which consists of pearls. Enoch resides in the fourth white gold heaven. Aaron is in the fifth silver heaven. And the sixth and seventh are reserved for Moses and Abraham.

The rest of those saved enjoy happy days in 'the Garden', which is a perfect environment where all desires (including sexual) are granted. Muslims finally get to drink alcohol, as 'rivers of wine' flow in paradise. Perpetual virgins are awarded to the faithful. That is, irrespective of how many times one of these women engage in sex, they become a virgin once again (LOL). The 72 virgins are strictly reserved for martyrs who died in jihad, but regular Muslims receive 40 each.

In addition to the 'honour', 72 virgins is quite the carrot on the stick for young frustrated men? Interestingly, these virgins are 'dark eyed'. Apparently, martyrdom is the only way to dodge judgement day, and go straight to the garden. It's contentiously the best way to ensure salvation.

Like the Islamic heaven, the Muslim hell is made up of seven levels. The first level is purgatory, which some Muslims will have to pass through. It's recalled, Catholics have the same safety net. Christians are confined to the second level. Jews are relegated to the third level. The fourth level is for the Sabaeans. The fifth level is for Zoroastrians, the sixth is for idolaters, and the seventh is for hypocrites.

Humans are eternally punished in hell by demons. So, it's probably better to adhere to Muhammad's rules? Life is a flash in the pan compared to eternity. But what if these law-abiding religious people are barking up the wrong tree? And they live these restricted lives to no avail. If they're not saved, surely indulging in sex, drugs and rock and roll is more fun? No question.

It's also pertinent to note, God insists in both the Old and New Testament, not to add or take away from His word. God's word is infallible. Yet Muhammad added his own spin to scripture. Thus, it stands to reason, that Jews and Christians gave his teachings a wide berth. God is not Allah, and Isa is not Jesus. It's like, Rasta's have their spin. And Jehovah Witnesses and Mormons have their spin, which similarly rejects the trinity. As mentioned, the Illuminati introduced these ideologies to cause confusion in the church.

Jesus forewarned us about false prophets. And Paul cautioned in Galatians 1:8, 'But even if we or an angel out of heaven should preach a gospel to you contrary to what we have proclaimed to you, let him be accursed'. So, that's subsequent prophets and angels. The Bible tells us we need to test the spirits, and if they deny Jesus is God, they are not from God. But rather this is the spirit of antichrist. Thus, perhaps we can wonder about the prophet Muhammad and the angel 'Gabriel'? Perhaps Muhammad was deceived by an 'angel of light' to start a new world deception?

It's like an angel came to Joseph Smith, and gave him the revised Mormon version of events, namely, 'The Book of Mormon: Another Testament of Jesus Christ'. Smith reiterated Lucifer's lies that men can be gods, of their own universe no less, and inhabit a planet along with their spouses. Smith said, 'God himself was once as we are now, and is an exalted man, and sits enthroned in yonder heavens'.

The angel Smith met, named Moroni, directed him to a hill near his home in New York, which is where he received the inscribed 'golden plates'. The angel forbade him to show the plates to anyone until they had been translated from their original 'reformed Egyptian language'. When the translation was complete, Smith returned the plates to the angel, and they've never been seen since? The Book of Mormon was published in 1830. Like Muhammad, Joseph Smith was a prophet, but for these 'latter days'.

It's also noted, that Muhammad was genuinely freaked out by Gabriel, who apparently shook him and scared him. It seems Gabriel was less than pleased that Muhammad was illiterate. Apparently, the angel squeezed Muhammad forcefully to the limit of his endurance (he couldn't breathe), stating 'read', but as Muhammad was unable to read, he had to learn to repeat the Revelation.

Like, the first five verses in the First Revelation, which states, 'Read in the name of your Lord, the Creator, Who creates man from a clot of blood! Read! Your Lord is merciful, For he has taught men by the pen, And revealed the mysteries to them!' Once Muhammad was able to repeat correctly, the angel disappeared, and so it continued for twenty years. Hence, the Koran is called the recitation.

The angel alleged this was God's word, which was believable. The Arabs knew Muhammad was illiterate. It was therefore unlikely that he could have produced such eloquent words. It's also highlighted, the Koran is written in many places like poetry, suggesting a demon. Pre-Islamic Arabs believed in poetry demons. People are inspired to write poetry.

Apparently after Muhammad's 'First Revelation', when he got home, tired and frightened, he turned to Khadijah for comfort. She told her cousin about the encounter, who was a Bible scholar, and he confirmed the visitor must have been angel Gabriel who visited Moses.

Apparently, Muhammad became suicidal and wondered if he might be possessed. Each time he went up to a mountain to top himself, Gabriel would appear and tell him he is Allah's prophet. It's highlighted however, that no one is depressed or suicidal in the Bible having seen angels. Furthermore, Muhammad experienced visions from five years old, and apparently his wet-nurse believed he was demon possessed. It's also noted, whilst Allah is represented by the moon, Muhammad is represented by the star, which is a reference to Lucifer?

Interestingly, Jeremiah 23:15 tells us, false prophets will be fed with bitterness and given poison, and in 23:34, their family will be punished. And apparently Muhammad was poisoned, and his male kids died. So, he was accursed?

In addition to orthodox Sunni and Shia Islam, unorthodox mystical Sufism surfaced. The word Sufi is derived from Sofia meaning wisdom, and Sufism was undoubtedly influenced by Gnosticism and Neo-Platonism. Thus, whilst Sufis obey Islamic law, they pertain to the divine spark within. Like the Gnostic, the Sufi says, 'look into your own hearts, for the kingdom of God is within you'. Some sects endorse reincarnation, viewing the grave as a metaphor. It's said that only initiated Sufis believe in reincarnation, because they 'know' better? Sufi Muslims seek to find the truth of divine love and knowledge through direct personal experience of God.

Rather than the dogmatic paternalistic tendency in Islam, Sufism is gentler and more 'feeling'. They use repetitive words to reach the state of connecting with Allah. And further, whilst music and dance as methods of worship are forbidden in mainstream Islam, Sufis view music and dance as more fruitful exercises in praising God. Their sensual methods, which include sacred Sufi ritualistic dances, lead to a state of ecstasy (dhikr) and becoming 'one with the unity of God'. Interestingly, mainstream Islam believes this ecstatic phenomenon was experienced only by Muhammad and nobody else can ever experience it. As it transpires, spiritual morphine is offered in various religions, like kundalini yoga.

Sufism's claim to universality is founded on recognising there is only one God, the God of all people and all true religions. God is regarded as essence, creative power, and cosmic mind. Classical Sufi scholars have defined Sufism as 'a science whose objective is the reparation of the heart and turning it away from all else but God'. The essential truth is the presence of divine reality. Sufism is about realising the current of love that runs throughout life, the unity behind forms. Only 'presence' can awaken us from our enslavement to the world and our own psychological processes. Presence is the state of being consciously aware and existing in selfless love.

For Sufi's, life is a journey of the heart. The emphasis is on truth. And the endeavour is to free our true or higher self from our false self (which is inauthentic). In essence, we need to bin our ego. Remembering God is the beginning of remembering ourselves. It seems we are God, which contradicts mainstream Islam.

Like, the mystical Sufi poet Rumi, (who has attracted millions to Sufism), said, 'Everything in the universe is within you. Ask all from yourself'. And also, 'Stop acting so small. You are the universe in ecstatic motion'. It's said Sufism is the esoteric heart of exoteric Islam. Like, it's purported the cabala is the esoteric heart of Judaism, and Gnosticism is the esoteric heart of Christianity. The unifying core of all esoteric religions is that we are God, or little gods.

As it transpired, not all Muslims considered Muhammad the 'seal of the prophets'. As more prophets surfaced, introducing more versions of Islam. Like, the Baha'i faith, which came about in the 19th century. Arabic 'Baha' means glory or splendour. Bab (the gate), the holy man of Baha'i, interpreted new meaning to Islamic law and longed for the coming of the next prophet.

Bab's successor, Baha'u'llah, which means Glory of God in Arabic, was thus the real founder of the faith. He got a vision at age forty composed of Baha'i scripture. Baha'i believers regard Baha'u'llah (1817-1892) as the most recent in a long line of 'Divine Messengers' that includes Moses, Buddha, Jesus and Muhammad. God has sent his messengers to teach us how we can know and love God.

Thus, whilst Baha'i's believe the Koran is the word of God, they have their own holy book, namely, the Book of Laws (Kitabi Aqdas). So, it's an independent religion, separate from Islam. The Baha'i doctrine is based on three core principles, namely, the unity of God, religion, and humanity. They advocate that all religions are divine, from the same one God. God is the imperishable, uncreated being who is the source of all existence.

Like the cabala, they see Satan, not as an evil demon, but the promptings of our own lower nature. Demons, jinn and fallen angels are aspects of ourselves. And heaven and hell are spiritual states, not physical, which reflect how close or far we are from God.

Baha'i's believe we're all created equal, and diversity of race and culture are to be appreciated. Their principle is humanity is a single race. But moreover, (in tandem with this principle), Baha'u'llah wrote of the need for world government. Hence, the Baha'i community supports the UN and the UN officially supports the Baha'i faith. This is one of the fastest growing religions. It's also said however, that it was introduced to corrupt Islamic belief and (further) divide Muslims.

Whilst it seems Judaism and Luciferianism began at the same time, i.e. with regards to Team Abraham and Team Nimrod post-Flood, it's often said Hinduism is the oldest religion. Hinduism is the third biggest religion in the world. It began in India and entails a richly diverse collection of beliefs and practices. Hindu notably means Indian, and most Indians are Hindus.

Hinduism is free of absolute or formal doctrine and is instead a cultivation of mystic and transcendent experiences. The description of Hindu priests' rituals and techniques corroborate with the magical abilities of sorcerers, magicians, and shamans of old. As discussed, Nimrod's religion went global after the fiasco at Babel. Hence, ancient or traditional religions are essentially the same serpent and sun worship. It seems Hinduism is a version of the Mystery Babylon religion.

As it transpires, the 'gods' revealed the Vedas ('knowledge') to Hindu priests or 'rishis'. The Four Vedas are the most ancient books of Hinduism, and they form the basis of Hinduism. So, they were written by Vedic seers circa 1500-1000BC (the Vedic period), but they're 'not of human agency'. They're called 'sruti' (what is heard), which distinguishes them from other religious texts which are called 'smriti' (what is remembered). Sruti is primary scripture, and smriti is secondary scripture. Rishis get srutis in deep meditation. They hear from the 'gods' and they're able to express the inexpressible through poetry. Rishis experience God. They have gnosis?

The Vedic scholar David Frawley explains the Vedas reveal the earliest royal bloodlines of India, the priest kings (Nagas) who arrived from a place across the sea. As mentioned, Nagas are nephilim. Nagas (Sanskrit for serpent) are demigods, half human and half serpent. Apparently, they came from Ethiopia. According to the Vedas, warriors from outside of India invaded, so called Aryans, and these shapeshifting bloodline adepts were initiated into the ancient knowledge.

Whilst it's purported that Hinduism is the religion of an ancient people known as Aryans (who were Caucasian), others maintain Aryans mixed with Indians to create the Hindu religion. Followers of the Vedas are called Arya, which refers to a person of noble birth or an upper caste person. The term Aryan comes from Arya. So, Aryans instituted the caste system ('caste' comes from casta meaning race or lineage), which is the heart of Hinduism. Blood does matter.

Early Hinduism, as seen in the Vedas, is mostly nature-worship consisting of prayers, chants, and sacred formulas. The individual verses contained in the Veda compilations are known as mantras (some selected Vedic mantras are recited as prayers). Stress was placed on blood sacrifice to appease the gods.

It's noted, whilst the majority of practicing Hindus today don't participate in animal sacrifices (and Hindu scriptures, like the Bhagavad Gita, actually forbid it), some sects do partake in this horrendous ritual (it's particularly common in Nepal). Thousands of animals, usually goats, are decapitated and the blood is offered to the deities/gods. The three methods used by Hindus to slaughter animals are decapitation, piercing the heart with a spike, and asphyxiation. For some Hindus, the spilling of blood is also necessary to appease the evil spirits. Worshippers believe the animal sacrifice brings them luck and prosperity. Apparently in some parts of the Hindu world, human sacrifices are offered.

However, whilst the earliest Hindu worship was animistic, it came to be centred on one supreme impersonal cosmic being known as Brahman. Hindus believe there is only one Supreme Being and he is the god of all religions. Brahman is the soul or inner essence of all things i.e. pantheism. Brahman is the ultimate reality, which is formless, eternal, and everywhere.

Whilst popular Hinduism is polytheistic i.e. millions of gods, reformed theistic Hinduism conceives of God as comprising a triad of Brahma the Creator, Vishnu the Preserver, and Shiva the Destroyer. Brahma was the first created living entity in the universe. Like, Logos was the first emanation according to Gnosticism. Thus, these gods manifest, unlike unmanifest Brahman. Like, Shiva is movement, dance, and vibration. He partakes in the dance of destruction (as featured at CERN).

Vishnu has many incarnations including Krishna, who is often depicted as seducer of wives and daughters. Krishna means all attractive, and he was the eighth avatar of Vishnu. Avatar is notably a Hindu word which means incarnation of God. Russell Brand (2014) said, 'I've always liked Krishna as a god because he's jolly, dresses cool, hangs around in fields and forests with fit women and animals, plus he's blue' (LOL) p.232. Apparently, the blue colour is their aura.

Like Krishna, the blue Hindu goddess Kali is also popular. Hence, people stick their tongue out like her? Or they're possessed by her? Kali is apparently Shiva's wife. As mentioned, she's associated with end times, illness, death, violence, and sexuality. The seventh avatar of Vishnu was Rama, which means, 'He who gives transcendental pleasure to those who know him'. Some Hindus believe Jesus was an avatar of Vishnu, and some liken Him to Krishna. Thus, there's many Hindu gods (330 million), but Brahma, Vishnu and Shiva are the main ones, the so-called Holy Trinity.

Different gods serve different purposes. Like, Ganesh is popular, as this Lord of Success grants success, prosperity, and protection against adversity. As mentioned, he looks like an elephant-man. He has an elephant head, a big belly and four arms, which suggests he's one of those pre-Flood hybrids? It seems he exists in the second heaven, with the rest of these smurfs?

Thus, Hindus pick a god, presumably the one they like best. And they chant before an image or statue of whatever god and offer flowers, incense, special oils etc. As mentioned, Yahweh specifically warns against making idols. Indeed, one of the Ten Commandments is not to worship other gods. So, these gods are not the same as Yahweh, but rather people could be inadvertently worshipping demons?

It's noted, that Deuteronomy 4:16-19 states, 'So do not corrupt yourselves by making a physical image in any form – whether of a man or woman, an animal or bird, a creeping creature or a fish. And when you look up into the sky and see the sun, moon and stars – all the forces of heaven – don't be seduced by them and worship them'.

And in Romans 1:21-25 we're told, 'For although they knew God, they neither glorified Him as God nor gave thanks to Him, but their thinking became futile and their foolish hearts were darkened. Although they claimed to be wise, they became fools and exchanged the glory of the immortal God for images made to look like a mortal human being and birds and animals and reptiles'.

So, God let them do whatever things their hearts desired, which led them to indulge in vile and degrading things with each other's bodies. 'Instead of believing what they knew to be the truth about God, they deliberately chose to believe lies, so they worshipped the things made by God but not the creator Himself'.

Reincarnation is a central doctrine. The Bhagavad Gita, the premiere holy book or sacred text of Hinduism, states 'as the embodied soul continually passes, in this body from childhood, to youth, to old age, the soul inhabits another body at the time of death'. The same soul lives on, hence the concept of 'old souls'. It's said personalities change but the soul remains constant throughout successive lives. So, 'people' don't really matter since these physical bodies come and go?

It's recalled that Satan taught 'ye shall not surely die'. This was the first sermon ever preached upon the immortality of the soul, and this lie has been accepted into almost every faith. As discussed, reincarnation has ancient roots, and it's a common denominator of esoteric world faiths e.g. Cabalists, Freemasons, Rosicrucian's, Rasta's, Scientology, Gnostics, Spiritism, Jainism.

The Bhagavad Gita is epic mythology which centres on truth, duty, and spirituality. Or maybe it's not mythology, but rather stories from the pre-Flood world, hence Ganesh? There's a seamless succession of teachings through the concept of 'divine incarnation' (god's assuming flesh). However, regardless of the myriad deities, everything is different manifestations of the same ultimate reality Brahman. Brahman is thus represented though people, plants, animals, birds. And since everything is God, means that everything can be worshipped as God or having God in it, which includes us.

Brahman is however beyond concepts and images. This gives Hinduism its monastic character despite numerous gods and goddesses. Thus, we don't pray to Brahman as this impersonal force won't respond, unlike the 'gods'. Alternatively, people mediate and chant mantras ('vain repetitions') to induce trance states to communicate with the gods. They cultivate a telepathically receptive 'state'.

But moreover, it seems Brahman is playing a game with us? It seems we're bewitched by Maya, which is the appearance of the physical world. In tandem with atomic physics, we're not separate but rather a collective mass of pulsating energy. The physical reality is illusory?

The Supreme Being, God or consciousness, partakes in a molecular dance of separation. It takes on shapes and forms, but everything is the same God essence. But disguised by millions of expressions and forms, begs the question if someone or something is playing a game with form? This divine game is called Lila. So, God becomes the world, and this creative play is known as Lila, but under the spell of Maya means not to know this.

Part of Maya includes the illusion of the physical self, which gives rise to a separate soul separate from Brahman. Such separation is an illusion based on avidya, or ignorance, produced under the spell of Maya. [Contrary to avidya, vidya means knowledge or insight]. Tolle (2011) notes, that in the present day, human consciousness is completely identified with its disguise. It only knows itself as form, and this is the egoic mind. But we are not our ego. We are the stillness underneath the noise. We are Brahman?

It's asserted that we're locked into physical consciousness. And most people are not conscious of their higher self (spirit body), beyond ego identity. The Hindu truth is thus, there is no separate identity, and consciousness is God essence expressing itself in form. We are a point of consciousness. We're a point of light, a divine spark?

The manifestation of Brahman in the human soul is atman. The atman is therefore the true or real self. It's envisaged as a reflection of Brahman, a transpersonal and universal soul into which everything merges. So, we can understand the nature of Brahman from within the atman, to realise our Brahman nature. Like, we can know the soul of the world through our soul. The realisation is that God dwells within me as me, and God dwells within you as you. Hence, people say Namaste to greet 'god' in each other.

Thus, beyond the veil of form and separation, we are God, the eternal One life underneath all forms of life. Enlightenment means to become conscious of the absolute oneness of the universe. It's like DMT? Hindus gain 'moksha' when their soul merges with God. They realise their god self and become one with everything in the universe

At death, the atman departs through a particular chakra (spiritual channel) which is determined by spiritual progress. Hindus believe that cremation helps dissolve the bond between the atman and the physical body, thereby allowing the atman to have a smooth transition into the next incarnation. Black (2010) highlights, 'To the ancients *all* life was involved in a pulse, rhythm or breath. They saw all human lives as breathed temporarily into the world of *Maya*, or illusion, then breathed out again, a process repeated through the ages' (p.176). Like, God gives us breath and then takes it away.

The physical body is transitory and seen as neither beginning nor ending. Death is nothing to be feared, since we reincarnate, but the endeavour is not to. The blessed hope is to escape rebirth. It's relayed that humanity has been cast into a long cycle of repetitive incarnations known as Samsara (the seas of suffering), but if we achieve enlightenment we can bail. Moksha is the end of the death and rebirth cycle.

However, only the elite Brahmins (top caste) can be enlightened and dodge rebirth. Thus, Hindus have to work their way up through the caste system (through reincarnations). The aim is to live an ethical life to move up the proverbial ladder. So, this religion also conditions us into behaving.

The emphasis is thus on personal and spiritual development to enable freedom from the life-death cycle. The burden of life rests with working out karma from our current lives and past incarnations. Karma is the moral law of retribution for deeds done, which causes rebirth into this same world. But karma is itself an impartial principle of cause and effect.

In the world of the Gita, 'karma is the force of creation, where from all things have their life.' It's the 'principle of causality', whereby the whole ethical consequence of one's acts are considered as fixing one's lot in the future existence. In plainer words, we reap what we sow. Thus, if people are born into a crap life, (like they're disabled and live in the slums), it's their own fault. This perspective undermines compassion?

Eastern philosophy maintains that souls emanate from the Supreme Spirit and must strive to be free of guilt and contamination. It's about liberating the self from the self, which comes from liberating self from desires. Thus, we need to discipline ourselves?

As discussed, yoga ('union with god') is the path we assume to reach Brahman, and there are many yoga's/paths. Basic physical training and various disciplines are designed for different spiritual levels. The term atman notably comes from the word for breath. Hence, the significance of breathing exercises in yogic and meditative practices (which includes hyperventilating to achieve ASC). Through yoga, the yogin or mystic adept can stop the process of Lila or play of God, thereby transcending the illusion of Maya. The aim is direct mystical experience of reality. The illusory self disappears upon union with Brahman.

As mentioned, all yoga postures are sun and moon salutations. They're bowing down and worshipping the sun and moon, with body, mind and soul. Postures (and breathing) are offered to the gods, which people hope will be accepted by them. So, they're not merely 'exercise', but rather saluting Lucifer. They're designed to open oneself up to 'god' or demons? The triune sun god has three phases on its course. Thus, at sunrise the sun god is worshipped as Brahma, at noon he's Shiva, and at sunset he's Vishnu.

As also mentioned, when Hindu mystics meditate, they can receive siddhis, which are typically defined as 'a magical or spiritual power for the control of self, others and the forces of nature'. In Hinduism, the 'eight great perfections' or siddhis are: reducing one's body to the size of an atom; expanding one's body to an infinitely large size; becoming infinitely heavy; becoming almost weightless; having unrestricted access to all places; realising whatever one desires; possessing absolute lordship; and the power to subjugate all.

However, according to Krishna (in the Bhagavata Purana), there's other 'secondary' siddhis which include moving the body wherever thought goes (i.e. astral projection), assuming any form desired, and entering the bodies of others. Another yogic siddhi is human invisibility. As discussed, the endeavour is to activate and control the spirit body. By calling on the gods, demons can bridge (unite) our soul and spirit bodies.

Like, OM is a sacred spiritual incantation or spell to evoke the gods. OM is the prime mantra of the higher self or atman. It's 'soul technology', which attunes us with our true nature. It is the sound of the creator, preserver, and destroyer of the universe. It reflects both the manifest and unmanifest Brahman. It's said that beyond the subatomic realm, there's a unified field which is no-thing, which is the unmanifest, or one-ness. And through transcendental meditation people can experience this one-ness.

But moreover, the divine union is with the 'Serpent of Light'. The point of deep meditation (including breathing, posture, chanting mantras), is to awaken the sleeping serpent to bestow the state of yoga. As discussed, kundalini energy or 'serpent power' rises up through the (alleged) chakras to reside at the top of the head or crown chakra, producing a profound mystical experience. People report feeling like an electric current is running along the spine, and when the snake bites (behind the bridge of the nose) it releases an ecstatic bolt of lightning.

The serpent's blinding light lights up the third eye, and they're enlightened. People experience mystical oneness or an OBE. With the latter, their light body emerges from their crown chakra. Like DMT, people report having visions of non-physical beings, serpents and gods, when this energy is activated. Their eyes are opened to see another dimension. They're born again? They're possessed by the kundalini serpent? As touched on, Hindus are waiting for their messiah/coming world leader, namely, Kalki, who is the tenth incarnation of Vishnu. Interestingly, he's depicted as riding a white horse.

And then Buddhism landed with Prince Gautama Siddhartha (563-483BC), who was born in Nepal but came from India. Buddhism was an offshoot of Hinduism, but Buddha binned the caste system. Early Buddhist scripture defined purity as determined by one's own state of mind, and refer to anyone who behaves unethically, of whatever caste, as 'rotting within', or a 'rubbish heap of impurity'. Thus, contrary to Hinduism, in Buddhism anyone can enter nirvana no matter how lowly. Prince Siddhartha was given the title Buddha, which means enlightened one.

Like King Solomon, Prince Siddhartha also shows par excellence how we're never truly satisfied. He was shielded from the world and enjoyed the life of luxury. He had it all, including a wife and kid, but like many materially satiated, he recognised the futile, empty, and vacuous nature of his existence.

So, he left the palace at 29 years young to live a nomadic and reflective life. Having observed human suffering, he vowed to become holy, to pursue the life of a holy man involving deprivation and asceticism. He sought to find a solution to the problem of human suffering. Buddha was not curious about the divine but rather human frustrations and sufferings. So, to that end, he tortured his body yogi fashion. This involved munching seeds, grass and even dung. He wore a hair shirt, lay on thorns, and slept among rotten corpses.

After seven years of strenuous discipline in forests, he sat beneath a Bodhi tree (near Nepal) in deep meditation (he ate the figs, which some allege were comprised of LSD properties) and made a vow not to move until he attained true liberation. Then on the morning of the seventh day, he opened his eyes and looked out to the morning star, (which is a curious reference to Lucifer?). At that moment he became enlightened absorbing the truth of Dharma, the laws underlying Buddhism and Hinduism. Dharma means 'right way of living' and 'path of righteousness'.

Apparently, Buddha decided to keep his enlightenment a secret but then Brahma appeared, and he changed his mind. This Hindu god of creation pleaded, 'the world will be lost, the world will not have a chance' (cited in Vernon, 2012 p.130). Perhaps we can wonder about this 'god' Brahma, who effectively convinced Buddha to create another religion, for more division?

As it transpires, we don't need 'gods' for salvation. Indeed, there are no gods. Hence, Buddha condemned ritual animal sacrifices. Buddha taught there is no ultimate being with the power to bring each person to nirvana (enlightenment) but rather we all possess our own enlightenment. We are our own guru. He said, 'I teach suffering, its origin, cessation and path. That's all I teach'.

Thus, during his travels, Prince Siddhartha came up with Four Noble Truths. The first Noble Truth is all existence is dukkha, which translates to suffering. The Buddha's insight was that our lives are a struggle, and we do not find ultimate happiness or satisfaction in anything we experience.

The second Noble Truth is the cause of dukkha is desire. Suffering has a cause, which is craving and attachment. Thus, we desire certain worldly things and suffer when we can't have them (e.g. people, drugs, status). We also suffer through ignorance i.e. wrong views.

The third Noble Truth is dukkha diminishes with the cessation of craving. The Buddha taught the way to extinguish desire, which causes suffering, is to liberate oneself from attachment.

The fourth Noble Truth is there is a path that leads to the cessation of dukkha. And this path is the Noble Eightfold Path. This is Buddha's prescription for self-realisation and the end to all (perceived) suffering. He taught methods through which we can change our perspective, which transcendentally alters our relationship with our otherwise material world.

As mentioned, Buddha was the first CBT therapist, asserting we create our reality through our thoughts. It's more about our perception of events, as opposed to the events themselves, that affects us. And we can choose not to be affected? Perspective is paramount because ignorance (wrong views) gives rise to suffering. In essence, it's about self-discipline and true awareness. The Buddha's way is not to end suffering but to find release within it.

Regarding perspective, we can consider the 'Mustard Seed' story. Thus, a grieving mother, who's looking for medicine/divine intervention for her dead child, is told by the Buddha to obtain mustard seeds from one home that hasn't lost a friend, child, husband or parent. As it transpires, this is impossible, which elucidates the truth that acceptance is key to suffering.

But moreover, Buddha realised there's a right way to live. He concurred with Socrates' deduction, that happiness is doing the right thing. How could we be happy 'deep down' if we know what we are doing is wrong?

The emphasis is on love and compassion, as this propels 'right' thinking and action. Namely: proper views, resolve, speech, action, livelihood, effort, mindfulness, and concentration. These eight behaviours define a path or way of being. They're significant dimensions of our thoughts and actions, and they support and reinforce each other.

The Buddha described the Eightfold Path as a means to enlightenment. It's like a raft for crossing the river, where once one has reached the opposite shore, one no longer needs the raft and can leave it behind. We have to self-regulate and manage our emotions, until its second nature.

The Buddha is often compared to a physician. Thus, in the first two Noble Truths he diagnoses the problem (suffering) and identifies its cause (attachment). The third Noble Truth is the realisation that there is a cure (don't form attachments), and the fourth Noble Truth provides the prescription (the way to achieve release from suffering). Buddhist philosophy endorses the doctrine of no sin, good or evil, but rather only suffering and ignorance. Buddha was therefore clearly tripping, as pure evil exists.

Since happiness is the cessation of suffering, and suffering comes from thoughts, Buddhists work towards stilling the mind. Like mindfulness, the mind has to be trained to stop thinking and being confused. Indeed, the mind needs to be bypassed because the mind is the problem. Buddhists use the term 'monkey mind' to refer to the never quiet, always gibbering part of the mind that distracts us from spiritual realities.

Meditation is thus a tool of enlightenment. Cessation is often equated with Nirvana, the goal of spiritual practice. Nirvana is a state of freedom from suffering, desire, and ignorance. But moreover, it's a transcendent state, in which false notions of a separate self disappear. It's the 'Samadhi' state.

Like his predecessors, Buddha conceded that all physical life is illusory. He was an idealist. As discussed, if only consciousness exists, physical objects and the material world exist only as projections of our conscious state. One of the best-known ancient Buddhist texts, the Heart Sutra, states 'Form is emptiness, and emptiness is form'. Like, the atomic realm?

Empty things are seen as transcending existence and non-existence. He observed that 'all things arise and pass away'. Life is transitory and there is no self or ego. It's Maya or illusion. There's a Buddhist saying, 'if there were no illusions, there would be no enlightenment'.

So, life is suffering when bewitched by Maya. But Maya can be transcended and dispelled. We can reach nirvana, which is a kind of utopia that means 'no place'. That is, beyond the illusions of time and space, there's nothing. We can attain a state of non-being, whereby we lose our identity and become nothing. We dissolve. It's like blowing out a candle.

This can be regarded as the biggest difference between Hinduism and Buddhism, namely, in Hinduism the ultimate reality is all things are divinely united, whereas in Buddhism the ultimate reality is nothingness. So, while Hindus become one with everything in the universe, Buddhists gain nirvana by detaching from everything until nothingness remains. Nirvana is passionless peace. Vernon (2012) concedes, 'Nirvana is not a peak experience, akin to psychotropic drugs' (p.129). So, it's not spiritual morphine, a kundalini serpent shock?

Rather than understanding Brahman from within the atman, for Buddhists it's about finding anatman or 'not soul' or 'no self'. Thus, Buddha rejected the prevailing religious doctrines at the time, including the eternal inner man or atman.

As mentioned, Buddha was the first bundle theorist i.e. there is no self but rather a bundle of neurological processes happening at the same time. There is no inner me or you. It's an illusion. Buddha said, 'every moment you are born, decay, and die'. Which is interpreted to mean that every moment, the illusion of 'self' renews itself and therefore every moment we need to remind ourselves of the illusion. Not only is nothing carried over from one life to the next, but nothing is carried over from one moment to the next.

However, having no self seems to contradict reincarnation, which Buddhism espouses. Buddhism accepts karma driven birth, and nirvana as the cessation of rebirth. Thus, it seems we're a soul that reincarnates until we're not? Buddha claimed that by becoming aware (at any time) that we are experiencing an illusion, the soul is elevated to a higher place and avoids the constant cycle of birth and rebirth.

Thus, the power to attain Samadhi is a precondition of attaining release from the cycle of death and rebirth (samsara). False notions of a separate self disappear, and this transcends the vicious cycle of bondage to karma. So, we can stop the madness. In Buddhism, release from karma becomes possible by the suppression of all desires, and when one has ceased to think of good and evil, and has risen above them both. We need to transcend, which is spiritual attainment.

It's suggested that Buddha's doctrine of anatman can be interpreted to mean there is no self that is distinct from the Buddhist void, where the void has the attributes of Brahman. Ergo, God is the void. However, it's also said 'God of the void' is a Hindu concept as Buddha didn't believe in God. It's said this controversy of Buddha's no self can be resolved by understanding the problem in Hinduism.

Thus, in Hinduism there has been debate over the centuries regarding what is reincarnating, and there are two opposing camps. There are those who believe that the soul of the person is the same as Brahman, whereas others believe we have individuated and distinctly separate souls. So, there's either a single undivided and indivisible soul that becomes embodied in a sequence of separate lives, or there's myriad souls transmigrating. Either way, it still reincarnates, until it doesn't?

It's also noted, since Buddhists don't worship or follow the gods, Buddhism is not a religion, but rather the Teachings of Buddha. Whilst some don't believe gods exist, others believe they exist but they're not worthy of worship as they're also stuck in the illusion of the world and cannot guide anyone out. It's posited that gods and demons are also caught up in the rebirth cycle.

The 'wheel of life' has six realms which are divided into three higher realms and three lower realms. The three higher realms consist of the god realm, demigod realm and human realm, and the three lower realms consist of the hell realm, animal realm and hungry ghost realm. The 'three poisons' of ignorance, attachment and aversion give birth to karma, which results in one of these realms. Ignorance is however known as the root poison because it gives birth to the other two. The solution is becoming a Buddha (by awakening true Buddhahood), so we don't need to reincarnate.

Suffice to say, it's assumed Buddha achieved his aim and didn't reincarnate. Buddha died aged eighty, and the earliest Buddhist scriptures were written about four hundred years after his ministry (until then his teachings were passed down orally). The collection of Buddha's sacred scriptures is known as the Pali Canon or more traditionally, the Tri-pitaka or 'three baskets' of teachings.

Whilst at its core Buddhism is exactly the same, some eighteen schools surfaced after Buddha (due to various interpretations of his teachings). But over a period of time, these schools gradually merged into two main schools, namely, Theravada and Mahayana. Theravada is the most ancient and orthodox form of Buddhism.

It's believed Prince Siddhartha was the temporal form of the eternal Buddha nature. And regarding his fat gut, apparently he didn't eat all the pies, but rather his belly (solar plexus) inflates with spiritual energy, which is code for demons? It's understood that demons attach to the solar plexus, the belly brain (soul).

Ironically, whilst Buddha taught no dependence upon one Supreme Being, it nevertheless transpired that he himself came to be deified and worshipped. Like, the Mahayanists pray to god and believe Buddha is a god, which contrasts to Theravada Buddhists, who insist there are no gods and Buddha is not a god. Thus, some Buddhists meditate, whereas others make offerings to images. Most Mahayanists observe vegetarianism. Buddha notably denied he was a god. He couldn't perform miracles and had no supernatural powers.

The same thing happened with Mahavira, founder of Jainism, who also taught that there was no object of worship, and that no deity should be prayed to or even talked about. And yet his followers defied him and worshipped his image. Jainism (founded in India sixth century BC) also teaches salvation by perfection through successive lives. They see moksha and nirvana as the same thing.

The 'three jewels' aka guiding principles in Jainism are right belief, knowledge and conduct. And the supreme principle is non-violence. Jainism is renowned for its ascetics. This translates to a regimented life with strict rules and trying our best to do the right thing, to prevent dreaded reincarnation? There's more dukkha in the post. How wonderful it would be, if someone divine could forgive our wrongdoings? Like, the Godman? However, I digress.

Numerous other deities are worshipped today by the majority of Buddhists. Buddha was also adopted as an incarnation of Vishnu. However, many Buddhists don't believe that Buddha is an avatar of Vishnu and instead believe that Hindu priests made that claim to stem the spread of Buddhism, which threatened Hinduism. It's understood, religion is a business. Like, in Nepal, for example, it's cheaper to be a Hindu than a Buddhist, as people have to contribute to temples, and prayers for the dead etc. So, finance determines religion? Salvation is not a free gift?

It's noted, the Big Five are like primary colours which birth secondary colours. Like, Sikhism, the fifth largest organised religion, is a mixture of Islam and Hinduism. Nanak, who founded Sikhism, was also deified by his followers. He became God, the supreme Brahma. Apparently, Nanak was taken in a vision (astral trip) to God's presence. And like, Santeria is a hybrid of Catholicism and shamanism. They venerate the saints but also partake in shamanic rituals (religious customs), including a trance and divination system for communicating with ancestral spirits and deities, animal sacrifice, and sacred drumming and dance. The Devil's portrait of religion is colourful.

But moreover, in addition to Theravada and Mahayana Buddhism, Vajrayana Buddhism subsequently developed, which is believed to be the hidden teachings of Buddha. Whilst based on the same teachings, Vajrayana provides a quicker path to enlightenment. It's purportedly the esoteric heart of Buddhism, like the other esoteric hearts of exoteric religion. And contrary to what Buddha taught, the central tenet is that everyone is God.

One of the spiritual practices of this kind of Buddhism is called 'deity yoga', where the aspirant attempts through various disciplines to realise himself or herself as God. It's like I AM meditation? The emphasis is on rituals, chanting and tantra techniques, which includes kundalini yoga. Vajrayana Buddhism is thus also known as Tantric Buddhism.

The Sanskrit word Tantra is roughly translated as 'expansion leading to liberation'. Tantric devotion is a supremely focussed sexuality as a pathway to unity with the Absolute. Through sexual union, (and harnessing mystical kundalini), male and female energy can be reunited i.e. dualism. It's duly noted, Sting popularised Tantric Buddhism, with his seven-hour tantric sex sessions. Tantric is as ancient as the Vedas, and apparently the Aryans and their rishis were particularly interested in these practices. It's asserted that people essentially invite demons into their bed. So, it gets infernally ecstatic.

As mentioned, Buddhists are eagerly awaiting the appearance of the Maitreya, who will initiate the emergence of a new spiritual world order. Buddha Gautama said, 'I am not the first Buddha (awakened one) who has come upon the earth, nor will I be the last. In due time another Buddha will rise in the world, a holy one, a supreme enlightened one, endowed with auspicious wisdom embracing the universe, an incomparable leader of men, a ruler of gods and mortals'.

'He will reveal to you the same eternal truths which I have taught you. He will establish his law (religion), glorious in its origins, glorious at the climax and glorious at the goal in the spirit and the letter. He will proclaim a righteous life wholly perfect and pure, such as I now proclaim. His disciples will number many thousands, while mine number many hundreds. He will be known as the Maitreya'.

Whilst not one of the 'Big Five' per se, but given its contemporary influence in the west, it seems pertinent to mention Taoism, founded by Lao-Tzu in the sixth century BC in China. Lao-Tzu is also regarded as a deity. The term Tao refers to 'way' or 'path', and Taoism means 'teachings of the way'. The guiding spirit of Tao flows in and around all living things. Tao is both the source of, and the force behind, everything that exists. It's both the creator and sustainer/preserver. Tao is the Uncreated Source, the Supreme Reality, Brahman, the Absolute or Godhead of the aeons etc.

Tao means eternal being. It was the Prime Mover, but it remains unmoved. This un-manifested presence or being is the life within every form, the inner essence of all that exists. It's the source of energy, which enables the manifested (world of form). But unlike energy which moves, the un-manifested is still. Energy is the link between the un-manifested and the physical universe.

Lao-Tze says, 'Tao is one. It was in the beginning. It will remain forever. It is impersonal, eternal, immutable, omnipresent, bodiless, immaterial. It cannot be perceived by the senses. It is nameless. It is indescribable. It is the first cause from which all substances take their origin and all phenomena flow. The great Tao is all-pervading. All things depend on it for life. It is the mother of all phenomena, of heaven and earth. It existed before the personal God. It is the father of God. It is the producer of God. It is the originator of heaven and earth. It is the mother of all things'.

So, Taoism is pantheism. Lao-Tze taught that Tao is everywhere. It is in the ant. It is in the grass. It is in the earthen-ware vessel. It is in excrement. It is everywhere yet appears to be nowhere. The central text of Taoism is the 'Tao Te Ching', 'the Canon of Reason and Virtue'. It contains 81 short poems or chapters, which consist of wise sayings and generalisations.

In essence, life is illusory and through emptiness we can connect with the universe. Emptiness is behind all things i.e. the material illusion is made up of empty space. All creatures and all things must eventually return to the source: 'All things vanish into the Tao. It alone endures'.

Tao thus preceded the creation of the cosmos. And from this One, came two basic principles or forces, namely, yin and yang. As touched on, the term 'dualistic monism' refers to how the one is two, and the two are one. The duality of yin and yang is an indivisible whole. The yin is the feminine or negative principle and is characterised as dark, wetness, cold, and passivity. The yang is the masculine or positive principle and is characterised by light, warmth, dryness, and activity. Yin is earth and yang is heaven, and from the yang force arises shen, the celestial portion of the human soul, and from the yin force comes kwei, the earthly part.

However, rather than being opposite or contrary forces, they are inherently complementary, interconnected, and interdependent. The definition of one requires the definition of the other to be complete. For example, day becomes night then night becomes day; the long and the short impart from and to each other; the high and the low comply with each other; existence and non-existence produce each other. Yin and yang represent every conceivable pair of opposites i.e. birth and death, growth and decay, health and illness, good and evil. The 'universe' comes into play through their interaction. These two polar energies combine/fuse to become physical matter.

Existence is perceived like flowing water, as energy continually flows between the poles of yin and yang. The aim of Taoist ethics is thus to find deliverance from this cosmic tension by a return to Tao. Lao Tzu described it as a river flowing home to the sea i.e. the 'river of energy' unites yin and yang and flows into the sea of energy.

Taoism notably pertains to the great separation. It maintains that thousands of years ago, life was like the Garden of Eden. Humankind lived in harmony with the natural world, and telepathically communicated with the animals, plants, and other life forms. Eating animals or killing them for 'sport' was unthinkable. Apparently, we worked alongside the earth angels and nature spirits. It seems the physical and spiritual world were one.

In tandem with the antediluvian world, it's purported the earth's atmosphere was very different, with a great deal more vegetation supporting moisture. And human life span was many times longer than what it is today. So, life became harsh. Lao Tzu recognised 'Nature is unkind'. It appears we lost our way. Hence, we need to rediscover our 'way'.

But moreover, there's two kinds of Taoism, namely, philosophical and mystical. The philosophical concerns attaining peaceful oneness and stilling the mind, and the mystical entails many gods and demons to be feared, and who's followers use magic and rituals to harness power (Te).

Mystical Taoism has roots extending to ancient shamanism. Thus, mystical Taoists are essentially pagans. They're au fait with the spirit world, and their polytheistic occultism includes animism. They also believe spirits reside in the organs, where they have access to cosmic energy, hence they perform exorcisms etc. Some mystical Taoists use the I Ching for divining and fortune telling.

Mystical Taoists also seek to secure immortality, which has led to the development of curatives and elixirs. The search for immortality has taken either this external alchemy path of ingesting elixirs in the hope of prolonging life, or the internal alchemy path to connect with that aspect of ourselves that survives the death of the body. So, unlike the former, which aspires to never die, the latter involves transferring our awareness from the physical into the more subtle aspects of our being. Thus, when our body dies, 'we' will 'consciously' remain. We obtain the philosopher's stone.

But furthermore, Taoism reveres women. The Tao Te Ching describes Tao as 'infinite, eternally present, the mother of the universe'. Thus, the Queen of Heaven (Semiramis) is being worshipped as mother of God. Lao Tze recognised that females are the mothers of all things and all human beings, and believed that without females or mothers, there was nothing else in the world. The goddess or divine mother has two aspects, namely, she gives life and takes life. The goddess is in everything and everything is part of the goddess. So, we're also the goddess? As it transpires, God is a woman?

It's noted, the goddess has been infused with new life in the New Age. Like, Greek goddess 'Gaia', the ancestral mother of all life. Great Mother Gaia is credited with giving birth to Earth and the entire universe, including the heavenly gods. Gaia is the personification of Earth, and we're testing her limits, hence her revenge? Whilst the 'Sacred Feminine' concept recognises God is beyond form and duality, (ergo God's neither male nor female), the term helps to redress the historical sexist imbalance. It's time for the divine feminine principle to shine. It's time to revere Baphomet, and get initiated into Sophia's wisdom?

New Age philosophies tend to be feminine in nature, which is seen as a backlash to patriarchy, a reaction against sexism. And contrary to Father God, who is associated with rigour and discipline, Mother Goddess has no doctrine of sin. There's no talk of hell but rather going back to her soul, her bosom even. Then we might reappear. Sex and customs are generally freer because they're part of nature and cannot be considered the fruits of evil. Nature worship is more important than sacred books. Hence, pagans celebrate the environment.

So, after millennia of male domination, we're returning to the cult of Great Mother. We're returning to witchcraft. As mentioned, Wicca is the fastest growing religion in the west. And why not cast a love spell, for example? Like, bake a cake for your desired lover and add menstrual blood to the ingredients. Magic is alluring because we can get power? And all that heightens power is good?

As touched on, the New Age landed in the sixties with these eastern imports. In addition to the sexual revolution, there was a spiritual revolution. The world was ready for Crowley's, Blavatsky's, Bailey's, and Jung's teachings? Good and evil are two sides of the same coin. There is no distinction between God and Satan? Ignorance is dispelled by enlightenment. We can achieve Christ consciousness, ergo there's no need for the cross. The Age of Aquarius promised peace, free love, and unity. It's noted, the hippy peace symbol is actually an upside cross with broken arms. Society no longer cared for Yahweh. Foreign gods seemed better, less constraining?

Mysticism and mystical experiences, including through drugs like LSD, were far more appealing than boring irrelevant church. As discussed, it seems people went to church but they didn't believe in God? They didn't really believe in the spirit world, yet they were up for some serpent power? Like, Jim Morrison became the Lizard king who could do anything. It's noted, the Doors were named after Aldous Huxley's 'The Doors of Perception' (1954), which are opened by mescaline. Apparently, the Lizard King was Morrison's alter ego. He claimed he could control lizards with the power of his mind, and he was their king. And mind control victim Jim Morrison was cool?

Transcendental Meditation (TM) was notably brought to the west by Maharishi Yogi in the fifties. He taught the Beatles this Hindu (Vedic) practice in the sixties, which popularised it. Just as 'celebrities' promote the occult agenda today. As highlighted, it's not random that people are increasingly migrating towards spiritual practices, like meditation and yoga. The influencers make it look cool, like the cabala. Hence, (as mentioned) popstar Katy Perry was invited to the Vatican to speak about TM. Which further supports the prospect that Pope Francis is a black pope?

TM is a simple (silent) mantra meditation technique in which a Sanskrit word is repeated. The Maharishi explains that with each repetition, awareness deepens, which enables moving closer to the unconscious source of thought. The idea is thus to get 'beyond thought to the source of thought'. Repeating the mantra essentially results in a hypnotic state, and people report feeling peaceful and more energised after meditation. The idea is to dissociate.

It's propagated that TM is an inward journey where faith has no object. It's promoted as a non-religious method for relaxation, stress reduction and self-development. And it's been popular because this discipline's been sold as void of dogma. But as it transpires, Maharishi admits that mantras are not meaningless but rather they're the names of Hindu gods. People are energised by these gods? Like, OM evokes demons (like theurgy). TM comes from the Vedic traditions of India.

It's also said there's no such thing as 'vital energy' invigorating the body that comes from proper breathing. The vital energy of prana (the so-called life force) in yoga, is talking about spirit i.e. demon spirits. As mentioned, entities are behind energies. Furthermore, TM is being introduced into schools, the workplace, and prisons etc to prepare the world for the New World Religion.

Steven Bancarz notably highlights the dark side of meditation. He cautions the dangers are not reported. Indeed, they're actively hidden. Thus, we're told meditation improves sleep and reduces stress etc, but clinical research proves otherwise. Negative side effects include fear, anxiety, panic, paranoia, depression, pain, sleep disorders, headaches/head pressure, suicidal ideation, hallucinations, sleep paralysis, nightmares, OBEs, confusion. These increase with long term meditation (i.e. years) and after meditation retreats.

Bancarz also pertains to the meditation teacher for Actualised Org, who concedes that if people meditate for longer than a year, they experience more suicidal thoughts. This teacher warns followers that it can get weird and dark. Like, people feel weird energy moving in their body. It's like their body is controlled by a puppet master. It's like they're possessed. He states that waves of insanity and madness, being out of control, nightmares and weird dreams, ESP, astral projection, OBEs, and seeing spirits, angels, demons, gods, insects, and aliens, are all common. In short, people can have a kundalini awakening.

The New Age movement is best defined as eclectic. It appeals to those disillusioned by organised religion and western rationalism. As highlighted, materialism doesn't fill our spiritual void. We know there's something missing. But we want to choose for ourselves from the buffet. It's highlighted that the New Age industry bridges the gap between materialism and spiritualism. Like, people can buy dolphin music, crystals, and angel cards. We can pay for Reiki healing. We can let therapists impart the kundalini spirit so that we see colours and get healings? We can take DMT. It seems there's something for everyone?

As touched on, one of the most popular occult practices is astral projection, and people are increasingly partial to spirit guides. Whilst New Age is an umbrella term for over a thousand occult practices, it's essentially repackaged Hinduism.

In essence, Nietzsche's declaration that God is dead has been transformed into 'everyone is God'. Rhonda Byrne, author of The Secret (2006), for example, states, 'You are God in a physical body. You are Spirit in the flesh. You are Eternal Life expressing itself as You. You are a cosmic being. You are all power. You are all wisdom. You are all intelligence. You are perfection. You are magnificence. You are the creator, and you are creating the creation of You on this planet' (p.164). And we like this idea? Why would anyone want to believe in old judging Yahweh if we don't have to? It seems our natural narcissism is pandered to?

Worldly wisdom tells us (we're continuously told) we need to love ourselves before we can love anyone else. Yet God's word tells us, to love God first, then our neighbour. Love is not about self. We don't put ourselves first. This is an inversion of Bible truth. Love is serving others. Like, Jesus came to serve, not to be served. He put others first and was sacrificed for us. So, love is putting others first, and even sacrificing our life for them? That's real love. Like, if push came to shove and someone had to take a bullet, most parents would sacrifice themselves for their kids?

It's highlighted that we are our own gods, and our lives are characterised by pride, self-exaltation and independence from God. However, as Dr Neil Anderson, author of the Bondage Breaker (1990) asserts, the problem with being our own gods is that we were never designed to occupy that role. The New Age movement is all about self, whereas with God, we look away from self.

As mentioned, it seems we're more self-obsessed than ever before? Indeed, we are the great I AM. So, the ultimate mystical goal is that our true identity is God. We're all God gazing out upon ourselves, and this cosmic integrated oneness is the foundation of a unified world view.

CS Lewis summarised, there's essentially two religions, namely, Hinduism (paganism) and Christianity. And these two religions are incompatible. As mentioned, pantheism and theism are mutually exclusive. So, we either believe we're God or we're not God. We either embody God's Holy Spirit or the antichrist spirit. Yogi Ramacharaka said, 'Hinduism is the fount from which all the world's mystics have drunk whether they realise it or not. It is the oldest source of the idea that latent in each of us is the self that is God'.

As discussed, Gnosticism, Hermeticism, Cabalism, Sufism, Hinduism, Buddhism, Luciferianism are essentially the same Mystery Babylon religion. And modern science is on the same mystical page, supporting the hermetic principle 'All is Mind'. 'God' is an impersonal energy force. Or He's our Father and loves us?

Contrary to the 'broad road' approach to God, pushed by the Vatican, Jesus tells us, (in Matthew 7: 14), 'But small is the gate and narrow the road that leads to life, and only a few find it'. Jesus came for everyone. He won't turn anyone away, and even the worst person can be forgiven. But it seems our instinct is to reject God of the Bible? Which is partly due to pride, because we can't humble ourselves before Almighty God? We struggle to say sorry for our sin aka poor choices that have hurt others including God.

It's also noted, that contrary to the Bible, the issue of sin is undermined in every other religion. But it's asserted that our problem is sin (moral), rather than alienation or separation from pure consciousness. Thus, the solution is not cessation of self but forgiveness. With religion, the emphasis is on salvation through works or self-salvation through gnosis. So, there's legalism, which is said to be the worst demonic doctrine. And there's experiencing the kundalini spirit, the counterfeit Holy Spirit. Or there's relationship with God through Jesus and the Holy Spirit.

But moreover, it's highlighted the powerful kundalini spirit is infecting churches. Like, evangelical pastor Benny Hinn, for example, knocks people down with the alleged Holy Spirit, like gurus do in ashrams. Sometimes people are touched on the head, but equally waves of people fall to the ground, as he waves his jacket at them. Like, being hypnotised? Multimillionaire Hinn has every-hinn, including private jets. He's also been exposed as a charlatan with regards to alleged healings. It's understood Satan has infiltrated protestant churches, as well as the Catholic Church.

Kenneth Copeland also imparts the 'Holy Spirit', (like other so-called charismatic preachers), and has his own fleet of private planes. He's apparently the richest pastor in the US. As mentioned, he's worth some $800 million. He notably wants to reconcile Protestantism with Catholicism to 'unify' the church. He thinks the Pope's a 'good guy'. Like, 'trendy' Hillsong (that was founded by a paedo) operates in the kundalini spirit, and it supports the unification of Protestantism and Catholicism, and Chrislam (Allah and God are the same). It promotes one world religion and is kosher with LGBTQ peeps. 'Trendy' Bethel church also operates in the kundalini spirit.

Maybe these pastors are not serving God of the Bible? Jesus said, 'It is easier for a camel to go through the eye of a needle than for a rich man to enter the kingdom of God' (Mark 10:25). So, that stings for rich men. They may prefer their temporary riches? Other trendy pastors are slated for wearing $5000 trainers and Rolex's etc. Is there any need when God's kids are starving?

It's notably alleged that Copeland is a Luciferian. He's a wolf in sheep's clothing. And he looks like one? Apparently, he's a 33rd degree mason like multimillionaire pastors Billy Graham, Oral Roberts and Pat Robertson. As mentioned, Graham was tight with American presidents, from Truman to Trump. Hence, he was called America's pastor. He was ecumenical and held the Pope in high regard. In an interview in 2005 with Larry King, he said Masonic Pope John Paul II is 'the most influential voice for morality and peace in the world in the last 100 years'. Pope John Paul II kissed a Koran.

Oral Roberts is considered the godfather of the charismatic movement, which believes in using spiritual gifts ('charismata') e.g. the gift of tongues, healings, visions, revelations, and prophecy. This movement was accepted by mainstream Protestantism and Roman Catholicism in the sixties. It contrasts with 'Cessationism', which is the doctrine that spiritual gifts ceased with the apostolic age (they ceased with the apostles). Rather than 'continuationism', cessationism advocates that miracles were used to testify that Jesus is God and promote the gospel. But rather than signs, the focus has since been on faith.

But it gets more haunted, as its alleged that SRA took place at Oral Roberts University, the prestigious Bible school that Graham helped launch. According to Fritz Springmeier, there's a programming centre underneath the prayer tower. Furthermore, apparently Phillip Eugene de Rothschild informed David Icke that satanic Oral Roberts succeeded in hijacking contemporary American Christianity to worship a different Jesus under the power of a different holy spirit. So, that's dodgy.

Like, it's argued that some leaders in the 'Word of Faith' movement and churches associated with the Toronto Blessing promote the false idea of being 'drunk in the spirit' or being filled with 'drunken glory'. Toronto Airport Christian Fellowship Church is known for its ecstatic worship, and supposed outpouring and anointing of the Holy Spirit. Worshippers have been overcome with outbreaks of laughter, (so-called 'holy laughter' is a hallmark manifestation), dancing, crying, groaning, shaking, falling, 'drunkenness', and stuck in positions of paralysis. So, this holy intoxication is kosher, unlike kundalini intoxication?

There's also the phenomenon of gold dust, which miraculously appears on people's heads and hands, and gold fillings. The Toronto Airport Christian Fellowship reported over three hundred people received gold and silver fillings during one conference, and in some cases up to ten per mouth. It's noted, there's countless stories of healings coupled with gold fillings and gold dust worldwide (from Mexico to South Africa to Canada to the UK). In the UK, the BBC posted an article entitled 'God fills in for dentists' (LOL).

A pastor I know experienced the gold dust phenomenon at a church service she attended. She said there was loads of gold dust everywhere, which they had to sweep up (she cellotaped some flecks onto her Bible). The same pastor also spoke about a godly man they called 'oily hands'. Apparently, he prayed a lot and oil would seep from his palms. He was literally anointed with oil. Like, some saints exude the finest perfumed oil.

Apparently Christian missionary Heidi Baker, who's renowned for being drunk in the spirit, received the Holy Spirit impartation from the Toronto Blessing. She also notably wants to unite Catholicism and Protestantism. And drunk is drunk. She literally staggers around with slurred speech. So, there's spiritual drunks and spiritual junkies.

Like, Jeannie Morgan, in her book, 'Encounter the Holy Spirit' (2011), spoke about a particularly wonderful experience. She said, 'Looking around, it seemed that God was not only working in me, but in the rest of the congregation. Some people were rolling on the floor laughing; others were falling about all over the place like they were drunk. A lady, normally confined to a wheelchair due to severe multiple sclerosis, was pushing her husband around in her wheelchair, grinning from ear to ear! Some were shaking uncontrollably, others were receiving the gifts of tongues and many other healings were taking place. It was bizarre to watch but also amazing' (p.40).

Christians speak about being 'slain in the spirit', which is when an individual falls to the floor whilst experiencing religious ecstasy. It's 'falling down under the power'. It may occur in a variety of settings, often when a minister lays hands on someone, but also praying in solitude. People experience their legs feeling weak and find they can no longer stand up properly, and overwhelmed they fall down, and often fall asleep.

I notably experienced this once at a church service, but I didn't fall asleep. People were praying over me, and I remember really reaching out to God in my heart and mind, earnestly trying to connect, really feeling the love, and the next thing I knew I passed out. And I remember thinking (feeling) it was the most amazing experience I'd ever had. It felt like I'd necked 100 disco pills (when disco biscuits were good). I was absolutely buzzing and almost drowning in love.

Pretty much everyone in the room was 'slain in the spirit', which includes my mum's mate, who's a spiritualist. My friend didn't conk out but instead literally cried no end. She was blessed with the 'gift of tears'. I remember surmising that an onlooker would be disturbed by the scene. It was like we were thoroughly minced at a party, (shaking, groaning, and passed out), with some preacher shouting about 'fire'.

It's noted, this spiritual buzz can be addictive. Like, Russell Brand likened kundalini yoga with crack cocaine. When attending such services, my mum would literally be the first in line (LOL). People are supposedly overcome by the Holy Spirit. But others insist we are to experience God soberly. 'Self-control' is one of the fruits of the spirit (as we'll get to). It's asserted that being slain in the spirit isn't in the Bible, nor is holy laughter. And convulsing is associated with demonic possession.

Heidi Baker, (who also bangs on about fire), refers to being possessed by the Holy Spirit. Regardless of the source, the fact is spiritual morphine exists. Our bodies can produce the best heroin ever through spiritual means. We're designed to experience overwhelming love.

Steven Bancarz notably advised that he was oppressed by the kundalini spirit at a hyper-charismatic church service he attended, and he had to be delivered. It's like people have been oppressed from New Age festivals, like 'Burning Man' and 'Coachella' in the US. When the party's over, they don't return alone. Thus, we have to be mindful regarding what we expose ourselves to. As discussed, this includes music etc.

Like, we have to be super careful who we allow to put their hands on us. Like, Reiki therapists imparting 'healing energy'. And like, so-called Christians who impart something dark into our being through praying for us. In the Bible, we're told God's people prayed and laid hands on one another to impart the Holy Spirit, but then there's this counterfeit rot to contend with. Hence, we need God's gift of discerning spirits. The devil's a trickster. 1 Timothy 4:1 warns us that in the last days, there will be a rise in those paying attention to deceiving spirits and doctrines of demons. So, we're here? It's said the great apostasy before Jesus returns could be due to seducing spirits.

With regards to being filled with the Holy Spirit to the point of shaking, it seems pertinent to mention the Quakers, founded by George Fox (1624-1691). Fox wanted to find a 'real' religion, to find the real God, but he didn't find Him in the churches he attended. And furthermore, he felt that people were just playing at being Christians. So, he roamed the fields for many years, floundering with his thoughts.

He said his Christian life began when he heard a voice speak to him. He felt the experience had brought him into direct contact with Jesus. The voice said, 'There is one, even Christ Jesus, that can speak to thy condition'. And when he heard it, his 'heart did leap for joy'. And so, he began proclaiming that we can have a direct experience of the love of God and we could know we were forgiven.

Like the reformers, he regarded ordained clergy men as superfluous. There was no need for pomp or splendour. He said, 'the Lord showed me, so that I did see clearly, that he did not dwell in these temples which men had commanded and set up, but in people's hearts...his people were his temple, and he dwelt in them'. God's church is His people, His bride.

So, Fox began a career of open-air preaching that resulted in the growth of a Christian movement that numbered some 50,000 within a few years and about 100,000 by the end of the century. People were aware of a special force in his words, unlike the formal and lifeless sermons of many minsters. It's highlighted the church lost her power when the Roman Empire perverted her in the fourth century.

As it transpired, Fox encountered opposition, and he was brought before the magistrates. The result was a sixth month stint inside. The judge mockingly nicknamed Fox and his followers the Quakers as they sometimes shook with emotion.

'The Friend's Church' deployed a system of quietism. The idea is 'let your words be few' and only speak if rumbled by the Holy Spirit. Fox advised, 'Be still and cool in thine own mind and spirit'. Sometimes a great rush of wind, the Holy Spirit, would swoosh through the room where they held their meetings, where besides the shaking, they would speak in tongues. It's also noted, the Quakers were the first to speak and act against slavery. They were friends with Native Americans and Eskimos, considering them equals, and they were also pro-women.

So, there's shaking, but then there's behaviours, like at the Toronto Blessing, that have been described as a 'cross between a jungle and a farmyard', with people roaring like lions and barking like dogs. Which seems weird? Another 'manifestation of the spirit' encountered at these meetings is vomit-like heaving, and actual vomiting, as people are cleansed of their sin. These experiences are attributed to the Holy Spirit entering people's bodies, as physical manifestations of the Holy Spirit's presence and power. It's like the shamanic initiate being cleansed of evil spirits?

The intense shouting, screaming, vigorous jerking, dancing, passing out, crying, howling, emotional outbursts, speaking in tongues, and healing, observed at 'Christian' churches, can be seen across the board in paganism, shamanism and mediumistic religious practices, voodoo religion, Hindu gurus etc.

Wheeler (2009) also spoke about the bizarre happenings at the Toronto Blessing. She said, 'Men barking and crawling around church platforms on all fours, being led on dog leashes, women howling from the pulpit like wild wolves, crowded auditoriums erupting in crazed laughter, with people going bonkers and running around whooping and hollering like chickens with their heads cut off'. And further, 'You'll also witness the grotesque fruits of the Brownsville and Toronto Revivals. People laughing hysterically, dancing and prancing around, some struck dumb, others jerking and shaking violently and falling down, still others slithering around the floor like serpents; all giving God the 'credit' for their ungodly performances' (p.248).

Russell Brand (2014) notably spoke about his experience at an African church, which he described as 'Christianity with a voodoo twist'. The people were speaking in tongues and he likened the jerking to a 'pre-ejaculatory' James Brown (LOL). He also compared that church with a typical Anglican church. Thus, he wrote,

'When the worship is at its peak, its wild, emphatic, orgiastic, juddering, shrieking, spasming peak, I wonder how will they ever climb down from this summit of selflessness? How will this animalistic holy frenzy segue into people shaking hands and stacking chairs? At some Anglican sermon in Surrey, the 'file down the aisle, handshake, smile' ending is the energetic climax of proceedings. After a polite rendition of 'Jerusalem' (in which Blake was apparently being sarcastic) or 'All Things Bright and Beautiful' (which Stewart Lee breaks down beautifully) there isn't a moment of post-coital awkwardness where everyone thinks, 'Fuck me, we really let ourselves go there'; the hymns, the prayers, the sermon and the departure never interrupt the frequency of neat obedience' (p. 59).

It's understood that healing, prophecy, speaking in tongues, and the ability to interpret tongues, are gifts from God. And Satan has his counterfeit versions, including all kinds of ESP. But critically, it seems Christians are being deceived into believing the kundalini spirit is the Holy Spirit?

Regarding the Holy Spirit, and as touched on, Jesus instructed His followers to wait in Jerusalem until they were given the Holy Spirit. This happened on the Day of Pentecost, which is a Jewish holiday that celebrates 50 days after Passover. Jesus told His people the Great Counsellor would come after He left. And He chose this time, seven weeks after He resurrected.

Acts 2:1-13 states, 'When the day of Pentecost arrived, they were all together in one place. And suddenly a sound like the blowing of a violent wind came from heaven and filled the whole house where they were sitting. They saw what seemed to be tongues of fire that came to rest on each of them. All of them began to speak in other tongues as the spirit enabled them'.

'Now there were dwelling in Jerusalem Jews, devout men from every nation under heaven. And at this sound the multitude came together, and they were bewildered, because each one was hearing them speak in his own language. And they were amazed and astonished, saying, 'Are not all these who are speaking Galileans? And how is it we hear, each of us in his own native language?'

'Parthians and Medes and Elamites and residents of Mesopotamia, Judea and Cappadocia, Pontus and Asia, Phrygia and Pamphylia, Egypt and the parts of Libya belonging to Cyrene, and visitors from Rome, both Jews and proselytes, Cretans and Arabians – we hear them telling in our own tongues the mighty works of God. And all were amazed and perplexed, saying to one another, 'What does this mean?' But others mocking said, 'They are filled with new wine'.

Paul notably tells us in 1 Corinthians 14:13-14, 'So anyone who has the gift of speaking in tongues should pray also for the gift of interpretation in order to tell people plainly what has been said. For if I pray in tongues, my spirit is praying, but I don't understand what I'm saying'.

Like, one night when I was at church, someone stood up and spoke in some foreign language, and then about ten minutes later, someone else interpreted as they knew that language. Pastor Dean Odle mentioned an occasion when someone in his church spoke in tongues, namely, Mandarin, and that night a Chinese brother just happened to be visiting, who was able to interpret what was said. For another example, I heard about a woman who couldn't comprehend that God loves her, and the Christian woman she was with, who was praying for her, began speaking in tongues, which happened to be Russian, which the woman knew as she could speak Russian. Thus, God reached the otherwise unreachable woman through His intervention.

God literally communicates with His kids through the gift of tongues and the gift of interpretation of tongues. It's understood God's gifts, including tongues, are to edify the church. So, we don't have to rely on faith alone? It's said that speaking in tongues helps non-believers, whereas prophesy strengthens believers.

However, unlike at Pentecost, when God enabled His people to speak in different languages to preach the gospel, it's highlighted that glossolalia practiced today is often unintelligible to everyone including the person. As mentioned, xenoglossia is the ability to speak fluently an unknown language and glossolalia is an unintelligible 'heavenly' language. It seems for the most part, people are babbling. Yet Paul said, it's better to be silent than babble in vain.

Preachers like Copeland, Hinn and Baker also speak in tongues. It makes people appear more spiritual? Moreover, I heard a story about a pastor who was speaking in tongues, and some bloke who was visiting the church understood the language and told him to stop. Apparently, the pastor was saying the vilest things about God, evidencing he was not operating in the Holy Spirit. So, there's legitimate charismatic churches, which honour God, and there's haunted charismatic churches. And it seems discernment is a challenge?

Before we finish here, it seems pertinent to mention Scientology, founded in 1954 by science fiction writer and haunted sex pest L Ron Hubbard (as mentioned he worked on occult projects with Jack Parsons). Hubbard defined Scientology as 'knowing how to know'. Prior to the launch of his religion, Hubbard had developed Dianetics, which he claimed was the science to improve mental health. He coined the term Dianetics from dia, which is Greek for 'through' and 'nous' for mind.

Hubbard was inspired by Freud and similarly presumed there are unconscious mental processes at play. He concurred that we're psychologically shaped by early life experiences and that these influence later behaviour. Dianetics uses a counselling technique known as 'auditing' to unlock or 'clear' minds. People are hooked up to an 'electropsychometer' (like a polygraph) and asked questions which source past trauma. The idea is to expose and remove painful memories to free the individual. The process is called 'clearing'. It centres on abreaction, a psychoanalytical concept Freud introduced, which is defined as the 'process of bringing to consciousness'. Jung was impressed with the instrument, stating, 'Aha, a looking glass into the unconscious'.

As it transpired however, psychiatry spurned his new psychotherapeutic tool/method, and apparently deemed Hubbard a paranoid schizophrenic. So, he changed Dianetics into a religion. It's noted, Scientology is vehemently opposed to psychiatry. Indeed, they refer to psychiatry as 'an industry of death' and 'brainwashing Nazi pseudoscience'. Hubbard created the anti-psychiatry organisation 'Citizens Commission on Human Rights' which has created campaigns to stand against psychiatric treatments including ECT, lobotomy, and psychotropic drugs like Ritalin and Prozac. It has also exposed abuses in the psychiatric profession.

For scientologists, the onus is on the individual to take responsibility for their own happiness and wellbeing. It's said our capabilities are unlimited, and these can be realised. We can solve our own problems by increasing the powers of rationality, and accomplish our own goals. This self-help philosophy is based on the maxim 'God helps those who help themselves'. So, that sounds good?

But Hubbard was haunted. He was a black magician and skilled hypnotist. He was partial to mescaline and coca, and he knew the spirit world is real. Apparently, he had a revelatory NDE. Moreover, when practitioners of Dianetics reported experiences which they believed had occurred in past-lives, he took these reports seriously.

He deducted that we're an immortal spiritual being or soul, which he termed Theta (which is Greek for spirit/thought). The thetan is our true identity, which is intrinsically good, omniscient and capable of unlimited creativity. And thetans are reborn, reincarnated, through a process called 'assumption'. Scientologists posit a causal relationship between the experience of earlier incarnations and our present life. So, it's like Hinduism?

Hubbard advised that he had been many people including Cecil Rhodes. He also said, heaven is a 'false dream' and a 'very painful lie', which convinces people they only have one life. In reality, there is no heaven and there was no Christ. So, he was antichrist, like his bum-bud Parsons.

At the higher levels of initiation, the levels above 'Clear', the church imparts its mystical teachings. Thus, initiates find out that 75 million years ago billions of disembodied souls were brought to our planet and attached to our bodies. So, we're not just a single person but rather we're a collection or 'cluster' of hundreds of different entities. We're literally infested and need to be exorcised as these thetans are the source of our troubles i.e. they cause confusion and internal conflict. This is the real purpose of CLEAR, namely, to expel or clear the 'alien psyches' from our bodies.

Apparently, we need to talk to these body-thetans, telepathically, to make them go away. Initiates are told to close their eyes and try to locate an entity, and they're forewarned they will feel pressure on various parts of their bodies e.g. top of their heads. These pressures are the entities to be audited. A former Scientologist, who progressed to the secret upper levels, advised that it's chiefly involved with the exorcism of demons.

According to Hubbard's son, Ron de Wolf, the controversial church is a dangerous cult that exists to make money. Membership is sealed by a one-billion-year pledge to symbolise their eternal commitment, and members have to pay a ton of money to progress through the levels. De Wolf explained that his father was 'deeply involved in the occult and black magic'. And he tried to evoke the Devil for power and practices. He notes however, that his father didn't worship Satan but rather believed that he was Satan.

He informs that 'black magic is the inner core of Scientology' and his father was into mind control, which involved various incantations, drugs, hypnosis, and pain. He claims his father had a volcanic-type temper, and that he regularly battered his mum. Apparently, de Wolf was the result of an abortion (he was born weighing two pounds and two ounces), as a result of some haunted ritual. And he recalls, when he was six years old, a vivid scene of his father performing an abortion ritual on his mother using a coat hanger. He also advised that as a child, his father would feed him and his sister bubble-gum mixed with Phenobarbital, and try to put them in hypnotic trances to create what he called a 'moon child'.

De Wolf however followed in his father's footsteps, and was up there with the heads and chiefs of Scientology (he said he was high on drugs when delivering many of his lectures). He states that in addition to conning people out of their money, the drugs and black magic, he participated in orgies with his father and female followers.

Apparently, his dad's theory was that 'one has to open or crack a woman's soul in order for the satanic power to pour through it and into him'. De Wolf said, 'It got kind of far out, culminating in a variety of sex acts. Dad also had an incredibly violent temper. He was into S&M and would beat his mistresses and shoot them full of drugs'.

He further advised that his dad was involved in organised crime including drug smuggling, and the women serving him were very good at doing the dirty work, at running money and drugs back and forth. Presumably, they were mind control victims? De Wolf abruptly left the church in 1959, and never did see his father again.

He concluded, 'It's a money-and-power game, period. It's who's got all the money, who can step on whom to climb up higher, who can control the most number of people, who's got the best 'stats'. It's a mad scramble up the pyramid, and let's see who we can trample in the climb'. It seems however that Scientology is losing its Hollywood sparkle, as people are realising this religion is haunted?

In summary, many people claim to show the way. Like, Buddha and his four Noble Truths. But only Jesus said, 'I Am the way'. Contrary to popular opinion that we're God, Jesus told us God is not an impersonal cosmic force, but rather our Father. And He made us to be in relationship with Him. So, He's not the void or Brahman or Tao or moon god Allah or Lucifer. Yahweh revealed Himself to His people, and even spoke on occasions. Like, when Jesus was baptised, God said (from heaven), 'This is my Son, whom I love; with Him I am well pleased' (Matthew 3:17). He's not far away.

It's also noted, that Jesus spoke more about hell than heaven. He was clear that it's a real place of torment. So, that's worth considering. It's always possible Jesus really is our saviour. Furthermore, it appears there are no second chances with Yahweh i.e. purgatory or reincarnation. We either know Him or we don't. And we're given a certain time to figure this out. Then God takes His breath back like a thief in the night.

CS Lewis said, 'Christianity is a statement which, if false is of no importance and if true is of infinite importance. The one thing is cannot be is moderately important'. This resonates with Kierkegaard, who said, whether or not Christianity is true is the most important question of our lives, because it's literally a matter of life and death. Truth is truth, and there can only be one truth? Like, Jesus is God or He's not.

'As a face is reflected in the water, so the heart reflects the person'. Proverbs 27:19.

'For as he thinks in his heart, so he is'. Proverbs 23:7

20

Battle for the Mind

Life is mental. Not least because, all we do is think. I am therefore I think? As soon as our conscious mind comes online, we're thinking thoughts, processing awareness and registering feelings. We entertain about 60,000 thoughts every day. We talk to ourselves about everything and anything. There's no switch off button, and as Tolle (2011) said, 'not to be able to stop thinking is a dreadful affliction' (p.12). Indeed, sometimes a lobotomy doesn't seem like a bad idea.

And from our thoughts, come our actions and behaviours. Jesus said, in Mark 7:20, 'It is the thought life that defiles you. For from within, out of a person's heart, comes evil thoughts, sexual immorality, theft, murder, adultery, greed, wickedness, deceit, eagerness for lustful pleasure, envy, slander, pride and foolishness. All these vile things come from within and make you unacceptable to God'.

And omniscient God knows all our hearts, just as He knew what Lucifer was thinking back in the day. In Acts 1:24, Paul writes, 'You know every heart'. And Jeremiah 17:9 states, 'the heart is more deceitful than all else and is desperately sick; who can understand it?' So, maybe we need a new heart?

Or maybe we need a new brain? Since the contemporary emphasis is on the brain not the heart. We associate thoughts with the brain, as opposed to the heart. But maybe Paracelsus was right, that there's more going on with the heart than pumping blood around the body. Maybe the heart is the seat of the soul? Contrary to the materialist assumption, maybe we are an embodied soul with a heart full of desires? It seems meds can temporarily alter the brain, but they can't change the heart?

As discussed, chemicals do not generate thoughts but rather moods. Thoughts trigger feelings, and feelings trigger thoughts, hence the medical fix. But it seems we entertain our thoughts? Or maybe our thoughts entertain us? Maybe we're obsessed or possessed with certain thoughts. As also discussed, people are increasingly struggling with their thought life. Like, we increasingly idealise suicide? And we can catch disorders from society, like BDD? We can inadvertently give ourselves mental health problems.

Like, an eleven year old girl I read about, who was slagged off at school for cutting her hair into a bob, went on to develop mental illness. Something as minor as a haircut changed her life. Feeling helpless, and thus as a means to take control, she told herself that if she did certain OCD rituals, she would be safe the next day. She said it started off as a game, but she became obsessed with negative thoughts and began self-harming. She advised that it felt like a rush and provided a way of letting her anger out. She wanted to check out, but fortunately got help instead.

We can literally drive ourselves crazy with our thoughts. Like, we can develop psychosis if we're depressed enough, or stressed enough, or overindulge in drink and drugs enough. Anxiety can rule our life. Or perhaps we can't help our explosive anger?

It seems mental health problems equates to being victims of our own thoughts? As it transpires, it's not easy to select our thoughts like our clothes, discarding those not befitting. And we don't always want to take responsibility for our choices, like listening to our thoughts? It's preferable to attribute blame elsewhere, including genes and chemical imbalances?

Or as Buddha advocated, we can change our perspective. We can learn to control our emotions? We can accept life is suffering and suck it up? We could dissociate, and not really live or love? Or we could avoid life. It's safer indoors? Or we could partake in some funky rituals to make us safe? As discussed, it's contended insanity is a normal reaction to the absurdity. And in the absence of meaning, mental health services will never catch up with demand.

As Jung argued, meaninglessness is at the root of almost all psychological problems. The materialist philosophy, that we're indoctrinated with, births nihilism. At the end of the day, there is no point? If we're not happy, we might as well exit the theatre, and end the drama. Our narrative results in Big Pharma cashing in, and a bunch of lost and bewildered sheep. Or maybe the solution to our soul sickness is yoga and meditation? Yet it seems promoting yoga and meditation for improved psychology is like opening a can of worms or serpents?

Neither problem nor solution is accidental. On the contrary, it appears our education has paid off. But for those wise to the serpent's deception, it's understood his evil endeavour is to hide God and dement us. He wants us to be permanently separated from our Father, who made us from the beginning (we're not an accident). He wants to take us down in every way.

But moreover, maybe we don't always choose our thoughts, but rather these are thrust upon us? Like, haunted daemons whisper all manner of garbage into our lughole. Maybe our minds are not inviolate to mental suggestions, statements, or threats, from ethereal others? Maybe we are prey in a spiritually hostile world? Like, Martin Luther asserted, the devil throws hideous thoughts into the soul, hatred of God, blasphemy, and despair.

As mentioned, neuroscientists advise that we can't control what comes into our minds e.g. to kill or rape someone, but we are responsible for acting on them. We have a 'conscious veto'. So, maybe these thoughts are given to us? It's understood that thinking involves a battle, between what we should do and what we want to do. Like, the id and superego standoff. Thus, what about morality? Each one of us has the potential to embody the very best and the very worst of human nature. As Russian writer Alexsandr Solzhenitsyn said, 'The dividing line between good and evil cuts through every human heart'.

As discussed, it seems God uses Earth (physical existence) as a breeding ground to cultivate souls, and we do the cultivating? We 'become' through our choices. We become good or evil? We choose our choice, which includes loving God and our neighbour, or not. Black (2010) wrote, 'The goodness in good people will shine out of them, while the faces and bodies of evil people will be moulded by the animal passions that dominate them'.

In the Native American legend, The Tale of Two Wolves, a Cherokee elder was teaching his grandson about life. Thus, he said to the boy, 'A fight is going on inside of me'. 'It is a terrible fight, and it is between two wolves. This battle that goes on between the two wolves is inside us all. One wolf is Evil. He is anger, envy, jealousy, sorrow, regret, greed, arrogance, self-pity, guilt, resentment, inferiority, lies, false pride, superiority, and ego'. He continued, 'The other is Good. He is joy, peace, love, hope, serenity, humility, kindness, benevolence, empathy, generosity, truth, compassion, and faith'. The grandson thought about it for a minute and then asked his grandfather: 'Which wolf will win?' Wisely, the grandfather smiled and replied, 'The one you feed'.

So, we're the feeders. We choose who wins, in a battle of good versus evil? Thus, we'll consider thought life, which includes morality. It's always possible life is a moral experiment? And we'll consider psychos, who fail miserably. And we'll consider the natural and supernatural context within which thoughts take place, and the literal power of thought. And we'll consider battles of the mind, including sexual and gender identity, given their contemporary prevalence. People endure untold anguish. Life would be a lot easier if they were 'normal'. And fundamentally, thoughts are as real as we believe them to be?

It's biblically understood that we inherit a sinful nature, freewill, and a conscience. This resonates with Freud's theory, namely, our superego and id are in battle, and our ego decides who wins. Pleasure is at stake. However, rather than the id, but likened to it, the Bible pertains to our flesh. Like the id, our flesh is self-centred and inseparable from the body. It's our basic nature or principle that operates in us from the time we're born. It's basically lazy, predisposed to sin, and wants its own way.

Thus, the id translates to flesh, and we're tempted very regularly by the 'id'? The Bible notably tells us about three temptations, namely, Lust of the Flesh, Lust of the Eyes, and the Pride of Life. Pride, the original sin, is regarded as the worst sin because it's the summit of self-love and is directly opposed to submission to God. So, our flesh is proud? Pride 'feels good'. Like, satisfying or cathecting our desires feels good.

Or the id is the monster that tempts our flesh? Rather than the id, ego and superego paradigm, the biblical version of events is that our flesh is tempted by demons, and we hear from God through our spirit (our moral instinct kicks in). Our soul is our ego, encased in flesh. It's our personality that chooses its choice. And we have God given morality until we don't?

We're told that in His grace, God preserved the inner witness of conscience, the basic awareness of right and wrong. God wrote the Ten Commandments on our heart, before He wrote them on tablets. Like, the Golden Rule (always treat others as you would like to be treated) is a universal phenomenon, unless we're psychos? As Paul highlights, when gentiles do the right thing, it is a testimony to this moral instinct.

In Romans 2:14-15, he states, 'When gentiles, who do not have the law, by nature do what the law requires, they are a law to themselves, even though they do not have the law. They show that the work of the law is written on their hearts, while their conscience also bears witness, and their conflicting thoughts accuse or even excuse them'.

Like Socrates insisted, we innately know what's right and wrong 'deep down'. The moral law 'speaks within us'. Thus, we don't need God to be ethical, as Dawkins insists, as values and ethics are engraved on our heart. God made us this way. Psalm 40:8 states, '...for your law is written on my heart'.

Dawkins would however attribute our conscience to evolution. We evolved to become moral agents, or ironically religion made us moral? Like, Jesus introduced humanism. Qualities like empathy help society survive. It wouldn't work if everyone was psychos? Dawkins rightly asserts that we don't need religion to make us decent. And religion can be used to excuse indecent behaviour. Thus, the phenomenon of 'conscience' can be rendered a social construction?

Thus, we can be spiritually dead but morally adept. Those with an active conscience can have humane feelings for others i.e. compassion and empathy. Which suggests there is a right and a wrong? Like, abusing animals and kids is (a priori) not okay. Yet it appears that concepts such as absolute right and wrong are dying a cultural death. What was wrong a generation ago is kosher today. Indeed, anything goes today, including sexualising children and popularising cannibalism? It seems we're devolving?

It also seems we like to rationalise and live in bad faith? We do know better? We choose to disobey our conscience. It's noted, our rebellious nature is realised early on. Like, the notorious 'testing twos', when the psycho-politics begins? And we start lying at about four years old. It's difficult to lie at three, because we know lying is wrong?

I watched this experiment whereby researchers/psychologists left kids alone in a room with a big bowl of sweets. The kids were explicitly told not to eat the sweets (they were filmed). Then a wee while later, the researchers returned and quizzed the children if they ate the sweets. Most three-year olds couldn't lie and instead would cry etc, whereas most four-year olds were able to lie and insist they hadn't touched the sweets.

As Scott Peck highlights, the primary motive for the cover up is fear. Or maybe it's less hassle. And while lying betrays the conscience, lying also suggests some rudimentary form of conscience as why lie? Lying is also associated with intelligence, (and theory of mind), as we have to reflect how our lies will go down. Lies are crafty.

Research has further shown that lied-to children are more likely to cheat and lie. There's a connection between adult dishonesty and children's behaviour, with kids who have been lied to more likely to cheat and then lie to cover up the transgression. Ironically, most of these adults' value honesty. These parents seem to think their lies don't have any impact on their child's honesty. Like, white lies are okay? Like, our government and media lie but they act in our best interest? So, kids learn lying from their parents, and inconsistency, since they say one thing and do another. Monkey see, monkey do.

It's said the one distinctive thing about human lying is that we understand that the lie itself is wrong. And this corroborates with the ninth commandment written on our heart, namely, don't bear false witness. Whilst we're probably all guilty of breaking at least this Commandment, it's understood that we don't like being lied to. Lies are hurtful and confusing.

It's also noted, there's something very powerful about truth, much like love and light. Hence, psychotherapy is called the honesty game. We can't get better unless we're honest with ourselves? And there's something potent about confessing and unloading psychological baggage. There's a certain freedom that comes from telling the truth. It's recalled that Jesus said, 'I Am the truth', and being made in His image, suggests we're designed to be honest? We're not okay otherwise?

Moreover, do we feel guilty for lying? As touched on, it's asserted that consciences are a necessary adaptation for society's survival. With basic guilt, (an affective state i.e. we feel bad), we learn from our mistakes, preventing bad behaviour and facilitating greater cooperation with others. Guilt suggests we know an action is wrong, and it can be a powerful emotion. Albeit, it's said only the good feel guilty.

So, there's psychos at one end of the spectrum, who relish in skinning victims alive and eating their psychedelic pain. Like, those who run the world, and kill people for profit (and depopulation). And at the other extreme, others experience excessive guilt resulting in neuroses. People can want to check out because of guilt. Guilt can consume people; devour them. Sometimes we need to be forgiven, as it's the only way to alleviate the guilt. Forgiveness is a powerful action, but we'll get back to this. Apparently 'shame' is the number one cause of suicide, which is different from guilt. Shame underpins pride?

Guilt notably plays an important role in OCD. Guilt plagues those who experience a conflict between what they haven't done and need to, and conversely, what they've done but shouldn't have. It's a neurotic nightmare. Interestingly, some therapists advise OCD sufferers to see their OCD as a bully and not to listen to him or her. This separates the person from their thoughts, as the bully generates the thoughts. It's said that fighting the bully is like fighting a monster. It's interesting because ethereal entities could be the monster? They could be responsible for torturing people with guilt-laden thoughts?

It appears the Ten Commandments are instinctive (by virtue of being written on our hearts) but we also have to learn the rules? Like, we instinctively know that lying and cheating is wrong, but we also learn that it's wrong? And we instinctively know that murder is wrong unless we're soldiers or jihadists? As highlighted, we don't have a natural inclination to kill. It makes soldiers physically sick until they get used to it.

Scott Peck notably asserts, 'Human killing is not instinctual but protection is. What replaces species-wide instincts in human beings is learned individual choice. We can reject what society says. We can choose celibacy despite sex being one of the few instincts we do have or kill ourselves for martyrdom' (People of the Lie, p.280).

In tandem with our innate disdain for lies, we have an innate sense of justice? Or we also learn this? Like, an eight year old boy I worked with, who had ADHD and behavioural problems, subsequently learned that he had to adhere to society's rules like everyone else. Like, he learned that it's not okay to skip the queue, and would shout at anyone else doing it (LOL). We all have to play by the rules or it's not fair? So, much of life isn't fair. Which includes the bodies and families we're born into, which in turn brings the benevolence of God into question?

It also seems pertinent to note, we're not the only creatures who lie, and equally have a sense of justice. Like, chimpanzees and apes often deceive each other. Capuchin monkeys, for example, make false alarm calls, signalling a predator approaching, so they can snaffle bananas from their elders, who otherwise hog the bananas. Apes have sneaky affairs. As explicated, animals are very clever. They know what they're doing?

Regarding equality, in a 'fairness experiment', two capuchin monkeys were taught to hand over pebbles in exchange for cucumber slices. And they were happy with their payment. But then the researcher randomly offered one monkey a grape for a pebble, which is a better deal because monkeys love grapes, in sight of the other monkey. The researcher then returned to the other monkey, but presented just a cucumber for the pebble, which the monkey threw back in disgust (LOL).

The monkey was not at all happy, which shows they care deeply about fairness. What mattered to them was not just what they received but also what others got. It also seems some animals can feel guilty? Like, dogs' sheepish demeanour when they've done something wrong. Or they're scared, as wrong actions merit punishment?

It's understood that lying undermines the conscience. And if we can lie once, we can lie again. We can also lie to ourselves because it's more palatable, although Sartre would not consent. We can deceive ourselves and others. But that's not integrity, and we value integrity? Or no one cares these days. Values and morals are arbitrary.

It's also noted, that lying can become pathological, which is an illness? Like, compulsive stealing is an illness? Like lying, if we can steal once, we can steal again. And cheat, as the old adage goes, 'once a cheater, always a cheater'. And abusers don't abuse once, as a one off? And, if we can rape and murder once, we can do it again? We might feel bad the first time, but less the second time, and so forth. We can develop a behaviour pattern. It seems we can erode our conscience; on the premise one was instilled in the first place. We can degenerate into psychos, which is supported by research that shows the more bad we do, the less guilt we feel.

Eric Fromm, psychoanalyst who studied the evil of Nazism, stated, 'Our capacity to choose changes constantly with our practice of life. The longer we continue to make the wrong decisions, the more our heart hardens; the more often we make the right decision our heart softens – or perhaps, better, comes alive (cited in Scott Peck, 'People of the Lie', 1983 p.91).

Fromm was apparently the first to identify an evil personality type. And he spoke about the genesis of evil. That is, we're not good then become evil overnight. But rather, it's a developmental process. We 'become'. So, we can become evil, which suggests evil is a real thing? Like, love is a real thing.

As mentioned, there's no reference to evil in the DSM, because good and evil are value judgements. We can't say murderers and paedophiles are evil. But rather they have Antisocial Personality Disorder (a clever obfuscation?). As mentioned, with ASPD, the person never shows remorse, has no interest in the feelings or rights of others, and is happy to lie, cheat and could murder.

So, we can choose to make right decisions, but we don't always want to. And regarding any God-given conscience, we can be tempted (by our flesh or the id) not to care? We can defend our ego by rationalising despondency? Praise the Lord however for preserving our conscience, as most 'normal' people have some kind of conscience, however fractured. We experience a tension between what we should do, and what we want to do? We're not narcissistic psychos?

But then there's kids from dysfunctional homes, for example, who fail to develop a conscience? Like, Fred West, whose twisted childhood included incest and bestiality. It's arguably no surprise he became a psycho, and together with his wife Rose, who also had a depraved childhood, tortured, raped and murdered at least twelve young women, including their own family members. Fred hung himself before going to trial, and Rose was imprisoned for life.

Or like, Richard Kuklinski aka Iceman had an abusive childhood. Kuklinski was nicknamed Iceman for his methods of freezing his victims to outfox forensic experts, as freezing victims' masks the time of death. This professional hitman murdered more than two hundred people, and brutality and torture often preceded his victim's demise. Like, he would cause his victims to bleed, and then tie them up in a rat-infested area, and the rats, attracted by the smell of blood would eventually eat the men alive. Apparently, he learned to torture animals in childhood. Psychiatrists say Kuklinski suffered from a paranoid personality disorder, and it's likely he inherited ASPD from his abusive parents.

It seems pertinent to acknowledge, that animal cruelty is psychopathic (like the fur industry and vivisection). And kids can be particularly cruel. Like, a group of teenagers bought a hamster from a pet shop in Cambridge, attached it to a firework with an elastic band, and blew it up. Can you imagine how terrified the hamster would be?

And I read a story about a dog that was tied up to a railway line and chewed off its own paws to get free. There's countless stories about cats and dogs being set on fire, shot, scalded with boiling water, and battered. Poor vulnerable animals have sustained brain damage and been left paralysed. It's heart-breaking. Such actions beg the question, how do we treat other living beings that similarly feel pain?

Mahatma Gandhi said, 'The greatest of a nation and its moral progress can be judged by the way its animals are treated'. And Immanuel Kant said, 'He who is cruel to animals becomes hard also in his dealings with men. We can judge the heart of a man by his treatment of animals'.

As a general rule, we tend to grow out of evil and narcissism, so perhaps we can admonish ruthless kids who have yet to learn? And others, who are similarly inauthentic, like fishing for fun as opposed to dinner (how can getting a hook in your eye be fun). Like, eating factory farmed animals. However, I digress.

And presumably Ivan became terrible for a reason? Ivan IV Vasilyevich (1530-1584) aka Ivan the Terrible was prone to rages and episodic bouts of insanity. So, maybe it's not his fault he butchered so many, including his son, in a particularly evil manner? He was unwell? Its 'sick' that he delighted in letting his dogs and bears devour the mutilated bodies of those he killed in the public square?

Maybe something got into him. Like, an autonomous complex took control? He became possessed by an archetype looking for fulfilment, or a monster. Which negates his culpability? As Jung contended, people become insane when usurped by a complex. We can't be responsible for what the unconscious unleashes. It seems evil is insanity, but not all the time, as sane evil people exist?

Apparently, Ivan would order women to be hanged at their own doors, and husbands were forced to go in and out under the swinging and festering corpses of those they had loved and cherished. He forced husbands to have dinner with their murdered wives. That is, dead wives and children, all dressed up for dinner no less, were fastened in their seat at the dinner table. He also made children watch their parents get dismembered.

But moreover, Ivan assumed the manner of one inspired, claiming divine powers. And people loved this maniac. Like, people loved Hitler and Stalin, who're presumably burning in hell? As discussed, it's widely believed that Hitler was possessed (he was harbouring demons). Apparently, Stalin was inspired by Ivan, and Ivan was inspired by Vlad the Impaler (the royal family's ancestor).

Besides an unfortunate start to life, it's purported we can inherit psycho-genes (so-called warrior genes). Apparently, there's primary and secondary psychos i.e. genetically caused or environmentally caused. It's like primary and secondary depression. And like the depression gene, which doesn't need to express itself with a loving environment, predisposed psychos don't have to become psychos with a loving and stable environment. Psychology is nature versus nurture?

It's noted, whilst the terms 'psychopath' and 'sociopath' are often used interchangeably, there's some difference. Sociopath replaced psychopath in the 1930s to emphasise the damage they do to society but more recently researchers have returned to using the term psychopath. Psychopath seems to refer to a more serious disorder, linked to genetic traits, whereas sociopath tends to refer to less dangerous people who are seen more as social products.

Robert 'Hare's Psychopathy Checklist' is a diagnostic tool used to assess the presence of psychopathy in individuals (he developed it in the 1970s). It rates a person's psychopathic or antisocial tendencies using a twenty-item inventory of perceived personality traits. In essence, psychos are characterised by superficial charm, pathological lying, egotistical narcissism, and diminished capacity for remorse. But the key trait is no conscience. Hence, they're cunning and manipulative, and genuinely don't care about anyone but themselves. Apparently, this is an incurable disorder (illness?).

It's also noted, whilst psychopathy is not the official title of any diagnosis in the DSM, the category of psychopath is included within ASPD. As mentioned, ASPD includes a 'callous unconcern for the feelings of others', which applies to psychos, but apparently only 1:5 people with ASPD are psychopaths. It seems those with a psychopathy personality disorder are worse, albeit no judgement.

Apparently, psychos don't experience emotions like 'normal people'. However, whilst psychos evidence a stunning lack of empathy, research has shown that they can empathise if they choose to. It's like a switch they can turn off and on. Psycho criminals were placed in a brain scanner and shown videos of one person hurting another. When they were asked to empathise with the individual in pain, the area relating to pain lit up. But without instruction, they showed reduced activity in the regions of the brain associated with pain.

It's noted, we use the same machinery (pain matrix, group of cells) when we're in pain and watching others in pain, which suggests we've been designed for empathy? Perhaps that's why porn's so successful? And movies in general, as these trigger myriad emotions i.e. we can experience other's ecstasy and agony. So, empathy can be willed. Psychos could learn the golden rule. Thus, it's said a cat can learn to become a mouse. But why would they want to, if they don't care?

Apparently 1-2% of the general population meets the clinical criteria for psychopathy. Hence, besides psycho killers who brutally rape and torture, psychos are everywhere i.e. in business, law, medicine, politics, TV, media, but particularly banking. Apparently, there's more psychos in banking than any other profession.

Corporate psychos, motivated by status and power, can make hard decisions that others would feel bad about making because they don't care. Like, 'Fred the Shred' (banker), who was knighted by the Queen (until he wasn't). Apparently 1:25 business leaders have psychopathic traits. Success is associated with grandiose, driven, ambitious, competitive, and ruthless individuals.

So, psychos have a personality disorder? Yet they can be devilishly charming. It seems grim to note, that according to psychologists, women are attracted to the 'dark triad'. This combines the self-obsession of narcissism, the impulsive, thrill seeking and callous behaviour of the psychopath, and the deceitful and exploitative nature of Machiavellianism. In other words, research shows that we're attracted to A-holes.

Or could psychos, including paedophiles, be possessed by demons? Maybe there's some spirit attachment? Like, Satanists, who appear sane, have demonic attachments? Like, Father George Bush and Jimmy Savile, who otherwise seemed like nice men? It seems the issue is whether people are evil or insane? As highlighted, there's a fine line between mad and bad.

Like, Ian Brady, who was responsible for the Moors murders, was diagnosed as a psychopath and declared criminally insane in 1985. It was insane that he aspired to 'commit the perfect murder'? Together with his partner in crime, Myra Hindley, who was referred to as 'the most evil woman in Britain', they sexually assaulted and murdered five children aged between ten and seventeen.

It's noted, that Brady repeatedly asked permission to die and was on hunger strike for fifteen years (he was force-fed daily to keep him alive). He tried to retract his admission that he was mentally unwell at the time of the crimes, but psychiatrists insisted he was mad. They maintained he had a serious personality disorder.

Or take, Norwegian psycho, Anders Behring Breivik, who was responsible for the Utoya island massacre in 2011, which resulted in 77 killings. He maintained, 'I am not a psychiatric case. I am sane. I am of sane mind'. He also said, 'young people were literally paralysed with fear and begging for their lives'. And 'there were a hundred voices in my head saying 'Don't do it. Don't do it'. Presumably, that was his conscience, God's voice, or the voice of angels? Maybe he was demonically possessed?

Psychiatrists initially diagnosed him as having paranoid schizophrenia, but following widespread criticism, he was re-diagnosed as having narcissistic personality disorder. So, he went from being clinically insane to sane, and therefore guilty. He was not deemed psychotic during the attacks. It seems ironic that psychiatry can 'change its mind' to accommodate popular opinion?

It's also reported that serial killing can become addictive. And psychos become bolder, as they seek their sadistic buzz. Like the Hillside Stranglers, Ken Bianchi and his cousin Angelo Buono, initially targeted prostitutes before moving onto middle class women and girls (the females ranged from twelve to twenty-eight). Apparently, they started out as pimps before they began their murderous career, which entailed sexually abusing and torturing at least ten women before murdering them. They notably posed as cops. They had fake badges and drove about in 'unmarked cars'.

They were sentenced to life in prison, so they were bad as opposed to mad? Apparently Buono boasted to his buds about raping and sodomising girls when he was fourteen years old, so that was bad? But what made him so bad?

Interestingly, Bianchi, (who testified against his cousin to avoid the death penalty), initially denied he was responsible for the crimes. He claimed his alternate personality 'Steve' was. 'Steve' emerged when he was in a trance, when psychiatrists hypnotised him. This sadistic alter took responsibility for the murders. It's said however that Bianchi acted like he had MPD. He was well versed in MPD and apparently seen the movie 'Sybil' many times.

As it transpired, psychiatrists rumbled his ruse and he confessed. Psychiatrists tricked him by saying at least three personalities were required for a diagnosis of MPD, and he subsequently went onto develop another personality, which led them to believe he was acting. He was eventually diagnosed with ASPD with sexual sadism.

Bianchi's adoptive parents notably described him as deeply troubled from a young age (his biological mother, who was an alcoholic and prostitute, gave him up two weeks after birth). He was described as a compulsive liar, and besides being quick to lose his temper, was his penchant for trance-like daydreams. He was diagnosed with petit mal seizures, the term given to 'staring spells', when he was five. Apparently 'absence seizures', which usually last less than fifteen seconds, are due to abnormal electrical activity in the brain. It seems this disturbance is attributed to an autonomous complex taking over? Bianchi was diagnosed with passive aggressive disorder by ten years old.

Or take James Holmes, who killed twelve and injured seventy during his mass shooting at the Batman screening in Colorado in 2012. He pleaded not guilty by reason of insanity. His lawyers said he had a psychotic episode during the attack, but his notebook revealed his obsession to kill ten years prior to the shooting, as well as detailed plans for the shooting. Hence, it was premeditated.

A second psychiatrist testified that Holmes was mentally ill but legally sane during the shooting. Apparently, Holmes suffers from schizoaffective disorder. It's also said however, that Holmes was a victim of mind control, and programmed to commit that atrocity. As discussed, it's purported that many lone shooters are CIA MK Ultra victims. So, they're not guilty?

And we can't always blame families for their haunted offspring, as we choose our choice? Like, misogynist Elliot Rodger, who's seemingly decent parents had no idea their kid was a blood thirsty psycho. Rodger advised it was tortuous being a virgin at twenty-two years old, and secured what he called his 'retribution'. He declared 'I will destroy all women', and went on a rampage in California in 2014, killing six people (including his two flatmates and one of their friends) and injuring fourteen, before killing himself.

He said, 'College is the time when everyone experiences those things such as sex and fun and pleasure. Within those years, I've had to rot in loneliness. It's not fair. You girls have never been attracted to me. I don't know why you girls aren't attracted to me, but I will punish you for it. It's an injustice, a crime'. He said, 'How could an inferior, ugly black boy be able to get a white girl and not me? I am beautiful, and I am half white myself. I am descended from British aristocracy. He is descended from slaves'.

He also said, 'I am the ideal, magnificent gentleman'. 'I am more than human. I am superior to them all. I am Elliot Rodger... Magnificent, glorious, supreme, eminent... Divine! I am the closest thing there is to a living god. 'Everyone will fear me as the powerful god I am'. Whilst he was never diagnosed with a mental illness, it would appear he was at least narcissistic and deluded.

It's said the most common theme among psychos who go on killing sprees is revenge. Like Rodger, who planned his retribution, they collect perceived injustices and payback. Like, Eric Berne's game, 'Now I've Got You, Son of a Bitch'. It's understood Rodger was lonely, rejected and bullied. Apparently kids once taped his head to his desk when he fell asleep. [Nice]. So, maybe it's not Rodger's fault that he became deranged? Or was he sane? Maybe he was demon possessed?

As Paracelsus said, devils may take possession of a living man, and make a weak man act as they please, and cause him to commit all sorts of foolishness and crime. It's understood, demons literally use people for evil. So, psychos could be victims? As mentioned, when people are possessed by demons, they want to kill and harm others. They enjoy it.

But moreover, often psychos report hearing voices which guide their actions. So, they're not psychos but rather schizophrenic. Like, serial killer David Berkowitz was diagnosed with paranoid schizophrenia. Berkowitz claimed his neighbour, Sam Carr, was the devil and his demon possessed dog passed on his messages. Berkowitz advised he was commanded to kill, stating, 'He told me to kill. Sam is the devil. I had to obey'. He alleged that Sam was a demon who lived six thousand years ago. And Sam needed blood to stay alive. Thus, he killed to provide him with blood. Berkowitz said, 'I am a monster. I am the son of Sam'.

But moreover, it seems Berkowitz enjoyed toying with the police, as he left handwritten notes at the crime scenes, taunting and insulting them. So, it seems he was mentally ill, but knew what he was doing? Although he was considered mentally unstable, Berkowitz pleaded guilty at his trial. He confessed to his crimes, including six murders and nearly 1,500 fires he set in and around New York City.

However, as it transpired, Berkowitz later retracted his possessed dog 'Son of Sam' story, claiming 'It was all a hoax, a silly hoax'. Berkowitz claims he was a member of a violent satanic cult that orchestrated the murders along with fellow cult members John and Michael Carr, the sons of Sam Carr. He claims he was demon possessed but he has since been freed through Jesus. He has become an evangelical Christian. He got a new heart?

For a less high profile example, my friend told me about a time when her brother was staying at his girlfriend's (parents) house, and the next day when he got up, he found the family dog dead in the garden. Apparently, his girlfriend's dad has schizophrenia, and he was told by Satan to kill his wife. He had to make a sacrifice, so instead of killing the wife, he killed the dog. So, he's mad because that couldn't be real? Or it's possible that people are hearing demonic voices. Maybe threatening and commanding voices are from an outside source, beyond so-called complexes.

Fortunately, 'schizophrenia' rarely occurs in childhood, but as mentioned, attachments can make us 'ill'. Like, Alex was severely damaged due to perverse primary attachments. Alex was dubbed 'Little Miss Evil'. Yet it seems wrong to label kids evil? In 'The Trouble With Alex: A Child Too damaged To Love' (2008), Melanie Allen reveals her story.

Thus, Alex was adopted at five years young and her new parents couldn't believe their good fortune. Alex seemed to be a dream child, heartbreakingly beautiful and affectionate. However, as the months passed, her parents began to see a very different side to their perfect daughter. This child seemed inherently evil. Indeed, her (adoptive) mother mused that she was some evil person reincarnated.

Alex was described as calculated and extremely manipulative. She did whatever it took to be the centre of attention, complete with bizarre and insidious tactics. Like, she walked strangely, stared fixedly, and tapped her feet incessantly. She dressed completely inappropriately, often with clothes back to front, or inside out. It seems she embodied the law of reversal?

Allen explains that looking in her eyes, there was nothing there. She seemed to be void of emotion yet filled with underlying hate. She was highly defiant and subsequently lied about acts when challenged. Alternatively, she played 'innocent'. She would mirror anyone she talked to and mirror their attitude. She could be superficially charming, knowing exactly what others wanted to hear. Her mother described her as a 'consummate actor', steely and controlled.

It appears Alex had Reactive Attachment Disorder, which is characterised by a lack of conscience, compassion and empathy; lack of eye contact except when lying (which includes crazy lying and they can lie very convincingly); very manipulative; don't respond to reason or logic; defiant behaviour; unable to recognise right or wrong; false allegations of abuse; indiscriminate affection towards strangers; lack of affection towards new parents/care-givers; rage; fear; destructive to self, others, animals and property; no impulse control; superficial charm; unusual eating patterns e.g. hoarding, gorging or refusal to eat; unsuccessful peer relationships; incessant chatter in order to control; very demanding; unusual speech patterns e.g. talking very softly except when lying, robotic speech and mumbling; learning delays and disorders, depressed IQ scores.

Whilst such kids choose their choice, it's understood they're damaged. So, it's not their fault they're psychos. They're not freely choosing? And it's always possible, as Black asserted, the abuse they suffered created a rent in their psyche, enabling spirits to come through? It's possible they have spirit attachments? Like, sodomising children arouses the kundalini spirit, or rather invites it in. It's highlighted that evil spirits are often behind evil thoughts.

As it transpired, by eight years young, Alex had a voice in her head which told her what to do and what not to do. In response to parental commands, like saying thank you, she would advise that she was ordered not to. The voice demanded total secrecy, forbidding her to reveal this entity to anyone. The voice in her head talked about death and threatened to kill others. It was filled with hate. It seems she developed schizophrenia? Maybe we should take imaginary friends seriously, since they could be spirit guides or real monsters?

It seems pertinent to note, the New Age Movement refers to children who possess paranormal abilities as 'indigo children'. The colour indigo is associated with psychic ability. These kids are invariably 'challenging' but they're considered 'special' and 'gifted' because they can communicate with the spirit world. Some regard these children (usually born after 1980) as more evolved. They're viewed as having an ancient and noble purpose. Others however claim 'indigo children' is the preferred term for ADHD. Unlike ADHD, indigo is a positive label?

Apparently, indigos feel like an 'old soul', (which is interesting?), and they're more prone to addictions, depression, and suicidal ideation. They bore easily, bristle at authority and have little patience. Simple acts like waiting in line drives them crazy. They have extremely high self-esteem. Indeed, it's said they act like royalty and have no guilt. Maybe these kids are haunted?

It seems the crux of the matter is 'free' choice. How much is freely willed? As people can come from horrific homes, and somehow aren't psychos. Yet others who seemingly received 'good enough' parenting become horror shows. Like, Rodger? People can enjoy being bad because they're psychos, which could be genetic, or not? Being bad can be enjoyable? Maybe, like two year olds, people don't care for rules. If there is no God, who cares? Being good's a snore.

It seems for as long as we can remember (i.e. from early childhood), we've always had the choice to choose the right or wrong action? We're always thinking, and have intentions and motives. Like, the kids who were challenged (tempted) with a big bowl of sweets knew what they were doing. And they knew they were lying when they lied.

Like, Nicola, (who I read about in a magazine), freely chose to be a bad egg or maybe she was born a bad egg? Nicola was described as having no empathy from a young age. Nicola's brother, Tom, advised 'Nicola seemed to enjoy turning people against each other'. He relayed that she was always in trouble at school, and parents stopped their kids from playing with her because she was a bad influence. Nicola's mum consulted a psychologist, but they advised Nicola was 'normal'. Tom said, 'Nicola was good at faking sanity'.

By eleven years old, Nicola was uncontrollable and disappeared for days at a time. She also got into drugs. As it transpired, things went from bad to worse over the years, and she subsequently killed her mum in a psychotic rage. She was sectioned and diagnosed as having schizophrenia. As it further transpired, when she was released from the secure psychiatric centre, she detrimentally spiralled into freefall relapse which resulted in killing another (she used a meat cleaver) and attempting to kill others.

However, despite her diagnosis, the judge said, 'You are manipulative and exceptionally dangerous. You made your choice. These were terrible acts for which you must take responsibility'. So, she was bad as opposed to mad, or both? Maybe an autonomous complex aka demon was activated?

Apparently, she left a note which detailed a list of condemned people, those she planned to kill. Her mum's name was on the top, which was scored out, and Tom's name was next. Tom accepts his sister suffers from a mental illness and personality disorder, but he doesn't believe this absolves her from responsibility for the killing of two women. Interestingly, at one stage, Nicola joined an evangelical church as she was convinced, she was surrounded by demons. Maybe that's why she got diagnosed with schizophrenia?

Thus, unlike those who don't know any better (like Little Miss Evil?), perhaps we can choose to become evil? We can develop evil hearts, by listening to the immoral voice rather than the moral voice inside our heads. As Fromm highlighted, choices are progressive. Like, A-holes (unchecked) turn into sadistic A-holes, who turn into psychos? As mentioned, if kids with 'conduct disorder' are left untreated, they become adults with ASPD (hence, the emphasis on early intervention).

It's also noted, that whilst some psychos are clever, other psychos often have lower IQs and deficits in problem solving. Thus, there's a difference between having an anger problem and poor self-management skills, and enjoying others' pain? Evil is more than ignorance. It also seems hard drugs, like crack and heroin, can erode our conscience. Perhaps they provide an opening for demons to come in. Like, Nicola?

Moreover, maybe we should call out evil, rather than skirting about psychiatric terms like personality disorders? Maybe we could rate evil on a scale of 1-10. The DSM could introduce Evil Spectrum Disorder. Scott Peck boldly asserts that certain people are evil, but he insists that evil should be considered a psychiatric illness. He states many evil people are diagnosed as having ambulatory schizophrenia, but alternatively he suggests classifying evil as a variant of narcissistic personality disorder. So, contrary to popular psychiatric opinion, they're sane, not insane. They're evil? Like, people who rape and kill children are evil.

In Peck's opinion, evil people are chronic scapegoaters. They're accusers. They can't face self-reproach and instead attribute blame to others. Since they can't face their own failures, they project these onto others through scapegoating. He considers unbridled narcissism to be the principal precursor of this psycho-spiritual illness. So, fear and pride (the devils favourite sin) contribute to evil. These characteristics prevent people from acknowledging their shadow (dark hidden side), which manifests as evil? For Jung, human evil was not the shadow itself, but 'refusal to meet with this shadow'.

Peck explains evil (malignant narcissism) is characterised by self-absorption, an un-submitted will and a remarkable power in controlling others. In his book, 'People of the Lie', he states, 'In addition to the abrogation of responsibility that characterises all personality disorders', 'evil' is distinguished by: 'consistent destructive, scapegoating behaviour, which may often be quite subtle; excessive, albeit usually covert, intolerance to criticism and other forms of narcissistic injury; pronounced concern with a public image and self image of respectability, contributing to a stability of lifestyle but also to pretentiousness and denial of hateful feelings or vengeful motives; intellectual deviousness, with an increased likelihood of mild schizophrenia like disturbance of thinking at times of stress' (p.146).

In short, evil people lie to themselves and others. Peck advised that 'People of the Lie' go to extreme lengths to preserve their egos. But moreover, Peck pertained to feeling repulsed by evil. He describes how this repulsion emanates at a physical and soul level. Furthermore, as mentioned, he attended exorcisms, so he knows evil is real. And it's not always human.

So, people can be possessed by evil? We can become possessed by our shadow, the evil part of us that we deny. But we can also be possessed by evil 'archetypes', which are independent of the physical brain? Thus, beyond simply facing the contents of our own personal unconscious, there could be spirit invaders. Maybe angels and demons do put thoughts into our hearts and minds? And God talks to us in a still, small voice?

As touched on, whilst Freud often wrote about his disenchantment with religion, apparently he was a cabalist and studied the mystical texts (including the Zohar) in private. David Bakan, author of 'Sigmund Freud and the Jewish Mystical Tradition' (1958), asserts Freudian psychology is rooted in the cabala. Freud's contribution is a contemporary secularised version of ancient Jewish mysticism. Apparently, Freud had his own inner circle or Secret Committee, which consisted of his most trusted psychoanalysts. Freud the cabalist was part of the cabal.

Black (2010) concedes that Freud was deeply interested in the cabala, and his idea of consciousness having a structure is essentially cabalistic. Freud's model of mind i.e. superego, ego and id can be seen as a materialised version of the tripartite cabalistic model. Black expounds, '...the very notion that there are impulses independent of our point of consciousness, but which may impinge upon it from outside, is a secularised, materialistic version of the esoteric account of consciousness. In Freud's scheme of life these hidden forces should be interpreted as sexual rather than spiritual. Freud later reacted against the esoteric roots of his ideas and stigmatised as mad the ancient form of consciousness out of which they had grown' (p.524).

Unlike Jung who espoused the daemonic, Freud materialised it and thought life became impervious to outside forces. As Black (2010) highlights, 'Today we tend to be very proprietorial about our thoughts. We want to take credit for originating them, and we like to think that our private mental space is inviolate, that no other consciousness can intrude on it' (p.56). But maybe not. Maybe the schizophrenics know better?

As discussed, the portions of the auditory cortex that light up when we hear real voices, is the same when hallucinating. Hence, they're received and processed like other voices. Some psychologists notably depart from orthodoxy and accept their patient's voices are real, rather than 'delusions' and 'hallucinations'. These voices do belong to monsters.

It's also noted, that 'Tourette Syndrome' is described as being like two people. Thus, there's the person and the 'tourettes'. Tourette syndrome is associated with tics, which are uncontrolled sudden, repetitive muscle movements and sounds. Tics can notably be a side effect of amphetamine drugs given to kids (nice). But moreover, coprolalia is a typical symptom, which entails excessive and uncontrollable use of foul or obscene language. Victims shout out derogatory remarks, refer to genitals, excrement, and sexual acts. These words or complex phrases do not necessarily reflect the thoughts, beliefs, or opinions of the person. So, that's a puzzling condition?

As discussed, whilst the demonic can literally make themselves known and felt, it's alleged these spirits largely operate by communicating with us through our thoughts. So, it's possible they're responsible for the Negative Automatic Thoughts we entertain? They nurture the negative mindsets we develop. Our entrenched patterns of thought, behaviour and habit are not so much self-sabotage? It's understood we can become slaves to our minds e.g. eating disorders, addictions, most mental afflictions. So, maybe they have something to do with it? Maybe demons are tempting our flesh?

It's also noted, that people often refer to their addictions as demons. Like, Russell Brand (2012) said recovering drunks and addicts, when clean, tell him 'how they continue to cope with an external world that will not submit to their imagined demands and an ego that is defined by its insatiability, this restless demon that forever wants more, that lingers like a tapeworm at the gateway to the soul, devouring and rejecting according to its needs' (p.45).

It seems the issue is whether we're the source of the demon, i.e. our id. Or we're the flesh and the id is an external demon? According to the Bible, demons know us intimately and tempt the flesh by capitalising on the desires of our heart. It appears the heart is paramount because thoughts come from the heart. The neurons in our heart communicate with the neurons in our brain, and our belly brain?

However, before we get to alleged daemonic warfare, aka the craziness that lurks behind the material veil, it seems pertinent to reiterate regarding thought life in the material (natural not supernatural) sense. And before we abscond from responsibility?

So, we think thoughts, our voice in our head. Which may include recycling the same old self-deprecating and paralysing thoughts because we're masochists? But then there's hearing our own voice tell us to do something, so not an external voice as such, but it seems misplaced? Like, on one occasion, I heard my own voice repeatedly say, when I was on the fourth floor in a hotel, to 'jump over the balcony'. Whilst I was insistent that there was no way I was going to jump off the balcony (I was not in the least depressed), the voice in my head, my voice, annoyingly continued 'jump over the balcony'. I surmise that was a demonic attack.

It seems we can be obsessed with ideas, like 'OCD'. We can't stop thinking about something, but rationally we could? So, we're still rational. We're still in touch with reality? We recognise that we need to take the bully on, or try to ignore him? Distract ourselves? It's understood that thoughts grow with attention and seem more important, but the truth is thoughts don't change a thing. There's no power in them, other than what we give them?

But then, there's hearing 'external' voices, which isn't normal. Such people are not in touch with reality. Or they are, but they also happen to hear voices from invisible personalities that no one else hears. As mentioned, whilst hearing voices suggests a neurological or psychological problem, many people function normally, which suggests they're not 'ill'? It just so happens they hear voices.

Like, mediums and psychics consult spirits, and they're sane? They're not necessarily tormented by voices, like paranoid schizophrenics who can be paralysed by fear and condemning thoughts. At any rate, the herd are placated there is no spirit world. Psychics and psychotics are merely party to their own unconscious?

Moreover, and fundamentally, we are what we think. 'We' are the result of an insane amount of thoughts and choices. Which includes conquests or defeats of moral battles? As Jesus taught, man's problem is his heart and nature. He didn't say we could blame demons or society for our inauthenticity. On the contrary, we're accountable. Thus, our flesh is a bind. Like, the spiritual battle we're immersed in. It's also noted, Jesus gets it (being fully man). He just didn't sin, which makes Him exceptional.

Jesus said, 'each tree is recognised by its own fruit'[32]. The biblical metaphor is that we're like trees that produce good or rotten fruit. Thoughts bear fruit and we reap what we sow. It's said, 'sow a thought reap an action; sow an action reap a habit; sow a habit reap a lifestyle; sow a lifestyle reap a destiny'. So, thoughts are more than just self-talk. They grow trees that seem difficult to uproot.

However, it's also understood that others, including 'society', can plant seeds into minds and hearts. Indeed, we're arguably programmed. What people say can affect us and become self-fulfilling? Like, what we're told growing up e.g. tell someone they're good or no good, and they may live up to that? Like, parents calling their young daughters sluts may precipitate slut behaviour. Albeit, who cares, as there's no judgement regarding sluts. Society says, 'knock yourself out'. Or calling sons a waste of breath, may encourage them to give up their breath?

Apparently 70% of gays were slagged off for being gay when they were young, which may or may not have impacted on their sexual orientation? Like, a couple of people suggested I was gay, as a late teenager, because I rarely had a boyfriend. And whilst I wasn't attracted to women, it brought my sexuality into question. Maybe I was gay? Or I rarely meet someone I like. It seems others affirm us? Like, we're not okay. Sartre said, 'words are more treacherous and powerful than we think', and 'words are loaded pistols'. As it transpires, sticks and stones may break our bones, but names can also harm us.

For an example, a mum I worked with, (she was a heroin user and neglecting her five year old daughter), had a younger brother (17 years old) who became 'unwell' through potent words. He was changing his niece, her daughter, and the mum's friends taunted him, claiming he was a paedophile. And six months later he was sectioned in the mental hospital believing he was a paedophile. This is a remarkably common fear.

Thus, we can develop mental illness, because of others? We can allow certain thoughts to take root, which engineers our downfall. It's understood we 'become' through the medium of society. But we can't blame society because we're held in bondage due to a certain perverse way of thinking. We can't blame society that we're born into a crazy world that serves no point. Or maybe the world is serving someone?

So, we increasingly don't know if we're okay? Maybe we're a paedophile? Maybe we're a tree? Or maybe some 'thought being' is attached to us making us think that? As discussed, the social psychological principle is, we believe what we hear ourselves say. And we can believe things that aren't true? As discussed, the DSM is bursting with diagnoses to explain our not-okay life position. Society is not okay, hence, the increase in mental cases.

Lest we forget, the deliberate assault on identity. It seems identity is an existential crisis? Who are we, and where do we fit in the world? Which tribe do we identify with? We're obsessed with ourselves, and we're bombarded with different messages. Identity politics has taken over? It's duly noted, that sexual and gender identity is part of this mine field. And this is by design because it ensnares our mind with no end of doubt and confusion. As mentioned, Satan is renowned as the author of confusion.

---

[32] See Luke 6:43-44, Matthew 12:33, Romans 11:24, John 15:1.

Thus, clearly differentiated gender roles have died a death, and 'traditional relationships' have been usurped by tri-sexuals, who try anything for sexual gratification. As discussed, society is hyper-sexualised, and people love porn. And in our gender fluid culture, no one cares what sex people are, it's about the person? We fall in love with people not genitals?

As also discussed, Kinsey 'liberated' sexual inhibition, or rather encouraged the masses to become depraved like him? And Freud reduced humankind to animals born with sexual instincts. They agreed that we're born bisexual. The extent of our homosexual tendencies can be determined by Kinsey's 'Heterosexual-Homosexual Rating Scale', which plants this supposition.

It's noted, that unlike those who have always inherently felt gay, so-called 'primary' homosexuality, others can be gay by default, so-called 'secondary' homosexuality. Like, in prisons, or same sex schools, or convents and monasteries, people may bat for the other side. And in the absence of people, people may bat the sheep? It's highlighted that women are more liberal, and more inclined to help each other out at the weekend.

It's also noted, that marketing sex undermined the value of intimacy and love. Instead of being sacred, sex became cheap. People became cheap? Trivialising sex trivialised relationships, and ultimately the family, which is the idea? The plan was always to destroy the family.

As discussed, we've been groomed to be sex pests (hence, Disney's contribution with its subliminal messages). It's said sexual deviancy is one of Satan's favourite ways to take people into sin. He capitalises on our sexual desires and suggests fantasies? Besides sex and porn addictions, affairs invariably break families up, and honey traps work well for blackmail. And sexual abuse is evil. But moreover, besides transforming society into Sodom and Gomorrah, it's purported the dark agenda is to confuse young people about gender.

It's understood that 'environmental factors' can confuse sexual and gender orientation, our biology? Like, people can be locked into a gay expression of sexuality on account of childhood sexual abuse. Whilst some boys who have been sexually abused become gay, others become homophobic, and others denigrate women as sexual objects. And the same applies to girls who have been sexually abused. People can also become gay after realising how crap the opposite sex is.

So, people can be made gay, like paedos? Often paedos were sexually abused as kids. The prey becomes the predator. Or maybe gays and paedos are born that way? There's notably no gene for either. There's no conclusive proof that sexual orientation is biological and fixed at birth. David Icke (2007) notably pertained to a gay woman who became heterosexual after she was transplanted with the heart of a teenage girl (p.18). So, she inherited a new heart with new desires.

As mentioned, homosexuality ceased being a mental illness in 1967. And it was promoted? People can take pride in being gay. People can be proud to be part of the LGBTQ+ community. There is no shame in sodomy and dressing up as the other sex. It can be fun for kinky heterosexuals? It's normal. Men enjoy pretending to be women, (in the privacy of their own homes), as a form of escapism. It seems femskins (female rubber-suits complete with breasts and feminine fur), takes cross dressing to a new fetish level? They're like actors? Being the opposite gender is like an alter ego, but unlike DID, people do it consciously.

Again, it seems to be about choice and freewill, as opposed to compulsion. There's a difference between cross-dressing for funsies and undergoing surgery to look like the opposite sex. With the latter, it's propagated that people are born in the wrong body. Kids who express a strong desire to live as the opposite gender are described as gender-variant. And kids can demonstrate cross-gender behaviours as young as two i.e. the clothes and toys they choose. It seems we're boxing kids into made up boxes?

Whilst statistically, transgenderism is not common (less than 1%), it's mainstream. It's highlighted there's an epidemic of gender dysphoria, particularly for young people. In the UK there's been a 2000% increase in referrals for those under 18 since 2009, and a 400% increase for those under 6. Changing sex seems to be a new fad? People weren't chopping off healthy body parts en masse fifty years ago. It's more accessible now?

It's noted, that such disorders generate untold 'wealth for health' providers e.g. surgery, meds/hormones, therapy etc. It's profitable that we're not OK, on many levels. Thus, it bodes well that hormone blockers, (especially when given to kids), increases thoughts of suicide and self-harm. It helps curb population size? It's contended the widespread push of transgender ideology has been detrimental to kids. It's said they're more confused than ever. And some young kids are frightened by it. Like, they worry they'll somehow magically become the opposite sex.

But moreover, apparently after puberty the majority of kids (75%-95%) outgrew their confusion. And people are increasingly reporting sex-change regret (apparently 1:10 change their minds). Thus, doctors are condemned for intervening too early, like providing hormones and blockers etc, which can lead to sterility. It seems doctors are over a barrel, as early intervention is usually better?

Whilst there's an argument for affirming kids, there's a counter argument that it's not helpful. It's also highlighted that kids are increasingly partial to dressing up as drag queens. Maybe they're inspired by the LGBTQ+ community? Drag queens are fabulous?

According to God however, it's an abomination for men to dress like women and vice versa (Deuteronomy 22:5). God designed humankind in His image, not the world's image. We're given a picture of what Godly men and women look like i.e. their strength of character. It's about the inside not the outside.

So, people can get their identity from religion or society. Like, Christians get their identity from Christ, not the world. And Muslims get their identity from the Koran. And worldly people get theirs from 'Vogue' (LOL). It's also recalled, it was the Watchers who inspired our vanity and introduced makeup etc.

As discussed, (besides the cross-dressing), Father God's not okay with fornication, adultery, homosexuality, bestiality, incest, or anything else perverted. Despite how normalised anal sex is, and with all due respect to those partial to that part of our anatomy, it's perverted to want to stick anything in there (on a scale of 1-10). The same applies to smear campaigns.

It's notably rumoured the aim is to have paedos under the same rainbow LGBTQ banner, because they're allegedly born that way. It seems adopting the rainbow is like giving God the bird? Perhaps trans-species people, who identify as another species e.g. they think they're dogs, belong to this queer community? Or that's a step too far. It's okay for people to dress up and act as dogs, on the premise they're wearing full bondage attire. Those queer folks can be part of the queer community but not those who actually believe they're a dog. That's not normal?

It seems a paradox that gender dysphoria is not considered a mental illness, yet trans-species people are considered delusional. Unlike gender dysphoria, identifying with animals, so called 'clinical lycanthropy', is a rare psychiatric disorder. So, it's okay to be the wrong gender, but not the wrong species? It's like kinky adults dressing up and acting as babies is okay, but not if they actually think they're babies? That's delusional. It's like believing we're a tree. So, trans-people are 'normal'. They're in touch with reality. It's not delusional to believe we're the wrong gender.

However, many trans-people succumb to mental ill health because of their identity affliction. Like, they would rather kill themselves than live another day trapped in the wrong body. They can't continue to live a lie? Which is ironic if they're believing a lie? Suicide rates are obscene for transgenders (circa 40%). Essentially, in their desperate attempt to feel better, their dilemma is whether to check out or undergo irreversible surgeries coupled with ongoing hormone injections? And that's just the medical side.

And the tragic part is, they'll never really be the opposite sex, because they're not. We're biologically male or female. That's it. It's binary or bind-ary. Like, men can physically alter the outside to look female, but inside they're XY. And more often than not, their masculine attributes betray their feminine persona e.g. man hands and feet.

And the same goes for women, who endeavour to look like men. They want to look how they feel. They want to reconcile the outside with the inside. And inside they feel like a man, which is not to be confused with butch lesbians who strut about like John Wayne. Trans women are not Tom boys who haven't learned how to be feminine, and don't want to. But rather they are Tom?

It's also highlighted that changing sex isn't entirely helpful, as suicide rates are equally high afterwards (circa 40%). So, surgery is not a cure? Gender dysphoria tears people's lives upside down and inside out. It's a battle of the mind that people could be done without? People can't stop thinking that they're the wrong sex, because they are the wrong sex? It's like people can't help being gay? And people can't help being a paedo?

Unlike homosexuality however, gender dysphoria is not sexually motivated but rather it's an identity disorder. But like primary homosexuality, gender identity is not a choice. Furthermore, changing gender can entail changing sexual identity. Like, men who become women want sex with men, because they're now a woman? Which seems gay? Or they're gay if they want sex with a woman. And vice versa for women who become men.

But moreover, some people have partial gender dysphoria e.g. some men identify as women, so they get breast implants, and dress like women, but they're happy to keep their penis. So, this contrasts with those who hate their penis, and can't wait to get rid of it. Thus, it's not that straight forward that people feel trapped in the wrong body. Apparently, men who have sex with lady-boys don't consider themselves gay. And men want alleged 'women' to use their penis. It's said 'gender' is a misnomer.

No one knows exactly what makes someone transgender. It's suggested that mistimed hormones during foetal development could be the culprit. Thus, it's a medical not psychiatric disorder? However, according to a twins study in 2013, in the majority of cases (more than 70%) only one twin had gender identity issues. Twins have the same DNA and prenatal hormones. So, this refutes the idea of being born in the wrong body. Like, homosexuality and paedophilia, there is no predisposing gene.

It's also understood, that gender bending chemicals in our water supply aren't helping. And neither are pesticides. Like, Atrazine which changes the sex of frogs. Male frogs literally turn into female frogs and can lay eggs. Male frogs also become gay. Similar results are found with other amphibians and animals. It's also reported that sperm counts are plummeting, which implicates chemtrails and cell-phones in pockets? It's all part of depopulation.

Or maybe trans-genderism is a developmental disorder, as Walt Heyer, author of 'Gender, Lies and Suicide: A Whistleblower Speaks Out' (2013), insists. Heyer, who became Laura at forty-two and lived as her for eight years, insists trans-people are not born that way. He began cross-dressing as a small child and had the desire to change gender. Heyer concedes that affirming kids as trans, as he was, is harmful. And he asserts that many trans-people were sexually abused as kids, as he was. This can distort the otherwise 'normal' trajectory people are on.

Regarding psychology's takeaway, Freud viewed gender identity as a process of identification and reinforcement by models i.e. social learning. Like, girls identified with females, and boys with males. And now kids identify with gender fluid influencers on TV? Like, singer Sam Smith, who's gay and identifies as Non-Binary Gender Queer. As mentioned, sometimes he feels like a man, and sometimes he feels like a woman. And that's okay. There's no rules, but rather innumerable gender identities, orientations and persuasions. Apparently, there's 100 different genders. Identity is a buffet. We're not governed by our genitals. On the contrary, we can choose our sexual and gender orientation?

As mentioned, existentialist Simone de Beauvoir insisted that one is not born a woman but becomes one. She proposed there's a critical (sensitive) period between 18 months and three years, during which sex roles or gender identities are socialised. This corroborates with gender imprinting in the early years. Apparently, sexual imprinting is the process whereby mate preferences are affected by learning at a very young age (it's assumed there's a critical period), usually using the parent as a model.

According to Jung, a child's awareness of its gender is established by eighteen months. He proposed that we create our gender identity by enhancing qualities which characterise our gender, and repress those that don't i.e. we hide unwanted gender traits in the shadow. It's assumed the personality naturally takes on the gender role and persona we're born with. But those repressed qualities are still within us i.e. the feminine qualities within the man, and the masculine qualities within the woman. We are therefore inherently androgynous, regardless of our gender. Men have an anima (feminine side) and women have an animus (masculine side), which reside in our unconscious. So, our conscious self is one sex, and our unconscious is the opposite.

Jung explains the anima and animus are archetypes that are stored in the collective unconscious. And as per, archetypes seek fulfilment and as a result we form personal complexes, which are hidden in the shadow. Jung explains the anima and animus are distinct sub-personalities within the psyche, intrinsically separate from the known. So, inside every man, there's an intact female personality (i.e. attitudes/behaviours), and inside every woman there's a male personality. It's recalled that anima is Latin for soul, and according to Jung, our soul is God, which is androgynous. The integration of the anima/animus is often called androgyny.

Thus, in tandem with his theory of making the unconscious conscious, the endeavour is to integrate our opposite gender, as we're in danger of being possessed by it, like an autonomous complex? He surmised that gay men are psychologically identified with the anima, and gay women the animus. They're possessed with the intrusion of the anima or animus. Hence, they adopt feminine and masculine identities respectively. So, trans people are an extension of gay people? Some older gay men notably claim they would have changed sex if they were a kid today. So, they're gay but also female? They liked playing with dolls and fairies.

But moreover, it's purported there's a 'Baphomet agenda' underpinning the transgender explosion. As discussed, Crowley promoted Baphomet and introduced the ideal of androgyny. Thus, we're brainwashed to be both male and female, hermaphrodite deities, and insatiable sex pests. It's also asserted, that the transgender ideology precedes the trans-human ideology. Changing sex inspires us to upgrade our bodies with technology. *Welcome to the machine?*

As touched on, sodomy is promoted, maybe to create weird astral entities for Lucifer's kingdom? And to violate God's command (Leviticus 18:22), that homosexuality is an abomination? It's highlighted that society normalised anal sex for women, as an incremental step towards anal sex being normal for men i.e. who cares if the sphincter belongs to a woman or a man.

It's also purported there's efforts towards sexualising young people, to pave the way for accepting paedophilia. Part of this agenda relies on portraying young people as mature. Like, there's no real difference between adults and teenagers, and even kids? They drink, take drugs, and have sex, the same way adults do. The focus is on sexual pleasure from a young age, as pioneered by Kinsey's horrific research. Hence, a UN report (2009) advocates teaching masturbation to five-year olds. Five-year olds are taught that 'touching and rubbing one's genitals is called masturbation' and that private parts 'can feel pleasurable when touched by oneself'.

As mentioned, schools are introducing masturbation into sex education, as this practice has historically been more taboo than the mechanics of procreation. So, kids are taught graphic sex education from a young age. Is there any need? And children as young as nine are told about the safety of legal abortions. The 'International Technical Guidance on Sexuality Education' is based on evidence from heavily pro-abortion groups like Planned Parenthood and LGBT advocacy groups. Compulsory sexual education is part of a global campaign by the UN.

As discussed, the societal message is sex and the city is good fun, getting wrecked and getting herpes? And if pregnancies arise, they can be terminated. Thus, kids literally can't wait to have sex and get spoiled with porn? Seedy minds and depraved sex addictions are the products of social engineering. People are led to believe they're free, but they're not?

Contrary to society's liberalism, God reserved sex as a gift for marriage. It's His wedding present that lasts a lifetime, til death do us part. Having made a covenant, witnessed by God, two people become one flesh. Two souls connect. They belong to each other, and their covenant is sealed with a blood oath. It's a beautiful design. We fall in love, (one of the best feelings in the world), and we get married. Marriage is security. God's a family man (we can remarry if our spouse dies). And as it transpires, real love is better than promiscuity. Furthermore, our rectum was not designed for sex.

It's also noted, the church has been massively divided regarding homosexuality. But the popular vote prevailed, like it did in 1967. Thus, sodomy is fine? Gay marriage was legalised in 2014. Or maybe sexual practices, like incest, adultery, sodomy, fornication, and bestiality, open us up to the spirit realm? Maybe we can open our third eye through our brown eye? Like, Crowley conjured up deities from his homosexual experiences, and Semiramis and Nimrod opened their third eye through incest.

At the very least, soul-ties are created by sexual encounters. When we become one flesh with others, we're bonded to them. Through sex, we create a spiritual opening, which can lead to spirit attachment. It's said this explains why people become obsessed with others. Thus, we need to break the soul ties. It's understood that sex is a powerful spiritual activity, hence the devil is using it for his own purposes, which includes destroying family life and creating blood sacrifices through abortion?

So, sexual and gender identity is being manipulated by cult-ure? But moreover, it's purported that spiritual warfare is behind the gender fluid immersion. It's possible that spirit beings insert untruths into our minds i.e. telling us who we think we are? Like, convincing us we're the wrong gender? It's always possible, as the spirit release experts insist, that spirit attachments account for the incline to change sex or sexual orientation, the desire to cross dress, and the insatiable need to masturbate.

And whilst we're all vulnerable to spiritual attachment, some are more vulnerable e.g. due to childhood abuse including sexual. It's possible a rent can be created in the psyche enabling spirits to come through. Like, drugs and occult practices create entrances. Apparently, some people have become gay with Reiki 'therapy'.

As discussed, spirit attachments are held responsible for all kinds of mental malaise. Like, suicidal thoughts, mood swings, addictions (including chronic masturbation), self-harm, paranoia, fear, anxiety, hearing voices, multiple personalities, nightmares, sleep paralysis. It seems the majority of mental illness can be attributed to spirits?

Or that's crazy? We can't attribute mental illness to spirit attachment? People slithering on the floor like snakes, or growling and barking like dogs, is evidence of trans-species? They're taken over with animal archetypes?

It seems pertinent to reiterate, that as a general rule, we need to open ourselves up to the spirit world through occult and sexual practices. As Mary Pytches, Christian author/counsellor, pitches in, demonization is usually the result of deliberate rebellion, occult involvement or long-term involvement in perverted activity. She cautions that unless there is obvious demonic manifestation, it should never be assumed that a person's problems are caused by demonization.

On the contrary, there's myriad other reasons why we're not okay. Like dysfunctional environments, genes, and chemicals. And our reaction to stress is paramount since it can propel a ton of chemicals not conducive to mental health. Genes can be triggered into action because of unusual social pressure. Thus, the majority of mental ill health has nothing to do with demons? But they can oppress us with counterproductive thoughts? And they arouse our tendency towards self-destruction. Like, Freud's Thanatos instinct?

Moreover, spirits can be cast out, which evidences a spiritual condition not a medical condition. Meds don't cast out spirits, but they might help dull their voices? Like, sprit release experts (including Dr Wickland) actually cure people (which is not profitable). As discussed, there's degrees of oppression leading up to full blown possession, which requires deliverance and exorcism. Oppression is being oppressed by spirits, and possession is being possessed by them.

Thus, it's said God's people can be oppressed but not possessed. And if we are experiencing anything untoward, like sleep paralysis or alien abduction, we can call on the Lord. The world is however kept in the dark regarding spiritual forces. It's not real. Anything untoward is from a faulty brain. And regarding thoughts, or lies, we're responsible for believing them?

As discussed, the devil is the Father of Lies. Like, with Eve, he told her she wouldn't die if she ate the fruit. So, he lies. He's a deceiver. And the greatest trick he ever pulled is convincing the world he doesn't exist, and his degenerate family?

Satan's methods are principally temptation, accusation, and deception. So, he tempts us through our weaknesses e.g. crack pipe, cheesecake, sheeps' furry butts, gambling. Then, having succumbed to temptation, we succumb to guilt. The tempter becomes the accuser. He condemns us. And we beat ourselves up on the premise we have a conscience. Thus, we need to tell him, 'the bully', to beat it. As touched on, guilt can destroy people. Like, addictions (temptations) can destroy people. If only we could be set free of such thoughts?

Rather than the id, it's biblically understood the devil is permitted to test mankind, to see if we choose evil or good. We can choose to put our desires above the needs of others, or we can show love, kindness, grace, forgiveness, and mercy to all, including our enemies. It's recalled that Jesus (God) commanded us to love each other, and these actions come from love. Mark Twain (1835-1910), US author, said 'kindness is the language which the deaf can hear and the blind can see'.

However, the worst tactic is deception, and believing things that aren't true. Like, we're a dreadful human being who deserves to die. We're held in bondage to the lies we believe. Like, believing the material paradigm places our soul in grave danger. Believing lies can lead to damnation. Like, foolishly believing there is no God, and we evolved from bacteria. And we don't want to be victims of deception, particularly if heaven and hell are at stake?

We're told Satan's agenda is to steal, kill and destroy. And his power centres on lying. It comes from us believing his lies. Hence, he's awfully good at it. It's said super intelligent Satan invented the power of suggestion. He casts aspersions. And he has an army of demons and fallen angels at his disposal. Thus, he assigns demons to whisper all manner of trash, including criticism and judgement, into our minds. They plant all kinds of unfruitful seeds (including through people). So, our minds are not inviolate to suggestions. On the contrary. 1 Peter 5:8 tells us, 'Be careful! Watch out for attacks from the Devil, your great enemy. He prowls around like a roaring lion, looking for some victim to devour'.

The exponential growth of mental health problems and illness evidences that people do not have 'peace of mind'. Minds are full of crap we'd rather not think about i.e. condemning thoughts, blasphemous thoughts, suicidal thoughts, homicidal thoughts. And it's possible haunted spirits are responsible for this dastardly onslaught? Hence, depression is likened to an unpleasant gremlin that sits on our shoulder and tells us lies. Depression is a liar. And they're responsible for tormenting people with 'hallucinations'. They're behind the voices people hear, and the 'ghosts' people see?

Paracelsus said devils influence men according to their qualities. They watch them, increase and deepen their faults, find excuses for their mistakes, cause them to wish the success of evil actions, and gradually absorb their vitality. As discussed, demons are spiritual parasites. So, it seems spiritual warfare is being passed off as mental health problems i.e. chemical imbalances? The spiritual context has been replaced with a medical context, complete with massive financial profits. Spiritual issues have been psychologised?

Pastor Joyce Meyer, in her book 'Battlefield of the Mind' (1994), highlights how our minds are continually bombarded with nagging thoughts, suspicions, doubts, fears, wonderings, reasoning and theories. She observes that the devil exploits our personality quirks, nature/genetic dispositions, and lust of the flesh to conspire against us. He knows our personalities, our insecurities, weaknesses, fears, and what bothers us most.

So, he plants seeds of doubt and fear. And he puts thoughts into our minds about what we already desire. He capitalises on what is already going on in our heart. Like, self-harm, adultery, bestiality. He takes the desires we have and uses them for his purpose. But we can't blame the devil for our choices, because that's as crap as Sartre's bad faith.

Like Scott Peck, Meyer affirms the devil has no power except in his lies. She explains how Satan works hard on our minds, building strongholds that prevent us from facing the truth. He sets about building these dysfunctional mindsets (which includes addictions) from early on to keep us in the wilderness. He targets the kids?

So, we're trapped by our mindsets. Like, we have to check the locks three times, or wash our hands for the millionth time. Or maybe we don't have to. And maybe we don't have to gouge chunks out our flesh. And maybe we don't have to drink, or lie in bed all day, or starve ourselves? We don't have to be scared there's a lion outside. We think a certain way, which has fundamentally been given to us? We have fixed ideas about the world and our place in it? We're being set up to fail?

Meyer explains that Satan can use any human sin or weakness e.g. pride, greed, and any tactic e.g. seduction, cajolery, flattery, intellectual argument, to engineer our fall. But his principal weapon is fear because that literally stops us in our tracks. She highlights that FEAR is a big part of the deception. And FEAR is False Evidence Appearing Real. She states that many are paralysed by fear, lies and oppression, which is so strong that whilst we can make the correct choices, we think we can't so we don't. It's also understood, (like eroding our conscience), that nobody loses control to Satan overnight. But rather it's a gradual process of deception and yielding.

Thus, since spiritual forces include fear and deception (lies), we must truthfully look at our thought patterns, habits, and behaviours. We can revise our thinking? We don't have to be plagued, consumed and tormented by negative destructive lies, whether we're responsible for them i.e. they're NATs from our underlying core beliefs, or the devil. We don't have to be trapped by miserable mindsets. In theory, we could liberate ourselves with the truth. And the truth is we're OK, unless someone has a gun to our head?

Like CBT instructs, we need to take each thought captive and examine it rationally for cognitive errors e.g. maybe we're not rubbish, and maybe life's not so bad? But as warriors in a spiritual battle, we take our thoughts captive to God and ascertain whether or not they're true to the obedience of Christ. Whilst we might feel like a car crash and a waste of time, God loves us (see God's love letter). We're important and do matter.

So, we can change our thinking by replacing the lies with truth about ourselves and what God says about us. The truth sets us free. God's word is powerful. It changes people. It soaks into our soul and gives us peace. Thus, we care for what God says, not the world. Indeed, God tells us not to care what the world thinks of us. The world belongs to Satan. It's legally his. Moreover, we're warned the world will despise Christians, rendering us bigots. God's word is not cool like Crowley's.

However, being cut off or separated from God, we identify with the world. Rather than getting the truth from God, the world tells us what to think and how to act. What to wear, and style our hair, our gender and sexual identity? We get our values and morals from society, like lying and cheating? Rather than focussing on God, the focus is firmly fixed on self. The cult of self dominates our culture. Satan's primary aim is to promote self-interest.

So, we're deceived into believing there is no God. And thus, our godless society is pleasure seeking. We've been given the misguided belief or illusion that wealth, fame, personal style and celebrating our image will make us happy. As discussed, we need to tick all the boxes (society imposes on us) to be happy. And we blame ourselves for not being able to achieve unachievable happiness?

It's asserted the consumer culture and cult of self is by design to control, manipulate and distract us. And the programme's working, as we've never been so self-absorbed, and obsessed with garbage that doesn't matter. Like, social media, football and soul destroying TV. We're obsessed with our identity and how we want to define ourselves. As mentioned, it was foretold that in the last days, we'd be consumed with the love of self and money. And that mankind's character will decline, given over to a reprobate mind, and evil will wax worse and worse.

The consumer culture is thus, not simply to entertain us with BS, (and make money), but to drain us emotionally and confuse us about our identity. Satan has deceived us into thinking that we are serving ourselves, when in fact we are serving the world, the flesh, and the devil. The sheep have never seemed so lost?

In Galatians 5:19-21 Paul asserts, 'The acts of the flesh are obvious: sexual immorality, impurity and debauchery; idolatry and witchcraft; hatred, discord, jealousy, fits of rage, selfish ambition, dissensions, factions and envy; drunkenness, orgies, and the like. I warn you, as I did before, that those who live like this will not inherit the kingdom of God. This behaviour is not acceptable to God'.

John reminds us, in 1 John 2:15-16, 'Do not love the world, nor the things in the world. If anyone loves the world, the love of the Father is not in him. For all that is in the world, the lust of the flesh and the lust of the eyes and the boastful pride of life, is not from the Father'. Paul states, 'do not conform any longer to the pattern of this world, but be transformed by the renewing of your mind' (Romans 12:12).

And 2 Peter 2:19 states, 'You're a slave to whatever controls you'. The Bible seems to regard addictions as slavery. We're in bondage. In Proverbs 11:27, we're told, 'If you search for good, you will find favour; but if you search for evil, it will find you'. It seems evil doesn't require much persuasion to come into our life? Indeed, id wants to come in.

As touched on, legalism works against our psychology, because we want what we can't have? It's reverse psychology, as everything is reversed with the devil. As Paul acknowledged, (in Romans 7:7-8), whilst the law is not sinful, it stirs up sinful passions. He submitted that he wouldn't have known what sin was had it not been for the law. He said, 'For I would not have known was coveting really was if the law had not said, "You shall not covet". But sin, seizing the opportunity afforded by the commandment, produced in me every kind of coveting'.

Hence, religion is legalistic? Like, it was a strategic move to introduce celibacy for catholic priests, for example, to covertly tempt them with each other and children? Apparently Semiramis promoted celibacy (which is unbiblical) for priests. Besides the Ten Commandments, the seven deadly sins, namely, pride, sloth, envy, gluttony, wrath, lust, and greed, were used from early times to educate and instruct Christians concerning fallen humanity. And it seems the world increasingly embodies these attributes? But we blame our genes rather than Satan e.g. alcohol gene, fat gene, psycho gene?

Fundamentally, we need a heart transplant since our desires come from our heart. Sin comes from the heart so we can't blame our brain? And we need to be spiritually born again to get a new heart. In Ezekiel 36:26

we're told, 'A new heart I will give you, and a new spirit I will put within you, and I will remove from your body the heart of stone and give you a heart of flesh'.

Jesus was crystal that you can only heal man by giving him an inner transformation, a new nature. He instructed that we need to die to self and be born again into a new self (because sin has distorted us and we're a mess). To be spiritually born again, means getting to know God personally. If we ask God into our lives, through Jesus, we encounter the Holy Spirit. And so, our relationship with God begins.

But moreover, we need to be washed clean first (because we're a mess). We need to be forgiven for our sins. Thus, bonus, at the heart of God is the desire to forgive, and forgive some more. We can always be forgiven if we truly repent. If we can get over ourselves, (our pride), and humble ourselves and ask for forgiveness. We need to come clean to become clean. We need to play the honesty game with our Father.

As touched on, being forgiven is transformative and liberating, as unresolved guilt can be painful. People with crosses to bear, can be freed from guilt. We can offload that weight (guilt inducing demon?) from our back. We can be set free. As discussed, some people, who can see beyond the veil, report seeing demons on people's backs. No danger. Father God doesn't want us to be plagued by guilt. Satan is the accuser not God. God wants us to learn and put the sin to bed. Love is not controlling, whereas guilt can be manipulated to control people (like religion).

So, God forgives us. He's paid for our sin. But part of the deal is we also have to forgive. When Jesus was asked how many times we should forgive others, He said, 'I do not say to you, up to seven times, but up to seventy times seven' (Matthew 18:21). Apparently 70x7 is a perfect number, where the name 70x7 is synonymous with God's eternal forgiveness. So, that bodes well, as there's literally no end to our sin.

But we further have to love and pray for our enemies. We're to bless those who mistreat us. Like, Jesus forgave and prayed for those who crucified Him. It's said that loving our enemies and forgiveness is the most striking feature of Christianity. Plato conceded that loving enemies is more challenging than the golden rule. It's also noted, that forgiveness begins in the will, because we don't always feel like forgiving (it's alleged our feelings catch up with our thoughts).

Forgiving others heals us. If we hold resentment to another, we're bound to that person by an emotional link. Forgiveness is the power to release, to dissolve that link. Thus, it's psychologically healthy to forgive and be forgiven, to become better not bitter. Forgiveness underpins strength. It's said, true power is the strength to forgive. And it's not condoning but rather letting it burn.

Mahatma Gandhi said, 'The weak can never forgive. Forgiveness is the attribute of the strong'. And Martin Luther King Junior said, 'He who is devoid of the power to forgive is devoid of the power to love'. George Herbert said, 'He who cannot forgive others destroys the bridge over which he himself must pass'. And something I've had to learn along the way is self-forgiveness. Whilst we know God forgives us, sometimes we need to forgive ourselves.

So, we ask God into our lives, and the Holy Spirit begins the process of transforming our heart to be filled with love. As Paul wrote, in 2 Corinthians 5:17, 'Therefore if any person is in Christ he is a new creation; the old has passed away'. And in 1 Corinthians 2:16, '...but we have the mind of Christ and do hold the thoughts of His heart'. We become Christos-like as cultivated by the Holy Spirit, which is reflected by increasing compassion and love for one another. In essence, we're alchemised.

In Galatians 5:22-23, Paul wrote, 'But when the Holy Spirit controls our lives, He will produce in us, love, joy, peace, patience, kindness, goodness, faithfulness, gentleness and self-control'. These are the fruit of the Holy Spirit. Holiness is following the Holy Spirit. It's recalled that Jesus said, 'Blessed are the pure of heart for they shall see God'. Like, kids are pure of heart until we ruin them.

It also seems pertinent to note, that Paul, in particular, talks about the battle between the flesh and the Spirit. He understood temptation. In Romans 7:14 he wrote, 'I don't understand myself at all, for I really want to do what is right but I don't do it. I do the very thing I hate'. He warned us not to be governed by our sensual nature or to obey the impulses of our flesh, the thoughts of our carnal minds.

In Romans 8:5, he states, 'For those who live according to the flesh set their minds on the things of the flesh, but those who live according to the Spirit set their minds on the things of the Spirit'. And in Romans 8:7-8, 'The mind that is set on the flesh is hostile to God; it does not submit to God's law, indeed it cannot; and those who are in the flesh cannot please God'.

And in Galatians 5:16-17, 'But I say, walk by the Spirit, and you will not gratify the desires of the flesh. For what the flesh desires is opposed to the Spirit, and what the Spirit desires is opposed to the flesh, for these are opposed to each other, to prevent you from doing what you want'. The flesh cannot however be eradicated until we receive our transformed resurrection bodies.

So, we have a relationship with God. We talk to our Father, although listening is more of a challenge? And we learn about Him and His-Story through His word. His word is living and speaks to us. [Like, spirits speak to people through the I Ching and Tarot cards]. The Holy Spirit dwells within Christians, and convicts us through truth, which nurtures our spiritual growth. Jesus provides the mirror, and the Holy Spirit reveals our cracks. So, we walk with God, and sometimes He carries us. And yet we let Him down a lot.

But moreover, in addition to becoming a loving and forgiving soul, we finally acquire meaning to this otherwise meaningless reality. And life gets a whole lot more interesting and crazy. However, we're not to be burdened. But rather, we're specifically told to take each day as it comes, and cast our cares on God. He's big enough to take it. We don't have to worry about anything. There's no need for anxiety? As Paul said, (in Romans 8:31), 'If God is for us, who can be against us?' And who better to have our back. And we don't have to freak out about what happens after death, because if we're with God, we'll be enjoying that marriage feast in heaven.

But furthermore, we also get power to trample on powers of darkness. When we join God's army, we become armed and equipped to call evil out from its hiding place. We're authorised to tell demons to beat it, in Jesus' name, (which includes aliens). As mentioned, Jesus told His followers to cast out demons and heal people in His name (there was no Big Pharma). It's also noted, that children were not immune to demonic possession. Like, those who have been sexually abused? We're all vulnerable to demonic attacks but inviting the occult into our lives is literally asking for it.

In her said book, Meyer speaks about a sick man looking for healing, but he began to doubt. God opened his eyes to the spirit world, and he saw a demon speaking lies to him, discouraging and disputing the word of God.

The man also saw that each time he confessed the word, light would come out of his mouth like a sword, and the demon would cower and fall backwards (p.106).

The weapons of spiritual warfare are thus not physical, but verbal, which is psychophysical? In the spiritual world, God's word is 'living and active, and sharper than any two-edged sword' (Hebrews 4:12). It seems thoughts or words are fiery darts?

As mentioned, Jonathan Welton was given the gift to see the spirit world. Like Dr Wickland and La-Sala, he sees snakes writhing about, and some of them are massive. But he further claims he sees objects lodged in people, like spears, swords, and arrows. Thus, there's literal weapons? He highlights how certain pains, like shoulder or back pain, are due to swords wedged there. As highlighted, our battle is not with flesh and blood, but spiritual wickedness, dark powers, and principalities. And knowledge of scripture is armour.

In Ephesians 6:14-17, Paul instructs us, 'Stand your ground, putting on the sturdy belt of truth and the body armour of God's righteousness. For shoes, put on the peace that comes from the Good News, so that you will be fully prepared. In every battle you will need faith as your shield to stop the fiery arrows aimed at you by Satan. Put on salvation as your helmet, and take the sword of the Spirit, which is the word of God'.

Paracelsus concedes that astral influence may act on wo/men unless we know how to protect ourselves. Like, Max Spiers conducted certain protective rituals, which worked until they didn't? It's noted, when Jesus was tempted by the devil during His forty days in the desert, He used scripture to shoot the devil down. Prayer, praise, and God's word are weapons in spiritual warfare, and it seems something happens when we use our weapons.

Whilst we can't see our prayers, (indeed, we can't see any of this), apparently they're very effective. A former dark high priest said, 'fervent prayers thwart Satan's activity like nothing else'. Prayers seem to inhibit and dispel demonic powers. My friend told me about a couple from church, who having moved into their new home, were told from the neighbour upstairs that they were interfering with her communication with the spirit world. And I heard about a psychic mum who told her son to quit praying as it was disturbing her 'aura'.

Doreen Irvine said spells wouldn't touch some of the most holy. She spoke about a godly man, who despite their malevolent efforts towards him, seemed to have an invisible shield, a 'hedge of protection', protecting him from satanic influence. So, God protects His kids. Jesus said, 'Lo, I am with you always' (Matthew 28:20). And we can call on Him 24/7.

It's noted, we can pray silently (we can speak to God in our heads), just as others can meditate silently to communicate with their gods. It's a spiritual connection. God knows our hearts, and why we're seeking His divine intervention. Our relationship with God is the most intimate relationship, and it deepens through prayer and spending time with Him.

It's also noted, that sons and daughters of men, (as opposed to God), often feel misunderstood. It's quite the contemporary ail. No one really understands them, when the truth is God understands us exactly. God knows our hearts and minds intimately. The mystery of consciousness is that God is privy to it. God's supreme mind knows all minds. He's consciously aware of everyone's consciousness, including all His creatures' consciousness. So, there's nothing private about our mental space (LOL). Moreover, Father God wants us to open the door of our heart and invite Him in for supper.

It seems pertinent to interject regarding the potency of thoughts and words, as it seems thoughts have some kind of substance to them. As mentioned, according to yogis who astral project, great volumes of thought clouds are seen rising up from cities. It seems electrically charged thoughts, (energy waves), travel through our electric universe? Hence, yogis report seeing thin lines of bright light, like electric sparks?

According to Paracelsus, the thoughts of mortals appear visible and material to spirits, as long as they're not too refined and spiritual in character to discern. And apparently DMT enables seeing auras around thoughts. Thus, some DMT partakers try their hardest to entertain positive thoughts, because they've seen what they look like, compared to crap negative thoughts.

Paracelsus explains that if we hold onto a thought, we create a form in our inner world. Thus, a good thought produces a good form, and an evil thought produces an evil form. The same energy that expresses itself in the form of evil, can express itself in the form of good. So, thoughts are energy? Like, energy is mass? So, prayer and worship are energy? Like, we give 'energy' to idols at concerts, who report feeling a surge of energy emanating from the crowd. We give 'love energy' to God and He reciprocates it?

Paracelsus explains that thoughts grow as they're nourished by thought and imagination i.e. we pay attention to particular thoughts and they blossom, for better or worse. Maybe thought forms correlate with neural pathways? As discussed, we create our reality through our thoughts. Rhonda Byrne concedes, 'We become what we think about most and attract what we think about most. Actions are powerful words, or thoughts, and nothing can come into existence without persistence of thought'. It seems we inadvertently create thought forms, and grow trees?

It's also recalled that 'thought forms' are deliberately constructed i.e. through visualisation, concentration and will. Thoughts can be actively bestowed with 'energy' for a nefarious purpose. It seems spiritual weapons are thought forms? As also discussed, Paracelsus recognised the importance of faith and imagination. These two pillars hold up the temple of magic.

It's understood there's something very potent about faith, much like truth, love and light. Like, we could move mountains with faith the size of a mustard seed? By our faith, we can be healed? We could have faith that we're okay?

It's highlighted that doubt comes in the form of thoughts that are in opposition to the word of God. Take Peter, for example, who was walking on the Sea of Galilee to meet JC, but as he began to doubt, he began to sink and cried out, 'Lord, save me!' (which is a picture for us?). Jesus caught him and said, 'you of little faith, why did you doubt?' Those in the boat notably worshipped Jesus, saying, 'Truly you are the Son of God' (Matthew 14:25-33).

With regards to the potency of thought and will, we can also consider Dr Masaru Emoto's (1943-2014) research. This shows the affect of human consciousness, the affect of words, thoughts, and emotions, on physical matter. Like, he evidenced how we can affect the molecular structure of water by projecting good or evil thoughts towards it.

Thus, he placed water into two beakers, which were subjected to either good or evil thoughts, then frozen to form crystallisations. And the results were astounding. The good thoughts e.g. hope, love, gratification, formed beautiful patterns, and the bad thoughts e.g. aggression, fear, hate and evil, formed horrible disjointed patterns. It's said love increases the energy level and stabilises the pattern, whereas hate decreases the energy level and causes havoc. Apparently, prayers make beautiful patterns. It's duly noted, we consist largely of water.

It's purported that emotions/thoughts vibrate at frequencies, from high and fast to low and slow. Apparently, love is the highest frequency. So, every time we think and feel something, we broadcast waves that vibrate to that particular thought or emotion. Thus, hate contaminates us and everything we're in contact with. And love enriches us and everything we're in contact with. Black (2010) relays Dante's point, namely, 'everything we do or think materially alters our universe' (p.375). Emotional states directly affect matter outside of our body as well as inside.

In his rice experiment, Dr Emoto placed portions of cooked rice into two containers. On one container he wrote 'thank you' and on the other 'you fool'. He then asked school children to say the labels on the jars out loud every day when they passed by them. After thirty days, the rice in the container with positive thoughts had barely changed, whereas the other was mouldy and rotten.

Dr Emoto was also the first person to record musical impressions on water in 1995. Heavy metal music (unsurprisingly) formed grim patterns, whereas classical music was peachy, and the Christmas carol 'Silent Night' formed a particularly beautiful crystallisation.

Experiments have also shown that water exposed to vibrations from mobile phones is dire, as is water subjected to microwaves etc. Our chemically treated water also produces grim patterns, which contrasts with water samples from untouched parts of the world, which produced the most beautiful crystallisations. Apparently, water that has not been touched by humans is most pure. And water has memory, as it receives and makes an imprint of whatever it is in contact with (hence homeopathy).

So, it makes sense to bless the water we drink. And being truly thankful for the food we receive? It's also said, it's not so much about the words but the intent behind them. Black (2010) states, 'In an idealist universe if two people perform exactly the same action in exactly the same circumstances, but one in a good-hearted way and the other not, the consequences are very different' (p.290). It seems we emit what we really feel. Our heart betrays our acting abilities? [Research shows our heart's field changes distinctly as we experience different emotions].

As Jesus said, in Matthew 5:28, 'But I say unto you, That whosoever looketh on a woman to lust after her hath committed adultery with her already in his heart'. He explained that it wasn't just what you did on the outside that was a sin, but even what you were thinking about on the inside, where wrong thoughts entail condemnation. Sin originates in the heart. But moreover, Jesus likened hate to murder. Hatred literally poisons people. Proverbs 14:39 tells us, 'a peaceful heart leads to a healthy body, but jealousy is like cancer in the bones'.

Jesus was adamant that we have to love our siblings regardless of how evil they are. And it appears loving others is doing something positive at some level. It also seems our thoughts are like exhaled breath i.e. we breathe them out to the ether. But unlike our breath, our thoughts are all recorded somewhere i.e. Akashic records? The Bible tells us about the 'Book of Remembrance'.

So, thoughts and words are powerful. They affect us. Like, oaths are binding? And God's word is alive and full of power. It energises us and changes us. It heals us emotionally, physically, and spiritually. As mentioned, we get peace, which the world is screaming for. Peace of heart is a gift from God. As Paul tells God's kids in Philippians 4:7, 'the peace of God, which transcends all understanding, will guard your hearts and your minds in Christ Jesus'.

So, words are important, and they're spiritual. Like, Jesus used words to cast out demons. And there's power in the name of Jesus. Lest we forget, God 'spoke' creation into existence. And the cabalists are obsessed with the inherent power in words and numbers, the codes of creation. There's 'words of power' in the spirit world, and 'passwords' to access different spiritual dimensions or zones. It seems language does indeed set us apart from the animals?

In summary, God knows what's going on behind the veil. What the battle between good and evil looks like? What the battlefield of the mind looks like? It seems warfare is happening, but for the most part we're none the wiser? Like, the angel we never see sitting beside us, but we trust is there? And how many angels have we met that we didn't realise were angels?

Moreover, whilst Jesus and His apostles lived in an age where evil spirits were a given, and they regularly attributed illness, both physical and mental, to demonic influence, not anymore. For psychiatry, this is crazy talk. It's delusional, as there is no spiritual world. There's no devil or demons, but it's always possible there's aliens from outer-space?

Psychology adequately explains our thought life e.g. depression, anxiety. Hearing voices suggests schizophrenia, and possession resonates with DID. And it's possible some alters have ESP or super strength, and can speak different languages? Any mysteries can be attributed to the curious unconscious. Like, poltergeist activity and levitation? And there's no such thing as evil, but rather personality disorders? So, there's nothing to see here folks, move along.

It's also duly noted, the world is a far nicer place because of drugs and lobotomies. Like, a service user I worked with, who was diagnosed with schizophrenia, was much nicer after two lobotomies, and heavily placated on meds. However, whilst she was amiable for the most part, every now and then, her 'rage' would make an appearance. Like, sometimes we see venomous flashes of anger in people, which could be construed as evil? It's like something wicked takes over, like an autonomous complex? It's said the eyes are the window to the soul, and if looks could kill?

Thus, for the most part, people are nicer on drugs, including kids. We can be very pleasant when pumped full of morphine or cocaine. Our reality hasn't changed. It just seems better through the lens of lithium. Life's better down the K-Hole. Huxley's soma works. The masses are happier drugged. Drugs are like a cosy blanket. And it would be crazy if there were no drugs to placate the maniacs. Imagine the suicides on behalf of the depressed.

But drugs don't really address the problem because our problem is our heart? And lack of meaning? Drugs merely subdue the passions of our wild heart and contain our reaction to the absurdity. The person is not a new creation through drugs. Like taking meths, doesn't remove our desire for heroin? We need this desire to be removed. We need a new heart that births new thoughts that are for us, not against us. We need God's help to deliver us from our poisons.

It's also noted, whilst the mind is fickle, as we can talk ourselves into and out of things, the heart is more like our nature i.e. it's consistent. It's our character. And contrary to psychiatry's fated assumption, we can change.

There's many a reformed jailbird who attests to the transformative power of the Holy Spirit. Untold lives have been turned around (like Berkowitz). The cure for otherwise incurable psychopathy is a new heart.

So, the desires of our heart can change. And we can be set free from sin. Like, we no longer want to sleep around with Tom, Dick and Harry. It makes us cringe. We recoil when we think of our past sinful behaviour. It's the opposite of cool. And we no longer want to look at porn and play with ourselves because it's grim (and sad). And we no longer want to take drugs because they're shit. Like, being a drunk is rubbish. And otherwise gay people don't want to have sex with same sex people, because it doesn't feel good. On the contrary, we want to worship God. We love fellowshipping with our Father. It's awesome, and the only thing that makes us truly happy.

With regards to Big Pharma then, it seems drugs can control symptoms but they're not a cure? As discussed, drugs can be very helpful for some, and very unhelpful for others. And therapy is more helpful than not. But it's possible the picture is far bigger than we've been led to believe. Like, our mind is couched in spiritual warfare. Thus, when it comes to mental health, maybe we shouldn't discount the spiritual realm? Particularly since many people who hear voices, hear things that are of a demonic nature, and often schizophrenics want spiritual help.

Moreover, clinical terms seem too reductive when accompanied by growling, devilish grimaces, and women speaking in rough male voices, stating they're not leaving the said person's body? As mentioned, how do psychiatrists rationalise deliverance sessions where people get thrown about the room or 'patients' writhe about in a snakelike fashion. It seems too ironic that psychiatrists are swimming in de-Nile. How do they explain apports?

Scott Peck notably explains the difference between DID and possession. Thus, with DID the core personality is unaware of the existence of the other personalities, whereas with possession the person is usually aware of the 'alien' personality. Thus, a true dissociation exists with DID. And with DID, personalities are not necessarily evil, whereas with possession, people are possessed by evil demons. He observed, that when the demonic spoke, 'an expression appeared on the patient's face that could be described only as satanic. It was an incredibly contemptuous grin of utter hostile malevolence' (People of the Lie, p.196). As mentioned, demons can also bestow supernatural knowledge, whereas the mentally ill never exhibit clairvoyance.

Dr Peck, Dr Wickland and Dr Sanderson etc aside, psychiatry insists the brain generates all behaviours, however weird. Thus, the litmus test is taking authority in Jesus' name and if it works, the problem is not neurological. And if it works, bonus for the mental health services budget. Employing a holistic approach i.e. ascertaining whether one's problems are physical, psychological, or spiritual, could do wonders to alleviate the stress on the NHS.

It's also highlighted however, that the main body of the protestant church, (in the last two hundred years), has relegated the demonic to personal temptation, and left medicine to deal with 'illness'. It's not okay to suggest demons have anything to do with illness (mental or physical). Talking about demons freaks us out? It's almost like they don't exist? And yet the Catholic Church is conducting more exorcisms than ever. There's been a dramatic rise in demonic possession and attacks, because we're living in the age of witchcraft and Satanism?

It's also recalled that pharmacy comes from pharmakeia which means sorcery. And pharmakeia was predicted to be rampant in the end days. It's said the spirit of pharmakeia is behind Big Pharma. Lest we forget that drugs do more than they say on the tin. Like, encourage suicidal ideation and produce tics. Some psychiatrists, like Dr Andrew Kaufman, claim psychiatric drugs don't help at all.

Despite the scepticism of orthodox psychiatry, (which is also ironic since they conjure up so many alleged 'diseases'), Scott Peck maintains, 'There are enough hints about human spiritual behaviour to constitute a science of sorts, and a wealth of happenings that cannot be explained without resorting to 'The God Theory' (Along the Road Less Travelled and Beyond, 1997 p.245). He also insists that possession, exorcism, and prayer, needs to be studied scientifically. For Peck, psychiatry has not only neglected but actively ignored the issue of spirituality. He states they fail to encourage healthy spirituality, and equally fail to combat unhealthy spirituality or false theology.

In essence, psychiatry would be better equipped to deal with 'mental illness' if they were versed in theology and the spiritual realm, and improved their listening skills. Peck states, 'Were psychiatry to enter into the field of spiritual research, I believe we would witness a most exciting and badly needed renaissance of personality theory' (Further Along the Road Less Travelled, 1990 p.254).

Controversial psychiatrist Laing said, 'I believe that if we can begin to understand sanity and madness in existential terms, we, as priests and physicians, will be enabled to see more clearly the extent to which we confront common problems' (p.96).

Like spiritual forces, good and evil are invisible but can be seen as manifested in others. It's like God is the most revealed yet most secret. And 'God is love, and all who live in love live in God, and God lives in them' (1 John 4:16). We're designed to love and be loved (it's instinctive). We can have a heart full of love, or a heart full of poison. We can let 'life' get the better of us. We can let Satan and his demons destroy us, steal our freedom and joy, and our ticket to heaven. It can happen to the best of us, through no fault of our own? Jesus said love is most important, which corroborates with those who have nearly died, who claim (at the end of the day) love is the only thing that matters.

As Peck asserts, the absence of love is the major cause of mental illness. He believes that healing is a function of love (and good psychotherapy can combat lies). Evil can only be conquered by love. Martin Luther King Junior said, 'Darkness cannot drive our darkness; only light can do that. Hate cannot drive out hate; only love can do that'.

So, we can win the battle for the mind (heart and soul) with God's love? It seems life is a moral experiment, and God's testing our character? It seems we either take God and the devil seriously or we don't? This is the meaning of life?

God's Love Letter

My child,

You may not know me, but I know everything about you. Psalm 139.1. I know when you sit down and when you rise up. Psalm 139.2. I am familiar with all your ways. Psalm 139.3. Even the very hairs on your head are numbered. Matthew 10:29-31. For you were made in my image. Genesis 1:27. In me you live and move and have your being. Acts 17:28. For you are my offspring. Acts 17:28. I knew you even before you were conceived. Jeremiah 1:4-5.

I chose you when I planned creation. Ephesians 1:11-12. You were not a mistake, for all your days were written in my book. Psalm 139:15-16. I determined the exact time of your birth and where you would live. Acts 17:26. You are fearfully and wonderfully made. Psalm 139: 14. I knit you together in your mother's womb. Psalm 139: 13. And brought you forth on the day you were born. Psalm 71:61. I have been misrepresented by those who don't know me. John 8: 41-44. I am not distant and angry, but am the complete expression of love. 1 John 4:16. And it is my desire to lavish my love on you. 1 John 3:1. Simply because you are my child and I am your father. 1 John 3:1.

I offer you more than your earthly father ever could. Matthew 7:11. For I am the perfect father. Matthew 5:48. Every good gift you receive comes from my hand. James 1:17. For I am your provider and I meet all your needs. Matthew 6:31-33. My plan for your future has always been filled with hope. Jeremiah 29:11. Because I love you with an everlasting love. Jeremiah 31:3. My thoughts toward you are countless as the sand on the seashore. Psalm 139:17-18. And I rejoice over you with singing. Zephaniah 3:17.

I will never stop doing good to you. Jeremiah 32:40. For you are my treasured possession. Exodus 19:51. I desire to establish you with all my heart and all my soul. Jeremiah 32:41. And I want to show you great and marvellous things. Jeremiah 33:3. If you seek me with all your heart, you will find me. Deuteronomy 4:29. Delight in me and I will give you the desires of your heart. Psalm 37:4. For it is I who gave you those desires. Philippians 2:13. I am able to do more for you than you could possibly imagine. Ephesians 3:20. For I am your greatest encourager. 2 Thessalonians 2:16-17.

I am also the Father who comforts you in all your troubles. 2 Corinthians 1:3-4. When you are broken-hearted, I am close to you. Psalm 34:18. As a shepherd carries a lamb, I have carried you close to my heart. Isaiah 40:11. One day I will wipe away every tear from your eyes. Revelation 21:3-4. And I'll take away all the pain you have suffered on this earth. Revelation 21:3-4. I am your Father, and I love you even as I love my son, Jesus. John 17:23. For in Jesus, my love for you is revealed. John 17:26. He is the exact representation of my being. Hebrews 1:3. He came to demonstrate that I am for you, not against you. Romans 8:31. And to tell you that I am not counting your sins. 2 Corinthians 5:18-19. Jesus died so that you and I could be reconciled. 2 Corinthians 5:18-19. His death was the ultimate expression of my love for you. 1 John 4:10. I gave up everything I loved that I might gain your love. Romans 8:31-32. If you receive the gift of my son Jesus, you receive me. 1 John 2:23. And nothing will ever separate you from my love again. Romans 8:38-39. Come home and I'll throw the biggest party heaven has ever seen. Luke 15:7.

I have always been Father, and will always be Father. Ephesians 3:14-15. My question is...Will you be my child? John 1:12-13.

I am waiting for you. Luke 15:11-32.

Father God

"Sometimes people don't want to hear truth because they don't want their illusions destroyed".
Nietzsche

Conclusion

The truth is arguably insane. Like, God and the devil are real, and there is a battle for our souls. And Satanists rule the world. And they're preparing to take on God. But it's more insane not to believe it? It's truly insane (delusional) to believe the universe and everything in it came from nothing, and for no reason. It's insane that people think we're on a spinning globe, that's zipping through the universe at insane speeds. It highlights the power of 'education'. And pride? Because people don't want to believe in Father God and His awesome Son Jesus.

The fact is, life is crazy, and then we die. And fundamentally, we don't know anything. It's all speculation. And God knows what happens when we die. But I'm of the opinion that it's the most important question because eternity is a long time. And it frankly amazes me why people don't think about it more. Sheep is the best metaphor for us. But deep down, at some intuitive level, we know there's truth? Life is One Big Existential Crisis if you think about it. And ignorance is arguably a choice in our age of information.

But moreover, we've not been abandoned like helpless sheep. We have this book, called the Holy Bible, which is alleged to be the infallible Word of God. It has the answers to the meaning of life. It literally explains everything, from our cosmology to our psychology. So, do we take a chance and trust that this sacred book is God given truth? And we've been given the roadmap to heaven. God said, 'Ye shall seek me and find me, when ye shall search for me with all your heart' (Jeremiah 29:13)

The fact is, we're here now. We're breathing, until we're not. So, whilst we're still breathing, we have a choice to know Father God, or not. Like, Pascal's wager, it makes sense to believe in God? Bugger going to hell. It sounds horrendous. We wouldn't want anyone to go there, not even our worst enemy.

If we go by the fruit of the tree, Jesus is unlike any other. There's no one like Him. He's the Godman. And He said He is the Truth. So, do we trust Him and invite Him in, when He knocks on the door?

Napoleon said, 'I know men; and I tell you that Jesus Christ is not a man. Superficial minds see a resemblance between Christ and the founders of empires, and the gods of other religions. That resemblance does not exist. There is between Christianity, and whatever other religions, the distance of infinity…

Everything in Christ astonishes me. His spirit overawes me, and His will confounds me. Between Him and whoever else in the world, there is no possible term of comparison. He is truly a being by Himself. His ideas and sentiments, and the truth which He announces, His manner of convincing, are not explained either by human organisation or by the nature of things…

The nearer I approach, the more carefully I examine, everything is above me – everything remains grand, of a grandeur which overpowers. His religion is a revelation from an intelligence which is certainly not of man… One can absolutely find nowhere, but in Him alone, the imitation or the example of His life… I search in vain in history to find the similar to Jesus Christ, or anything which can approach the gospel' (cited in Roger Carswell, 1993 p.98).

As CS Lewis said, 'As in arithmetic – there is only one right answer to a sum; but some of the wrong answers are much nearer being right than others'. Many philosophies and religions resonate with God's word, and we might prefer to believe them. We lie to ourselves in bad faith? But truth is absolute. And half-truths actively add confusion. As English poet Lord Tennyson said, 'a lie which is half a truth is ever the blackest of lies'. Thus, people get deceived by the serpent.

But moreover, the Bible is the playbook for Satanists. His-Story is unfolding because they're making it unfold. They're preparing the way for their antichrist messiah. Evil will come in the name of love. They're preparing the sheeple, politically and spiritually. And we're a heartbeat away from being chipped with the mark of the beast. It's also noted, that some people come to faith in God when they realise Satan is real and the satanic agenda is real. They deduct that if Satan and demonic spirits are real, Jesus has to be real. This is the good news.

As perverse as it may seem, there's part of me that wants to see how it all unfolds. Whilst I appreciate it will be the worst time ever to live, I'd quite like to see the sky rolled up like a scroll and the stars fall from heaven. I'm curious about the looming alien deception. And the giants and hybrids that wait in anticipation for the green light. Like, the sleeper agents wait to be activated. And like the astral entities, who're chomping at the bit to get out from behind the veil. The lying signs and wonders, including holograms, will be immense. And we could be the generation that sees it unfold?

Moreover, having read about the reality of our existence, 'you can't not know, what you know'. So, you have no excuse for not knowing. Welcome to my world (LOL). As Joshua 24: 15 states, '… choose for yourselves this day whom you will serve'. Jesus said (Matthew 10:32-34), 'If anyone acknowledges me publicly here on earth, I will openly acknowledge that person before my Father in heaven. But if anyone denies me here on earth, I will deny that person before my Father in heaven'.

I'll be seeing you?

XXXXXXX

'Ecclesiastes' by King Solomon circa 931 BC

Appendix

Everything is Meaningless

'Everything is meaningless' says the teacher, 'utterly meaningless!'

What do people get for all their hard work? Generations come and go, but nothing really changes. The sun rises and sets and hurries around to rise again. The wind blows south and north, here and there, twisting back and forth, getting nowhere. The rivers run into the sea, but the sea is never full. Then the water returns again to the rivers and flows again into the sea. Everything is so weary and tiresome! No matter how much we see, we are never satisfied. No matter how much we hear, we are not content.

History merely repeats itself. It has all been done before. Nothing under the sun is truly new. What can you point to that is new? How do you know it didn't already exist long ago? We don't remember what happened in those former times. And in future generations, no one will remember what we are doing now.

The Futility of Wisdom

I, the teacher, was king of Israel, and I lived in Jerusalem. I devoted myself to search for understanding and to explore by wisdom everything being done in the world. I soon discovered that God has dealt a tragic existence to the human race. Everything under the sun is meaningless, like chasing the wind. What is wrong cannot be righted. What is missing cannot be recovered.

I said to myself, 'Look I am wiser than any of the kings who ruled in Jerusalem before me. I have greater wisdom and knowledge than any of them.' So I worked hard to distinguish wisdom from foolishness. But now I realise that even this was like chasing the wind. For the greater my wisdom, the greater my grief. To increase knowledge only increases sorrow.

The Futility of Pleasure

I said to myself, 'Come now, let's give pleasure a try. Let's look for the 'good things' in life.' But I found that this, too, was meaningless. 'It is silly to be laughing all the time,' I said. 'What good does it do to seek only pleasure?' After much thought, I decided to cheer myself with wine. While still seeking wisdom, I clutched at foolishness. In this way, I hoped to experience the only happiness most people find during their brief life in this world.

I also tried to find meaning by building huge homes for myself and by planting beautiful vineyards. I made gardens and parks, filling them with all kinds of fruit trees. I built reservoirs to collect the water to irrigate my many flourishing groves. I bought slaves, both men and women, and others were born into my household. I also owned great herds and flocks, more than any of the kings who lived in Jerusalem before me. I collected great sums of silver and gold, the treasure of many kings and provinces. I hired wonderful singers, both men and women, and had many beautiful concubines. I had everything a man could desire!

So I became greater than any of the kings who ruled in Jerusalem before me. And with it all, I remained clear-eyed so that I could evaluate all these things. Anything I wanted, I took. I did not restrain myself from any joy. I even found great pleasure in hard work, an additional reward for my labours. But as I looked at everything I had worked so hard to accomplish, it was all so meaningless. It was like chasing the wind. There was nothing really worthwhile anywhere.

The Wise and the Foolish

So I decided to compare wisdom and folly, and anyone else would come to the same conclusions I did. Wisdom is of more value than foolishness, just as light is better than darkness. For the wise person sees, while the fool is blind. Yet I saw that wise and foolish people share the same fate. Both of them die. Just as the fool will die, so will I. So of what value is all my wisdom? Then I said to myself, 'This is all so meaningless!' For the wise person and the fool both die, and in the days to come, both will be forgotten.

The Futility of Work

So now I hate life because everything done here under the sun is so irrational. Everything is meaningless, like chasing the wind. I am disgusted that I must leave the fruits of my hard work to others. And who can tell whether my successors will be wise or foolish? And yet they will control everything I have gained by my skill and hard work. How meaningless!

So I turned in despair from hard work. It was not the answer to my search for satisfaction in this life. For though I do my work with wisdom, knowledge and skill, I must leave everything I gain to people who haven't worked to earn it. This is not only foolish but highly unfair. So what do people get for all their hard work? Their days of labour are filled with pain and grief; even at night they cannot rest. It is all utterly meaningless.

So I decided there is nothing better than to enjoy good food and drink and to find satisfaction in work. Then I realised that this pleasure is from the hand of God. For who can eat or enjoy anything apart from him? God gives wisdom, knowledge and joy to those who please him. But if a sinner becomes wealthy, God takes the wealth away and gives it to those who please him. Even this, however, is meaningless, like chasing the wind.

A Time for Everything

There is a time for everything, a season for every activity under the sun. A time to be born and a time to die. A time to plant and a time to harvest. A time to kill and a time to heal. A time to tear down and a time to rebuild. A time to cry and a time to laugh. A time to grieve and a time to dance. A time to scatter stones and a time to gather stones. A time to embrace and a time to turn away. A time to search and a time to lose. A time to keep and a time to throw away. A time to tear and a time to mend. A time to be quiet and a time to speak up. A time to love and a time to hate. A time for war and a time for peace.

What do people really get for all their hard work? I have thought about this in connection with the various kinds of work God has given people to do. God has made everything beautiful for its own time. He has planted eternity in the human heart, but even so, people cannot see the whole scope of God's work from beginning to end. So I concluded that there is nothing better for people than to be happy and to enjoy themselves as long as they can. And people should eat and drink and enjoy the fruits of their labour, for these are gifts from God.

And I know that whatever God does is final. Nothing can be added to it or taken from it. God's purpose in this is that people should fear him. Whatever exists today and whatever will exist in the future has already existed in the past. For God calls each event back in its turn.

The Injustices of Life

I also noticed that throughout the world there is evil in the courtroom. Yes, even the courts of law are corrupt! I said to myself, 'In due season God will judge everyone, both good and bad, for all their deeds.'

Then I realised that God allows people to continue in their sinful ways so he can test them. That way, they can see for themselves that they are no better than animals. For humans and animals both breathe the same air, and both die. So people have no real advantage over the animals. How meaningless! Both go to the same place – the dust from which they came and to which they must return. For who can prove that the human spirit goes upward and the spirit of animals goes downward into the earth? So I saw that there is nothing better for people than to be happy in their work. That is why they are here! No one will bring them back from death to enjoy life in the future.

Again I observed all the oppression that takes place in our world. I saw the tears of the oppressed, with no one to comfort them. The oppressors have great power, and the victims are helpless. So I concluded that the dead are better off than the living. And most fortunate of all are those who were never born. For they have never seen all the evil that is done in our world.

Then I observed that most people are motivated to success by their envy of their neighbours. But this, too, is meaningless, like chasing the wind.

Foolish people refuse to work and almost starve. They feel it is better to be lazy and barely survive than to work hard, especially when in the long run everything is futile.

The Advantages of Companionship

I observed yet another example of meaningless in our world. This is the case of a man who is all alone, without a child or a brother, yet who works hard to gain as much wealth as he can. But then he asks himself, 'Who am I working for? Why I am giving up so much pleasure now?' It is all so meaningless and depressing.

Two people can accomplish more than twice as much as one; they get a better return for their labour. If one person falls, the other can reach out and help. But people who are alone when they fall are in real trouble. And on a cold night, two under the same blanket can gain warmth from each other. But how can one be warm alone? A person standing alone can be attacked and defeated, but two can stand back-to-back and conquer. Three are even better, for a triple-braided cord is not easily broken.

The Futility of Political Power

It is better to be a poor but wise youth than to be an old and foolish king who refuses all advice. Such a youth could come from prison and succeed. He might even become king, though he was born in poverty. Everyone is eager to help such a youth, even to help him take the throne. He might become the leader of millions and be very popular. But then the next generation grows up and rejects him! So again, it is all meaningless, like chasing the wind.

The Importance of Fearing God

As you enter the house of God, keep your ears open and your mouth shut! Don't be a fool who doesn't realise that mindless offerings to God are evil. And don't make rash promises to God, for he is in heaven, and you are only here on earth. So let your words be few.

Just as being too busy gives you nightmares, being a fool makes you a blabbermouth.

So when you make a promise to God, don't delay in following through, for God takes no pleasure in fools. Keep all the promises you make to him. It is better to say nothing than to promise something that you don't follow through on. In such cases, your mouth is making you sin. And don't defend yourself by telling the Temple messenger that the promise you made was a mistake. That would make God angry, and he might wipe out everything you have achieved.

Dreaming all the time instead of working is foolishness. And there is ruin in a flood of empty words. Fear God instead.

The Futility of Wealth

If you see a poor person being oppressed by the powerful and justice being miscarried throughout the land, don't be surprised! For every official is under orders from higher up, and matters of justice only get lost in red tape and bureaucracy. Even the king milks the land for his own profit!

Those who love money will never have enough. How absurd to think that wealth brings true happiness! The more you have, the more people come to help you spend it. So what is the advantage of wealth – except perhaps to watch it run through your fingers!

People who work hard sleep well, whether they eat little or much. But the rich are always worrying and seldom get a good night's sleep.

There is another serious problem I have seen in the world. Riches are sometimes hoarded to the harm of the saver, or they are put into risky investments that turn sour, and everything is lost. In the end, there is nothing left to pass on to one's children. People who live only for wealth come to the end of their lives as naked and empty-handed as on the day they were born.

And this, too, is a very serious problem. As people come into this world, so they depart. All their hard work is for nothing. They have been working for the wind, and everything will be swept away. Throughout their lives, they live under a cloud – frustrated, discouraged, and angry.

Even so, I have noticed one thing, at least, that is good. It is good for people to eat well, drink a good glass of wine, and enjoy their work – whatever they do under the sun – for however long God lets them live. And it is a good thing to receive wealth from God and the good health to enjoy it. To enjoy your work and accept your lot in life – that is indeed a gift from God. People who do this rarely look with sorrow on the past, for God has given them reasons for joy.

There is another serious tragedy I have seen in our world. God gives great wealth and honour to some people and gives them everything they could ever want, but then he doesn't give them the health to enjoy it. They die, and others get it all! This is meaningless – a sickening tragedy.

A man might have a hundred children and live to be very old. But if he finds no satisfaction in life and in the end does not even get a decent burial, I say he would have been better off born dead. I realise that his birth would have been meaningless and ended in darkness. He wouldn't even have had a name, and he would never have seen the sun or known of its existence. Yet he would have had more peace than he has in growing up to be an unhappy man. He might live a thousand years twice over but not find contentment. And since he must die like everyone else – well, what's the use?

All people spend their lives scratching for food, but they never seem to have enough. Considering this, do wise people really have any advantage over fools? Do poor people gain anything by being wise and knowing how to act in front of others?

Enjoy what you have rather than desiring what you don't have. Just dreaming about nice things is meaningless; it is like chasing the wind.

The Future-Determined and Unknown

Everything has already been decided. It was known long ago what each person would be. So there's no use arguing with God about your identity.

The more words you speak, the less they mean. So why overdo it?

In the few days of our empty lives, who knows how our days can best be spent? And who can tell what will happen in the future after we are gone?

Wisdom for Life

A good reputation is more valuable than the most expensive perfume. In the same way, the day you die is better than the day you are born.

It is better to spend your time at funerals than at festivals. For you are going to die, and you should think about it while there is still time.

Sorrow is better than laughter, for sadness has a refining influence on us.

A wise person thinks much about death, while the fool thinks only about having a good time now.

It is better to be criticised by a wise person than to be praised by a fool! Indeed, a fool's laugher is quickly gone, like thorns crackling in a fire. This also is meaningless.

Extortion turns wise people into fools, and bribes corrupt the heart.

Finishing is better than starting. Patience is better than pride.

Don't be quick tempered, for anger is the friend of fools.

Don't long for "the good old days", for you don't know whether they were any better than today.

Being wise is as good as being rich; in fact, it is better. Wisdom or money can get you almost anything, but it's important to know that only wisdom can save your life.

Notice the way God does things; then fall into line. Don't fight the ways of God, for who can straighten out what he has made crooked?

Enjoy prosperity while you can. But when hard times strike, realise that both come from God. That way you will realise that nothing is certain in this life.

The Limits of Human Wisdom

In this meaningless life, I have seen everything, including the fact that some good people die young and some wicked people live on and on. So don't be too good or too wise! Why destroy yourself? On the other hand, don't be too wicked either – don't be a fool! Why should you die before your time? So try to walk a middle course – but those who fear God will succeed either way.

A wise person is stronger than the ten leading citizens of a town!

There is not a single person in all the earth who is always good and never sins.

Don't eavesdrop on others – you may hear your servant laughing at you. For you know how often you yourself have laughed at others.

All along I have tried my best to let wisdom guide my thoughts and actions. I said to myself, 'I am determined to be wise.' But it didn't really work. Wisdom is always distant and very difficult to find. I searched everywhere, determined to find wisdom and to understand the reason for things. I was determined to prove to myself that wickedness is stupid and that foolishness is madness.

I discovered that a seductive woman is more bitter than death. Her passion is a trap, and her soft hands will bind you. Those who please God will escape from her, but sinners will be caught in her snare.

'This is my conclusion', says the Teacher. 'I came to this result after looking into the matter from every possible angle. Just one out of every thousand men I interviewed can be said to be upright, but not one woman! I discovered that God created people to be upright, but they have each turned to follow their own downward path.'

How wonderful to be wise, to be able to analyse and interpret things. Wisdom lights up a person's face, softening its hardness.

Obedience to the King

Obey the king because you have vowed before God to do this. Don't try to avoid doing your duty, and don't take a stand with those who plot evil. For the king will punish those who disobey him. The king's command is backed by great power. No one can resist or question it. Those who obey him will not be punished. Those who are wise will find a time and a way to do what is right. Yes, there is a time and a way for everything, even as people's troubles lie heavily upon them.

Indeed, how can people avoid what they don't know is going to happen? None of us can hold back our spirit from departing. None of us has the power to prevent the day of our death. There is no escaping that obligation, that dark battle. And in the face of death, wickedness will certainly not rescue those who practice it.

The Wicked and the Righteous

I have thought deeply about all that goes on here in the world, where people have the power to hurt each other. I have seen wicked people buried with honour. How strange that they were the very ones who frequented the Temple and are praised in the very city where they committed their crimes! When a crime is not punished, people feel it is safe to do wrong. But even though a person sins a hundred times and still lives a long time, I know that those who fear God are better off. The wicked will never live long, good lives, for they do not fear God. Their days will never grow long like the evening shadows.

And this is not all that is meaningless in our world. In this life, good people are often treated as though they were wicked, and wicked people are often treated as though they were good. This is so meaningless!

So I recommend having fun, because there is nothing better for people to do in this world than to eat, drink, and enjoy life. That way they will experience some happiness along with all the hard work God gives them.

In my search for wisdom, I tried to observe everything that goes on all across the earth. I discovered that there is ceaseless activity, day and night. This reminded me that no one can discover everything God has created in our world, no matter how hard they work at it. Not even the wisest people know everything, even if they say they do.

Death Comes to All

This, too, I carefully explored: Even though the actions of the godly and wise people are in God's hands, no one knows whether or not God will show them favour in this life. The same destiny ultimately awaits everyone, whether they are righteous or wicked, good or bad, ceremonially clean or unclean, religious or irreligious. Good people receive the same treatment as sinners, and people who take oaths are treated like people who don't.

It seems so tragic that one fate comes to all. That is why people are not more careful to be good. Instead, they choose their own mad course, for they have no hope. There is nothing ahead but death anyway. There is hope only for the living. For as they say, 'It is better to be a live dog than a dead lion!'

The living at least know they will die, but the dead know nothing. They have no further reward, nor are they remembered. Whatever they did in their lifetime – loving, hating, envying – is all long gone. They no longer have a part in anything here on earth. So go ahead. Eat your food and drink your wine with a happy heart, for God approves of this! Wear fine clothes, with a dash of cologne!

Live happily with the woman you love through all the meaningless days of life that God has given you in this world. The wife God gives you is your reward for all your earthly toil. Whatever you do, do well. For when you go to the grave, there will be no work or planning or knowledge or wisdom.

I have observed something else in this world of ours. The fastest runner doesn't always win the race, and the strongest warrior doesn't always win the battle. The wise are often poor, and the skilful are not necessarily wealthy. And those who are educated don't always lead successful lives. It is all decided by chance, by being at the right place at the right time.

People can never predict when hard times might come. Like fish in a net or birds in a snare, people are often caught by sudden tragedy.

Thoughts on Wisdom and Folly

Here is another bit of wisdom that has impressed me as I have watched the way our world works. There was a small town with only a few people living in it, and a great king came with his army and besieged it. There was a poor, wise man living there who knew how to save the town, and so it was rescued. But afterward no one thought any more about him. Then I realised that though wisdom is better than strength, those who are wise will be despised if they are poor. What they say will not be appreciated for long. But even so, the quiet words of a wise person are better than the shouts of a foolish king. A wise person can overcome weapons of war, but one sinner can destroy much that is good.

Dead flies will cause even a bottle of perfume to stink! Yes, an ounce of foolishness can outweigh a pound of wisdom and honour.

The hearts of the wise lead them to do right, and the hearts of the foolish lead them to do evil. You can identify fools just by the way they walk down the street!

If your boss is angry with you, don't quit! A quiet spirit can overcome even great mistakes.

There is another evil I have seen as I have watched the world go by. Kings and rulers make a grave mistake if they give foolish people great authority, and if they fail to give people of proven worth their rightful place of dignity. I have even seen servants riding like princes – and princes walking like servants.

When you dig a well, you may fall in. When you demolish an old wall, you could be bitten by a snake. When you work in a quarry, stones might fall and crush you! When you chop wood, there is danger with each stroke of your axe! Such are the risks of life.

Since a dull axe requires great strength, sharpen the blade. That's the value of wisdom; it helps you succeed.

It does no good to charm a snake after it has bitten you.

It is pleasant to listen to wise words, but the speech of fools brings them to ruin.

Since fools base their thoughts on foolish premises, their conclusions will be wicked madness.

Foolish people claim to know all about the future and tell everyone the details! But who can really know what is going to happen?

Fools are so exhausted by a little work that they have no strength for even the simplest tasks.

Destruction is certain for the land whose king is a child and whose leaders feast in the morning. Happy is the land whose king is a nobleman and whose leaders feast only to gain strength for their work, not to get drunk.

Laziness lets the roof leak, and soon the rafters begin to rot.

A party gives laughter, and wine gives happiness, and money gives everything!

Never make light of the king, even in your thoughts. And don't make fun of a rich man, either. A little bird may tell them what you have said.

Generosity and Diligence

Give generously, for your gifts will return to you later. Divide your gifts among many, for you do not know what risks might lie ahead.

When the clouds are heavy, the rains come down.

When a tree falls, whether south or north, there it lies.

If you wait for perfect conditions, you will never get anything done.

God's ways are as hard to discern as the pathways of the wind, and as mysterious as a tiny baby being formed in a mother's womb.

Be sure to stay busy and plant a variety of crops, for you never know which will grow – perhaps they all will.

Advice for Old and Young

Light is sweet; it's wonderful to see the sun!

When people live to be very old, let them rejoice in every day of life. But let them also remember that the dark days will be many. Everything still to come is meaningless.

Young man, it's wonderful to be young! Enjoy every minute of it. Do everything you want to do; take it all in. But remember that you must give an account to God for everything you do. So banish grief and pain, but remember that youth, with a whole life before it, still faces the threat of meaninglessness.

Don't let the excitement of youth cause you to forget your Creator. Honour him in your youth before you grow old and no longer enjoy living. It will be too late then to remember him, when the light of the sun and moon and stars is dim to your old eyes, and there is no silver lining left among the clouds. Your limbs will tremble with age, and your strong legs will grow weak. Your teeth will be too few to do their work, and you will be blind, too. And when your teeth are gone, keep your lips tightly closed when you eat! Even the chirping of birds will wake you up. But you yourself will be deaf and tuneless, with a quavering voice. You will be afraid of heights and of falling, white haired and withered, dragging along without any sexual desire. You will be standing at death's door. And as you near your everlasting home, the mourners will walk along the streets.

Yes, remember your Creator now while you are young, before the silver cord of life snaps and the golden bowl is broken. Don't wait until the water jar is smashed at the spring and the pulley is broken at the well. For then the dust will return to the earth, and the spirit will return to God who gave it.

'All is meaningless', says the Teacher, 'utterly meaningless.'

Concluding Thoughts

Because the Teacher was wise, he taught the people everything he knew. He collected proverbs and classified them. Indeed, the Teacher taught the plain truth, and he did so in an interesting way.

A wise teacher's words spur students to action and emphasise important truths. The collected sayings of the wise are like guidance from a shepherd.

But, my child, be warned: There is no end of opinions ready to be expressed. Studying them can go on forever and become very exhausting!

Here is my final conclusion: Fear God and obey his commands, for this is the duty of every person. God will judge us for everything we do, including every secret thing, whether good or bad.

References

The Bible

The Book of Enoch

The Book of Giants

The Book of Jasher

The Book of Jubilees

The Lost Gospels

Corpus Hermeticum

Shaun Attwood, 'American Made: Who Killed Barry Seal? Pablo Escobar or George H W Bush?' (2016) Gadfly Press

Edward Albee, 'Who's Afraid of Virginia Woolf?' (1967) Atheneum

Alan Alford, 'Gods of the New Millennium' (1996) Eridu Books

Neil Anderson, 'The Bondage Breaker' (1990) Harvest House Publishers

Sue Atkinson, 'Climbing out of Depression' (2005) Lion Books

Simone De Beauvoir, 'The Second Sex' (1949) Penguin

Eric Berne, 'Games People Play' (1964) Grove Press

Jonathan Black, 'The Secret History of the World' (2010) Quercus Publishing

Helena Blavatsky, 'The Secret Doctrine' (1888) Penguin

Russell Brand, 'Revolution' (2014) Penguin

Derren Brown, 'Tricks of the Mind' (2006) Channel 4

Rebecca Brown, 'Prepare for War' (1987) Whitaker House

Lorna Byrne, 'Angels in my Hair' (2008) Arrow

Rhonda Byrne, 'The Secret' (2006) Atria Books

Bill Bryson, 'A Short History of Nearly Everything' (2003) Black Swan

Fritjof Capra, 'The Tao of Physics' (1975) Shambhala Publications

Roger Carswell, 'Grill a Christian' (2011) 10 Publishing

Noam Chomsky, '9-11' (2001) Seven Stories

John Coleman, 'Conspirator's Hierarchy: The Story of the Committee of 300' (1993) Bridger House Publishers

Milton William Cooper, 'Behold a Pale Horse' (1991) Windrush Publishers

Douglas Coupland, 'Generation X' (1991) St Martins Press

Phillip Day, 'The Mind Game' (2002) Credence Publishing

Michael Drosnin, 'The Bible Code' (1997) Atria

Erving Goffman, 'Stigma: Notes on the Management of Spoiled Identity' (1990) Penguin

Erving Goffman, 'The Presentation of Self in Everyday Life' (1990) Penguin

Melody Green, 'No Compromise: The Life Story of Keith Green' (1989) Thomas Nelson

Bill and Judy Guggenheim, 'Hello From Heaven!' (1995) Watkins

Sam Harris, 'The End of Faith' (2004) WW Norton and Company

Thomas Harris, 'I'm OK, You're OK' (1972) Arrow

Stephen Hawking, 'A Brief History of Time' (1988) Bantam Books

Henry Heydt, 'A Comparison of World Religions' (1967) Christian Literature Crusades

Alexander Hislop, 'The Two Babylons' (1858) CreateSpace Independent Publishers

Patrick Holford and Jerome Burne, 'Food is Better Medicine than Drugs: Your Prescription for Drug-free Health' (2006) Piatkus Books

Aldous Huxley, 'Brave New World' (1931) Chatto and Windus

David Icke, 'The David Icke Guide to the Global Conspiracy' (2007) Bridge of Love

David Icke, 'The Trigger, the Lie that Changed the World – Who Did It and Why' (2019) David Icke Books

Doreen Irvine, 'From Witchcraft to Christ' (1973) Kingsway

David Jacobs, 'Alien Encounters: First-hand Accounts of UFO Abductions' (1992) Virgin Books

Irvine Kirsch, 'The Emperor's New Drugs: Exploding the Antidepressant Myth' (2011) Bodley Head

Ronald David Laing, 'The Divided Self' (1960) Penguin

CS Lewis, 'Mere Christianity' (1952) Harper Collins

Hal Lindsey, 'Satan is Alive and Well on Planet Earth' (1972) Zondervan

Hal Lindsey, 'The 1980s: Countdown to Armageddon' (1981) Westgate Press

Texas Marrs, 'Dark Majesty: The Secret Brotherhood and the Magic of a Thousand Points of Light' (2004) Living Truth Publishers

Paul McKenna, 'The Paranormal World according to Paul McKenna' (1996) Faber and Faber

Paul McKenna and Hugh Willbourn, 'How to Mend Your Broken Heart' (2003) Bantam Press

Joyce Meyer, 'Battlefield of the Mind' (1994) Warner Faith

Thomas Moore, 'Dark Night of the Soul' (2004) Piatkus

Jeannie Morgan, 'Encounter the Holy Spirit' (2011) Monarch Books

Frederick Nietzsche, 'Beyond Good and Evil: Prelude to a Philosophy of the Future' (1886) Aziloth Books

George Orwell, '1984' (1948) Secker and Warburg

Siddhaswarupananda Paramahamsa, 'Reincarnation Explained' (1987) Crystal Clarity Publishers

Scott Peck, 'People of the Lie' (1983) Simon and Schuster

Scott Peck, 'Along the Road Less Travelled and Beyond' (1997) Penguin

Scott Peck, 'Further Along the Road Less Travelled' (1998) Pocket Books

Albert Pike, 'Morals and Dogmas of the Ancient and Accepted Scottish Rite of Freemasonry' (1872) Martino Fine Books

Besant Puri and Hilary Boyd, 'The Natural Way to Beat Depression' (2005) Hodder

Yogi Ramacharaka, 'Fourteen Lessons in Yogi Philosophy and Oriental Occultism' (1983) Cosimo Classics

The 'Readers Digest', 'Mysteries of the Unexplained', 'How Ordinary Men and Women Have Experienced the Strange, the Uncanny, and the Incredible (1989)

Valery Rees, 'From Gabriel to Lucifer' (2013) Bloomsbury Publishers

Carl Rogers, 'Person to Person' (1967) Souvenir Press

Carl Rogers, 'On Personal Power' (1977) Delacorte Press

Elizabeth Kubler-Ross, 'The Wheel of Life: A Memoir of Living and Dying' (1997) Simon and Schuster

Bertrand Russell, 'In Praise of Idleness' (1935) Allen and Unwin

Peter Sedgwick, 'Psycho Politics' (1982) Unkant

Rupert Sheldrake, 'The Science Delusion' (2012) Hodder and Stoughton

Grant and Jane Solomon, 'The Scole Experiment: Scientific Evidence for Life After Death' (1999) Campion Books

Lionel Shriver, 'We Need to Talk About Kevin' (2003) Counterpoint

Lee Strobel, 'The Case for Christ' (1998) Zondervan

Thomas Szasz, 'The Myth of Mental Illness' (1961) Harper

Thomas Szasz, 'The Untamed Tongue: A Dissenting Dictionary' (1990) Open Court Publishing

Laurie Taylor and Stanley Cohen, 'Escape Attempts: The Theory and Practice of Resistance in Everyday Life' (1976) Routledge

Eckhart Tolle, 'The Power of Now' (2011) Namaste Publishing

Richard Velleman, 'Counselling for Alcohol Problems' (2002) Sage Publications

Mark Vernon, 'The Big Questions: God' (2012) Quercus

Barbara Ward, 'Healing Grief: A Guide to Loss and Recovery' (1993) Vermillion

Gary Wayne, 'The Genesis 6 Conspiracy: How Secret Societies and the Descendants of Giants Plan to Enslave Humankind' (2016) Trusted Books

Irvine Welsh, 'Ecstasy' (1996) Vintage

Irvine Welsh, 'Trainspotting' (1993) Harvill Secker

Cisco Wheeler, 'Behold a White Horse' (2009) Xulon Press

Ellen White, 'The Great Controversy' (1995) James White

Carl Wickland, 'Thirty Years Among the Dead' (1924) White Crow Books

About the Author

I was born in Zambia in 1977, and moved to Ayrshire, Scotland, when I was four. My parents subsequently divorced, and my mum (who got custody of my brother and I) moved up to Aberdeen, where I have lived since I was seven. My dad returned to Africa, so I have been back and forth there all my life. I went to Aberdeen University when I left school and did a MA degree in psychology. After that, I did a MSc in economics, and worked in investment banking for a year. Then I did a MSc in applied social studies and worked as a social worker for a few years. I also trained in transactional analysis psychotherapy. Then I decided to travel to beloved Africa, so I quit my job and studies. When I returned, I worked in mental health for a couple of years, which I loved. And then I quit that to write my book. And here we are in 2020, and it's finally complete. Woo hoo!

www.ingramcontent.com/pod-product-compliance
Lightning Source LLC
Chambersburg PA
CBHW081341230426
43667CB00017B/2695